Siemens NX 9
Design Fundamentals

Jaecheol Koh
ONSIA Inc.

ONSIA

Siemens NX 9
Design Fundamentals
A Step by Step Guide

ISBN-10: 1500739146
ISBN-13: 978-1500739140

ONSIA Inc., Seoul, Republic of Korea
Phone: +82-70-8232-0341
Fax: +82-2-6918-4602
E-Mail: onsia@e-onsia.com

Author: Jaecheol Koh
Publisher: ONSIA Inc., Republic of Korea

Download Files for Exercises

Visit our homepage www.e-onsia.com. You can download the files for exercises without any limit. This textbook is written in NX 9 and the files are available in NX 6.0 with some exceptions.

Download Files for Exercises

Visit our homepage www.e-onsia.com. You can download the files for exercises without any limit. This textbook is written in NX 9 and the files are available in NX 6.0 with some exceptions.

Preface

This textbook explains how to create solid models, assemblies and drawings using Siemens NX 9. NX is a three dimensional CAD/CAM/CAE software developed by Siemens PLM Software Inc., Germany. This textbook is based on NX 9. Users of earlier releases can use this book with minor modifications. We provide files for exercises via our website. Almost all files are in NX 6.0 so readers can open the files using NX 6.0 and later releases.

It is assumed that readers of this textbook have no prior experience in using Siemens NX for modeling 3D parts. This textbook is suitable for anyone interested in learning 3D modeling using Siemens NX.

Each chapter deals with the major functions of creating 3D features using simple examples and step by step, self-paced exercises. Additional drawings of 3D parts are provided at the end of each chapter for further self exercises. The final exercises are expected to be completed by readers who have fully understood the content and completed the exercises in each chapter.

Topics covered in this textbook

- Chapter 1: Basic components of Siemens NX 9, options and mouse operations.
- Chapter 2: Basic step by step modeling process of NX 9.
- Chapter 3 and 4: Creating sketches and sketch based features.
- Chapter 5: Usage of datums to create complex 3D geometry.
- Chapter 6: Additional modeling commands such as fillet, chamfer, draft and shell.
- Chapter 7: Modification of 3D parts to take advantage of parametric modeling concepts.
- Chapter 8: Copying features, modeling objects and bodies.
- Chapter 9: Additional modeling commands such as trim body, tube, sweep along guide, emboss and various commands in synchronous modeling.
- Chapter 10: Advanced sketch commands.
- Chapter 11: Measuring and verifying 3D geometries.
- Chapter 12 and 13: Constructing assembly structures and creating or modifying 3D parts in the context of assembly.
- Chapter 14 and 15: Creating drawings for parts or assemblies.
- Appendix A: Selecting Objects

This page left blank intentionally.

Table of Contents

Chapter 6
Additional Modeling 235

Chapter 9
Additional Modeling 373

Chapter 13
Assembly Design II 499

Chapter 14
Creating Drawing Views 545

Chapter 15
Dimension, Annotation and Assembly Drawing. 593

This page left blank intentionally.

Chapter 1

Starting NX

■ **After completing this chapter you will understand**

- general information about NX.
- how to run NX.
- user interfaces in NX.
- the basic operations in NX.
- how to set the modeling environment in NX.

1.1 Introducing NX

NX is a three dimensional CAD/CAM/CAE software developed and sold by Siemens PLM Software. NX was first developed in 1969 as UNIAPT by the US company United Computing. The company purchased the ADAM (Automated Drafting and Machining) software code from MGS in 1973 and released a commercial CAD/CAM software known as Unigraphics in 1975.

The following year, United Computing was acquired by the aerospace company McDonnell Douglas, who created new CAD/CAM divisions, including the Unigraphics Group. Finally, in 1980, Unigraphics was released, marking the group's first true 3D modeling hardware and software offering.

In 1991 the Unigraphics Group was acquired by EDS and the software business was branded EDS Unigraphics. Eventually, in 1997 EDS set up its Unigraphics division as a wholly owned subsidiary called Unigraphics Solutions.

Since then, Unigraphics Solutions has purchased many industrial software companies such as Applicon and SDRC, and the company changed its name to UGS Corporation. In 2003 UGS received a license to the MSC Nastran source code and branded its own engineering analysis software as NX Nastran.

NX is a universal CAD, CAM and CAE software which originates from UGS, SDRC and MSC Nastran, respectively, in their ideas of design, manufacturing and engineering analysis.

1.2 Versions of NX

This textbook was written in NX 9.0.1.3. Readers using any version of NX 9.0 will have no problems with reading this textbook. However, it is recommended that NX 9.0.1 or a later version is used to avoid programming bugs. You can identify the version of NX by choosing **Help > About NX** in the **File** tab.

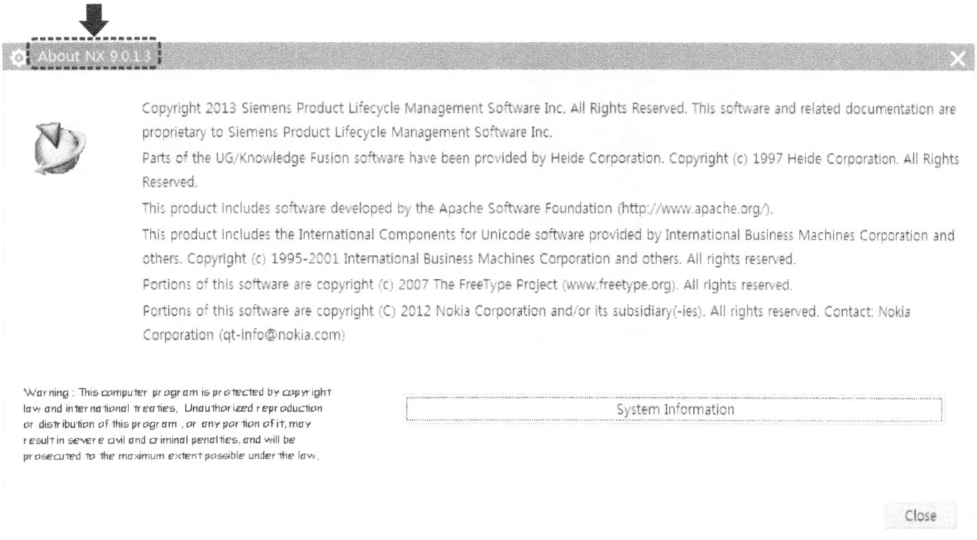

Fig 1-1 Identifying the Version of NX

QRM

The third digit in the NX version number such as 9.0.0.25 is called the QRM (Quick Response Maintenance) version. This is a type of patch program to enhance the software's functionality and to eliminate programming bugs.

1.3 Executing NX

To execute NX you can choose **Start > All Programs > Siemens NX 9.0 > NX 9.0**. Fig 1-3 shows the icon of NX 9.0.

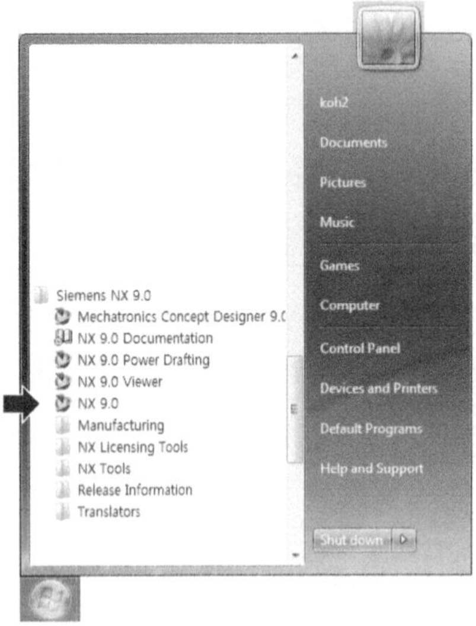

Fig 1-2 Executing NX 9

Fig 1-3 NX Icon

You may either double click the icon in the background of **Windows** or click the fast executing facility.

Fig 1-4 NX Icon in Windows Wallpaper

Fig 1-5 NX Icon in Fast Access Area

Fig 1-6 shows the start window of NX 9.0. In this window, you can open an existing part file or create a new file.

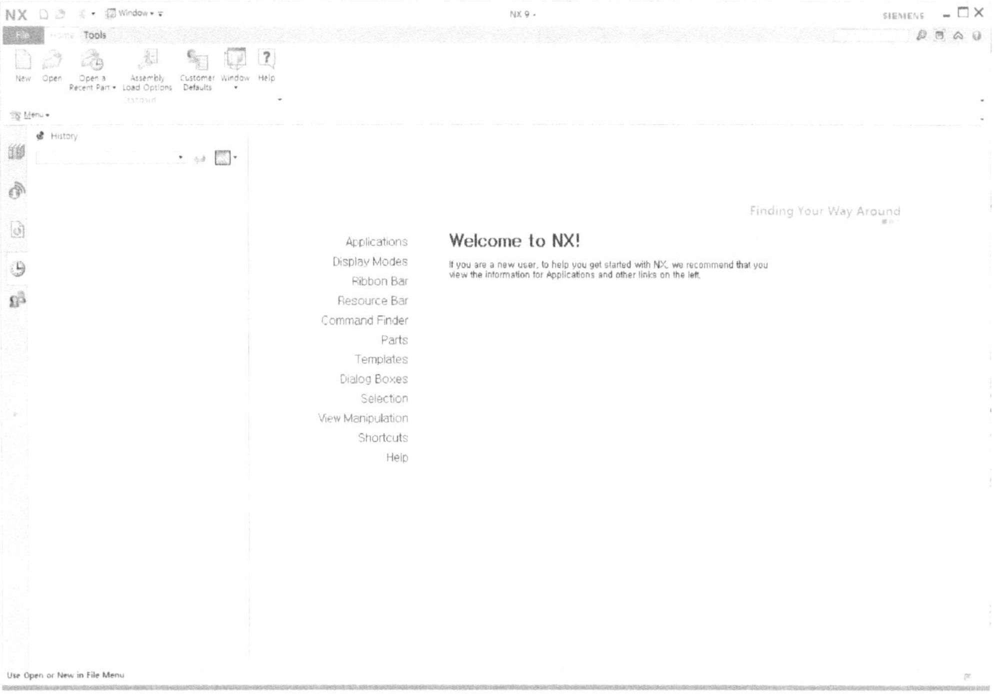

Fig 1-6 Start Window of NX

Some basic instructions on how to use NX are explained in the main window. If you click on text such as **Application, Roles, Customize,** etc. their meanings and basic usages are explained on the right. Fig 1-7 shows an explanation of the dialog boxes.

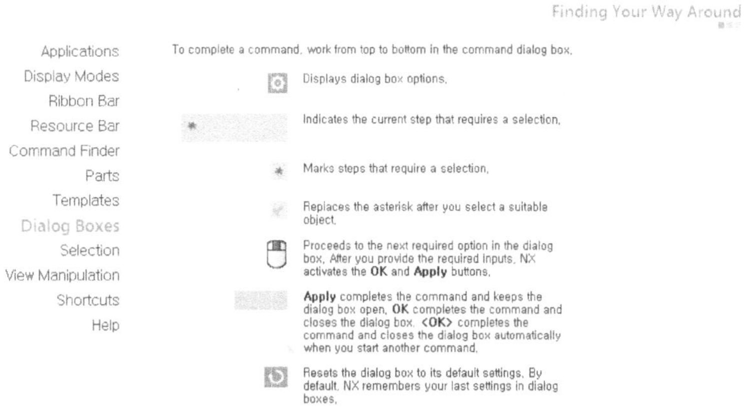

Fig 1-7 Explanation on the Dialog Boxes

If you click the **New** icon in the **Home** tab, the **New** dialog box is invoked as shown in Fig 1-8. Click the **Model** tab and select **Model** in the **Templates** option to create your first model file. Designate your folder for creating the NX part file by clicking the button on the right of the folder input area, then enter the file name. You should keep in mind that two bytes characters such as Chinese, Japanese or Korean characters are not allowed when naming the folder or part file.

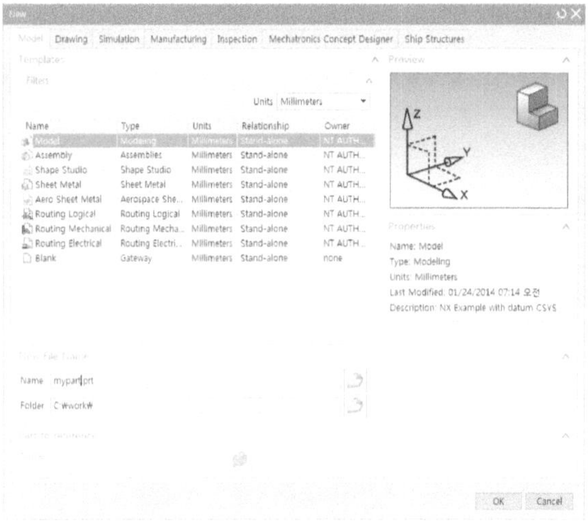

Fig 1-8 New Dialog Box

If you click **OK** in the **New** dialog box after designating the template, folder and file name, the **Modeling** application is invoked as shown in Fig 1-10.

Note that the part file will not have been created in the designated folder unless you save the file. If you click the **Save** button in the **Quick Access** toolbar, the part file will be created in the designated folder. You can close the file by choosing **File > Close > All Parts** in the **File** tab. If you try to close the file without saving it, the information box as shown in Fig 1-9 is invoked. You can **Save and Close** the file or **Close** the file without saving or **Cancel** the **Close All Parts** command.

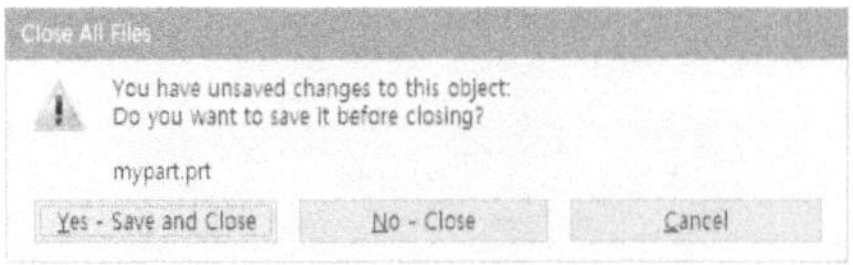

Fig 1-9 Information Box

1.4 User Interface of NX

Fig 1-10 shows the screen of NX 9 **Modeling** application which appears after creating a new part file with the **Model** template.

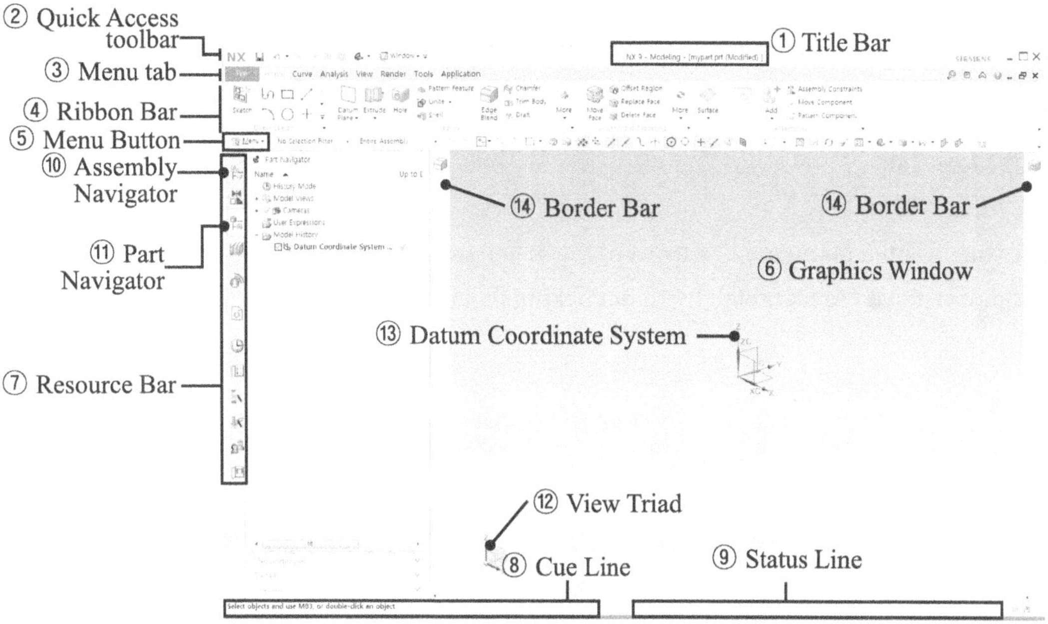

Fig 1-10 Screen Shot of NX 9.0 Modeling Application

① Title Bar

Shows the name of the displayed or work part file. When a part file is modified, it is marked as (Modified) in the title bar. You may save the file before exiting the file if necessary.

Fig 1-11 Title Bar of a Modified Part

② Quick Access Toolbar

You can register frequently used icons in the **Quick Access** toolbar. You can register an icon in the **Quick Access** toolbar by right clicking and choosing **Add to Quick Access Toolbar** in the popup menu as shown in Fig 1-13. Fig 1-12 shows the **Quick Access** toolbar where the **Extrude** icon is registered.

Fig 1-12 Quick Access Toolbar

Fig 1-13 Adding an Icon

③ Menu Tab

If you click the **Menu** tab, the icons of the menu group appear in the **Ribbon** bar. You can add or remove the **Menu** tab by right clicking on an empty ribbon bar area.

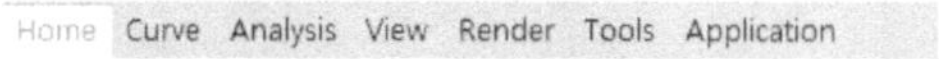

Fig 1-14 Menu Tab

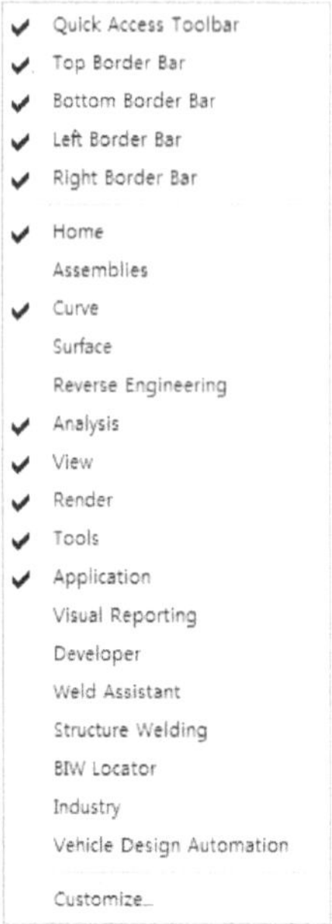

Fig 1-15 Displaying Option

④ Ribbon Bar

If you click a Menu tab, the icons are displayed in the ribbon bar. Fig 1-16 shows the icons in the ribbon bar of the **Home** tab.

Fig 1-16 Ribbon Bar of the Home Tab

⑤ Menu Button

If you click the **Menu** button, commands of the current NX application are displayed. You can choose a command in the **Menu** button instead of clicking an icon in the **Ribbon** bar.

Fig 1-17 Menu Button

⑥ Graphics Window

The open part is displayed in the graphics window. You can select the geometry of the part shown in the graphics window.

⑦ Resource Bar

Tools such as **Part Navigator** and **Assembly Navigator** which you will use during the modeling or assembly process are arranged as respective pages.

⑧ Cue Line

Users are prompted to perform an action to accomplish a command option. Fig 1-18 shows an example of a cue line message which is displayed when you click the **Sketch** icon in the **Home** tab.

Select object for sketch plane or double click axis to orient

Fig 1-18 An Example of the Cue Line Prompt

⑨ Status Line

This line displays the message explaining the result of a command. Fig 1-19 shows an example of a status line message after saving a file.

Part file saved

Fig 1-19 An Example of the Status Line Message

⑩ Assembly Navigator

Fig 1-20 shows the **Assembly Navigator** which shows the structure of an assembly part.

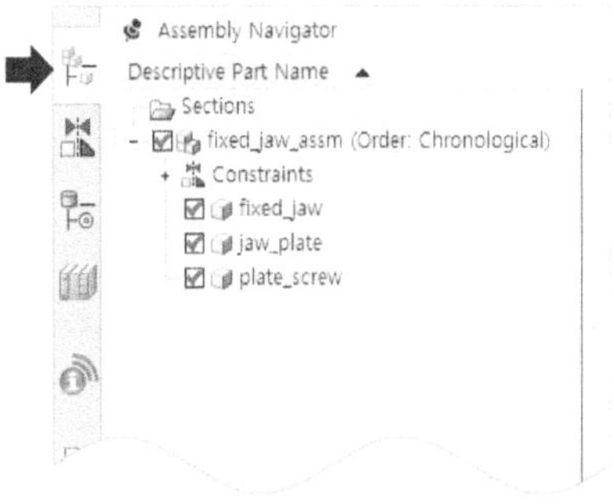

Fig 1-20 Assembly Navigator

⑪ Part Navigator

Fig 1-21 shows the **Part Navigator** which shows the modeling history of a part. Users can modify a feature of a part in the **Part Navigator**.

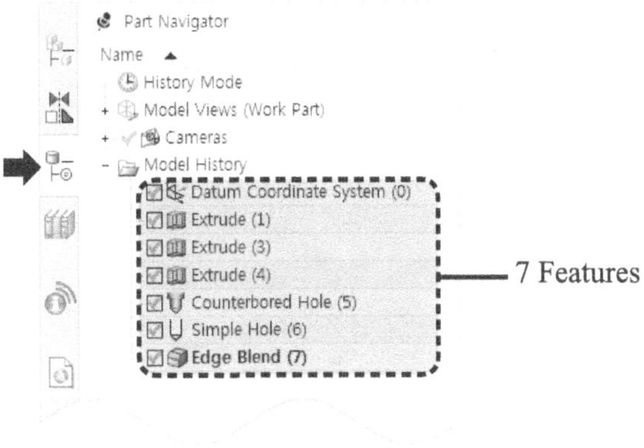

Fig 1-21 Part Navigator

⑫ View Triad

View triad designates the direction of an absolute coordinate system of the modeling space.

Fig 1-22 View Triad

⑬ Datum Coordinate System

The datum coordinate system is a feature that consists of three objects which are used for various purposes. You can create a sketch on a datum plane. Datums are explained in Chapter 5.

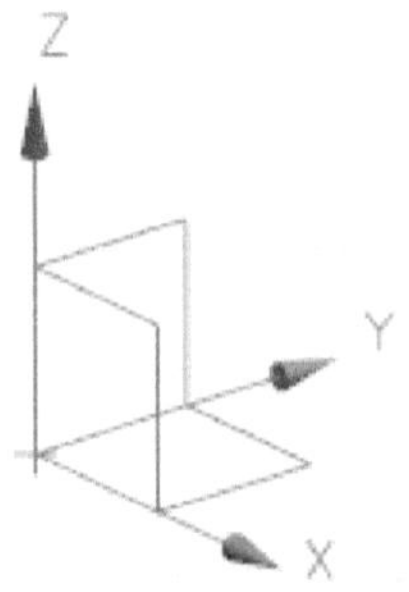

Fig 1-23 Datum Coordinate System

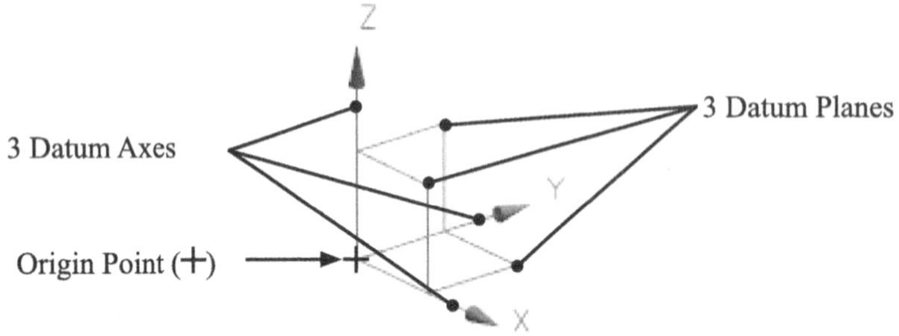

Fig 1-24 Three Objects Composing Datum Coordinate System

Selecting a Point

You may encounter difficulties in selecting the point at the origin of the datum coordinate system. Points are not magnified even when you zoom in on the model. You have to rely on either the snap symbol beside the mouse pointer or the quick pick utility to select an existing point.

⑭ Border Bar

You can register icons in the **Border Bar** areas that are located in thc four sides around the graphics window. You can place icons in the top, bottom, left or right border bar by right clicking and choosing in the popup menu as shown in Fig 1-13. You can remove icons by right clicking on the icon in the border bar.

1.5 Roles

With the help of **Roles**, users can restore a pre-defined user interface suitable to their modeling skill level or depending on their industrial area. We will use the Essentials role in this textbook.

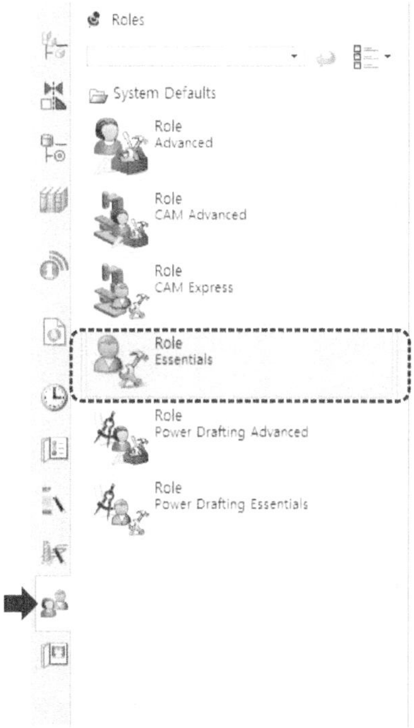

Fig 1-25 Roles

1.6 Mouse Operations

Fig 1-26 shows the button names on a wheel mouse. This textbook assumes that you are using a wheel mouse.

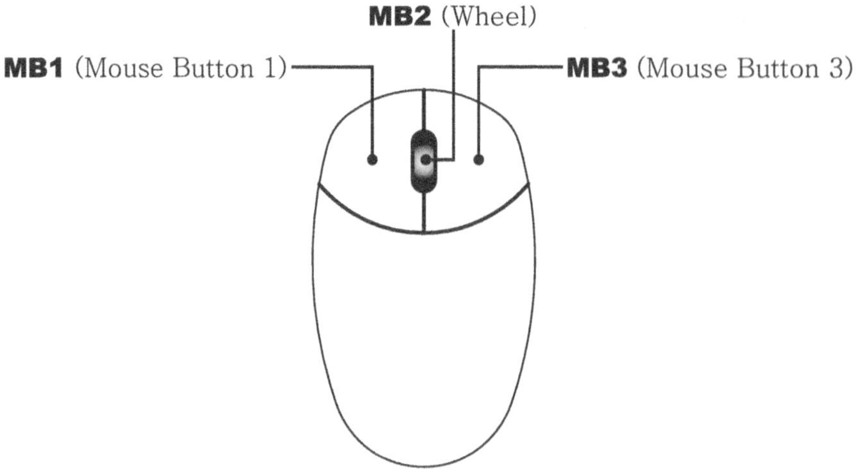

Fig 1-26 Name of Mouse Buttons

Each mouse button is referred to as MB1, MB2 and MB3 respectively for convenience. The following table explains the functions of each mouse button.

Keyboard	Mouse Operations		Function
	Button	Operation	
N/A	MB1	Click	Select objects
Shift		Click	Add object selection or deselect
N/A	MB2 (Wheel)	Click	Same as OK in the dialog box
		Click and Drag	Rotate the model view
		Rotate	Zoom In/Out the model view
Ctrl		Click	Same as Apply in the dialog box
		Click and Drag	Zoom In/Out the model view
Shift		Click	Pan the model view
Alt		Click	Same as Cancel in the dialog box
N/A	MB3	Click	Invoke the popup menu
N/A		Click and Drag	Invoke the radial popup menu
Ctrl + Shift	MB1 MB2 MB3	Click	Radial Toolbar 1 Radial Toolbar 2 Radial Toolbar 3

Table 1-1 Mouse Usage

① Click MB1: Select objects

You can select modeling objects as shown in Fig 1-27. The color of the selected object turns to orange and the shortcut menu appears.

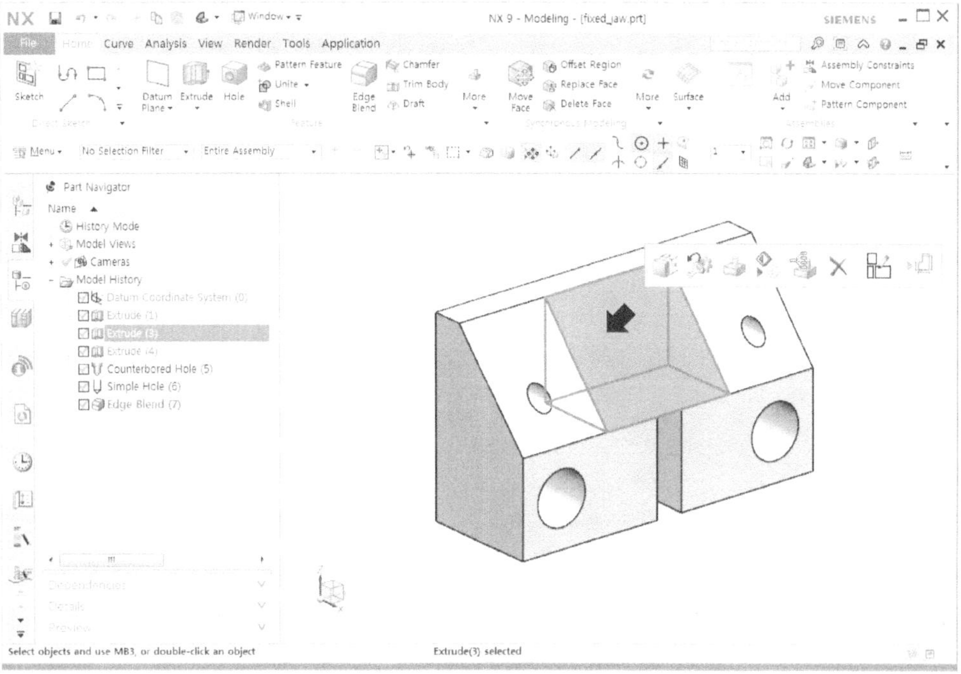

Fig 1-27 Selecting the Extrude Feature

If you click MB1 on the background of the graphics window, the **View** shortcut toolbar is available as shown in Fig 1-28 and you can use commands in the toolbar.

Fig 1-28 View Shortcut Toolbar

② Press the Shift key and click MB1: Deselect an object

You can deselect objects by pressing the **Shift** key and clicking MB1 on the selected object. If you want to deselect all the selected objects, just press the **ESC** key.

③ Click MB2: Same as proceeding to the next recommended step in a dialog box.

For example, clicking MB2 in the dialog box as shown in Fig 1-25 is the same as pressing the **OK** button which is highlighted in green as the next recommended step.

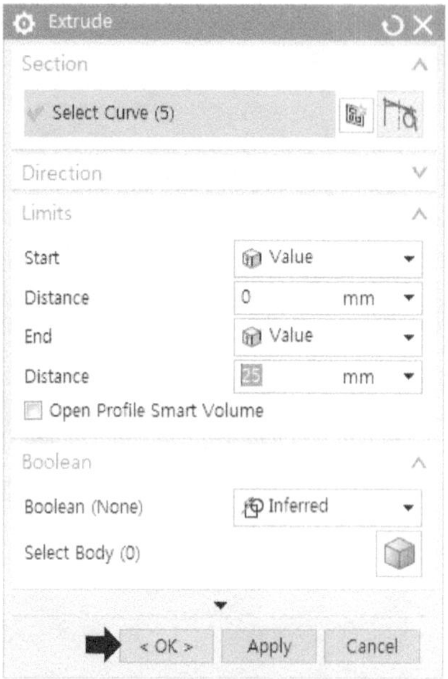

Fig 1-29 OK Button in the Extrude Dialog Box

④ Press MB2 and Drag: Rotate the model view

Press MB2 on the graphics window and drag the mouse. You can rotate the model view.

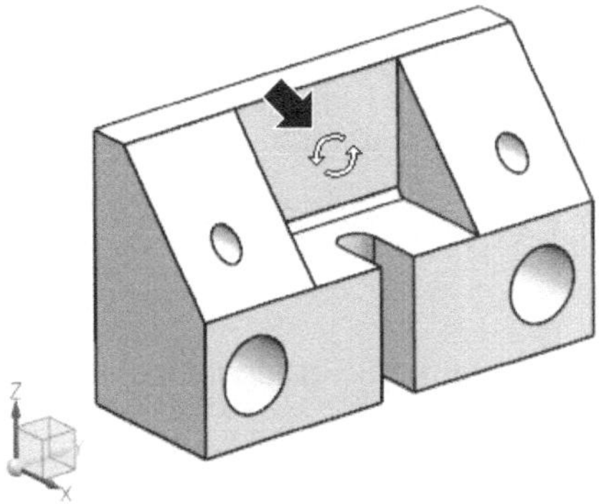

Fig 1-30 Mouse Cursor of View Rotate

⑤ Rotating the wheel: Zoom In/Out the model view

The model view can be zoomed in or out by rotating the wheel of the mouse. The view is zoomed depending on the current location of the mouse pointer. Fig 1-31 shows the direction of wheel rotation to zoom in or out on the model view.

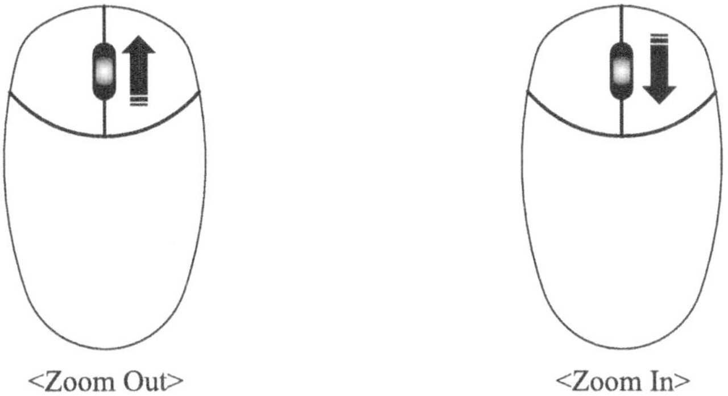

Fig 1-31 Wheel Rotation

⑥ Press the **Ctrl** key and click MB2: Same as pressing **Apply** in the dialog box

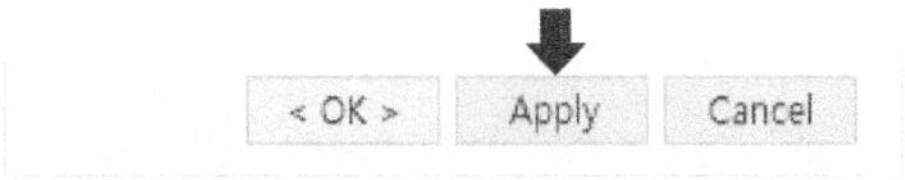

Fig 1-32 Apply Button in a Dialog Box

⑦ Press the **Ctrl** key and drag MB2: Zoom In/Out the model view

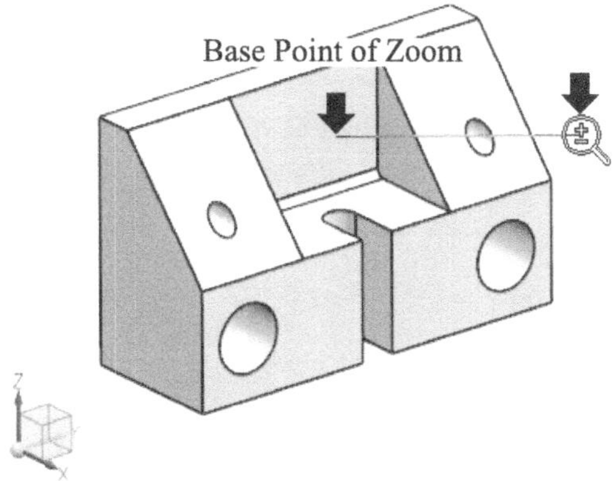

Fig 1-33 Mouse Cursor of Zoom and the Zoom Base Point

⑧ Press the Shift key and click MB2: Pan the model view

Model view is panned while the view angle is fixed.

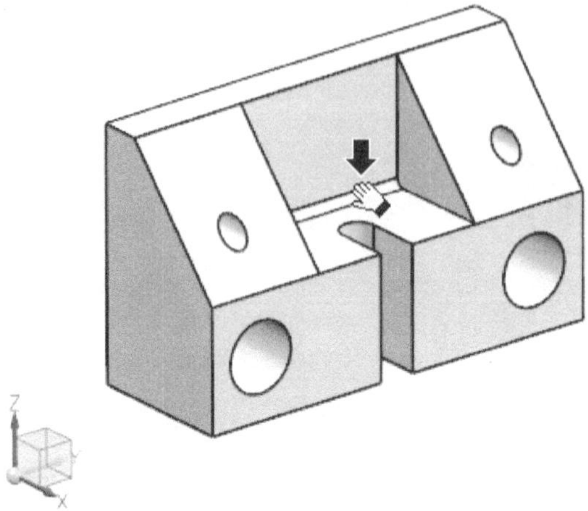

Fig 1-34 Mouse Cursor of View Pan

⑨ Press the **Alt** key and click MB2: Same as pressing **Cancel** in the dialog box

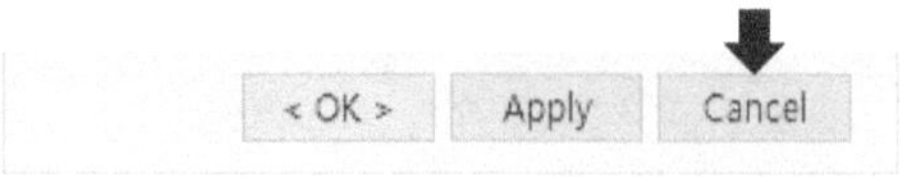

Fig 1-35 Cancel Button in a Dialog Box

⑩ Click MB3: Invoke the popup menu

Several types of popup menus are available by clicking MB3. If you click MB3 on in the background of the graphics window, the **Selection** shortcut toolbar and the **View** popup menu are invoked as shown in Fig 1-36.

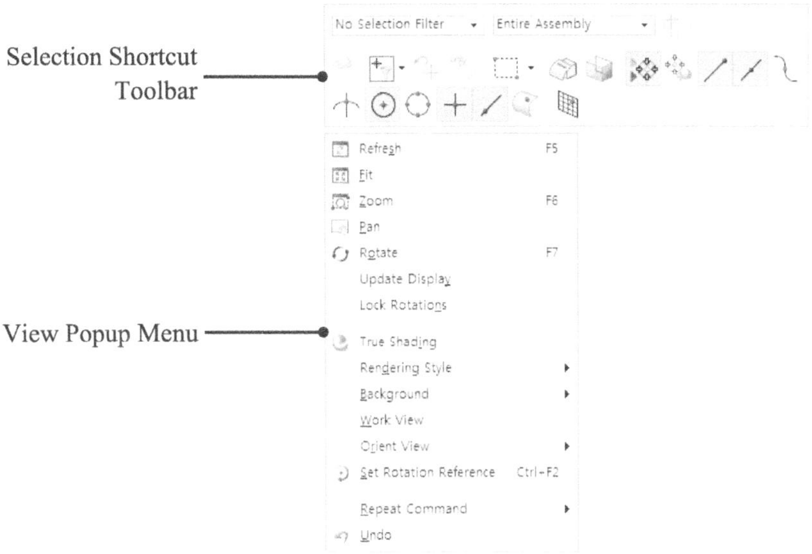

Fig 1-36 Popup Menu

Click MB3 on a modeling object. A popup menu as shown in Fig 1-37 is invoked according to the type of object.

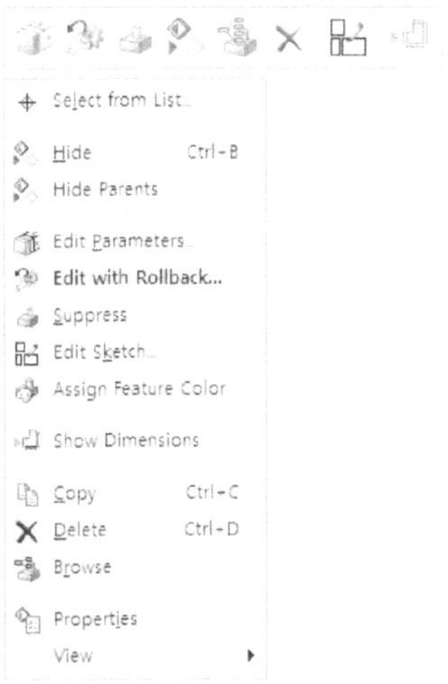

Fig 1-37 Popup Menu on the Extrude Feature

⑪ Press and hold MB3: Invoke the radial popup menu

Press and hold MB3 on an empty area in the graphics window. After a while the radial view popup menu is invoked as shown in Fig 1-38. You can switch the model view style quickly by dragging the mouse cursor over the icon.

Fig 1-38 Radial View Popup Menu

Press and hold MB3 on a modeling object. Other types of icons are available in the radial popup menu according to the type of object as shown in Fig 1-39.

Fig 1-39 Radial Popup Menu for a Sketch Feature

⑫ Press the Ctrl and Shift key and press and hold MB1, 2 or 3: Invoke radial toolbar

Press the **Ctrl** and **Shift** key at the same time while the mouse cursor is in the graphics window and press MB1, MB2 or MB3. The radial toolbars shown in Fig 1-40 are available which enables you to apply function icons quickly.

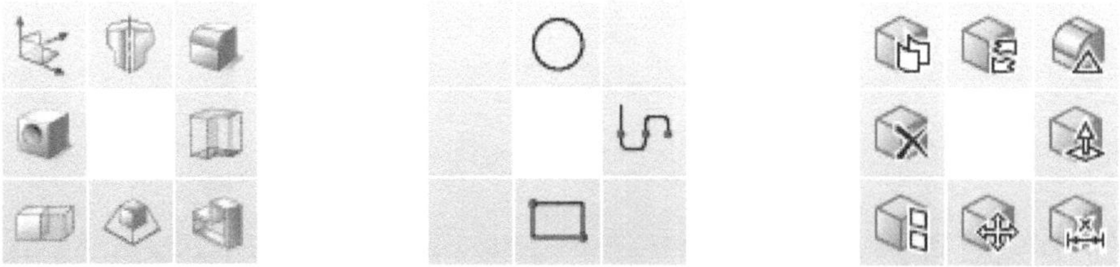

Ctrl + Shift + MB1 | Ctrl + Shift + MB2 | Ctrl + Shift + MB3

Fig 1-40 Radial Toolbar

1.7 View Popup Menu

In the **View** popup menu, you can access the frequently used view commands quickly by clicking MB3 on an empty area of the graphics window.

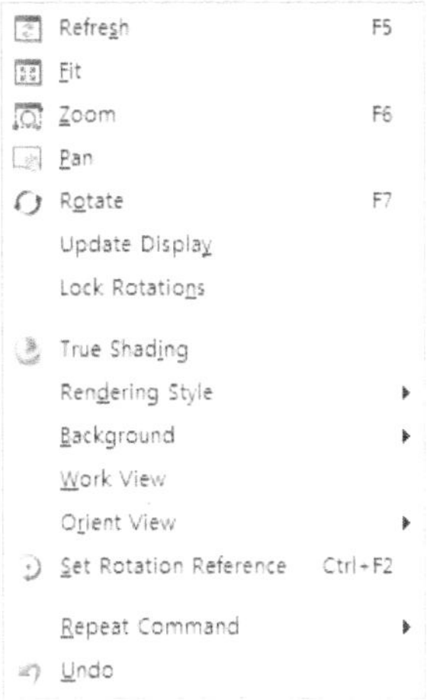

Fig 1-41 View Popup Menu

① Refresh

You can erase temporary afterimages such as asterisk or vector arrows that appear during the modeling process.

Fig 1-42 Asterisk

② Fit

The model geometry is displayed fitted in the graphics window. You can adjust the fit percentage by accessing **Preferences** > **Visualization** in the **Menu** button in the **View/ Screen** tab.

This setting is applicable only in the current session. That is to say, if you exit the NX, the default fit percentage of 100% is restored.

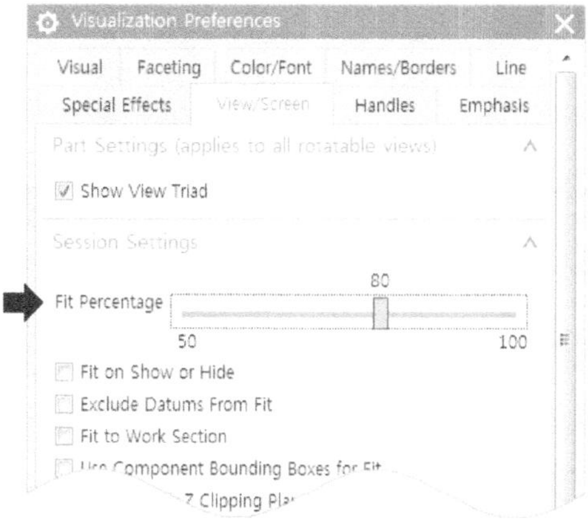

Fig 1-43 Fit Percentage Option

Fig 1-44 shows different views for respective fit percentages. A fit percentage of 80% is recommended.

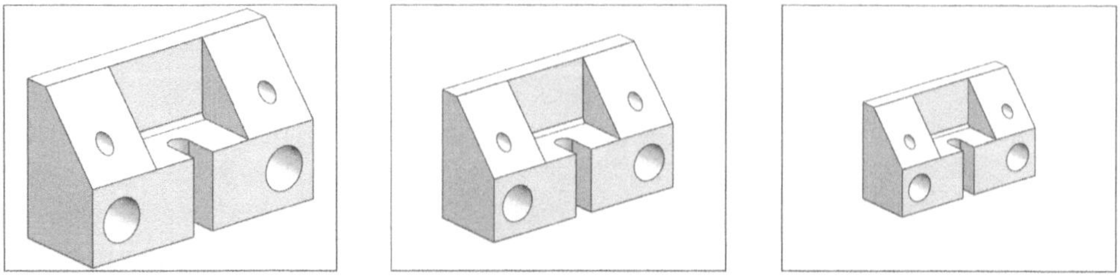

Fit Percentage=100% Fit Percentage=80% Fit Percentage=60%

Fig 1-44 View Fit

③ Zoom

You can designate the rectangle window to magnify the region.

④ Rotate

You can rotate the view by selecting this icon and pressing MB1 and dragging.

⑤ Pan

You can pan the view by selecting this icon and pressing MB1 and dragging.

⑥ True Shading

A realistic rendering is available by pressing this icon.

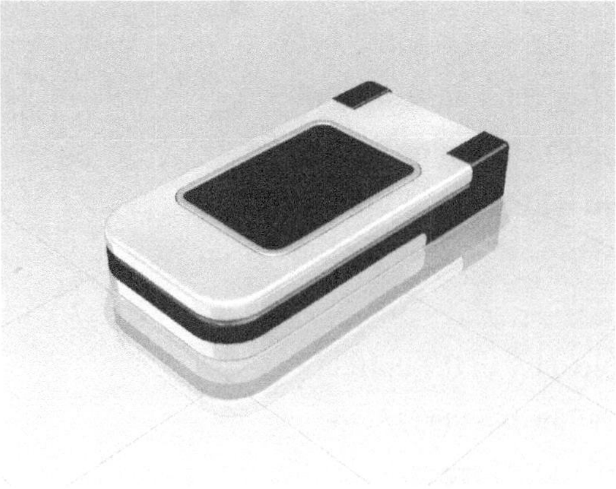

Fig 1-45 True Shading Rendering Style

⑦ Rendering Style

Apply a display type to the model geometry. The **Shaded with Edges** style is used in general and you can switch to another rendering style if necessary.

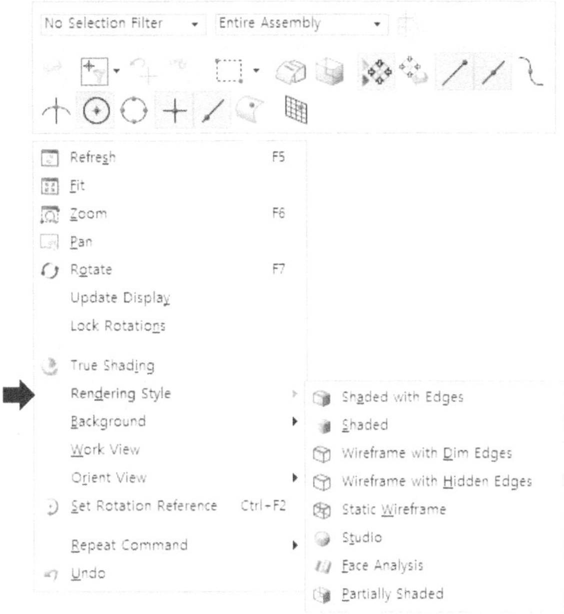

Fig 1-46 Rendering Style

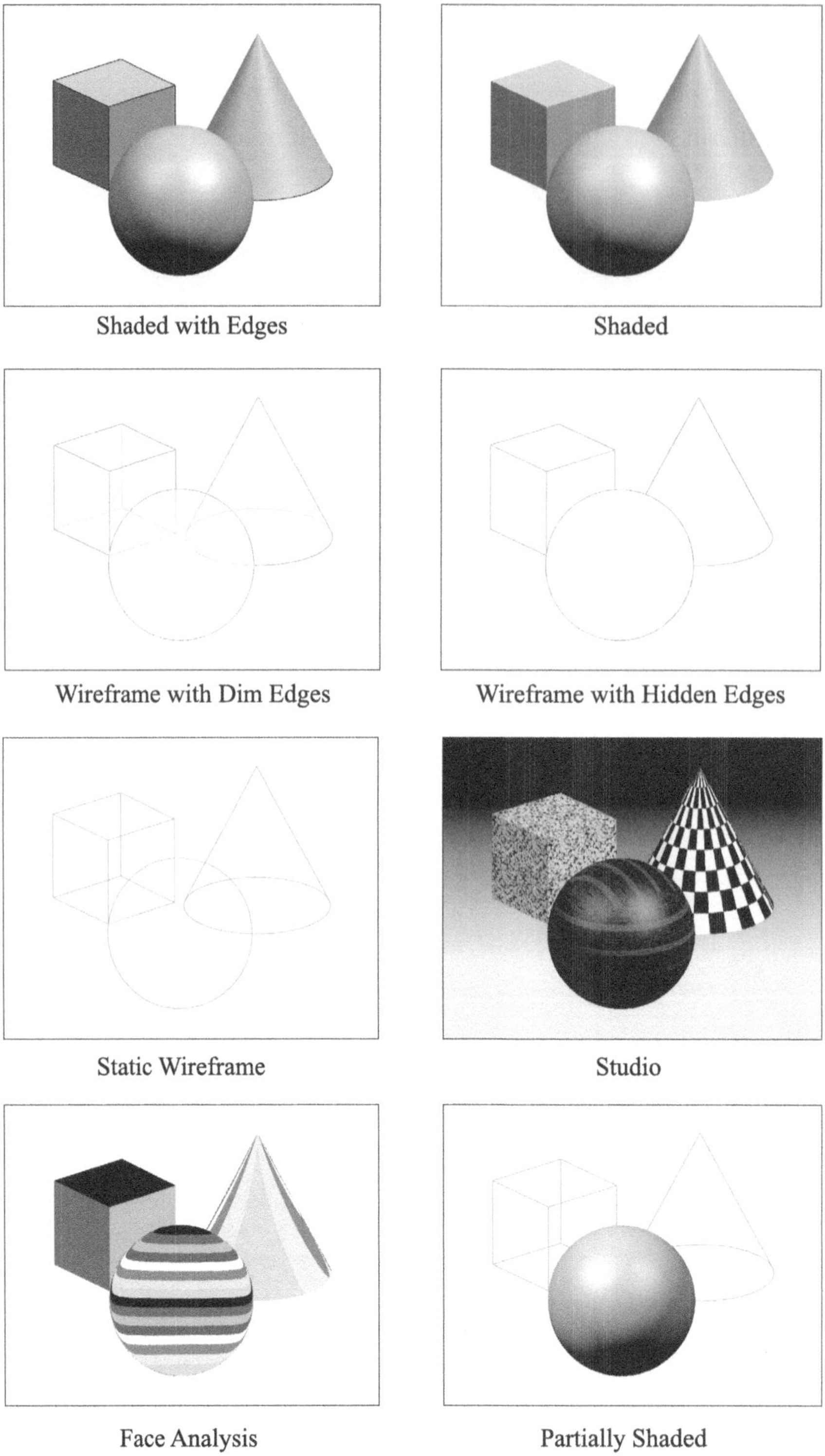

Fig 1-47 Rendering Style

⑧ Orient View

You can apply a pre-defined view direction. Either the **Trimetric** or **Isometric** view orientation is appropriate to recognize the 3D shape. You can apply the **Trimetric** view orientation by pressing the **Home** key in the keyboard.

Fig 1-48 Orient View

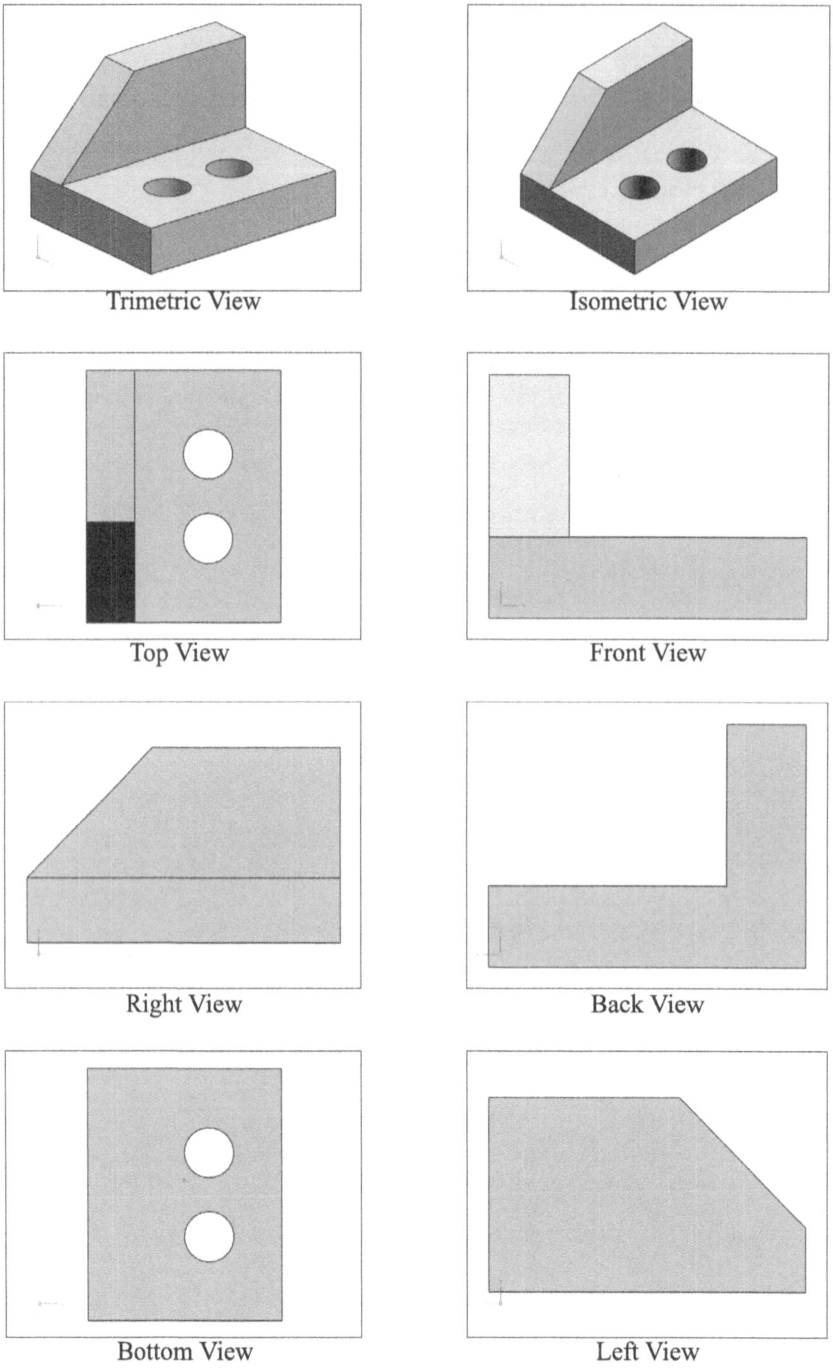

Fig 1-49 Orient View

⑨ Set Rotation Reference

Set the rotation reference when you rotate the model view. You can examine the geometry carefully by rotating the model around the rotation reference.

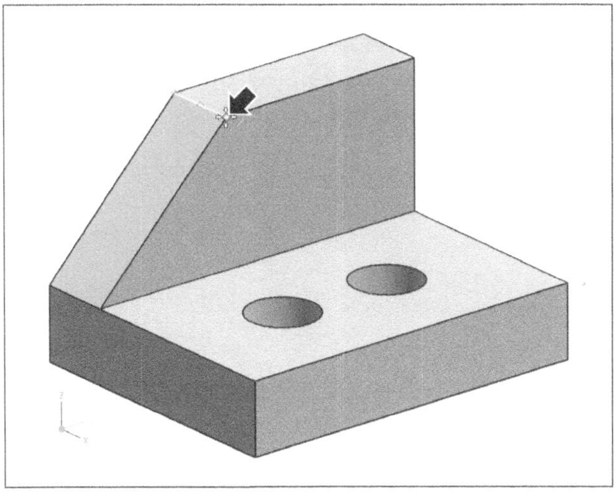

Fig 1-50 Setting the Rotation Reference at a Vertex

⑩ Clear Rotation Reference

Clear the rotation reference.

⑪ Undo

Undo the last operation.

1.8 Customer Defaults

In this section, we will set the customer defaults that will be applied whenever you execute NX. Remember that after setting the customer defaults, you have to re-execute the program.

Menu Button > File > Utilities > Customer Defaults

Fig 1-51 Customer Defaults

1.8.1 Fit Percentage

Set the view fit percentage to 80 %.

Gateway > Visualization > View/Screen > Fit View > Fit Percentage

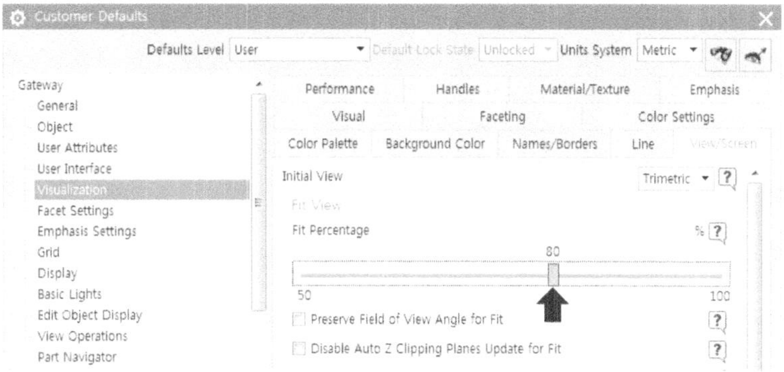

Fig 1-52 Fit Percentage

1.8.2 Distance Tolerance

You can set the distance tolerance to 0.01mm or another value according to your design condition. A smaller distance than the tolerance is considered as zero.

Modeling > General > Tolerances/Scales > Distance

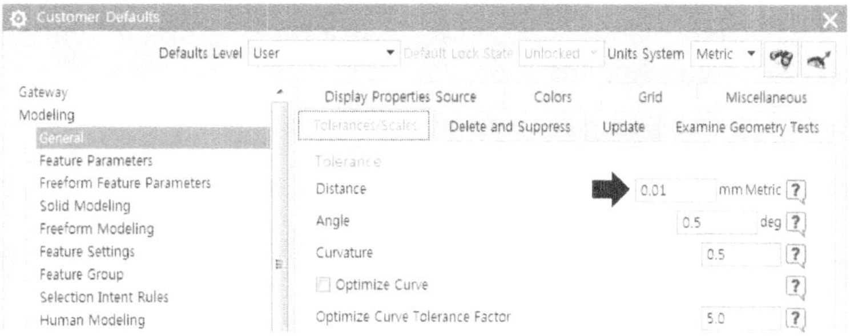

Fig 1-53 Distance Tolerance

1.8.3 Double Click Action for Sketches

Define the action when you edit a sketch.

Modeling > General > Miscellaneous > Double Click Action for Sketches
Modeling > General > Miscellaneous > Edit Sketch Action

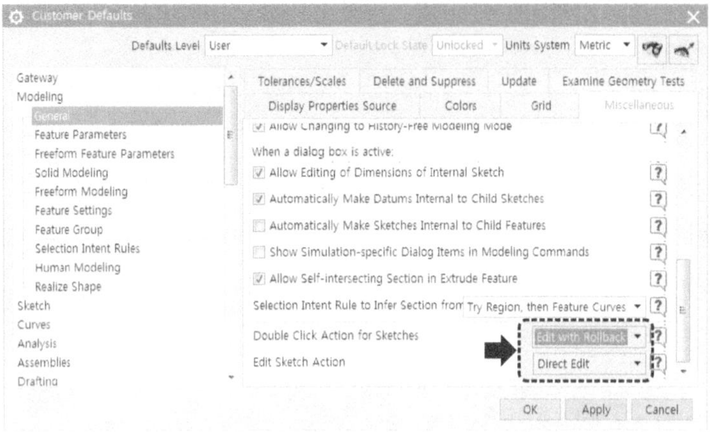

Fig 1-54 Double Click Action for Sketches / Edit Sketch Action

1.8.4 Continuous Auto Dimensioning in Design Applications

Uncheck the **Continuous Auto Dimensioning in Design Applications** option so that auto dimensioning is not applied when you draw a sketch.

Sketch > Inferred Constraints and Dimensions > Dimensions > Continuous Auto Dimensioning in Design Applications

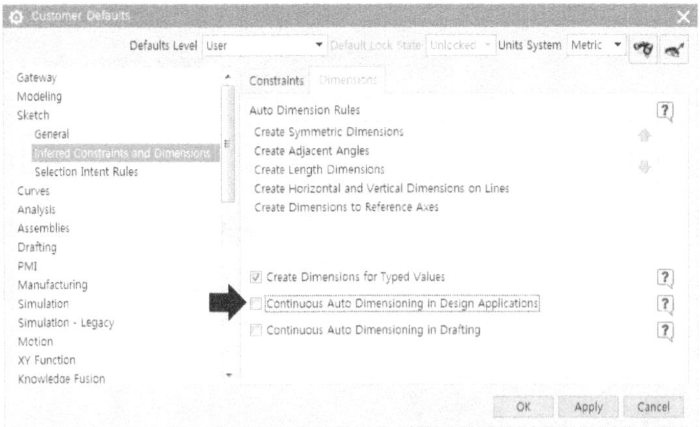

Fig 1-55 Continuous Auto Dimensioning in Design Applications

1.8.5 Tracking the Changes and Deleting

You can track the changes of the customer defaults by clicking the **Manage Current Settings** button in the **Customer Defaults** dialog box.

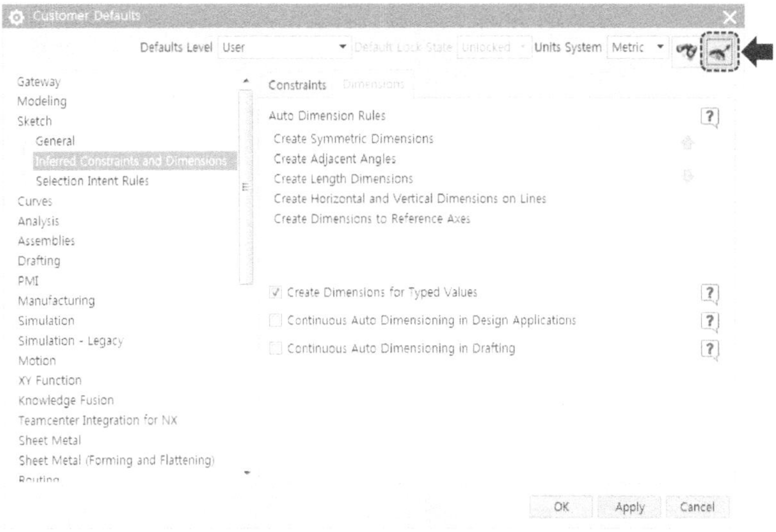

Fig 1-56 Manage Current Settings Button

You can export or import the customer defaults in the **Manage Current Settings** dialog box and delete the item to remove changes of setting. If you delete the item, the default setting is restored and applied when you re-execute NX.

Fig 1-57 Manage Current Settings Dialog Box

1.9 User Interface

You can set the user interface by choosing **Preferences > User Interface** in the **Menu** button. Modification of the user interface is ***not*** recommended for new users of NX.

Fig 1-58 User Interface Menu

1.9.1 Resetting the Information Message

When information messages are not displayed after choosing the "Don't display this message again" option in the dialog box, you can show the messages again by resetting the option in the **General** tab in the **User Interface Preferences** dialog box as shown in Fig 1-59.

1.9.2 Resetting the Window Position

The types and location of toolbars can be reset in the **Layout** tab in the **User Interface Preferences** dialog box. If you press the **Reset Window Position**, the location of the NX sub-windows such as **Resource Bar, Selection Bar**, etc. is reset. You can set the location and type of the **Resource Bar** by using the option in the **Display Resource Bar** dropdown.

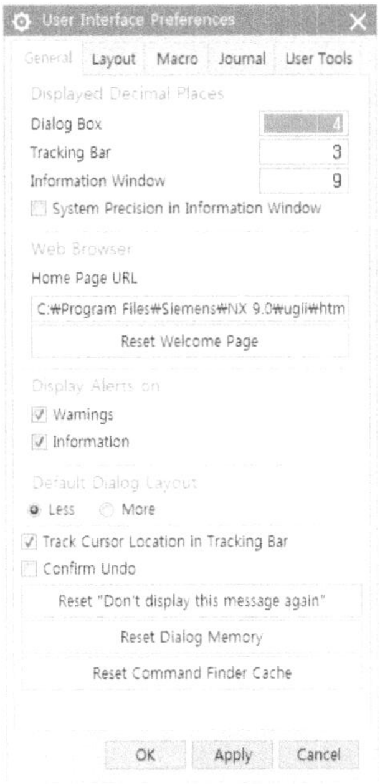

Fig 1-59 General Tab

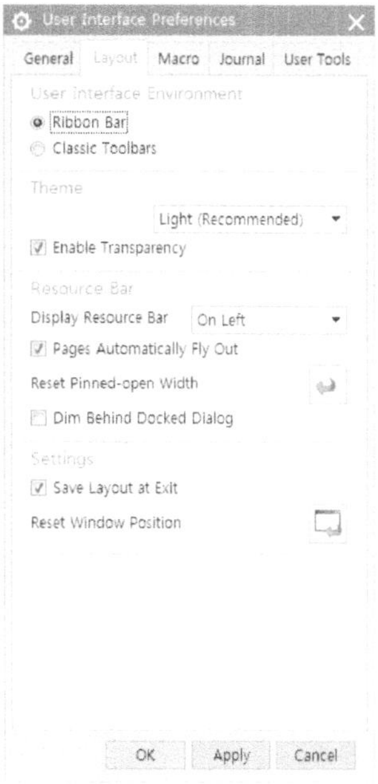

Fig 1-60 Layout Tab

This page left blank intentionally.

Chapter 2

Modeling Process with NX

■ After completing this chapter you will understand

- key concepts of three dimensional modeling.
- the modeling process of NX.

2.1 Terms and Concepts

2.1.1 Three Dimensional Modeling

All objects in the real world are three dimensional. However thin an object may be, it has thickness and therefore volume. Three dimensional shapes cannot be realized in two dimensions. We cannot create three dimensional shapes on a sheet, but we can draw a shape so it appears to be three dimensional.

With the development of computers and graphic processors, we can now establish three dimensional shapes in a virtual space on our computer system. We can define a surface from wireframes and we can define the volume with closed surfaces. Creating three dimensional shapes on a computer is called three dimensional modeling. With the help of various three dimensional design software, we can create automobiles, airplanes, home appliances and other objects in a graphic space. We can move, rotate and zoom the model in and out in a virtual three dimensional space just as we do in real space.

2.1.2 Feature Based Modeling

Three dimensional models can be created by combining many basic features. A feature defines a basic shape through a command operation. You can define a feature using a command and several options in the feature definition dialog boxes. Therefore, a feature is understood to be the smallest unit of modeling that can be defined and modified individually. Creating three dimensional models based on the accumulation of many features is called feature based modeling.

Fig 2-1 shows some basic features which can be created by extruding or revolving wireframes. (A) and (B) can be created by extruding a rectangular or circular wireframe along one direction. (C) and (D) can be created by revolving a rectangular or circular wireframe around an axis.

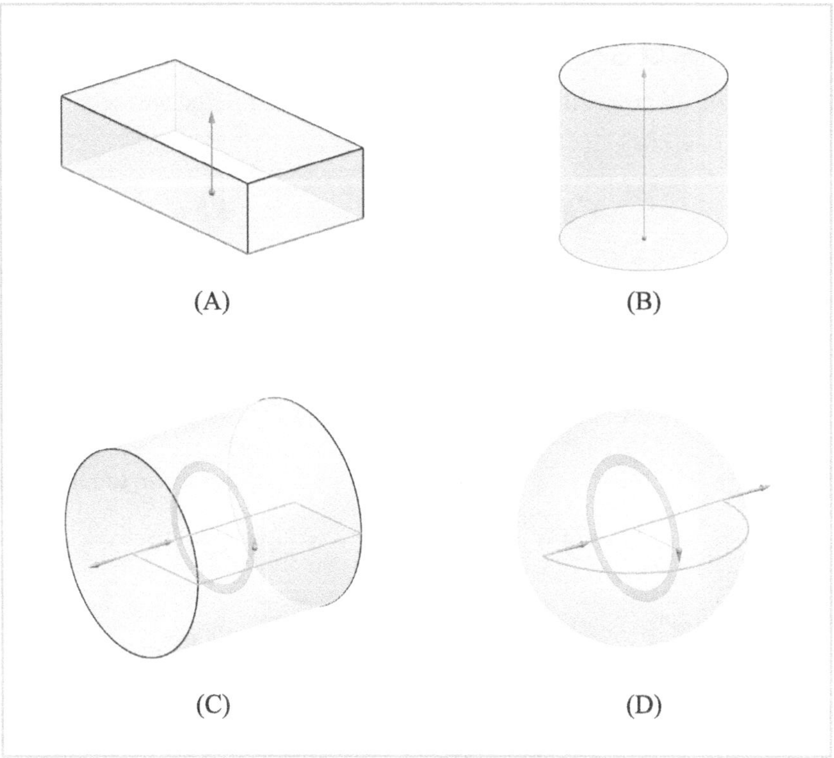

Fig 2-1 Some Basic Features

2.1.3 History Based Modeling

Features created in NX are grouped in the Part Navigator in order. Looking at the Part Navigator, you can understand the modeling history of a part. You can also modify the feature definition options by accessing the feature definition dialog box. This is called history based modeling. Fig 2-3 shows each modeling step of a part with the Part Navigator. The following explains each step.

① Create a sketch on the xy plane.
② Extrude the sketch along the Z direction with the **Extrude** command.
③ Create a second sketch on the top planar face of the geometry.
④ Extrude the sketch with the **Extrude** command and unite to the existing body.
⑤ Apply fillet to the edges.
⑥ Hollow out the body with the **Shell** command.
⑦ Create a third sketch on a side wall.
⑧ Extrude the sketch and subtract from the body.

The order of feature creation is very crucial in creating the desired model. If you apply the **Shell** command (step ❻ in Fig 2-3) before applying the **Edge Blend** (step ❺ in Fig 2-3), you will not be able to create the proper thickness for the filleted surface.

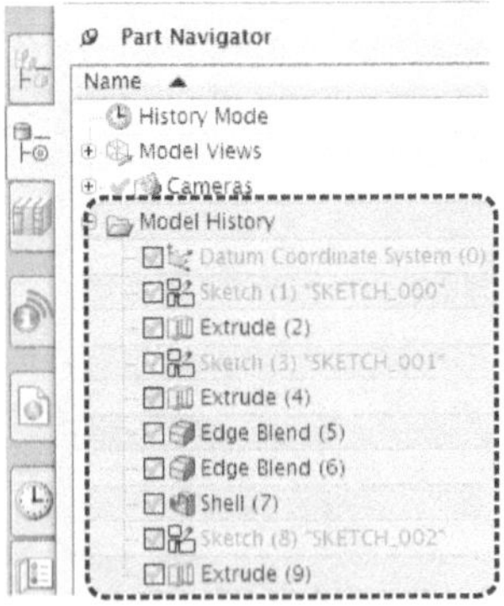

Fig 2-2 Model History

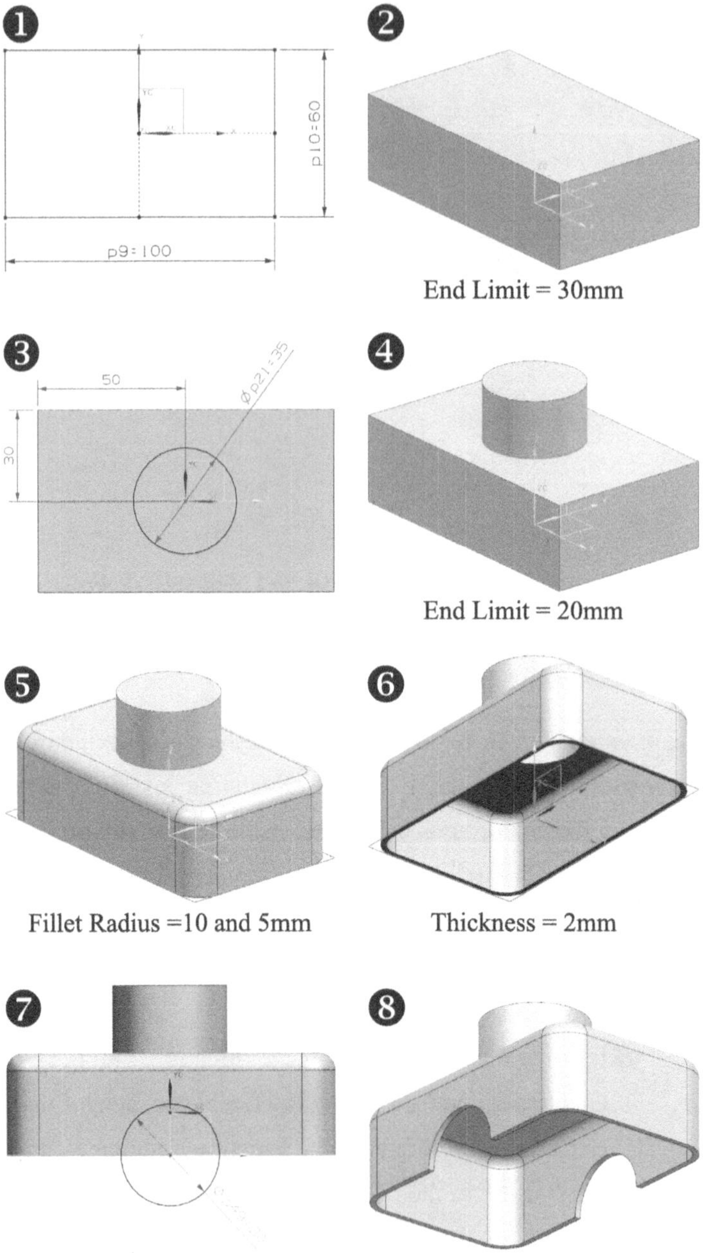

Fig 2-3 Modeling History

2.2 Introduction to NX 9.0 Modeling Process

In this section, we will learn the general process of modeling with NX 9.0 by following the steps illustrated in Fig 2-3.

2.2.1 Creating a Part File

1. Execute NX 9.0 and press the **New** icon.

Fig 2-4 New Icon

2. Select the **Model** template in the **Templates** group in the **New** dialog box.

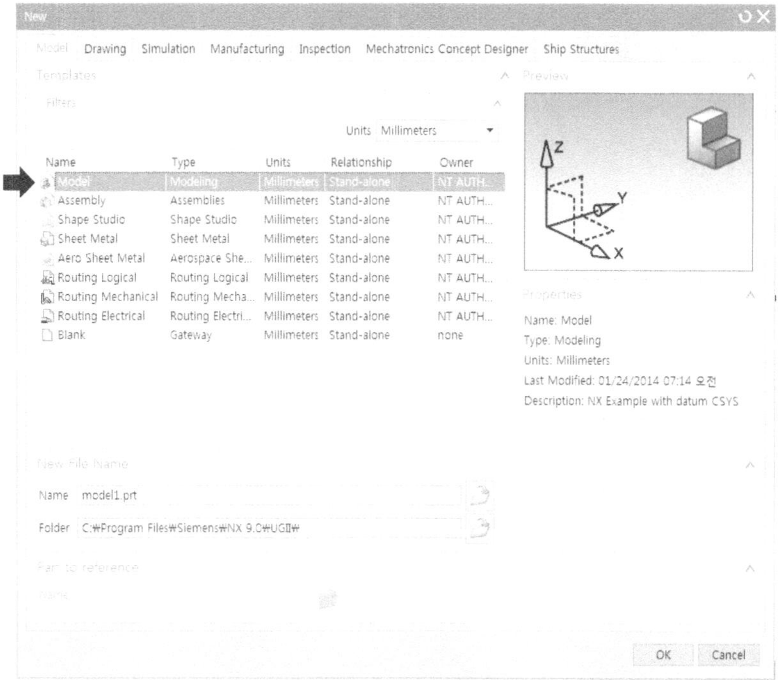

Fig 2-5 Model Template

3. Press the OK button in the lower part of the dialog box.

Fig 2-6 OK Button

A part file with a Datum Coordinate System is created as shown in Fig 2-7.

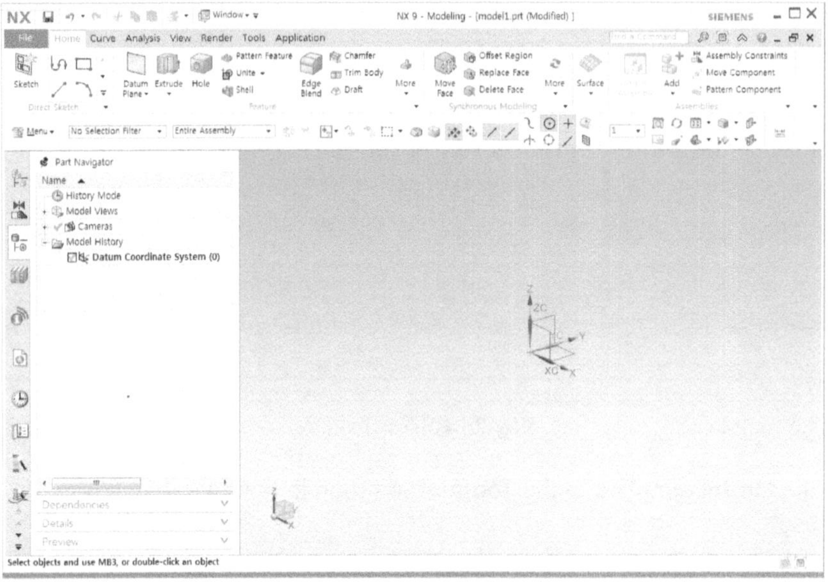

Fig 2-7 A New Part File

2.2.2 Creating the First Sketch (Step ❶ in Fig 2-3)

1. Click the **Sketch** icon in the **Home** tab.

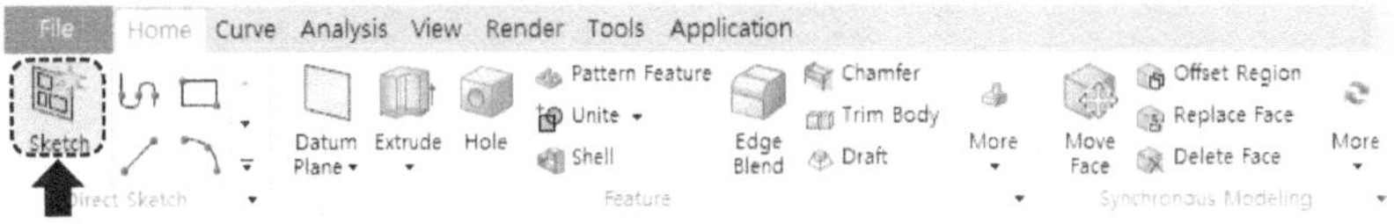

Fig 2-8 Sketch Icon

2. Press the **Reset** button in the **Create Sketch** dialog box as shown in Fig 2-9.

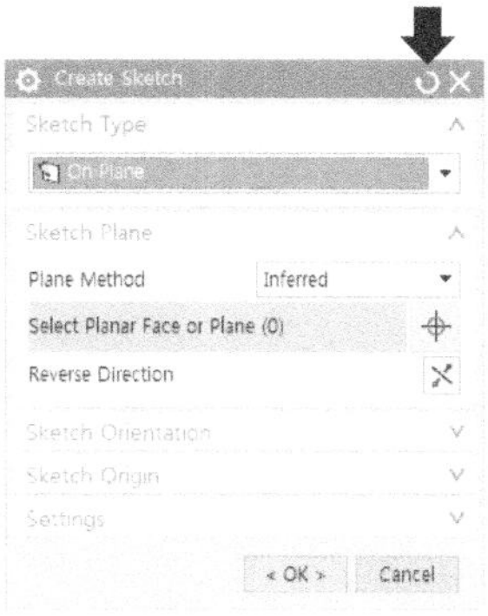

Fig 2-9 Create Sketch Dialog Box

3. Press the **OK** button in the dialog box.

Fig 2-10 OK Button

4. Confirm that the sketch plane is aligned as shown in Fig 2-11.

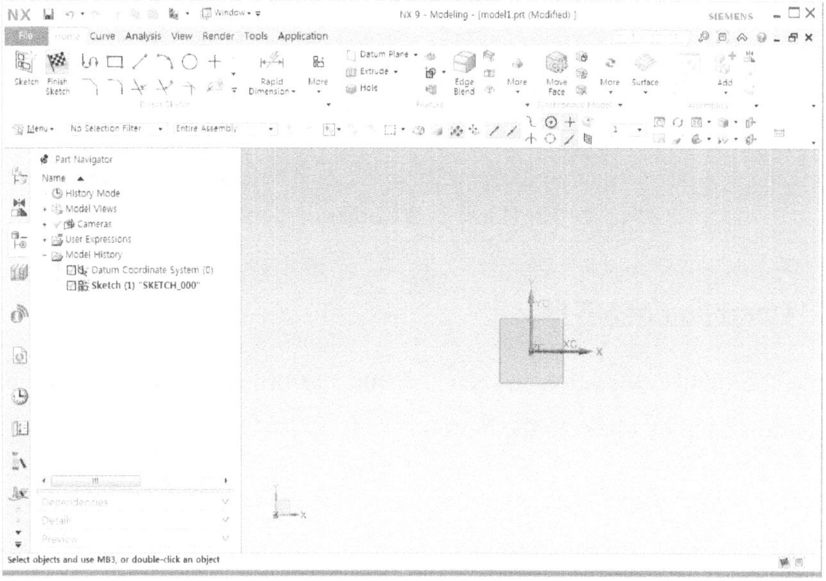

Fig 2-11 Screen of Sketch Environment

5. Click the **Rectangle** icon in the **Direct Sketch** icon group as shown in Fig 2-12.

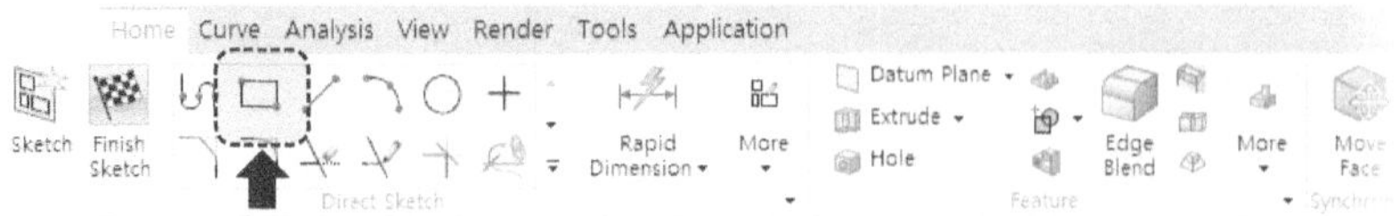

Fig 2-12 Rectangle Icon in Direct Sketch Group

6. Move the mouse pointer around the location specified by the arrow in Fig 2-13 and click MB1. The location may be different according to the reader.

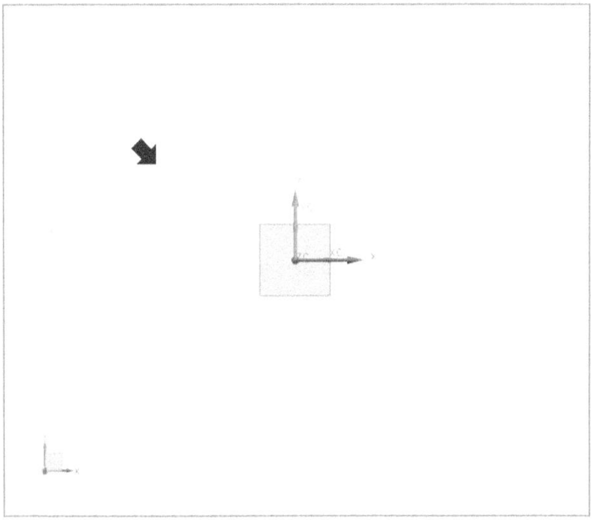

Fig 2-13 Upper Left Corner of the Rectangle

Operation of MB1

Note that the mouse operation in step 6 is not performed by dragging or holding mouse button 1 but by clicking the button.

7. Move the mouse pointer around the location specified in Fig 2-14 and click MB1.

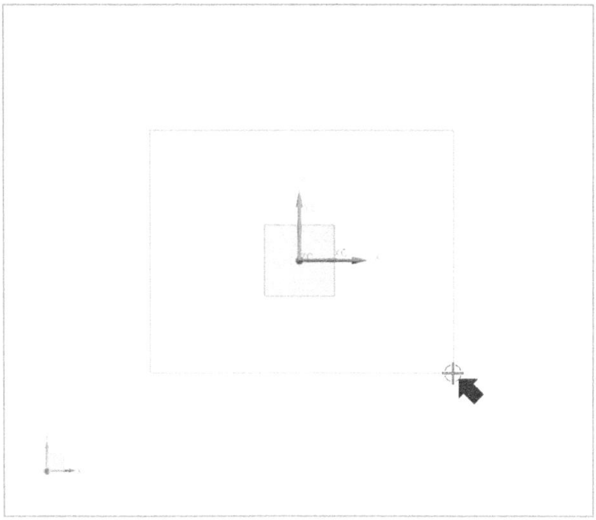

Fig 2-14 Lower Right Corner of the Rectangle

8. Confirm that a rectangle is created as shown in Fig 2-15.

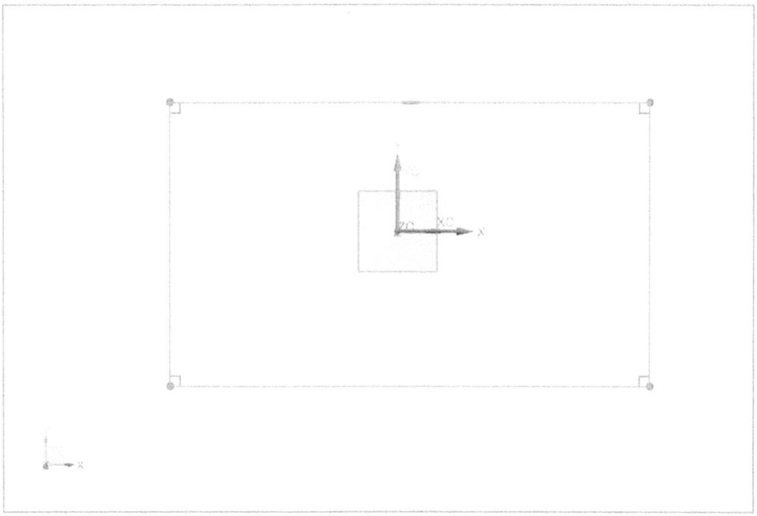

Fig 2-15 A Rectangle Created

Automatic Dimensioning

If dimensions are created automatically in Fig 2-15, uncheck the **Continuous Auto Dimensioning in Design Applications** option as explained in Section 1.8.4 on Page 30. Note that you have to exit NX and execute it again.

9. Click the **More** button in the **Direct Sketch** icon group in the **Home** tab and click the **Geometric Constraints** icon.

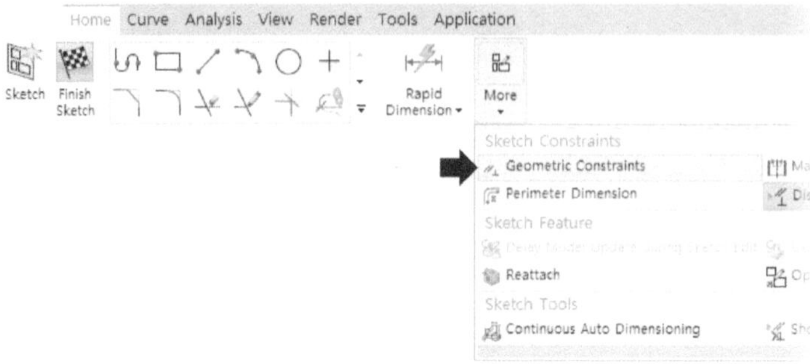

Fig 2-16 Geometric Constraints Icon

10 Press OK in the information box shown in Fig 2-17.

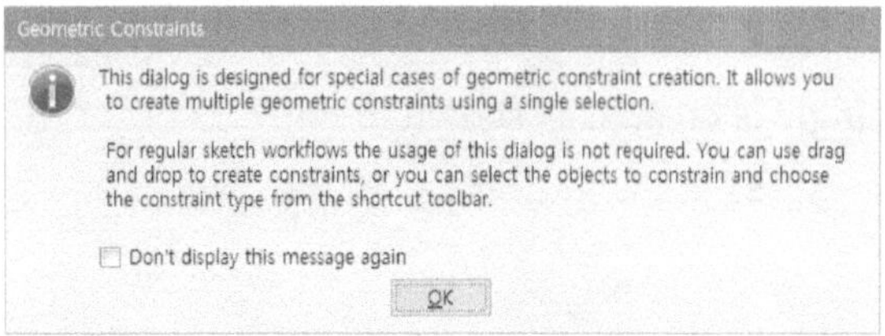

Fig 2-17 Information Box

11. Click the Midpoint button in the Geometric Constraints dialog box as shown in Fig 2-18.

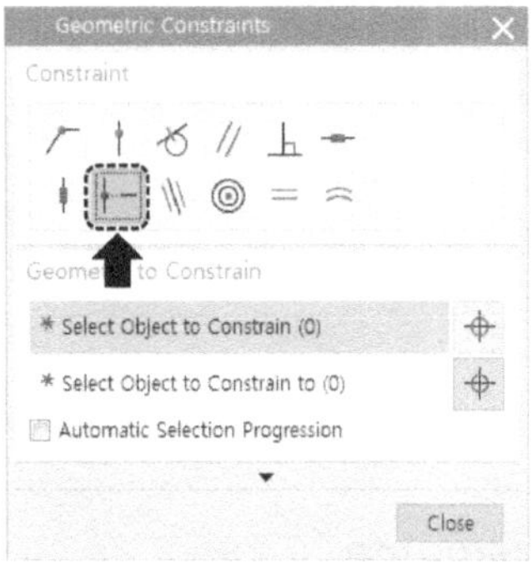

Fig 2-18 Geometric Constraints Dialog Box

12. Select the line specified by the arrow in Fig 2-19 and click MB2(mouse button 2 or the wheel).

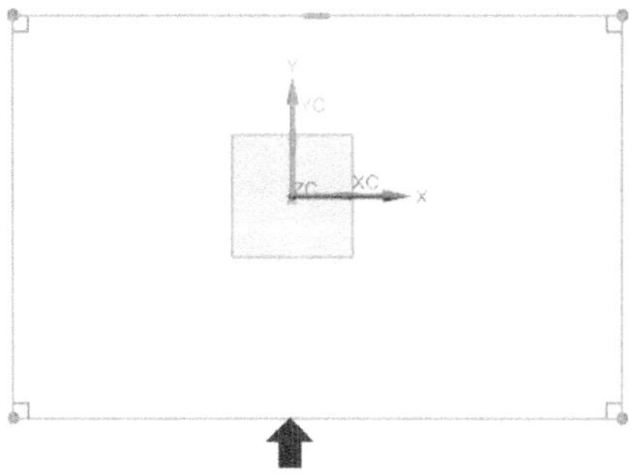

Fig 2-19 Selecting the Line

13. Select the origin as specified by the arrow in Fig 2-20. The Midpoint constraint is applied and the line moves to satisfy the given geometric constraint as shown in Fig 2-21.

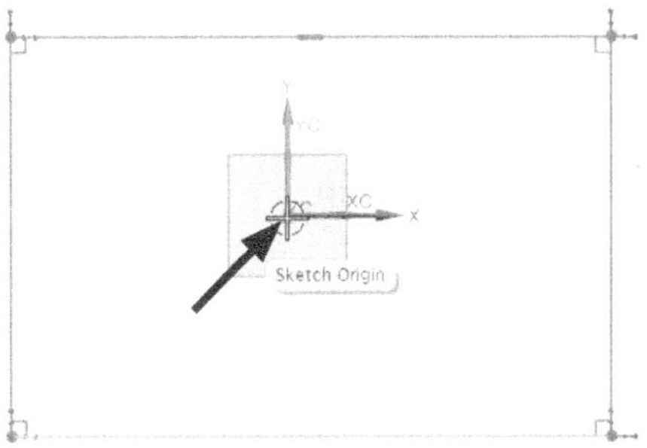

Fig 2-20 Location of Origin

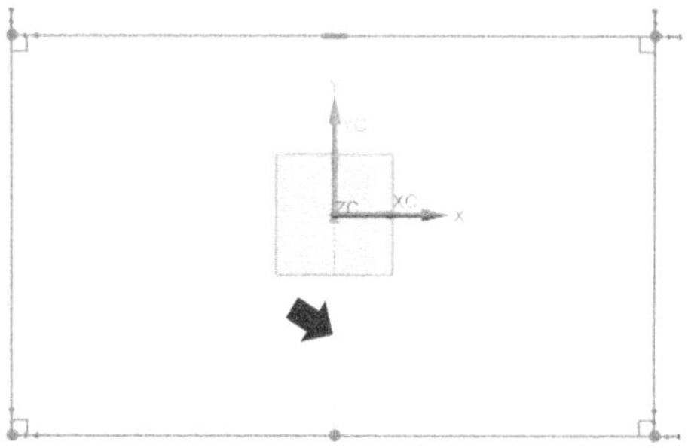

Fig 2-21 Result of Midpoint Constraint

14. Note that the Geometric Constraint dialog box is not closed. If you have closed the dialog box, click the Geometric Constraint icon to re-open it.
15. Click the Midpoint button in the dialog box and select the vertical line as specified in Fig 2-22. If the information box shown in Fig 2-17 appears, check the option "Don't display this message again."

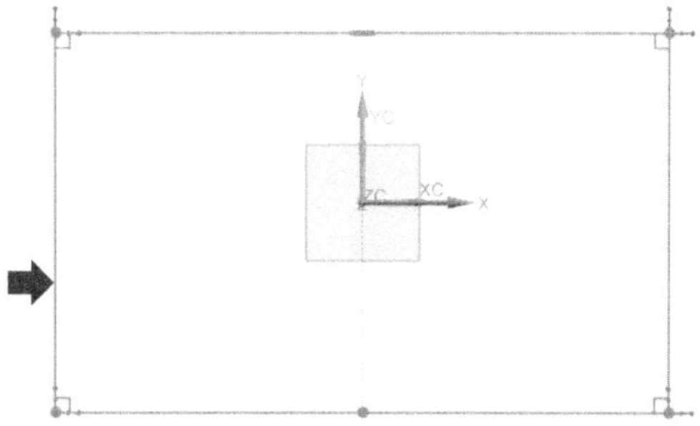

Fig 2-22 Selecting the Vertical Line

16. Click the middle button of the mouse or the wheel (MB2).

17. Select the origin as the object to constrain to. The Midpoint constraint is applied as shown in Fig 2-23.

18. Close the Geometric Constraint dialog box by pressing the Close button in the dialog box.

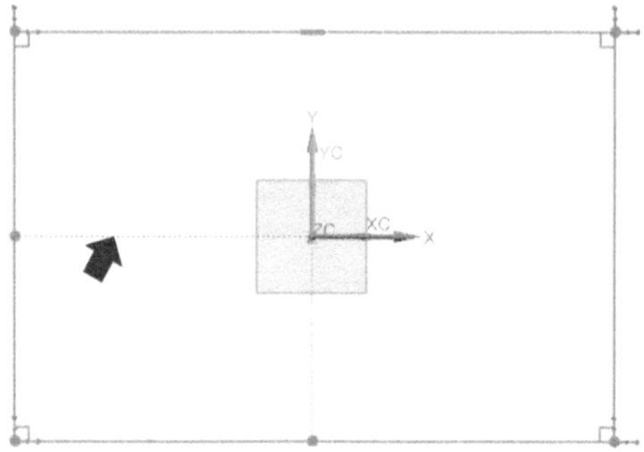

Fig 2-23 Result of the Second Midpoint Constraint

19. Click the Rapid Dimension icon in the Direct Sketch icon group.

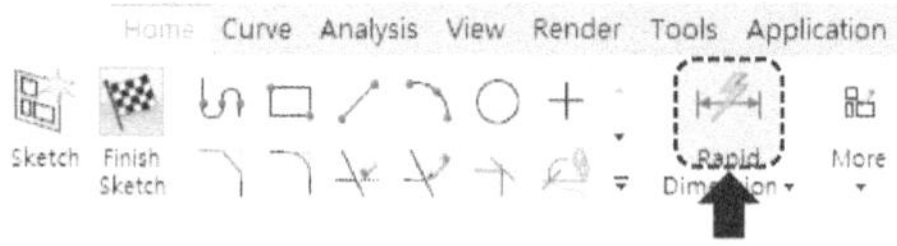

Fig 2-24 Rapid Dimension Icon

20. Select the two lines specified by ❶ and ❷ as shown in Fig 2-25.

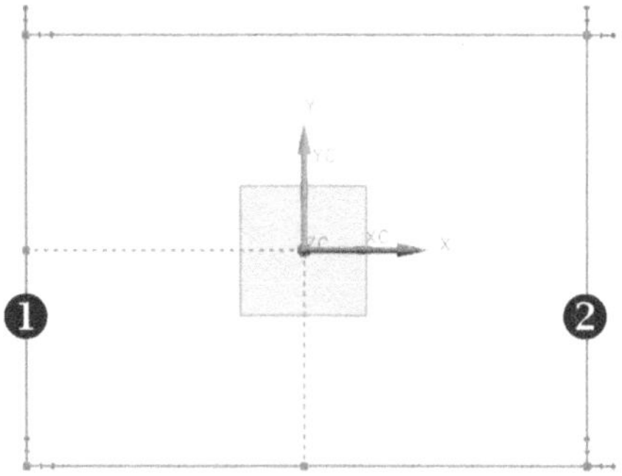

Fig 2-25 Selecting the Two Lines

21. Note that a dimension value appears on the mouse pointer. Move the dimension text under the lower horizontal line as shown in Fig 2-26.

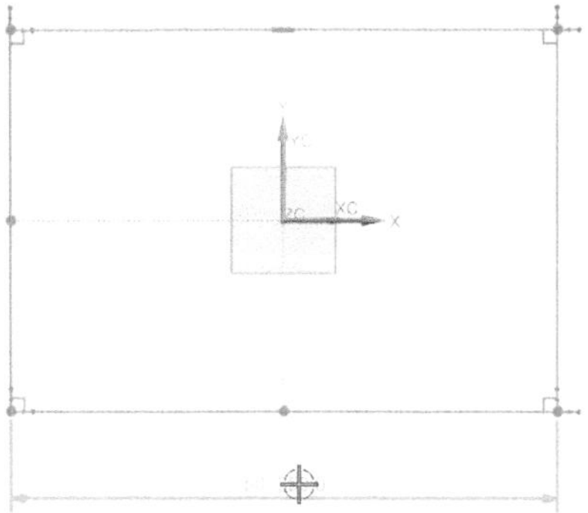

Fig 2-26 Location of the Dimension Value

22. Click MB1 to specify the location of the dimension as shown in Fig 2-32.
23. Modify the value to 100 in the input box and press the **Enter** key on the keyboard.
24. Confirm that the horizontal distance between the two lines has been modified to the specified value.

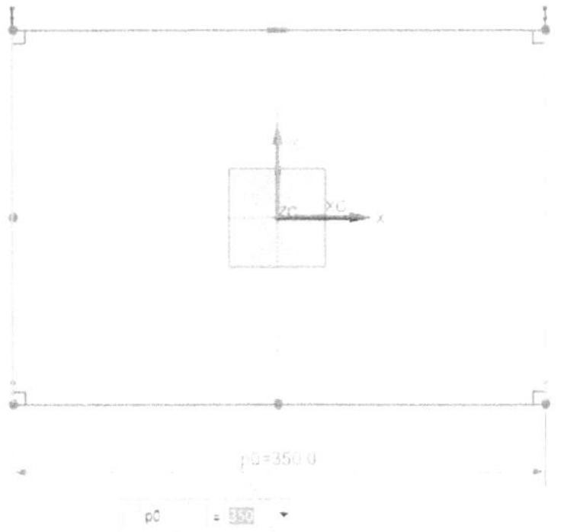

Fig 2-27 Locating the Dimension

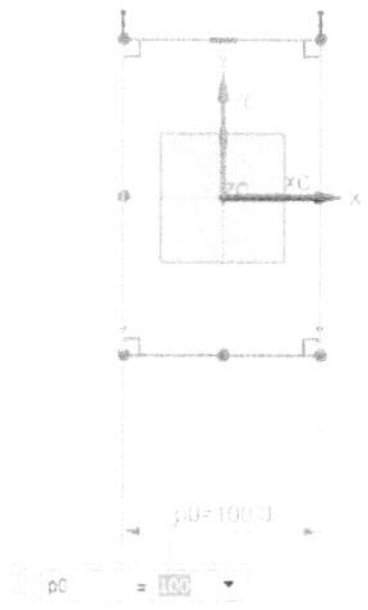

Fig 2-28 Modifying the Value

! *p0 = 350*

Note that the dimension is expressed in p0=350. p0 is the name of the parameter and 350 is its value. Your parameter name and value may be different from those in the textbook.

! *Press the Enter Key after Modifying a Value*

Pressing the **Enter** key allows you to preview the result of the modification. When you modify a value in the dialog box, it is recommended that you press the Enter key before pressing the **OK** button.

25. Repeat steps 19 through 24 to define a 60mm vertical distance between the two lines as shown in Fig 2-29.
26. Close the **Rapid Dimension** dialog box.

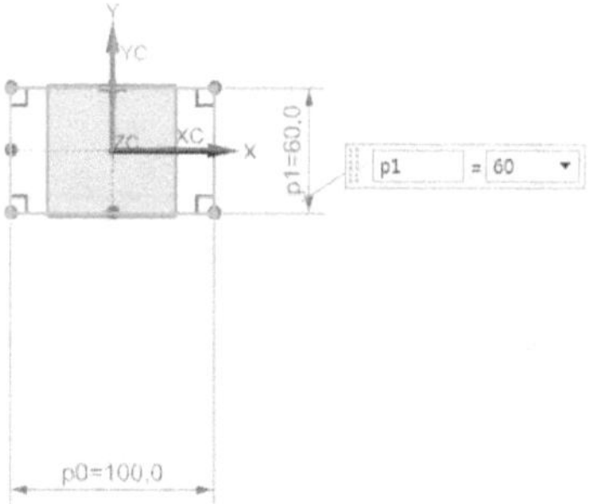

Fig 2-29 Vertical Dimension

27. Drag the dimensions to a new location as shown in Fig 2-30.
28. Press Ctrl + F to fit the model.

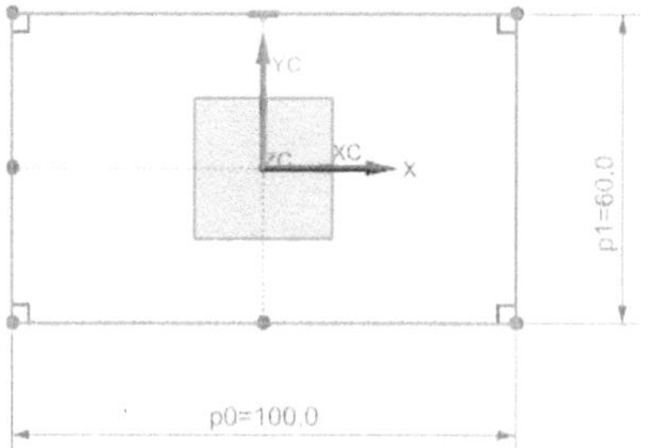

Fig 2-30 Sketch Completed

29. Press the **Finish Sketch** icon in the **Direct Sketch** icon group.

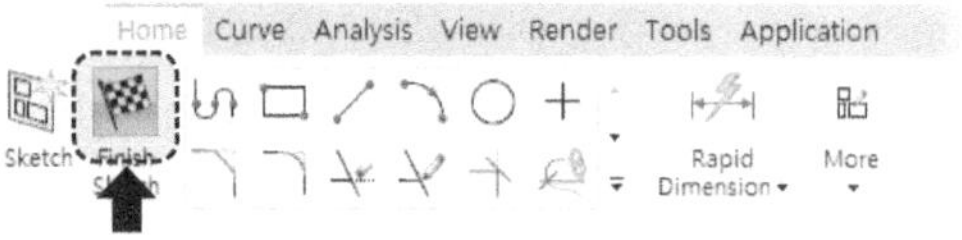

Fig 2-31 Finish Sketch Icon

30. Press the **Home** key on the keyboard.

Note that the model view rotates as shown in Fig 2-32. You can recognize the sketch feature in the Part Navigator as shown in Fig 2-33.

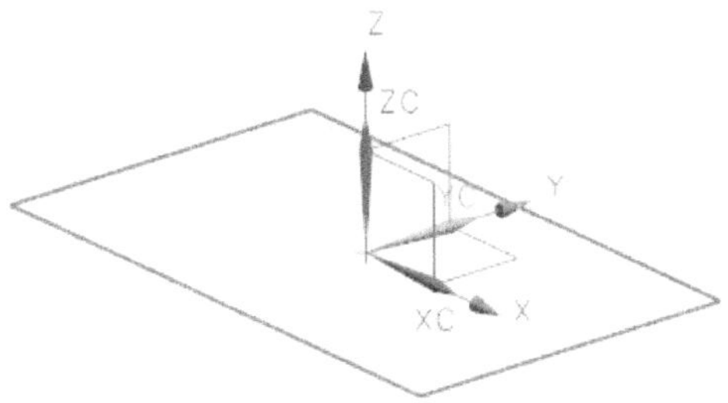

Fig 2-32 First Sketch Completed

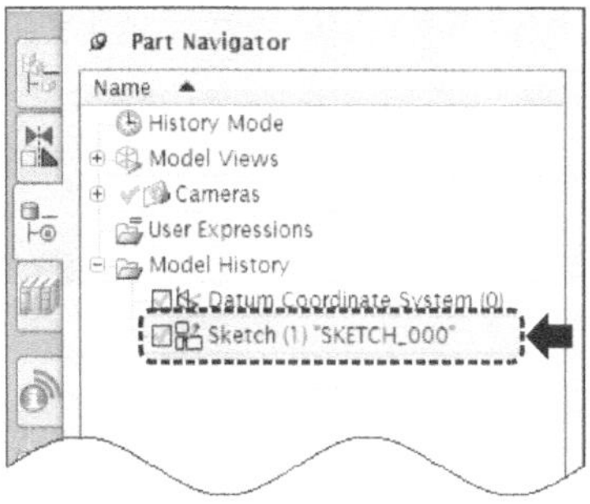

Fig 2-33 Sketch Feature

2.2.3 Extruding the Sketch (Step ❷ in Fig 2-3)

1. Click the **Extrude** icon in the **Feature** icon group.

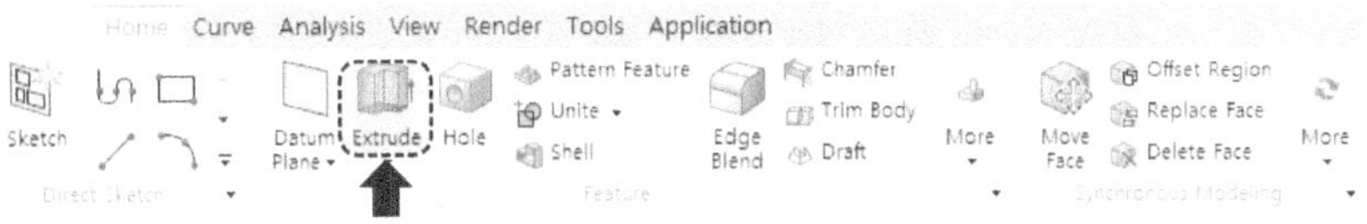

Fig 2-34 Extrude Icon in the Feature Icon Group

2. Press the **Reset** button in the **Extrude** dialog box.

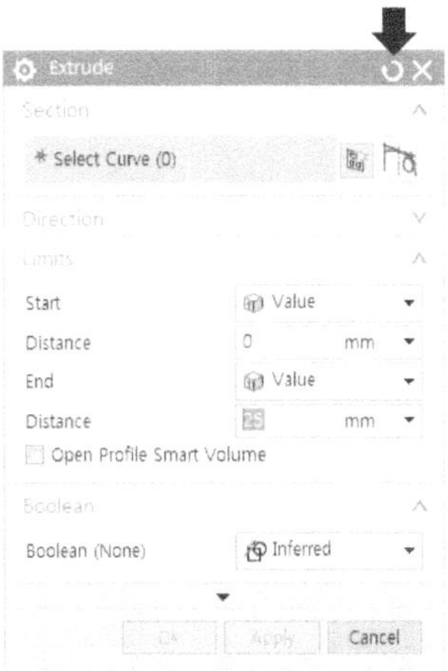

Fig 2-35 Reset Button in the Extrude Dialog Box

3. Select one of the four sketch lines shown in Fig 2-36.

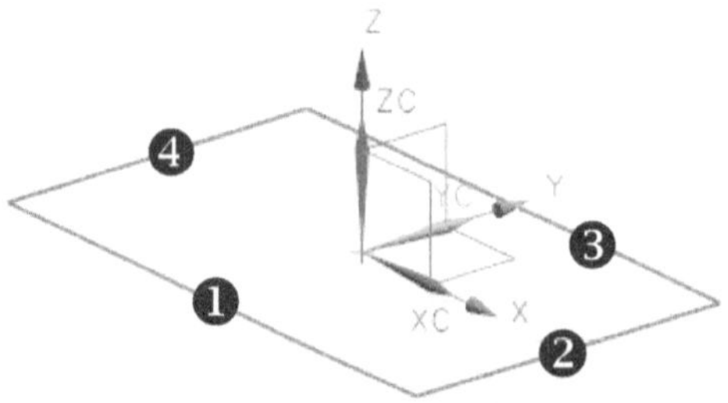

Fig 2-36 Four Lines

4. A preview of the extruded feature is displayed with the sketch dimensions as shown in Fig 2-37.

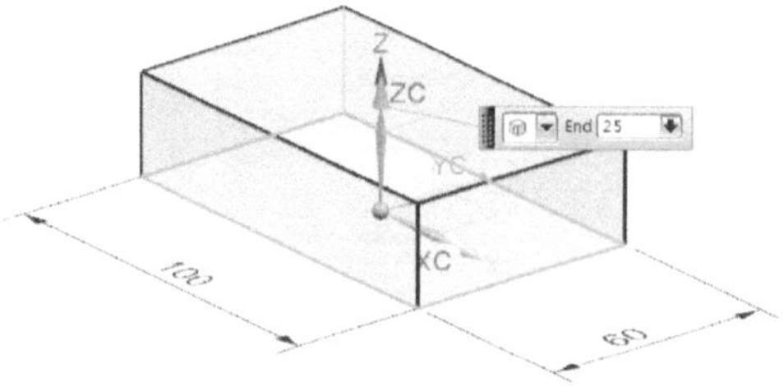

Fig 2-37 Preview of Extrude Feature

5. Enter 30 in the **Distance** input box as shown in Fig 2-38 and press the **Enter** key.
6. Press the **OK** button in the **Extrude** dialog box.

A solid body is created as shown in Fig 2-39.

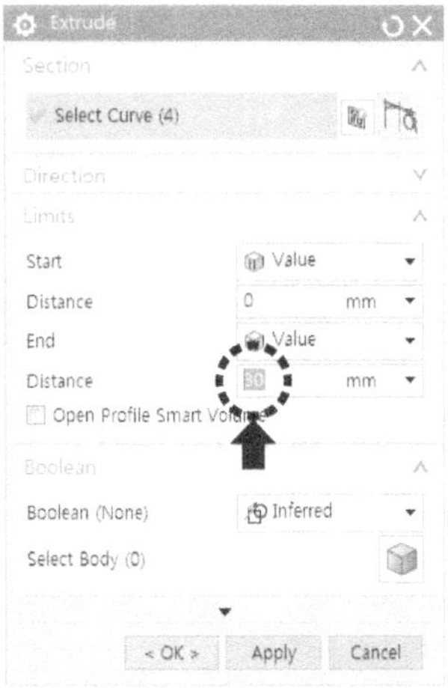

Fig 2-38 30mm of End Distance

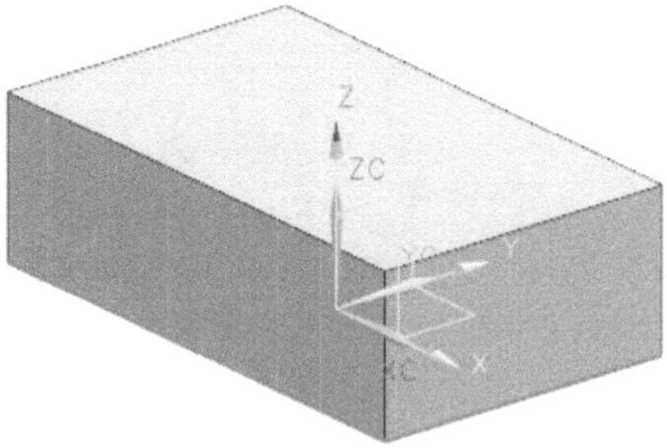

Fig 2-39 A Solid Body Created

2.2.4 Creating the Second Sketch (Step ❸ in Fig 2-3)

1. Click the **Sketch** icon in the **Direct Sketch** icon group.

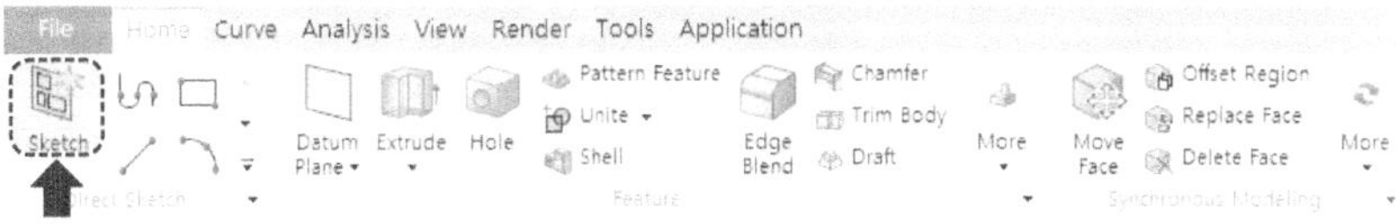

Fig 2-40 Sketch Icon

2. Select the upper plane of the hexahedron specified in Fig 2-47 as the sketch plane.

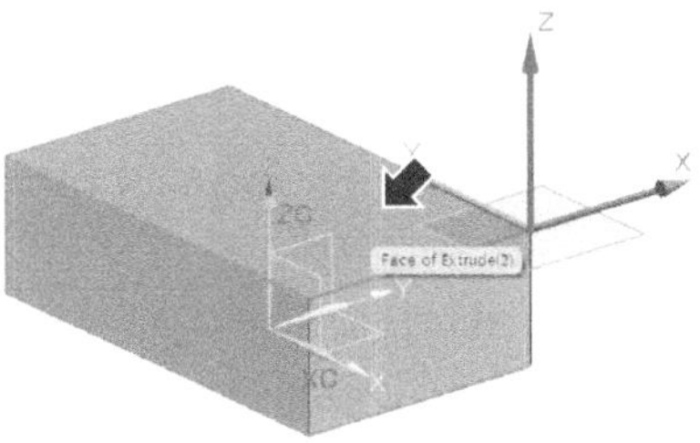

Fig 2-41 Sketch Plane

3. Press the **OK** button in the **Create Sketch** dialog box. The direct sketch is invoked. Press Ctrl + F on the keyboard.
4. Click the **Circle** icon in the **Direct Sketch** icon group.

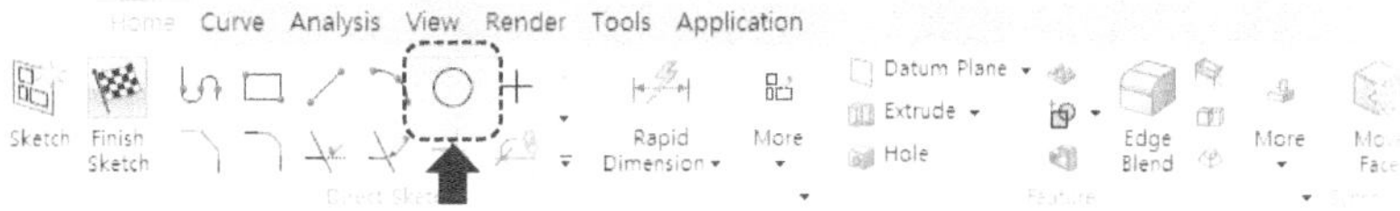

Fig 2-42 Circle Icon

5. Let's change the rendering to **Static Wireframe**. Place the mouse pointer on an empty area of the graphics window and click MB3 for two or three seconds. The radial pop-up is invoked as shown in Fig 2-43. Drag the mouse pointer to the left while pressing MB3 pressed and release the mouse.

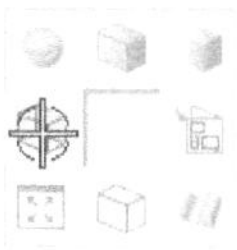

Fig 2-43 Changing the Rendering Style

6. Place the mouse pointer on the origin as shown in Fig 2-44 and click MB1 when the mouse pointer changes as pointed out by the arrow. The point is selected.

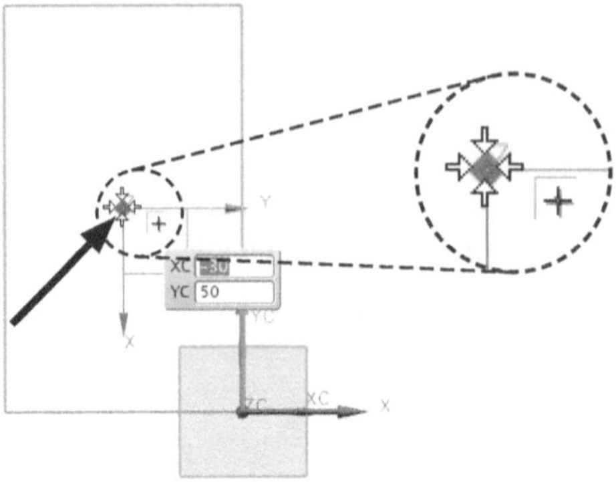

Fig 2-44 Selecting the Origin Point as the Center of the Circle

7. Create a circle and specify a 30mm diameter. You can create a diametral dimension by clicking the **Rapid Dimension** icon in the **Direct Sketch** icon group and choosing **Diametral** in the **Measurement** option.

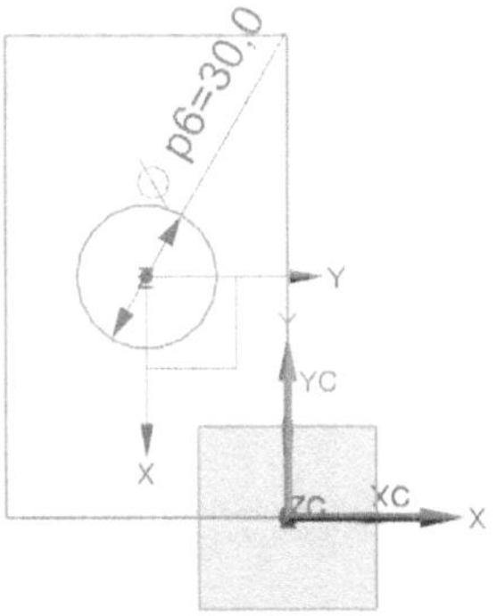

Fig 2-45 Circle Created

2.2.5 Extruding the Sketch (Step ❹ in Fig 2-3)

1. Finish the sketch and create a cylindrical geometry as shown in Fig 2-46. Click the **Extrude** icon in the **Feature** icon group and select the circle.
2. Set the **Distance** and **Boolean** options as shown in Fig 2-47.
3. Press the **OK** button in the dialog box.

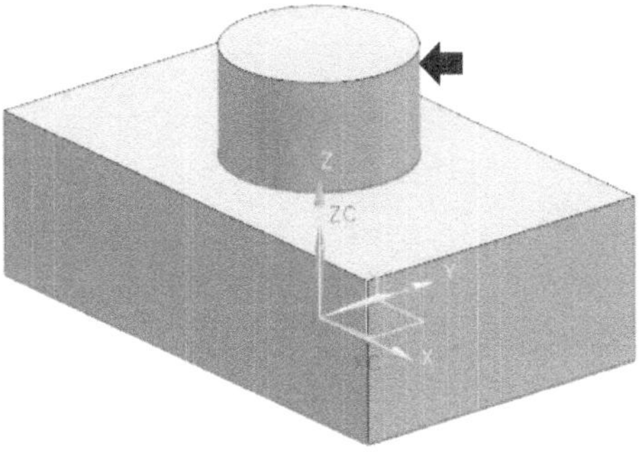

Fig 2-46 Cylindrical Geometry

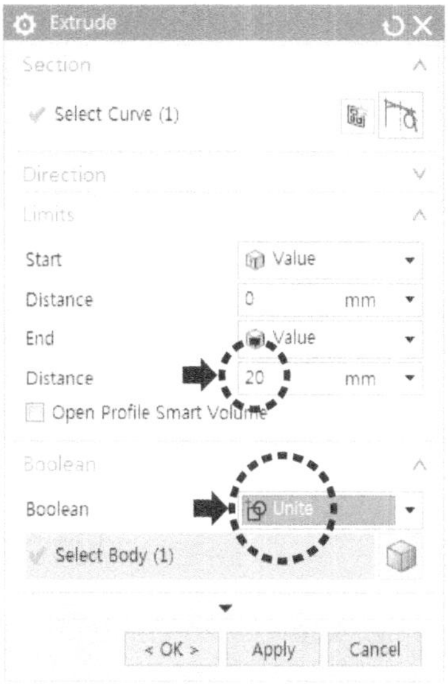

Fig 2-47 Options in Extrude Dialog Box

2.2.6 Rounding Edges (Step ❺ in Fig 2-3)

1. Click the **Edge Blend** icon in the **Feature** icon group.

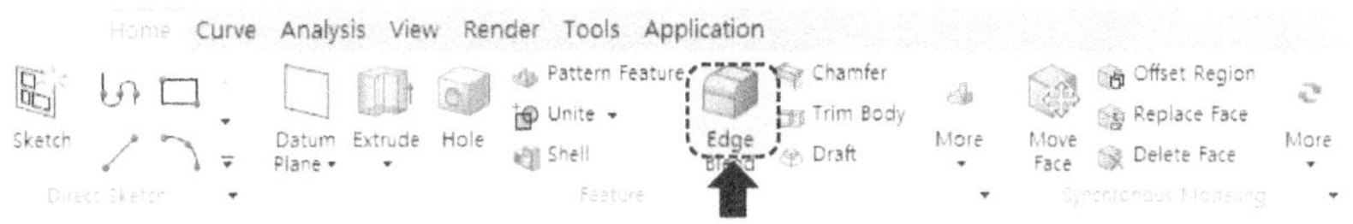

Fig 2-48 Edge Blend Icon in Feature Group

2. Reset the dialog box.
3. Enter 10 in the **Radius 1** input box and press the **Enter** key.

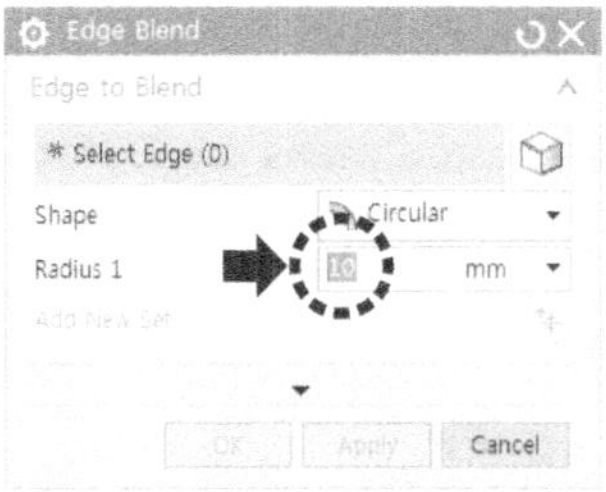

Fig 2-49 Radius 1 Value

4. Select the 4 edges specified in Fig 2-50 regardless of the order. You have to rotate the model view to select the hidden edge or change the rendering style to **Static Wireframe**.

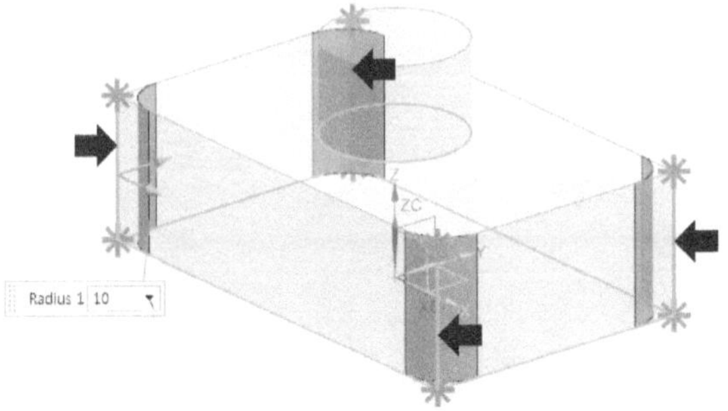

Fig 2-50 Four Edges to Select

5. Press the **Apply** button in the **Edge Blend** dialog box.
6. The 4 edges are rounded. This kind of operation is generally called a fillet. Note that the **Edge Blend** dialog box is still active.

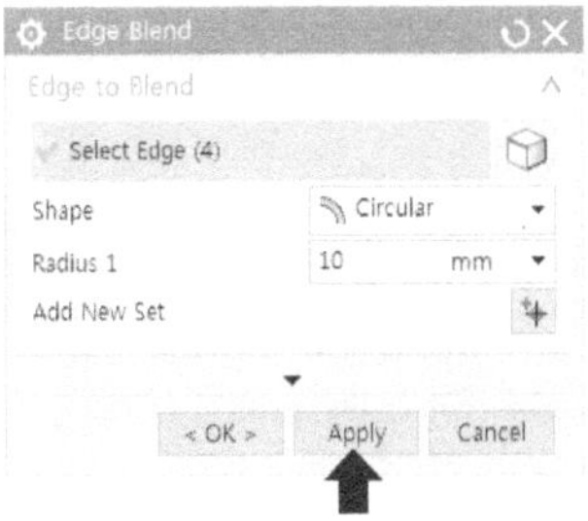

Fig 2-51 Apply Button in Edge Blend Dialog Box

! Apply

If you press the **OK** button, the dialog box is closed. Press the **Apply** button if you want to perform the command consecutively.

7. Enter 5 in the **Radius 1** input box and press the **Enter** key.
8. Select the edge specified by the arrow in Fig 2-52.

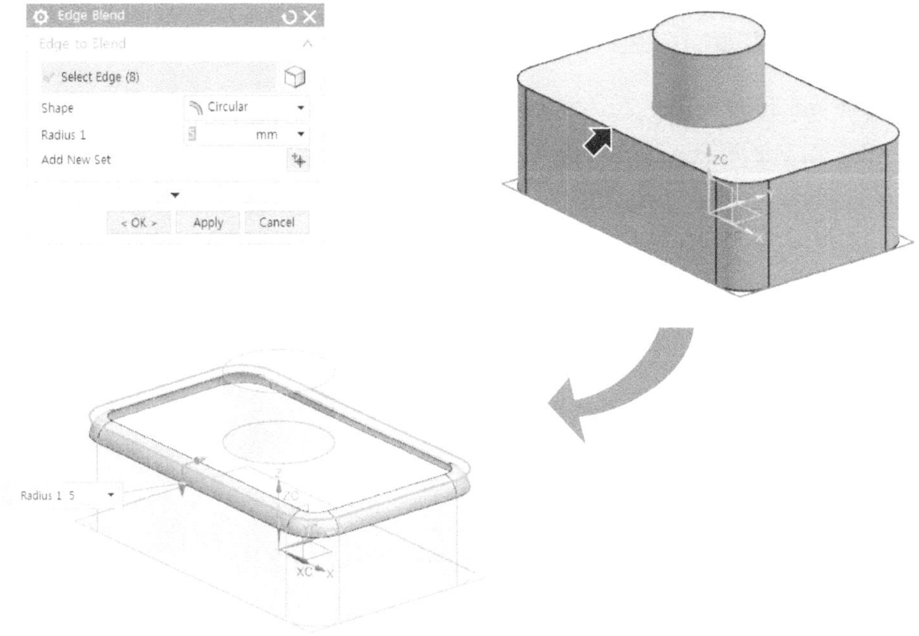

Fig 2-52 Edges to Select

9. Press the **OK** button in the **Edge Blend** dialog box.
10. Confirm that the edges are filleted as shown in Fig 2-53.

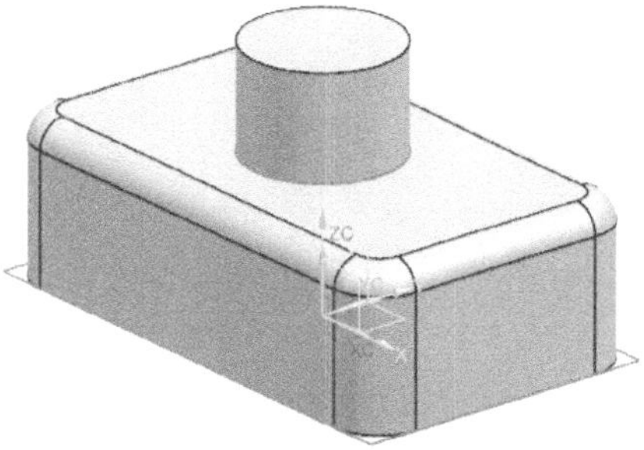

Fig 2-53 Result of Edge Blend

Curve Rule: Tangent Curves

The option specified in Fig 2-54 is called a **Curve Rule**. With the **Tangent Lines** curve rule, all curves that are tangent connected to the selected curve are selected together as shown in Fig 2-52.

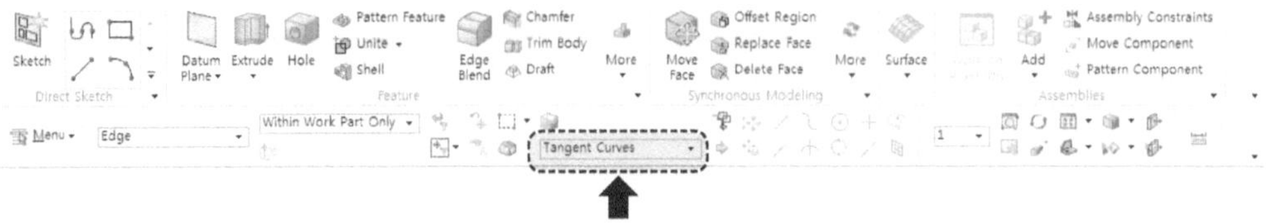

Fig 2-54 Curve Rule: Tangent Curves

2.2.7 Hollowing Out the Solid Body (Step ❻ in Fig 2-3)

1. Click the **Shell** icon in the **Feature** icon group.

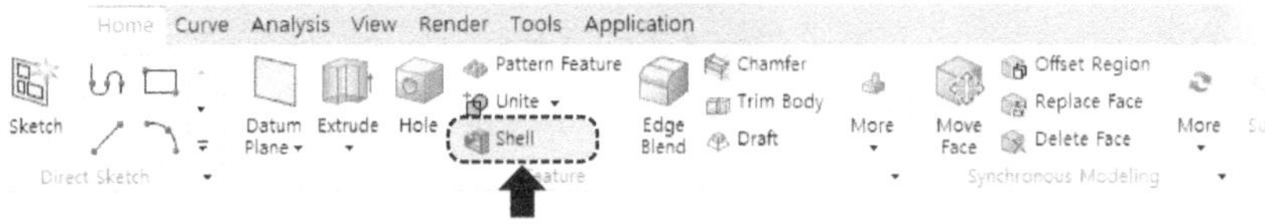

Fig 2-55 Shell Icon in Feature Icon Group

2. Reset the **Shell** dialog box.
3. Enter 2 in the **Thickness** input box in the **Shell** dialog box and press the **Enter** key.

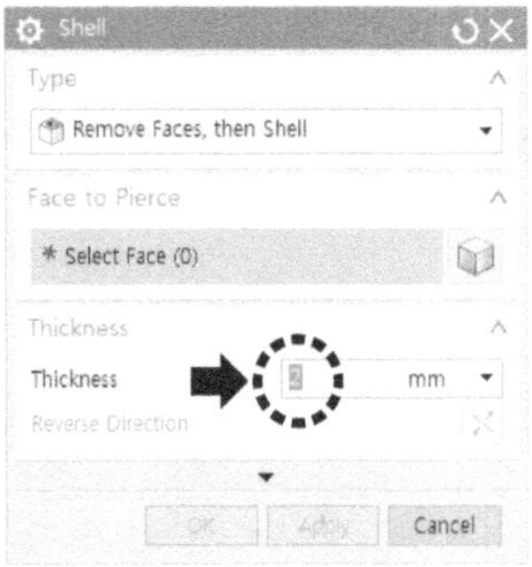

Fig 2-56 Thickness Option

4. Rotate the model view as shown in Fig 2-57 and select the bottom face specified by the arrow. The result of 2mm thick wall is previewed as shown in Fig 2-58.

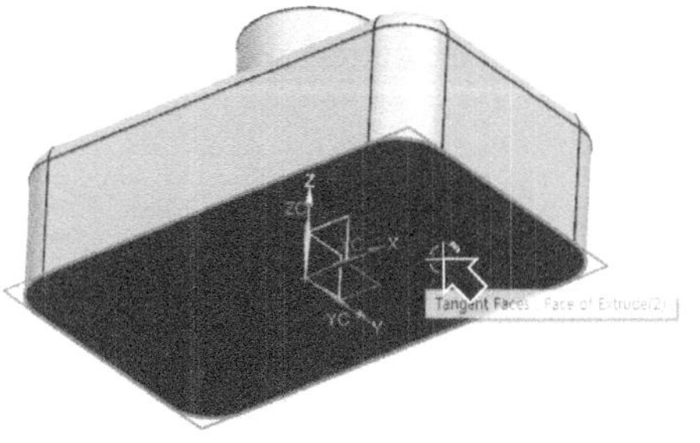

Fig 2-57 Face to Remove

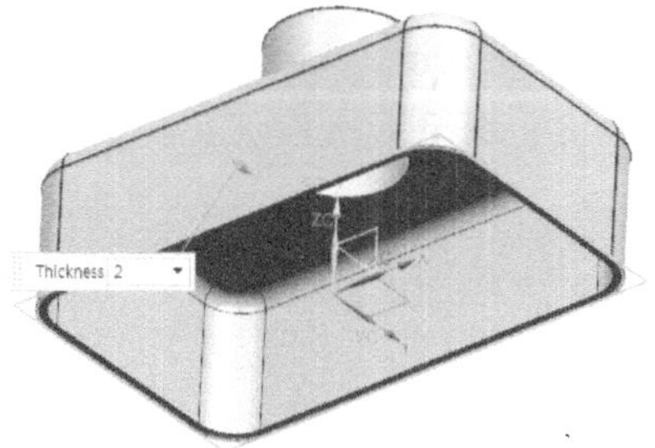

Fig 2-58 Preview of Shell

5. Press the **OK** button in the **Shell** dialog box. The Shell feature is created as shown in Fig 2-59

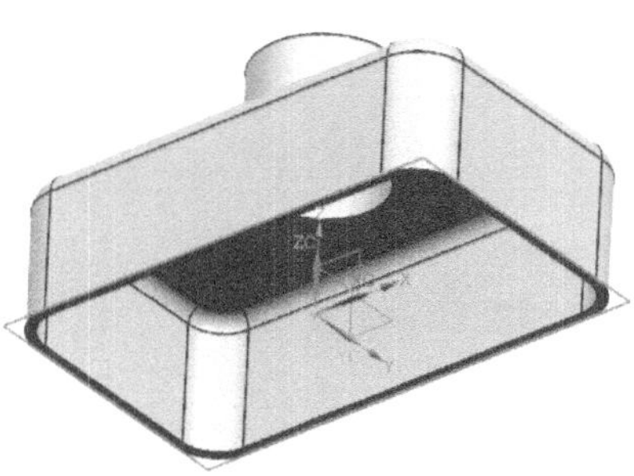

Fig 2-59 Result of Shell

2.2.8 Subtracting with a Cylinder (Steps ❼ and ❽ in Fig 2-3)

1. Press the **Home** key on the keyboard.
2. Create a sketch on the side plane as shown in Fig 2-60. Note that the center of the circle is at the midpoint of the lower edge (refer to the modeling hint on page 58).

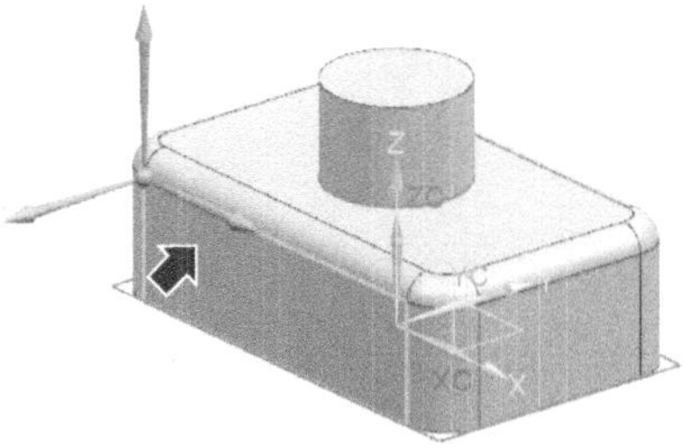

Fig 2-60 Sketch Plane

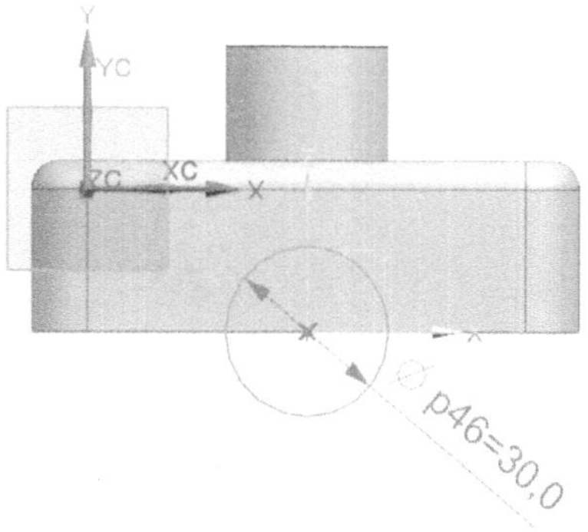

Fig 2-61 Sketch

Hint !

Change the rendering style to **Static Wireframe** and create a circle. To specify the center of the circle, click MB1 at the origin when the mouse cursor snaps the existing point as specified in Fig 2-62.

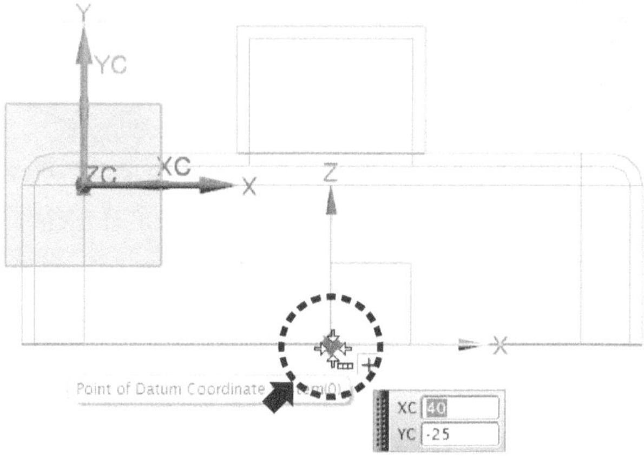

Fig 2-62 Center of Circle at the Origin

3. Extrude the circle to create a model as shown in Fig 2-74 (refer to the modeling hint below).

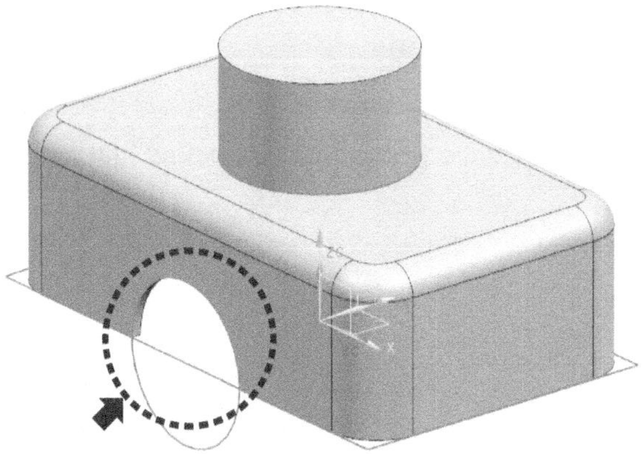

Fig 2-63 Completed Model

Hint !

Option to remove the cylinder is shown in Fig 2-64.

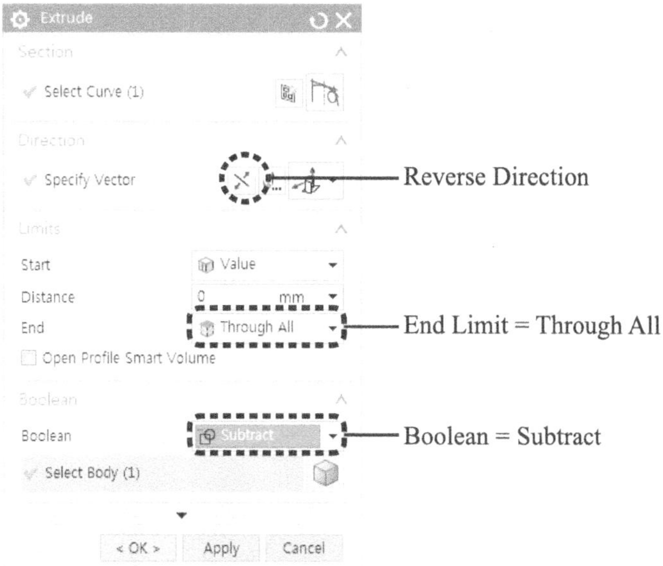

Fig 2-64 Extrude Option

2.2.9 Saving and Closing the Part File

1. Press the **Save** icon in the **Quick Access** toolbar.

Fig 2-65 Save Icon

2. Press the folder icon ( ) in the **Name Parts** dialog box as shown in Fig 2-66.
3. Designate the folder as C:\Work. If the folder does not exist, create one.
4. Enter file name as mypart.prt and press **OK** in the dialog box.

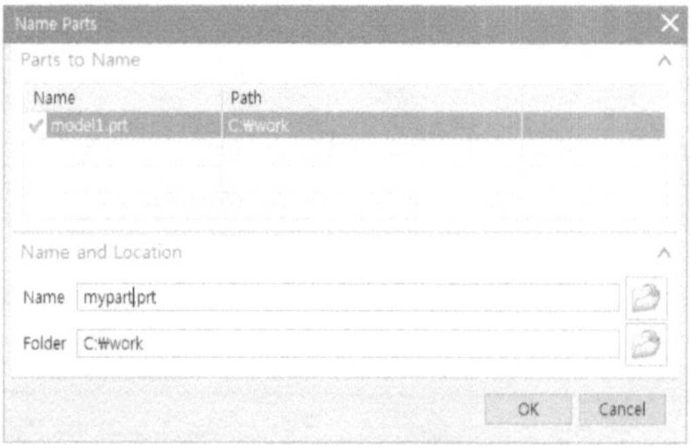

Fig 2-66 Name Parts Dialog Box

5. Press the **File** tab and choose **Close > All Parts**. The start window of NX appears as shown in Fig 2-68. Note that **History** is selected in the resource bar on the left. The recent part files are shown in the list and you can open a part file by clicking it.

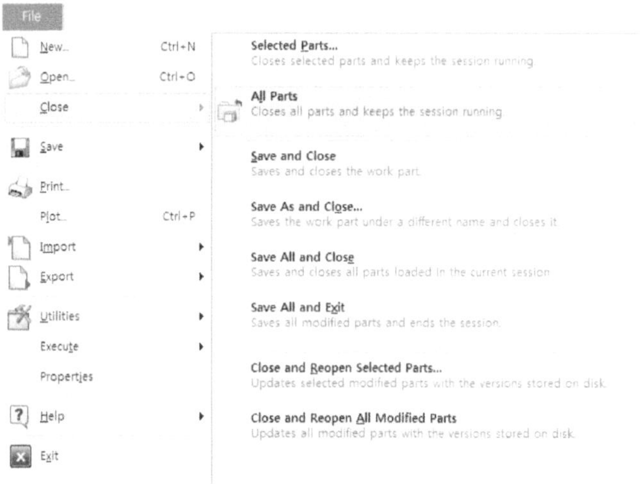

Fig 2-67 File > Close > All Parts

6. Right click on an empty area in the **History** window.

7. Choose **Clear History** in the pop-up menu as shown in Fig 2-69. The file list is cleared without deleting the file itself.

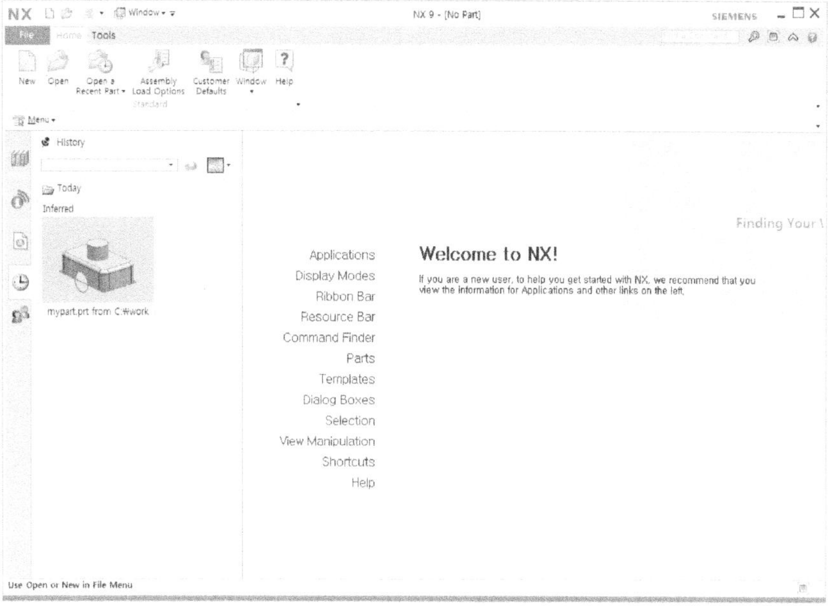

Fig 2-68 Start Window of NX

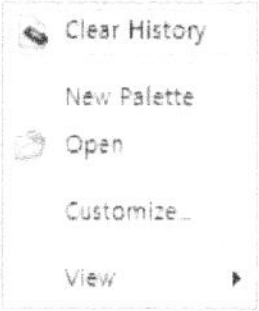

Fig 2-69 Clearing the File History

2.3 Summary of the Modeling Process

If a 3D model consists of many pads, pockets and other features, keep in mind the following guidelines to create models while avoiding mistakes.

1. Create a sketch.
   - Define the sketch plane.
   - Create the sketch curves and define their shape with constraints.

2. Create 3D geometry.
   - Create features using the **Extrude** or **Revolve** command to add or remove volumes.

3. Detail Modeling
   - Complete the model by applying commands such as **Edge Blend** and **Shell** that modify edges or faces.

In step 2 and 3, it is recommended that you create all features that add material to the body and then create features that remove material from the body. Additional features are recommended to be created at the final step. However, this is just a guideline. In practical modeling, the three steps are applied repeatedly as required. Note that if the modeling order is not properly followed, the result may differ from your desired outcome.

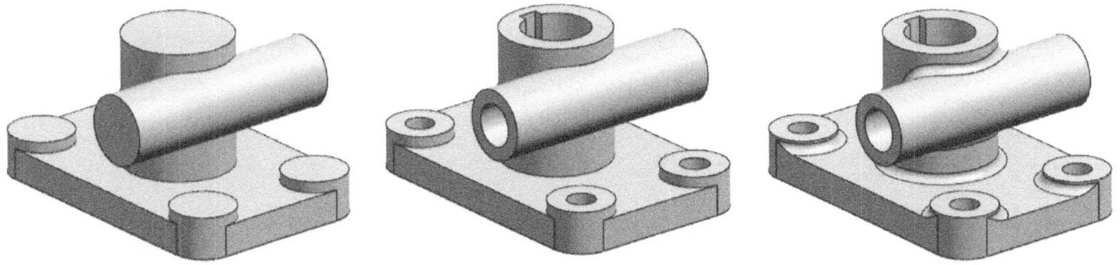

(a) Unite Bodies (b) Remove Bodies (c) Detail Modeling

Fig 2-70 General Modeling Process

Chapter 3

Sketch

■ **After completing this chapter you will understand**

- the process to create sketches.
- how to modify sketches.
- various functions for creating sketch curves.
- how to constrain sketch curves.
- how to create sketches using tools in direct sketch.

3.1 Introduction

A sketch is a feature that consists of points and curves on a plane.

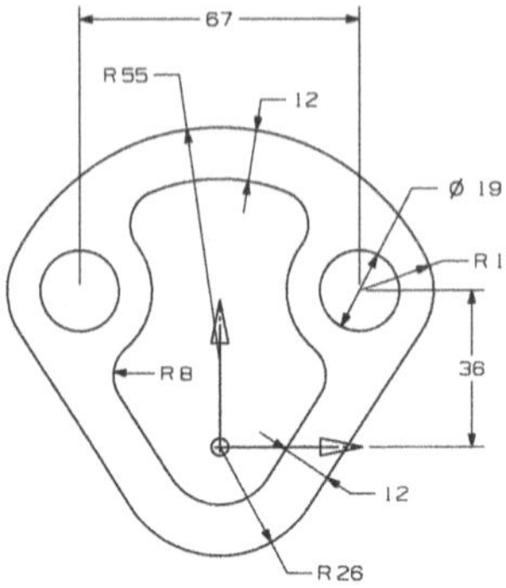

Fig 3-1 Example of a Sketch

Sketch curves are used to define a section, and the section is used to create three dimensional geometry with the **Extrude** and **Revolve** commands.

Example of using a sketch in the **Extrude** command.

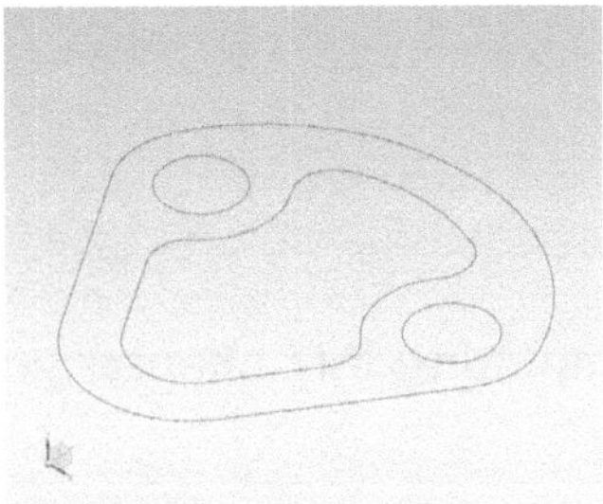

Fig 3-2 Sketch for Extrusion

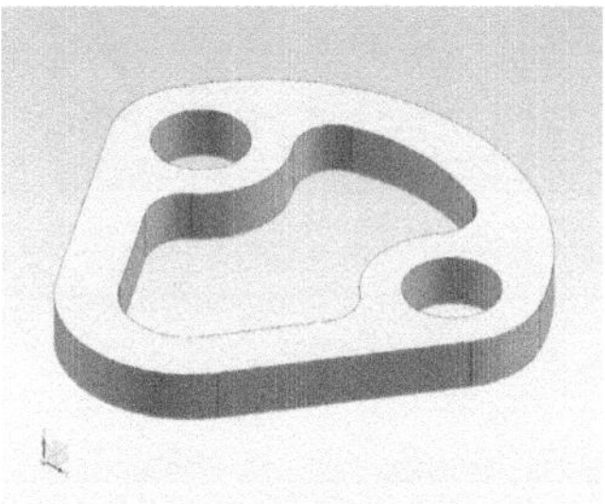

Fig 3-3 Extruded Geometry

Example of using a sketch in the **Revolve** command.

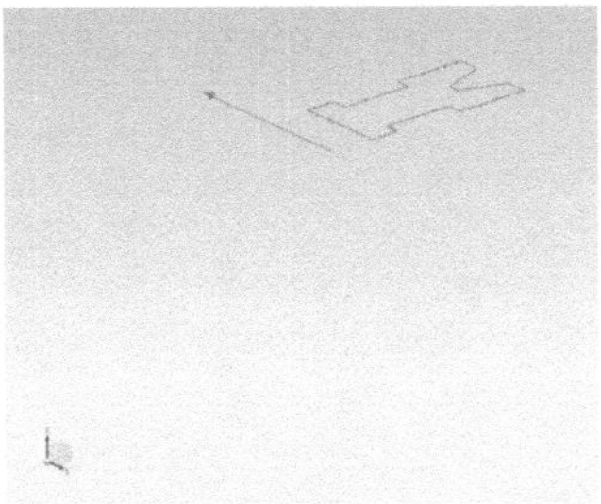

Fig 3-4 Sketch for Revolution

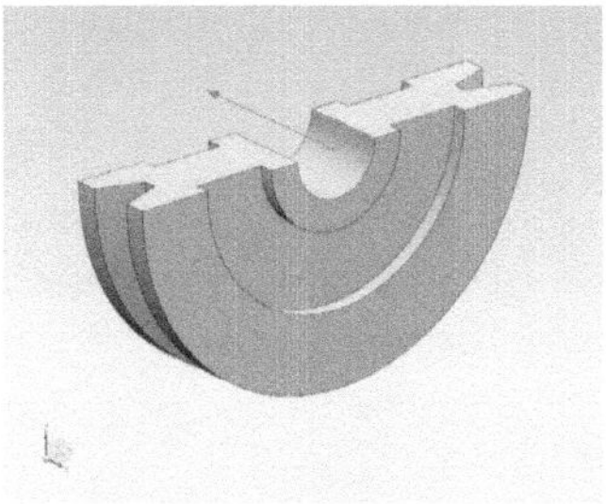

Fig 3-5 Revolved Geometry

3.2 Creating a Sketch

You can create a new sketch by clicking the **Sketch** icon in the **Direct Sketch** icon group in the **Home** tab.

Fig 3-6 Sketch Icon

Creating a New Sketch on the XY Plane — Exercise 01

1. Execute NX and click the **New** icon in the **Home** tab.

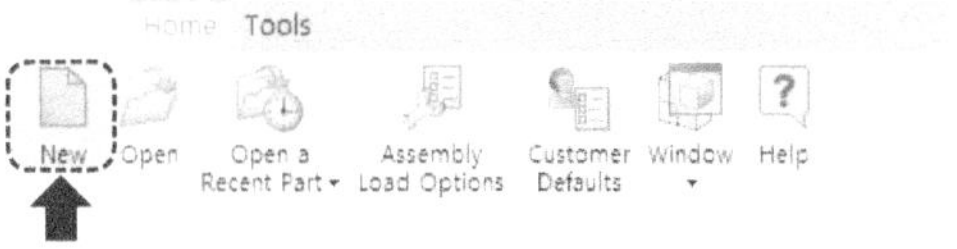

Fig 3-7 New Icon

2. Confirm that the **New** dialog box is invoked as shown in Fig 3-8.

3. Select **Model** in the **Templates** option as designated by Ⓐ in Fig 3-8.

4. Enter the part name in the **New File Name** option (Ⓑ in Fig 3-8). Note that only one part will be created in the part file.

5. Click the **Choose Directory** button on the right of the **Folder** input box (Ⓒ in Fig 3-8) to specify the folder. Note that two byte characters such as Chinese, Japanese and Korean characters are not allowed as the file name or the folder name.

6. Click **OK** in the **New** dialog box.

The **Modeling** application is invoked as shown in Fig 3-9. Note that the **Datum Coordinate System** has been created automatically. This is because you have used the **Model** template.

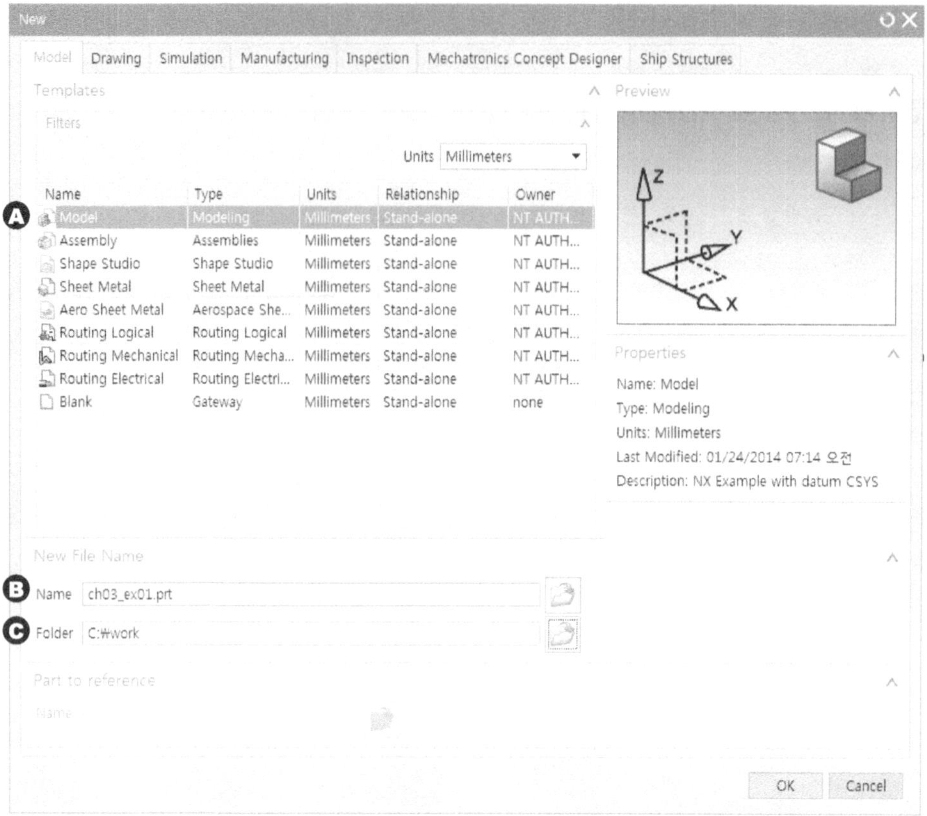

Fig 3-8 New Dialog Box

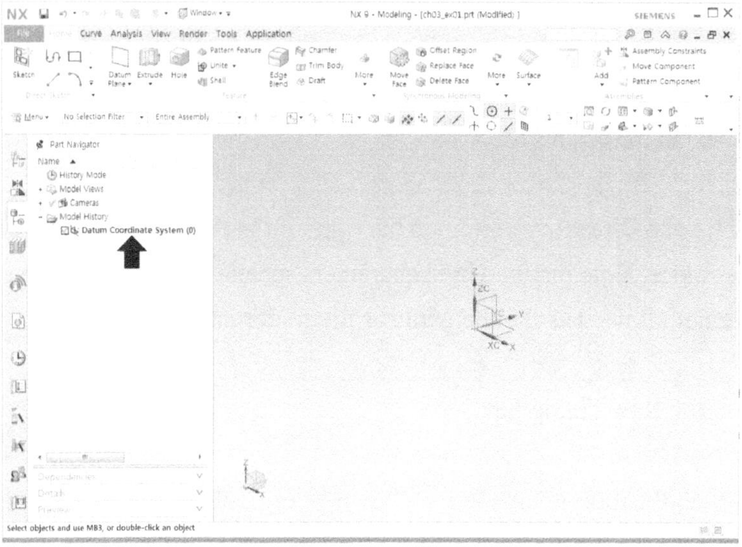

Fig 3-9 Screen of Modeling Application

7. Click the **Sketch** icon in the **Feature** icon group.

8. Press the **Reset** button in the **Create Sketch** dialog box.

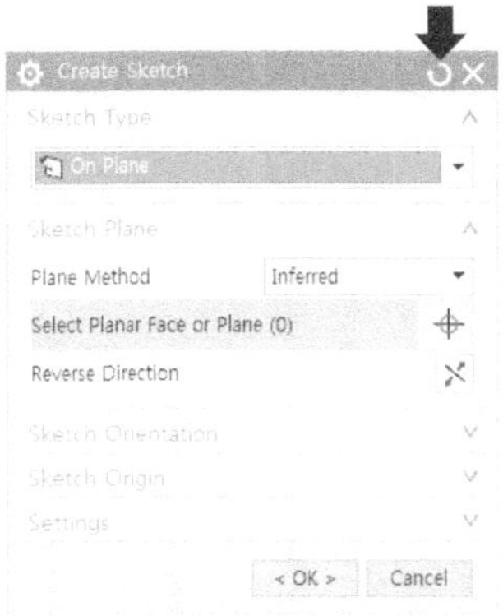

Fig 3-10 Reset Button

9. Confirm that the XY plane is highlighted in blue to notify that the plane will be used as the sketch plane.

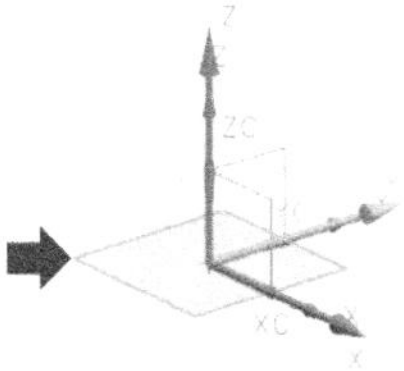

Fig 3-11 Preselected Sketch Plane

10. Press the **OK** button in the **Create Sketch** dialog box.

Fig 3-12 OK Button

11. The sketch commands are activated and you will create curves using the tools in the **Direct Sketch** icon group as shown in Fig 3-13.

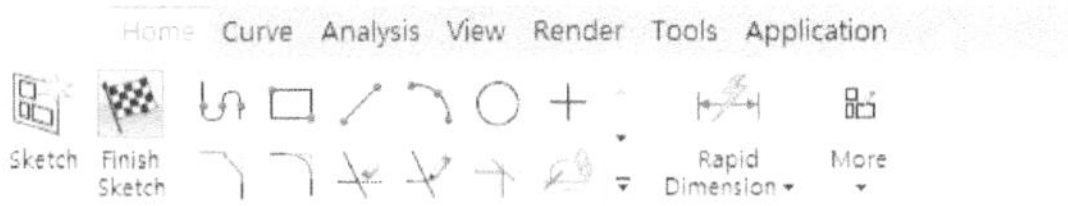

Fig 3-13 Direct Sketch Icon Group

The model view is rotated to align the sketch plane to the screen. The sketch plane is defined on the XY plane and you are ready to create sketch objects.

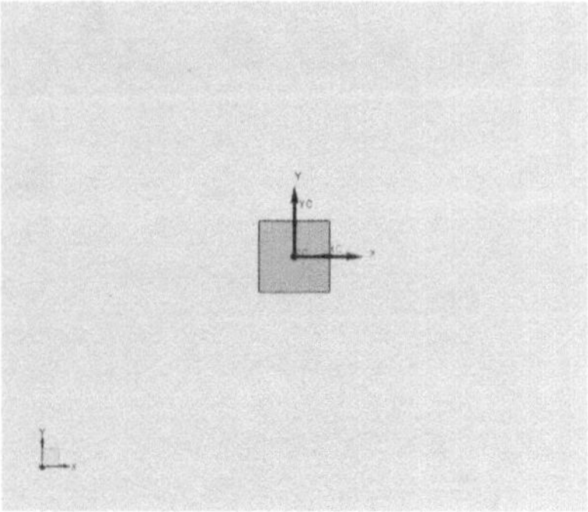

Fig 3-14 Graphics Window

12. You can exit the sketch by clicking the **Finish Sketch** icon. A shortcut key is available; **CTRL + Q**.

Fig 3-15 Finish Sketch Icon

END of Exercise

Orient View to Sketch

You can rotate the model view by pressing MB2 and dragging. To restore the sketch view orientation press MB3 on an empty area of the graphics window and select **Orient View to Sketch** in the popup menu.

3.3 Deleting a Sketch Feature

A sketch is recorded in the **Part Navigator** as a feature. To delete a sketch feature, just select it in the **Part Navigator** and press the **Delete** key.

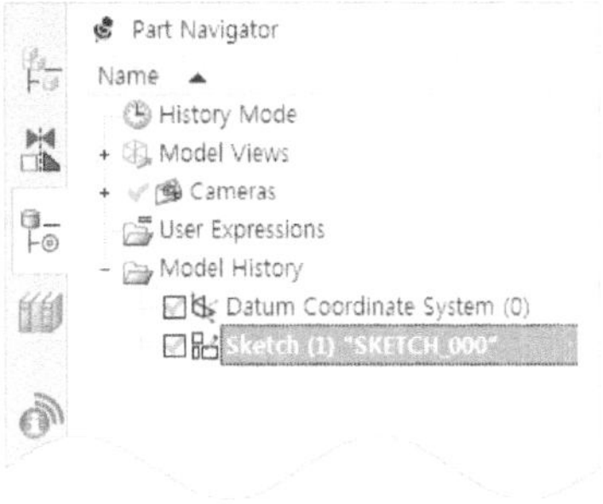

Fig 3-16 Selecting a Sketch Feature

Do not Create Empty Sketch Features

Beginners usually click the **Sketch** icon to modify an existing sketch, but this creates a new sketch feature instead. You can detect empty sketch features because they are not highlighted when you select them in the **Part Navigator**. It is highly recommended that the empty sketch features are deleted.

3.4 Sketch Procedure

Let's learn about the general procedure of creating a sketch.

3.4.1 Defining the Sketch Plane

If you click the **Sketch** icon in the **Direct Sketch** icon group, you are prompted to select the sketch plane. If you place the mouse pointer on a plane, the **X**, **Y**, **Z** axes and the origin of the sketch are displayed as shown in Fig 3-17. If you press the OK button, the sketch feature is created.

View orientation in Fig 3-17 can be attained by pressing the **Home** key which is a shortcut for a **Trimetric View**. The Z axis indicates the normal direction to the sketch plane.

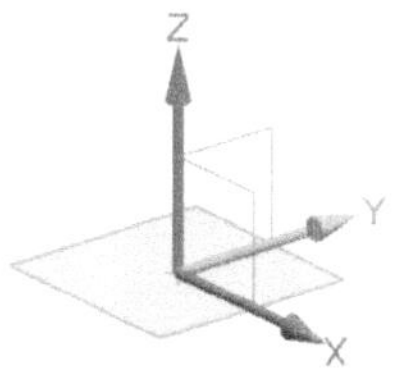

Fig 3-17 Sketch CS

3.4.2 Creating Sketch Curves

After defining the sketch plane, you will create sketch curves using the commands in the **Direct Sketch** icon group. At this stage, you can create the curves roughly, but the size and shape of the sketch should be as similar as possible to the desired outcome

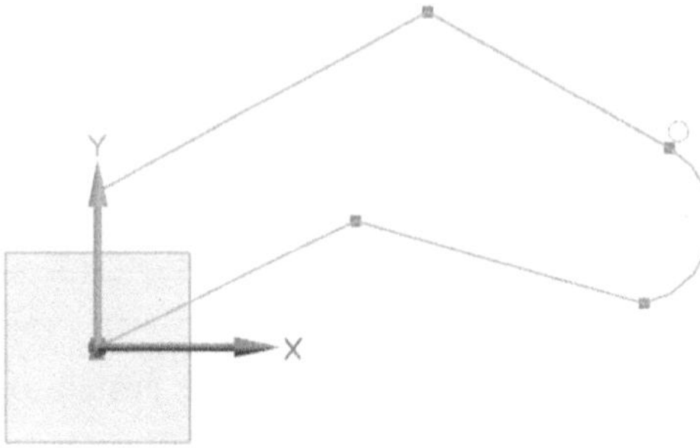

Fig 3-18 Rough Sketch

3.4.3 Constraint

Define the sketch curves exactly as you want using constraints. Fig 3-19 shows a sketch that is defined fully.

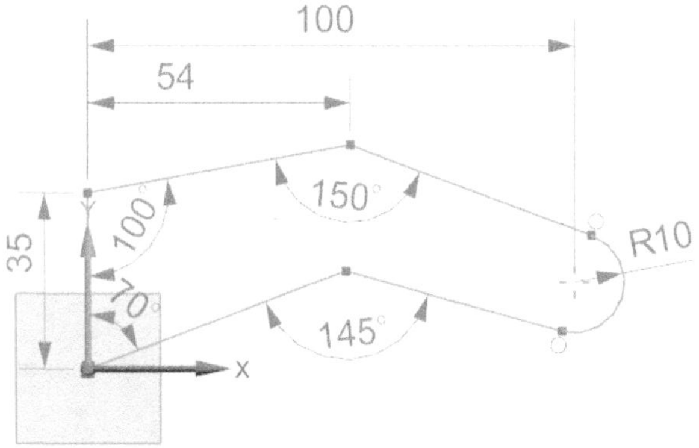

Fig 3-19 Fully Defined Sketch

3.4.4 Finish the Sketch

Click the **Finish Sketch** icon after completing the sketch.

Create sketches shown in Fig 3-20 through Fig 3-27. You have to create individual part files with the **Model** template for each sketch. You can specify the location arbitrarily.

(1) Point

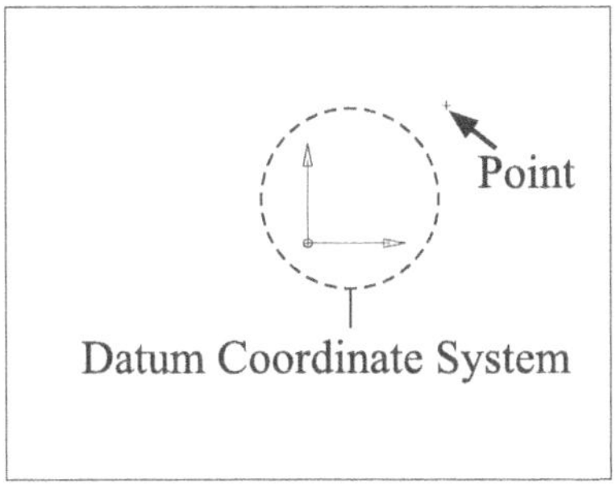

Fig 3-20 Point

(2) Horizontal Line

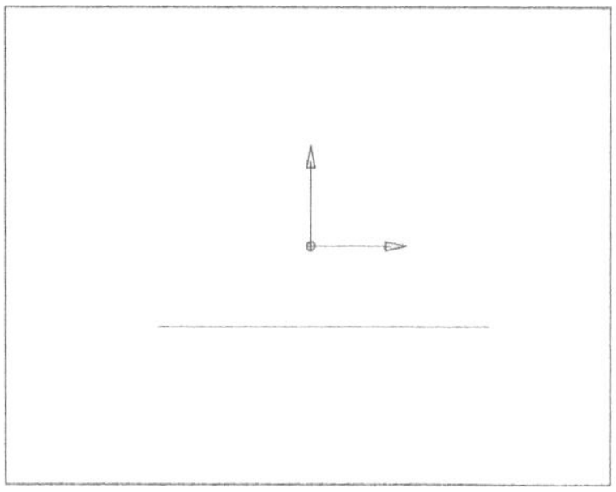

Fig 3-21 Horizontal Line

(3) Vertical Line

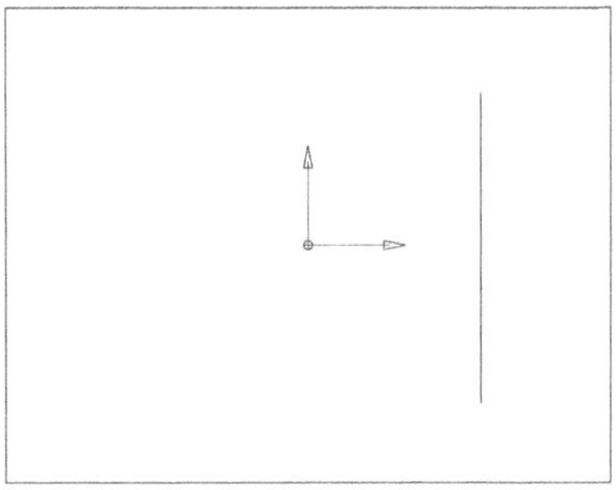

Fig 3-22 Vertical Line

(4) Diagonal Line

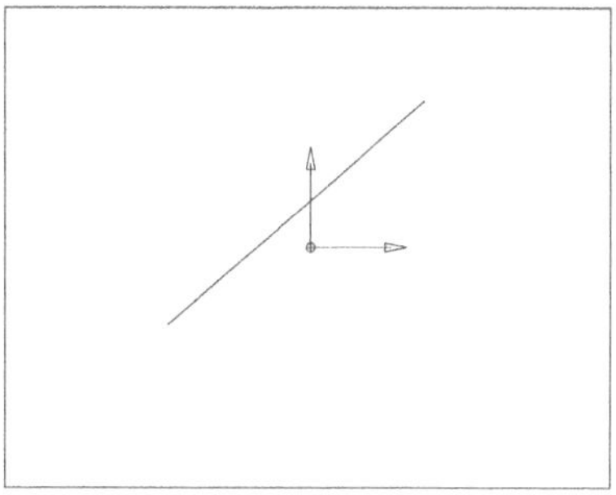

Fig 3-23 Diagonal Line

(5) Connected Lines

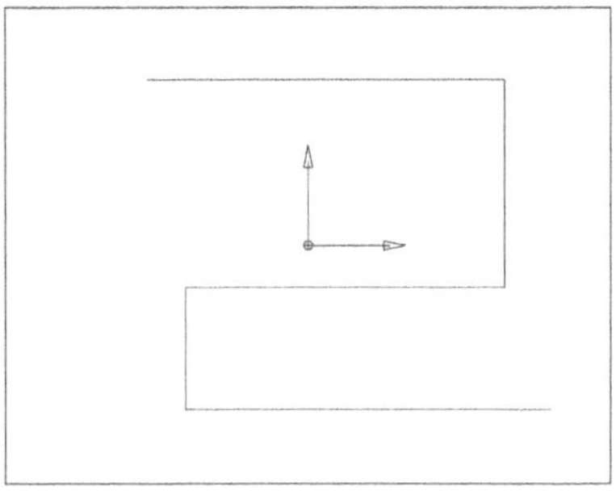

Fig 3-24 Connected Lines

(6) Arc

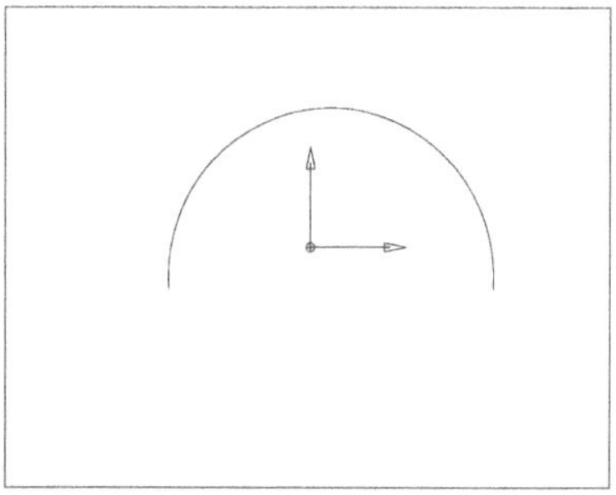

Fig 3-25 Arc

(7) Circle

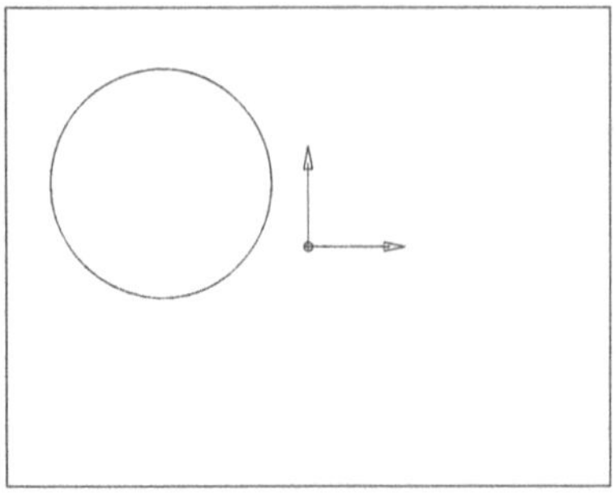

Fig 3-26 Arc

(8) Rectangle

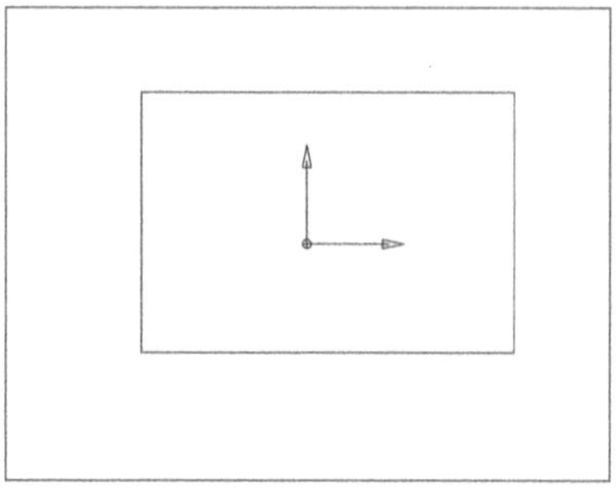

Fig 3-27 Rectangle

END of Exercise

Drawing an Arc and a Rectangle

1. Follow either of the steps shown in Fig 3-28 to create an arc.
2. The default method to create a rectangle is shown in Fig 3-29. Be careful not to drag the mouse, but click in order.

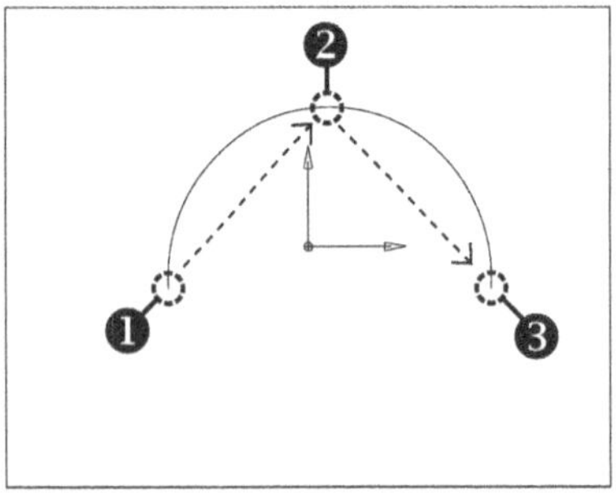

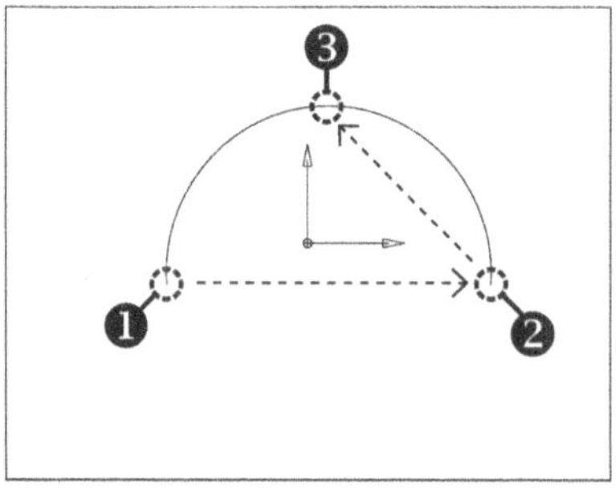

Fig 3-28 Drawing an Arc

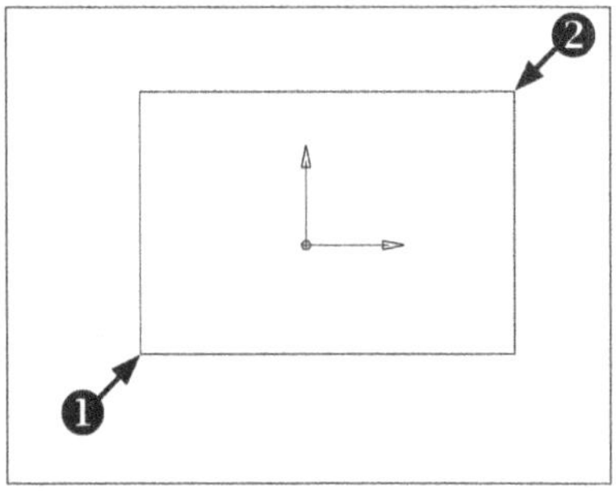

Fig 3-29 Drawing a Rectangle

3.5 Profile

Using the **Profile** command in the **Direct Sketch** icon group, you can draw lines and curves consecutively.

<u>Profile command can be terminated by the following method.</u>

1. Press the **ESC** key twice.
2. Click MB2 twice while the constraint symbol is not appearing.
3. Click the other command icon.

<u>Identifying Current Part File and Closing Part File</u>

You can identify the current part file and switch to the other part file in the **Window** menu. You can switch the part file in the **Window** tab and in the **Quick Access** toolbar. Fig 3-30 shows several part files that were created in Exercise 02.

Fig 3-30 Identifying Part Files

To close all part files choose **File > Close > All Parts** in the **Menu** button. You can close files by clicking the file menu as shown in Fig 3-31.

Fig 3-31 Closing Parts

Exercise 03 Using the Profile Command

Let's draw curves as shown in Fig 3-32 using the **Profile** command. The curves may not appear exactly the same as that given in the example. Just create lines and arcs consecutively.

Fig 3-32 Rough Sketch Created by the Profile Command

1. Click the **New** icon.
2. Specify the folder and define the name of the part file.

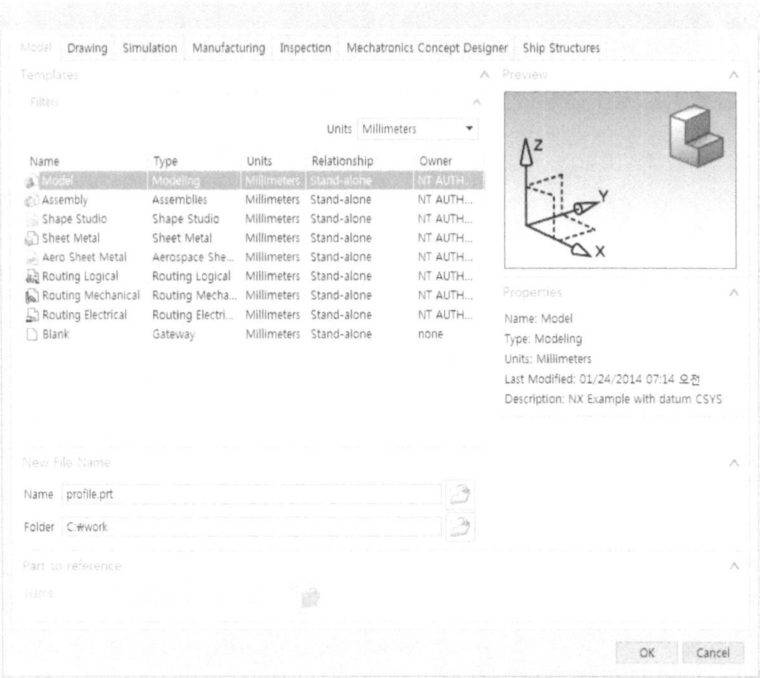

Fig 3-33 Creating a New Part File

3. Press the **W** key in the keyboard. **WCS** is hidden as shown in Fig 3-34.

Fig 3-34 Hiding WCS

! *WCS?*

WCS (Work Coordinate System) is used as a reference when you create a model. You can refer to WCS to specify a location. WCS can be hidden or shown by pressing the 'W' key on the keyboard which is the shortcut to display or show the WCS.

4. Click the **Sketch** icon.

5. Reset the **Create Sketch** dialog box and press the **OK** button in the **Create Sketch** dialog box.

6. Click the **Profile** icon in the **Direct Sketch** icon group.

Fig 3-35 Profile Icon

7. Select the four points in order as specified in Fig 3-36. Start the point ❶ at the origin. Three lines are created consecutively.

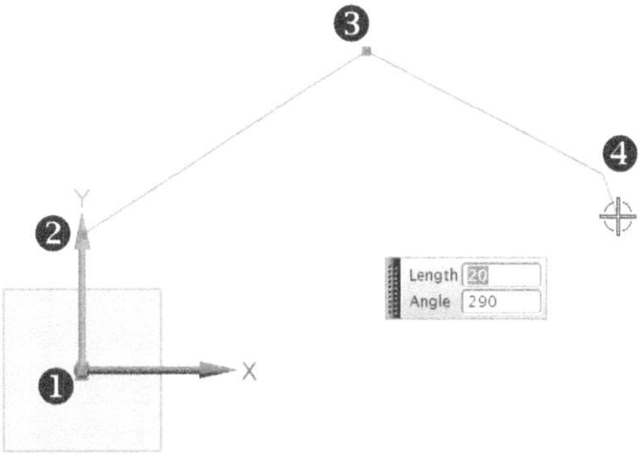

Fig 3-36 Creating Consecutive Lines

8. Select the **Arc** button in the **Profile** option bar. An arc is previewed as specified by Ⓐ in Fig 3-37.

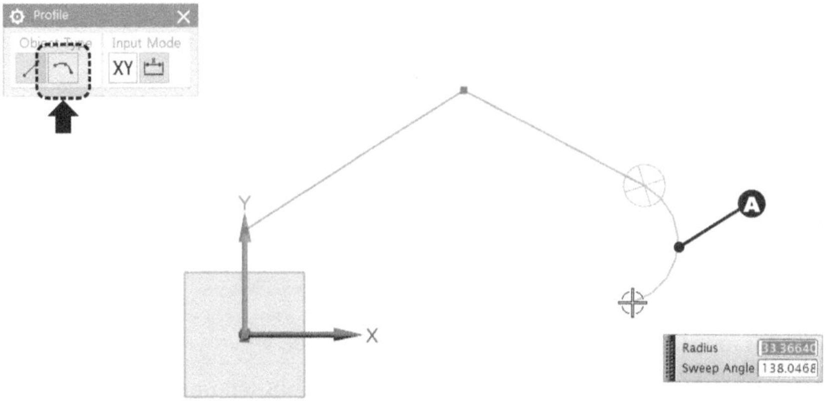

Fig 3-37 Switching to Arc

9. Select the location ❺, ❻ and ❼ in order as shown in Fig 3-38. Point ❼ has to be defined at the same location as point ❶ in Fig 3-36 to close the profile.
9. Press the **ESC** key twice to terminate the **Profile** command.
10. Click the **Finish Sketch** icon to exit the **Direct Sketch**.

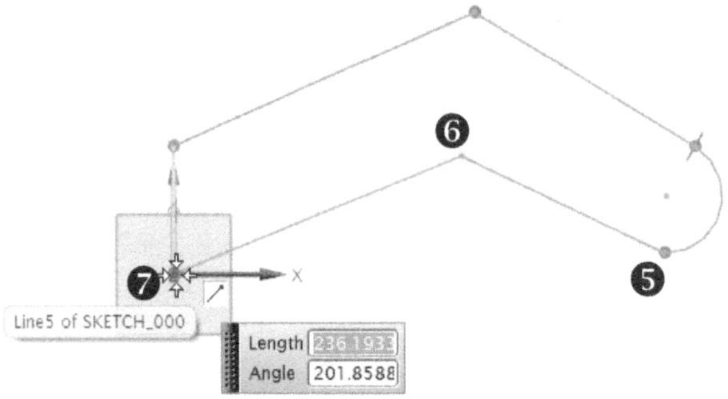

Fig 3-38 Creating Line and Arc Consecutively

END of Exercise

Changing Arc Direction

An arc may be created differently from the one shown in Fig 3-37. You can change the direction of the arc according to the following steps.

1. Pressing the **Arc** button in the **Profile** option bar, the arc is previewed as Fig 3-39 (a).
2. Move the mouse pointer to the center of symbol as shown in Fig 3-39 (b).
3. Drag the mouse for the desired direction among the four regions in symbol as shown in Fig 3-39 (c).

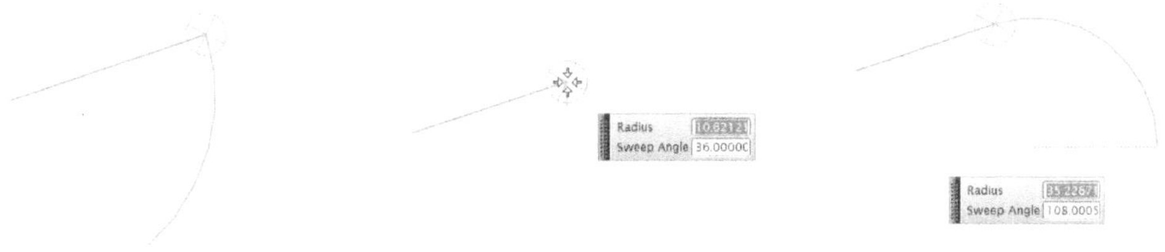

(a) (b) (c)

Fig 3-39 Changing the Arc Direction

3.6 Snap Point Option

The snap point option is available when you define a point location. You can snap on a curve, edge, vertex, existing point etc. Note that the snap point option is always available whenever you define a point location even outside of the sketch environment.

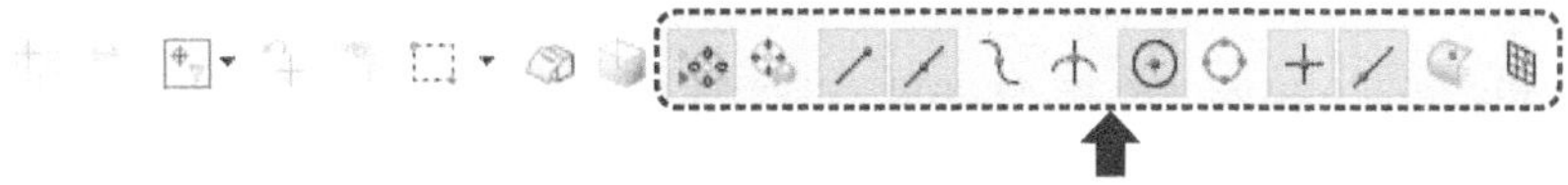

Fig 3-40 Snap Point Option

Fig 3-41 shows the symbol of the mouse pointer when it is snapped. Click MB1 to define the location when the symbol appears. Location is defined and the relevant constraint is applied. Suppose that you have defined an end point of a line on the mid point of an existing line. The end point will still be on the mid point even though you extend the existing line.

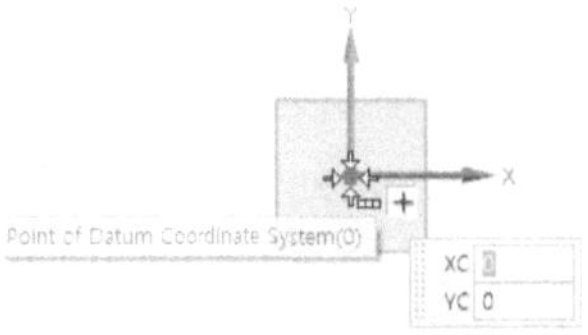

<Existing Point>

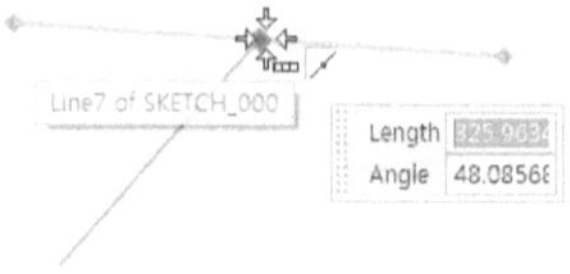

<Midpoint>

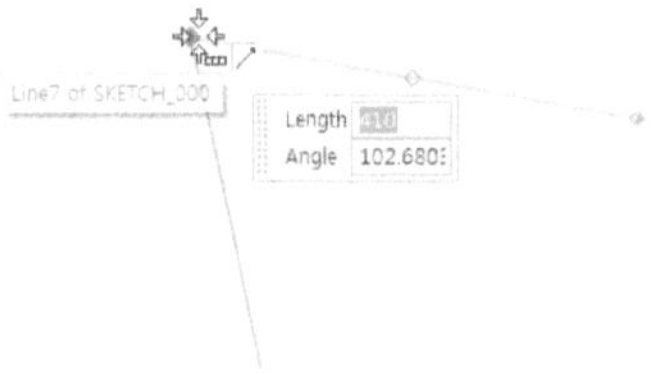

<End Point>

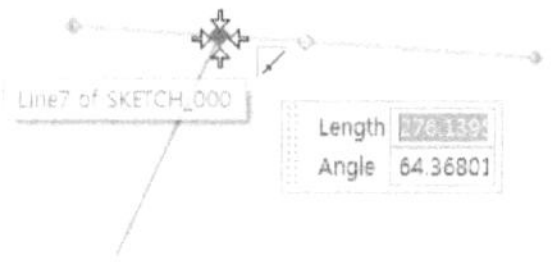

<Point on Curve>

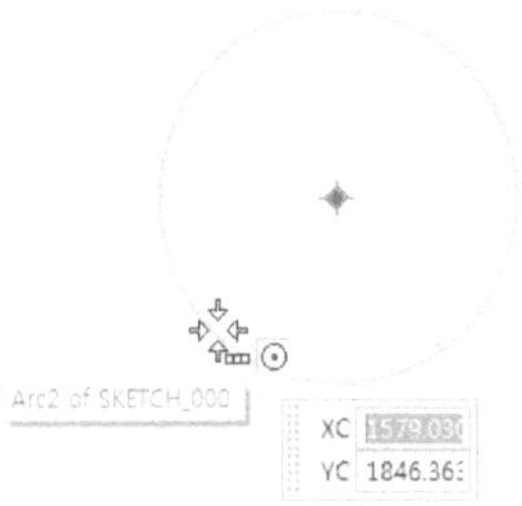

<Arc Center>

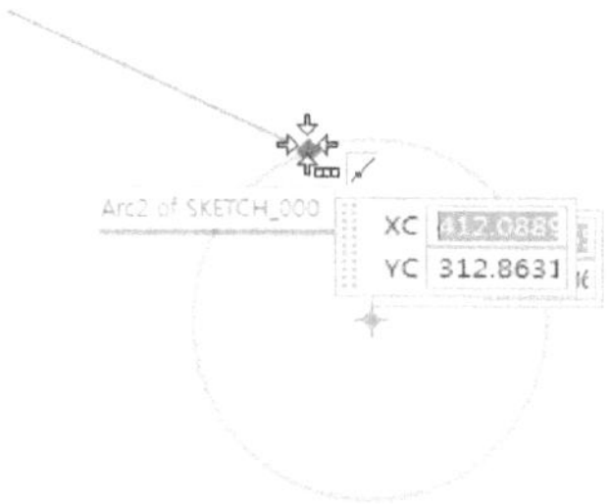

<Point on Curve>

Fig 3-41 Snapped Symbol of the Mouse Pointer

3.7 Constraining Sketch Curves

Up until now, you may have created sketch curves arbitrarily. However, a sketch that is not defined exactly as required or desired has no meaning in mechanical design. We have to define the size and shape of sketch curves exactly as we want and then use them to extrude or revolve to create 3D features.

In parametric modeling software such as NX, you can precisely define the sketch by using two types of constraints; **Geometrical Constraint** and **Dimensional Constraint.**

3.7.1 Dimensional Constraint

With dimensional constraints, you will use numerical values to define the distance, length, radius, diameter, angle, etc.

Fig 3-43 shows the icons used to define dimensional constraints. If you click the upper part of the Rapid Dimensions icon as designated in Fig 3-43, you can apply various types of dimensional constraints. The shortcut key for the Rapid Dimension command is 'D'.

If you reset the dialog box, the default Method in the Measurement option group is Inferred. The type of dimension is determined according to the selected objects. For example, if you select two parallel lines, you can apply the Perpendicular dimension. If you select two angled lines, you can apply the Angular dimension. If you select a circle or an arc, you can apply the Diametral or Radial dimensions, respectively.

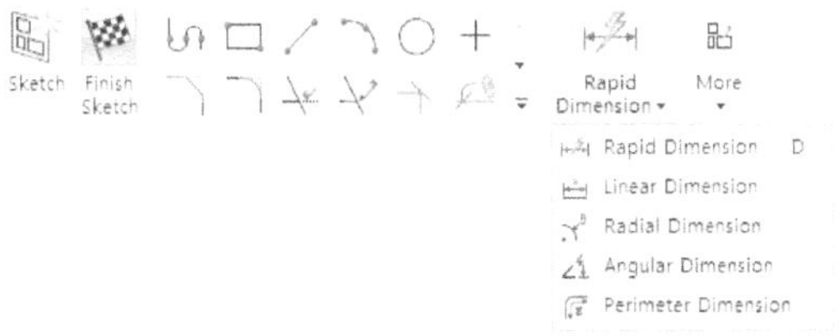

Fig 3-42 Dimensional Constraints

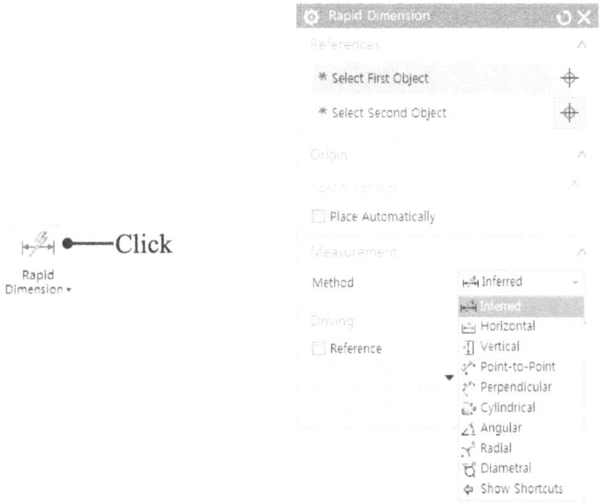

Fig 3-43 Rapid Dimensional Icon and Dialog Box

After creating the dimension with the Inferred method, you can identify the type of dimension by double clicking the dimension.

To apply a specific type of dimension, you have to select the corresponding icon under the **Rapid Dimensions** icon in the dropdown shown in Fig 3-44. For example, if you want to create a radial dimension for a circle or an arc, click the **Radial Dimension** icon in the dropdown and select the circle or arc. Because the default method for the radial dimension is **Inferred**, the diametral dimension is created by selecting a circle. You can create a radial dimension for a circle by selecting **Radial** in the **Method** dropdown.

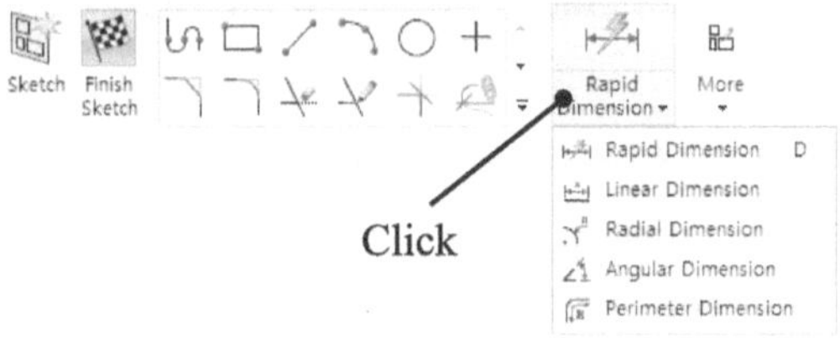

Fig 3-44 Specific Types of Dimension

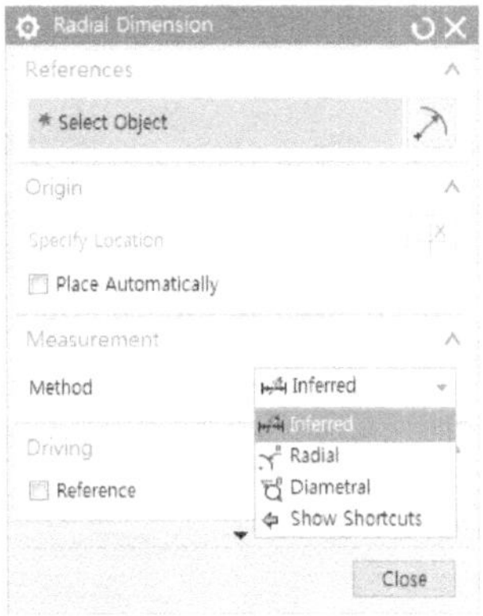

Fig 3-45 Radial Dimension Dialog Box

If you check the **Place Automatically** option in the **Origin** option group, the location of the dimension is determined automatically. If you modify the dimension value while creating the dimension or by double clicking the dimension after creating, the shape of the sketch curves is adapted. This type of dimension is called the driving dimension. If you select the **Reference** option in the **Driving** option group, you cannot modify the dimension value.

The **Settings** option is available by clicking the **More** button at the lower part of the dia-

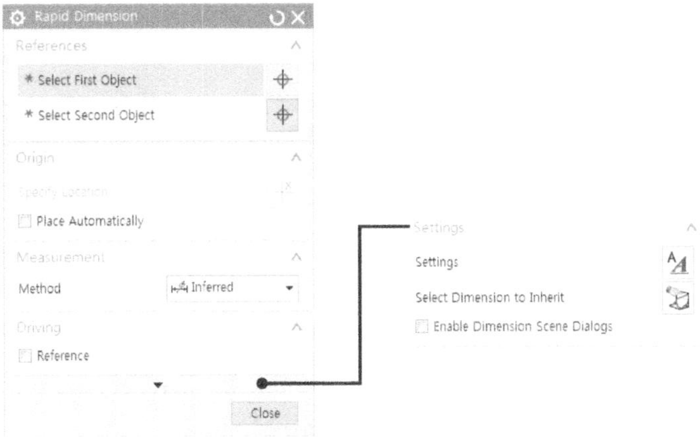

Fig 3-46 Settings Option

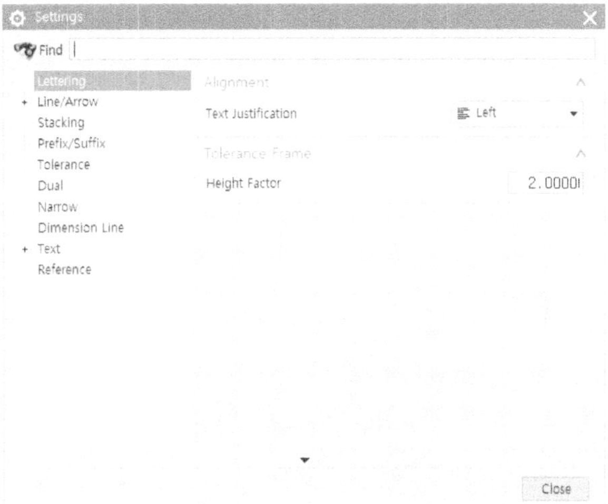

Fig 3-47 Settings Dialog Box

log box and you can set the appearance of the dimensions. Details for this option are explained in Chapter 15. If you want to change the appearance of a dimension, press MB3 on the dimension and choose the **Settings** option in the pop-up menu as shown in Fig 3-48.

The appearance of the dimension can be inherited by choosing the **Select Dimension to Inherit** button in the **Settings** option of the **Rapid Dimension** dialog box.

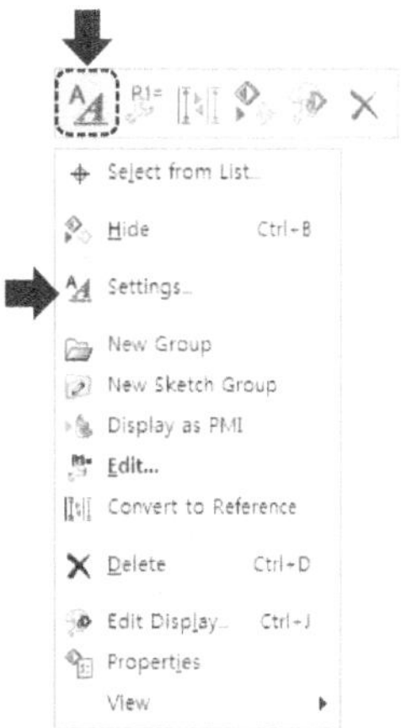

Fig 3-48 Settings Menu

3.7.2 Geometric Constraint

With geometrical constraints, you will define the shape of the curves by defining their relationship with other sketch objects such as coincidence, concentric, collinear, equal radius, equal length, etc. The geometrical constraints are used to define the shape of curves without entering a value.

You can apply the geometric constraints either by clicking the **Geometric Constraints** icon or by selecting the sketch objects. The **Geometric Constraints** icon is available in the **Direct Sketch** icon group by pressing the **More** button.

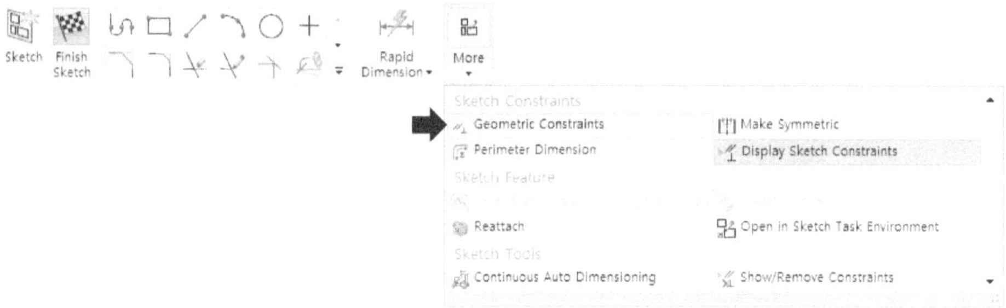

Fig 3-49 Geometric Constraints Icon in the More Option Group

To add a large icon, click the symbol marked by a circle in Fig 3-50 and select **Geometric Constraints**. The icon is added in the **Direct Sketch** icon group as shown in Fig 3-51. The shortcut key for **Geometric Constraints** is 'C'.

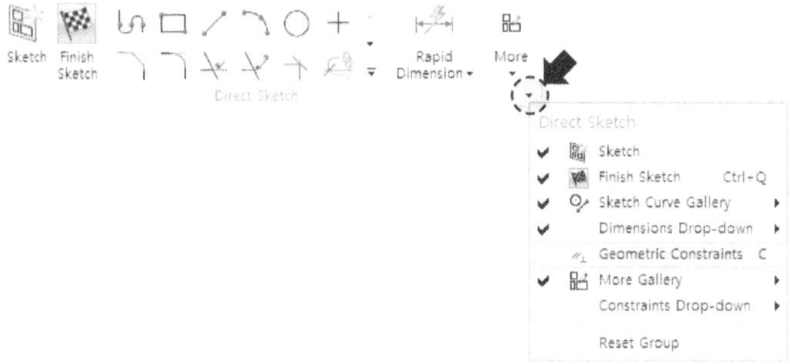

Fig 3-50 Adding a Large Icon

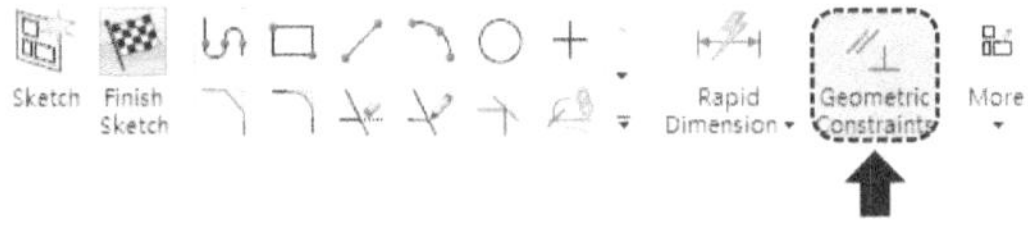

Fig 3-51 Geometric Constraints Icon

If you click the **Geometric Constraints** icon, the information shown in Fig 3-52 is displayed, which explains that you do not need to invoke the **Geometric Constraints** dialog box. You can apply the geometric constraints by dragging and dropping the sketch curves or points or by selecting the sketch objects first and choosing a proper constraint to be applied. The **Geometric Constraints** dialog box is useful when you are applying the same type of constraint repeatedly.

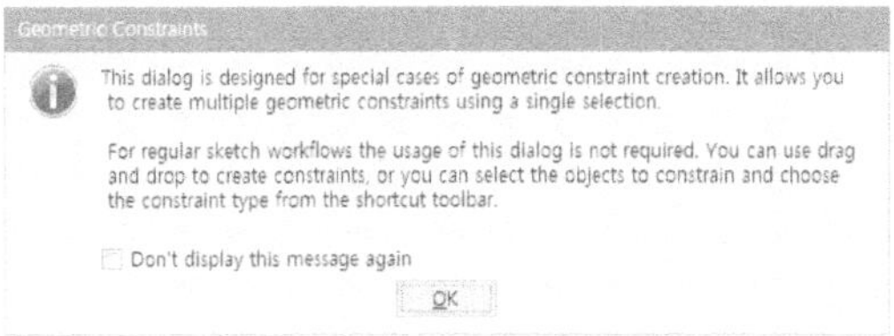

Fig 3-52 Information for Geometric Constraints

If you press the **OK** button in the information box, the **Geometric Constraints** dialog box is invoked as shown in Fig 3-53. Select the type of constraint in the **Constraint** option area and select the objects to apply the constraint. Note that the type of object is filtered according to the type of constraint specified in the **Constraint** option area. For example, if you select the **Point on Curve** constraint in the **Constraint** option area and have selected the curve for the **Object to Constrain**, then you can select only the point for the object to constrain to. This is because you can apply the **Point on Curve** constraint between a curve and a point.

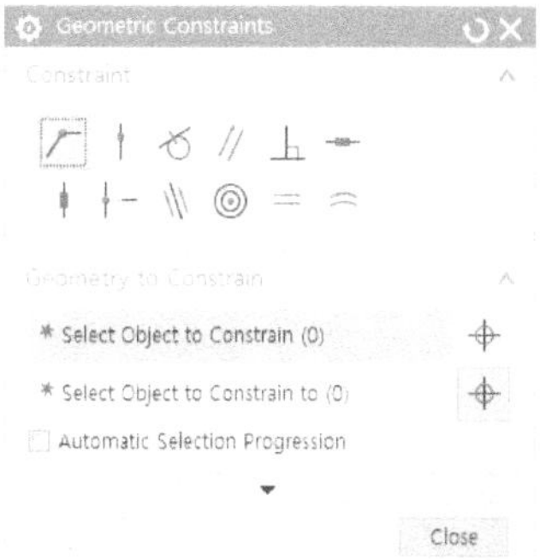

Fig 3-53 Geometric Constraints Dialog Box

If you click the **More** button in the dialog box, the **Settings** option is available and you can set the types of geometric constraints that you can apply in the dialog box. The checked types of geometric constraints are applicable as the buttons in the **Constraint** option area. If you select the **Automatic Selection Progression** option, the selection step is progressed automatically.

You can delete dimensional constraints and geometric constraints by selecting the symbols and pressing the **Delete** key on the keyboard.

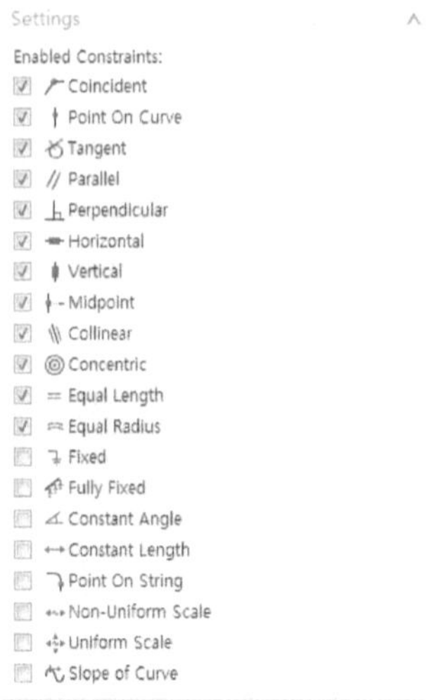

Fig 3-54 Settings Option in the Geometric Constraints Dialog Box

Types of geometrical constraints available for the selected objects are listed in the **Constraint** option bar.

Icon	Name	Description	Symbol
	Horizontal	A line is constrained to horizontal. (Parallel to the X axis)	
	Vertical	A line is constrained to vertical. (Parallel to the Y axis)	
	Coincident	Points or end points become coincident.	
	Point On Curve	A point is defined on an existing line or curve.	
	Midpoint	A virtual line normal to an existing line at the center passes through the specified point.	
	Collinear	Lines become collinear.	
	Parallel	Lines become parallel.	
	Perpendicular	Lines or curves become perpendicular.	
	Tangent	Two curves become tangent.	

	Equal Length	Lengths of lines become equal.	
	Concentric	Centers of arcs or circles become coincident.	
	Equal Radius	Radiuses of arcs or circles become equal.	

You can apply geometric or dimensional constraints by selecting the objects first instead of clicking their corresponding icons. The toolbar options shown in Fig 3-55 are available when you have selected two lines. If you select a circle, the toolbar options shown in Fig 3-56 are available. Note that you can apply the radial or the diametral dimension in the shortcut toolbar by selecting the circle.

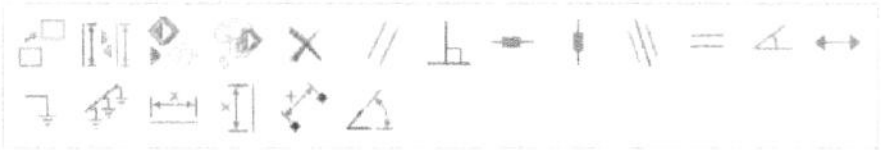

Fig 3-55 Shortcut Toolbar when Two Lines are Selected

Fig 3-56 Shortcut Toolbar when a Circle is Selected

You can drag the unconstrained sketch curves by selecting them with MB1 and the geometric constraints can be applied while you are dragging the sketch objects. Fig 3-57 shows the process of applying the tangent constraint by dragging the line and snapping to the circle.

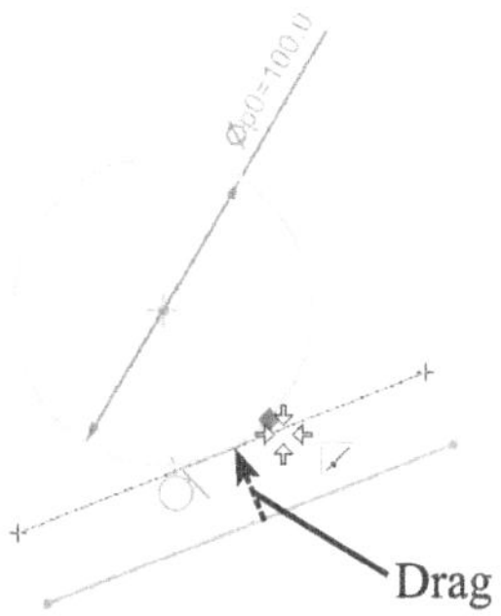

Fig 3-57 Applying the Geometric Constraint While Dragging

Applying Constraints in Combination

Two types of constraints are combined to fully define the shape and size of sketch objects. If the geometry changes abruptly by applying a constraint, you will have to undo the constraint and try another constraint.

3.7.3 Make Symmetric

This constraint makes two sketch curves symmetric against a line or axis. Location and size are constrained to symmetric. Click the **Make Symmetric** icon in the **Direct Sketch** icon group, and select the **Primary Object**, **Secondary Object** and **Symmetry Centerline** in order. Fig 3-60 shows the result of applying the **Make Symmetric** constraint between the two circles after creating each circle.

Fig 3-58 Make Symmetric Icon

Fig 3-59 Make Symmetric Dialog Box

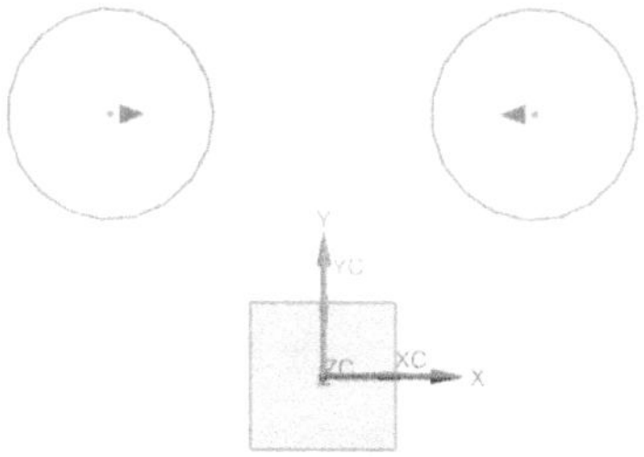

Fig 3-60 Symmetric Constraint between Two Circles

Do not apply Fixed or Fully Fixed constraint.

Fixed or **Fully Fixed** constraint among the geometrical constraints are not used to define the shape of the sketch curves. They are used to fix sketch objects that are imported from another CAD system. Sometimes you may fix some sketch objects temporarily to evaluate the status of constraint of other sketch objects. You have to delete the **Fixed** constraint after its temporary use.

3.8 Status of Constraint

There are four types of sketch constraints. A sketch is strongly recommended to be fully constrained. Over constrained or conflicting constraints must be strictly avoided.

No.	Status	Description	Color
1	Partially Constrained	Some points or curves are not constrained.	Medium Maroon
2	Fully Constrained	All curves and curves are constrained exactly.	Deep Green
3	Over Constrained	An additional constraint which is the same as the existing constraint has been applied to the fully constrained sketch object.	Red
4	Conflicting Constraint	An additional constraint which conflicts with the existing constraint has been applied to the sketch object.	Magenta

Let's study each case by constraining a rectangle.

(1) Partially Constrained

Fig 3-61 Partially Constrained

The lower left corner is constrained and the two lines are constrained to have equal length. Vertical constraints are applied between the connected lines.

However, length of the sides is not defined.

The color of the partially constrained object turns to medium maroon while applying constraints. You can drag the partially constrained sketch object after releasing the constraint or dimension icon.

Fig 3-62 Status Bar Message

(2) Fully Constrained

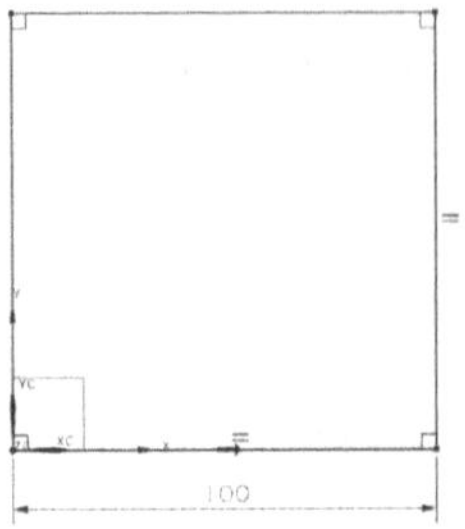

Fig 3-63 Fully Constrained

If you apply a distance dimension to the sketch in Fig 3-62 the rectangle is fully constrained.

Status bar message reads as shown inFig 3-64.

Color of the fully constrained object turns to deep green when the constraint or dimension icon is pressed.

You cannot drag the fully constrained sketch object after releasing the constraint or dimension icon.

Fig 3-64 Status Bar Message

(3) Over Constrained

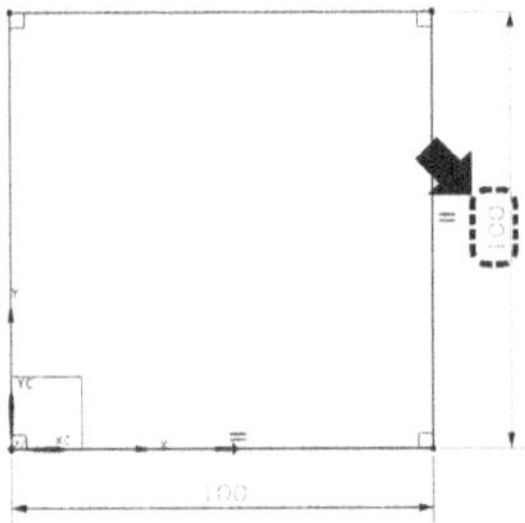

Fig 3-65 Over Constrained

If you apply an additional distance dimension to the sketch in Fig 3-63, the rectangle is over constrained and the color turns to red.

Status bar message reads as shown in Fig 3-66.

You cannot drag the over constrained sketch objects or modify the size to the input value.

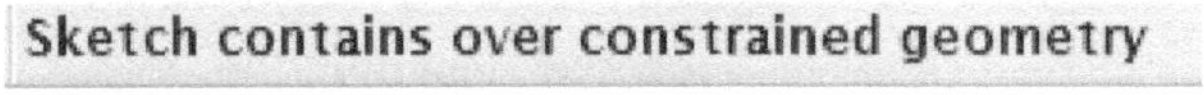

Fig 3-66 Status Bar Message

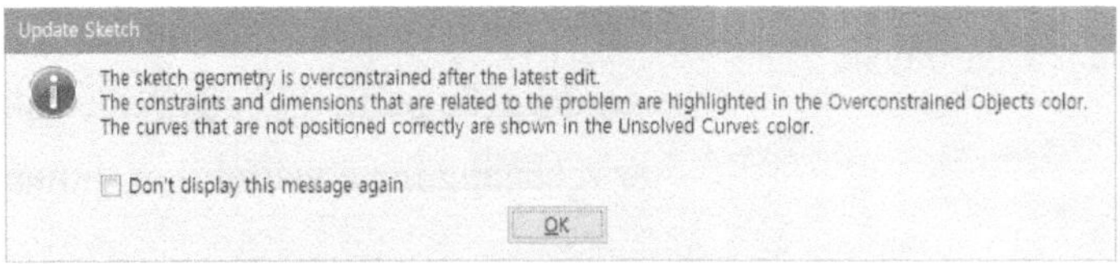

Fig 3-67 Overconstrained Message

(4) Conflicting Constraint

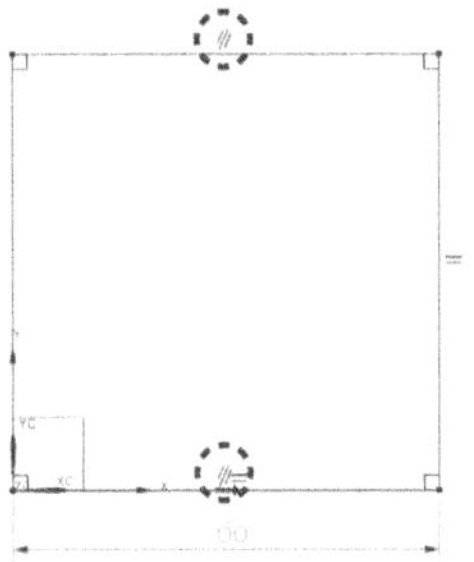

Fig 3-68 Conflicting Constraint

If you apply a collinear constraint to the upper and lower line in Fig 3-68, it conflicts with the existing equal length constraint and the color turns to magenta.

Status bar message reads as shown in Fig 3-69.

You cannot drag the sketch objects with conflicting constraints or modify the size to the input value.

Fig 3-69 Status Bar Message

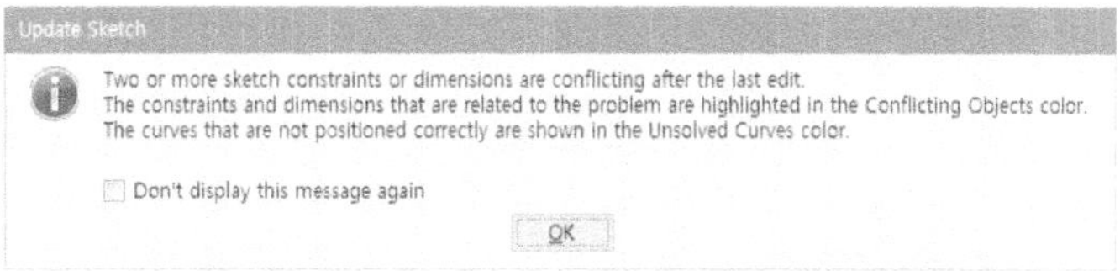

Fig 3-70 Message of Conflicting Constraint

3.9 Evaluating Sketch Status by Dragging

If you click the constraint or dimension icon, you can identify the status of the sketch by its color. A partially constrained sketch displays one or more DOF arrow as designated by the arrow in Fig 3-71, which means that the point can be dragged along the direction.

Note that you can drag the partially constrained sketch object after releasing the constraint or dimension icon.

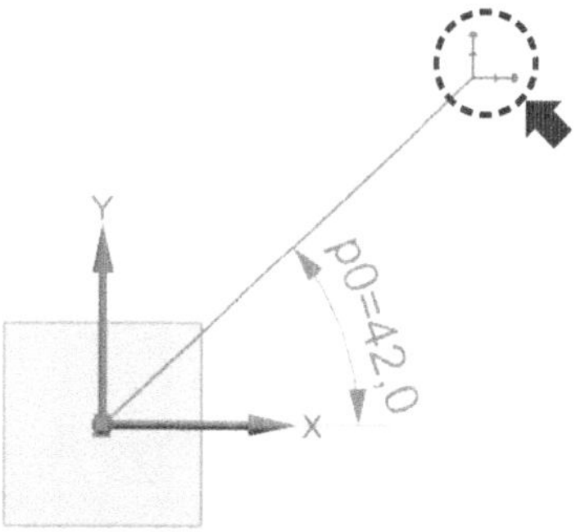

Fig 3-71 DOF Arrow

3.10 Open in Sketch Task Environment

Creating a sketch by clicking the **Sketch** icon in the **Home** tab is called **Direct Sketch**. The direct sketch is created in the **Modeling** application, and other commands in the **Modeling** application are available while creating the sketch.

The **Sketch** task environment is available in the **Modeling** application of NX. You can use only the sketch commands in the **Sketch** task environment and you can select only the sketch objects. You have to be aware that you can delete other objects in the **Direct Sketch**.

If you click the **Open in Sketch Task Environment** icon in the **Direct Sketch** icon group, the **Sketch** task environment is invoked as shown in Fig 3-73.

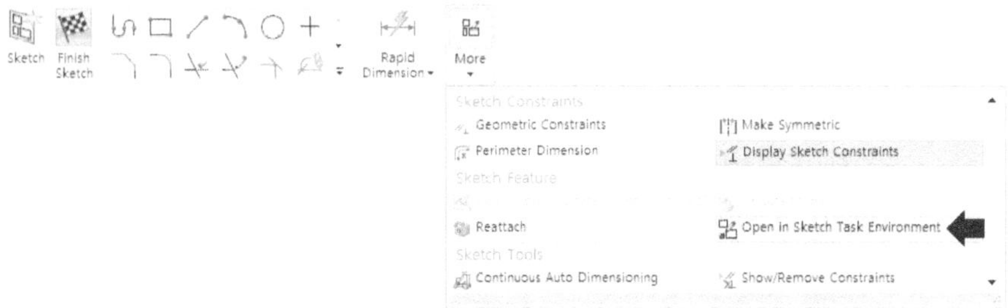

Fig 3-72 Open in Sketch Task Environment Icon

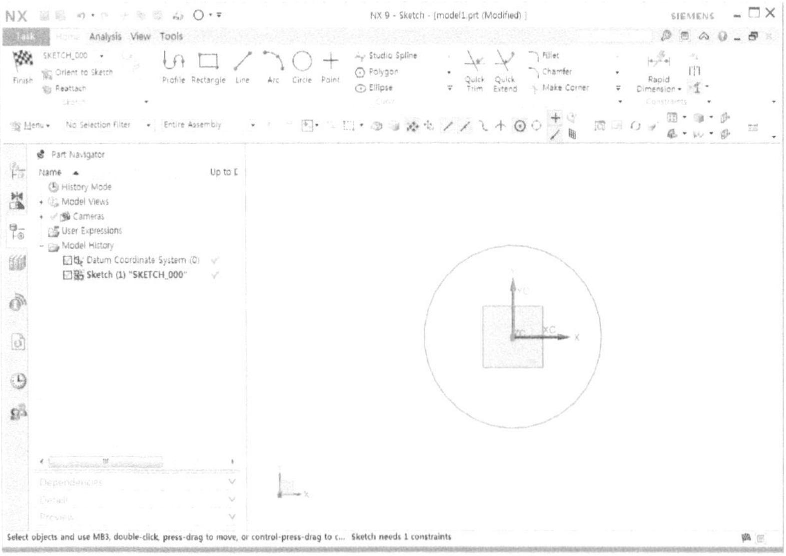

Fig 3-73 Sketch Task Environment

Let's create a 45 ° slanted line against the X axis and fully constrain it. Name the part file Exercise 04.prt and define a sketch on the XY plane.

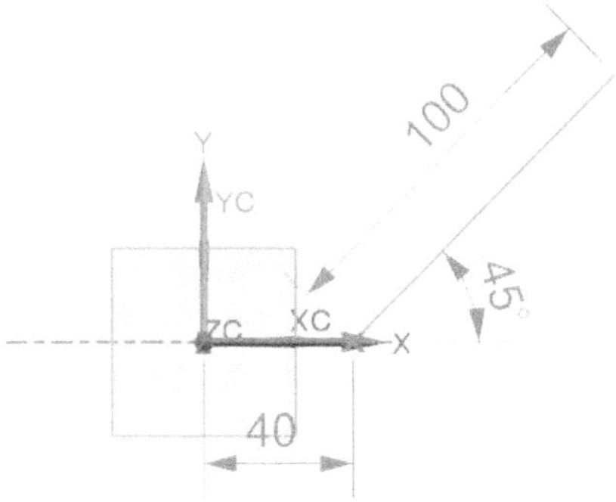

Fig 3-74 Slanted Line

Creating a Line

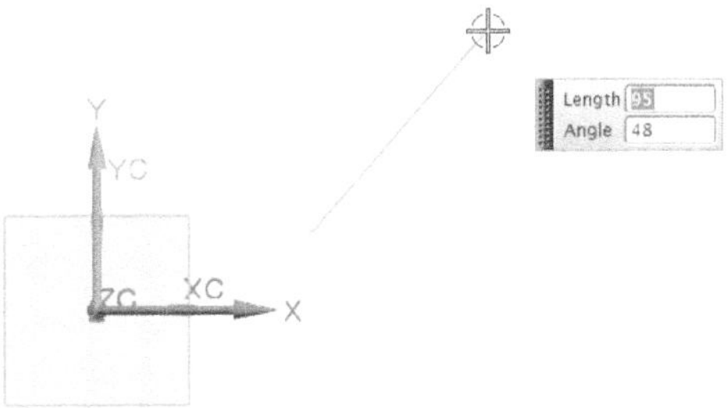

Fig 3-75 Creating a Line

1. Draw a line with the **Profile** command as shown in Fig 3-75.
2. Press the **ESC** key twice to terminate the **Profile** command.

Applying Constraints

1. Click the **Geometric Constraints** icon. You can press '**C**' as a shortcut key. Check the option 'Don't display this message again' in the **Geometric Constraints** information box and press OK.

2. Reset the dialog box and click the **Point on Curve** button in the **Constraints** option area. (❷ in Fig 3-76).

3. Select the end point ❸ of the line. Make sure that you click MB1 when the end point is snapped as shown in the figure.
4. Click MB2
5. Select the X axis.

The end point of the line moves onto the X axis and the **Point on Curve** symbol appears.

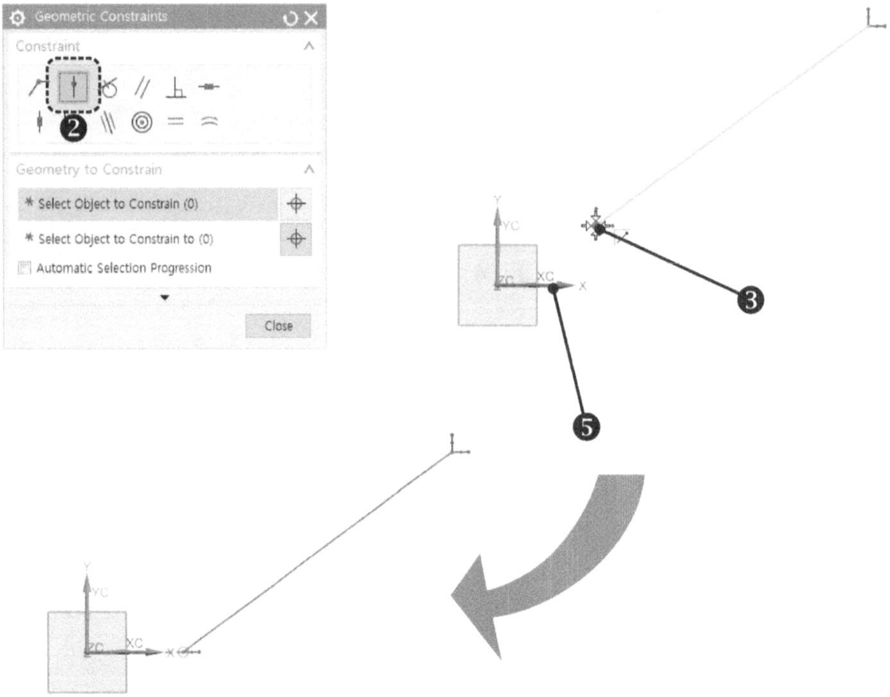

Fig 3-76 Applying Point on Curve Constraint

Dragging

1. Be sure that the **Geometric Constraints** icon is pressed and notice the DOF arrow at one end of the line.
2. Press the **Close** button in the **Geometric Constraints** dialog box.
3. Select the end point of the line (Ⓐ in Fig 3-77) and drag along the dotted arrow direction.

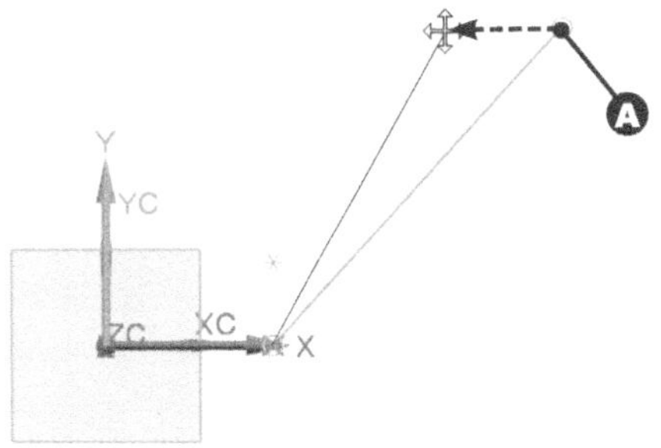

Fig 3-77 Dragging the End Point

Angular Dimension

1. Click the **Rapid Dimension** icon. You can press '**D**' as a shortcut key.
2. Select the line and the X axis.
3. Move the mouse pointer between the line and the axis and click MB1 to create the angular dimension.
4. Enter 45 in the input box and press the **Enter** key. Confirm that the angle of the line is adopted to the specified value.

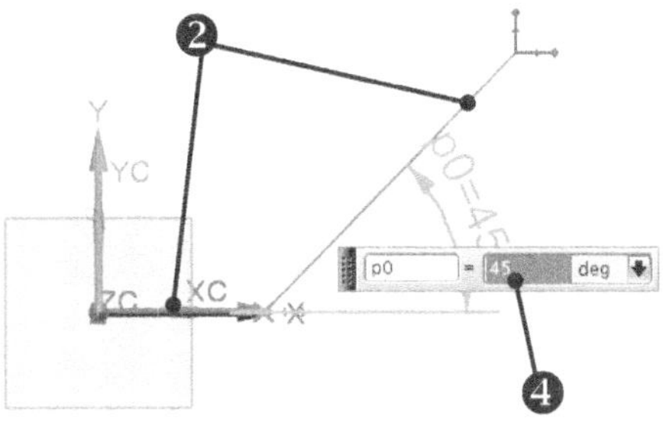

Fig 3-78 Creating Angular Dimension

Length Dimension

1. Be sure that the **Rapid Dimension** icon is pressed and select the line.
2. Move the mouse pointer above the line and click MB1 to create a length dimension as shown in Fig 3-79.
3. Enter 100 in the input box and press the **Enter** key. Confirm that the length is adopted to the specified value.
4. Press the **Close** button in the **Rapid Dimension** dialog box.

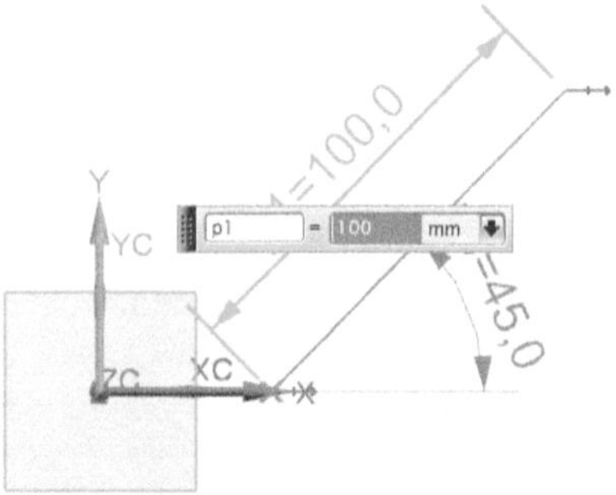

Fig 3-79 Creating Length Dimension

Verifying the Sketch Status

Looking at Fig 3-79, you can identify a DOF arrow at the end of the line which implies that the line can be dragged horizontally. You can constrain this DOF by defining the horizontal distance between the Y axis and an end point of the line.

1. Click the **Rapid Dimensions** icon.
2. Select the Y axis and the lower end point of the line.
3. Specify the location of the dimension as shown in Fig 3-80. Enter 40 for its distance and press the **Enter** key.

Confirm the following four statuses.

- Color of curves is yellow green.
- No DOF arrows are found.
- The line is not dragged after releasing the dimension icon.
- Status bar message reads "Sketch is Fully Constrained".

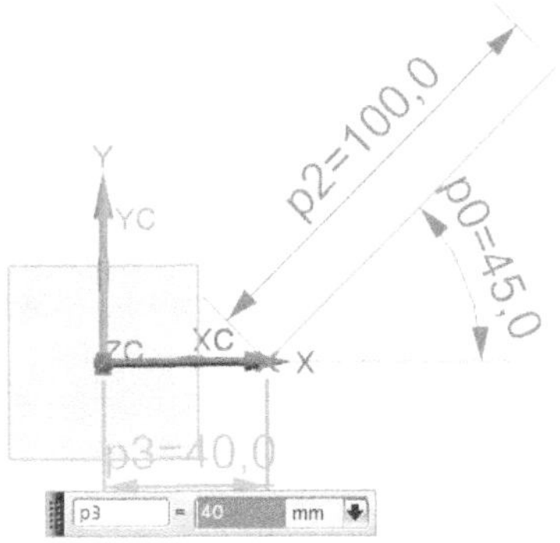

Fig 3-80 Creating Distance Dimension

Finish Sketch

1. Click the **Finish Sketch** icon. You can press '**Q**' as a shortcut key.
2. Save the file. Name of part is Exercise 04.prt.

END of Exercise

Color of Sketch Objects

Do you recognize that the color of the sketch line changes when you exit the sketch? The color of an active sketch is medium moss. If you exit the sketch, the color turns to blue. Note that you cannot drag curves out of an active sketch.

Reference of Constraint

You can see three types of coordinate systems. The WCS can be identified by the XC, YC and ZC axis which cannot be selected because they are not modeling objects. The sketch axis can be identified by the X (red), Y (green) and Z (blue) axis. The datum coordinate system can be identified by the X, Y and Z axis. You can constrain the sketch objects with reference to the sketch and datum coordinate system. You cannot use the WCS as the reference of the constraints because it is not the modeling object.

Curves in other sketch features, objects of 3D geometry and three dimensional curves can be used as the reference of a sketch constraint. Note that the curves in other sketch features are colored in blue.

3.11 Deleting and Modifying Sketch Objects

3.11.1 Modifying Sketch

There are two approaches in accessing a sketch feature to modify sketch objects.

(1) Using the Direct Sketch

Right click on the sketch feature in the Part Navigator and select **Edit** in the pop-up menu. The **Direct Sketch** is invoked and the sketch is activated as shown in Fig 3-81. You can modify the sketch dimensions by double clicking them. To finish the **Direct Sketch**, just click the **Finish Sketch** icon in the **Direct Sketch** icon group. You can press the '**Q**' button in the keyboard.

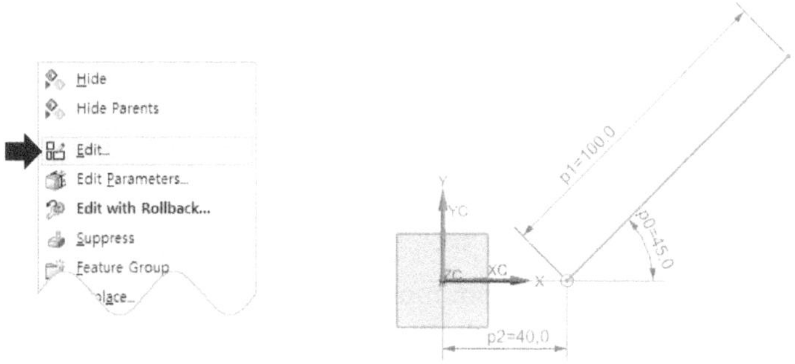

Fig 3-81 Modifying Sketch in Direct Sketch

(2) Edit with Rollback

Double click or right click on a sketch in the Part Navigator and choose **Edit with Rollback** in the pop-up menu. You will be invoked in the **Sketch** task environment where you can delete sketch curves or modify constraints. You can finish the sketch by pressing the **Finish Sketch** icon or you pressing the '**Q**' button in the keyboard. Note that the action of executing the **Edit** and **Edit with Rollback** command may be different in your setting. Refer to **"1.8.3 Double Click Action for Sketches"** for detail.

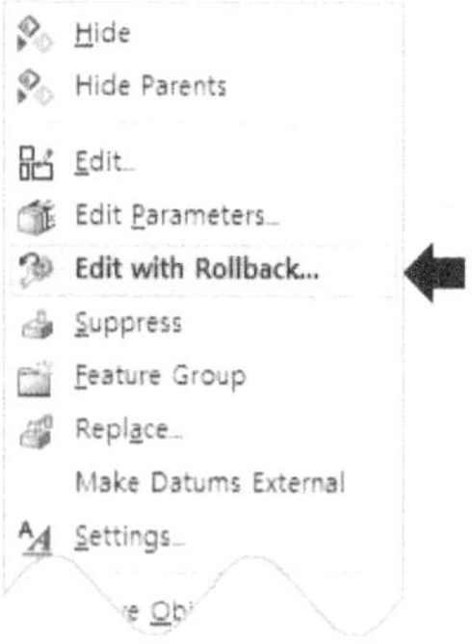

Fig 3-82 Edit with Rollback Option

3.11.2 Deleting Sketch Feature or Objects

You can delete the sketch features in the **Part Navigator** by selecting the features and pressing the **Delete** key.

Individual sketch objects can be deleted in the **Direct Sketch** or **Sketch** task environment. You can delete sketch curves, points, geometrical constraints or dimensional constraints by selecting them and pressing the **Delete** key.

Modifying Sketch **Exercise 05**

Let's modify the sketch that has been completed in Exercise 04. Delete the **Point on Curve** constraint that has been applied between the lower left end of the line and the X axis, and apply a 40mm dimension as shown in Fig 3-83 to fully constrain the line.

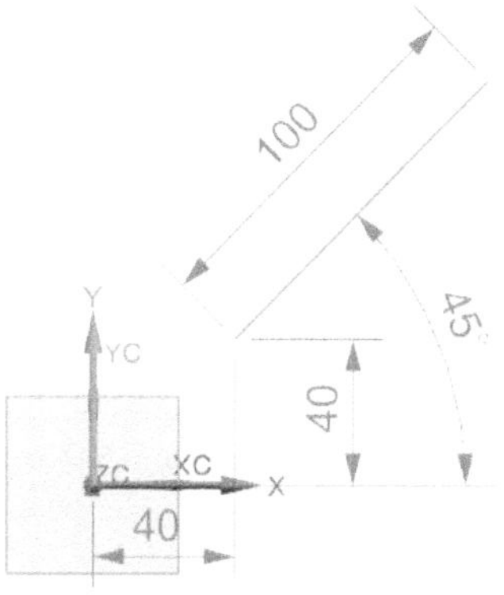

Fig 3-83 Modified Sketch

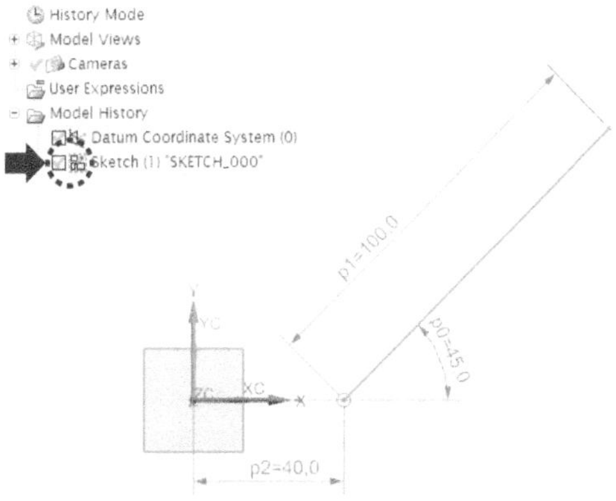

Fig 3-84 Entering Sketch Environment

Invoking the Sketch

1. Double click the sketch in the **Part Navigator**.

Note that the sketch symbol **Part Navigator** is changed as designated by the arrow in Fig 3-84. The sketch is aligned to the screen.

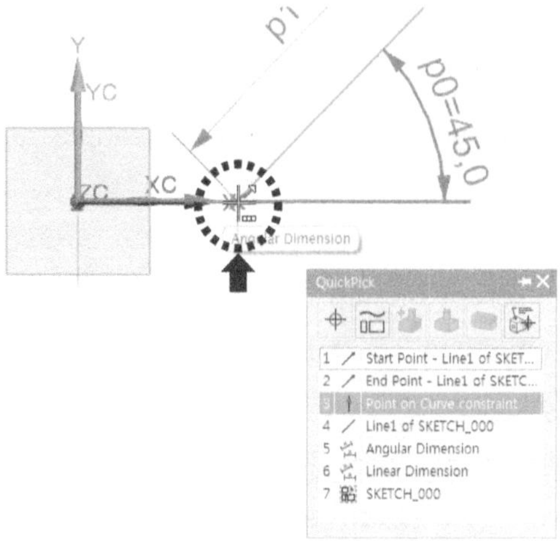

Fig 3-85 Deleting Geometrical Constraint

Deleting the Geometrical Constraint

1. Place the mouse pointer on the lower end of the line.
2. Click MB1 when the mouse pointer changes as designated by the arrow in Fig 3-85. The **Quick Pick** dialog box is invoked.
3. Click MB1 on the **Point on Curve Constraint** in the **Quick Pick** dialog box.
4. Press the **Delete** key.

The constraint symbol is deleted and the sketch status changes to partially constrained.

Adding Dimension

1. Drag the line as shown in Fig 3-86.
2. Press the **Inferred Dimensions** button and apply a 40mm vertical dimension as shown in Fig 3-87.
3. Press the **Q** key to finish the sketch.

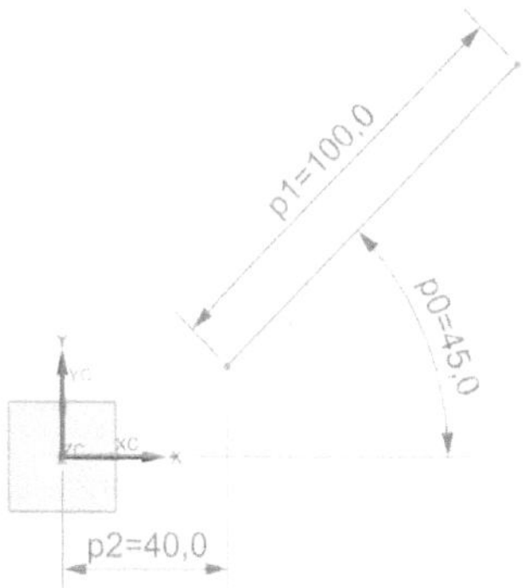

Fig 3-86 Dragging the Line

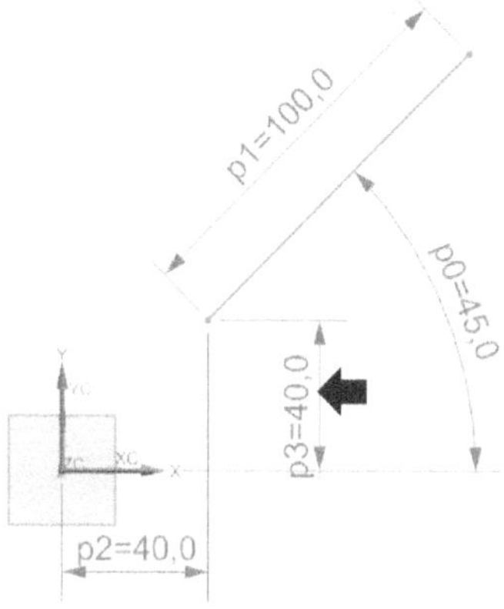

Fig 3-87 Creating Distance Dimension

END of Exercise

Creating a Rectangle Symmetric to the X and Y Axis (Make Symmetric Constraint) — Exercise 06

Let's create a rectangle that is symmetric to the X and Y axis as shown in Fig 3-88. Name the part file Exercise 06.prt and define a sketch on the XY plane.

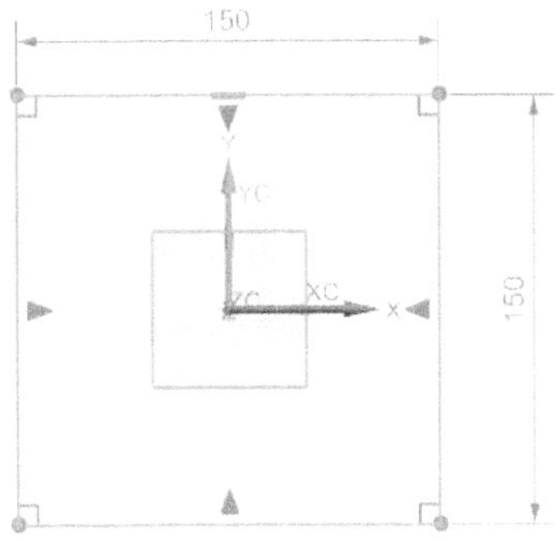

Fig 3-88 Rectangle Symmetric to the X and Y Axis

Create a Rectangle

1. Create a rectangle as shown in Fig 3-89 using the **Rectangle** icon in the **Direct Sketch** icon group.

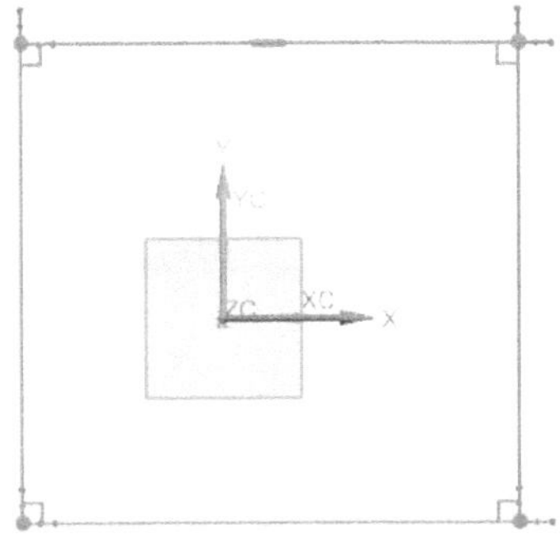

Fig 3-89 Rectangle

Confirm that the **Horizontal** and **Perpendicular** symbols are shown.

Apply Symmetric Constraint against the Y Axis

1. Press the **Make Symmetric** icon.
2. Select the primary object (A in Fig 3-90).
3. Select the secondary object (B in Fig 3-90).
4. Select the Y axis as the symmetry centerline (C in Fig 3-90).

A symmetric symbol appears as designated by the arrow in Fig 3-90.

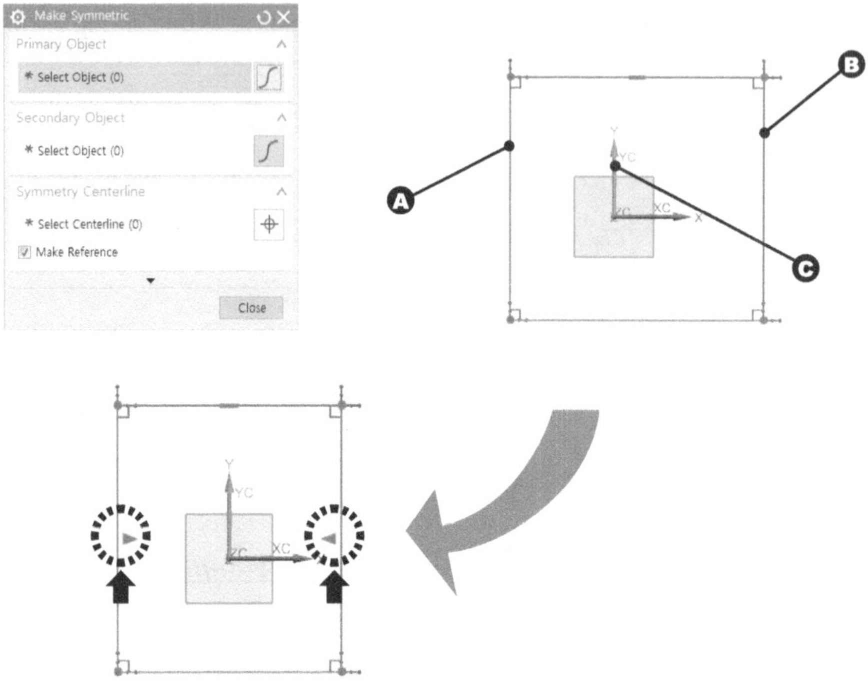

Fig 3-90 Applying Symmetric Constraint

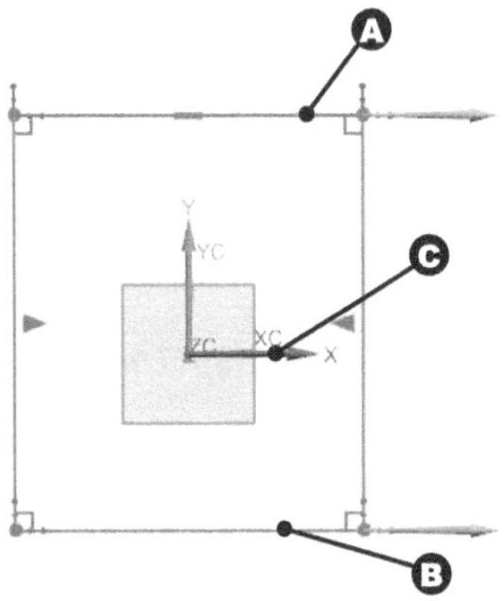

Fig 3-91 Applying Symmetric Constraint

Apply Symmetric Constraint against the X Axis

1. Press the **Reset** button in the **Make Symmetric** dialog box.
2. Apply the symmetric constraint by selecting Ⓐ, Ⓑ and Ⓒ in order as shown in Fig 3-91.
3. Close the **Make Symmetric** dialog box.

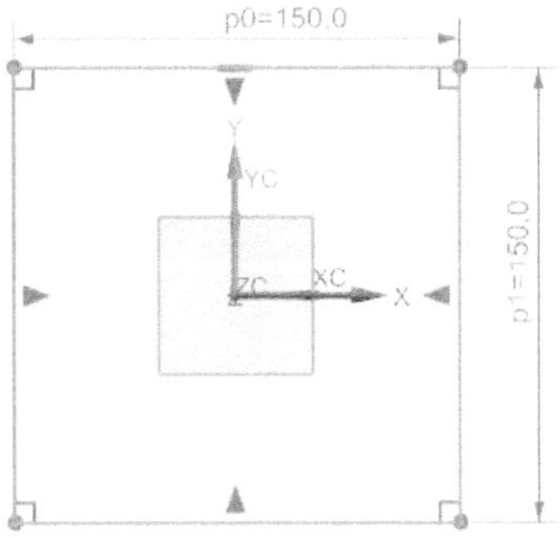

Fig 3-92 Applying Dimension

Applying Dimensions

1. Press the **Rapid Dimensions** icon and apply dimensions as shown in Fig 3-92.
2. Press the **Q** key to finish the sketch.

END of Exercise

Displaying Only the Dimension Values

1. Finish the direct sketch and choose **Preferences > Sketch** in the **Menu** button.

2. Select **Value** in the **Dimension Label** dropdown list.

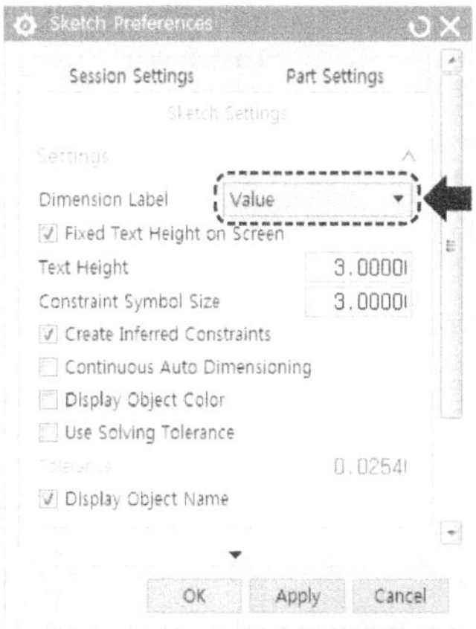

Fig 3-93 Sketch Style Dialog Box

This option applies for sketches that are created afterwards. If you want to apply the option for the existing sketches double click the sketch in the Part Navigator to invoke the **Sketch** task environment and choose **Task > Sketch Settings** in the **Menu** button.

! *Resetting*

You may encounter a situation that requires you to reset the various NX conditions.

1. Resetting the Ribbon bar and menus
Use the Role. The default role is "**Essentials**".

2. Resetting the dialog boxes
Use the **Reset** button in the dialog box.

3. Resetting the model view
Press the **Home** key on the keyboard. The **Trimetric View** is restored and the model is fitted in the graphics window.

4. Default rendering style
Drag the mouse upward while right clicking on the background of the graphics window. The default rendering style of "**Shaded with Edges**" is attained.

5. Resetting the customer defaults
   ① Choose **File > Utilities > Customer Defaults**
   ② Press the **Manage Current Settings** button in the **Customer Defaults** dialog box.
   ③ Delete changes of the customer defaults.

Refer to "1.8.5 Tracking the Changes and Deleting" on Page 31.

6. Resetting NX windows
   ① Choose **Preferences > User Interface** in the **Menu** button.
   ② Press the **Reset Window Position** button in the **Layout** tab.

Refer to "1.9.2 Resetting the Window Position" on Page 32.

Creating a Rectangle Symmetric to the X and Y Axis (Midpoint Constraint)

Exercise 07

Let's create a rectangle that is symmetric to the X and Y axis as shown in Fig 3-99. We will use the **Midpoint** constraint. Name the part file Exercise 07.prt and define a sketch on the XY plane.

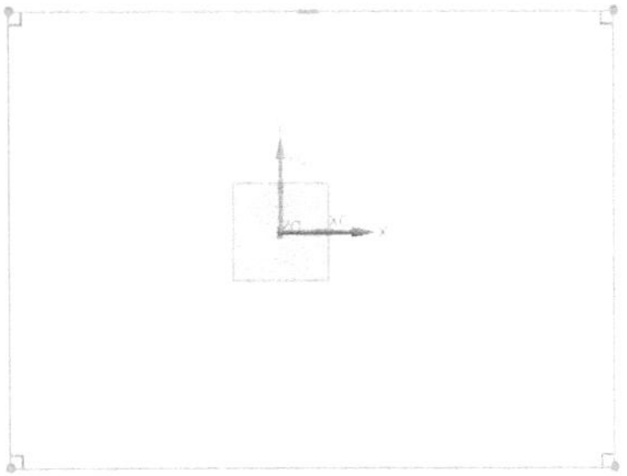

Fig 3-94 Rectangle

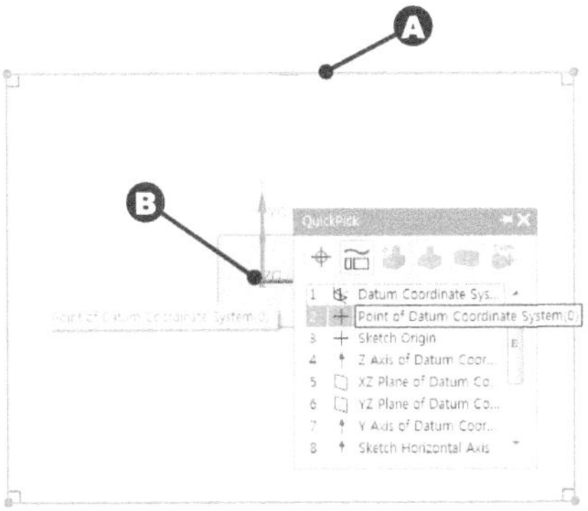

Fig 3-95 Selecting Objects

Fig 3-96 Shortcut Toolbar

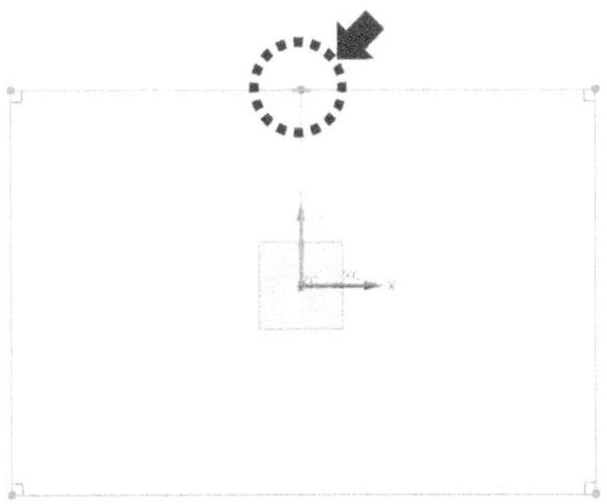

Fig 3-97 Applying Midpoint Constraint

Create a Rectangle

1. Create a rectangle as shown in Fig 3-94 using the **Rectangle** icon in the **Direct Sketch** icon group.

Confirm that the **Horizontal** and **Perpendicular** symbols are shown.

Applying Midpoint Constraint

1. Select the line **A** shown in Fig 3-95.
2. Select the point **B** shown in Fig 3-95. You may suffer difficulty in selecting the origin point. You can use the **QuickPick** utility.
3. Choose Midpoint in the shortcut toolbar as shown in Fig 3-96.

You can see the **Midpoint** symbol as designated by the dotted circle in Fig 3-97.

4. Apply a midpoint constraint between the horizontal line and the origin point as shown in Fig 3-98.

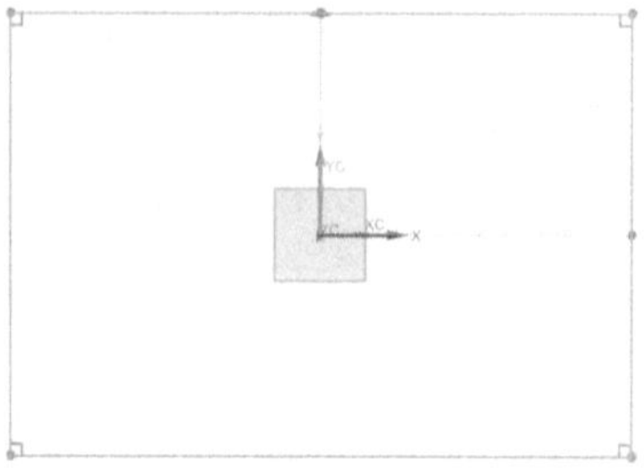

Fig 3-98 Midpoint Constraint Applied

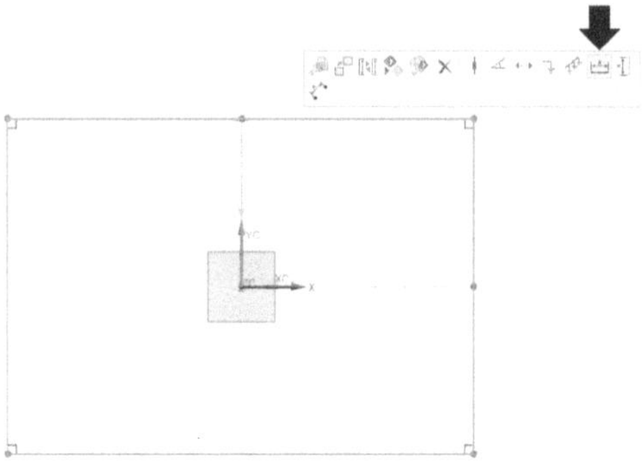

Fig 3-99 Dimension

Applying Dimensions

1. Select the horizontal line, choose **Horizontal Dimension** in the shortcut toolbar and modify the value to 150.
2. Apply the vertical dimension in the same way.
3. Finish the sketch.

END of Exercise

3.12 Other Sketch Commands

This section explains other useful sketch commands.

3.12.1 Quick Trim

You can trim sketch curves with respect to an intersecting curve. The **Point on Curve** constraint is created between the trimmed end point and the trimming line. Fig 3-101 shows the trimming a portion of a circle.

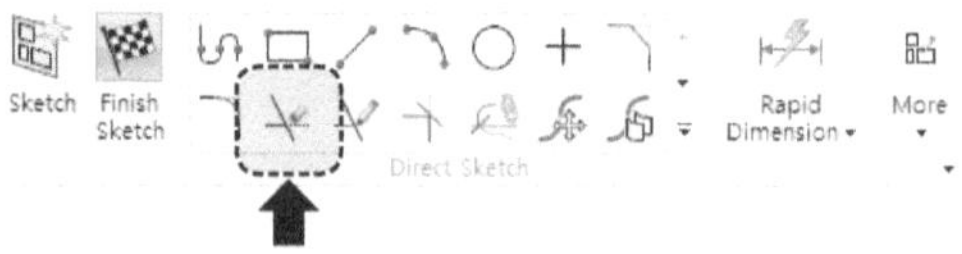

Fig 3-100 Quick Trim Icon

Fig 3-101 Before and After the Quick Trim

You can trim out several lines by using the crayon function as shown in Fig 3-102. Click the **Quick Trim** icon and drag the mouse on the curves to trim out while pressing MB1. The mouse pointer changes as shown in Fig 3-102 and the curves crossed by the path are trimmed out against the boundary curves that are met.

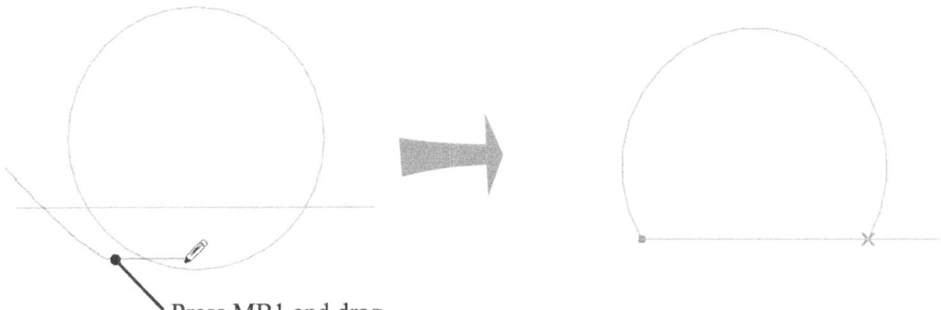

Fig 3-102 Trimming with the Crayon Function

3.12.2 Fillet

Connect two curves smoothly using an arc. The **Tangent** constraints are applied automatically. Press the **Fillet** icon in the **Direct Sketch** icon group. A Fillet option bar is invoked as shown in Fig 3-104 and you can specify the **Fillet Method**. If you select the **Trim** button, the remaining portion of the connected curve is trimmed out.

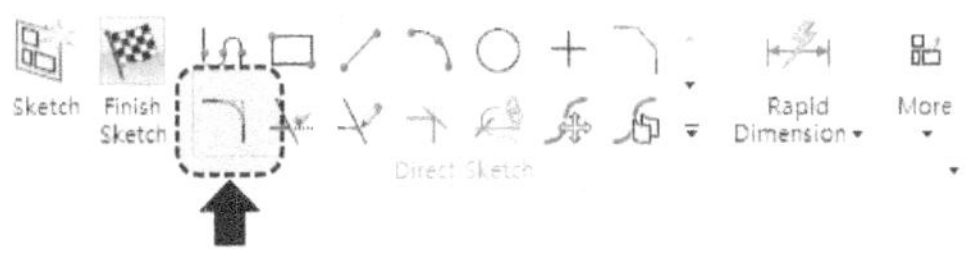

Fig 3-103 Fillet Icon

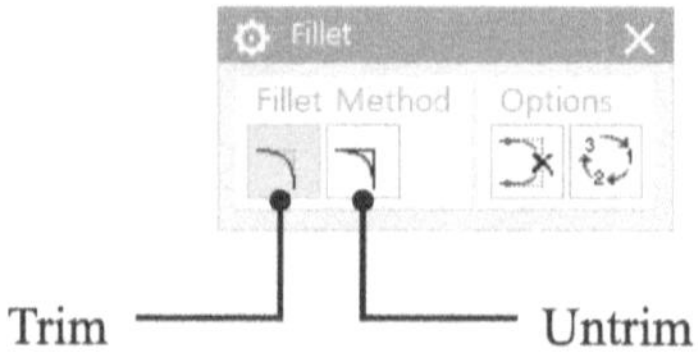

Fig 3-104 Fillet Method

Fig 3-105 shows the results of a fillet with the **Trim and Untrim** option.

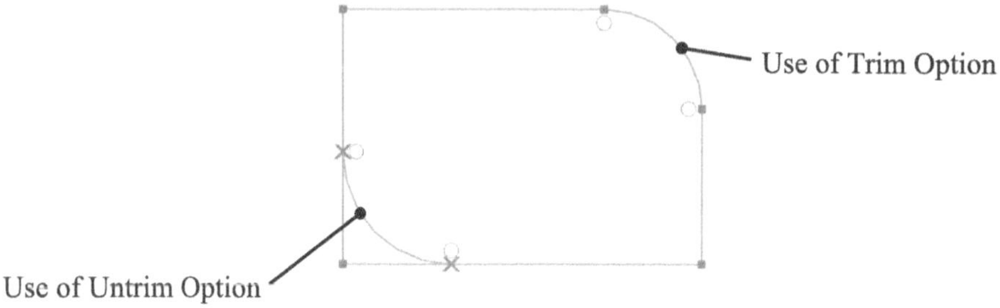

Fig 3-105 Results of Each Fillet Method

Press the **Fillet** icon and drag the mouse across the two curves to connect while pressing MB1. The **Crayon** function is completed and a fillet is applied.

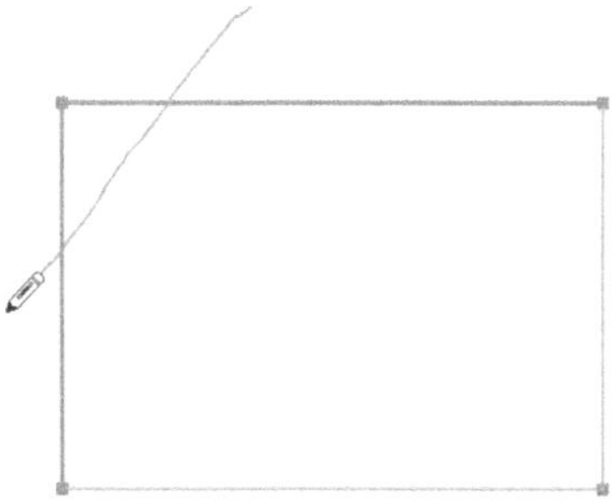

Fig 3-106 Use of Crayon Function

3.12.3 Mirror Curve

You can mirror sketch curves against a specified symmetric line. In case you have created curves that are not symmetric, but you want to make them symmetric, apply the **Symmetric Constraint**. Note that you can apply the **Symmetric Constraint** for a respective set of symmetric curves one by one.

Fig 3-107 Mirror Curve Icon

Fig 3-108 shows mirroring a circle with respect to the Y axis. The **Mirror** symbol appears.

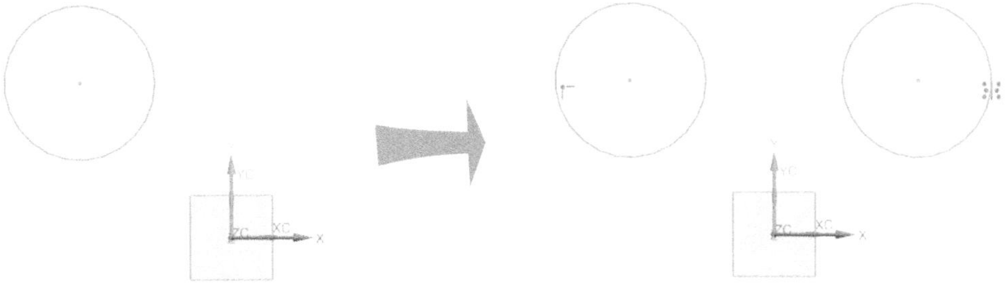

Fig 3-108 Mirroring with Mirror Curve Command

Creating a Horizontal Line **Exercise 08**

Create a horizontal line and fully constrain it so that the center passes through the origin to be collinear with the X axis.

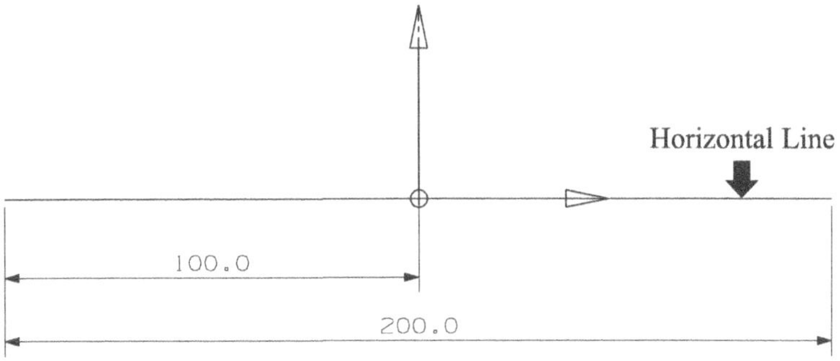

Fig 3-109 Horizontal Line

Procedure

1. Create a line below the X axis using the **Line** command.
2. Apply the **Collinear** and **Midpoint** constraints referring to the following table.

No	Object to Select		Geometrical Constraint
1	Line	X axis	Collinear
2	Line	Point at the Origin	Midpoint

3. Apply either a 100mm or 200mm dimension.

END of Exercise

Caution!

You must not apply two dimensions in Fig 3-109. When you apply only one dimension, the sketch is fully constrained because the other distance is constrained by the **Midpoint** constraint. If you apply both dimensions, the sketch will be over constrained.

Selecting Object in the QuickPick Dialog Box

The **QuickPick** dialog box can be invoked to facilitate selecting a specific object among several overlapped objects. Place the mouse pointer on the objects and wait for a few seconds. When the mouse pointer changes as shown in Fig 3-110, click MB1. The **QuickPick** dialog box as shown in Fig 3-111 appears and you can select the desired object in the dialog box.

Fig 3-110 QuickPick Indicator

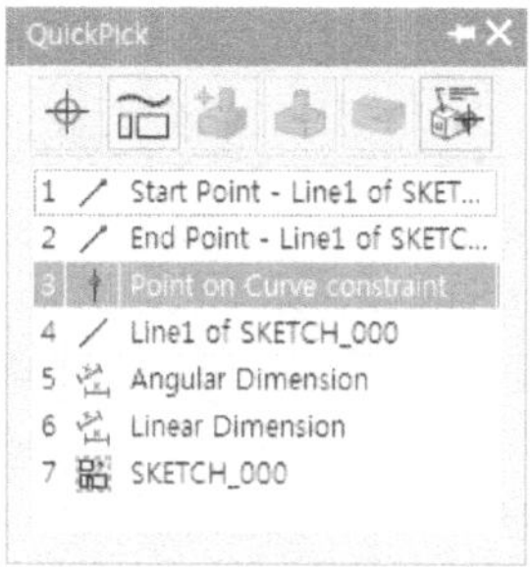

Fig 3-111 Quickpick Dialog Box

Create a closed half circle whose center is at the origin as shown in Fig 3-112 and fully constrain the sketch.

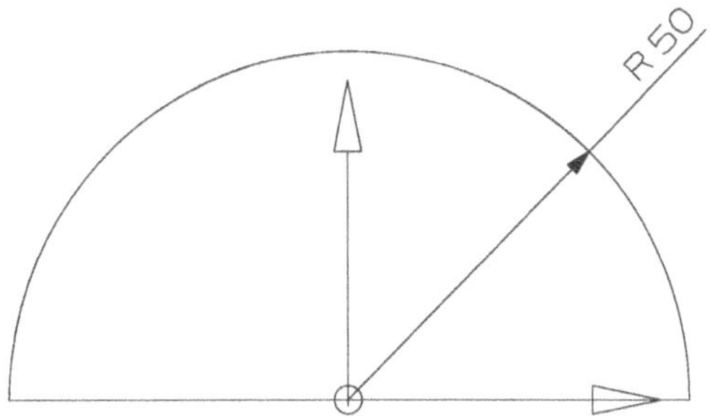

Fig 3-112 Closed Half Circle

Procedure

1. Create a circle whose center is constrained at the origin point.
2. Press the **Alt** key and create a horizontal line under the X axis and across the circle.
3. Apply the **Collinear** constraint between the X axis and the horizontal line.
4. Trim out the lower portion of the circle at the line beyond the circle.
5. Apply the radius dimension.

If the sketch is not fully constrained, apply appropriate additional constraints.

END of Exercise

Exercise 10 Creating a Regular Triangle

Create a triangle and fully constrain it as shown in Fig 3-113. The lower side line is collinear with the X axis and the center of the lower side is at the origin.

Caution!

Do not apply the dimension (50) in the figure. The half distance will be constrained by the 100mm dimension and the **Midpoint** constraint between the horizontal line and the origin.

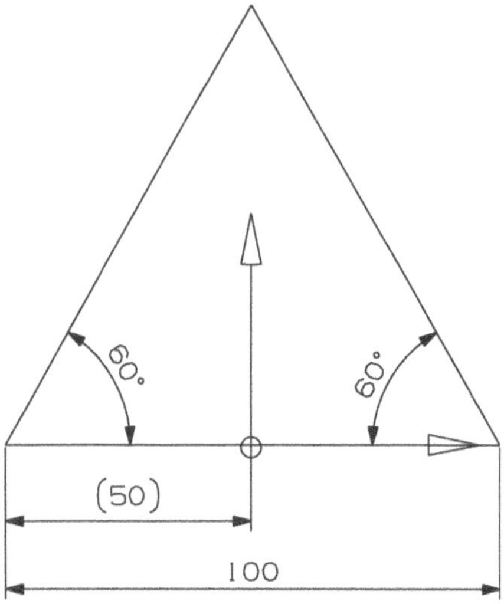

Fig 3-113 Regular Triangle

Hints!

1. Create a triangle with the **Profile** command.
2. Create a horizontal line under the X axis. Be sure that the **Horizontal** constraint is snapped.
3. Refer to Exercise 08 to constrain the lower horizontal line.
4. Apply the **Equal Length** constraint for the three side lines.

END of Exercise

Create a rectangle and apply a fillet at the corners as shown in Fig 3-114. The sketch has to be fully constrained.

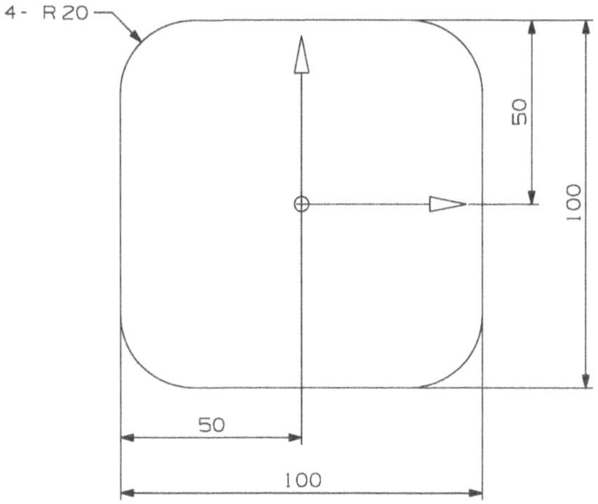

Fig 3-114 Rounded Rectangle

Procedure

1. Create a rectangle so that the origin is located in the middle of the rectangle.
2. Press the **Fillet** icon in the **Direct Sketch** icon group.
3. Select the two lines specified in Fig 3-115.
4. Move the mouse pointer around the location shown in Fig 3-116.

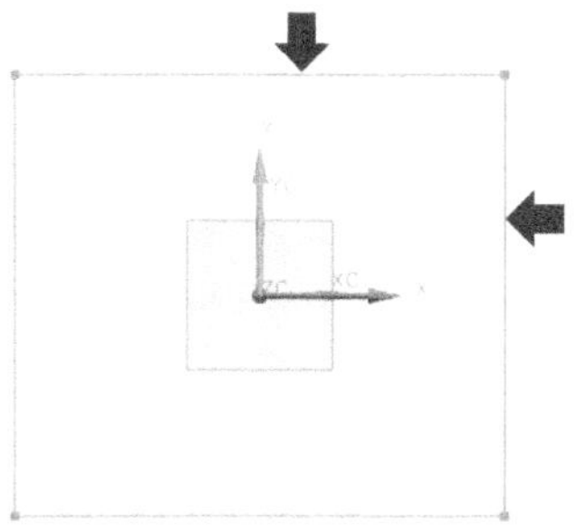

Fig 3-115 Selecting Two Lines

5. Click MB1 to create a fillet as shown in Fig 3-117.

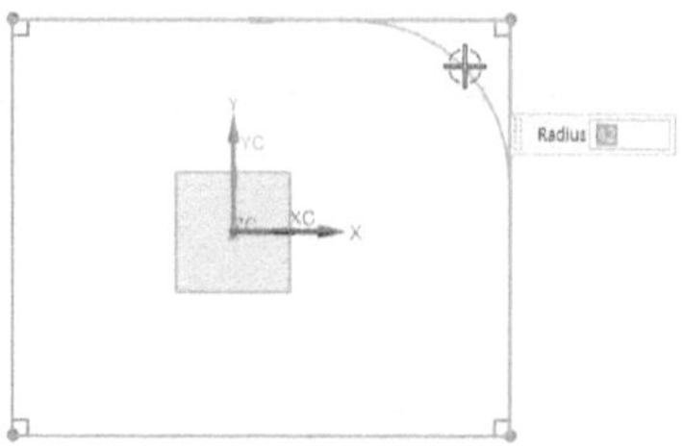

Fig 3-116 Location of the Mouse Cursor (⌖)

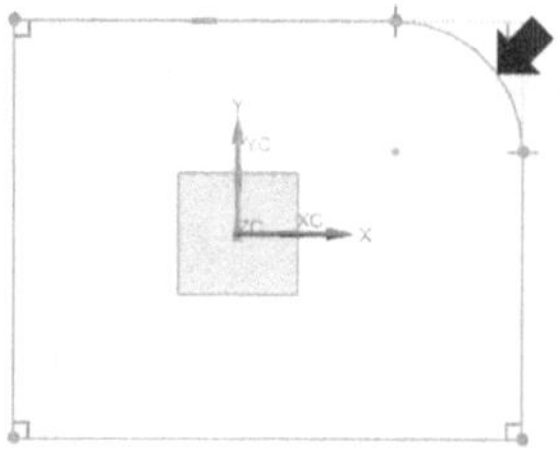

Fig 3-117 Fillet Created

6. Create fillets for the other three corners as shown in Fig 3-118. You can use the crayon function as shown in Fig 3-119.

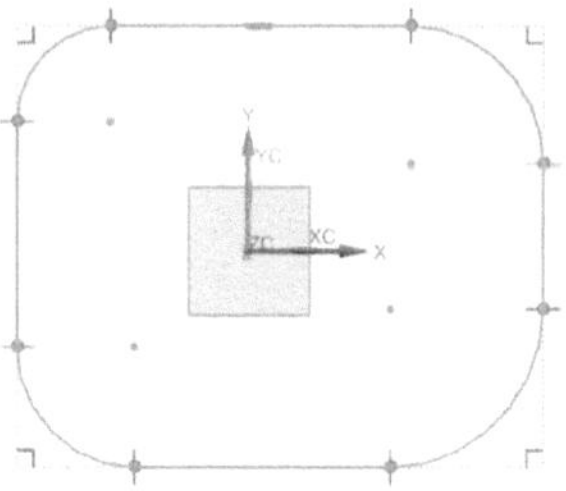

Fig 3-118 Rounded Corners

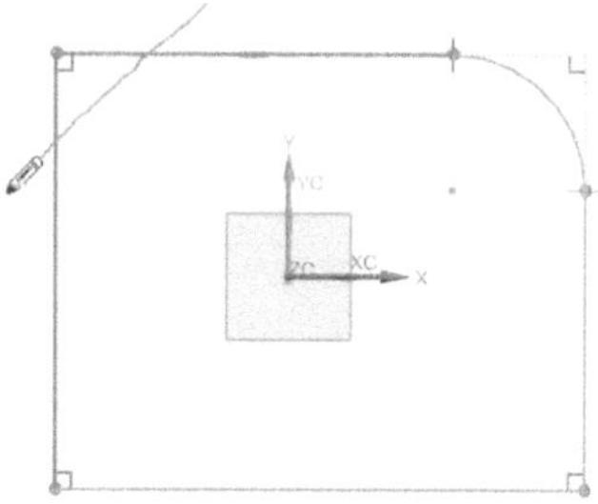

Fig 3-119 Using the Crayon Function

7. Apply geometrical constraints (**Midpoint**, **Equal Length**, **Equal Radius**) and dimensional constraints (horizontal and radius dimension) to fully constrain the sketch.

END of Exercise

Caution!

1. If you drag the mouse while the **Rectangle** icon is pressed, the **Rectangle Method** is changed to the second rectangle as shown in Fig 3-120. In this case, press the first icon in the dialog bar.

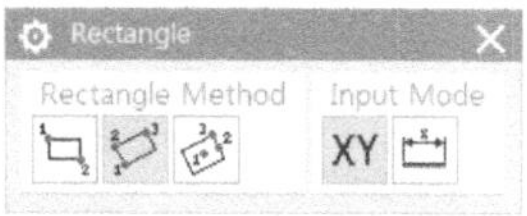

Fig 3-120 Rectangle Method

2. If you apply the **Midpoint** constraint first and then create a fillet with the **Trim** option, the **Midpoint** constraint will be deleted.

Create a sketch as shown in Fig 3-121and fully constrain it.

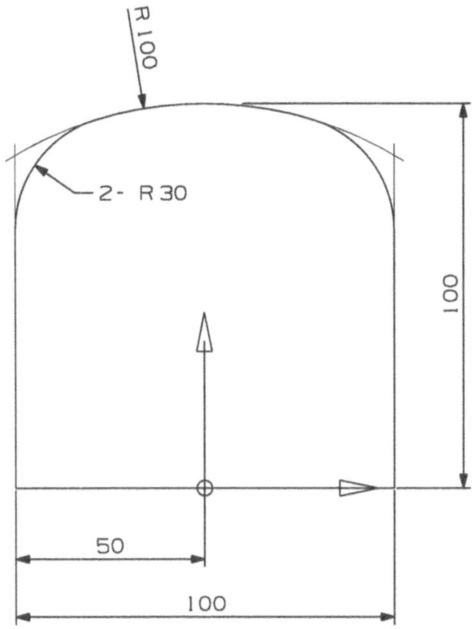

Fig 3-121 A Sketch with Fillet

Hints!

Follow the procedure shown in Fig 3-122 to draw curves and apply appropriate constraints.

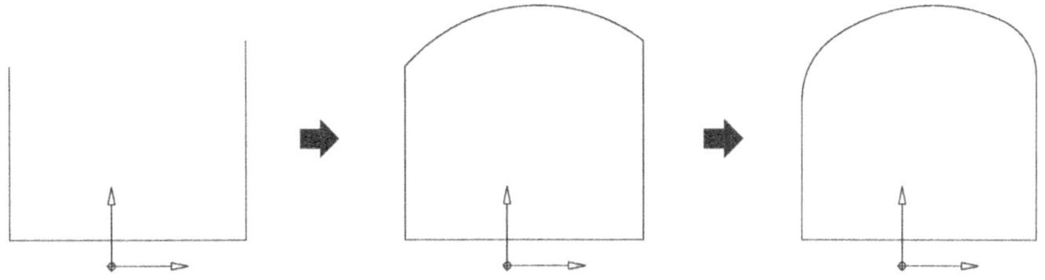

Fig 3-122 Drawing Curves

END of Exercise

Exercise 13 Creating Symmetric Sketch

Let's create a sketch that is symmetric with respect to the Y axis and fully constrain it as shown in Fig 3-123. Note that the sketch consists of three pairs of symmetric arcs.

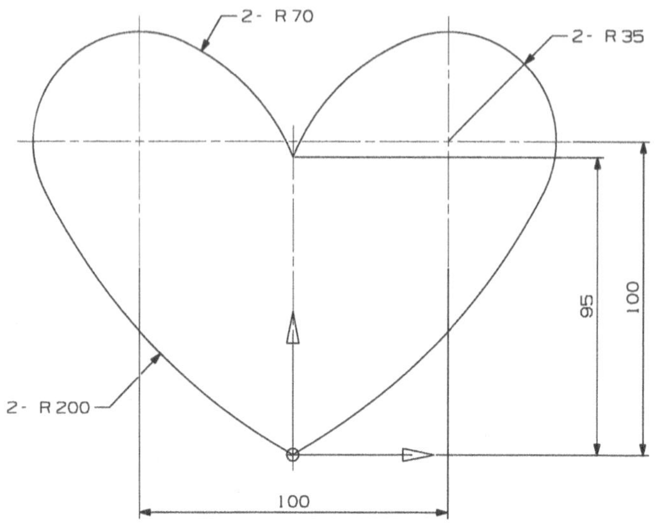

Fig 3-123 Symmetric Sketch

Procedure

1. Create a circle and two arcs as shown in Fig 3-124 and apply geometrical constraints.

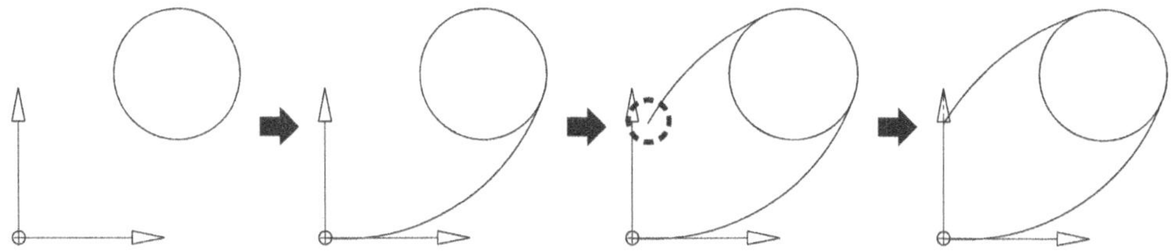

Fig 3-124 Creating a Circle and Two Arcs

Hints!

Apply the **Point on Curve** constraint between the end of the arc designated by the dotted circle in Fig 3-124 and the Y axis. Be sure to select the end of the arc so it is located in the circular mouse cursor. If you have selected the end point successfully, a small asterisk is displayed at the end of the arc.

2. Select the **Mirror Curve** icon in the **Direct Sketch** icon group.

Fig 3-125 Mirror Curve Icon

Drop-down Button

You can select the **Mirror Curve** icon by clicking the **Sketch Curve** dropdown button (Ⓐ in Fig 3-126).

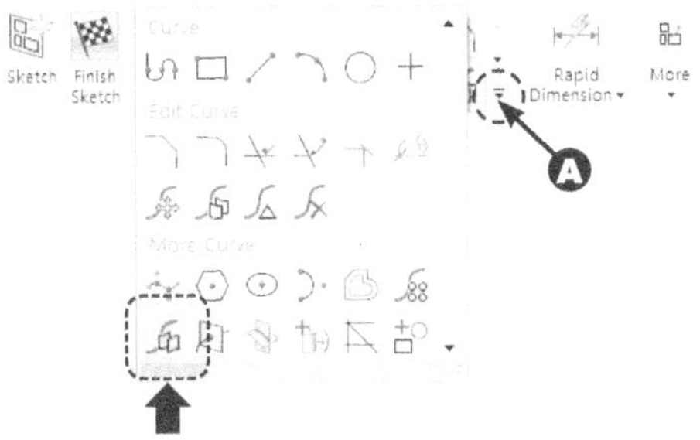

Fig 3-126 Drop-down button

The **Mirror Curve** dialog box appears as shown in Fig 3-127.

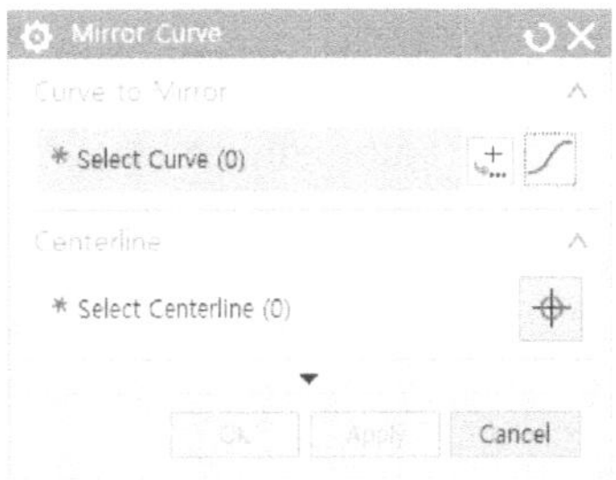

Fig 3-127 Mirror Curve Dialog Box

3. Select the curves (one circle and two arcs).
4. Press MB2.
5. Select the Y axis. You can select either the datum axis or the sketch axis.

6. Press the **OK** button in the **Mirror Curve** dialog box. Curves are mirrored as shown in Fig 3-128 and the mirror symbol appears on the curves.

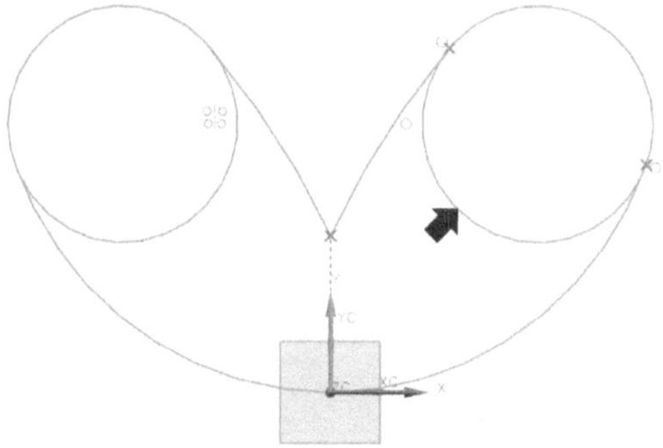

Fig 3-128 Mirrored Curved

7. Trim out the portion of the circle designated by the arrow in Fig 3-128.
8. Apply dimensional and geometrical constraints as required to fully constrain the sketch.

Order of Constraints

In general, geometrical constraints are applied first to shape the sketch and then the dimensional constraints are applied. However, you do not need to stick to this order all the time. When you encounter abrupt changes to the sketch as a result of a constraint, undo it by pressing **Ctrl + Z** and try other constraints.

Quick Extend

When a curve is created short as shown in Fig 3-129, you can extend the end of the curve by using the **Quick Extend** command. You may apply the **Point on Curve** constraint between the end point of the curve and the circle.

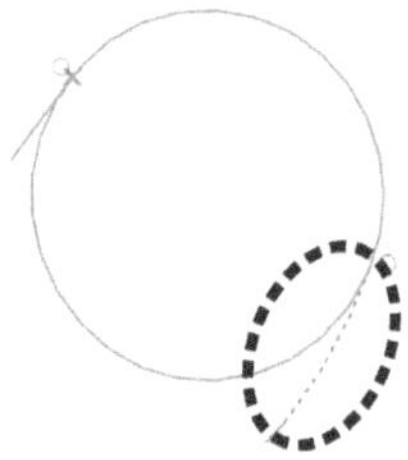

Fig 3-129 Arc Created in Short

Fig 3-130 Result of Quick Extend

END of Exercise

3.13 Reference Dimension and Curve

You can create a reference dimension or you can convert a driving dimension into a reference dimension. The reference dimensions do not work in evaluating the constraints network but just show the current dimension value as a result of other constraints.

If you convert a curve into a reference curve, you cannot use the curve in defining the section to create 3D geometry. Reference curves are used to define other sketch curves.

Fig 3-131 shows a fully constrained sketch. If you apply a regular driving dimension on the slanted line, the sketch will be over constrained. If you apply a reference dimension or convert the driving dimension into a reference dimension as shown in Fig 3-132, the sketch is not over constrained and the dimension is displayed in another color (Color ID 191: Strong Stone).

You can create a reference dimension when you apply the dimension, but this method is not recommended. Instead, convert a driving dimension to a reference dimension after creation as shown in Fig 3-132. Note that you cannot modify the dimension by double clicking the reference dimension.

If you want to convert a reference dimension to a driving dimension (Color ID 134: Medium Royal), press MB3 on the reference dimension and select **Convert to Driving** in the popup menu.

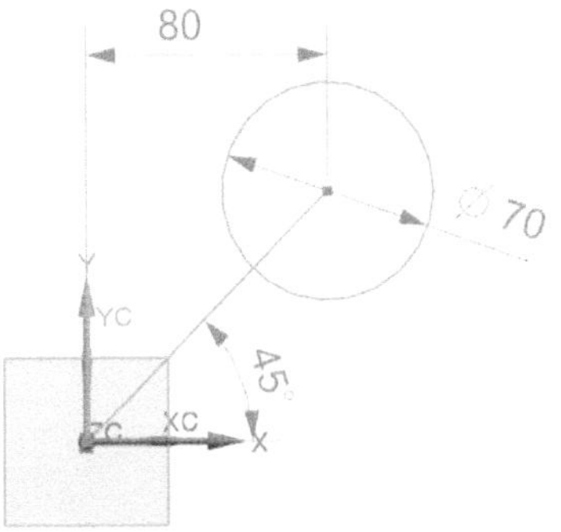

Fig 3-131 Fully Constrained Sketch

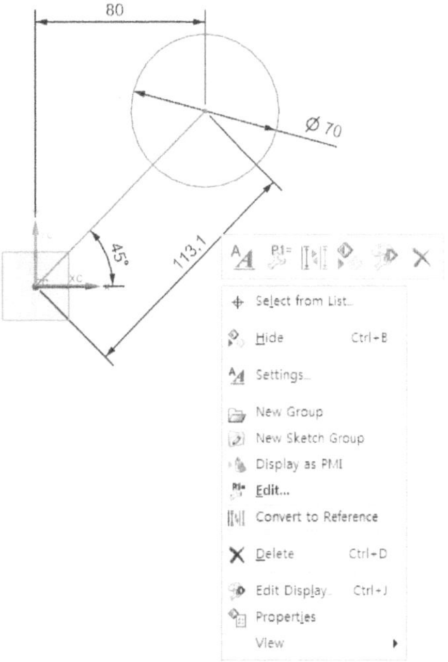

Fig 3-132 Convert to Reference Option

The slanted line in Fig 3-131 is created to apply an angular dimension. In this case, you can convert the line into a reference curve. Place the mouse pointer on the line and press **MB3 > Convert to Reference**. The reference curve is displayed in a phantom line. Note that the reference curves cannot be selected to define the section to create 3D geometry.

If you want to convert the reference curve into an active curve, press MB3 on the curve and select **Convert to Active** in the popup menu.

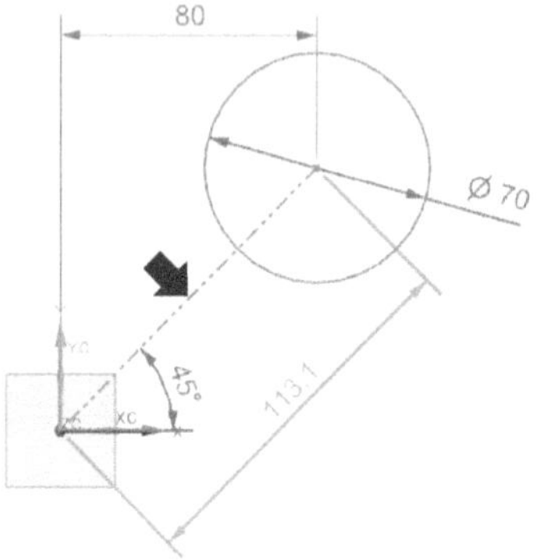

Fig 3-133 Reference Curve

Create Reference Dimension Option

You can create a reference dimension while you are creating dimensional constraints, by checking the **Reference** option in the dialog box. Note that the option has to be turned off to create driving dimensions afterwards. You cannot modify the dimension value when the dimension is created in reference.

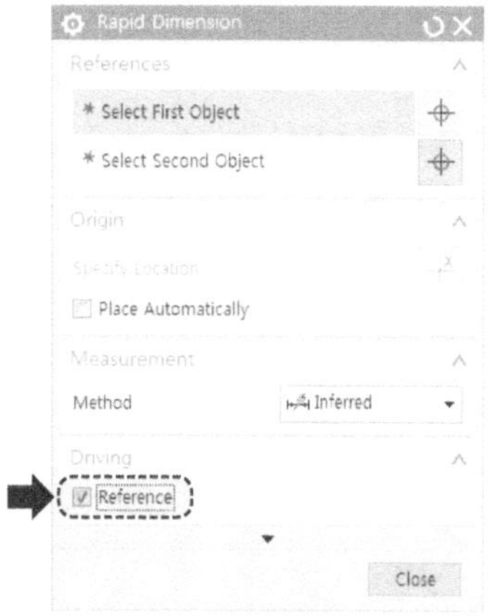

Fig 3-134 The Reference Option

Create a sketch and fully constrain as shown in Fig 3-135.

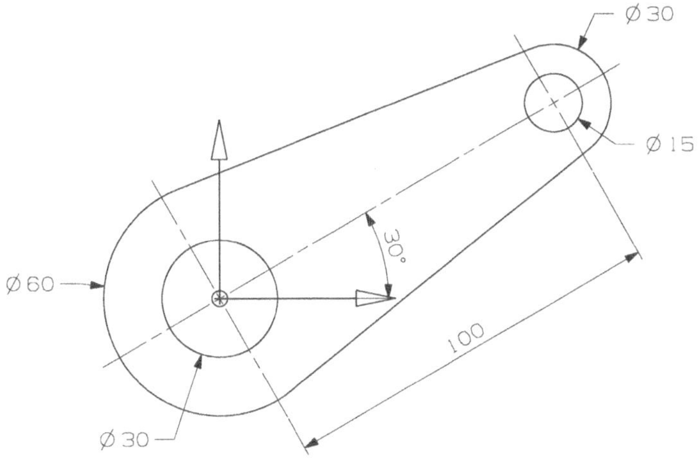

Fig 3-135 Sketch to Create

Procedure

1. Create a sketch as shown in Fig 3-136.

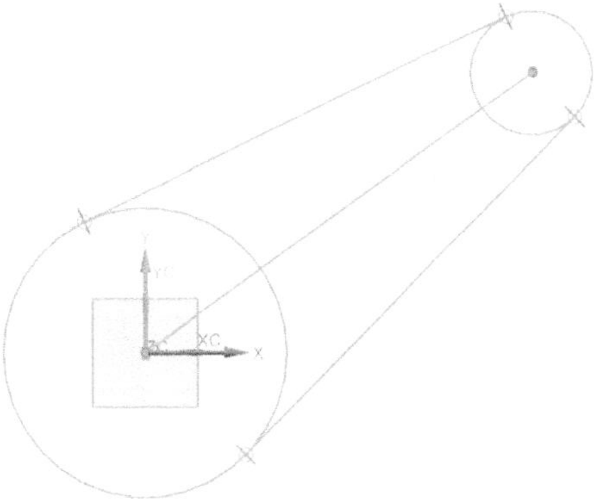

Fig 3-136 Creating Sketch Curves

2. Trim unnecessary curves as shown in Fig 3-137.
3. Create two circles as shown in Fig 3-138.

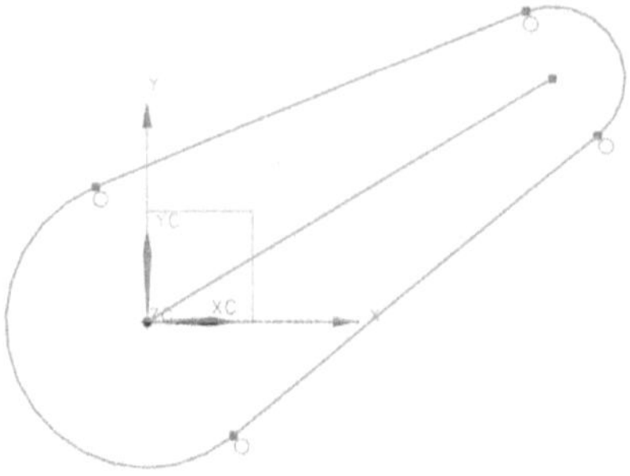

Fig 3-137 Applying Quick Trim

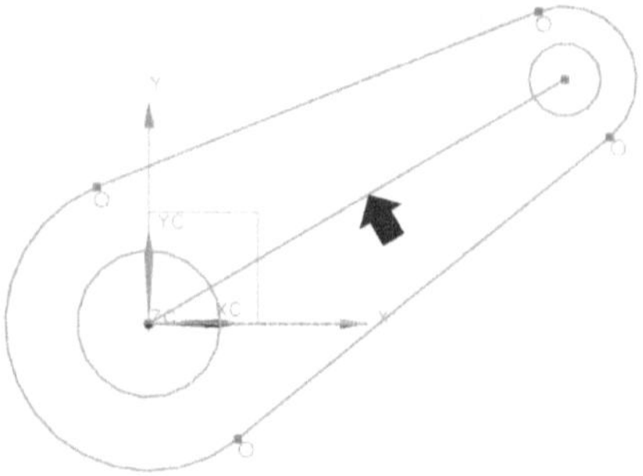

Fig 3-138 Creating Circles

4. Place the mouse pointer on the line specified by the arrow in Fig 3-138 and press MB3.
5. Select **Convert to Reference** in the popup menu shown in Fig 3-139. The line is converted to a phantom line.

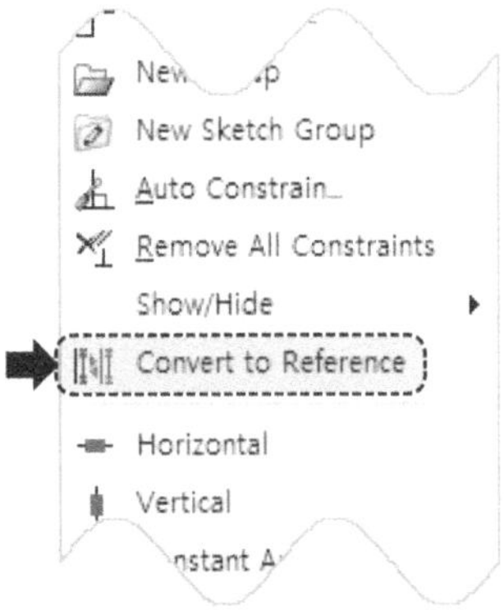

Fig 3-139 Convert To Reference Option

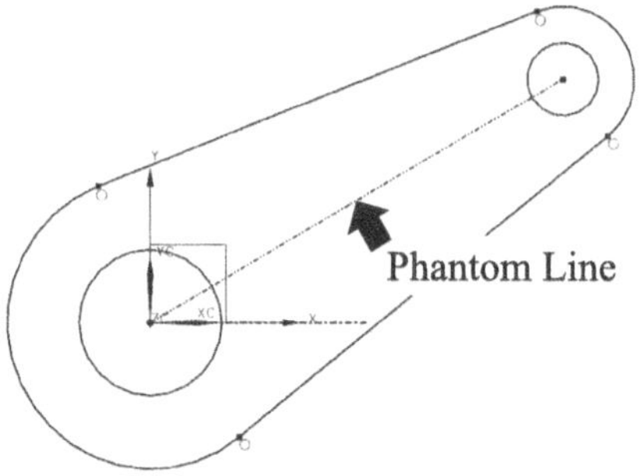

Fig 3-140 Reference Line

6. Apply dimensional constraints to fully constrain the sketch and finish the sketch.

END of Exercise

3.14 Understanding Continuous Auto Dimensioning

Up until now, we have created the sketch with the auto dimensioning option turned off. In this section, let's create the sketch in Exercise 14 in the **Direct Sketch** after turning on the **Continuous Auto Dimensioning** option.

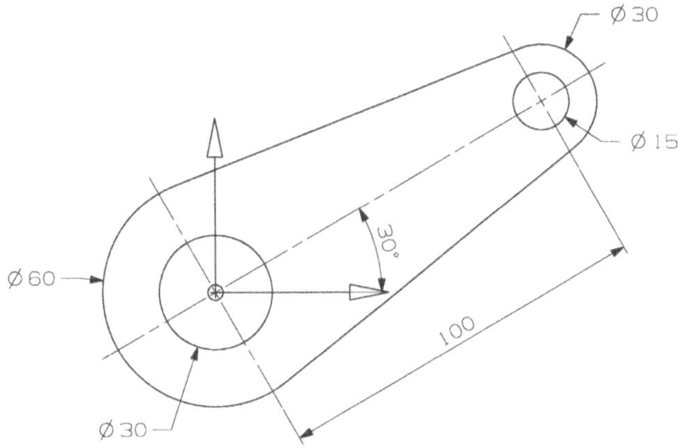

Fig 3-141 Sketch to Create

1. Create a new part file.
2. Select **Preferences > Sketch** in the **Menu** button.
3. Check the **Continuous Auto Dimensioning** option in the **Sketch Settings** tab in the **Sketch Preferences** dialog box shown in Fig 3-142 and click OK.

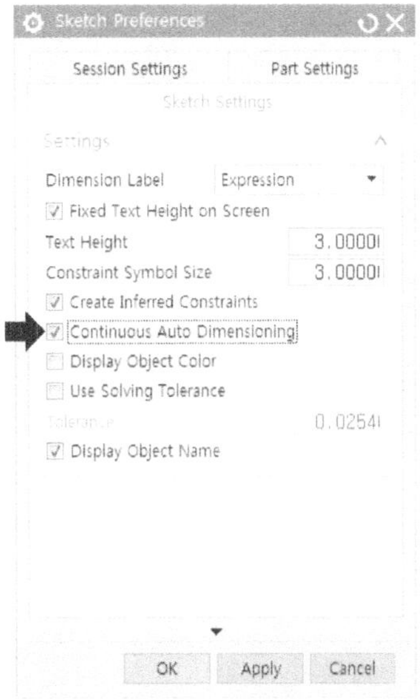

Fig 3-142 Continuous Auto Dimensioning Option

4. Press the **Sketch** icon in the **Direct Sketch** icon group.

5. Reset the **Create Sketch** dialog box and click **OK** in the dialog box. The sketch plane is defined on the XY plane and the sketch axes are aligned on the screen.

6. Create a sketch as shown in Fig 3-143 using the icons available in the **Direct Sketch** icon group. The dimensions that are automatically created may be different from that shown in Fig 3-143.

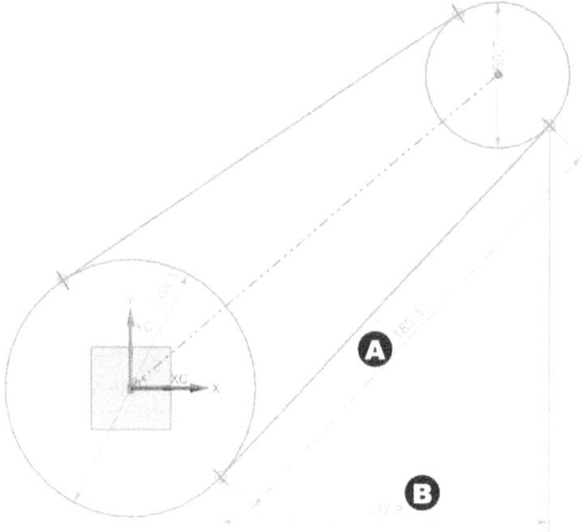

Fig 3-143 Sketch with Autodimensioning

Dimensions Ⓐ and Ⓑ specified in Fig 3-143 cannot be deduced from the drawing shown in Fig 3-141. The auto dimensions have to be constituted by other conditions to fully constrain. Let's apply the angle and length dimension.

7. Click the **Rapid Dimension** icon in the **Direct Sketch** icon group.

8. Create the angular and length dimensions of the reference line as shown in Fig 3-144.

Confirm that the auto dimensions Ⓐ and Ⓑ in Fig 3-143 disappear.

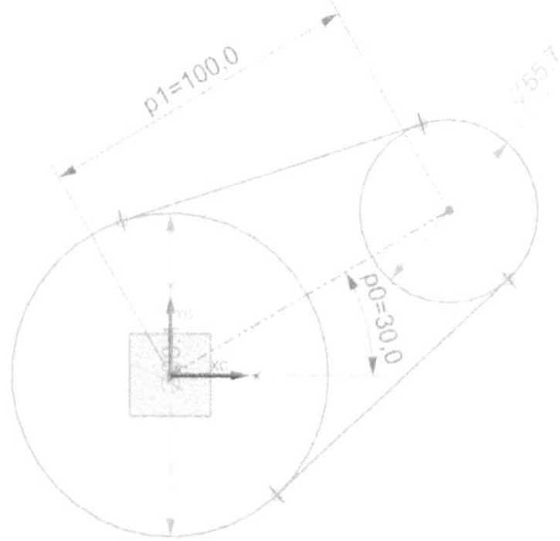

Fig 3-144 Dimension

Continuous Auto Dimensioning Option

Scope of the **Continuous Auto Dimensionig** option depends on with which menu you have set the option.

1. If you have set the option in **File > Utilities > Customer Defaults** in the **Menu** button, the option is applied whenever you execute NX.
2. If you have set the option in **Preferences > Sketch** in the **Menu** button, the option is applied for all sketches in the current NX session after setting the option. It has precedence over the **Customer Defaults** settings.
3. If you turn on or off the **Continuous Auto Dimensioning** button in the **Direct Sketch** icon group or in the **Sketch** task environment, the option applies for only the sketch. It has precedence over settings in **Preferences** or **Customer Defaults**.

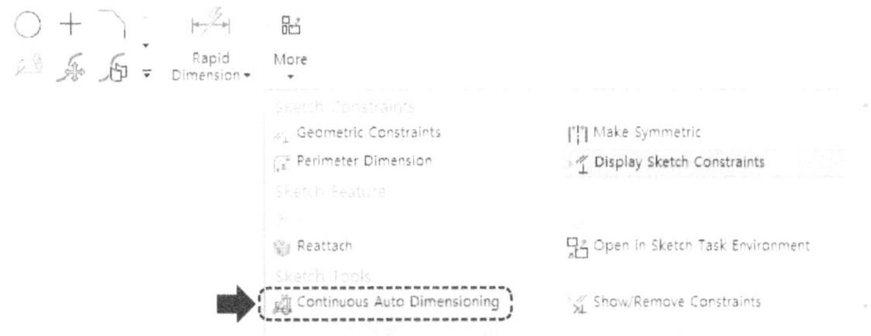

Fig 3-145 Continuous Auto Dimensioning option in the Direct Sketch Icon Group

When the **Continuous Auto Dimensioning** option is turned on, you cannot delete the auto dimensions. If you want to delete the auto dimension, you have to turn off the **Continuous Auto Dimensioning** option in the **Direct Sketch** or in the **Sketch** task environment.

9. Press the **ESC** key to cancel the **Rapid Dimension** command. The status line message reads as shown in Fig 3-146.

Fig 3-146 Status Line Message

Note that the sketch curves with auto dimensions can be dragged. You have to enter exact dimension values for the auto dimension. It implies that you have to regard the fully constrained sketch with auto dimension as not really fully constrained.

10. Double click the diameter dimension and enter the exact value. The colour of the dimension changes to blue which is a driving dimension.

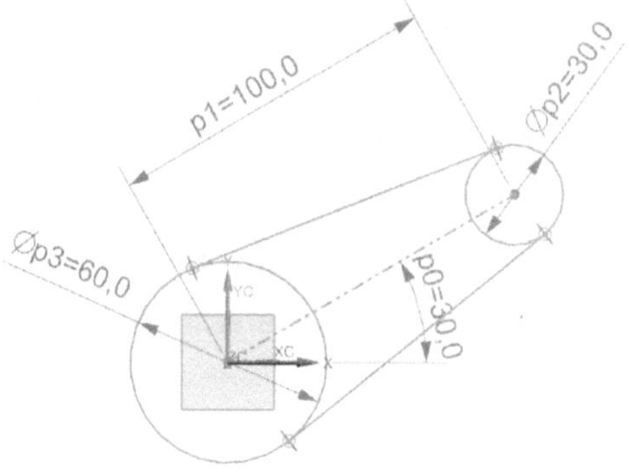

Fig 3-147 Fully Constrained Sketch

11. Complete other constraints and trim out the unnecessary curves and finish the sketch.

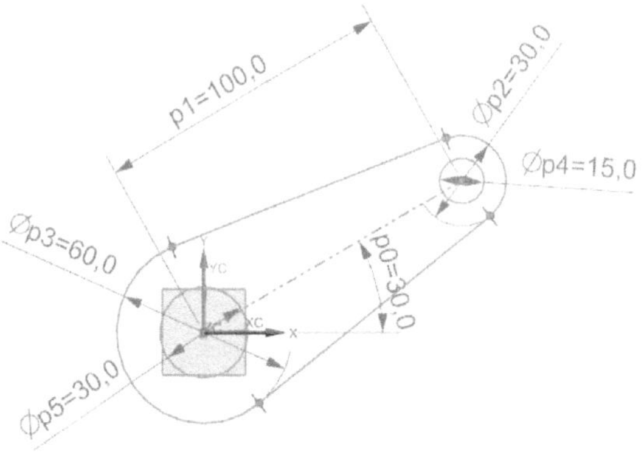

Fig 3-148 Completed Sketch

Create the sketch shown in Fig 3-149.

Caution!

1. The dimensions in the drawing do not mean that they all have to be applied as the dimensional constraint.
2. Fully constrain the sketch.
3. Locate the sketch origin (⊕) at the origin of the coordinate system.

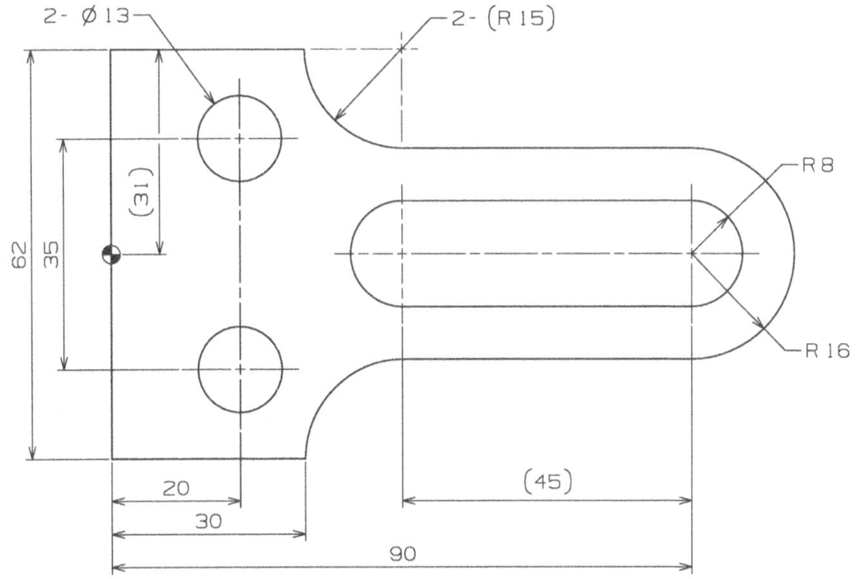

Fig 3-149 Bracket

Defining the Sketch Origin

Depending on the location of the sketch, constraining can become easier or more difficult. Therefore, you have to be prudent in defining the sketch origin. A general guideline is to define the origin on the symmetric line or at the center of a circle.

END of Exercise

Exercise 16 Flat Pin

Create the sketch shown in Fig 3-150.

Caution!

1. The dimensions in the drawing do not mean that they all have to be applied as the dimensional constraint.
2. Fully constrain the sketch.
3. Locate the sketch origin (⊕) at the origin of the coordinate system.

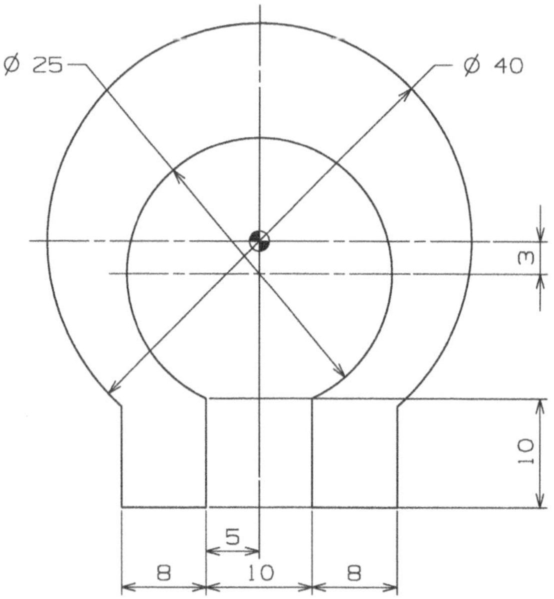

Fig 3-150 Flat Pin

END of Exercise

Create the sketch shown in Fig 3-151.

Caution!

1. The dimensions in the drawing do not mean that they all have to be applied as the dimensional constraint.
2. Fully constrain the sketch.
3. Locate the sketch origin (⊕) at the origin of the coordinate system.

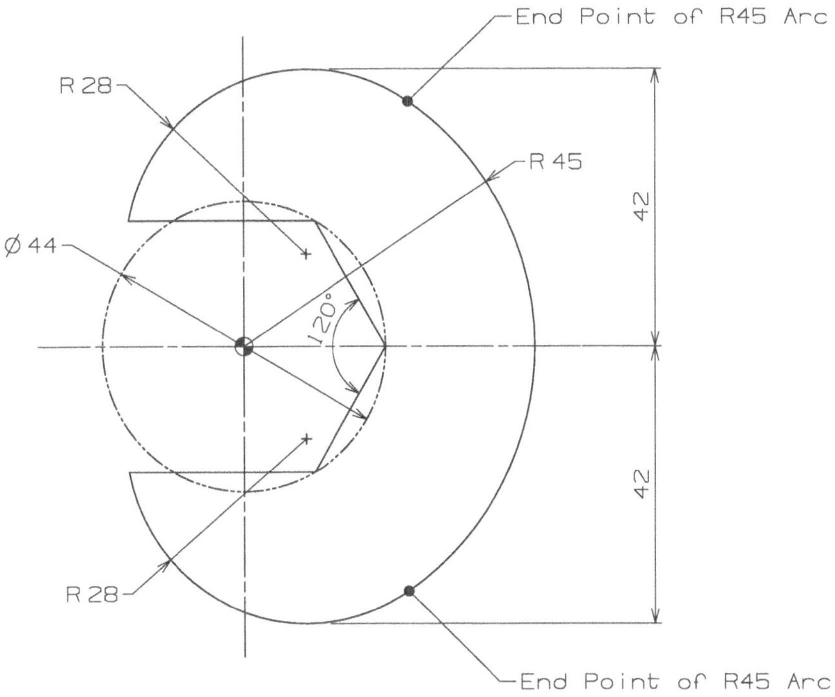

Fig 3-151 Spanner Head

END of Exercise

Hints!

Create sketch curves and constrain them according to the following steps.

❶

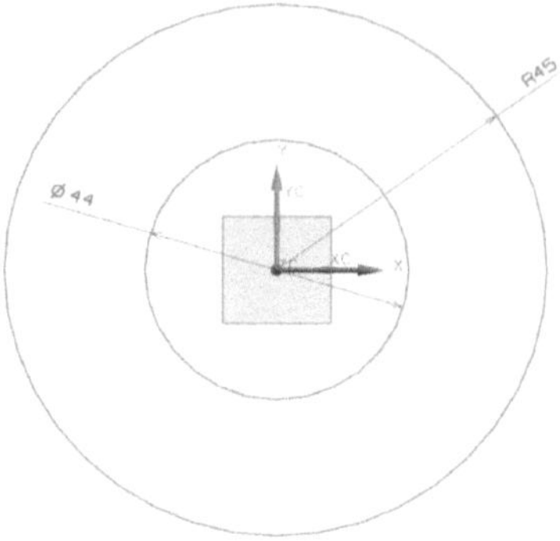

❷

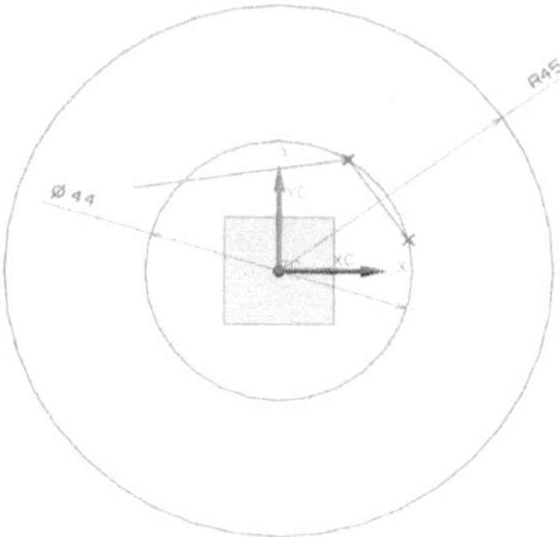

❸

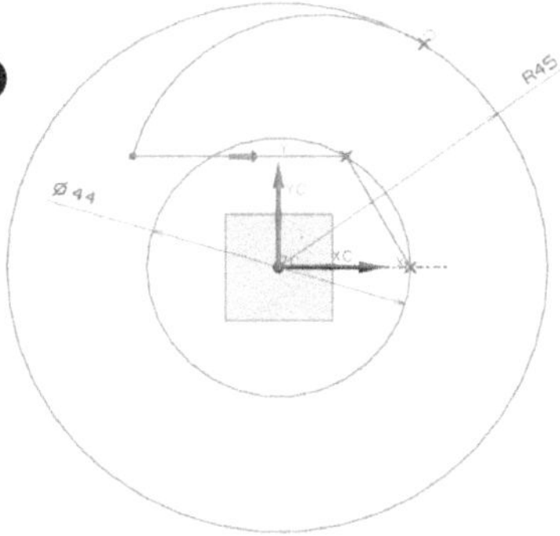

❹

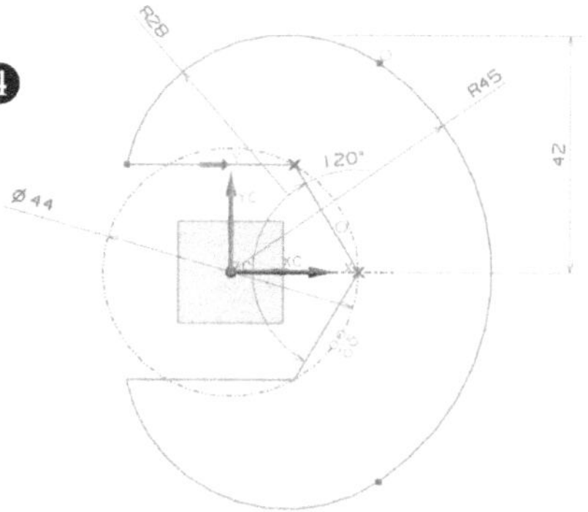

END of Exercise

Create the sketch shown in Fig 3-152.

Caution!

1. The dimensions in the drawing do not mean that they all have to be applied as the dimensional constraint.
2. Fully constrain the sketch.
3. Locate the sketch origin (⯐) at the origin of the coordinate system.

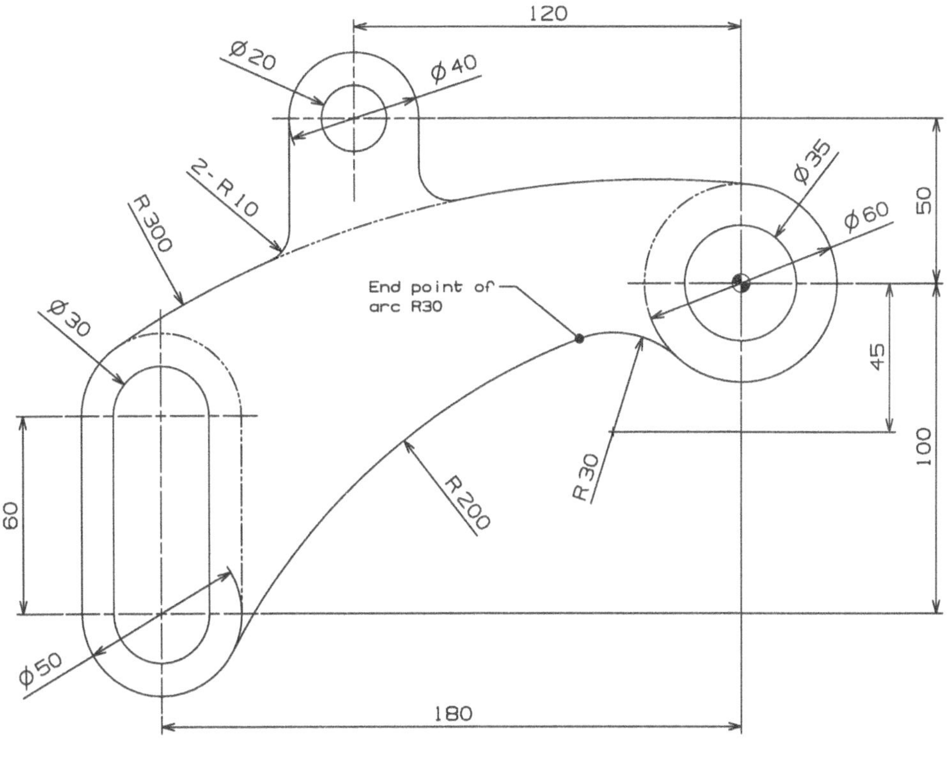

Fig 3-152 Link

Hints!

Create sketch curves and constrain them according to the following steps.

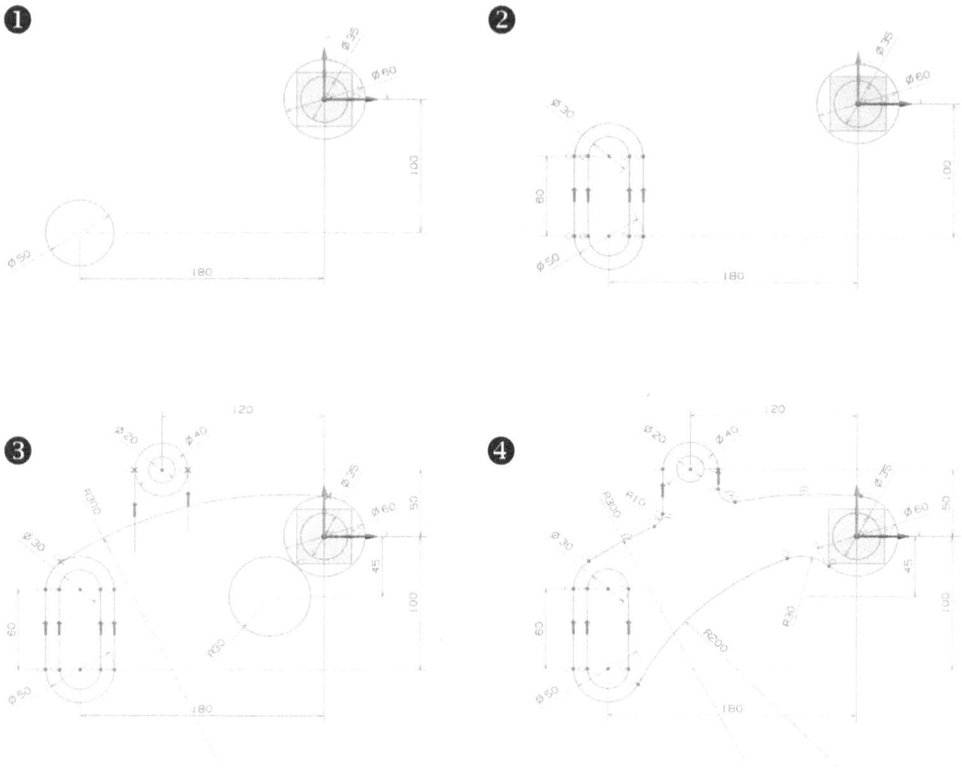

END of Exercise

Chapter 4

Creating 3D Geometry

■ After completing this chapter you will understand

- the definition and condition of a **Section**.
- various options in **Selection Intent**.
- options in **Extrude**.
- how to modify the color of objects.
- usage of **Revolve** and conditions of the section and revolve axis.
- how to create holes using the **Hole** command.
- how to create bosses using the **Boss** command.

4.1 Extruding

You can create a three dimensional feature by extruding a section along a specified direction. Fig 4-2 shows a 3D geometry created by extruding the section defined by the sketch shown in Fig 4-1.

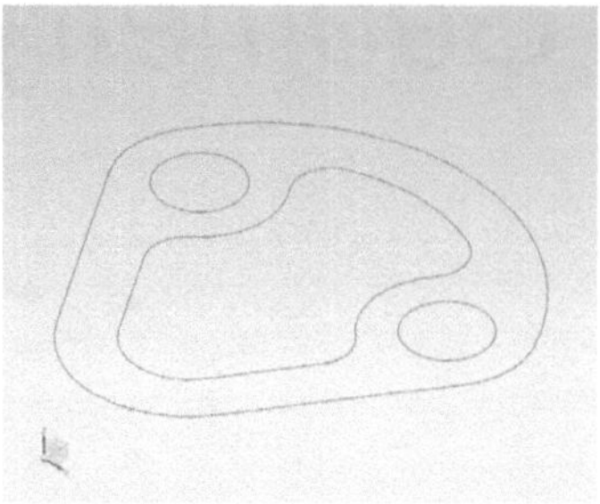

Fig 4-1 Profile of a 3D Model

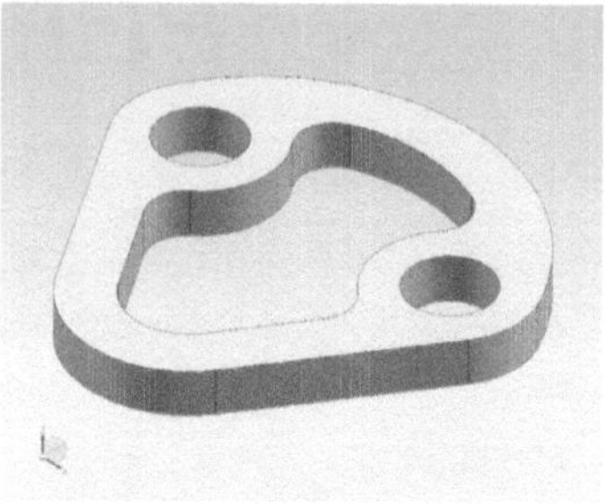

Fig 4-2 Extruded Feature

Procedure

1. Press the **Extrude** icon in the **Feature** icon group. You can press the **X** key as a shortcut.
2. Define the section.
3. Press the **Reset** button in the **Extrude** dialog box.
4. Set the options such as **Limits** and **Boolean** and press **OK**.

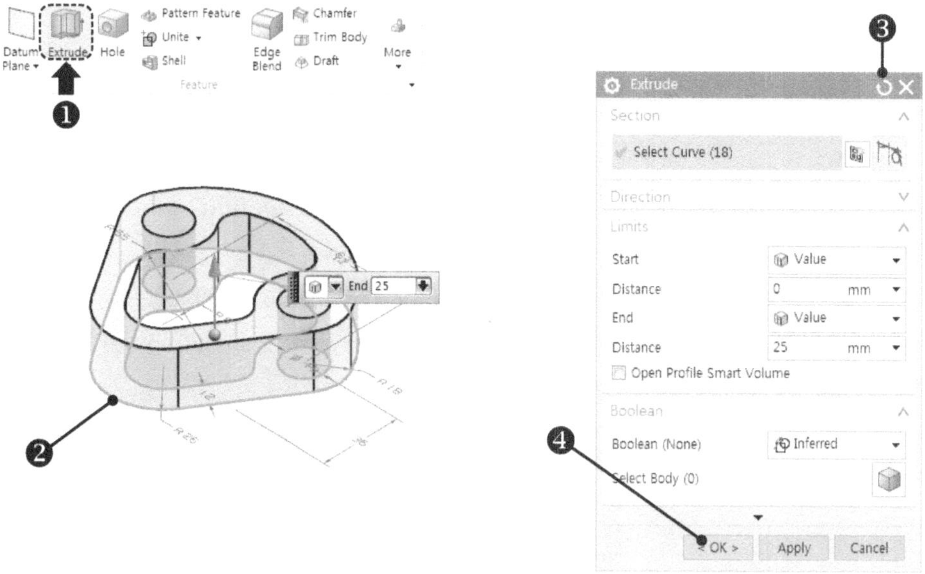

Fig 4-3 Process of Extruding

4.2 Understanding Sections

You can create 3D geometry shown in Fig 4-5 by extruding the rectangle among the curves in Fig 4-4. The set of curves contributing to constructing the 3D geometry is called a **Section**.

When you define a section using curves, the **Curve Rule** becomes available. You can select a set of single curves as a section or you can select all the curves in a sketch as a section.

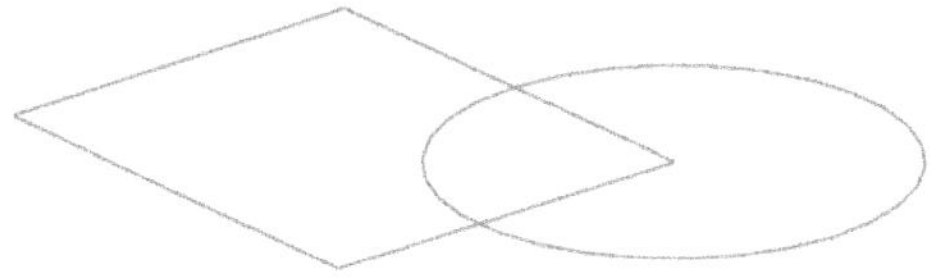

Fig 4-4 Sketch

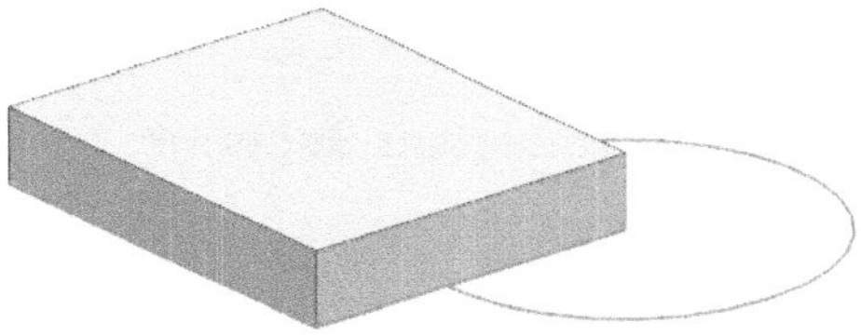

Fig 4-5 Extruded Rectangle

4.2.1 Condition of a Section

To create a single solid body, the following conditions have to be met.

① The section has to be planar.
② The section has to be closed. Internal loops are allowed.
③ The section curves cannot intersect each other.

Allowing Self-Intersecting Sections

Self-intersecting sections had been not allowed until NX 6. However, self-intersecting sections are allowed in extrude by default since NX 7.5. It is highly recommended to not allow this type of section to better understand the nature of the section. You can uncheck the **Allow Self-intersection Section in Extrude Feature** option by pressing the **Menu** button **File > Customer Defaults > Modeling > General > Miscellaneous** tab. Note that you have to exit NX and execute it again.

What is a Solid Body?

There are two types of bodies in NX. A solid body is a geometry that has volume. If a geometry is closed by surfaces, you can define the material inside the surface provided that the geometry is a solid body. Note that geometry closed by surfaces cannot constitute a solid body.

The other type of body is a sheet body which does not have volume. A geometry closed by surfaces but not filled with material is called a sheet body. Modeling with a sheet body is outside of the scope of this textbook.

4.2.2 Inconsistent Sections

Examples of inconsistent sections are as follows.

① Three Dimensional Section

If you extrude a section defined by selecting three dimensional curves, a sheet body is created as shown in Fig 4-7 even though the section is closed.

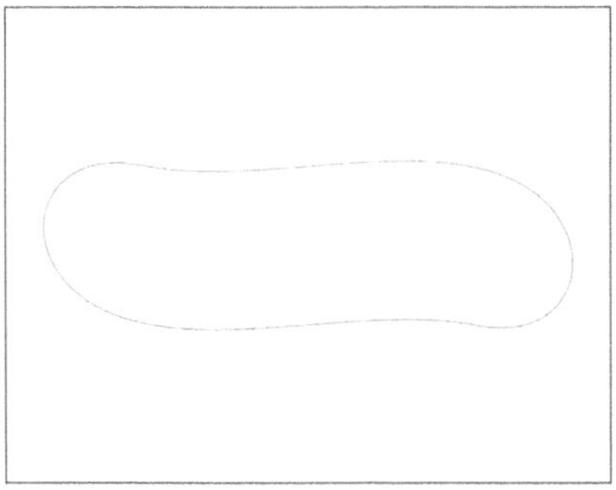

Fig 4-6 3D Curve

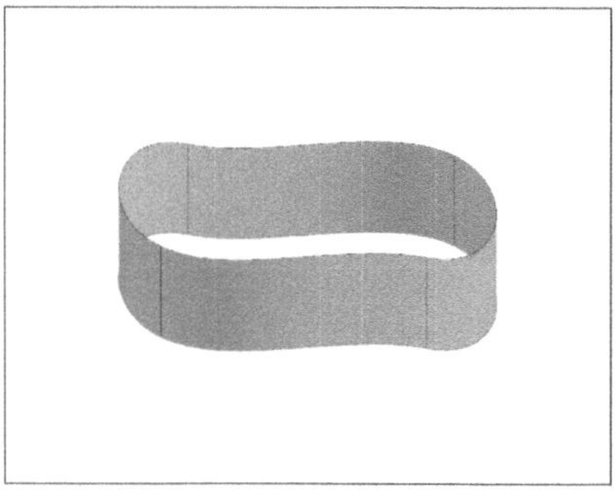

Fig 4-7 Sheet Body Created

② Open Section

A connected open section constructing a sheet body as shown in Fig 4-9. If the section curves are disconnected, several sheet bodies are created. Note that the solid body will not be created if you do not define a closed section for an **Extrude** operation, even though you have created a closed sketch.

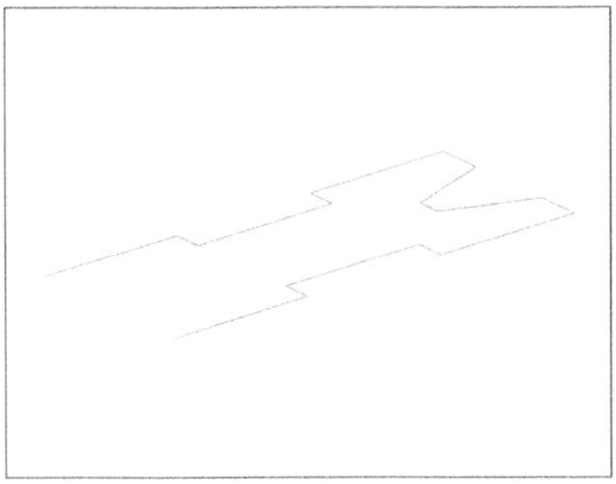

Fig 4-8 Open Section

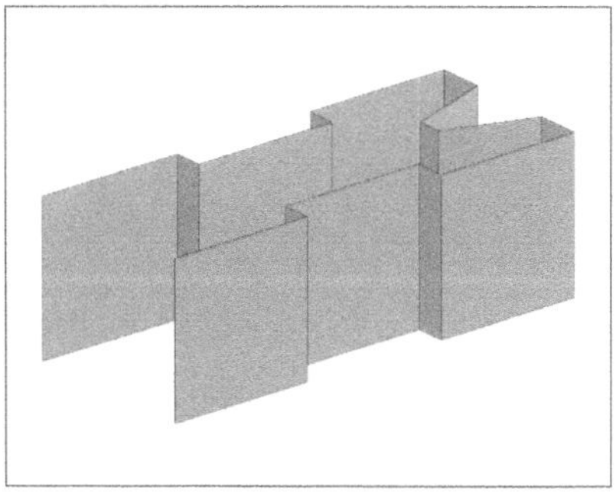

Fig 4-9 Sheet Body Created

③ Self-intersecting Section

If you select all the sketch curves shown in Fig 4-10 as a section, three solid bodies and four sheet bodies are created as shown in Fig 4-11.

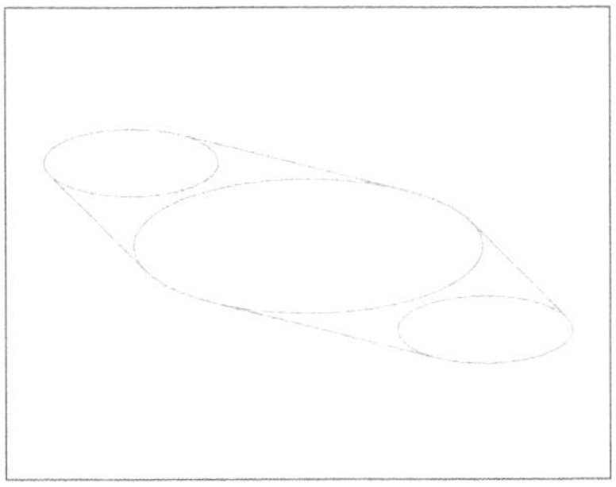

Fig 4-10 Self-Intersecting Section

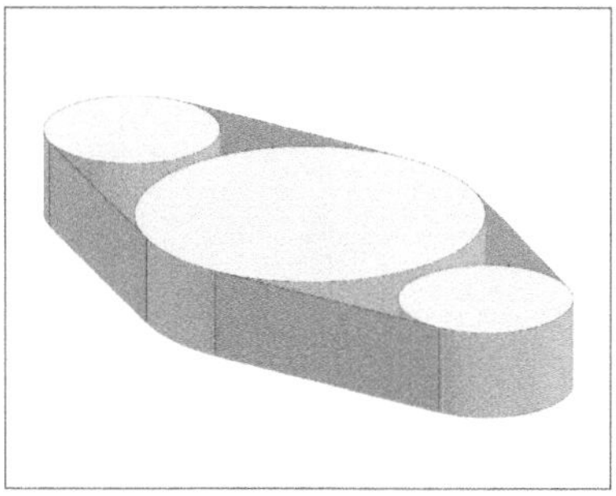

Fig 4-11 Solid Body and Sheet Body Created

! *Closed Loops*

You can extrude several closed loops that do not intersect each other. If there is a closed section within another closed section, the internal area is created as an empty volume as shown in Fig 4-12. If the closed sections are separated from each other, each loop is created as multiple solid bodies as shown in Fig 4-13.

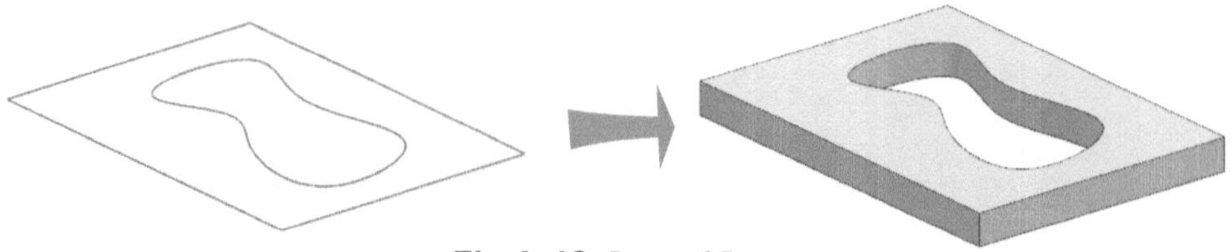

Fig 4-12 Internal Loop

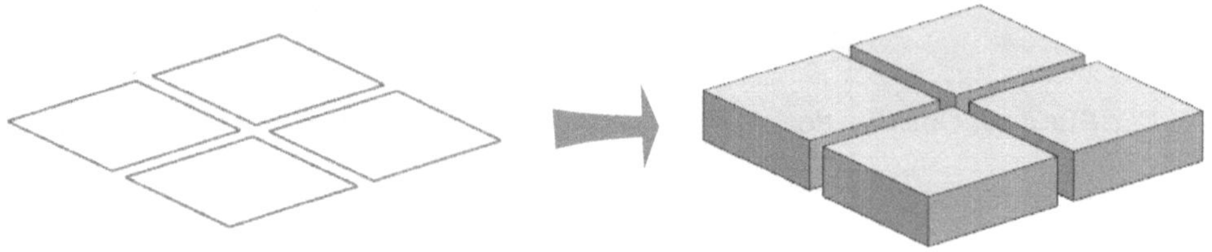

Fig 4-13 Separated Loops

4.3 Selection Intent

You can construct a consistent section by selecting sketch curves or edges appropriately by using the **Selection Intent** options which is available in the **Selection Bar**. Selection intent is always available when you select objects such as points, curves or faces in the model.

Fig 4-14 Selection Intent

4.3.1 Curve Rule

Curve rules are available with some additional options whenever you are at a step that allows you to select curves or edges during a command process.

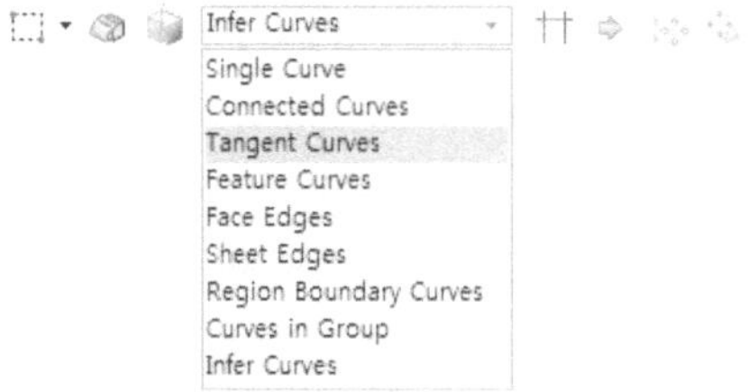

Fig 4-15 Curve Rule

! *Curve Rule and Snap Point Option*

The **Curve Rule** option is always available whenever you have to select curves. Remember that the **Snap Point** option is activated whenever you select points.

① **Single Curve**: You can select a single curve or single edge by pressing MB1.

② **Connected Curves**: If you select a curve or edge, all the curves connected end by end are selected by chain.

③ **Tangent Curves**: Tangent connected curves or edges are selected by chain.

④ **Feature Curves**: All curves in a feature are selected as a section at a single pick.

⑤ **Infer Curves**: An appropriate curve rule is applied by NX depending on the type of the first pick object. For example, if you select a curve in a sketch, all curves in the sketch are defined as a section.

4.3.2 Stop at Intersection

The section chain stops at the intersection of the curves to prevent selecting a self-intersecting section.

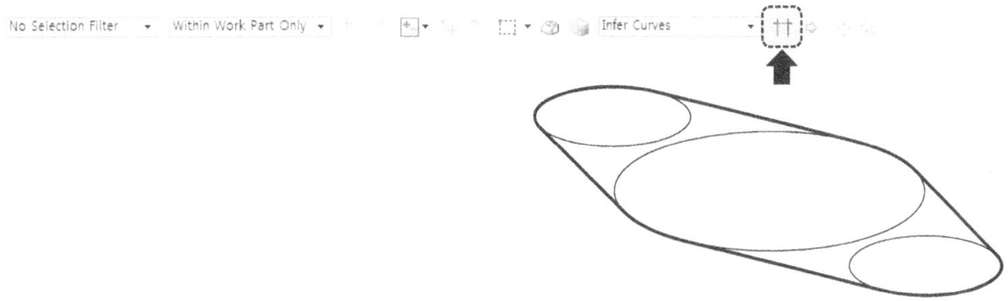

Fig 4-16 Valid Outer Section (Thick Lines)

4.3.3 Follow Fillet

When two curves are filleted and either the **Connected Curves** or **Tangent Curves** curve rule is selected, the section chain follows the fillet curve.

4.3.4 Chain within Feature

Limits the scope of stopping at the intersection and following the fillet to within the same feature as the first pick object.

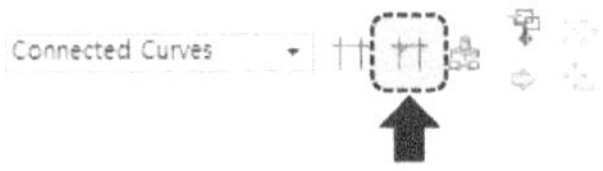

Fig 4-17 Follow Fillet Option

Fig 4-18 Chain within Feature Option

Exercise 01 Basic Usage of Extrude Command

Let's learn the basic usage of the **Extrude** command by modeling a block.

1. Create a new part as ch05_ex01.prt.
2. Draw a sketch as shown in Fig 4-19. Enter p0 in the **p1** input box. P1 dimension is linked to p0 and has the same value. Apply the **Midpoint** constraint to fully constrain the sketch as shown in Fig 4-20.
3. Press the **Q** or **Ctrl + Q** key to finish the sketch.

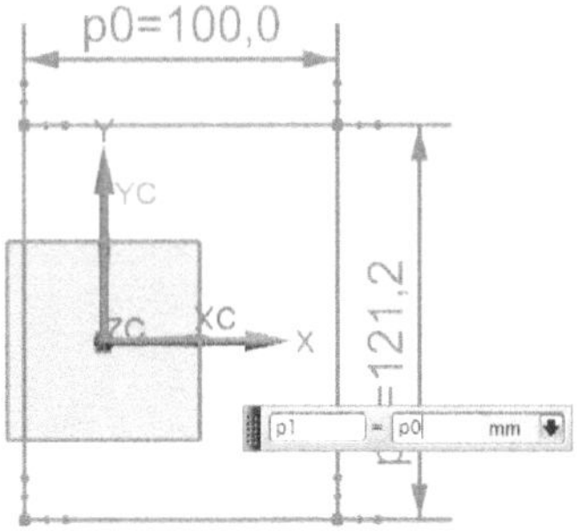

Fig 4-19 Linking Dimension Value

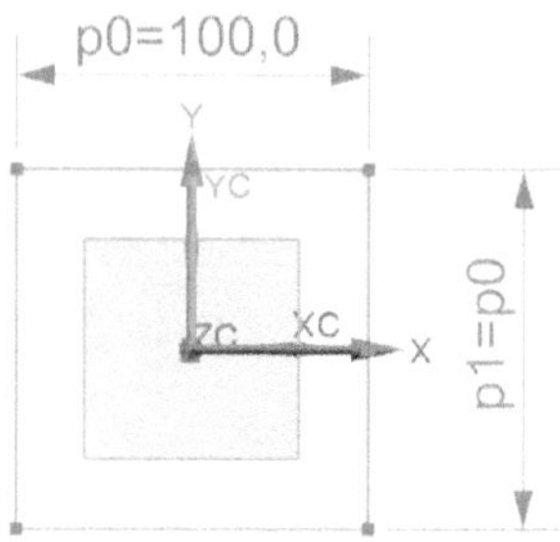

Fig 4-20 Fully Constrained

4. Press the **Extrude** icon in the **Feature** icon group.
5. Reset the dialog box by pressing the **Reset** button in the dialog box.

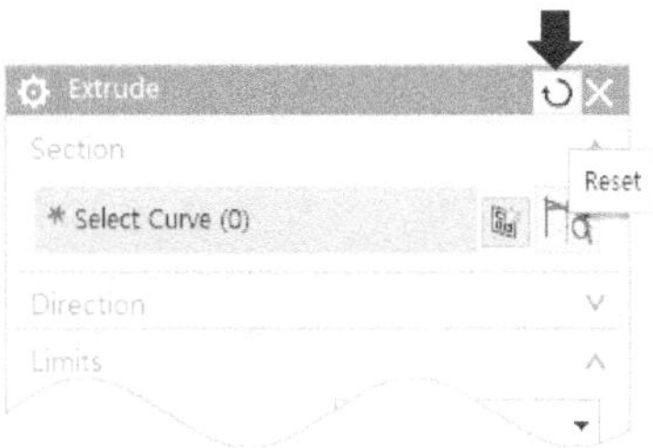

Fig 4-21 Reset Button

Resetting the Dialog Box

It is highly recommended to reset the dialog box before setting the options. If you reset the **Extrude** dialog box after selecting a section, the section is deselected and the curve rule is reset to **Infer Curves**.

6. Look at the **Extrude** dialog box. You can identify which step you are at in the command flow.

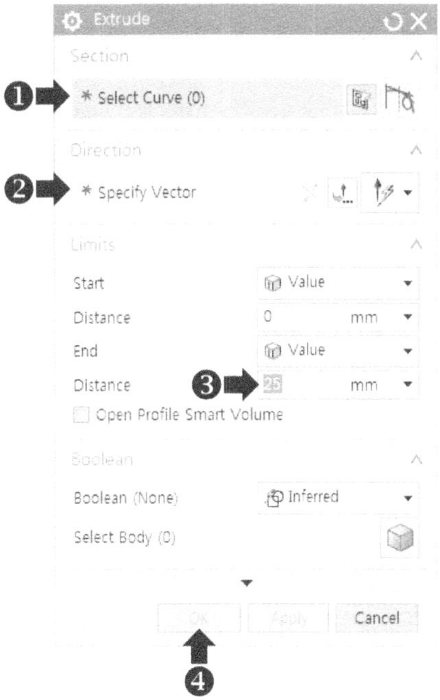

Fig 4-22 Extrude Dialog Box

① The orange highlighted option is the current step to select object(s). The **Type Filter** shows the type of objects that can be selected.

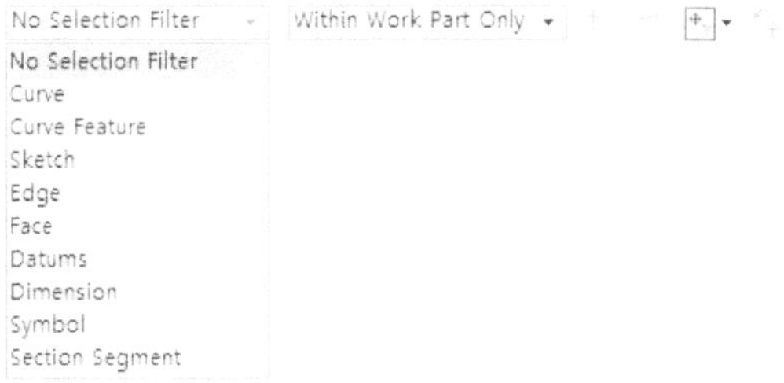

Fig 4-23 Type Filter

② The red asterisk(*) implies the option that you must define by selecting an object. If the option is defined, the mark changes to a green check.

③ The default value for the end limit is 25 mm. You can modify the value and press **Enter** to preview the result.

④ The **OK** or **Apply** button is not available because the options with the red asterisk are not defined yet.

7. Verify that the default curve rule is as shown in Fig 4-24.

Fig 4-24 Default Curve Rule

8. Select one of the sketch curves. All four curves are selected as the section and the extrude feature is previewed as in Fig 4-25.

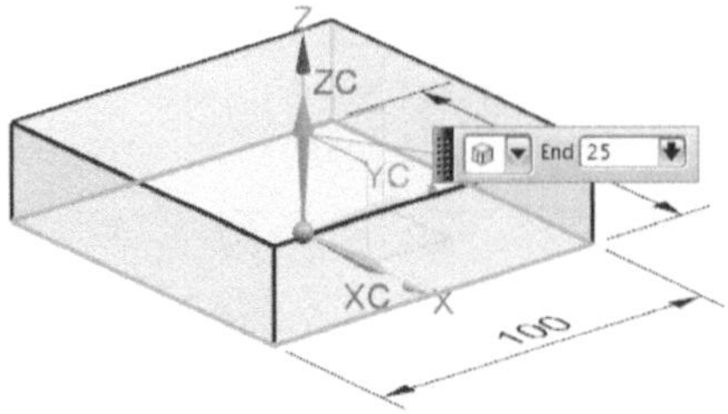

Fig 4-25 Preview of Extrude

9. Let's simplify the model in the graphics window.

① Select **Format > WCS > Display** in the **Menu** tab.
② Press the **Show and Hide** button in the **View** group in the **Top** border bar (❷ in Fig 4-26).
③ Click the (-) symbol (❸ in Fig 4-26) in the **Show and Hide** dialog box. The datum coordinate system is hidden. Fig 4-27 shows the model with the WCS and datum coordinate system hidden.

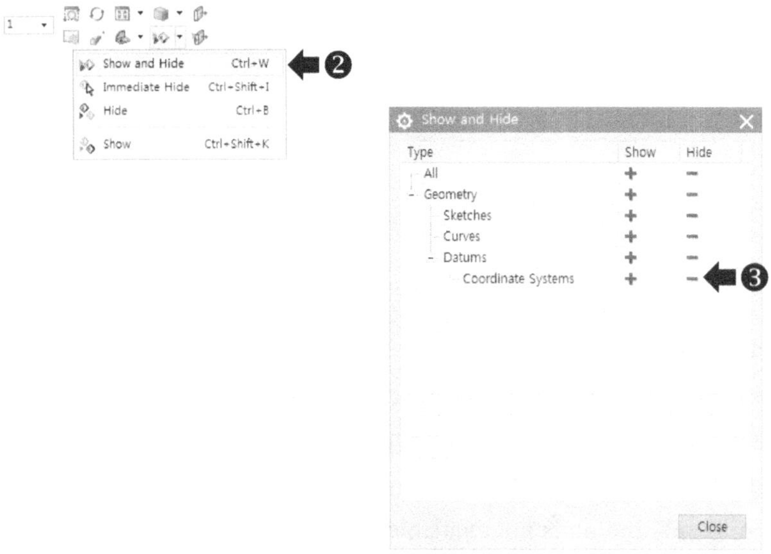

Fig 4-26 Hiding Datum

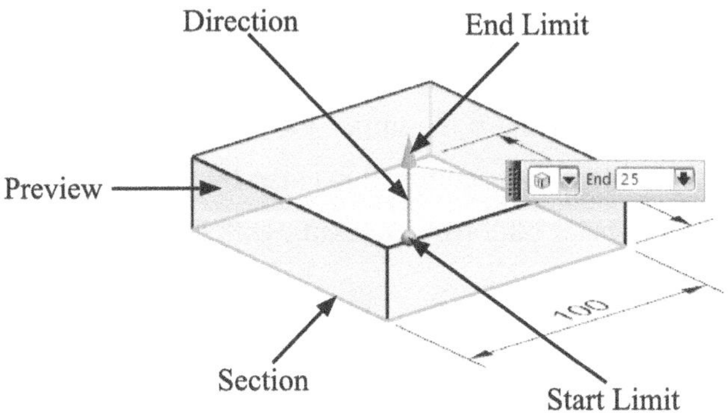

Fig 4-27 Preview of Extrude

Quiz !

Why are all four lines selected? You can answer this by considering the meaning of the **Infer Curves** curve rule. As the **Feature Curves** curve rule is inferred, all curves in the sketch feature are selected.

10. Let's review the changes to the dialog box.

Two asterisks are changed into green check marks and the **OK** and **Apply** buttons are activated.

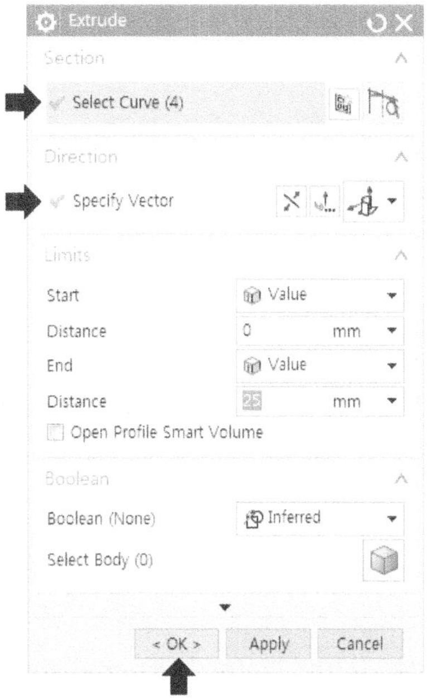

Fig 4-28 Extrude After Defining Section

Meaning of the Highlighted Button

The highlighted button in the dialog box implies the next recommended step in the command flow. You can accept the recommended step by clicking MB2. Of course, you can activate other options or buttons by clicking with MB1.

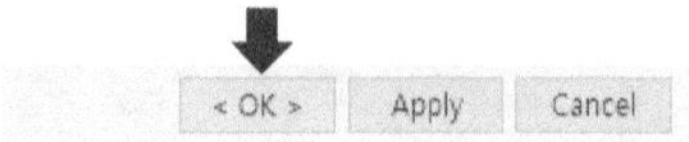

Fig 4-29 OK Button Highlighted

11. Input 25 in the **Distance** input box and press **Enter**. Fig 4-30 shows the preview of the **Extrude** feature.

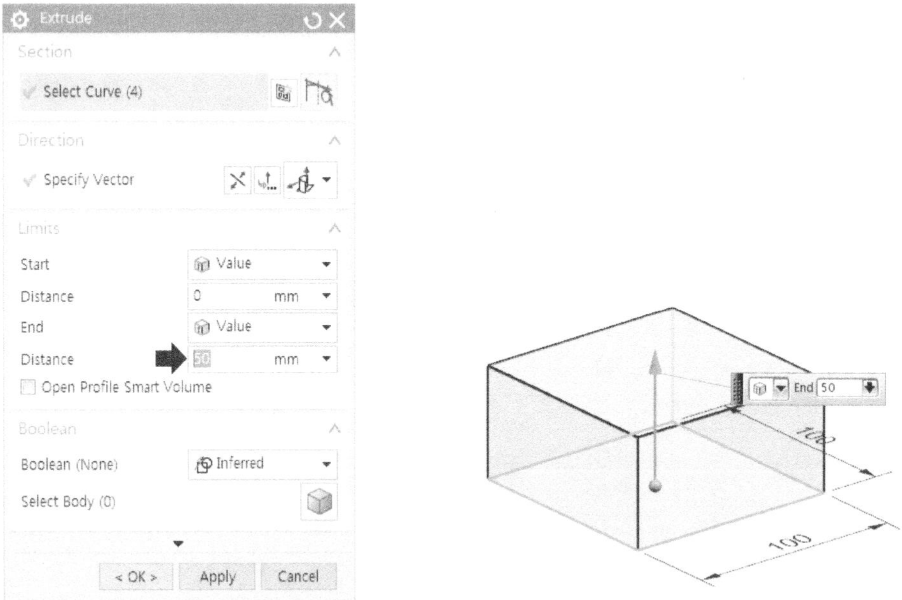

Fig 4-30 Modifying End Distance

Previewing the Feature

1. A preview is shown when the minimum requirements are met for the current feature.
2. When you modify a value in the dialog box, you have to press the **Enter** key to update the preview.

12. Press **OK** in the dialog box. You can click MB2. A solid body 50 mm extruded by the rectangular section is created as shown in Fig 4-31.

Fig 4-31 Solid Body Created

END of Exercise

Hide and Show

The sketch feature is still shown in the graphics window after extruding. You can hide the sketch feature with the **Hide** command in the **View** tab. You can hide features by pressing **MB3 > Hide** on the feature in the **Part Navigator** or in the graphics window. Hidden features can be shown by pressing **MB3 > Show** on the hidden features in the **Part Navigator** or using the **Show** command in the **View** tab.

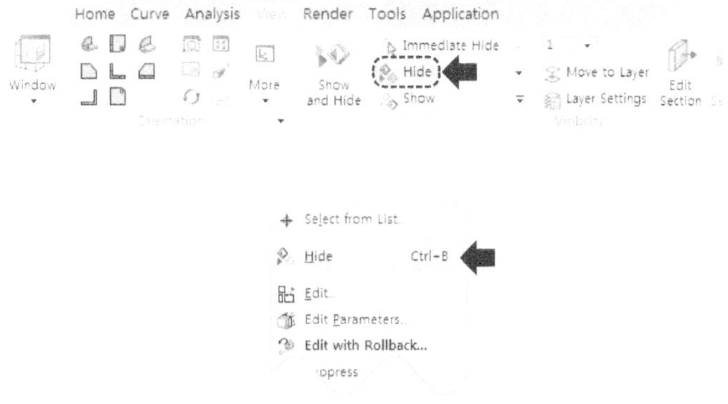

Fig 4-32 Hide Option

4.4 Boolean Option

Boolean options are available for the second and later solid features. There are three types of boolean operations.

① **Unite**: Unite current solid feature to the exiting solid body.

② **Subtract**: Subtract current solid feature from the existing solid body.

③ **Intersect**: Create an intersect solid body between the current solid feature and the existing solid body.

The **None** option in the **Boolean** dropdown list creates a separate body. A part has one solid body in general in a file. Therefore, the solid body created by the **None** option is operated with other solid bodies after completing the respective body modeling.

Fig 4-33 Boolean Option in Extrude Dialog Box

The following requirements have to be met to perform a boolean operation in solid modeling.

① The target and tool bodies have to be solid.

② The solid bodies to be operated on must have a common volume. If you try a boolean operation between separate solid bodies, an error message is displayed as shown in Fig 4-34.

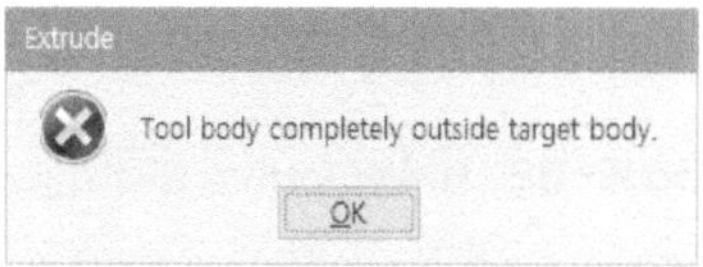

Fig 4-34 Error Message

4.4.1 Unite

Current solid feature is united to an existing solid body. When several solid bodies exist, you have to select one. Fig 4-38 shows an example of the **Unite** boolean operation.

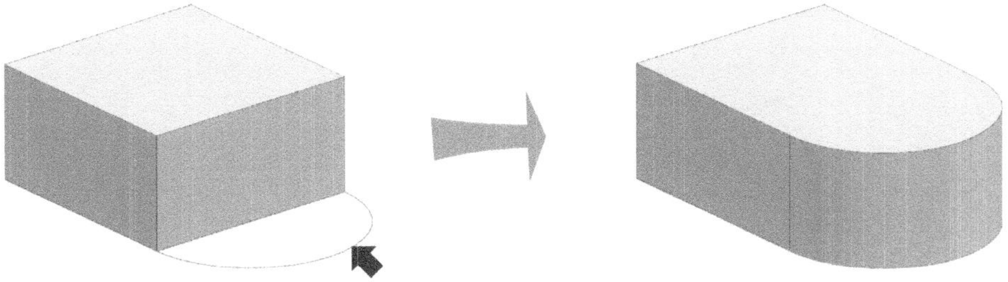

Fig 4-35 Before and After Unite

4.4.2 Subtract

Common volume between an existing body and current solid feature is removed from the existing body. Fig 4-39 shows the result of the **Subtract** boolean operation.

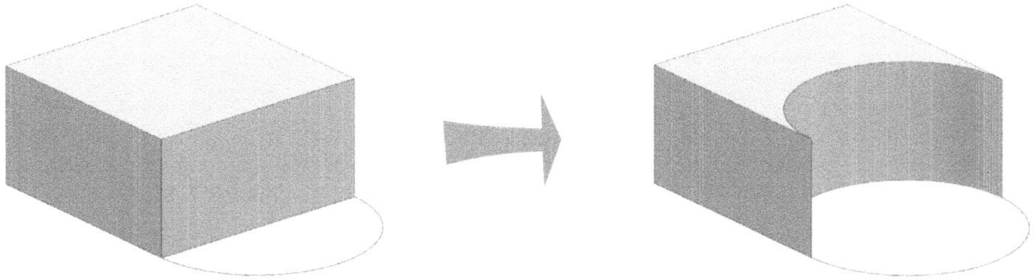

Fig 4-36 Before and After Subtract

4.4.3 Intersect

Common volume between an existing body and current solid feature remains as the result body.

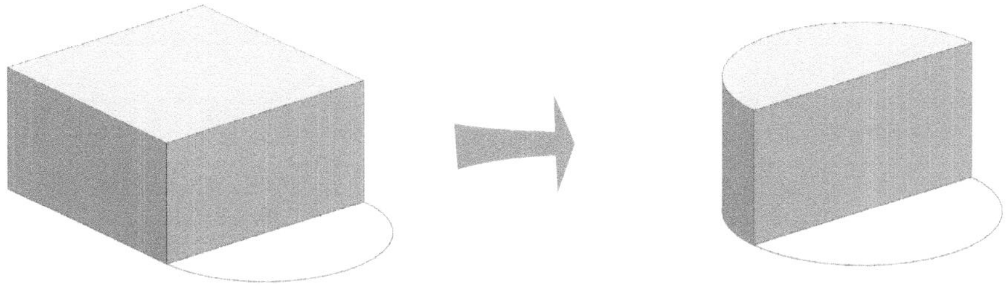

Fig 4-37 Before and After Intersect

4.4.4 None

Create a new solid body which has a separate volume. The existing body and the new body have their respective volumes.

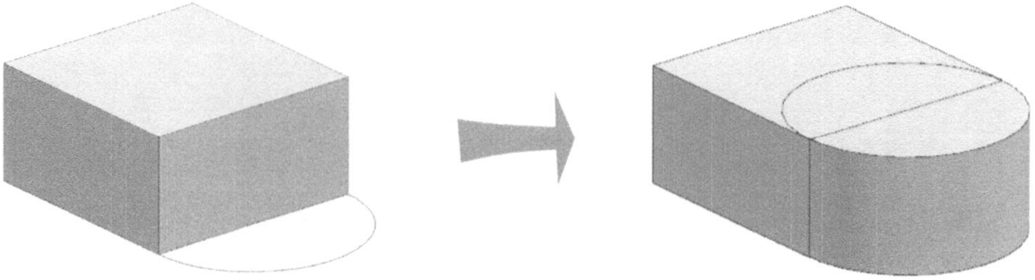

Fig 4-38 New Solid Body Created

4.4.5 Boolean Operation Between Bodies

A boolean operation between solid bodies can be performed in the **Feature** icon group. Note that you can select only a solid body as the target and tool bodies.

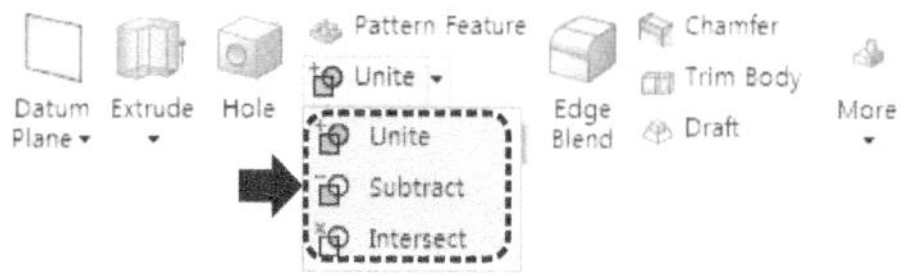

Fig 4-39 Boolean Icons

Procedure

1. Press the boolean button in the **Feature** icon group.
2. Select a target body. You can select only one solid body and the command option flows to the next step.
3. Select tool bodies.
4. Press **OK**.

Properties of the result body are inherited from the target body. For example, if the color of the target body is red, the result body is colored red.

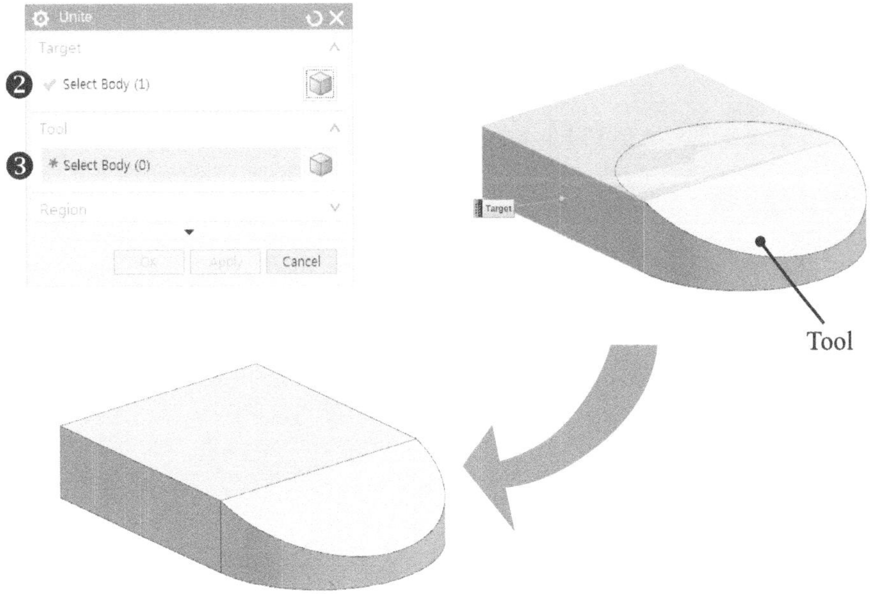

Fig 4-40 Boolean Between Bodies

How to count the number of solid bodies?

You need to verify the number of solid bodies to make sure that you have a single solid body. If there is more than one solid body, you have to perform a boolean operation. Keep to the following procedure to count the number of solid bodies.

1. Set the **Type Filter** to **Solid Body**.

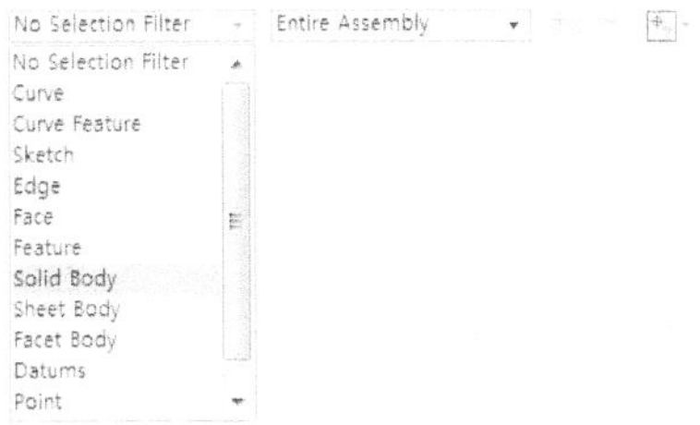

Fig 4-41 Type Filter

2. Press **Ctrl + A** on the keyboard. This selects all filtered objects.
3. Read the status bar message where the number of selected objects is displayed.

Exercise 02 Creating a Solid Body

Create the solid model shown in Fig 4-42.

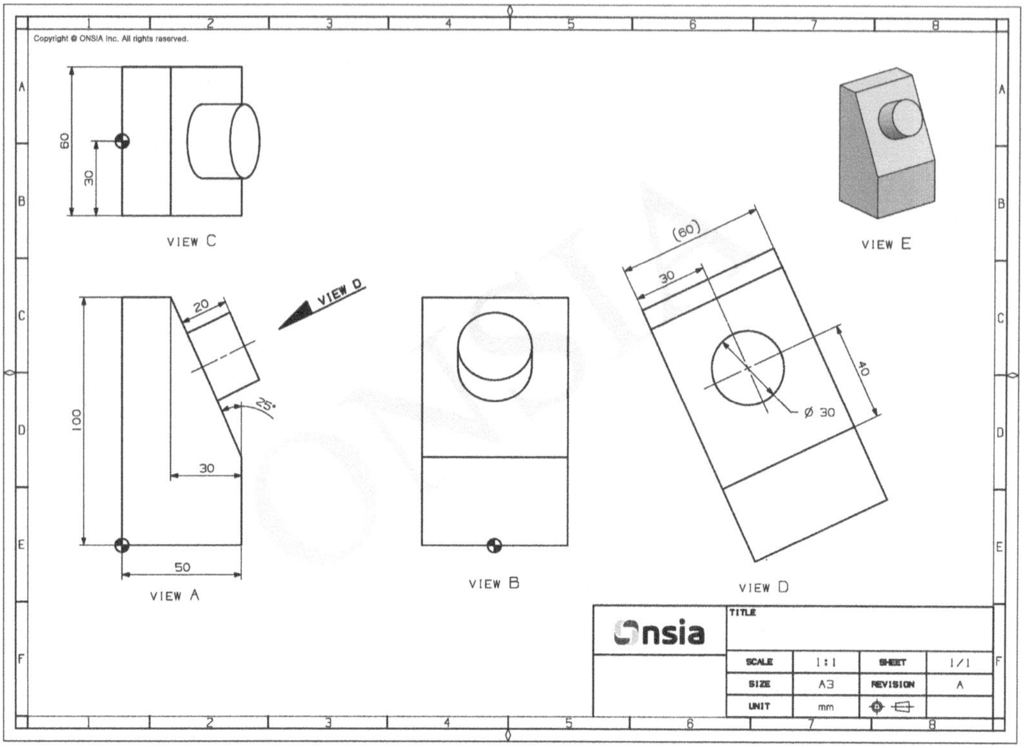

Fig 4-42 Drawing for Exercise 02

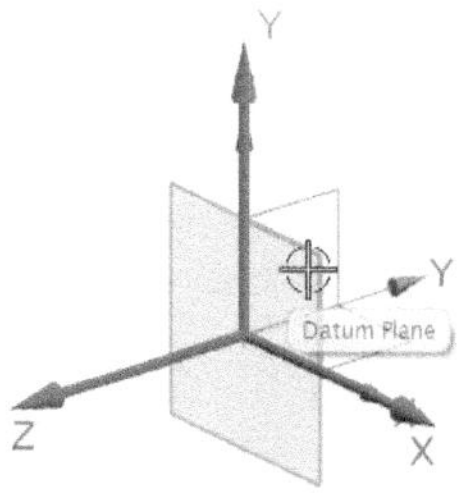

Fig 4-43 Sketch Plane

Creating a File and the Sketch

1. Create a part file named ch04_ex02.prt.
2. Press the **W** key to hide WCS.
3. Press the **Sketch in Task Environment** icon and select the XZ plane as the sketch plane.
4. Create the sketch as shown in Fig 4-43 and fully constrain it.
5. Finish the sketch.

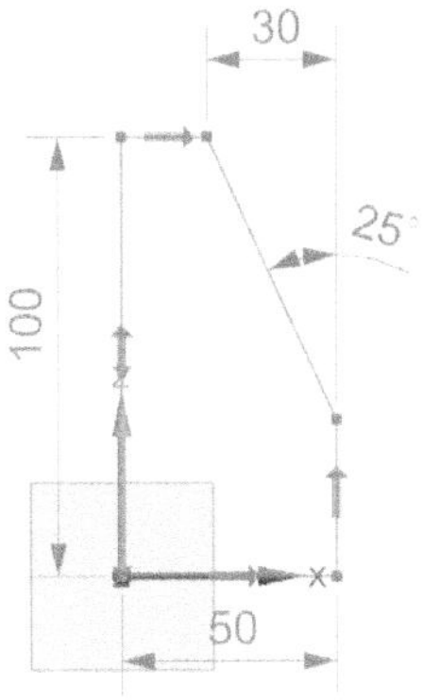

Fig 4-44 First Sketch

Extruding

1. Press the **Extrude** icon.
2. Press the **Reset** button in the dialog box.
3. Select the line Ⓐ specified in Fig 4-45 to define the section.
4. Select **Symmetric Value** as the **End** limit and enter 30 in the **Distance** input box.
5. Press **Enter**.
6. Check the preview and press **OK** in the dialog box.

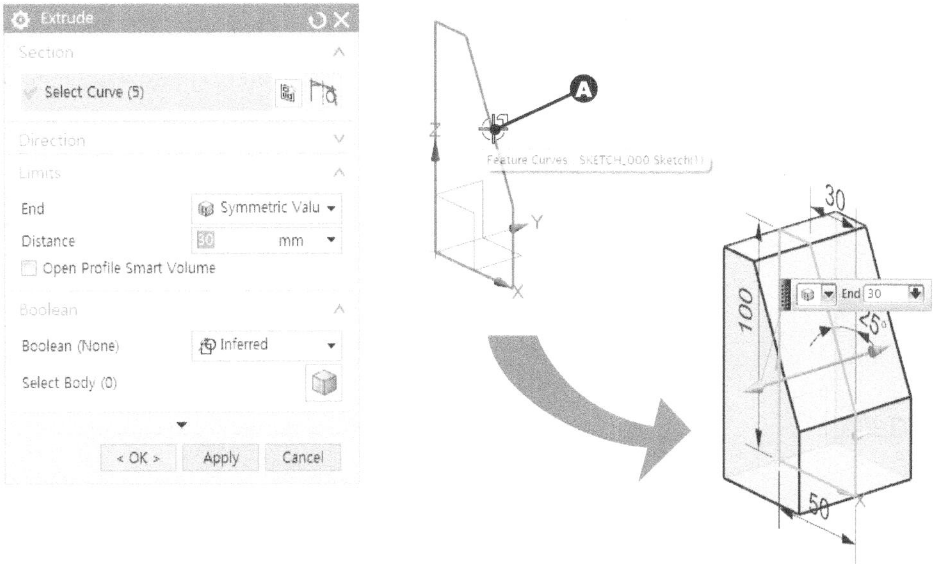

Fig 4-45 Extruding the First Sketch

Creating the Second Sketch

1. Press the **Sketch in Task Environment** icon and select the face Ⓑ in Fig 4-46 as the sketch plane. Align the sketch coordinate system as the figure. Note that the sketch origin is changed depending on the location of the mouse pointer on the sketch plane.
2. Create a circle and fully constrain it as shown in Fig 4-47. Then finish the sketch.

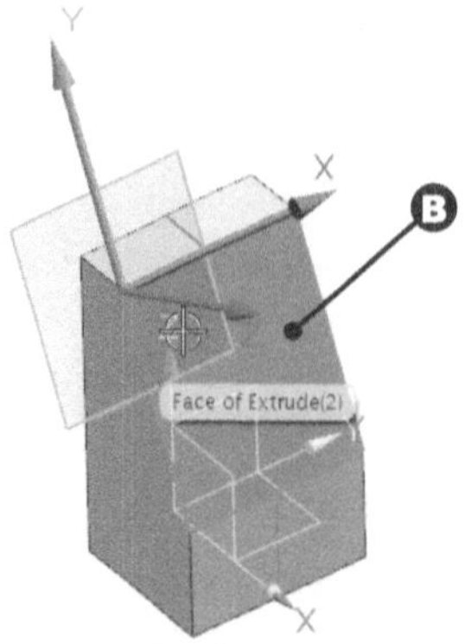

Fig 4-46 Sketch Plane for the Second Sketch

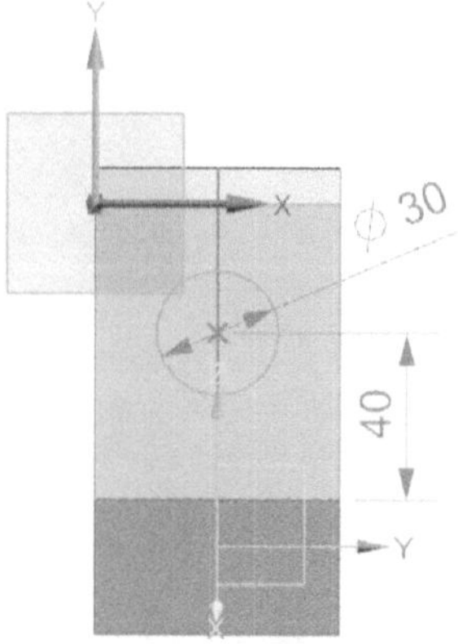

Fig 4-47 Second Sketch

Selection Scope

When you apply constraints after creating sketch curves, you can specify the selection scope. The default selection scope is Within Active Sketch Only which means that you can select objects only within the current active sketch. If you want to select curves in other sketch feature or edges, you have to change the selection scope to Within Work Part Only.

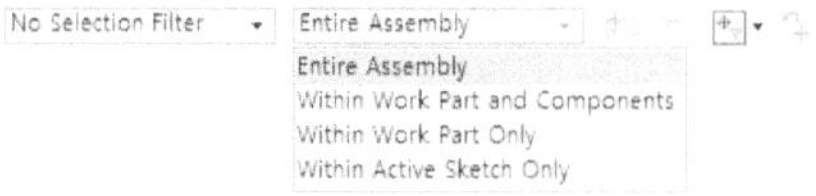

<Selection Scope>

Extruding

1. Press the **Extrude** icon.
2. Select the second sketch as the section.
3. Enter 0 in the **Start** limit and 20 in the **End** limit input box and press **Enter**.
4. Check the preview in the graphics window.

Why do you sketch on the XZ plane?

The trimetric view is displayed as in Fig 4-49 when you create the first sketch on the XZ plane. The trimetric or isometric view is located at the upper right region of the drawing.

5. Select **Unite** in the **Boolean** dropdown list.

6. Press **OK** in the **Extrude** dialog box.

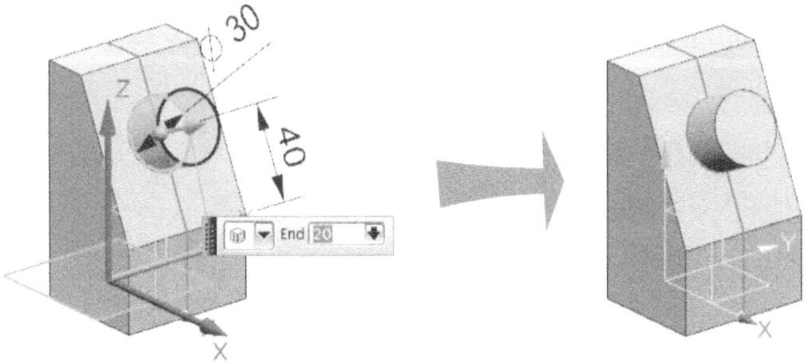

Fig 4-48 Extruding the Second Sketch

Hiding Unnecessary Objects

1. Press the **Show and Hide** icon in the **View** tab.

2. Click the '-' symbol for **All** in the **Show and Hide** dialog box. All types of objects are hidden.

3. Click the '+' symbol for **Solid Bodies** in the **Show and Hide** dialog box. Only the solid body is shown.

4. Press the **Home** key on the keyboard. Trimetric view is displayed.

5. Save the part file and close by choosing **File > Close > All Parts**.

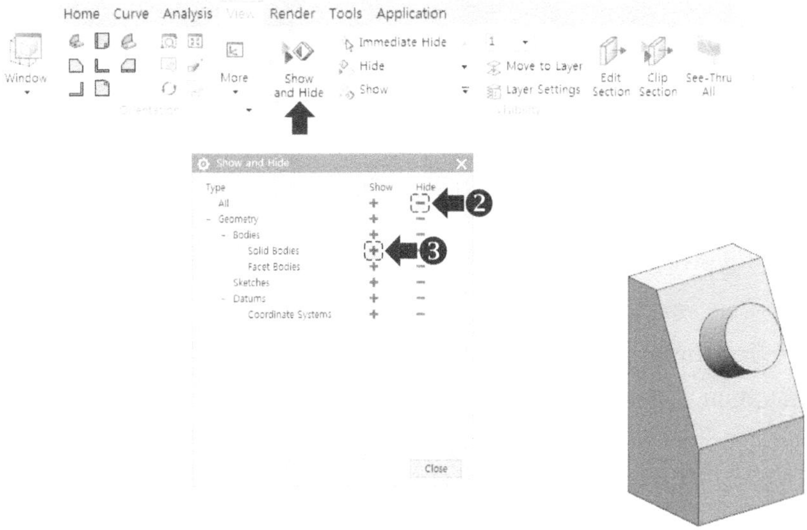

Fig 4-49 Hiding or Showing Objects

END of Exercise

4.5 Sketch Coordinate System

Press the **Sketch** icon and place the mouse cursor on a plane. The sketch coordinate system is previewed. Each axis can be used in constraining sketch points or curves.

- ► X Axis is the horizontal reference.
- ► Y Axis is the vertical reference.
- ► Z Axis is normal to the sketch plane.

Sketch origin can be set in the **Sketch Origin** option in the **Create Sketch** dialog box. You can specify the origin by selecting the end point of an edge as shown in Fig 4-51.

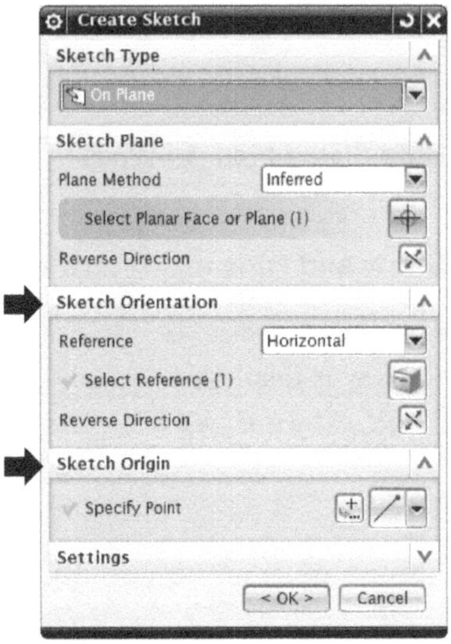

Fig 4-50 Create Sketch Dialog Box

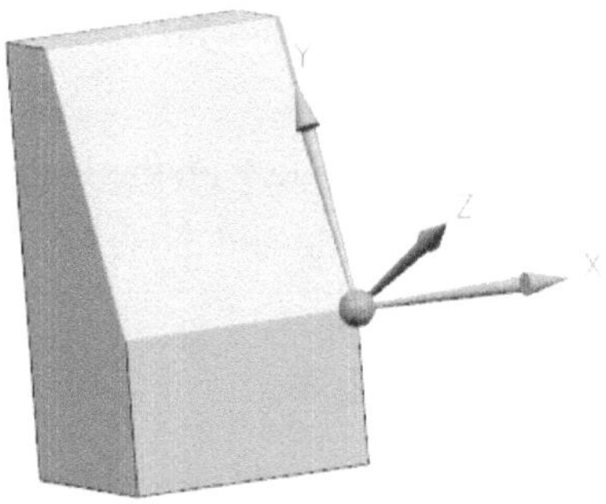

Fig 4-51 Selecting Sketch Origin

You can modify the horizontal or vertical direction of the sketch coordinate system according to the following procedure.

① Select **Horizontal** or **Vertical** in the **Reference** dropdown list in the **Sketch Orientation** option.
② Click the **Select Reference** option.
③ Select linear object (Ⓐ in Fig 4-52) for reference. You can reverse the direction by clicking the **Reverse Direction** button or by double clicking the arrow head.

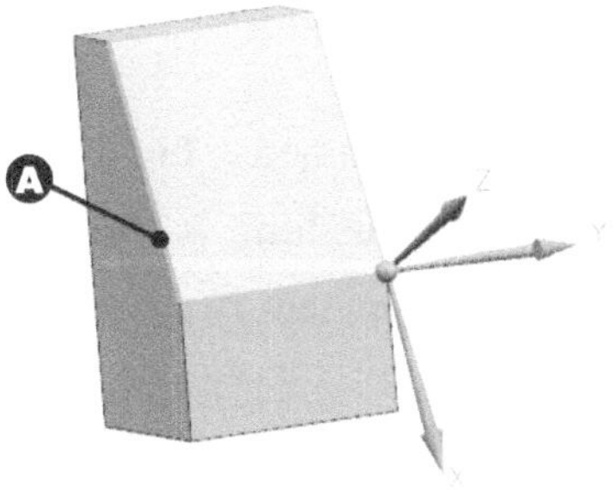

Fig 4-52 Setting the X Direction

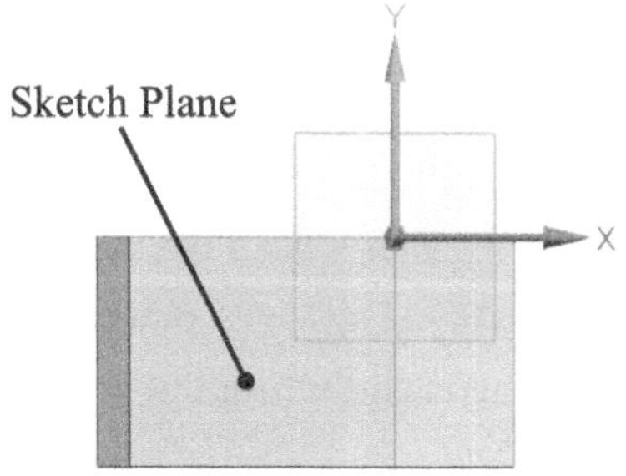

Fig 4-53 Aligned Sketch Plane

④ Press **OK**. The sketch plane is aligned as shown in Fig 4-53. Note that the **Z** axis is aligned normal to screen.

4.6 Direction Option of Extrude

Extrude direction is set automatically normal to section plane. Positive direction is the same as the sketch Z axis which is defined when you select the sketch plane. You can specify another direction for extrude by clicking the **Specify Vector** option and selecting reference direction or defining a vector.

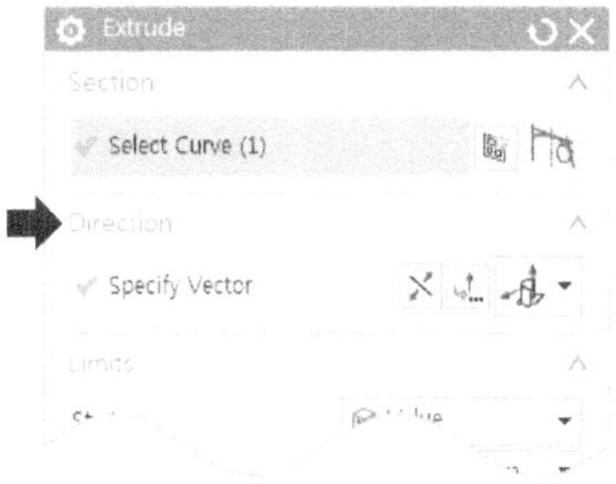

Fig 4-54 Direction Option

4.7 Limit Option

The extrude limit can be defined by value or by selecting the geometry. Fig 4-55 shows the options to define the start and end limits of extrude. The start limit is designated by a small sphere at the arrow start point and the end limit is designated by the arrow head. You can drag each limit in the graphics window.

Fig 4-55 Limits Option

4.7.1 Symmetric Value

You can extrude symmetrically about the section plane. Note that you have to enter half of the total extrusion value. The section plane is located at the center of the extrude feature.

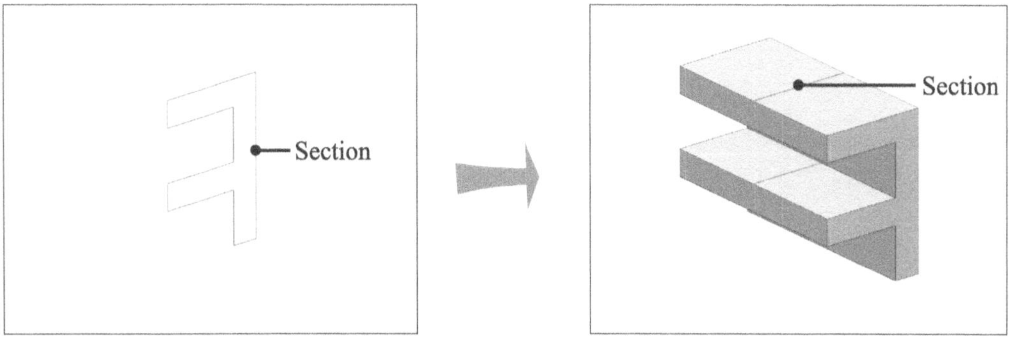

Fig 4-56 Extruding 200mm Along Both Sides

Fig 4-57 Symmetric Value as Limit Option

4.7.2 Until Next

Limit is defined by the geometry first met along the extrusion direction. The limit of the feature has to be fully encosed by the first geometry it meets. Note that limiting by geometry is available only for the solid extrude feature.

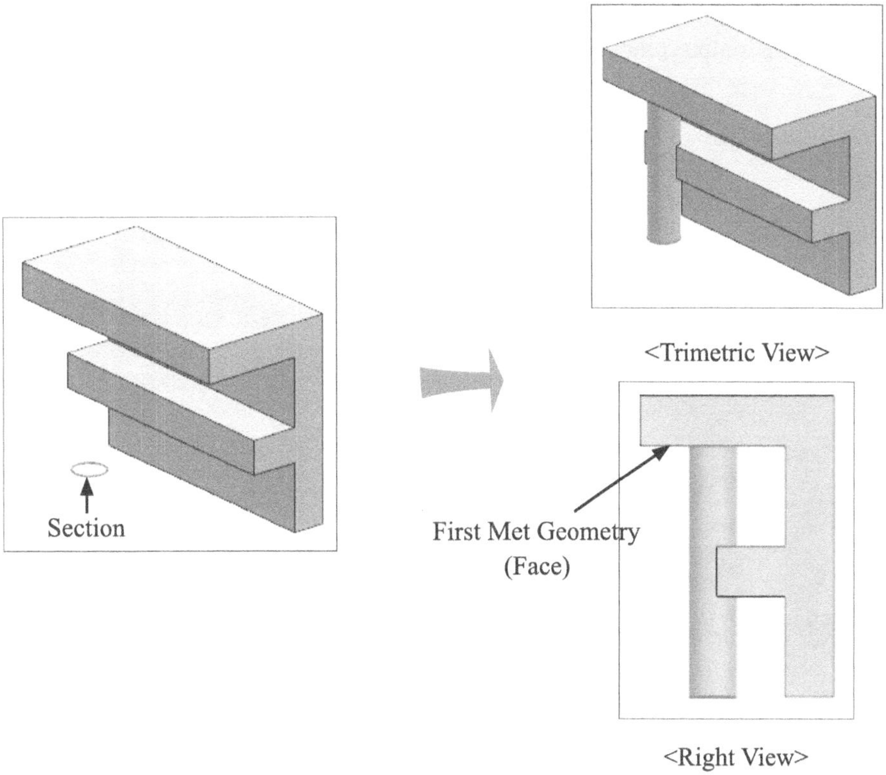

Fig 4-58 Until Next as the End Limit Option

Fig 4-59 Until Next Option

4.7.3 Until Selected

The limit is defined by selecting an object in the 3D geometry. When the limit object is modified after extrusion, the extrude limit will be updated. The limit has to be fully enclosed by the selected object. You can select a face, datum plane, solid body or sheet body as the limiting object. As the datum plane has no boundary, the limit of the extrusion is always valid with the datum plane.

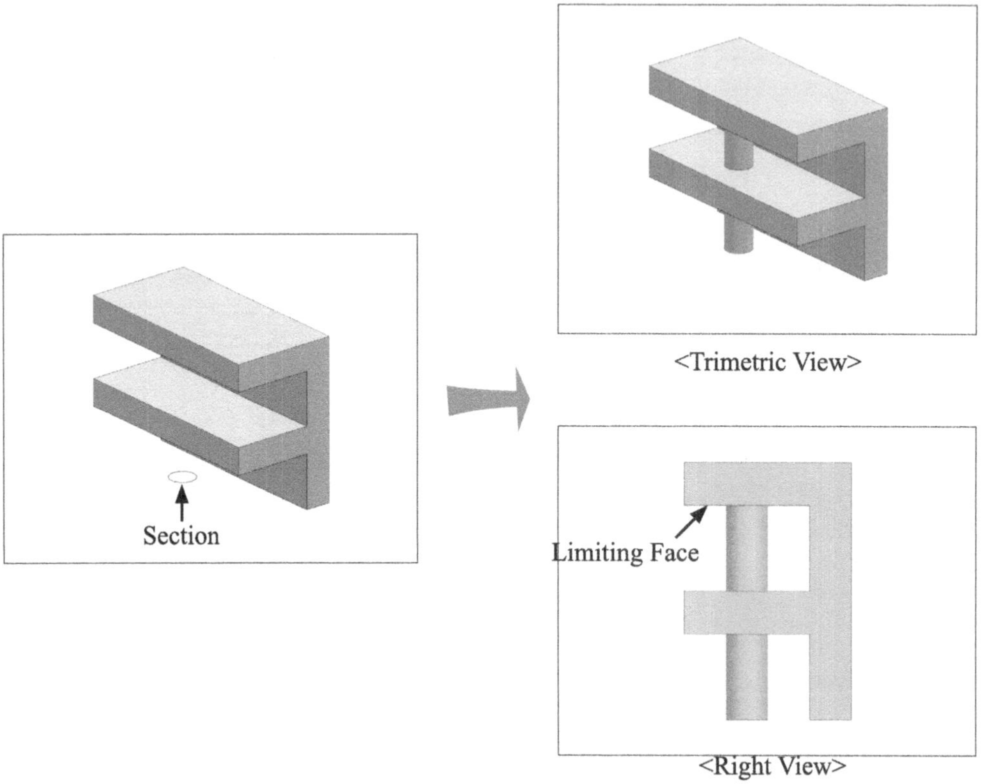

Fig 4-60 Until Selected as the End Limit

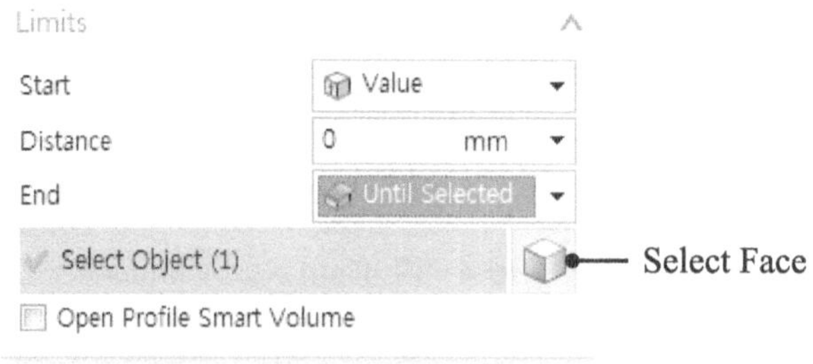

Fig 4-61 Until Selected Option

4.7.4 Until Extended

The limit is defined by selecting an object in the 3D geometry. The geometry is extended when the limit of extrusion is not fully enclosed by the selected geometry.

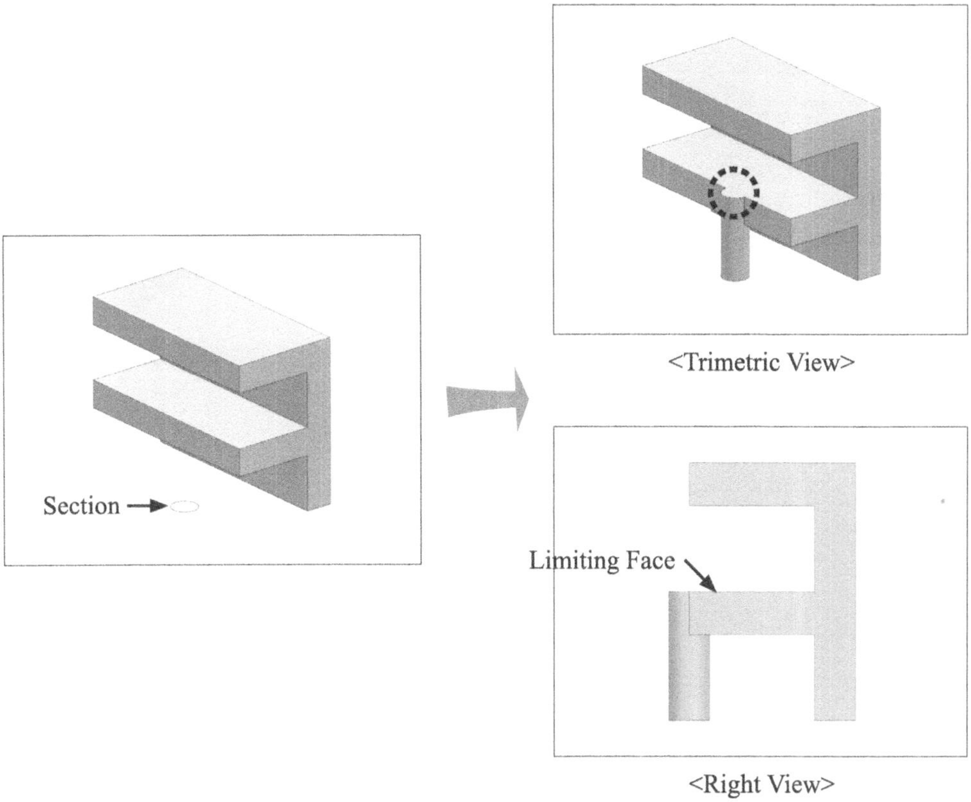

Fig 4-62 Until Extended as the End Limit

> **! *Differrence Between Until Selected and Until Extended***
>
> If the start and/or end limit of an extrude feature is defined by selecting an object, the limit has to be fully enclosed by the object. Otherwise an alert message is invoked as shown in Fig 4-63. With the **Until Extended** limit option, the limiting object will be extended so that the limit can trim the extrude feature.
>
> 
>
>
> **Fig 4-63** Alert Message

4.7.5 Through All

The section is extruded until the end of the selected geometry. Fig 4-64 shows the result of removing the extrude feature from the existing body by extruding through the geometry.

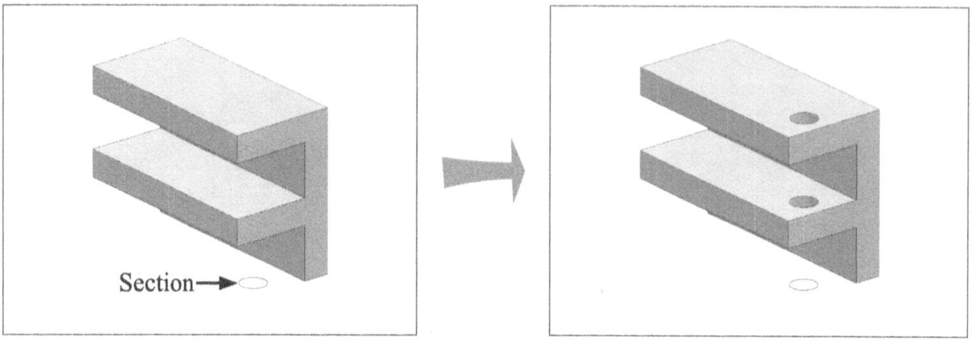

Fig 4-64 Through All as the End Limit

Fig 4-65 Limits and Boolean Option

4.8 Other Options in Extrude Command

4.8.1 Draft

Side faces of the extrude feature are slanted about the extrusion direction by the specified angle.

Fig 4-66 Draft Option

Quiz !

Six types of limiting options are available for extruding a closed section. Which options request you to enter numerical values?

Fig 4-67 Extruding with the Draft Option

4.8.2 Offset

Section can be offset while extruding. With the **Two-Sided** offset option, you can create an extrude feature as shown in Fig 4-68.

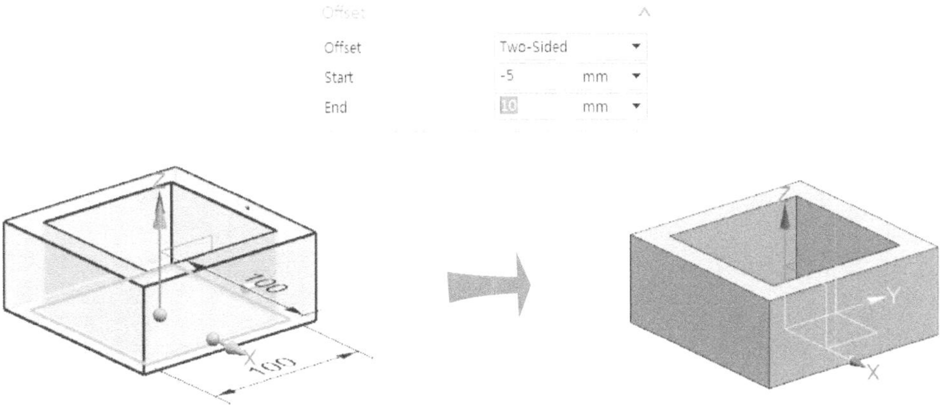

Fig 4-68 Extruding with the Offset Option (Two-Sided)

4.8.3 Open Profile Smart Volume

You can extrude an open section and regard it as a solid body by specifying the direction. You can apply a boolean operation with the existing solid body.

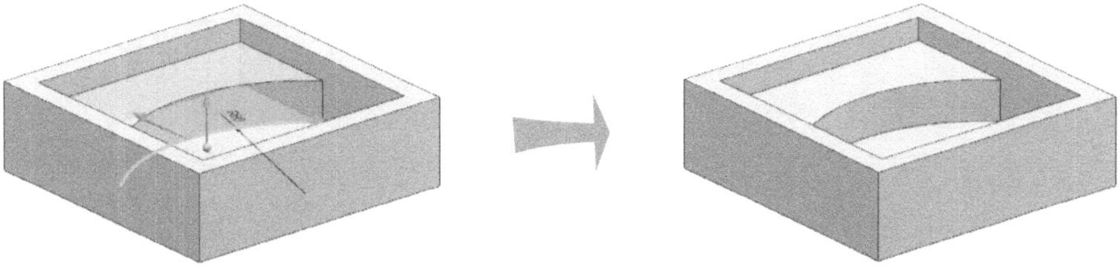

Fig 4-69 Uniting with the Open Profile Smart Volume Option

Exercise 03 Guide Block

Requirements

① Feature **A** is always extruded until face **B**.

② Feature **C** always remove all through the body.

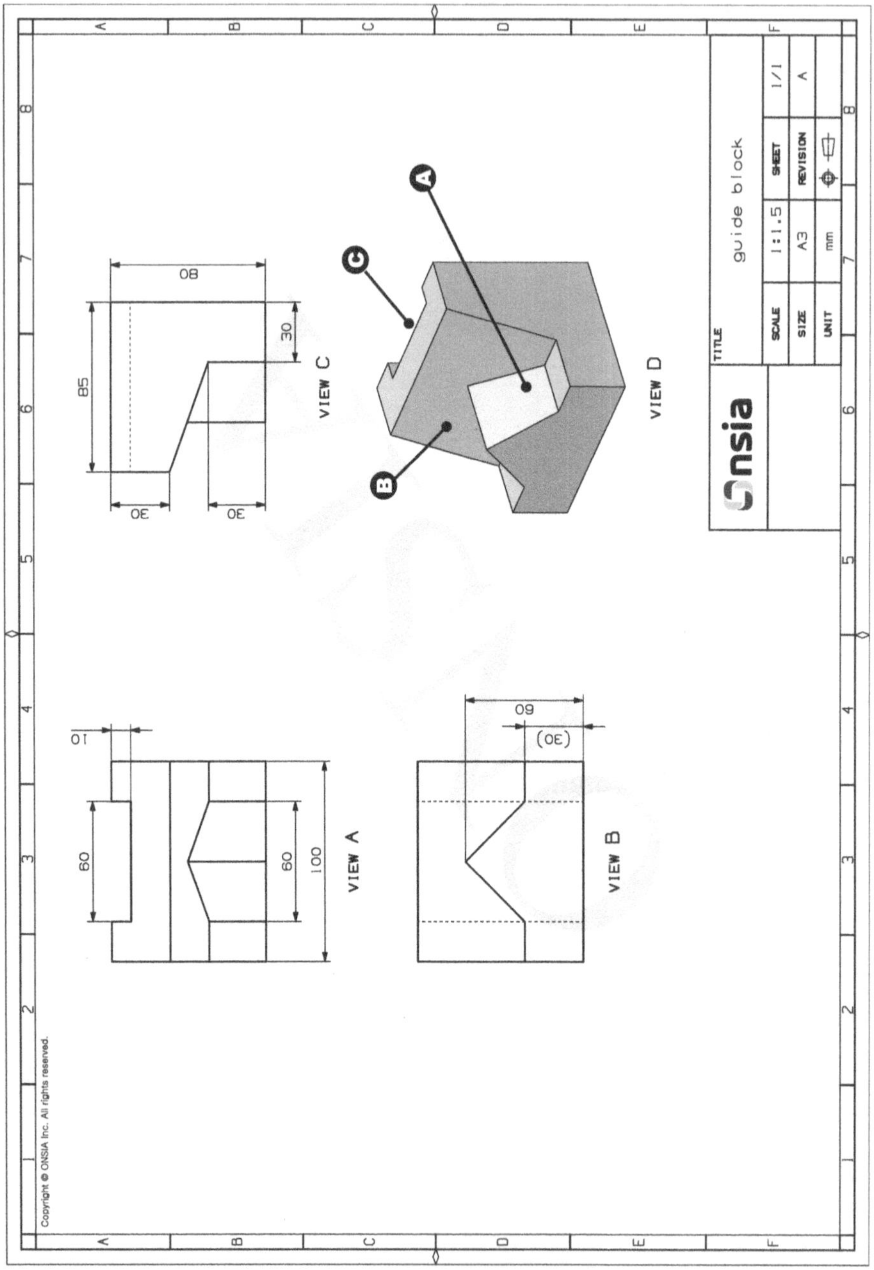

Fig 4-70 Drawing for Guide Block

4.9 Editing Object Display

You can edit the color, line font, line width, face translucency, etc. using the **Edit Object Display** icon in the **View** tab according to the following procedure.

1. Click the **Edit Object Display** icon in the **Visualization** icon group in the **View** tab. The **Class Selection** dialog box appears as shown in Fig 4-72, where you can select objects with the help of various selection methods.

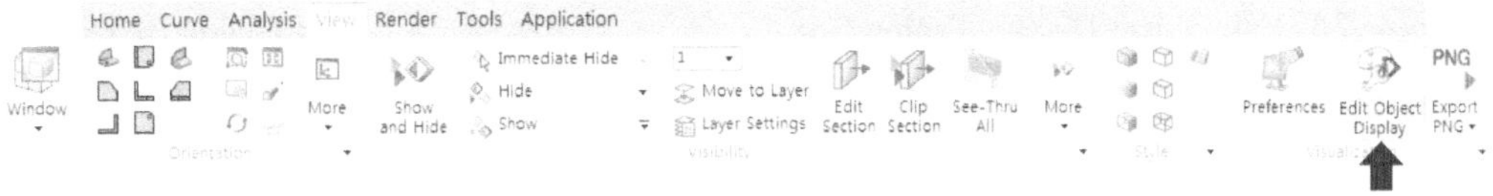

Fig 4-71 Edit Object Display Icon

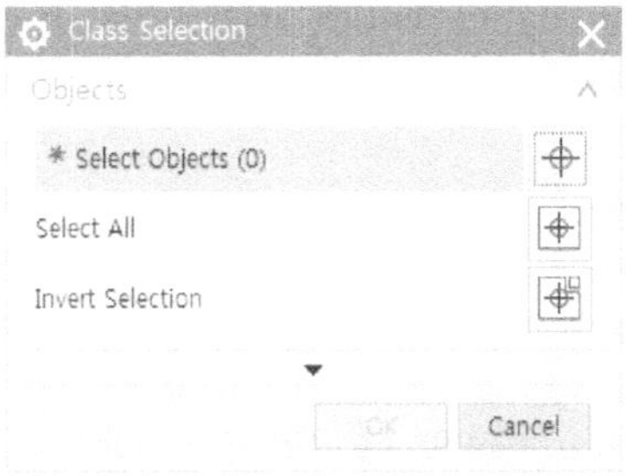

Fig 4-72 Class Selection Dialog Box

2. Select the object to edit the display and press **OK**. Fig 4-73 shows various types of objects available.

Fig 4-73 Type Filter

3. Click the color block (**A** in Fig 4-74) in the **Edit Object Display** dialog box.
4. Select the desired color in the dialog box and press **OK**.
5. Press the **OK** button in the **Edit Object Display** dialog box.

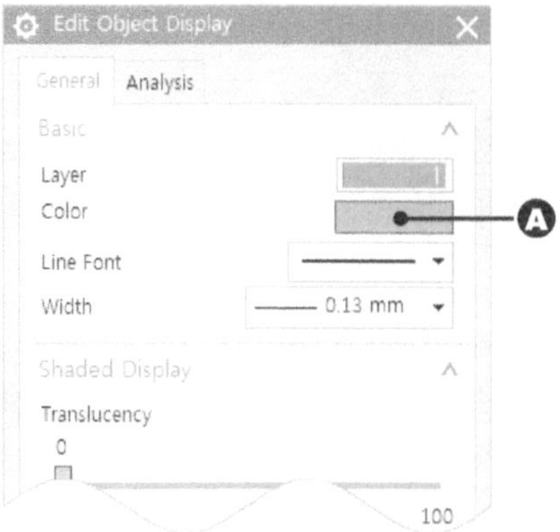

Fig 4-74 Edit Object Display Dialog Box

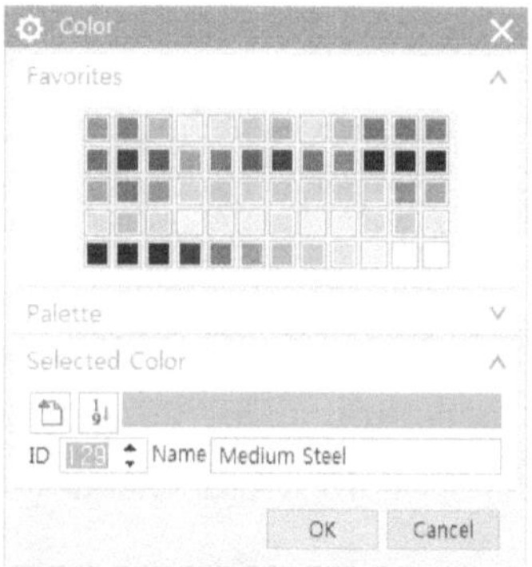

Fig 4-75 Color Dialog Box

4.10 Revolve

You can create a solid body by revolving a section around an axis. Revolve axis can be defined by selecting a linear object or datum axis.

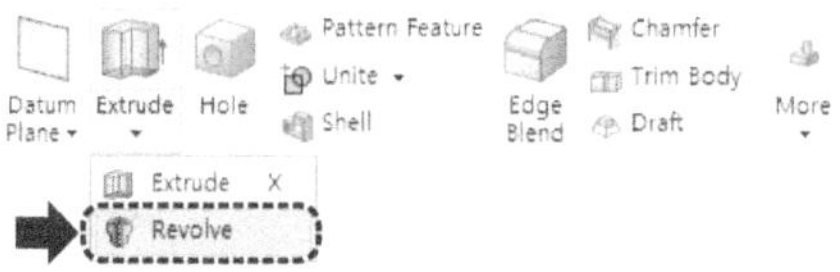

Fig 4-76 Revolve Icon

Procedure

1. Press the **Revolve** icon.
2. Reset the **Revolve** dialog box.
3. Define a section.
4. Click MB2.
5. Select a revolution axis.
6. Specify limit option, boolean option etc. and press **OK**.

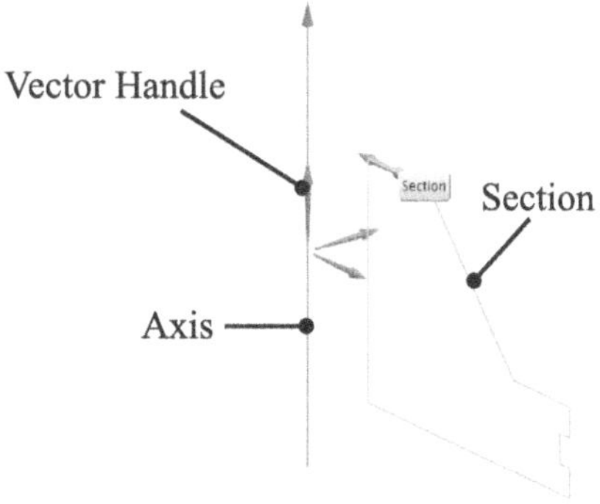

Fig 4-77 Section and Axis

When you select the vector handle, you have to specify the point to pass through. The vector handle specifies only the direction of the rotation axis. Note that you can drag the symbol of the vector handle.

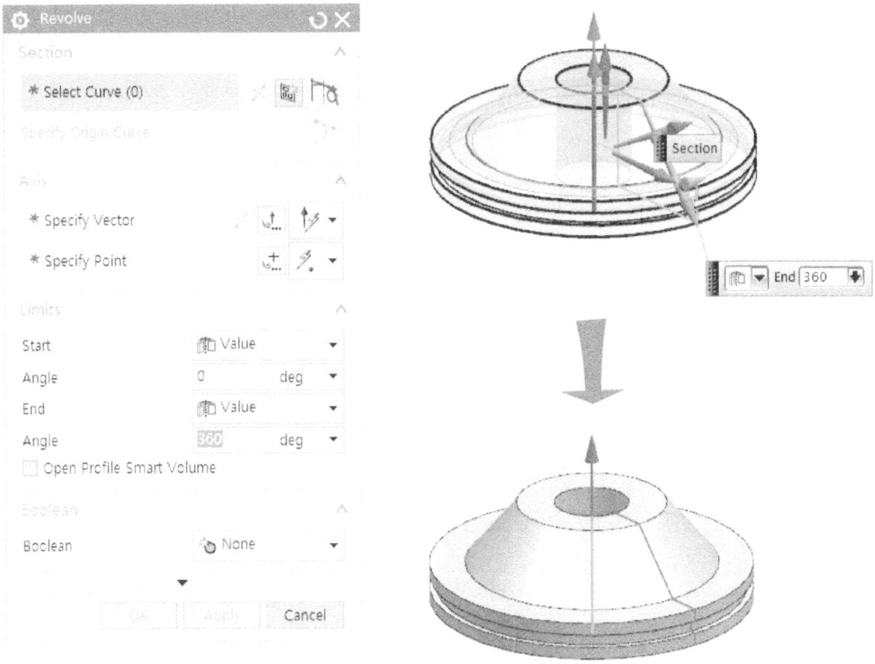

Fig 4-78 Revolving a Section

4.10.1 Section and Axis of Revolve

Keep in mind the following conditions when defining the section and axis for revolve.

① Section has to be closed to create a solid body.
② The revolution axis cannot be defined across the section.
③ The revolution axis cannot be normal to the section plane.

If you select the three dotted lines of the rectangle shown in Fig 4-79 as the section and specify the other side as an axis to revolve 180°, you will obtain a sheet body.

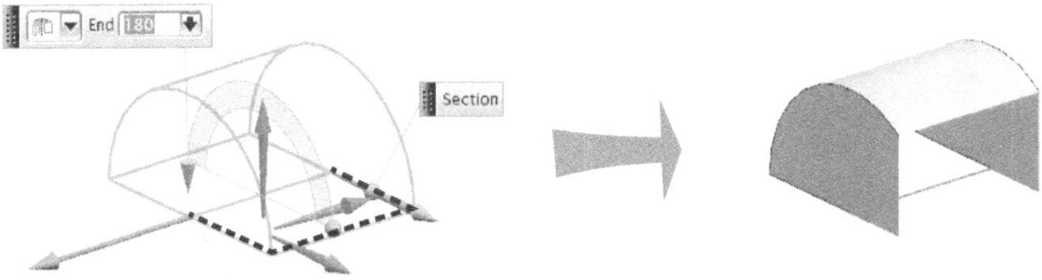

Fig 4-79 Revolving an Open Section

When the revolve axis is defined across the section or the axis is normal to the section plane, an alert message is invoked as shown in Fig 4-80.

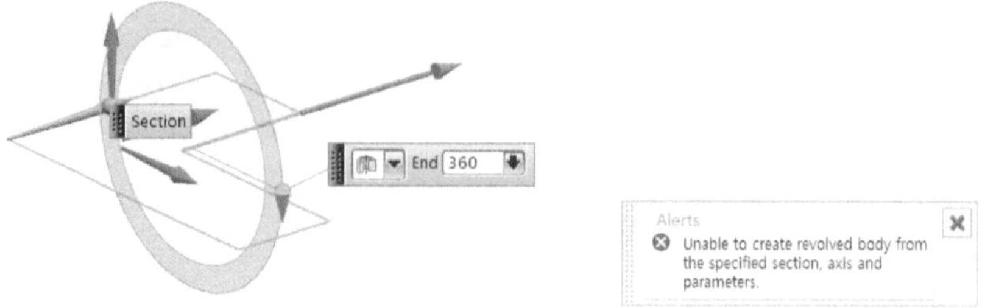

Fig 4-80 Axis Defined Across the Section

! Displaying Cross Section

A cross section of a 3D model as shown in Fig 4-81 can be attained with the **Edit Work Section** icon.

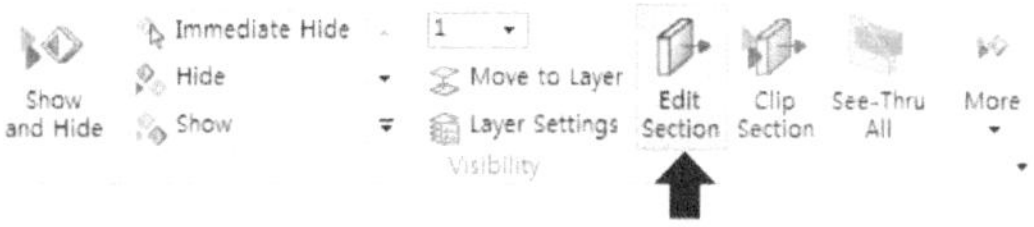

Fig 4-81 Edit Work Section Icon

The sectioning plane is defined normal to the **X** direction by pressing the **X** button in the **View Section** dialog box. You can move the sectioning plane by dragging the arrow head.

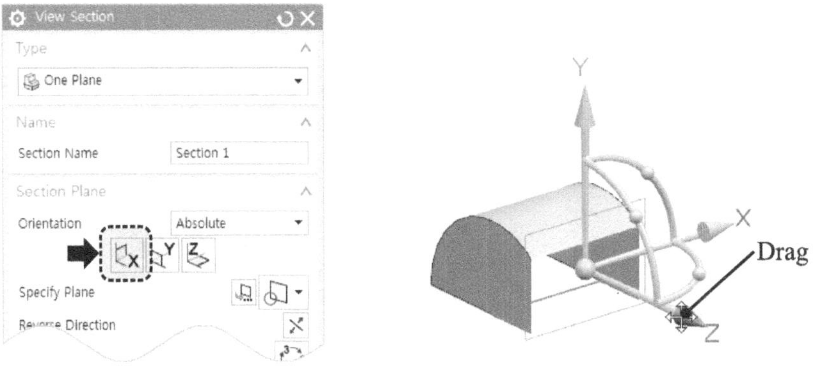

Fig 4-82 Defining Sectioning Plane

Looking Up a Command

You can look up a command using the **Command Finder**.

Fig 4-83 Command Finder Icon

Only a portion of the command text can work. You can execute the command by clicking in the search result.

Fig 4-84 Result of Command Finder

Creating a Sketch while Defining a Section

Select a plane when you are prompted to select curves to define a section for an extrude or revolve feature. The sketch environment is invoked and you can create the sketch. You can press the **Sketch Section** button to define the sketch plane and create the sketch.

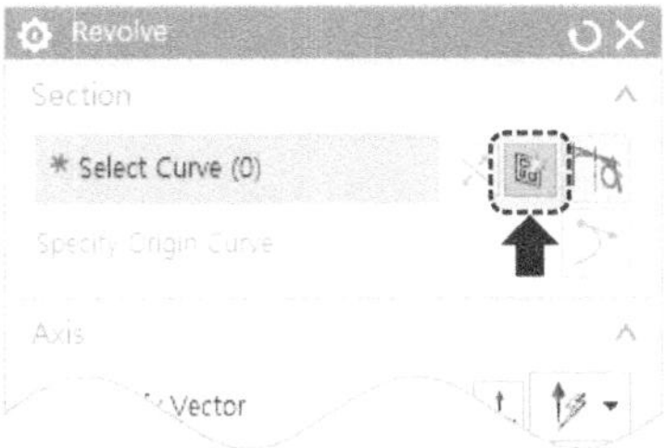

Fig 4-85 Sketch Section Button

4.11 Creating Holes

You can create holes using the **Hole** command. You have to specify the location of the hole centers and define their shape. Note that the snap point option is available in selecting the location of the hole centers. You can create the point in the sketch environment.

Procedure

1. Press the **Hole** icon in the **Feature** icon group.

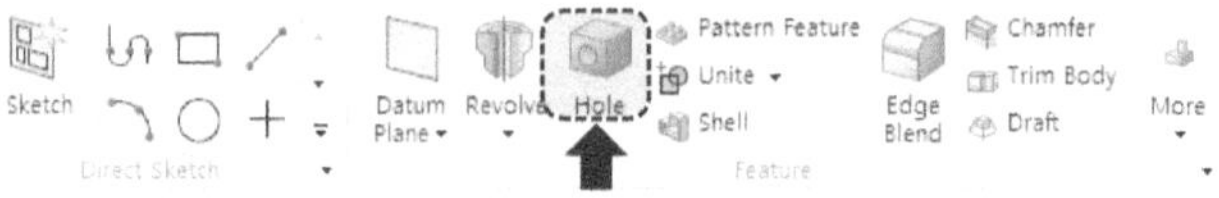

Fig 4-86 Hole Icon

2. Reset the dialog box.
3. Select the type of holes.
4. Specify hole centers.
5. Set other options such as **Direction** and **Form and Dimensions** and press **OK**.

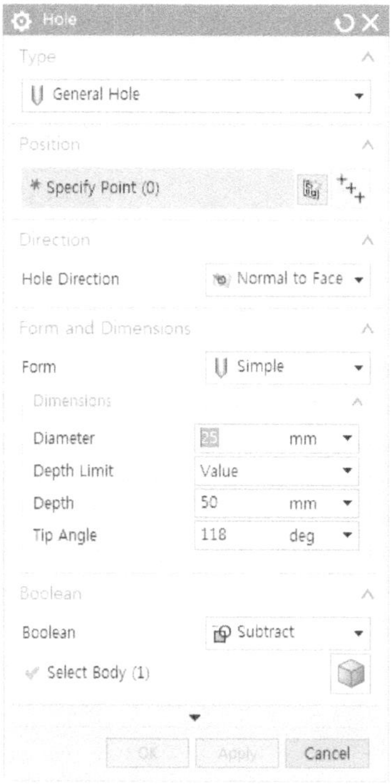

Fig 4-87 Hole Dialog Box

Direction is set as **Normal to Face** by default which means that the holes will be created normal to the face to which the points belong. When the point is out of a surface beyond the allowance, you have to specify the direction explicitly.

Options in the **Form and Dimensions** group define the type of the hole and its dimension.

Hole features can be created as solid bodies which will be used as tool bodies for subtraction afterwards.

4.11.1 General Type Holes

Fig 4-88 through Fig 4-91 shows a cross section of general type holes.

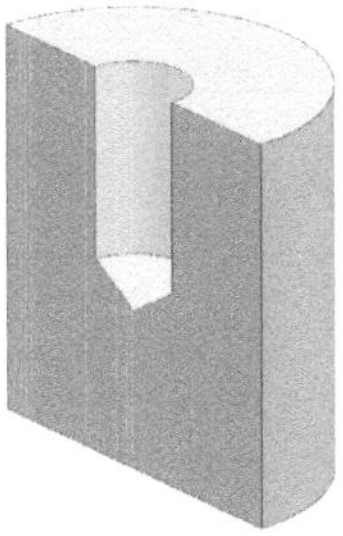

Fig 4-88 Simple Hole

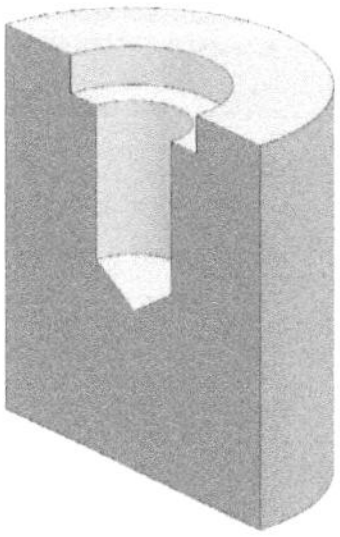

Fig 4-89 Counterbored Hole

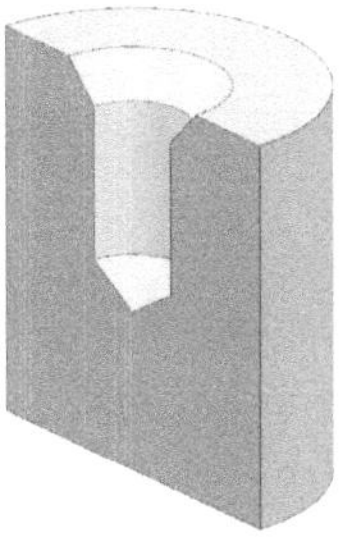

Fig 4-90 Countersunk Hole

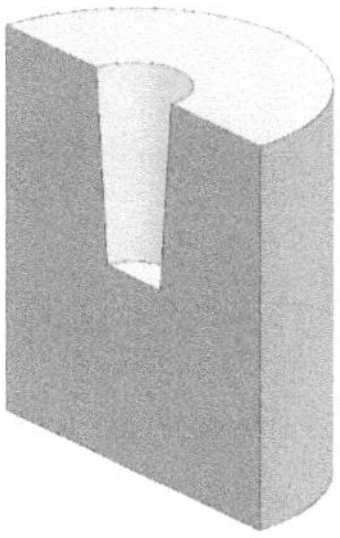

Fig 4-91 Tapered Hole

Fig 4-92 and Fig 4-93 show the cross section and dimensions of a counterbored hole and a countersunk hole, respectively. The numbers in the cross section corresponds to the numbers in the dialog box.

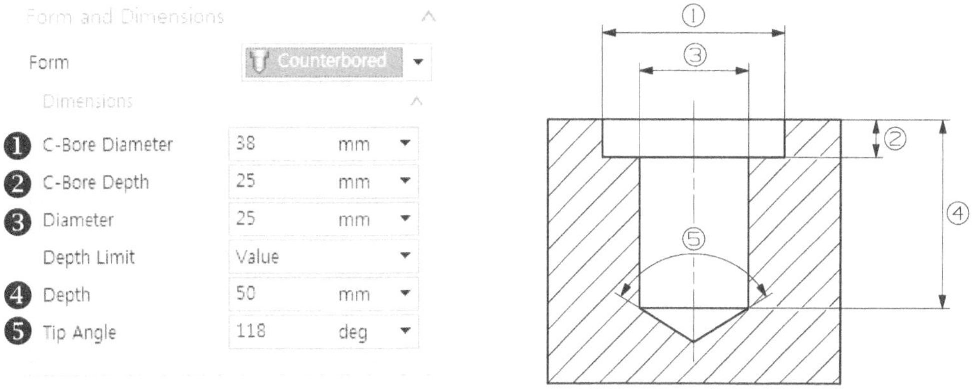

Fig 4-92 Dimensions of Counterbored Hole

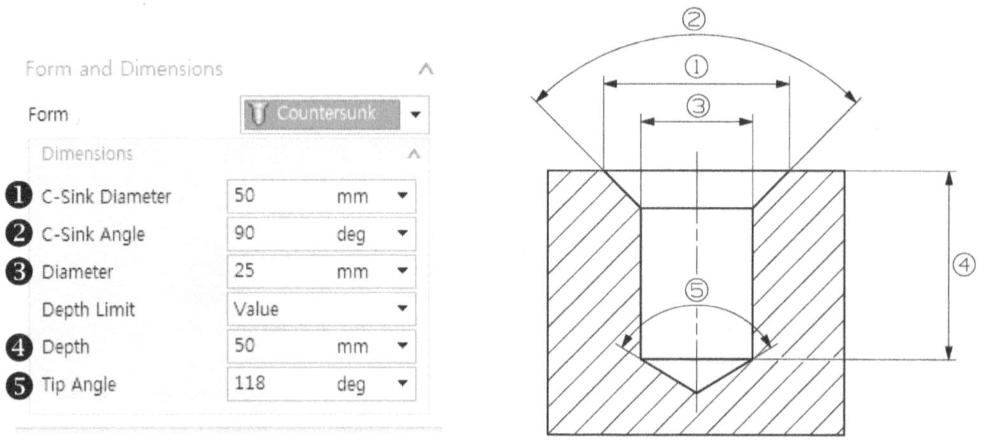

Fig 4-93 Dimensions of Countersunk Hole

4.11.2 Threaded Type Holes

Fig 4-94 and Fig 4-95 show cross section of a threaded hole and the dialog box for the type of **Threaded Hole**. You can specify thread dimensions which can be associated to the hole annotation in the drawing.

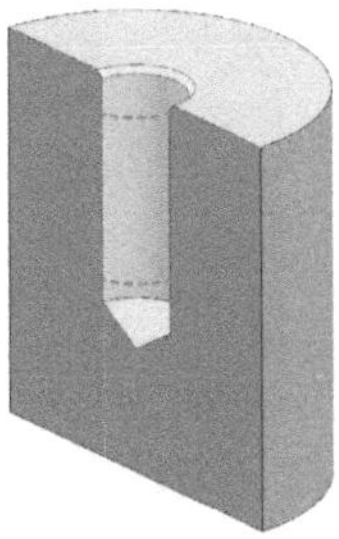

Fig 4-94 Threaded Hole

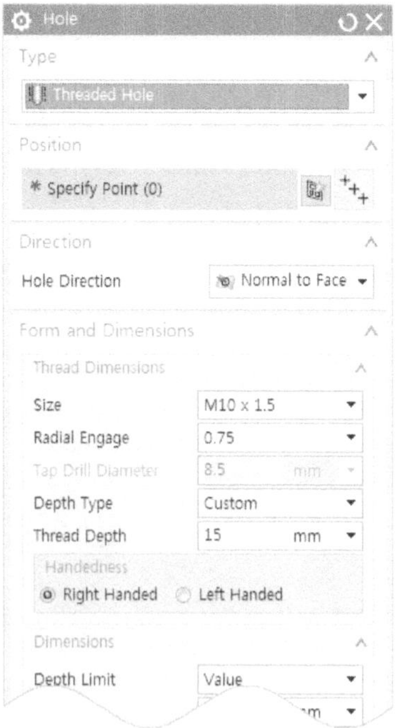

Fig 4-95 Dialog Box for Threaded Hole Type

Let's learn how to define the position and dimension of a simple hole.

Creating a Base Feature

1. Create a file named ch04_ex04.prt and extrude the sketch shown in Fig 4-96. The sketch is created on the XY plane.
2. Extrude the section 20mm as shown in Fig 4-97.

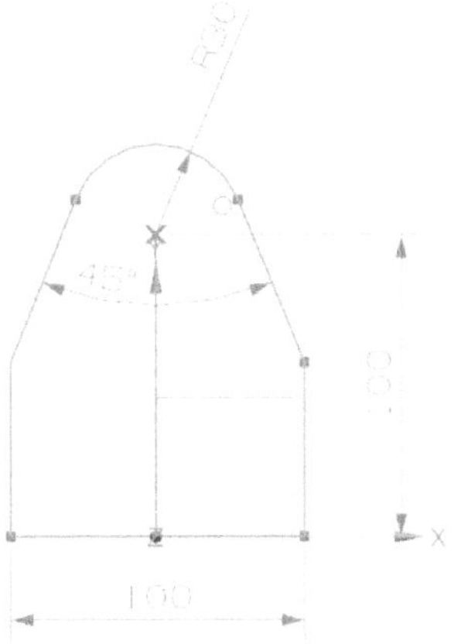

Fig 4-96 Sketch

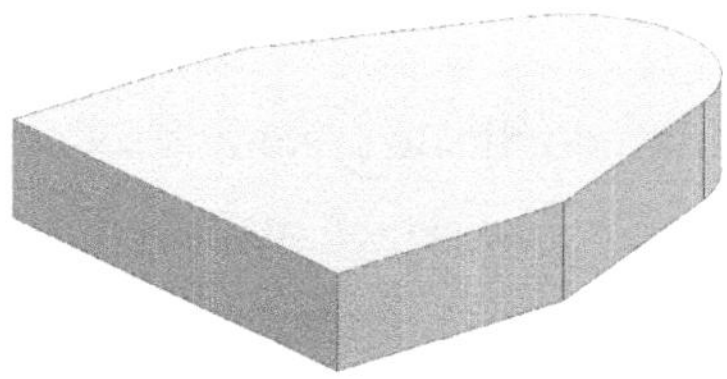

Fig 4-97 Extrude

Executing the Hole Command

1. Click the **Hole** icon in the **Feature** icon group.
2. Reset the dialog box.
3. Confirm that the default type is **General Hole**.
4. Confirm that the **Specify Point** option is highlighted.

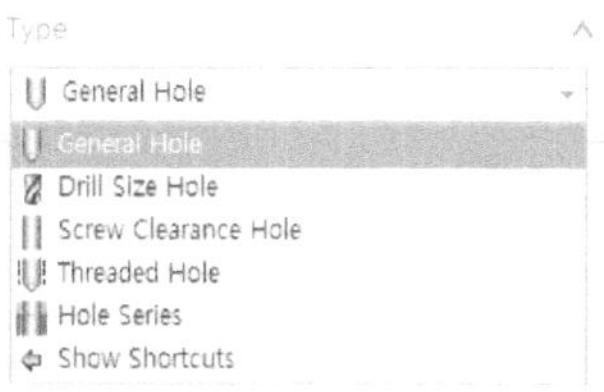

Fig 4-98 General Hole Type

5. Click the **Sketch Section** ( )icon in the **Specify Point** option group. The **Create Sketch** dialog box is invoked and you are prompted to select an object for the sketch plane.

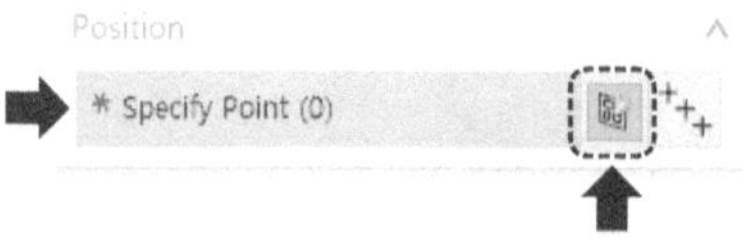

Fig 4-99 Position Group in Hole Dialog Box

6. Select the upper plane around the region designated by the arrow in Fig 4-100.

Fig 4-100 Selecting the Sketch Plane

The sketch coordinate system is set as shown in Fig 4-101. Do not press OK yet. If you press OK, the sketch plane will be aligned as shown in Fig 4-102, which is inconvenient when constraining the sketch.

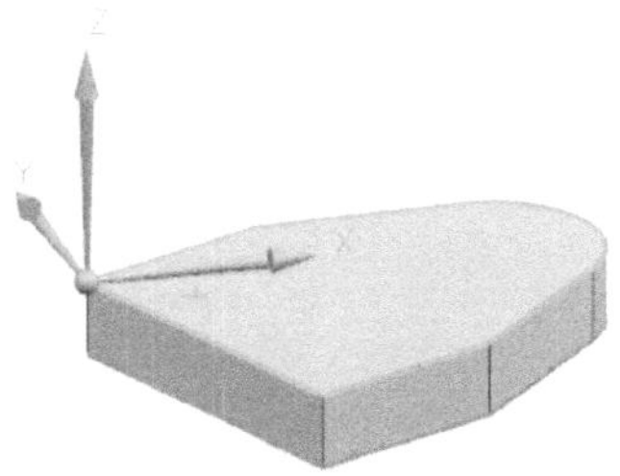

Fig 4-101 Sketch Coordinate System

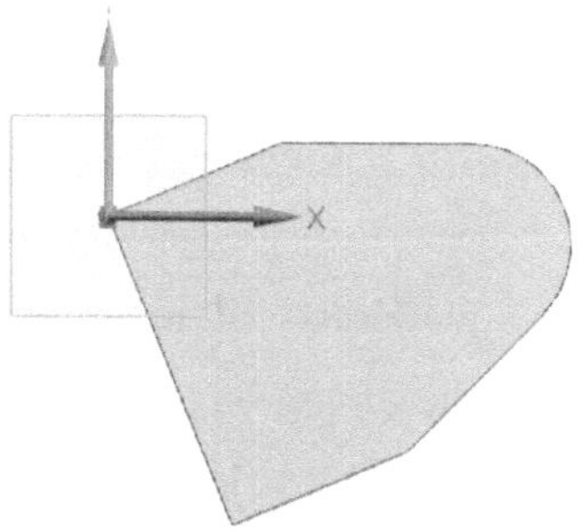

Fig 4-102 Aligned Sketch Plane

Orienting Sketch Plane

1. Expand the **Sketch Orientation** option group in the **Create Sketch** dialog box.
2. Note that the **Reference** dropdown list is **Horizontal** and click the **Select Reference** option.
3. Select the edge around the region designated by the arrow in Fig 4-105.

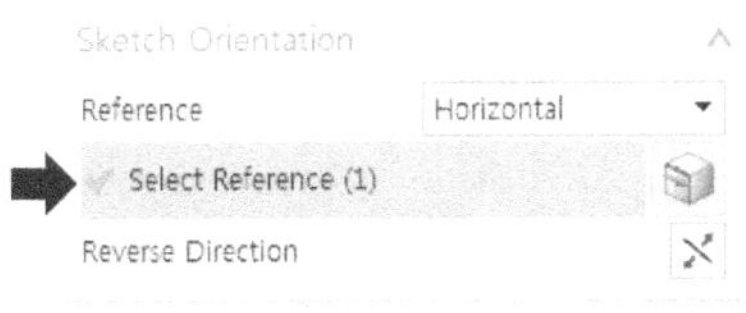

Fig 4-103 Select Reference Option

Fig 4-104 Selecting Edge

The horizontal axis of the sketch coordinate system is aligned to the selected edge. If the X axis is reversed, press the **Reverse Direction** button in the dialog box.

4. Press **OK** in the **Create Sketch** dialog box. The **Sketch Point** dialog box is invoked and you are prompted to specify the location of a point.

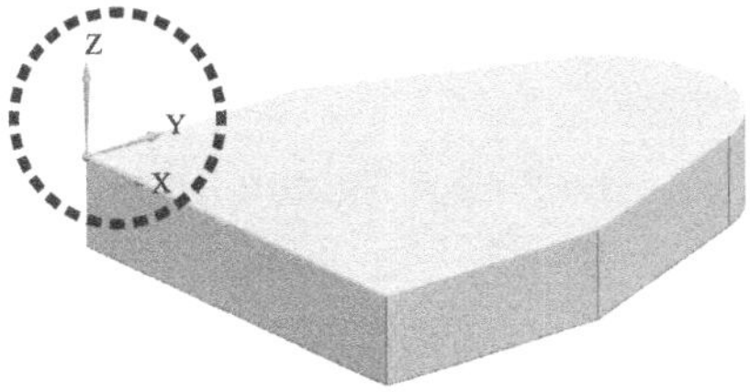

Fig 4-105 Horizontal Sketch Axis Aligned to the Edge

Creating a Point and Constraining

1. Select the location designated by the arrow in Fig 4-106.

A point is created as shown in Fig 4-107. Note that the point is smaller than the one marked in the figure.

2. Close the **Sketch Point** dialog box.

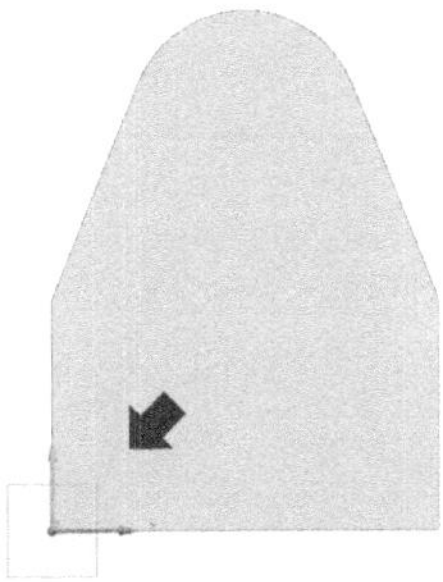

Fig 4-106 Location to Pick

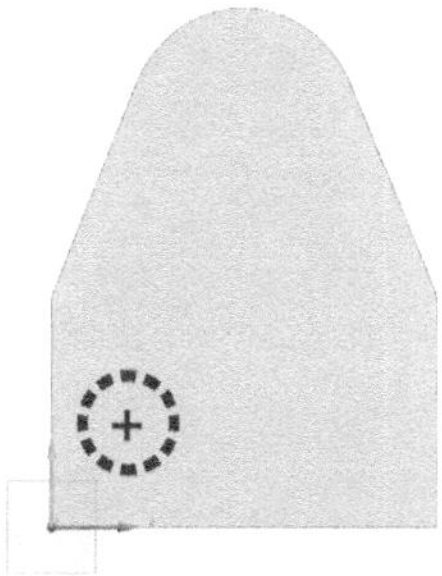

Fig 4-107 Point Created

3. Fully constrain the point as shown in Fig 4-110.

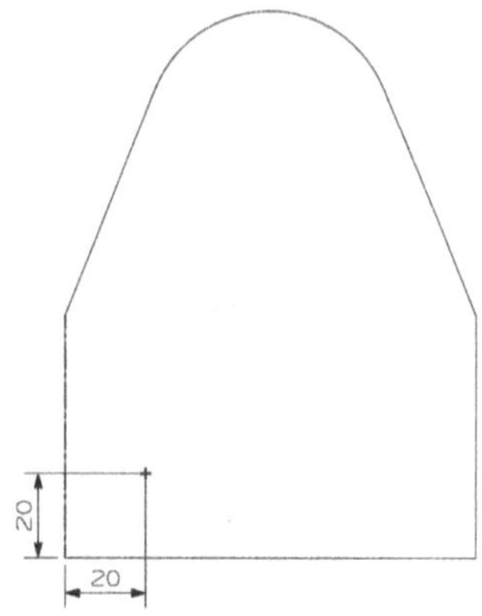

Fig 4-108 Constrain the Point

4. Finish the sketch by clicking the **Finish Sketch** icon. (Finish Sketch) Default sized hole is previewed.

5. Enter the **Form and Dimensions** option as shown in Fig 4-109.

Dimensions	Values
Diameter	10
Depth Limit	Value
Depth	15
Tip Angle	118

Fig 4-109 Dimension Values

Note that you have to press **Enter** to preview the result. Fig 4-110 shows the preview of the hole.

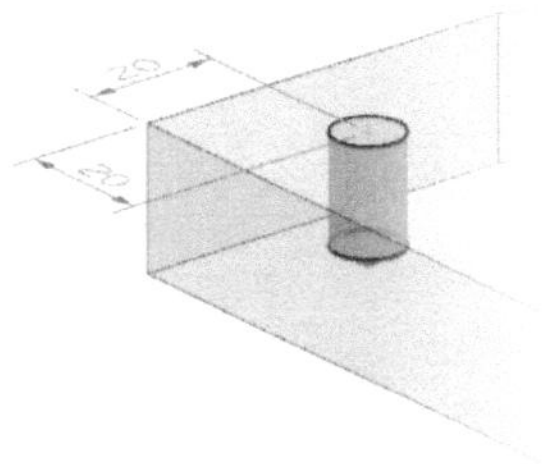

Fig 4-110 Preview of Simple Hole

Tip Angle

Note that the tip angle of the drill is 118 °. Therefore, the default tip angle of the hole is set to 118 °. If you want to create a flat hole, enter 0 in the **Tip Angle** input box.

Fig 4-111 Drill Tip Angle = 118 °

6. Press **OK** in the **Hole** dialog box. A hole is created as shown in Fig 4-112 and the sketch for the hole position disappears.

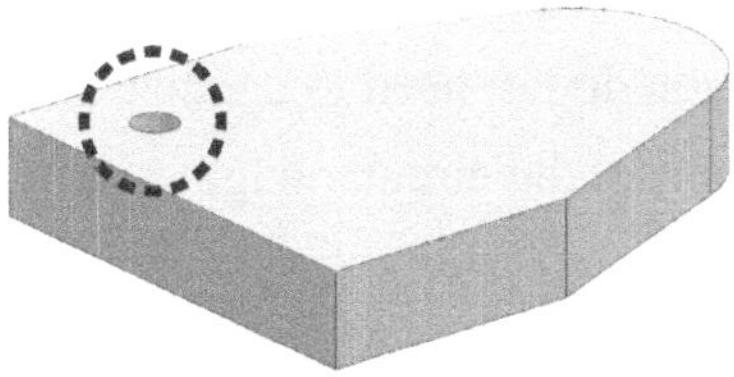

Fig 4-112 Simple Hole Created

7. Do not close the file and go on to Exercise 05.

END of Exercise

Identifying Hole Type in Part Navigator

You can identify the type of hole by looking at the **Part Navigator**.

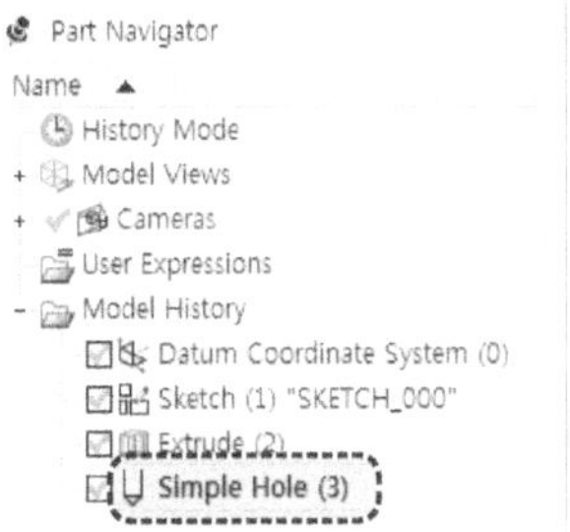

Fig 4-113 Simple Hole Feature

Exercise 05 Creating a Simple Hole (Position by Snap Point Option)

Create a through hole with a diameter of 20mm on the part as shown in Fig 4-114.

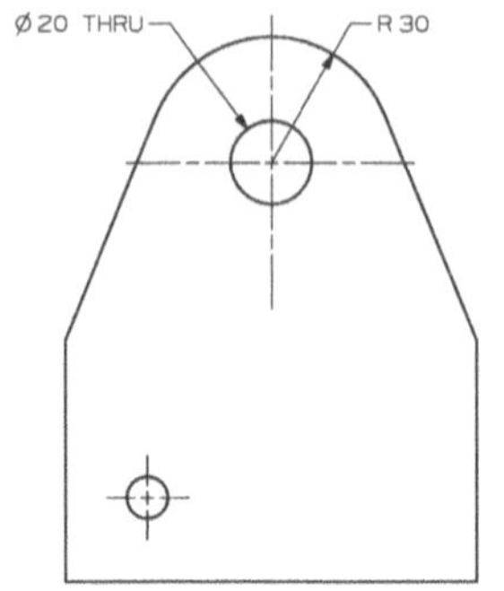

Fig 4-114 Dimension of the Through Hole

Hint !

1. To specify the position, you do not need to create a sketch.
2. Click MB1 when the center of the circular edge is snapped as shown in Fig 4-115.

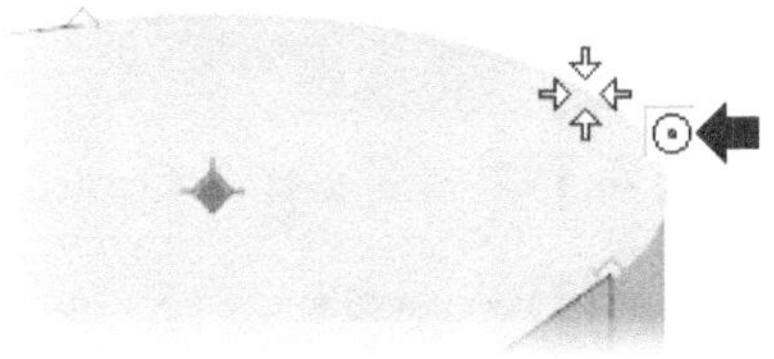

Fig 4-115 Arc Center

3. Specify the type as **General Hole** and set the **Form and Dimensions** option as shown in Fig 4-116.

Fig 4-116 Form and Dimensions Option

END of Exercise

4.12 Creating a Boss

Using the **Boss** command, you can create a cylindrical geometry on a plane and unite to the existing body.

Usage of Boss Command **Exercise 06**

Let's learn the basic usage of the **Boss** command through an exercise.

Creating Base Feature

1. Create a file named ch04_ex06.prt and extrude the sketch shown in Fig 4-117. The sketch is created on the XY plane.
2. Extrude the section 20mm as shown in Fig 4-118.

You can use the result of the previous exercise by deleting the hole features.

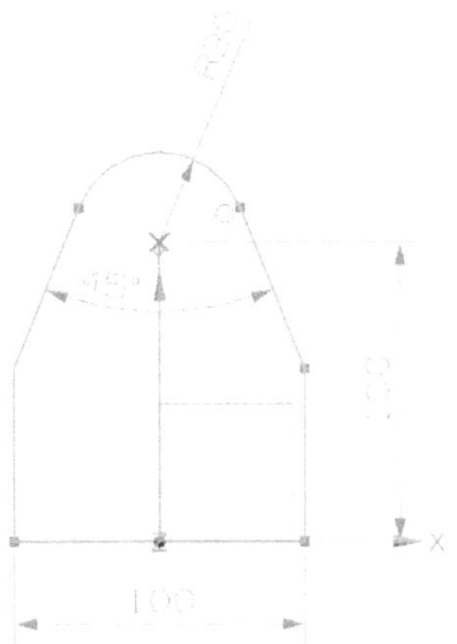

Fig 4-117 Sketch

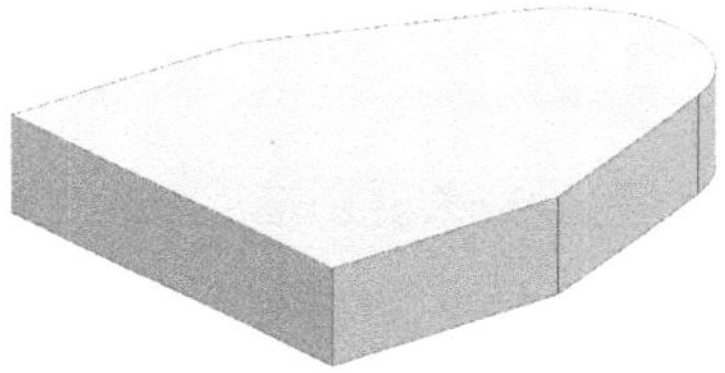

Fig 4-118 Extrude

Executing the Boss Command

1. Click the triangular icon in the **Feature** icon group as shown in Fig 4-119 and select **More Gallery > Design Feature Gallery > Boss**. The **Boss** icon is available when you click the **More** button in the **Feature** icon group.

Fig 4-119 Adding the Boss Icon

2. Click the **Boss** icon by pressing the **More** button in the **Feature** icon group. You can choose **Insert > Design Feature > Boss** in the **Menu** button.
3. Select the plane around the location designated by the arrow in Fig 4-120. A cylinder is previewed as shown in Fig 4-121. Enter the dimension values as shown in Fig 4-122.

Fig 4-120 Placement Face

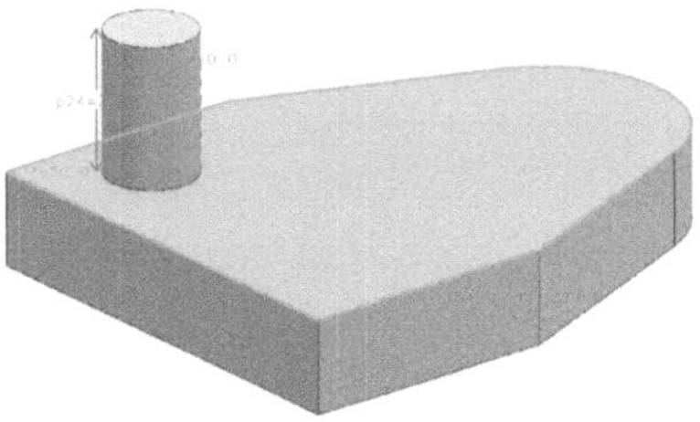

Fig 4-121 Preview of the Boss

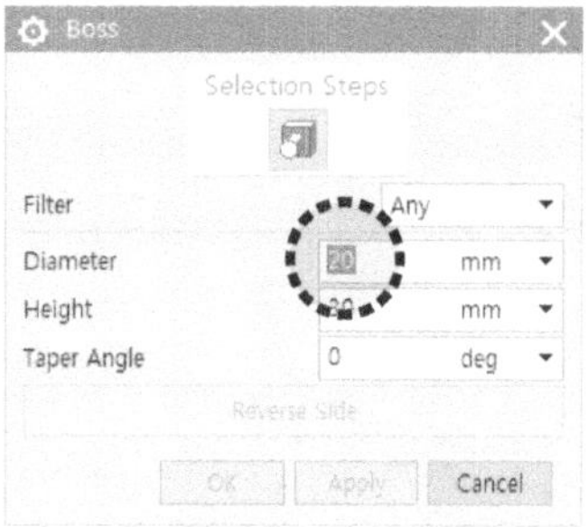

Fig 4-122 Boss Dialog Box

4. Press **OK** in the **Boss** dialog box. The **Positioning** dialog box appears as shown in Fig 4-123. Note that the **Perpendicular** icon (❹) is selected.

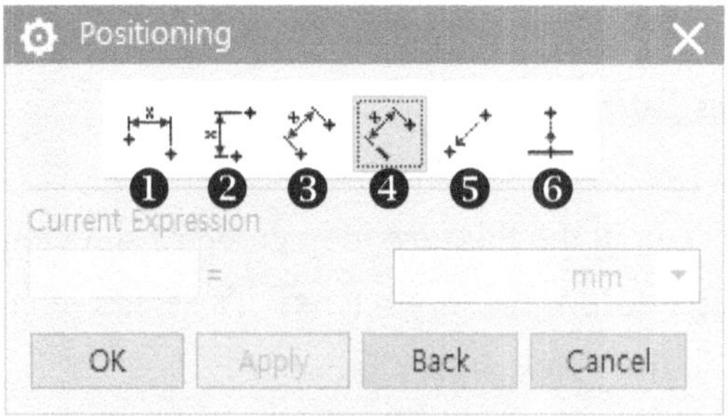

Fig 4-123 Positioning Dialog Box

❶ **Horizontal**: Apply horizontal dimension between the boss center and a point in the body.

❷ **Vertical**: Apply vertical dimension between the boss center and a point in the body.

❸ **Parallel**: Apply parallel dimension between the boss center and a point in the body.

❹ **Perpendicular**: Apply perpendicular dimension between a line and the boss center.

❺ **Point onto Point**: Position the bottom center of the boss feature onto a point in the body. An arc center can be detected.

❻ **Point onto Line**: Position the bottom center of the boss feature on a line.

5. Select the edge designated by the arrow in Fig 4-124.
6. Enter 20 in the input box as shown in Fig 4-125 and press **Enter** on the keyboard.

The distance dimension is modified as shown in Fig 4-126.

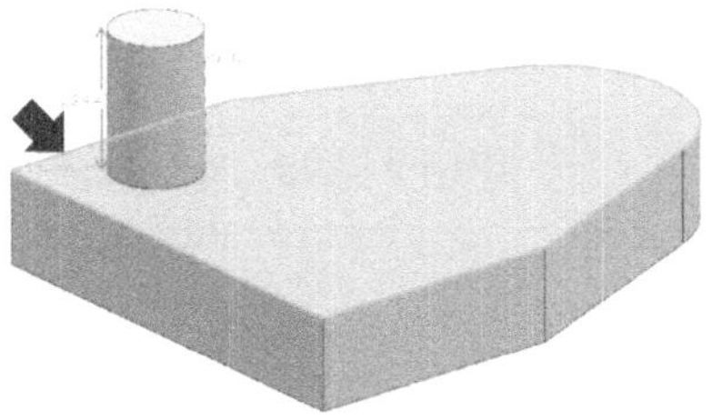

Fig 4-124 Edge to Select

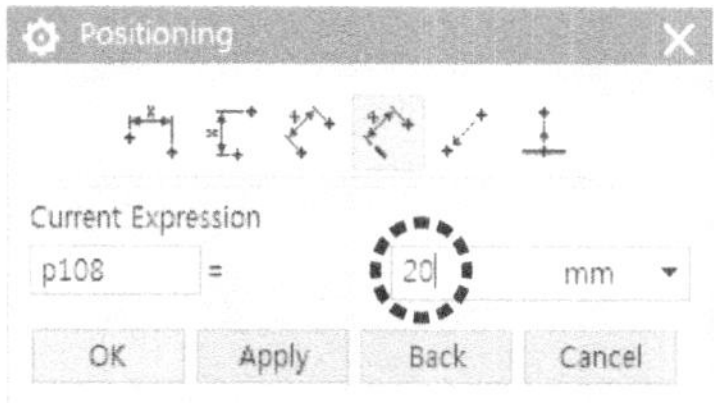

Fig 4-125 Distance Value

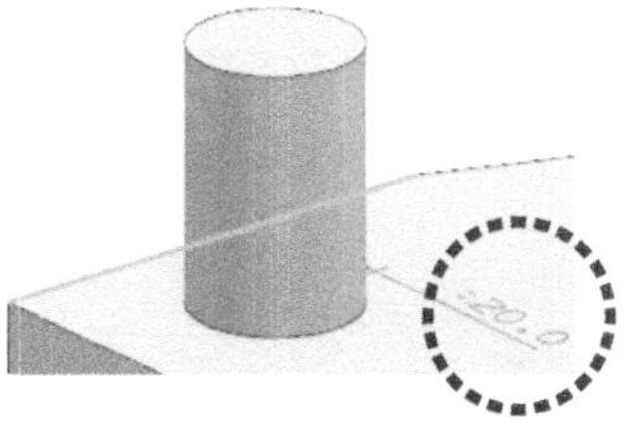

Fig 4-126 Distance Dimension

7. Select the edge specified in Fig 4-127.
8. Enter 20 in the input box and press **Enter** on the keyboard.
9. Press the **OK** button in the **Positioning** dialog box. A boss feature is created as shown in Fig 4-128.

<u>Go on to Exercise 07.</u>

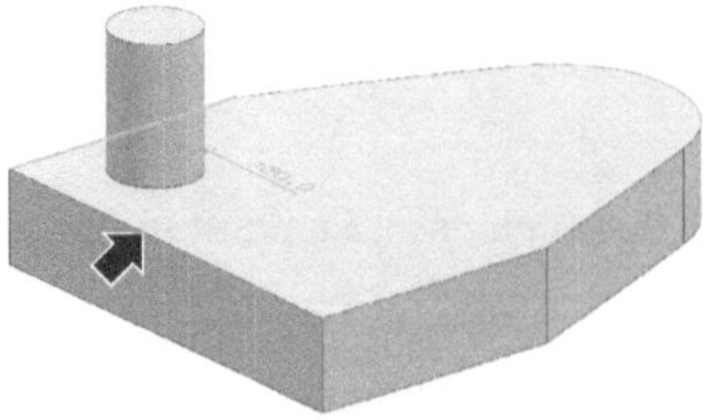

Fig 4-127 Edge to Select

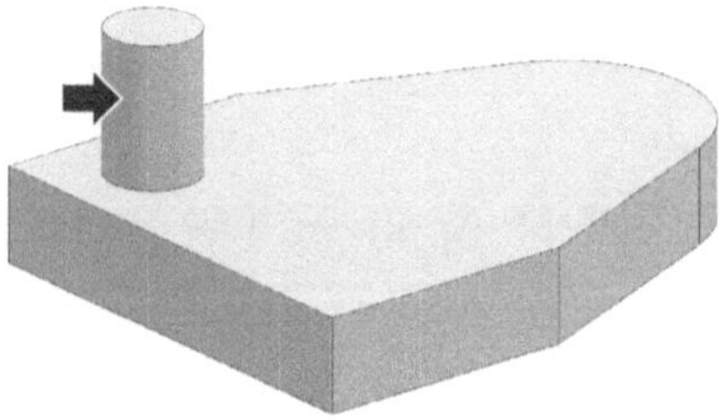

Fig 4-128 Boss Created

END of Exercise

Positional Form Feature

Features such as boss, pocket, pad, etc. which are available in **Insert > Design Feature** in the **Menu** button are called **Positional Form Features**. Their dimensions are defined first and the location is defined later and is not based on the sketch.

Fig 4-129 Positional Form Feature

Modifying the Position

Place the mouse pointer on the boss feature, press MB3 and select **Edit Positioning** in the pop-up menu. Note that you cannot modify the position of the boss by double clicking the feature.

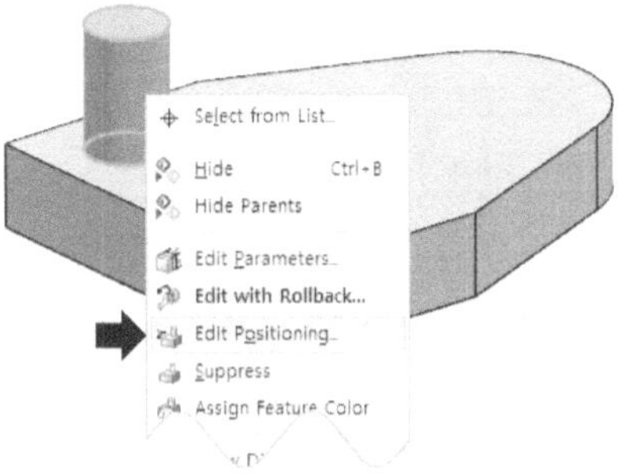

Fig 4-130 Edit Positioning Menu

Reusing the Recent Command

You can apply a recent command in various ways.

1. Use the **Quick View** toolbar by clicking MB1 in an empty area in the graphics window.

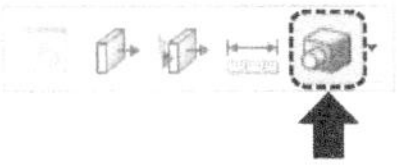

Fig 4-131 Quick View Toolbar

2. Use the recent command in the **Quick Access** toolbar.

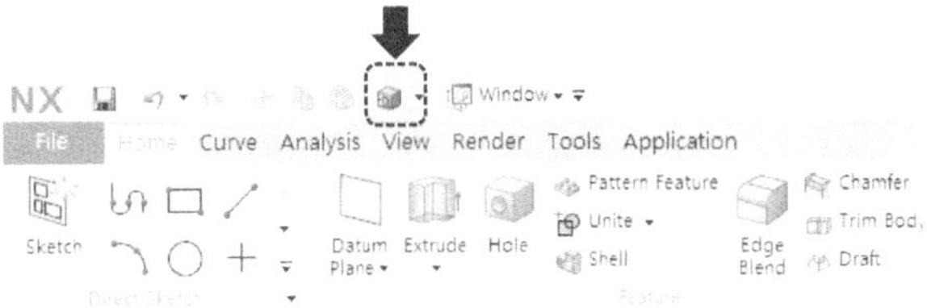

Fig 4-132 Quick Access Toolbar

3. Use the recent command in the pop-up menu by clicking MB3 in an empty area in the graphics window.

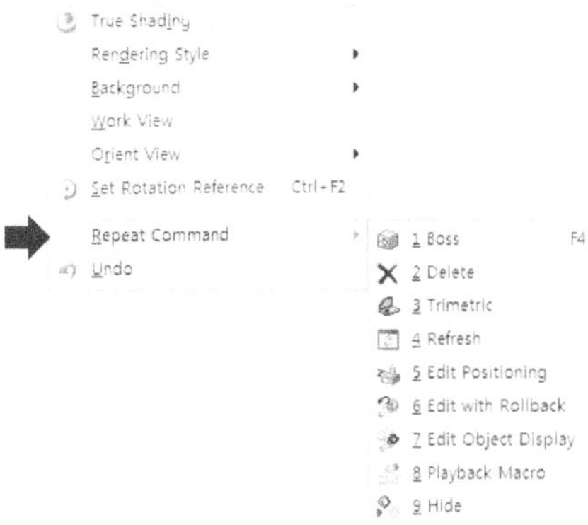

Fig 4-133 View Pop-up menu

Exercise 07 Creating a Boss (Point onto Point)

Create a boss of 20 mm diameter and 30 mm height as shown in Fig 4-134. The center of the bottom center of the boss is coincident with the center of edge Ⓐ.

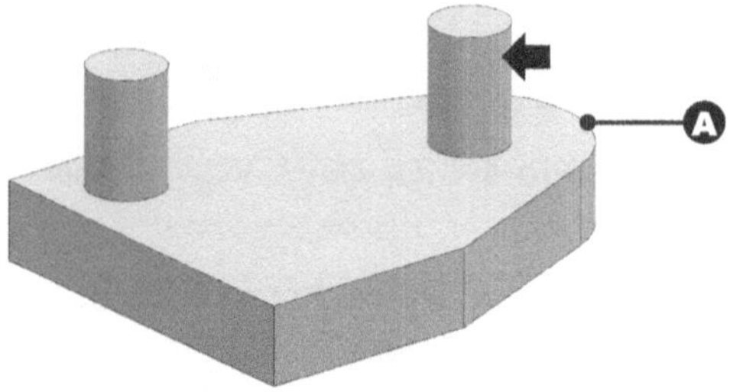

Fig 4-134 Boss to Create

Hint !

1. Choose the **Point onto Point** () positioning method and select the edge Ⓐ.
2. Choose the **Arc Center** in the **Set Arc Position** dialog box.

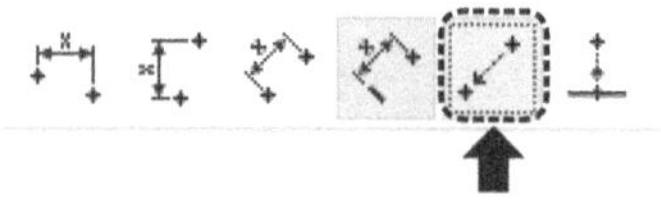

Fig 4-135 Point onto Point Positioning Method

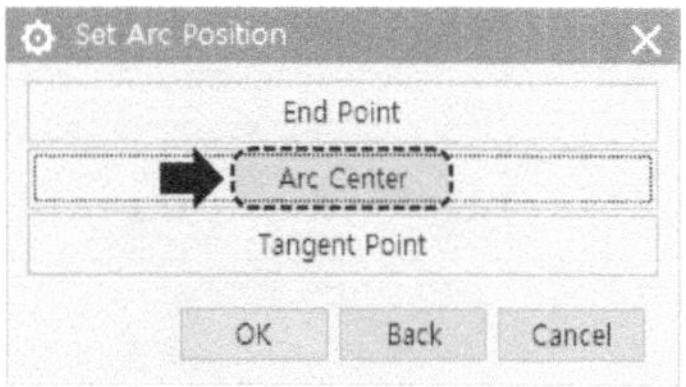

Fig 4-136 Arc Center Option

END of Exercise

Create a solid model referring to the drawing in Fig 4-137.

1. All sketches have to be fully constrained.
2. You should not use the **Fix** constraint.

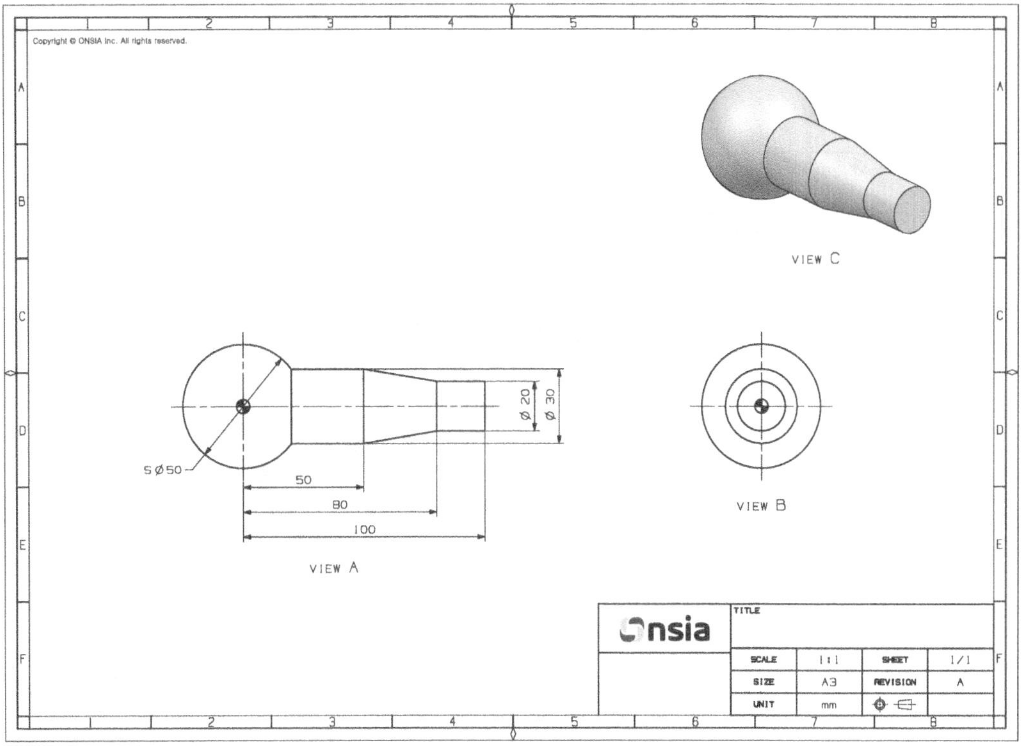

Fig 4-137 Drawing for Exercise 08

Exercise 09 Creating a Revolved Body

ch04_ex09.prt

Create a solid model referring to the drawing in Fig 4-138.

1. All sketches have to be fully constrained.
2. You should not use the **Fix** constraint.

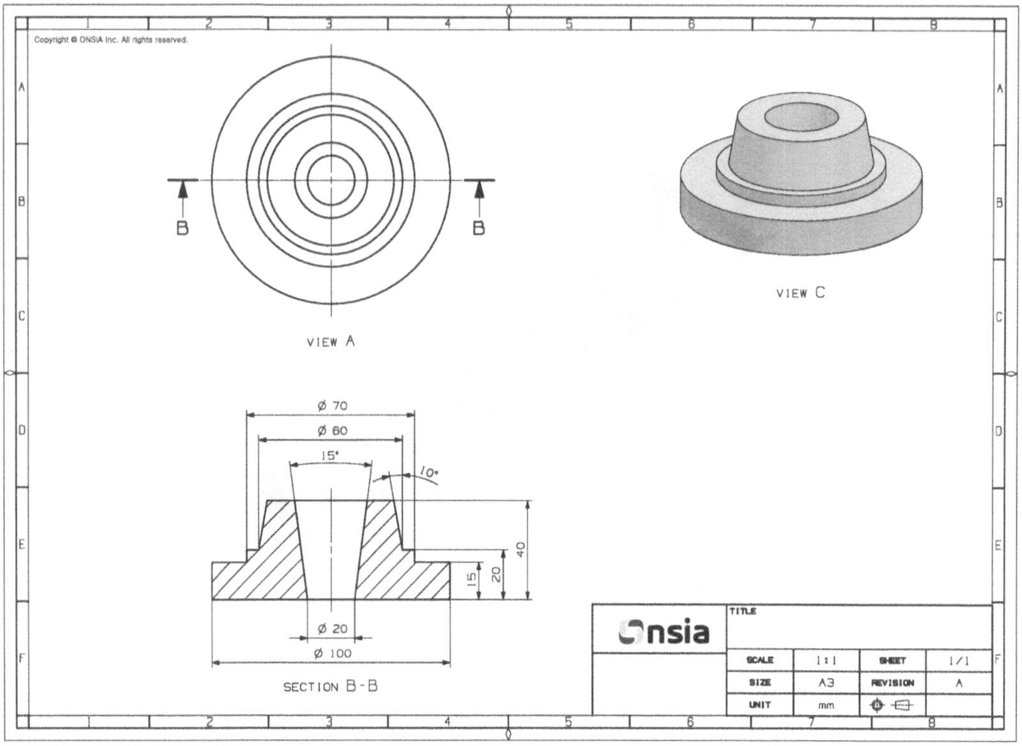

Fig 4-138 Drawing for Exercise 09

Create a solid model referring to the drawing in Fig 4-139.

1. All sketches have to be fully constrained.
2. You should not use the **Fix** constraint.
3. Use the **Hole** command to create holes.

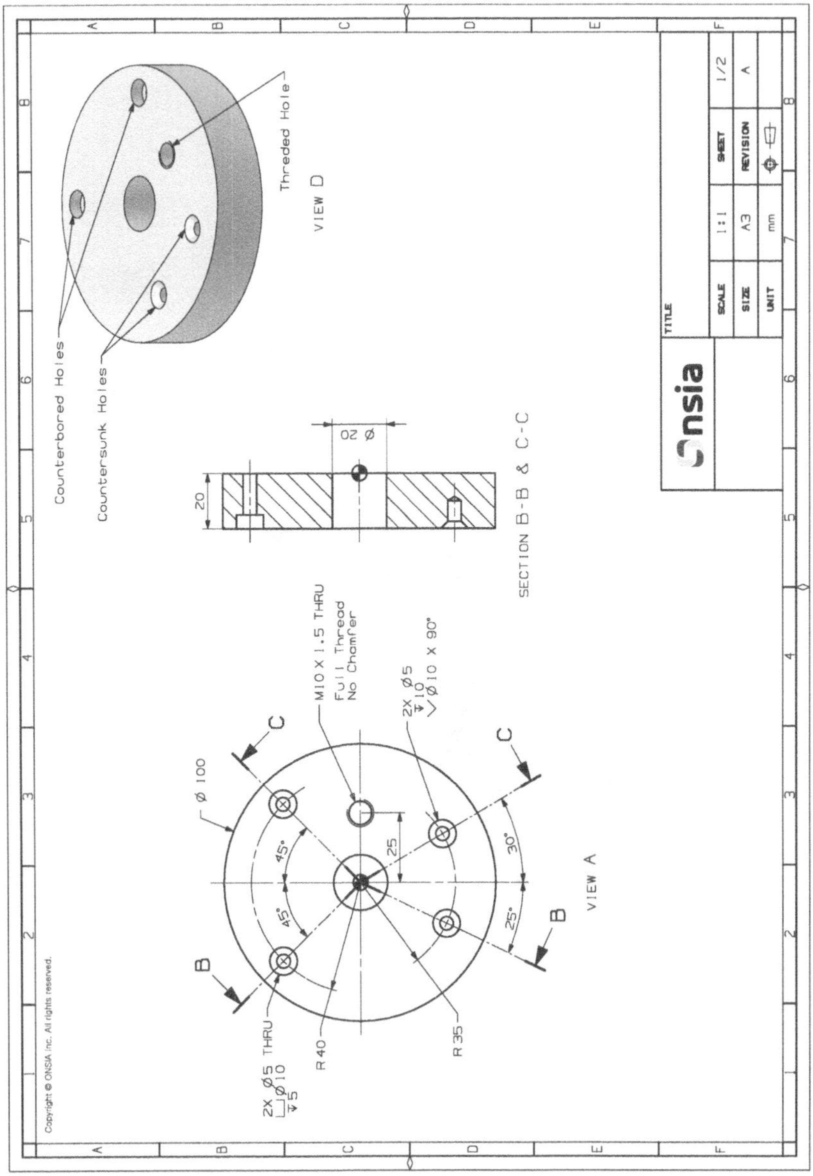

Fig 4-139 Drawing for Exercise 10

Hints !

1. Create a model referring to the following procedure.

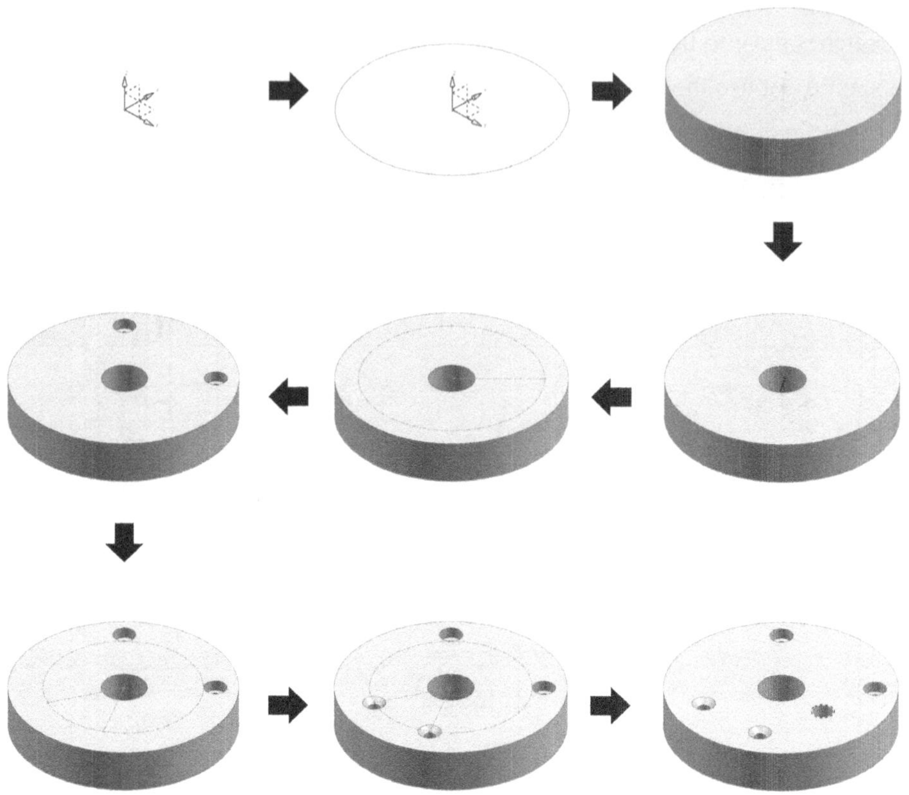

2. Refer to Fig 4-140 and Fig 4-141 to enter the dimensions of the counterbored holes and countersunk holes.

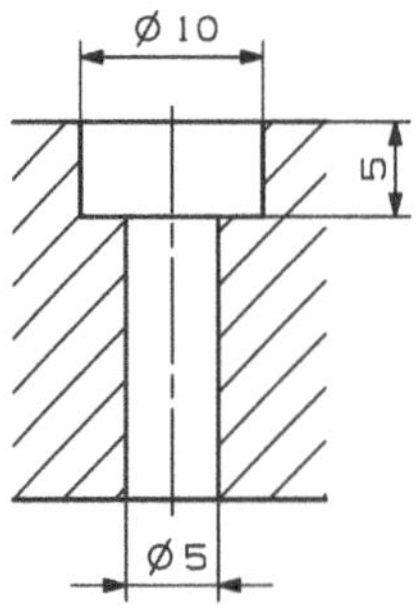

Fig 4-140 Counterbored Hole

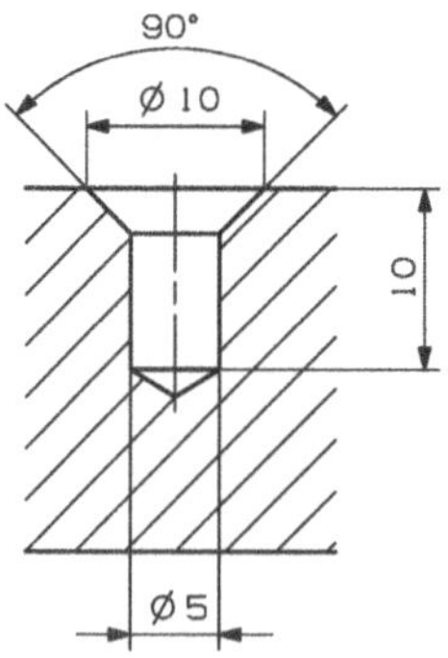

Fig 4-141 Countersunk Hole

Create a solid model referring to the drawing in Fig 4-142.

1. Use the **Hole** command to create holes.
2. Result model has to be a single solid body.

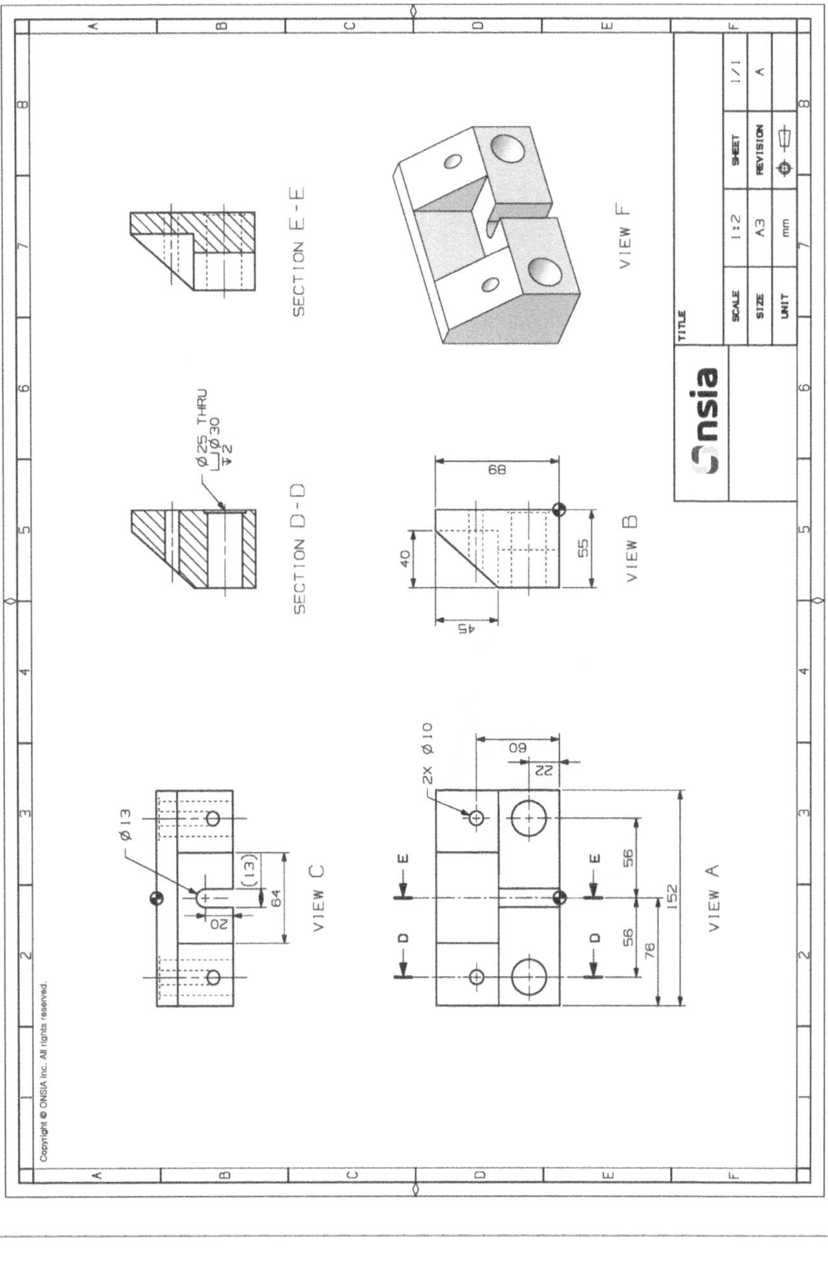

Fig 4-142 Drawing for Exercise 11

Hint !

Create a model referring to the following procedure.

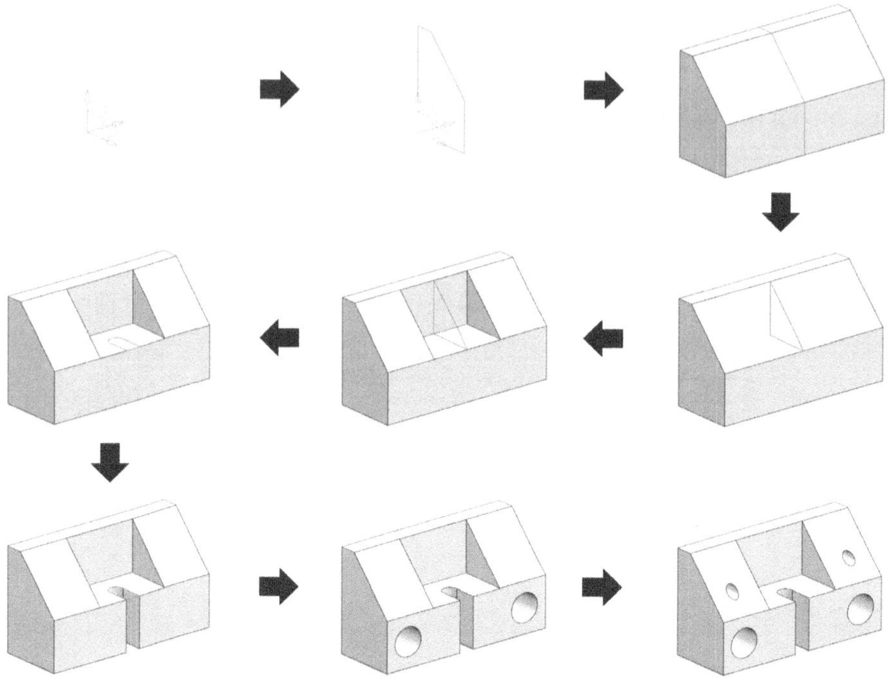

Create a solid model referring to the drawing in Fig 4-143.

1. Use the **Hole** command to create holes.
2. Result model has to be a single solid body.

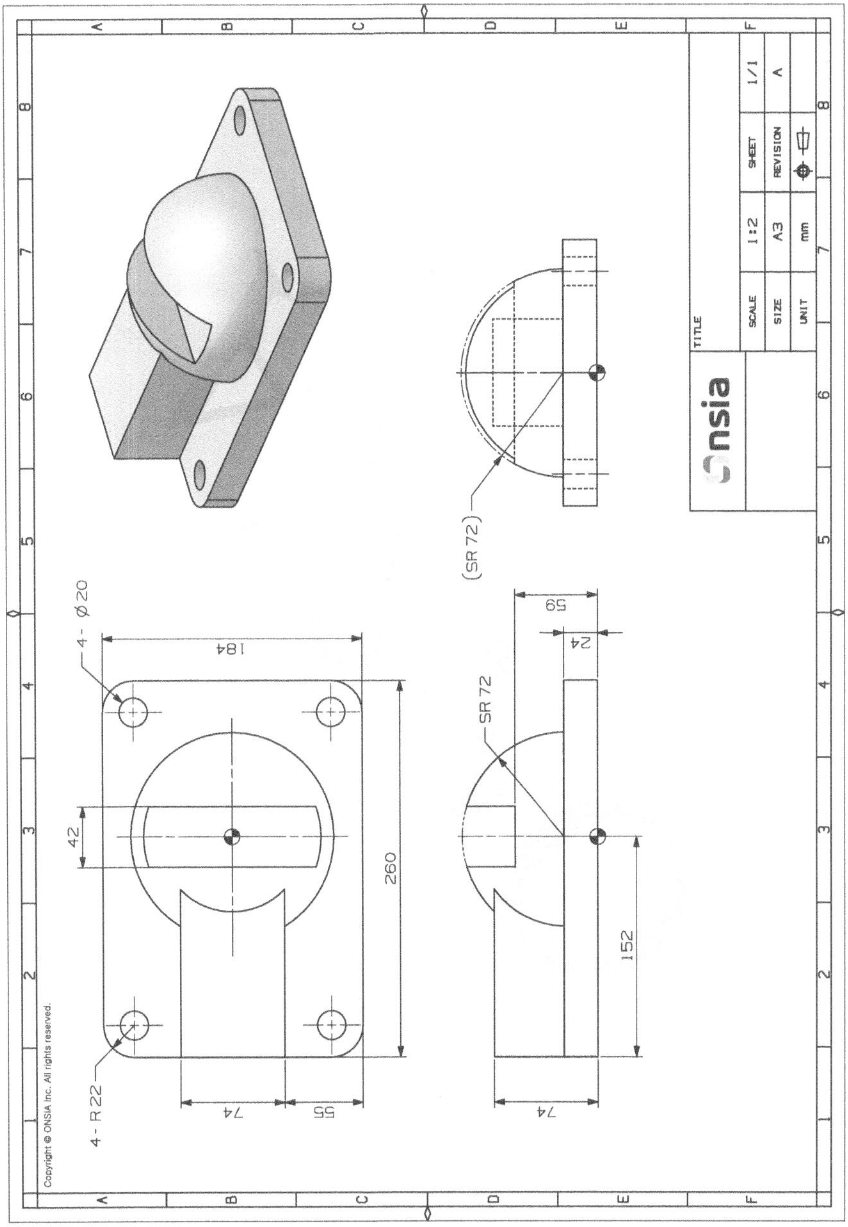

Fig 4-143 Drawing for Exercise 12

Hint !

Create a model referring to the following procedure.

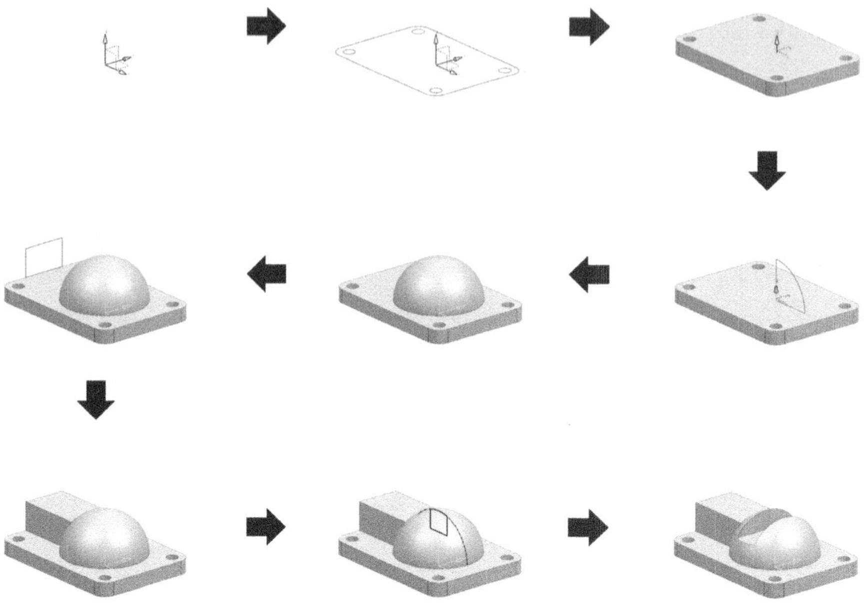

Chapter 5

Datums

■ After completing this chapter you will understand

- the characteristics of datum objects.
- how to create various types of datum planes and the usage.
- how to create various types of datum axes and the usage.
- that the datum coordinate system consists of datum planes, axes and a point.
- how to create various types of datum coordinate systems.

5.1 Datums

Up to Chapter 4, we used planes, lines and points for the following purposes.

► ***Planes***: for defining sketch planes and for limiting planes using the **Extrude**, **Revolve** , and Hole commands

► ***Lines***: for defining a direction using the **Extrude** and **Hole** commands. Revolution axis of **Revolve** command

► ***Points***: for defining the location of holes. Passing a point in defining a vector

That is to say, we selected planes, linear edges or points for cases where the modeling process required us to select those elements to define a feature. We have been able to select a planar face onto which to create a sketch. We have been able to select a plane to define the limit of **Extrude**, **Revolve** or **Hole** features.

The cases where we have to select an object to define the direction, we have been able to select a linear edge, plane (to select a normal direction) or cylindrical face (to select an axial direction). If we need to select a point, we have been able to select a vertex or a point created in the sketch.

However, what do we do if there is no exact object for what we want to select? For such cases, we have to create the required plane, point or line with reference to the existing geometry. The geometry elements that are created for this purpose are called **Datums**.

Datums are defined with reference to existing geometries maintaining associativity with them. Therefore, if the parent geometries are changed parametrically, the reference elements will be updated. You can create datums without associativity if required.

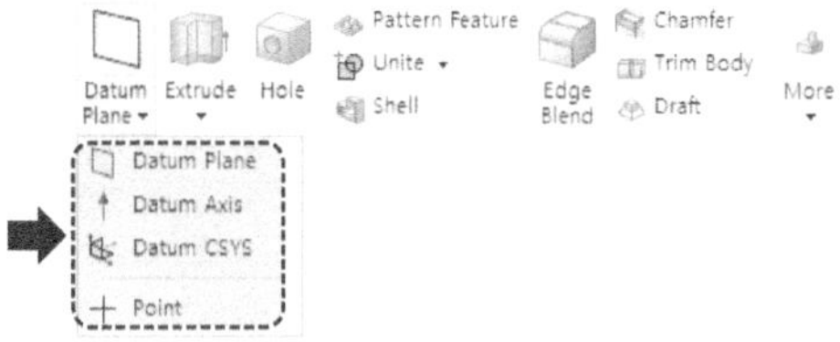

Fig 5-1 Datum Icons

5.2 Datum Plane

The planes designated by arrows in Fig 5-2 and Fig 5-3 are called datum planes.

Fig 5-2 Datum Plane

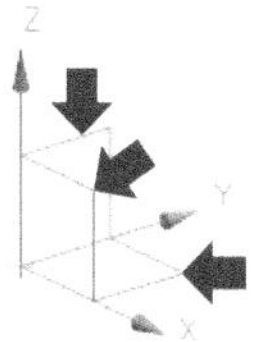

Fig 5-3 Datum Plane

Datum planes are frequently used on which to define a sketch plane. They are also used to limit extrude or revolve features.

Datum planes have the following characteristics.

▸ A datum plane does not have area or thickness.

▸ A datum plane does not have a boundary. It is an infinite plane. The rectangle shown in the part geometry is simply a symbol to show the existence of the datum plane. You can select the datum plane on the rectangular symbol.

If you choose the **Datum Plane** button from the **Feature** icon group, the **Datum Plane** dialog box as shown in Fig 5-4 appears. There are many methods for defining the datum plane in the **Type** dropdown list. Other options in the dialog box are changed according to the selected type.

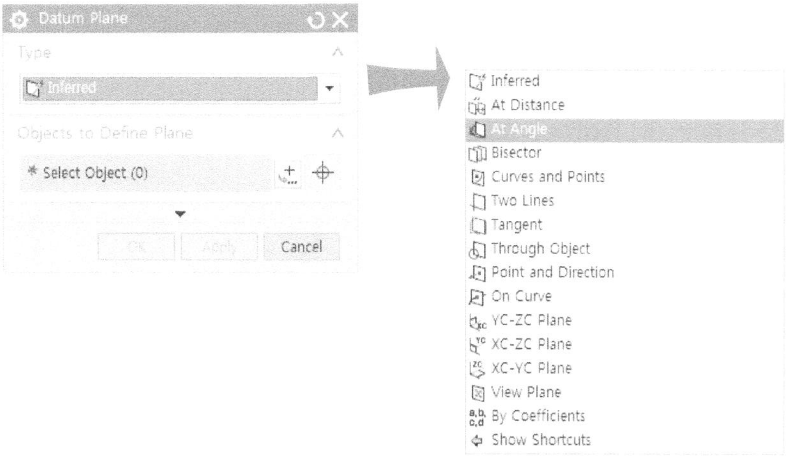

Fig 5-4 Datum Plane Dialog Box

5.2.1 Usages of a Datum Plane

The following are three typical usages of datum planes.

① Sketch Plane

The feature designated by the arrow in Fig 5-5 is created by extruding a sketch defined on a datum plane slanted 45 degrees from the yz plane.

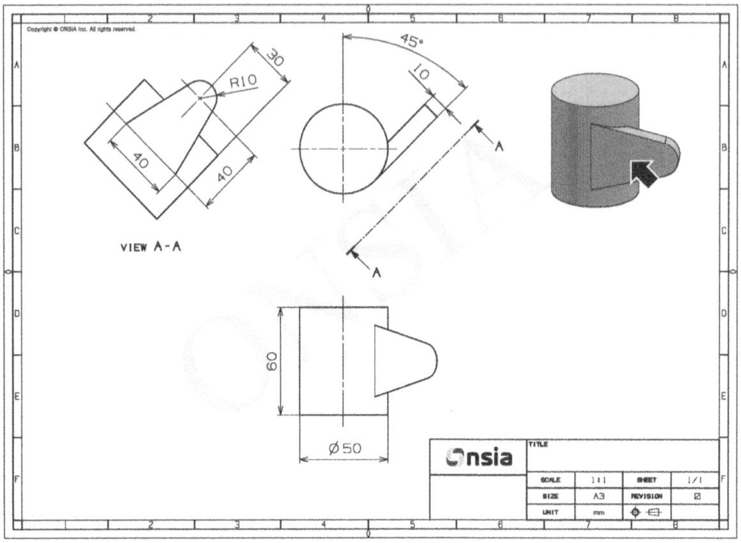

Fig 5-5 An Example of a Sketch Plane Defined on a Datum Plane

② Control the Size of a Feature

If you define the datum planes as shown in Fig 5-6, you can define the size of a feature. You can either constrain sketch curves with reference to the datum plane or select the datum plane to limit the **Extrude** feature.

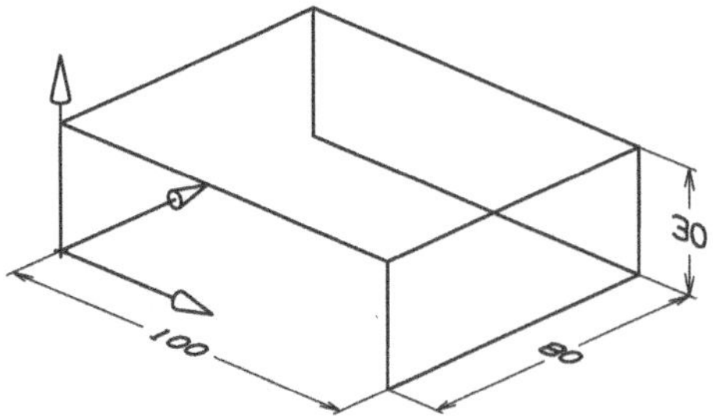

Fig 5-6 Three Reference Planes Defined at a Distance

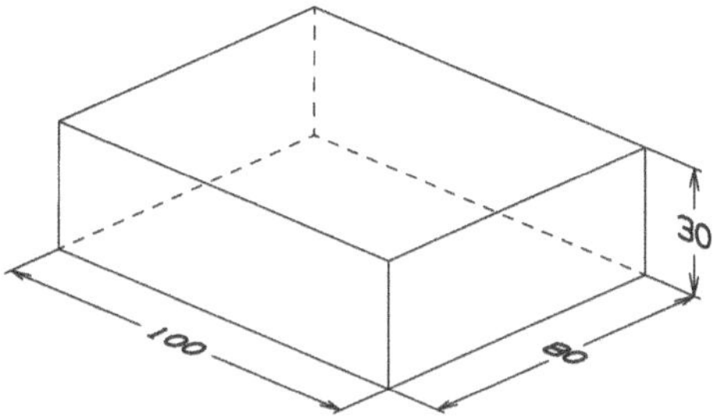

Fig 5-7 An Extrude Feature

③ Tool Object of the Split Command

The cut plane designated by the arrow in Fig 5-8 is created with the **Trim Body** command. You can select a datum plane as the trimming tool.

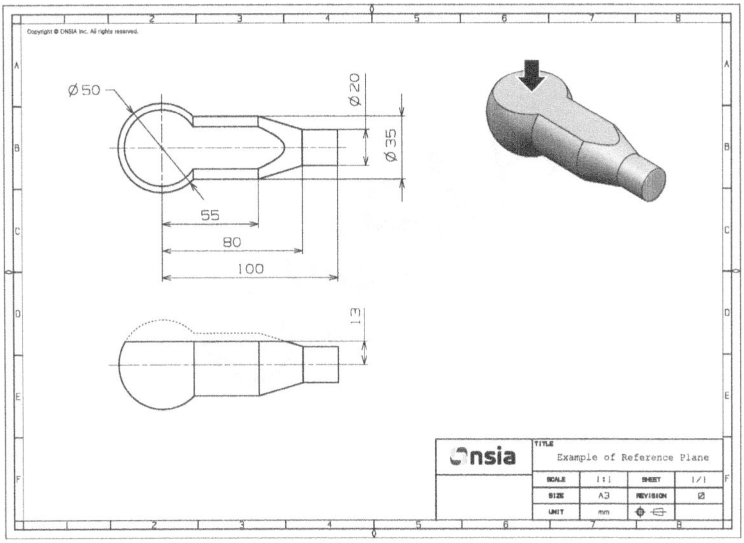

Fig 5-8 Trimming a Solid Body with a Datum Plane

Fig 5-9 and Fig 5-10 show the process for trimming a body with a datum plane.

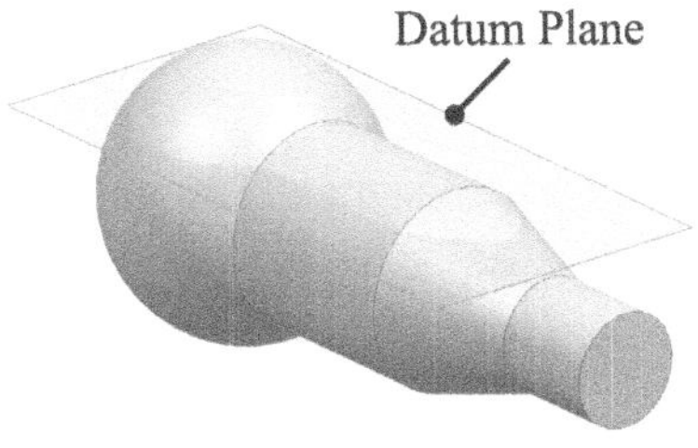

Fig 5-9 Before Trimming

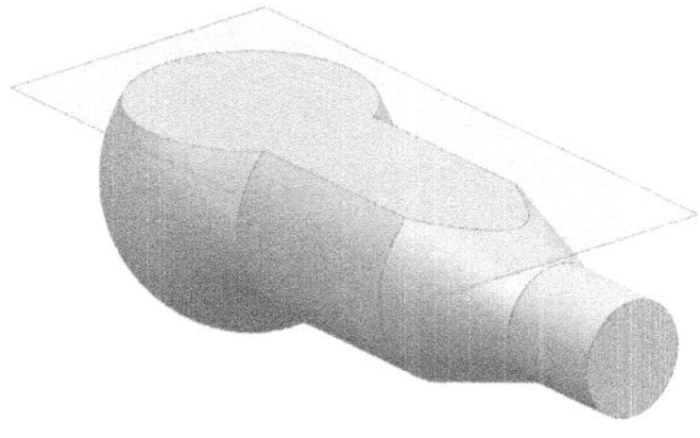

Fig 5-10 After Trimming

! ***Other Usages of Datum Plane***

- Placement face of **Positional Form Features** such as **Boss** and **Pad** command
- Mirror plane of **Mirror Body** or **Mirror Feature** command

5.2.2 Types of Datum Plane

You can identify various types of datum planes in the **Datum Plane** dialog box. If you select a type in the dropdown list, other options in the dialog box will change accordingly. You can define a datum plane by carefully reading the cue line messages for the corresponding options.

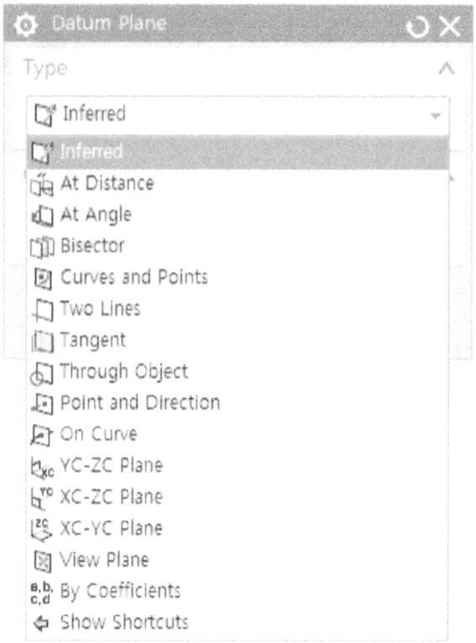

Fig 5-11 Types of Datum Plane

Exercise 01 At Distance Type Datum Plane

With the **At Distance** type, you can create a datum plane at a distance from an existing planar face or another datum plane. Let's learn how to create the **At Distance** type datum plane.

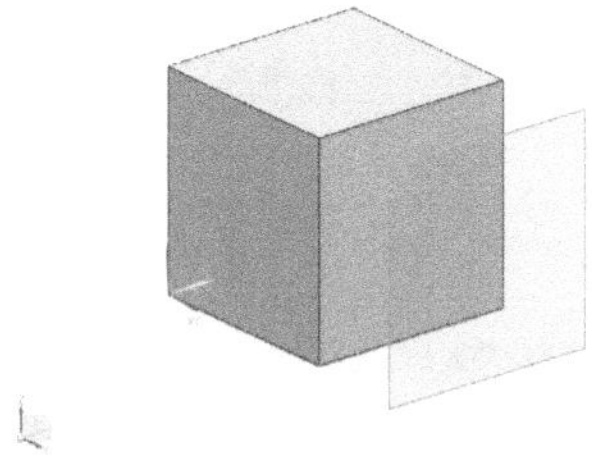

Fig 5-12 Datum Plane (At Distance Type)

Creating a Block

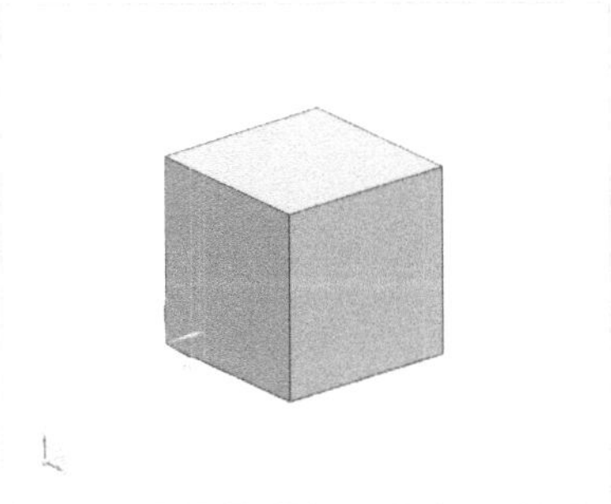

Fig 5-13 A Block

1. Create a new part file and give it an arbitrary name.
2. Choose **Insert > Design Feature > Block** in the **Menu** button.
3. Press the **Reset** button in the **Block** dialog box and press **OK**.

Creating a Datum Plane

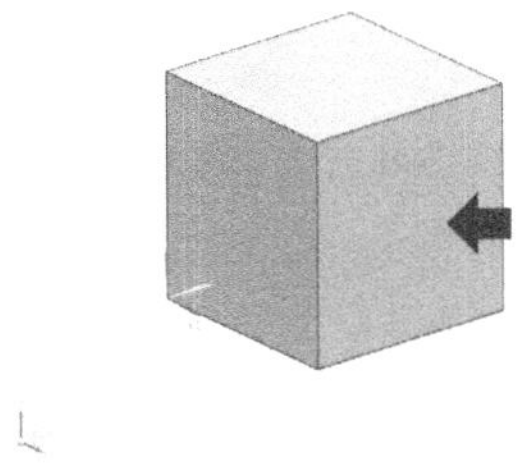

Fig 5-14 Face to Select

1. Click the **Datum Plane** icon in the **Feature** icon group.
2. Reset the dialog box.
3. Select **At Distance** in the **Type** drop-down list.
4. Select the plane designated by the arrow in Fig 5-14.
5. Enter 50 in the **Distance** input box in the **Offset** option group and press the **Enter** key. A preview is shown as in Fig 5-16.

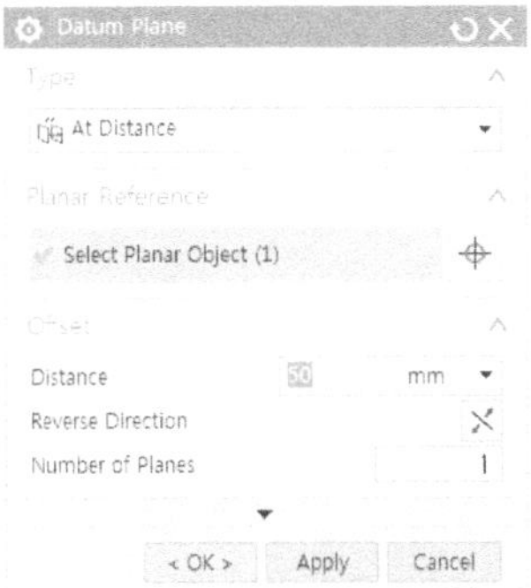

Fig 5-15 Datum Plane Dialog Box

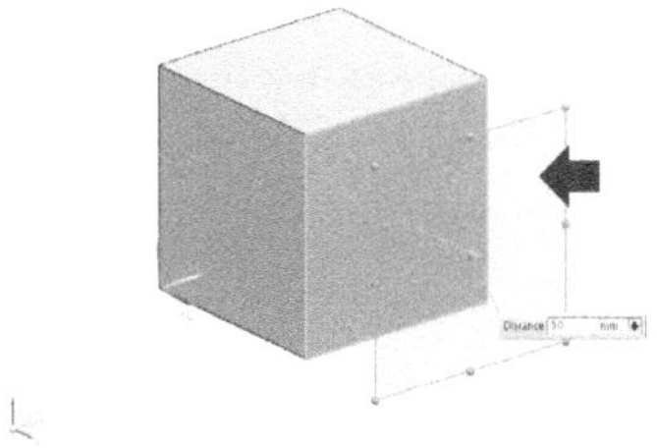

Fig 5-16 Preview

6. Press **OK** in the **Datum Plane** dialog box. The datum plane is created as shown in Fig 4-17. Now, let's modify the size of the block.

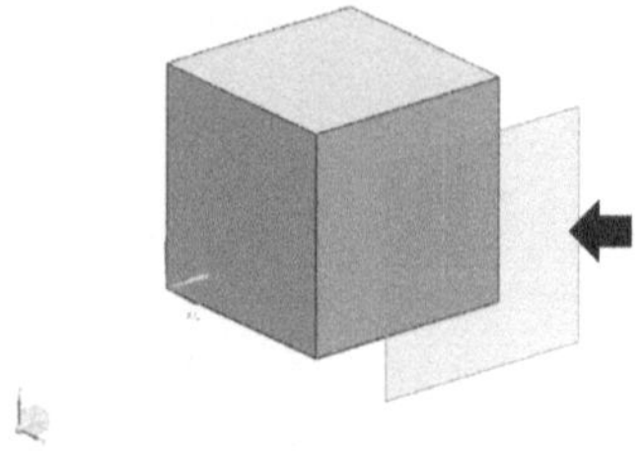

Fig 5-17 Datum Plane Created

Modifying the Size of the Block

1. Double click the block feature in the **Part Navigator** or in the graphics window.
2. Modify the **Length** of the **Block** as shown in Fig 4-18 and press the **Enter** key.
3. Press the **OK** button in the **Block** dialog box. Confirm that the distance between the side plane of the block and the datum plane is maintained to 50 mm.

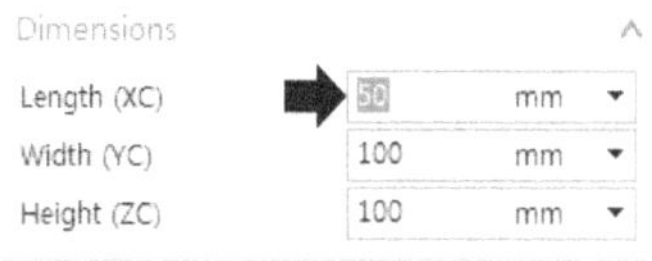

Fig 5-18 XC Length of Block Feature

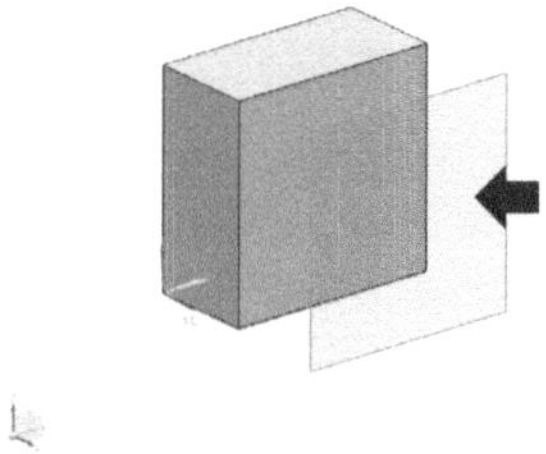

Fig 5-19 Modified Block Feature

4. Close without saving the file.

END of Exercise

With the **Inferred** type, you can create a datum plane by selecting objects. The type is determined depending on which objects you have selected. Let's create a datum plane with the **Inferred** type and identify by which type it has been created.

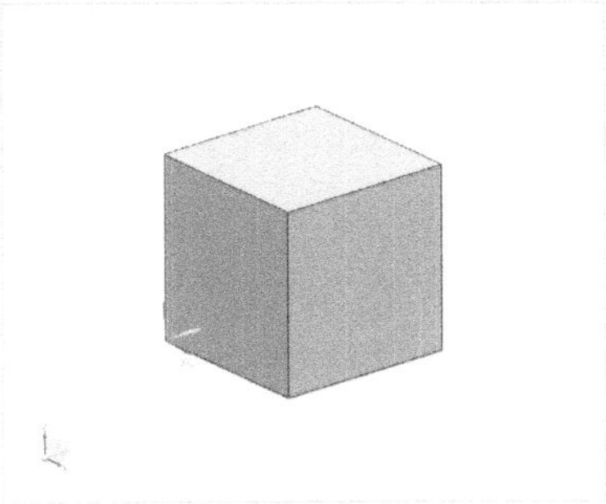

Fig 5-20 A Block

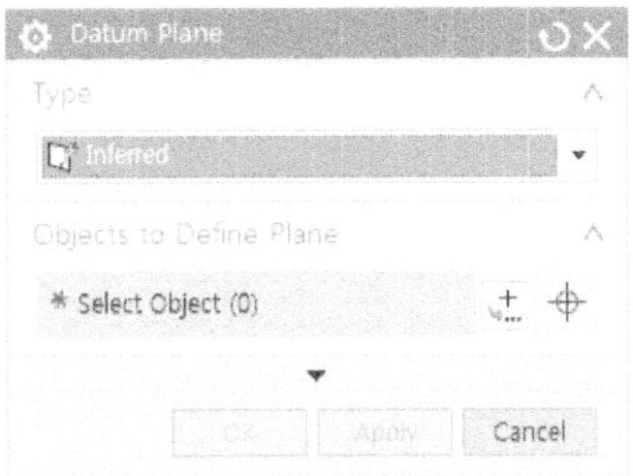

Fig 5-21 Inferred Type

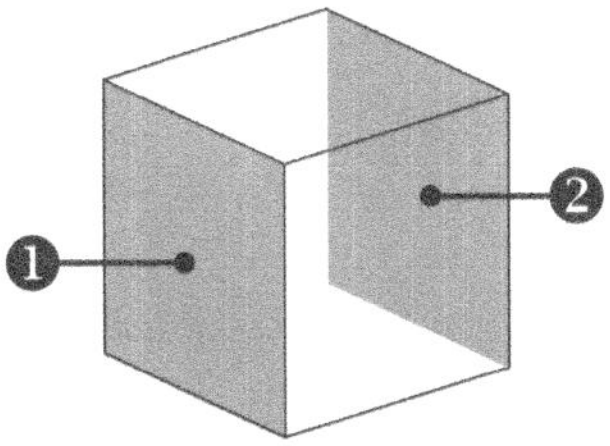

Fig 5-22 Two Faces to Select

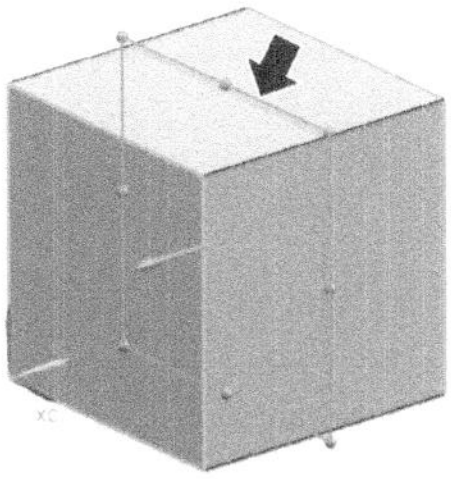

Fig 5-23 Preview

Creating a Block

1. Create a new part file and give it an arbitrary name.
2. Choose **Insert > Design Feature > Block** in the **Menu** button.
3. Press the **Reset** button in the **Block** dialog box and press **OK**.

Creating a Datum Plane

1. Click the **Datum Plane** icon in the **Feature** icon group.
2. Reset the dialog box. Type is set to **Inferred**.
3. Select the two faces ❶ and ❷ shown in Fig 5-22. Note that you have to rotate the model to select the face ❷. You may switch the rendering style to **Static Wireframe** or you can use the **QuickPick** utility.

The datum plane in the middle of the two planes is previewed as shown in Fig 5-23.

4. Press **OK** in the **Datum Plane** dialog box to create the datum plane.

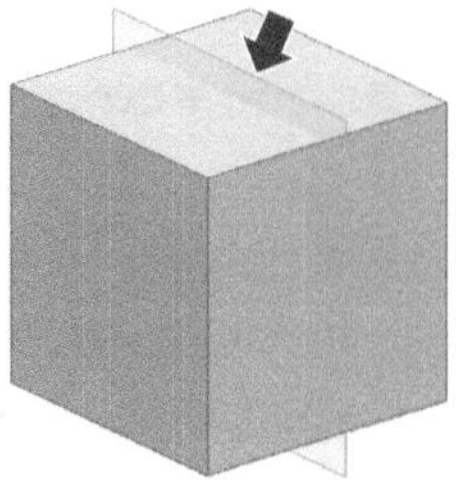

Fig 5-24 Datum Plane Created

Fig 5-25 Type of Datum Plane

Identifying Type

The **Inferred** type determines the specific creating type depending on the selected objects. You can identify the creating type in the dialog box.

1. Double click the datum plane feature in the part navigator or graphics window.

The type is set to **Bisector** in the dialog box as shown in Fig 5-25.

2. Close without saving the file.

END of Exercise

'Bisector' Type Datum Plane

When you create a **Bisector** type datum plane, the two planes do not need to be parallel.

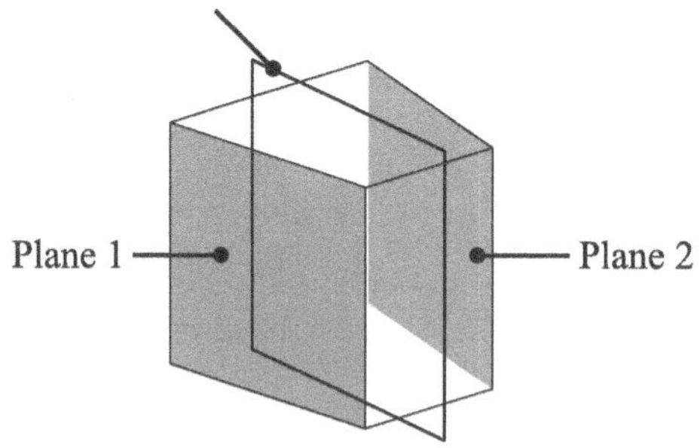

Fig 5-26 Bisector Datum Plane Between Non-Parallel Planes

Let's create a model by defining an angled datum plane.

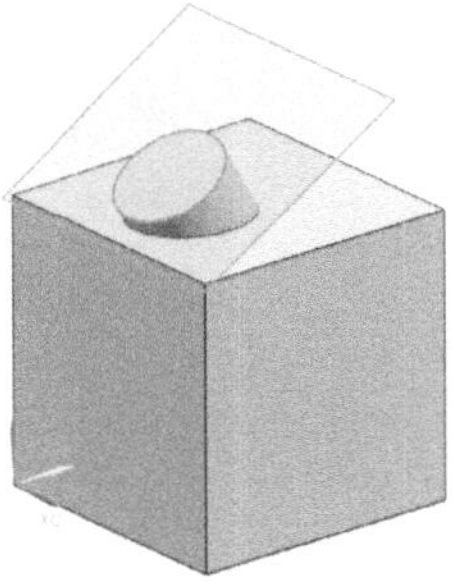

Fig 5-27 Model to Create

Creating a Block

1. Create a new part file and give it an arbitrary name.
2. Choose **Insert > Design Feature > Block** in the **Menu** button.
3. Press the **Reset** button in the **Block** dialog box and press **OK**.

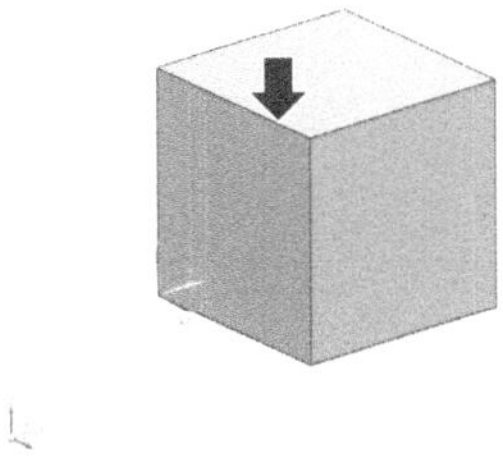

Fig 5-28 Edge to Select

Creating a Datum Plane

1. Click the **Datum Plane** icon in the **Feature** icon group.
2. Reset the dialog box.
3. Select the edge around the location designated by the arrow in Fig 5-28. Be sure not to snap the midpoint or end point of the edge.

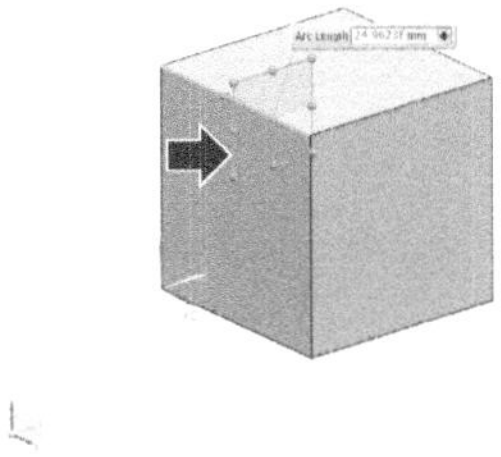

Fig 5-29 Preview

A datum plane that is normal to the edge is previewed as shown in Fig 5-29.

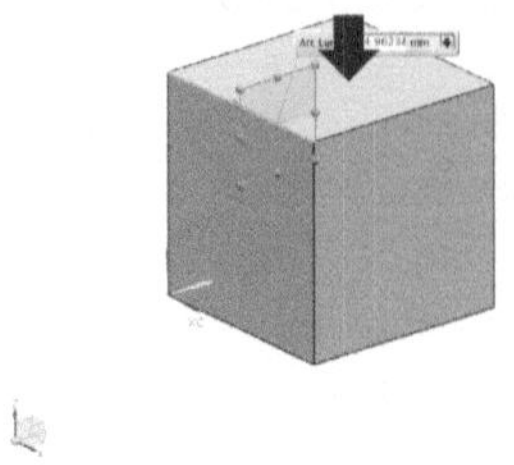

Fig 5-30 Plane to Select

4. Select the upper plane designated by the arrow in Fig 5-30. A preview is shown as Fig 5-31. The plane is 90° angled from the plane about the edge.
5. Enter 45 in the **Angle** input box in the dialog box as shown in Fig 5-32 and press **Enter**. Fig 5-33 shows the preview of the 45° angled datum plane.

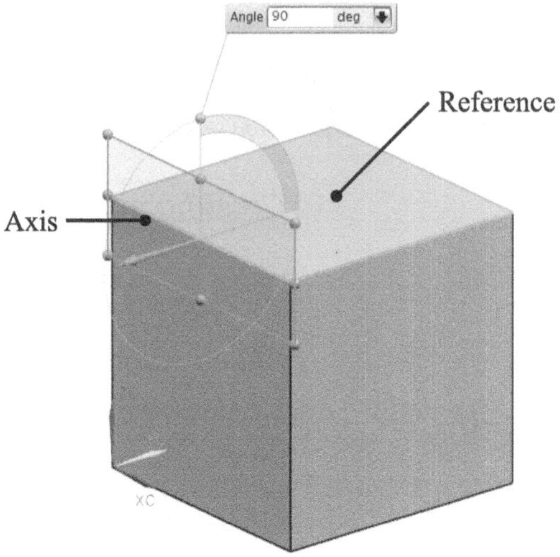

Fig 5-31 Preview of the 'At Angle' Type Datum Plane

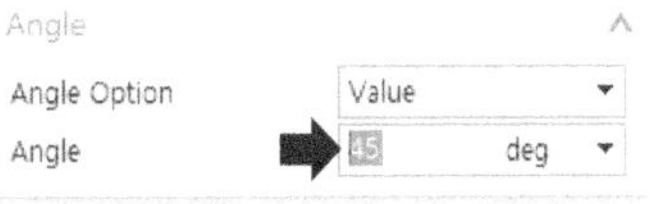

Fig 5-32 Modified Angle

Fig 5-33 45° Angled Datum Plane

'At Angle' Type Datum Plane

The **At Angle** type datum plane can be created by selecting a planar reference plane as the start angle and a linear object as the through axis.

Fig 5-34 Datum Plane Created

Fig 5-35 Type of Datum Plane

6. Press **OK** in the dialog box to create the datum plane.
7. Double click the datum plane and verify the type of creating as shown in Fig 5-35.

Modeling with Datum Plane

1. Create a circle and fully constrain it by defining a sketch plane on the datum plane as shown in Fig 5-37.

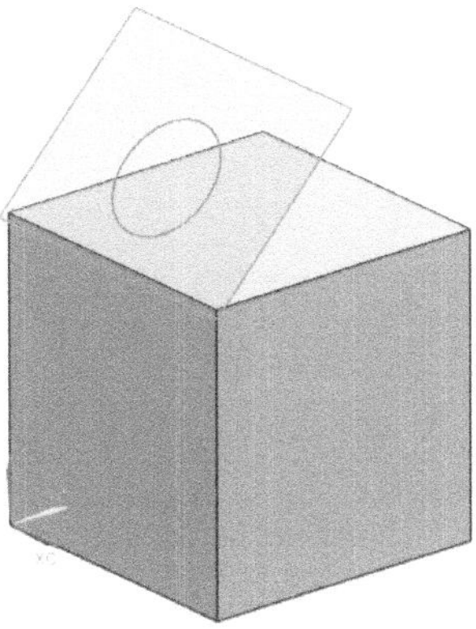

Fig 5-36 Sketch Created on the Datum Plane

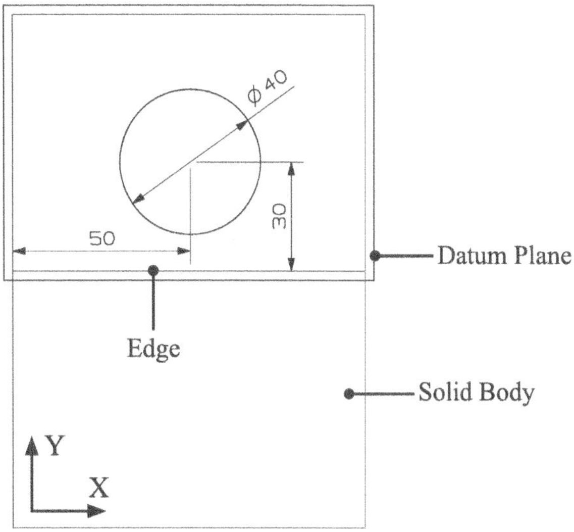

Fig 5-37 Constraining the Sketch

Caution!

Note that you cannot select the rectangular boundary of the datum plane to define an inplane dimension. You can select the linear edge of the body although it is not on the sketch plane.

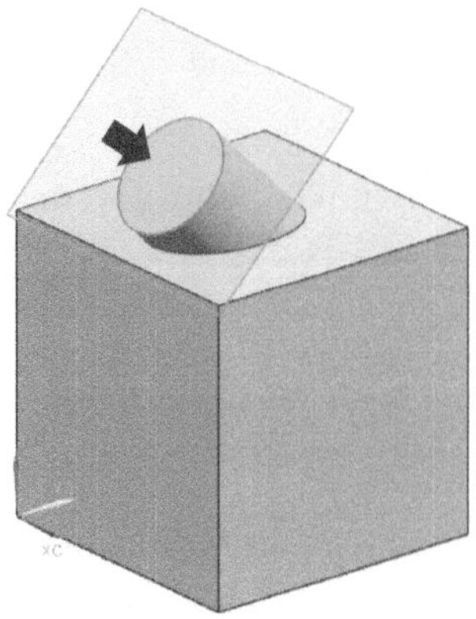

Fig 5-38 Result of Extrude

2. Extrude by selecting the sketch as shown in Fig 5-38. Choose **Until Next** as the end limit and **Unite** as the **Boolean** option.

Modifying the Model

1. Expand the **Details** panel below the **Part Navigator** (click the title designated by the arrow in Fig 5-39).
2. Select the datum plane in the graphics window.
3. Double click the line of p6=45 in the **Expression** column in the **Datails** panel. The variable p6 may vary reader by reader.

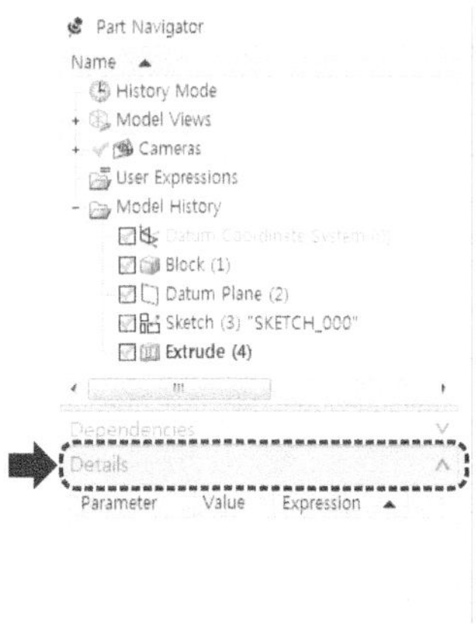

Fig 5-39 Details Panel

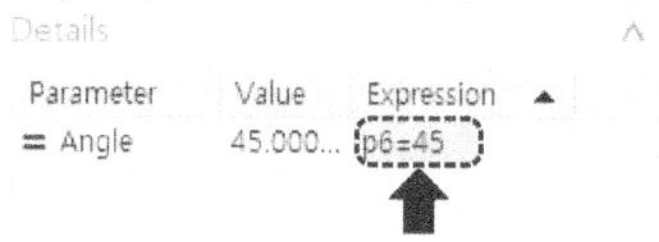

Fig 5-40 Double Click

4. Enter 30 instead of 45 in the input box and press **Enter**. The model is modified as shown in Fig 5-42.
5. Press the **ESC** key on the keyboard to deselect the datum plane.
6. Close without saving the file.

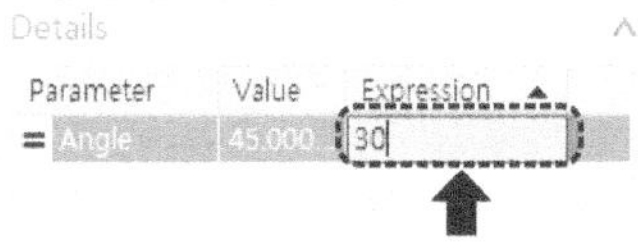

Fig 5-41 Modified Value

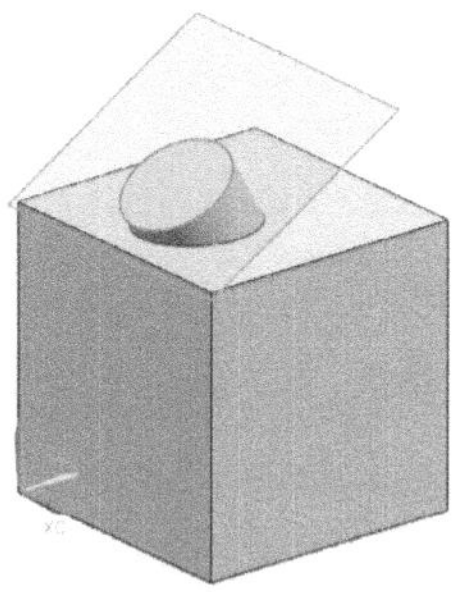

Fig 5-42 Result of Modification

END of Exercise

Most Efficient Way to Modify a Dimension Value

You can modify the parameter values in the **Details** pannel instantly. Bear in mind the following restrictions.

► The input value has to be a number. If you double click an expression such as p6=45/2, the **Expression** dialog box is invoked.
► You have to select one feature only to display the variables in the **Details** panel. If you select two or more features in the part navigator, nothing will appear in the **Details** panel.

Resizing the Symbol of the Datum Plane

1. You can resize the symbol of the datum plane for modeling convenience by dragging the eight sizing handles which are marked by the dotted circles in Fig 5-43.

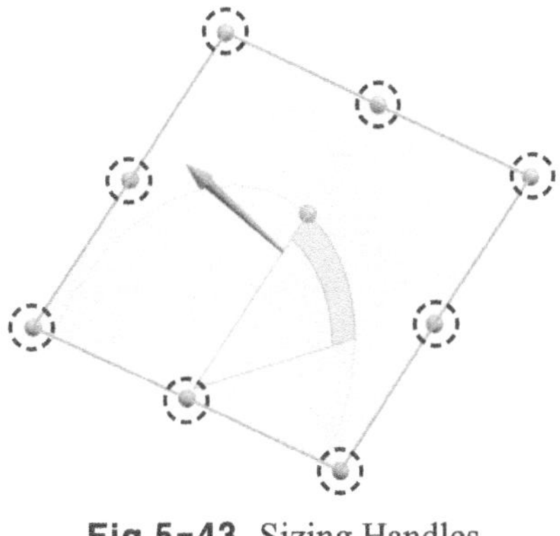

Fig 5-43 Sizing Handles

2. Snapping can be ignored by pressing the **Alt** key while dragging the sizing handle.
3. If you have already created the datum plane, just double click it to resize the symbol of the datum plane.
4. Press MB3 on the sizing handle. You can reset the size of the symbol and you can resize it symmetrically.
5. If the sizing handle is not available by double clicking, choose **Edit > Feature > Resize Datum Plane** in the **Menu** button.

Exercise 04 At Angle Type Datum Plane - 2

Let's create a datum plane passing through the centerline of a cylinder. Then we will create a 45° angled datum plane with respect to the plane. Assume that there is no datum coordinate system at the origin.

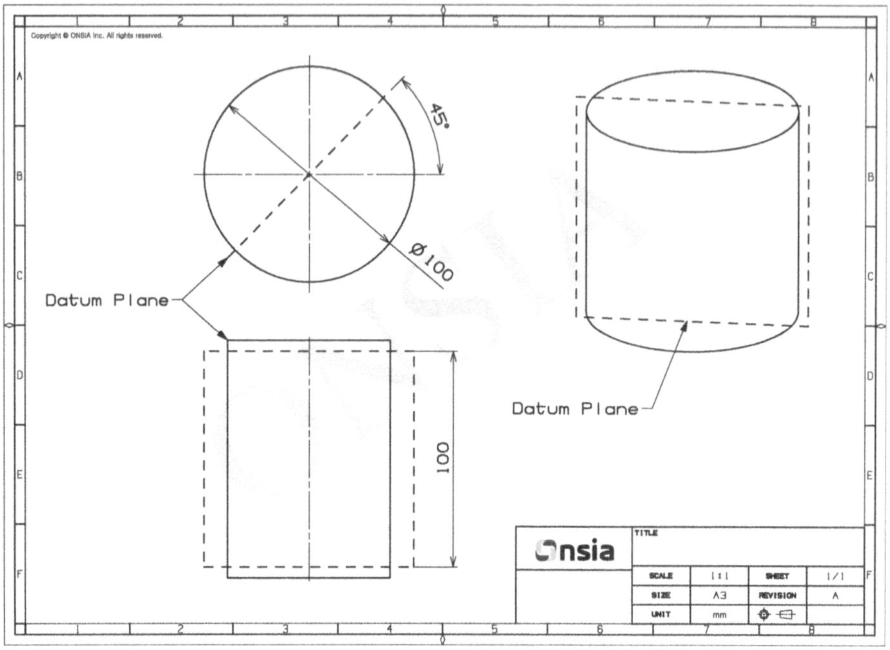

Fig 5-44 Drawing for Datum Plane

Creating a Cylinder

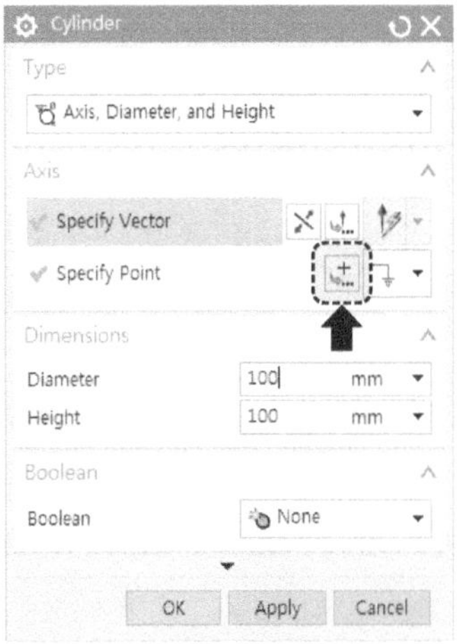

Fig 5-45 Cylinder Dialog Box

1. Create a new part file and give it an arbitrary name. Hide the **WCS** and datum coordinate system.
2. Choose **Insert > Design Feature > Cylinder** in the **Menu** button.
3. Reset the **Cylinder** dialog box and press the **Point Dialog** button designated by the arrow in Fig 4-45.
4. Enter the values in the **Point** dialog box as shown in Fig 5-46 and press **OK**.

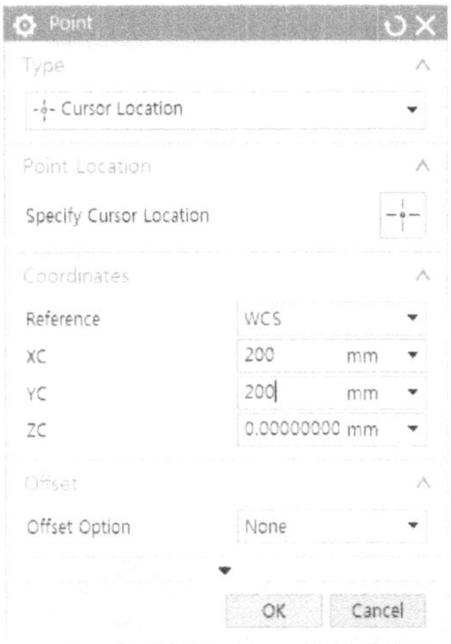

Fig 5-46 Point Dialog Box

Fig 5-47 Cylinder Created

5. Enter 100 in the **Diameter** input box in the **Cylinder** dialog box and press **OK** to create a cylindrical body.

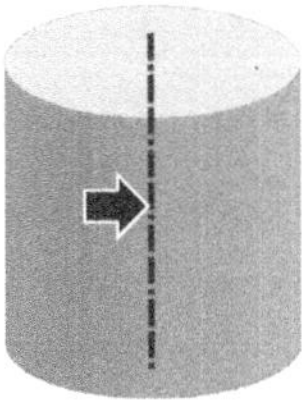

Fig 5-48 Centerline

Creating a Datum Plane

1. Click the **Datum Plane** icon in the **Feature** icon group.
2. Reset the dialog box.
3. Place the mouse cursor on the cylindrical face.

Fig 5-49 Datum Plane Created

The centerline of the cylinder is highlighted as designated by the arrow in Fig 5-48.

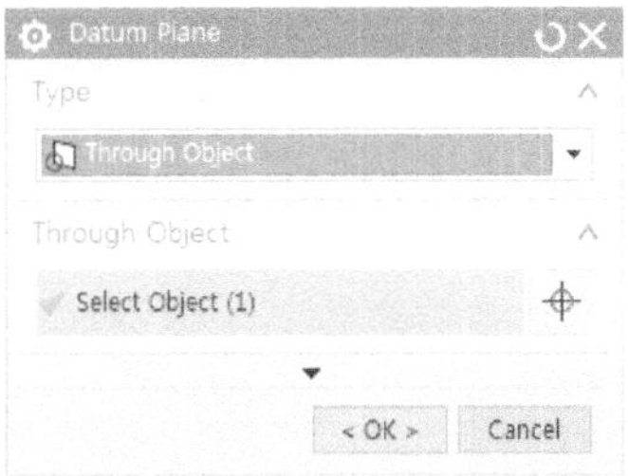

Fig 5-50 Type of Datum Plane

4. Move the mouse cursor over the centerline and select it. The datum plane is previewed.
5. Press **OK** to create the datum plane.
6. Double click the datum plane and verify the type of datum plane as shown in Fig 5-50.

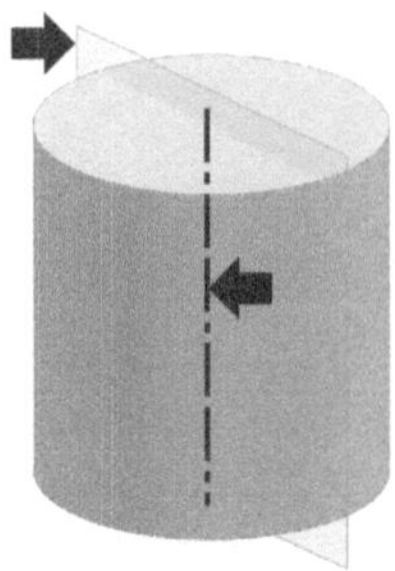

Fig 5-51 Objects to Select

Creating 45° inclined Datum Plane

A 45° angled datum plane can be created with reference to the datum plane which has been created on the centerline.

1. Click the **Datum Plane** icon and reset the dialog box.
2. Select the centerline and the datum plane specified in Fig 5-51 in any order.
3. Enter 45° in the **Angle** input box and press the **OK** button in the dialog box. The datum plane is created as shown in Fig 5-52.
4. Double click the datum plane to check the type.

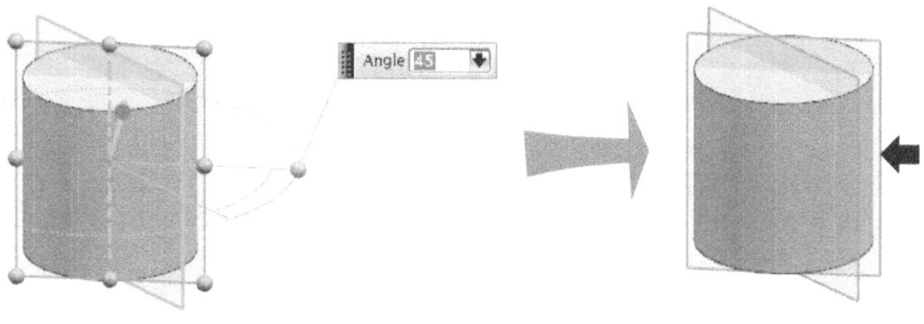

Fig 5-52 45° Angled Datum Plane

5. Close without saving the file.

END of Exercise

Let's create a datum plane that is tangent to a cylindrical face and passes through a specific point.

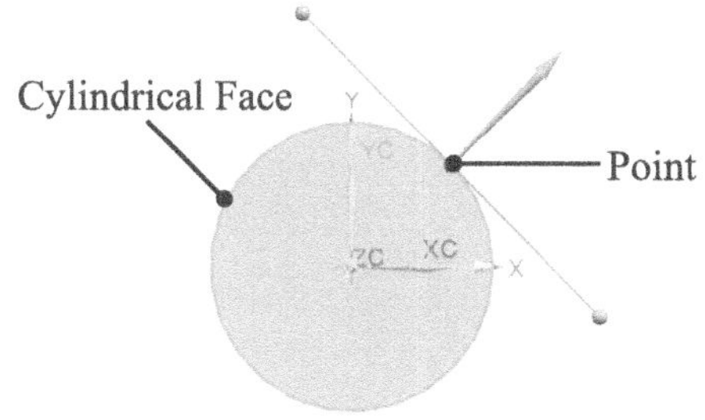

Fig 5-53 Datum Plane to Create

Creating a Cylinder

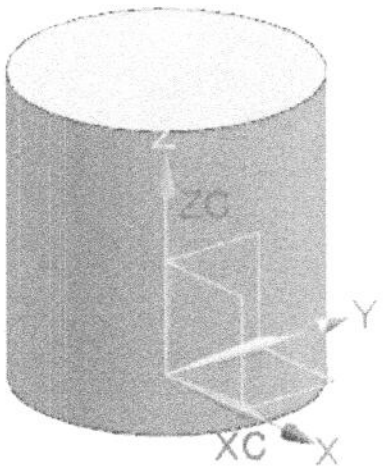

Fig 5-54 A Cylinder

1. Create a new part file and give it an arbitrary name.
2. Choose **Insert > Design Feature > Cylinder** in the **Menu** button.
3. Reset the **Cylinder** dialog box and enter 100 as the diameter.
4. Press **OK** to create a cylindrical body.

Creating a Point

1. Click the **Point** icon in the **Feature** icon group.
2. Select **Point on Curve/Edge** in the **Type** dropdown list.

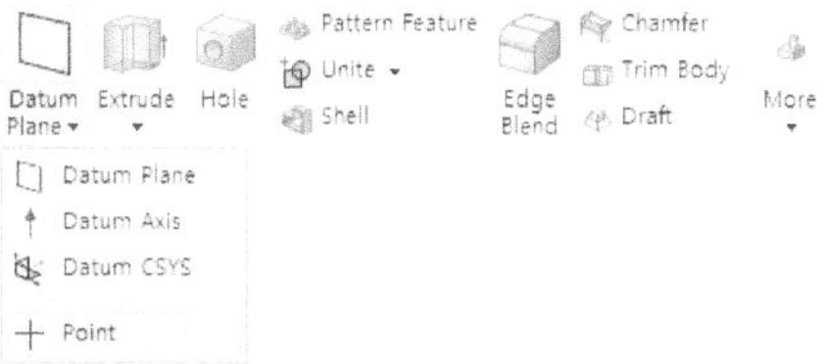

Fig 5-55 Point Icon

Fig 5-56 Point Option and the Edge to Select

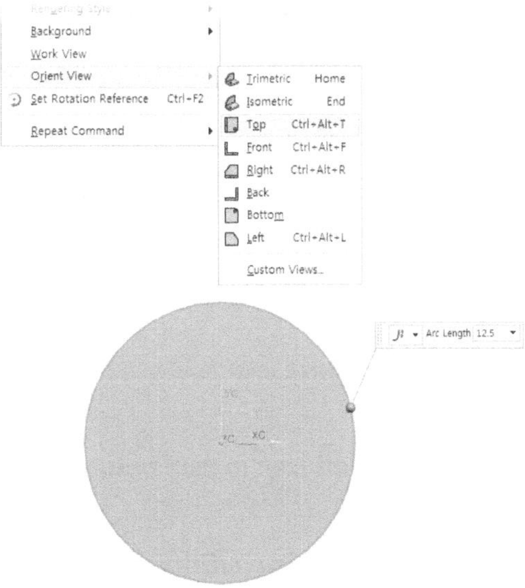

Fig 5-57 Location of the Point

3. Select the edge Ⓐ specified in Fig 5-56.
4. Click MB3 on an empty area in the graphics window and choose **Orient View > Top** in the pop-up menu.
5. Set the **Location on Curve** in the **Point** dialog box as shown in Fig 5-56 and press **Enter**. A preview of the point is shown as in Fig 5-57.
6. Press **OK** in the dialog box to create the point.
7. Press the **Home** key to change the model view to Trimetric.

Creating a Datum Plane

1. Click the **Datum Plane** icon in the **Feature** icon group.
2. Reset the dialog box.

3. Select the point and the cylindrical face regardless of the order.

4. Click MB3 on an empty area in the graphics window and choose Orient View > **Top**. A preview is shown as in Fig 5-59.

5. Press **OK** to create the datum plane as shown in Fig 5-60.

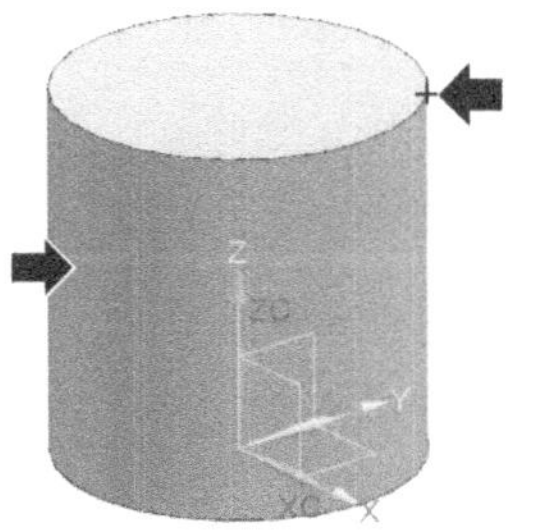

Fig 5-58 Selecting Point and Face

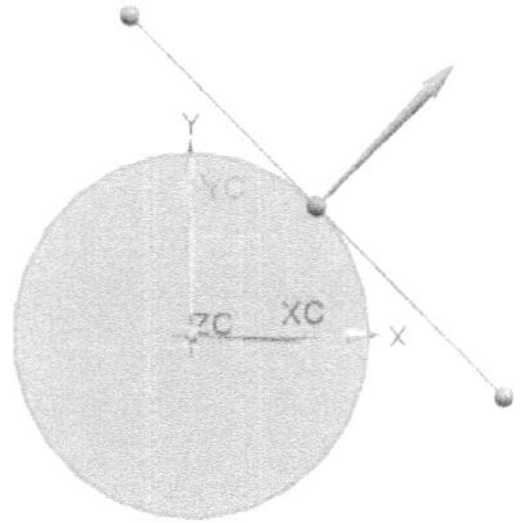

Fig 5-59 Preview

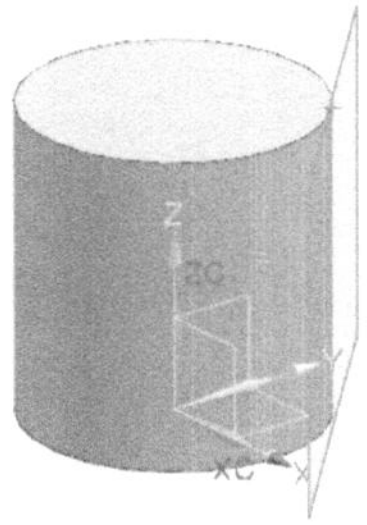

Fig 5-60 Datum Plane Created

Identifying Type

1. Double click the datum plane just created.

The creation type of the datum plane is shown as in Fig 5-61. Note that there are several subtypes available in creating a **Tangent** type datum plane. The subtype is set to **Through Point** which means the datum plane is created tangent to the selected cylindrical face and passes through the specified point.

2. Close without saving the file.

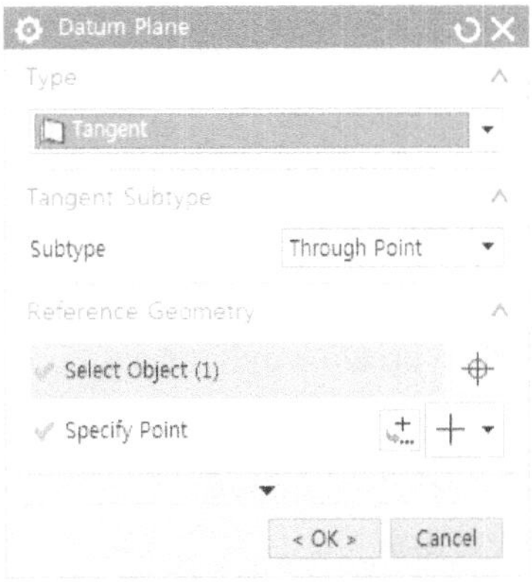

Fig 5-61 Type of Datum Plane

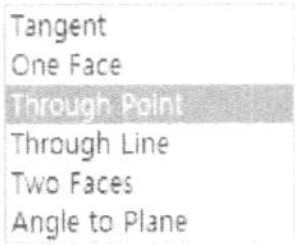

Fig 5-62 Subtype

END of Exercise

Exercise 06 Tangent Type Datum Plane - 2

Let's create a datum plane that is tangent to a cylindrical face and angled with respect to a plane.

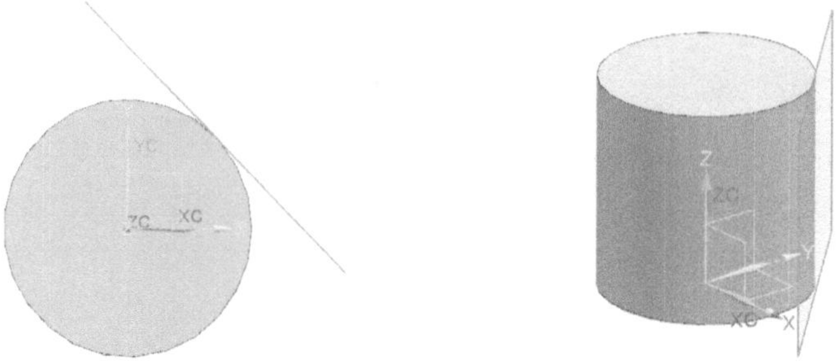

<Top View> <Trimetric View>

Fig 5-63 Datum Plane to Create

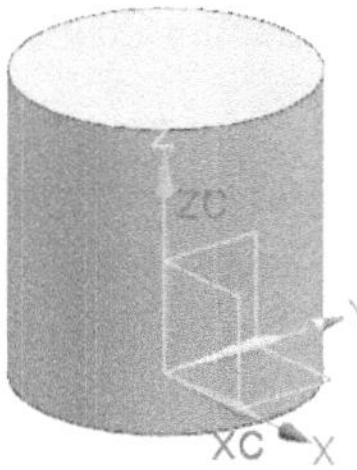

Fig 5-64 A Cylinder

Creating a Cylinder

1. Create a new part file and give it an arbitrary name.
2. Choose **Insert > Design Feature > Cylinder** in the **Menu** button.
3. Reset the **Cylinder** dialog box and enter 100 as the diameter.
4. Press **OK** to create a cylindrical body.

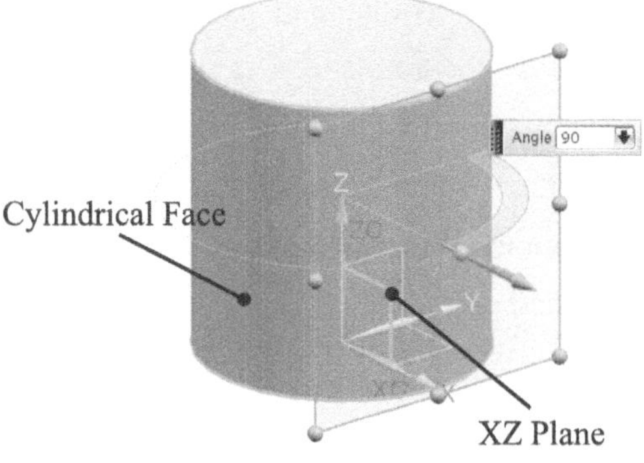

Fig 5-65 Objects to Select

Creating a Datum Plane

1. Click the **Datum Plane** icon in the **Feature** icon group.
3. Select the **XZ** plane in the datum coordinate center.
4. Click MB3 on an empty area in the graphics window and choose **Orient View > Top** in the pop-up menu.

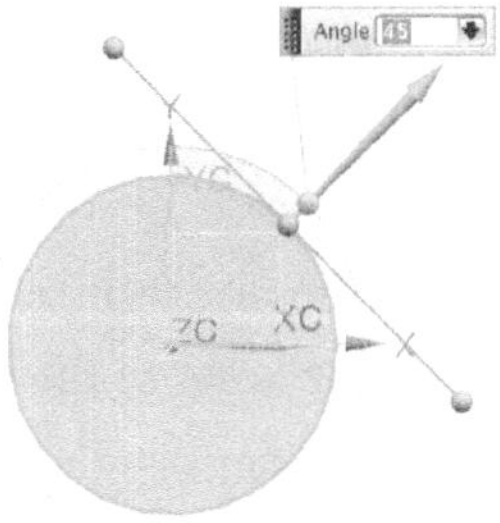

Fig 5-66 Top View

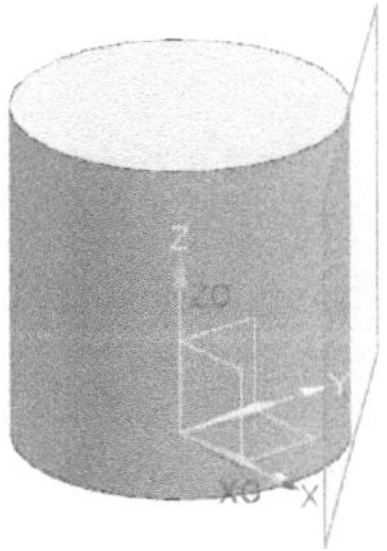

Fig 5-67 Datum Plane Created (Trimetric View)

Fig 5-68 Type of Datum Plane

5. Enter 45° in the **Angle** input box so that the top view is shown as Fig 5-66.
6. Press **OK** in the **Datum Plane** dialog box.

Identifying Type

1. Double click the datum plane just created.

A dialog box is shown as Fig 5-68. Note that the plane has been created with the **Angle to Plane** subtype among the Tangent types.

2. Close without saving the file.

END of Exercise

5.3 Point

When you are prompted to select points, but the snap point option for the location is not available, you have to create points at the desired location. A command flow option where you have to select points make the **Point Dialog** button available (refer to Fig 5-45). You can create points using the **Point** command in the **Feature** icon group.

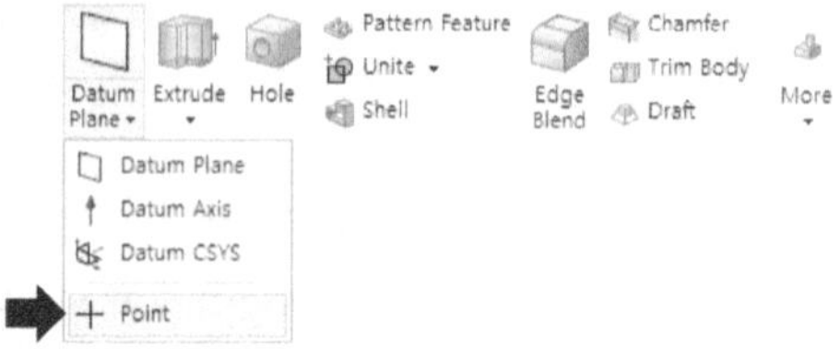

Fig 5-69 Point Icon

Various types of point creation methods are available in the **Type** dropdown list as shown in Fig 5-70. The types are similar to the **Snap Point** option. If you choose the **Inferred** type, the **Snap Point** option is activated and you can create points turning the appropriate **Snap Point** option on or off.

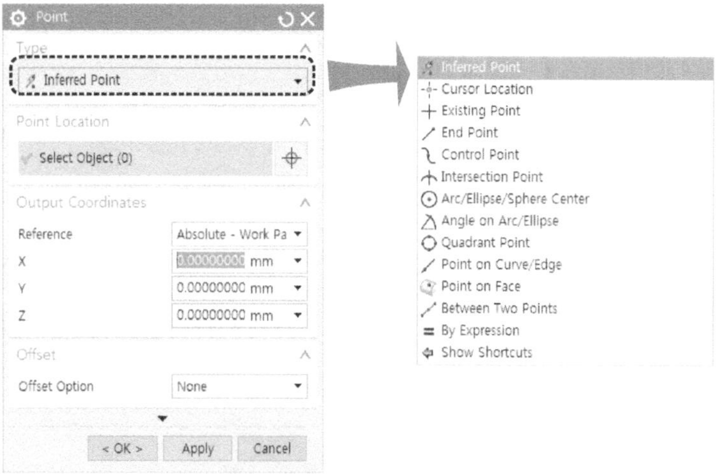

Fig 5-70 Point Dialog Box

5.3.1 Output Coordinates

When you define a point by selecting the model geometry, the coordinate values are displayed in the dialog box. Choose **Inferred** in the **Type** dropdown list, and then you can enter the required coordinate value in the input box.

5.3.2 Offset

After selecting a point location, you can create a new point by offsetting the selected point.

Procedure

1. Click the **Point** icon.
2. Select a point using an appropriate **Type** option.
3. Select an appropriate offset option and enter the offset values.
4. Press **OK** in the dialog box.

Fig 5-71 Offset Option

5.3.3 Associative Option

Datums are defined with reference to existing geometries maintaining associativity with them. You can turn off the **Associative** option when you create datums. If you turn off the **Associative** option, the datums will not be updated even though you modify the defining geometries.

A datum plane that is created without associativity is recorded as a **Fixed Datum Plane** in the **Part Navigator** as shown in Fig 5-72. If you create a point without associativity, the point is not recorded in the **Part Navigator** and you cannot modify the location of the point later.

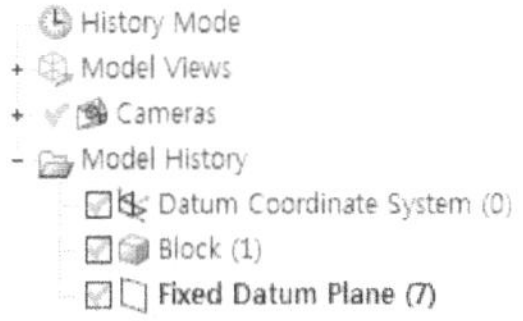

Fig 5-72 Datum Plane without Associativity

5.4 Datum Axis

The axes designated by arrows in Fig 5-73 and Fig 5-74 are called datum axes.

Fig 5-73 Datum Axis

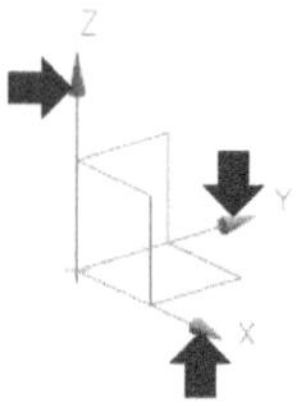

Fig 5-74 Datum Axis

If the modeling flow requires you to select an axis but there are no linear objects in the existing geometry, you can create the axis by using the **Datum Axis** command in the **Feature** icon group. The command flow option makes the **Vector Dialog** button available and you can create a datum axis during the command flow. Compared to lines which are created in a sketch, the datum axis can be defined in the 3D space.

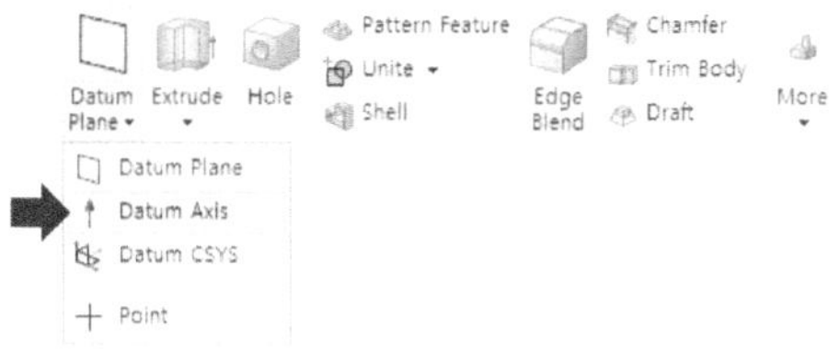

Fig 5-75 Datum Axis Icon

5.4.1 Characteristics of a Datum Axis

Note that the datum axis has restricted characteristics of a line. You can define a dimension or geometrical constraints with reference to a datum axis as shown in Fig 5-73 and Fig 5-74, but you cannot select the datum axis when you define a section. The datum axis does not have length but only specifies direction and location.

5.4.2 Usage of Datum Axis

The following are three typical usages of datum axis.

① Axis of Revolve

Fig 5-76 shows a **Revolve** feature created by selecting the datum axis as the revolution axis.

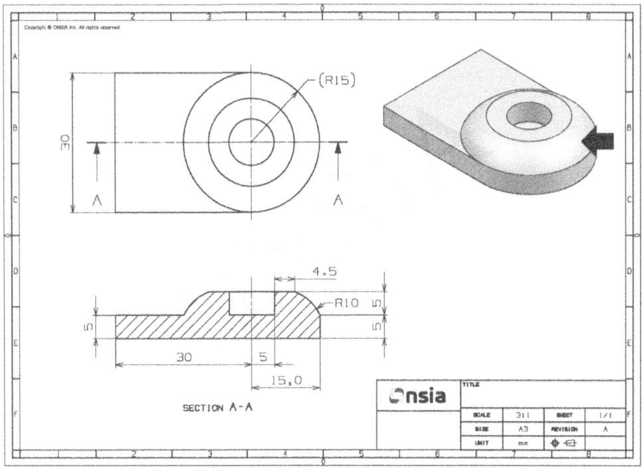

Fig 5-76 Revolve Feature

② Rotation Axis of Circular Pattern Command

Fig 5-77 shows the **Circular** type of **Pattern Feature** created by selecting the datum axis as the rotation axis.

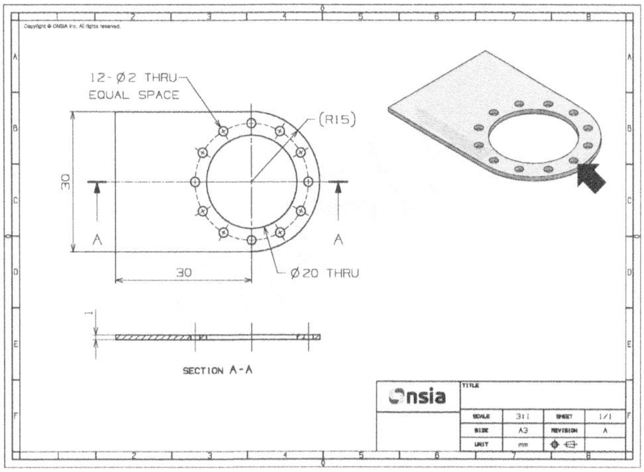

Fig 5-77 Circular Pattern Feature

② Direction of Linear Pattern Command

Fig 5-78 shows the **Linear** type of **Pattern Feature** created by selecting the datum axis as the direction of array.

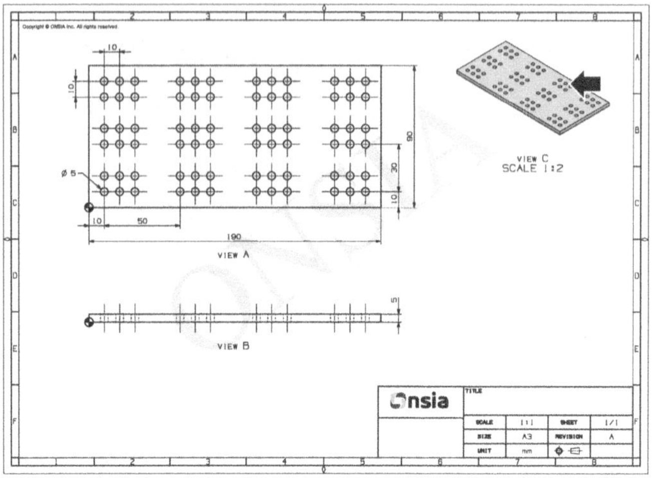

Fig 5-78 Linear Pattern Feature

5.4.3 Types of Datum Axis

You can identify various types of datum axes in the **Datum Axis** dialog box. If you select a type in the dropdown list, other options in the dialog box are changed accordingly. You can define a datum axis by carefully reading the cue line messages for the corresponding options.

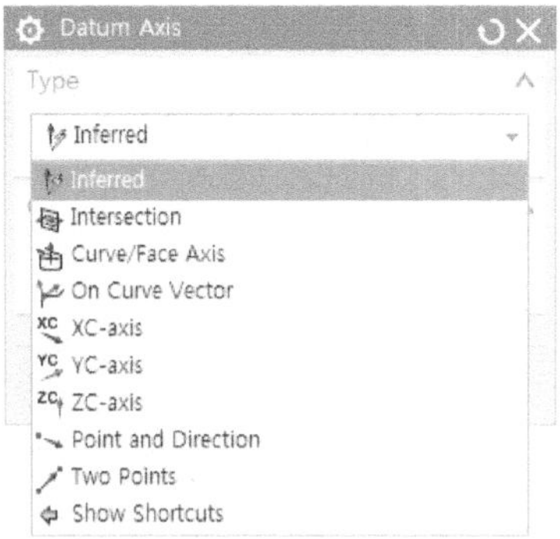

Fig 5-79 Types of Datum Axis

Create a datum axis that passes through a point and copy a feature using the **Circular** type of **Pattern Feature**. Copying features will be explained in Chapter 6 in detail.

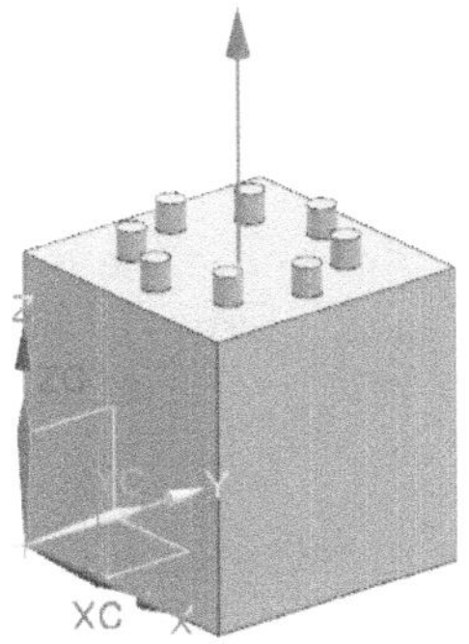

Fig 5-80 Model for Exercise

Creating a Block and Datum Planes

1. Create a part and give it an arbitrary name.

2. Choose **Insert > Design Feature > Block** in the **Menu** button.

3. Reset the **Block** dialog box and press **OK**.

4. Create the two **Bisector** type datum planes as shown in Fig 5-82.

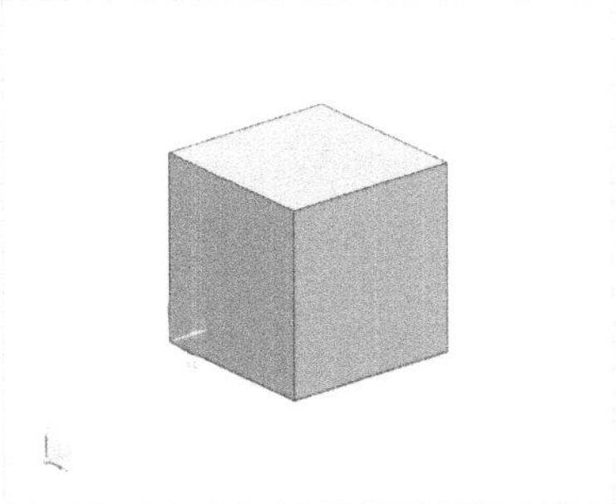

Fig 5-81 A Block

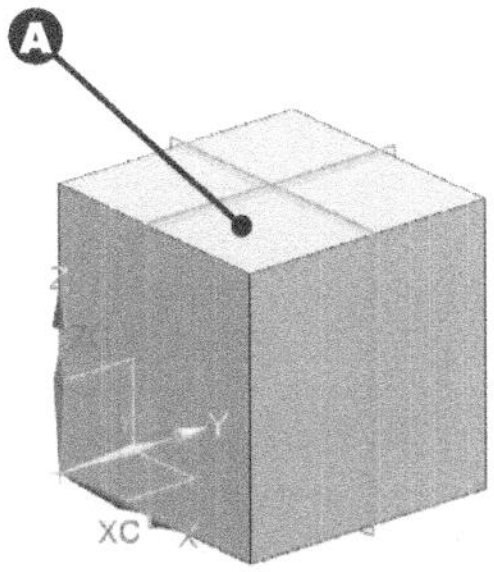

Fig 5-82 Datum Planes

Creating a Boss

1. Choose **Insert > Design Feature > Boss** in the **Menu** button.

2. Select the upper plane designated by **A** in Fig 5-82 and enter the values in the **Boss** dialog box as shown in Fig 5-83.

3. Press **OK** in the **Boss** dialog box. The **Positioning** dialog box as shown in Fig 5-84 is invoked.

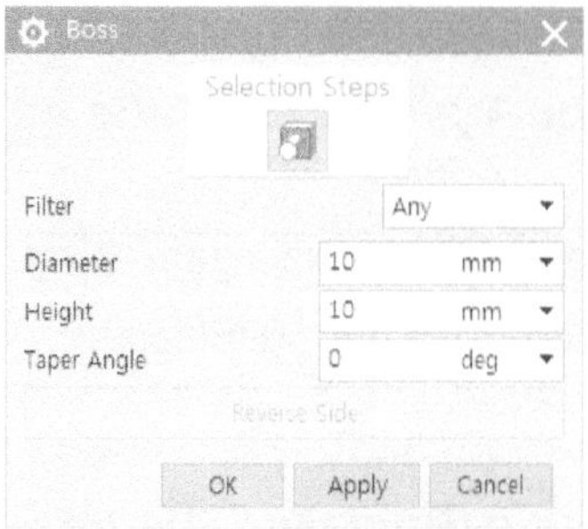

Fig 5-83 Boss Dialog Box

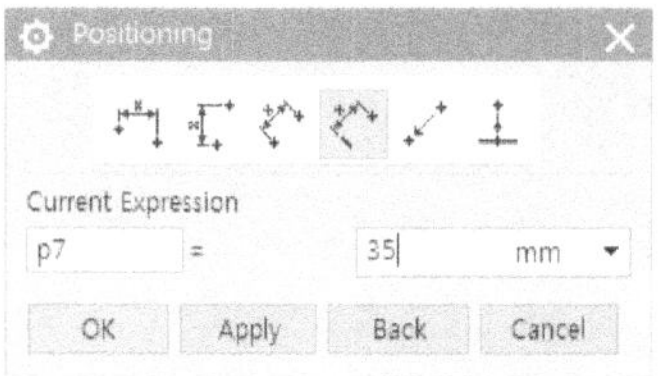

Fig 5-84 Positioning Dialog Box

4. Select the datum plane Ⓐ designated in Fig 5-85.

5. Enter 35 in the input area in the positioning dialog box and press the **Apply** button.

6. Press the **Point onto Line** button in the **Positioning** dialog box.

7. While the **Point onto Line** is invoked, select the datum plane Ⓑ designated in Fig 5-85.

8. Press **OK** in the **Positioning** dialog box.

A **Boss** feature is created at 35 mm distance from the datum plane Ⓐ and on the intersection line between the placement face and datum plane Ⓑ.

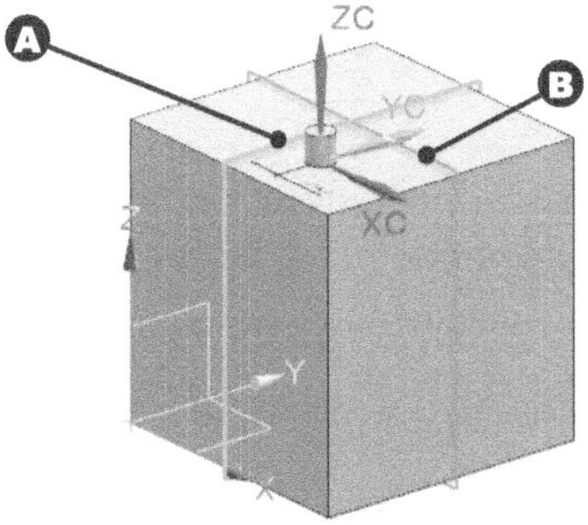

Fig 5-85 Selecting Datum Planes

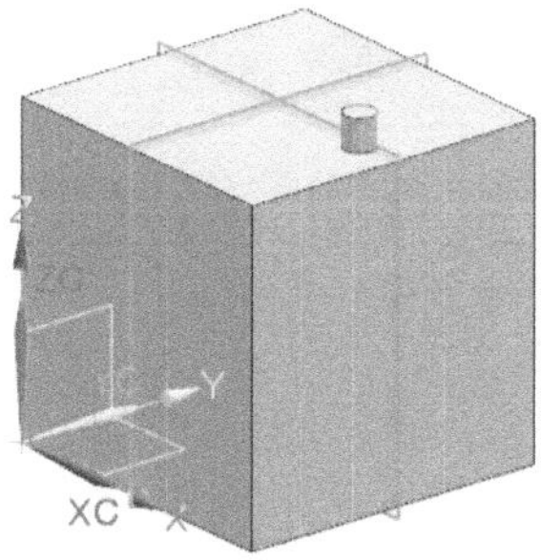

Fig 5-86 Boss Feature Created

A datum plane can be considered as a line.

We have defined the center of a boss on a datum plane. The **Boss** feature is always defined on a planar placement face. Therefore, the datum planes Ⓐ and Ⓑ are considered as lines when they are viewed from the placement face.

Creating a Datum Axis

We will create an axis that is normal to the upper plane and passes through the center of the plane.

1. Hide the two datum planes.
2. Click the **Datum Axis** icon in the **Feature** icon group.
3. Select **Point and Direction** as the type.
4. Press the **Point Dialog** button designated by the arrow in Fig 5-87.
5. Select **Point on Face** as the type of point.
6. Select the upper face and enter the **U** and **V** parameters as shown in Fig 5-88.
7. Press **OK** in the **Point** dialog box.
8. Check that the **Direction** option is set to **Face/Plane Normal** as shown in Fig 5-89 and press **OK**.

The datum axis is created as shown in Fig 5-90.

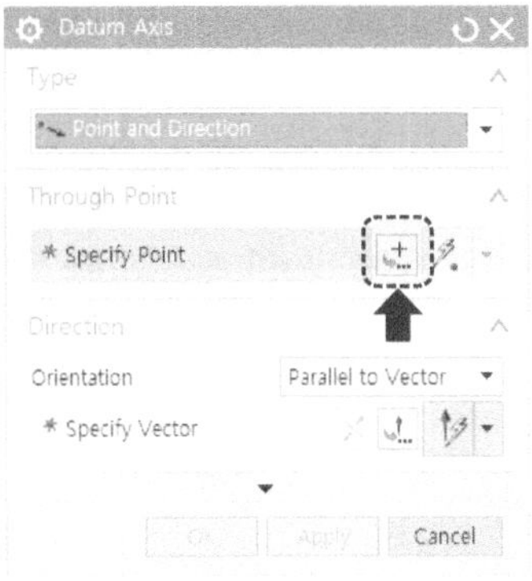

Fig 5-87 Type of Datum Axis

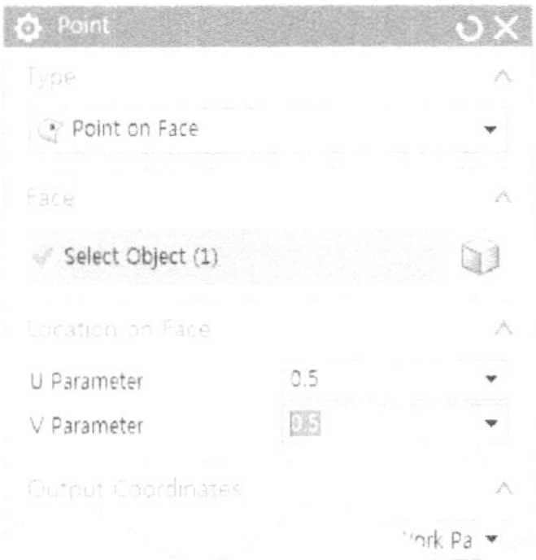

Fig 5-88 Type of Point

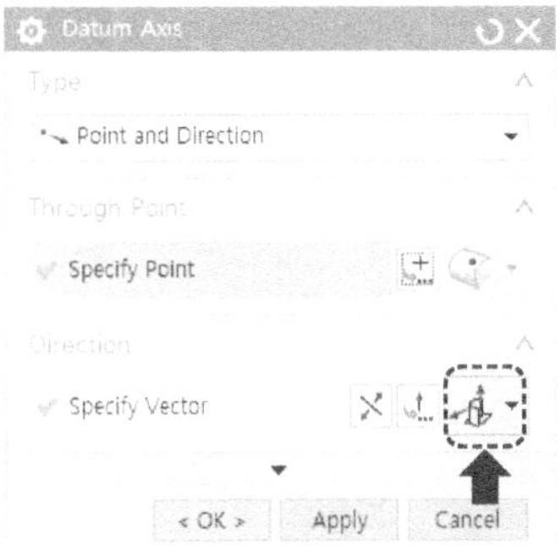

Fig 5-89 Datum Axis Options

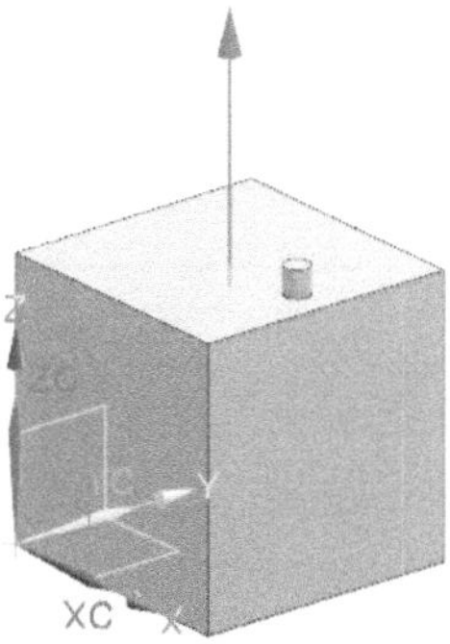

Fig 5-90 Datum Axis Created

! *Creating a Point in Advance*

In this exercise, we create a point while creating the datum axis. You can create a point in advance by clicking the **Point** icon in the **Feature** icon group.

Creating a Circular Pattern

Copying features will be explained in Chapter 6 in detail. However, it is recommended that you follow the below introduction to copying features. The numbers in Fig 5-91 correspond to the step numbers.

1. Click the **Pattern Feature** icon in the **Feature** icon group and reset the dialog box.
2. Select **Circular** as the **Layout** option.
3. Select the **Boss** feature and click MB2.
4. Select the datum axis created.
5. Set the **Angular Direction** option and press **OK** in the dialog box.
6. Close without saving the file.

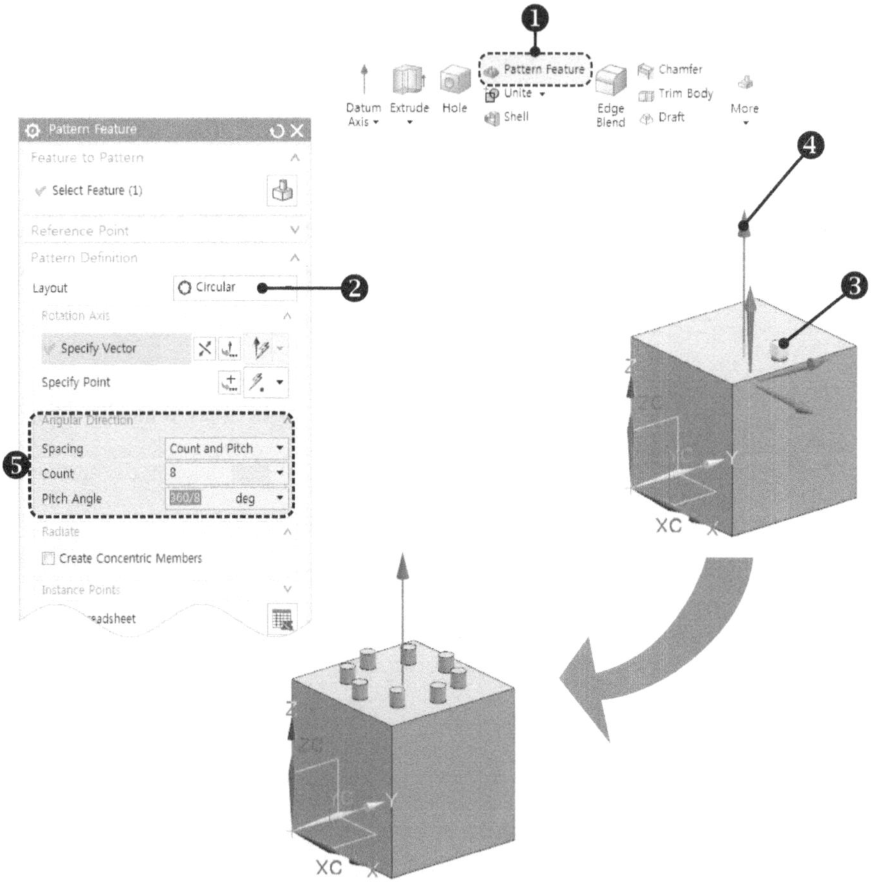

Fig 5-91 Process of Pattern Feature

END of Exercise

Let's create a datum axis by intersecting two planes and create a revolve feature.

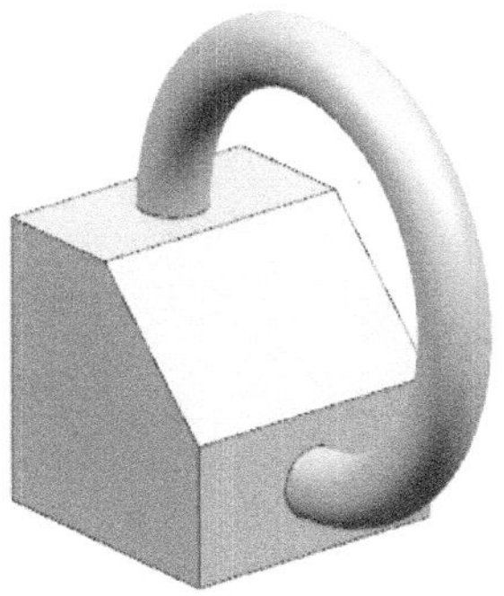

Fig 5-92 Model for Exercise

Creating a Block

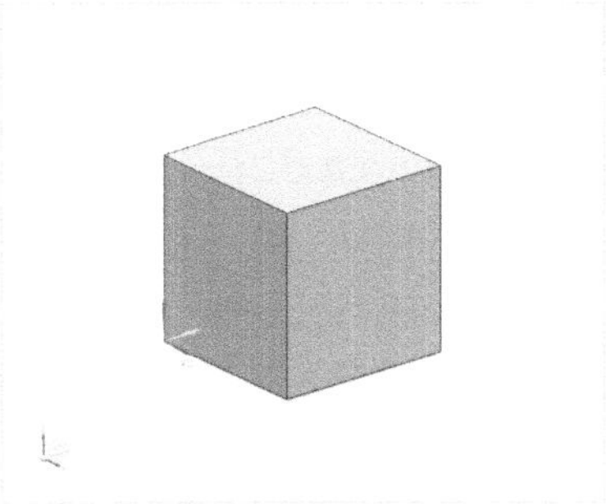

Fig 5-93 A Block

1. Create a new part file and give it an arbitrary name.
2. Choose **Insert > Design Feature > Block** in the **Menu** button.
3. Press the **Reset** button in the **Block** dialog box and press **OK**.

Creating a Chamfer

The **Chamfer** command will be explained in Chapter 7. Follow the below steps as an introduction to this command.

1. Click the **Chamfer** icon in the **Feature** icon group and reset the dialog box.
2. Select the edge Ⓐ shown in Fig 5-94.
3. Enter 50 in the **Distance** input box and press **Enter** key.
4. Press **OK** in the **Chamfer** dialog box.

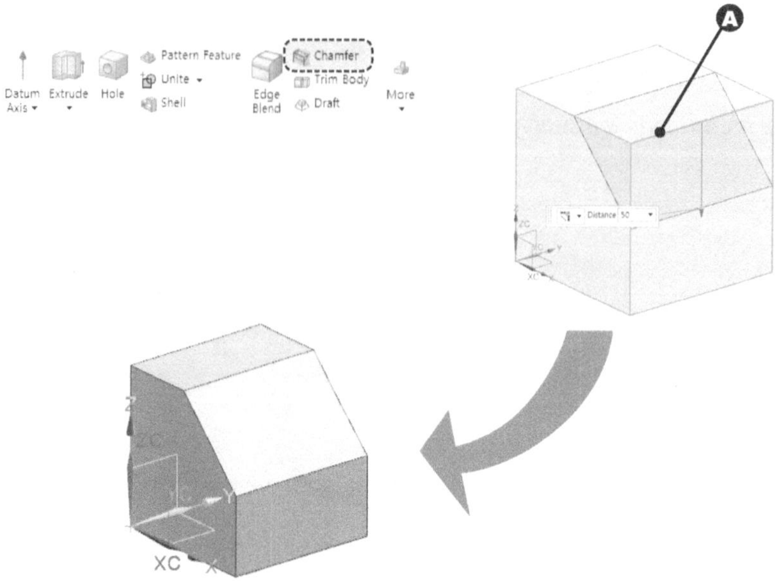

Fig 5-94 Creating a Chamfer

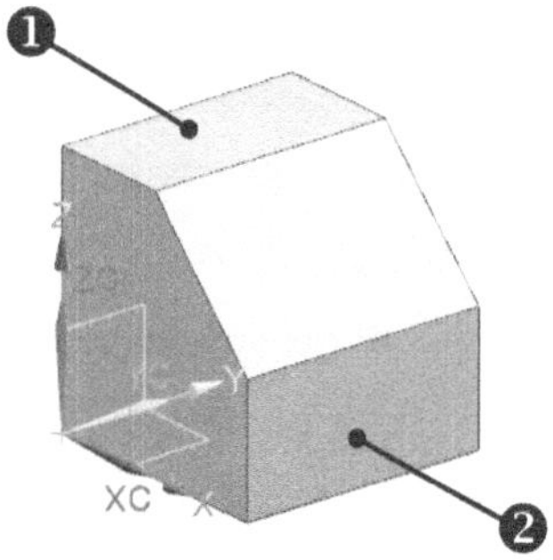

Fig 5-95 Faces to Select

Creating a Datum Axis

1. Click the **Datum Axis** icon in the **Feature** icon group.
2. Reset the dialog box.
3. Select the faces ❶ and ❷ specified in Fig 5-95 regardless of the order.
4. Press **OK** to create the datum axis as shown in Fig 5-95.

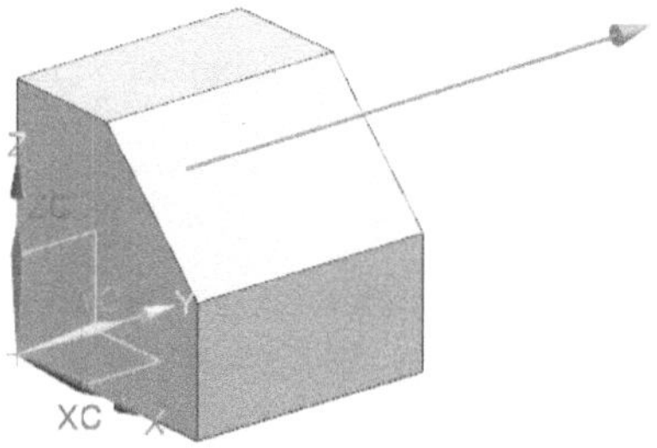

Fig 5-96 Datum Axis Created

Creating a Sketch

Create a sketch as shown in Fig 5-97 using the tools in the **Direct Sketch** icon group. The location is constrained by the **Midpoint** constraint. Do not finish the sketch.

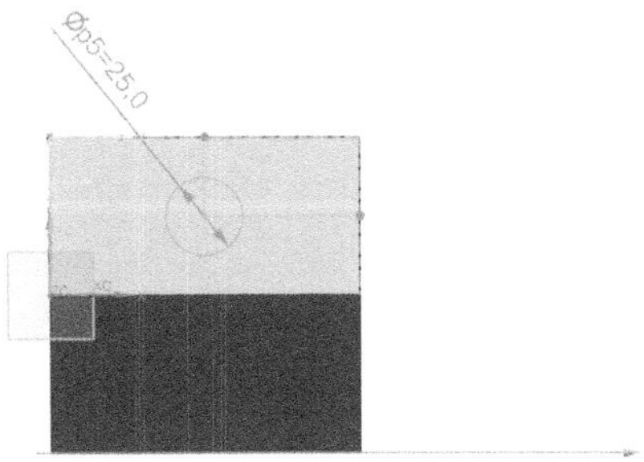

Fig 5-97 Sketch

Creating a Revolve Feature

1. Click the **Revolve** icon. The sketch is selected as a section.
2. Press MB2.
3. Select the axis (❸ in Fig 5-99).
4. Select **Until Selected** as the end limit (❹ in Fig 5-98).
5. Select the face Ⓐ shown in Fig 5-99.
6. Choose **Unite** as the **Boolean** option.
7. Press **OK**. The **Revolve** feature is created as shown in Fig 5-100.

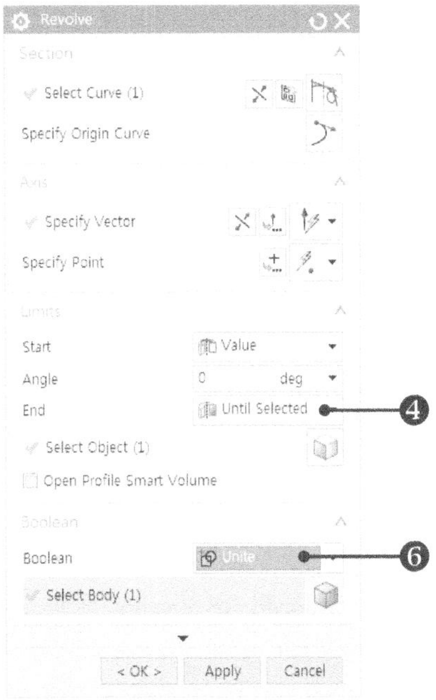

Fig 5-98 Revolve Dialog Box

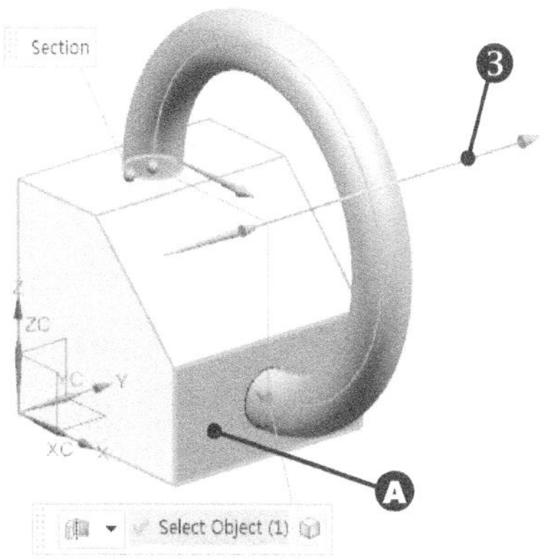

Fig 5-99 Preview of Revolve Feature

! Direct Sketch

You can click the **Revolve** or **Extrude** icon without finishing the direct sketch. Note that all curves in the sketch are selected as the section.

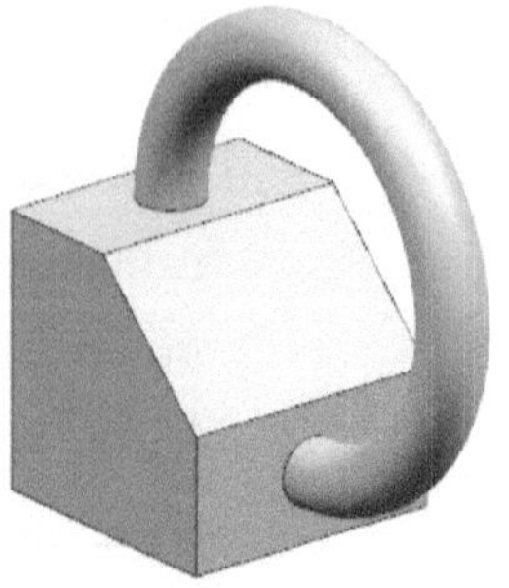

Fig 5-100 Completed Model

END of Exercise

5.5 Datum Coordinate System

The modeling object shown in Fig 5-101 is called a **Datum Coordinate System**.

A datum coordinate system consists of three datum planes, three datum axes and one point at the origin. You can define seven modeling objects that can be used during the modeling process by creating a datum coordinate system. A datum coordinate is automatically created when you create a part file with the **Model** template.

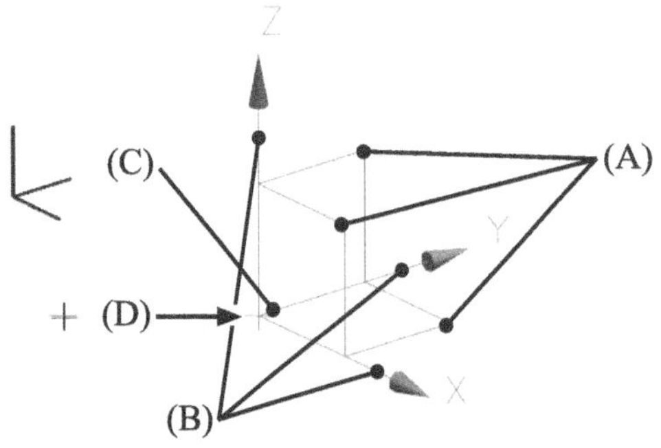

(A) Datum Plane: 3
(B) Datum Axis: 3
(C) Coordinate System: 1
(D) Point: 1

Fig 5-101 Datum Coordinate System

Click the **Datum CSYS** icon in the **Feature** icon group. The **Datum CSYS** dialog box shown in Fig 5-103 is invoked and you can create various types of datum coordinate systems. Note that the **Associative** option in the **Settings** option group is not available when you select **Dynamic** in the **Type** dropdown list.

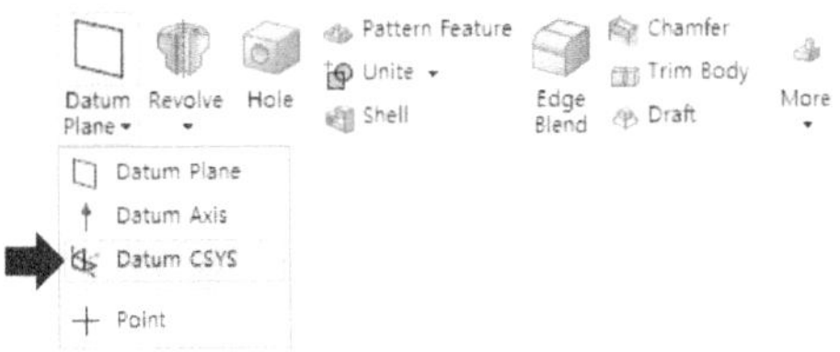

Fig 5-102 Datum CSYS Icon

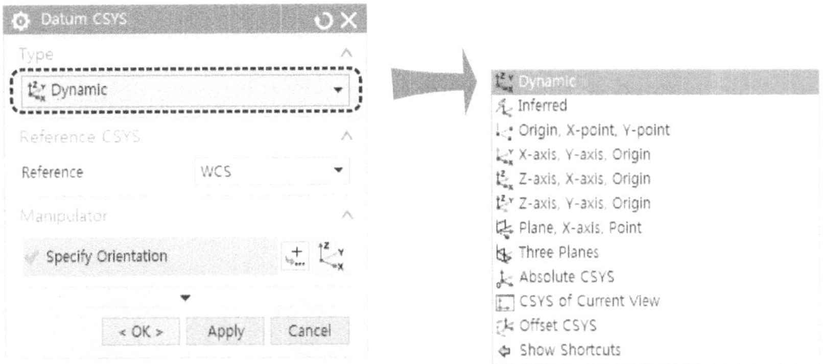

Fig 5-103 Datum CSYS Dialog Box

Exercise 09 Creating a Datum Coordinate System

Create a 100 x 100 x 100 block and create a datum coordinate system according to the following requirements. The requirements have to be met even though you will modify the Y dimension to 200 mm.

Requirements

1. The origin of the datum coordinate system is located at the center of the upper face.
2. The X axis is aligned to the diagonal direction.
3. The Z axis is always normal to the upper face.

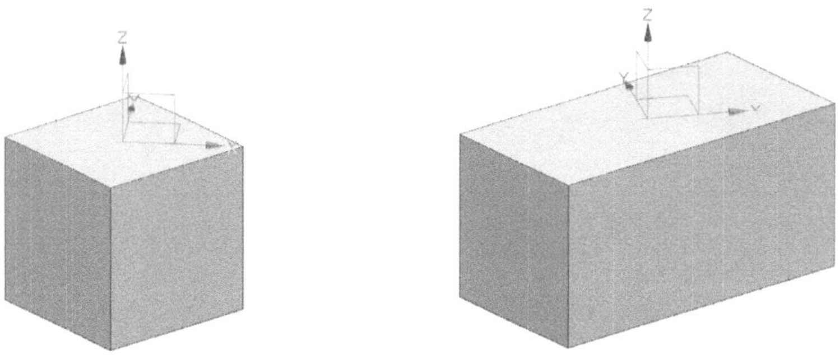

Fig 5-104 Creating a Datum Coordinate System

Hint!

You can specify the origin point and the Z axis while you are creating a datum coordinate system of the type shown in Fig 5-105.

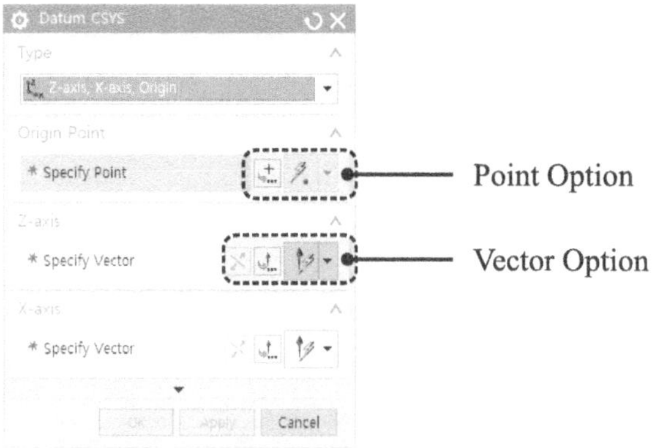

Fig 5-105 Datum CSYS Options

END of Exercise

Create a solid model referring to the drawing in Fig 5-106.

Requirements

1. All sketch objects have to be fully constrained.
2. Do not use the **Fix** constraint.
3. The final result has to be a single solid body.

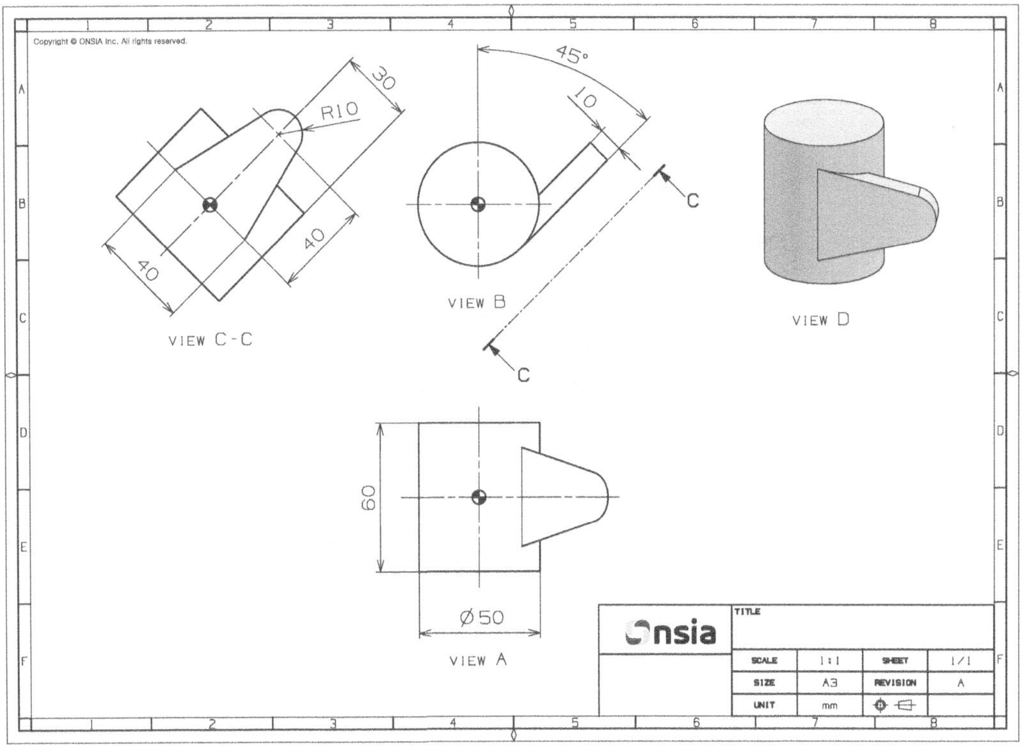

Fig 5-106 Drawing for Exercise 10

Hint!

Create the model referring to the following procedure.

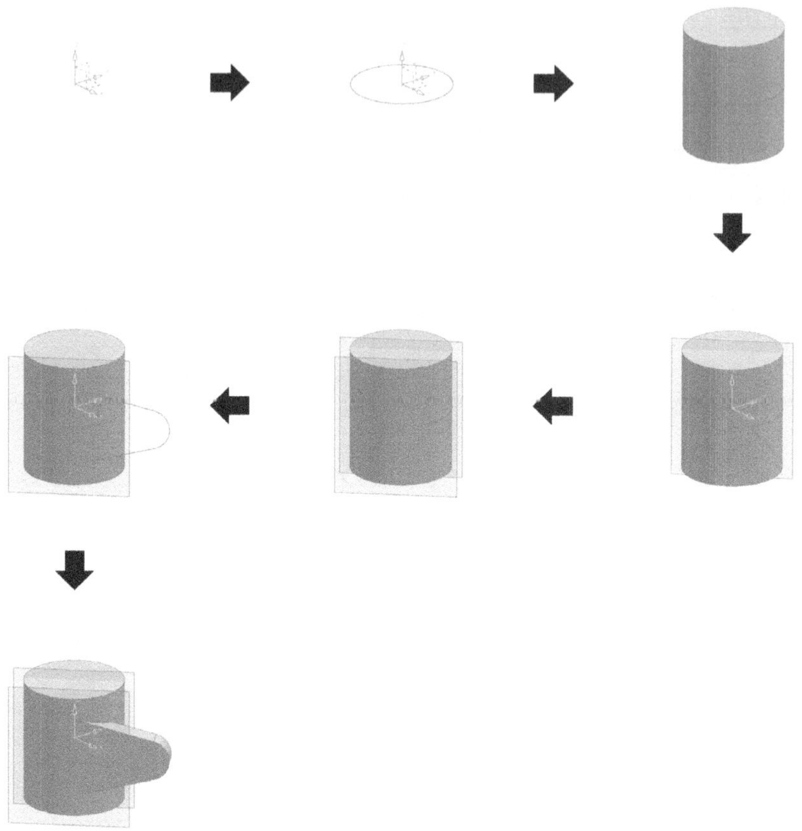

Create a solid model referring to the drawing in Fig 5-107.

1. All sketch objects have to be fully constrained.
2. Do not use the **Fix** constraint.
3. The final result has to be a single solid body.

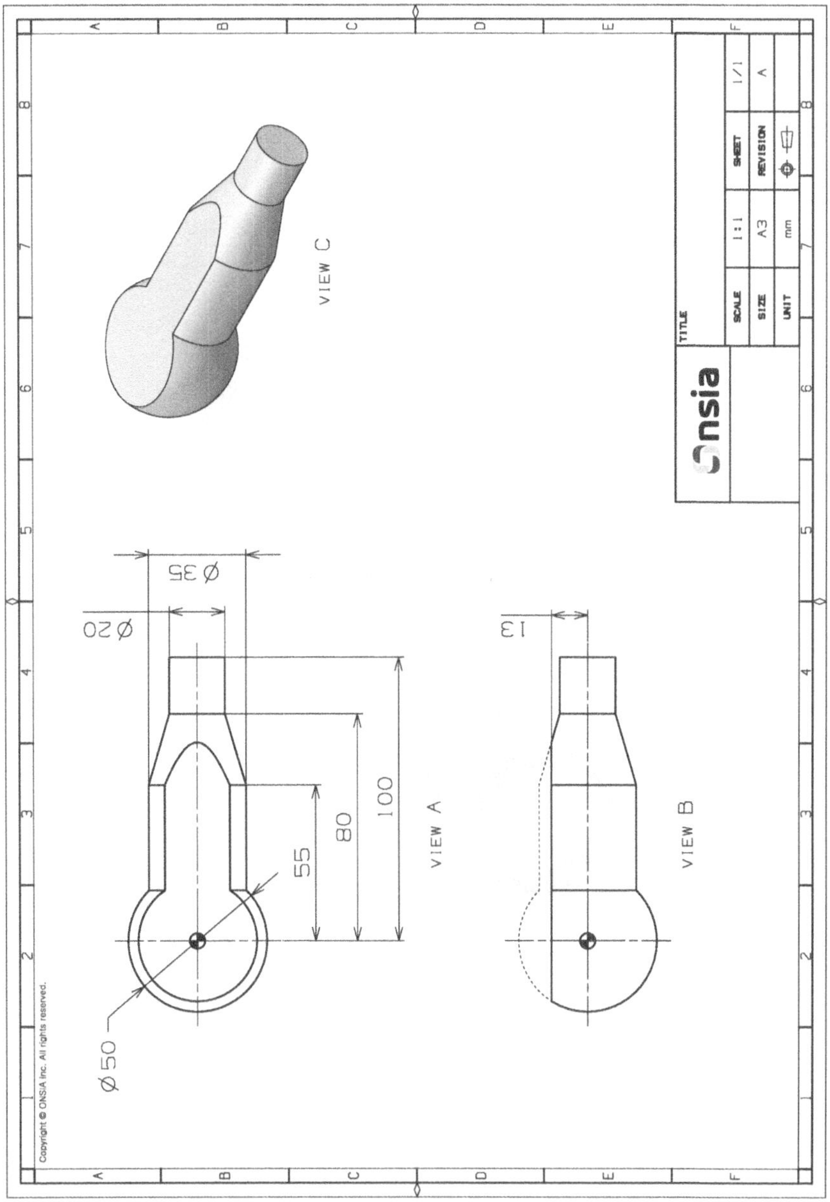

Fig 5-107 Drawing for Exercise 11

Hint!

Create the model referring to the following procedure.

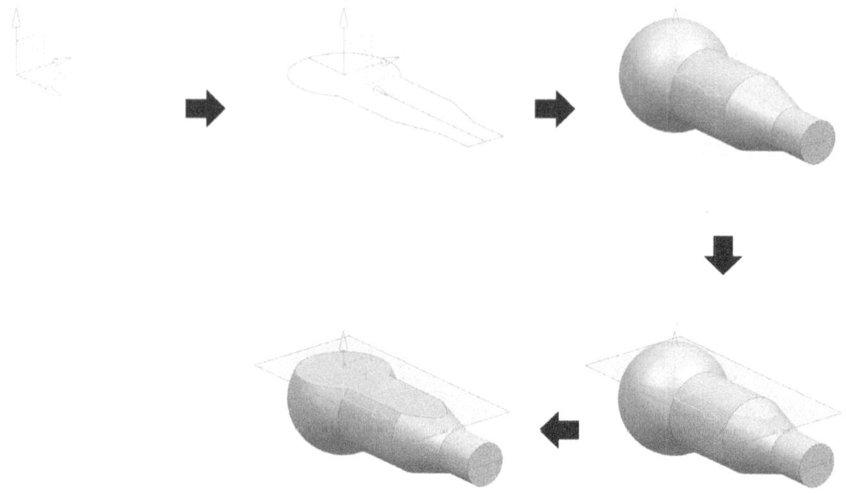

Trim Body

Use the **Trim Body** command for donig Exercise 10. Keep to the following procedure.

1. Click the **Trim Body** icon in the **Feature** icon group.

2. Select a solid body or a sheet body as the target
3. Click MB2.
4. Select the datum plane.
5. Determine the side to trim out.
6. Press the **OK** button.

Create a solid model referring to the drawing in Fig 5-108.

1. All sketch objects have to be fully constrained.
2. Do not use the **Fix** constraint.
3. The final result has to be a single solid body.

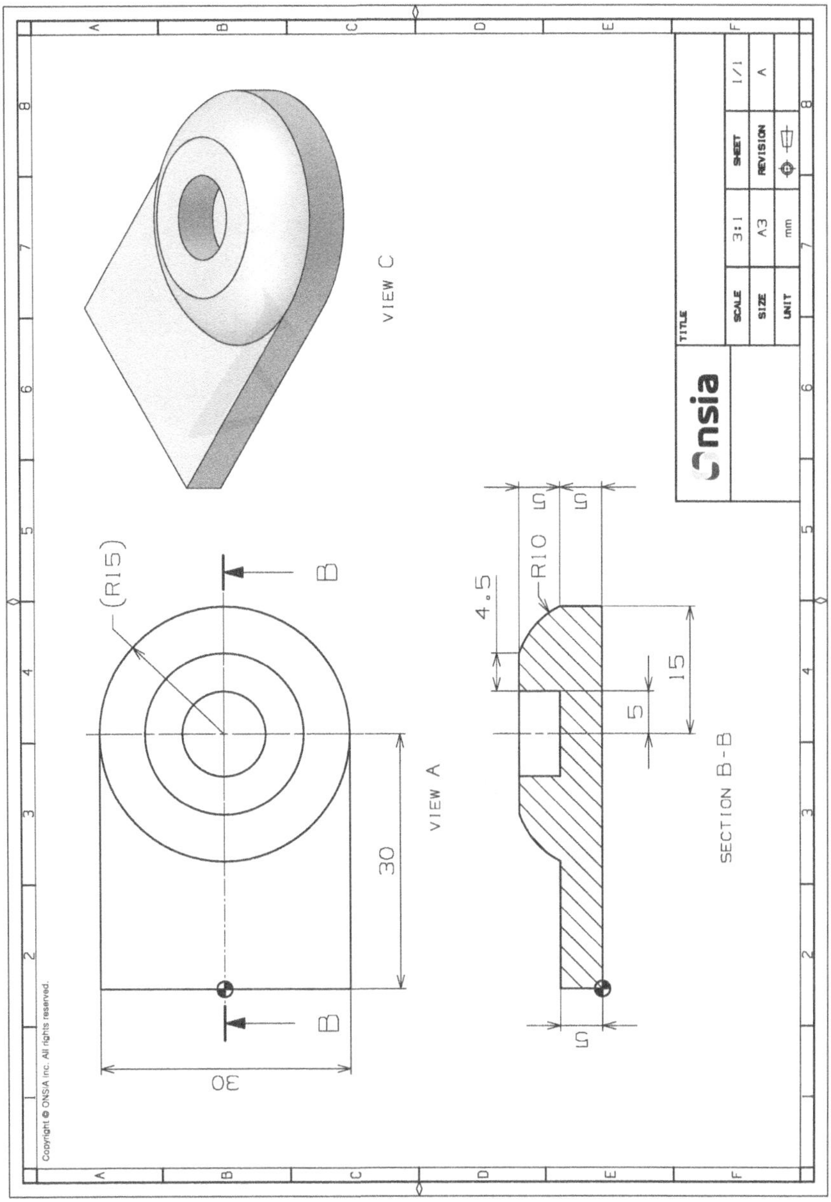

Fig 5-108 Drawing for Exercise 12

Hint!

Create the model referring to the following procedure.

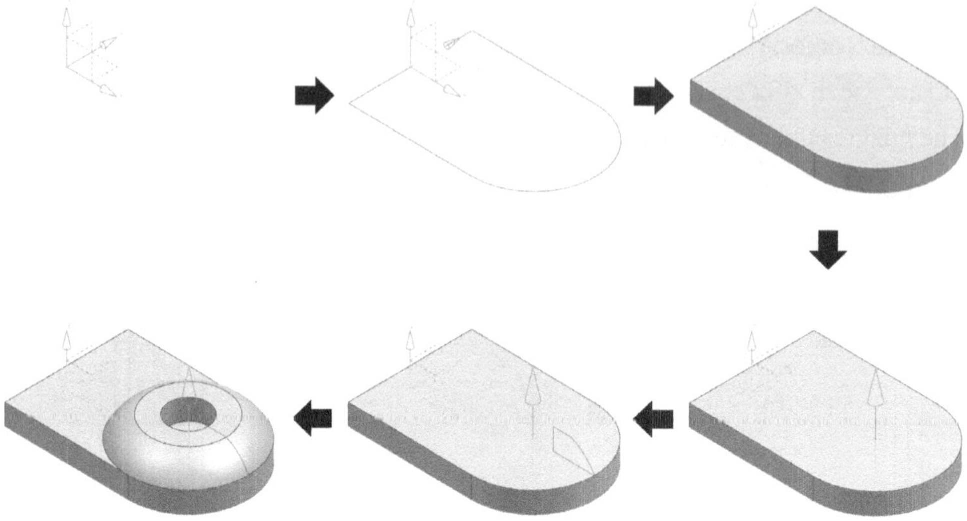

Create a solid model referring to the drawing in Fig 5-109.

1. The final result has to be a single solid body.
2. Use the **Hole** command to create holes.

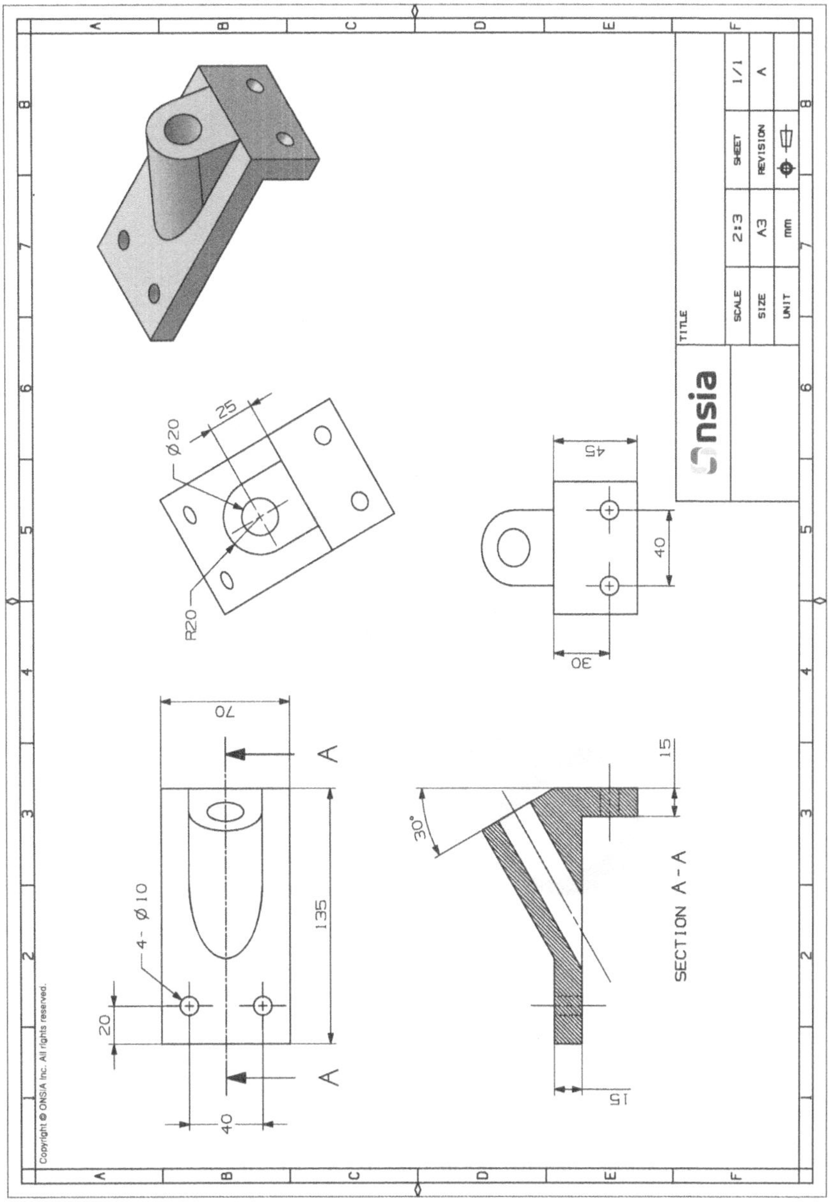

Fig 5-109 Drawing for Exercise 13

Exercise 14 Creating a Datum Coordinate System

Create a solid model referring to the drawing in Fig 5-110.

1. The final result has to be a single solid body.
2. Use the **Hole** command to create holes.

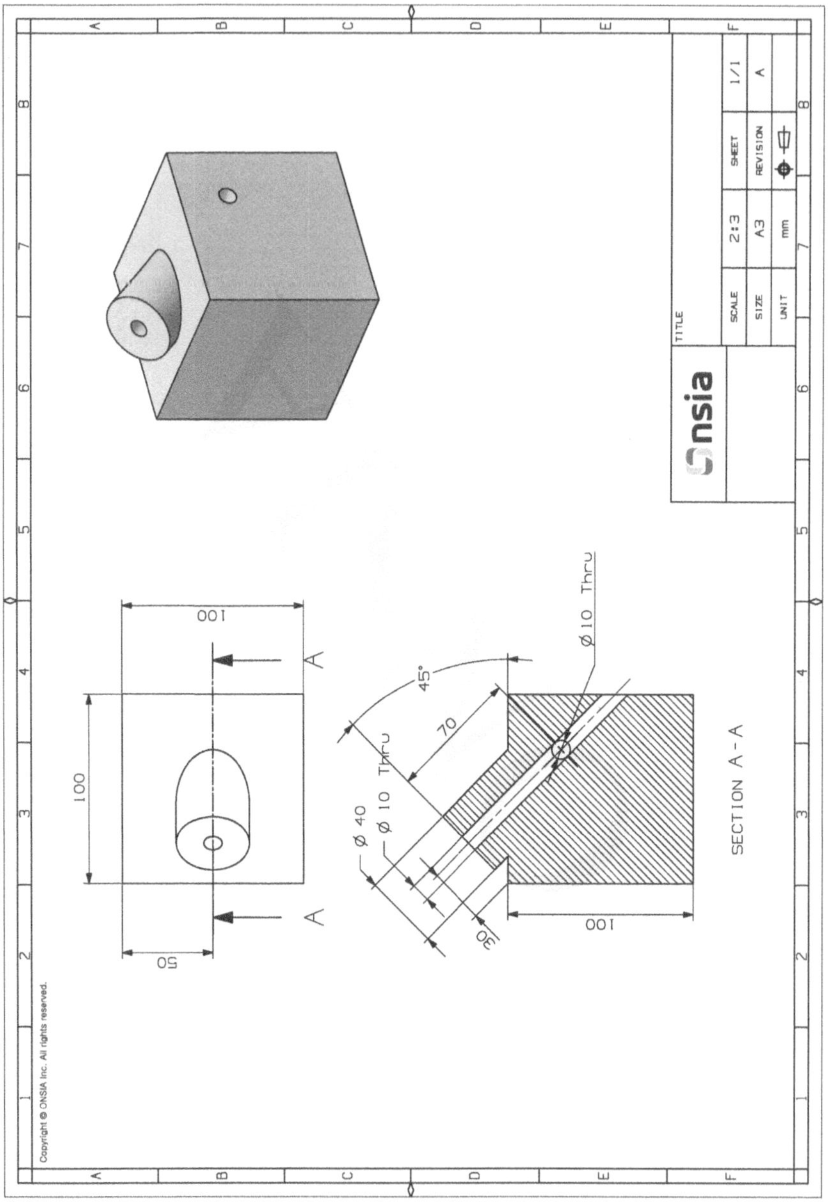

Fig 5-110 Drawing for Exercise 14

Chapter 6

Additional Modeling Commands - Part I

After completing this chapter you will understand

- the types and procedure of **Edge Blend**.
- how to create **Chamfer** on an edge.
- designer's requirements of **Draft**.
- various types and options of **Draft**.
- how to apply wall thickness by using the **Shell** command.

6.1 Detail Modeling

Recall the general modeling process introduced in "2.3 Summary of the Modeling Process" on Page 59.

1. Create a sketch.
   - ► Defi ne the sketch plane.
   - ► Create the sketch curves and defi ne their shape with constraints.

2. Create 3D geometry.
   - ► Create features using the **Extrude** or **Revolve** command to add or remove volumes.

3. Detail Modeling
   - ► Complete the model by applying commands such as Edge Blend and Shell that modify edges or faces

In this chapter, we will learn commands that are used in the third step.

There are four commands that can be classifi ed in detail modeling: **Edge Blend**, **Chamfer**, **Draft** and **Shell**. Detail modeling commands do not require a sketch. They can be applied on edges or faces that have already been created. Refer to "A.4 Selecting Points, Lines and Faces" on Page 636 for selecting edges, faces and points.

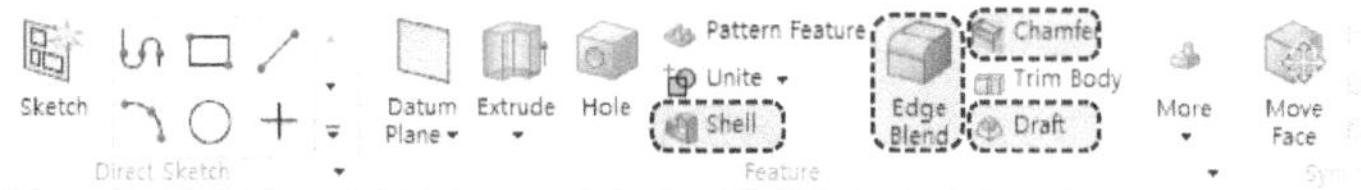

Fig 6-1 Icons for Detail Modeling

6.2 Edge Blend

Sharp edges can be rounded with the **Edge Blend** command which is generally called a fillet.

Fig 6-2 Before Edge Blend

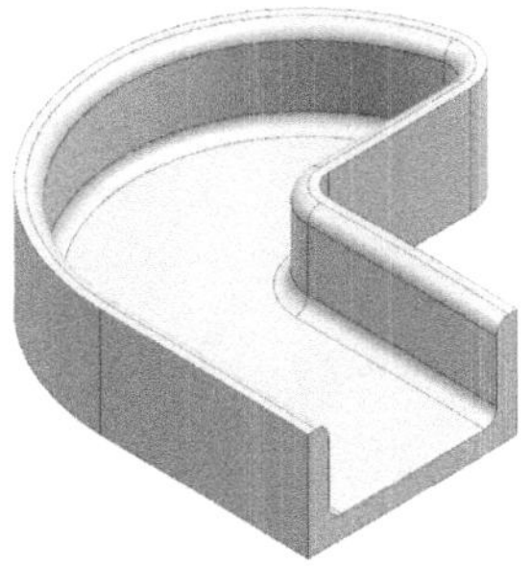

Fig 6-3 After Edge Blend

Edge fillets are applied to smoothen sharp edges. There are two types of sharp edges. Fig6-4 shows concave edges Ⓐ and convex edges Ⓑ.

When a part has been manufactured, convex edges can damage the parts, resulting in deterioration of product quality. They can even cause injury to people who deliver or handle the parts.

When a load is applied to a part, the stress will concentrate at the concave edges and a fracture may initiate from these edges. Using the **Edge Blend** command, you can create fillets on the concave or convex edges in the 3D model. Some types of fillets are created inevitably during the manufacturing process and some are required to improve the mechanical performance of the part.

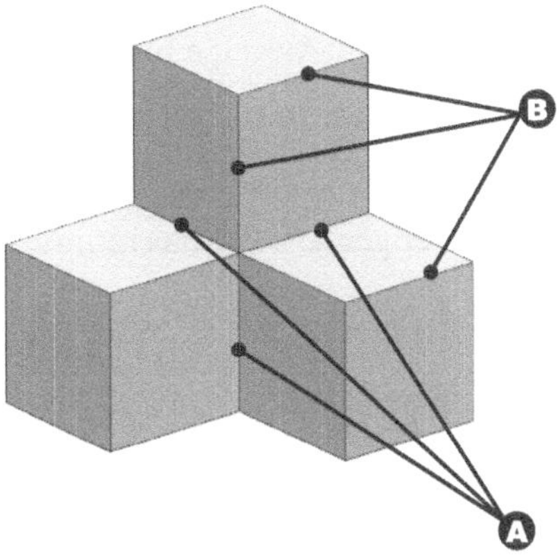

Fig 6-4 Types of Edges

6.2.1 Types of Edge Blend

In NX 8.5, there are four types of edge blends available as shown in Fig 6-5.

<General Blend>

<Variable Radius Blend>

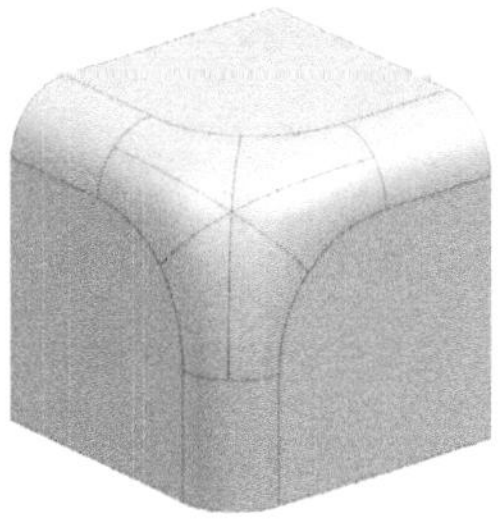

<Setback Blend>

<Limit Blend>

Fig 6-5 Types of Edge Blends

A setback blend can be applied on vertices where three or more edges meet. You can cre-atea smoother blend on vertices.

A limit blend is applied on edges where you cannot create a complete fillet on the edge due to the complexity of the geometry. An edge blend is limited to a portion of the edge by specifying the distance from one end of the selected edge.

You can also apply blends on an edge with various radiuses at the specified points.

This exercise explains how to create general edge blend.

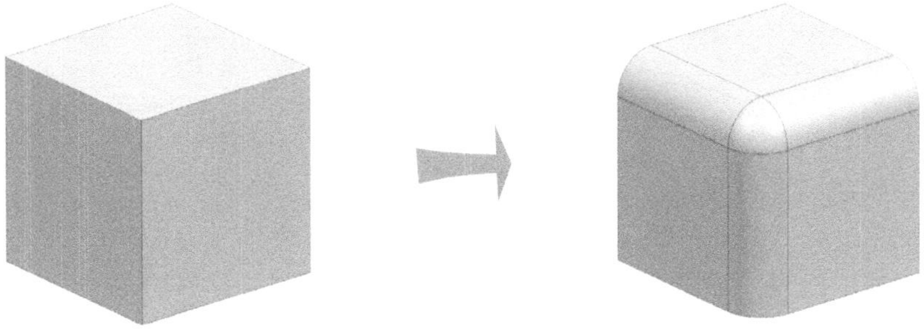

Fig 6-6 Before and After Edge Blend

Fig 6-7 A Block

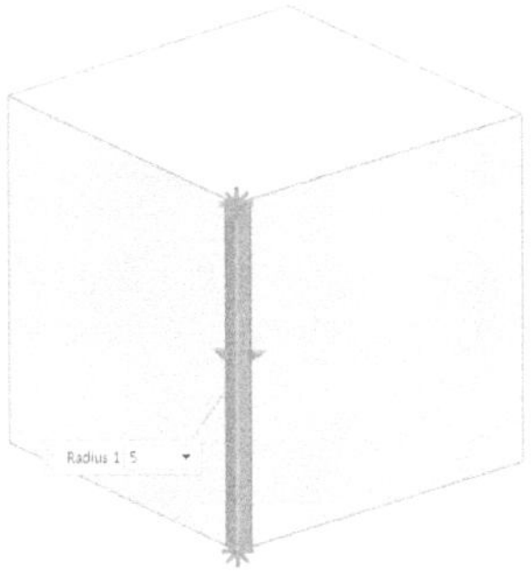

Fig 6-8 Preview of Edge Blend

1. Create a new part file and create a block as shown in Fig 6-7.
2. Click the **Edge Blend** icon in the **Feature** icon group.
3. Reset the dialog box.
4. Select the vertical edge designated by the arrow in Fig 6-7. You can see the preview of the 5 mm radius fillet as shown in Fig 6-8.
5. Delete the **Radius 1** value in the **Edge Blend** dialog box shown in Fig 6-9 and press the **Enter** key. You can see the preview of Radius 1 = 20 fillet in the graphics window. Press the **Apply** button in the dialog box.

The sharp edge is rounded as shown in Fig 6-9.

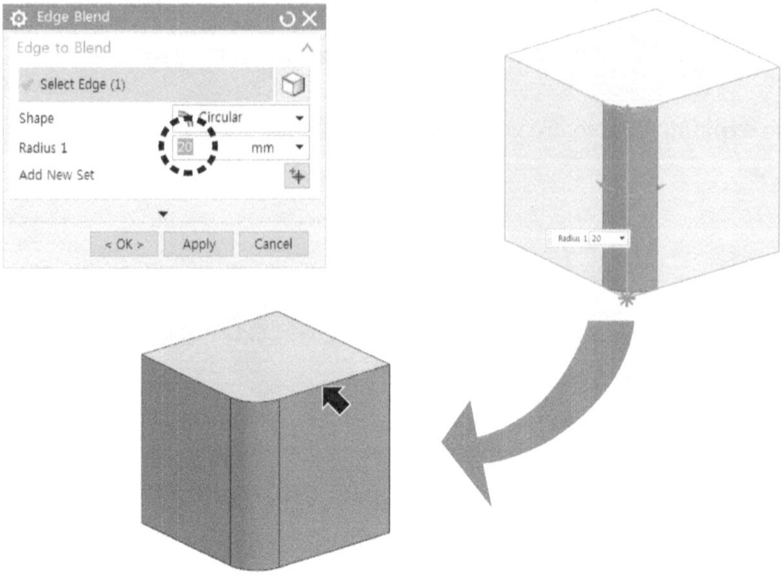

Fig 6-9 Creating R20 Edge Blend

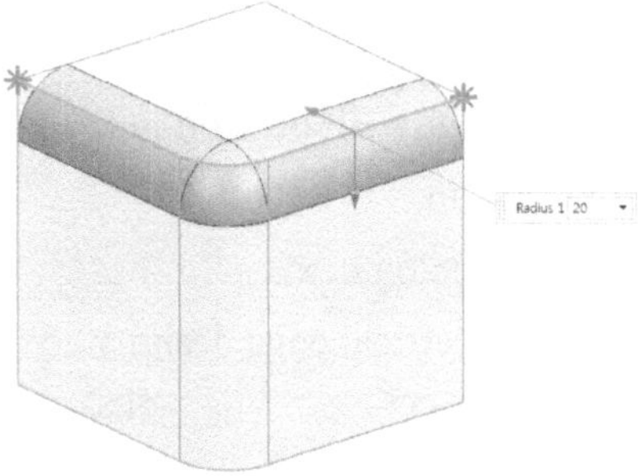

Fig 6-10 Preview of Edge Blend

6. Ensure that the **Radius 1** value is 20 and select the edge designated by the arrow in Fig 6-9.

All three edges are selected together as shown in Fig 6-10.

7. Press **OK** in the dialog box. A 20mm radius edge blend is applied on the three tangent connected edges as shown in Fig 6-11.

8. Close without saving the file.

Fig 6-11 Edge Blend Created

END of Exercise

Curve Rule

The Edge Blend is a command that can be applied on edges. Therefore, the Curve Rule is available at the selection step. The reason why the three edges are selected at the same time in Fig 6-10 is that the default curve rule for Edge Blend is Tangent Curves.

Fig 6-12 Curve Rule

Add New Set Exercise 02

You can define edge blends for several radiuses in a single **Edge Blend** feature. Let's learn how to add a new set of blend radiuses in the **Edge Blend** dialog box.

Fig 6-13 Edge Blend to Create

Fig 6-14 A Block

1. Create a new part file and create a block as shown in Fig 6-14.
2. Click the **Edge Blend** icon in the **Feature** icon group.
3. Reset the dialog box.
4. Enter 20 in the **Radius 1** input box and press the **Enter** key.
5. Select the vertical edge designated by the arrow in Fig 6-14.

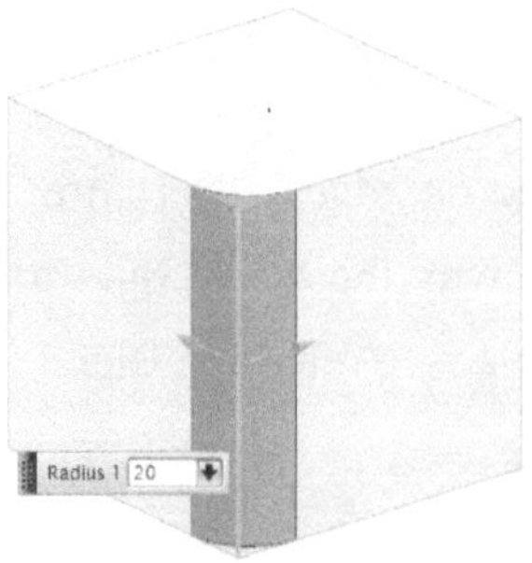

Fig 6-15 Preview of Edge Blend

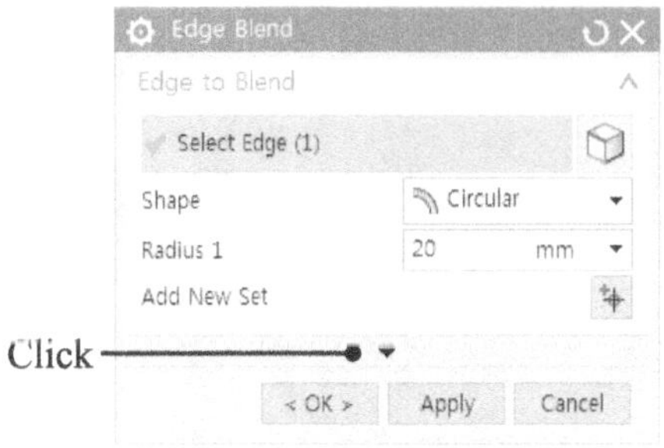

Fig 6-16 More Button

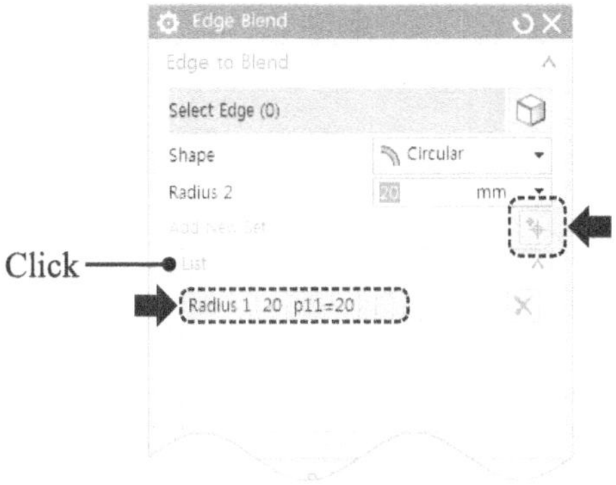

Fig 6-17 Edge Blend Defined

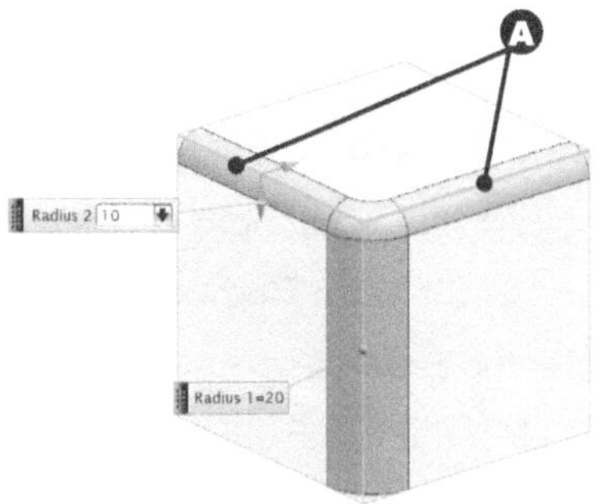

Fig 6-18 Edges to Select

A 20 mm radius edge blend is previewed as shown in Fig 6-15.

6. Click the **More** button to expand the dialog box as shown in Fig 6-16.
7. Expand the **List** area of the dialog box by clicking the title as shown in Fig 6-17.
8. Click the **Add New Set** icon as specified by the upper arrow in Fig 6-17.

The edge blend is defined in the **List** area and the title of the **Radius 1** input box changes to **Radius 2**.

9. Enter 10 in the **Radius 2** input box and press the **Enter** key.
10. Select the two edges designated by Ⓐ in Fig 6-18.
11. Press **OK** in the dialog box.

The edge blend is created as shown in Fig 6-13. Only one edge blend feature is recorded in the **Part Navigator** as shown in Fig 6-19.

12. Close without saving the file.

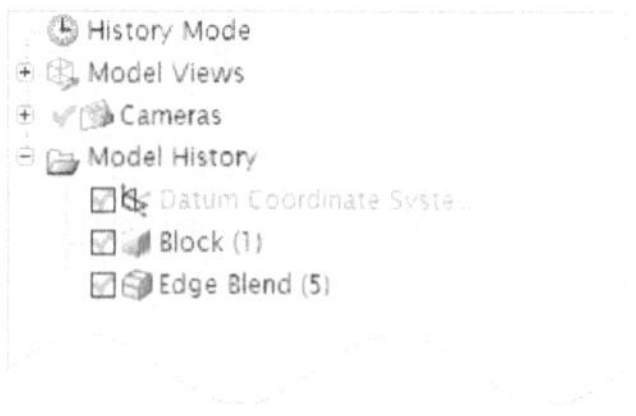

Fig 6-19 Part Navigator

END of Exercise

Quiz!

Why is the **Tangent Curves** curve rule not applied when selecting edges in Fig 6-18?

Answer: The edge blend of radius 20mm is not created yet but it is just a preview. Therefore, the two edges are not tangent connected.

6.2.2 Shape Option

The shape option defines the sectional shape of the blend surface. While the **Circular** type generates a constant curvature surface along the section line, the **Conic** type generates a variable curvature surface.

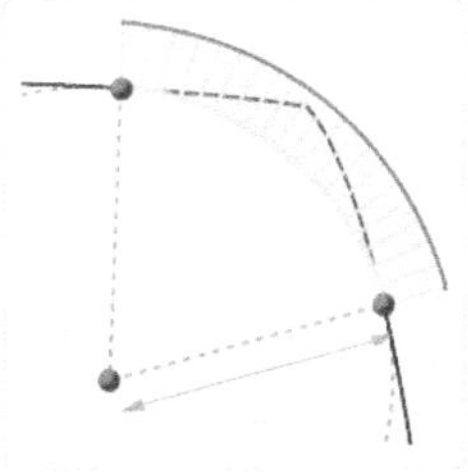

Fig 6-20 Curvature of Circular Type

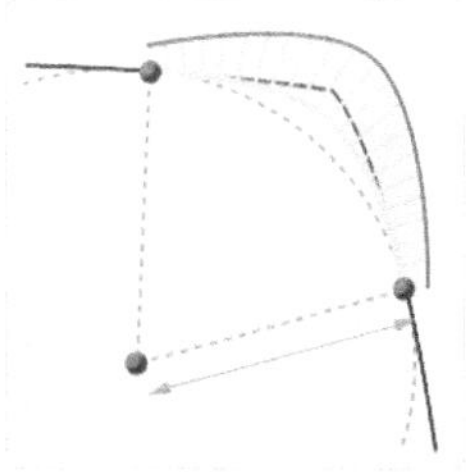

Fig 6-21 Curvature of Conic Type

If you choose the **Conic** type in the **Shape** option, other options are changed to define the variable curvature fillet.

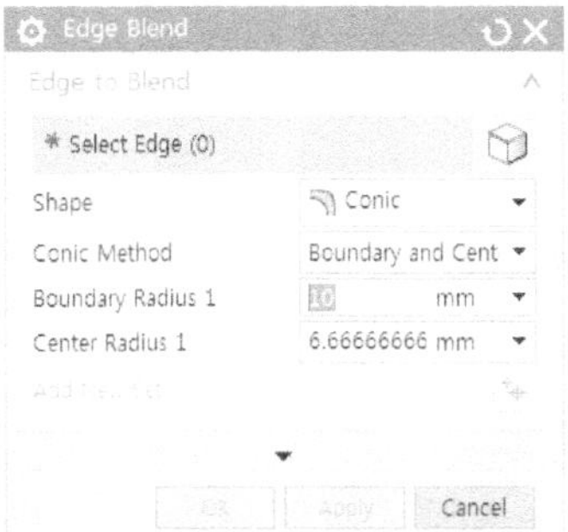

Fig 6-22 Options for Conic Blend

Exercise 03 **Variable Radius Edge Blend**

Let's learn the process of applying a variable radius edge blend.

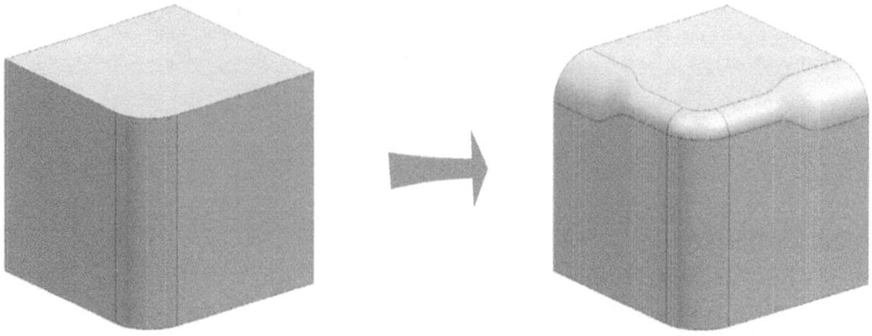

Fig 6-23 Before and After Variable Radius Edge Blend

Fig 6-24 A Block

1. Create an arbitrarily named part file and create a block feature.
2. Apply an R20 edge blend as shown in Fig 6-24.
3. Click the **Edge Blend** icon again.
4. Select the edges to apply the blend by clicking the edge designated by the arrow in Fig 6-25.
5. Expand the option group by clicking the title of **Variable Radius Points** as shown in Fig 6-26.

Fig 6-25 Edge to Select

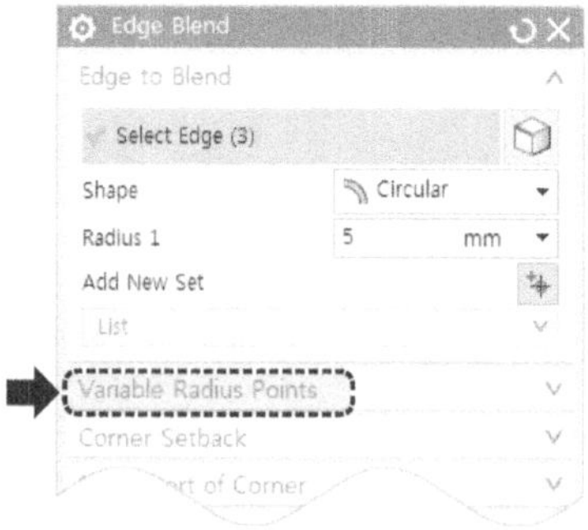

Fig 6-26 Variable Radius Points Option

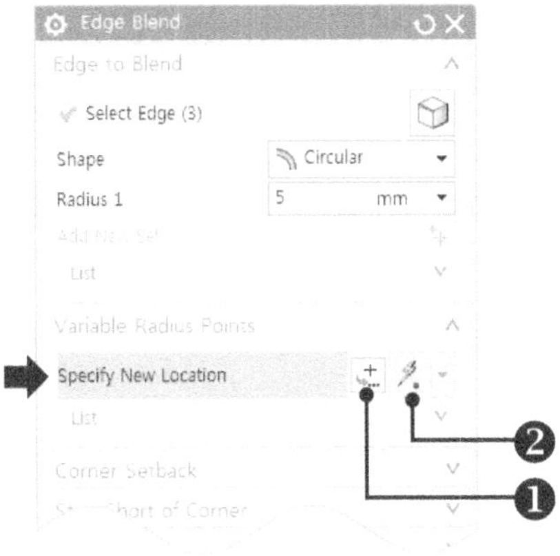

Fig 6-27 Specify New Location

6. Click the Specify **New Location** option as designated by the arrow in Fig 6-27.

7. Select the end point designated by the arrow in Fig 6-28. Be sure to click MB1 when the end point is snapped as shown in Fig 6-29. Any of the three edges that meet at the vertex may be highlighted.

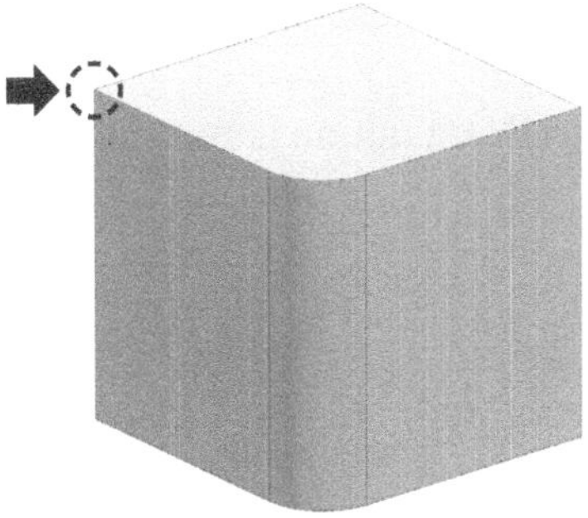

Fig 6-28 End Point of the Edge

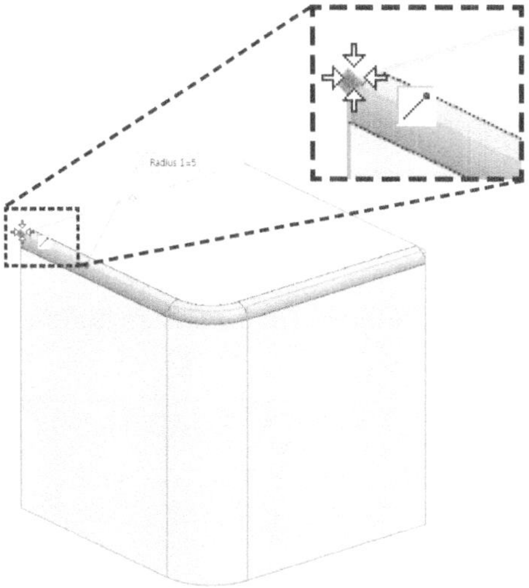

Fig 6-29 Snapped End Point

Caution!

Option buttons ❶ and ❷ specified in Fig 6-27 are the **Point Dialog** and **Snap Point** options, respectively. After clicking the title of the **Specify New Location** option, you can select points using the **Snap Point** option in the selection bar. The options ❶ and ❷ are used when you cannot select the desired points with the **Snap Point** option. Refer to "A.4 Selecting Points, Lines and Faces" on Page 636 for detail.

Fig 6-30 Snap Point Option

8. Delete the value in the **V Radius** input box shown in Fig 6-31 and type 20, then press the **Enter** key.

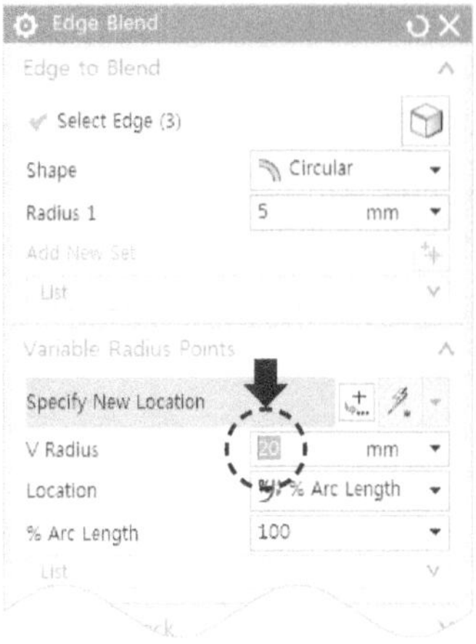

Fig 6-32 V Radius Value

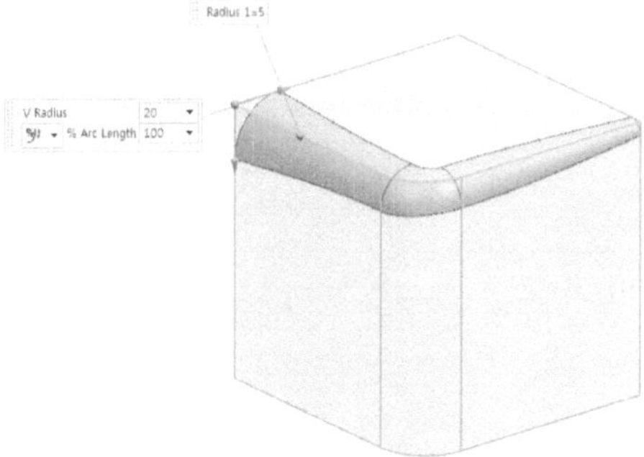

Fig 6-31 Preview of R20 Blend at the End Point

9. Ensure that the **Point on Curve** button in the **Snap Point** option is turned on as shown in Fig 6-33.

Fig 6-33 Point on Curve Option

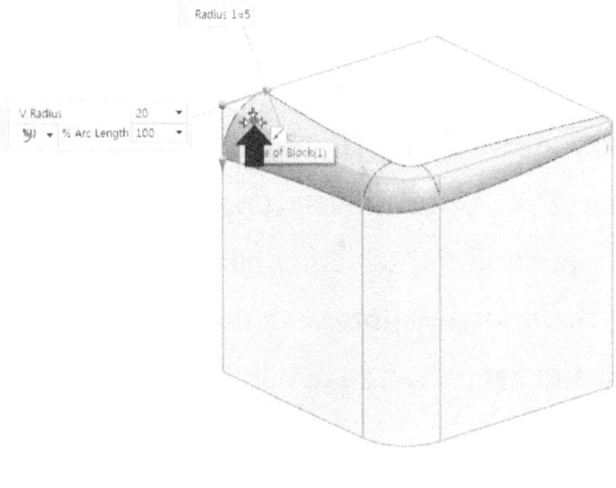

Fig 6-34 Specifying the Point Location

10. Select the point around the location specified in Fig 6-34. You may select a point around the middle because we will modify the % value.

11. Enter 65 in the **% Arc Length** input box designated by the arrow in Fig 6-35 and press the **Enter** key. The new location of V Radius = 20 mm point is previewed as in Fig 6-36.

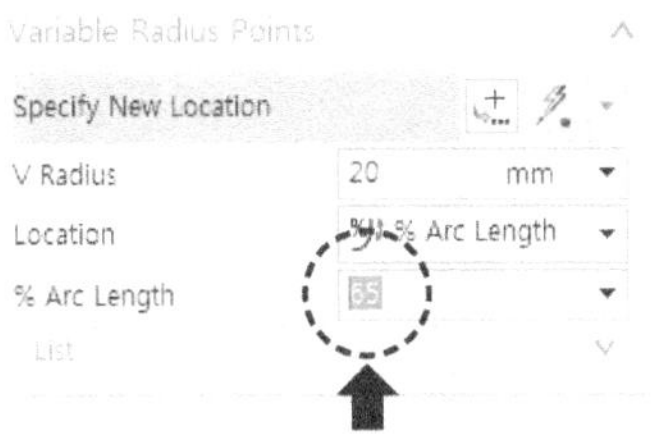

Fig 6-35 % Arc Length Value

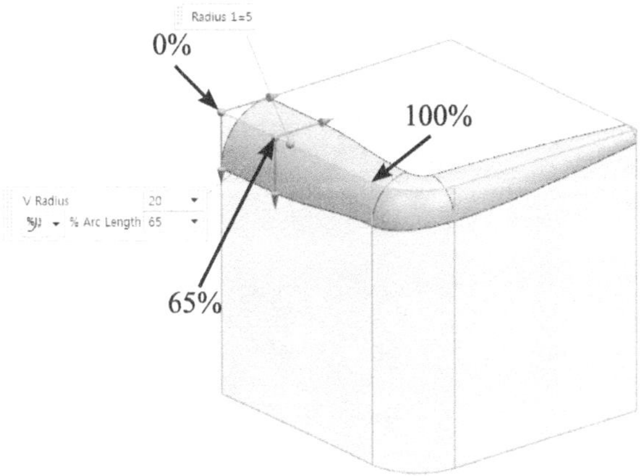

Fig 6-36 Location of % Arc Length

Caution!

The start and end of the **% Arc Length** is defined for each edge. Although three edges are selected for edge blend, the start and end of the **% Arc Length** is not defined as in Fig 6-37.

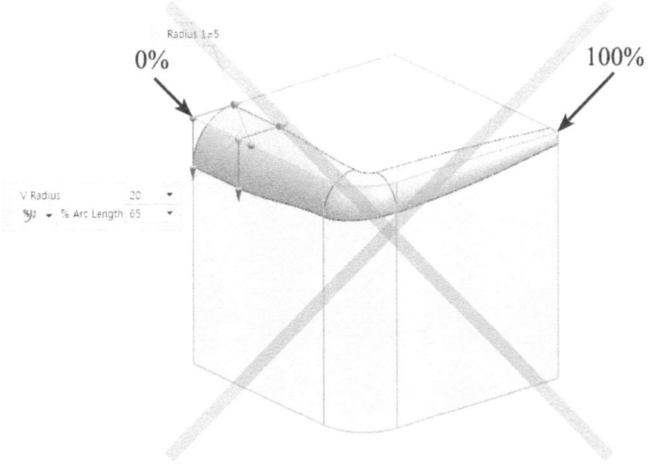

Fig 6-37 Wrong Understanding of % Arc Length

12. In the same manner as steps 9 to 11, define each radius for the four points specified in Fig 6-38. Note that you may have to enter different **% Arc Length** values for points 4 and 5 depending on the start point of the edge.

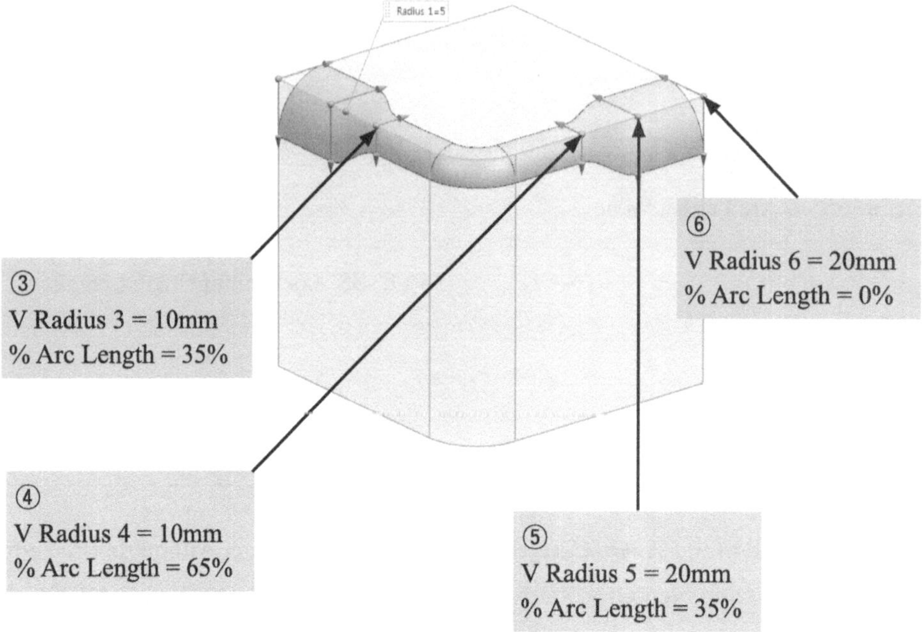

Fig 6-38 Values for Four Points

13. Press **OK** in the dialog box. Various radius edge blends are created as shown in Fig 6-39. Close without saving the file.

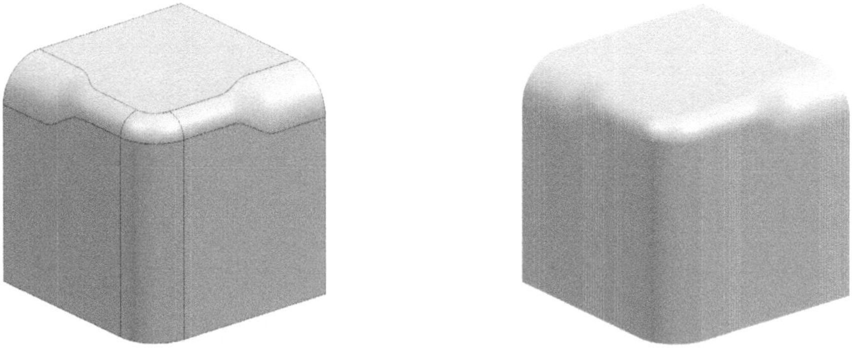

<Shaded with Edge> <Shaded>

Fig 6-39 Variable Radius Edge Blend Created

END of Exercise

Modifying Variable Radius Edge Blends

You can modify the values in a variable radius edge blend according to the following procedure. Refer to the numbers in Fig 6-40 for each step number.

① Double click the edge blend feature in the **Part Navigator**.
② Click the **List** title in the **Variable Radius Points** option group in the **Edge Blend** dialog box.
③ Select the item to modify.
④ Modify the **V Radius** and **Location** value.

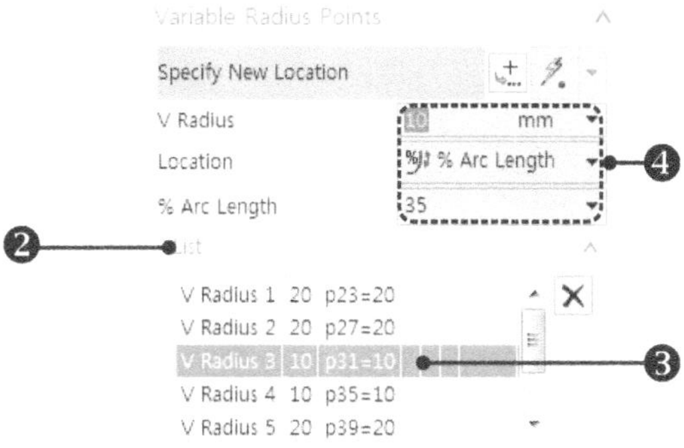

Fig 6-40 Modifying Variable Radius Edge Blend

6.2.3 Guideline for Applying Edge Blend

Quite often you will not be able to create a satisfactory edge blend for complex geometry. The following guidelines outline the steps to create edge blends successfully.

1. Apply the fillet for the larger radius first, and then proceed to the smaller ones.
2. Apply the fillet for the concentrated edges first by selecting the edges at the same time.
3. Apply fillets one by one, not as a single feature.
4. Apply the fillet for the separate edges first so that the edges to be selected later are tangent connected.

Exercise 04 Applying Edge Blend *ch06_ex04.prt*

Open the file ch06_ex04.prt and apply edge blend on all edges except the bottom face as shown in Fig 6-42. The blend radiuses for each edge are specified in Fig 6-43 and Fig 6-44.

Note that the edge blends are not the variable radius blend. Try to apply the blends one by one, not as a single feature.

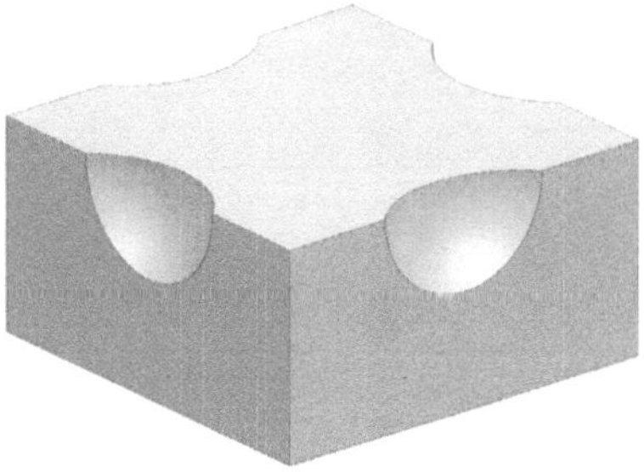

Fig 6-41 Before Edge Blend

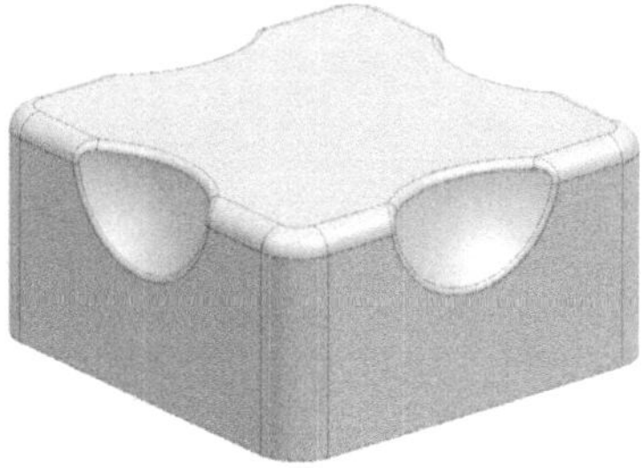

Fig 6-42 After Edge Blend

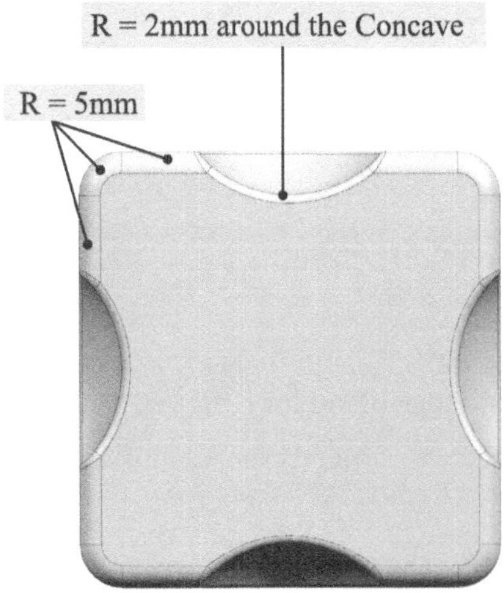

Fig 6-43 Top View

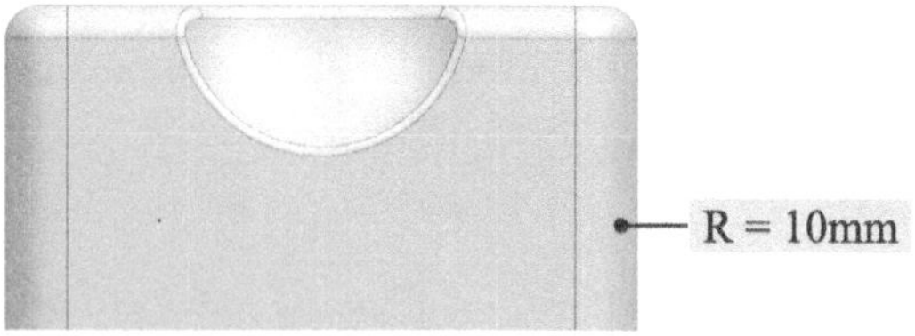

Fig 6-44 Front View

END of Exercise

Setback Blend - 1 Exercise 05

Let's learn the process of applying a setback blend on a vertex where three edges meet.

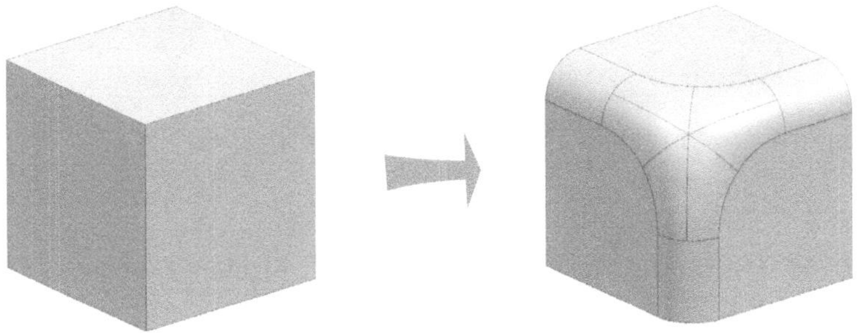

Fig 6-45 Before and After the Setback Blend

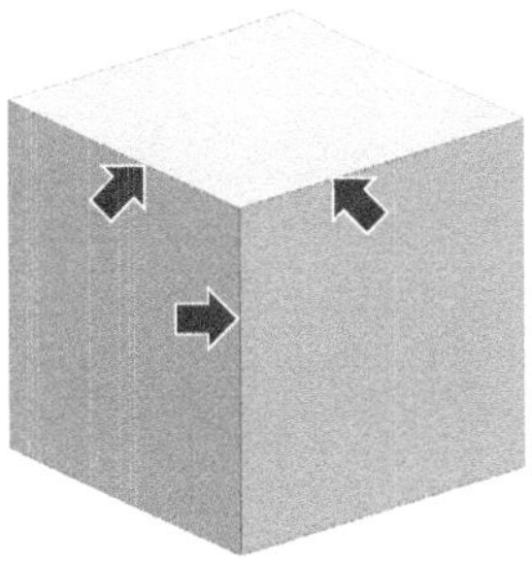

Fig 6-46 Edges to Select

Fig 6-47 Corner Setback Option

1. Create an arbitrarily named part file and create a block with a dimension of 100 x 100 x 100 mm.

2. Click the **Edge Blend** icon and reset the dialog box.

3. Select the three edges as specified in Fig 6-46.

4. Enter 20 in the **Radius 1** input box and press the **Enter** key.

5. Expand the **Corner Setback** option group by clicking Ⓐ specified in Fig 6.47 and click the **End Point** option as specified by Ⓑ in Fig 6-47.

6. Select the vertex Ⓒ shown in Fig 6-48.

7. Enter the setback values as shown in Fig 6-49.

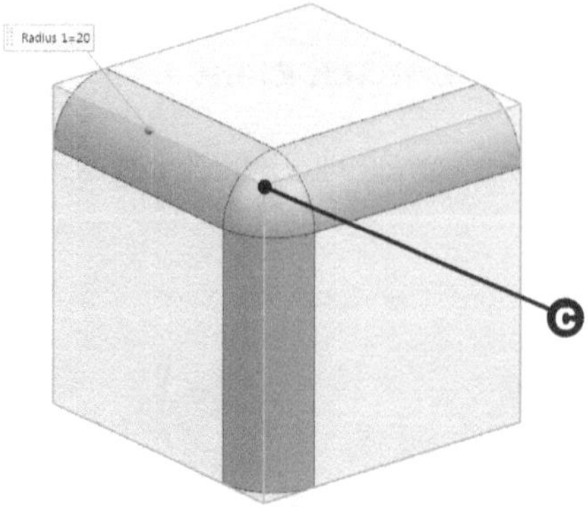

Fig 6-48 Corner to Select

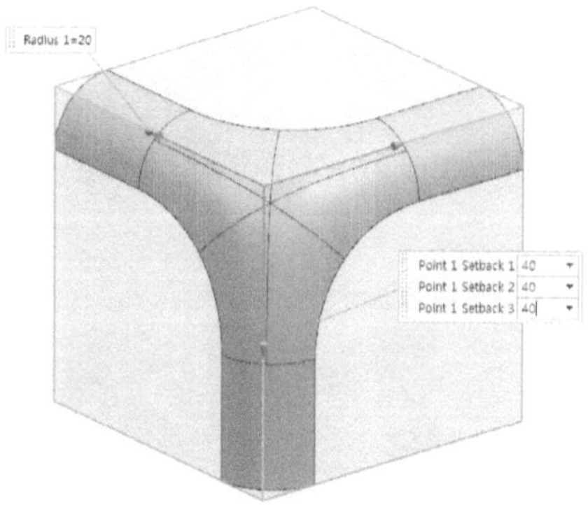

Fig 6-49 Setback Values

8. Click **OK** in the dialog box.

9. Close without saving the file.

END of Exercise

! *Point M Setback N*

Fig 6-50 shows the case of defining four setback points where three edges meet for each. Therefore, the number of setback handle is 12. Each setback value can be identified by the point and setback number as shown in Fig 6-51.

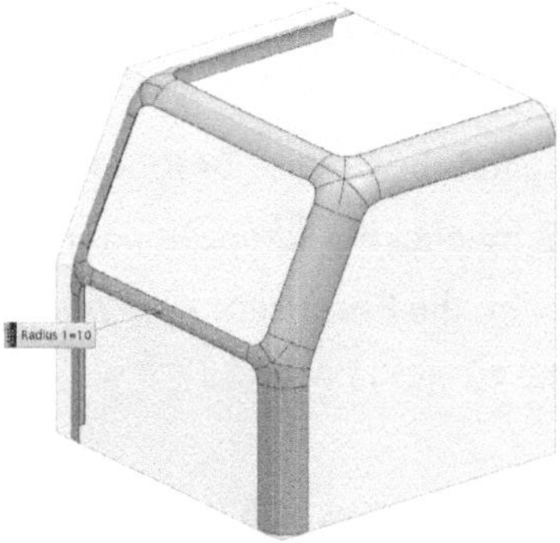

Fig 6-50 Four Setback Points

Fig 6-51 Point and Setback Number

Open the file ch06_ex06.prt and apply edge blend as shown in Fig 6-53. All fillet radiuses are 10 mm except for the one specified in Fig 6-52. Apply a setback distance for yourself.

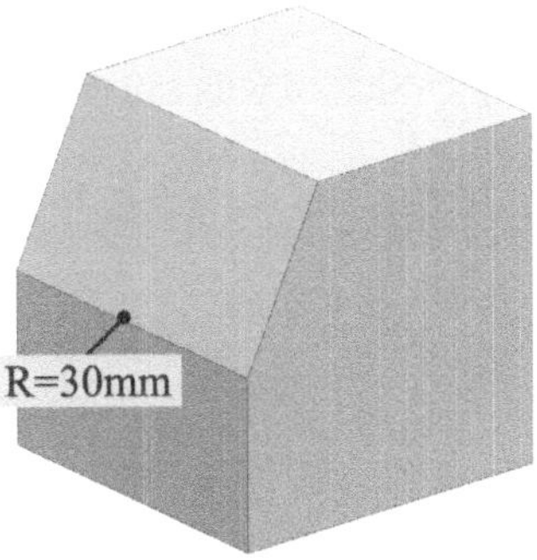

Fig 6-52 Before Edge Blend

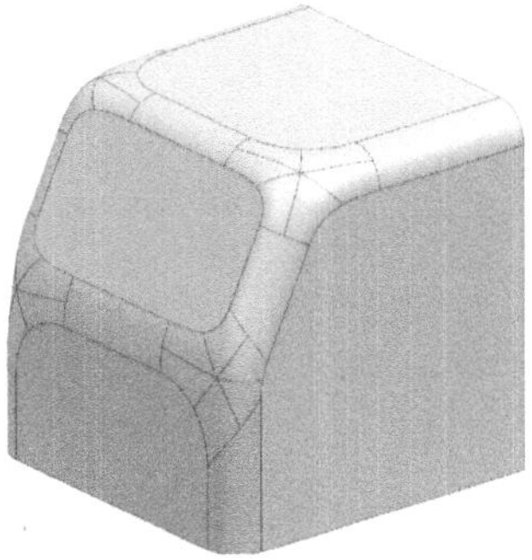

<Shaded with Edges>

<Shaded>

Fig 6-53 After Edge Blend

Hints!

1. You have to select all the contributing edges in a single edge blend feature. Use the **Add New Set** option to define the R30 blend in addition to the R10 blends.
2. Select the four corners to apply setback blends.

END of Exercise

Exercise 07 Setback Blend - 3

ch06_ex07.prt

Open the file ch06_ex07.prt and apply edge blend as shown in Fig 6-55. The fillet radius is 5 mm for all edges except the bottom. Apply 5 mm setback distances.

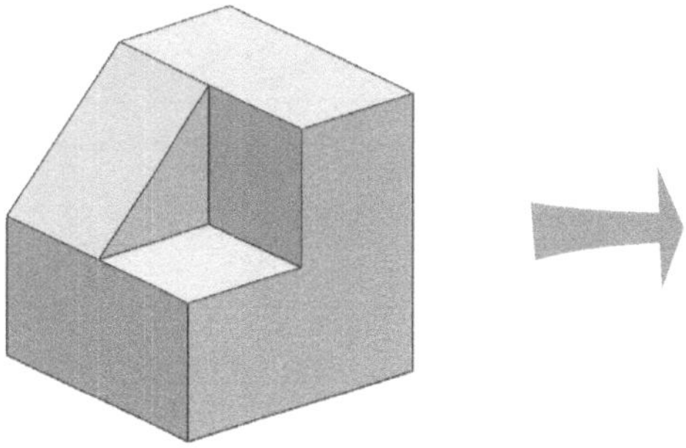

Fig 6-54 Before Edge Blend

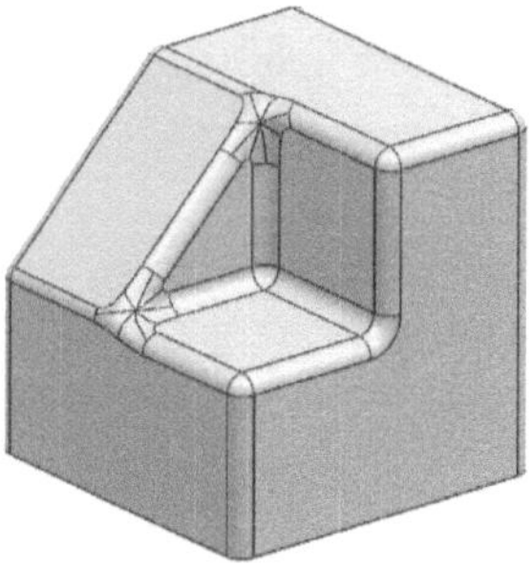

<Shaded with Edges>

<Shaded>

Fig 6-56 After Edge Blend

Hint!

Apply edge blend three times as shown in Fig 6-56.

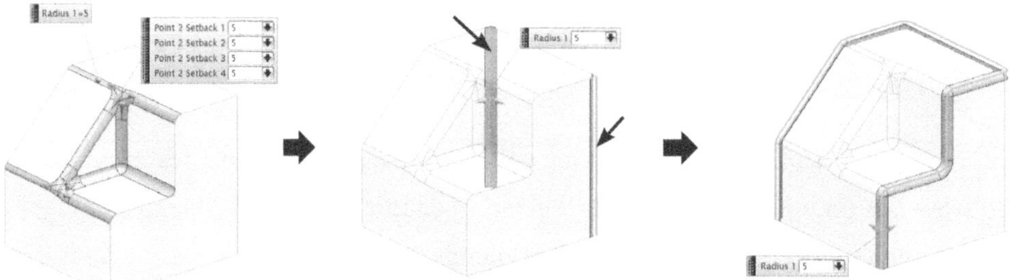

Fig 6-55 Applying Three Edge Blends in Sequence

END of Exercise

Selecting Hidden Edges in Shaded Rendering Style

Remember that you cannot select geometries such as edges, lines and faces that are not visible in the graphics window by default. When you select the edges or curves in a shaded rendering style, you have to rotate the model view or change the rendering style to **Static Wireframe**.

In NX, there is an option that allows you select hidden wireframes in the selection bar as specified in Fig 6-57. You can highlight the hidden edges when you move the mouse cursor on the edge.

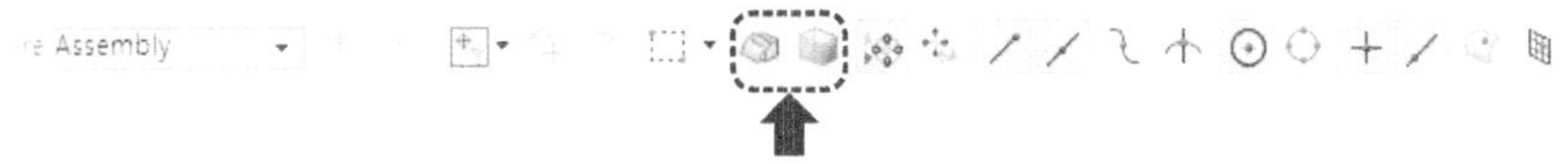

Fig 6-57 Options to Select Highlight Hidden Edge

Limit Blend Exercise 08

Let's learn the process of applying a limit blend on a portion of an edge.

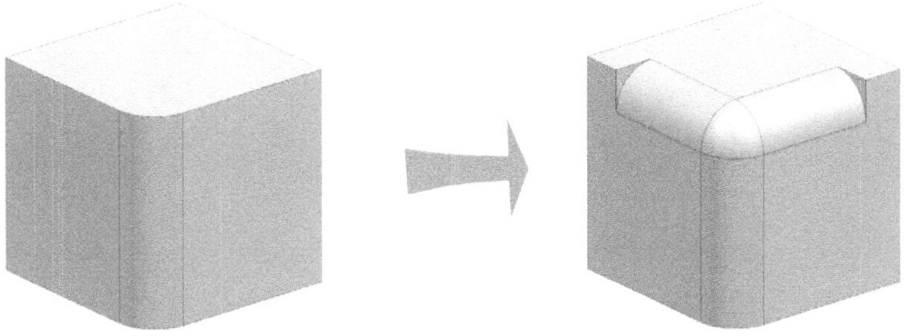

Fig 6-58 Before and After Applying Limit Blend

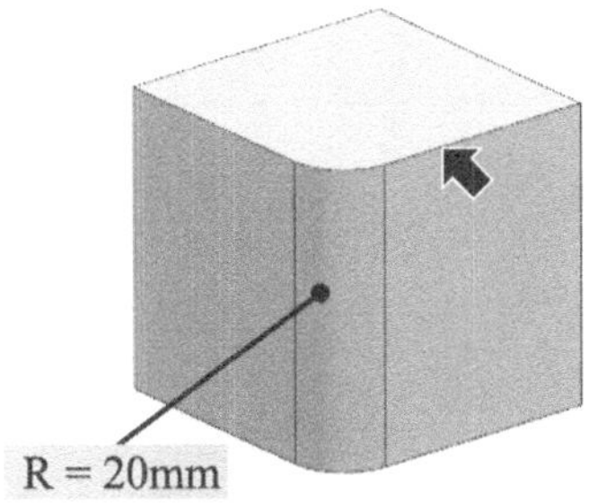

Fig 6-59 A Block

1. Create an arbitrarily named part file and create a block with a dimension of 100 x 100 x 100 mm.

2. Apply an R20 fillet on a vertical edge as shown in Fig 6-59.

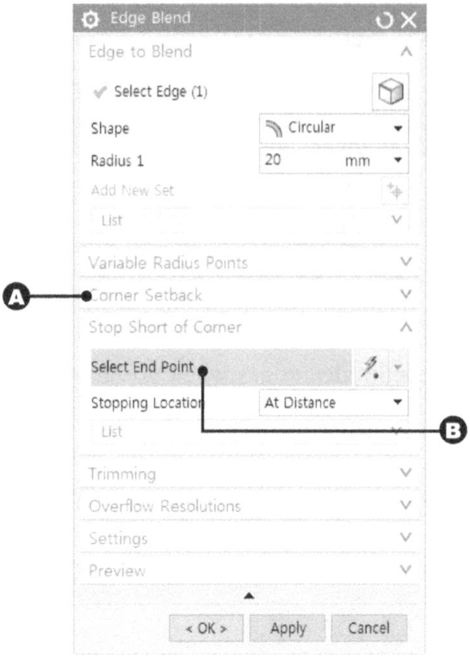

Fig 6-60 Stop Short of Corner Option

3. Click the **Edge Blend** icon again.

4. Select the edges to apply the limit blend as specified by the arrow in Fig 6-59.

5. Expand the **Stop Short of Corner** option group by clicking the title Ⓐ in Fig 6-60.

6. Click the **Select End Point** option (Ⓑ in Fig 6-60).

7. Select the vertex Ⓒ in Fig 6-61 and enter 20 in the **Arc Length** input box.

8. Define the limit blend for the vertex Ⓓ in the same way.

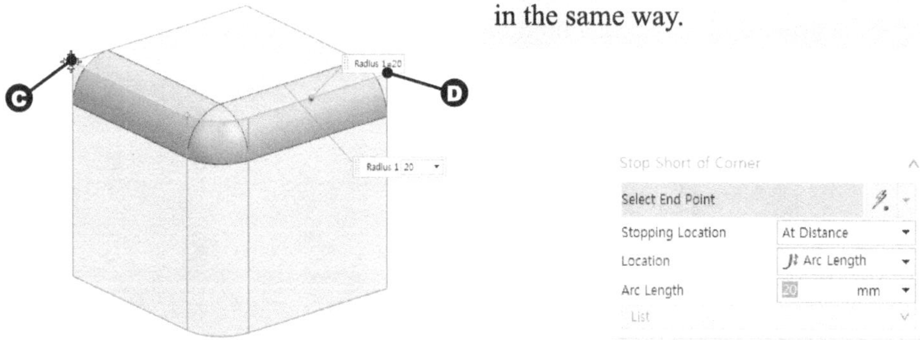

Fig 6-61 Selecting Corners

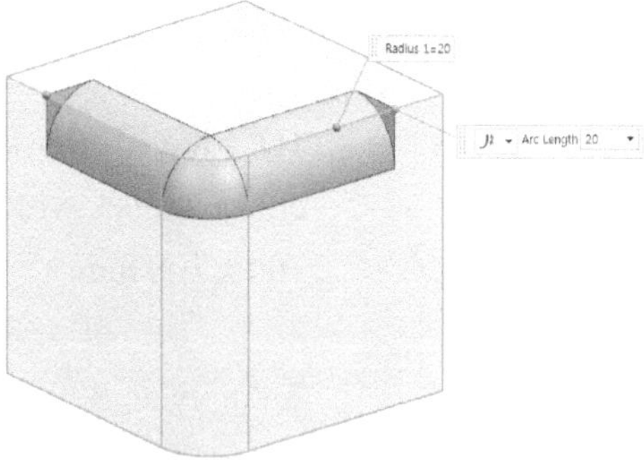

Fig 6-62 Preview of the Limit Blend

END of Exercise

Usage of Limit Blend

The corner specified by (+) in Fig 6-63 is the vertex where six edges meet which is a very complex geometry. You can create a more aesthetic surface at the corner by applying limit blends. Then create an **N-Sided Surface** and apply the **Patch** command to create the surface at the corner as shown in Fig 6-66.

Fig 6-63 Complex Vertex

Fig 6-64 Result of Limit Blend

Fig 6-66 Patch

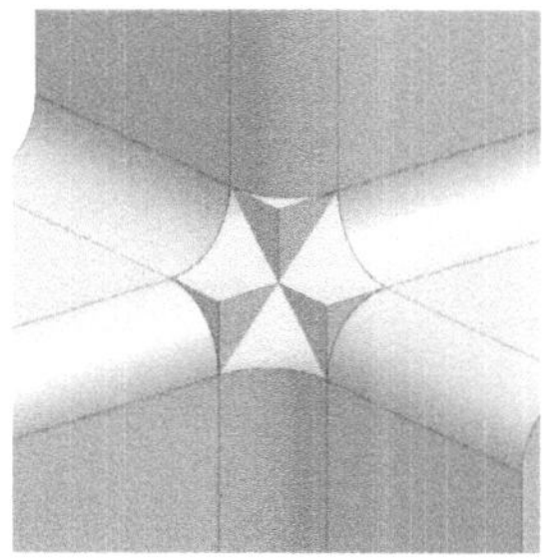

Fig 6-65 N-Side Surface

6.3 Chamfer

Sharp edges can be chamfered at a specified angle or by entering a distance from the sharp edge. Material can be removed or added to eliminate the sharp edge of a part. Fig 6-67 shows the case of removing material and Fig 6-68 shows the case of filling material.

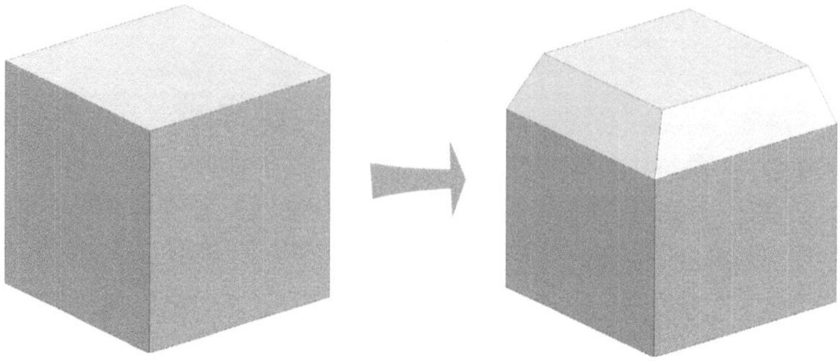

Fig 6-67 Removing Material by Chamfer

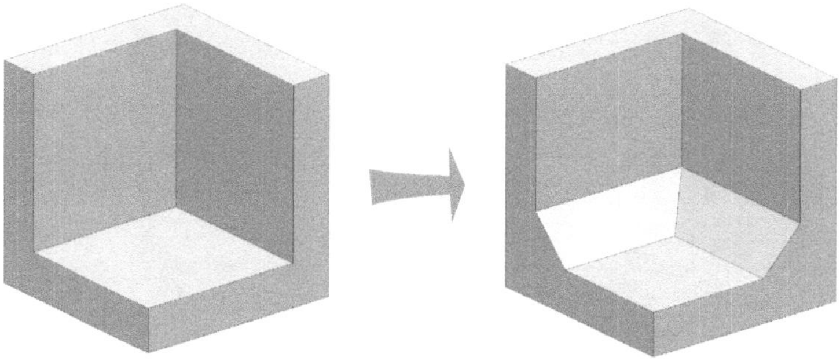

Fig 6-68 Adding Material by Chamfer

6.3.1 Procedure

Keep to the following procedure to apply chamfer on an edge. The step numbers correspond to the steps in Fig 6-69.

① Click the **Chamfer** icon in the **Feature** icon group.
② Select the edge to apply chamfer.
③ Set the **Offsets** option and press **OK**.

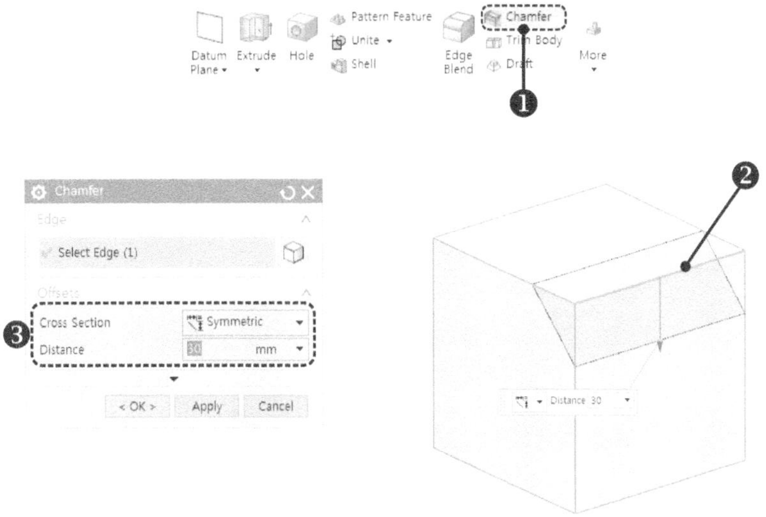

Fig 6-69 Procedure of Applying Chamfer

6.3.2 Cross Section Option

Symmetric

Chamfer is defined by entering a distance symmetrically from the edge to be chamfered as depicted in Fig 6-70. This method is the simplest and most widely used.

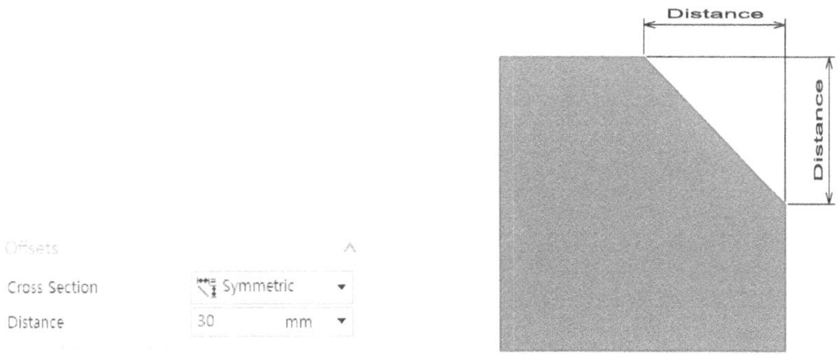

Fig 6-70 Symmetric Cross Section

Asymmetric

Chamfer distance can be defined asymmetrically along each face that shares the edge to be chamfered. If you click the **Reverse Direction** button in the dialog box, the chamfer distances along the face is switched.

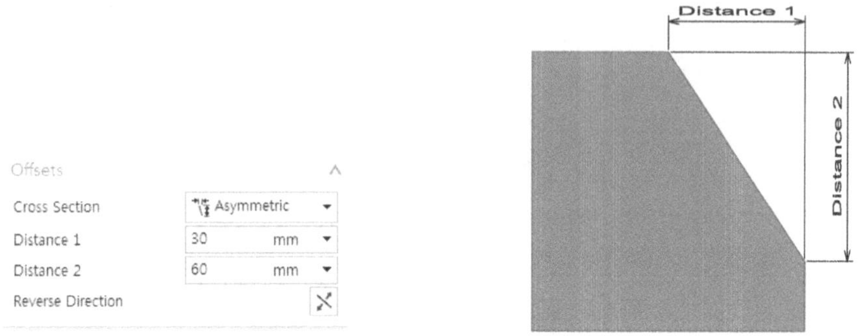

Fig 6-71 Asymmetric Cross Section

Offset and Angle

You can apply chamfer by defining a distance along a face and an angle from the face. If you click the **Reverse Direction** button in the dialog box, the distance is defined along the other face which shares the edge to be chamfered.

Fig 6-72 Offset and Angle Cross Section

6.3.3 Offset Method

Offset method can be set in the **Settings** option group which is available by expanding the dialog box.

Offset Edges along Faces

Chamfer can be applied accurately for simple geometry. Offset values are measured from the edge to be chamfered along each face that shares the edge.

Fig 6-73 explains the offset measurement schematically. Offset distances are measured starting from the edge to be chamfered (ⓐ) along each offset direction (ⓑ and ⓒ). Chamfer face (ⓓ) is created by connecting the offset edges defined on the faces that share the edge to be chamfered.

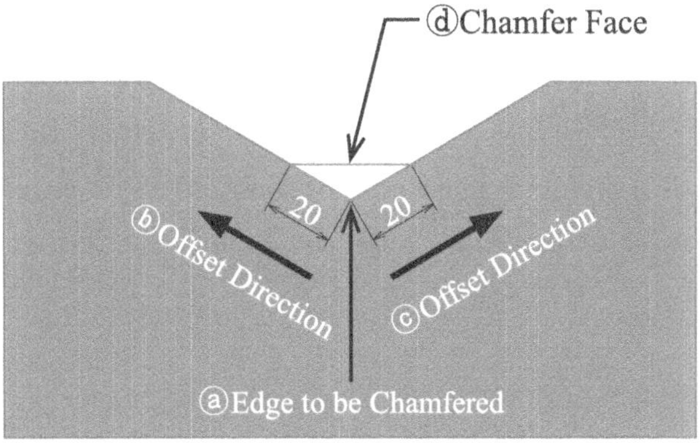

Fig 6-73 Offset Edges along Faces

Offset Faces and Trim

Chamfer face can be created for complex geometry. Offset distance is not measured from the edge to be chamfered but measured from the intersection of the two offset faces that share the edge to be chamfered.

Fig 6-74 explains the offset measurement schematically. The two faces are offset along the offset direction Next, project normal faces starting from the intersection (ⓒ) of the two offset faces (ⓑ) along the original face. Chamfer face (ⓓ) is created by connecting the edges constructed by the intersection of the normal faces and the original faces sharing the edge to be chamfered.

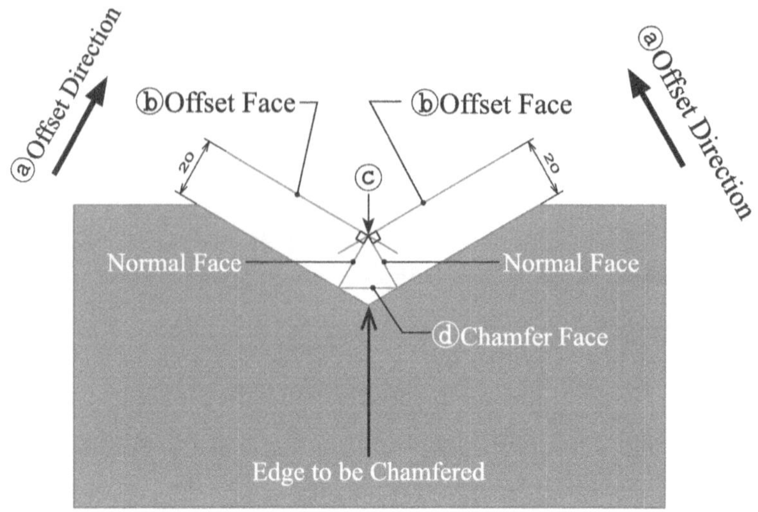

Fig 6-74 Offset Faces and Trim

Alerts while Applying Chamfer

When you apply chamfer on the upper edges of the model shown in Fig 6-75, an alert message shown in Fig 6-76 appears. You have to choose Offset Faces and Trim as the offset method.

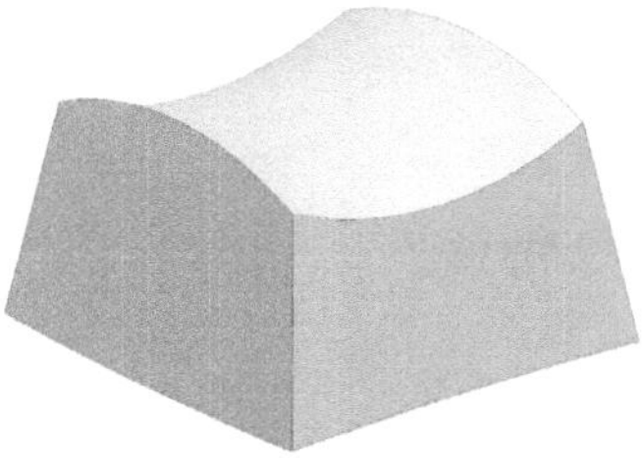

Fig 6-75 Example

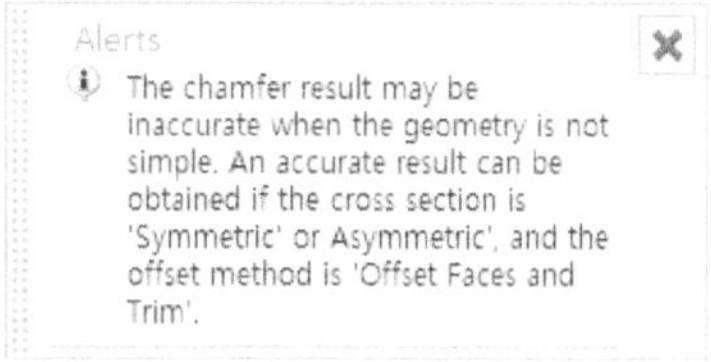

Fig 6-76 Alert Message

Removing Feature Alert Icon in the Part Navigator

Chamfer can be created by ignoring the alert message shown in Fig 6-76. However, an icon marked by 'i' appears in front of the chamfer feature in **Part Navigator** as designated by the arrow in Fig 6-77.

Fig 6-77 Information Alert Icon

Fig 6-78 Clear Information Alerts Option

This icon is called a feature alert icon. You can remove the feature alert icon by choosing the **Clear Feature Info Alerts** option in the pop-up menu as shown in Fig 6-78. The pop-up menu is available by clicking MB3 on an empty area in the Part Navigator as designated by ⓐ in Fig 6-77.

Note that, among the three types of feature alert icons (, and), you can only remove the Information Alert ( ).

6.4 Draft

You can apply draft on a face with reference to the pulling direction of the upper mold. If the side face is not guaranteed a proper draft angle, the part cannot be separated from the mold. Fig 6-79 shows the side face before and after draft, where the pulling direction is upward.

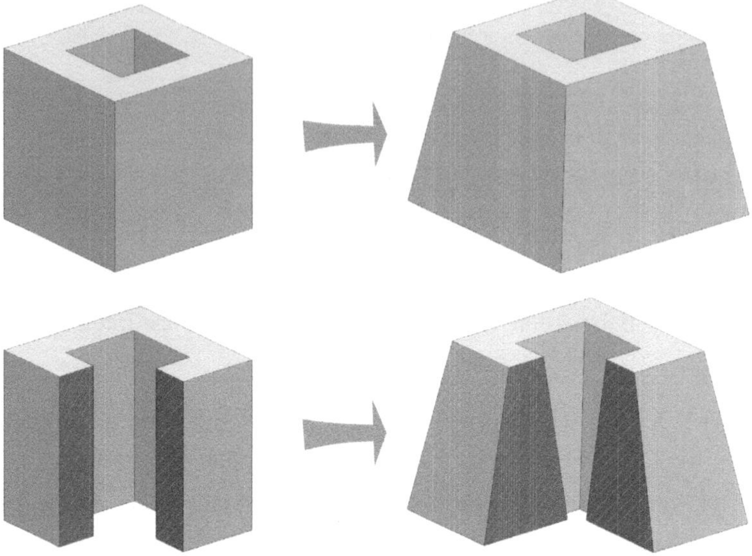

Fig 6-79 Before and After the Draft

Why does the side face of a part have to be slanted? This is a question that arises when you manufacture a part through a mold.

Fig 6-80 shows a part that will be manufactured out of plastic. You will design an upper mold (cavity) and the lower mold (core) as shown in Fig 6-81 and Fig 6-82 respectively.

The two molds are assembled as shown in Fig 6-83 where plastic resin will be injected into the vacant area as designated by ⓐ in Fig 6-83. Temperature is applied to the mold for a while and the resin will become cured as designated by the black area in Fig 6-84. When the part is cured sufficiently, the mold will be opened by pulling the upper mold upward to separate the part from the mold.

However, if the side face of the part or the corresponding face of the mold is parallel to the pulling direction, the side face will be damaged in the area designated by the arrows in Fig 6-85 because of the slip between the faces.

<Top> <Bottom>

Fig 6-80 Sample Part

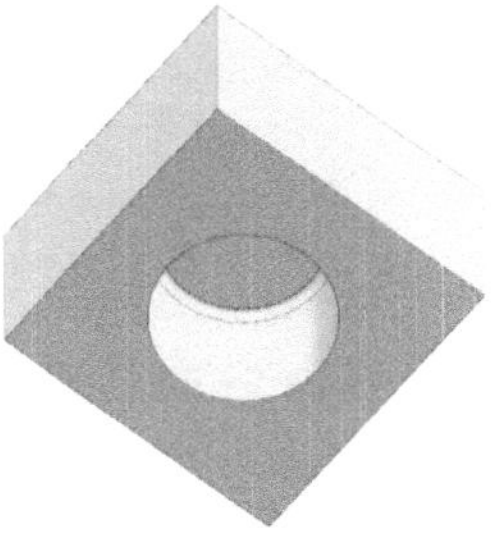

Fig 6-81 Upper Mold (Cavity)

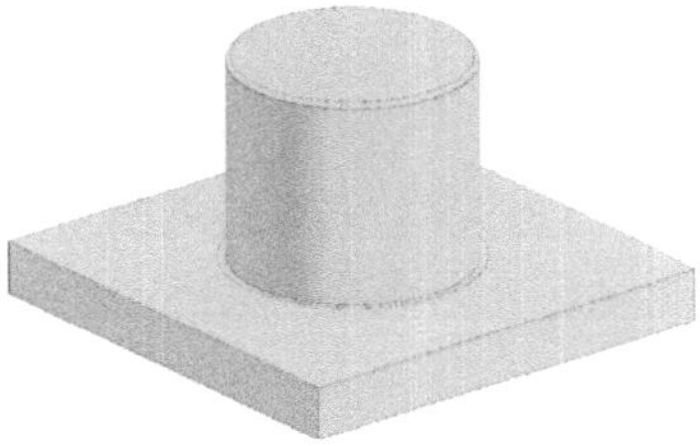

Fig 6-82 Lower Mold (Core)

Fig 6-83 Assembled Mold

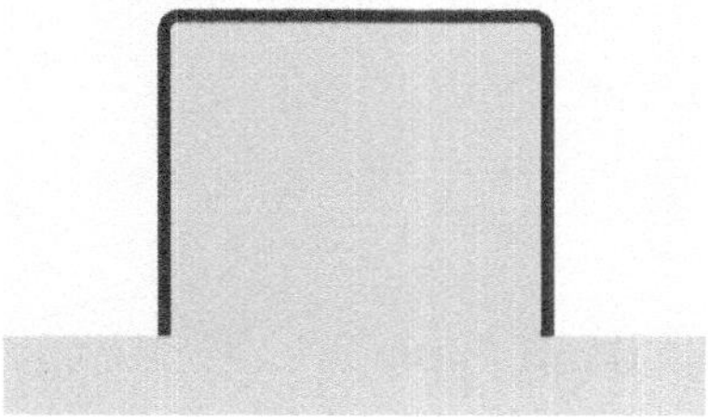

Fig 6-84 Cured Product (Black)

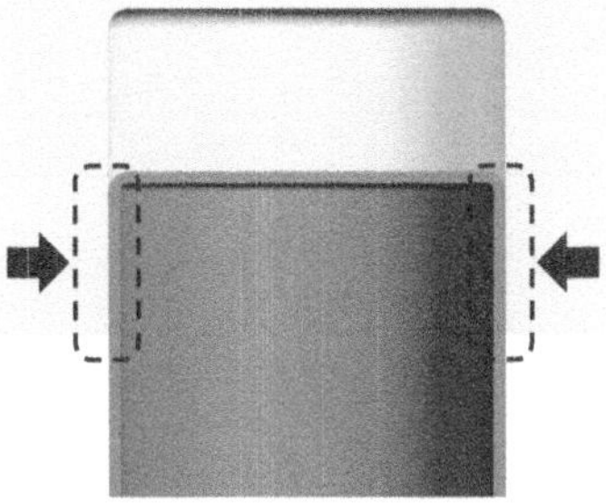

Fig 6-85 Side Face Where Slip Occurs

Damage to the side faces that occurs while the part is separated from the mold can be avoided by applying draft as shown in Fig 6-86. Positive angle draft means that the angle is applied so that the part can be separated easily as shown in Fig 6-87. If you apply a reverse angle draft, you cannot separate the part or the part will be broken.

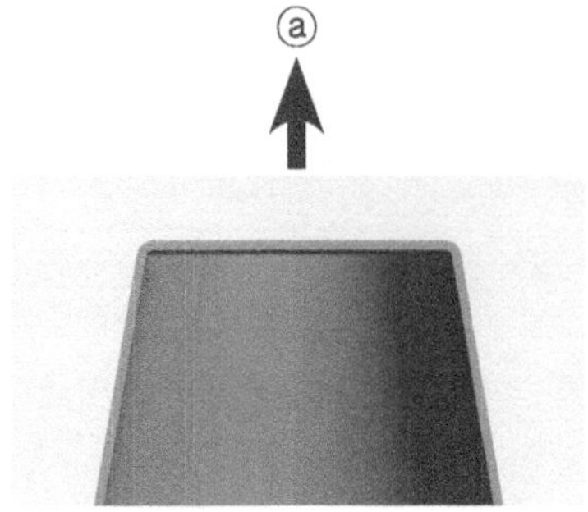

Fig 6-86 Part Applied with Draft Angle

Fig 6-87 Parting

Draw Direction (ⓐ in Fig 6-86)

The direction of movement of the upper mold (cavity) to separate the part from the mold is called a **Draw Direction**. Sometimes it is called a **Die Direction** or an **Eject Direction**.

6.4.1 Draft Type

Fig 6-88 shows four types of draft. This textbook explains how to apply three types of draft through step by step exercises: From Plane, From Edges and Tangent to Faces.

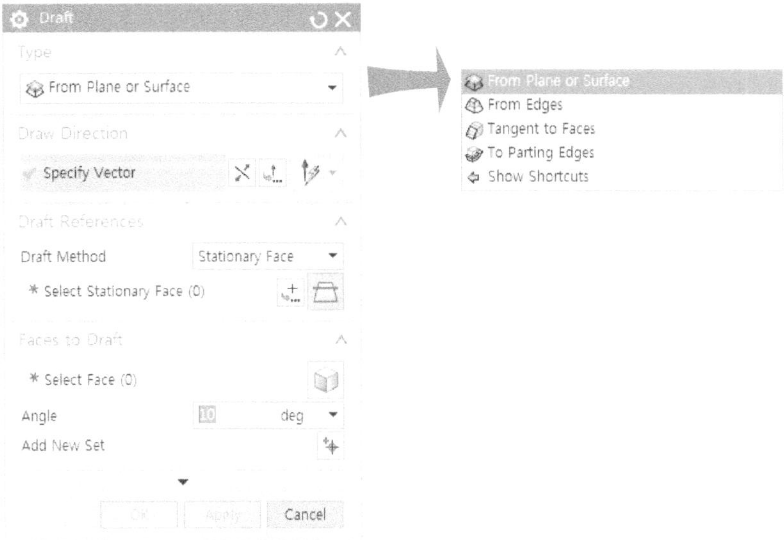

Fig 6-88 Types of Draft

ch06_ex09.prt **From Plane or Surface Type Draft** **Exercise 09**

If you choose **From Plane or Surface** as the type of draft, the **Draw Direction** and the **Stationary Plane** option become available. Drafting angle is applied starting from the stationary plane. The stationary plane does not need to be connected to the face to draft.

Open the given file and learn how to apply the **From Plane or Surface** type draft.

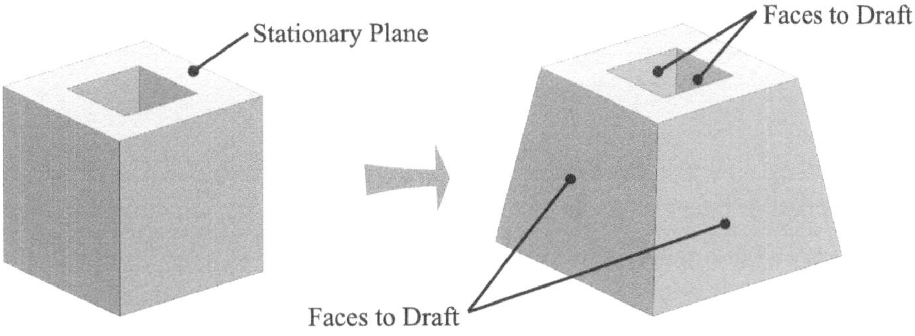

Fig 6-89 Applying "From Plane or Surface" Type Draft

1. Open the given file ch06_ex09.prt.

2. Click the **Draft** icon in the **Feature** icon group.

3. Reset the dialog box. Note that **From Plane** is the default type of draft.

The option **Specify Vector** in the **Draw Direction** option group is highlighted as designated in Fig 6-90. The Z direction is highlighted in the graphics window because the default draw direction is ZC of the WCS.

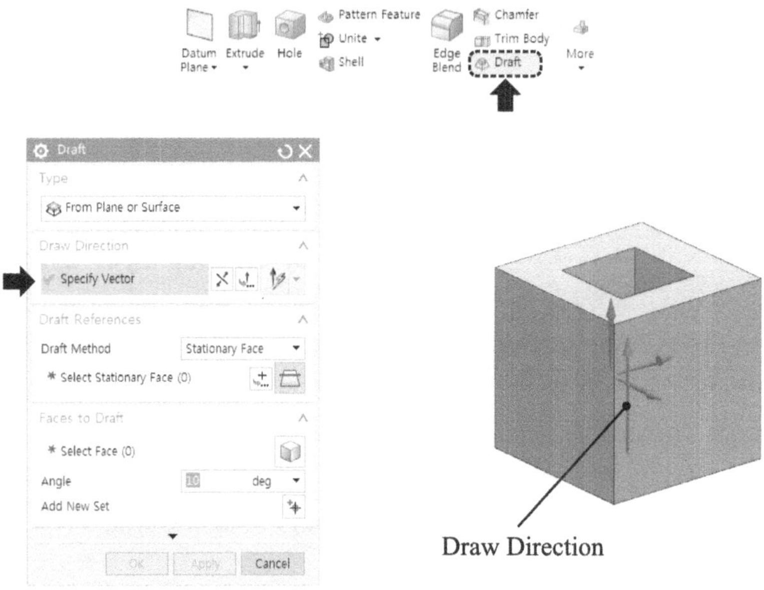

Fig 6-90 Specifying Draw Direction

4. Click MB2 because the draw direction is correct. If the direction does not correlate with the design intent, you can specify another direction by selecting an object. The **Stationary Plane** option is highlighted.

5. Select the face Ⓐ in Fig 6-91 as the stationary plane. The **Faces to Draft** option is highlighted.

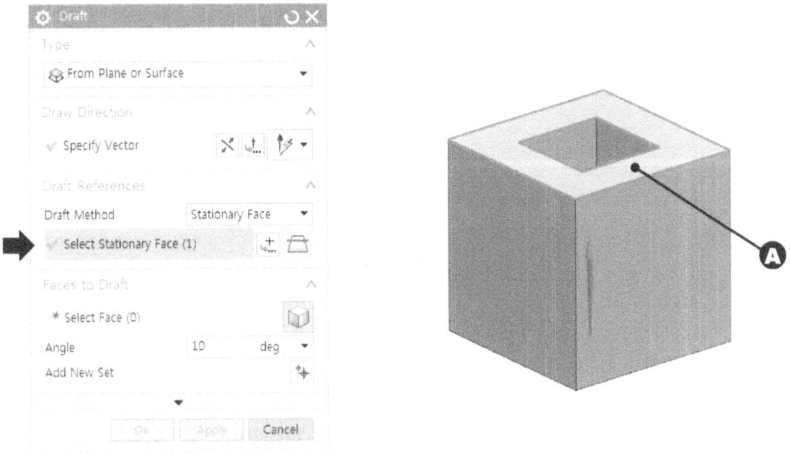

Fig 6-91 Selecting Stationary Plane

6. Select the four outer faces and four inner faces to draft as specified by **B** in Fig 6-92.

7. Enter 5 in the **Angle 1** input box and press the **Enter** key. The drafted face is previewed as shown in Fig 6-92.

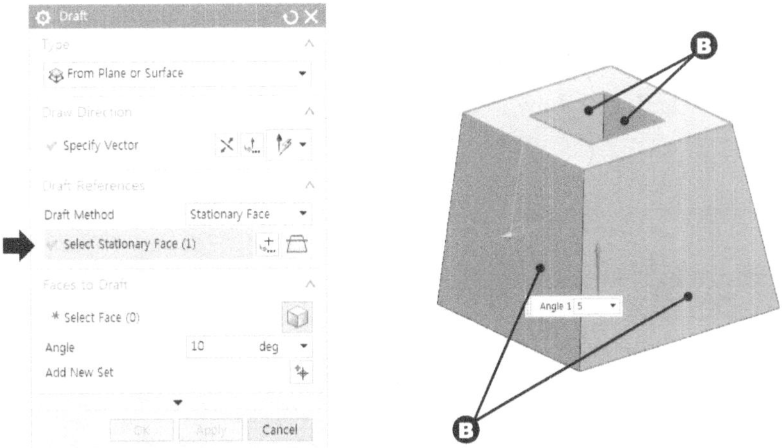

Fig 6-92 Selecting Faces to Draft

8. Press OK in the dialog box. Fig 6-93 shows the result of draft.

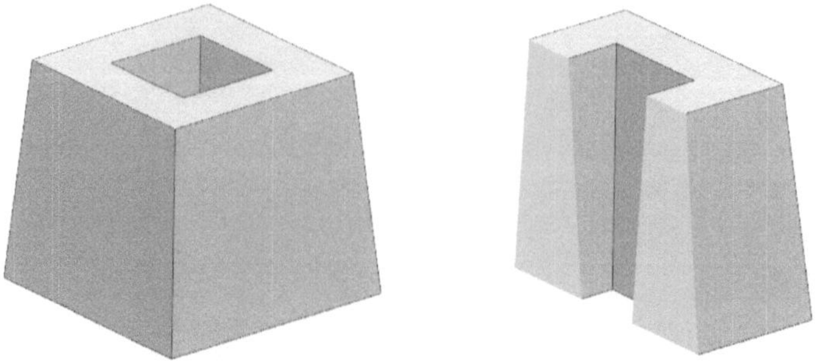

Fig 6-93 Completed Model

END of Exercise

Exercise 10 From Edges Type Draft

ch06_ex10.prt

If you choose **From Edges** as the type of draft, the **Draw Direction** and the **Stationary Edges** option become available. Drafting angle is applied from the stationary edges. Note that you do not need to select the faces to draft. Drafting is applied to the faces that share the stationary edges but do not guarantee the specified drafting angle.

Open the given file and learn how to apply the **From Edges** type draft.

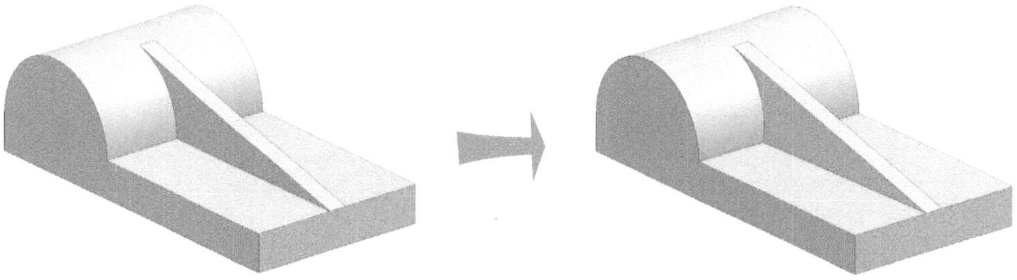

Fig 6-94 Applying "From Edges" Type Draft

1. Open the given file ch06_ex10.prt.

2. Click the **Draft** icon in the **Feature** icon group.

3. Reset the dialog box.

4. Select **From Edges** in the **Type** dropdown list. Make sure that the draw direction is set to +ZC direction of WCS and press MB2.

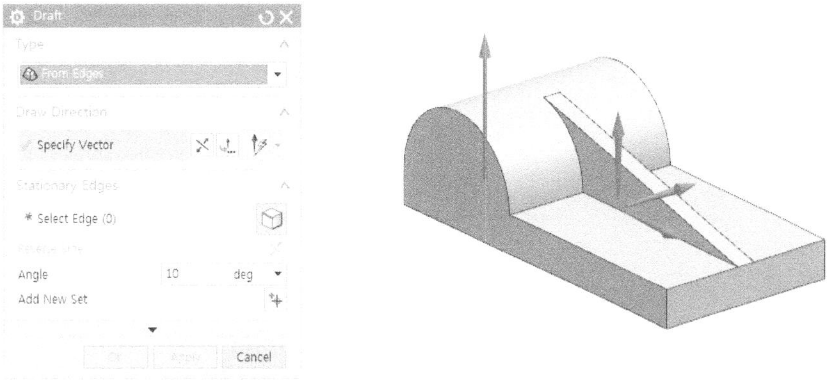

Fig 6-95 Specifying Draw Direction

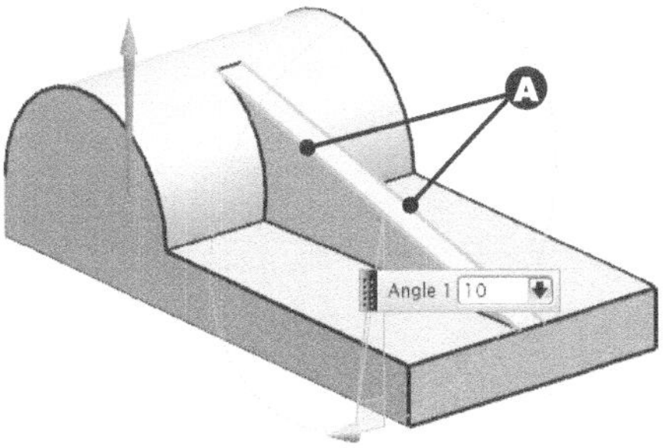

Fig 6-96 Selecting Stationary Edges

5. Make sure that the **Stationary Edges** option is highlighted and select the edge specified by Ⓐ in Fig 6-96. The draft result is previewed.

6. Press **OK**. Note that you do not need to select the faces to draft. Fig 6-97 shows the result of draft.

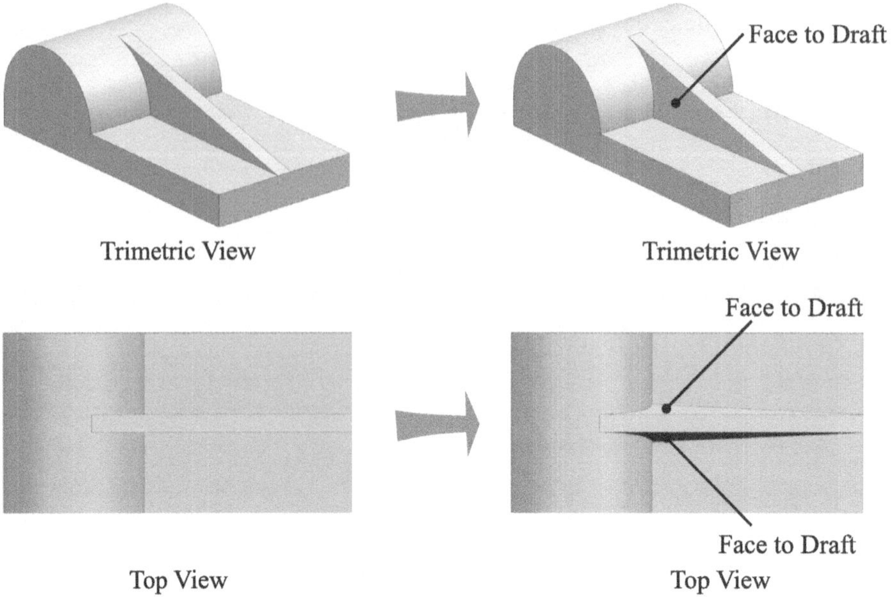

Fig 6-97 Completed Model

END of Exercise

Variable Draft Points

The **Variable Draft Points** option is activated when you apply draft with the **From Edges** type. You can define various draft angles for the specified points.

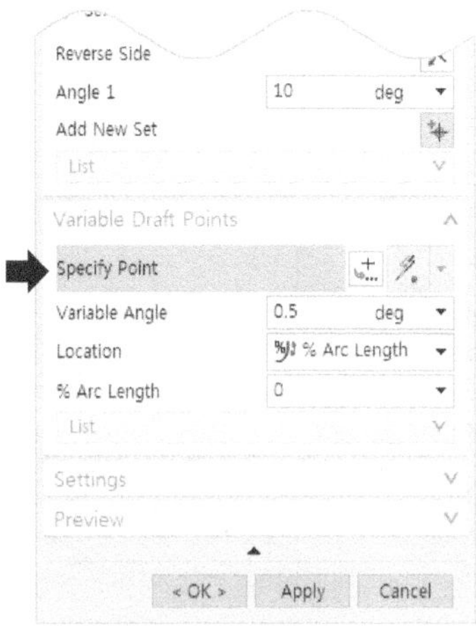

Fig 6-98 Variable Draft Points Option

Faces Ⓐ and Ⓑ in Fig 6-99 require draft. If you choose **Tangent to Faces** as the type of draft, the **Draw Direction** and the **Tangent Faces** option become available. Tangent face at the specified draft angle is created tangent to the selected face.

Open the given file and learn how to apply the **Tangent to Faces** type draft.

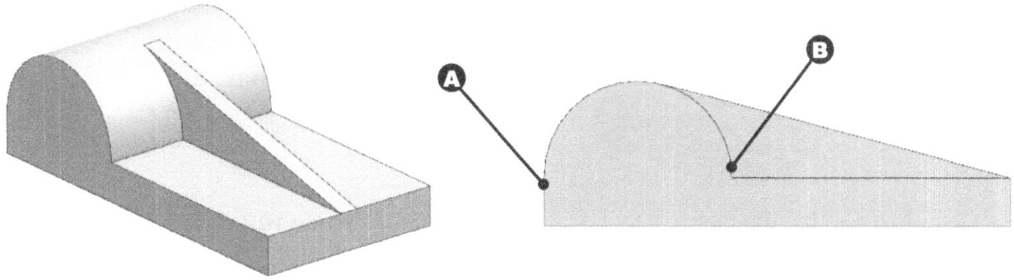

Fig 6-99 Face to Apply Draft

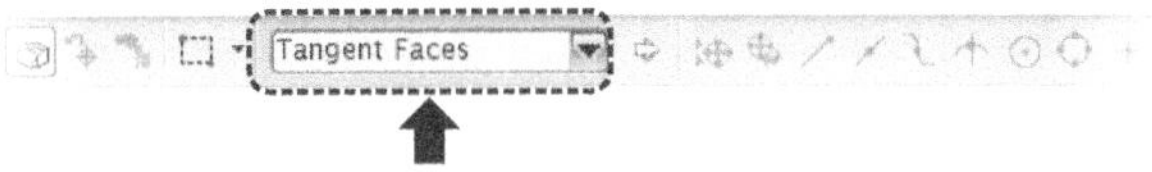

1. Open the given file ch06_ex11.prt.

2. Click the **Draft** icon in the **Feature** icon group.

3. Reset the dialog box.

4. Select **Tangent to Faces** in the **Type** dropdown list. Make sure that the draw direction is set to +ZC direction of WCS and press MB2.

5. Make sure that the **Tangent to Faces** option is highlighted. Note that the **Face Rule** option is set to **Tangent Faces**.

6. Select the cylindrical face specified in Fig 6-100.

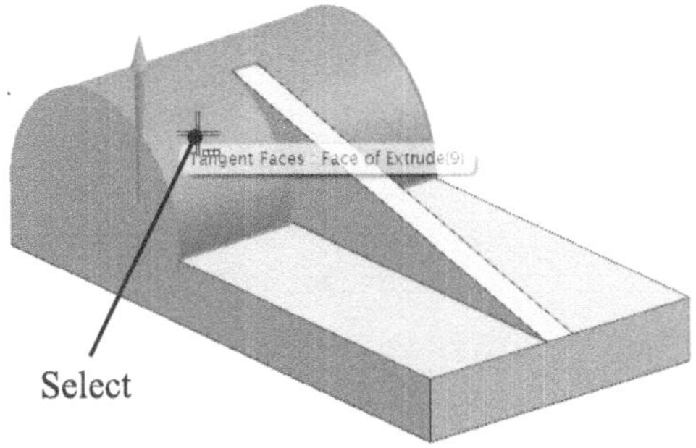

Fig 6-100 Selecting Tangent Face

7. Enter 20° in the **Angle 1** input box and press the **Enter** key. A preview is shown as Fig 6-101.

8. Press **OK** in the dialog box. Align the view to Front and confirm that the draft angle is applied correctly.

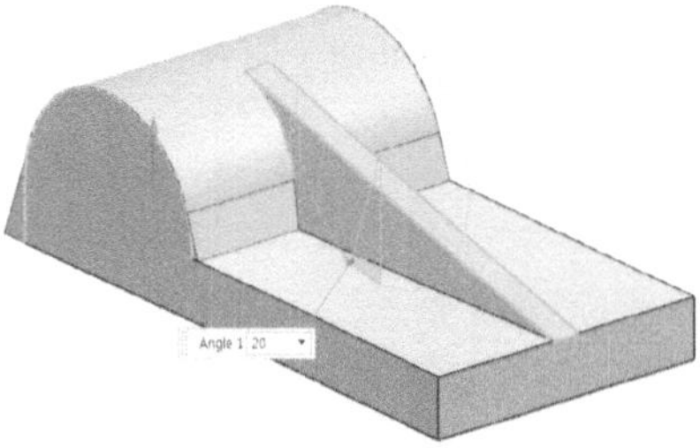

Fig 6-101 Preview

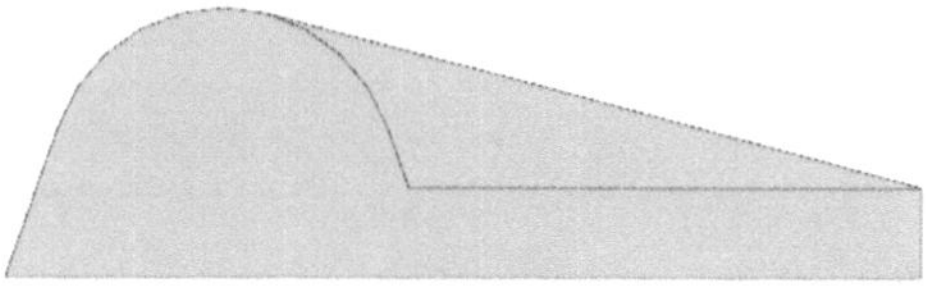

Fig 6-102 Front View

END of Exercise

! *Important!*

The key point in applying the Tangent to Faces type draft is that you have to select the faces ⓐ and ⓑ at the same time. Selecting face ⓒ does not affect the result because the face is normal to the draw direction.

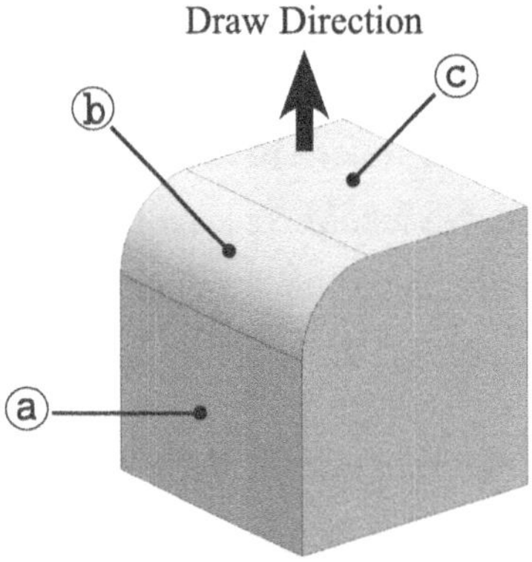

Fig 6-103 Faces in Model

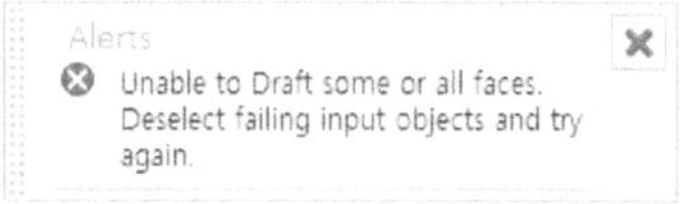

Fig 6-104 Alert Message

Note that if you select only face ⓐ, an alert as shown in Fig 6-104 will appear.

ch06_ex12.prt

Applying Draft Exercise 12

Open the given file ch06_ex12.prt and apply 10° draft for the faces as specified in Fig 6-105. The draw direction is parallel to the ZC axis of WCS.

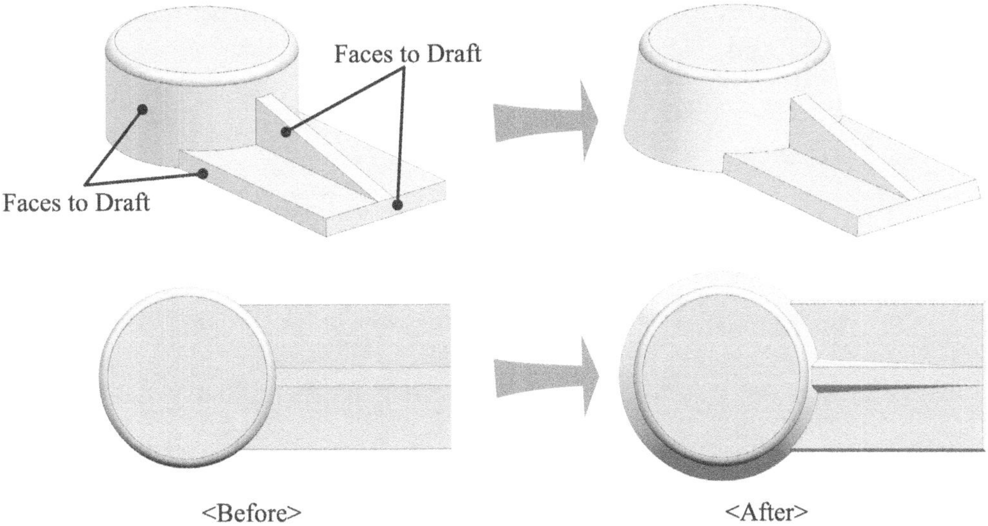

Fig 6-105 Before and After Applying Draft

! *Hint!*

1. Apply draft for all surfaces that are parallel to the draw direction. The faces to apply draft are displayed in yellow in the file for this exercise.
2. You have to use at least two types of draft.
3. When the completed model is viewed from the Top, the yellow faces should not be visible.

END of Exercise

6.4.2 Other Options in Draft

If you use the **Parting Face** method as the **From Plane or Surface** type draft, you can apply draft with respect to a face, datum plane or a point. Selecting a point as the draft reference, you are specifying a normal plane to the draw direction that passes through the selected point. The reference of the draft is defined at the intersection between the parting face and the faces to draft.

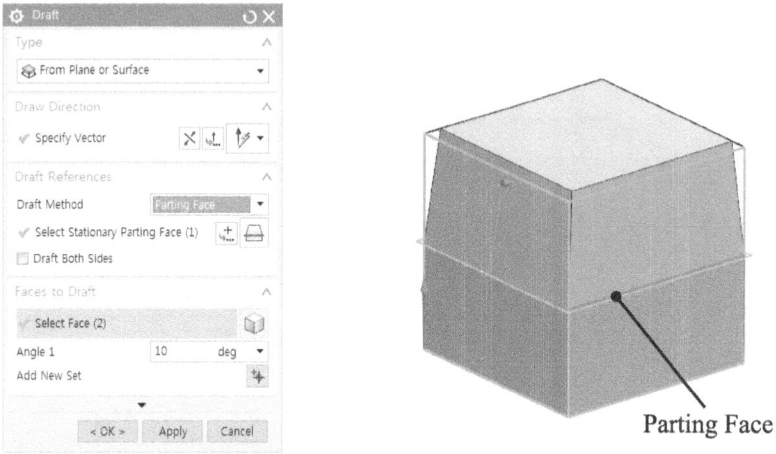

Fig 6-106 Parting Face Method

If you select the **Draft Both Sides** option, you can apply draft for both sides against the parting face. You can even apply a different draft angle for each side by unchecking the **Symmetric Angle** option.

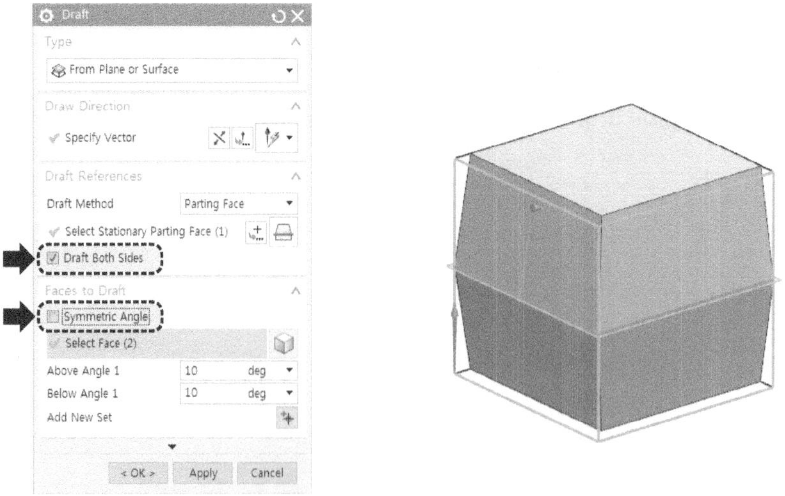

Fig 6-107 Draft Both Sides Option

If you use the **Stationary and Parting Face** method as the **From Plane or Surface** type draft, you can specify both the stationary face and the parting face. Note that the parting and the stationary faces are the same in the **Parting Face** method.

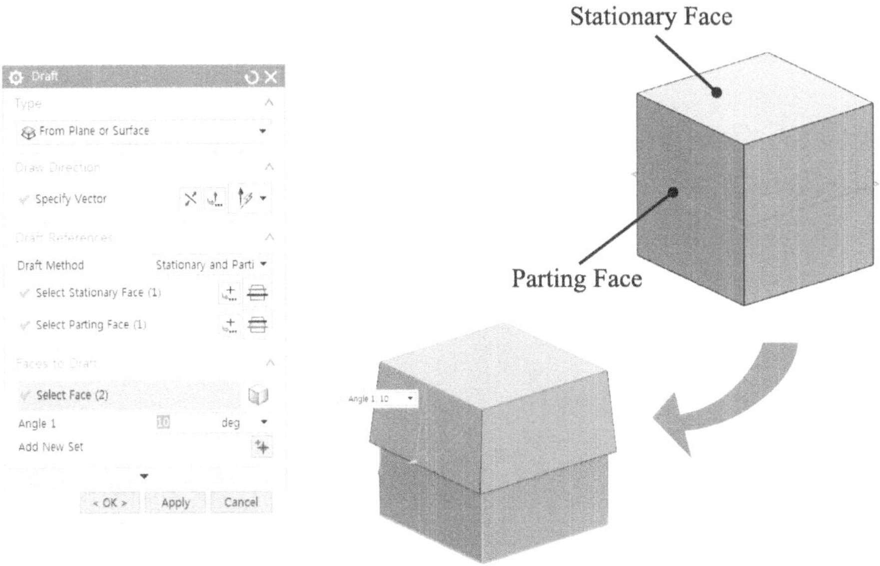

Fig 6-108 Stationary and Parting Face Method

If you use the **From Parting Edges** type draft, you can apply draft with respect to the pre-defined edges. The parting edges can be defined using the **Divide Face** command.

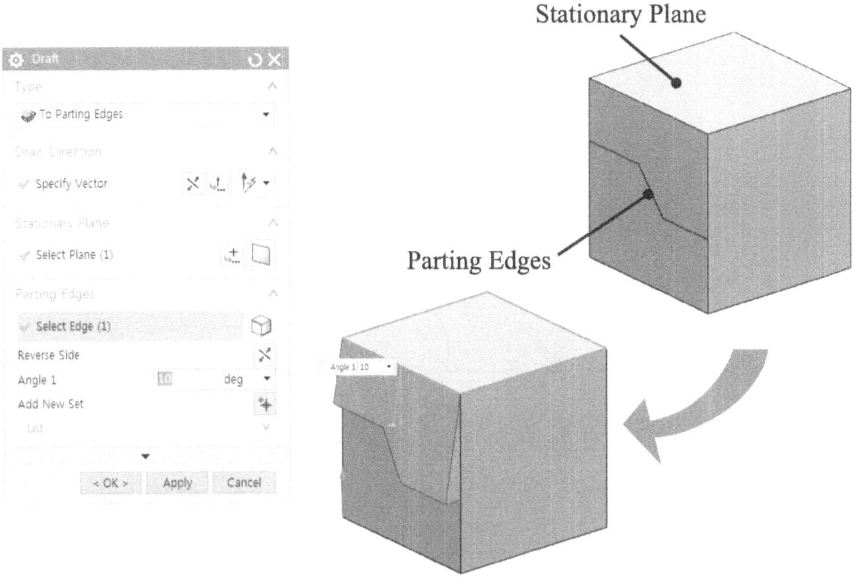

Fig 6-109 From Parting Edges Type

6.5 Shell

This command hollows out a solid body to create a thin wall.

Procedure

1. Click the **Shell** icon in the **Feature** icon group.
2. Reset the **Shell** dialog box.
3. Select the **Face to Pierce**.
4. Enter the thickness of the wall.
5. Press **OK** in the **Shell** dialog box.

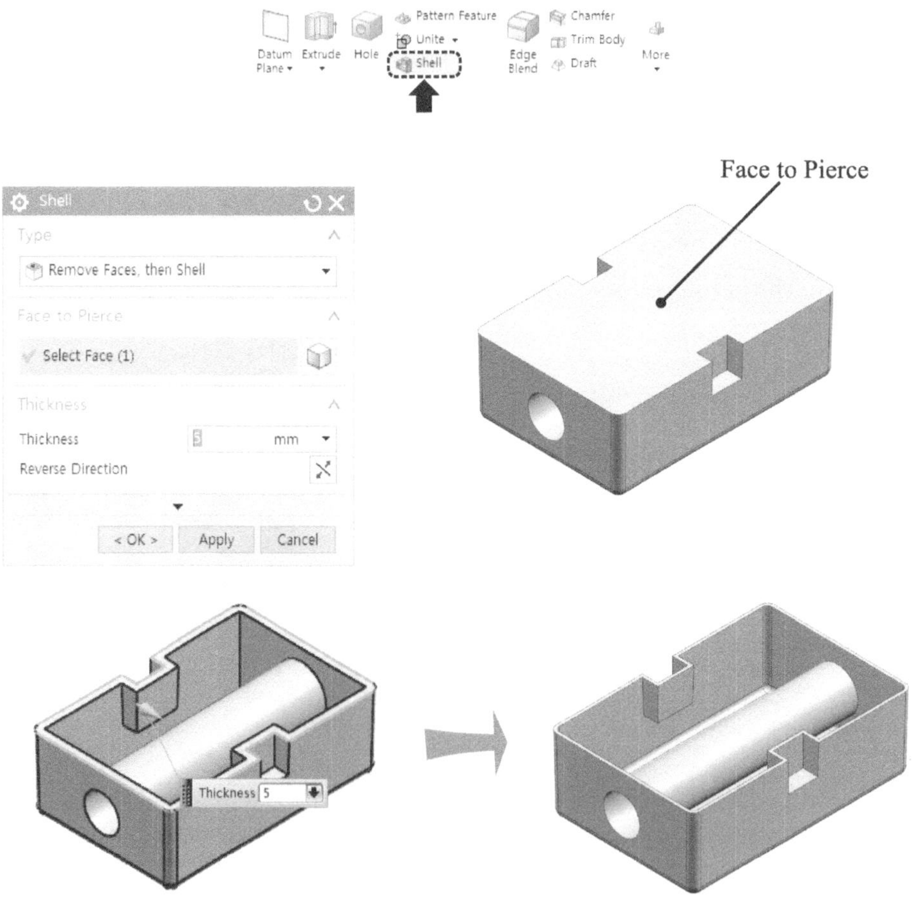

Fig 6-110 Procedure to Apply Shell

You can select as many faces to pierce as required provided that the original solid body is not divided into two or more solid bodies. Fig 6-107 shows an example of specifying several faces to be pierced.

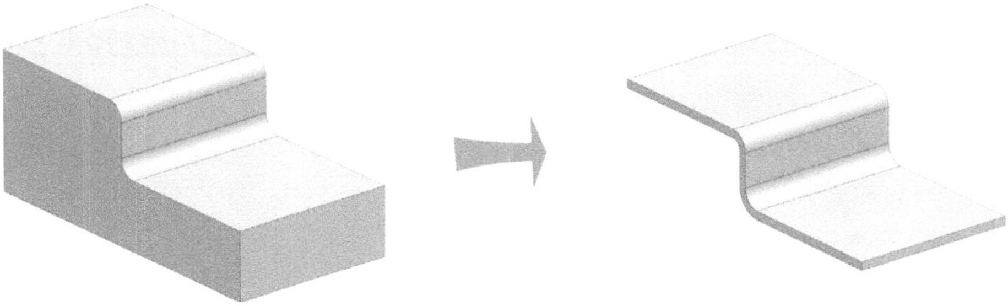

Fig 6-111 Specifying Several Faces to Pierce

6.5.1 Reverse Direction

Thickness of shell command is applied inward to the solid body by default. If you want to apply shell thickness outward, click the **Reverse Direction** option.

Fig 6-108 (a) shows the volume of liquid that will be filled in the bottle. If you want to create a bottle that has the inner volume maintained, you have to apply the **Shell** command by reversing the direction.

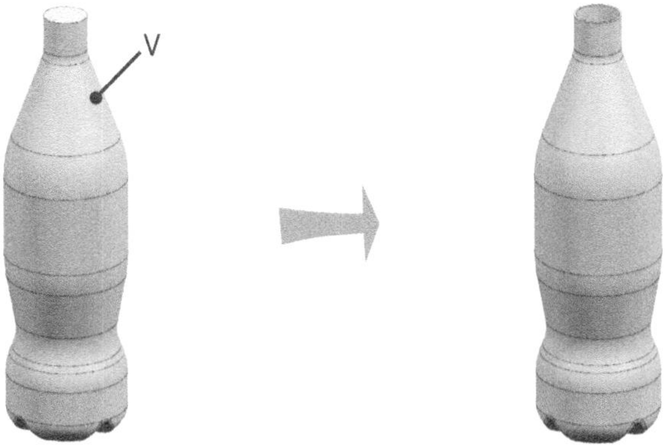

Fig 6-112 Reversing the Shell Thickness Direction

6.5.2 Alternate Thickness

You can apply various thicknesses for the specified faces.

Procedure (Step number corresponds to that in Fig 6-109 and Fig 6-110).

1. Click the **Shell** icon.
2. Reset the dialog box.
3. Select the face to be pierced.
4. Enter the thickness and press the **Enter** key.
5. Expand the **Alternate Thickness** option group (❺ in Fig 6-113).
6. Click the **Select Face** option and select the face to apply a different thickness (❻ in Fig 6-114).
7. Enterthe thickness in the **Thickness 1** input box and press the **Enter** key.
8. Click the **Add New Set** button and apply a different thickness for other faces if required.
9. Press **OK** in the dialog box.

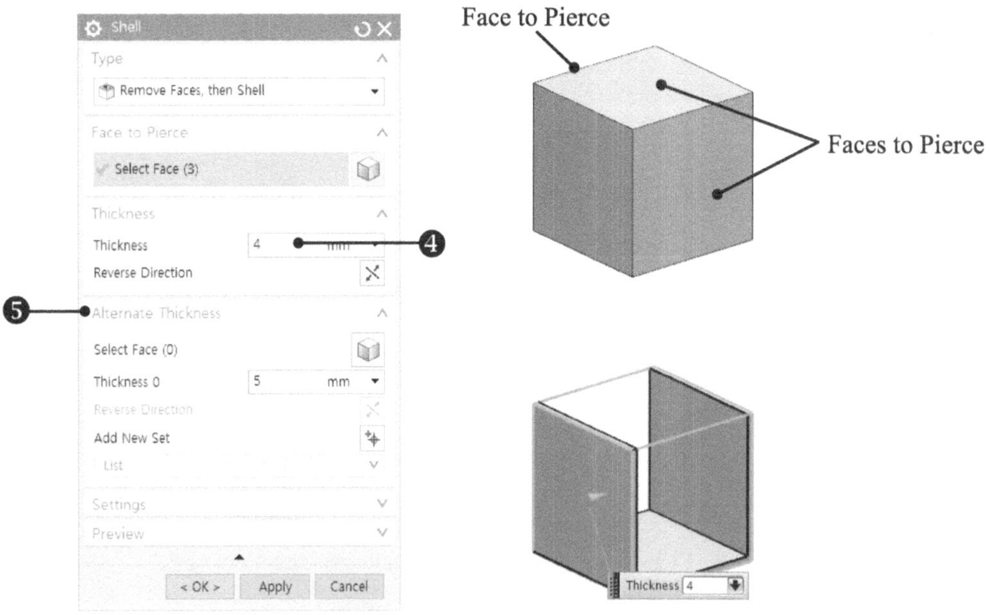

Fig 6-113 Procedure to Apply Alternate Thickness (1/2)

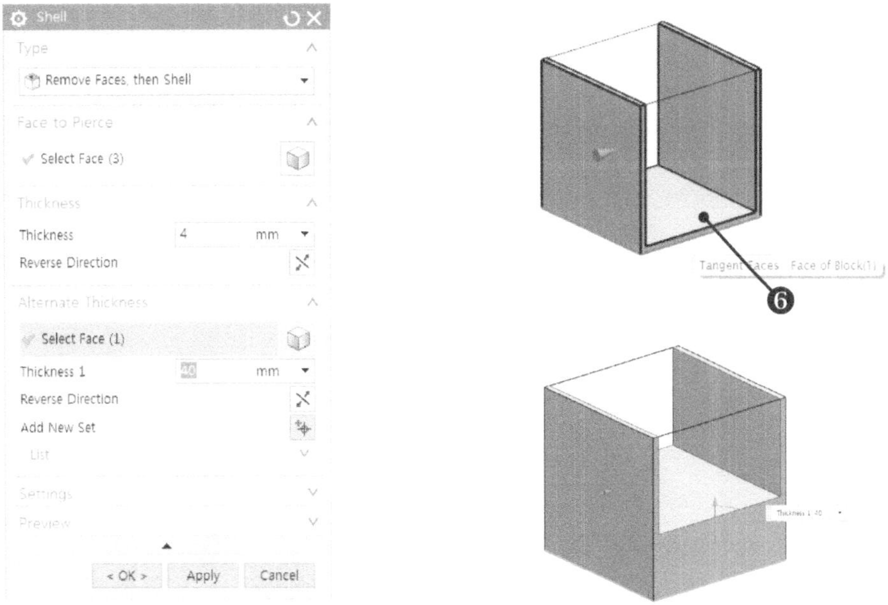

Fig 6-114 Procedure to Apply Alternate Thickness (2/2)

Note that you can apply the **Shell** command for the solid body even though it has already been applied by the **Shell** command. You can create the model shown in Fig 6-115 by applying additional **Shell** command to the resultant solid body shown in Fig 6-114.

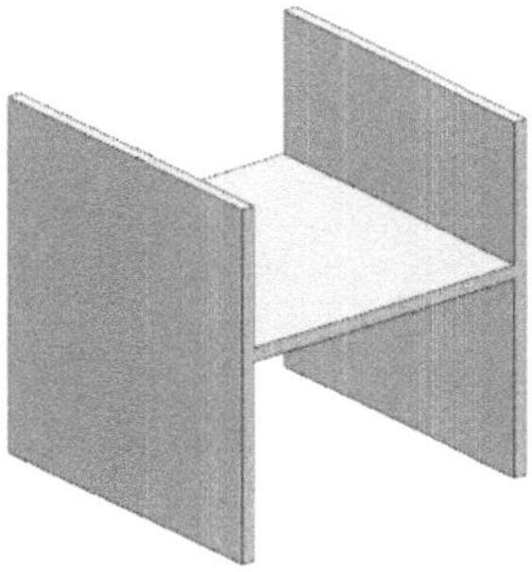

Fig 6-115 Applying Shell Twice

If the shell thickness is small enough with regard to the existing body, you can apply the **Shell** command to create the model as shown in Fig 6-116.

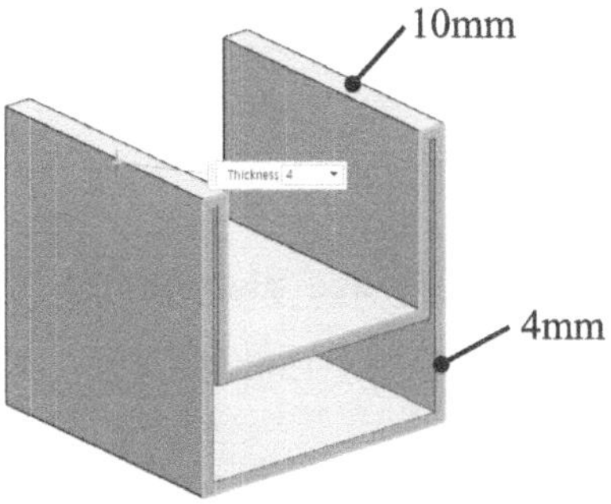

Fig 6-116 Applying Thickness

Exercise 13 Applying Fillet and Shell

ch06_ex13.prt

Apply a fillet and shell to the given model ch06_ex13.prt according to the following procedure.

① Apply R5 fillet to the specified fillet.
② Apply 3mm thickness uniformly by removing the bottom face.
③ Apply R3 Face Blend to the bottom edge.

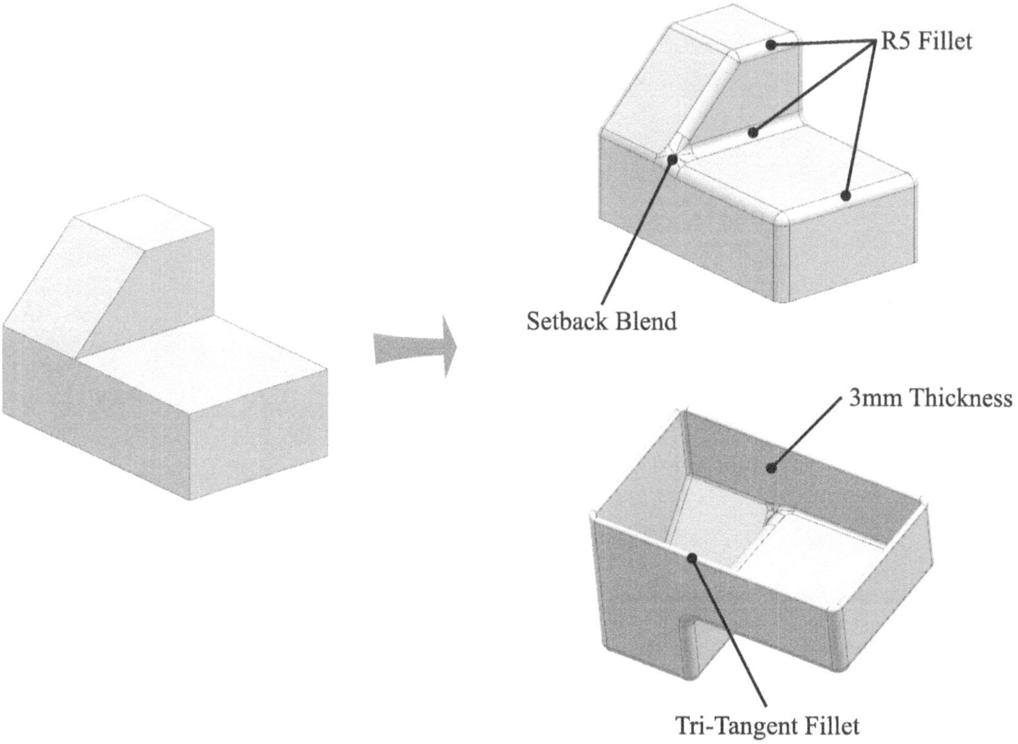

Fig 6-117 Applying Fillet and Shell

Tri-Tangent Fillet

Select **Insert > Detail Feature > Face Blend** in the **Menu** button and select **Three Defining Face Chains** as the type to apply the tri-tangent fillet.

END of Exercise

Apply draft, fillet and shell to the given model ch06_ex14.prt according to the following procedure.

① Apply 3° draft to all faces that are parallel to the draw direction which should be ZC axis of the WCS. The bottom plane and the face Ⓐ should not be changed.
② Apply fillet for all edges except the edges on the bottom face.
③ Apply 2mm thickness shell by piercing the bottom face.

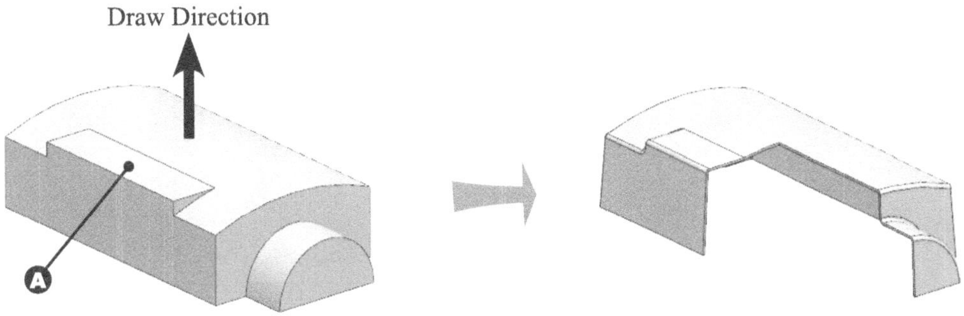

Fig 6-118 Applying Draft, Fillet and Shell

Hint!

Types of draft to be applied are **From Plane** and **Tangent to Faces**.

END of Exercise

Exercise 15 **Handle**

ch06_ex15.prt

Create the solid model referring to the drawing in Fig 6-119.

1. The result model has to be a single solid body.
2. All sketches have to be fully constrained with no **Fix** constraint.

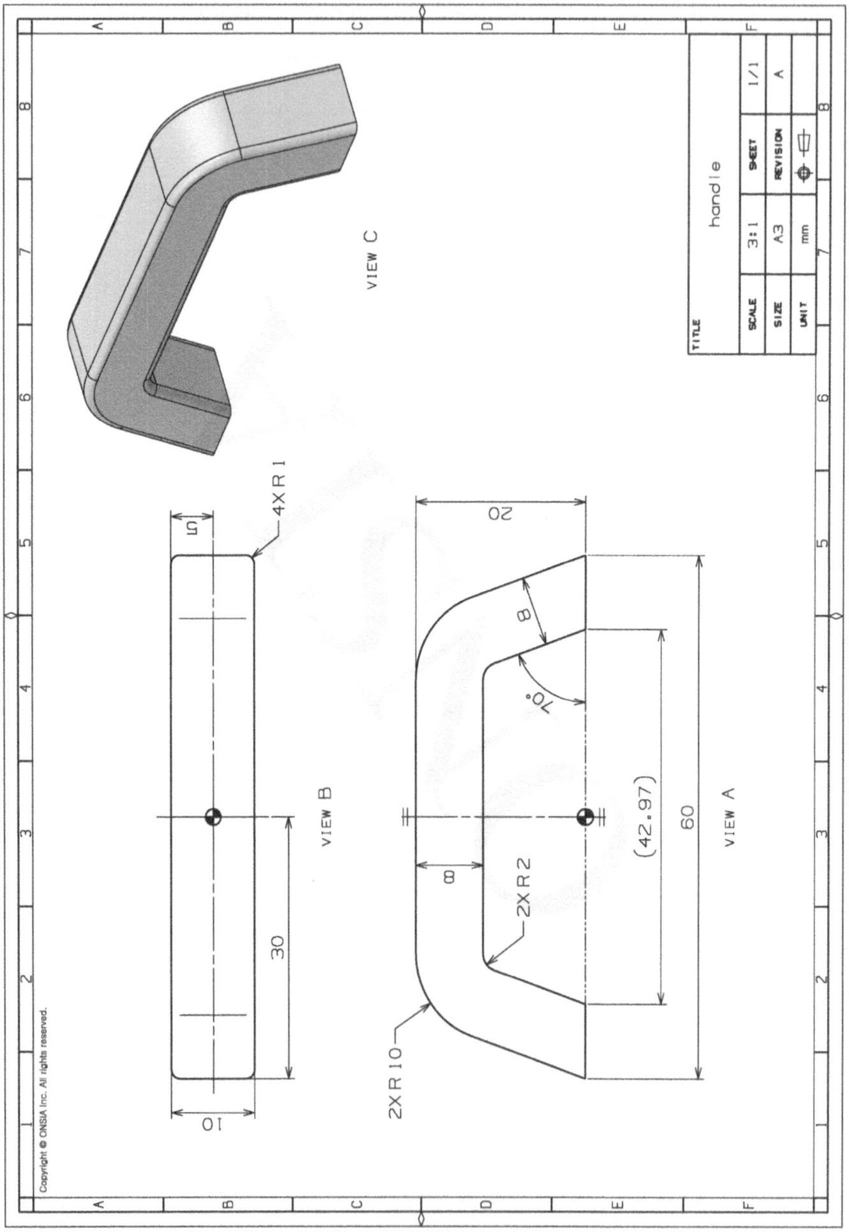

Fig 6-119 Drawing for Exercise 15

Create the solid model referring to the drawing in Fig 6-120.

1. The result model has to be a single solid body.
2. All sketches have to be fully constrained with no **Fix** constraint.

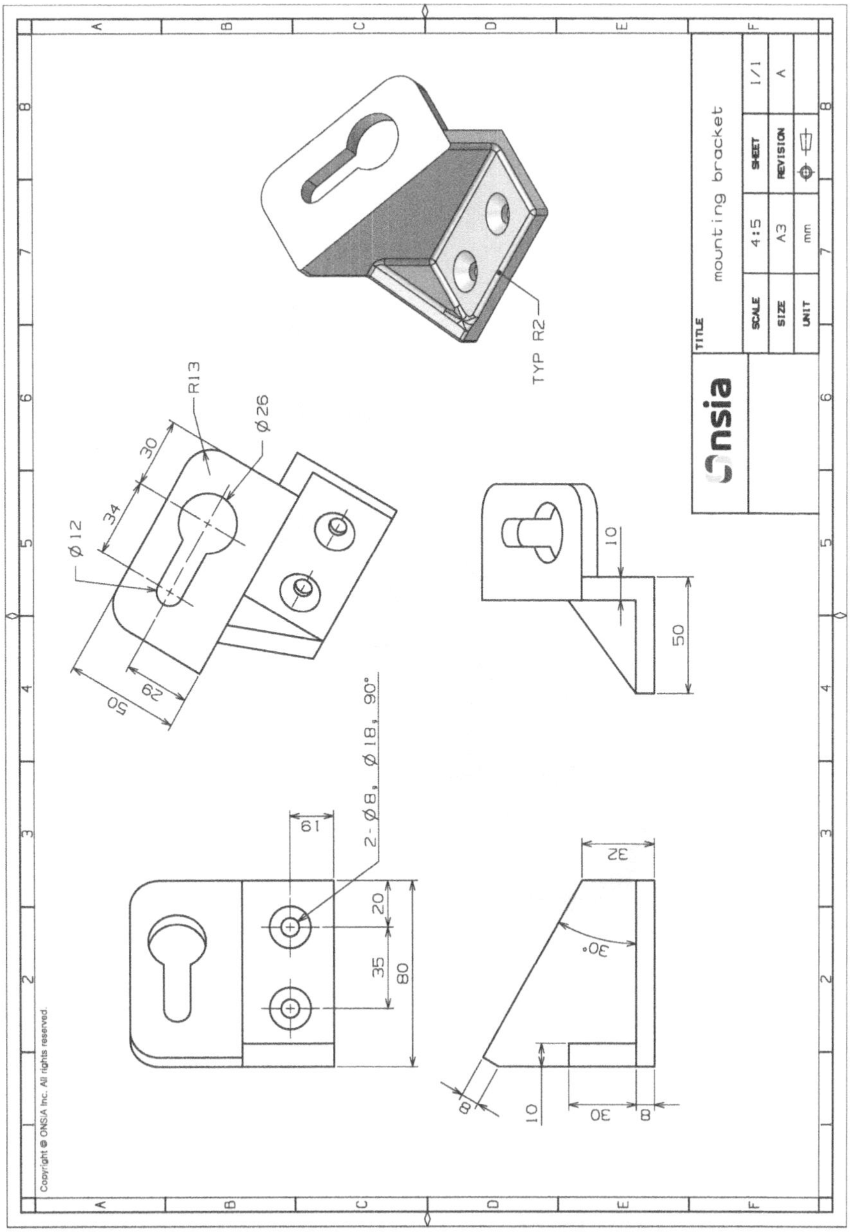

Fig 6-120 Drawing for Exercise 16

Exercise 17 Plastic Cover

ch06_ex17.prt

Create the solid model referring to the drawing in Fig 6-121.

1. Fillet radius is 3mm.
2. Draft for the faces designated by Ⓐ are created with the face Ⓕ as the stationary plane.
3. Draft for the faces designated by Ⓑ are created with the face Ⓖ as the stationary plane.
4. Apply draft for the cylindrical faces marked by Ⓒ (four places).
5. Shell thickness is 2mm uniform.

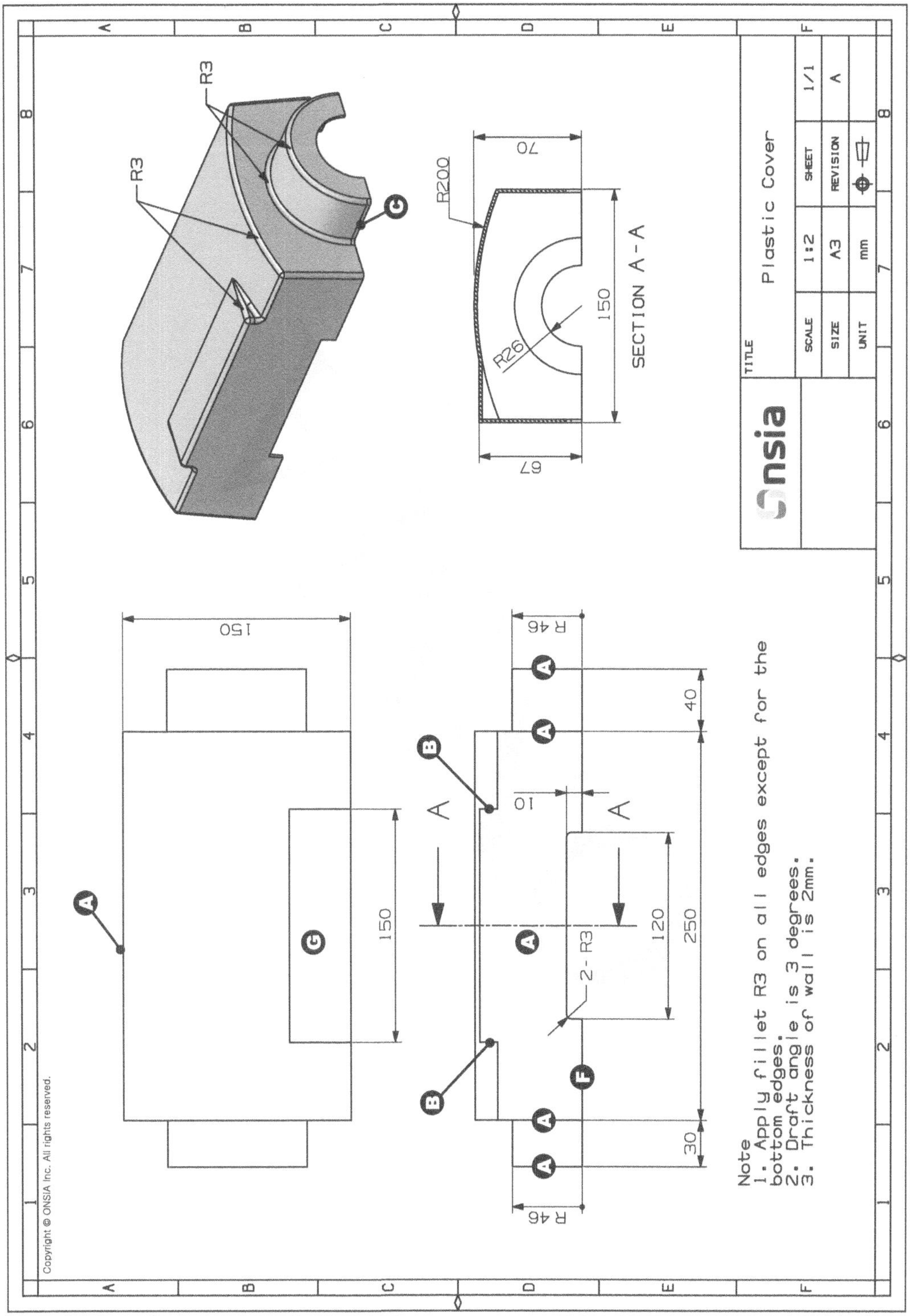

Fig 6-121 Drawing for Exercise 17

Exercise 18 **Guide Bracket**

ch06_ex18.prt

Create the solid model referring to the drawing in Fig 6-122.

Refer to the following guides for the general modeling procedure.

1. Create all features that add material.
2. Create features that remove material.
3. Apply fillet last.

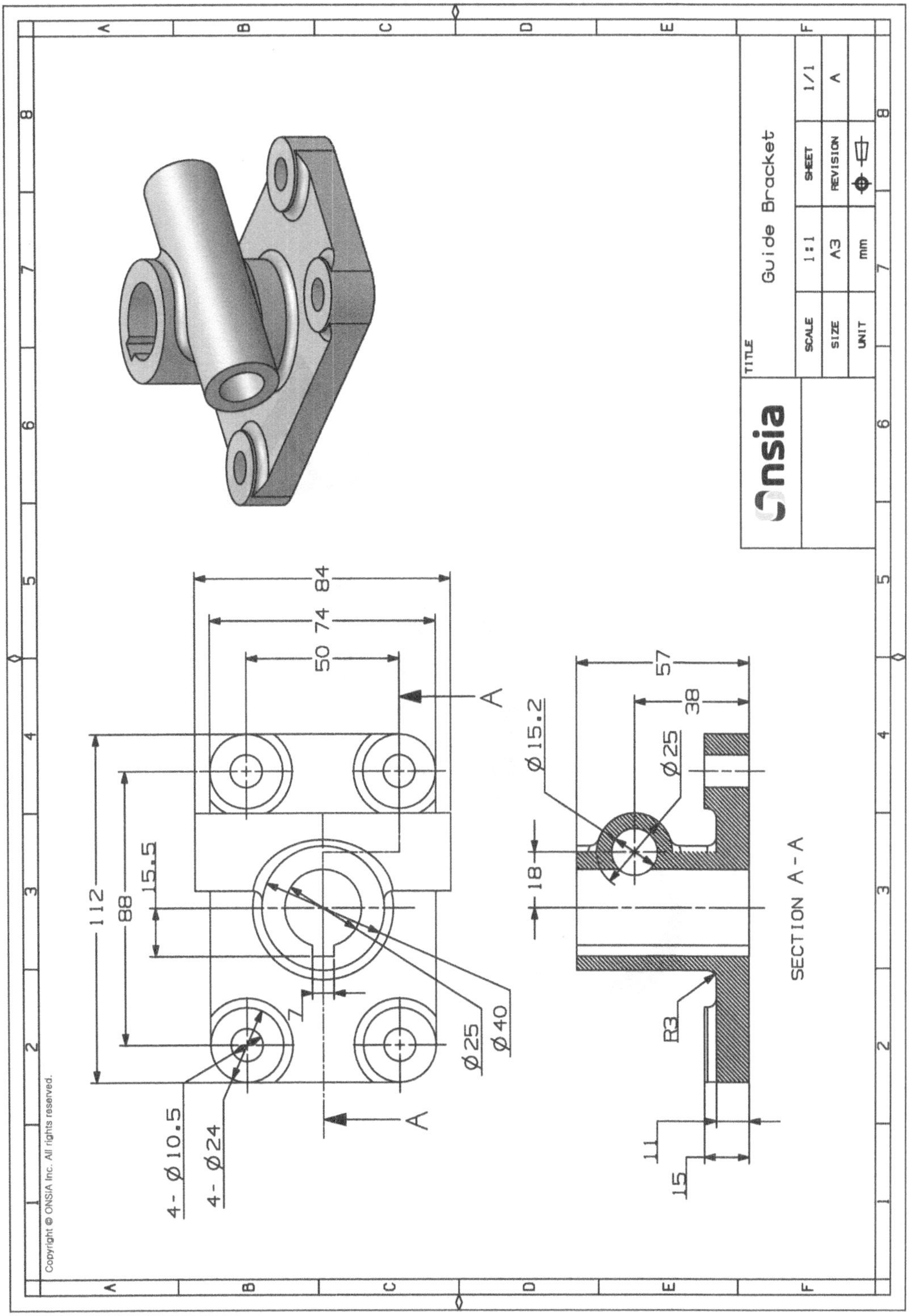

Fig 6-122 Drawing for Exercise 18

This page left blank intentionally.

Chapter 7

Parametric Modification

■ **After completing this chapter you will understand**

- the parent/child relationships between features.
- the importance of the modeling order.
- how to modify a sketch and section definition.
- how to modify feature definition parameters.
- how to re-select or re-define modeling objects.

7.1 Understanding Parametric Modification

If you discover during or after the modeling process that a part feature has been created incorrectly, you can take one of the following two approaches to correct this.

① Delete the feature and create it correctly.
② Modify the feature definition or section.

In parametric modeling software such as NX, the second approach is recommended as it best utilizes the characteristics of the software. The first approach should only be chosen when the second method is not available.

Fig 7-1 shows the impact of parametric modification. If you modify the slant angle of feature Ⓐ by modifying its sketch, the sketch plane of feature Ⓑ will be updated due to the associativity. In this chapter, we will learn how to modify features and consider the anticipated impact on the model. Note that we will encounter update errors because of associativities between the features. Therefore, we have to learn how to cope with errors that are generated when modifying the model.

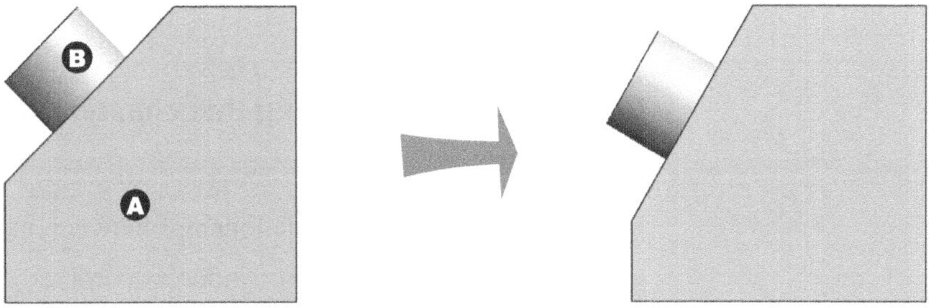

Fig 7-1 Impact of Feature Modification

7.1.1 Parent - Child Relationship of Features

If you have used an existing geometry to define a feature, an associativity is established between the features by default. Therefore, if you modify the existing geometry before defining a certain feature, the latter feature will be affected. The former feature is called a parent feature and the latter feature is called a child feature.

The associativity between features must be considered when you are modifying a feature because errors can be encountered on account of the loss of information. If you do not deal with the associativity properly, child features can be influenced to generate unexpected geometry. You can choose not to establish associativity when you create a feature or after creating a feature if the command provides the **Associativity** option.

Associativity between features in NX can be investigated by pressing MB3 on a feature in the part navigator. If you choose **Browse** in the pop-up menu as shown in Fig 7-2, a browser showing the relationships between features is invoked as shown in Fig 7-3.

The features on the left of the selected feature are the parent features and the features on the right are the child features. If you double click the **Extrude(4)** feature appearing in the browser, the **Extrude** dialog box is invoked and you can modify the parameters of extrude. Of course, you can modify parent or child features by double clicking them.

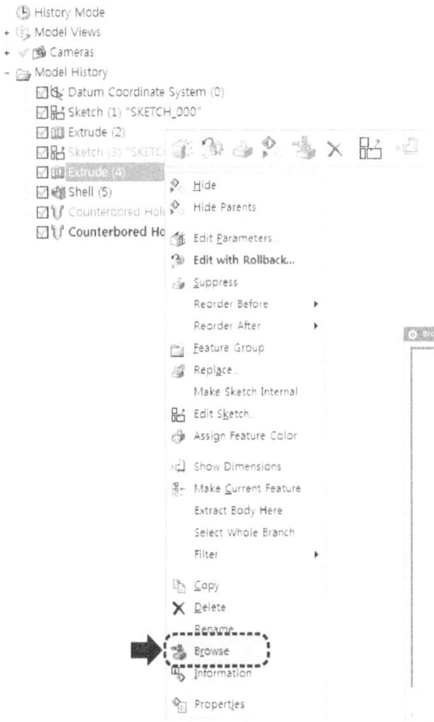

Fig 7-2 Pop-up Menu

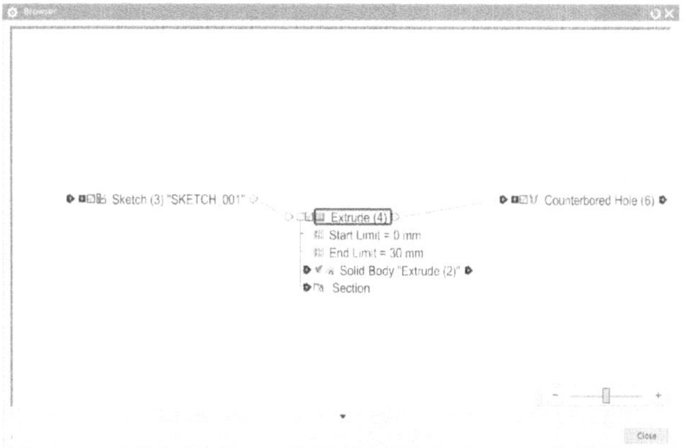

Fig 7-3 Browser

You can also identify parent or child features of the selected feature by the color shown in the part navigator. If you select a feature in the part navigator, the parent of the selected featurs is identified by red and the child of the selected feature are identified by blue. Note that if you delete a feature, the child features can be deleted together.

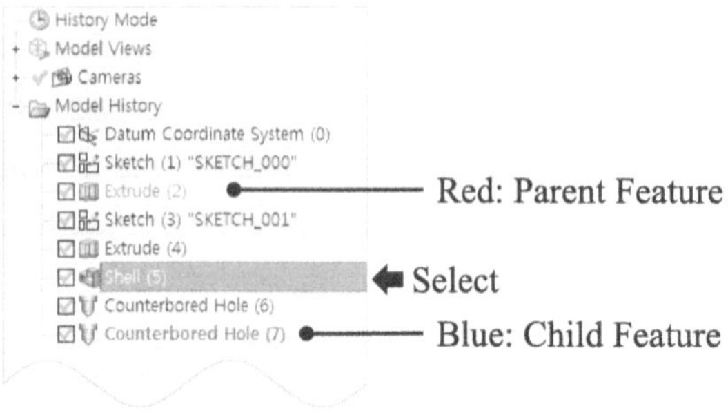

Fig 7-4 Parent-Child Relationship in Part Navigator

7.1.2 Deleting a Feature

When you delete a certain feature, you have to bear in mind that the child features may have problems in building. If you try to delete a feature, a notification message as shown in Fig 7-5 will appear to inform you of the impact of the deletion. The child features may also be deleted or have some problems in building correctly. Therefore, you have to minimize the deletion of a feature during modification.

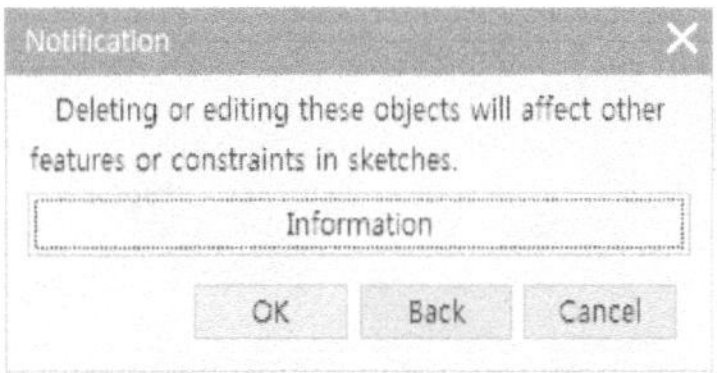

Fig 7-5 Notification

7.2 Modifying a Sketch

If you double click a sketch feature in the **Part Navigator** or double click on the sketch feature in the graphics window, you can modify the sketch in the sketch environment. Refer to "1.8.3 Double Click Action for Sketches" on 30 for setting the customer defaults.

Approaches to Modifying a Sketch

① Leave the sketch curves intact and modify the sketch dimensions or constraints. You can delete the constraints and re-define new ones.
② Delete the sketch curves or create new curves and fully constrain the curves.
③ Change the sketch plane and/or sketch axis.

You will take the first approach in most cases. The second approach may be taken when the first approach is not sufficient to obtain the desired sketch. The third approach is taken when you have to move the sketch plane to another plane or when you have to change the orientation and/or origin of the sketch plane.

ch07_ex01.prt **Modifying Sketch Dimensions** **Exercise 01**

Open the given part file ch07_ex01.prt and modify dimensions of sketch. Then examine how the child feature is influenced.

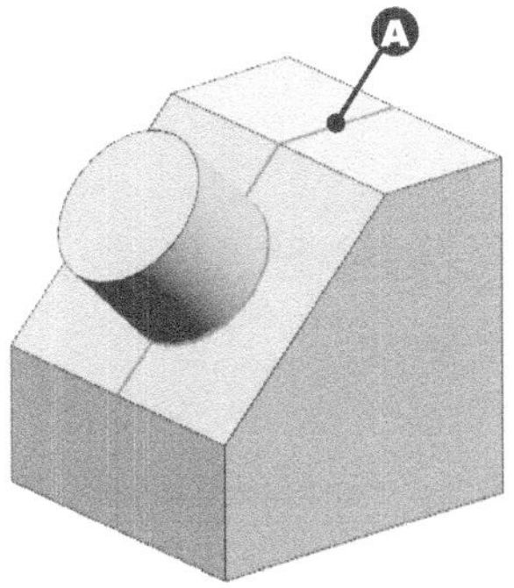

Fig 7-6 File for Exercise

1. Open the given part file ch07_ex01.prt.

2. Double click the feature Ⓐ specified in Fig 7-6.

The **Sketch** environment is invoked as shown in Fig 7-7.

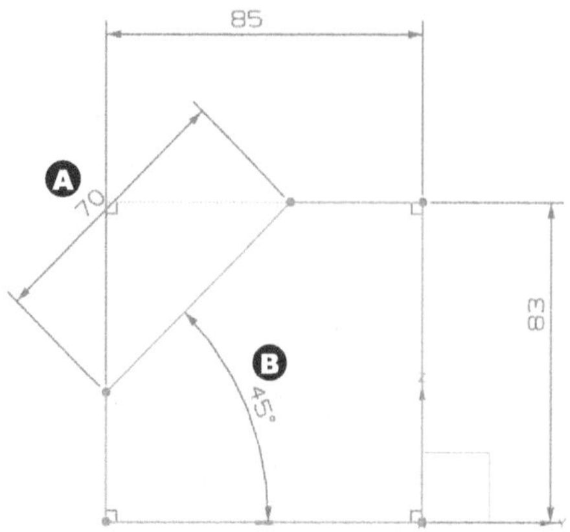

Fig 7-7 Sketch Activated

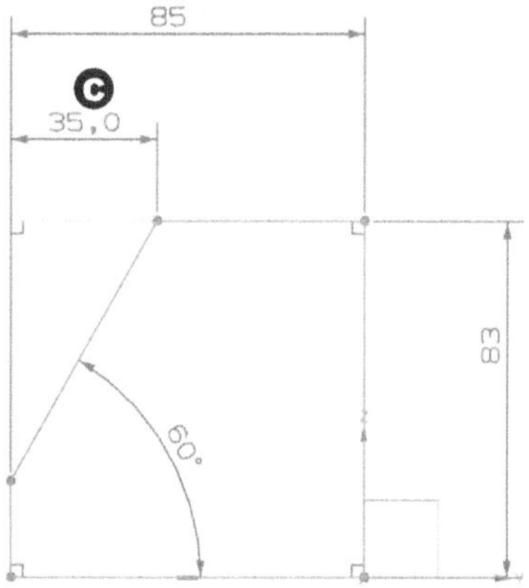

Fig 7-8 Dimension to Modify

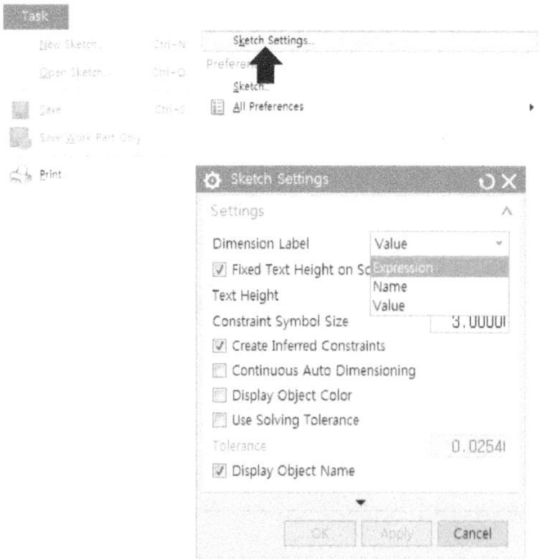

Fig 7-9 Dimension Label Option

3. Delete the dimension Ⓐ shown in Fig 7-7 and apply dimension Ⓒ as shown in Fig 7-8.

4. Double click the dimension Ⓑ shown in Fig 7-7 and modify to 60.

Let's display the dimension variables.

5. Click the **Task** tab and select **Sketch Settings** as shown in Fig 7-9.

6. Select **Expression** in the **Dimension Label** dropdown list.

Variables and values are displayed as shown in Fig 7-10.

7. Double click the dimension Ⓓ shown in Fig 7-10 and enter p9 in the input box Ⓔ as shown in Fig 7-10. Then press the **Enter** key. Note that the variable name for the dimension 85 is p9.

8. Modify the **Dimension Label** option to **Value** as shown in Fig 7-12.

9. Click the **Finish Sketch** icon to exit the sketch environment.

Fig 7-12 shows the modified model.

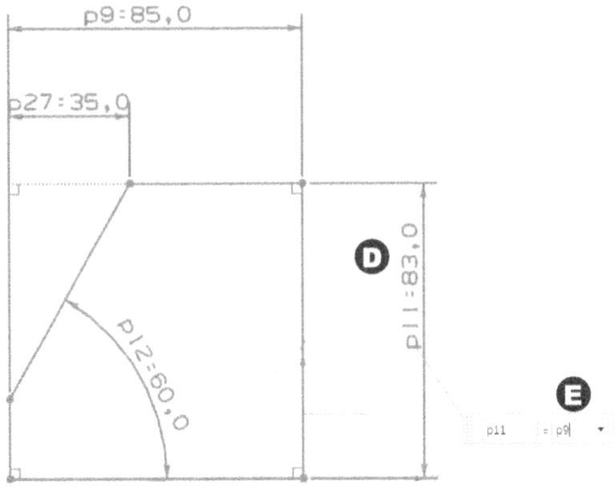

Fig 7-10 Linking the Dimension Variable

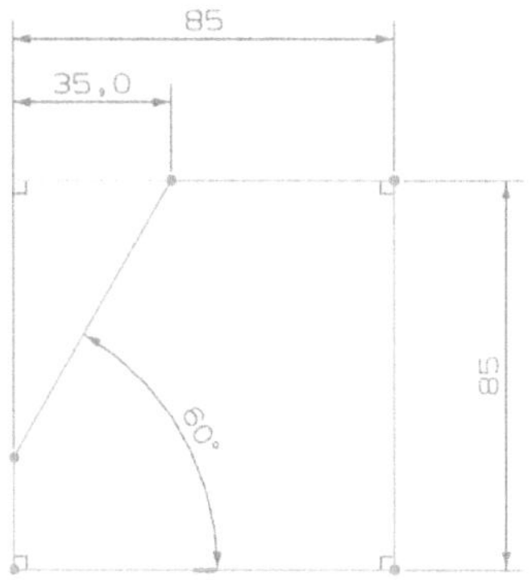

Fig 7-11 Sketch Modified

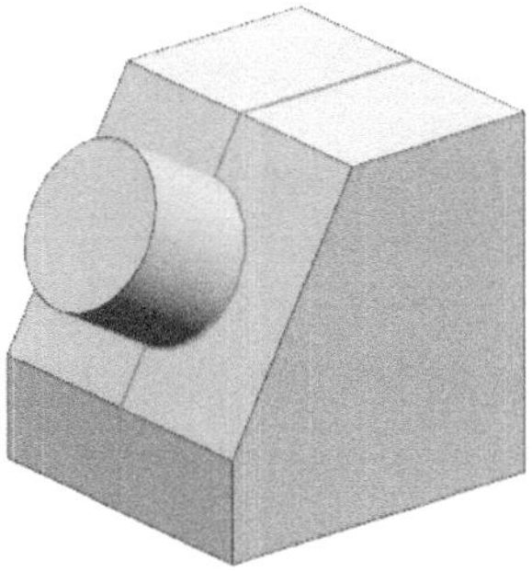

Fig 7-12 Completed Model

END of Exercise

7.2.1 Changing the Sketch Plane

You can change the sketch plane in the **Sketch** environment. Click the **Reattach** icon as shown in Fig 7-13. The **Reattach Sketch** dialog box, which is the same as what you have seen when you define the sketch, is invoked as shown in Fig 7-14 and you can change the sketch plane and redefine the sketch orientation and sketch origin.

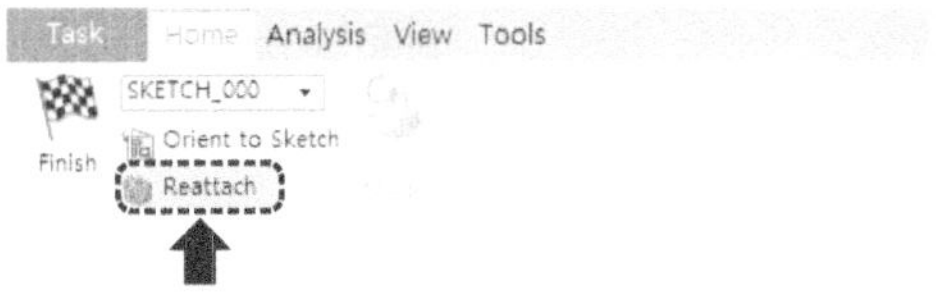

Fig 7-13 Reattach Icon

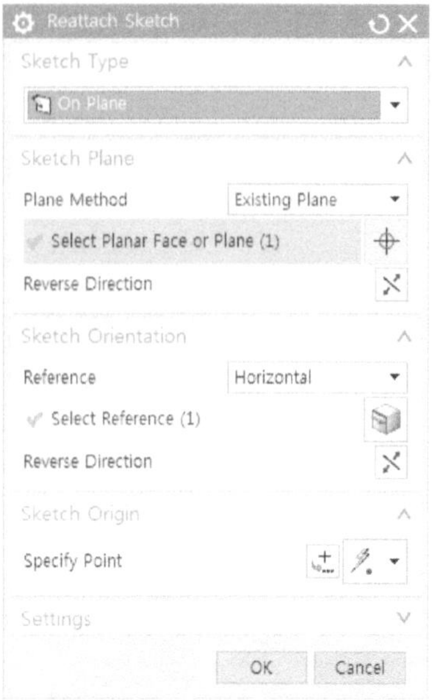

Fig 7-14 Reattach Sketch Dialog Box

When you are changing the sketch plane, bear in mind that the objects selected to fully constrain the sketch curves are held. That is to say, if you have applied a dimensional or geometrical constraint with regard to an edge or vertex, you have to redefine the constraint if an incorrect result is generated. You may need to modify the horizontal or vertical reference.

You can use the **Reattach** command in the direct sketch. Note, however, that you cannot select the datum plane that has been created after the sketch as the new sketch plane. This is because of the dependencies between the features, which is true when you are applying the sketch constraints.

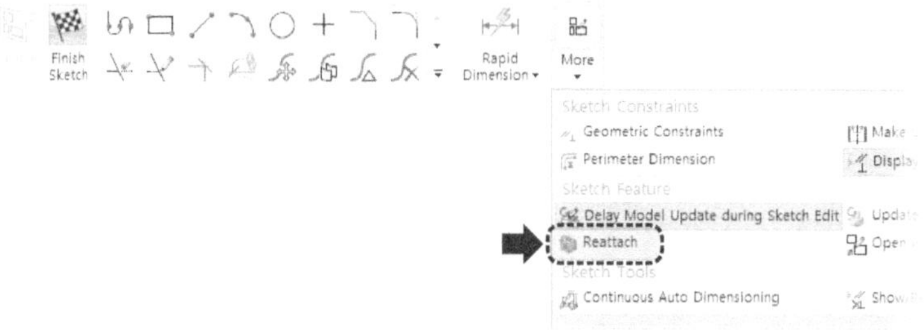

Fig 7-15 Reattach Icon in the Direct Sketch

! *Most Efficient Way to Modify a Dimension Value*

There is a **Details** panel on the lower part of the **Part Navigator** as shown in Fig 7-16. You can modify the dimension value most efficiently by expanding this panel and selecting a feature in the **Part Navigator**. Note the following restrictions when using the **Details** panel.

► The input value has to be a number. If you double click an expression such as p11=p9 (Ⓐ in Fig 7-16), the **Expression** dialog box is invoked as shown in Fig 7-17.

► You must select only one feature in order to display the variables in the **Details** panel. If you select two or more features in the part navigator, nothing will appear in the **Details** panel.

Fig 7-16 Details Panel

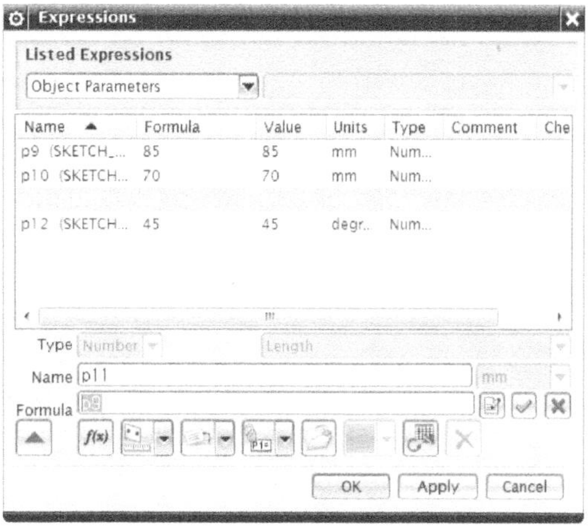

Fig 7-17 Expressions Dialog Box

7.3 Inserting a Feature (Make Current Feature)

You can insert a feature at a desired location in the part navigator. Press MB3 on a feature in the part navigator and select **Make Current Feature** as shown in Fig 7-18 (a). The part history rollbacks after the selected feature as shown in Fig 7-18 (b), and you can proceed with the modeling process. Fig 7-18 (c) shows the inserting of a datum plane after the feature **Extrude (2)**.

If you want to restore the final model, press MB3 on an empty region in the part navigator and select **Update to End** in the pop-up menu. Or you can press MB3 on the lowest feature and select **Make Current Feature** in the pop-up menu.

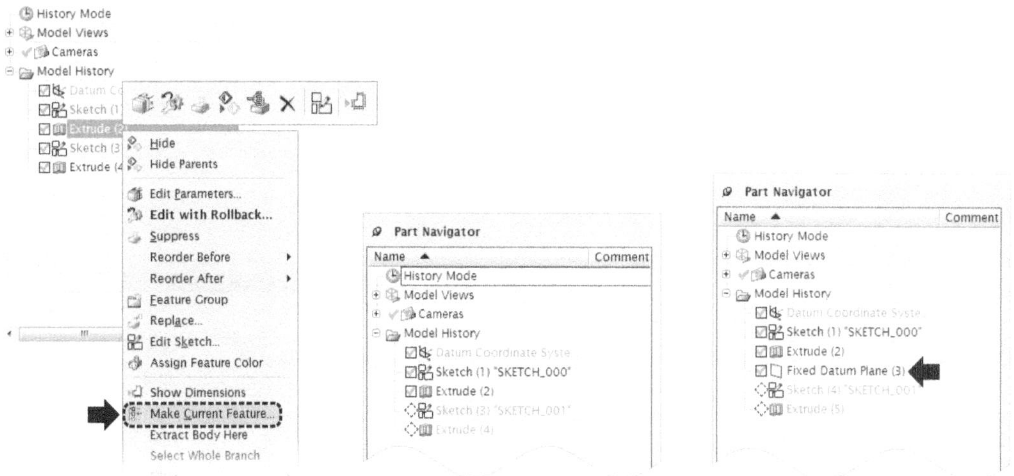

(a) (b) (c)

Fig 7-18 Inserting a Feature

In this exercise, we will practice the following modeling techniques.

1. Delete a sketch curve and create a new one.
2. Insert a datum plane after the desired feature and before the feature to use it.
3. Change the sketch plane to the inserted datum plane.

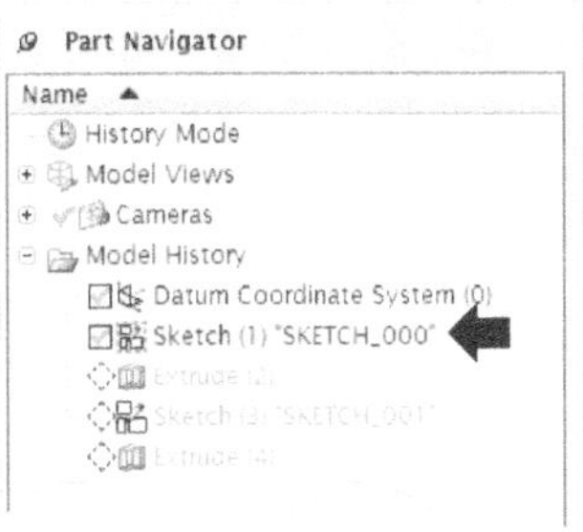

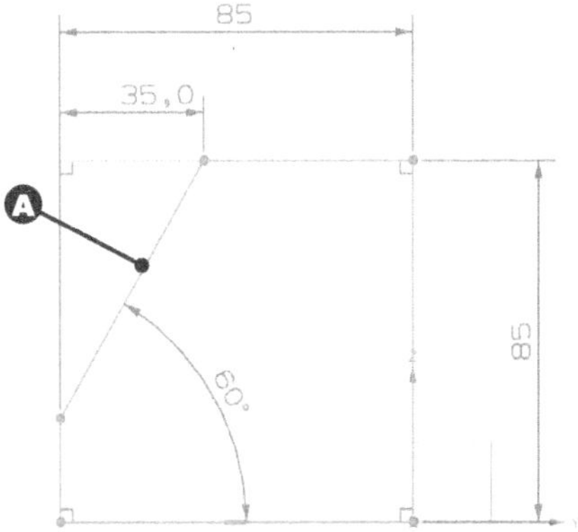

Fig 7-19 Sketch to Modify

Direct Sketch

If you feel using the direct sketch is convenient, you can activate the **Direct Sketch** by pressing MB3 on a sketch and choosing **Edit** in the pop-up menu.

Modifying Sketch

1. Open the given file ch07_ex02.prt.

2. Double click the sketch feature specified in Fig 7-19 to invoke the **Sketch** task environment.

3. Delete the line Ⓐ shown in Fig 7-19 and create an arc Ⓑ as shown in Fig 7-20.

4. Fully constrain the sketch as shown in Fig 7-20 and finish the sketch. Information is invoked as shown in Fig

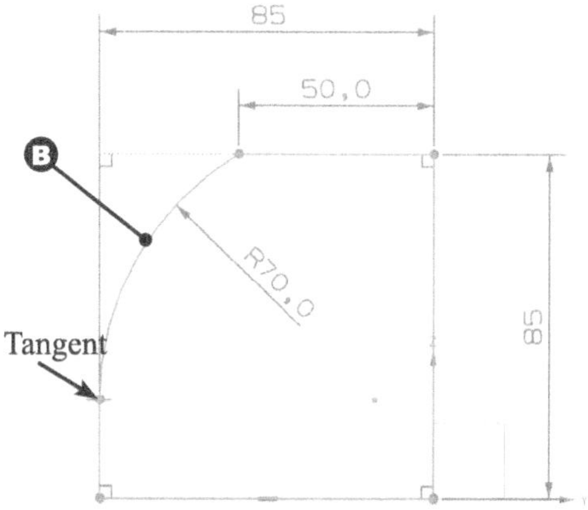

Fig 7-20 Modified Sketch

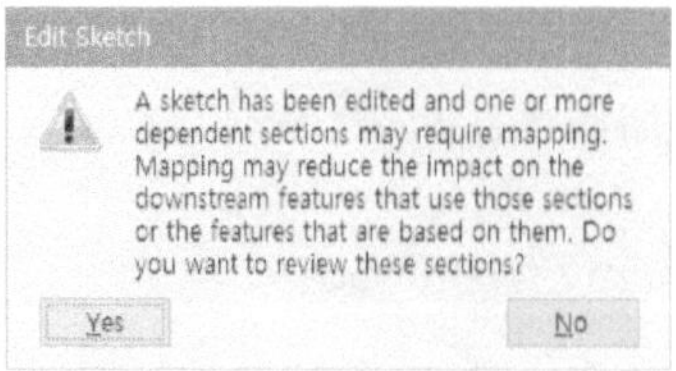

Fig 7-21 Edit Sketch Information

7-21. Note that mapping may reduce the impact on the downstream features that use the modified section.

5. Click **No** in the information dialog box.

An information window as shown in Fig 7-22 is invoked and the feature error symbols (⊠) are marked in the part navigator. Note that the erroneous features do not appear in the model.

Place the mouse cursor on the erroneous

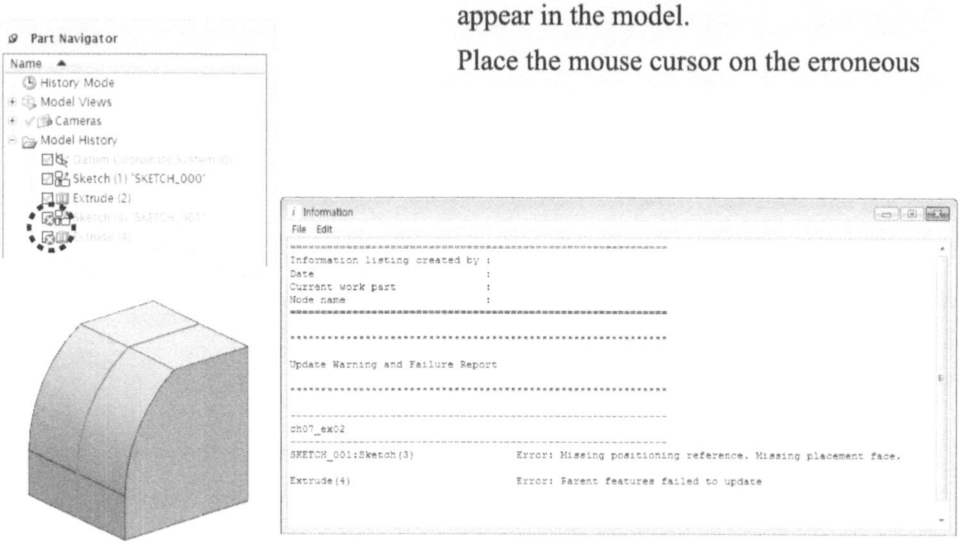

Fig 7-22 Feature Error Information and Symbol

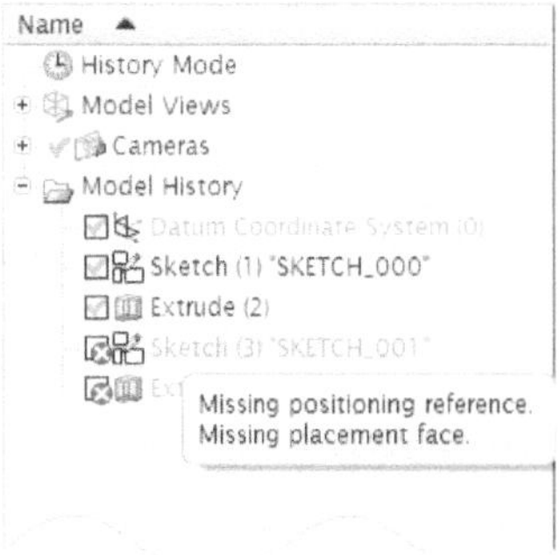

Fig 7-23 Causes of Error

feature and wait for some seconds. Causes of the error are shown as a balloon tip.

You have created the **Sketch (3)** on a plane extruded by a line. Now, the line is substituted by an arc and the sketch plane has disappeared, which has made an impact on the **Extrude (4)**.

Purpose of Exercise 02

Note that the purpose of this exercise is not to delete a feature but to modify the generated errors. Suppose that you have created a lot of features referencing the geometry of **Extrude (4)**. If you delete the **Sketch (3)**, all downstream features associated with **Extrude (4)** can be deleted.

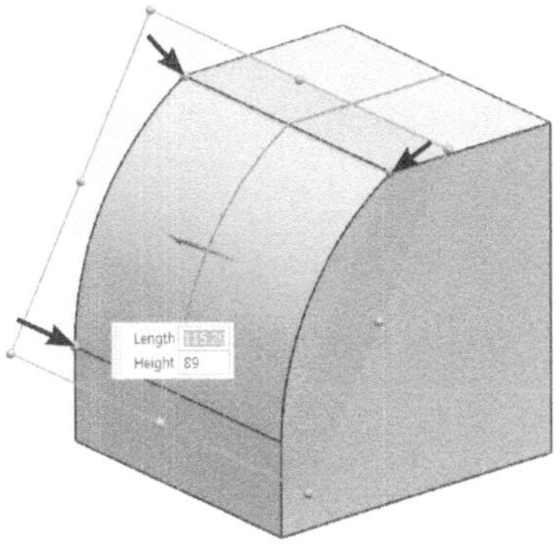

Fig 7-24 Datum Plane

Creating a Datum Plane

Let's insert a datum plane before the **Sketch (3)** feature and change the sketch plane onto the datum plane.

1. Press MB3 on **Extrude (2)** and choose **Make Current Feature** in the pop-up menu.

2. Create a datum plane passing through the three vertices designated by the arrows in Fig 7-24. Resize the datum plane by dragging the sizing handle.

3. Press MB3 on **Extrude (5)** and choose **Make Current Feature** as shown in Fig 7-25.

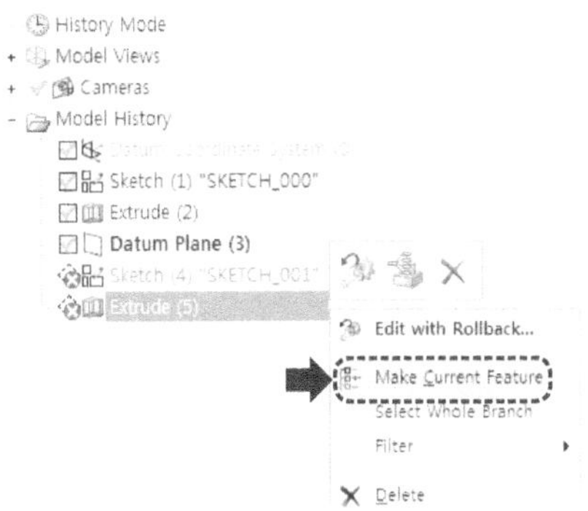

Fig 7-25 Make Current Feature

Errors are not resolved. Recall that you have just created a datum plane at the required location.

Changing the Sketch Plane

1. Double click the **Sketch (4)** feature and enter the sketch environment as shown in Fig 7-26.

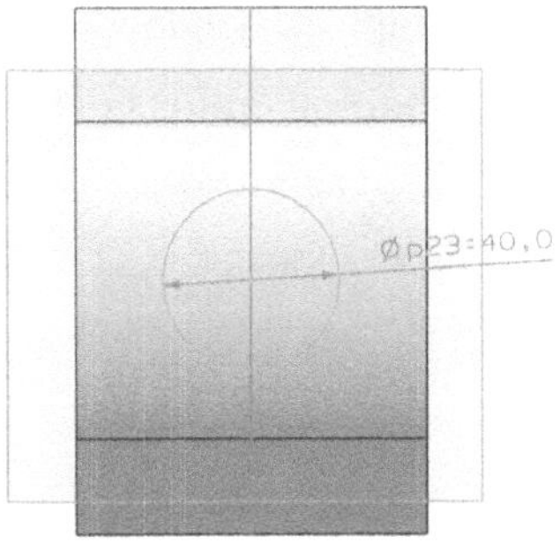

Fig 7-26 Sketch Environment

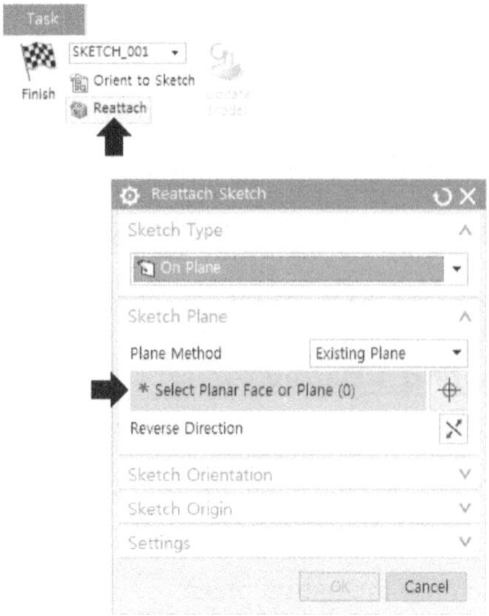

Fig 7-27 Reattach Sketch Dialog Box

2. Press the **Reattach** icon in the **Sketch** toolbar. The **Reattach Sketch** dialog box is invoked and you are prompted to select a planar plane or face. Be sure that nothing is chosen.

3. Select the datum plane.

4. Finish the sketch.

Fig 7-28 shows the part navigator and the model with the errors resolved.

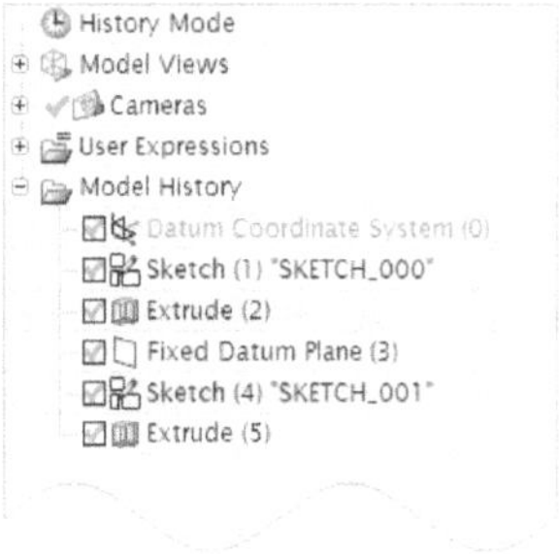

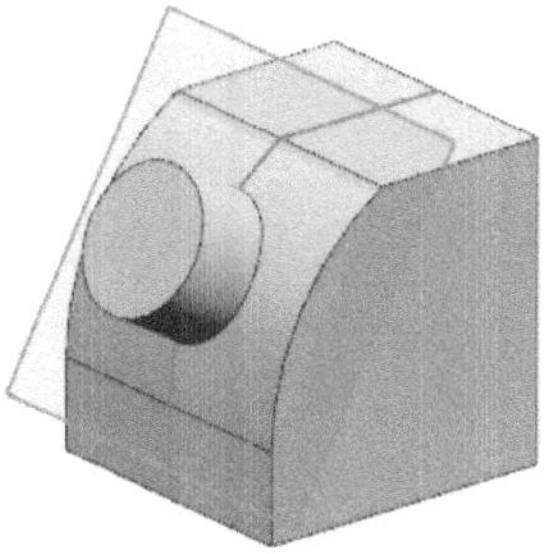

Fig 7-28 Completed Model

END of Exercise

7.4 Modifying Feature Definition

If you double click a feature in the part navigator or in the graphics window, the feature definition dialog box appears. You can modify the feature definition options in the dialog box. The types of modifying feature definitions can be classified as follows.

Approaches to Modifying Feature Definition Options

① Reselecting target objects such as sections and edges.
② Modifying values
③ Modifying other options such as direction and thickness options.

When you modify a section, you have to determine whether to map the sections or not. If you map an old section curve to a new one, the modeling impact on the child features can be reduced.

Let's think about modifying a rectangular section to a pentagon as shown in Fig 7-29. If you map the section curve Ⓐ to the line Ⓑ, the sketch on the plane Ⓒ will be defined on the new plane designated by Ⓓ automatically. An error will not occur for the sketch and extrude feature for the cylinder.

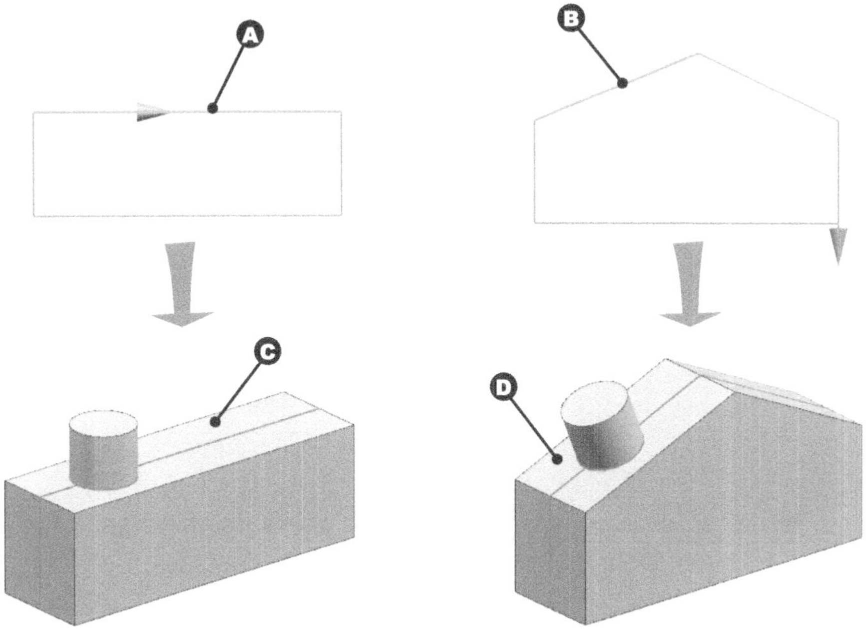

Fig 7-29 Understanding Mapping

7.4.1 Reselecting Target Objects

If you have created a feature on an existing geometry, you might have selected the geometry when you were applying a command. You can re-select geometry such as vertexes, edges and faces by invoking the feature definition dialog box. Examples of re-selecting objects for defining a feature are as follows.

① Limit element of **Extrude** and **Hole** feature
② Edges of **Edge Blend** or **Chamfer** features
③ Axis of **Revolve** or **Circular Pattern** features
④ Faces, edges and points that have been selected while creating a datum feature

⑤ A face that has been selected while creating a **Draft** or **Shell** feature

When you re-select a target object, you can click the option field in the dialog box and select other objects in the model. If you want to deselect objects, press the shift key and select the object.

Exercise 03 Modifying a Section

ch07_ex03.prt

Let's modify a section with and without section mapping and compare the modification process.

Modifying without Mapping

1. Open the given file ch07_ex03.prt.

2. Press MB3 on the **Extrude (2)** and choose **Make Sketch External** as shown in Fig 7-30. The sketch feature is got out of the extrude feature.

3. Double click the sketch and enter the **Sketch** task environment.

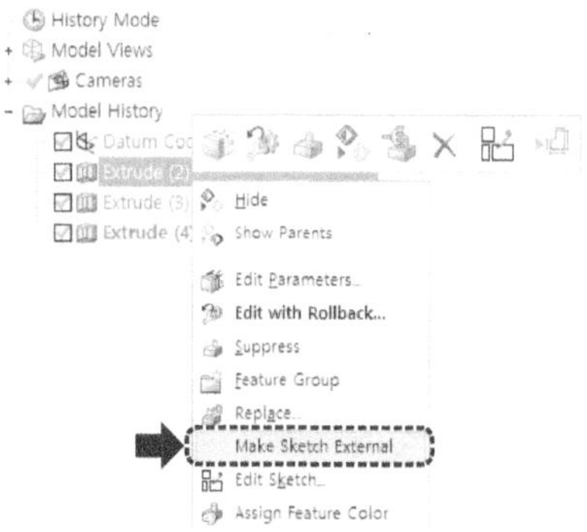

Fig 7-30 Make Sketch External Option

4. Modify the sketch as shown in Fig 7-31 and finish the sketch.

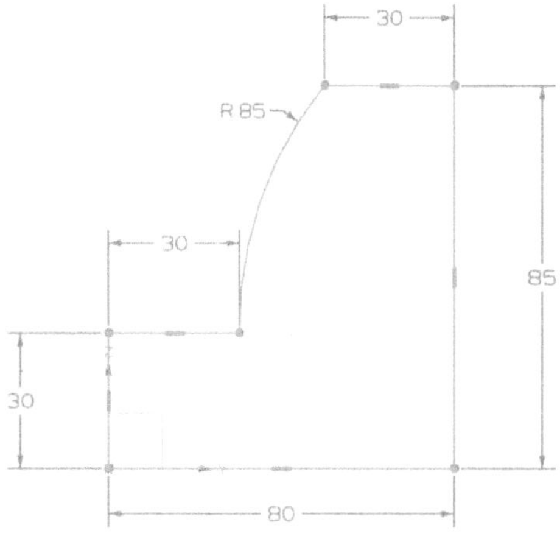

Fig 7-31 Modified Sketch

5. Press the **No** button in the **Edit Sketch** information box shown in Fig 7-32.

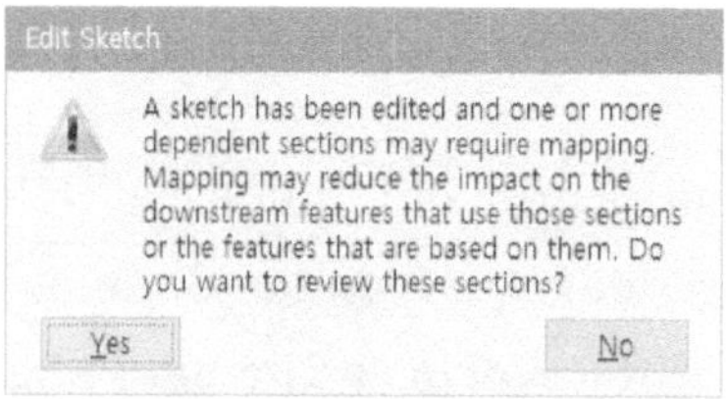

Fig 7-32 Edit Sketch Information Box

6. Close the information box. An error occurred as shown in Fig 7-33.

7. Double click the **Extrude (3)** feature.

8. The **Alerts** window is invoked as shown in Fig 7-34 which informs you that the limit is missing.

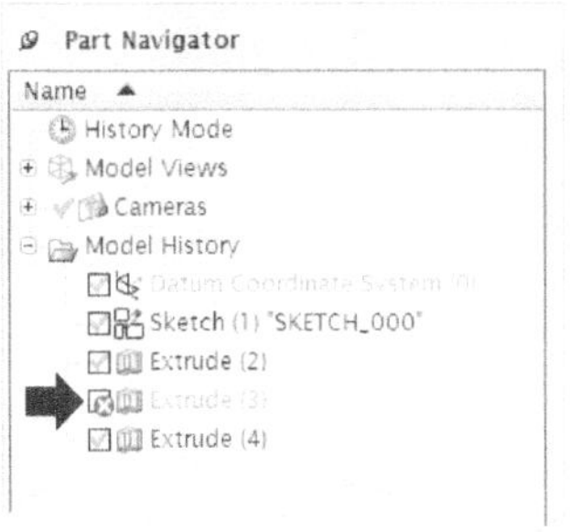

Fig 7-33 Erroneous Feature

Fig 7-34 Alerts Window

9. Make sure that the **Select Object** option field is highlighted as designated by the arrow in Fig 7-35. If not, click it.

10. Select the face Ⓐ specified in Fig 7-35.

11. Press **OK** in the dialog box.

The error in the extrude feature has disappeared and the modification is completed.

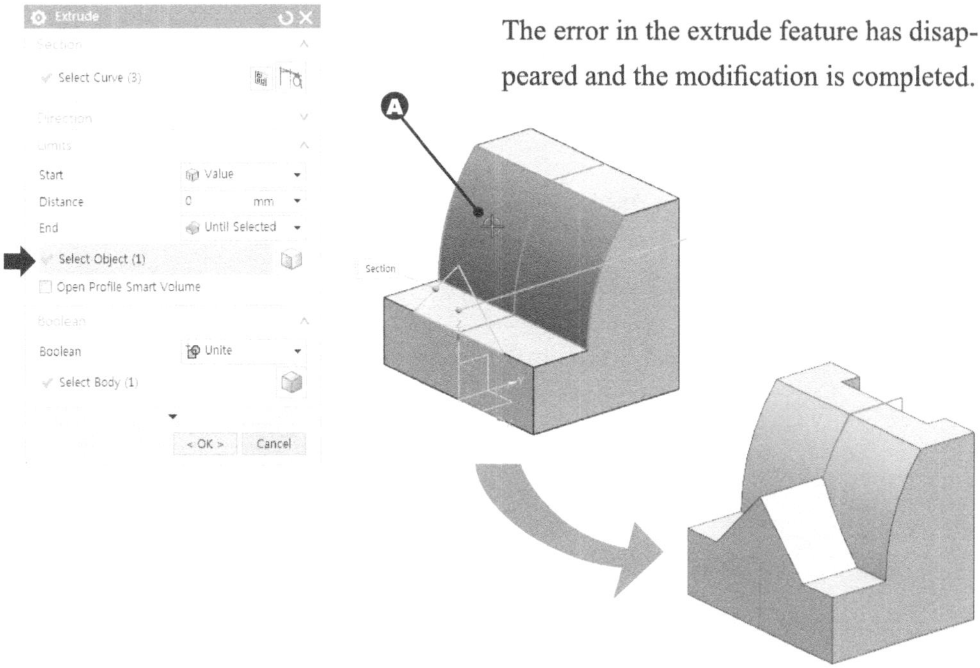

Fig 7-35 Modification Completed

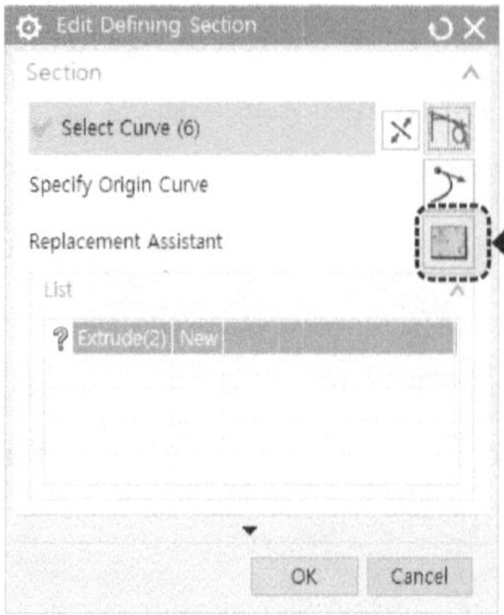

Fig 7-36 Edit Defining Section Dialog Box

Modifying with Mapping

1. Close without saving the file. Open the same file again.

2. Repeat the process of modifying without mapping up to step 4.

3. Press **Yes** in the information box shown in Fig 7-32.

4. Click the **Replacement Assistant** button in the dialog box shown in Fig 7-36.

The curve is mapped automatically and the question mark in the dialog box changes to a green check mark.

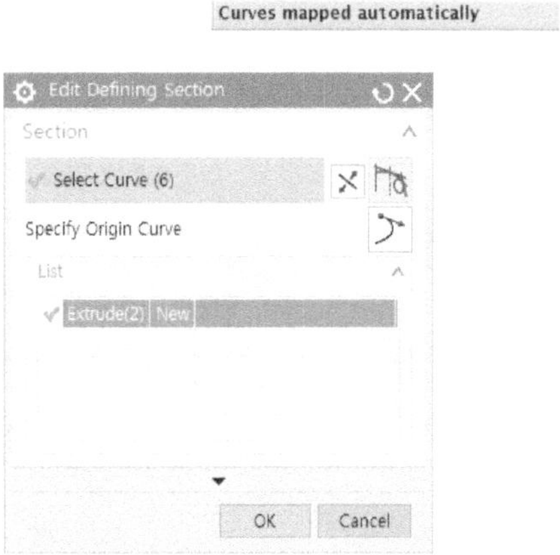

Fig 7-37 Mapping Completed

5. Press **OK** in the dialog box.

6. Finish the sketch.

An error does not occur and the modification is completed. This implies that the curved face has been chosen as the limit of the extrude feature.

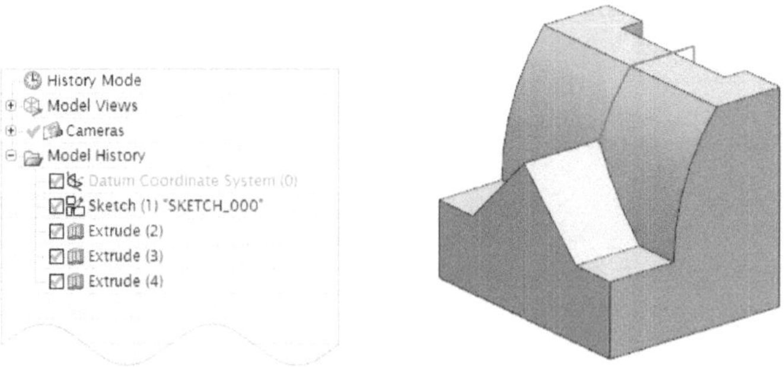

Fig 7-38 Modified Model

END of Exercise

In this exercise, you can practice selecting and deselecting edges for edge blend. We will not delete the edge blend feature, but modify the existing one.

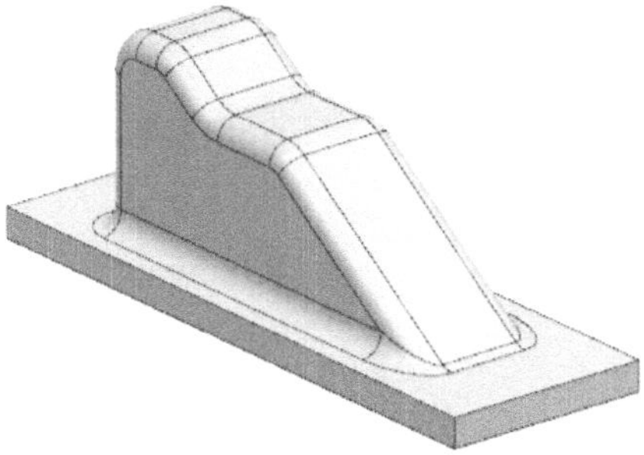

Fig 7-39 Model for Exercise

Reviewing Modeling History

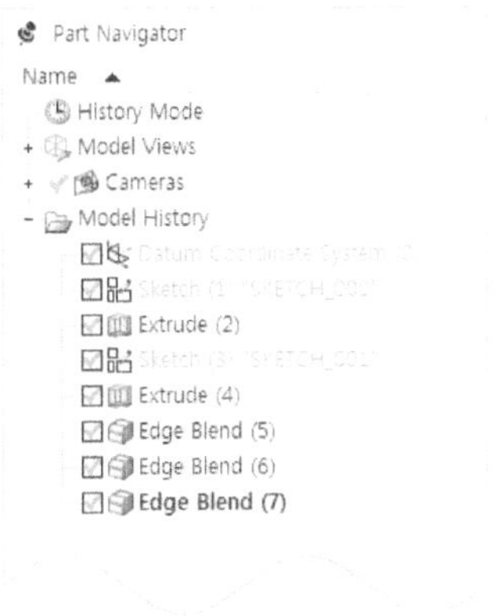

Fig 7-40 Modeling History

1. Open the given file ch07_ex04.prt.

2. Make the **Edge Blend (5)** a current feature.

Fig 7-41 shows the model up to the selected edge blend.

3. Review the modeling history by making **Edge Blend (6)** and **Edge Blend (7)** the current features one by one.

4. Update the model to the end.

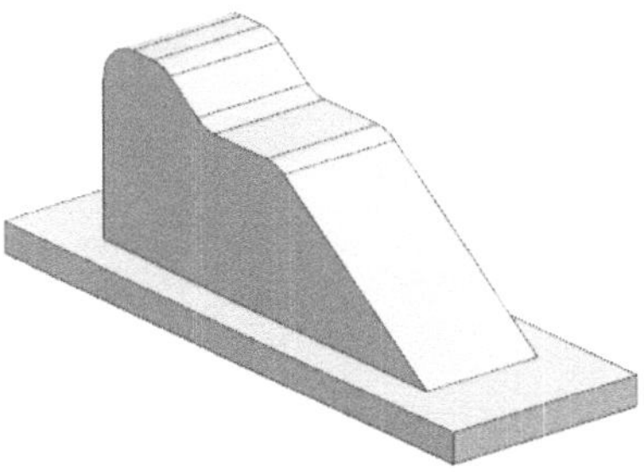

Fig 7-41 Rollback to Edge Blend (5)

Modifying the Sketch

1. Double click the **Sketch (3) "SKETCH_001"** and enter the sketch environment.

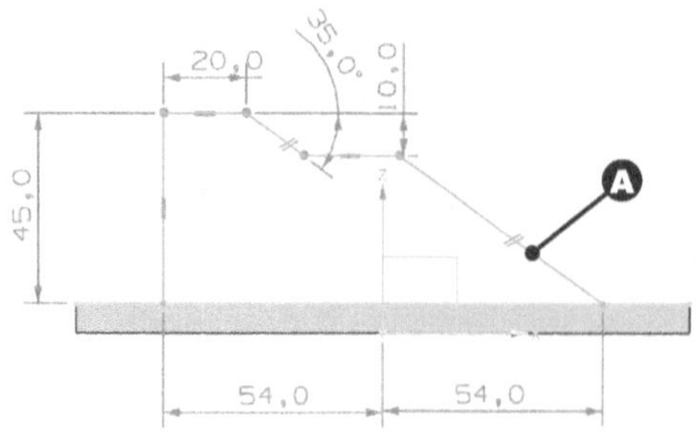

Fig 7-42 Original Sketch

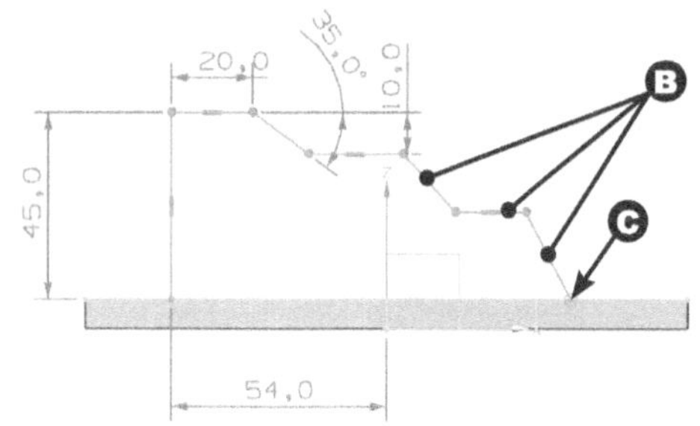

Fig 7-43 Modified Sketch

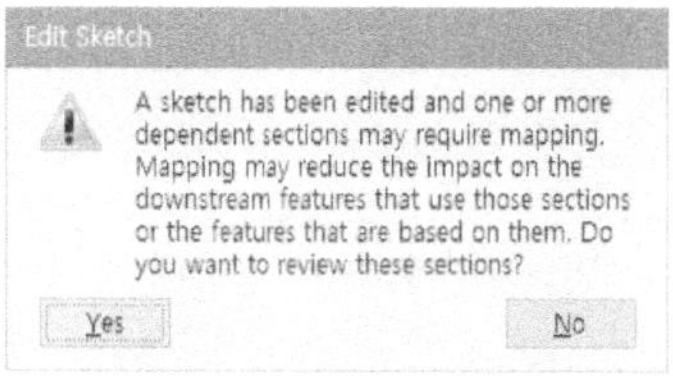

Fig 7-44 Edit Sketch Information Box

2. Delete the line Ⓐ shown in Fig 7-42 and create three curves specified by Ⓑ in Fig 7-43. The end point Ⓒ has to be on the edge. You can skip fully constraining the curves.

Errors are anticipated in the existing edge blend. We will resolve the error and add new edges to the edge blend feature. Recall that the purpose of this exercise is modifying the existing feature, not deleting and creating a new feature.

3. Finish the sketch.

4. Press **No** in the **Edit Sketch** information box.

Four errors are detected as shown in Fig 7-45.

5. Close the information window.

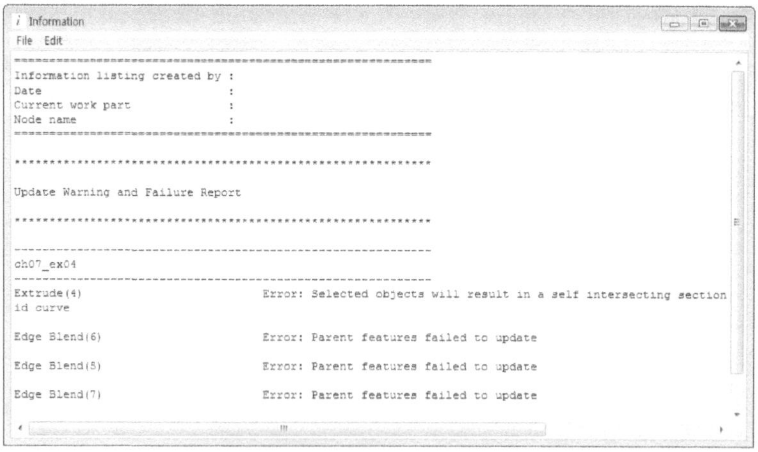

Fig 7-45 Information Window

Resolving the Error

1. Double click the first erroneous feature **Extrude (4)**.

Confirm the following in Fig 7-46:

① The **Select Curve** option field is highlighted in the **Extrude** dialog box.

② The **Alerts** message appears on the bottom right of the graphics window.

③ The section is highlighted in orange in the model.

Note that the section is self-intersecting. You have to modify the erroneous section.

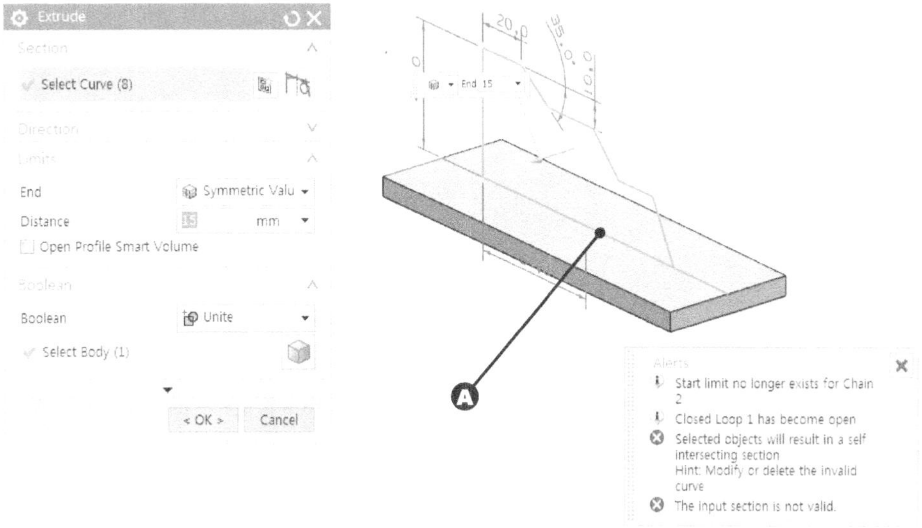

Fig 7-46 Cause of Error in Extrude

2. Press the **Shift** key and click MB1 on the line Ⓐ shown in Fig 7-46. The feature is previewed as in Fig 7-47.

3. Release the **Shift** key and select the line Ⓑ as designated in Fig 7-47.

The section is defined correctly as shown in Fig 7-48.

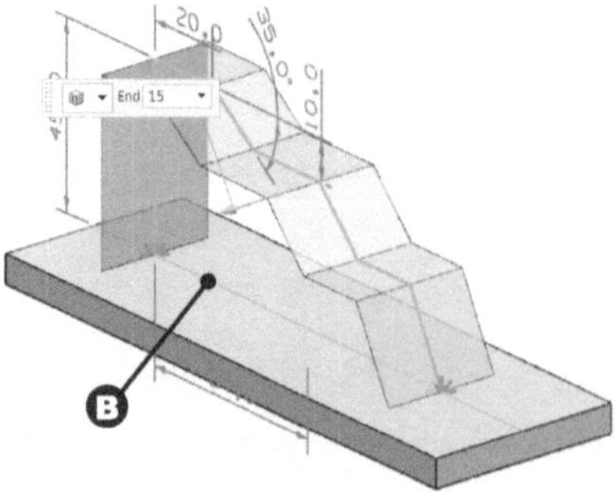

Fig 7-47 Section is Deselected

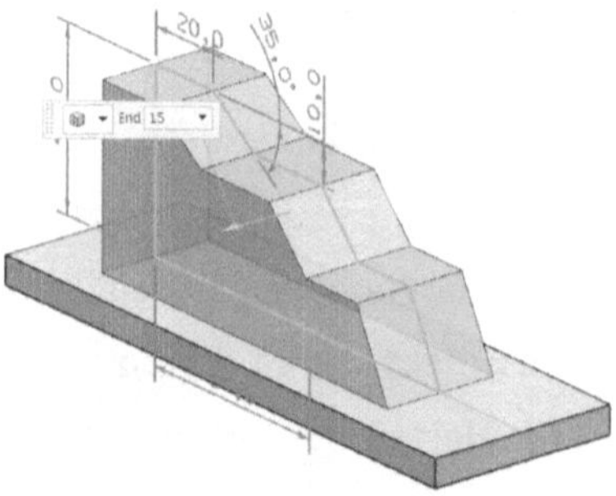

Fig 7-48 Corrected Section

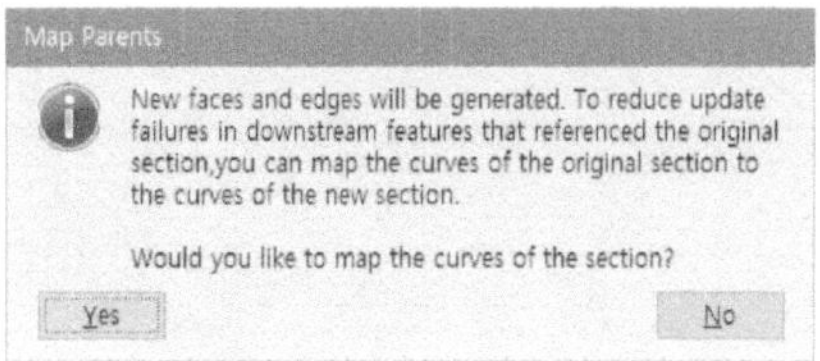

Fig 7-49 Mapping Dialog Box

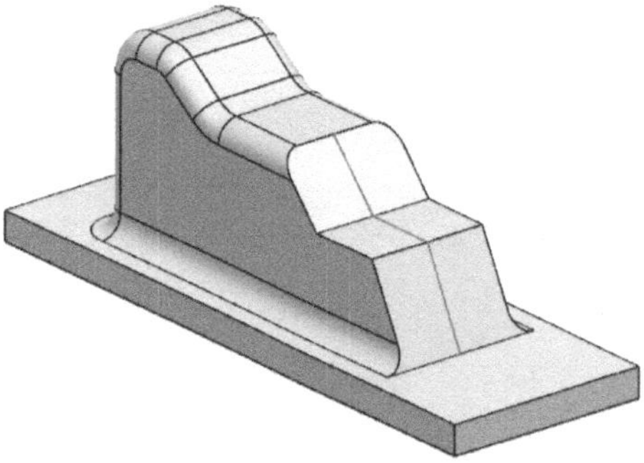

Fig 7-50 Incomplete Model

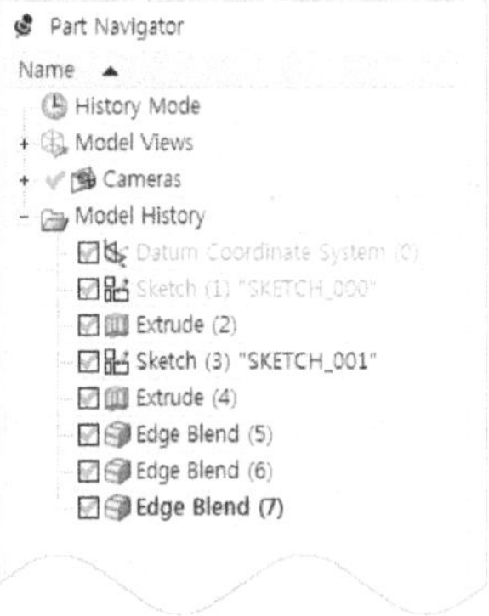

Fig 7-51 Modeling History

4. Press **OK** in the **Extrude** dialog box.

5. Press **No** in the **Map Parents** dialog box shown in Fig 7-49.

The model appears as shown in Fig 7-50. There is no error, but the edge blend is not complete.

Applying Edge Blend

1. Double click **Edge Blend (5)** in the part navigator.

2. Read the **Alerts** message as shown in Fig 7-52 and consider how to modify the edge blend feature.

3. Press the **Shift** key and deselect the edge **A** specified in Fig 7-52. The old edge has disappeared and a new one has been created. This step is deselecting the old edge. Note that the number of selected edges is (3) in the **Select Edges** option field.

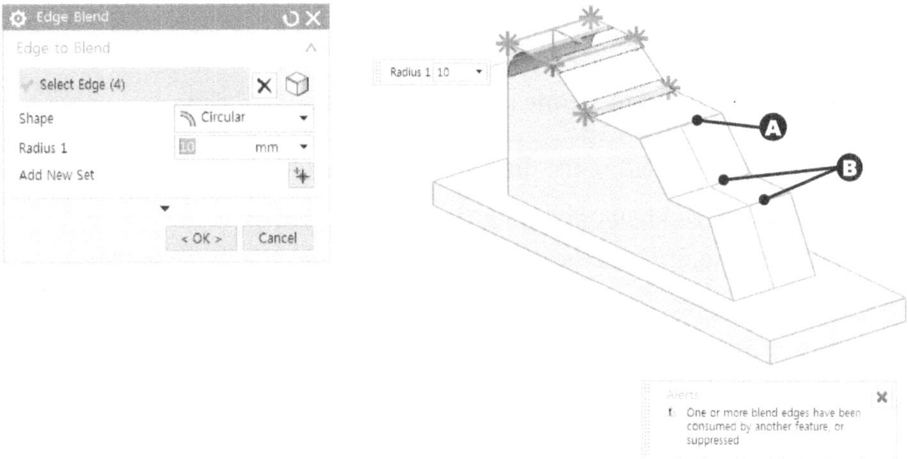

Fig 7-52 Alerts Message

4. Release the **Shift** key and select the newly created edges Ⓐ and Ⓑ designated in Fig 7-52. Use the **QuickPick** utility to select the newly created edge Ⓐ. Six edges are marked in the option field.

5. Press **OK** in the dialog box.

Modification is completed as shown in Fig 7-53.

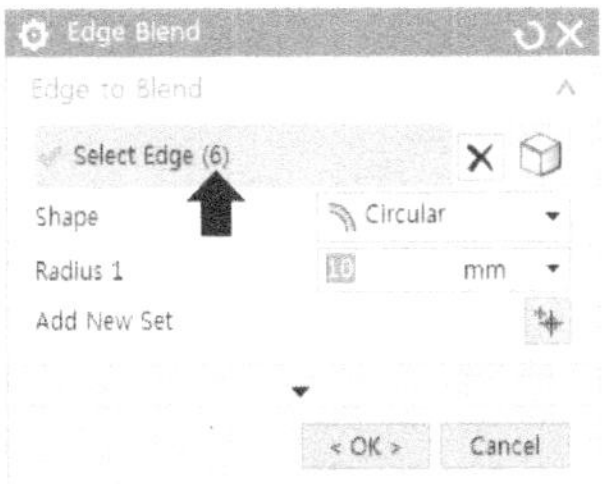

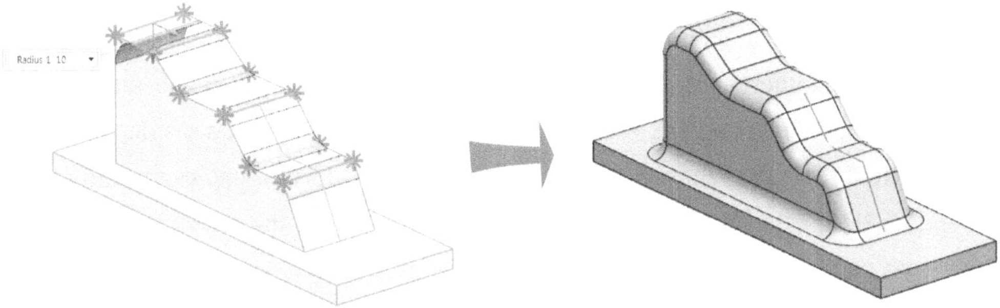

Fig 7-53 Adding Edges in Edge Blend

END of Exercise

Selecting and Deselecting Objects

You can select or deselect modeling objects in the following manner.

① While the selection field in the dialog box is highlighted, press the **Shift** key and click MB1 on the object to deselect objects.
② While the selection field in the dialog box is highlighted, release the **Shift** key and click MB1 on the object to select additional objects.

Bear in mind the following tips when you select objects. Refer to Appendix A on Page 633 for more topics on selecting objects.

① When the selection field in the dialog box is highlighted, the candidate object types are shown in the **Selection Filter** dropdown list. Fig 7-54 shows the selection bar when selecting edges for edge blend. Only the edges can be selected.
② The snap point option, curve rule and face rule are activated when you are selecting points, lines or faces, respectively, during the modeling process. Note that the curve rule and face rule are activated simultaneously when you can select both types of objects.

Fig 7-54 Selection Filter and Curve Rule

③ You cannot select objects that are not visible. Therefore, you cannot select edges or faces when the rendering style is either **Shaded with Edges** or **Shaded**. If you want to select unseen objects, rotate the model or change the rendering style to **Static Wireframe** or another style that can show the unseen objects. You can utilize the **Quick Pick** tool which appears when you place the mouse pointer on overlapped objects for a few seconds. When you select hidden edges or curves, you can turn on the two options designated by the arrows in Fig 7-55, which allow the selection of hidden wireframes and highlights them.

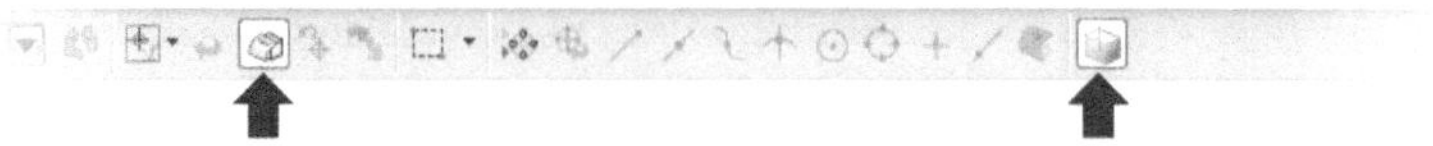

Fig 7-55 Options Available in Selecting Hidden Edges or Curves

7.5 Reordering a Feature

The modeling order has great effect in constructing a model. When the modeling order is not taken properly, you may have to repeat unnecessary modeling processes or you may not even be able to create the desired model.

When the modeling order is not correct, you can reorder the feature in the part navigator. If you press MB3 on a feature, the two options pointed out in Fig 7-56 become available, which allow moving the location of the feature before or after the target feature.

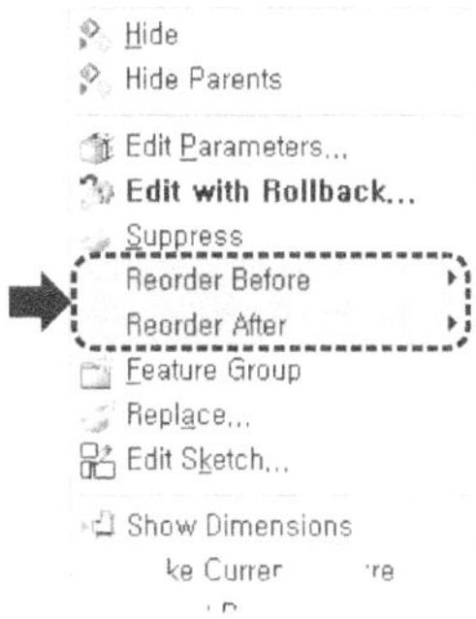

Fig 7-56 Reorder Options

You can reorder features using the drag and drop function. Fig 7-57 shows dragging the **Shell (5)** feature and dropping before **Extrude (4)**.

Bear in mind that, when you reorder features, you cannot move the features earlier before the parent feature and later after the child feature on account of the associativity between the features.

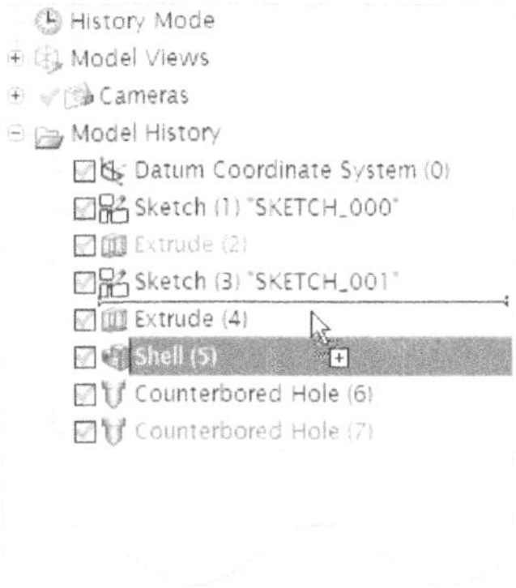

Fig 7-57 Drag and Drop of a Feature

Exercise 05 Reordering a Feature

ch07_ex05.prt

We will practice the following two exercises.

1. Reorder a feature and examine the modeling impact.
2. Add a feature and reorder, then examine the modeling impact.

Fig 7-60 Adding a Feature and Reordering

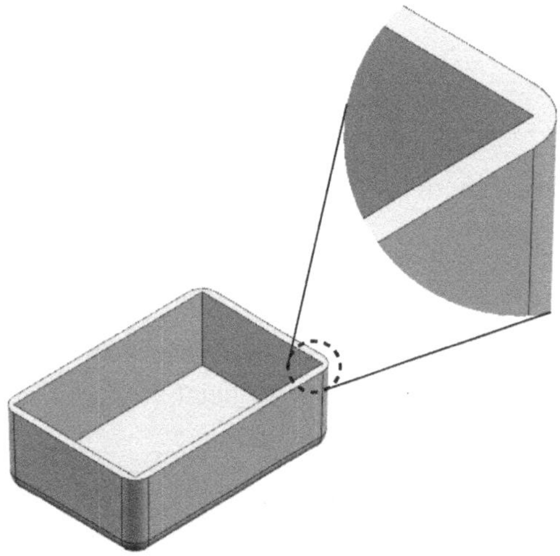

Fig 7-58 Examining the Modeling

Fig 7-59 Modeling History

Reordering a Feature

1. Open the given file ch07_ex05.prt.

2. Examine the portion as shown in Fig 7-59. Edge blend is not applied by the **Shell** feature.

3. Examine the modeling history in the part navigator.

Note that the **Edge Blend** is created after the **Shell**.

4. Click MB1 on the **Edge Blend** in the part navigator. The color of the **Shell** does not change which implies that there is no associativity between the **Edge Blend** and the **Shell**.

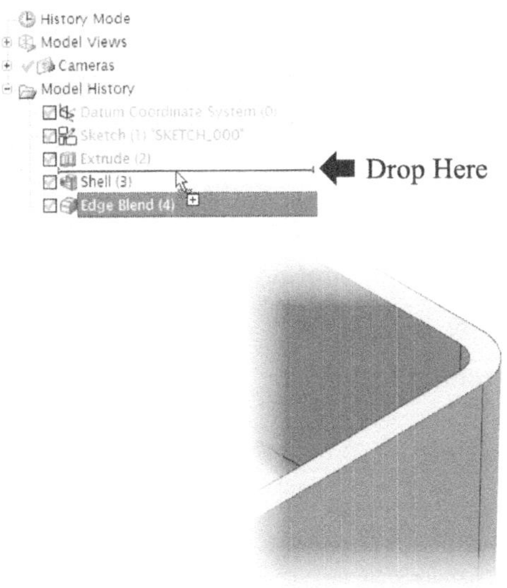

Fig 7-61 Reordering a Feature

5. Drag the **Edge Blend** feature and drop before the **Shell** feature as shown in Fig 7-61. The **Shell** command is applied for the edge blend face.

Adding a Feature

1. Create a point using in the **Direct Sketch** and constrain the point at the center of the face as shown in Fig 7-62. Apply two midpoint constraints with the upper edge and the blended edge as designated by the arrow. Note that you have to choose **Within Work Part Only** or **Entire Assembly** as the selection scope. Refer to "A.7 Selection Scope" on 642 for detail.

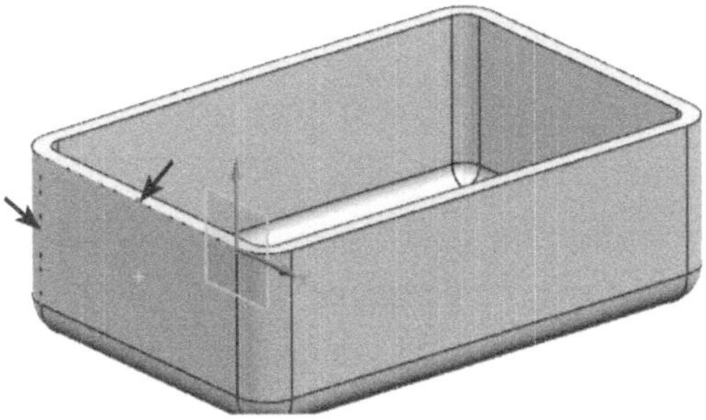

Fig 7-62 Creating a Point

2. Finish the direct sketch.

3. Click the **Hole** icon.

4. Select the point as the center of the hole.

5. Set the hole options as shown in Fig 7-63 and press **OK**.

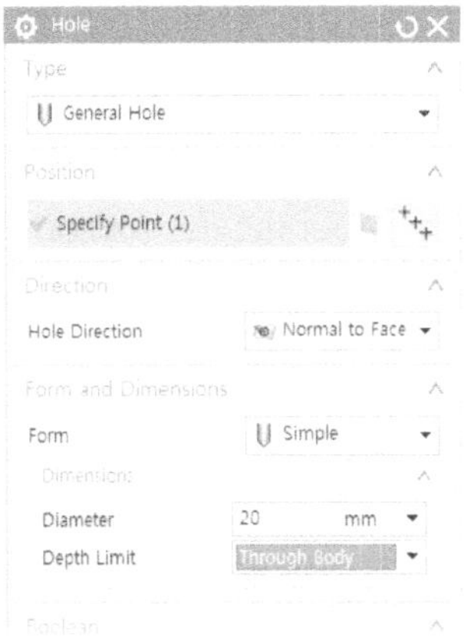

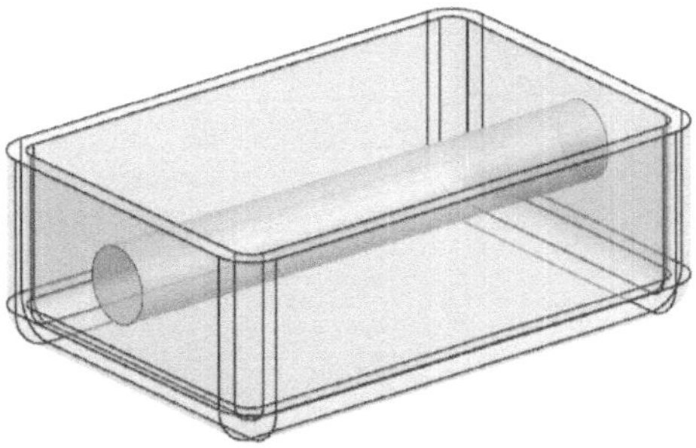

Fig 7-63 Creating a Hole

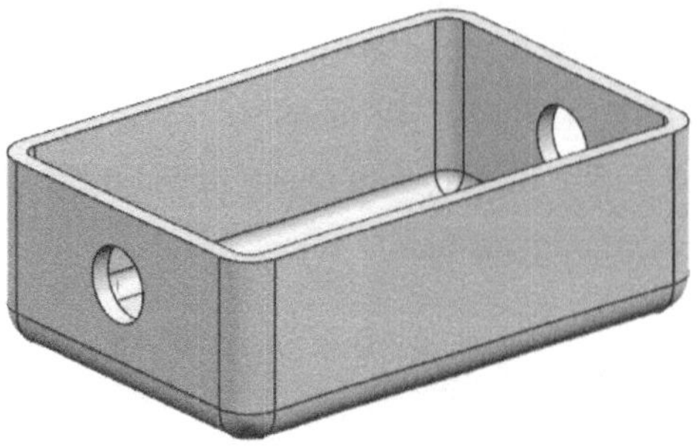

Fig 7-64 Hole Created

6. Select the sketch of the point in the part navigator and confirm that the **Extrude (5)** and **Edge Blend (3)** turn to red.

You can identify the parent features in the associativity browser shown in Fig 7-65 by pressing **MB3 > Browse on the Sketch (5)** feature.

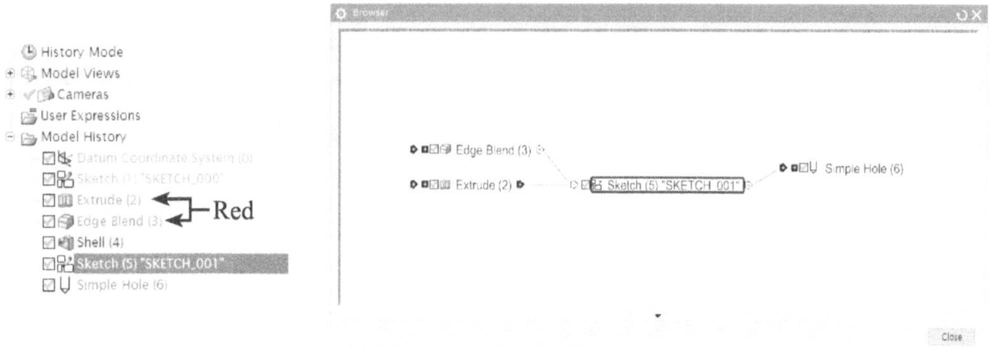

Fig 7-65 Identifying Associativity between Features

Reordering a Feature

1. Drag the **Simple Hole** feature and drop before the **Edge Blend**.

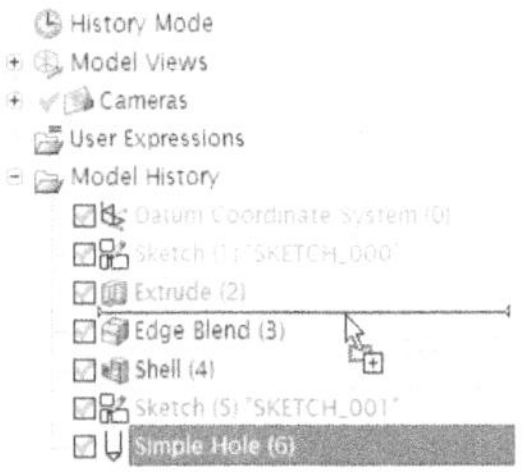

An error message is shown as in Fig 7-66. There is no direct associativity with the **Edge Blend** but the dependency is built by the sketch.

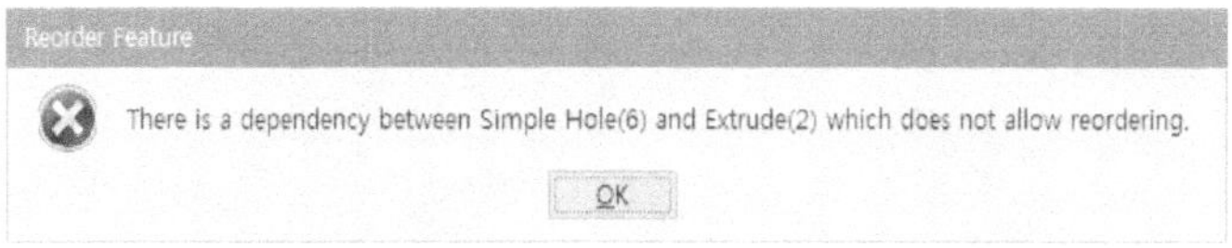

Fig 7-66 Dropping before Parent Feature

2. Press **OK** in the information box.

3. Drag the **Simple Hole** and drop before the **Shell** feature.

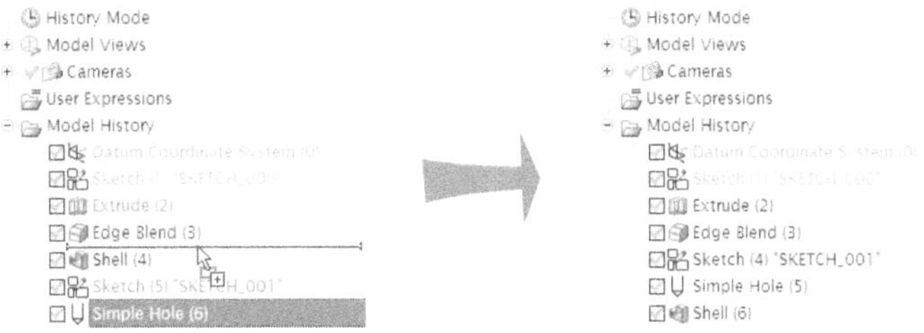

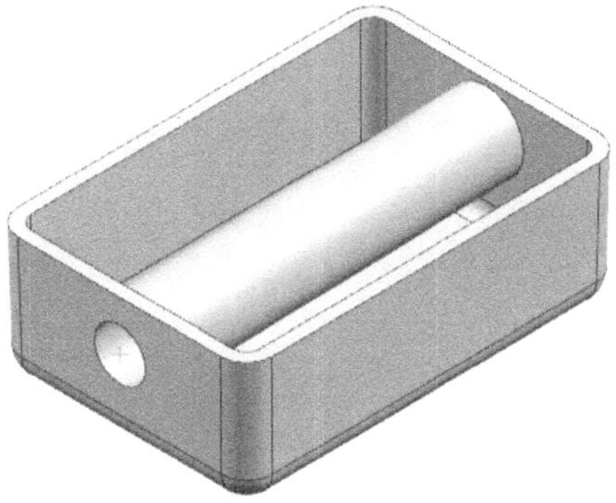

Fig 7-67 Reordered Simple Hole

END of Exercise

How to Reorder Before Edge Blend

You cannot reorder the **Simple Hole** feature before the **Edge Blend** because of the dependency. If you must reorder the feature, choose one of the following methods.

① Delete the dependency first and reorder. In the case of Exercise 05, delete the midpoint constraint that has been applied between the point and the blend edge and substitute with another constraint that has no relationship with the edge blend.

② Delete the **Simple Hole** feature and rollback the part before the **Edge Blend** by using the **Make Current Feature** option. Then you can create a hole before the edge blend.

Exercise 06 **Modifying a Section and Adding a Feature**

ch07_ex06.prt

Modify the given part as shown in Fig 7-68 keeping to the requirements.

Requirements

1. Do not create a new sketch.
2. Modify the section for the existing **Extrude** features.
3. You can add extrude or a hole feature at the desired location in the part navigator.
4. There should be no error in the completed model.

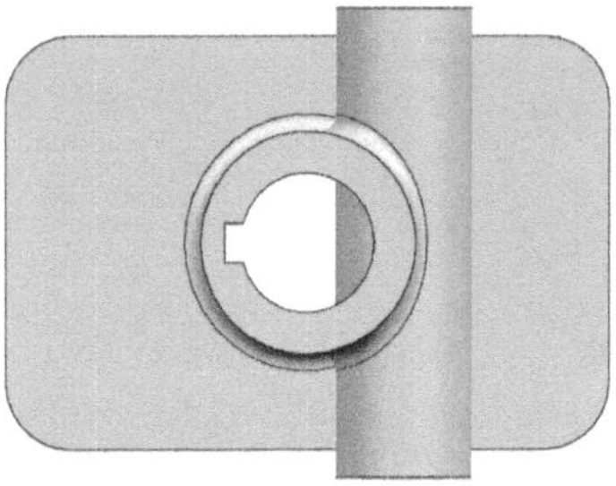

(Before Modification - Top View)

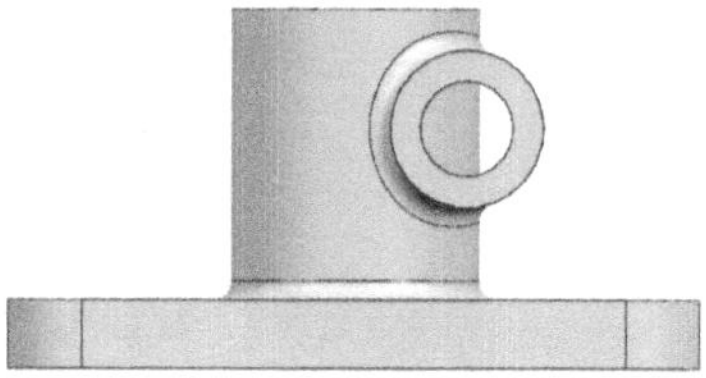

(Before Modification - Front View)

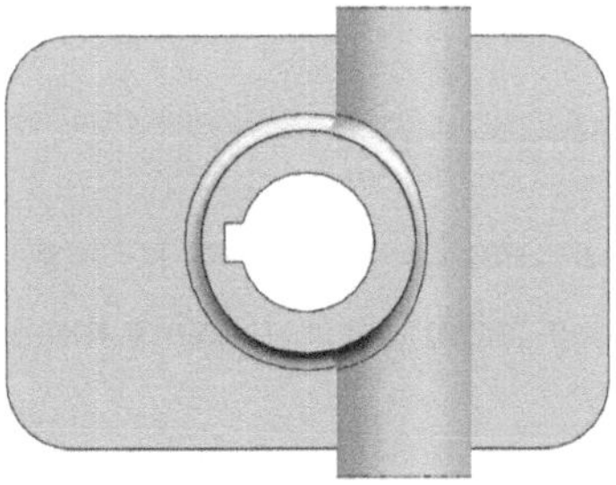

(After Modification - Top View)

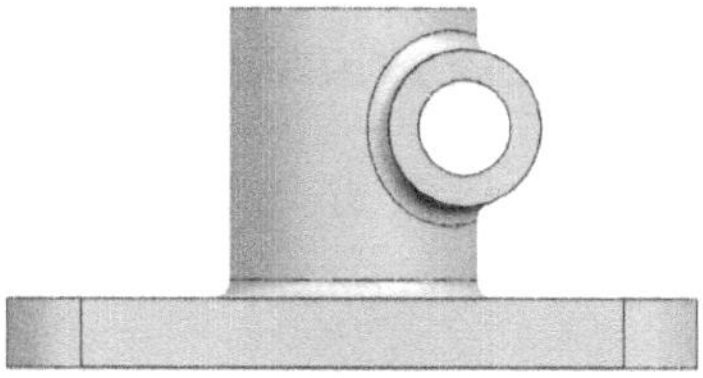

(After Modification - Front View)

Fig 7-68 Before and After the Modification

END of Exercise

Modify the given part according to the brief steps below. The purpose of this exercise is to modify a feature and resolve the downstream errors.

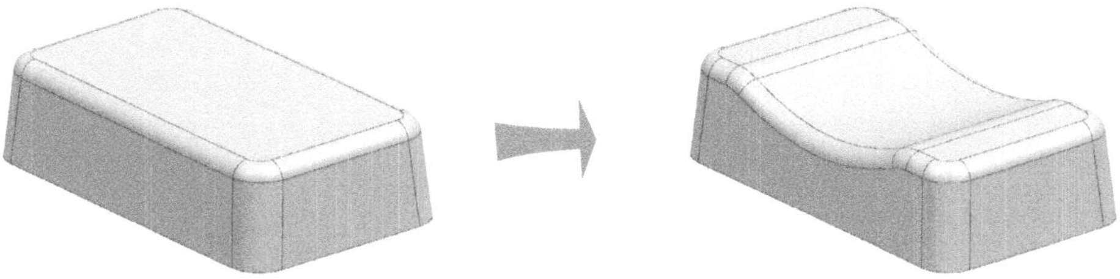

Fig 7-69 Before and After the Modification

Step 1

1. Make the **Extrude (3)** a current feature and create a sketch as shown in Fig 7-70.
2. Extrude the circle and subtract the body.

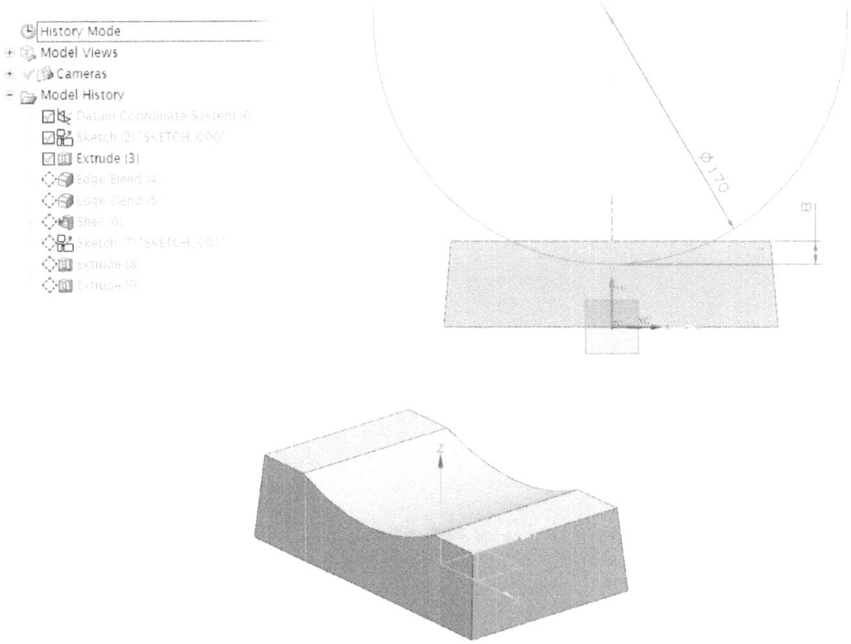

Fig 7-70 Modification Step 1

Step 2

1. Update the model to the end by choosing **MB3 > Make Current Feature** on the last feature. You can choose **Update to End** from the pop-up menu by pressing MB3 on an empty area in the **Part Navigator**.
2. Modify the section of **Extrude (10)** and **Extrude (11)** such that the model appears as shown in Fig 7-71.

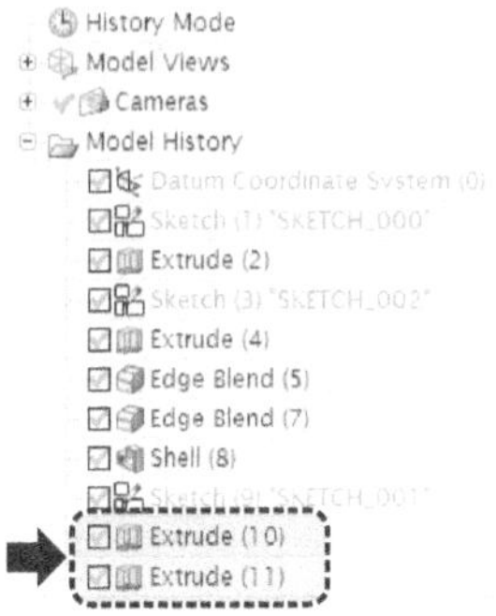

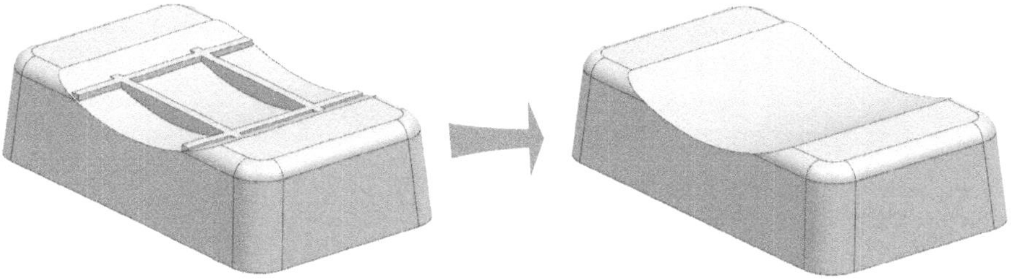

Fig 7-71 Modification Step 2

Step 3

1. Make the **Edge Blend (5)** a current feature.
2. Apply a 20 mm radius edge blend on the edge specified by **A** in Fig 7-72.
3. Update the model to the end.

Fig 7-73 shows the completed model. The cut model is to show the inside of the model.

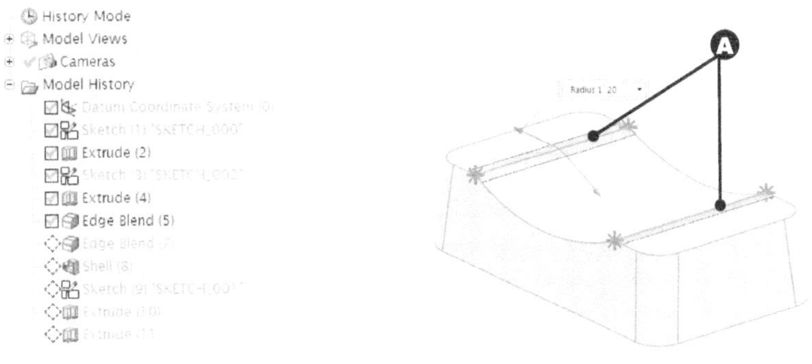

Fig 7-72 Modification Step 3

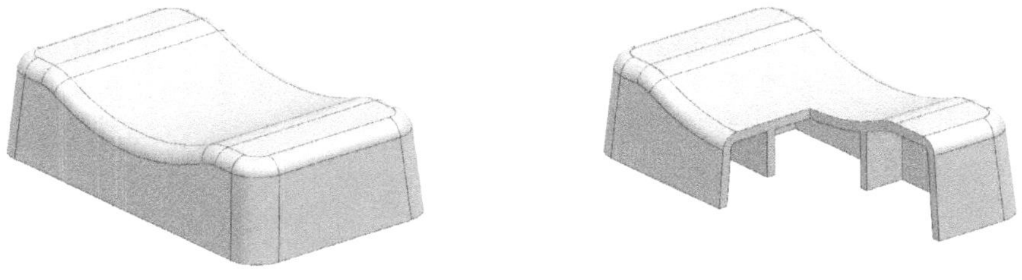

Fig 7-73 Completed Model

END of Exercise

Exercise 08 **Joint Part**

ch07_ex08.prt

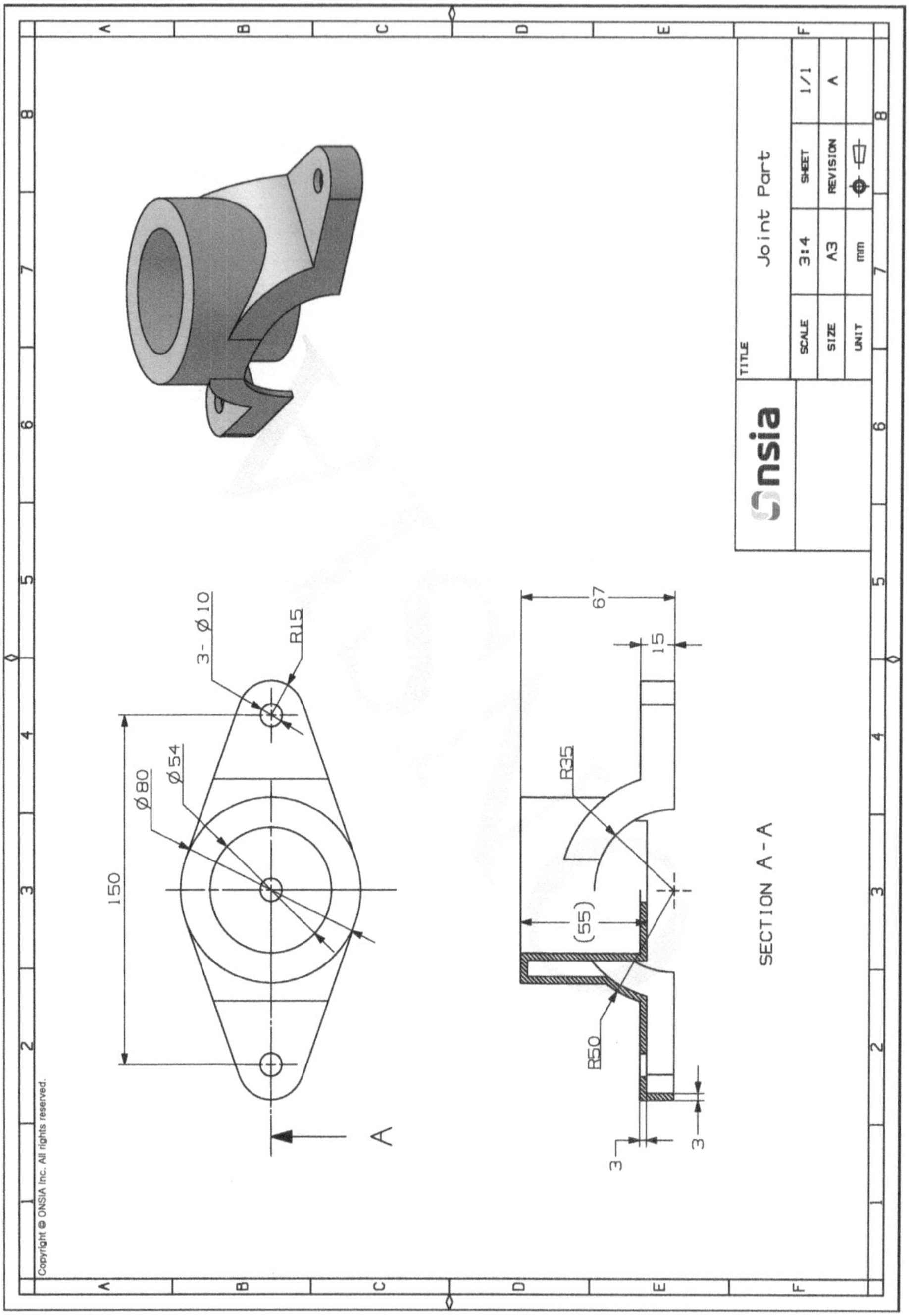

Fig 7-74 Drawing for Exercise 8

Hint!

Create the model referring to the following procedure.

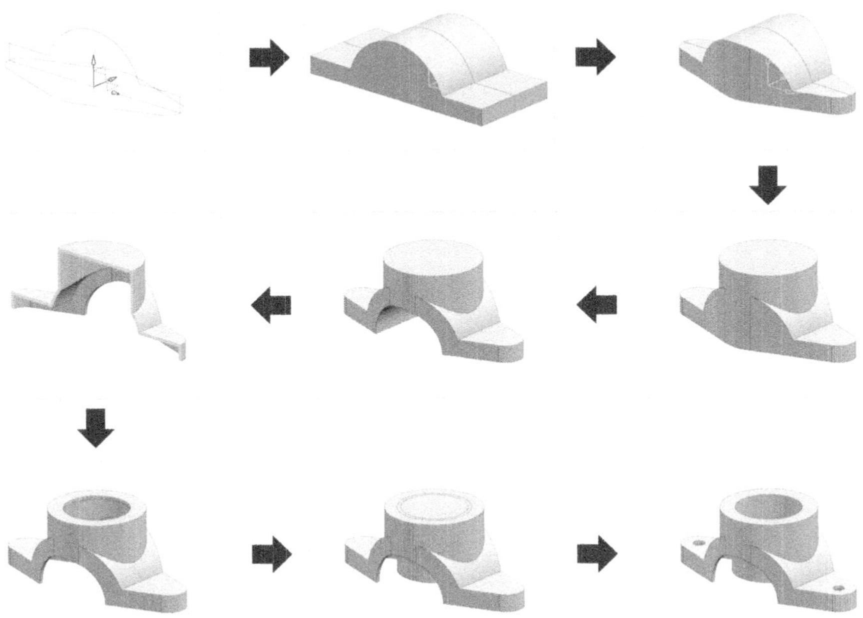

Note: The image capture in step 6 is to show the inside of the model. You do not need to split the model.

This page left blank intentionally.

Chapter 8

Copy of Objects and Features

After completing this chapter you will understand

- how to create patterns of features, faces and geometries using the **Pattern Feature**, **Pattern Face** and **Pattern Geometry** commands.
- how to use the **Mirror Feature**, **Mirror Face** and **Mirror Geometry** commands.
- how to copy and paste features.

8.1 Introduction

Repeating the same modeling process several times is time consuming and tedious. Once a feature or object is created, you can escape from tiresome modeling repetition by applying commands that copy features or objects. Moreover, you can modify the result of the copy by changing the copy options. Fig 8-1 shows copying a hole to create four holes. The number of instances can be changed to eight as shown in Fig 8-2 by modifying the corresponding copy option. If the size of the instanced hole is changed, the sizes of all instances are updated.

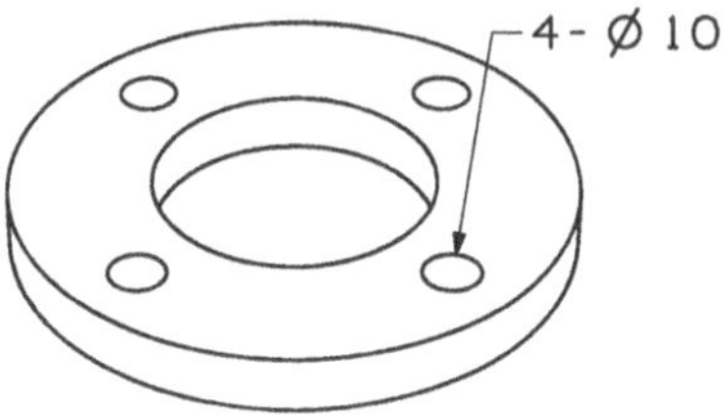

Fig 8-1 Four Holes

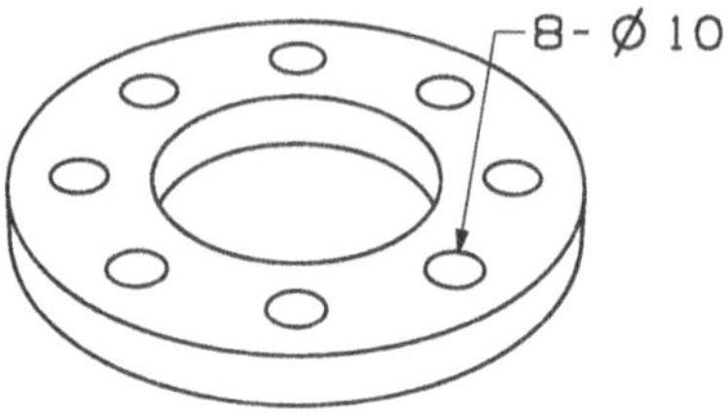

Fig 8-2 Eight Holes

8.2 Classifying Copy Commands

NX gives several copy commands. You have to apply the appropriate command according to your requirements. You can choose the required command correctly by remembering the following two guidelines.

① Types of copy source: Which to copy?
② Method of copy: How to copy?

Fig 8-3 shows the commands that can be applied to copy features, faces and geometries. You can access the commands in the **Menu** button by choosing **Insert > Associative Copy**. The commands are classified according to the types of source and method to copy. The patterning and mirroring methods will be covered in this textbook.

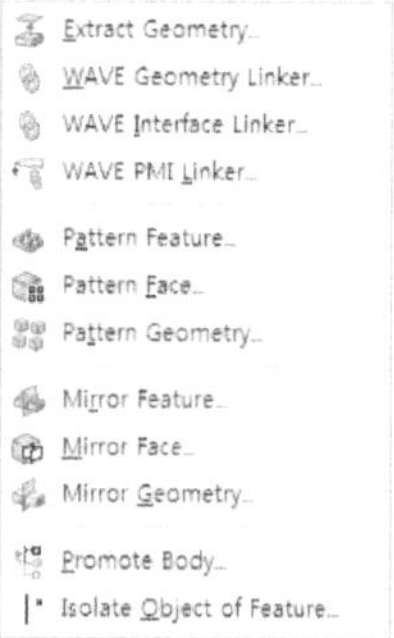

Fig 8-3 Copy Commands in NX

8.2.1 Source of Copy

When you apply a copy command, you have to always select the source of the copy. You can select the source in the part navigator or in the model. The types of source of copy can be identified in the **Type Filter** dropdown list. Refer to Appendix A on Page 633 for more topics on selecting objects.

Fig 8-4 and Fig 8-5 show the types of source of the **Pattern Feature** command, **Pattern Geometry** command, respectively.

Fig 8-4 Source of Pattern Feature Command

Fig 8-5 Source of Pattern Geometry Command

The source objects of the **Pattern Feature** and the **Mirror Feature** command are features. Note that the parameters that define the feature are also be copied. On the other hand, the **Pattern Geometry** and **Mirror Geometry** commands copy the geometry of the model. Therefore, construction options such as the **Boolean** operation and the limit options of a feature cannot be copied.

Fig 8-6 shows the copy commands in the **Feature** icon group. The **Pattern Geometry** command does not appear by default.

Fig 8-6 Copy Commands in the Feature Icon Group

8.2.2 Method to Copy

You can identify the method to copy in the Layout dropdown list in the patterning commands.

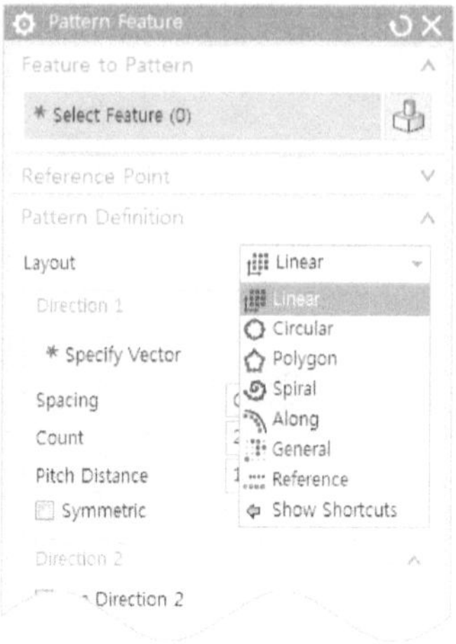

Fig 8-7 Layout Dropdown

Four types of copy methods will be covered in this textbook: **Linear Pattern, Circular Pattern, General Pattern** and **Mirror**.

Linear Pattern

Linear pattern copies features or geometries along one or two specified directions at a specified distance or pitch. Fig 8-8 shows patterning a solid body along the X and Y axis of the datum coordinate system.

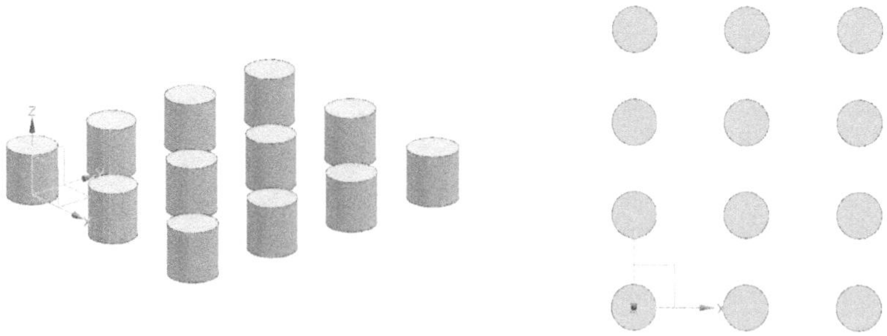

Fig 8-8 Example of Linear Pattern

Circular Pattern

Circular pattern copies features or geometries about a rotation axis at a specified angle. Fig 8-7 shows patterning a solid body about the Z axis.

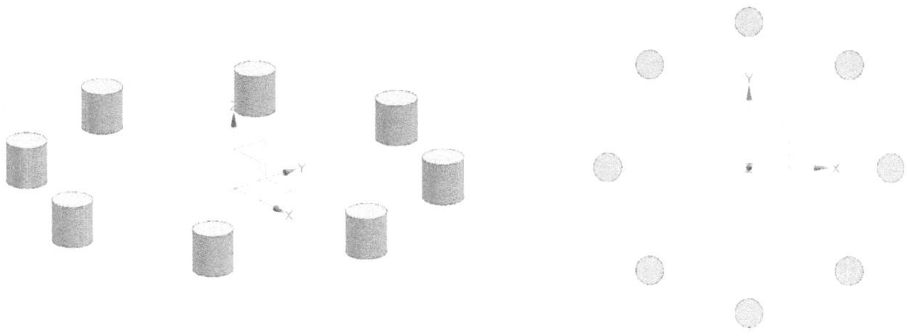

Fig 8-9 Example of Circular Pattern

Mirror

Mirroring method copies features or geometries about a symmetry plane. Fig 8-8 shows mirroring a feature about the datum plane. Note that you can choose the datum plane or the planar face of another body as the symmetry plane.

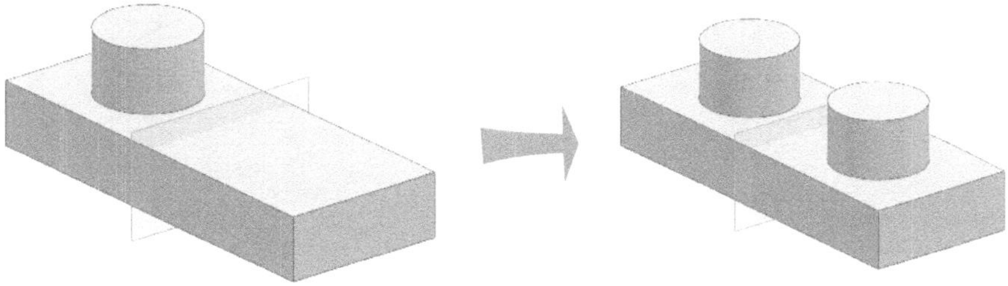

Fig 8-10 Example of Mirroring Method

General Pattern

You can copy features or geometries by selecting points on the location. Fig 8-11 shows coyping the cylindrical feature to the points defined in the sketch.

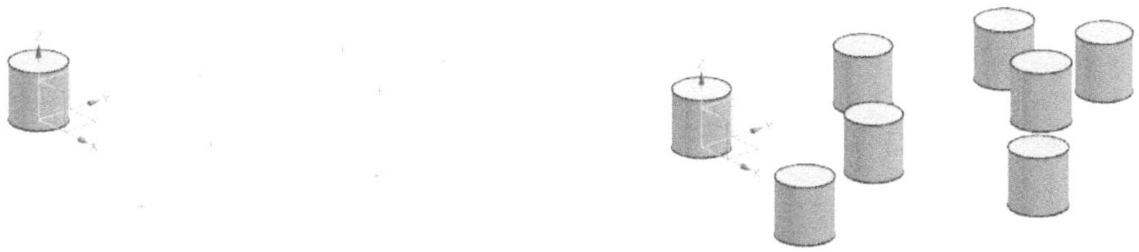

Fig 8-11 Example of General Pattern

8.3 Pattern Feature

You can apply several types of copy methods by selecting features as a source.

8.3.1 Linear Type

Procedure

① Click the **Pattern Feature** icon in the **Feature** icon group.
② Press the **Reset** button in the dialog box.
③ Select the source of pattern. Note that you can select several features at the same time, and the number of selected features is marked in the option field.
④ Select the **Layout** option in the dropdown list. You can define the copy method.
⑤ Specify the **Direction 1** option. You can define the direction of the linear pattern.
⑥ If you want to define another direction of the linear pattern, select the **Use Direction 2** option and set the option.
⑦ Press **OK** in the dialog box.

Fig 8-12 Pattern Feature Icon

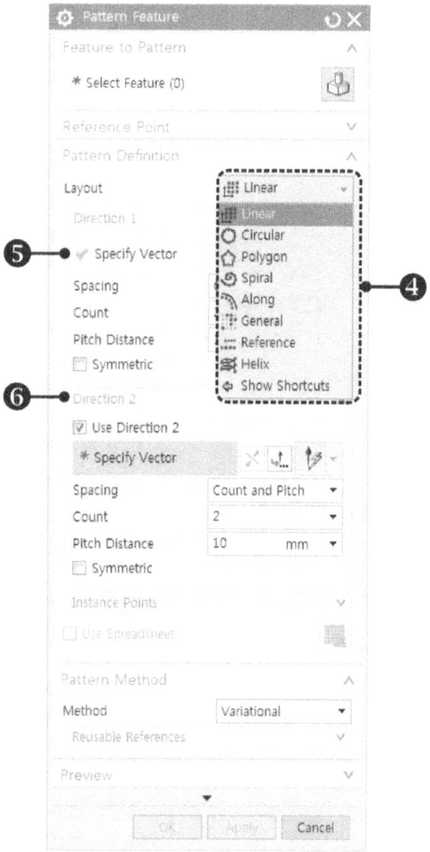

Fig 8-13 Pattern Feature Dialog Box

Spacing Option

Spacing option defines the patterning method of instances.

► **Count and Pitch**: Input the number of instances and spacing between instances. The total span is calculated.

► **Count and Span**: Input the number of instances and total span. The pitch is calculated.

► **Pitch and Span**: Input pitch between instances and total span. The number of instances is calculated.

► **List**: Input the number of instances and specify the spacing for each instance. You can specify variable spacing by pressing the **Add New Set** button.

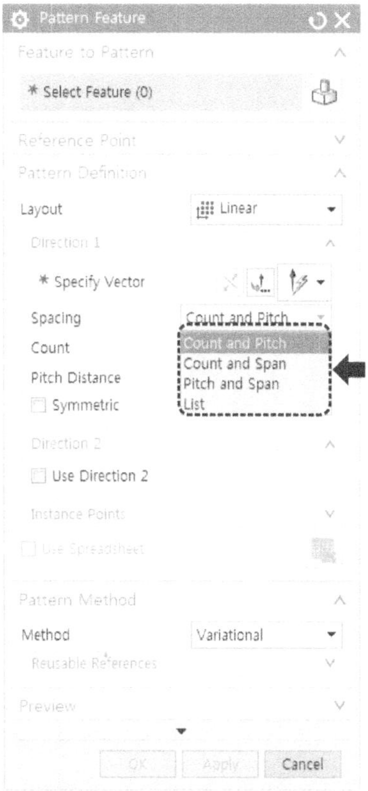

Fig 8-14 Spacing Option

Exercise 01 Linear Type Pattern

ch08_ex01.prt

Create a **Boss** feature and apply a rectangular pattern according to the suggested procedure.

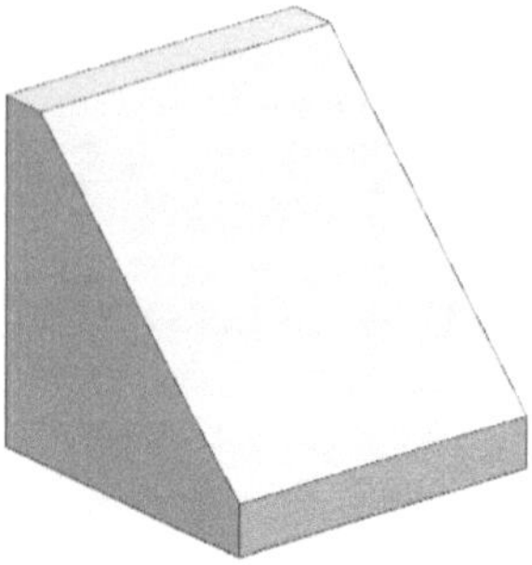

Fig 8-15 Model for Exercise

1. Open the given file ch08_ex01.prt.

2. Choose **Insert > Design Feature > Boss** in the **Menu** button.

3. Create a **Boss** feature as shown in Fig 8-16 (Diameter: 10 mm, Height: 20 mm).

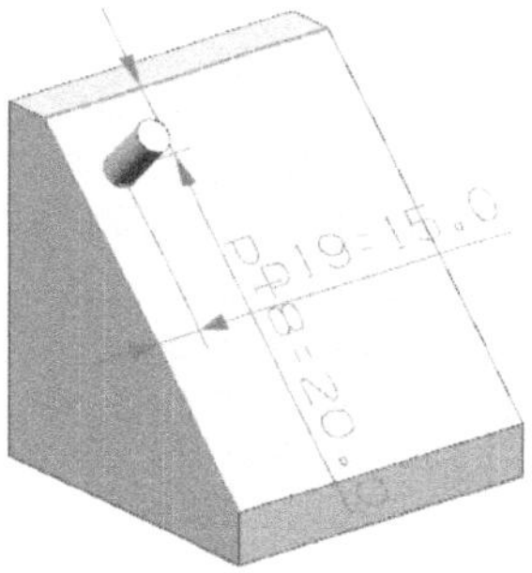

Fig 8-16 Creating a Boss Feature

4. Click the **Pattern Feature** icon in the **Feature** icon group and reset the dialog box.

5. Confirm that the **Select Feature** option is highlighted in the dialog box and select the **Boss** feature.

Fig 8-17 Specify Vector Option

6. Press MB2. The **Direction 1** option is highlighted and you are prompted to specify a vector as the first direction of the rectangular pattern.

7. Select the edge Ⓐ specified in Fig 8-18. Press the **Reverse Direction** button if the direction is reversed.

8. Specify the **Spacing** option as shown in Fig 8-18.

9. Press the **Enter** key in the keyboard. The result of the pattern is previewed as shown in Fig 8-18.

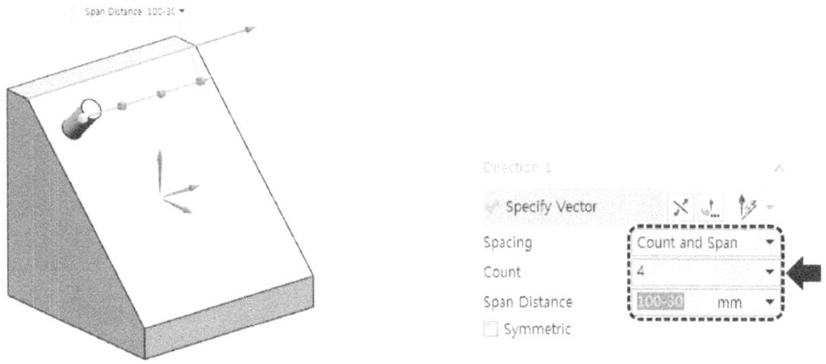

Fig 8-18 Direction 1 Option

10. Check the **Use Direction 2** option as shown in Fig 8-19. The **Specify Vector** option becomes available.

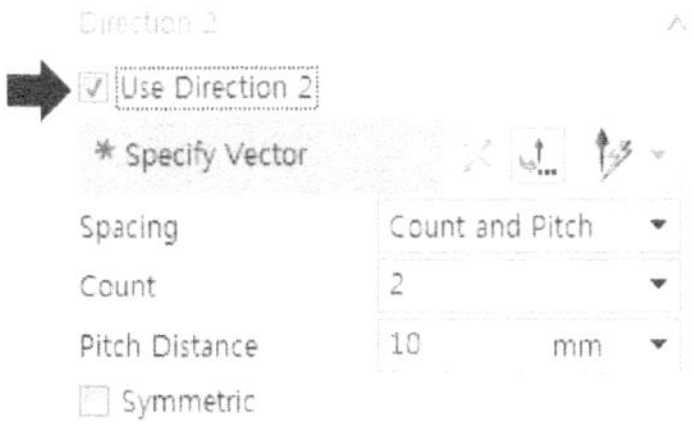

Fig 8-19 Direction 2 Option

11. Select the edge Ⓑ as shown in Fig 8-20.

12. Specify the **Spacing** option as shown in Fig 8-20.

13. Press **Enter** in the keyboard. A preview of the instances is shown in Fig 8-20.

14. Press **OK** in the dialog box. Fig 8-21 shows the result.

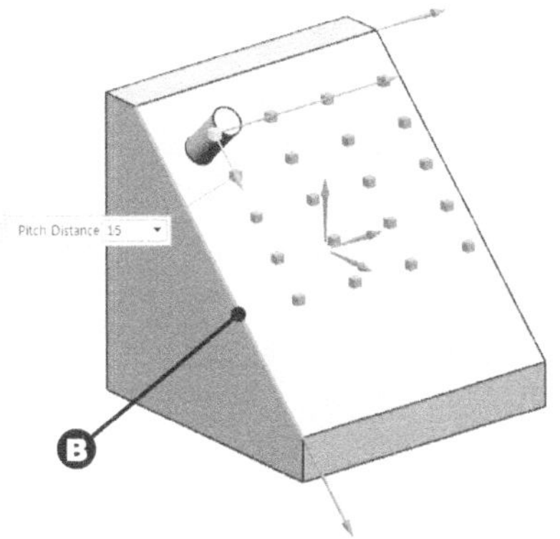

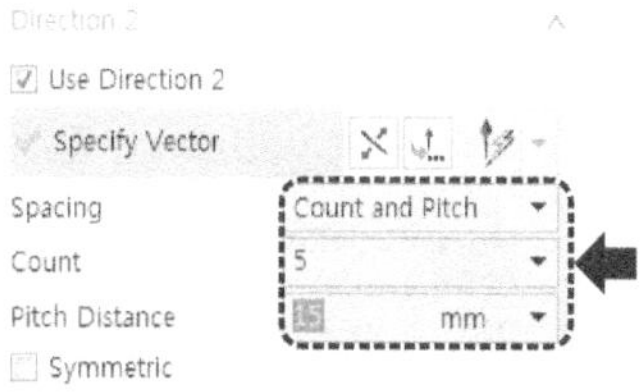

Fig 8-20 Direction 2 Option

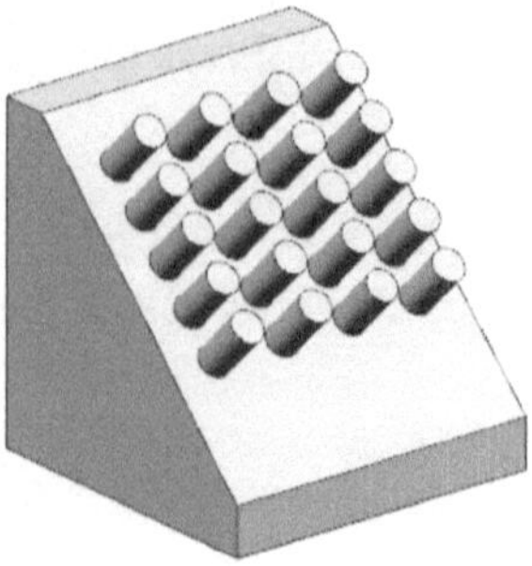

Fig 8-21 Completed Model

END of Exercise

Part Navigator

Fig 8-20 shows the part navigator and the result of the rectangular pattern. You can suppress an instance by unchecking the box in front of the instance in the part navigator. The location of instances is specified by the digits in [ ]. The first number implies the **Direction 1** location and the second number implies the **Direction 2** location.

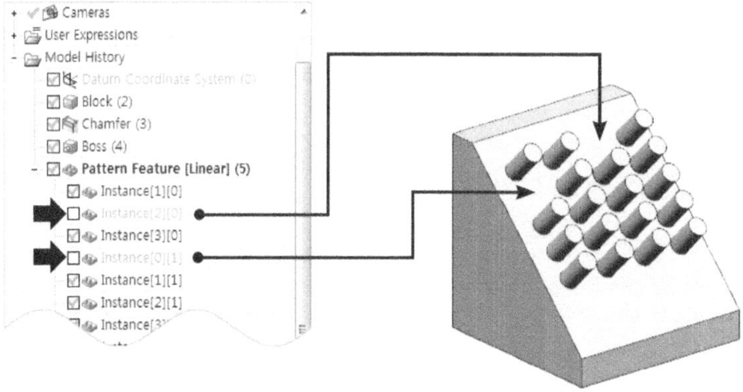

Fig 8-22 Suppressing Instances

Use of Expression

You have specified the values of the **Count and Span** of the **Spacing** option for direction 1 in Exercise 01 because you know the total span of the pattern. For direction 2, you can measure the span and use the measured value in the **Spacing** option.

A through hole is created in the given model. The location along the diagonal edge is defined arbitrarily. Let's create four holes symmetrically along the diagonal edge.

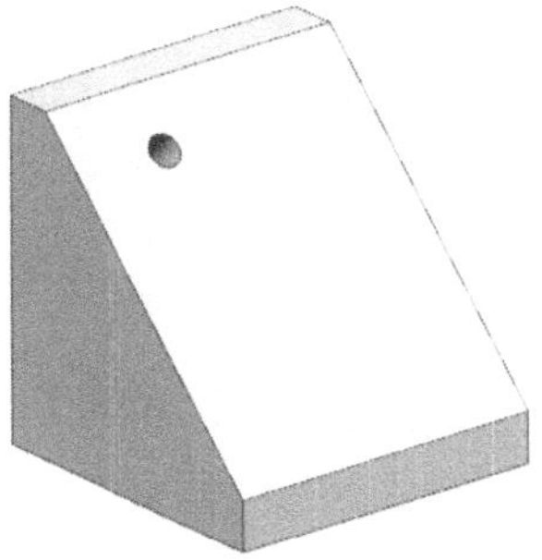

Fig 8-23 File for Exercise

Definition of Variable

1. Open the given file ch08_ex02.prt.
2. Choose **Tools > Expression** in the **Menu** button.
3. Select **All** in the **Listed Expression** dropdown list (❸ in Fig 8-24).
4. Enter "edge_to_hole" in the **Name** input box (❹ in Fig 8-24).
5. Click the **Measure Distance** icon in the dialog box (❺ in Fig 8-24).

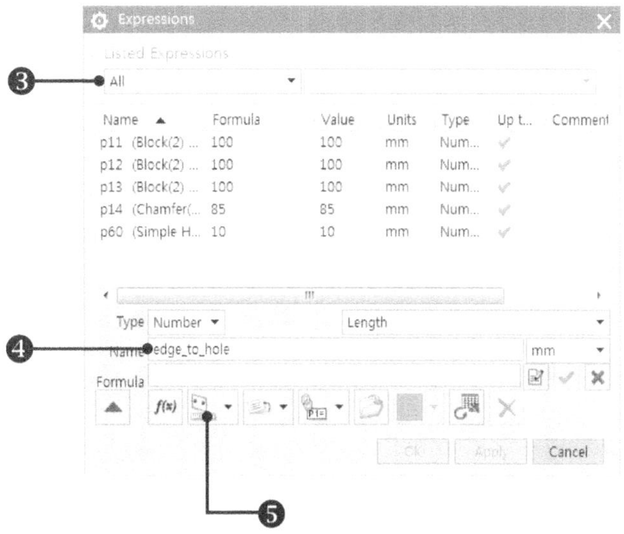

Fig 8-24 Expression Dialog Box

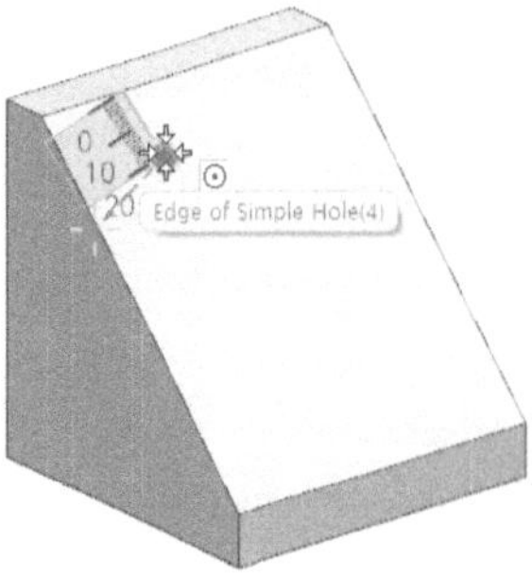

Fig 8-25 Measuring Distance

6. Measure the distance between the edge and the center of the hole as shown in Fig 8-25.

7. Press **OK** in the **Measure Distance** dialog box. The **Expression** dialog box is shown in Fig 8-26. Note that the measured distance value is allocated in another variable. The number may vary reader to reader.

8. Click the check button (❽ in Fig 8-26).

9. The variable “edge_to_hole” is defined as shown in Fig 8-26.

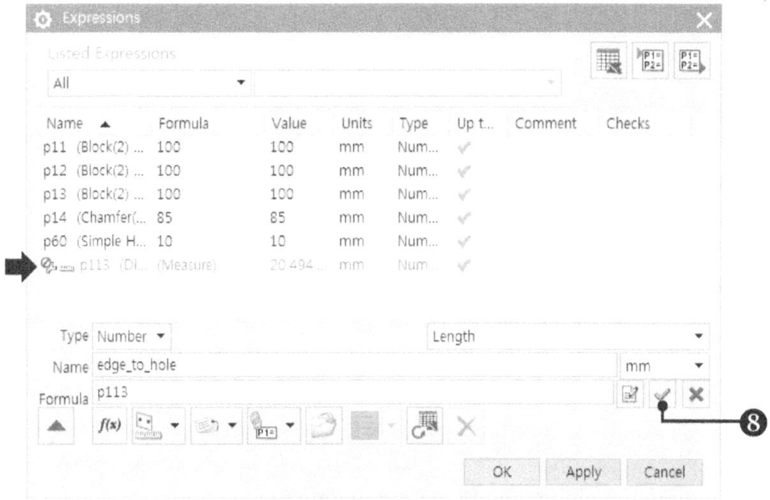

Fig 8-26 Result of Measure

10. Define a variable named “diagonal” and measure the length of the diagonal edge. Use the **Measure Length** option instead of **Measure Distance** (refer to Fig 8-28).

The **Expression** dialog box after defining the variable “diagonal” is as shown in Fig 8-29.

11. Press **OK** in the **Expression** dialog box.

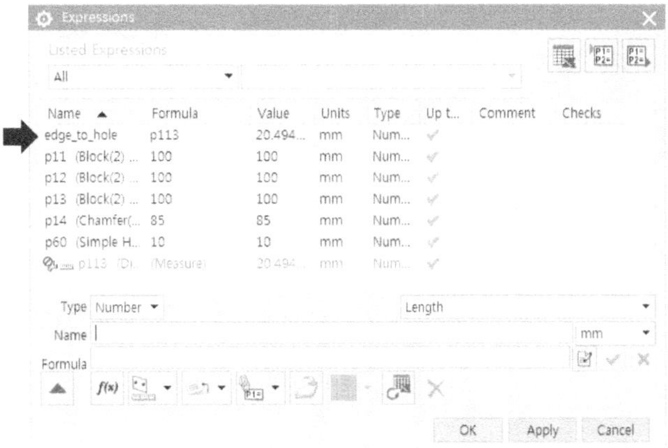

Fig 8-27 Defined Variable

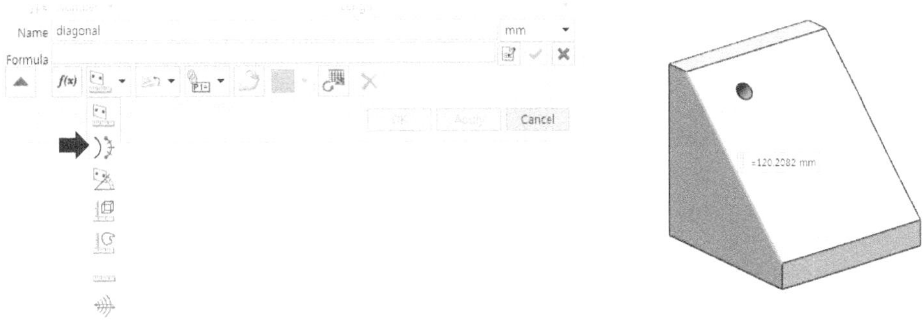

Fig 8-28 Measure Length Icon

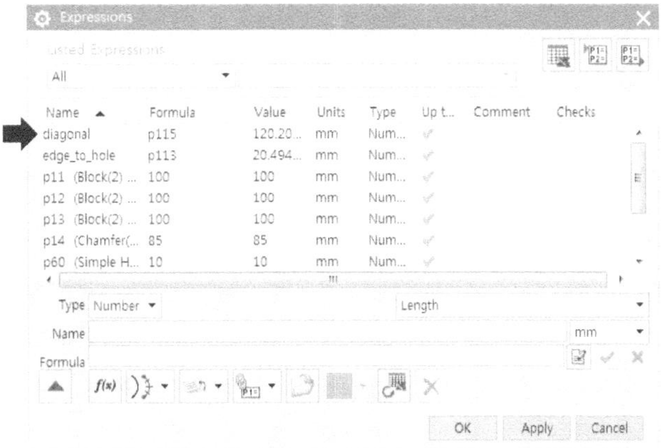

Fig 8-29 Completed Variable Definition

Creating a Pattern

1. Click the **Pattern Feature** in the **Feature** icon group.
2. Reset the dialog box.
3. Select the **Simple Hole** and press MB2.
4. Select the edge Ⓐ as shown in Fig 8-30.
5. Set the **Direction 1** option as shown in Fig 8-30 and press **Enter**. A preview of instances is shown as in Fig 8-30. Note that the base point is located at the center of the instances.

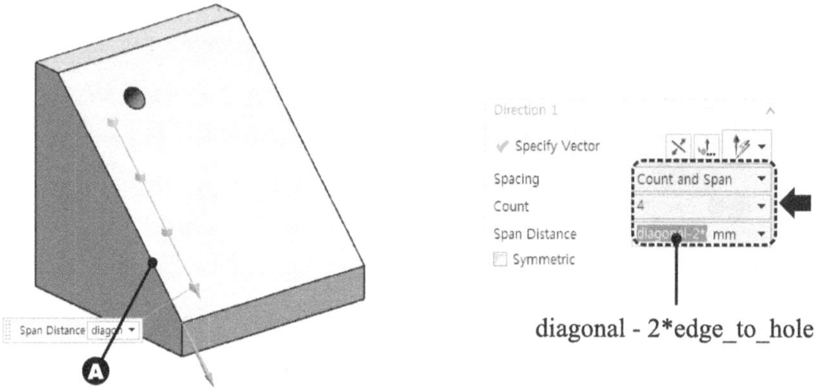

Fig 8-30 Direction 1 Option

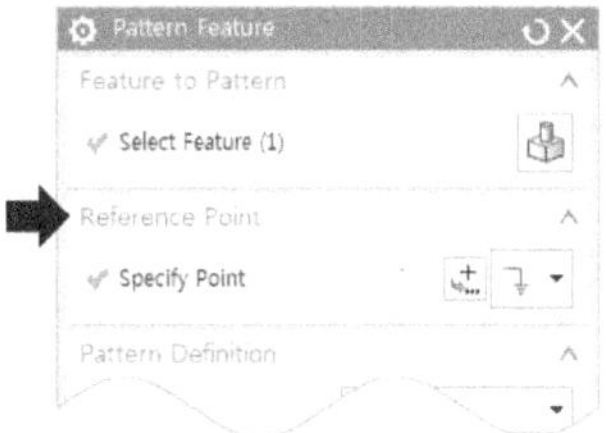

Fig 8-31 Reference Point Option

6. Expand the **Reference Point** option in the dialog box and click the **Specify Point** option.

7. Select the center of the hole edge.

A preview is shown as in Fig 8-32.

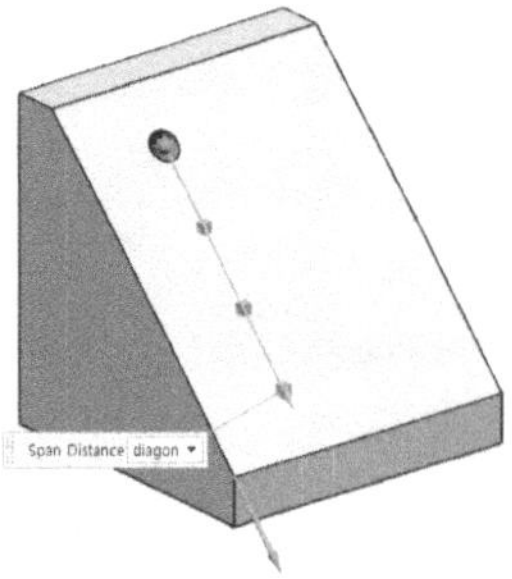

Fig 8-32 Preview of Pattern

8. Press **OK** in the **Pattern Feature** dialog box. Fig 8-33 shows the result.

9. Click the **Edit Section** icon in the **View** tab and show the model as in Fig 8-34. The instances are created as through holes.

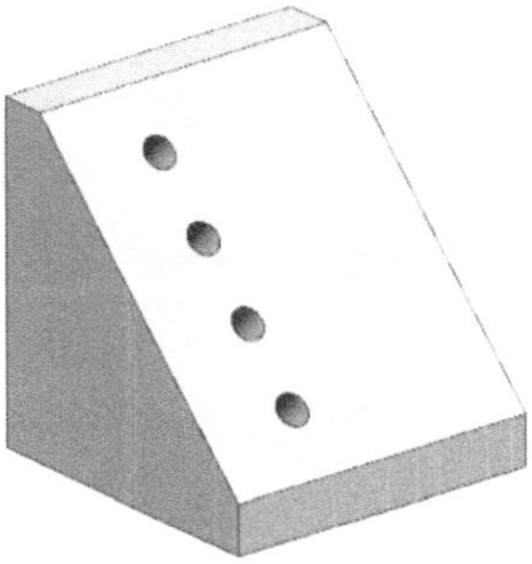

Fig 8-33 Completed Model

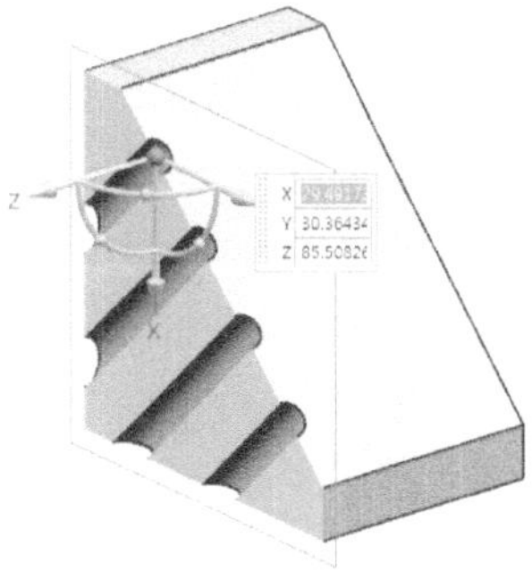

Fig 8-34 Work Section

END of Exercise

8.3.2 Cautions in Using the Pattern Feature Command

Pay attention when using the **Pattern Feature** command in the following aspect. The cautions are applied for another type of pattern.

① When you try to copy features such as a datum and sketch or the Boolean operations, an alert message as shown in Fig 8-35 is invoked. You cannot change the **Pattern Method** when you copy datum or sketch features.

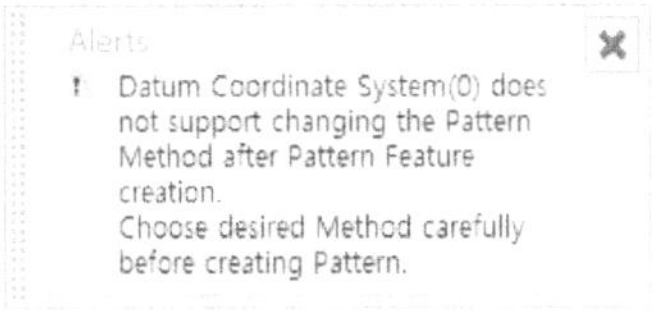

Fig 8-35 Alert Message

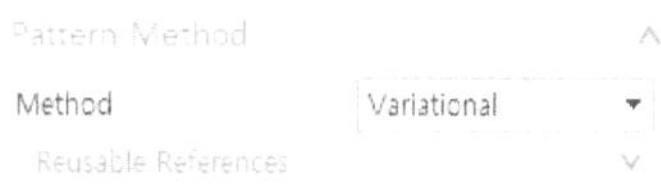

Fig 8-36 Pattern Method Option

② A boolean option is applied for instances. The fourth instance shown in Fig 8-37 cannot be formed because the solid body for creating the hole is outside of the target body.

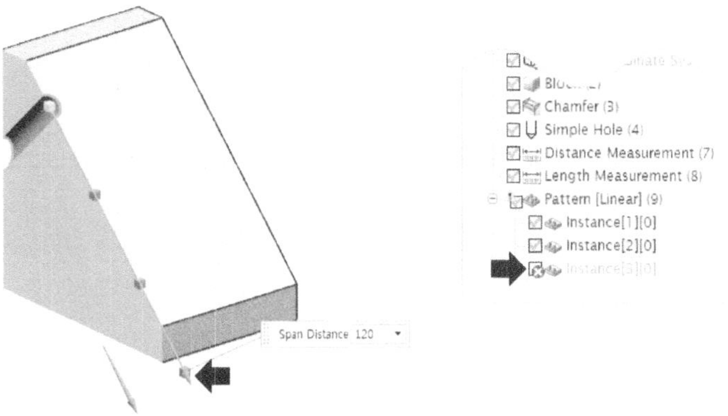

Fig 8-37 Erroneous Instance

③ Features such as a fillet or chamfer have to be patterned together with the parent features. If you select only the fillet or chamfer feature, an alert message as shown in Fig 8-38 is invoked.

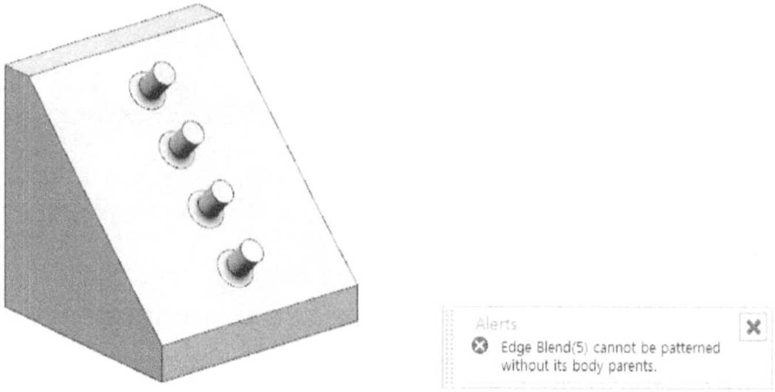

Fig 8-38 Pattern of Fillet

Exercise 03 Creating and Modifying Pattern *ch08_ex03.prt*

Perform the following modeling process according to the brief steps below.

1. Create a linear pattern.
2. Modify the option of the pattern.
3. Modify the geometry of the source feature.

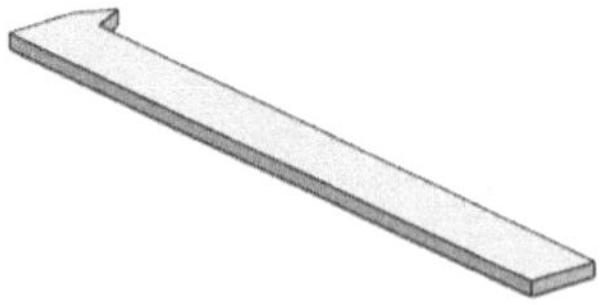

Fig 8-39 File for Exercise

Step 1

Create a linear pattern according to the information given in Fig 8-40. Note that you can select a feature in the part navigator.

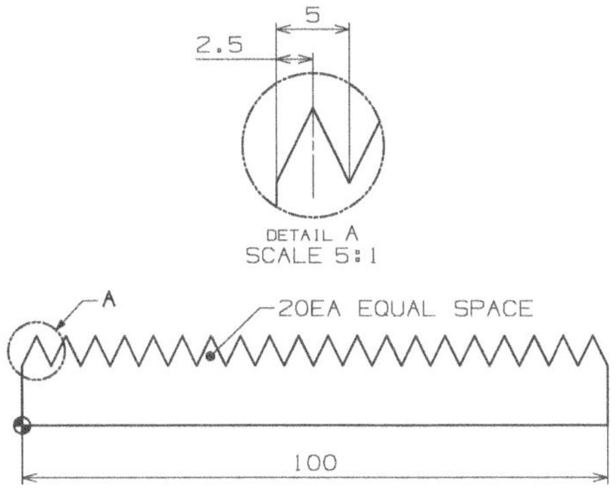

Fig 8-40 Information of Pattern

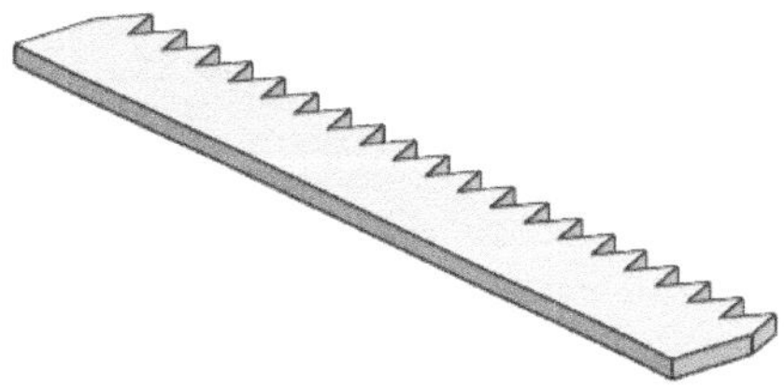
Fig 8-41 Result of Pattern

Step 2

Modify the number of teeth from 20 to 10 by double clicking the **Pattern** feature in the part navigator. The span has to be modified from 5 mm to 10 mm.

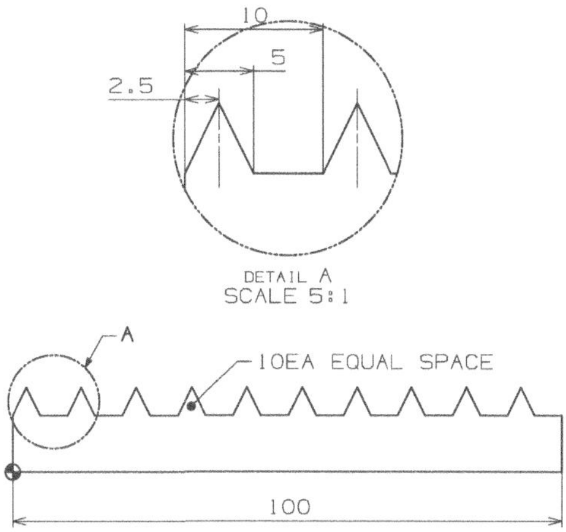

Fig 8-42 Information for Modification

Step 3

Show the sketch for the second extrude feature and modify its dimensions as shown in Fig 8-43. You can modify the sketch dimensions by pressing **MB3 > Edit Sketch** on the extrude feature. The direction option is the same as that of Step 1.

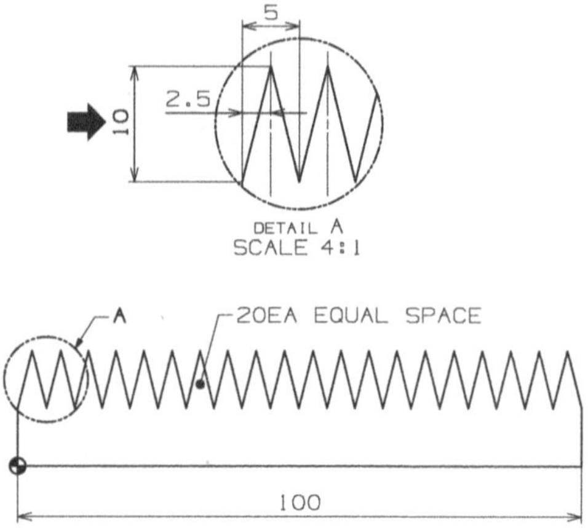

Fig 8-43 Information of Modification

END of Exercise

8.3.3 Circular Type

Procedure

① Click the **Pattern Feature** icon in the **Feature** icon group.

② Reset the dialog box.

③ Select the source feature. You can select several features at the same time.

④ Select the **Layout** option as **Circular** in the dropdown list.

⑤ Select a vector as the rotation axis (❺ in Fig 8-44).

⑥ Set the **Angular Direction** option (❻ in Fig 8-44) and press **OK** in the dialog box.

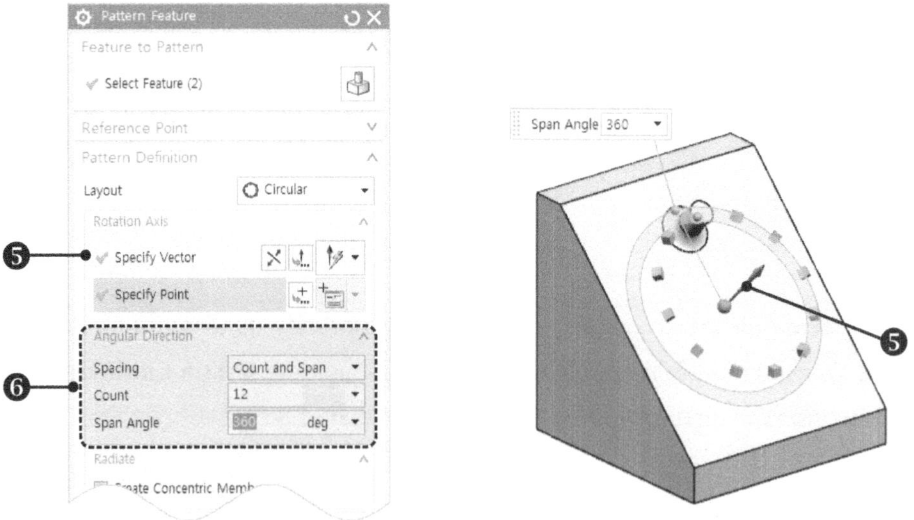

Fig 8-44 Procedure for Circular Type Pattern

Spacing Option

The spacing option defines the patterning method of instances.

► **Count and Pitch**: Input the number of instances and angular pitch. The total angular span is calculated.

► **Count and Span**: Input the number of instances and total angular span. The angular pitch is calculated.

► **Pitch and Span**: Input the angular pitch and total angular span. The number of instances is calculated.

► **List**: Input the number of instances and specify the angular spacing for each instance. You can specify variable spacing by pressing the **Add New Set** button.

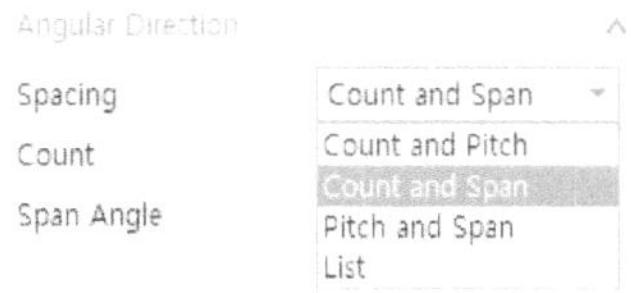

Fig 8-45 Spacing Option for Circular Pattern

ch08_ex04.prt **Circular Type Pattern** **Exercise 04**

Open the given file and create a circular type pattern after creating a datum axis.

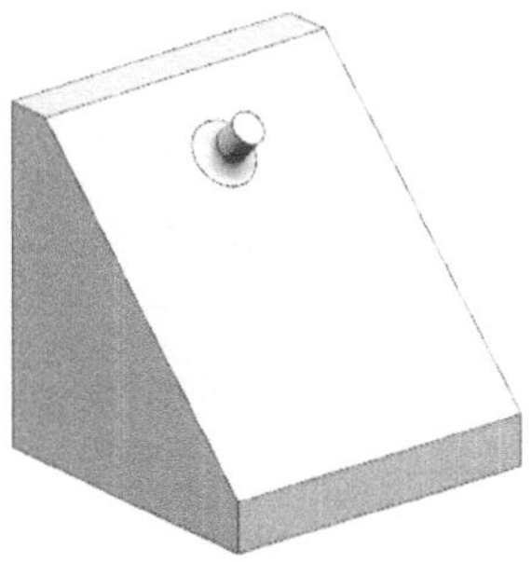

Fig 8-46 Model for Exercise

Creating a Datum Axis

1. Open the given file ch08_ex04.prt.

2. Click the **Datum Axis** icon in the **Feature** icon group.

3. Select **Point and Direction** in the **Type** dropdown list.

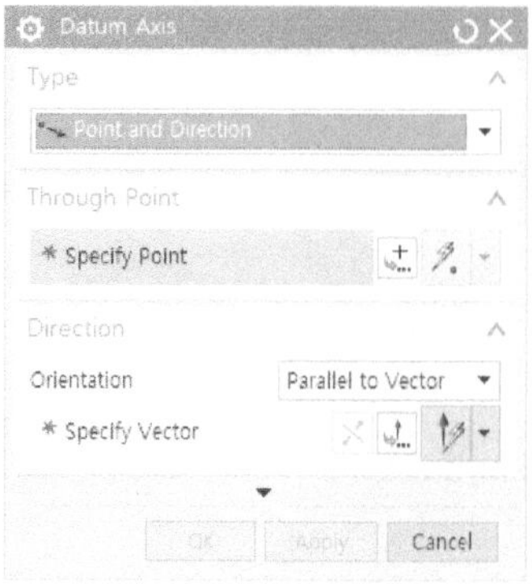

Fig 8-47 Datum Axis Dialog Box

4. Press the **Point Dialog** button in the **Datum Axis** dialog box as specified in Fig 8-47.

5. Select **Between Two Points** in the **Type** dropdown list.

6. Select the points Ⓐ and Ⓑ shown in Fig 8-48 in order and enter 50 in the **%Location** input box. The point is previewed as Ⓒ in Fig 8-48.

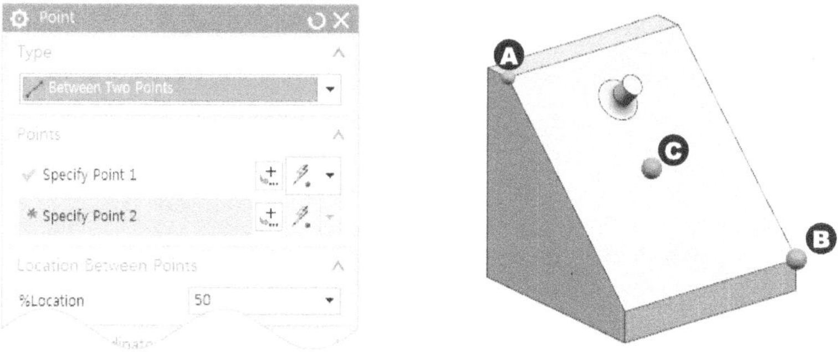

Fig 8-48 Point to Specify the Location of Datum Axis

7. Press **OK** in the **Point** dialog box.
8. Press MB2 to proceed to the **Specify Vector** option in the **Datum Axis** dialog box.
9. Select the plane Ⓓ shown in Fig 8-49 to specify the normal direction.
10. Press **OK** in the **Datum Axis** dialog box.

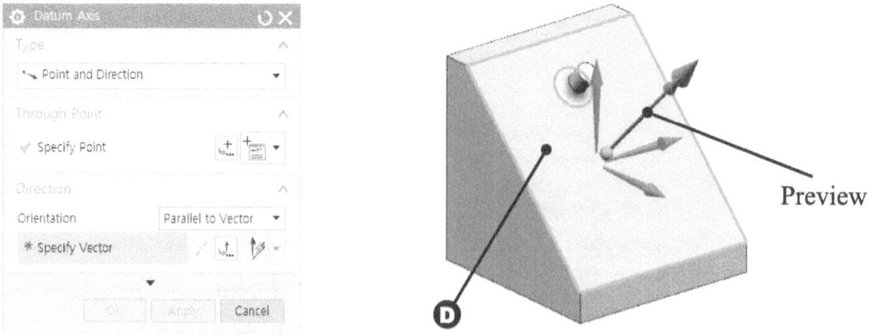

Fig 8-49 Direction of Datum Axis

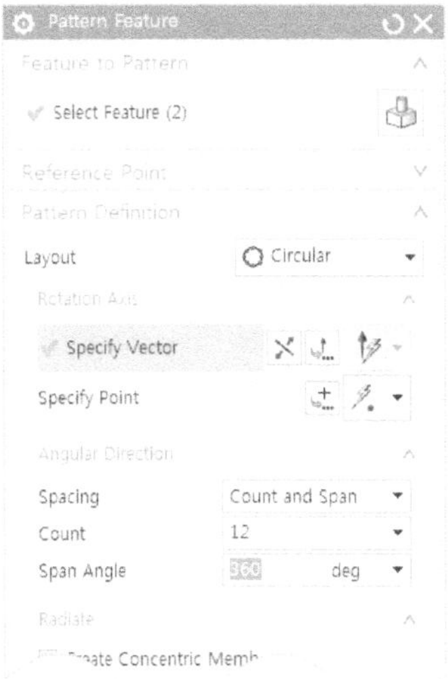

Fig 8-50 Options in Circular Type Pattern

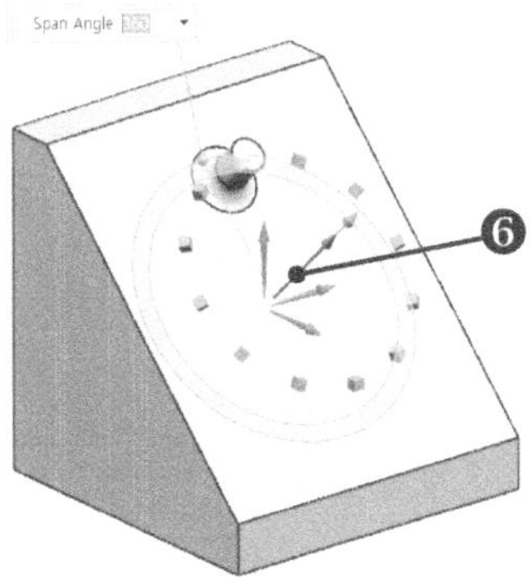

Fig 8-51 Preview of Circular Pattern

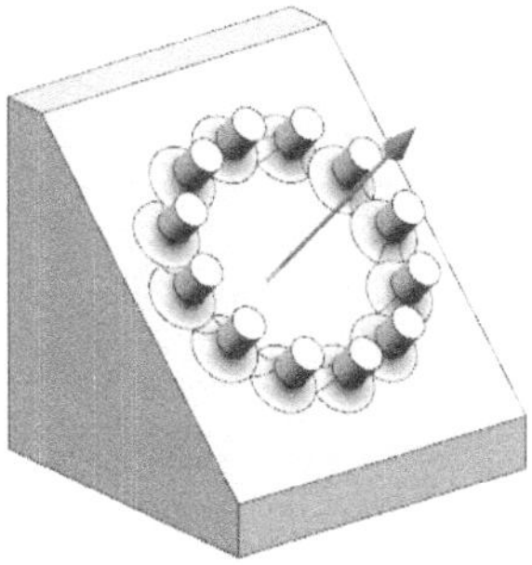

Fig 8-52 Unnatural Edge Blend

Creating a Circular Pattern

1. Click the **Pattern Feature** icon.

2. Reset the dialog box.

3. Select the **Boss** feature and the **Edge Blend** feature.

4. Select **Circular** in the **Layout** drop-down list.

5. Click MB2.

6. Select the datum axis as the rotation axis (❻ in Fig 8-51).

7. Set the **Angular Direction** option as shown in Fig 8-50 and press **Enter**. Fig 8-51 shows the preview of the circular pattern.

9. Press **OK** in the **Pattern Feature** dialog box.

The edge blends between the boss features are created unnaturally as shown in Fig 8-52.

Modifying Edge Blend

1. Delete the edge blend feature in the part navigator. Press **OK** in the **Notification** dialog box.

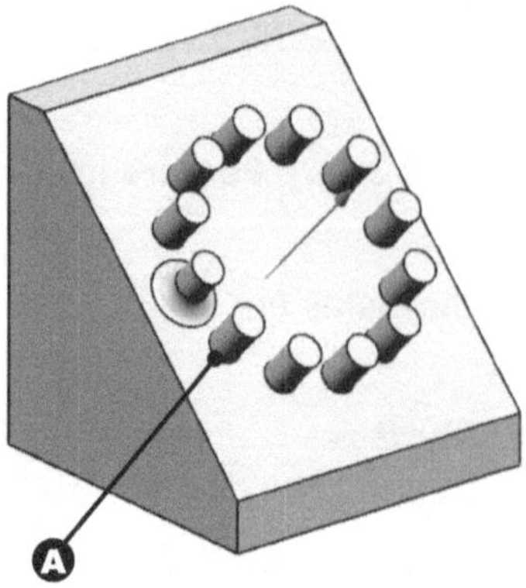

Fig 8-53 First Edge Blend

2. Create an R5 edge blend for a boss feature as shown in Fig 8-53.

3. Click the **Edge Blend** icon to apply an edge blend to a nearby boss feature.

4. Select the edge Ⓐ designated in Fig 8-53.

5. Expand the **Overflow Resolutions** option in the **Edge Blend** dialog box and click the option field Ⓑ in Fig 8-54.

6. Select the edge Ⓒ in Fig 8-54. The two edge blends meet naturally.

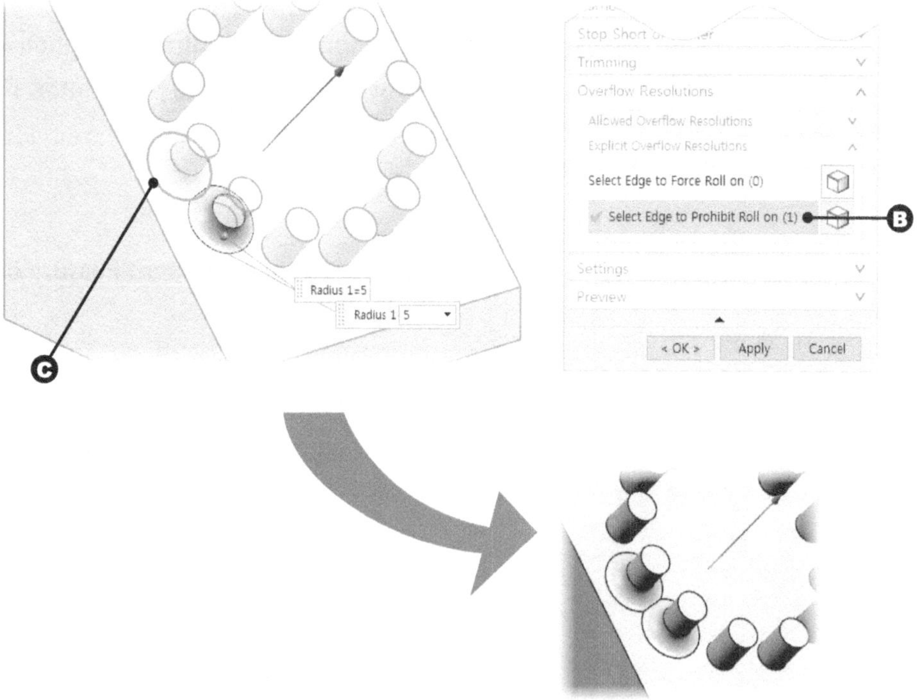

Fig 8-54 Second Edge Blend

7. Apply an R3 edge blend for the edge created between the two R5 edge blends as shown in Fig 8-55.

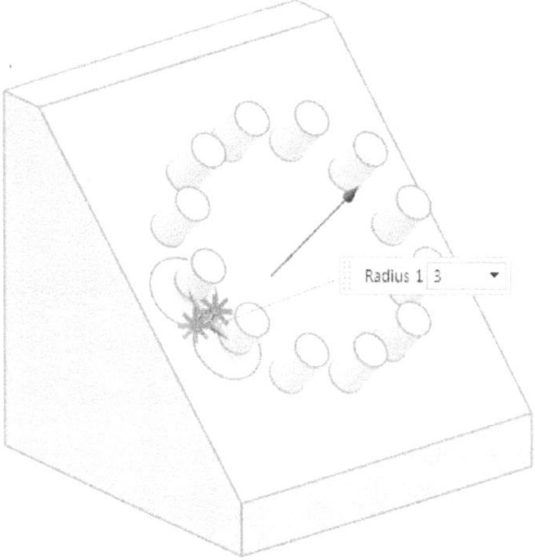

Fig 8-55 Applying R3 Edge Blend

8. Apply edge blends for the other boss features. Fig 8-56 shows the completed model in the **Shaded** rendering style.

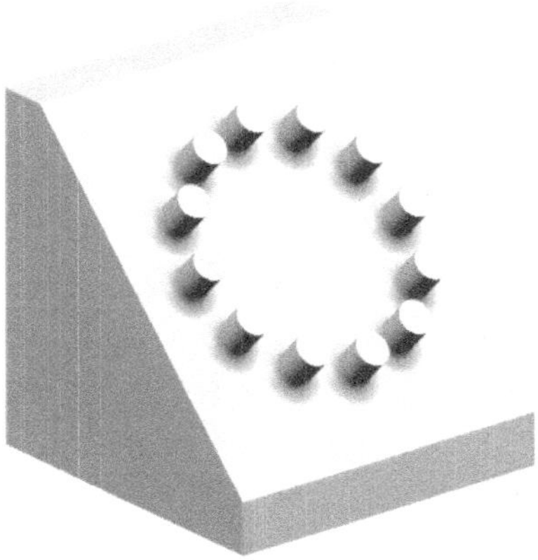

Fig 8-56 Completed Model

END of Exercise

Exercise 05 Creating Circular Pattern

ch08_ex05.prt

Open the given part ch08_ex05.prt and create a circular pattern as shown in Fig 8-57.

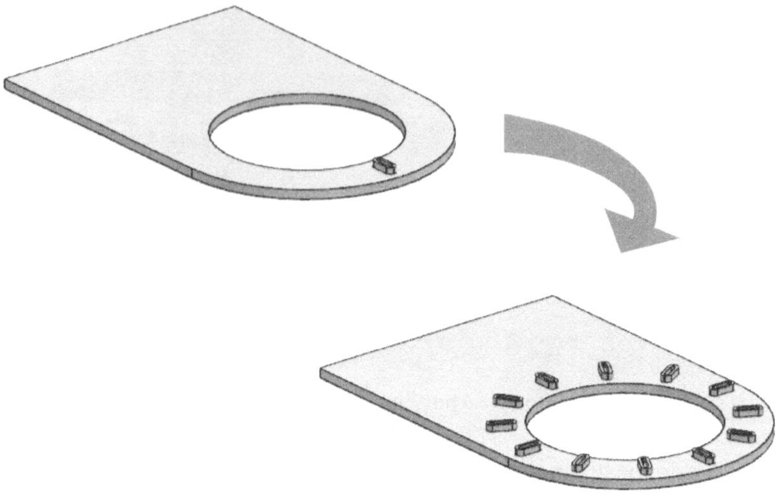

Fig 8-57 Circular Pattern

END of Exercise

! Defining Axis

If you select the planar face ❶ in Fig 8-58 in the Specify Vector option, the normal vector of the plane is defined as the vector of the axis. Choose the center point of the circular edge ❷ in the Specify Point option. Use the snap point option to select the center point of the edge.

Fig 8-58 Defining Axis

Orientation Option

The orientation of instances of the circular pattern may not be rotated according to the angular pitch of the pattern by setting the orientation option as shown in Fig 8-59. The **Orientation** option is available by clicking the **More** button in the dialog box.

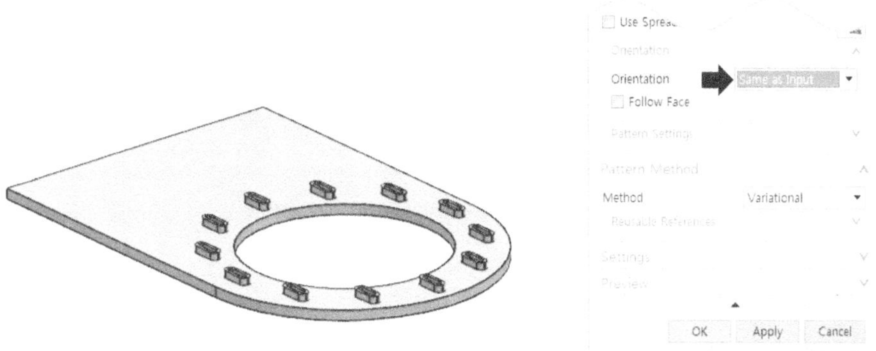

Fig 8-59 Orientation of Instances

Create Concentric Members Option

You can create a circular pattern on the different radius concentric circles as shown in Fig 8-60.

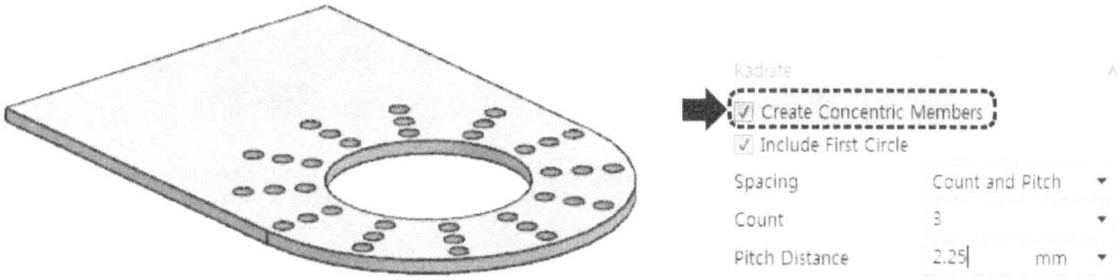

Fig 8-60 Circular Pattern on Concentric Circles

8.3.4 General Type

Procedure

① Click the **Pattern Feature** icon in the **Feature** icon group.

② Press the **Reset** button in the dialog box.

③ Select the source of pattern. Note that you can select several features at the same time, and the number of selected features is marked in the option field.

④ Select the **General** option in the dropdown list.

⑤ Specify a point in the **From** option field.

⑥ Select points as the target location in the **To** option field.

⑦ Press **OK** in the dialog box.

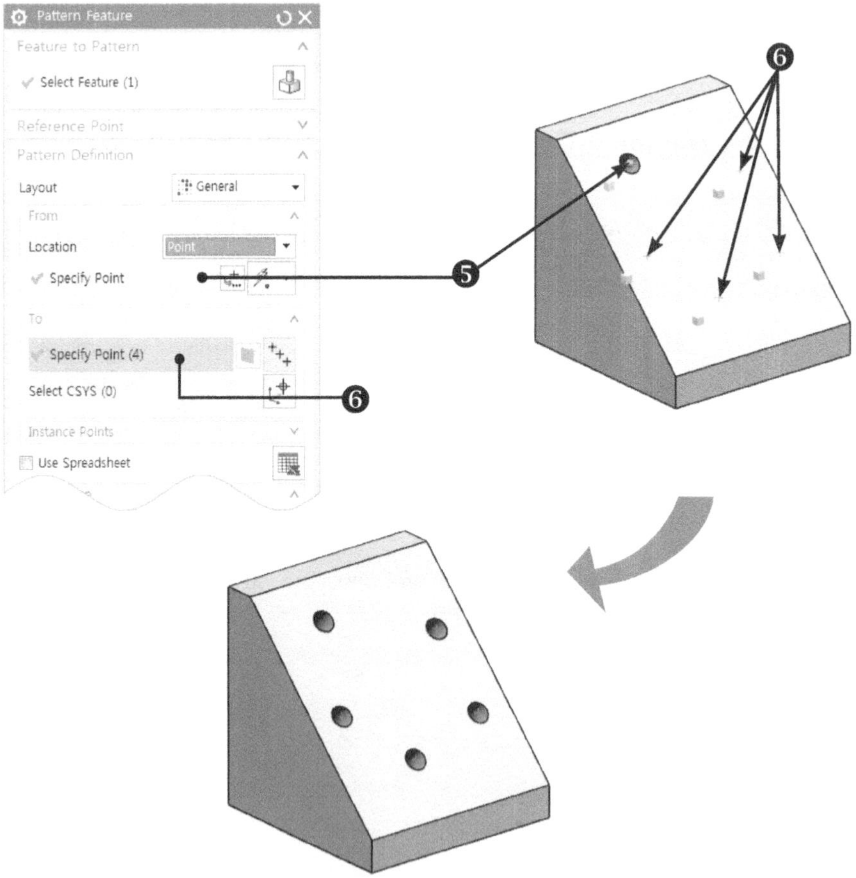

Fig 8-61 Procedure for General Type Pattern

8.4 Mirror Feature

You can copy features by mirroring with respect to a symmetric plane. You can select the datum plane or planar face as the mirror plane. Datum planes or sketch features cannot be mirrored. When the boolean option is applied for the source, the instances should not lie outside of the target body. You can copy several features in a single operation.

Fig 8-62 Mirroring a Feature

8.5 Copy of Geometries

You can copy general geometries using the commands **Pattern Geometry** and **Mirror Geometry**. Because the source objects are the general geometries which can be obtained as a result of the modeling process, you cannot select them in the **Part Navigator** but you can in the graphics window. However, you can select geometries without the part history.

8.5.1 Mirror Geometry

You can execute the **Mirror Geometry** command in the **Menu** button by choosing **Insert > Associative Copy > Mirror Geometry**. The type of geometry can be identified in the **Type Filter**. Note that you can copy a solid body or a sheet body using this command.

Fig 8-63 Mirror Geometry Dialog Box

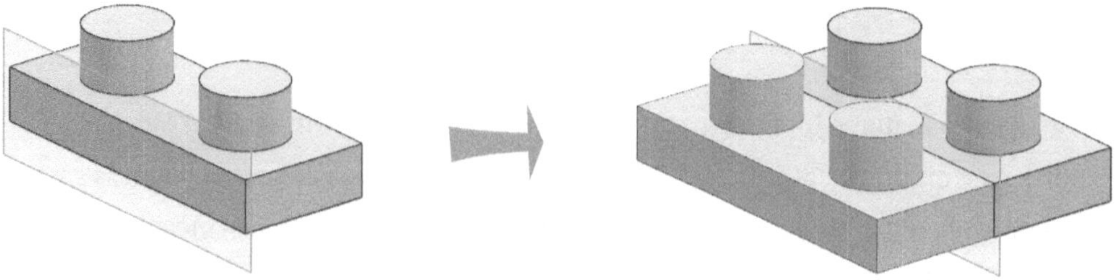

Fig 8-64 Mirroring Solid Body

8.5.2 Pattern Geometry

You can execute the **Pattern Geometry** command in the **Menu** button by choosing **Insert > Associative Copy > Pattern Geometry**. The method to copy is similar to the **Pattern Feature** command and the source of the copy is similar to the **Mirror Geometry** command. Because you can select both the curves and the faces, the **Curve Rule** and the **Face Rule** are available in the selection bar. When you select faces, you have to set the type filter to **Face** on account of the selection priority. Refer to "A.8 Selection Priority" on Page 643.

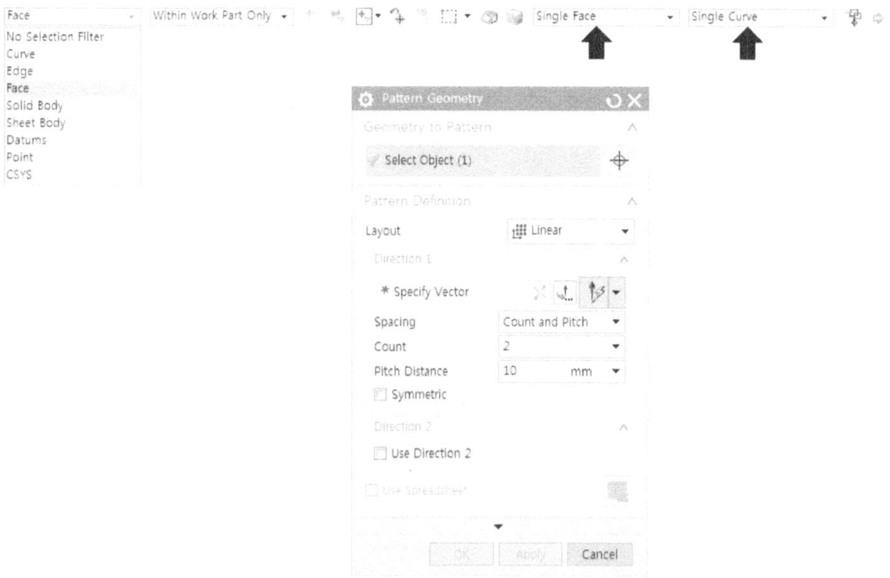

Fig 8-65 Pattern Geometry Dialog Box

ch08_ex06.prt

Mirroring Feature and Body Exercise 06

In this exercise, we will mirror a feature and body by opening the given file. Then, we will learn how the modification of the model impacts the result.

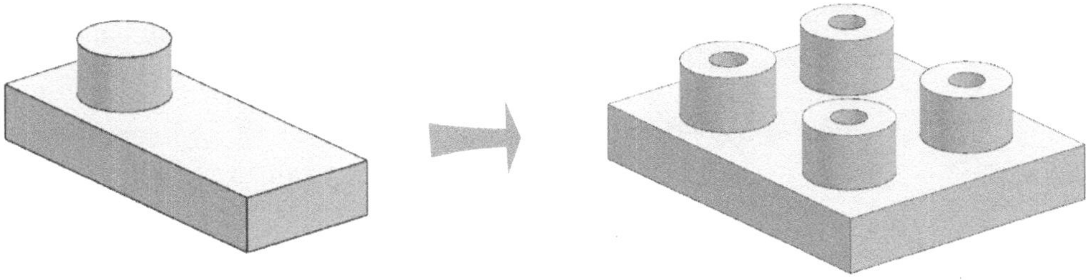

Fig 8-66 Mirroring Feature and Body

Mirror Feature 1

1. Open the given file ch08_ex06.prt.

2. Click the **Mirror Feature** icon in the **Feature** icon group and reset the dialog box.

3. Select the feature to copy (❸ in Fig 8-67). You can select the feature in the part navigator or in the model.

4. Click MB2.

5. Select the **Mirror Plane** (❺ in Fig 8-67).

6. Press **OK** in the dialog box.

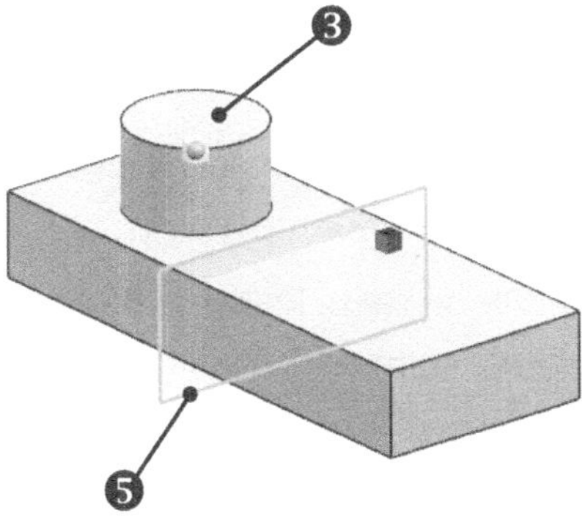

Fig 8-67 Selecting the Feature and Mirror Plane

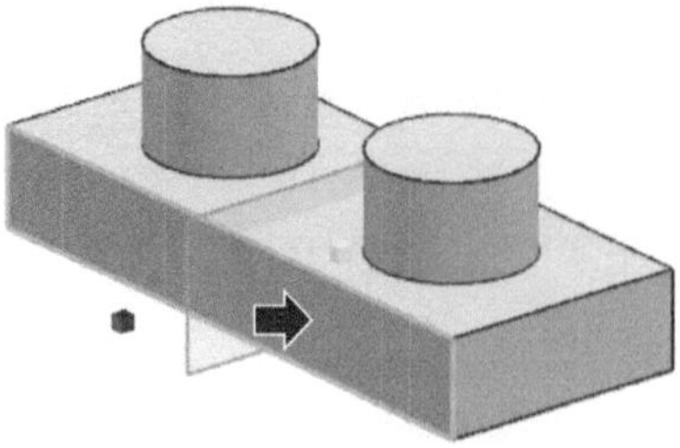

Fig 8-68 Mirror Plane

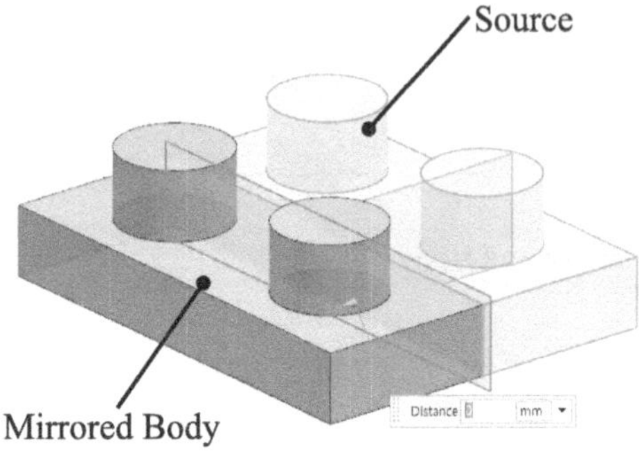

Fig 8-69 Preview

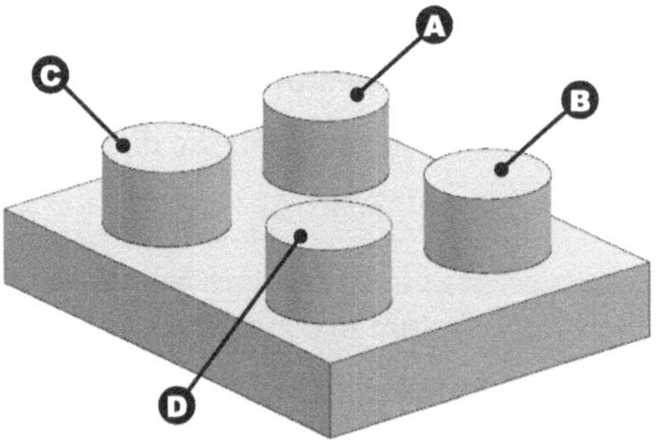

Fig 8-70 United Model

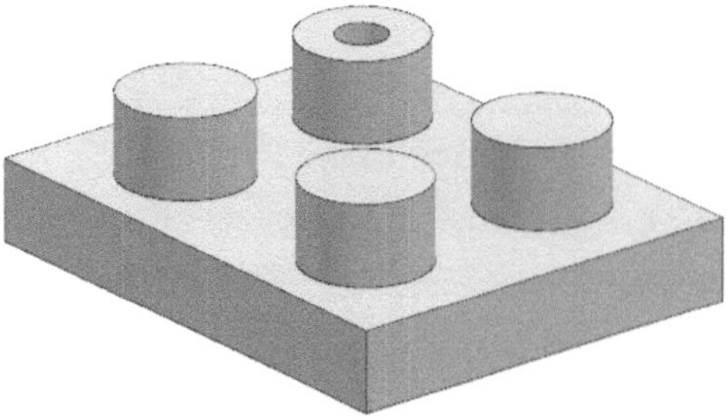

Fig 8-71 Creating a Hole

Mirror Geometry

Let's mirror a solid body using the **Mirror Geometry** command.

1. Choose **Insert > Associative Copy > Mirror Geometry** in the **Menu** button and reset the dialog box.

2. Select the source body as designated in Fig 8-69.

3. Click MB2.

4. Select the mirror plane designated by the arrow in Fig 8-68.

5. Press **OK** in the **Mirror Geometry** dialog box.

6. Unite the two bodies using the **Unite** command in the **Feature** icon group. Choose the source of mirror as the target of the **Unite** command. Cylindrical features are named as shown in Fig 8-70 for convenience.

Modification

1. Create a hole on feature Ⓐ in Fig 8-70 (Diameter: 70 mm, Depth: 10mm). A hole is created only on feature Ⓐ as shown in Fig 8-71.

The part navigator at this point is shown in Fig 8-72 (a).

Let's add the hole as the source of the mirror feature. Note that the **Simple Hole** should be created in advance of the mirror feature.

2. Drag the **Simple Hole** feature and drop it above the **Mirror Feature (6)**. The result of the **Mirror Geometry** is affected, but there is no change in the result of **Mirror Feature** command.

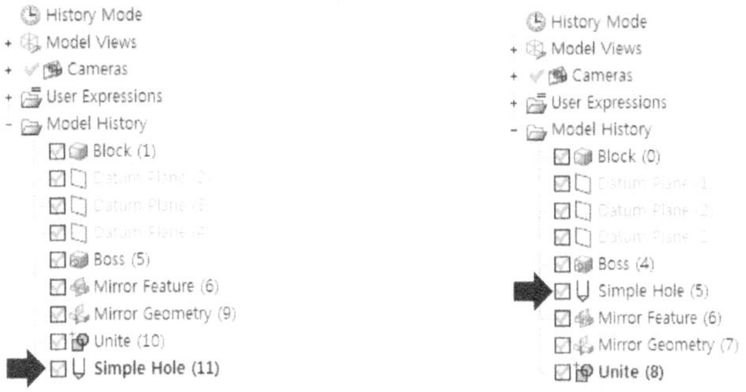

(a) (b)

Fig 8-72 Part Navigator

3. Double click the **Mirror Feature (6)** shown in Fig 8-72 (b). Confirm that the number of selected features in the **Mirror Feature** dialog box is 1.

4. Press the Ctrl key and select the **Simple Hole** feature in the part navigator. Confirm that the number of selected feature in the dialog box changes to 2.

5. Click OK in the **Mirror Feature** dialog box.

Fig 8-74 shows the result of modification.

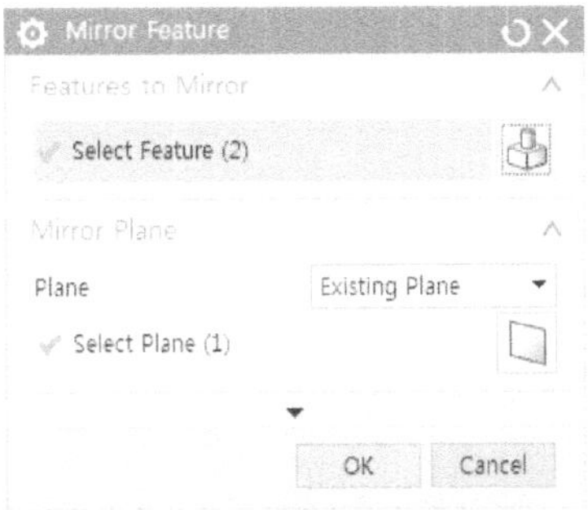

Fig 8-73 Two Simple Hole Features Selected

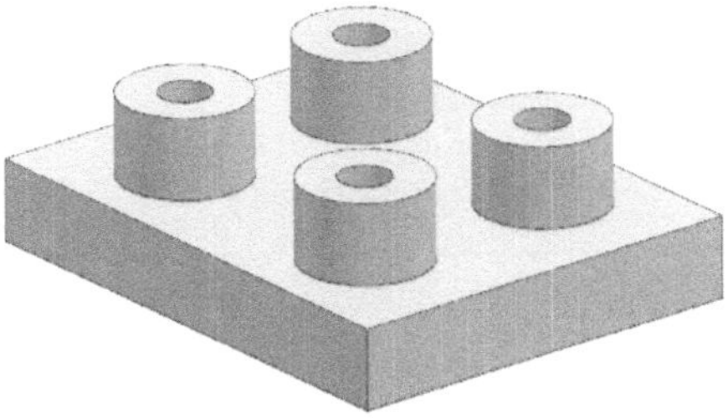

Fig 8-74 Completed Model

END of Exercise

8.6 Copy of Faces

You can copy faces using the **Pattern Face** and the **Mirror Face** commands. Note that you can select only faces as the source and that the solid property of the faces is copied together. This means that if the source face is a portion of a solid body, the resulting faces have to be the face of a solid body. This command can be applied on the geometry without the modeling history.

Fig 8-76 shows the result of the **Mirror Face** command after copying eight faces. Although you have copied only the faces, the inner volume of the mirrored faces is filled with solid. If the model is conditioned such that the mirrored faces cannot create a solid volume, the **Mirror Face** command fails.

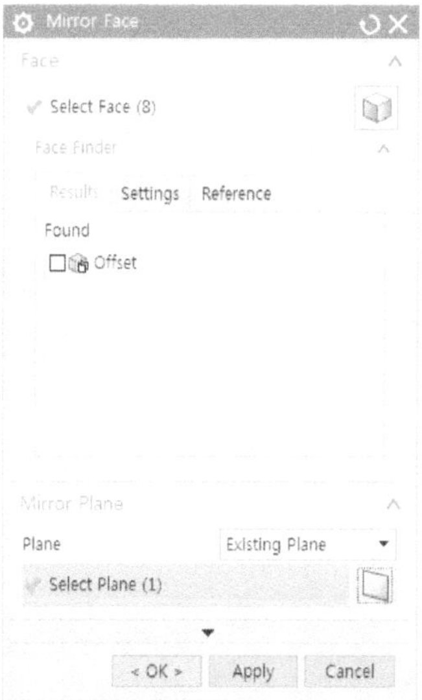

Fig 8-75 Mirror Face Dialog Box

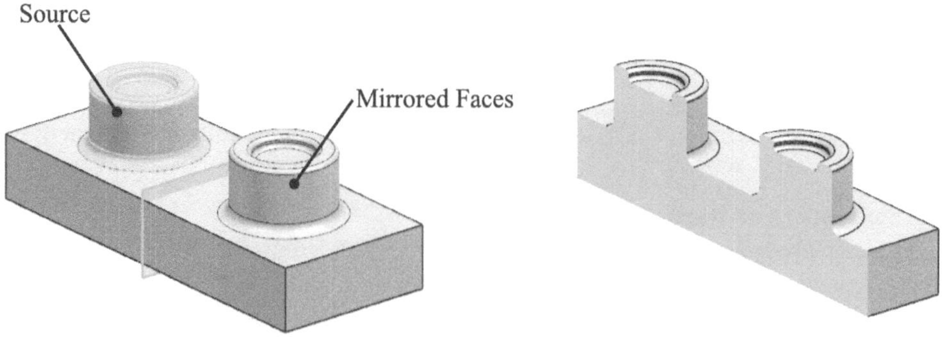

Fig 8-76 Result of the Mirror Face Command

ch08_ex07.prt **Instance Geometry** **Exercise 07**

Let's copy the faces with the **Instance Geometry** command. We will use the **Mirror** as the **Instance Type** option.

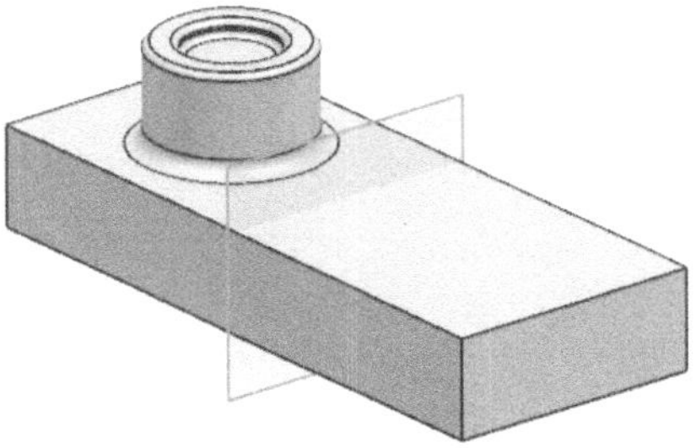

Fig 8-77 Model for Exercise

1. Open the given file ch08_ex08.prt.
2. Choose **Insert > Associative Copy > Mirror Geometry** in the **Menu** button.
3. Reset the **Mirror Geometry** dialog box.
4. Select **Face** in the **Type Filter**.
5. Select **Region Face** as the **Face Rule**.

The status line message prompts you to select a seed face.

Fig 8-78 Type Filter and Face Rule

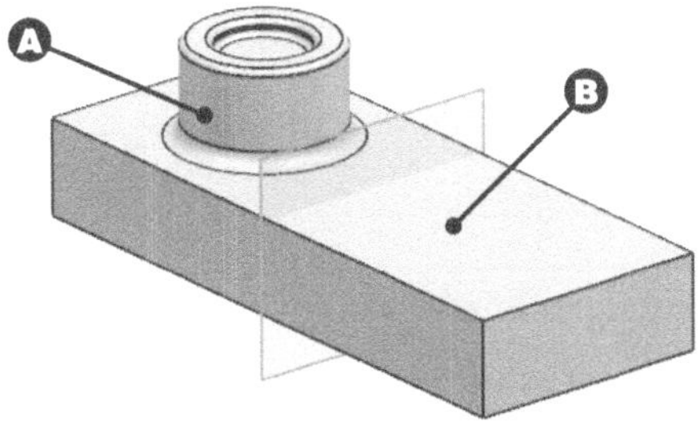

Fig 8-79 Seed Face and Boundary Face

! *Seed Face*

A seed face is a representative face among the faces which are isolated by the boundary face. All the faces on the side of the seed face with regard to the boundary face are selected at one time.

6. Select the face Ⓐ in Fig 8-79 as the seed face. The status line message prompts you to select a boundary face.

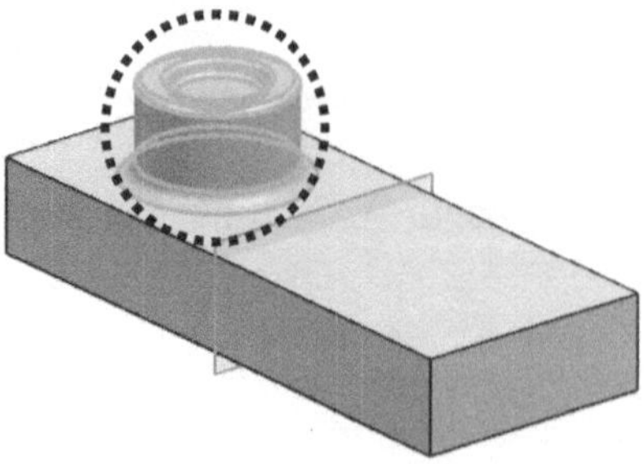

Fig 8-80 Selected Faces

7. Select the face B in Fig 8-79 as the boundary face.

8. Click MB2. All the faces on the side of the seed face are selected together as shown in the dotted circle in Fig 8-80. The number of selected faces (8) is marked in the **Select Face** option field.

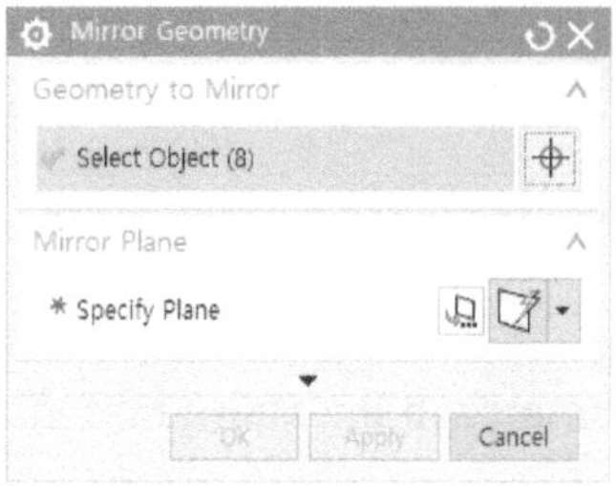

Fig 8-81 Mirror Geomery Dialog Box

9. Click MB2 again to proceed to the **Mirror Plane** option field.

10. Select the datum plane and press the **OK** button.

The work section is shown in Fig 8-83. Note that the interior of the copied faces is not filled with material.

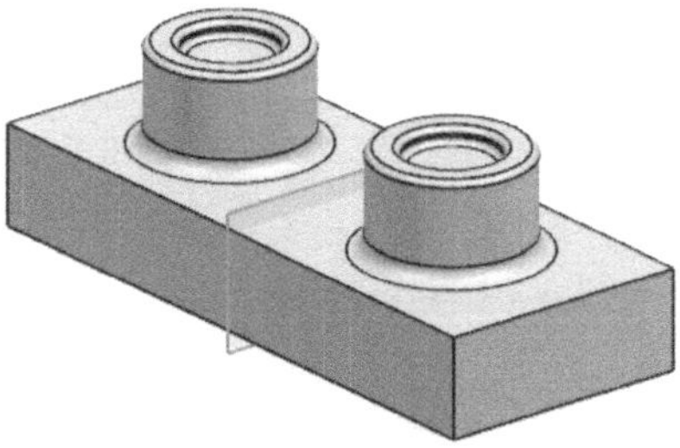

Fig 8-82 Completed Model

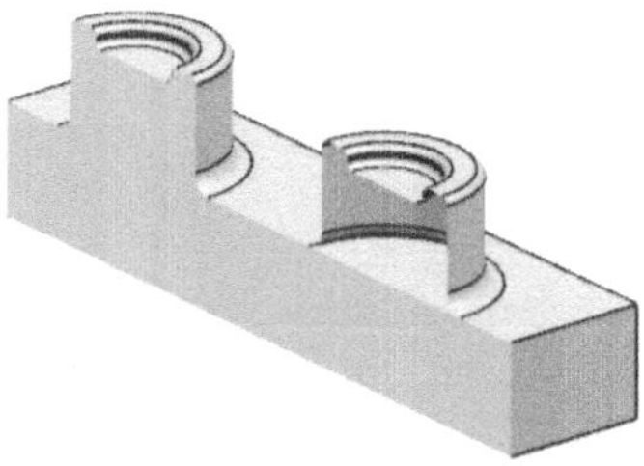

Fig 8-83 Work Section

! *Boundary Face*

With the **Region Faces** face rule, you can select faces connected to the seed face up to the boundary face. While only one face can be selected as the seed face, you can select as many faces as required to isolate the faces.

END of Exercise

8.7 Copy and Paste of Features

You can copy and paste features to avoid repetative modeling work when the formal feature copy commands are not available. For example, you can copy an edge blend feature on another edge and you can copy a sketch feature on another plane.

Remember when you paste a feature, you have to select the objects that are essential in defining the feature. For example, you have to select the edge in pasting the edge blend feature.

When you paste a sketch, you have to select a new sketch plane and define the horizontal and vertical references. You may have to reselect the reference objects to constrain the sketch correctly.

ch08_ex08.prt **Copy and Paste of Edge Blend** **Exercise 08**

Let's copy and paste an edge blend repeatedly.

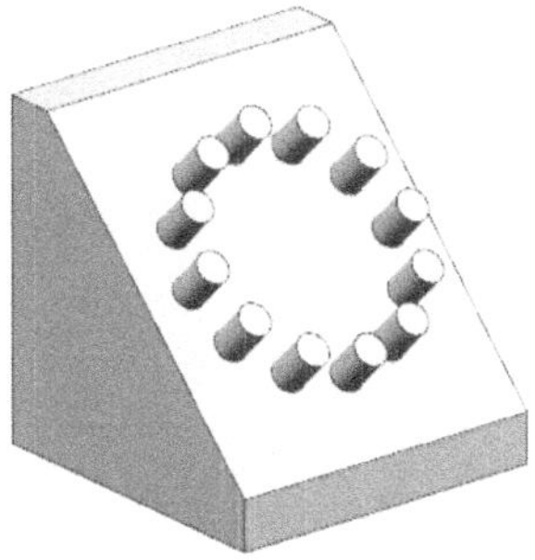

Fig 8-84 Model for Exercise

Creating an Edge Blend

1. Open the given file ch08_ex08.prt.

Looking at the part navigator, the instances of the circular pattern are a long listed as shown in Fig 8-85. Note that the pattern is created in NX 6. You can collect several features in a group.

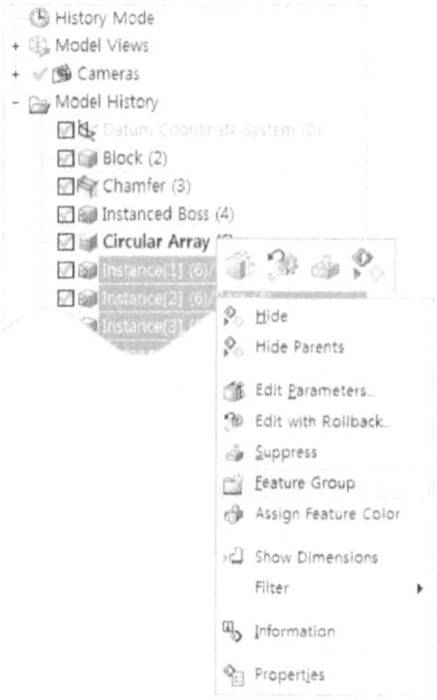

Fig 8-85 Feature Group Option

2. Select the instance features as shown in Fig 8-85 and press **MB3 > Feature Group** on one of the features.

3. Enter the name of the group in the **Feature Group** dialog box and press **OK**.

The modeling history is simplified as shown in Fig 8-87.

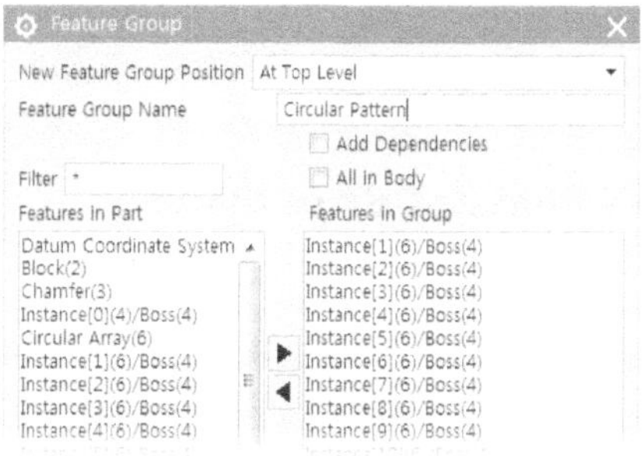

Fig 8-86 Naming Group

Fig 8-87 Simplified Features

4. Create an R5 edge blend on one edge as shown in Fig 8-88.

5. Click the **Edge Blend** icon again and select the edge **A** in Fig 8-89.

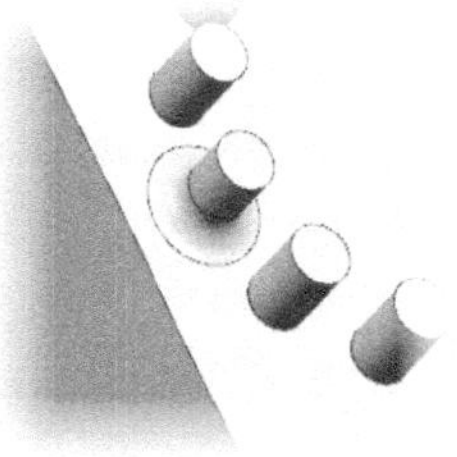

Fig 8-88 First Edge Blend

6. Expand the **Edge Blend** dialog box and click the **Select Edge to Prohibit Roll on** option field in the **Overflow Resolutions** option group as shown in Fig 8-90.

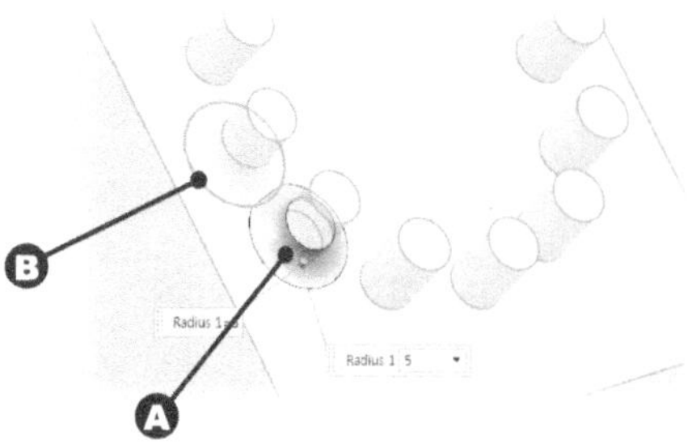

Fig 8-89 Second Edge Blend

7. Select the edge **B** in Fig 8-89.

8. Press **OK** in the dialog box.

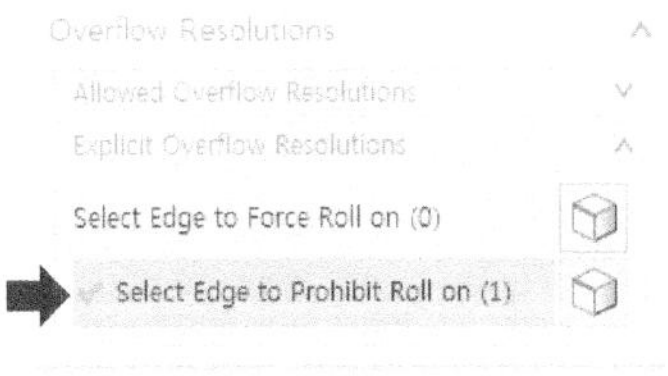

Fig 8-90 Overflow Option

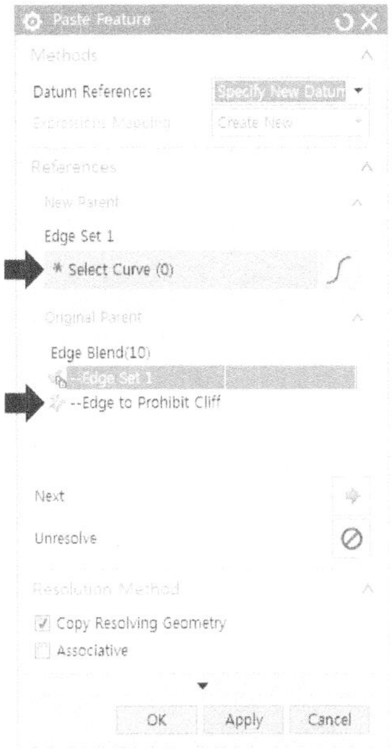

Fig 8-91 Paste Feature Dialog Box

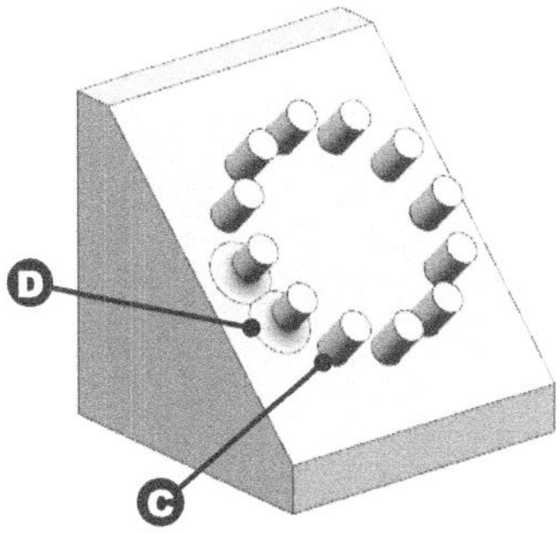

Fig 8-92 Two Edge Blends

Copy and Paste

We will create the remaining edge blends by copying the second one. Remember that you have to select the edge to prohibit roll on because you have set the option in Fig 8-90.

1. Select the second edge blend in the part navigator.

2. Press **Ctrl + C** in the keyboard.

3. Press **Ctrl + V**. The **Paste Feature** dialog box appears as shown in Fig 8-91 and the **Select Curve** option field is highlighted.

4. Select the edge **C** in Fig 8-92.

5. Click the **Edge to Prohibit Cliff** in the **Original Parent** list box shown in Fig 8-91.

Select **Curve** option field is highlighted again.

6. Select the edge **D** shown in Fig 8-92.

7. Click the **Apply** button in the **Paste Feature** dialog box. Edge blend is created on the third edge as shown in Fig 8-93.

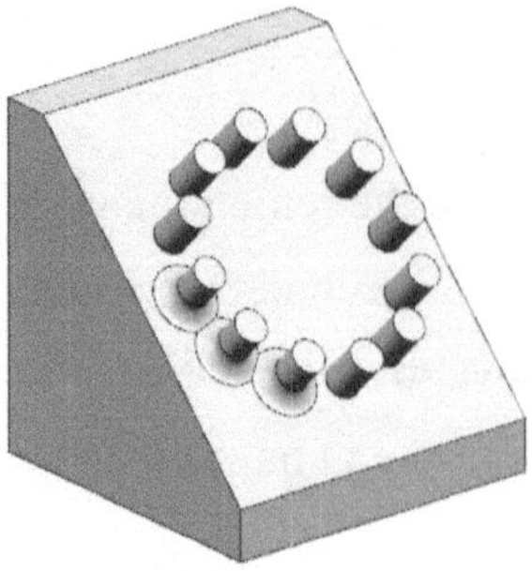

Fig 8-93 Third Edge Blend

8. Paste the edge blend feature on the remaining edges consecutively. Click the **Next** button to proceed to the next selection step in the **Original Parent** list box.

If you have clicked the **OK** button, you can press **Ctrl + V** to restart pasting.

Note that, for the last edge blend, you have to apply the **Edge to Prohibit Cliff** option for both edges. Fig 8-94 shows the completed model.

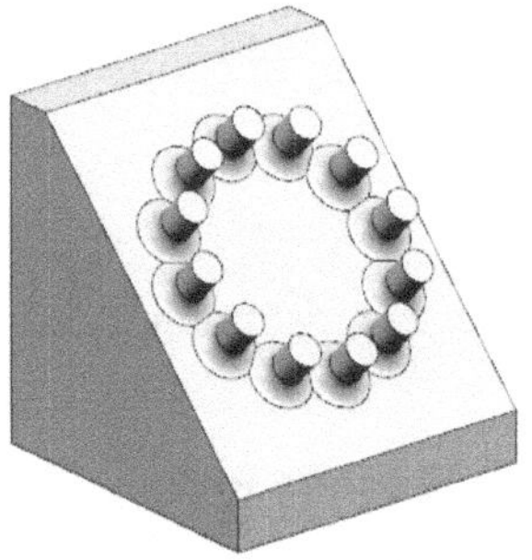

Fig 8-94 Completed Model

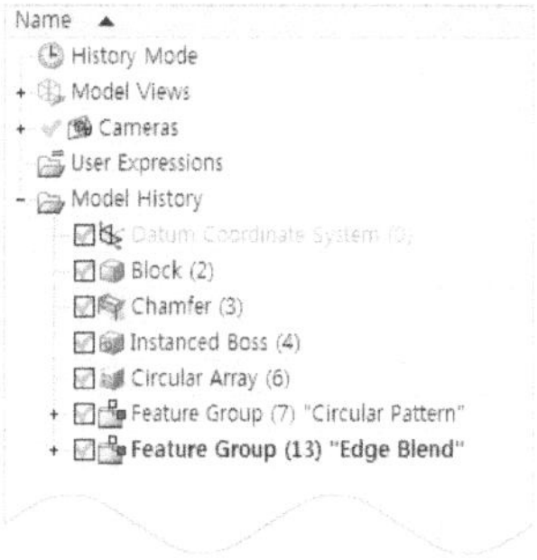

Fig 8-95 Part Navigator

END of Exercise

Referring to the suggested modeling steps, create the spanner model as shown in Fig 8-97. We will copy and paste the sketch feature for the head.

Step 1

Create a datum coordinate system on which to create the sketch for the large head of the spanner. The top view is shown in Fig 8-97. Offset the default datum coordinate system at the origin with the option shown in the dialog box.

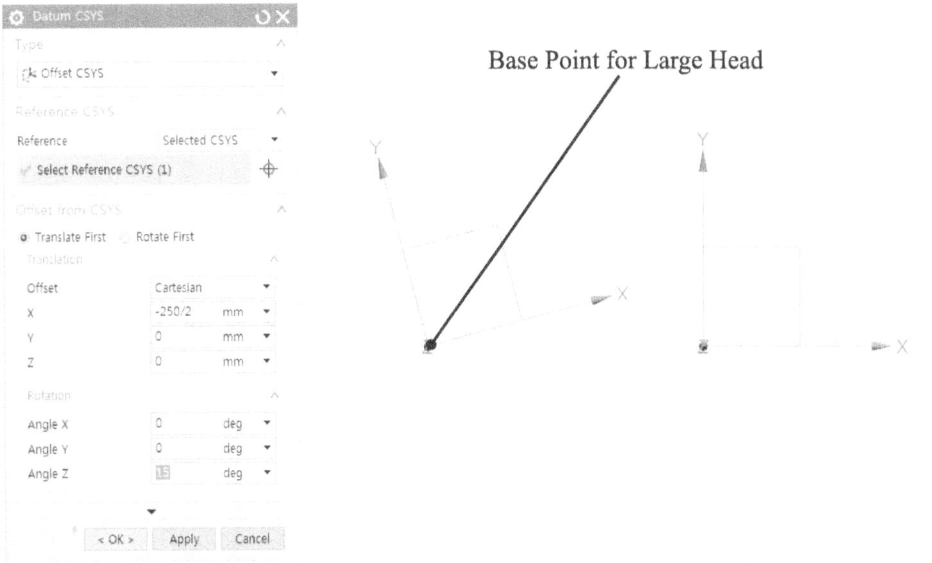

Fig 8-96 Datum Coordinate System for the Large Head

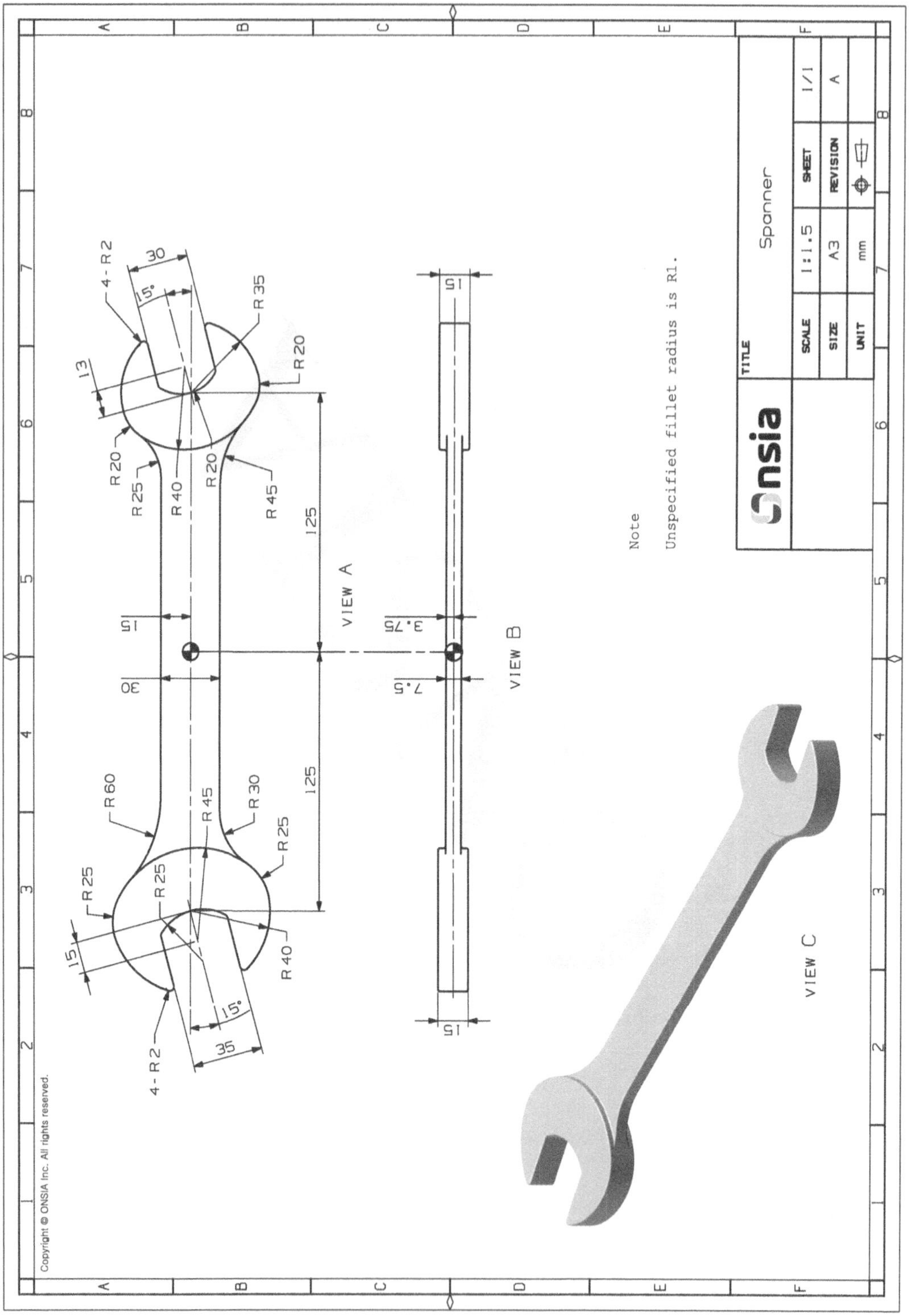

Fig 8-97 Drawing for Exercise 9

Step 2

Create a sketch for the large head on the XY plane of the datum coordinate system created in Step 1. Fully constrain the sketch only with regard to the offset coordinate system.

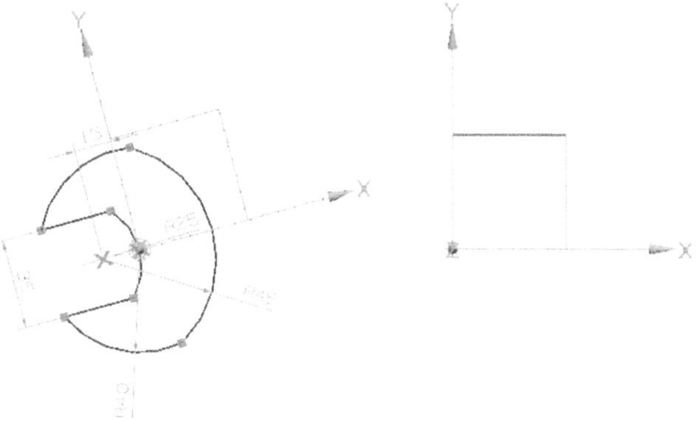

Fig 8-98 Sketch for the Large Head

Step 3

Create another datum coordinate system on which to create the sketch for the small head of the spanner. The top view is shown in Fig 8-99. Note that the X and Y axis have to be reversed with regard to the large head.

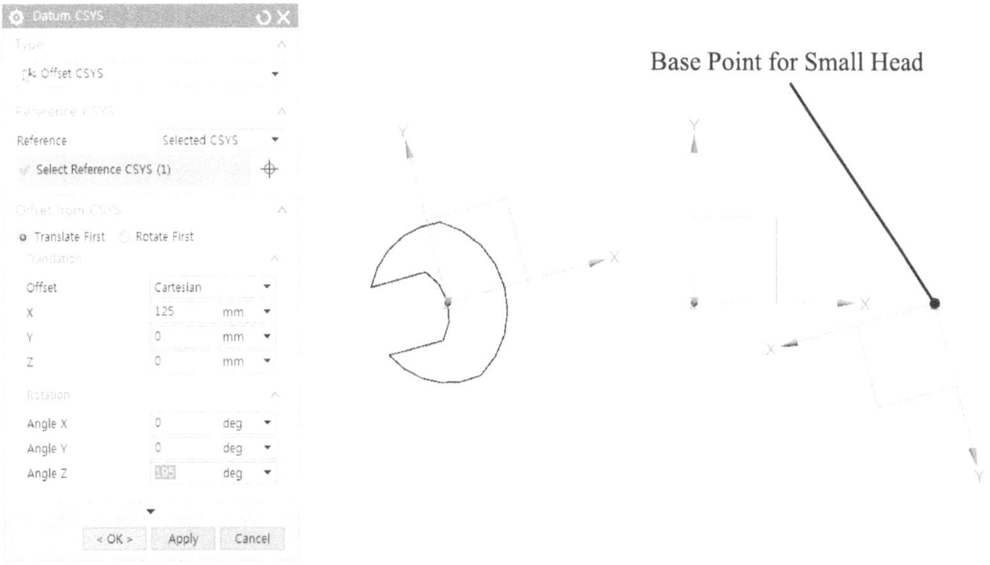

Fig 8-99 Datum Coordinate System for the Small Head

Step 4

Copy the sketch for the large head and paste on the datum coordinate system created in Step 3. Then, modify the dimensions for the small head according to the drawing in Fig 8-97.

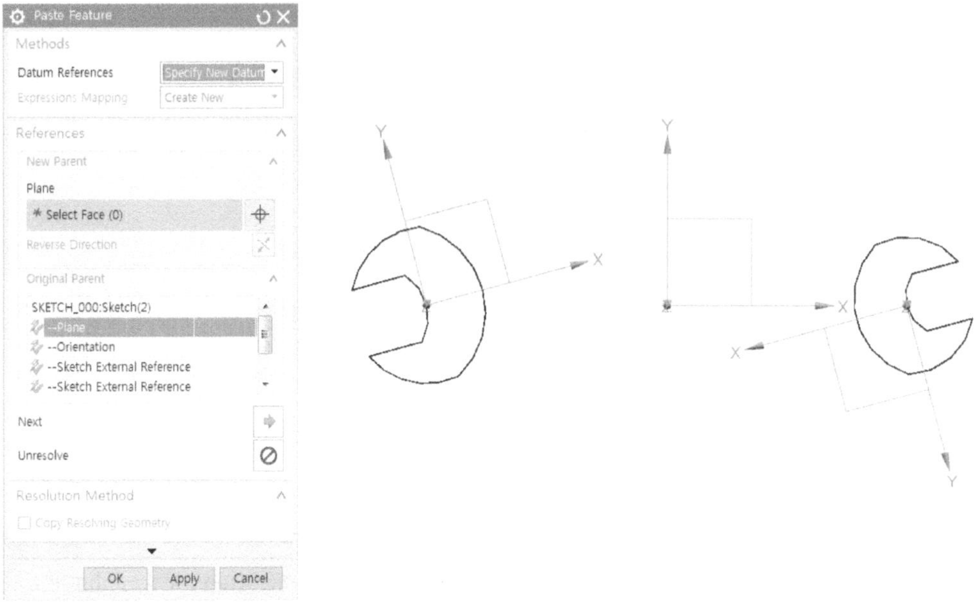

Fig 8-100 Pasting Sketch for Small Head

Step 5

Create the other features and apply R1 edge blend for all unspecified edges.

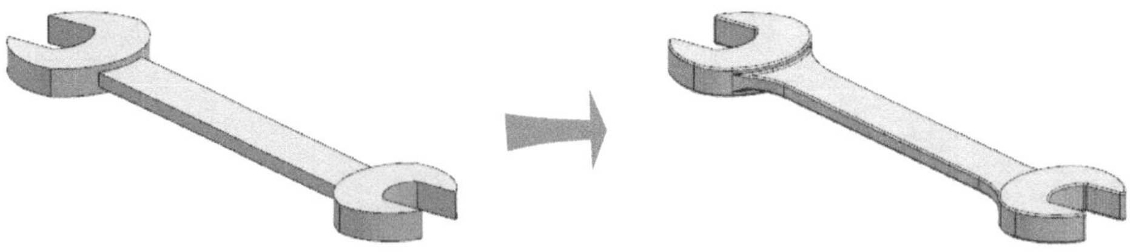

Fig 8-101 Completed Model

END of Exercise

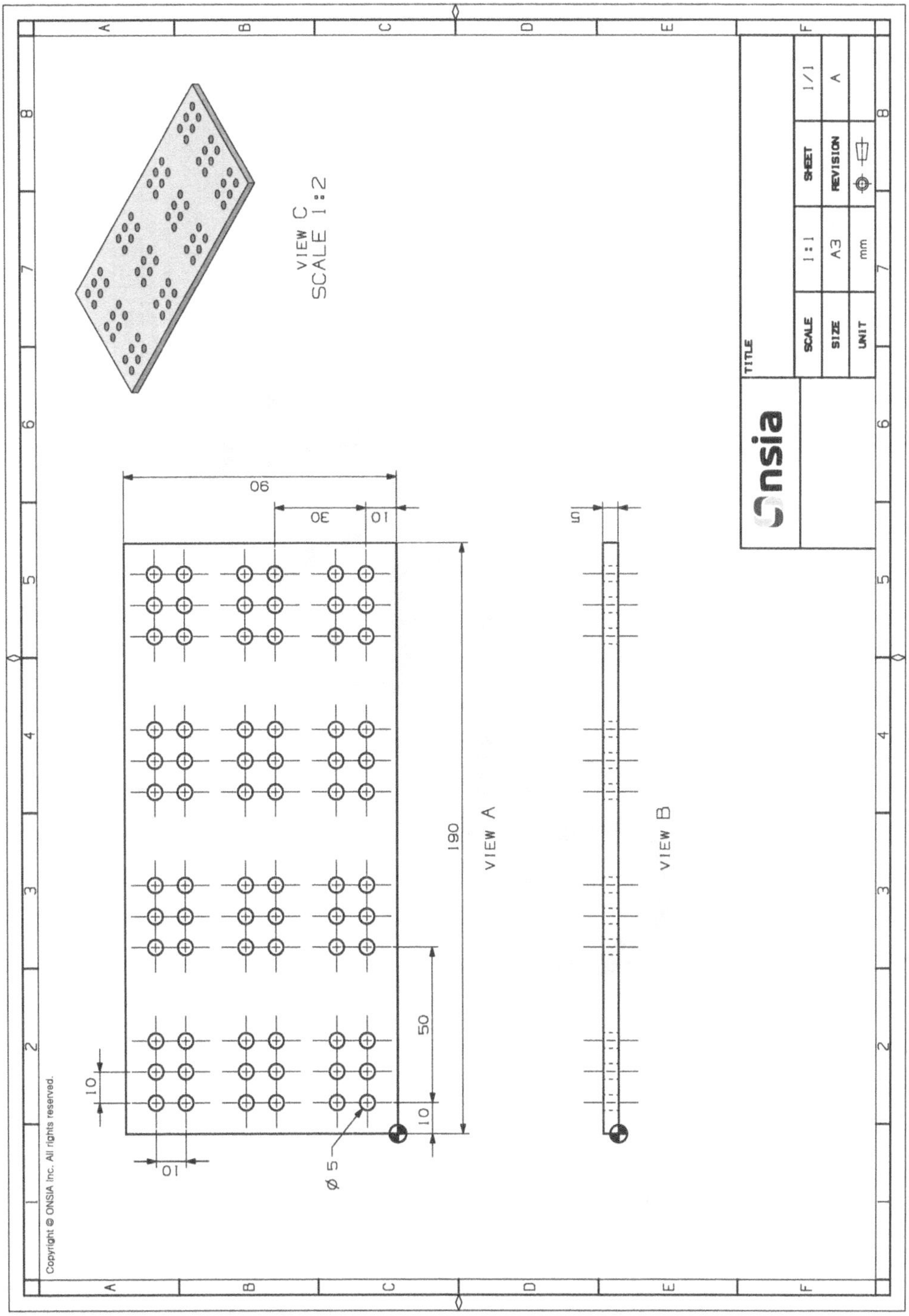

Fig 8-102 Drawing for Exercise 10

Exercise 11 Pattern Feature or Pattern Face

ch08_ex11.prt

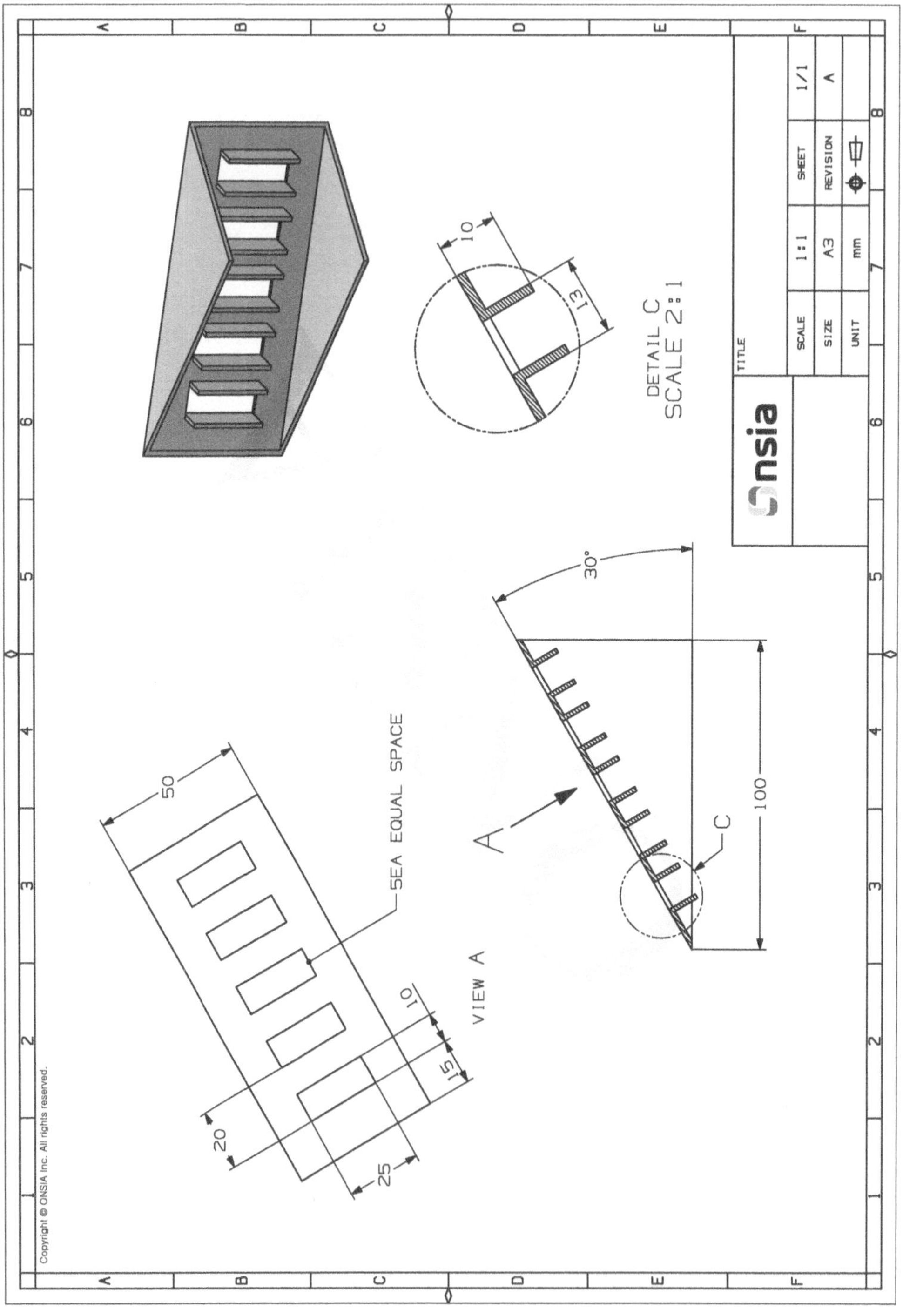

Fig 8-103 Drawing for Exercise 11

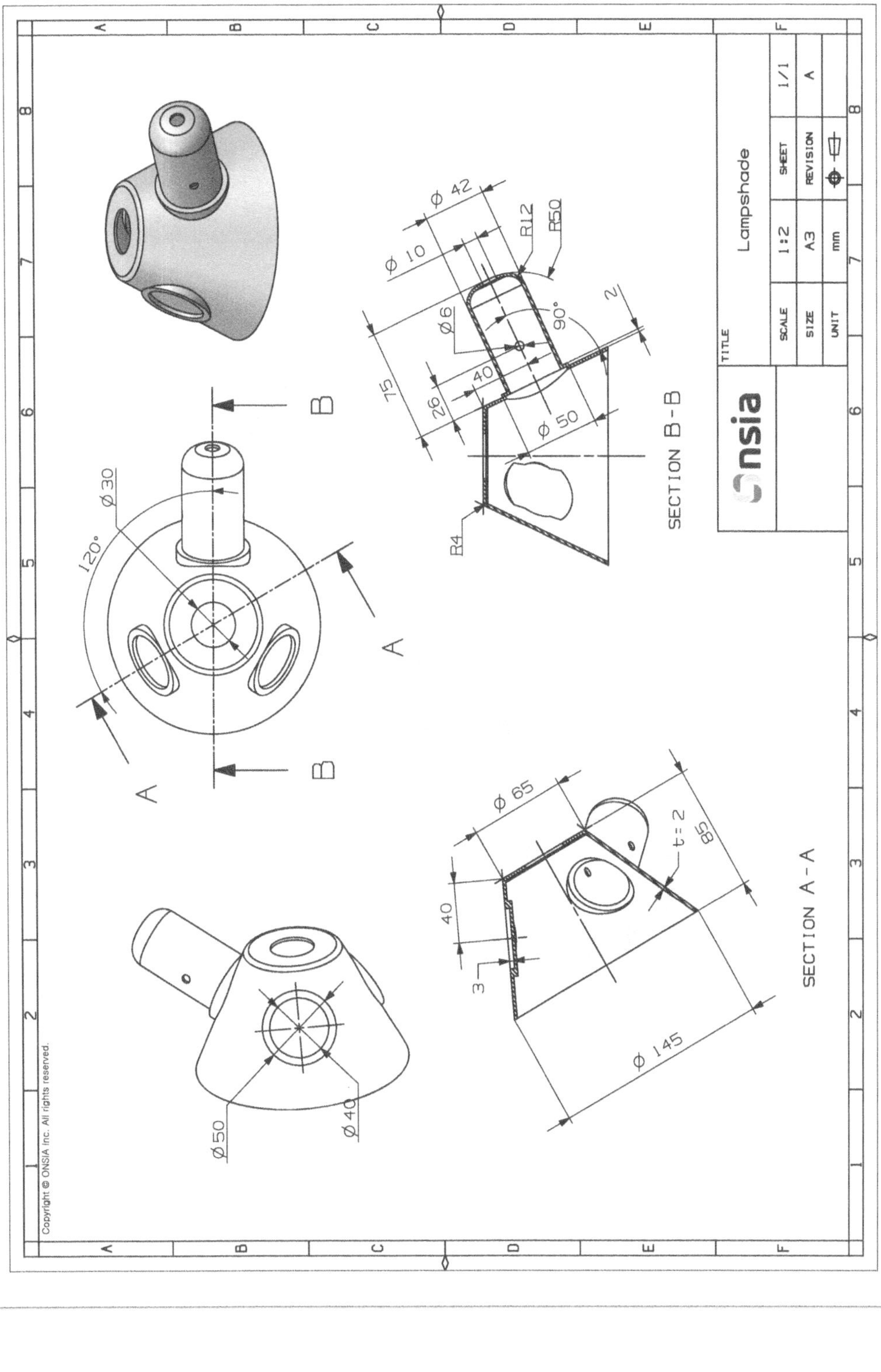

Fig 8-104 Drawing for Exercise 12

This page left bland intentionally.

Chapter 9

Additional Modeling Commands - Part II

■ **After completing this chapter you will understand**

- how to use the **Trim Body** command to trim a body.
- how to use the **Sweep along Guide** and **Tube** command.
- how to create an emboss.
- concepts of direct modeling and how to use the commands of synchronous modeling.

9.1 Trim Body

Cut out sheets or solid bodies with regard to the datum plane or the unselected face.

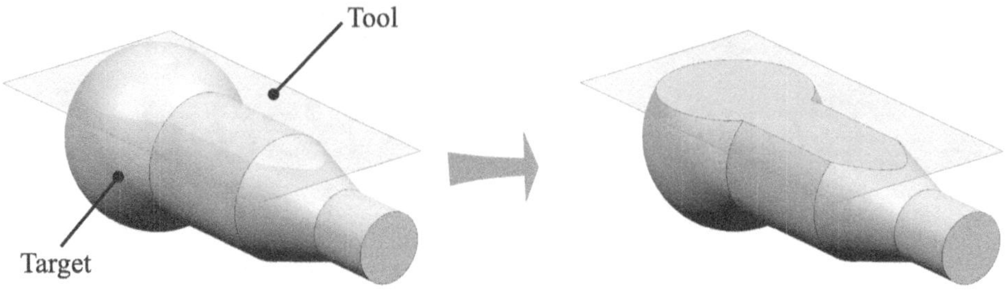

Fig 9-1 Trim Body Using Datum Plane as a Tool

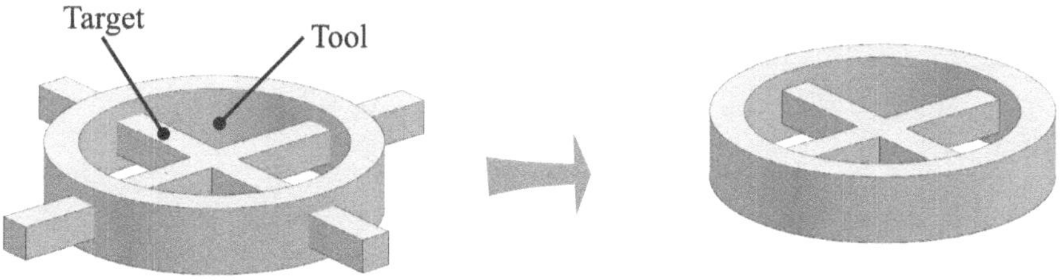

Fig 9-2 Trim Body Using Face as a Tool

9.1.1 Procedure

Keep to the following procedure to trim out a portion of the target bodies. The numbers in Fig 9-3 correspond to the step numbers.

① Click the **Trim Body** icon in the **Feature** icon group.
② Select the target body.
③ Select the tool body. You can create a new datum plane to use as a tool.
④ Press **OK** in the **Trim Body** dialog box.

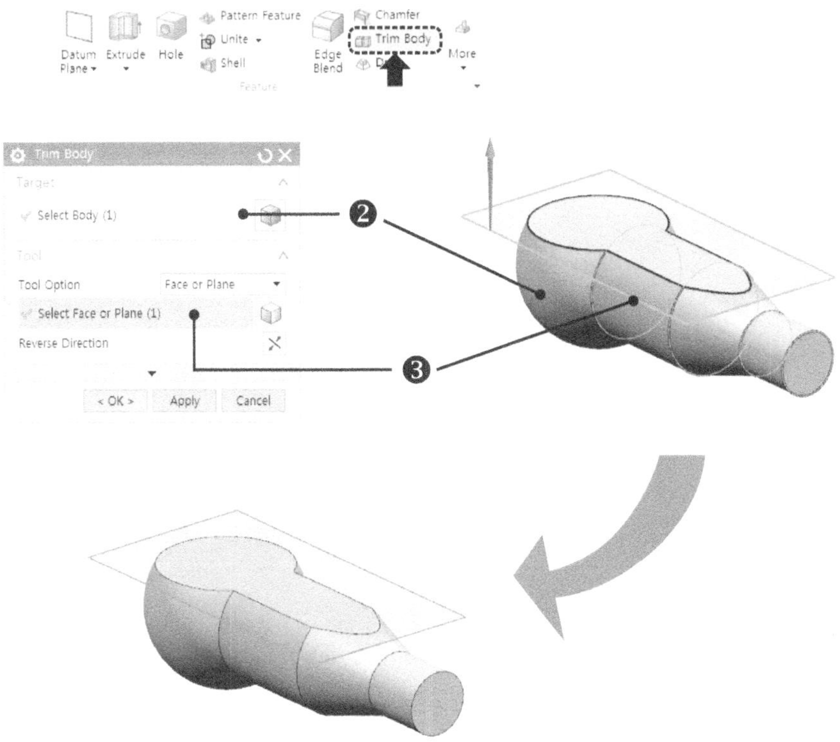

Fig 9-3 Using Trim Body Command

If you select **New Plane** in the **Tool Option** dropdown list, you can create a new datum plane to use as a tool. Click the **Plane Dialog** button. The **Plane** dialog box is invoked and you can define the datum plane as usual. In this case, the tool datum plane is not visible after the trim body operation.

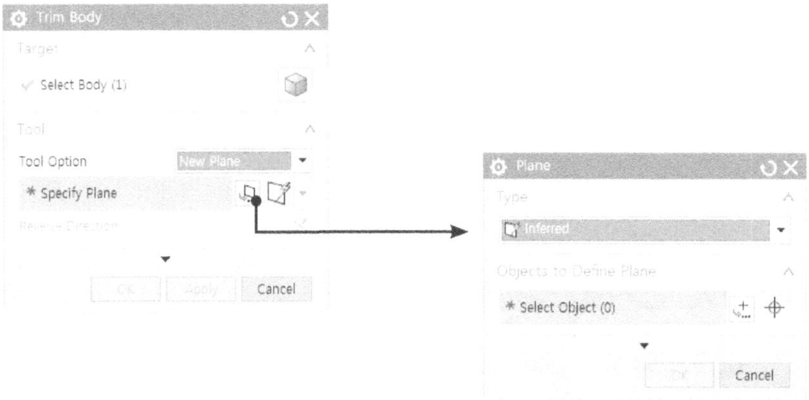

Fig 9-4 Creating a New Datum Plane

Exercise 01 Trim Body Using Face as a Tool

ch09_ex01.prt

Let's learn how to trim out a portion of a solid body with regard to the face of another body.

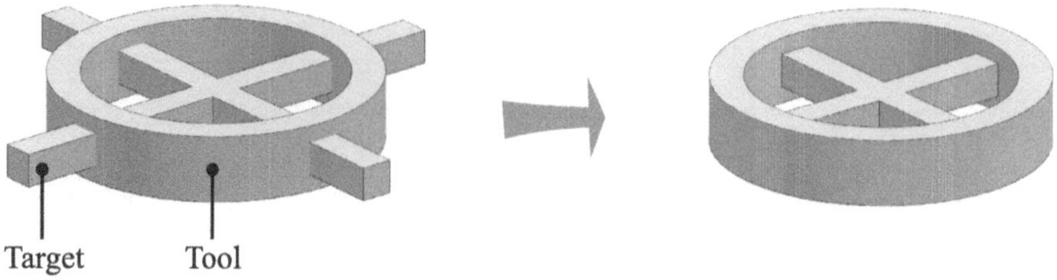

Fig 9-5 Before and After the Trim Body

1. Click the **Trim Body** icon in the **Feature** icon group.
2. Reset the dialog box.
3. Select the target body as specified in Fig 9-5.
4. Click MB2. The **Select Face or Plane** option field is highlighted.
5. Confirm that the face rule in the selection bar is set to **Body Faces**.
6. Change the face rule to **Single Face**.

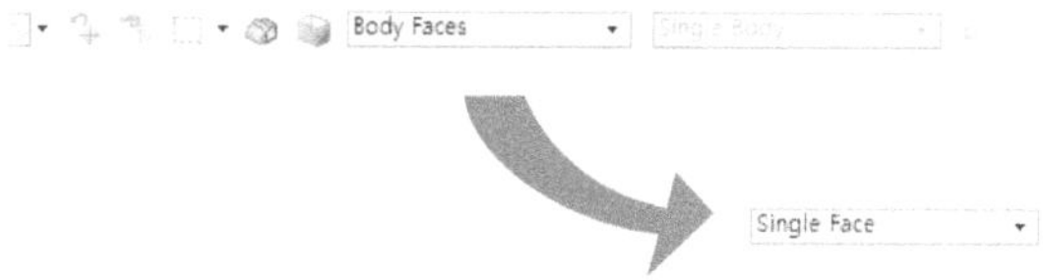

Fig 9-6 Changing the Face Rule

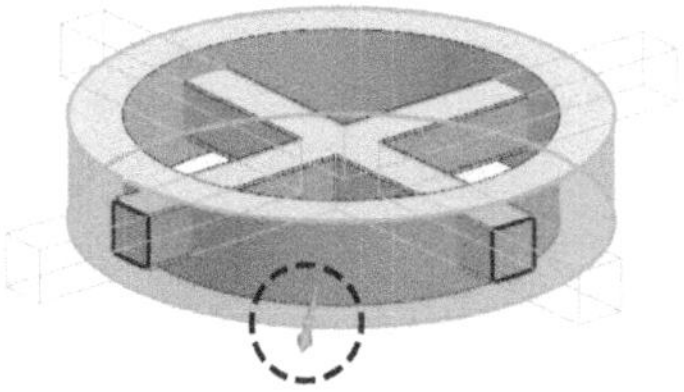

Fig 9-7 Preview

7. Select the face to use as a tool as specified in Fig 9-5.
8. Verify the preview. If the cut out direction is not correct, press the **Reverse Direction** button in the **Trim Body** dialog box.

! *Face Rule: Body Faces*

With the **Body Faces** face rule, all the faces of a body are selected at one time by selecting a face of the body. Bear in mind that the default face rule for the **Trim Body** is **Body Faces**.

Fig 9-8 Completed Model

9. Press **OK** in the dialog box.

Note that the model consists of two solid bodies.

10. Unite the two bodies. Fig 9-8 shows the completed model.

END of Exercise

Caution in Using Face as a Tool

Only the face of the unselected body can be selected as a tool of the **Trim Body** command. If you unite the two bodies first in Exercise 01 and then try to trim the resulting body, you cannot the select the tool face specified in Fig 9-5.

Trimming while Uniting

You can trim a region of a body during the **Unite** operation. Execute the **Unite** command by clicking the **Unite** icon in the **Feature** icon group and select the target and the tool body. Then select the **Define Regions** option in the **Region** option group. If you select the **Keep** option and select the region, the selected region of the body which can be separated by the faces of the other body is retained and united.

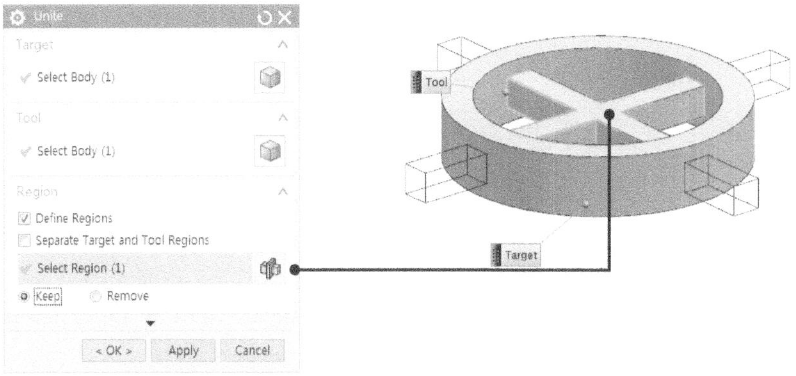

Fig 9-9 Region Option of the Unite Command

Exercise 02 Trimming a Body with a Face

ch09_ex02.prt

Open the given file and complete the modeling according to the suggested steps.

1. The resultant body has to be a single solid body.
2. The passage has to be open across the two pipes.

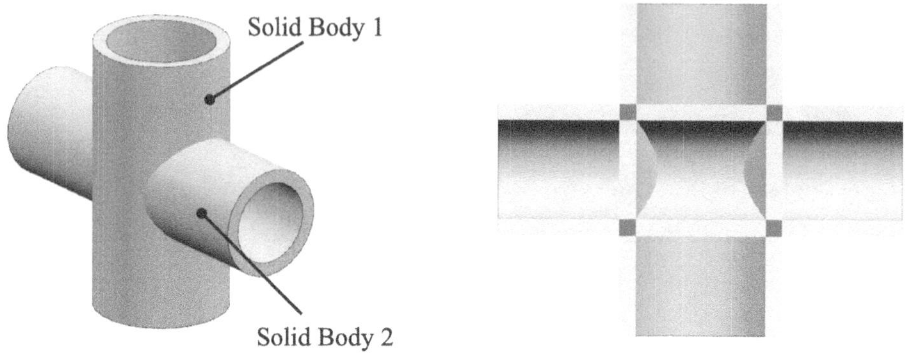

Fig 9-10 Model for Exercise

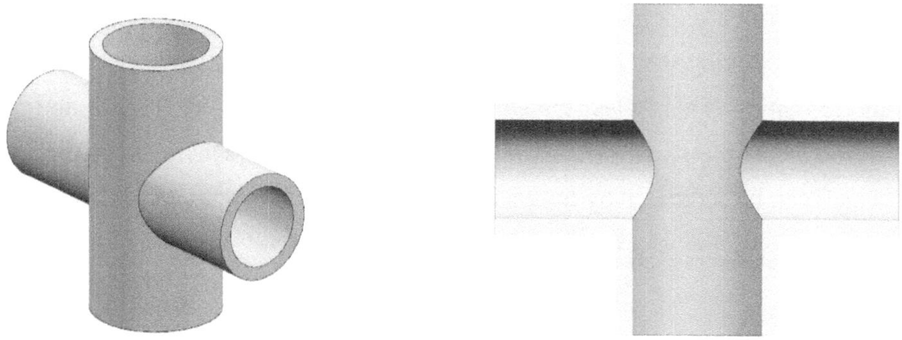

Fig 9-11 Completed Model

Step 1

Trim out solid body 1 as shown in Fig 9-12 with regard to the inner face of solid body 2.

Fig 9-12 Trimming out Solid Body 1

Step 2

Trim out solid body 2 as shown in Fig 9-13 with regard to the outer face of solid body 1. Solid body 2 is separated into two solid bodies.

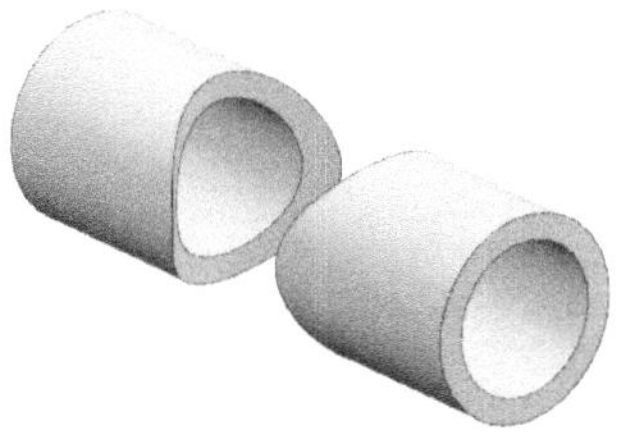

Fig 9-13 Trimming out Solid Body 2

Step 3

Unite the resultant three solid bodies. Note that you can select only one body for the target and as many bodies as you want for the tool.

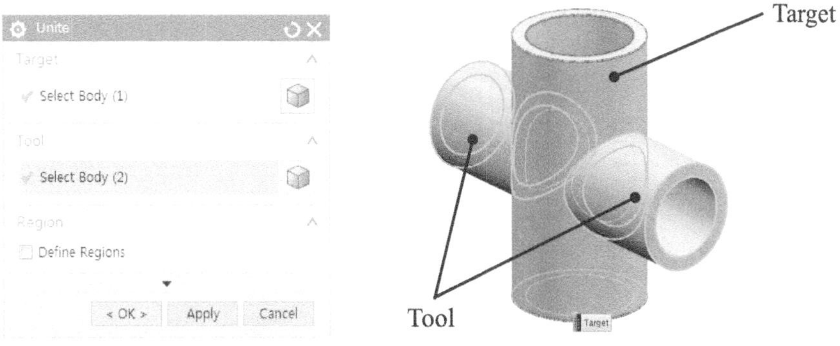

Fig 9-14 Unite

END of Exercise

9.2 Tube

Create a circular pipe along a path. Note that only the tangent continuous curves can be used as the **Path**.

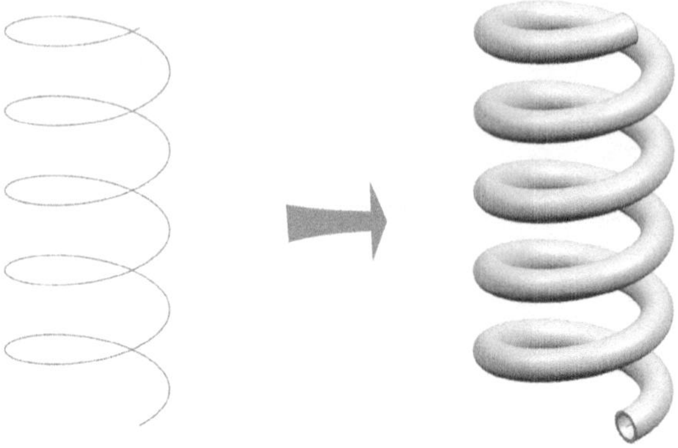

Fig 9-15 Tube

9.2.1 Procedure

Keep to the following procedure to trim out a portion of the target bodies. The numbers in Fig 9-17 correspond to the step numbers.

① Press the **More** button in the **Surface** icon group and click the **Tube** icon.

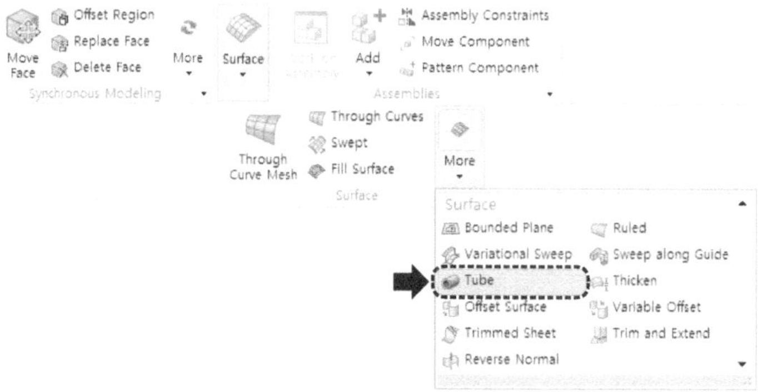

Fig 9-16 Tube Icon

② Reset the **Tube** dialog box.

③ Select the path.

④ Enter dimensions for the cross section.

⑤ Set other options and press **OK**.

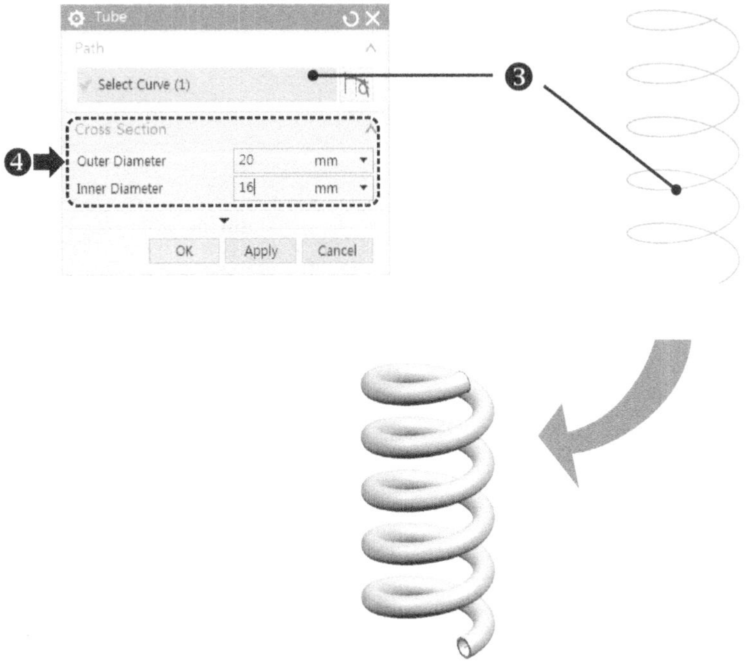

Fig 9-17 Using Tube Command

9.2.2 Output Option

You can set the **Output** option by expanding the **Settings** option group.

Fig 9-18 Output Option

Multiple Segments

The tube is created in many segments. The face is created through a simple calculation and it takes little time to generate the face.

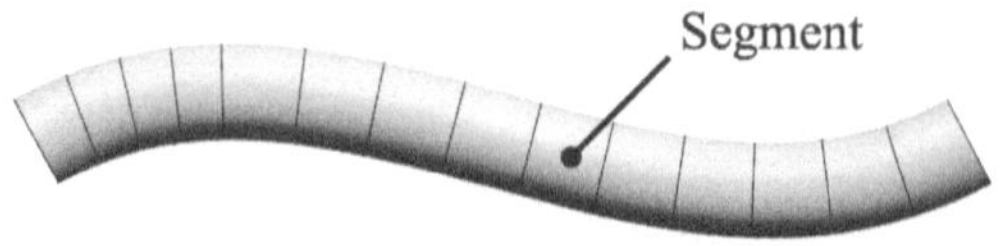

Fig 9-19 Multiple Segments

Single Segment

The tube is created in one segment. The face is created through a complex calculation and it takes a long time to generate the face.

Fig 9-20 Single Segment

9.3 Sweep along Guide

Sweep a section through a guide to generate the feature. It is a simple case of the **Swept** command which is in the scope of surface modeling.

Compared to the **Tube** command, you can create your own sketch and use it as the section. You can use an open or closed section. Multiple loops in the section are not allowed, but the section can have internal loops.

9.3.1 Procedure

Keep to the following procedure to trim out a portion of the target bodies. The numbers in Fig 9-21 and Fig 9-22 correspond to the step numbers.

① Press the **More** button in the **Surface** icon group and click the **Sweep along Guide** icon.

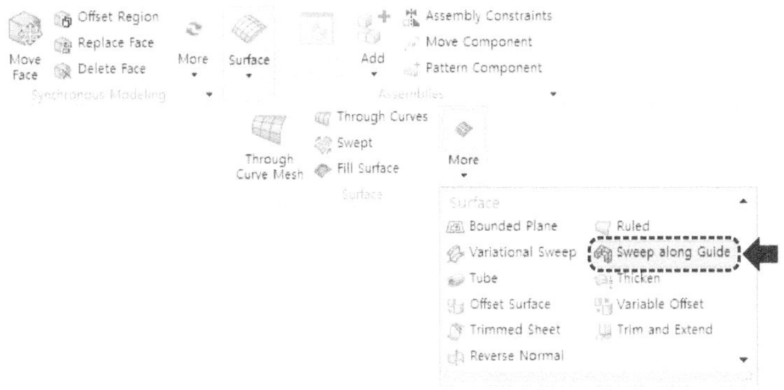

Fig 9-21 Sweep along Guide Icon

② Reset the **Sweep along Guide** dialog box.

③ Select the curves to use as a section. Choose a proper curve rule.

④ Press MB2 and select the curve to use as a guide.

⑤ Set other options and press **OK**.

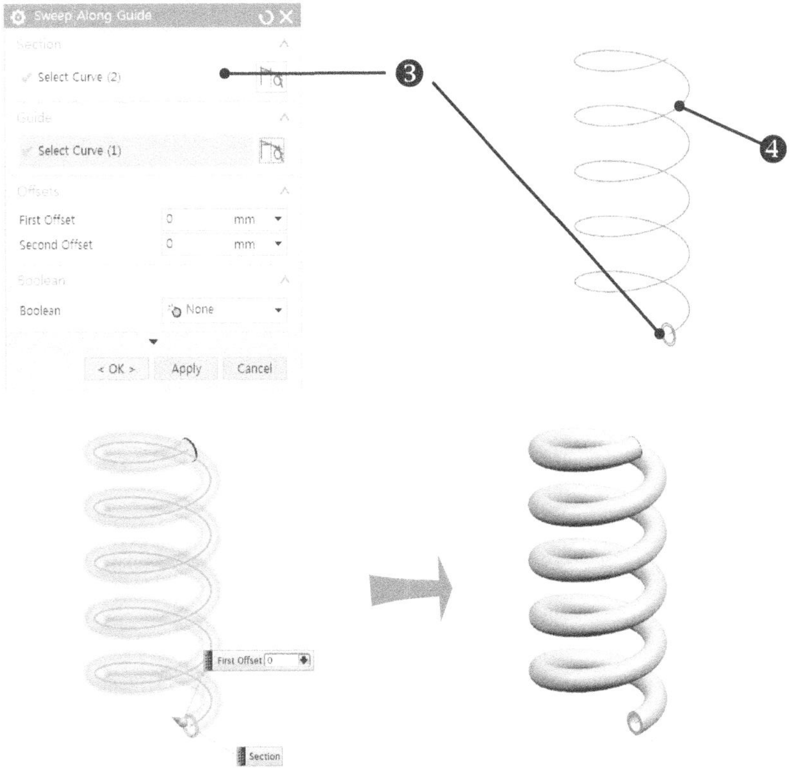

Fig 9-22 Using Sweep along Guide Command

9.4 Emboss

You can create engraved or embossed features as shown in Fig 9-23.

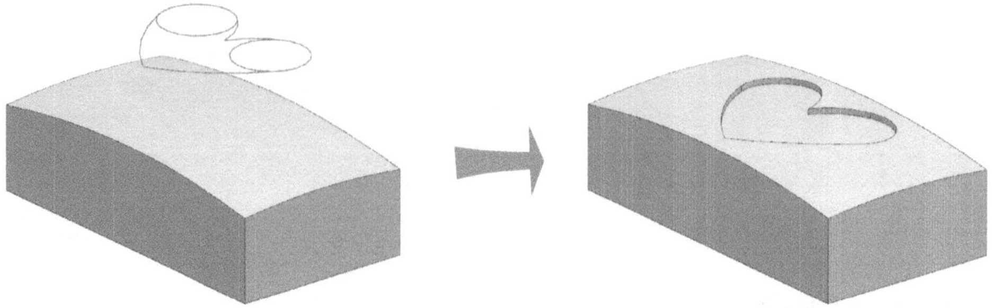

Fig 9-23 Emboss Feature

Exercise 03 Emboss

ch09_ex03.prt

Let's create an emboss feature that engraves the surface at a uniform depth.

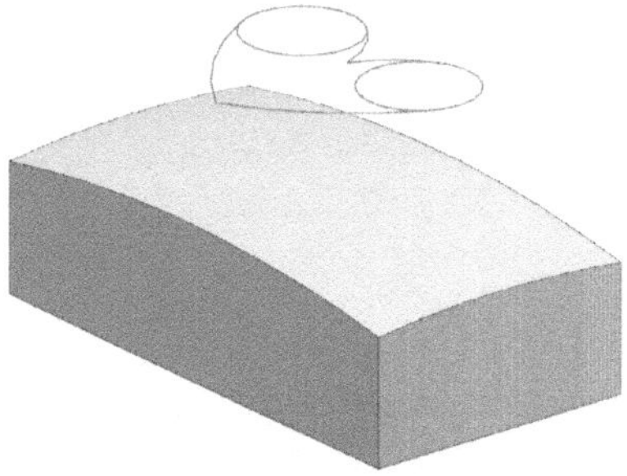

Fig 9-24 Model for Exercise

Fig 9-25 Emboss Menu

Executing Emboss Command

1. Open the given file ch09_ex03.prt.
2. Choose **Insert > Design Feature > Emboss** in the **Menu** button.
3. Reset the dialog box.
4. Change the rendering style to **Static Wireframe**.

Selecting Section and Face to Emboss

1. Confirm that curve rule is set to **Tangent Curves** and turn on the **Stop at Intersection** and **Follow Fillet** options.
2. Select the outer curves of the given sketch to form a heart.
3. Click MB2.
4. Change the face rule to **Single Face**.
5. Select the upper face as the **Face to Emboss**. Emboss is previewed as shown in Fig 9-26.

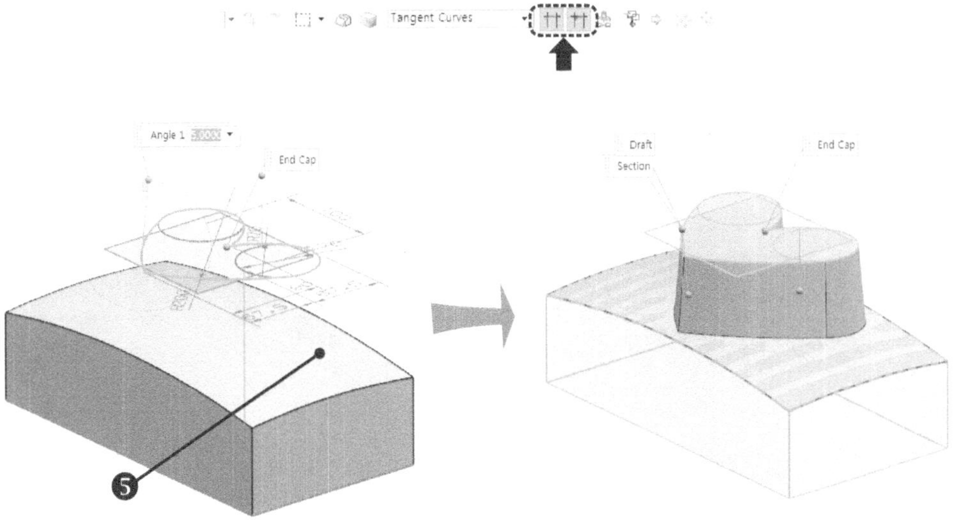

Fig 9-26 Selecting Section and Emboss Face

! Carving Characters

You can create texts as a set of curves by choosing **Insert > Curve > Text** in the **Menu** button. Then you can carve the texts using the **Emboss** command.

End Cap Option

1. Set the **End Cap** option (A in Fig 9-27).
2. Press the **Reverse Direction** button to turn emboss to engrave.
3. Expand the **Draft** option and enter 0 (B in Fig 9-27).
4. Press **OK** in the dialog box.

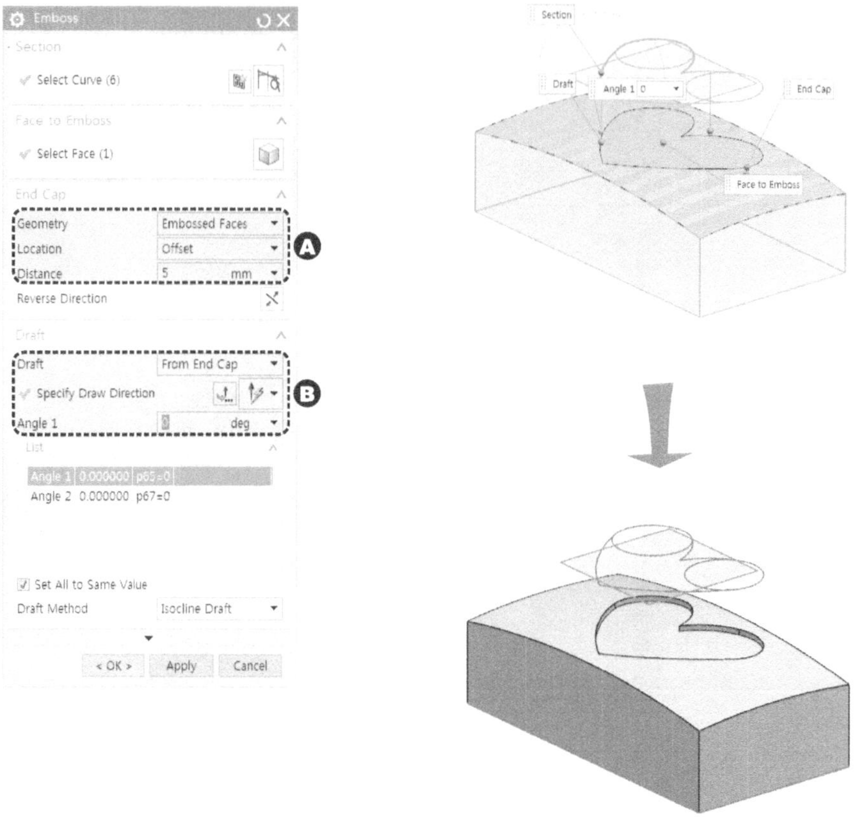

Fig 9-27 Emboss Feature Created

END of Exercise

Color of Heart

You can change the color of the embossed face using the **Edit Object Display** command. You have to set the type filter to **Face** to select only the desired faces.

9.5 Synchronous Modeling

Modeling and modification up until this chapter have been performed parametrically. That is to say, we have defined features in the dialog box and modified the parameters in the dialog box to modify the model geometry. As a result, when the model is created from another CAD system, the modification is restricted to some edge and face operations. However, using the synchronous modeling techniques, we can more flexibly modify geometries that do not have a model history. Fig 9-28 shows the **Synchronous Modeling** icon group.

Fig 9-28 Synchronous Modeling Icon Group

9.5.1 Move Face

You can select faces and move them according to the definite method.

ch09_ex04.stp **Move Face** **Exercise 04**

1. Open the given file ch09_ex04.stp. You have to choose **STEP Files** as the file type. It may take a while to translate the STEP file to part data.

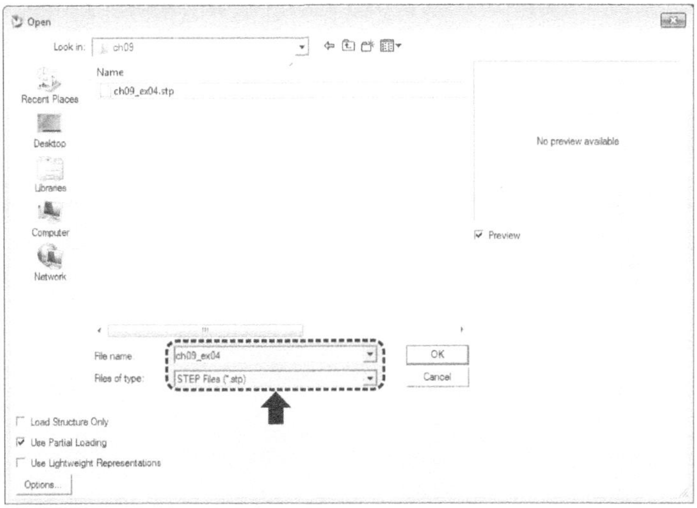

Fig 9-29 Opening the STEP File

Fig 9-30 Move Face Icon

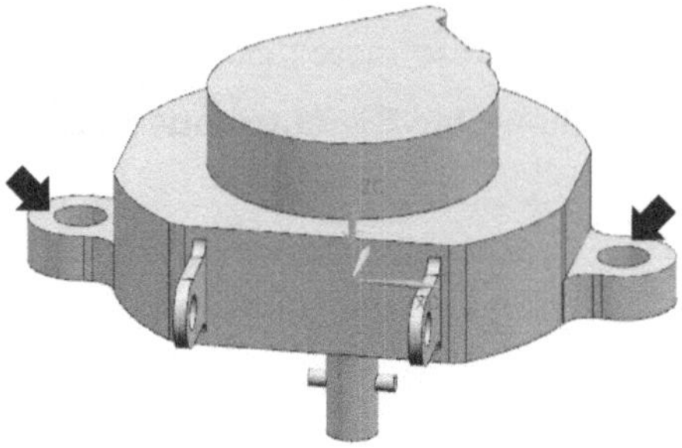

Fig 9-31 Faces to Select

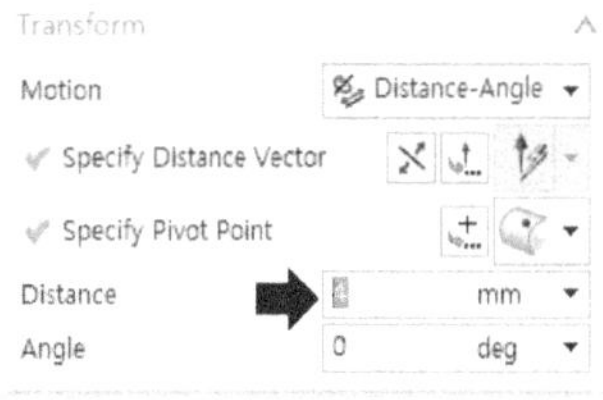

Fig 9-32 Move Distance

2. Click the **Move Face** icon in the **Synchronous Modeling** icon group.

3. Reset the **Move Face** dialog box.

4. Select the faces designated by the arrow in Fig 9-31.

5. Enter 4 in the **Distance** input box in the **Move Face** dialog box as shown in Fig 9-32 and press the **Enter** key. The moved face is previewed as shown on the left of Fig 9-33.

6. Press the **OK** button in the dialog box.

7. Close without saving the file.

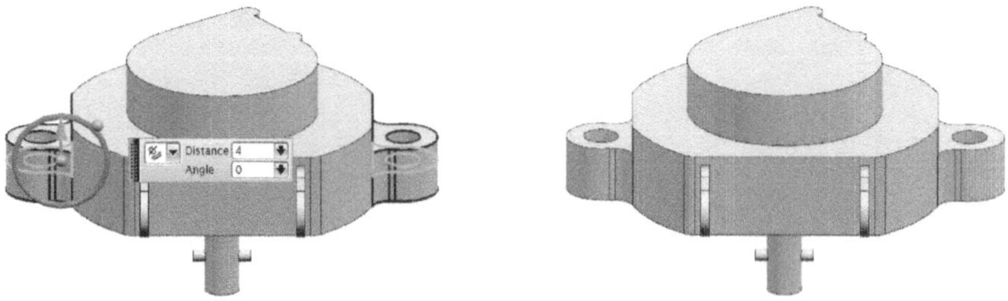

Fig 9-33 Result of Move Face

END of Exercise

9.5.2 Resize Blend

You can modify the radius of a blend surface without the edge blend parameters. Note that this command is applicable only for a cylindrical surface.

ch09_ex04_stp.prt **Resize Blend** **Exercise 05**

1. Open the file ch09_ex04_stp.prt. This file has been created automatically as a result of opening the STEP file in Exercise 04.

2. Press the More button in the **Synchronous Modeling** icon group and click the **Resize Blend** icon.

3. Reset the **Resize Blend** dialog box.

4. Select the four cylindrical faces as designated in Fig 9-35. The current radius of the face is entered in the **Radius** input box in the dialog box.

5. Enter 0.5 as the radius and press the **Enter** key. The resized blend is previewed as shown in Fig 9-36.

6. Press **OK** in the dialog box. The radius of the blend surface is modified on the right of Fig 9-37.

7. Close without saving the file.

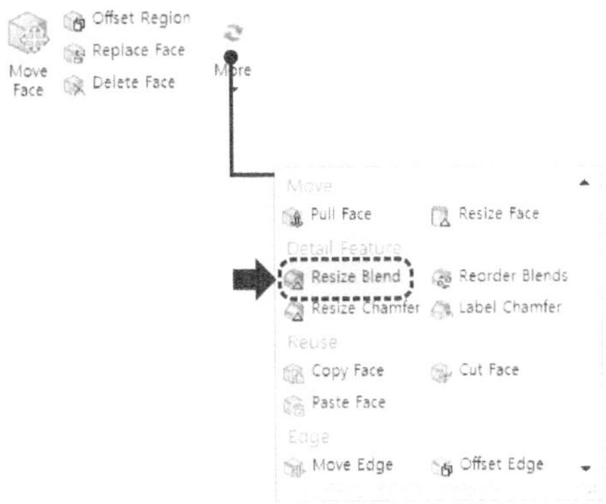

Fig 9-34 Resize Blend Icon

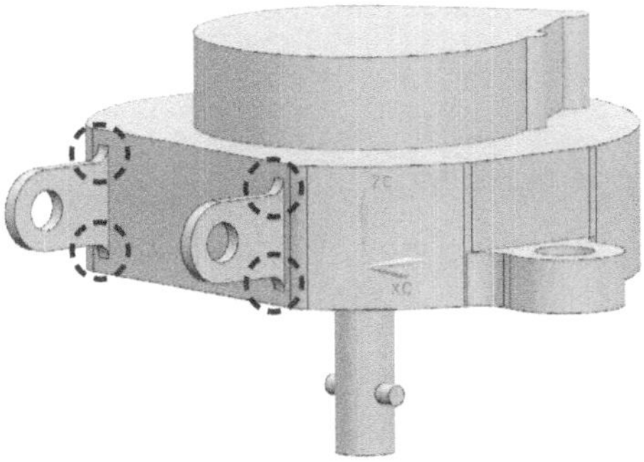

Fig 9-35 Faces to Select

Fig 9-36 Modified Radius

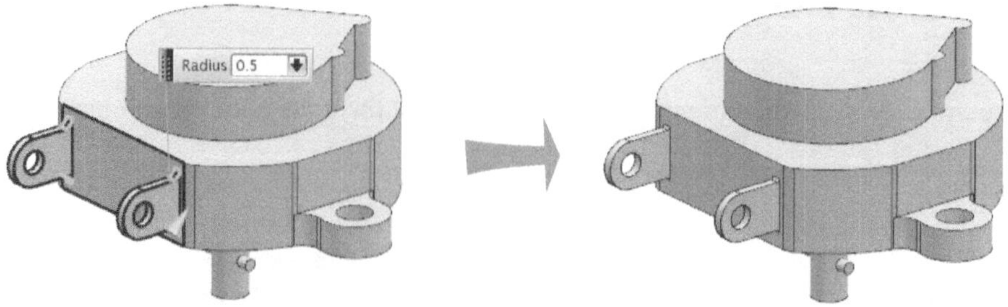

Fig 9-37 Result of Resize Blend

END of Exercise

9.5.3 Delete Face

You can delete faces when they are completely isolated from the remaining body.

Exercise 06 **Delete Face** *ch09_ex04_stp.prt*

1. Open the file ch09_ex04_stp.prt. This file has been created automatically as a result of opening the STEP file in Exercise 04.

2. Click the **Delete Face** icon in the **Synchronous Modeling** icon group.

3. Reset the **Resize Blend** dialog box.

4. Change the face rule in the selection bar to **Region Face**.

Fig 9-38 Region Face

Select seed face for region

Fig 9-39 Status Line Message

You are prompted in the status line to select a seed face as shown in Fig 9-39.

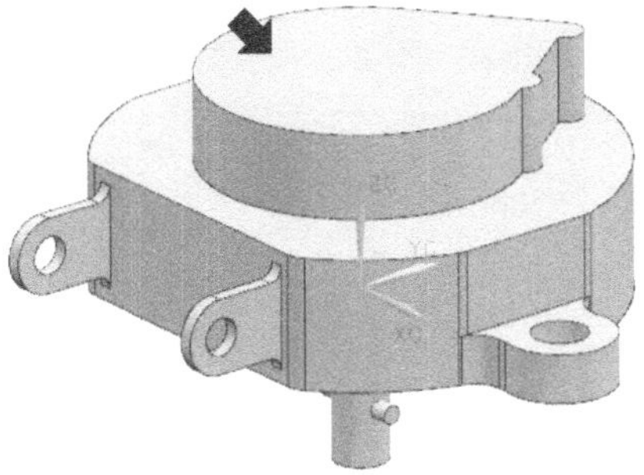

Fig 9-40 Seed Face

! *Seed Face*

A seed face is a representative face among the faces which are isolated by the boundary face. All the faces on the side of the seed face with regard to the boundary face are selected at one time.

Select boundary faces for region, or press MB2 to finish the region

Fig 9-41 Status Line Message

5. Select the face designated by the arrow in Fig 9-40 as the seed face. You are prompted in the status line to select a boundary face.

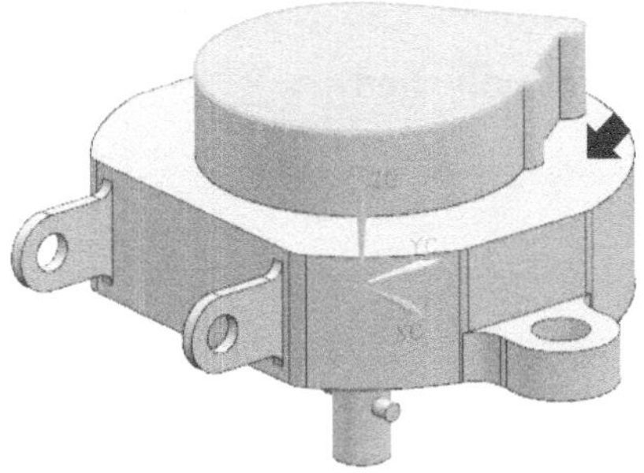

Fig 9-42 Boundary Face

6. Select the face designated in Fig 9-42 as the boundary face.

7. Click MB2. Six faces are selected as shown in Fig 9-43.

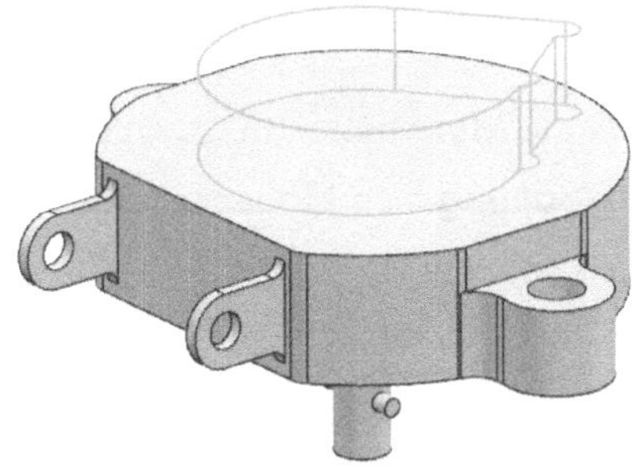

Fig 9-43 Selected Faces

8. Press **OK** in the dialog box. The selected faces are deleted as shown in Fig 9-44.

9. Close without saving the file.

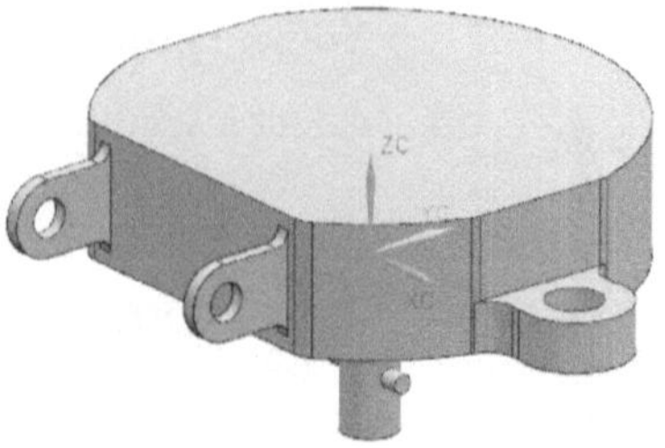

Fig 9-44 Result of Deleted Face

! Boundary Face

With the **Region Faces** face rule, you can select faces connected to the seed face up to the boundary face. While only one face can be selected as the seed face, you can select as many faces as required to isolate the faces.

END of Exercise

9.5.4 Copy Face

You can copy faces from a body. If you want to fill or remove a solid body by the copied faces, the faces have to be isolated from the faces of the solid body.

Exercise 07 **Copy Face** *ch09_ex04_stp.prt*

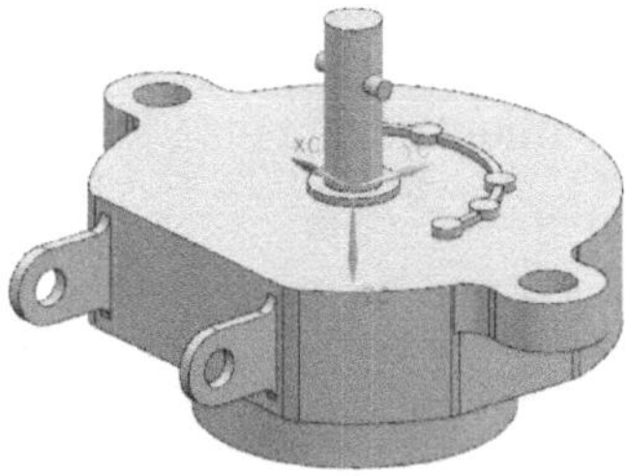

Fig 9-45 Model for Exercise

1. Open the file ch09_ex04_stp.prt. This file has been created automatically as a result of opening the STEP file in Exercise 04.

2. Press the More button in the **Synchronous Modeling** icon group and click the **Copy Face** icon.

3. Reset the **Copy Face** dialog box.

4. Rotate the model as shown in Fig 9-45.

5. Check the options in the **Settings** tab in the dialog box as shown in Fig 9-46.

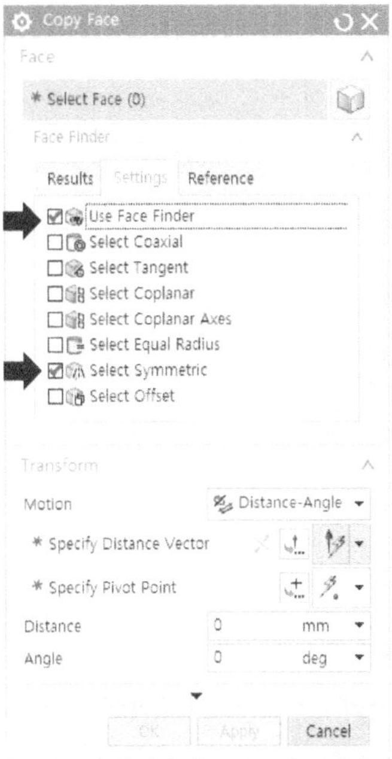

Fig 9-46 Settings Option

6. Select the two faces specified by Ⓐ in Fig 9-47.

The faces on the opposite side are selected because you turned on the **Select Symmetric** option in Fig 9-46.

7. Click the **Specify Distance Vector** option field in the dialog box as shown in Fig 9-46.

8. Select the vector Ⓑ shown in Fig 9-48.

9. Enter 5 in the **Distance** input box and press **Enter** in the keyboard. The copied faces are previewed as shown in Fig 9-49.

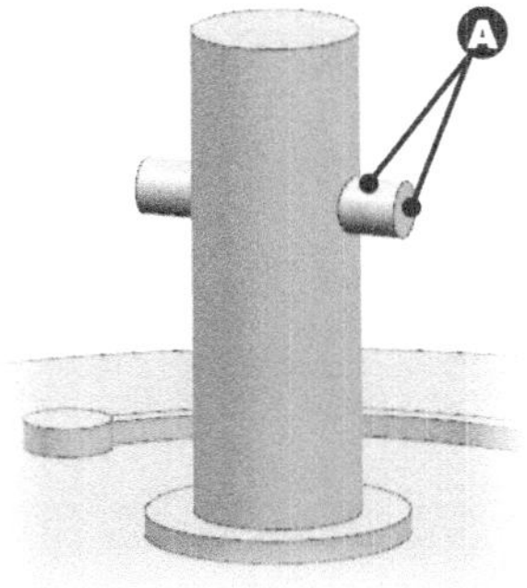

Fig 9-47 Faces to Copy

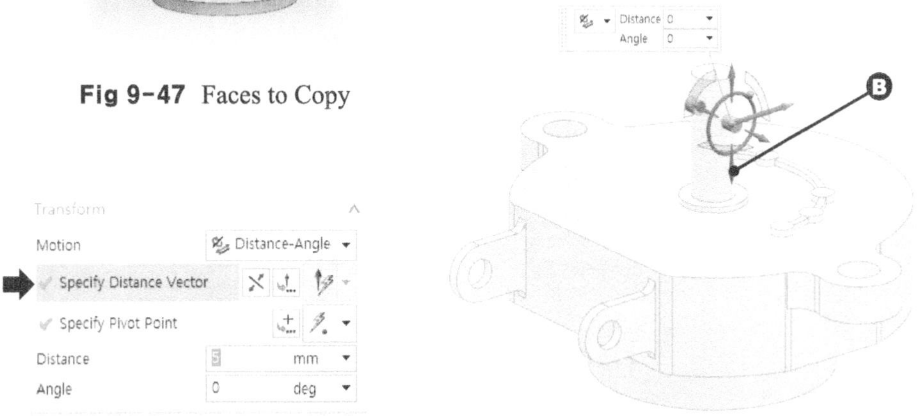

Fig 9-48 Option for Transform

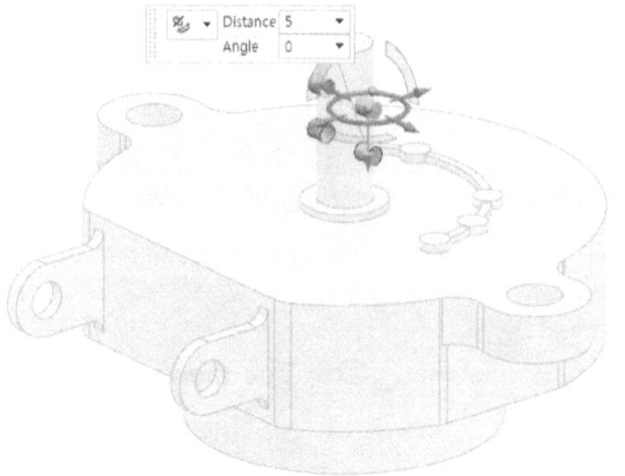

Fig 9-49 Preview

10. Check the **Paste Copied Faces** option in the **Paste** option group in the dialog box as shown in Fig 9-50.

Fig 9-50 Paste Option

11. Press **OK** in the dialog box. The faces for the boss are copied and the inside is filled with material.

12. Close without saving the file.

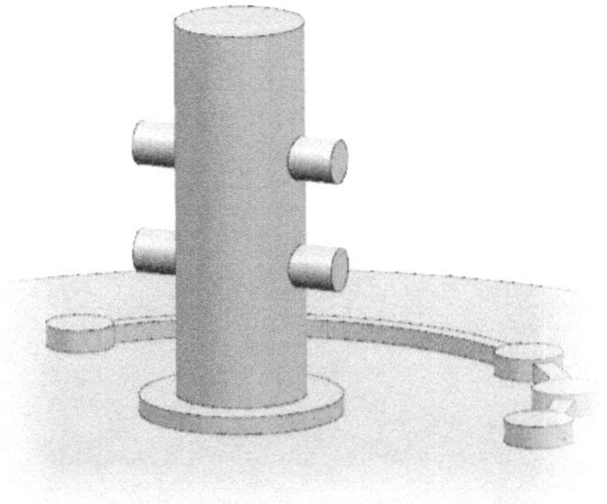

Fig 9-51 Result of Copy Face

END of Exercise

9.5.5 Make Coplanar

You can make a plane coplanar with a specific plane.

ch09_ex04_stp.prt **Make Coplanar** **Exercise 08**

1. Open the file ch09_ex04_stp.prt. This file has been created automatically as a result of opening the STEP file in Exercise 04.

2. Choose **Insert > Synchronous Modeling > History-Free Mode** in the **Menu** button.

3. Choose **Insert > Synchronous Modeling > Make Coplanar** in the **Menu** button.

4. Reset the **Make Coplanar** dialog box.

5. Rotate the model view as shown in Fig 9-52.

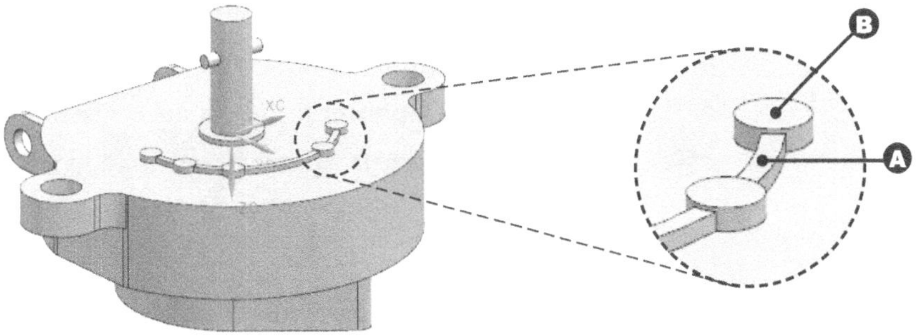

Fig 9-52 Faces to Select

6. Select the face Ⓐ specified in Fig 9-52 as the motion face. You can select only one motion face. Therefore, the **Stationary Face** option is automatically progressed.

7. Select the face Ⓑ specified in Fig 9-52 as the stationary face. The motion face becomes coplanar as shown in Fig 9-53, and an alert message is generated. The information symbol in the part navigator can be removed by pressing **MB3 > Clear Feature Info Alerts** on the **Coplanar** feature.

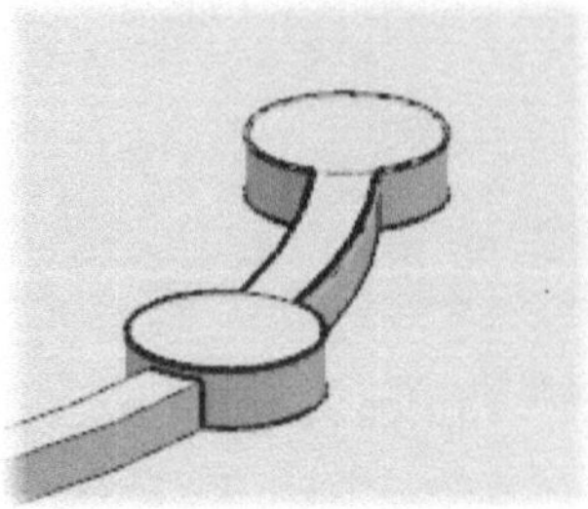

Fig 9-53 Preview

Fig 9-54 Alerts Message

8. Confirm that the **Select Face** option field in the **Motion Group** is highlighted and you are prompted to select faces to move with the motion face in the cue line.

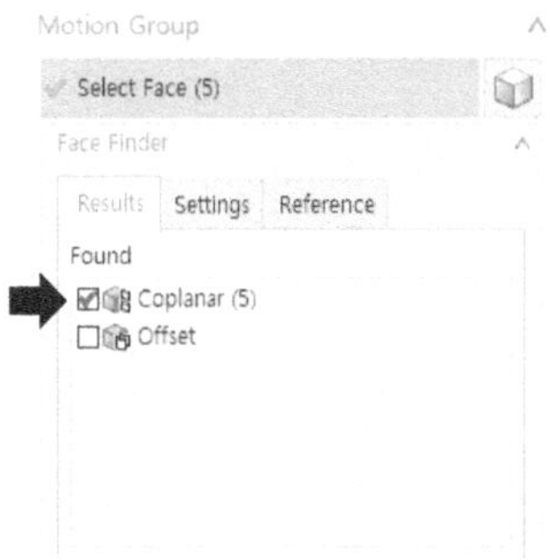

Fig 9-55 Coplanar Option

9. Check the **Coplanar** option in the **Face Finder** list box as shown in Fig 9-55.

10. Press **OK** in the dialog box. All faces coplanar with the motion face are made coplanar with the **Stationary Face** as shown in Fig 9-56. Note that the **Make Coplanar** feature is not registered in the **Part Navigator** because we have chosen the **History-Free Mode** option.

11. Close without saving the file.

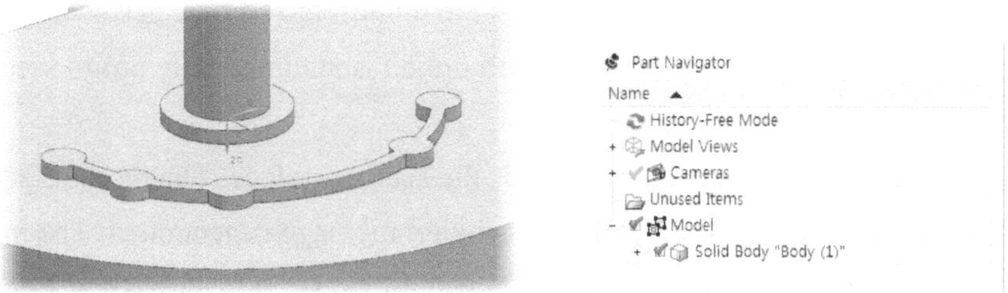

Fig 9-56 Result of Make Coplanar

END of Exercise

9.5.6 Linear Dimension

You can apply a linear dimension between planar objects such as edges and faces. Then you can modify the dimension value to modify the geometry.

ch09_ex04_stp.prt **Linear Dimension** **Exercise 09**

1. Open the file ch09_ex04_stp.prt.

2. Note that we have chosen a history-free mode of the **Part Navigator** in the previous exercise. Press MB3 on an empty area in the **Part Navigator** and select **Timestamp Order** option.

3. Create a datum coordinate system as shown in Fig 9-57 and rotate the model view.

4. Choose **Insert > Synchronous Modeling > Dimension > Linear Dimension** in the **Menu** button.

5. Select the YZ plane as designated by the arrow in Fig 9-58 as the **Origin Object**. The **Measurement Object** option is highlighted as shown in Fig 9-59.

6. Turn on the **Midpoint** in the snap point option and select the midpoint of the edge specified by the arrow in Fig 9-60. The dimension is displayed as shown in Fig 9-61.

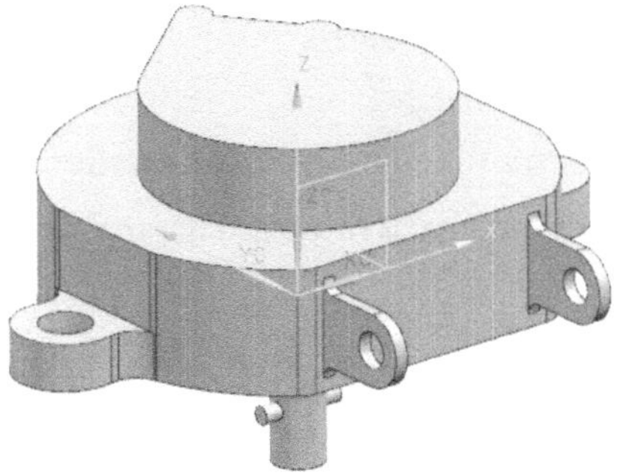

Fig 9-57 Model for Exercise

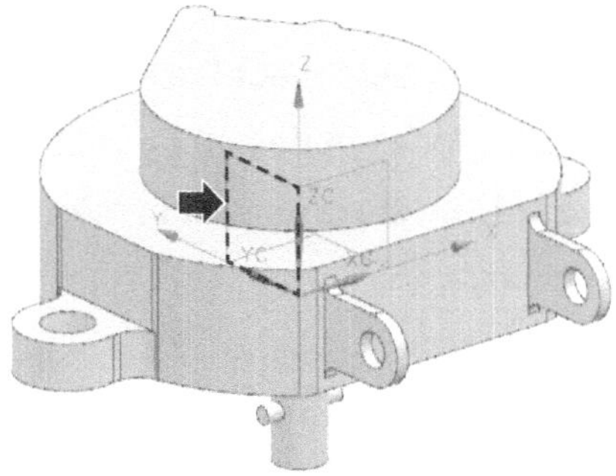

Fig 9-58 YZ Plane

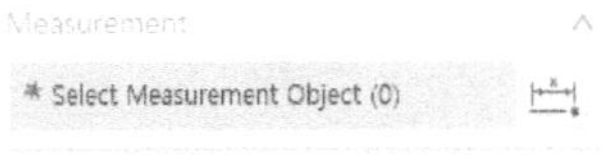

Fig 9-59 Measurement Option Group

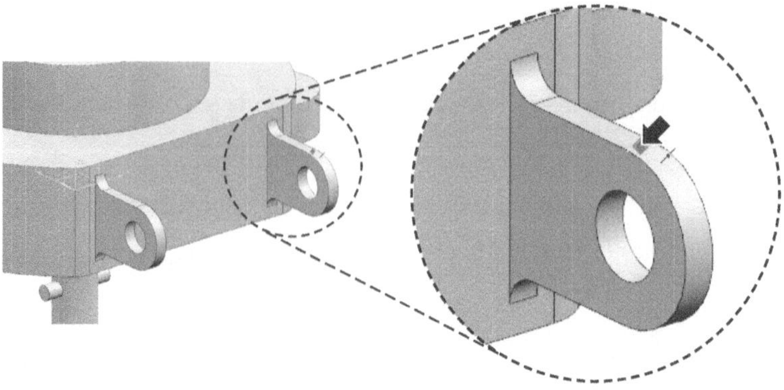

Fig 9-60 Selecting the Midpoint of an Edge

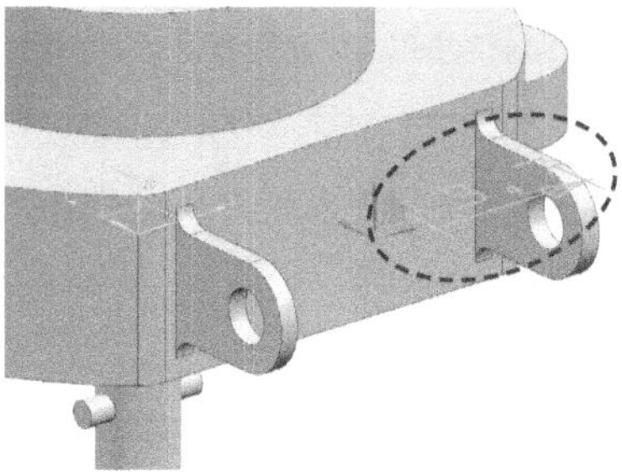

Fig 9-61 Measured Distance

7. Confirm that the **Specify Location** option field is activated as shown in Fig 9-62.

8. Click MB1 at a proper location to create the linear dimension as shown in Fig 9-64.

Fig 9-62 Specify Location Option

9. Confirm that the **Select Face** button in the **Face To Move** option group is highlighted and you are prompted to select the faces to move.

10. Change the face rule to **Boss or Pocket Faces** and press the **Include Boundary Blends** button as shown in Fig 9-63.

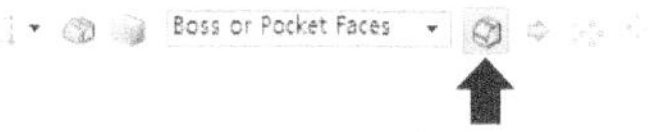

Fig 9-63 Face Rule and Option

11. Select the face Ⓐ in Fig 9-62. All the protruded faces are selected at one time.

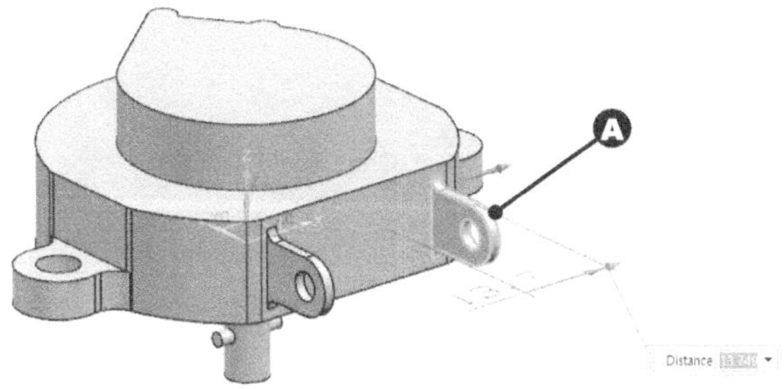

Fig 9-64 Selecting Faces

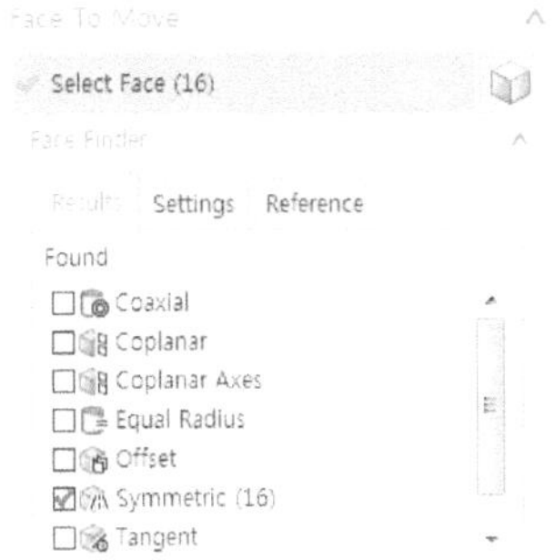

Fig 9-65 Symmetric Option

12. Check the **Symmetric** option in the **Face Finder** list box as shown in Fig 9-65. All the symmetric faces are selected together as shown in Fig 9-66.

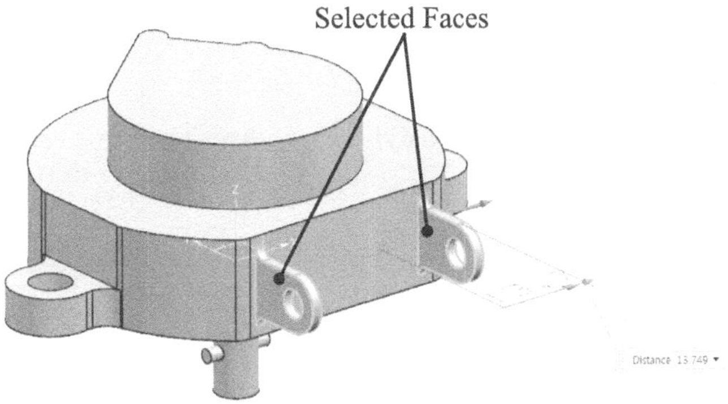

Fig 9-66 Faces to Move

13. Enter 10 in the **Distance** input box and press **Enter** in the keyboard. The geometry modification is previewed as shown in Fig 9-67.

14. Click **OK** in the dialog box. The geometry is modified as shown in Fig 9-68.

15. Close without saving the file.

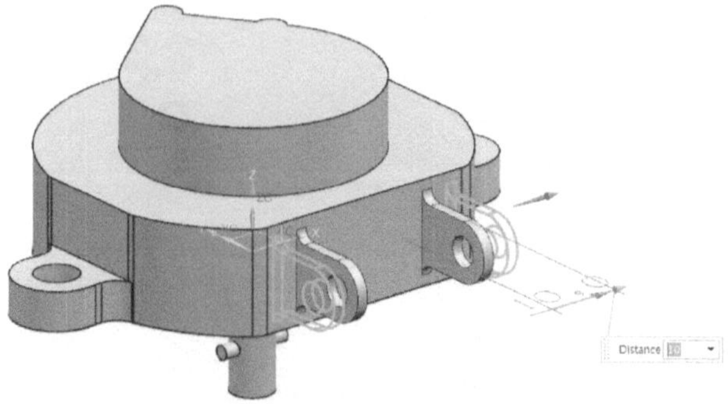

Fig 9-67 Preview

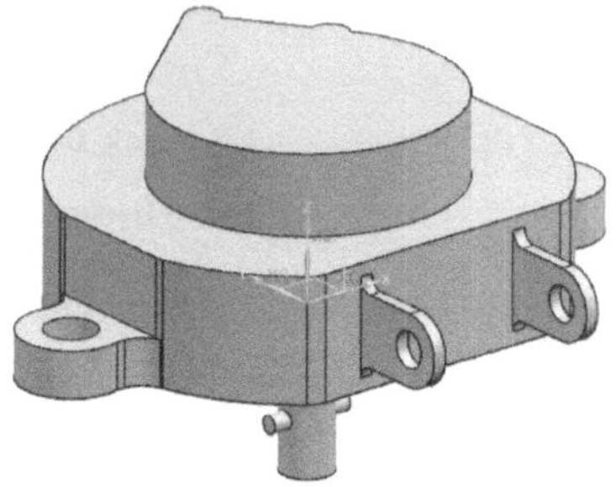

Fig 9-68 Result of Modifying Linear Dimension

END of Exercise

9.5.7 Radial Dimension

You can apply a radial dimension on the cylindrical face. Then you can modify the dimension value to modify the geometry.

Exercise 10 **Radial Dimension** *ch09_ex04_stp.prt*

1. Open the file ch09_ex04_stp.prt.

2. Choose **Insert > Synchronous Modeling > Dimension > Radial Dimension** in the **Menu** button and reset the dialog box.

3. Rotate the model view as shown in Fig 9-69.

4. Select the cylindrical face as designated by the arrow in Fig 9-69. The radius of the cylinder is identified in the **Radius** input box.

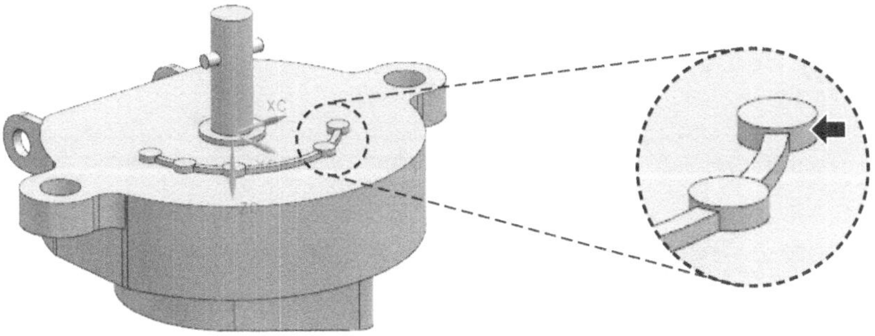

Fig 9-69 Face to Select

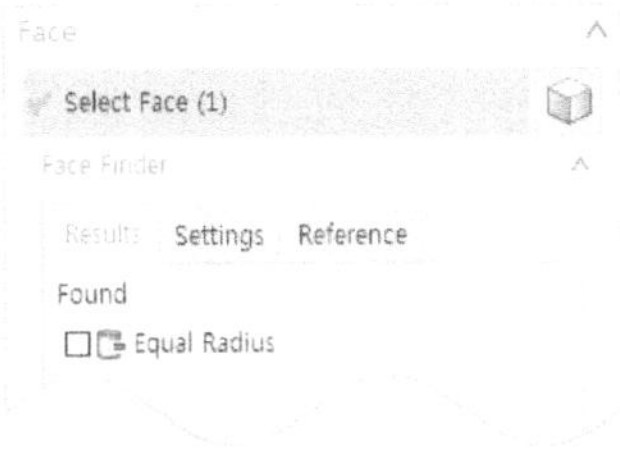

Fig 9-70 Equal Radius Option

5. Check the Equal Radius option in the Face Finder list box as shown in Fig 9-70. The list option changes as shown in Fig 9-71 and all the equal radius cylindrical faces are selected together as designated by the arrows in Fig 9-72.

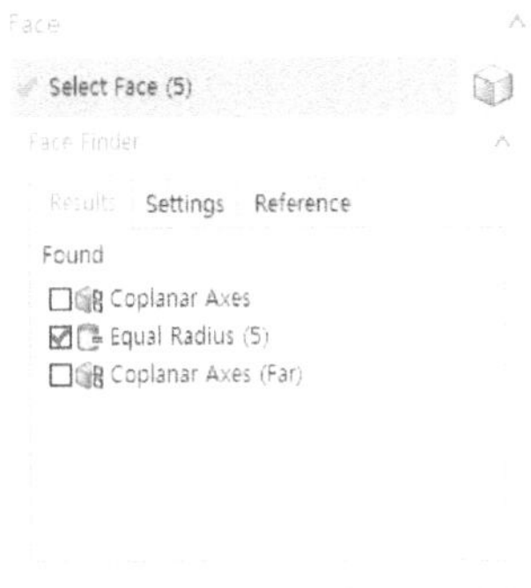

Fig 9-71 Equal Radius Option Checked

6. Enter 5 in the Diameter input box and press Enter.

7. Press OK in the dialog box. Fig 9-73 shows the result of modification.

8. Close without saving the file.

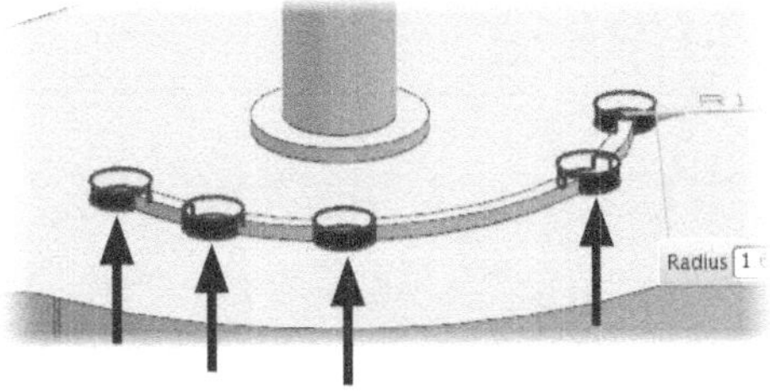

Fig 9-72 Selected Faces

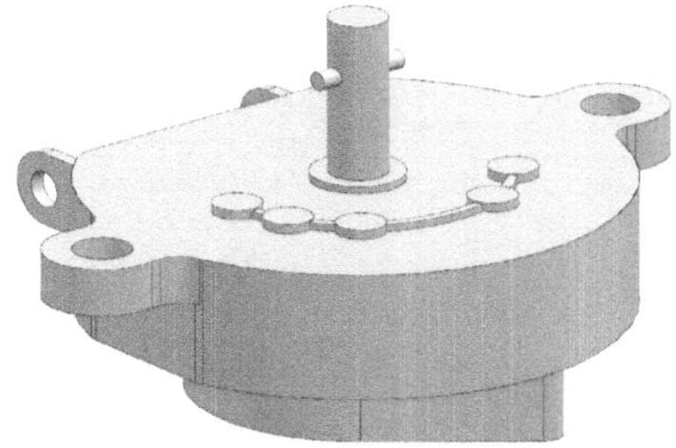

Fig 9-73 Result of Modifying Radial Dimension

END of Exercise

Exercise 11 **Toy Box Cover**

ch09_ex11.prt

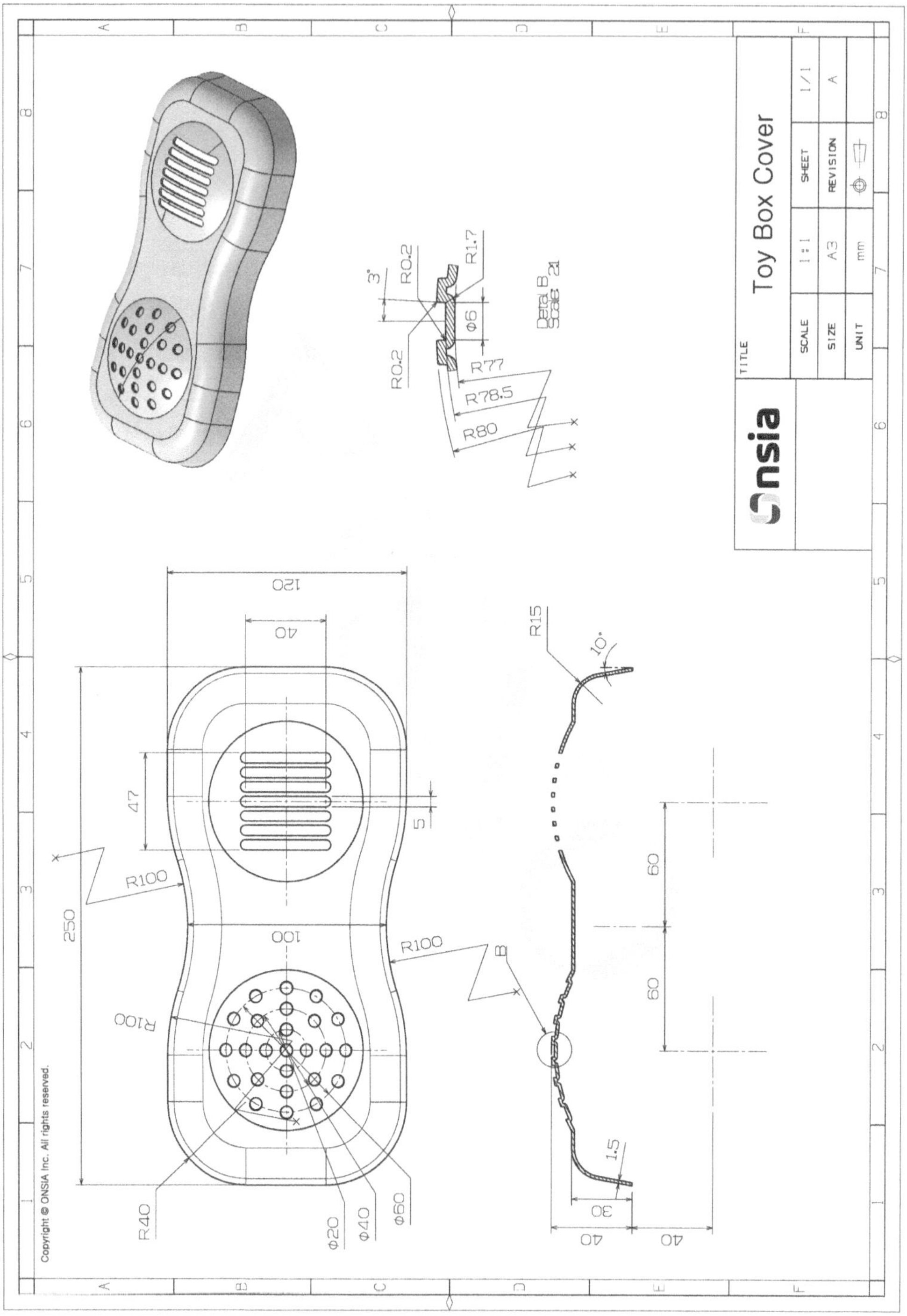

Fig 9-74 Drawing for Toy Box Cover

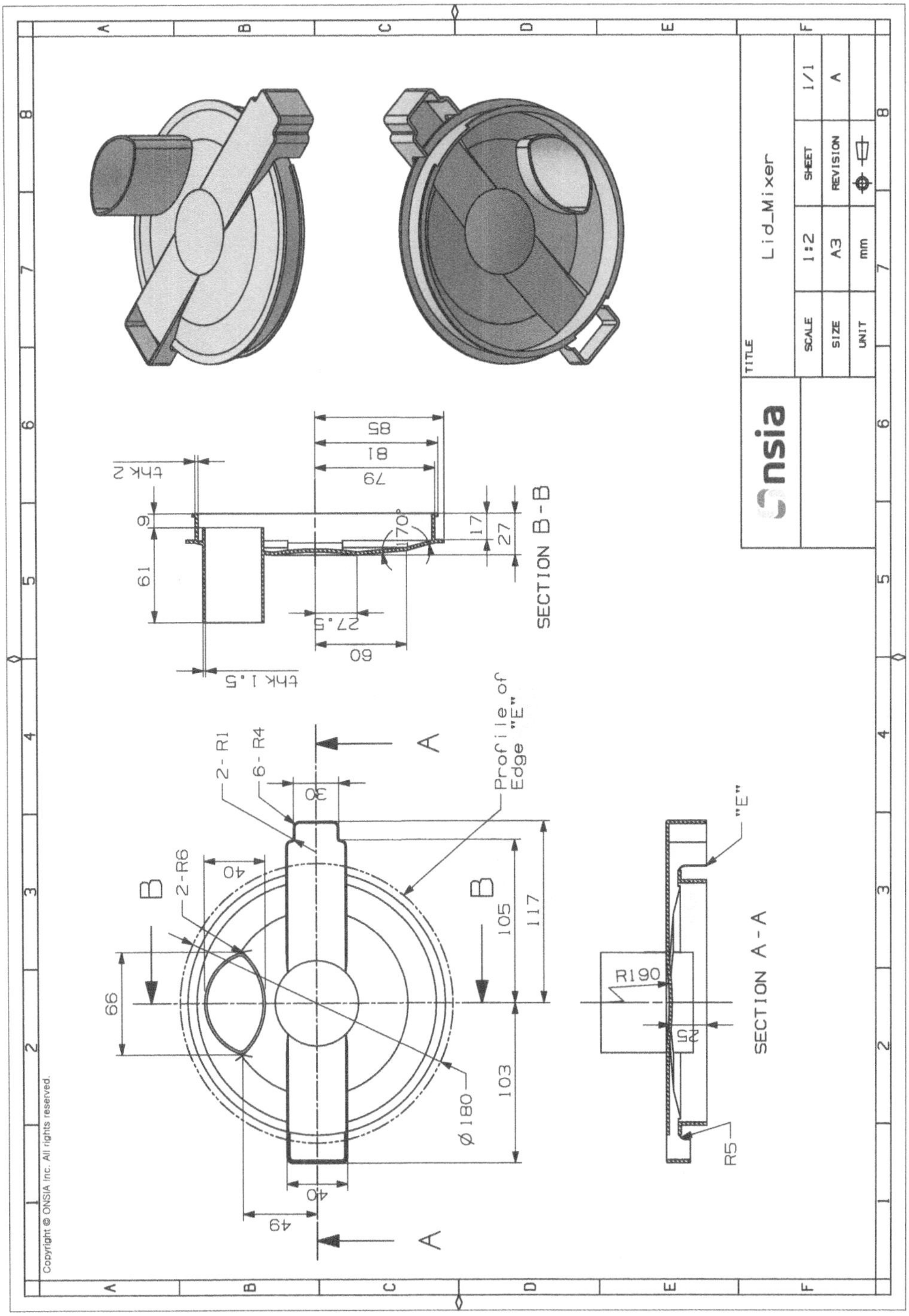

Fig 9-75 Drawing for Lid of Electric Mixer

This page left blank intentionally.

Chapter 10

Advanced Sketch

■ **After completing this chapter you will understand**

- how to create intersection points with the sketch plane.
- how to create intersection curves with the sketch plane.
- how to project a curve or edge on the sketch plane.
- how to trim recipe curves.
- how to offset sketch curves.

10.1 Intersection Point

You can create an intersection point with associativity between the current sketch plane and an edge or curve. Fig 10-2 shows an intersection point and the reference axis. Tangential and normal axes of the face at the intersection point are created automatically when the point is at an intersection with an edge.

Fig 10-1 Cylindrical Body

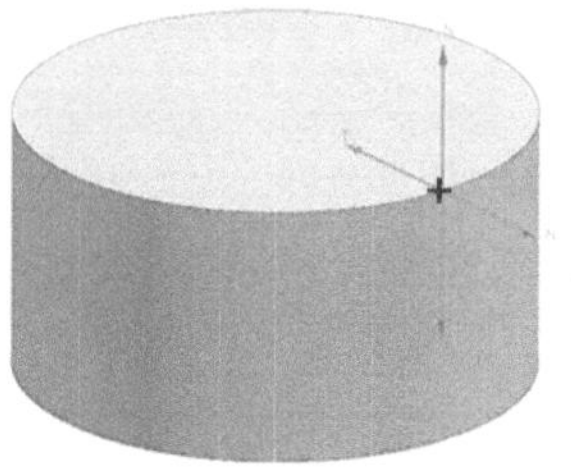

Fig 10-2 Intersection Point

The intersection point is created with associativity to the selected edge or curve. Therefore, the features referring to the intersection point are updated when the geometries associated with the intersection point are modified.

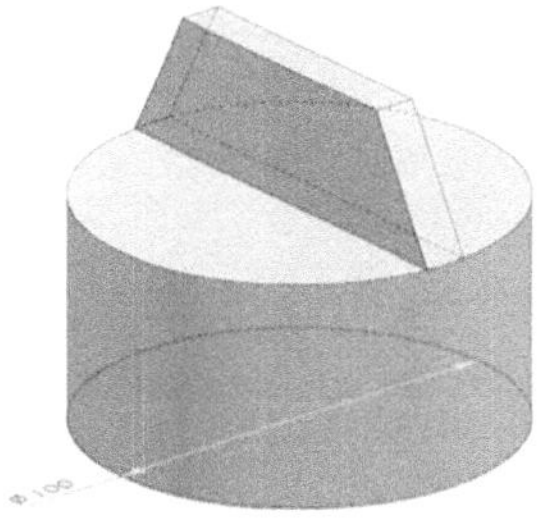

Fig 10-3 Diameter = 100mm

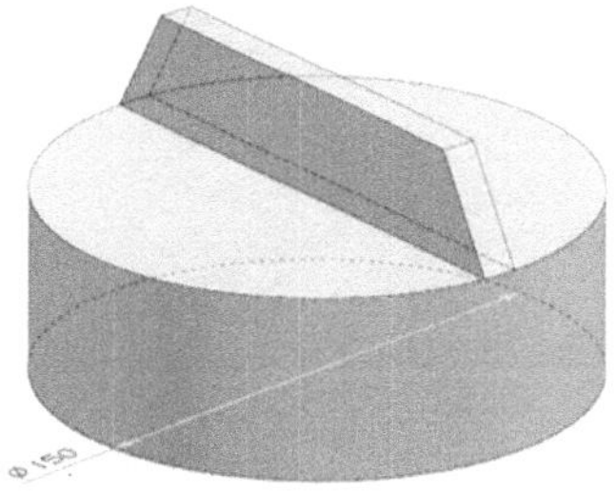

Fig 10-4 Diameter = 150mm

10.1.1 Executing the Intersection Point Command

You can execute the **Intersection Point** command by choosing **Insert > Sketch Curve > Intersection Point** in the **Menu** button. You can also execute this command by clicking the **Intersection Point** icon in the **Sketch Curve** icon list which can be expanded by clicking the down arrow symbol in the **Direct Sketch** icon group as shown in Fig 10-5.

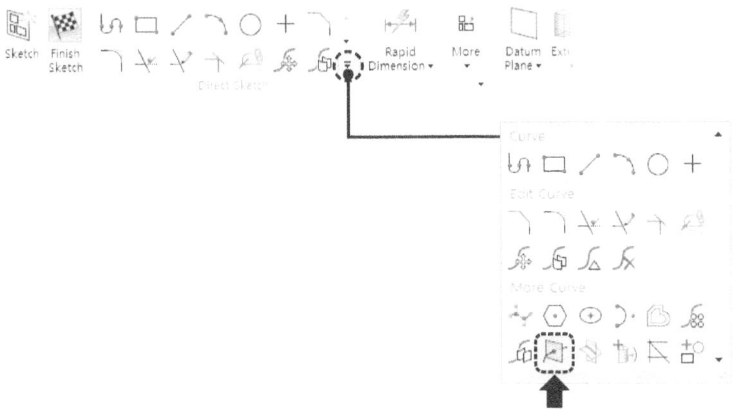

Fig 10-5 Intersection Point Icon

10.1.2 Intersection Point Dialog Box

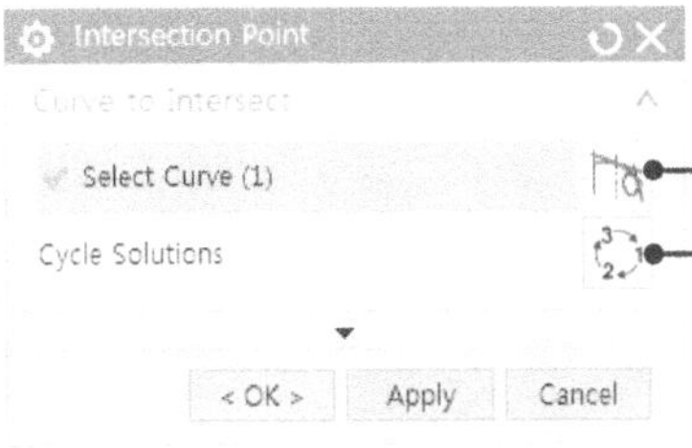

① **Curve**

Select curves or edges to make intersection with the sketch plane.

② **Cycle Solutions**

When more than one intersection point is available, you can select another possible intersection point.

Fig 10-6 Intersection Point Dialog Box

When you create a sketch on the ZX plane as shown in Fig 10-7, two intersection points with the circular edge are possible as designated by the arrow.

Note that you can create only one intersection with a single operation of the **Intersection Point** command. If you want two points as shown in Fig 10-7, you have to perform the command twice.

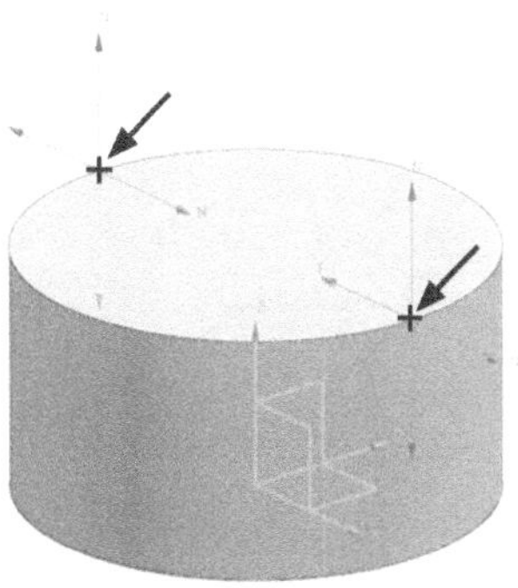

Fig 10-7 Two Intersection Points

Exercise 01 Creating an Intersection Point

ch10_ex01.prt

Let's create an intersection point using the given model.

Fig 10-8 Creating an Intersection Point

1. Open the given file ch10_ex01.prt.

2. Click the **Sketch** icon in the **Feature** icon group.

3. Change the model view to **Trimetric**.

4. Click the **Intersection Point** icon in the **Direct Sketch** icon group.

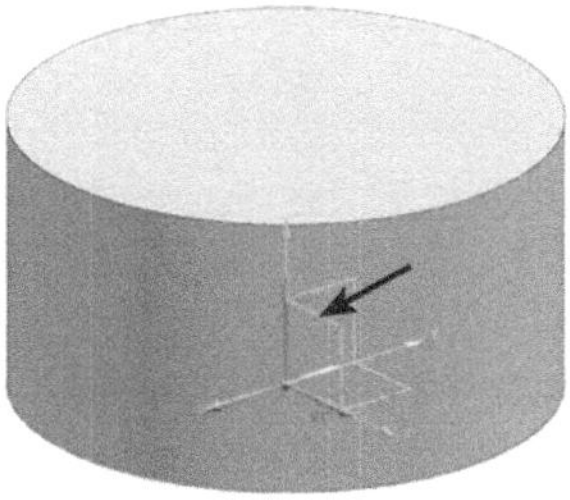

Fig 10-9 Sketch Plane

5. Select the circular edge specified in Fig 10-10. An intersection point is previewed as shown in the dotted circle of Fig 10-11.

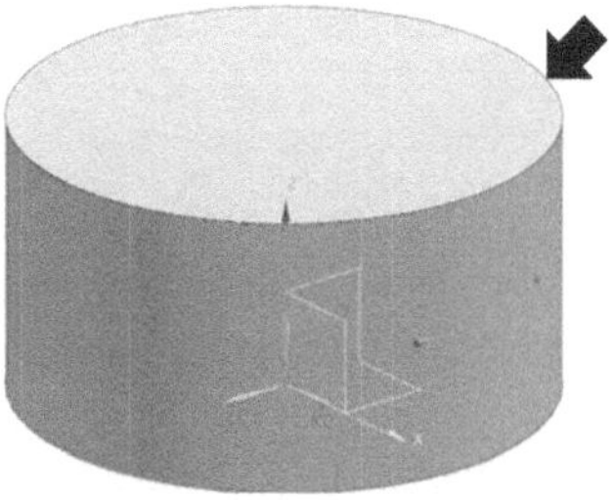

Fig 10-10 Edge to Select

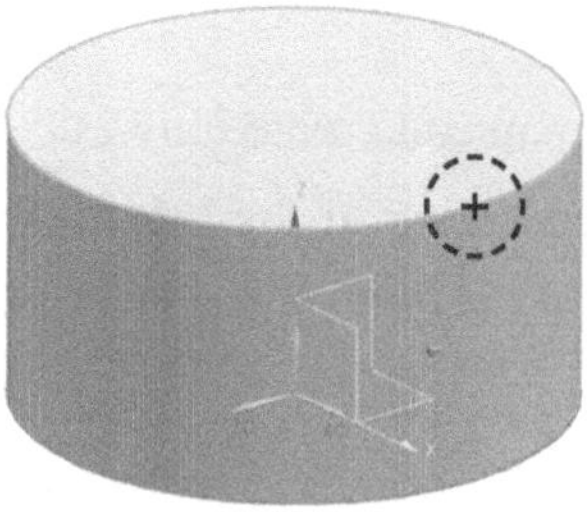

Fig 10-11 Preview

6. Click **OK** in the dialog box. One intersection point and four datum axes are created as shown in Fig 10-12.

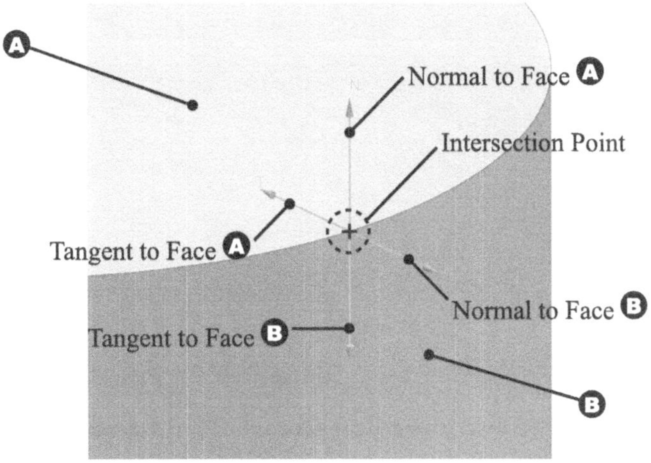

Fig 10-12 Result of Intersection Point

7. Finish the sketch. The intersection point is shown, but the datum axis are not shown. This implies that the datum axes can be used within the sketch where the intersection point is created.

8. Do not save the file and close.

END of Exercise

! *Datum Axis at Intersection Point*

1. You can constrain sketch curves with regard the tangent and normal datum axis to the face which possesses the intersection edge. When the intersection edge is shared by two faces, two pairs of the datum axis are created.

2. When you are creating an intersection point with curves, only the point is created.

10.2 Intersection Curve

You can create an intersection curve with associativity between the current sketch plane and faces. Fig 10-14 shows an intersection curve. Note that you can select connected faces to make the intersection.

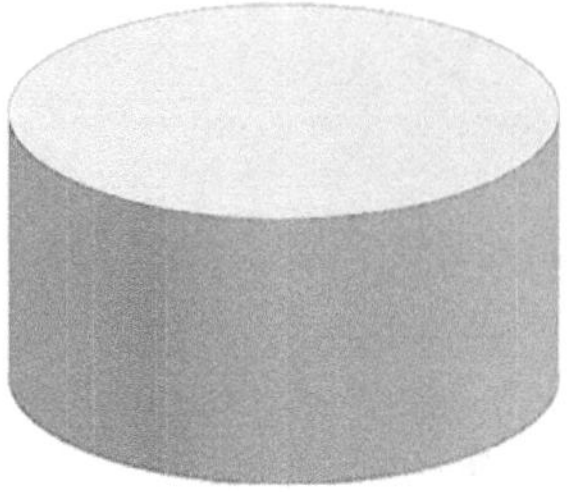

Fig 10-13 Cylindrical Body

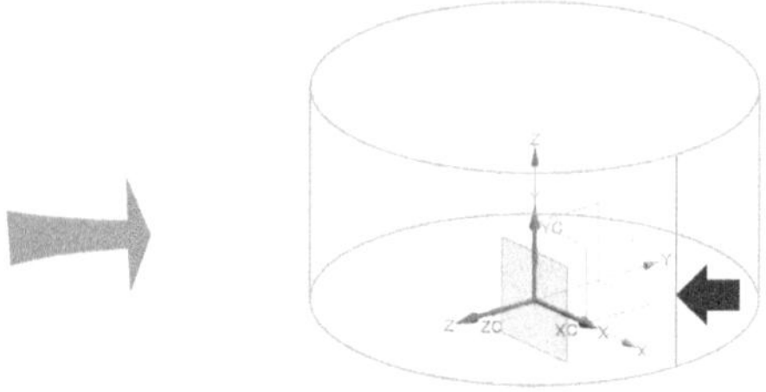

Fig 10-14 Intersection Curve

10.2.1 Executing the Intersection Curve Command

You can execute the **Intersection Curve** command by choosing **Insert > Sketch Curve > Intersection Curve** in the **Menu** button. You can also execute this command by clicking the **Intersection Curve** icon in the **Sketch Curve** icon list as shown in Fig 10-15.

Fig 10-15 Intersection Curve Icon

> **! *Changing the View Orientation***
>
> **Trimetric View** is recommended when you are creating an intersection point or intersection curve. You can return to the sketch view by pressing MB3 on an empty area and choosing **Orient View to Sketch** in the view popup menu.

10.2.2 Intersection Curve Dialog Box

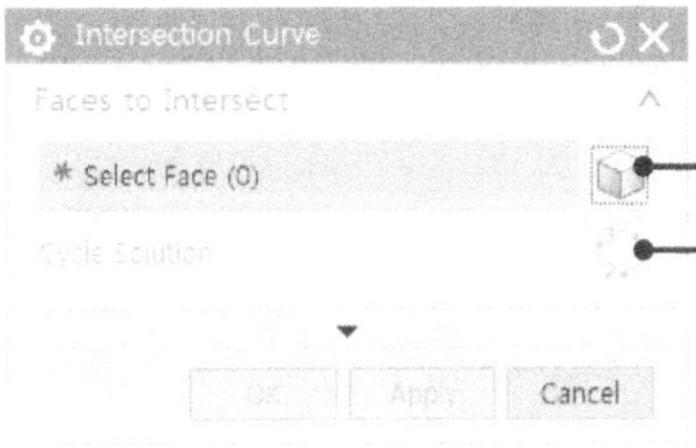

① **Face**
Select faces to make intersection with the sketch plane.

② **Cycle Solution**
When more than one intersection curve is available, you can select another possible intersection curve.

Fig 10-16 Intersection Curve Dialog Box

ch10_ex02.prt **Creating an Intersection Curve** **Exercise 02**

Let's create an intersection curve using the given model.

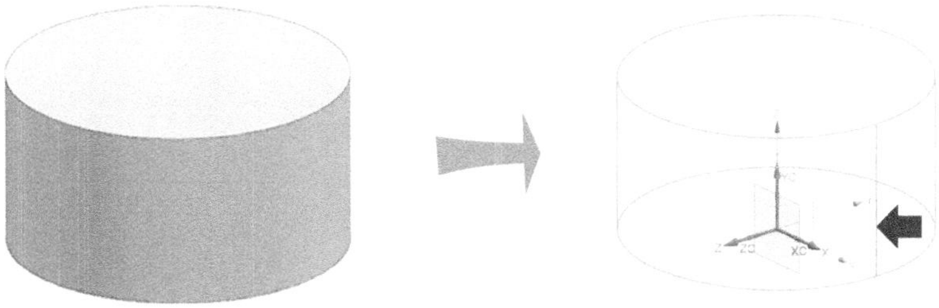

Fig 10-17 Creating an Intersection Curve

1. Open the given file ch10_ex02.prt.

2. Click the **Sketch** icon in the **Feature** icon group and select the ZX plane as the sketch plane.

3. Change the model view to **Trimetric**. You can change the model view by pressing MB3 on an empty area and choosing **Orient View > Trimetric** in the popup menu.

4. Choose **Insert > Sketch Curve > Intersection Curve** in the **Menu** button.

5. Select the cylindrical face pointed out by the arrow in Fig 10-18. Change the rendering style to **Static Wireframe**. A preview of the intersection curve is shown like in Fig 10-19.

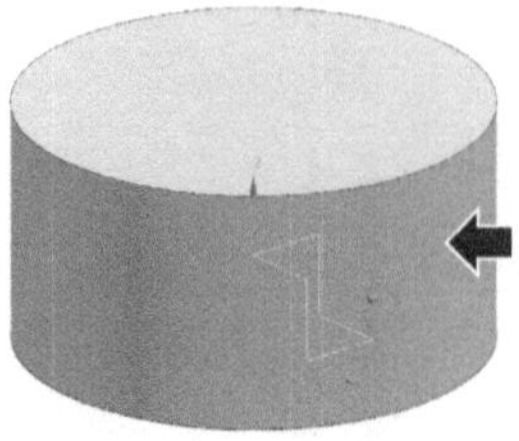

Fig 10-18 Face to Intersect

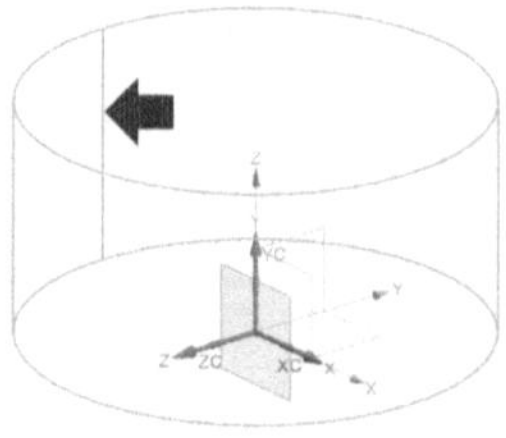

Fig 10-19 Preview

6. Press the **Cycle Solution** button in the **Intersection Curve** dialog box. Another possible intersection curve is previewed like in Fig 10-20.

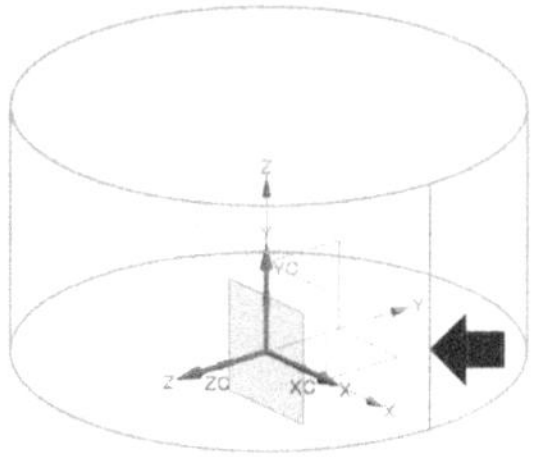

Fig 10-20 Preview of Other Solution

7. Press **OK** in the dialog box.

8. Finish the sketch.

9. Close without saving the file.

END of Exercise

Modifying Intersection Point and Intersection Curve

You can double click the intersection point or intersection curve in the sketch task environment to modify their definitions. You can reselect the curves or faces to intersect, or you can have another possible result.

10.3 Project Curve

You can project curves, edges or points on the sketch plane.

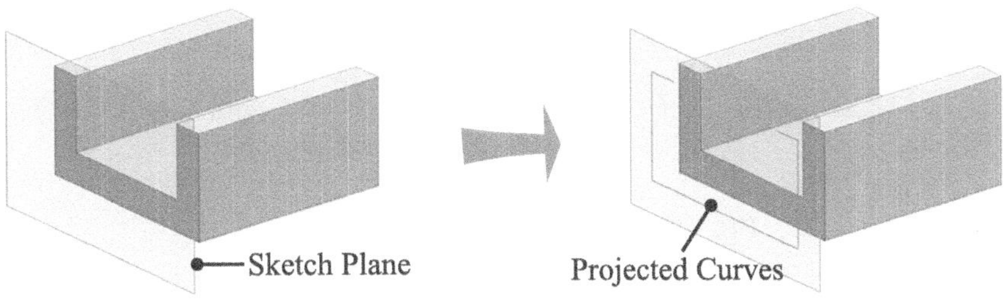

Fig 10-21 Sketch Plane　　**Fig 10-22** Projected Curve

10.3.1 Executing the Project Curve Command

You can execute the **Intersection Curve** command by choosing **Insert > Sketch Curve > Project Curve** in the **Menu** button. You can also execute this command by clicking the **Project Curve** icon in the **Sketch Curve** icon list as shown in Fig 10-23.

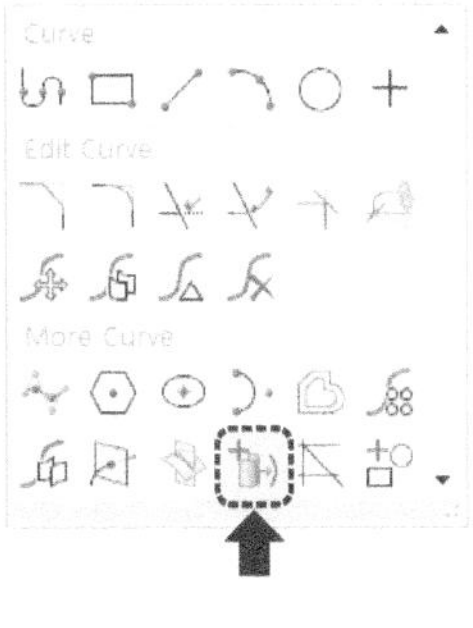

Fig 10-23 Project Curve Icon

10.3.2 Project Curve Dialog Box

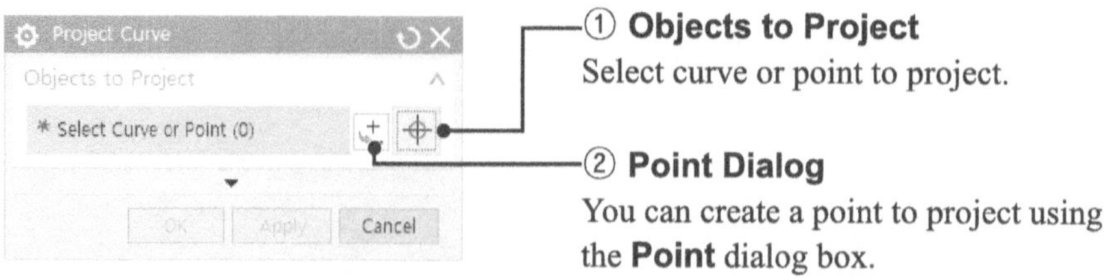

Fig 10-24 Project Curve Dialog Box

> **! *Projection Direction***
>
> The objects are projected normal to the sketch plane at all times.

Exercise 03 Projecting Curves

ch10_ex03.prt

Let's project curves on the sketch plane and use them in the following modeling process. We will use the **Project Curve** icon in the **Direct Sketch** icon group.

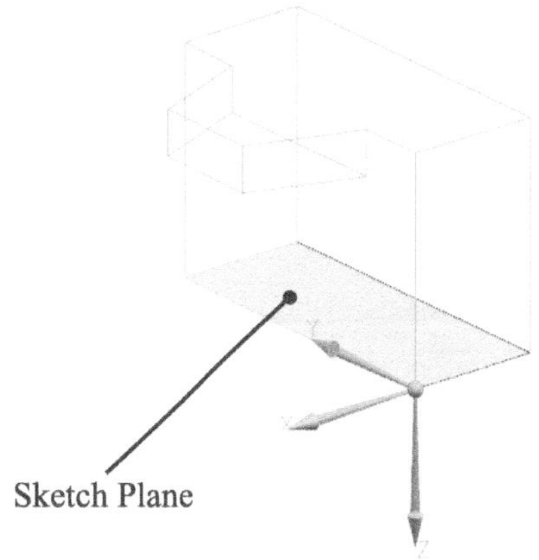

Fig 10-25 Sketch Icon and Sketch Plane

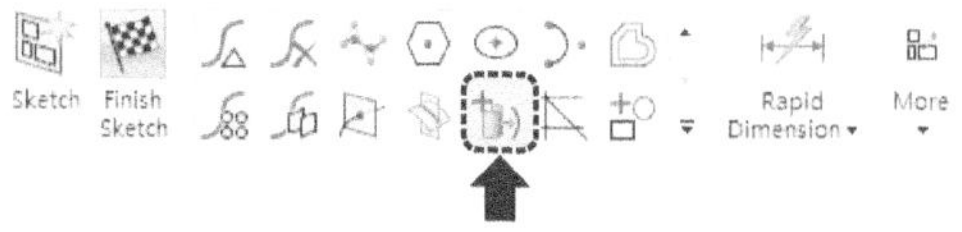

Fig 10-26 Project Curve Icon

Projecting Curves

1. Open the given file ch10_ex03.prt.

2. Click the **Sketch** icon in the **Direct Sketch** icon group. Choose the bottom face as the sketch plane as shown in Fig 10-25.

3. Press the **Home** key on the keyboard to restore the **Trimetric** view.

4. Click the **Project Curve** icon in the **Direct Sketch** icon group.

5. Select **Face Edges** as the **Curve Rule**.

6. Select the face Ⓐ shown in Fig 10-27. All four edges of the selected face are selected.

7. Press **OK** in the **Project Curve** dialog box. Four curves are projected on the sketch plane as shown in Fig 10-28.

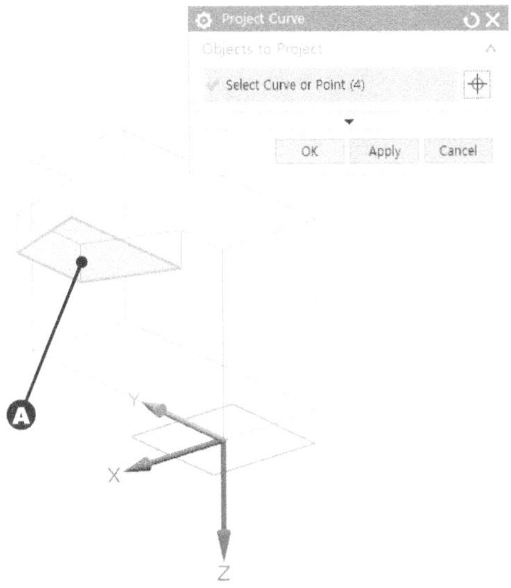

Fig 10-27 Face to Select

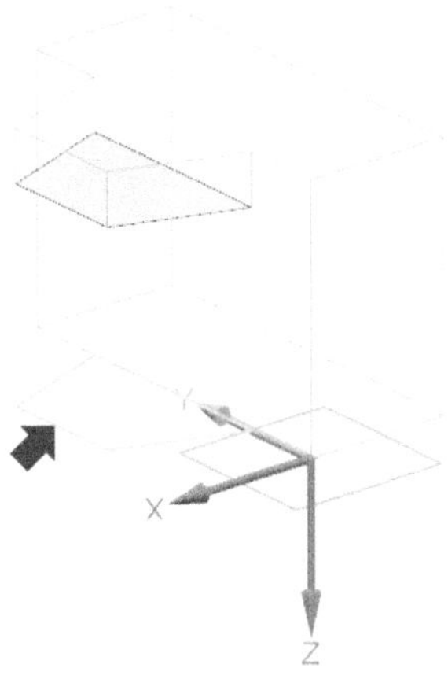

Fig 10-28 Projected Curves

Extruding

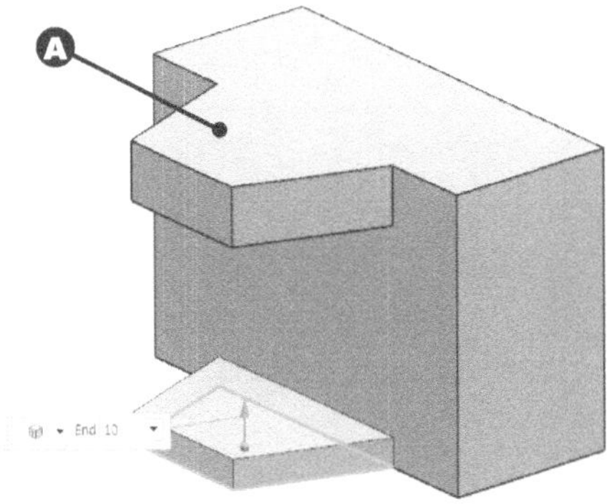

Fig 10-29 Extrude Feature

1. Press **Q** in the keyboard to finish the direct sketch.
2. Click **Extrude** in the **Feature** icon group.
3. Reset the dialog box and select the projected curves as the section.
4. Extrude the section by 10 mm and unite to the body as shown in Fig 10-29.

The section of the extrude feature is the same as the source of projection and the height is different from the upper feature.

Modifying the Source Sketch

1. Show the sketch for the feature **A** in Fig 10-30 and double click the sketch. Confirm that the **Sketch** task environment is invoked.

2. Modify the sketch as shown in Fig 10-30 and finish the sketch.

The geometry is modified as shown in Fig 10-31.

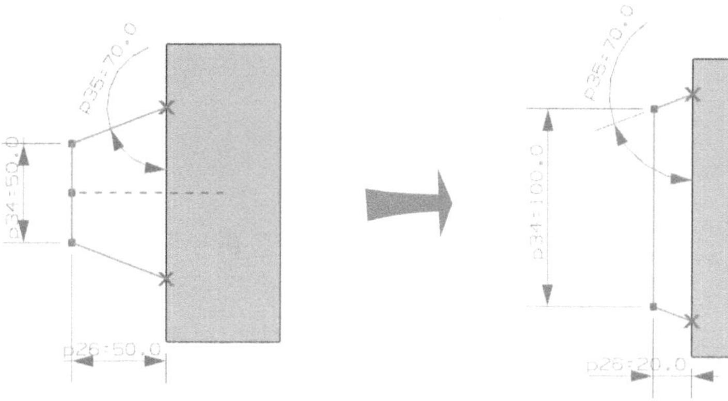

Fig 10-30 Modifying the Sketch

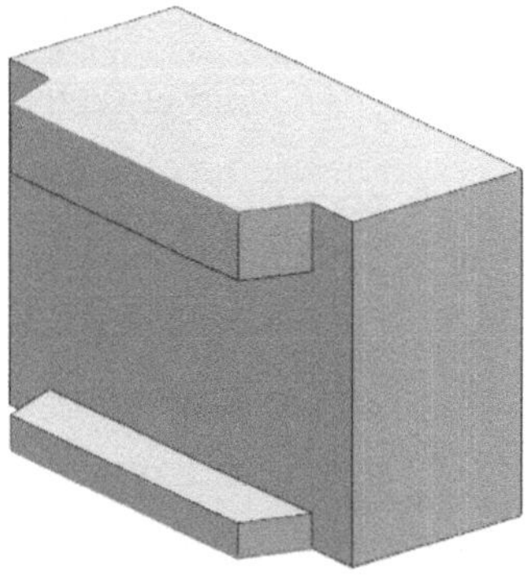

Fig 10-31 Completed Model

END of Exercise

Let's create intersection curves on the sketch plane and use them in the following modeling process. We will use the **Intersection Curve** icon in the **Direct Sketch** icon group.

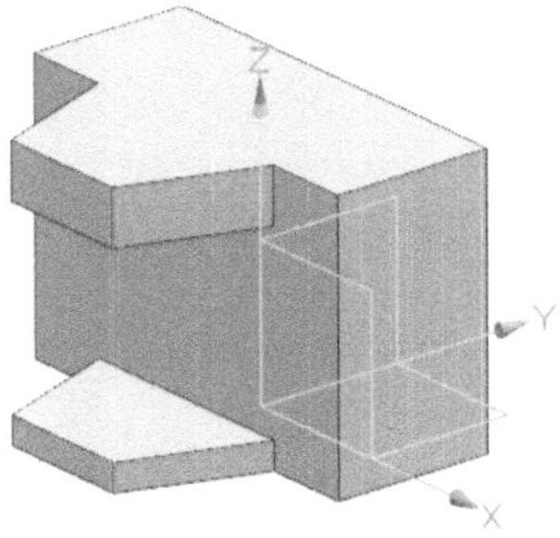

Fig 10-32 Model for Exercise

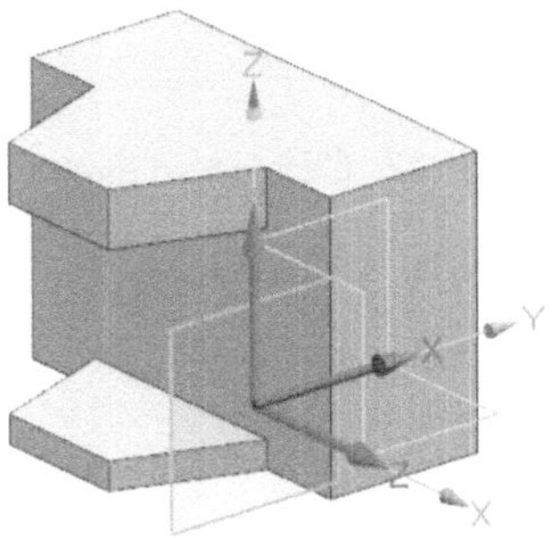

Fig 10-33 Direct Sketch

Creating a Sketch

1. Open the given file ch10_ex04.prt.
2. Show the datum coordinate system as in Fig 10-32.
3. Click the **Sketch** icon in the **Direct Sketch** icon group and select the YZ plane.
4. Press the **Home** key on the keyboard to restore the **Trimetric** view orientation as shown in Fig 10-33.
5. Click the **Intersection Curve** icon **Direct Sketch** icon group.
6. Select the face Ⓐ designated in Fig 10-34.

An intersection curve is created as shown in Fig 10-35.

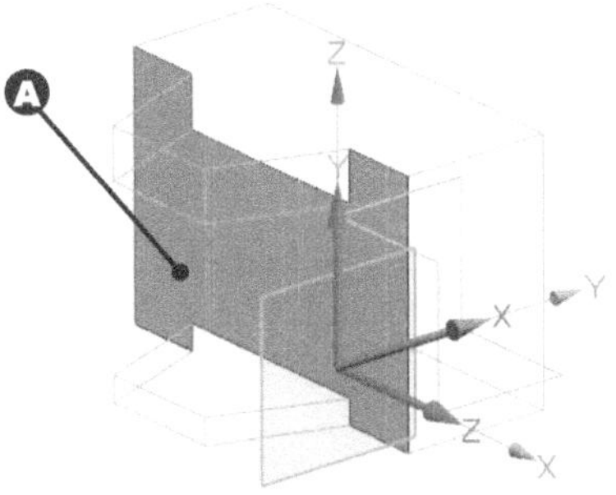

Fig 10-34 Face to Intersect

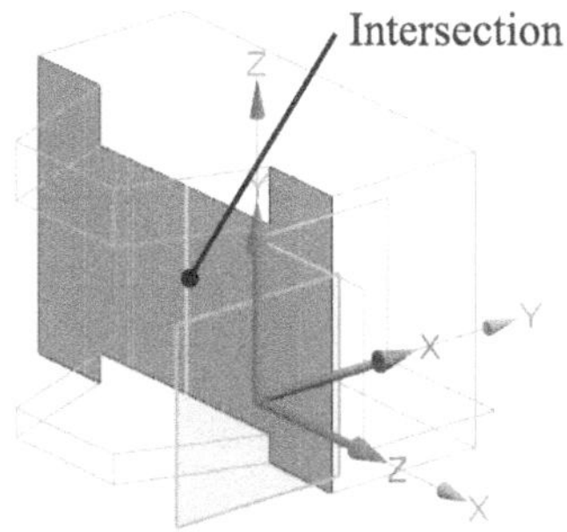

Fig 10-35 Intersection Curve

7. Create an intersection curve with the face **B** shown in Fig 10-36.

8. Click the **OK** button in the **Intersection Curve** dialog box.

9. Create line **C** shown in Fig 10-37 and complete the sketch. The end points of the line are at the midpoint of the two intersection points.

10. Finish the direct sketch.

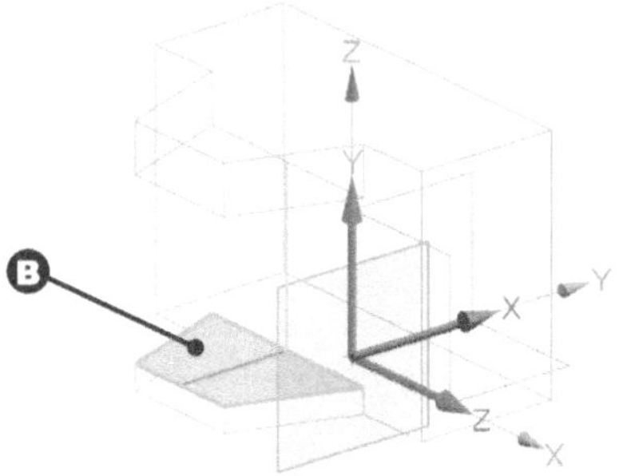

Fig 10-36 Intersection Curve

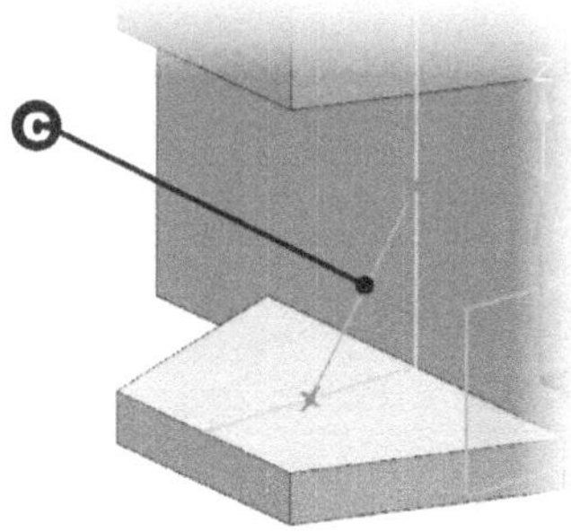

Fig 10-37 Completed Sketch

Extruding

1. Click the **Extrude** icon in the **Feature** icon group.

2. Reset the dialog box.

3. Turn on the **Stop at Intersection** button in the selection bar as shown in Fig 10-38.

4. Define a triangular section as shown in Fig 10-39.

5. Set the limit option as shown in Fig 10-39 and unite the extrude feature with the existing solid body.

6. Close without saving the file.

Fig 10-38 Stop at Intersection Option

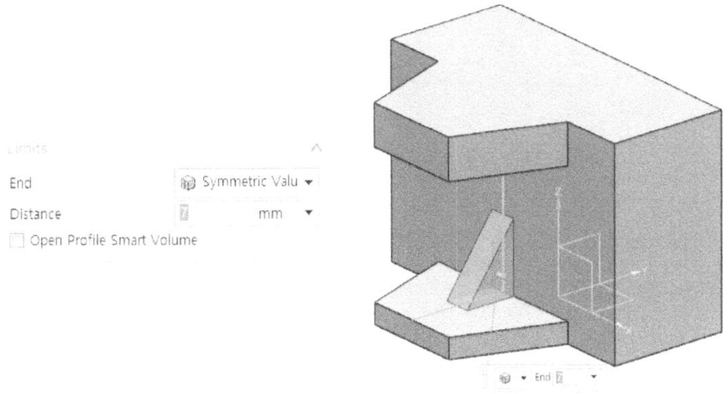

Fig 10-39 Creating an Extrude Feature

END of Exercise

10.4 Trimming Recipe Curve

You can trim recipe curves such as intersection curves and project curves using the **Trim Recipe Curve** command. Note that the **Trim Recipe Curve** command is available only in the sketch task environment.

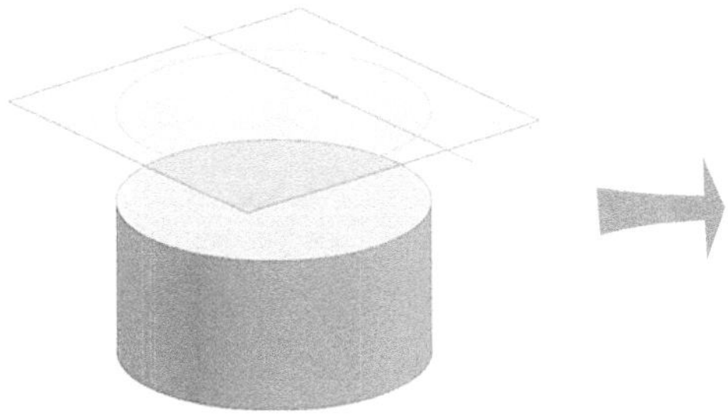

Fig 10-40 Before Trimming

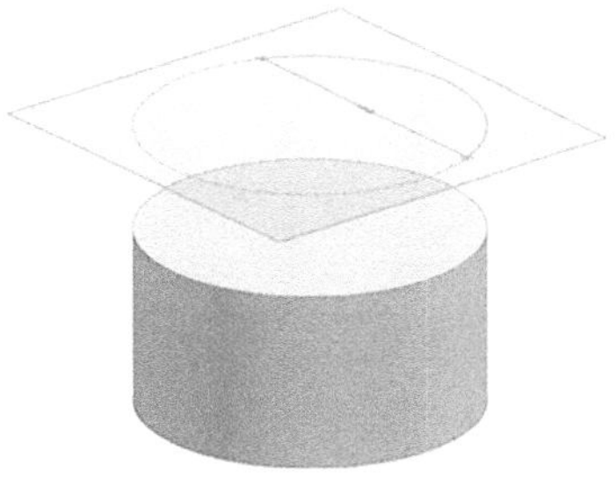

Fig 10-41 After Trimming

If you try to apply **Quick Trim** for the recipe curves, an information box is invoked as shown in Fig 10-42.

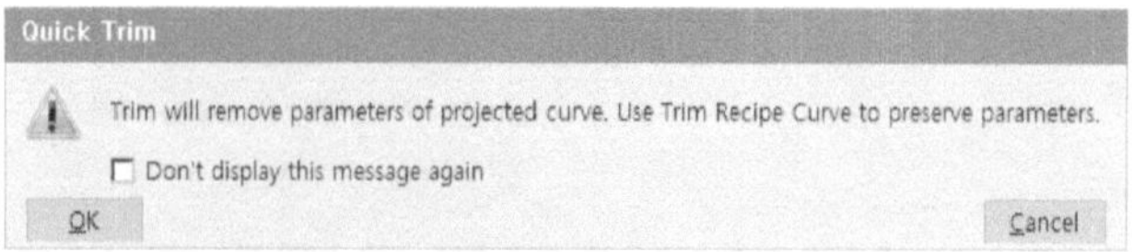

Fig 10-42 Quick Trim Information Box

You can trim the recipe curves with the **Quick Trim** command, but you cannot modify the definition of the recipe curves. The resultant curve of the **Quick Trim** turns to a general sketch curve, and you have to constrain it to define its shape and dimension.

10.4.1 Executing the Trim Recipe Curve Command

You can execute the **Trim Recipe Curve** command by choosing **Edit > Curve > Trim Recipe Curve** in the **Menu** button as shown in Fig 10-43. Remember that the **Trim Recipe Curve** command is not available in the **Direct Sketch**.

Fig 10-43 Trim Recipe Curve Menu

10.4.2 Trim Recipe Curve Dialog Box

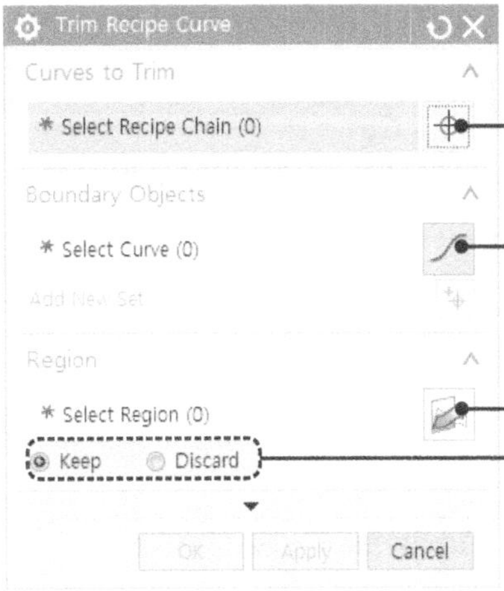

① **Recipe Curves to Trim**
Select the recipe curves to trim.

② **Boundary Objects**
Select the boundary objects which intersect with the recipe curves to trim.

③ **Region**
You can reselect the region to discard or keep.

④ **Keep/Discard**
Choose whether to keep or discard the selection region.

Fig 10-44 Trim Recipe Curve Dialog Box

ch10_ex05.prt **Trimming Recipe Curves** **Exercise 05**

Let's trim the recipe curve in the sketch task environment and use it in the following modeling process.

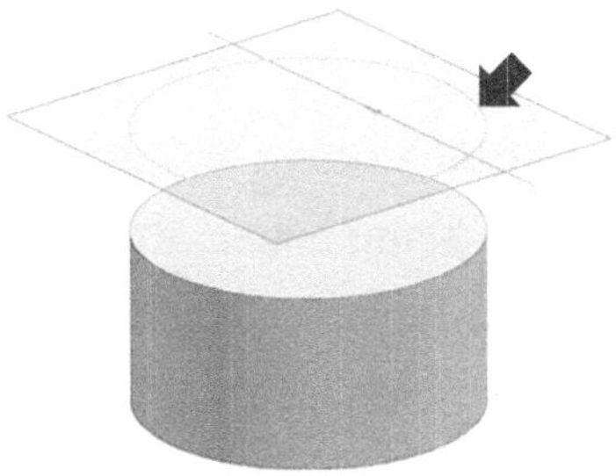

Fig 10-45 Model for Exercise

Trying Quick Trim

1. Open the given file ch10_ex05.prt.

2. Double click the sketch designated by the arrow in Fig 10-45. The **Sketch** task environment is invoked because of the setting in "1.8.3 Double Click Action for Sketches" on Page 30. If the **Direct Sketch** is activated, click the **Open in Sketch Task Environment** icon in the **Direct Sketch** icon group.

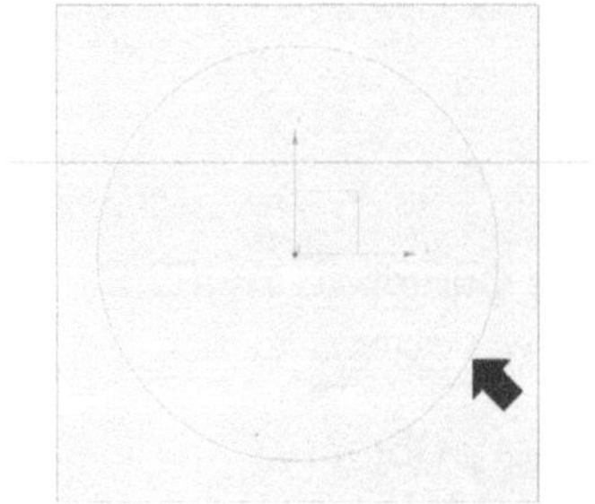

Fig 10-46 Hidden Solid Body

3. Hide the solid body as shown in Fig 10-46. You can hide the solid body by clicking the **Hide** button in the **View** tab or by pressing **Ctrl + B**.

4. Click the **Quick Trim** icon in the **Sketch Tools** icon group.

5. Select the recipe curve around the region designated by the arrow in Fig 10-46.

An information box is shown as in Fig 10-47.

6. Cancel the information box.

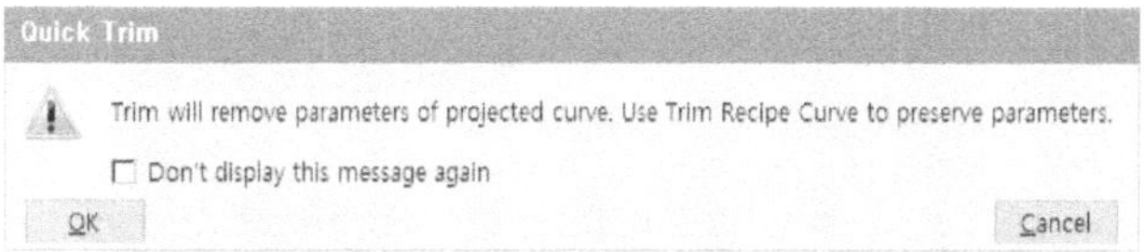

Fig 10-47 Quick Trim Information Box

7. Close the **Quick Trim** dialog box.

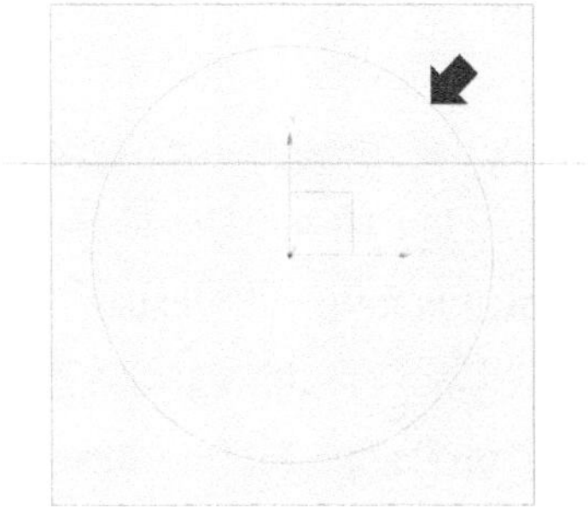

Fig 10-48 Selecting the Recipe Curve

Trimming Recipe Curve

1. Choose **Edit > Curve > Trim Recipe Curve** in the **Menu** button. Remember that the menu is available only in the sketch task environment.

2. Select the recipe curve around the region pointed out by the arrow in Fig 10-48.

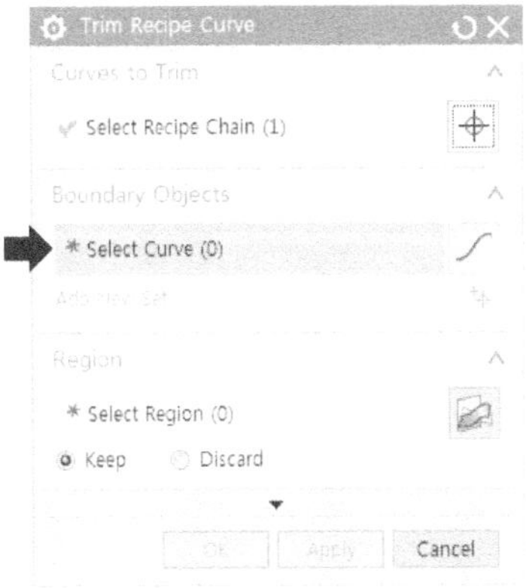

Fig 10-49 Boundary Objects Option

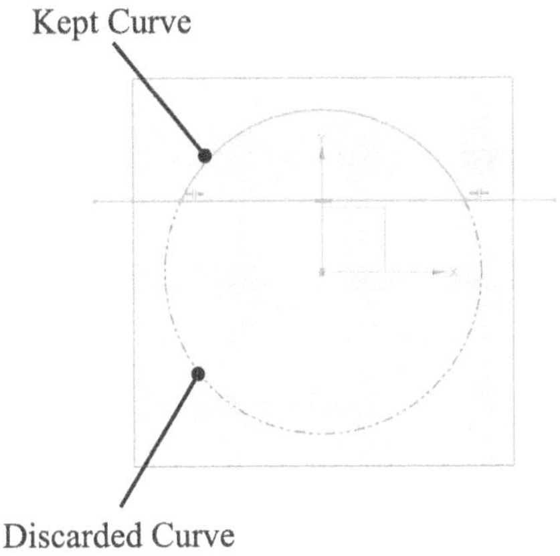

Fig 10-50 Trimmed Recipe Curve

3. Confirm that the **Select Curve** option field in the **Boundary Objects** option group is highlighted as shown in Fig 10-49.

4. Select the horizontal line.

5. Press **OK** in the dialog box.

The lower part of the recipe curve turns to phantom which is recognized as a reference curve.

6. Finish the sketch and extrude the sketch as shown in Fig 10-51.

7. Close without saving the file.

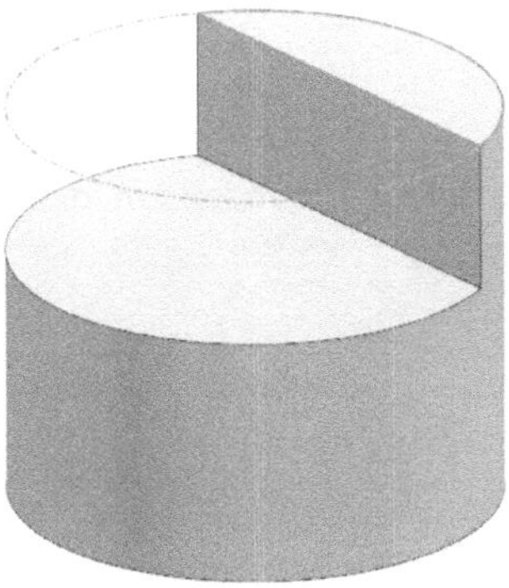

Fig 10-51 Completed Model

END of Exercise

10.5 Offset Curve

Offset curves or edges on the sketch plane.

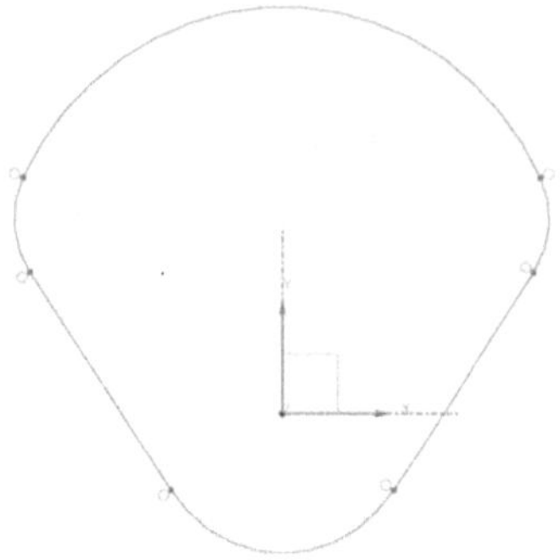

Fig 10-52 Sketch Curves

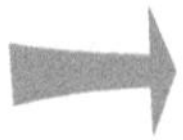

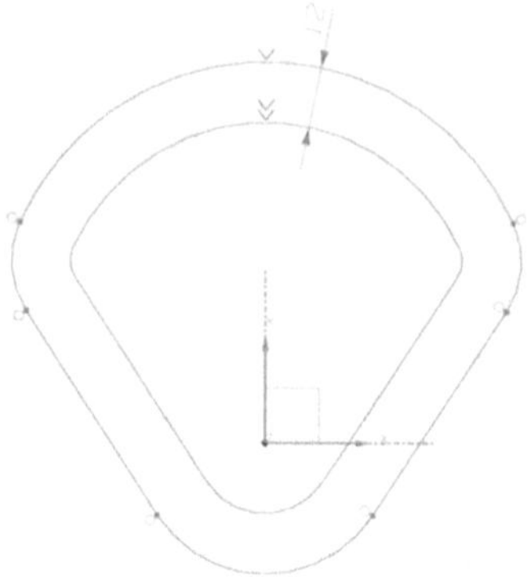

Fig 10-53 Offset Curves

10.5.1 Executing the Offset Curve Command

The **Offset Curve** icon is available both in the direct sketch and the sketch task environment. Fig 10-54 and Fig 10-55 show the **Offset Curve** icons in the direct sketch and the sketch task environment, respectively.

Fig 10-54 Offset Curve Icon in the Direct Sketch

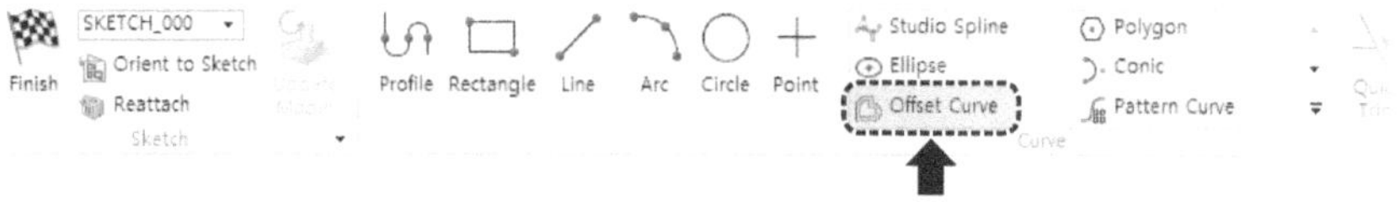

Fig 10-55 Offset Curve Icon in the Sketch Task Environment

10.5.2 Offset Curve Dialog Box

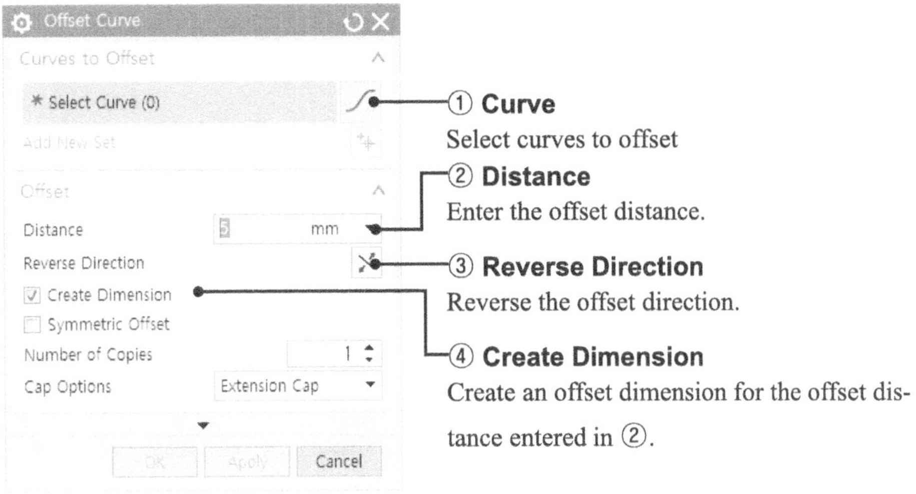

Fig 10-56 Offset Curve Dialog Box

ch10_ex06.prt **Creating Offset Curve** **Exercise 06**

Let's create offset curves using the fully constrained sketch curves.

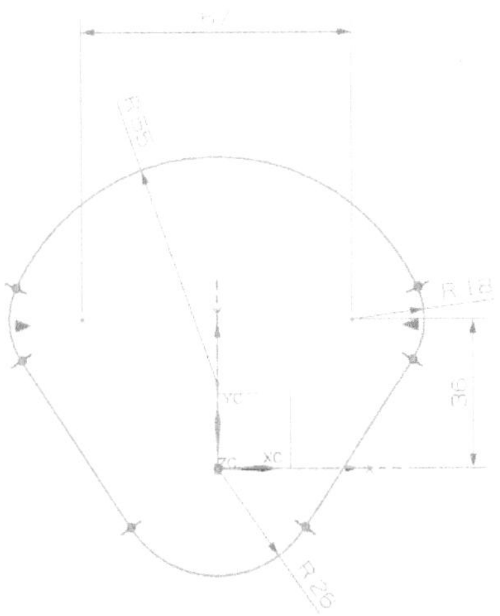

Fig 10-57 Sketch

1. Open the given file ch10_ex06.prt.

2. Press MB3 on the **Sketch** feature in the **Part Navigator** and choose **Edit** in the pop-up menu.

The direct sketch is activated as shown in Fig 10-57.

3. Click the **Offset Curve** icon in the **Direct Sketch** icon group and reset the dialog box.

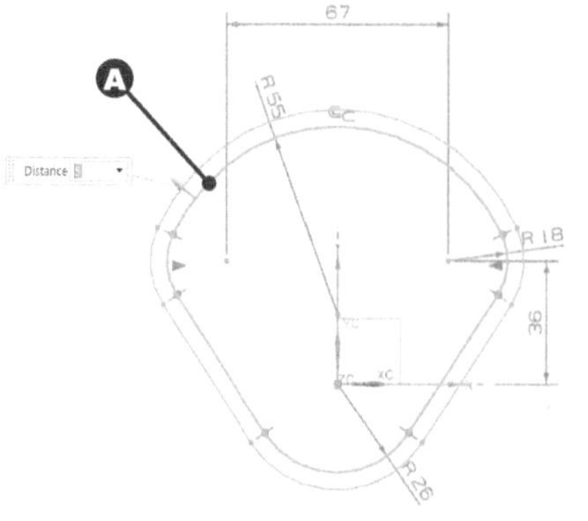

Fig 10-58 Preview of Offset Curve

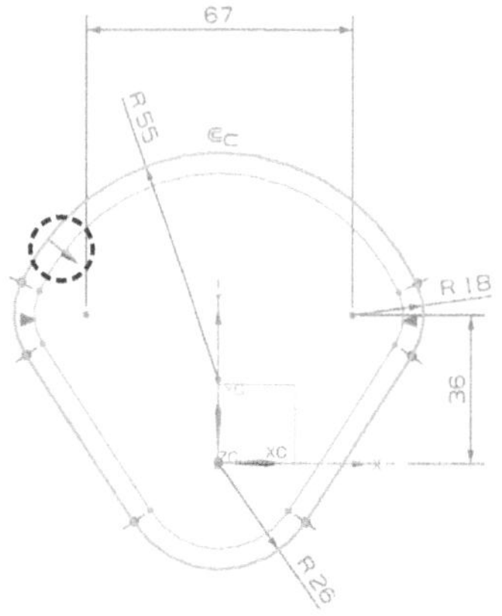

Fig 10-59 Reversed Offset Direction

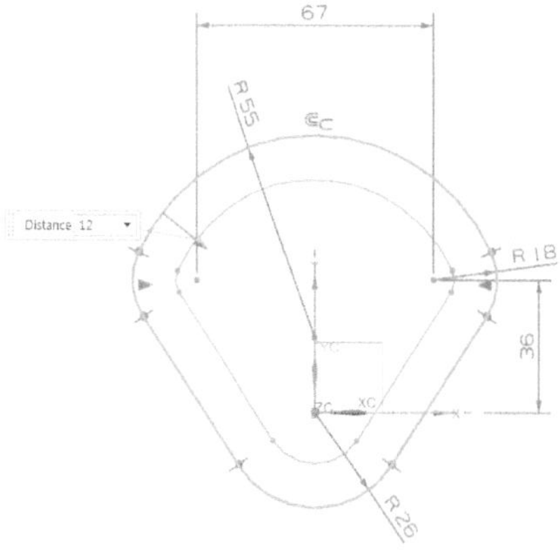

Fig 10-60 Modified Offset Distance

4. Select the curve Ⓐ designated in Fig 10-58. The curve is offset outward as shown in Fig 10-58.

Let's reverse the offset direction.

5. Click the **Reverse Direction** icon in the dialog box. The offset direction is reversed as shown in Fig 10-59.

6. Enter 12 in the **Distance** input box and press the **Enter** key. The offset curve is previewed as shown in Fig 10-60.

7. Click **OK** in the dialog box. The offset curves are constrained with the offset dimension as shown in Fig 10-61.

8. Finish the sketch.

9. Close without saving the file.

! *Curve Rule*

The default curve rule for offsetting curves is **Connected Curves**.

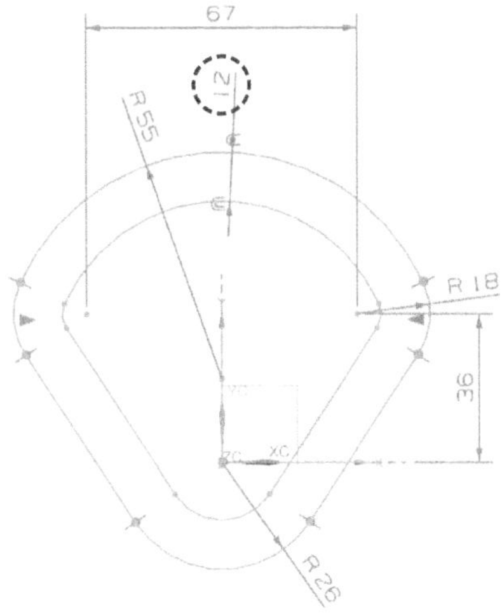

Fig 10-61 Offset Curve

END of Exercise

Symbol of Offset

You can identify the source and result of the offset by looking at the symbol shown in Fig 10-62.

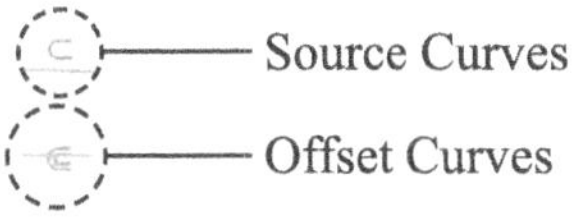

Fig 10-62 Offset Constraint

Exercise 07 **Stand Foot**

ch10_ex07.prt

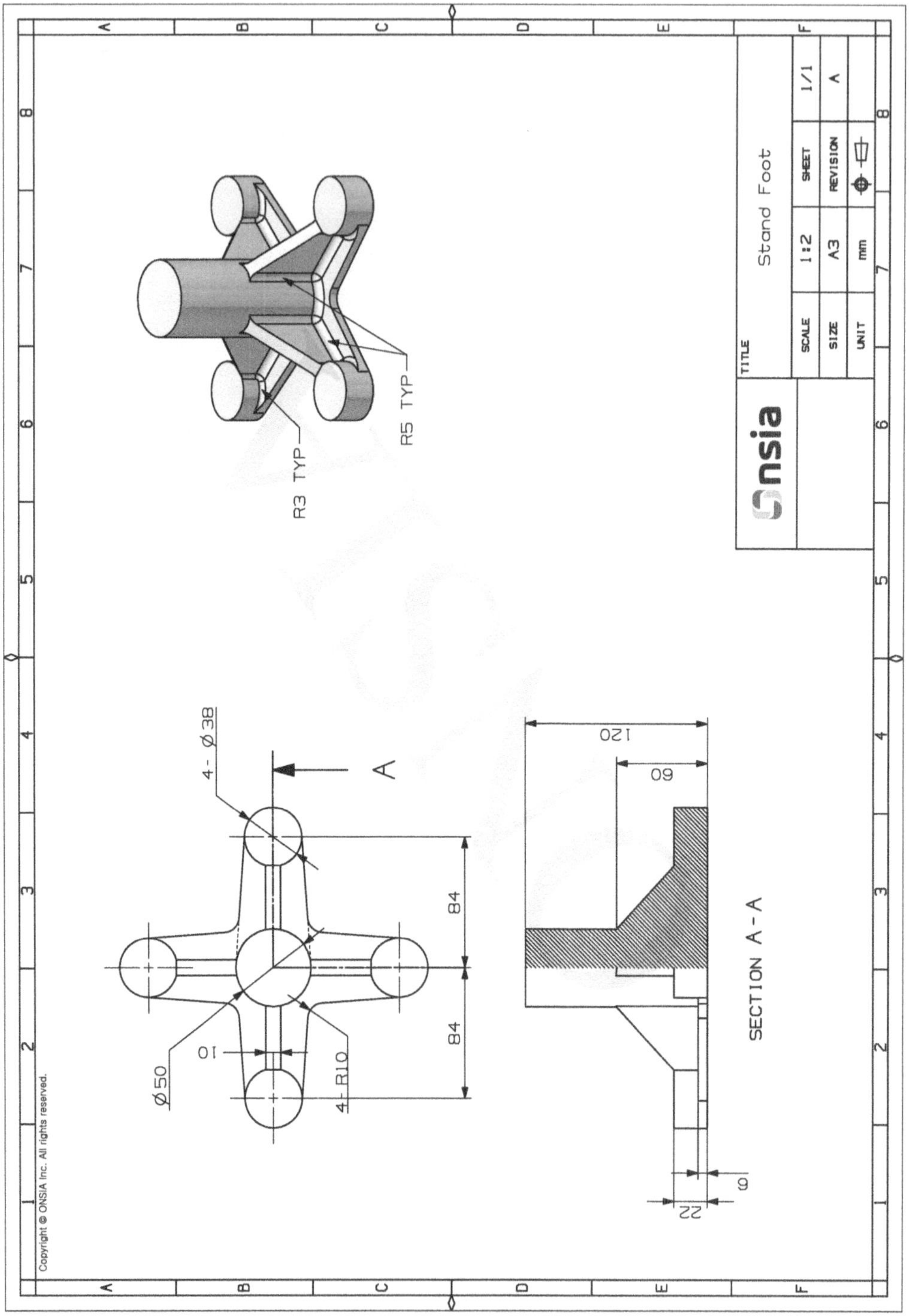

Fig 10-63 Drawing for Exercise 7

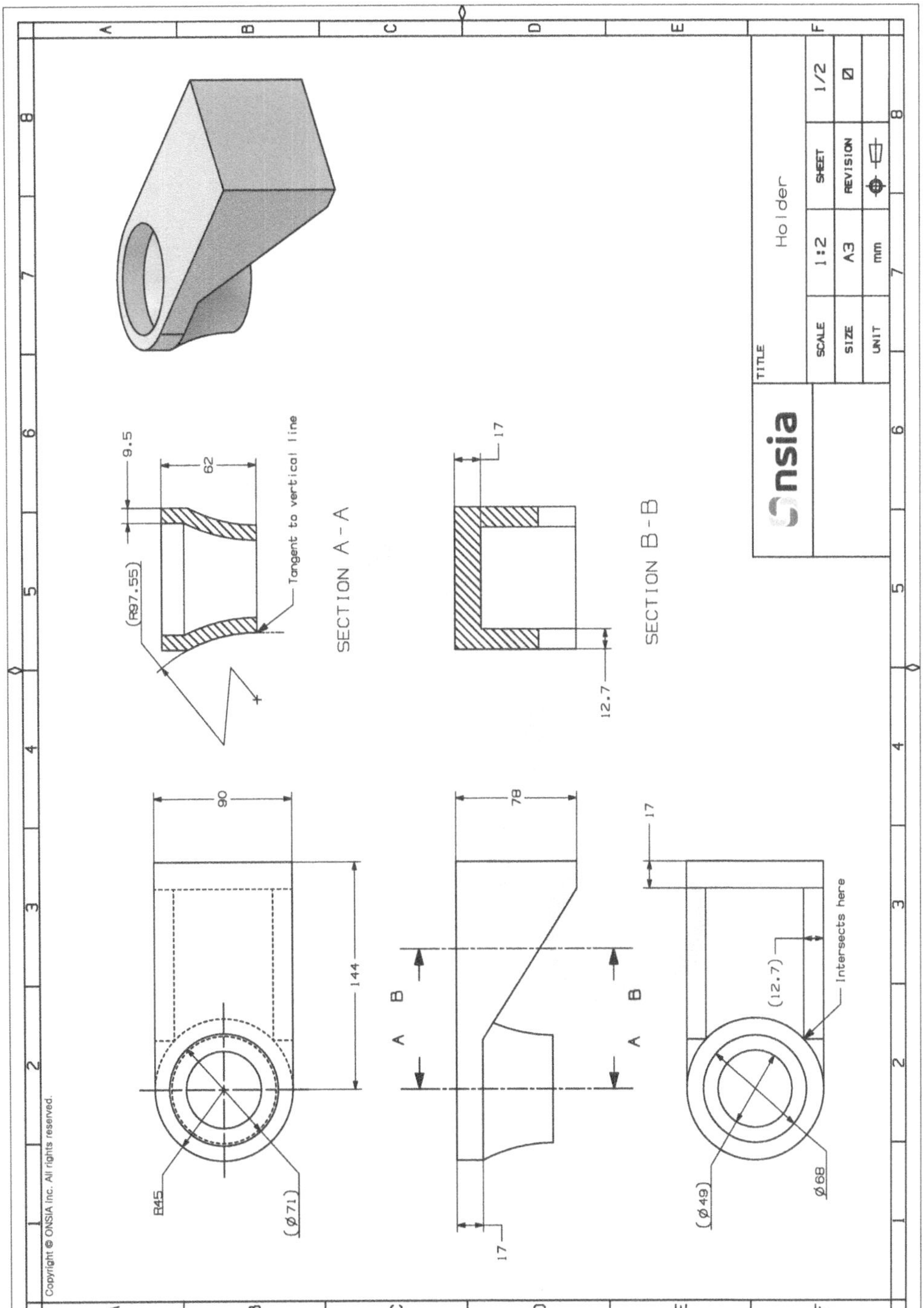

Fig 10-64 Drawing for Exercise 8

This page left blank intentionally.

Chapter 11

Measurements

■ **After completing this chapter you will understand**

- how to measure distance, length and radius using the **Measure Distance** command.
- how to measure an angle.
- how to measure the solid properties of a solid body.

11.1 Measure Distance

Measures distance, length, radius etc.

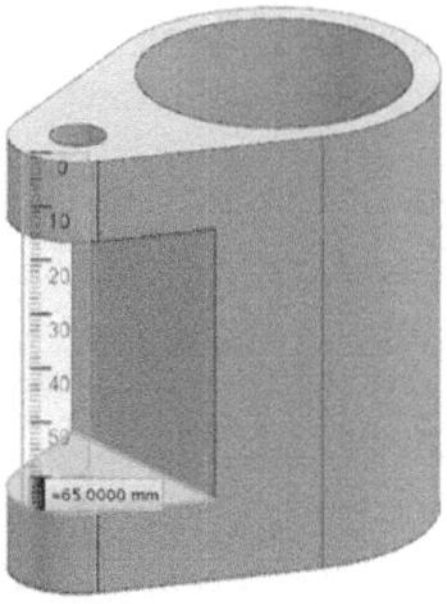

Fig 11-1 Distance

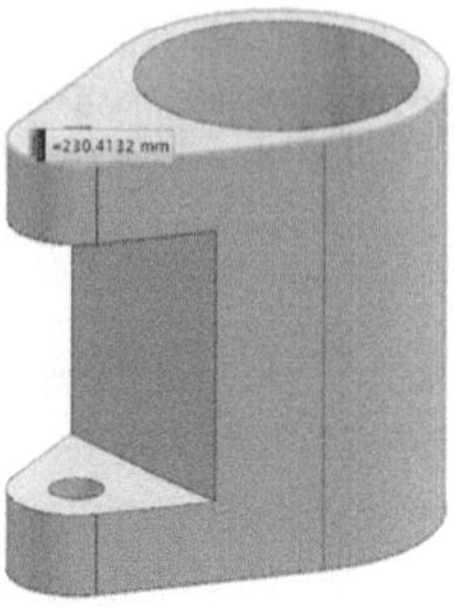

Fig 11-2 Length

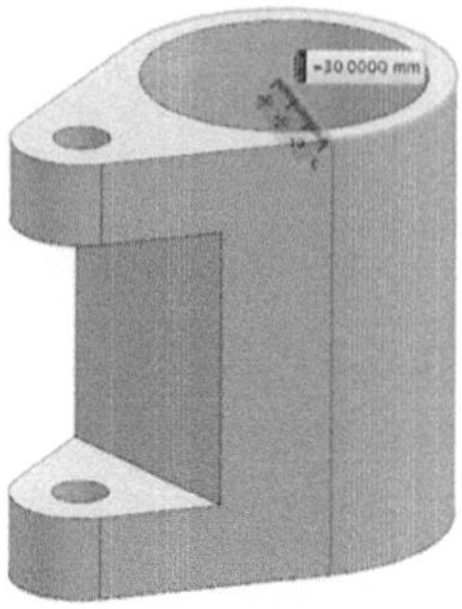

Fig 11-3 Radius

11.1.1 Measure Distance Dialog Box

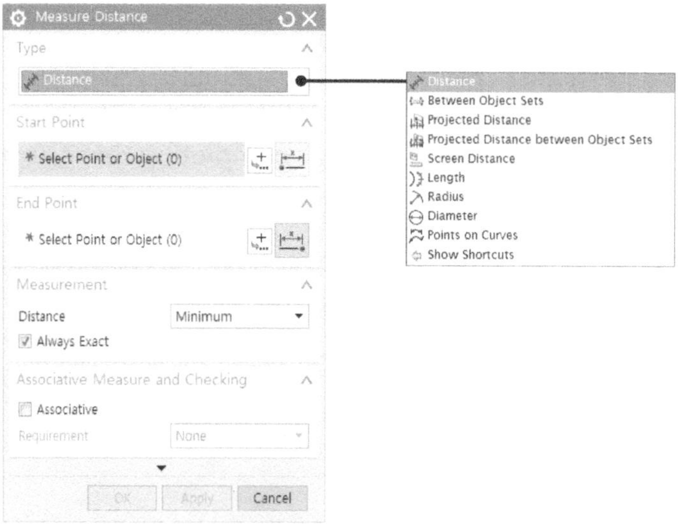

Fig 11-4 Measure Distance Dialog Box

11.1.2 Distance

You can measure the distance between two objects or points.

ch11_ex01.prt **Measuring Length** **Exercise 01**

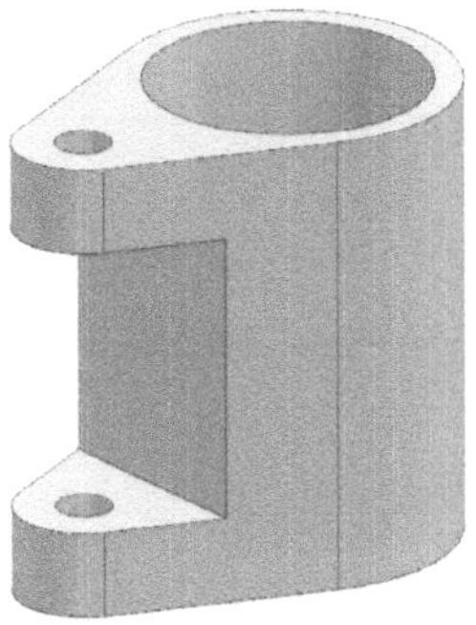

Fig 11-5 Model for Exercise

Distance Between Two Parallel Faces

1. Open the given file ch11_ex01.prt.

2. Click the **Measure Distance** icon in the **Analysis** tab as shown in Fig 11-6.

3. Confirm that the **Type** option is **Distance**.

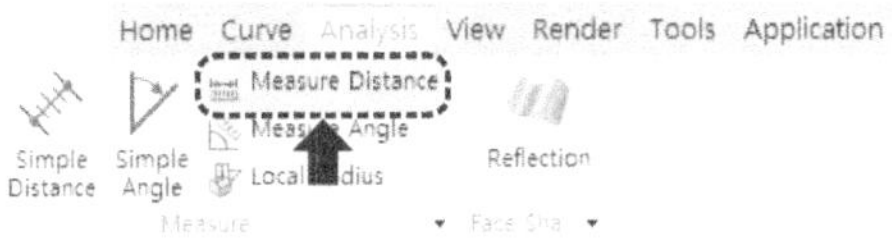

Fig 11-6 Measure Distance Icon

4. Select the two faces as shaded in Fig 11-7.

The distance value is labelled as shown in Fig 11-8.

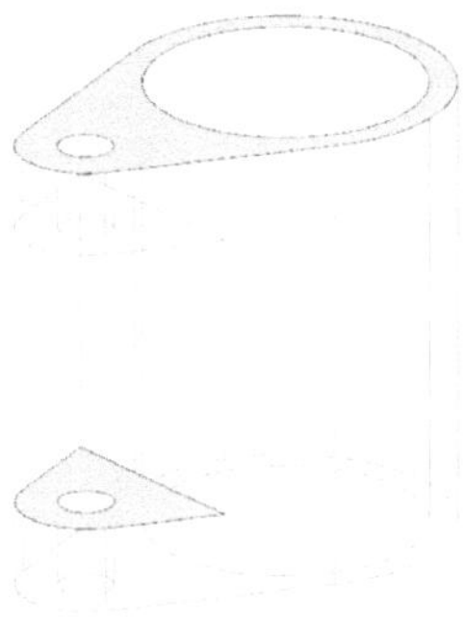

Fig 11-7 Faces to Select

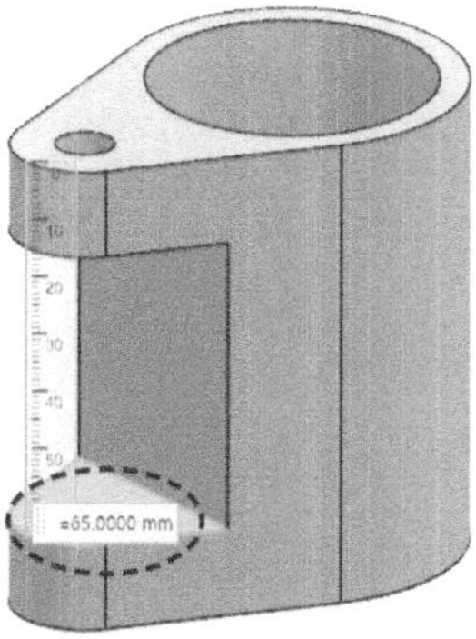

Fig 11-8 Measured Distance

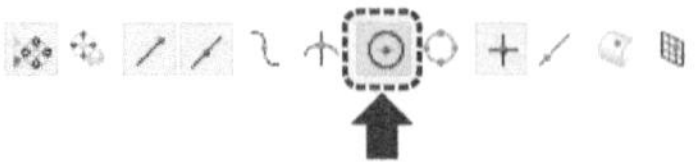

Fig 11-9 Arc Center Snap Option

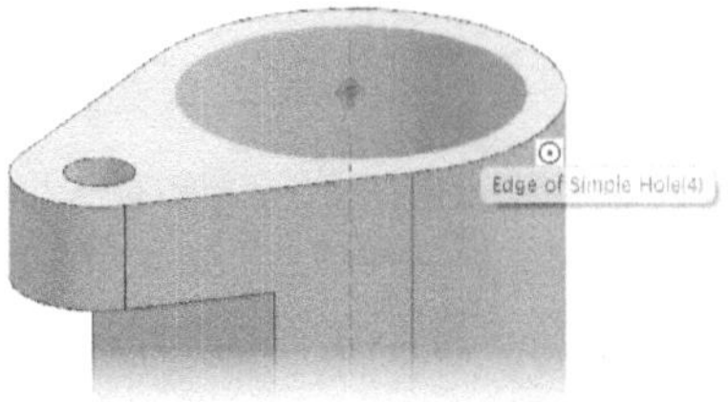

Fig 11-10 Selecting the First Point

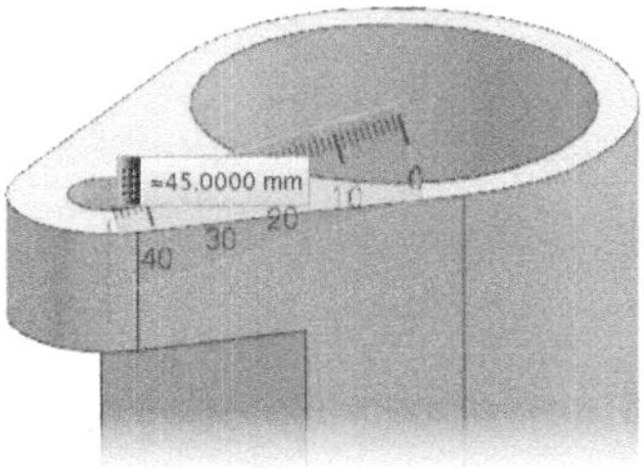

Fig 11-11 Selecting the Second Point

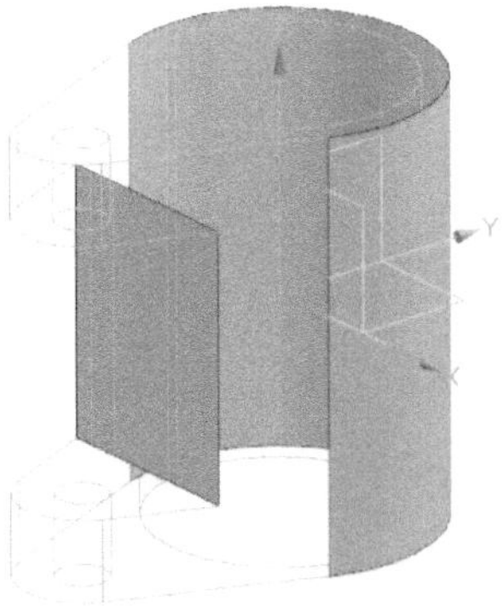

Fig 11-12 Faces to Select

Distance Between Two Points

1. Press the reset button in the **Measure Distance** dialog box.

2. Confirm that the **Arc Center** snap option is turned on as shown in Fig 11-9.

3. Select the center point of the larger hole as shown in Fig 11-10.

4. Select the center point of the smaller hole as shown in Fig 11-11.

The distance is measured as 45 mm.

Max Distance Between Two Faces

1. Press the reset button in the **Measure Distance** dialog box.

2. Select the two faces as shaded in Fig 11-12.

The minimum distance between the two faces is measured as shown in Fig 11-13.

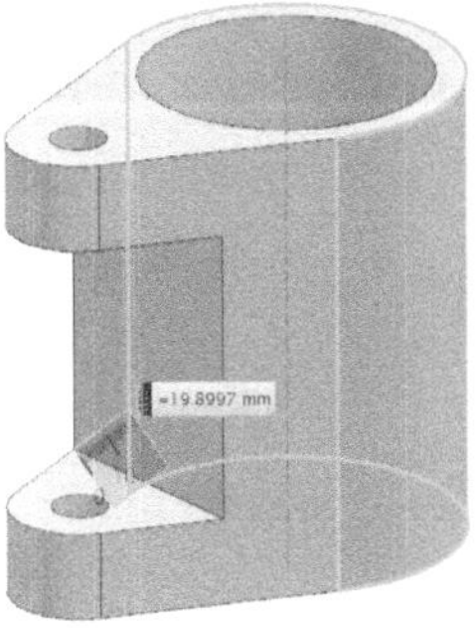

Fig 11-13 Minimum Distance

3. Change the distance option in the **Measurement** option group to **Maximum** as shown in Fig 11-14.

The maximum distance between the two faces is measured as shown in Fig 11-15.

4. Click the **OK** button in the **Measure Distance** dialog box.

5. Close without saving the file.

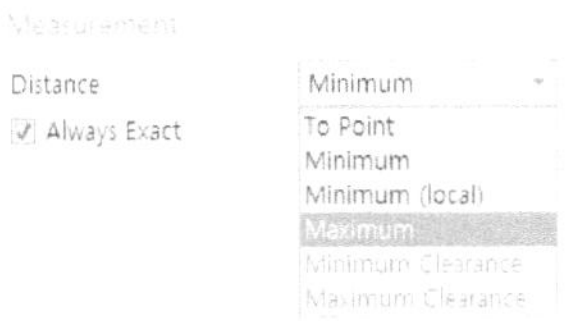

Fig 11-14 Distance Option

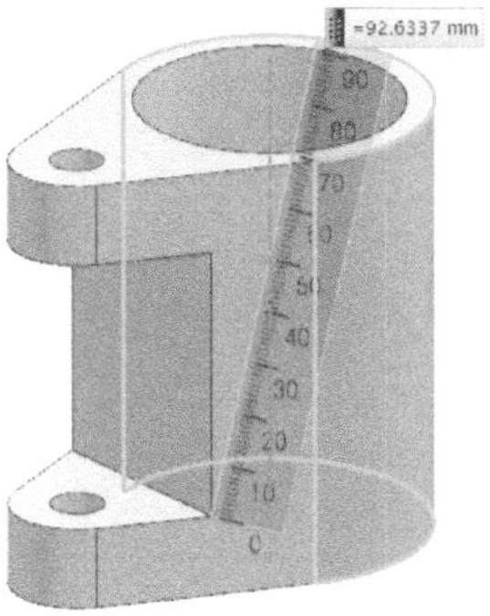

Fig 11-15 Maximum Distance

END of Exercise

! *Showing the Measurement Label*

If you click the **OK** button in the dialog box after measuring the distance, the label is cleared by default. You can show the label by choosing **Show Dimension** in the **Annotation** dropdown list as shown in Fig 11-16 and press **OK** or **Apply**. The dimension label can be cleared by pressing the **F5** key

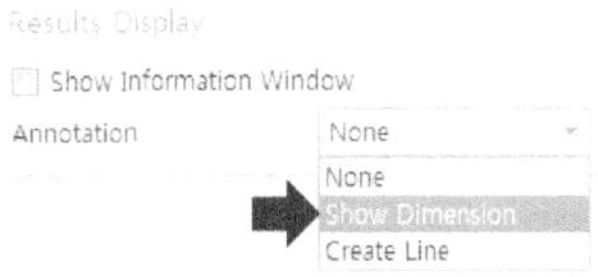

Fig 11-16 Show Dimension

11.1.3 Projected Distance

You can measure the distance projected onto the specified direction. You can measure the minimum or maximum distance. You can also measure the minimum or maximum clearance.

Exercise 02 **Measuring Projected Clearance** *ch11_ex02.prt*

Let's measure the maximum clearance between the two faces as shown in Fig 11-17.

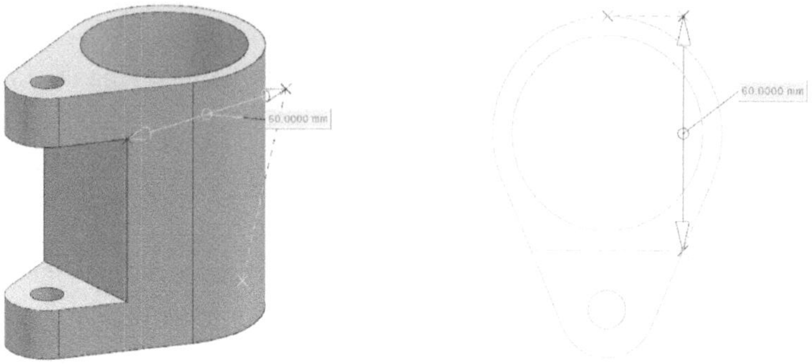

Fig 11-17 Distance to Measure

1. Open the given file ch11_ex02.prt.

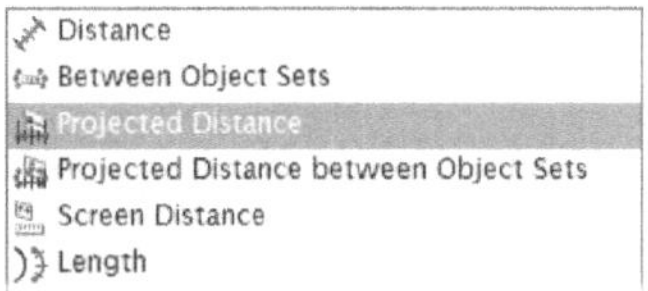

Fig 11-18 Projected Distance Option

2. Click the **Measure Distance** icon in the **Analysis** tab and reset the dialog box.

3. Select the **Projected Distance** in the **Type** dropdown list as shown in Fig 11-18.

The **Vector** option is available in the dialog box, and you are prompted to select a vector.

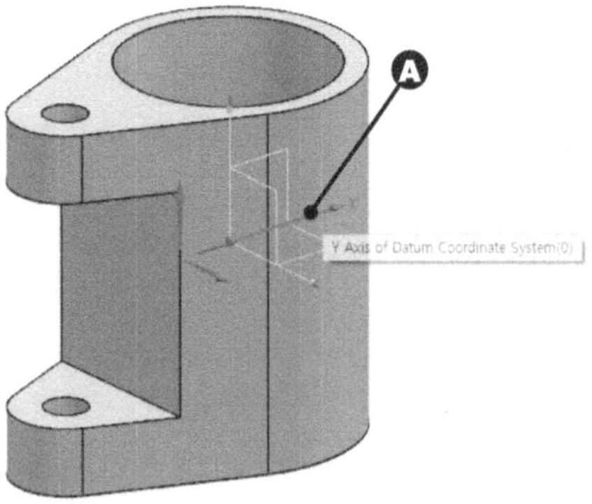

Fig 11-19 Projection Direction

4. Select the Y axis in the datum coordinate system as specified by **A** in Fig 11-19.

5. Select the two faces as shaded in Fig 11-20.

The minimum distance is measured as shown in Fig 11-21.

6. Choose **Maximum Clearance** in the **Distance** dropdown list as shown in Fig 11-22. The maximum clearance is measured as shown in Fig 11-23.

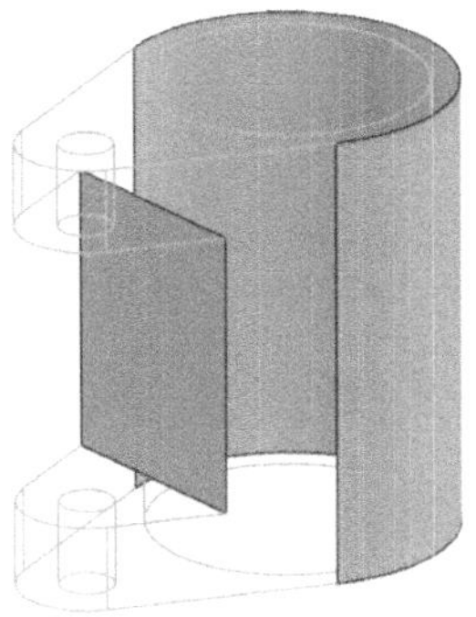

Fig 11-20 Faces to Select

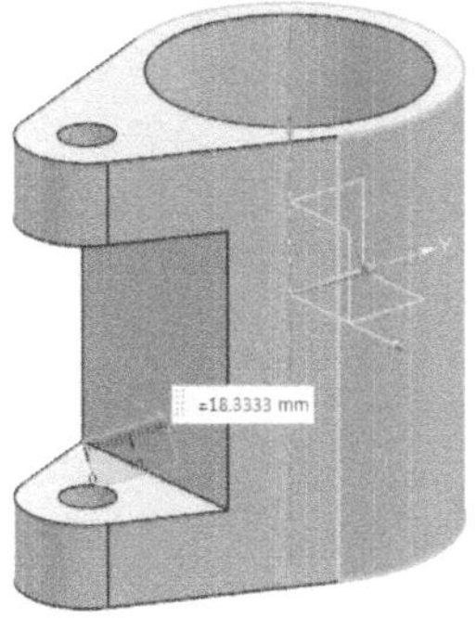

Fig 11-21 Minimum Distance

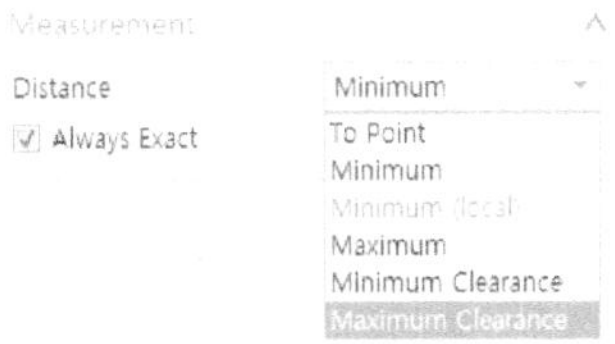

Fig 11-22 Maximum Clearance Option

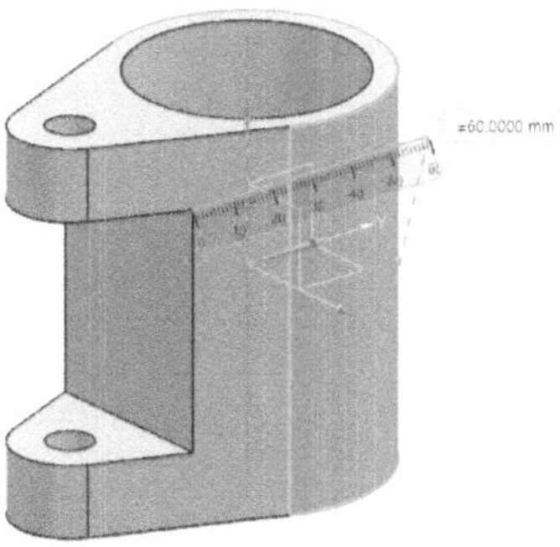

Fig 11-23 Measured Maximum Clearance

Now, let's show the measurement label in the model and in the part navigator.

7. Check the **Associative** option and choose **Show Dimension** in the **Annotation** dropdown list as specified by the arrow in Fig 11-24.

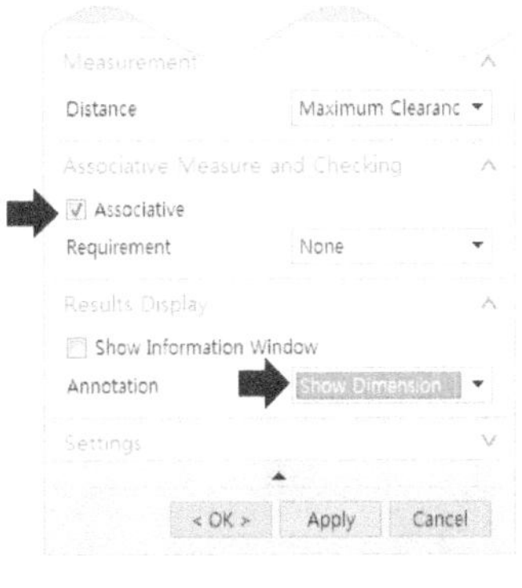

Fig 11-24 Associative and Annotation Option

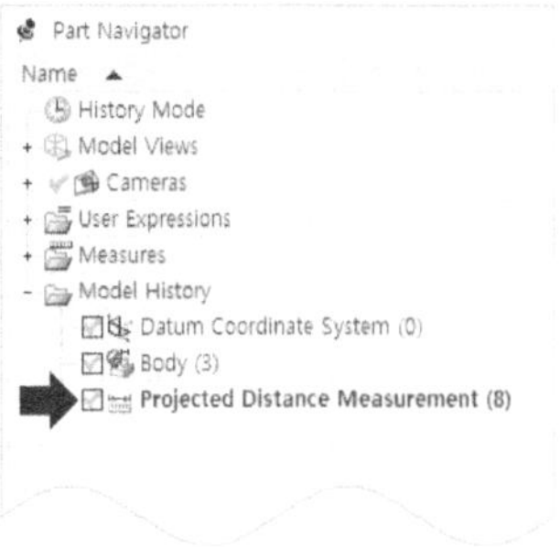

Fig 11-25 Measurement Recorded

8. Click the **OK** button in the dialog box.

Verify that the measurement result is recorded in the part navigator as shown in Fig 11-25.

9. Change the rendering style to **Static Wireframe** and rotate the model view to top as shown in Fig 11-26.

10. Close without saving the file.

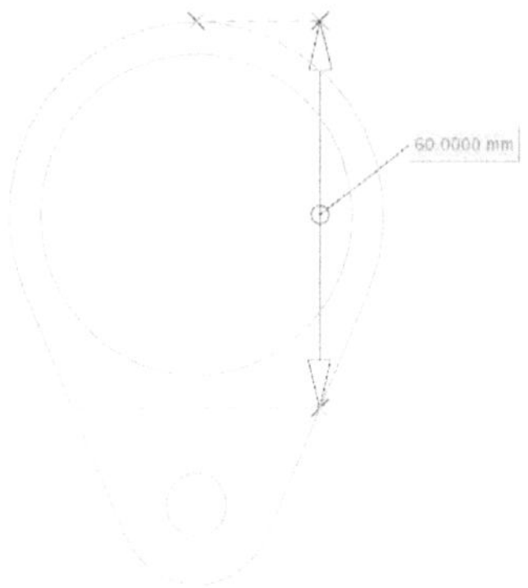

Fig 11-26 Measured Maximum Clearance

END of Exercise

11.1.4 Length Type

You can measure the length of the selected object. The curve rule becomes available.

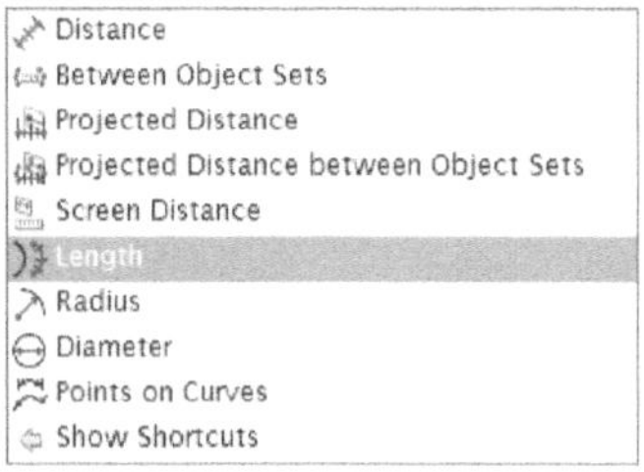

Fig 11-27 Length Type

If you want to measure the length of the single edge that is specified in Fig 11-28, you have to choose **Single Curve** in the **Curve Rule** dropdown list. Fig 11-29 shows the length of the measured single edge.

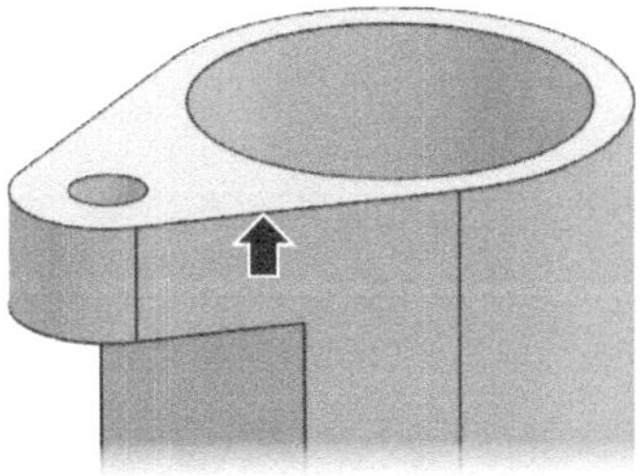

Fig 11-28 Selected Edge

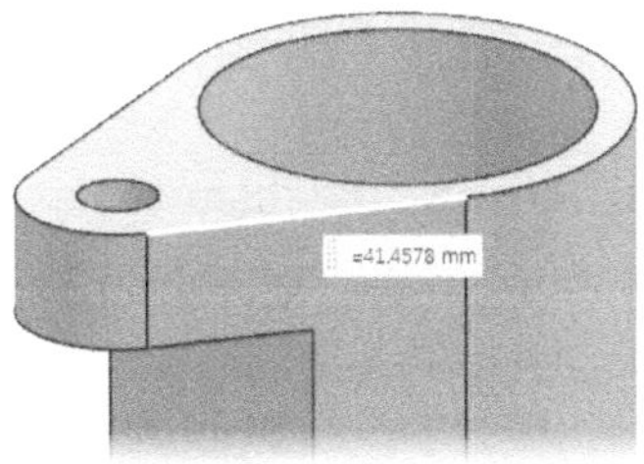

Fig 11-29 Measured Length

If you measure the length with the default curve rule, i.e. **Tangent Curves**, the full length of the tangent connected edges are measured as shown in Fig 11-30.

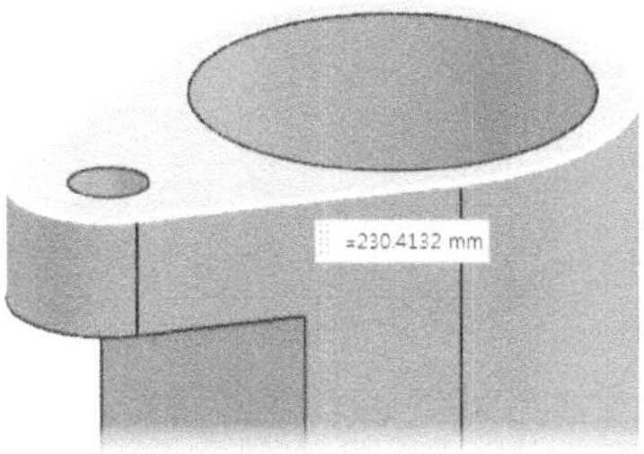

Fig 11-30 Measured Length of Tangent Connected Edges

11.1.5 Radius Type

You can measure the radius of the arcs, circular edges or cylindrical faces. Fig 11-31shows the measured radius of the cylindrical face.

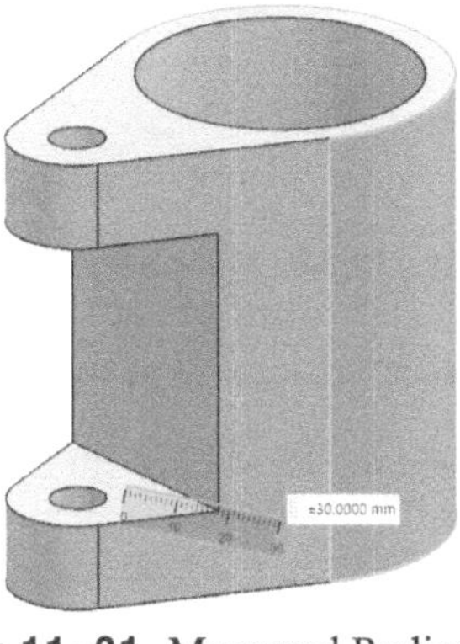

Fig 11-31 Measured Radius

11.3.1 Diameter Type

You can measure the diameter of the arcs, circular edges or cylindrical faces by selecting **Diameter** in the **Type** dropdown list in the **Measure Distance** dialog box. Fig 11-32 shows the measured diameter of the cylindrical face.

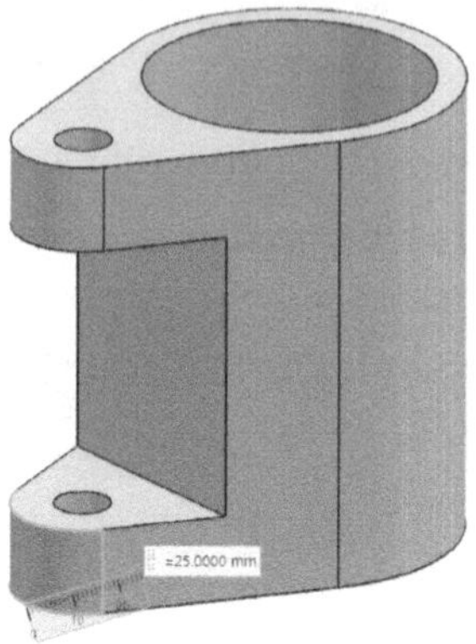

Fig 11-32 Measured Diameter

11.2 Measure Angle

You can measure the angle between linear or planar objects.

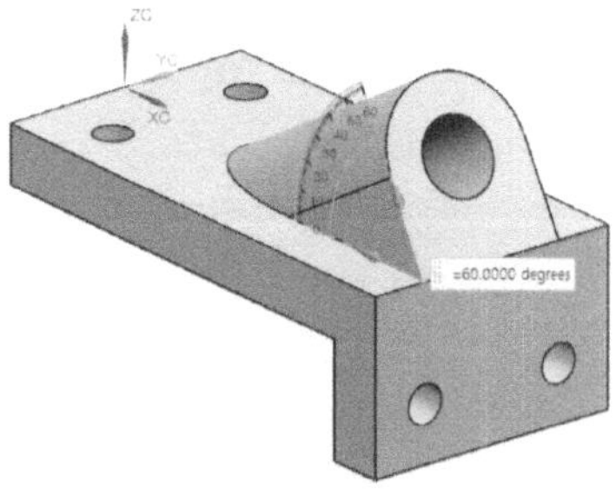

Fig 11-33 Measuring Angle

You can execute the **Measure Angle** command in the **Analysis** tab as shown in Fig 11-34 or in the **Menu** button by choosing **Analysis > Measure Angle**.

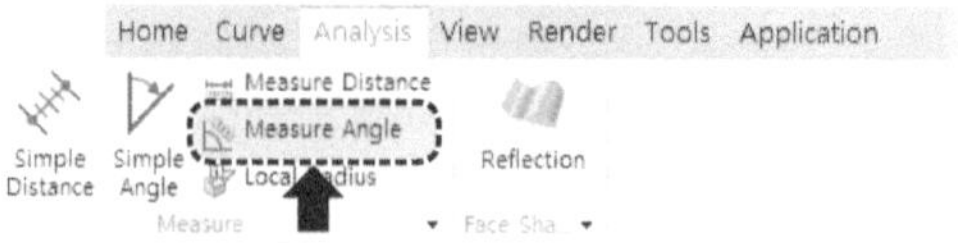

Fig 11-34 Measure Angle Icon

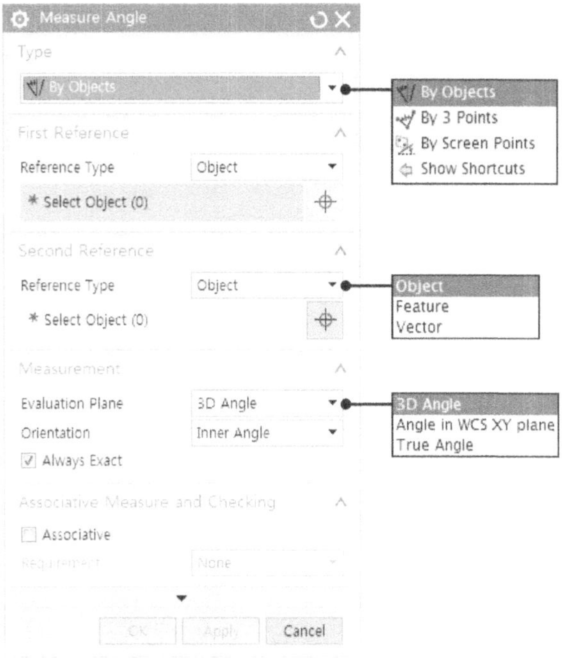

Fig 11-35 Measure Angle Dialog Box

11.3 Simple Distance and Simple Angle

With the **Simple Distance** command, you can measure the minimum distance between two selected objects. With the **Simple Angle** command, you can measure the angle between two selected vectors. Vectors are defined by selecting objects, features or by using the **Vector Dialog** tool.

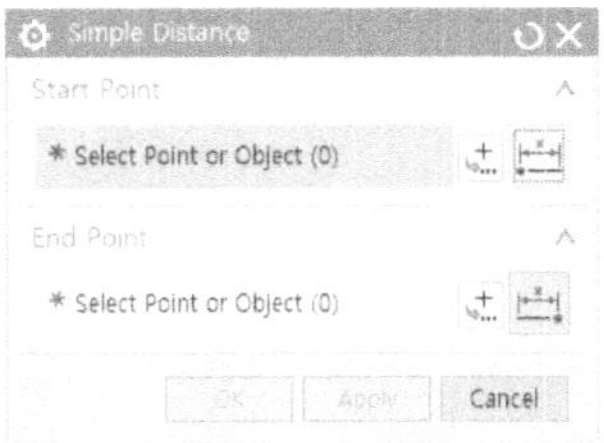

Fig 11-36 Simple Distance Dialog Box

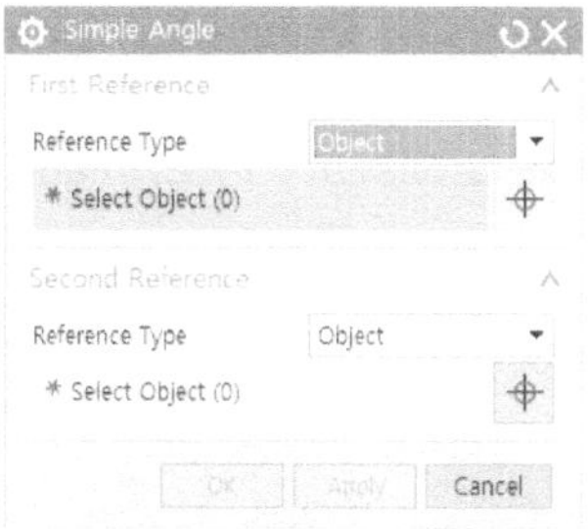

Fig 11-37 Simple Angle Dialog Box

Exercise 03 Measuring Angle

ch11_ex03.prt

Let's measure the angle viewed from the front as shown in Fig 11-38.

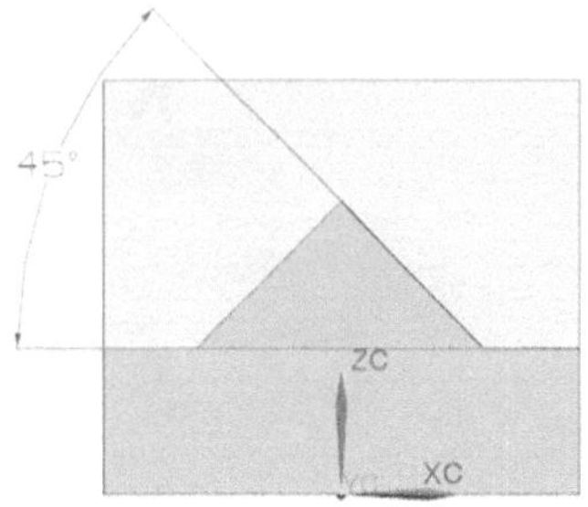

Fig 11-38 Measuring Angle

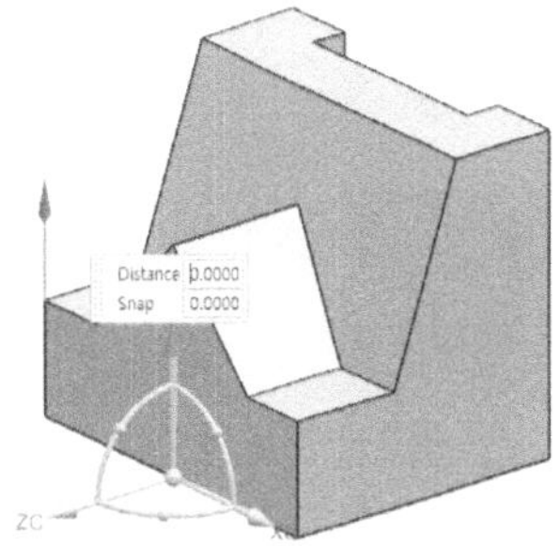

Fig 11-39 Aligning WCS

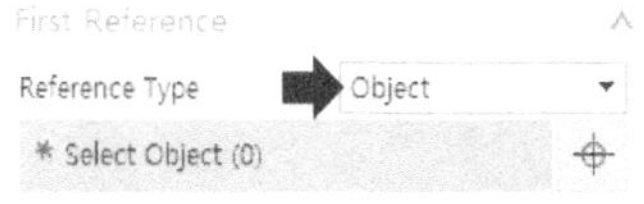

Fig 11-40 Reference Type: Object

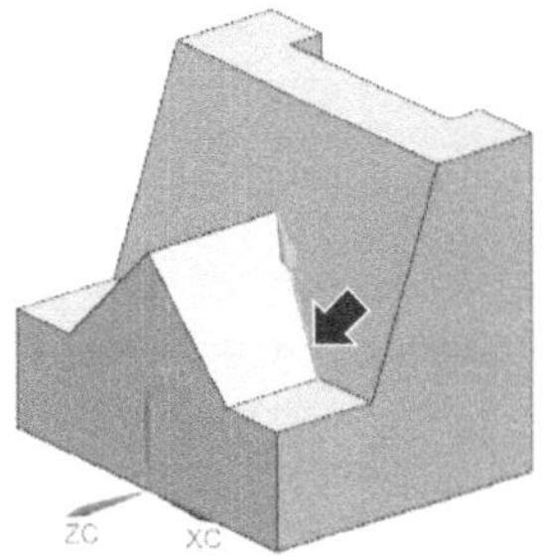

Fig 11-41 Edge to Select

1. Open the given file ch11_ex03.prt.

2. Double click the WCS in the screen and align the YC axis as shown in Fig 11-38.

3. Choose **Analysis > Measure Angle** in the **Menu** button.

4. Reset the **Measure Angle** dialog box.

5. Confirm that the default reference type is set to **Object** as shown in Fig 11-40.

6. Select the edge at the location designated by the arrow in Fig 11-41. If the arrow direction is not correct, click the first reference option field and select the edge correctly.

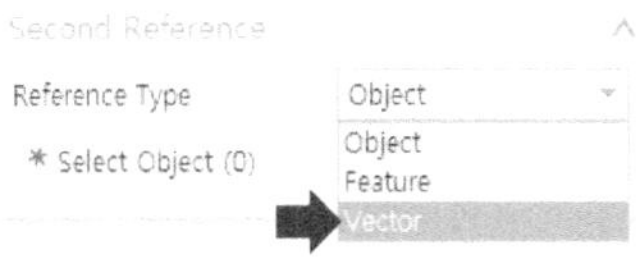

Fig 11-42 Reference Type: Vector

7. Choose **Vector** in the **Reference Type** dropdown list in the **Second Reference** option group as shown in Fig 11-42.

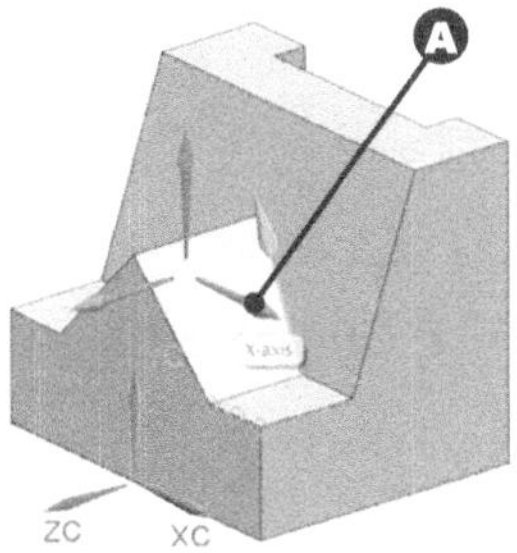

Fig 11-43 Selecting Vector

8. Click the X axis in the vector handle designated by **A** in Fig 11-43.

9. Press the **Reverse Direction** button.

The angle is measured on the plane that is formed by the two vectors as shown in Fig 11-44.

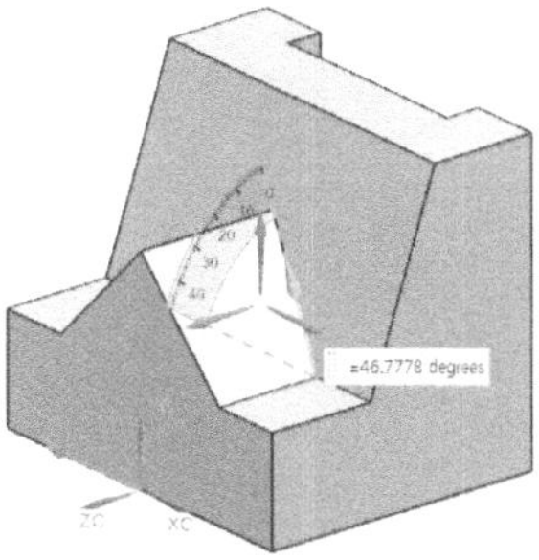

Fig 11-44 Measured Angle

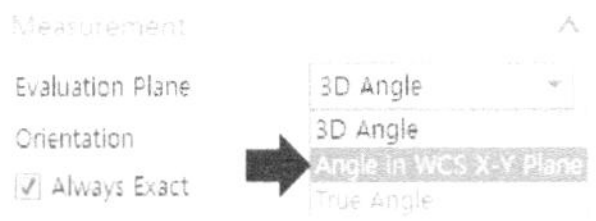

Fig 11-45 Evaluation Plane: Angle in WCS XY plane

10. Choose **Angle in WCS XY plane** in the **Evaluation Plane** dropdown list as shown in Fig 11-45.

The angle is measured as desired as shown in Fig 11-46.

11. Close without saving the file.

Fig 11-46 Measured Angle

END of Exercise

11.4 Measure Bodies

You can measure the volume, surface area, mass, radius of gyration, weight, etc. of a solid body.

11.4.1 Executing Measure Bodies Command

You can execute the **Measure Bodies** command by choosing **Analysis > Measure Bodies** in the **Menu** button.

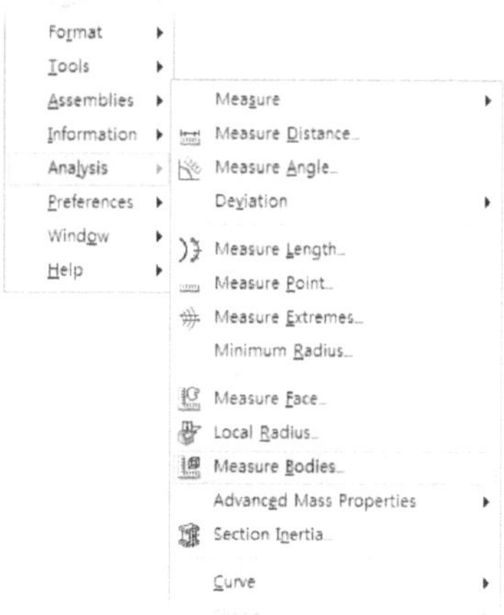

Fig 11-47 Measure Bodies Menu

11.4.2 Measure Bodies Dialog Box

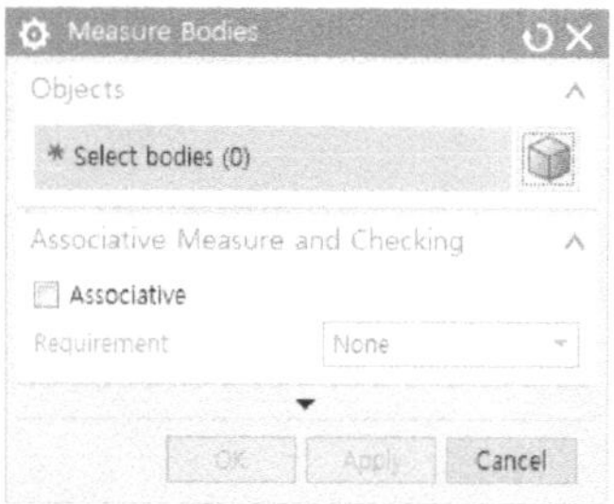

Fig 11-48 Measure Bodies Dialog Box

Let's measure the mass of the handle shown in Fig 11-48. Suppose that the handle is made of ABS resin. We will assign material to the part and measure the mass.

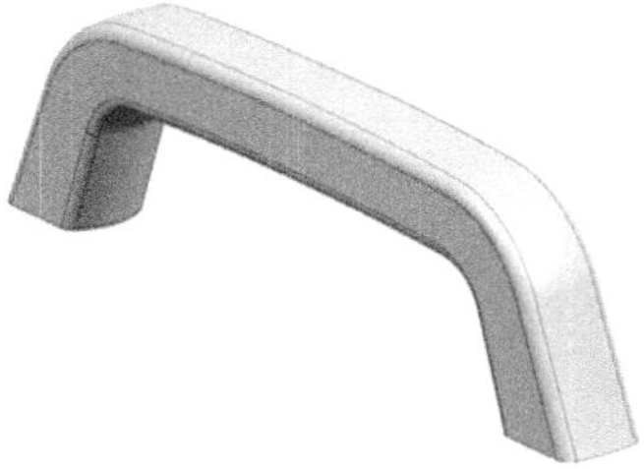

Fig 11-49 Part to Measure

1. Open the given file ch11_ex04.prt.

2. Choose **Tools > Materials > Assign Materials** in the **Menu** button.

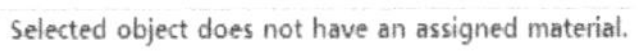

Fig 11-50 Message in Status Line

3. Select the body in the graphics window. The status line message informs that the part has no material assigned as shown in Fig 11-50.

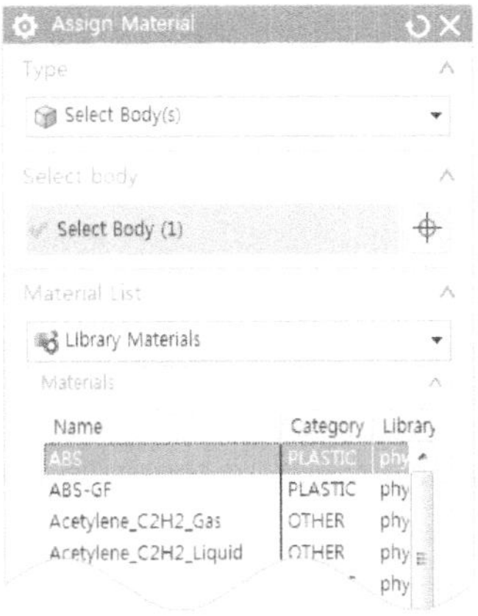

Fig 11-51 Assigning Material

4. Select ABS in the material list in the dialog box.

5. Click **OK** in the dialog box.

6. Choose **Analysis > Measure Bodies** in the **Menu** button.

7. Select the solid body in the graphics window.

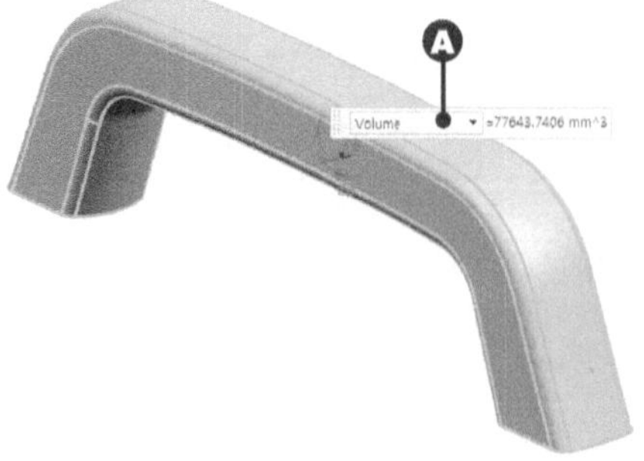

Fig 11-52 Measured Volume

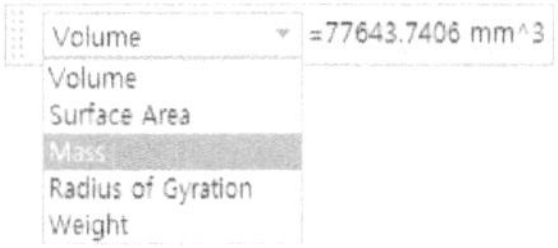

Fig 11-53 Choosing Mass

The volume is labelled in the model as shown in Fig 11-52.

8. Choose **Mass** in the dropdown list designated by Ⓐ in Fig 11-52. Confirm that the mass is measured to 81.53 g.

You can record the result of the measurement in the part navigator by checking the **Associative** option in the dialog box. If the measured value is recorded in the part navigator, the value is allocated to a variable. Then you can create a link with the variable to define another variable through an expression in the following modelling process.

9. Click **OK** in the dialog box.

10. Close without saving the file.

END of Exercise

11.4.3 Detailed Information

You can identify the detailed physical properties of the solid body by checking the **Show Information Window** option in the **Measure Bodies** dialog box as shown in Fig 11-54. Detailed information on the physical properties is shown in the **Information** window as shown in Fig 11-55.

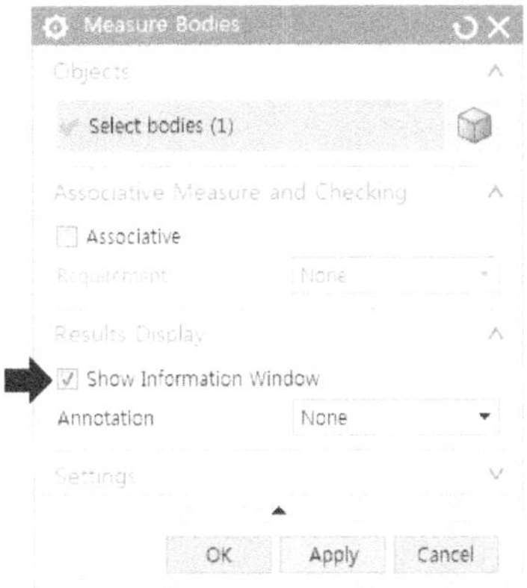

Fig 11-54 Show Information Window Option

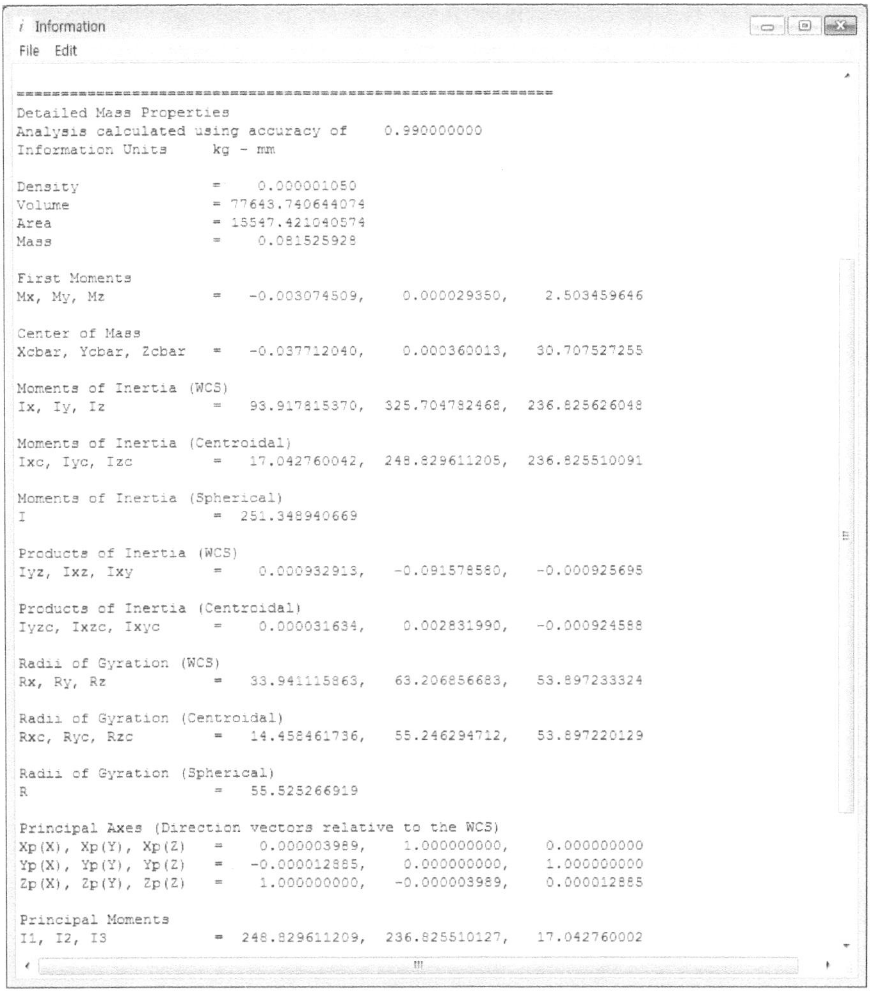

```
Information
File   Edit

============================================================
Detailed Mass Properties
Analysis calculated using accuracy of     0.990000000
Information Units      kg - mm

Density               =    0.000001050
Volume                = 77643.740644074
Area                  = 15547.421040574
Mass                  =    0.081525928

First Moments
Mx, My, Mz            =   -0.003074509,     0.000029350,     2.503459646

Center of Mass
Xcbar, Ycbar, Zcbar   =   -0.037712040,     0.000360013,    30.707527255

Moments of Inertia (WCS)
Ix, Iy, Iz            =   93.917815370,   325.704782468,   236.825626048

Moments of Inertia (Centroidal)
Ixc, Iyc, Izc         =   17.042760042,   248.829611205,   236.825510091

Moments of Inertia (Spherical)
I                     =  251.348940669

Products of Inertia (WCS)
Iyz, Ixz, Ixy         =    0.000932913,    -0.091578580,    -0.000925695

Products of Inertia (Centroidal)
Iyzc, Ixzc, Ixyc      =    0.000031634,     0.002831990,    -0.000924588

Radii of Gyration (WCS)
Rx, Ry, Rz            =   33.941115863,    63.206856683,    53.897233324

Radii of Gyration (Centroidal)
Rxc, Ryc, Rzc         =   14.458461736,    55.246294712,    53.897220129

Radii of Gyration (Spherical)
R                     =   55.525266919

Principal Axes (Direction vectors relative to the WCS)
Xp(X), Xp(Y), Xp(Z)   =    0.000003989,     1.000000000,     0.000000000
Yp(X), Yp(Y), Yp(Z)   =   -0.000012885,     0.000000000,     1.000000000
Zp(X), Zp(Y), Zp(Z)   =    1.000000000,    -0.000003989,     0.000012885

Principal Moments
I1, I2, I3            =  248.829611209,   236.825510127,    17.042760002
```

Fig 11-55 Information Window

Exercise 05 Using the Measured Value *ch11_ex05.prt*

Create the model shown in Fig 11-56 referring to the given steps. The dimension marked Ⓐ should always have the same value as the difference of the radius. We will formulate the difference by measuring the radiuses.

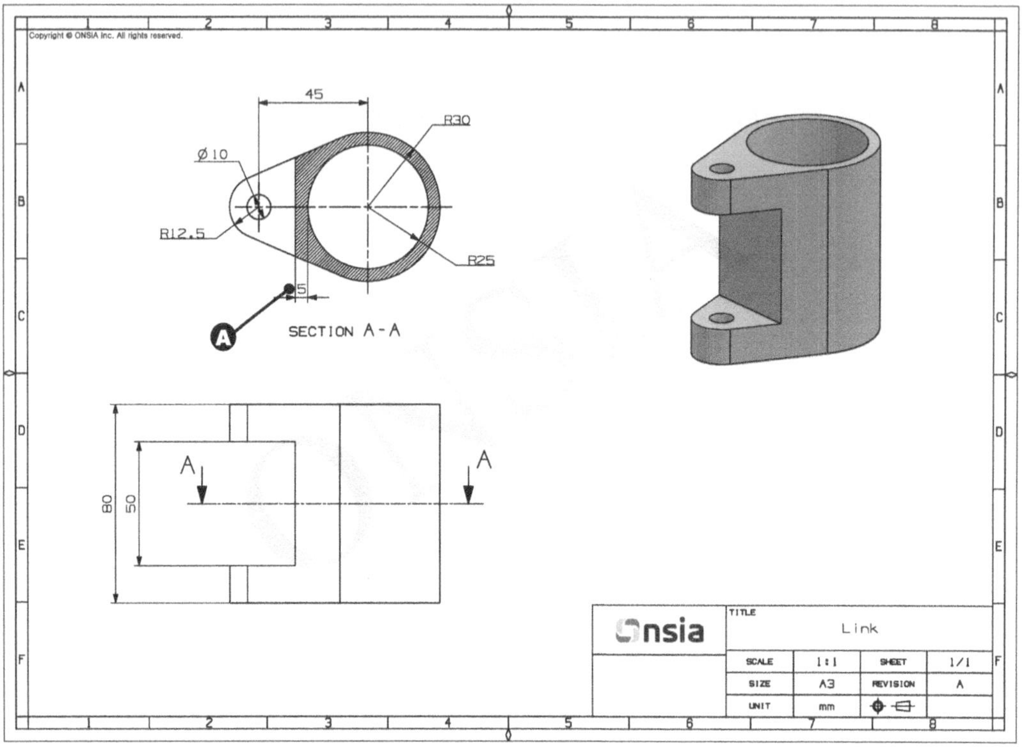

Fig 11-56 Drawing of Link

Step 1

1. Create the sketch viewed from the top on the XY plane of the datum coordinate system and extrude the outer section to create the base body as shown in Fig 11-57.
2. Create a through hole of diameter 50 as shown in Fig 11-58.

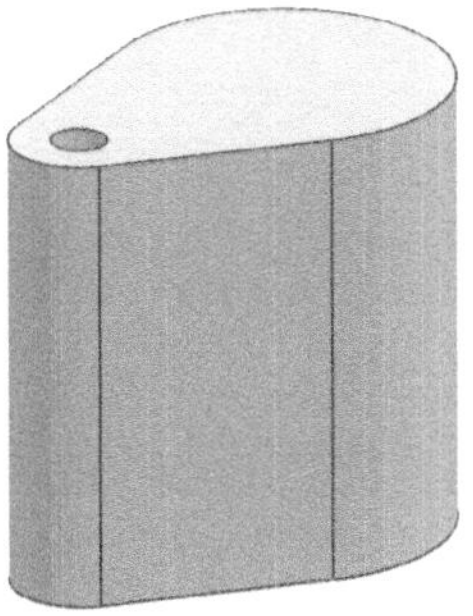

Fig 11-57 First Extrude

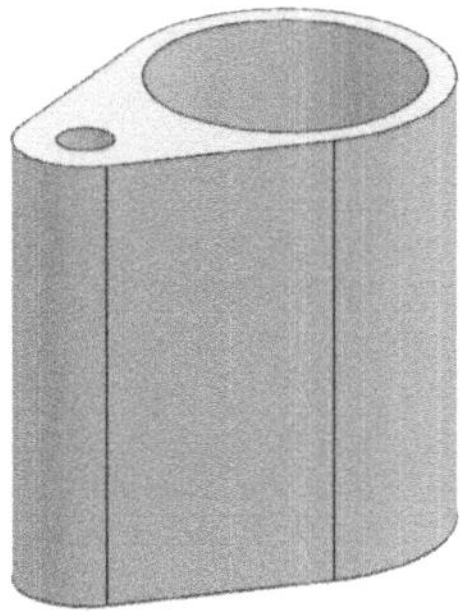

Fig 11-58 Creating a Hole

Step 2

1. Define a sketch on the YZ plane.
2. Create intersection curves by selecting the two shaded faces as designated by the arrow in Fig 11-59 and convert the intersection curve into a reference.
3. Create a rectangle as shown in Fig 11-60.

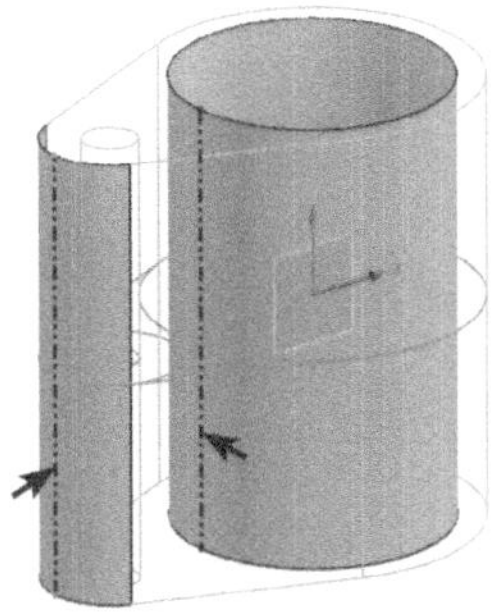

Fig 11-59 Intersection Curve

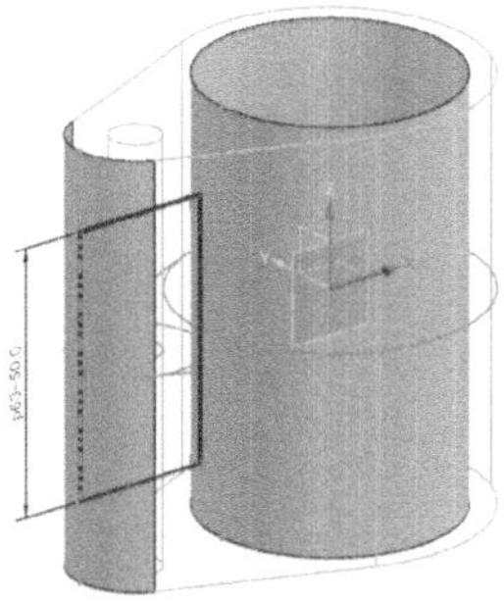

Fig 11-60 Sketch

Step 3

1. Create the dimension as shown in Fig 11-61.
2. Click the down arrow as designated by **B** in Fig 11-61.
3. Choose **Formula** in the dropdown list. The **Expression** dialog box is invoked.

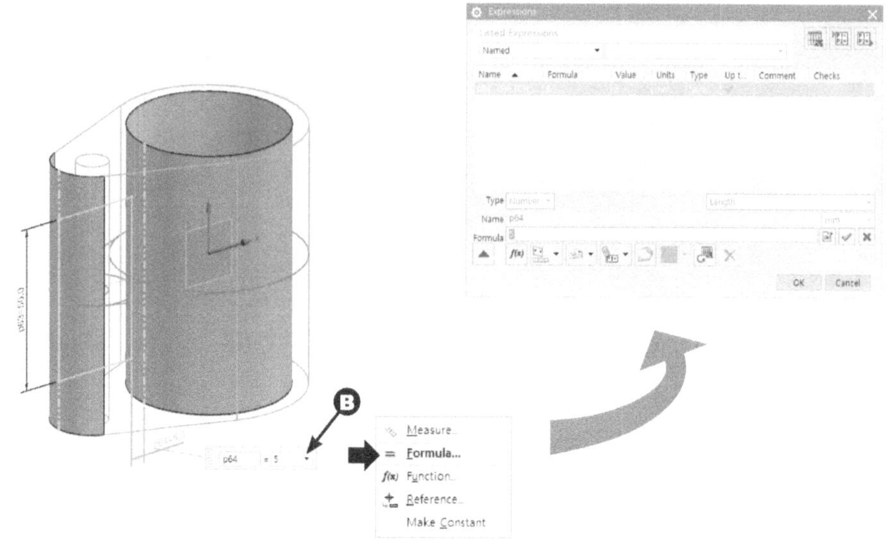

Fig 11-61 Activating Formula

Step 4

1. Click the **Measure Distance** icon in the dropdown list as designated by **C** in Fig 11-62.
2. Choose **Radius** in the **Type** dropdown list of the **Measure Distance** dialog box.
3. Select the outer cylindrical face of R30 to measure the radius and press **OK** in the **Measure Distance** dialog box.
4. Confirm that the measurement variable is entered in the **Formula** input box. The variable number can be different from yours.
5. Enter a minus symbol (-) after the variable as shown in the input box.

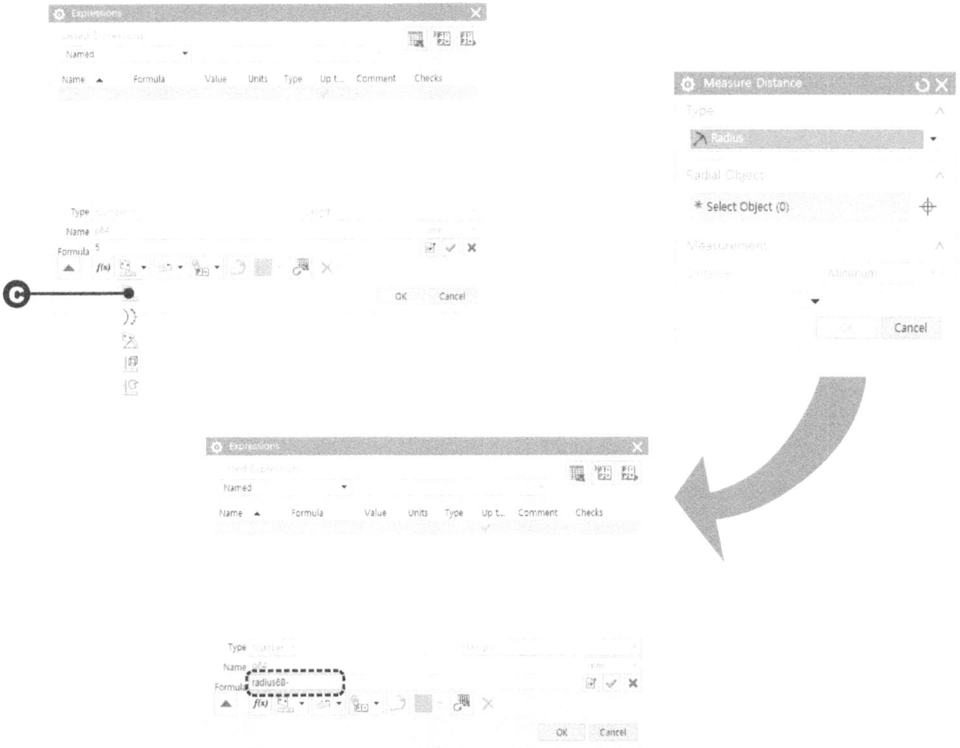

Fig 11-62 Entering the Measurement Result

Step 5

1. Click the **Measure Distance** icon in the dropdown list as designated by Ⓖ in Fig 11-62.
2. Measure the radius of the R25 hole and click **OK** in the **Measure Distance** dialog box.
3. Confirm that the measurement variable is entered in the **Formula** input box as shown in Fig 11-63. The variable number can be different from yours.
4. Click the green check button in the **Expression** dialog box and verify that the formula has been inserted as shown in Fig 11-64.
5. Press **OK** to close the **Expression** dialog box.

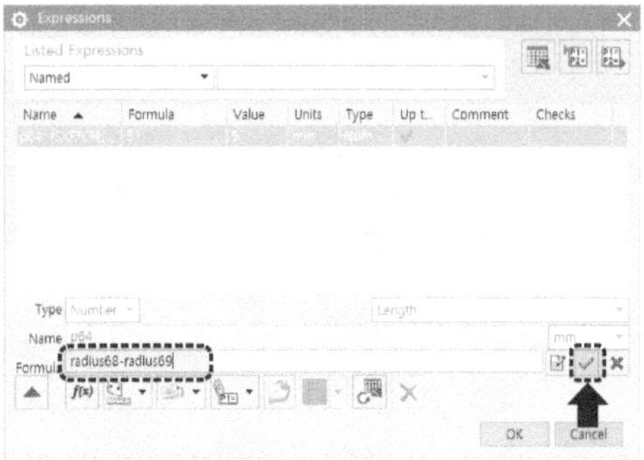

Fig 11-63 Entering the Formula

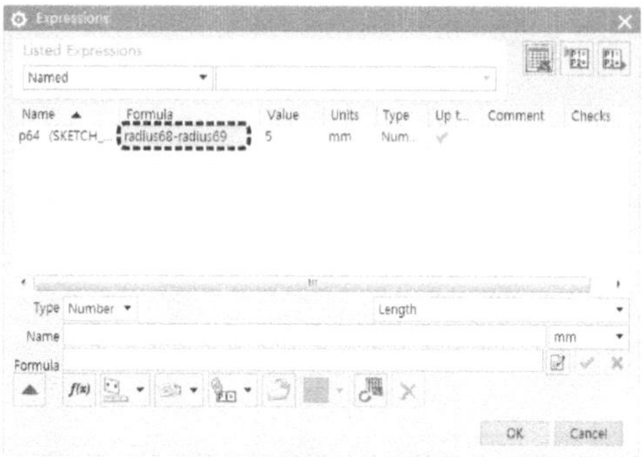

Fig 11-64 Compled the Formula

Step 6

Finish the sketch and extrude the rectangle to complete the model as shown in Fig 11-65.

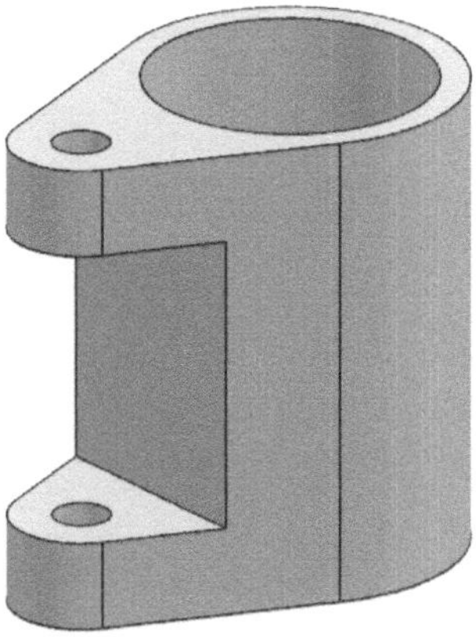

Fig 11-65 Completed Model

END of Exercise

Chapter 12

Assembly Design I (Bottom-Up Assembly)

■ After completing this chapter you will understand

- the terms and concepts of assembly design.
- how to create an assembly file and construct the assembly structure.
- how to move and constrain components.
- the meaning of a master part.
- the concept of the reference set.

12.1 Introduction

Products we use every day are in an assembled form. Up until Chapter 10, we have been creating individual parts using NX. After completing the part design, the parts will be manufactured in real life and then assembled so that they function as intended as a complete product. The products will undergo testing if required and then be sold to customers if they pass the tests.

Suppose that we are manufacturing individual parts just after completing the design. If there are problems in the actual assembly, it will take a lot of time, effort and money to correct the design mistakes.

On the other hand, we can replicate assembly on the computer for every part that constitutes the product. We can check interferences, the mechanism and basic physical characteristics such as weight, center of mass, etc. by using the tools in the **Assemblies** icon group. If design mistakes are found during the checking process, we can modify the design within the assembly context by making the part a work part.

12.2 Terms and Definitions

12.2.1 Component

If parts are assembled in the part file to construct an assembly, they are called components. Parts used as components do not contain information that defines the part geometry. Instead, the part components only show the resulting geometry and have their own independent appearance, position and orientation. Therefore, file size of the assembly part file is smaller than the summation of all the file sizes of the components.

A component can be an assembly which contains other part components. This type of component is called an assembly component to distinguish it from a part component.

12.2.2 Master Part

The information data for constructing a 3D model geometry is contained in a part file. Up until Chapter 10, we have been creating geometries in the part file. The part which is used as a component is called a master part to distinguish it from the component.

12.2.3 Sub-assembly

Sub-assembly is a general term to refer to an assembly that is used as a component.

12.2.4 BOM (Bill of Material)

BOM refers to a parts list which contains basic information on the parts that constitute a product.

12.2.5 Bottom-up Assembly Design

Bottom-up assembly design refers to an assembly process starting from the bottom of the assembly structure to construct the top assembly. Looking at Fig 12-1, parts A through F are designed in advance independently and assembled to construct sub-assemblies, and finally to construct the top assembly.

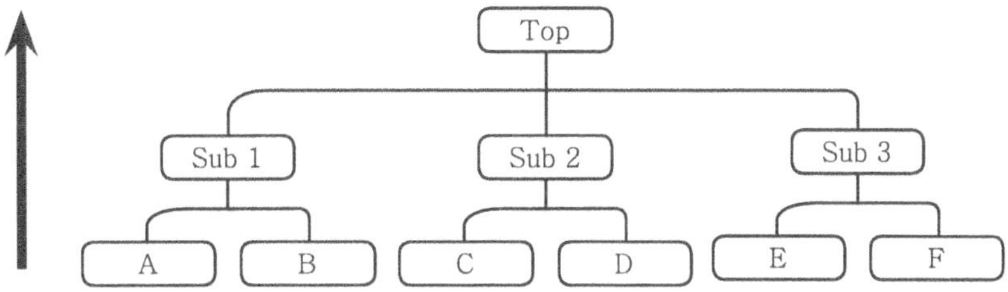

Fig 12-1 Concept Diagram of Bottom-Up Assembly Design

12.2.6 Top-Down Assembly Design

The process of creating certain parts in the context of an assembly is called a top-down assembly design. Referring to the diagram shown in Fig 12-2, the top assembly is constructed with the parts A, B, C, E and F and then the missing part D is created by making the master part a work part. You can also modify a part in the context of an assembly.

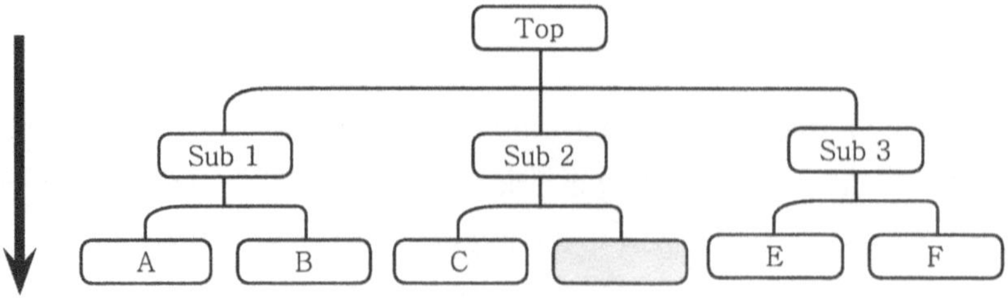

Fig 12-2 Concept Diagram of Top-Down Assembly Design

12.3 Key Functions in Assemblies

The following topics are key interests in assembly design.

① Constructing Assemblies: This is called bottom-up assembly design.

② Constraining: You will specify the position and orientation of components in an assembly.

③ Checking Interference: You will check if the components interfere with other components at their specified position and orientation.

④ Part Modeling: This is called top-down assembly design.

⑤ Disassembling: You can disassemble the components to create an assembly drawing.

12.4 Constructing an Assembly

In most cases constructing an assembly entails assembling components in the bottom-up assembly design. We will move or constrain the components to define their position and orientation.

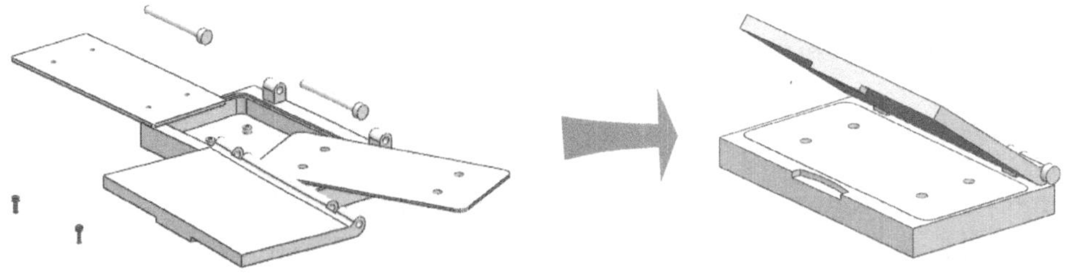

Fig 12-3 Constructing an Assembly

12.4.1 Creating Assembly File

The assembly file has the same extension .PRT as the part file. You will add the suffix _asm to the file name to distinguish the assembly part file from the geometry part file. The assembly file is created using the **Assembly** template.

Creating an Assembly File **Exercise 01**

1. Choose **File > New** in the **Menu** button.

2. Click the **Model** tab and select **Assembly** template as designated by ❷ in Fig 12-4.

3. Enter the assembly file name and specify the folder as designated by ❸ in Fig 12-4.

4. Press **OK** in the **New** dialog box.

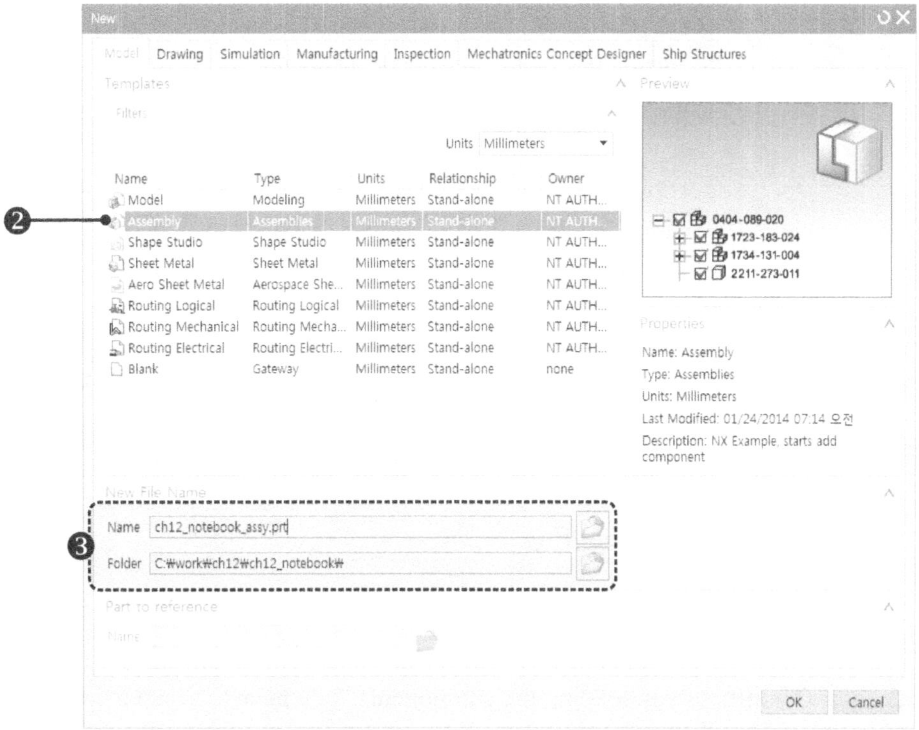

Fig 12-4 Creating a New Assembly File

The **Add Component** dialog box is invoked as shown in Fig 12-5.

5. Click **Cancel** in the dialog box.

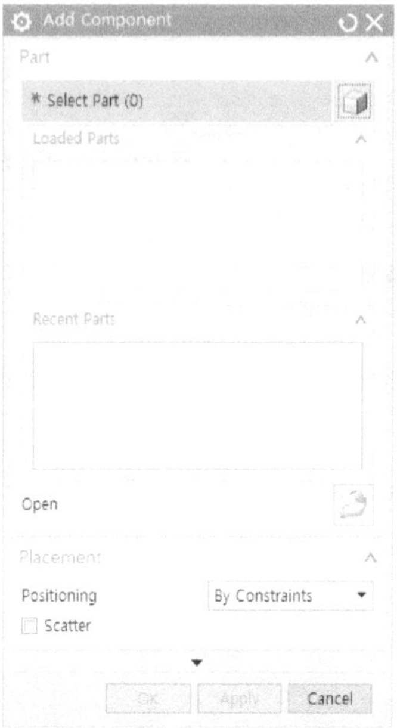

Fig 12-5 Add Component Dialog Box

END of Exercise

Folder of Assembly File

It is highly recommended to create the assembly part file in the same folder as the components. If you create the assembly file in a different folder from the components, you may suffer difficulty in loading the components. You have to select a proper load option.

12.4.2 Assembly Option

Fig 12-6 shows the NX window after creating a new part file with the **Assembly** template.

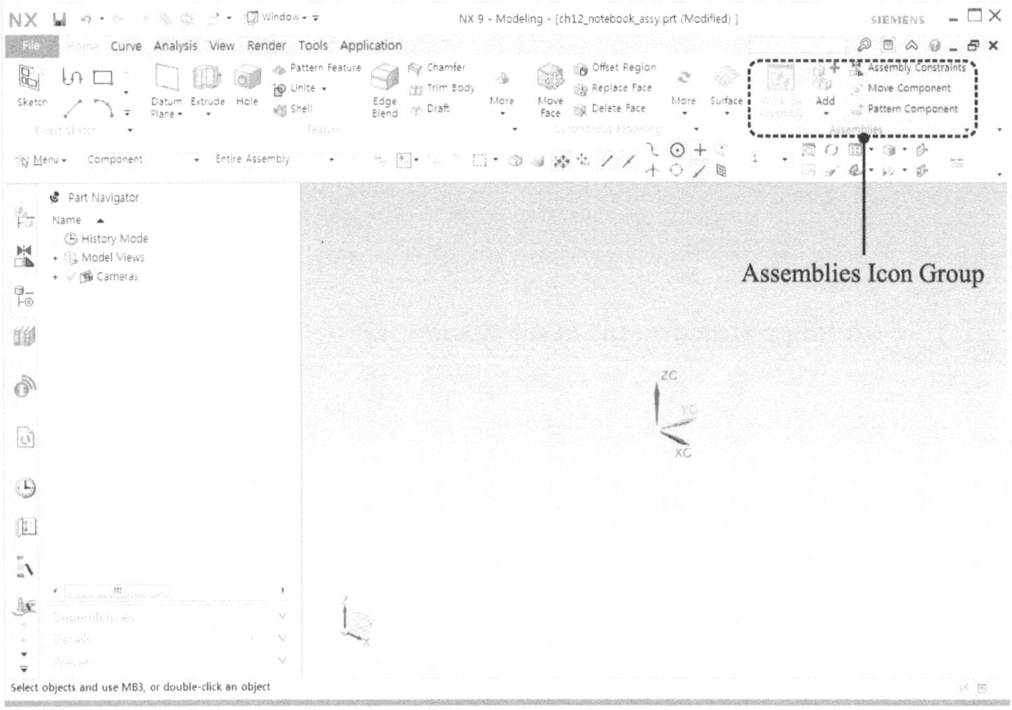

Fig 12-6 Assemblies Icon Group

You can hide or show the **Assemblies** icon group by choosing **Assemblies** in the **Application** tab of NX as shown in Fig 12-7. If you turn on the **Assemblies** functions, all the **Assemblies** menus in the **Menu** button become available.

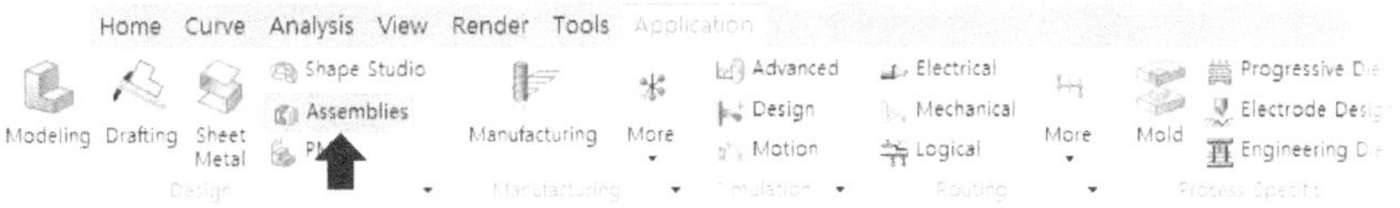

Fig 12-7 Activating Assemblies Commands

12.4.3 Adding Components

You can add components by clicking the **Add** icon in the **Assemblies** icon group.

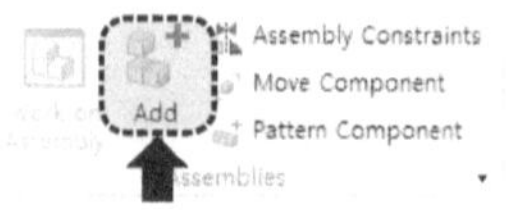

Fig 12-8 Add Icon

Exercise 02 Adding a Component in an Assembly

Let's learn the process of adding a component in an assembly.

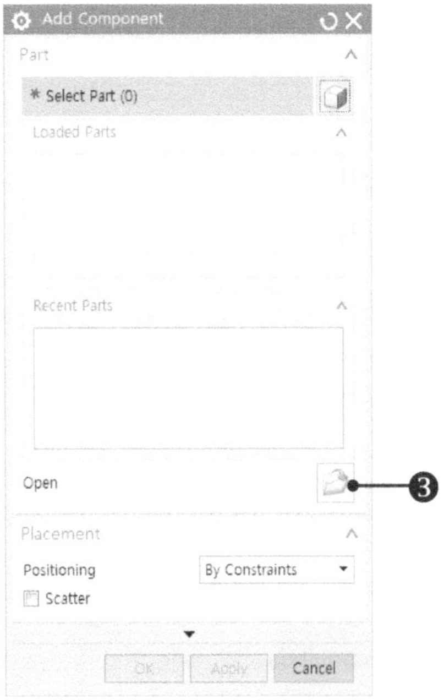

Fig 12-9 Add Component Dialog Box

1. Click the **Add** icon in the **Assemblies** icon group.

2. Reset the dialog box.

3. Click the **Open** button (❸ in Fig 12-9).

4. Select the **Deck** component. The name of the part file is shown in the **Loaded Parts** list box in the dialog box and the preview of the component is shown in the **Component Preview** window in the lower right corner.

5. Choose **Absolute Origin** in the **Positioning** dropdown list (❺ in Fig 12-10).

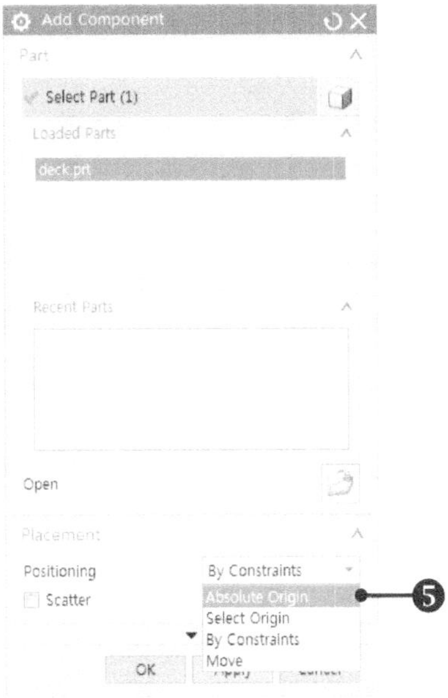

Fig 12-10 Positioning Option

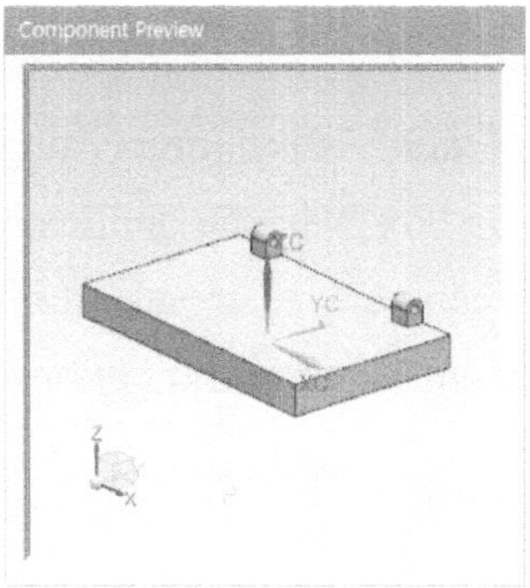

Fig 12-11 Preview of Component

6. Click the **Apply** button. The component file appears in the **Recent Parts** list box and the component geometry is shown in the graphics window.

7. Click the **Open** button again and add another component.

8. Close the **Add Component** dialog box after adding all the required components by clicking the **Cancel** button.

END of Exercise

Options for the **Add Component** dialog box are explained next.

① **Select Part**: You can select the existing component in the graphics window or in the assembly navigator.

② **Loaded Part**: The loaded parts are listed in this box and you can select them to add repeatedly.

③ **Duplicates**: This option is available after clicking the **More** button in the lower part of the dialog box. You can duplicate the selected component as much as required. The duplicated components are added in the same location. Therefore, you will use the **Scatter** option in the **Positioning** option group at the same time.

④ **Positioning**

► **Absolute Origin**: The absolute coordinate system of the component is added in coincidence with that of the assembly part file.

► **Select Origin**: If you click **Apply** or **OK** in the dialog box, the **Point** dialog box is displayed, and you can specify the location of the origin of the component.

► **By Constraints**: If you click **Apply** or **OK** in the dialog box, the **Assembly Constraint** dialog box is displayed, and you can apply constraints to fully constrain the component.

► **Move**: If you click **Apply** or **OK** in the dialog box, the **Point** dialog box is displayed, and you can specify the location of the origin of the component and then move the component with the dynamic orientation handle.

Fig 12-12 Options in Add Component Dialog Box

12.4.4 Saving Assembly File

The following options are available in the **File** tab in saving the assembly and master part file.

① **Save**: You can save the current work part and all the modified components and sub-assemblies.

② **Save Work Part Only**: You can save only the current work part. If you are working with an assembly part, the component master parts will not be saved even if they have been modified. If you are working with a master part, the parent assembly part will not be saved.

Fig 12-13 Save Menu

③ **Save As**: You can save the current work part as a new file. You can save the assembly file as a new file and the component master part as a new part file.

④ **Save All**: You can save all part files that are loaded in the current NX session.

Work Part

You make a component work part by pressing **MB3 > Make Work Part** on the component in the assembly navigator. The part history of the master part is available in the part navigator, and you can modify the part. You can make the assembly file by pressing **MB3 > Make Work Part** on the top assembly.

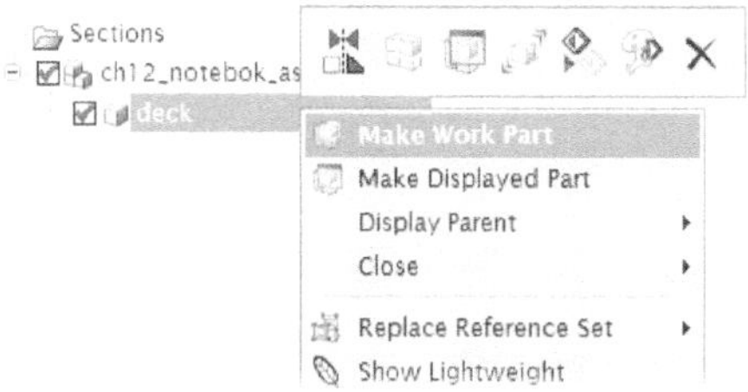

Fig 12-14 Making a Work Part

Exercise 03 Creating an Assembly and Saving

Folder: ch12₩ch12_notebook

Create an assembly according to the suggested process and save the assembly file.

Adding Deck Component

Let's add the **Deck** component with the **Absolute Origin** positioning option.

1. Click the **New** icon and create an assembly file with the name of ch12_notebook_assy.prt in the folder ch12\ch12_notebook.

2. Reset the **Add Component** dialog box.

3. Click the **Open** button in the **Add Component** dialog box.

4. Select deck.prt in the ch12_notebook folder.

5. Click **OK** in the **Part Name** dialog box. You will notice that deck.prt appears in the **Loaded Parts** list box.

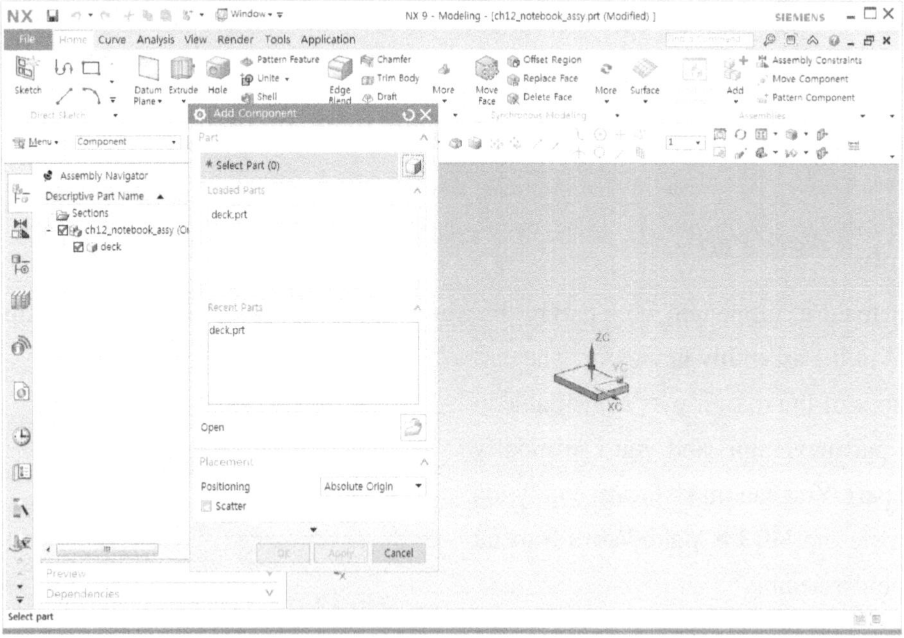

Fig 12-15 Adding Deck Component

6. Choose **Absolute Origin** in the **Positioning** dropdown list and click **Apply**. The **Deck** component is added to the assembly as shown in Fig 12-15.

Adding Top Component

Now, let's add the **Top** component with the **Move** option as the positioning.

1. Click the **Open** button in the **Add Component** dialog box.

2. Select top.prt and choose **Move** in the **Positioning** dropdown list.

3. Click **OK** in the **Add Component** dialog box. The **Point** dialog box will be displayed.

4. Select the midpoint of the edge as designated by Ⓐ in Fig 12-16. The **Move Component** dialog box will appear and the move handle is activated in the graphics window.

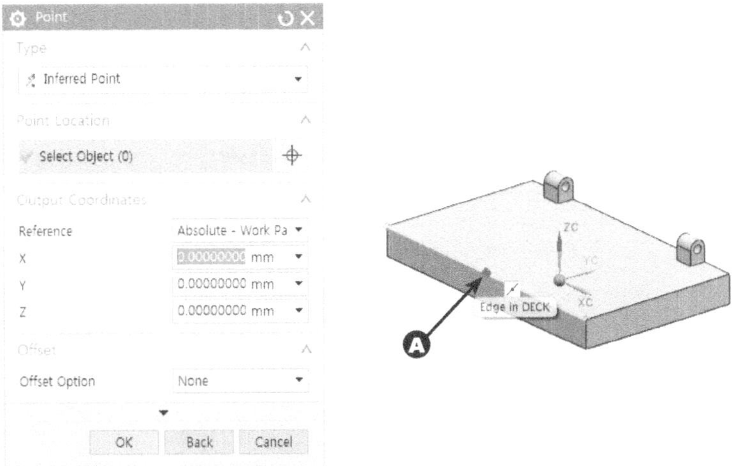

Fig 12-16 Specifying the Origin Point

5. Drag the heads of the move handles as shown in Fig 12-17 to locate the **Top** component.

6. Click **OK** in the **Move Component** dialog box.

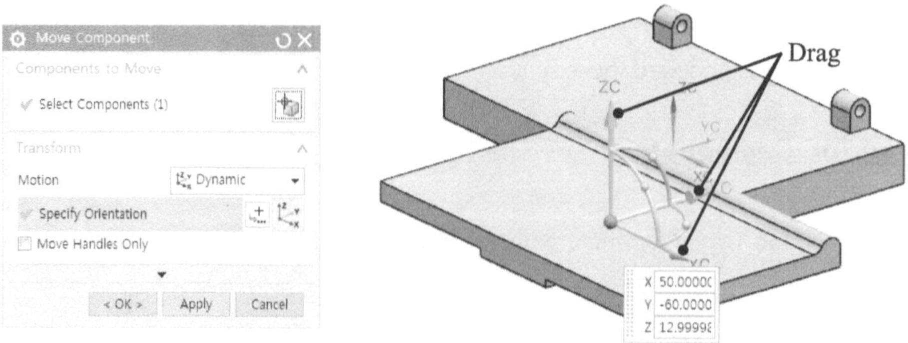

Fig 12-17 Moving Component

7. Choose **Save > Save** in the **File** tab.

8. Open the ch12_notebook folder with the file explorer.

9. Compare the size of the files as shown in Fig 12-13. You will notice that the size of the assembly file is smaller than the sum of those of the master parts.

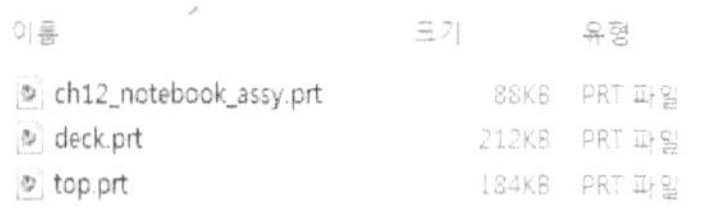

Fig 12-18 Comparing File Size

END of Exercise

Master Part

The component that is shown in the assembly file is showing just the geometry data that is defined automatically in modeling the part. Looking at the part navigator of the assembly file, you will notice that there is no modeling history available. The part history of the component is saved in the master part, and if you modify the master part, the component geometry will be updated. Making the component work part is the same as opening the part file of the component.

12.4.5 Closing Files

You can close files by choosing a proper **Close** menu in the **File** tab as shown in Fig 12-19. Several menus for closing files are explained next.

① **Selected Parts**: You can close the open or loaded files selectively.

② **All Parts**: You can close all loaded files in the NX session.

Fig 12-19 Close Menu

If you choose the **Selected Parts** in **File > Close**, the **Close Part** dialog box as shown in Fig 12-20 will be invoked. Each option numbered in Fig 12-20 is explained next.

① Select the parts to close.

② Specify whether to close only the selected assembly file or to close the assembly part file and all its components.

③ Closes all open parts. Clicking this button is the same as choosing **Close > All Parts** in the **File** tab.

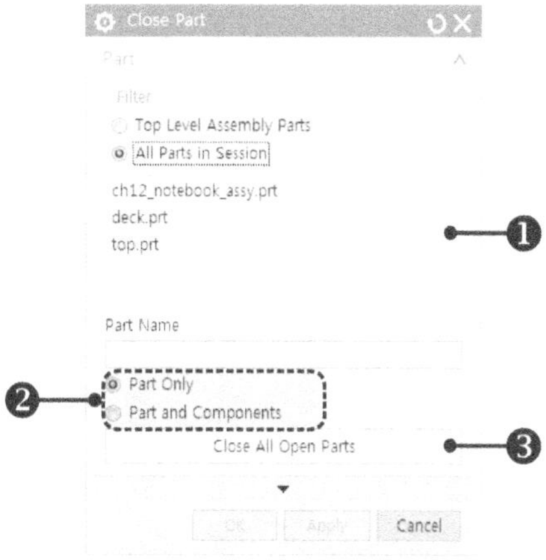

Fig 12-20 Close Part Dialog Box

Closing Displayed Part

If you close the part that is currently displayed in the graphics window, NX displays no parts in the graphics window. You can show the loaded part by choosing it in the **Window** menu in the **Quick Access** toolbar. If you choose **More** in the **Window** menu, you can display the component part.

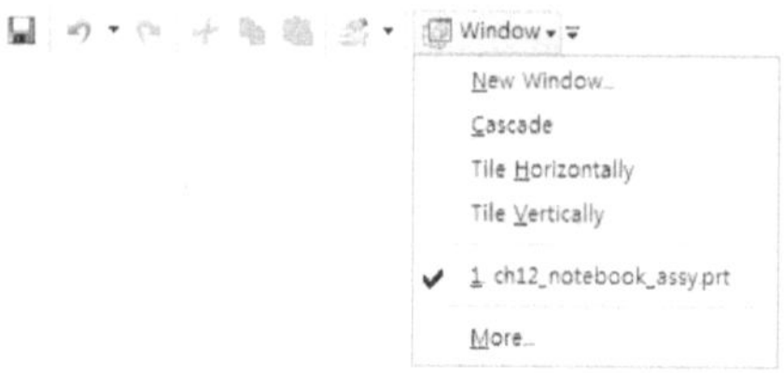

Fig 12-21 Window Menu

12.4.6 Opening Files

You can open an assembly file by choosing **File > Open** in the ribbon bar or in the **Menu** button. Options for opening files are explained next. The numbers correspond to those in Fig 12-22.

① **Load Structures Only**: Does not load the component geometry but shows only the structure of the assembly. You can load the component geometry selectively after opening the assembly file.

② **Options**: You can set the assembly load option while loading the assembly file.

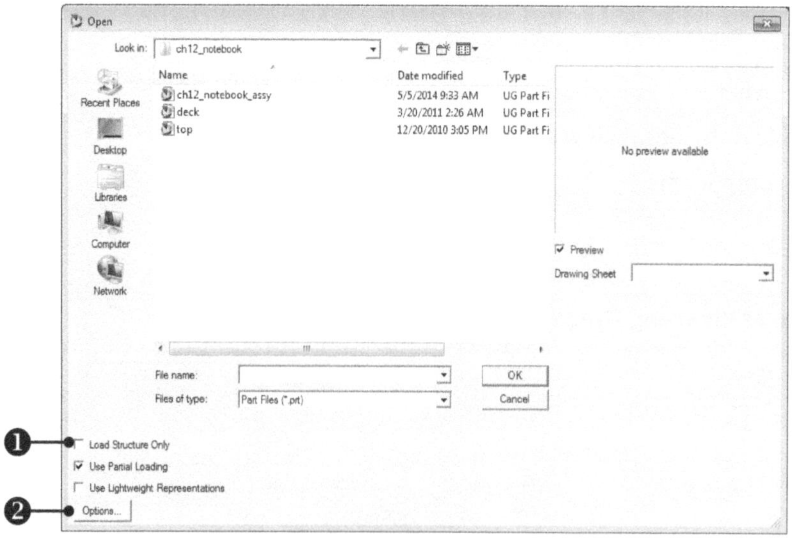

Fig 12-22 Opening an Assembly File

If you click the **Options** button in the dialog box, the **Assembly Load Options** dialog box is invoked as shown in Fig 12-23 and you can specify detailed load options.

③ **Part Versions** Option Group: Specifies where to search the master part of the components.

► **As Saved**: Searches components in the same folder as the assembly file was saved. The structure of folder has to be the same.

► **From Folder**: Searches components in the same folder as the assembly file. Sub-folders are not searched.

► **From Search Folders**: Searches components in the specified folder. You have to enter ... after the folder name to search the sub-folders.

④ **Scope** Option Group: Specifies the scope of the components to load.

► **All Components**: Loads all components.

► **Structure Only**: Loads the assembly structure only. Geometries of the components are not visible.

► **As Saved**: Loads components as the assembly file saved.

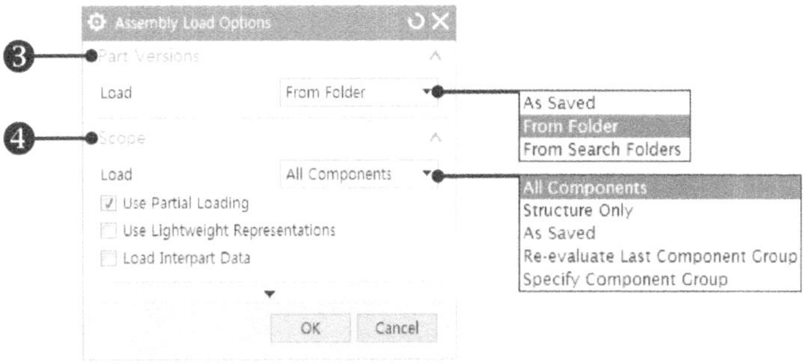

Fig 12-23 Assembly Load Options Dialog Box

Use Partial Loading and Load Interpart Data Option

► **Use Partial Loading**: Load components partially. You can load a component fully by pressing **MB3 > Open > Component Fully** on the desired components in the assembly navigator.

► **Load Interpart Data**: Loads part files needed to update interpart data, even if the part files would otherwise not be loaded.

Exercise 04 Opening the Assembly File

Folder: ch12_notebook
File: ch12_ex04_assy.prt

Let's open an assembly according to the suggested process and learn about the assembly load option.

Opening File

1. Choose **File** tab > **Close > All Parts** to close all loaded parts.

2. Create a folder named top_parts in the ch12_notebook folder and move the top.prt file into the top_parts folder.

3. Click **Open** in the **File** tab.

4. Select ch12_ex04_assy.prt and specify the assembly load option as shown in Fig 12-24.

5. Click **OK** in the **Open** dialog box.

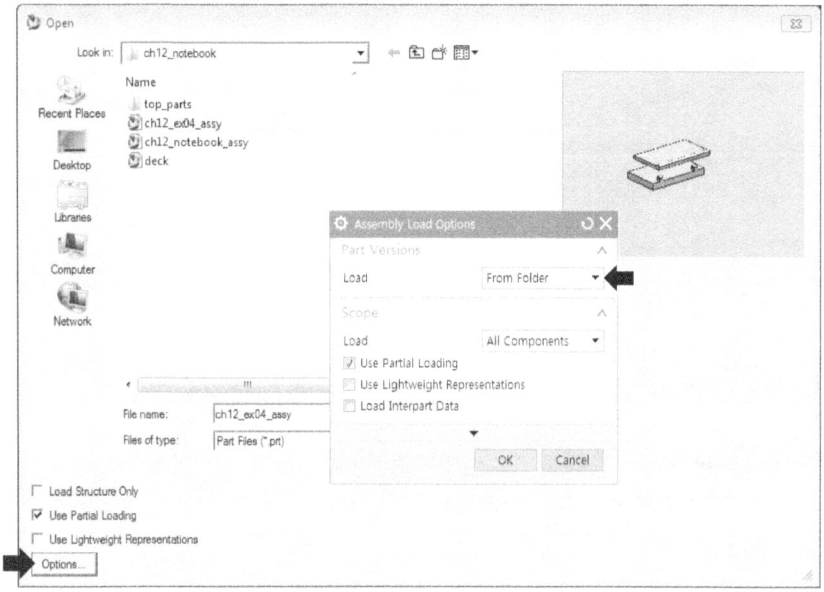

Fig 12-24 Opening an Assembly

A warning message as shown in Fig 12-25 is displayed. The load option is not the correct option to load the **Top** component.

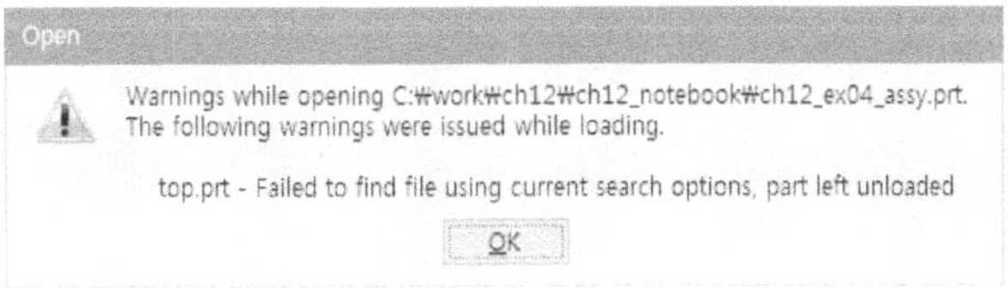

Fig 12-25 Warning Message

6. Click **OK** in the message box.

You will notice that

- Only the **Deck** component is shown in the graphics window.
- The **Top** component in the assembly navigator is not checked and dimmed.

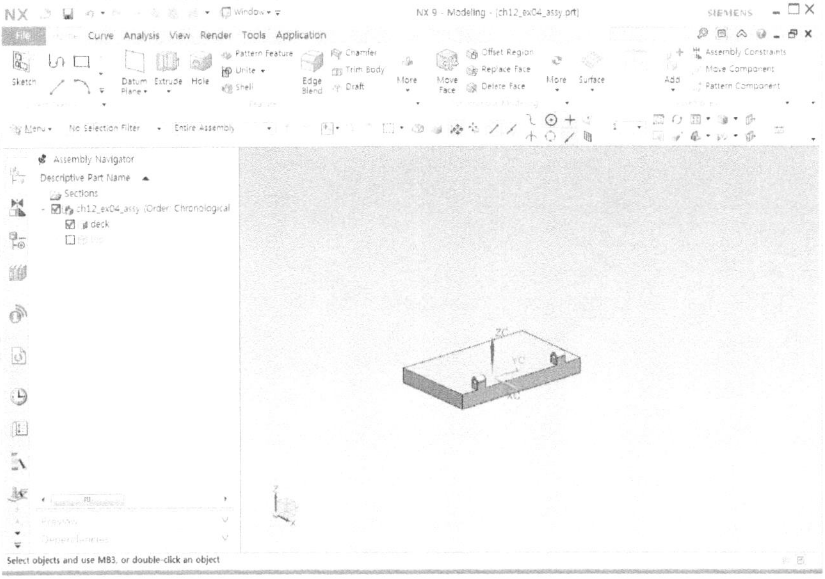

Fig 12-26 Opened Assembly

Changing Assembly Load Option

1. Click the check box in front of the **Top** component in the assembly navigator. The warning message still appears.

2. Click **OK** in the message box.

3. Choose **File > Options > Assembly Load Options** in the **Menu** button.

① Choose **From Search Folders** in the **Load** dropdown list.

② Specify the search folder by clicking the button ❷ designated in Fig 12-27. Make sure that you enter three dots after the name of the folder.

③ Press the **Enter** key. Confirm that the search folder has been added in the list area as shown in Fig 12-27.

Click the check box in front of the **Top** component in the assembly navigator. You will notice that the component is shown in the graphics window.

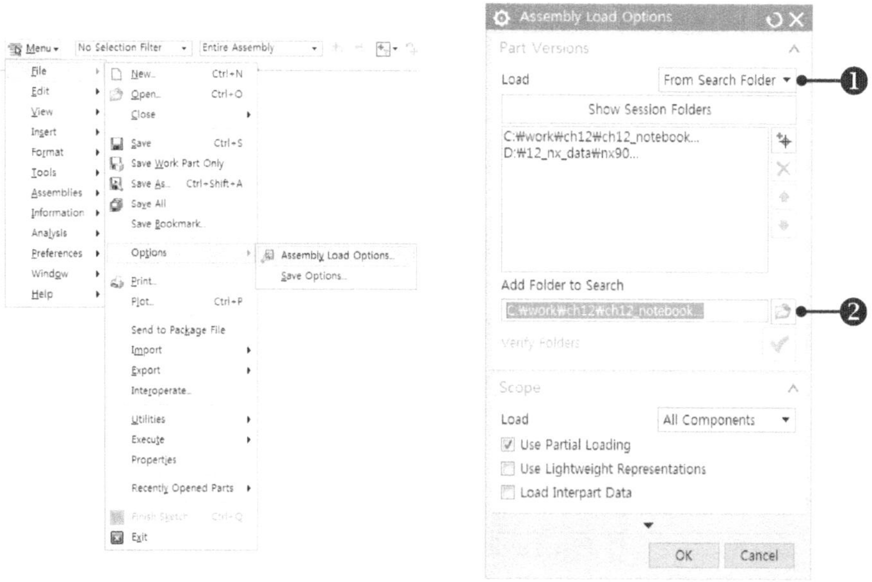

Fig 12-27 Assembly Load Option

4. Press **MB3 > Close > Part** on the **Top** component as shown in Fig 12-28.

5. Choose **File > Close > All Parts.**

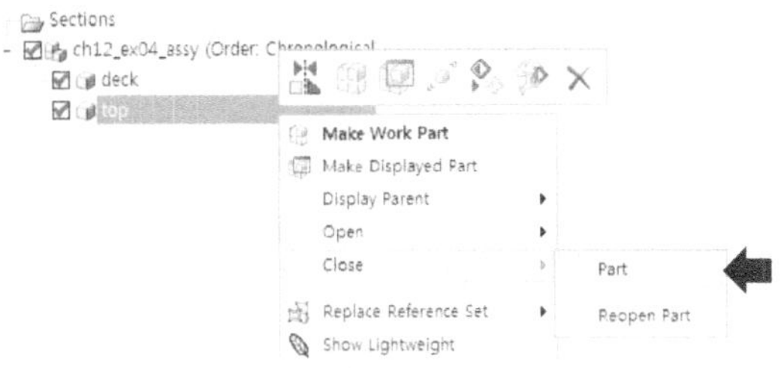

Fig 12-28 Closing a Component

END of Exercise

12.4.7 Using the Assembly Navigator

Column

You can make the assembly navigator wider as shown in Fig 12-29 by dragging the vertical boundary.

Ⓐ **Read-Only**: The diskette symbol means that you have write privilege to the part file. The lock symbol means that you cannot save the part file after modification. The dotted box means that the component is partially loaded and you cannot identify if you have write privilege to the file. You can load the component fully by pressing **MB3 > Open > Component Fully** on the component.

Ⓑ **Modified**: Informs you that the part file has been modified.

Ⓒ **Reference Set**: Informs you of the reference set that is used to display the component in the assembly.

Fig 12-29 Columns of Assembly Navigator

Pop-up Menu

Pop-up menus are available by pressing MB3 on the component.

Ⓐ **Hide**: Hide the selected components in the assembly. You can show the hidden components in the pop-up menu in the same way.

Ⓑ **Show Only**: Show only the selected components and hide all other components.

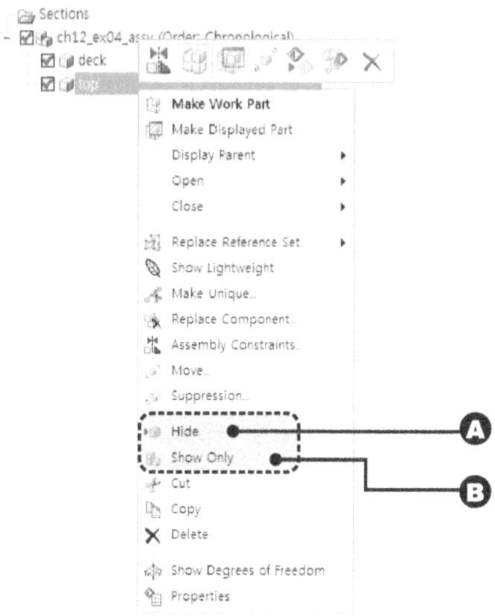

Fig 12-30 Pop-up Menu

12.4.8 Moving and Rotating Component

Using the **Move Component** icon in the **Assemblies** icon group, you can move or rotate the un-constrained components.

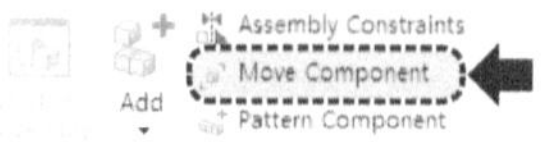

Fig 12-31 Move Component Icon

Folder: ch12_notebook
File: ch12_ex05_assy.prt

Moving and Rotating Component **Exercise 05**

1. Open the given assembly file ch12_ex05_assy.prt.

2. Click the **Move Component** icon in the **Assemblies** icon group. You are prompted to select components to move in the cue line.

3. Select the **Top** component in the part navigator or in the graphics window. The number of selected components is displayed in the option field ❶ in Fig 12-32.

4. Click MB2 or click the **Specify Orientation** option button specified by ❷ in Fig 12-32.

5. Confirm that the **Motion** option is **Dynamic.**

You will notice that the orientation handle is activated as shown in Fig 12-32. You can use the handle to move components in the following way.

Ⓐ Drag the move handle: You can move the selected component along the axis.
Ⓑ Drag the rotate handle: You can rotate the component about the normal axis to the plane.
Ⓒ Drag the origin handle: You can move the component to an arbitrary location.

6. Close all loaded files to proceed with the next exercise.

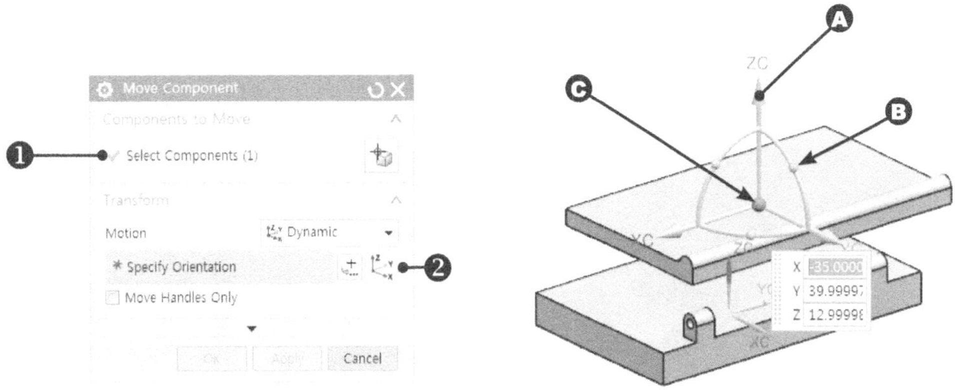

Fig 12-32 Moving Component

END of Exercise

You can specify how to move the component in the **Motion** dropdown list as shown in Fig 12-33.

You can copy the component while moving or rotating components or manually in the **Mode** dropdown list. The **Copy** option is available after clicking the **More** button on the lower part in the dialog box.

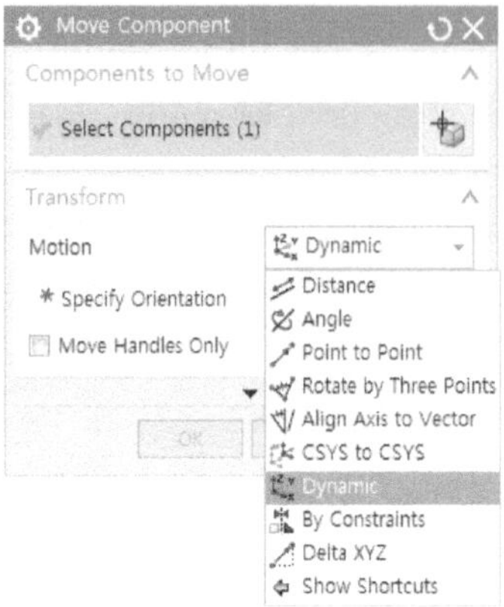

Fig 12-33 Motion Option

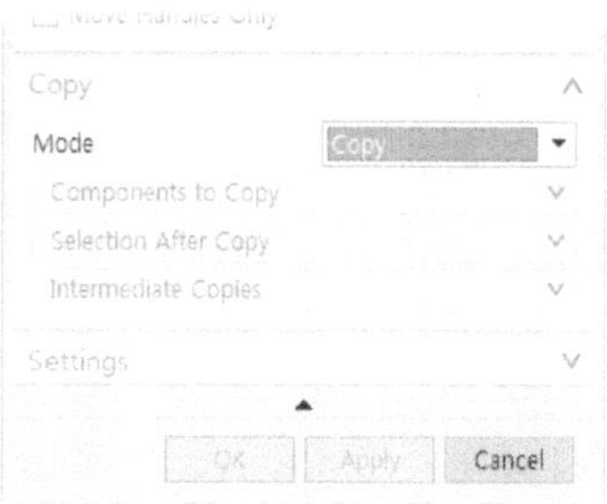

Fig 12-34 Copy Option

Exercise 06 Moving from Point to Point

Folder: ch12_notebook
File: ch12_ex06_assy.prt

Move the **Top** component using the **Point to Point** option from the point Ⓐ to Ⓑ shown in Fig 12-35.

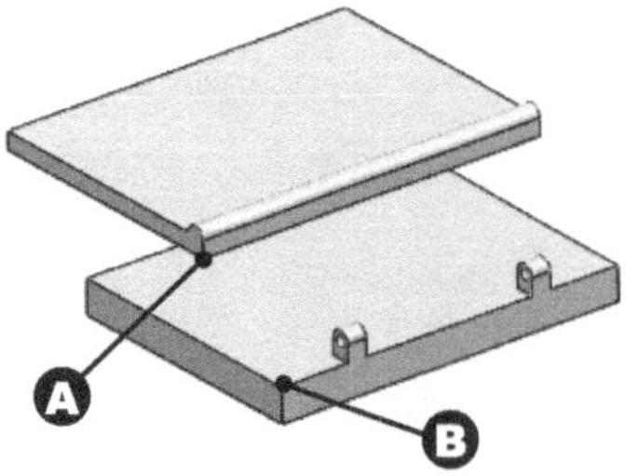

Fig 12-35 Before

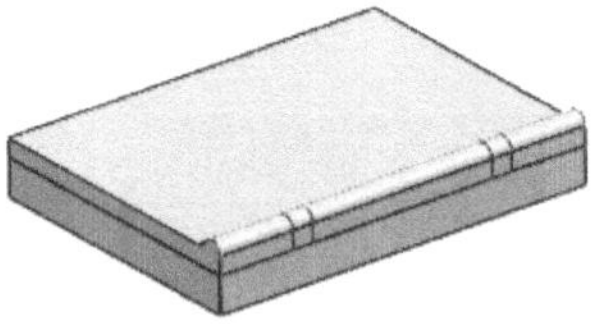

Fig 12-36 After

END of Exercise

12.4.9 Copy of Component

In most cases, you will add several components which point to the same master part. For example, many bolts and nuts of the same standard will be used to assemble an assembly. The geometry of each component will be the same, but each component can have its respective position, orientation and color in the assembly.

You can add a component that points to the geometry of the same master part through the following three methods.

Copy/Paste

1. Select the component in the assembly navigator.
2. Press **CTRL + C** in the keyboard to copy the components.
3. Click the assembly where to paste the components.
4. Press **CTRL + V** in the keyboard to paste the components.

Note that the components will be overlapped. Therefore, you are recommended to move the pasted component while the components are selected.

Add Icon

You can add components as many times as required using the **Add** command or you can specify the number of components to add in the **Duplicates** option. The **Duplicate** option is available after clicking the **More** button on the lower part of the dialog box.

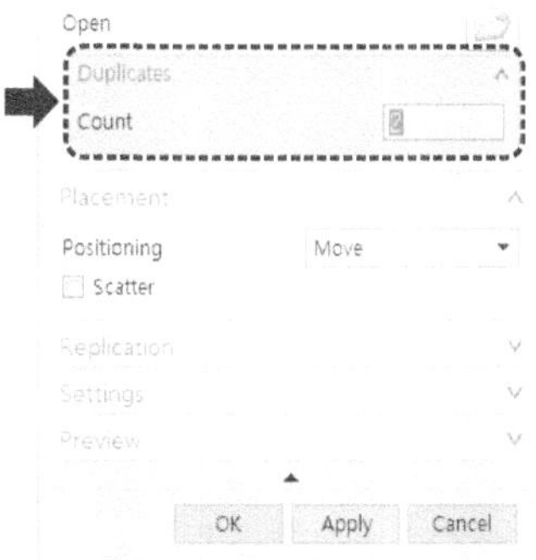

Fig 12-37 Duplicate Option

Copy Option in the Move Component Dialog Box

You can copy components while you are moving or rotating the component with the **Move Component** command.

12.5 Assembly Constraints

Using the **Assembly Constraints** icon in the **Assemblies** icon group, you can constrain the movement or rotation of components within an assembly. Remember that the position and orientation of an object in the space can be defined completely with six degrees of freedom, i.e. three translational and three rotational degrees of freedom.

Fig 12-38 Assembly Constraints Icon

When you are constraining components in an assembly, you have to specify the fixed component and then constrain the other components with respect to the fixed component.

You cannot move the fully constrained component with the **Move Component** command. If you try to move the fixed component, a message as shown in Fig 13-39 is invoked.

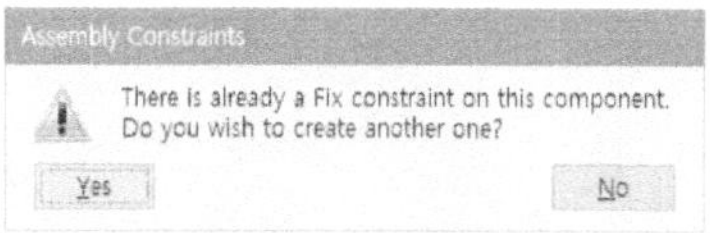

Fig 12-40 Assembly Constraints Message

Several types of assembly constraints are available in the **Type** dropdown list in the **Assembly Constraints** dialog box as shown in Fig 12-40.

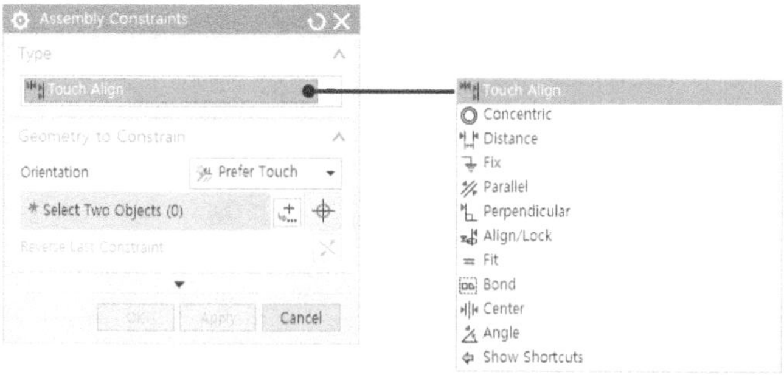

Fig 12-39 Types of Constraint

12.5.1 Fix

Fix one or more component at the current location. You can constrain another component with respect to the fixed component or other fully constrained components. Applied constraint is listed in the **Constraints** container in the assembly navigator as shown in Fig 12-41 and the symbol is marked in the component as shown in Fig 12-42.

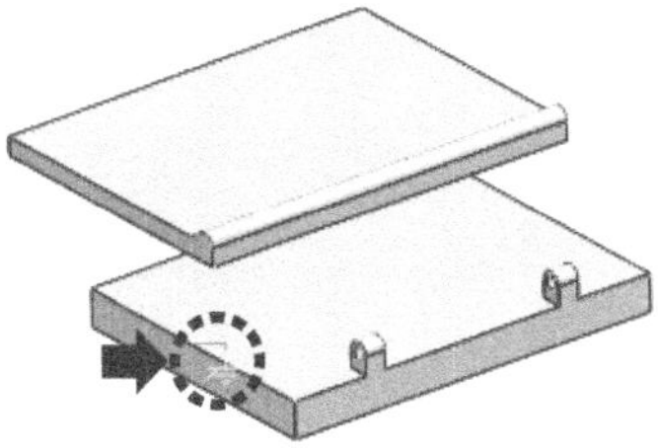

Fig 12-41 Fix Symbol

Fig 12-42 Fix Constraint in the Constraints Container

You can delete a constraint in the container or convert to other corresponding constraints by pressing MB3 on the constraint.

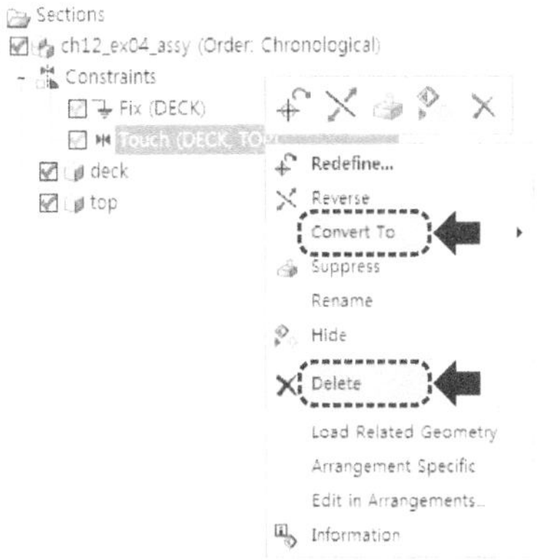

Fig 12-43 Pop-up Menu of Constraint

! *Moving the Fixed Component*

You can move the fixed component by pressing **Yes** in the message window shown in Fig 12-39. All other components constrained with respect to the fixed component will move to satisfy the applied constraint.

12.5.2 Touch/Align

You can apply a touch or align constraint between two lines, points or faces or in a combination of two objects allowed with the **Touch/Align** constraint. The **Orientation** options shown in Fig 12-44 are available.

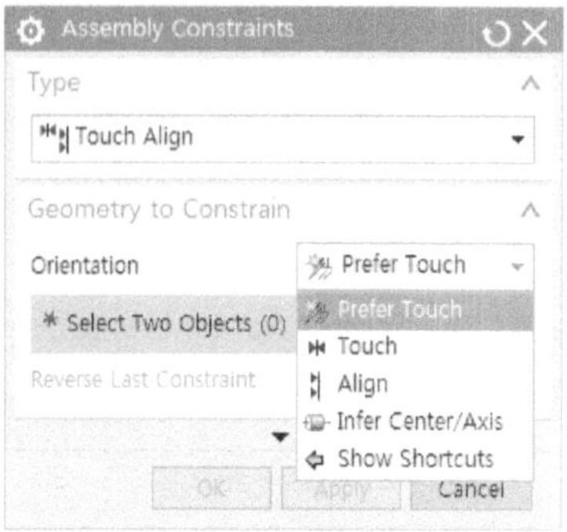

Fig 12-44 Orientation Option

Touch

The two objects are made coincident with the orientation vectors reverted. For example, the normal vectors of the two faces shown in Fig 12-45 are reverted while the two faces become coincident.

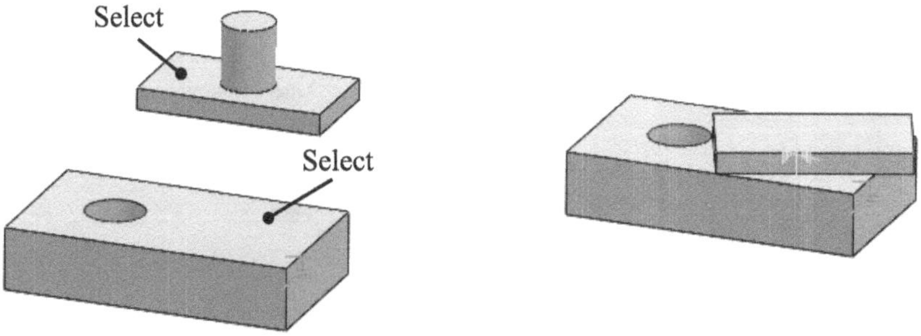

Fig 12-45 Applying Touch Constraint

Align

The two objects are made coincident with the orientation vectors aligned. For example, the normal vectors of the two faces shown in Fig 12-45 are aligned while the two faces become coincident.

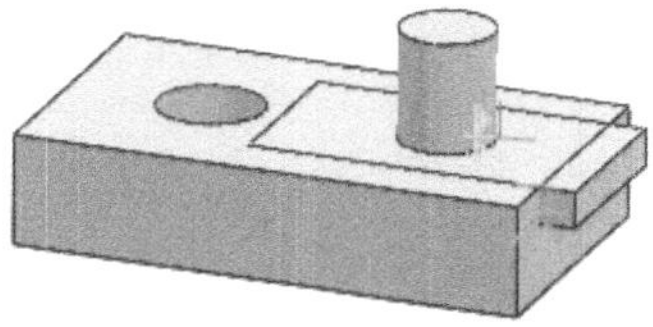

Fig 12-46 Applying Touch Constraint

Prefer Touch

When both the **Touch** and **Align** constraints are available, **Touch** is applied as a preference.

Infer Center/Axis

You can select the centerline of the cylindrical or conic faces by selecting the faces easily. If you do not use this option when aligning the centerlines, you have to select the centerline very carefully.

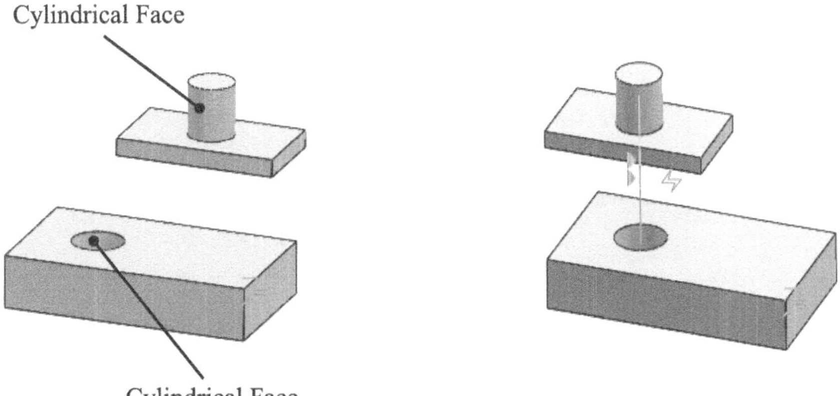

Fig 12-47 Aligning Centerlines with Infer Center/Axis Option

Reversing Touch and Align

You can convert **Touch** to **Align** and vice versa using the **Reverse Last Constraint** option in the dialog box or by choosing the **Reverse** option in the constraint pop-up menu as shown in Fig 12-48.

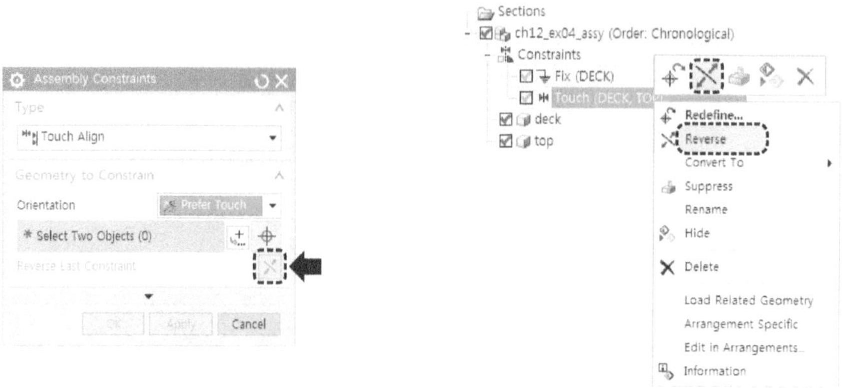

Fig 12-48 Converting Touch and Align

Note that constraint conflict may occur when reversing the constraint orientation. The conflicted constraints and components are marked with red x mark as shown in Fig 12-49.

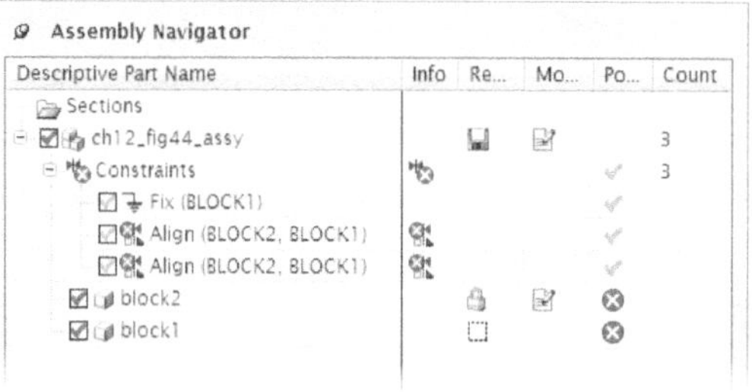

Fig 12-49 Conflicted Constraints and Components

Let's constrain the notebook assembly given in ch12_ex07_assy.prt. We will fix the **Deck** component and constrain the **Top** component with the **Touch/Align** constraint.

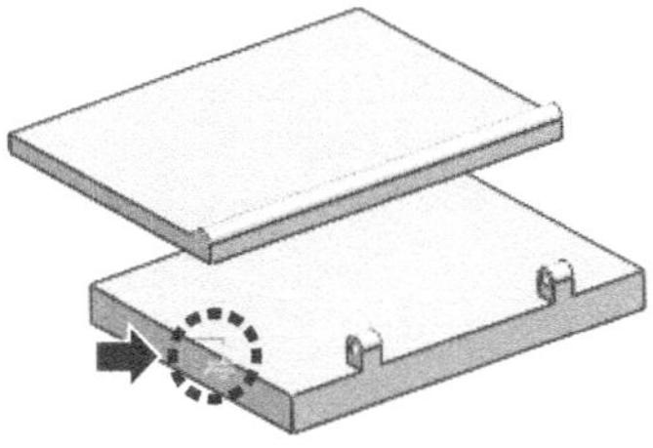

Fig 12-50 Fix Symbol

Fig 12-51 Fix Constraint

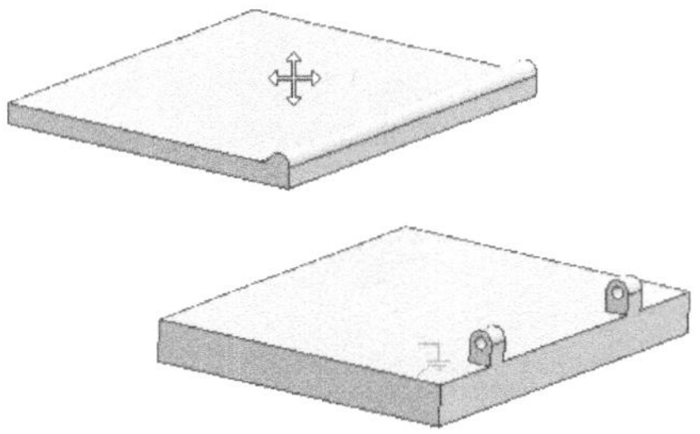

Fig 12-52 Dragging Component

Dragging Component

You can drag the unconstrained component **"while the Constraint dialog box is activated"**. Also, you can move the unconstrained component with the **Move Component** command.

Fix

1. Open the assembly file ch12_ex07_assy.prt in the ch12_notebook folder. Use the load option **From Folder**.

2. Click the **Assembly Constraints** icon in the **Assemblies** icon group.

3. Select **Fix** in the **Type** dropdown list.

4. Select the **Deck** component in the graphics window.

5. Click **Apply** in the dialog box. Identify the **Fix** symbol in the component and the **Fix** constraint in the **Constraints** container as shown in Fig 12-51.

Touch/Align - 1

1. The **Constraint** dialog box is still active. If it is closed, click the **Assembly Constraints** icon.

2. Select **Touch/Align** in the **Type** dropdown list.

3. Click the **Top** component with MB1 and drag as shown in Fig 12-52.

4. Select **Prefer Touch** in the **Orientation** dropdown list and select the two faces Ⓐ and Ⓑ as shown in Fig 12-53.

5. Click **Apply** in the dialog box.

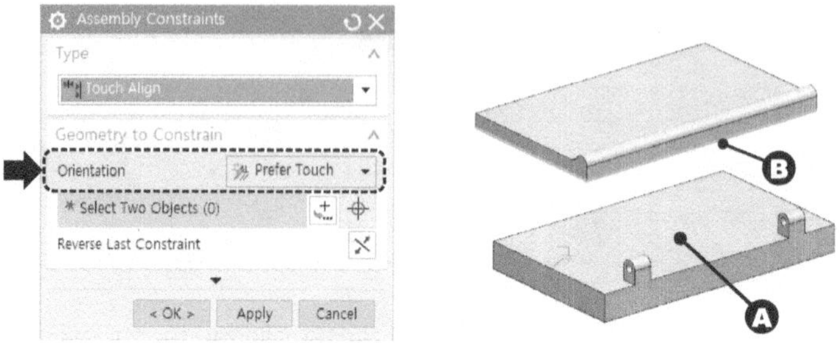

Fig 12-53 Selecting Faces

Verify that the **Touch** symbol is marked between the components and in the **Constraints** container in the assembly navigator.

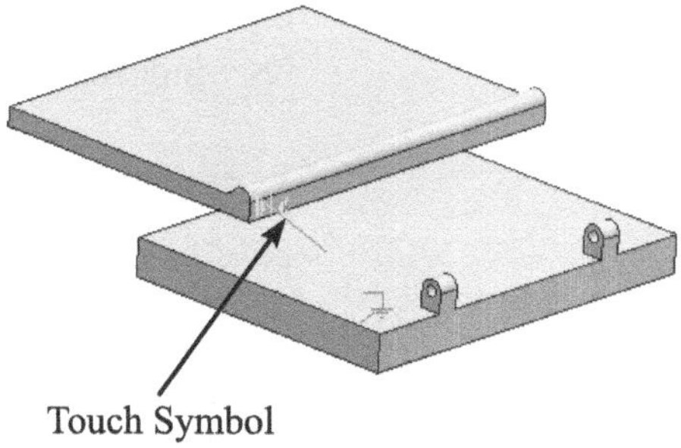

Fig 12-54 Touch Constraint

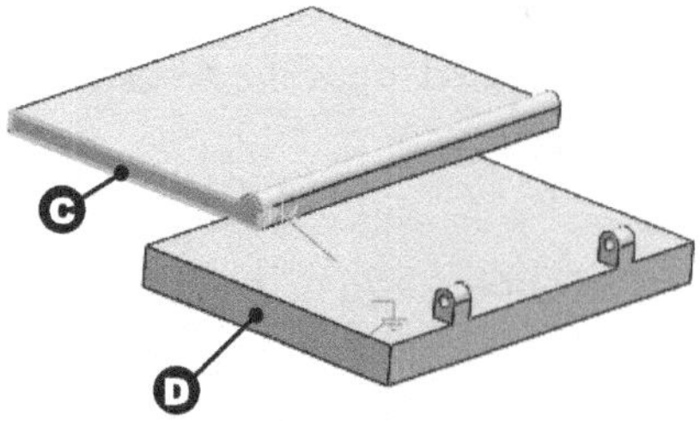

Fig 12-55 Selecting Faces

6. Select the faces Ⓒ and Ⓓ as shown in Fig 12-55. Note that the **Orientation** option is still **Prefer Touch**. The result is the **Align** constraint as shown in Fig 12-56.

7. Choose **Reverse Last Constraint** in the **Assembly Constraints** dialog box as shown in Fig 12-57.

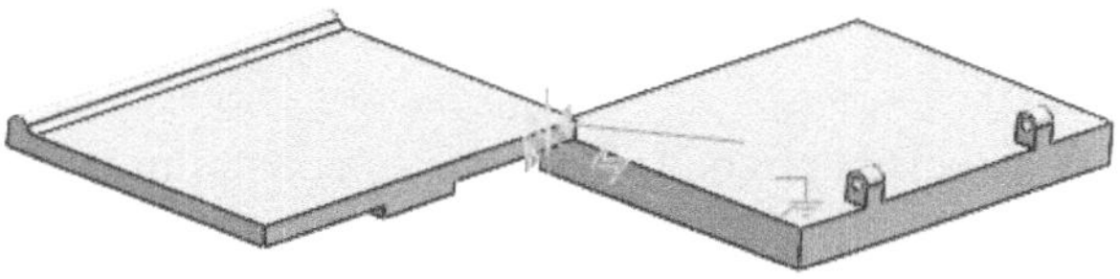

Fig 12-56 Result of Touch/Align

8. Confirm that the component faces are aligned as shown in Fig 12-58. This means that the **Touch** constraint has been reversed to the **Align** constraint.

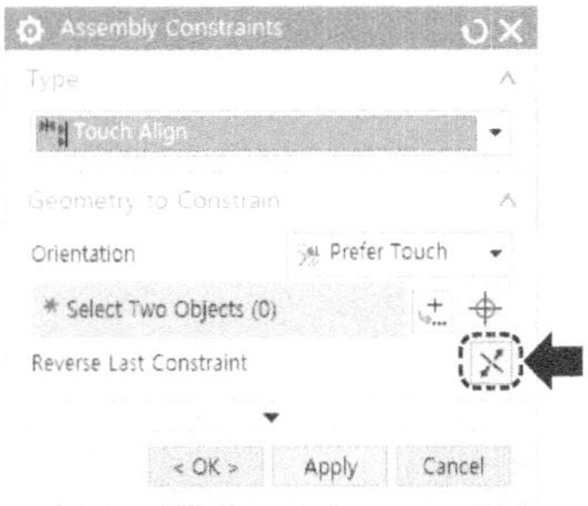

Fig 12-57 Reverse Option

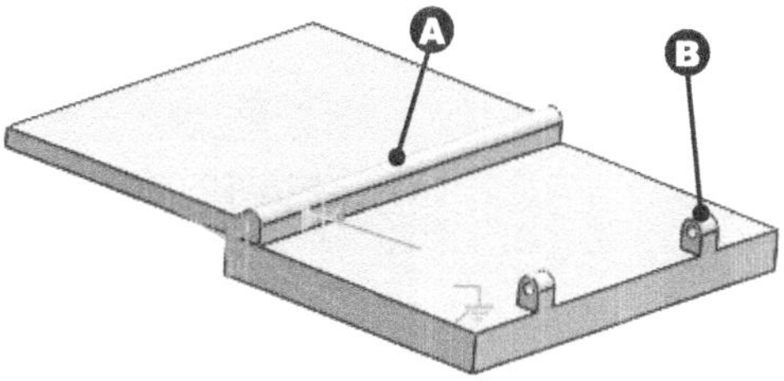

Fig 12-58 Reversed Constraint

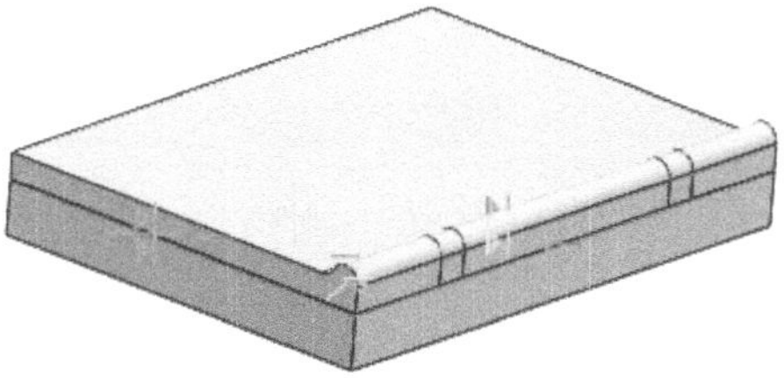

Fig 12-59 Fully Constrained Components

Touch/Align - 2

1. Choose **Infer Centerline/Axis** in the **Orientation** dropdown list of the **Assembly Constraints** dialog box.

2. Select the cylindrical faces **A** and **B** as shown in Fig 12-58. You can select the centerlines. The **Top** component is fully constrained as shown in Fig 12-59.

END of Exercise

12.5.3 Center

The center of the two objects is aligned. This type of constraint is used when the **Touch/Align** constraint is not available. Note that only one to one alignment is available with the **Touch/Align** constraint.

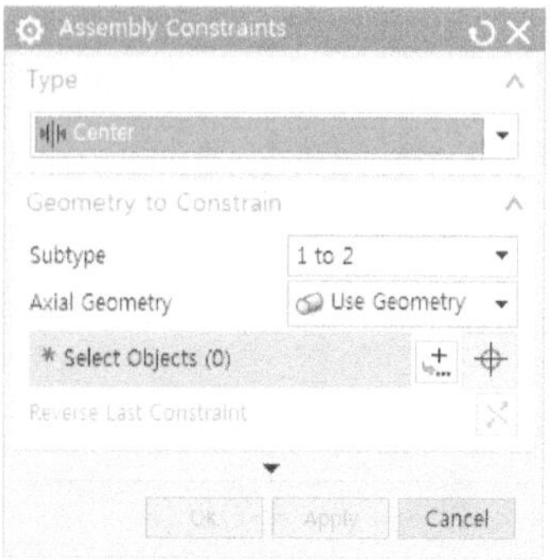

Fig 12-60 Options of Center Constraint

1 to 2

You can align the first object with the center of the second and third objects. Select the objects in the order designated in Fig 12-61.

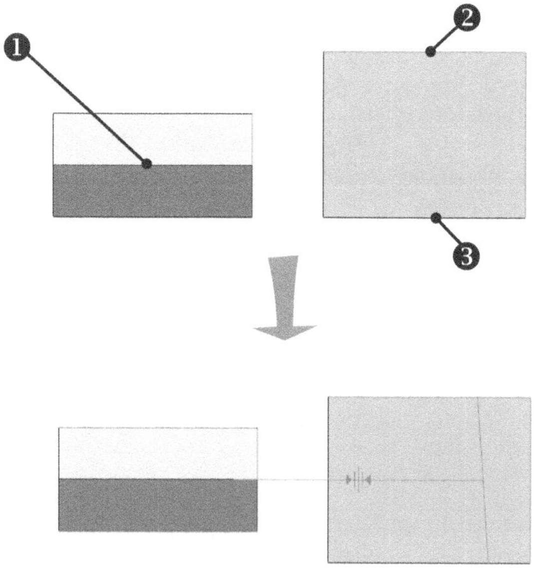

Fig 12-61 Center Constraint (1 to 2 Option)

2 to 1

You can align the center of the first and second objects with the third object. Select the objects in the order designated in Fig 12-62.

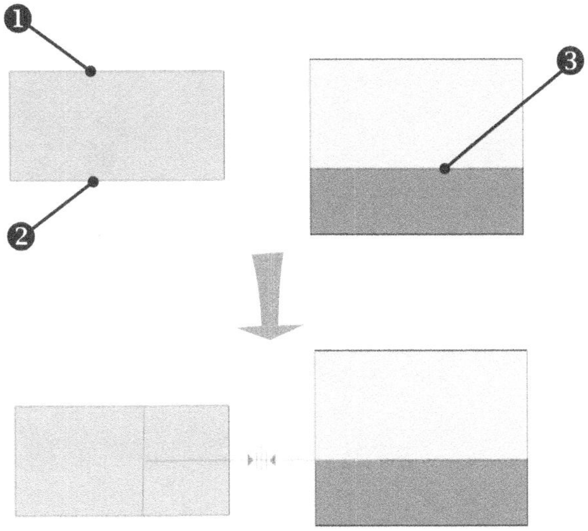

Fig 12-62 Center Constraint (2 to 1 Option)

2 to 2

You can align the center of the first and second objects with the center of the third and fourth objects. Select the objects in the order designated in Fig 12-63.

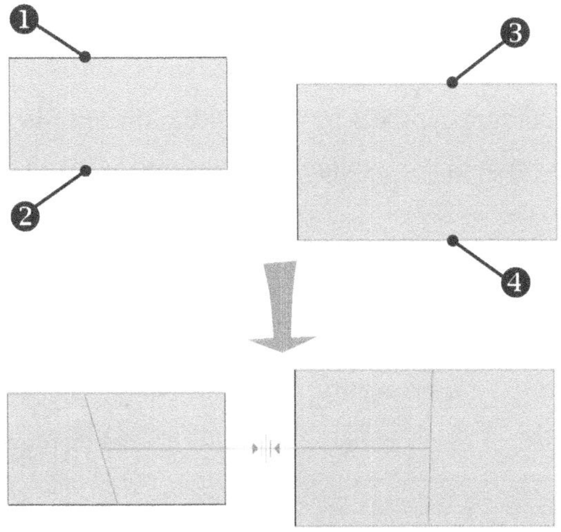

Fig 12-63 Center Constraint (2 to 2 Option)

Exercise 08 Center Constraint

Folder: ch12
File: ch12_ex08_assy.prt

Let's constrain the two components so that component Ⓐ is assembled on component Ⓑ at the center as shown in Fig 12-64. Fix component Ⓑ.

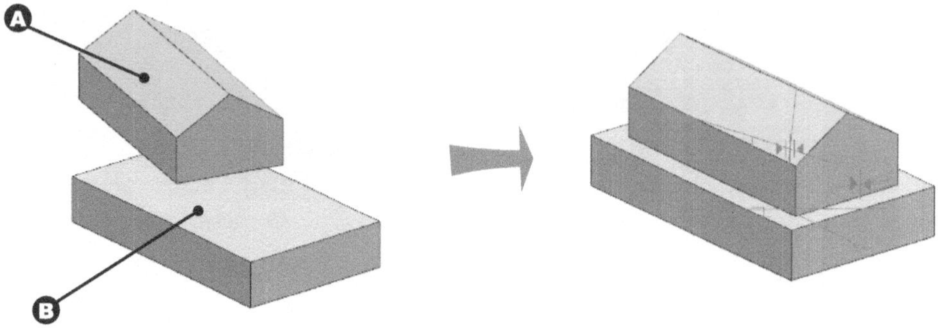

Fig 12-64 Constraining Center

Hints!

1. Use the **1 to 2** or **2 to 1** option to align the center edge with the longitudinal center of component Ⓑ.
2. Use the **2 to 2** option to align the lateral centers of the two components.
3. Use **Touch/Align** to make the faces touch each other.

END of Exercise

Hiding the Symbol of Constraints

You can hide all constraint symbols by unchecking the **Display Constraints in the Graphics Window** option that is available by pressing MB3 on the **Constraints** container.

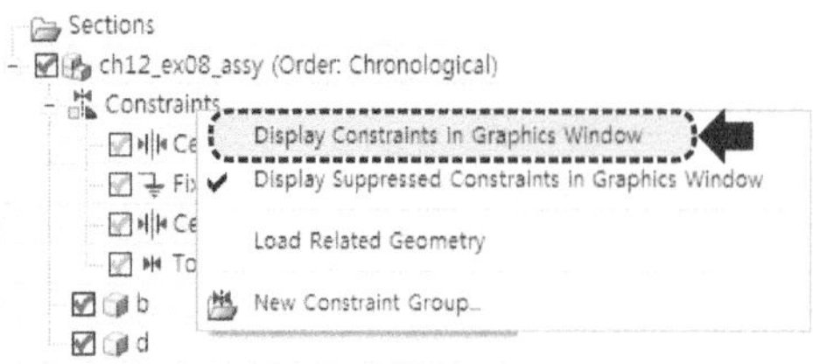

Fig 12-65 Pop-up Menu

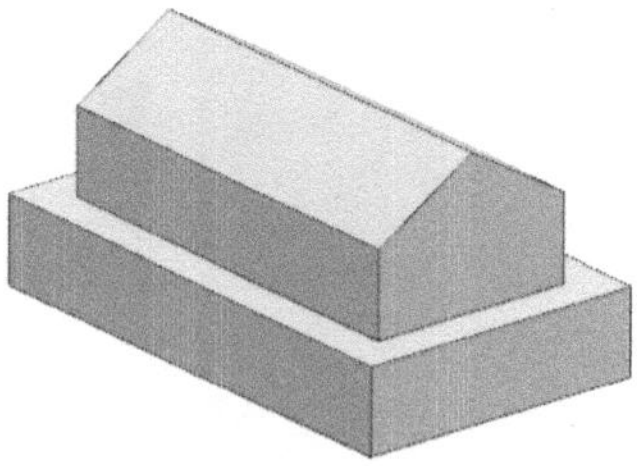

Fig 12-66 Constraints Symbol Hidden

12.5.4 Concentric

You can make the center of the planar circles aligned. The plane of the circle is also aligned or touched by choosing the **Reverse Last Constraint** button.

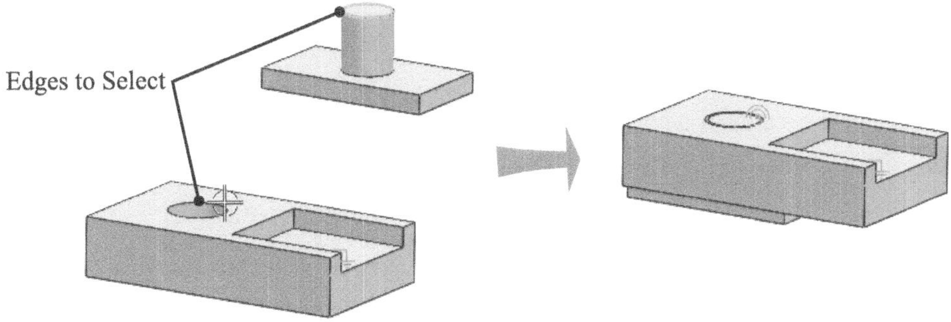

Fig 12-67 Applying Concentric Constraint

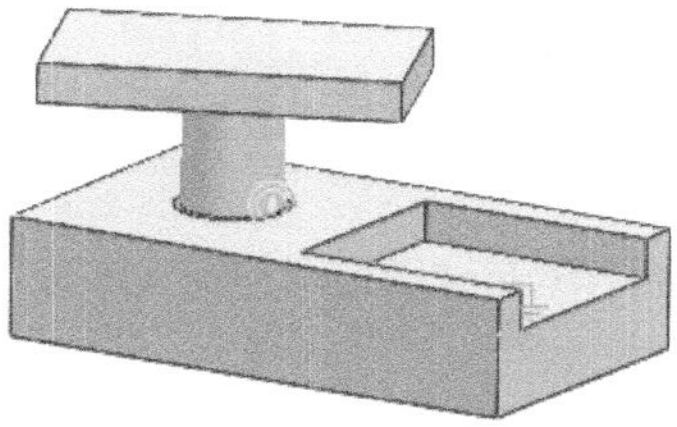

Fig 12-68 Reversed Concentric Constraint

12.5.5 Other Constraints

Angle

Applies angle between two objects.

Bond

The selected components are constrained with respect to each other as if they are bonded.

Fit

Brings together two cylindrical faces with equal radiuses. If the radiuses later become non-equal, the constraint is invalid.

Distance

Applies distance between two objects.

Parallel

Makes two planar or linear objects parallel to each other.

Perpendicular

Makes two planar or linear objects perpendicular to each other.

\

12.5.6 Verifying Constraint Status

You can verify the status of a constraint by looking at the **Position** column in the assembly navigator as shown in Fig 12-69. The **Position** column can be added by clicking MB3 on the title area and choosing **Columns** > **Position** in the pop-up menu.

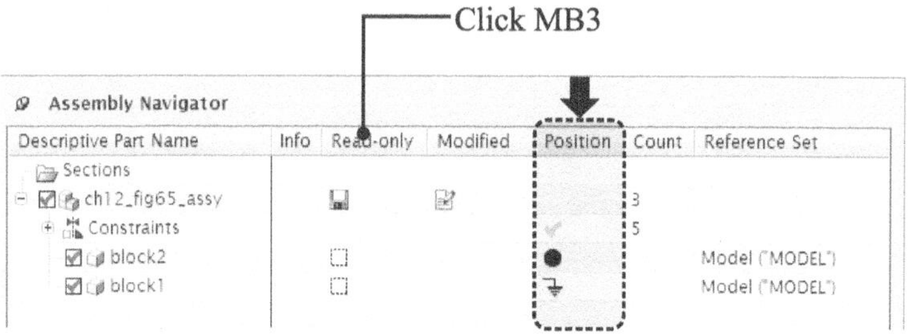

Fig 12-69 Verifying Status of the Assembly Constraint

Meaning of Symbols

○ No constraints are applied for the component.

◐ Some constraints are applied for the component but the component is not fully constrained.

● The component is fully constrained.

⏚ The component is fixed.

Note that you cannot make the components fully constrained when there is no fixed component. Therefore, you have to specify at least one component to be fixed and then constrain the other components with respect to the fixed components or to other fully constrained components.

Show Degrees of Freedom

By choosing **Show Degree of Freedom** on the component's pop-up menu, you can verify the number of unconstrained degrees of freedom and the type of DOF.

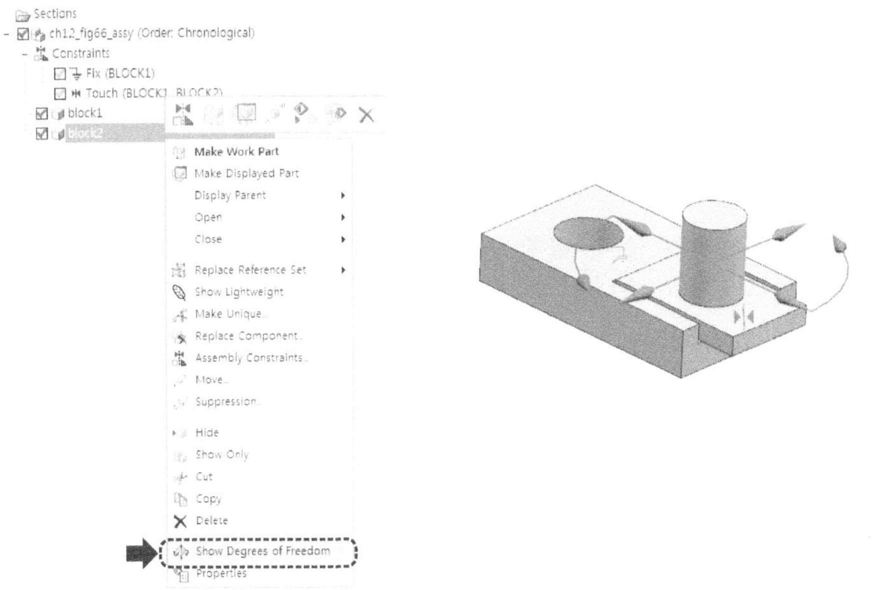

Fig 12-70 Identify the Types of Remaining DOF

12.5.7 Show and Hide Constraints

You can hide or show constraints by selecting the constraints according to the following methods.

- ▸ Use the **Show** or **Hide** icon in the **View** tab.
- ▸ Choose **Show** or **Hide** in the pop-up menu that is available by clicking MB3 on the desired constraints in the **Constraints** container in the assembly navigator.

In addition to the above mentioned methods, you can hide or show constraints that are defined between the selected components or that are connected to the selected components. You can execute the **Show and Hide Constraints** command by choosing **Menu** button > **Assemblies** > **Component Position** > **Show and Hide Constraints.**

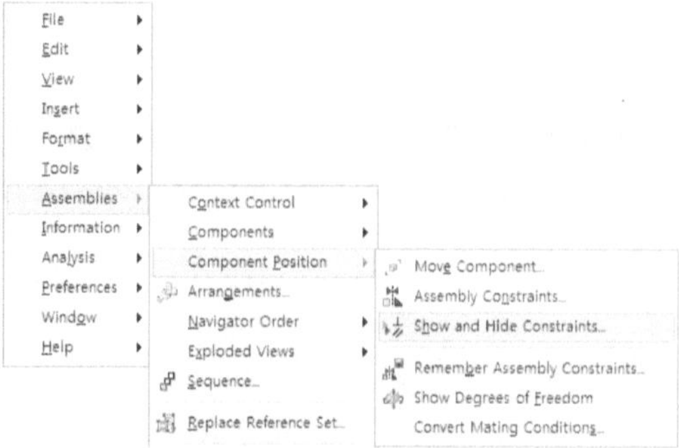

Fig 12-71 Show and Hide Constraints Icon

If you choose **Between Components** in the **Show and Hide Constraints** dialog box as shown in Fig 12-72, the constraints between the selected components are shown and all other constraints are hidden. If you check the **Change Component Visibility** option, other components in addition to the selected ones are also hidden.

If you select one or more components with the **Connected to Components** option, all constraints related to the selected components are shown.

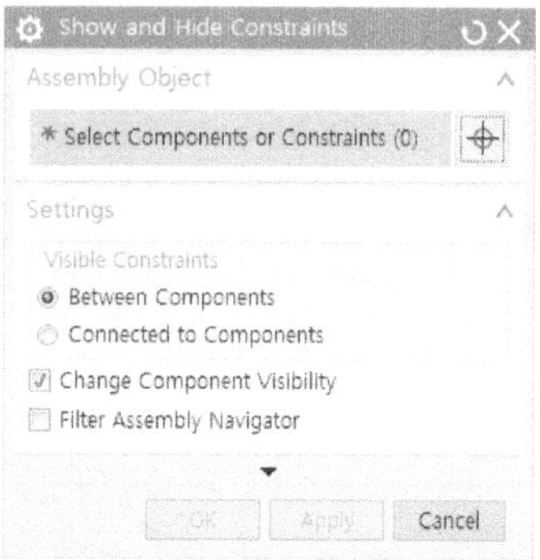

Fig 12-72 Show and Hide Constraints Dialog Box

Using the **Show and Hide Constraints** command, you can identify the interested constraints in the **Constraints** container in the assembly navigator and delete or modify the constraint.

12.5.8 Suppressing Constraints

You can suppress constraints by pressing **MB3 > Suppress** on the constraints as shown in Fig 12-73. The suppressed constraints are considered to be not applied. Therefore, you can move and drag the corresponding components.

You can unsuppress the constraints by pressing **MB3 > Unuppress** on the suppressed constraints.

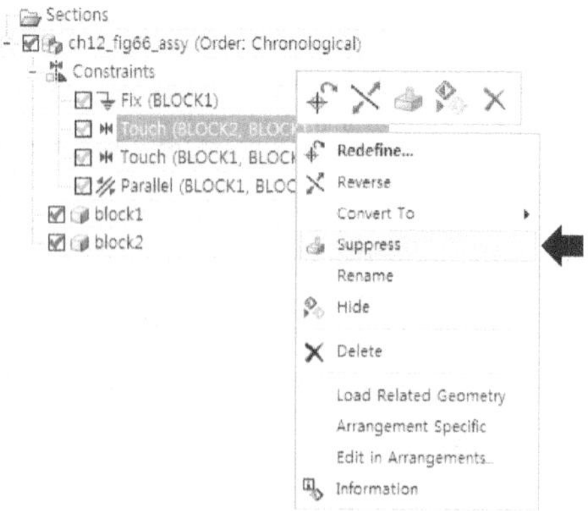

Fig 12-73 Suppress Menu

12.6 Reference Set

You have clearly created datum coordinate systems, datum planes, sketches, etc. when you are creating a part model as shown in Fig 12-74. However, the component displays only the solid body when they are added in an assembly as shown in Fig 12-75. The geometry that can be shown when the part is added to an assembly is defined in the **Reference Set** when modeling the part.

Fig 12-74 Bushing Part

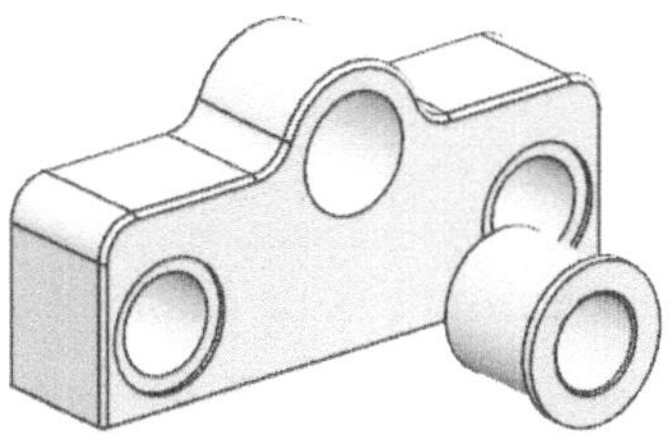

Fig 12-75 Bushing Component

The following three types of reference sets are defined by default when you create the model.

Model

Displays the sheet body and solid body.

Entire Part

Displays all modeling objects in the part model.

Empty

Displays nothing.

The reference set to apply for a component can be chosen in the **Add Component** dialog box as shown in Fig 12-76. The **Settings** option is available after clicking the **More** button on the lower part of the dialog box. Note that the default reference set is **Model** and only the solid body and sheet body in the master part has been displayed.

You can define your own reference set by choosing **Format > Reference Sets** in the **Menu** button during the part modeling.

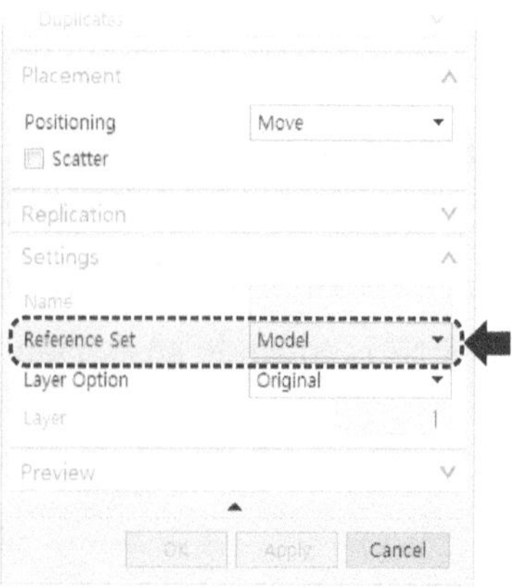

Fig 12-76 Add Component Dialog Box

The reference set can be changed after adding the components. Press MB3 on the components and choose the desired reference set in the pop-up menu as shown in Fig 12-77. Note that the current reference set is dimmed out in the pop-up menu.

After displaying all modeling objects in a component, you can use the datum planes, datum axes, sketches, etc. to constrain the component, or reference the objects in modeling another component part in top down assembly modeling.

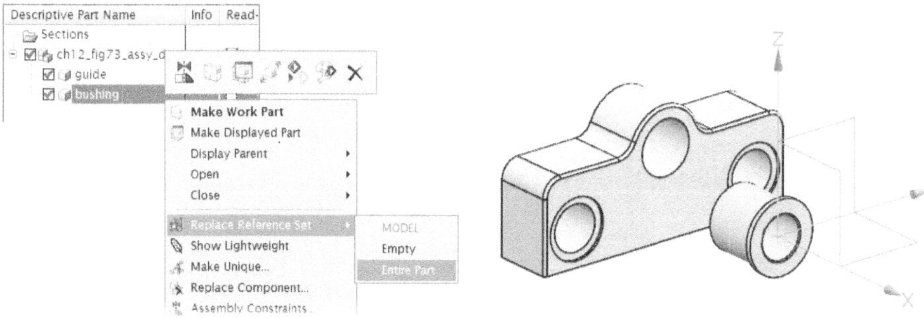

Fig 12-77 Changing the Reference Set

Let's constrain the **Bushing** component in the given assembly file. We will fix the **Guide** component and access the reference set to constrain the **Bushing**.

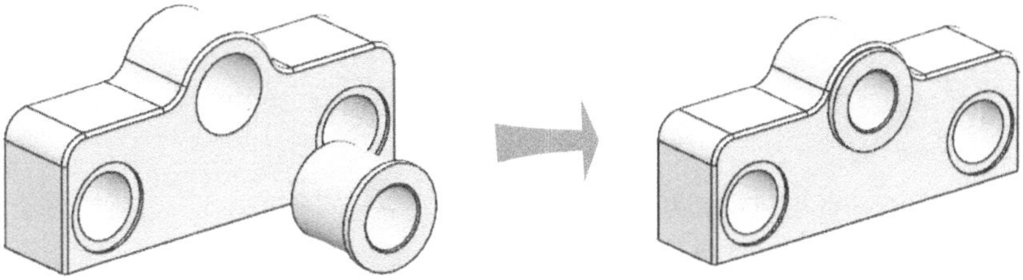

Fig 12-78 Assembly for Exercise

Concentric Constraint

1. Open the given assembly part file ch12_ex09_assy.prt.

2. Fix the **Guide** component.

3. Click the **Assembly Constraints** and choose **Concentric** in the **Type** dropdown list.

4. Select the circular edges **A** and **B** as shown in Fig 12-78. You do not need to rotate the **Bushing** component as shown in the figure.

5. Click **OK** in the dialog box.

Fig 12-80 shows the assembly after applying the **Concentric** constraint. Note that the **Bushing** component is not fully constrained yet.

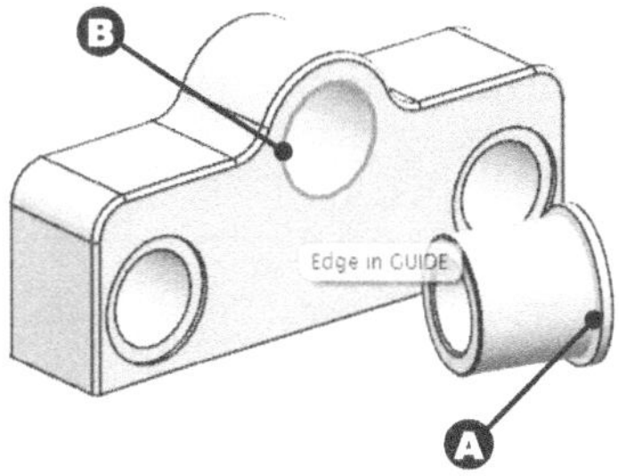

Fig 12-79 Edges to Select

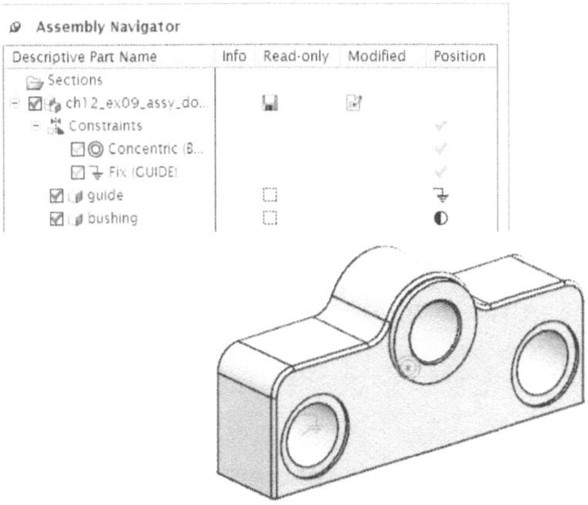

Fig 12-80 After Applying Concentric Constraint

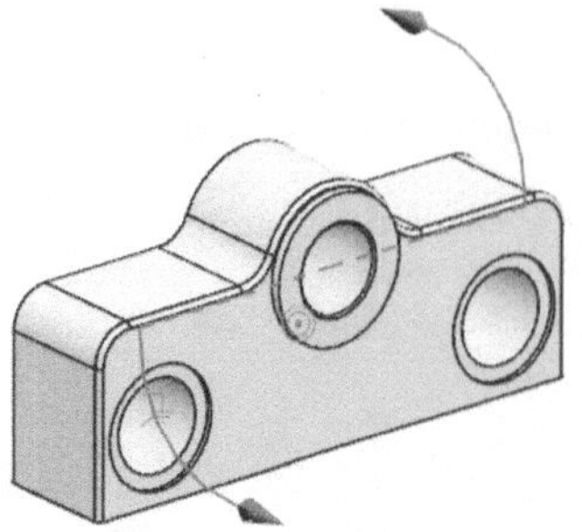

Fig 12-81 Verifying the DOF of Bushing Component

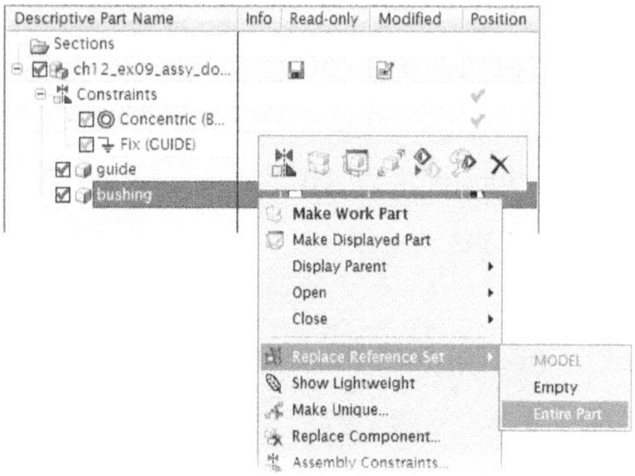

Fig 12-82 Changing Reference Set

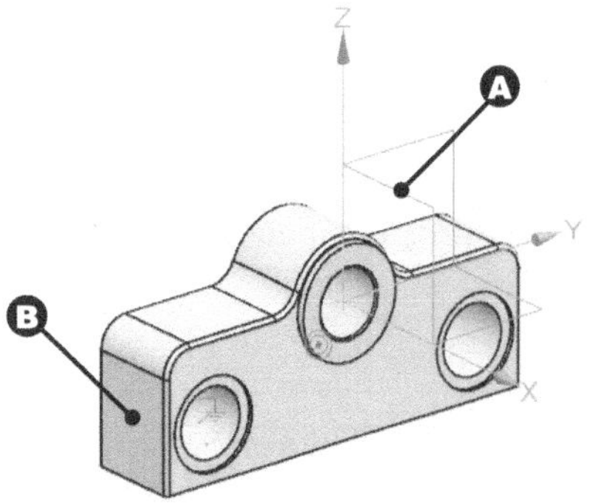

Fig 12-83 Selecting Planes

Verifying the DOF

1. Press **MB3 > Show Degrees of Freedom** on the **Bushing** component.

The remaining DOF is displayed as shown in Fig 12-81. Note that the component can rotate.

2. Press the **F5** key to remove the DOF display.

Change Reference Set and Constrain Rotational DOF

1. Press **MB3 > Replace Reference Set > Entire Part** on the Bushing component.

The datum coordinate system is shown like in Fig 12-83.

2. Click the **Assembly Constraints** icon in the **Assemblies** icon group.

3. Choose **Parallel** in the **Type** dropdown list.

4. Select the datum plane Ⓐ and the plane Ⓑ in the component as shown in Fig 12-83.

5. Click **OK** in the dialog box.

6. Confirm that the **Bushing** component is fully constrained in the **Positioning** column in the assembly navigator.

7. Change the reference set of the **Bushing** component to **Model**.

8. Uncheck the **Display Constraints in Graphics Window** option which is available by pressing MB3 on the **Constraints** container in the assembly navigator.

9. Close without saving the file.

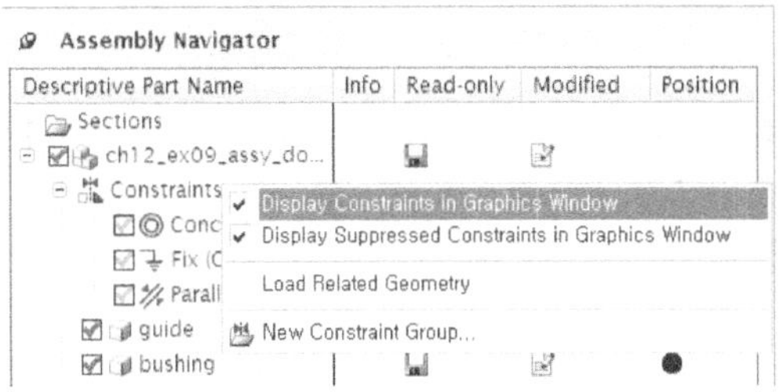

Fig 12-84 Hide Constraint Symbols

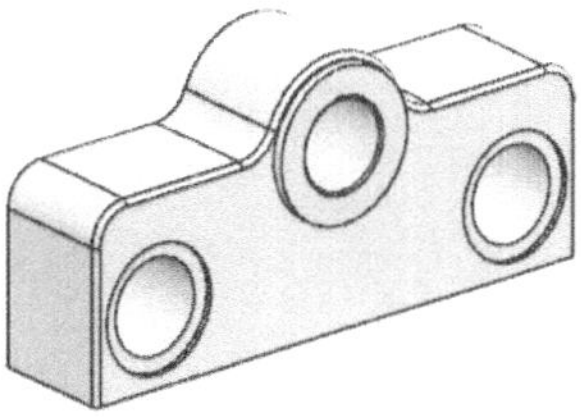

Fig 12-85 Completed Assembly

END of Exercise

Exercise 10 Creating Notebook Assembly

Folder: ch12_ex10

Create an assembly using parts given in the folder ch12_ex10. The name of the assembly file will be Notebook_assy.prt. Fix the **Deck** component and fully constrain all other components.

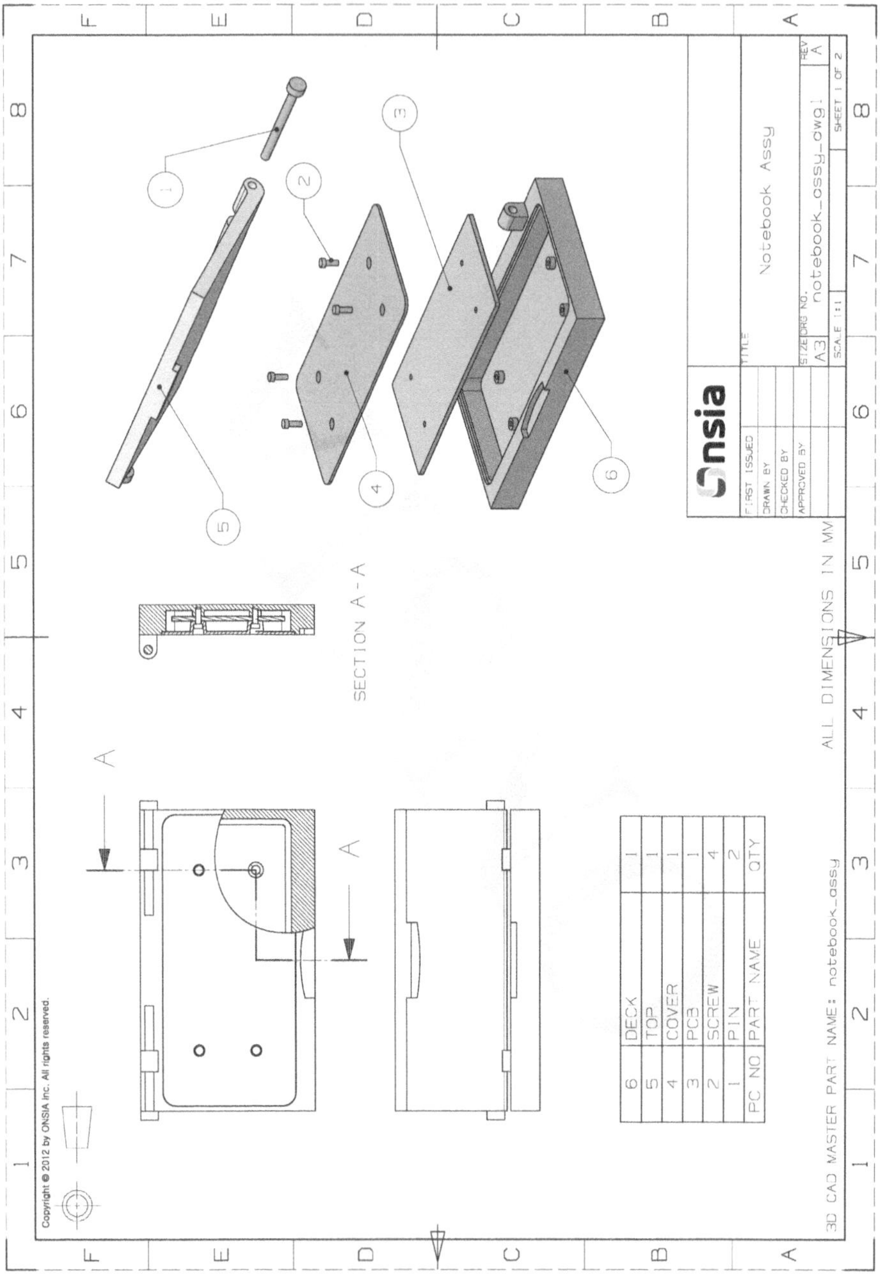

Fig 12-86 Notebook Assembly

Chapter 13

Assembly Design II (Top-Down Assembly)

■ **After completing this chapter you will understand**

- top-down modeling process.
- how to check for interference.
- how to modify a master part during the assembly process.
- how to create a new component in an assembly.
- various methods in displaying an assembly.

13.1 Context Control

The process of creating or modifying certain parts in the context of assembly is called **Top-Down Assembly Design**. When you are performing top-down assembly modeling, you need to understand exactly in which file you are doing which modeling process. The process of managing your work part and the displayed part is called **Context Control**. Fig 13-1 shows the sub-menus of context control in the **Menu** button.

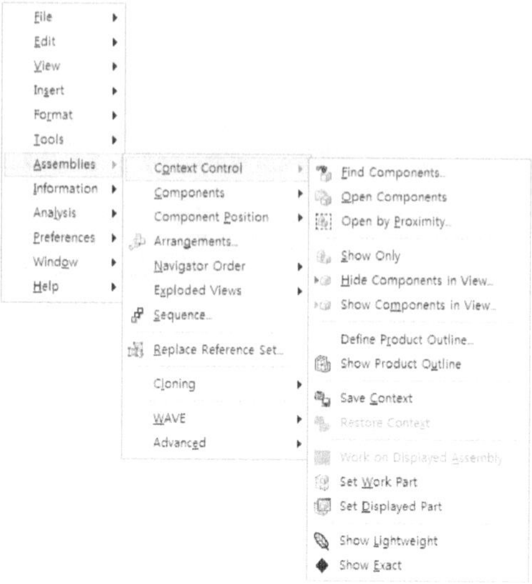

Fig 13-1 Context Control Menu

13.1.1 Closing Component

You can close a component or assembly by pressing MB3 on the corresponding item in the assembly navigator and choosing **Close** in the pop-up menu as shown in Fig 13-2. The closed component is unloaded, and you can identify the unloaded component in the assembly navigator as shown in Fig 13-3. Note that the assembly cannot show the geometry of the component unless it is re-loaded.

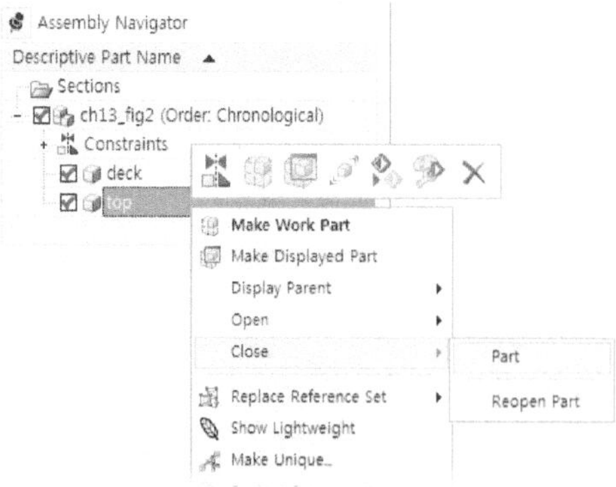

Fig 13-2 Close Menu

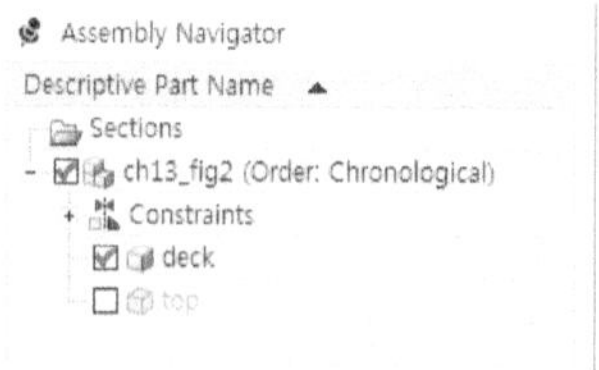

Fig 13-3 Closed Top Component

13.1.2 Opening Component

You can load the component geometry or sub-assembly by opening the part file as shown in Fig 13-4.

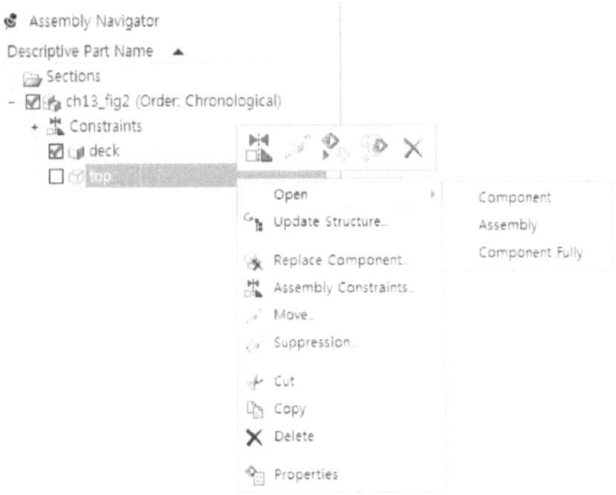

Fig 13-4 Open Menu

If you choose **Open > Component or Assembly** in the pop-up menu, the assembly shows only the geometry of the component. If you choose **Open > Component Fully**, you can load the attributes and link the information of the master part. If you do not have write privilege to the master part of the **Top** component, a lock symbol is marked in the **Read-only** column in the assembly navigator as shown in Fig 13-5.

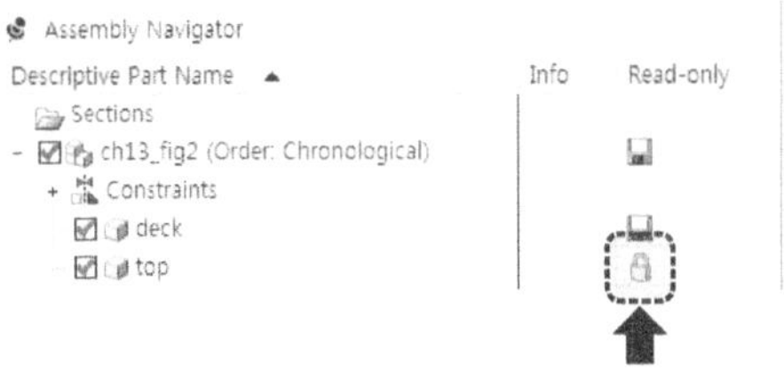

Fig 13-5 Lock Symbol

Other Symbols in Read-only Column

: You have write privilege to the part file of the component or sub-assembly.

: The component is not fully loaded. Write privilege is not identified.

You can acquire write privilege for the part file according to the following procedure.

1. Open the **Properties** dialog box and uncheck the **Read-only** option as shown in Fig 13-6.
2. Close the corresponding component in the assembly.
3. Open the component fully.

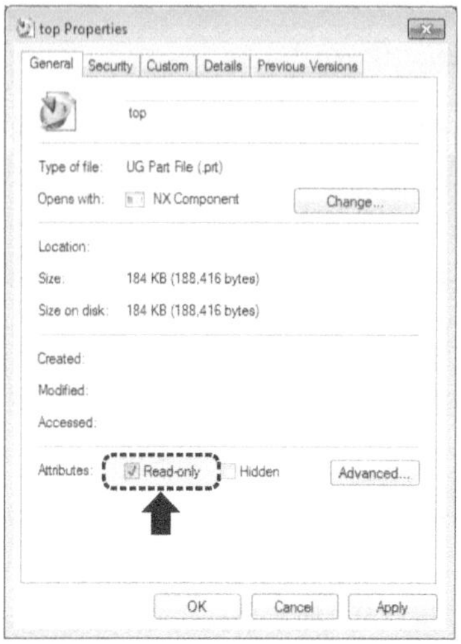

Fig 13-6 Read-only Option

13.1.3 Make Work Part

To modify the component geometry, you have to make the master part a work part. You can make the master part of the **Deck** component by clicking MB3 on the component and choosing **Make Work Part** in the pop-up menu as shown in Fig 13-7. Or you can make the component a work part by just double clicking the component in the assembly navigator.

If you make a component part a work part, the color of the other components become dimmed as shown in Fig 13-8. You can identify the work part in the assembly navigator by looking at the symbol. While the work part is symbolized in color, all other components are colored in gray wireframe as shown in the assembly navigator in Fig 13-8.

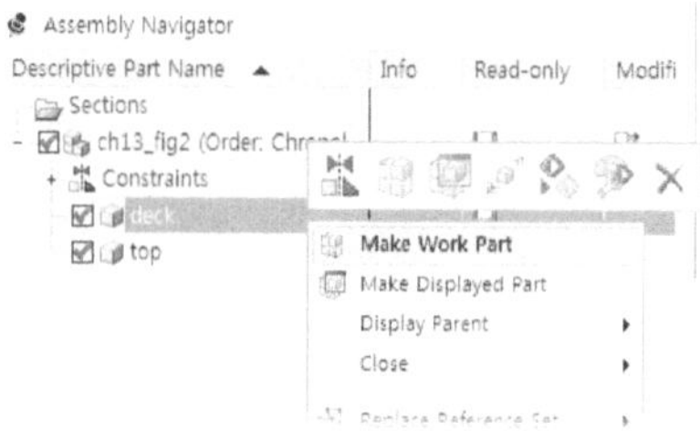

Fig 13-7 Make Work Part Option

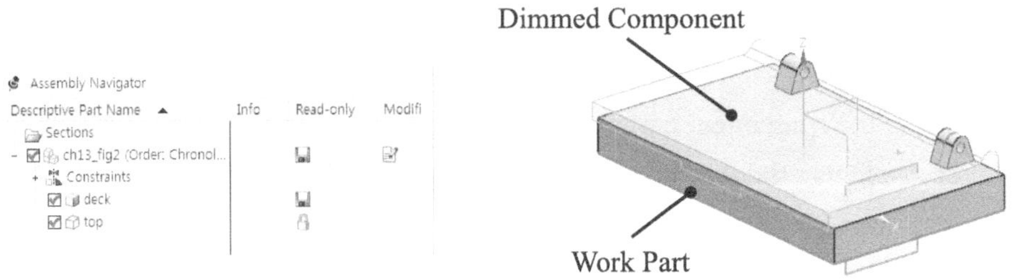

Fig 13-8 Identifying Work Part

Remember that making a component a work part means opening the master part of that component in the context of an assembly. The difference with opening the part file with the **File > Open** menu is that you can see other components in the assembly.

If you make a component a work part in an assembly, the modeling history of the component part is available in the part navigator. You will want to reference the part history because you are going to modify the master part.

If you make the read-only part a work part and try to modify its modeling history, the message shown in Fig 13-10 is displayed. You can modify the part by pressing the OK button. However, you cannot save the part.

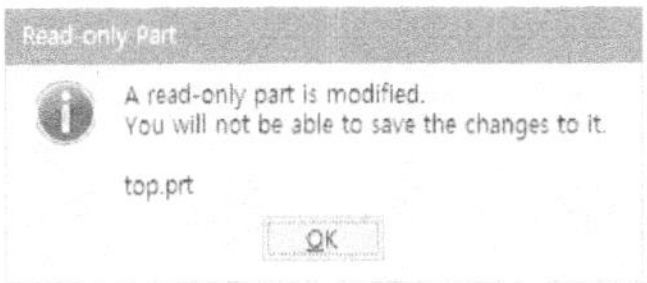

Fig 13-9 Read-only Message

Note that you have to make the assembly a work part after modifying the component part. Fig 13-10 shows the assembly navigator where the assembly is a work part. The icons are expressed in shaded color.

Fig 13-10 Assembly Part in Work

13.1.4 Make Displayed Part

You can display the component part or assembly in the graphics window. Fig 13-9 shows the result of displaying the assembly while the component part is a work part.

To display only the master part of the **Deck** component, press MB3 on the component and choose **Make Displayed Part**. The graphics window looks as if you have opened the part file as shown in Fig 13-12.

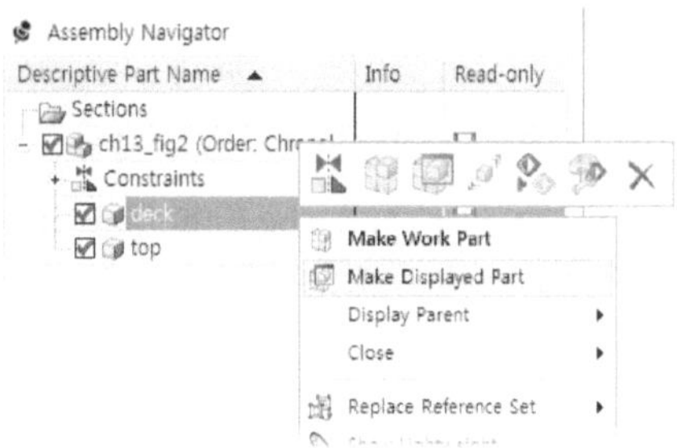

Fig 13-11 Make Displayed Part Menu

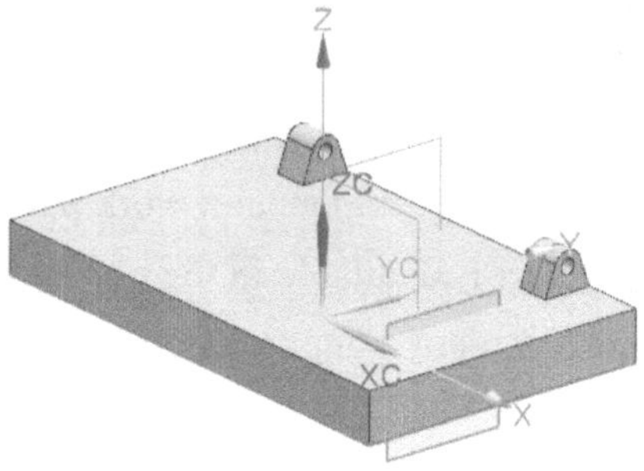

Fig 13-12 Displayed Deck Part

To display the assembly part in the graphics window as shown in Fig 13-14, click MB3 on the assembly file in the assembly navigator and choose **Display Parent > "name of assembly"** in the pop-up menu as shown in Fig 13-13. In this case, you have to remember that the **Deck** component is in the work part. To do the assembly related work such as constraining and interference check, you have to be sure to make the assembly part a work part.

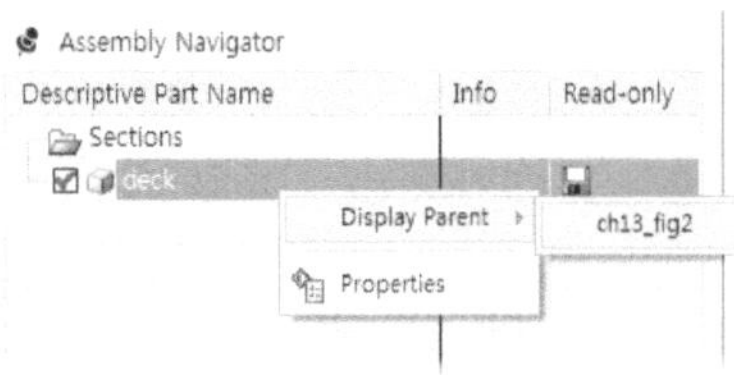

Fig 13-13 Making the Assembly a Displayed Part

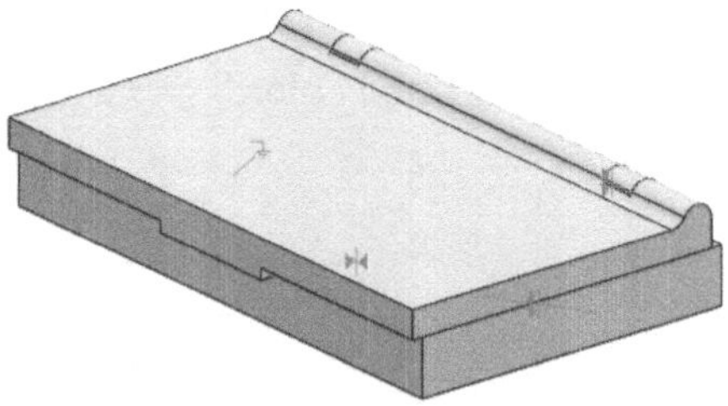

Fig 13-14 Displayed Assembly

What to do in which part?

To modify the geometry of the component part, you have to make the part a work part first. Because you are going to modify the master part, you will have to display the part navigator.

To do the assembly related work such as moving or constraining components and interference check, you have to make the assembly part a work part. You can do the assembly related work in the **Modeling** or **Gateway** application.

Folder: ch13_ex01
File: ch13_ex01_assy.prt

Modifying and Saving the Component Part — Exercise 01

The components in the given file have the same width, but the distance from edge to hinge center is different. Let's modify the geometry of the **Deck** component specified by Ⓐ in Fig 13-15.

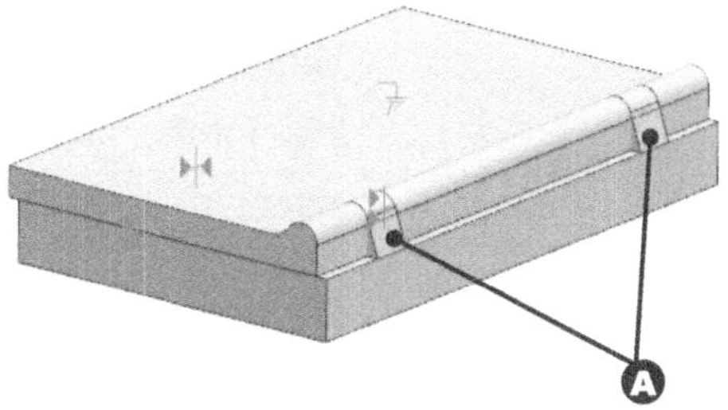

Fig 13-15 Geometry to Modify

Changing the Read-only Attribute

1. Open the assembly file given in the ch13_ex01 folder.
2. Select the two components and press **MB3 > Open > Component Fully** on one of the selected components.

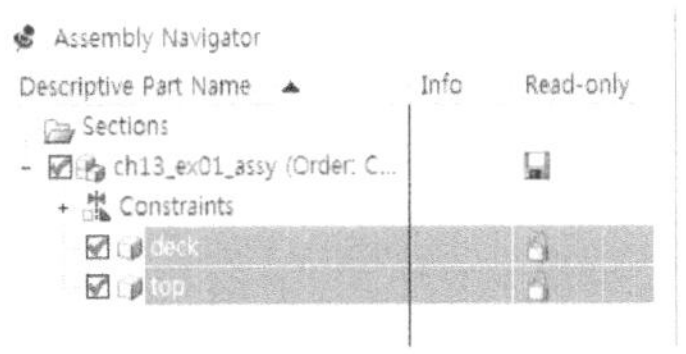

Fig 13-16 Assembly Navigator

Close the **Open** message box. Examine the read-only column in the assembly navigator and identify the lock symbol as shown in Fig 13-16.

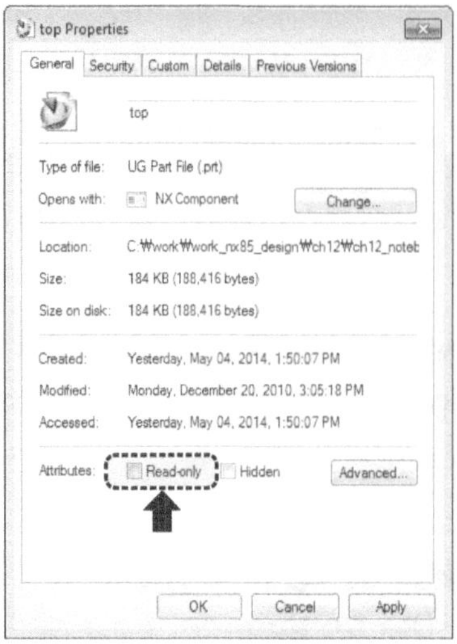

Fig 13-17 Read-only Attribute

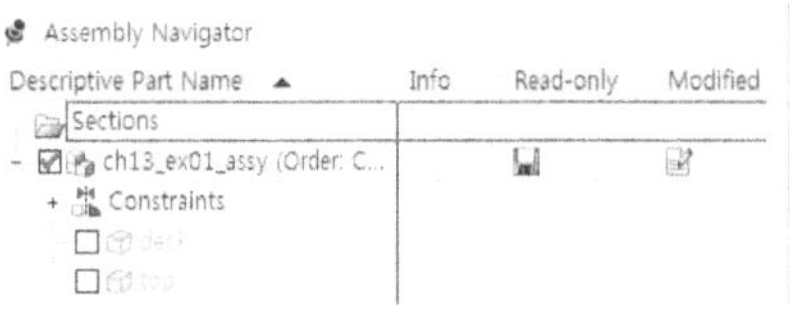

Fig 13-18 Assembly Navigator

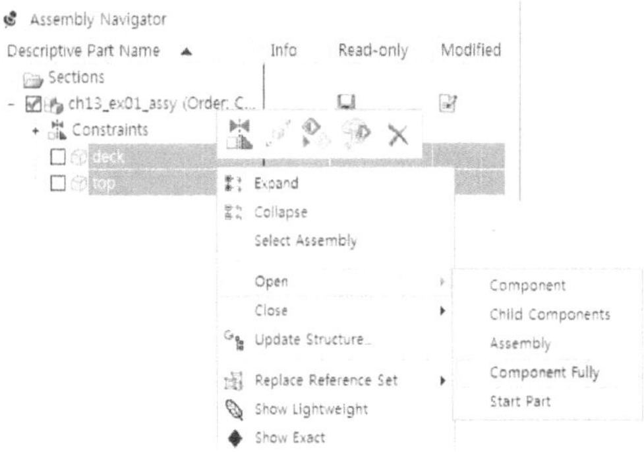

Fig 13-19 Opening Components Fully

3. Uncheck the **Read-only** attributes of the top.prt and the deck.prt file in the windows file explorer.

4. Press MB3 on the **Top** component and choose **Close > Part** in the pop-up menu.

5. Close the **Deck** component in the same way.

The assembly navigator at this step is shown as in Fig 13-18.

6. Select the two components and open the components fully in the way shown in Fig 13-19.

Verify that you have acquired write privilege for the part files in the assembly navigator.

Making the Deck Component a Work Part

1. Double click the **Deck** component to make it a work part.

The assembly navigator and the assembly are displayed as shown in Fig 13-20.

Fig 13-20 Making the Deck Component a Work Part

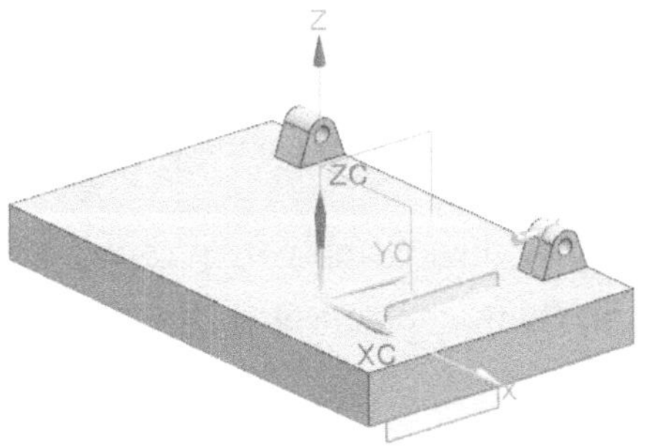

Fig 13-21 Displaying the Deck Part

Displaying only the Deck Part

Let's display only the **Deck** part in the graphics window.

1. Display the assembly navigator in the resource bar.
2. Press MB3 on the **Deck** component and choose **Make Displayed Part** in the pop-up menu.
3. Press the **Home** key. The deck part is displayed as shown in Fig 13-21.

Fig 13-22 Modeling History of Deck Part

Modifying the Sketch of the Deck Part

1. Display the part navigator as shown in Fig 13-22.
2. Double click the sketch designated by the arrow in Fig 13-22.
3. Press the **Home** key to display the **Tri-metric** view as shown in Fig 13-23.
4. Modify the two angular dimensions to 90° and finish the sketch.

Fig 13-24 shows the modified hinge boss.

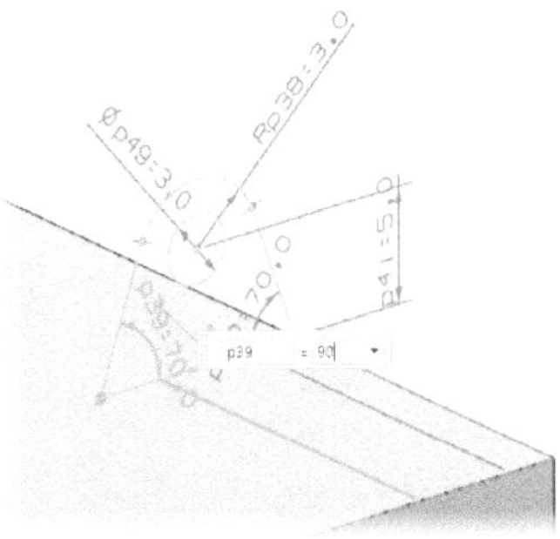

Fig 13-23 Sketch

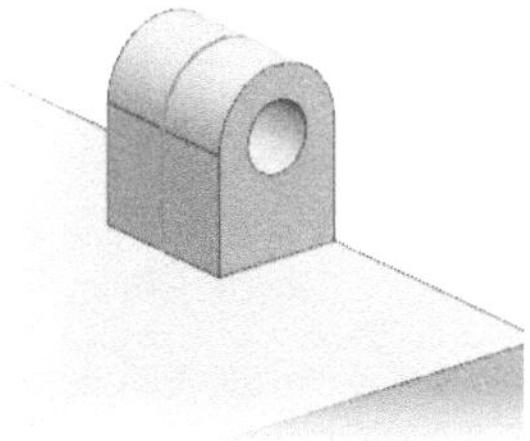

Fig 13-24 Modified Part

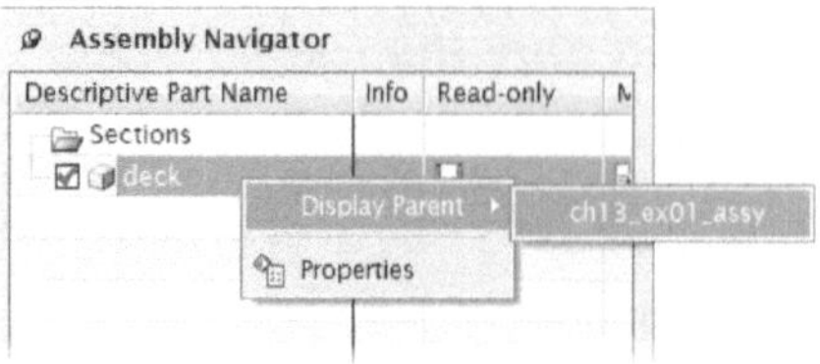

Fig 13-25 Displaying Assembly

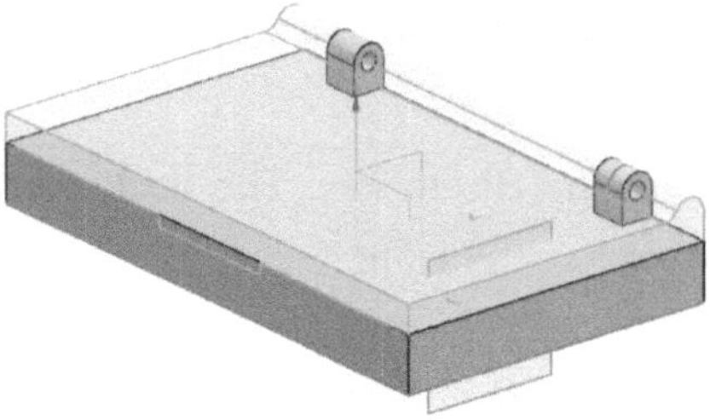

Fig 13-26 Displayed Assembly

Fig 13-27 Modified Column

Making the Assembly a Work Part

1. Display the assembly navigator.

2. Display the assembly by pressing MB3 on the **Deck** component as shown in Fig 13-25.

The assembly is displayed as shown in Fig 13-26.

3. Double click ch13_ex01_assy in the assembly navigator to make it a work part.

Save

1. Check the **Modified** column in the assembly navigator. You can see that the master part files are modified as shown in Fig 13-29.

2. Choose **File > Save > Save** in the **Menu** button. The assembly part file and all the modified component part files are saved.

3. Choose **File > Close > All Parts** in the **Menu** button.

END of Exercise

13.2 Interference Check

The purpose of assembling parts on a computer is to check for design errors before manufacturing the parts. The fundamental issue arising in checking an assembly is interference. We first assemble parts according to their design position and orientation and then check if the geometry of the part intrudes onto the volume of another part.

Component 1 in Fig 13-28 has a hole with a diameter of φ30 which is smaller than the outer diameter φ35 of Component 2. Therefore, we cannot assemble **Component 2** into the hole of **Component 1** using actual parts.

However, using 3D modeling software such as **Siemens NX**, we can assemble **Component 1** and **Component 2** irrespective of their sizes. Therefore, after assembling the components in their correct position, we need to check if they interfere with each other.

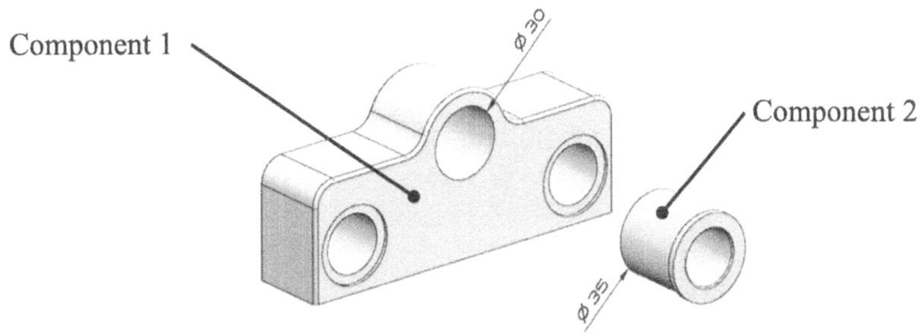

Fig 13-28 Assembly with Interference

13.2.1 Types of Interference

We can classify the status of interference into three types.

Hard

Fig 13-29 illustrates a hard state of interference. The volume of a component intrudes the volume of another component physically. In the case of a pressure fit, a very small amount of hard type interference can happen by intention. However, if this happens in a general assembly condition, you have to modify the parts to avoid interference.

Fig 13-29 Hard State

Touching

Two parts touch each other along the face, edge or vertex. You may or may not need to modify the parts depending on your design intent.

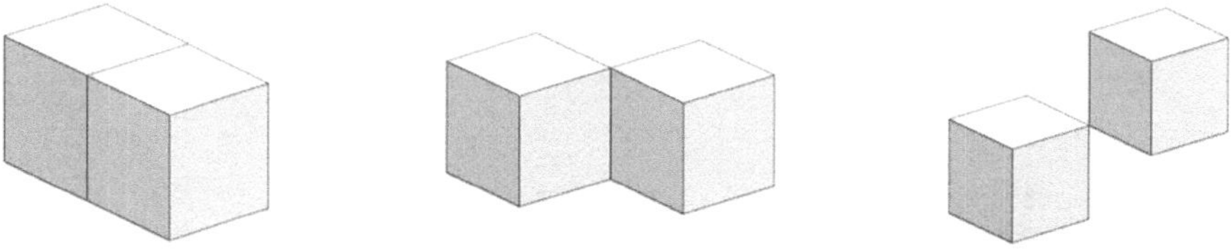

Fig 13-30 Touching State

Soft

You can regulate minimum clearance between components. If the minimum clearance is smaller than the intended design, you have to modify the parts.

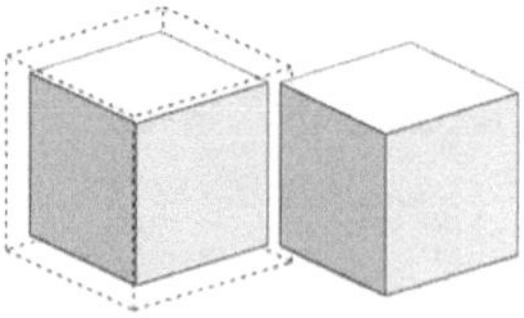

Fig 13-31 Soft State

Folder: ch13_ex02
File: ch13_ex02_assy.prt

Let's check interference between components in the given assembly.

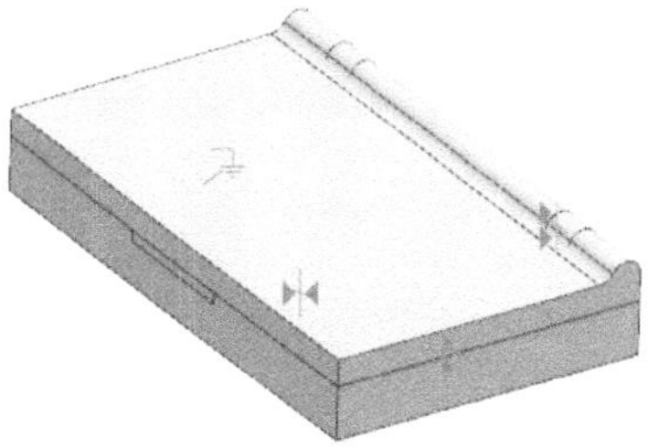

Fig 13-32 Assembly for Exercise

Fig 13-33 Clearance Browser Menu

1. Open the assembly file in the given folder.

2. Choose **Analysis > Assembly Clearance > Clearance Browser** in the **Menu** button.

3. Drag the **Clearance Browser** and dock above the graphics window as shown in Fig 13-34.

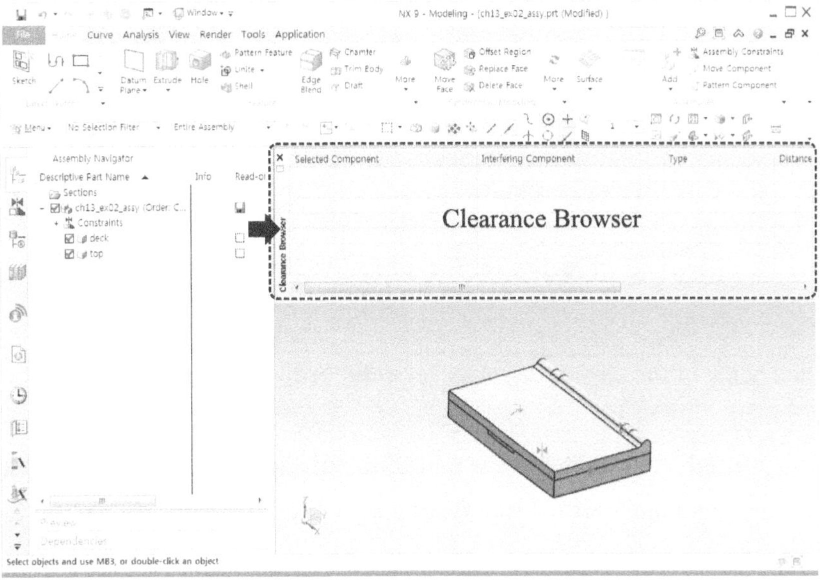

Fig 13-34 Docked Clearance Browser

Managing Clearance Browser

You can drag the clearance browser by clicking the title bar with MB1. You can undock the browser by dragging the portion designated by the arrow in Fig 13-34.

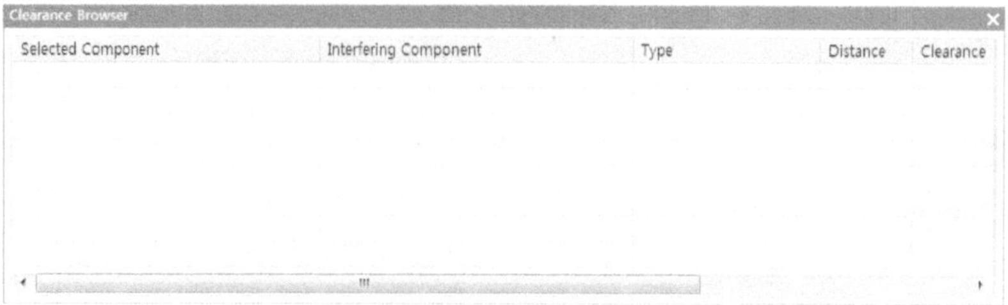

Fig 13-35 Undocked Clearance Browser

4. Click MB3 on the empty area in the **Clearance Browser** and choose **Clearance Set > New** in the pop-up menu as shown in Fig 13-36.

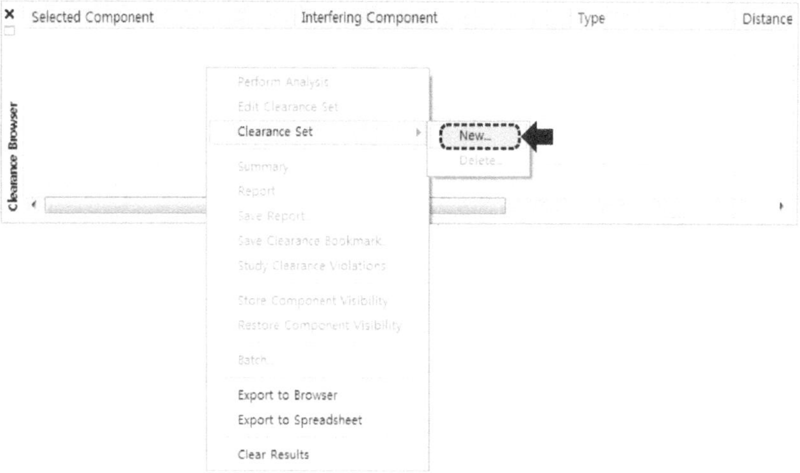

Fig 13-36 Creating a Clearance Set

5. Enter the name of the clearance set as **"check hard"** as shown in Fig 13-37.

6. Click the **More** button on the lower part of the dialog box, expand the **Settings** option group and press the **Interference Geometry** option button as shown in Fig 13-38.

7. Set the options in the **Interference Geometry** as shown in Fig 13-38.

► Check the **Save Interference Solids** option.

► Enter 100 in the **Layer** input box.

► Choose **Yellow** as the **Interference Color** (Color ID: 6)

8. Click **OK** in the **Clearance Properties** dialog box.

9. Click MB3 on the name of the clearance set, i.e. **"check hard"**, and choose **Perform Analysis** in the pop-up menu.

Interferences are displayed in the **Clearance Browser** as shown in Fig 13-39.

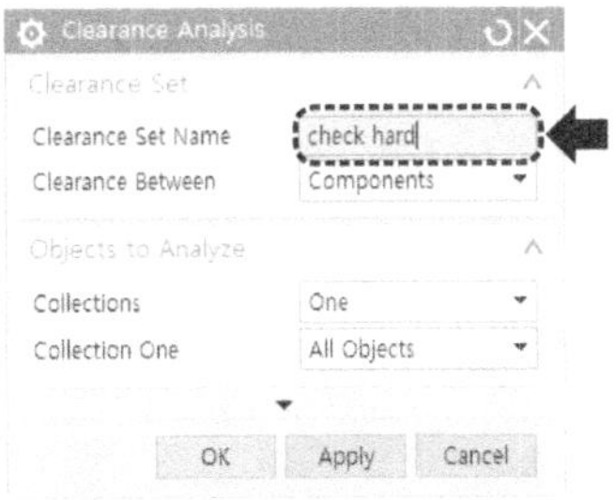

Fig 13-37 Set Name

Fig 13-38 Interference Geometry Option

Fig 13-39 Result of Analysis

Meaning of Interference Geometry Options

According to the options set in Fig 13-38, you will have solid bodies for the hard type of interference between the components. The solid bodies will be colored yellow and allocated to layer 100. Layer is a tool that can classify modeling objects.

Solid bodies for the interference are created as shown in Fig 13-40. You can identify the bodies in the part navigator as shown in Fig 13-41 Ⓐ.

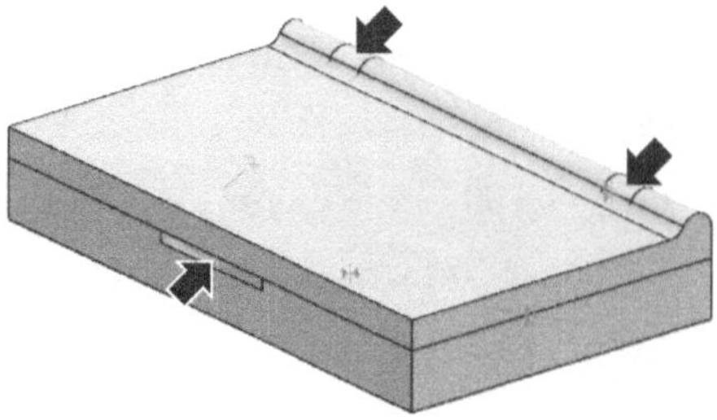

Fig 13-40 Solid Bodies

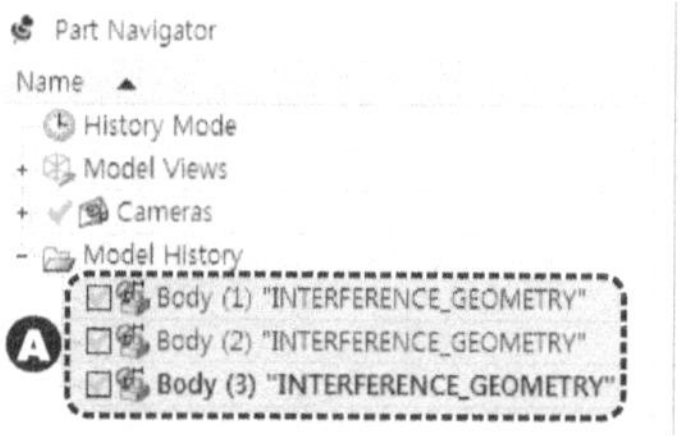

Fig 13-41 Part Navigator

9. Choose **Format > Layer Settings** in the **Menu** button.

10. Uncheck the box designated by the arrow in Fig 13-42. Confirm that the interference bodies disappear from the graphics window.

11. Click **Close** in the **Layer Settings** dialog box.

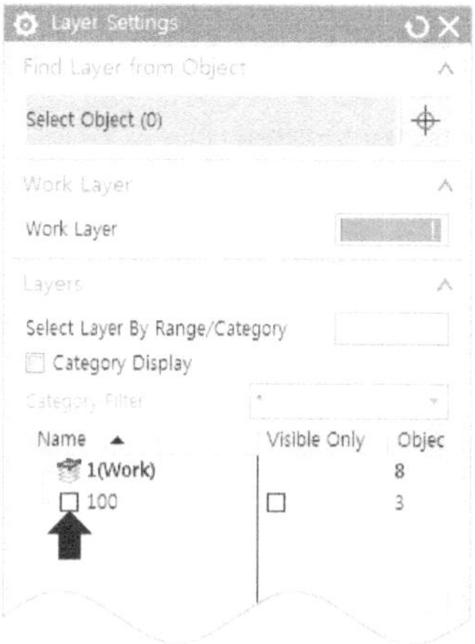

Fig 13-42 Hiding the Layer

12. Check the box in front of the interference item as designated by **B** in Fig 13-43. The interference is displayed in red as designated by the arrow in Fig 13-43.

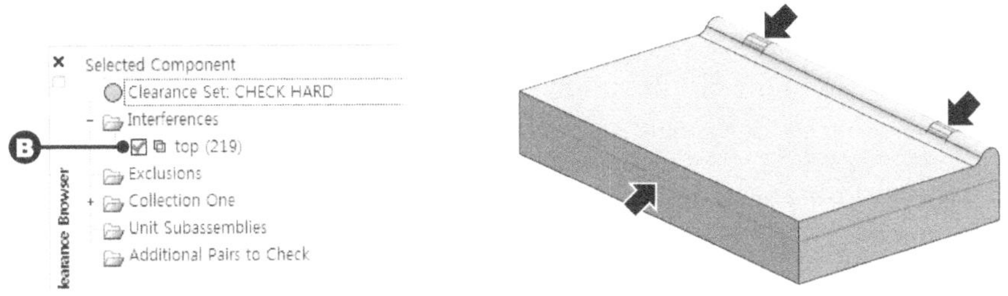

Fig 13-43 Displaying Interference

13. Click MB3 on the **"top"** at the location designated by **C** in Fig 13-44 and choose **Wireframe Lefg** in the pop-up menu. The component on the left, i.e. the **Top** component is displayed in wireframe as shown in Fig 13-44. Note that there maybe the **Deck** component on the left.

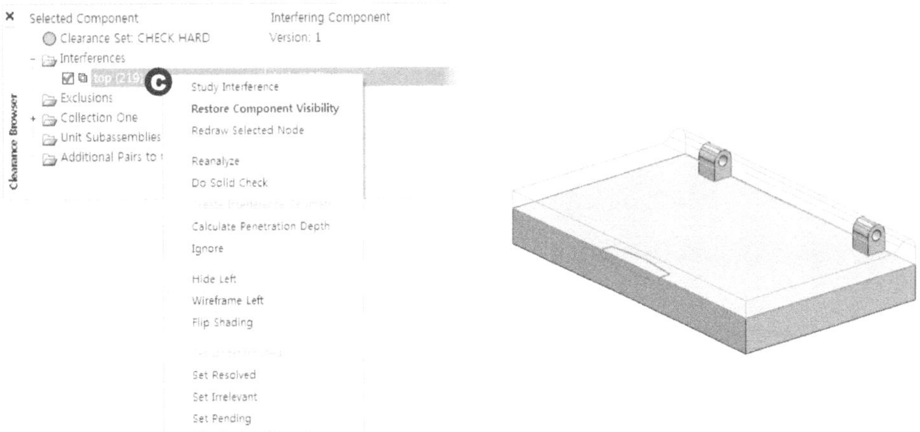

Fig 13-44 Changing the Rendering Style

! *Location of Clicking MB3*

If you click MB3 on the left component in the interference browser, the **Hide Left** and **Wireframe Left** menus can be applied. If you click MB3 on the right component in the interference browser, the **Hide Right** and **Wireframe Right** menus can be applied. If you choose **Flip Shading** you can flip the rendering style between the left and right components.

14. Finish the interference study by clicking the check box in front of the interference item. Or you can choose the **Restore Component Visibility** option in the pop-up menu in Fig 13-46. Or you can double click the list of the interference check.

15. Choose **Save As** in the **Menu** button.

16. Name the part file as ch13_ex02_assy_analyzed.prt in the same folder as the components, i.e. ch13_ex02.

17. Choose **File > Close > All Parts** in the **Menu** button.

END of Exercise

! *What happens?*

If you save the assembly file without finishing the interference study, a message box as shown in Fig 13-45 is displayed.

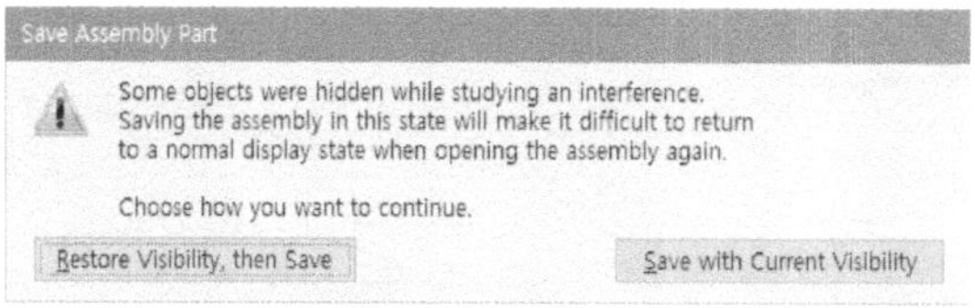

Fig 13-45 Save Assembly Part Message Box

13.3 Referencing Component Geometry

After checking for interference in an assembly, you will have to modify the part where the interference has been taken place. In this case, it will be convenient if you can see and reference the geometry or parameters of the counter component. You can modify a component by making the master part a work part and displaying the assembly. This kind of modeling process is called **Top-Down Assembly Design**.

Examples of modeling a part by referencing the geometry or parameter of other components are as follows.

① You can define a sketch plane on the plane of the component which is not in a work part.

② You can select the face of another component as the limiting object of Extrude. You can also select the component body as the tool of the boolean operation.

③ You can project or intersect geometry of other components.

④ You can define a parameter value by referencing the parameter of another component or assembly part.

13.3.1 Interpart Link

When you select geometry from another component to define a feature, you can turn on the **Create Interpart Link** option shown in Fig 13-48. As a result, the feature will update when the linked geometry is modified, or even when the position of the linked component is changed. Therefore, you must not move the component if you have referenced the geometry with the interpart link option.

In other words, if you want to move the referenced components after the top-down assembly design, you have to turn off the **Create Interpart Link** option. As a result, the modification of the linked geometry is not reflected to the referencing feature.

The **Interpart Link** option is activated when you are allowed to select objects from other components. For example, the option is activated when you choose **Until Selected** in the **Limit** option of **Extrude** or when you are projecting edges from other components. Fig 13-46 shows the **Interpart Link** button in the **Selection Bar**. Note that the **Interpart Link** button is activated when you have selected **Entire Assembly** in the **Selection Scope** dropdown list. In this textbook, we will not activate the **Interpart Link** option so that we can move components after constraining.

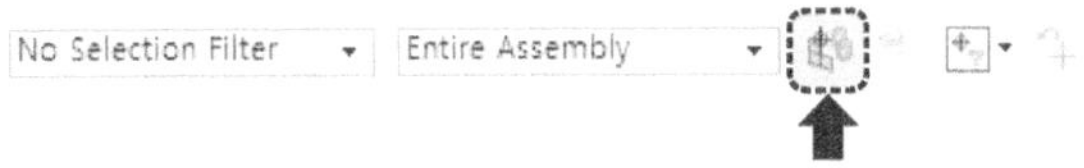

Fig 13-46 Interpart Link Option

13.3.2 Selection Scope

Selection scope defines the range where you can select geometry during the modeling process. Three levels of selection scope are available.

- **Entire Assembly**: You can select geometry from all components shown in the graphics window including the upper assembly.
- **Within Work Part and Components**: You can select geometry from the work part and from its components.
- **Within Work Part Only**: You can select geometry only from the work part.

Therefore, if you want to reference geometry from another component of an assembly, you have to choose either **Entire Assembly** or **Within Work Part and Component** in **the Selection Scope** dropdown list.

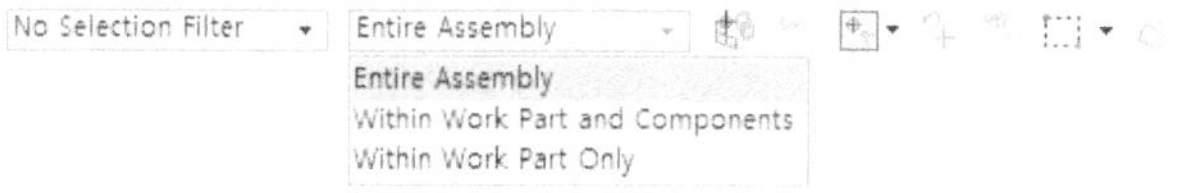

Fig 13-47 Selection Scope

Exercise 03 Modifying the Top Component

Folder: ch13_ex03
File: ch13_ex03_assy.prt

Let's modify the **Top** component in the given assembly and save the master part as a new part.

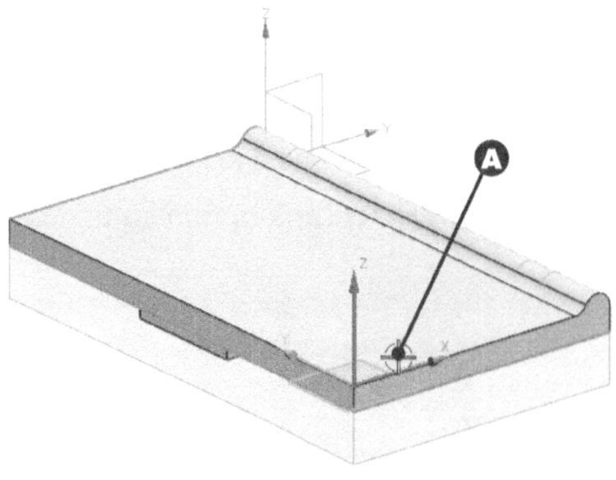

Fig 13-48 Sketch Plane

Preparing

1. Confirm that you are in the Modeling application and make the **Top** component a work part by double clicking it.
2. Click the **Sketch** icon around the location designated by Ⓐ in Fig 13-48 and reset the **Create Sketch** dialog box.

Fig 13-49 Hiding the Component

3. Press the **Home** key on the keyboard to display the **Trimetric** view.

4. Hide the **Top** component by clicking MB3 on the component as shown in Fig 13-49.

Creating Sketch

1. Click the **Project Curve** icon in the **Direct Sketch** icon group.

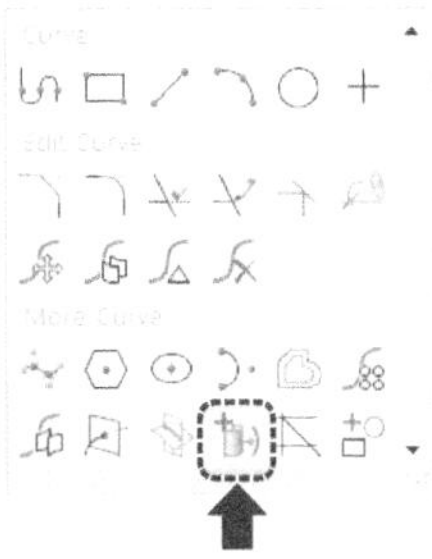

Fig 13-50 Project Curve Icon

2. Confirm that the selection scope is **Entire Assembly** and make sure that the **Create Interpart Link** button is released.

3. Choose **Single Curve** as the curve rule.

Fig 13-51 Selection Bar Options

4. Select the six edges of the hinge boss as designated by **B** in Fig 13-52.

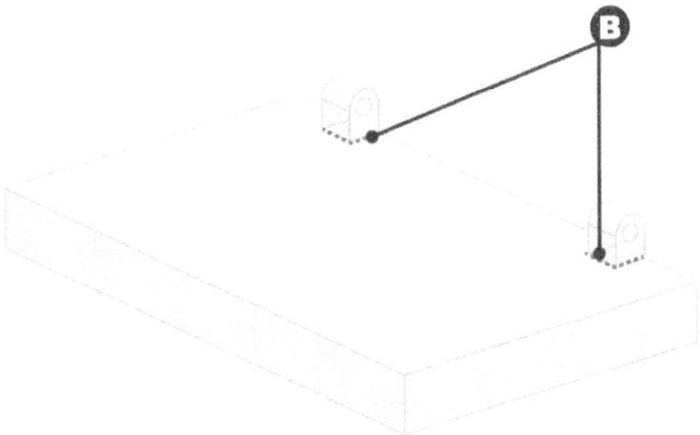

Fig 13-52 Edge to Project

5. Click **OK** in the **Project Curve** dialog box.

6. Click **Yes** in the message box shown in Fig 13-53.

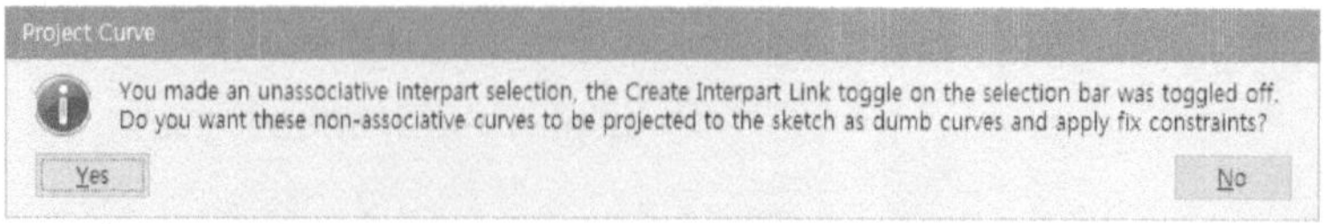

Fig 13-53 Non-associative Information Box

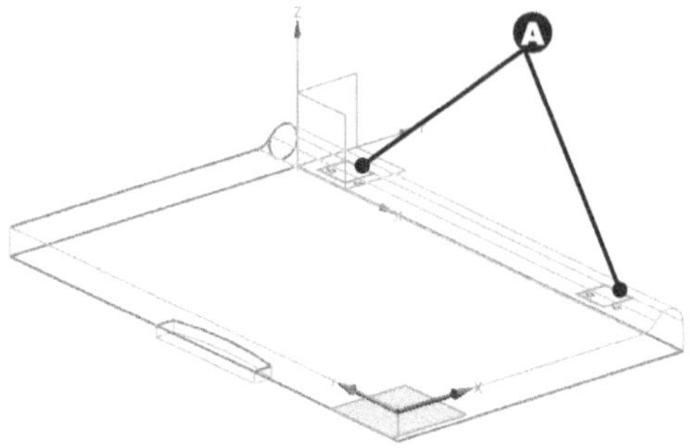

Fig 13-54 Completed Sketch

7. Show the **Top** component and hide the **Deck** component.

8. Change the rendering style to **Static Wireframe**.

9. Create a line as designated by Ⓐ in Fig 13-54 to complete the sketch.

Removing the Part

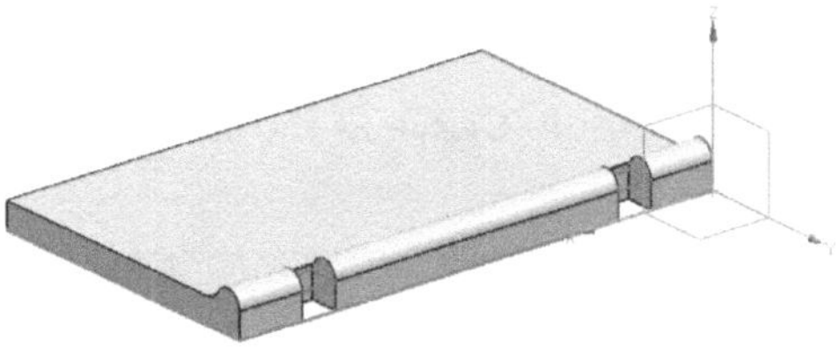

Fig 13-55 Modified Top Component

1. Finish the sketch.

2. Extrude the sketch to remove the hinge slot as shown in Fig 13-55.

Saving as a New File

Remember that top.prt is the current work part. You can save the component part file and the assembly part file as a new file according to the following process.

1. Choose **File > Save > Save As**.

2. Enter **"top_rev1"** in the file name input box as shown in Fig 13-56 and click **OK**.

Information window and another **Save As** dialog box appears. In this dialog box, you can designate a new assembly part file. If you want to overwrite the assembly file, you have to click **Cancel** in the second **Save As** dialog box.

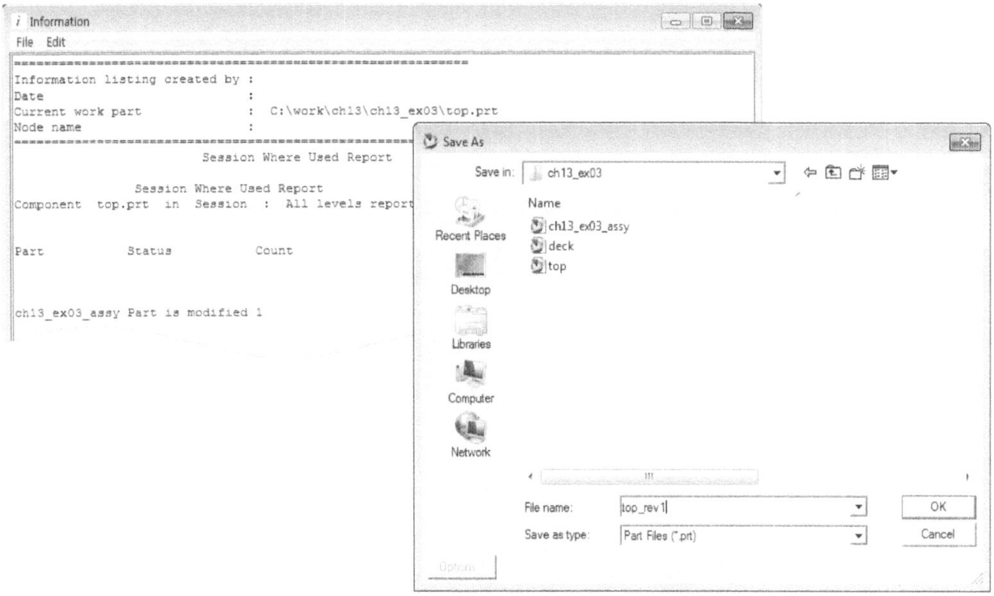

Fig 13-56 Saving as a New Part File

3. Enter a new assembly file name as shown in Fig 13-57 and click **OK**.

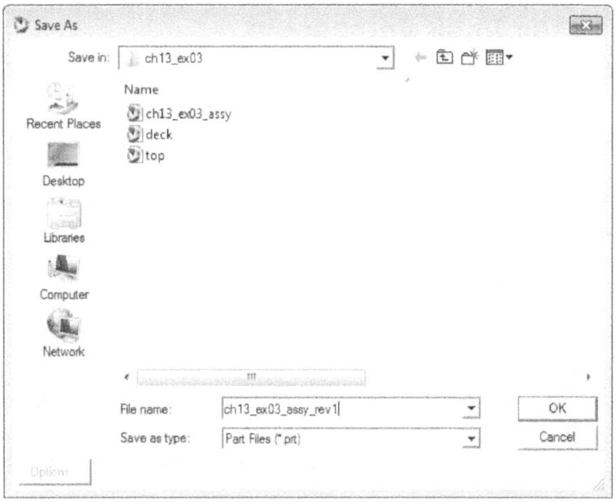

Fig 13-57 Saving as a New Assembly File

An information is displayed as shown in Fig 13-58 and the **Save As** dialog box is invoked.

4. Click **Yes** in the **Save As** dialog box.
5. Close the **Information** window.

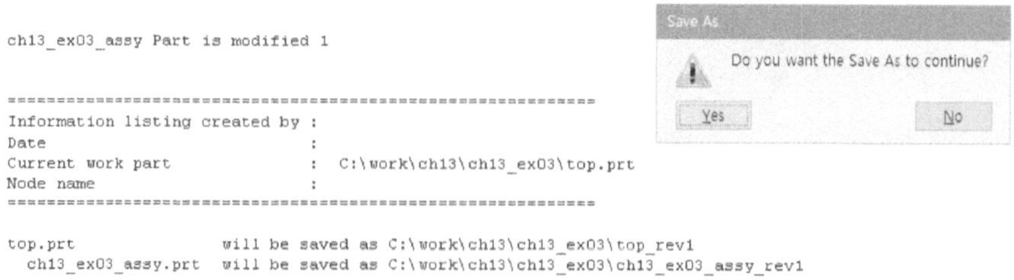

Fig 13-58 Executing the Save As Operation

Fig 13-59 Assembly Navigator

The assembly navigator is as shown in Fig 13-59. Confirm that the names of the **Top** component and the assembly file have been changed.

It is recommended to continue the next exercise to modify the **Deck** component part by following a similar procedure.

Exercise 04 Modifying the Deck Component and Checking Interference

Folder: ch13_ex03
File: ch13_ex03_assy_rev1.prt

Procedure

1. Modify the **Deck** component according to the suggested procedure. We will modify the portion specified by Ⓐ in Fig 13-60.
2. Check for interference between the components.
3. Modify the **Top** component.
4. Save the modified files.

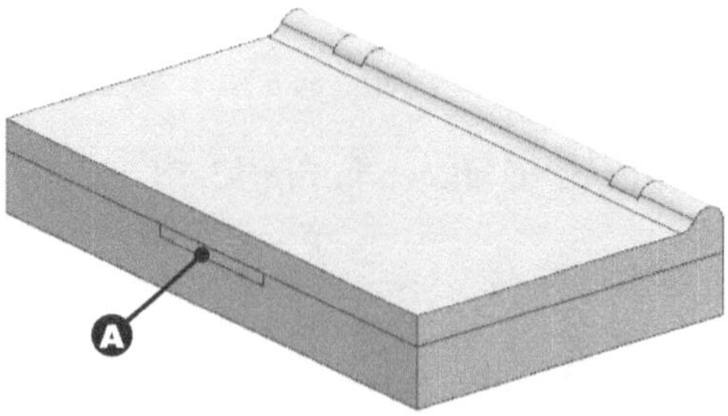

Fig 13-60 Portion to Modify

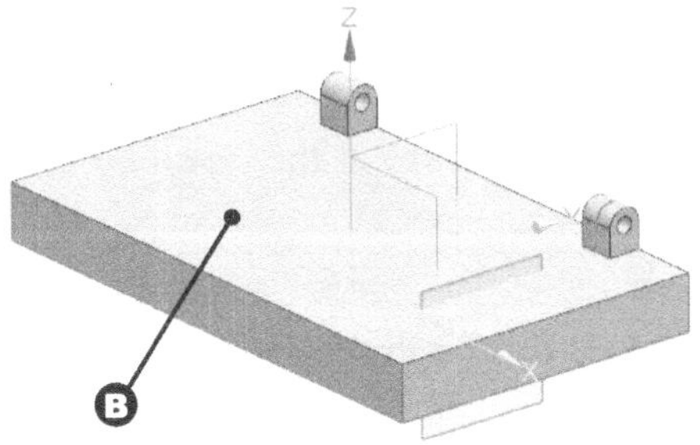

Fig 13-61 Sketch Plane

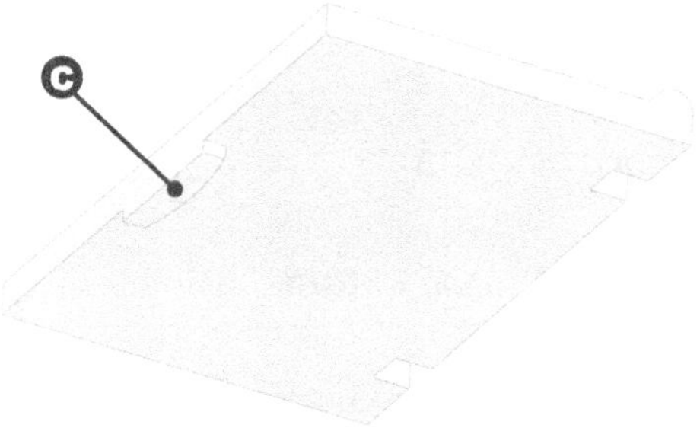

Fig 13-62 Face to Select

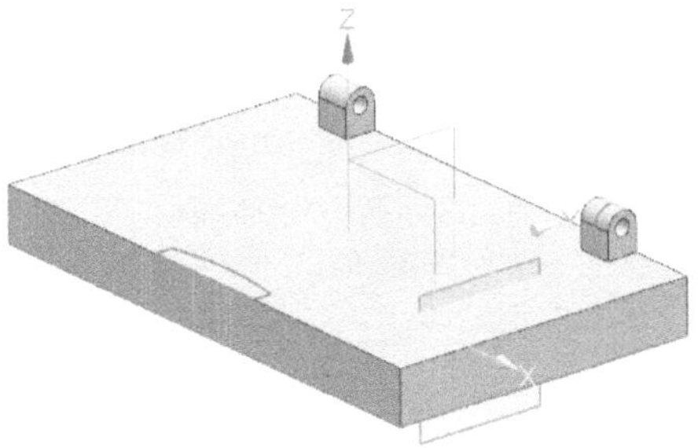

Fig 13-63 Created Sketch

Creating Sketch

1. Make the **Deck** component a work part.

2. Hide the **Top** component.

3. Click the **Sketch in Task Environment** icon and select the face B in Fig 13-61 as the sketch plane.

4. Hide the **Deck** component and show the **Top** component.

5. Click the **Project Curve** icon and select the edges constituting the face C in Fig 13-62. You can use the **Face Edges** curve rule.

6. Finish the sketch.

7. Show the **Deck** component and hide the **Top** component(Fig 13-63).

Removing Body

1. Click the **Extrude** icon and select the sketch curve as the section.

2. Show the **Top** component and hide the **Deck** component while the **Extrude** dialog box is open. Use the pop-up menu in the assembly navigator to hide or show the components.

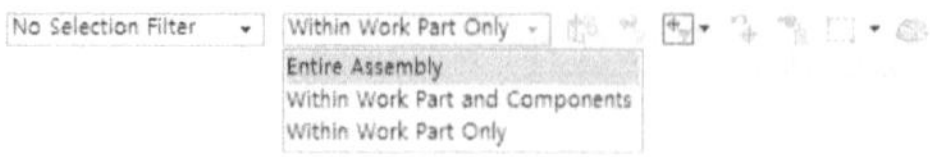

Fig 13-64 Selection Scope

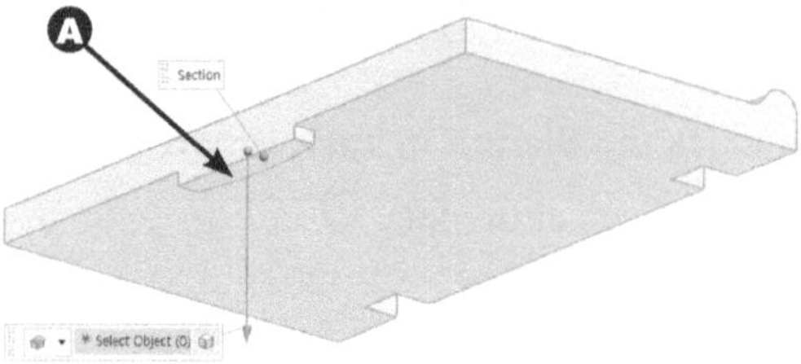

Fig 13-65 Selecting Limit

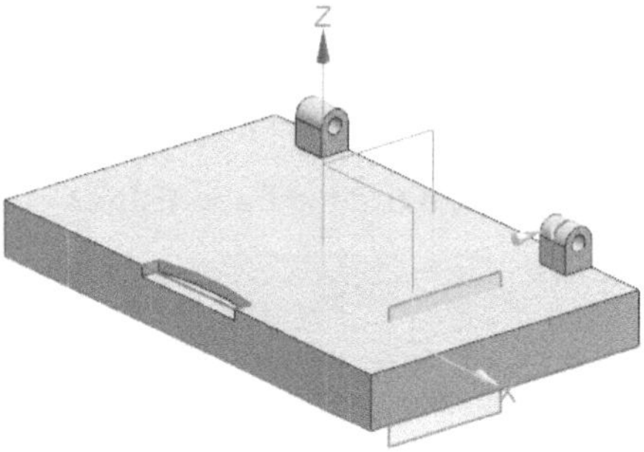

Fig 13-66 Modified Part

3. Reverse the direction of extrusion.

4. Choose **Subtract** in the **Boolean** drop-down list.

5. Choose **Until Selected** in the **End** drop-down list.

6. Choose **Entire Assembly** in the **Selection Scope** dropdown list in the selection bar as shown in Fig 13-64.

7. Select the face Ⓐ of the **Top** component specified in Fig 13-65.

8. Click **OK** in the **Extrude** dialog box.

9. Show the **Deck** component and hide the **Top** component.

Fig 13-66 shows the modified **Deck** component.

Saving as a New File

Remember that deck.prt is the current work part. You can save the component part file as a new file. We will overwrite the assembly file ch13_ex03_assy_rev1.prt.

1. Choose **File > Save > Save As**.

2. Enter **"deck_rev1"** in the **File Name** input box and click **OK** in the **Save As** dialog box.

3. Click **Cancel** in the second displayed **Save As** dialog box. Read the information message shown in Fig 13-67 and click **Yes** in the **Save As** information box.

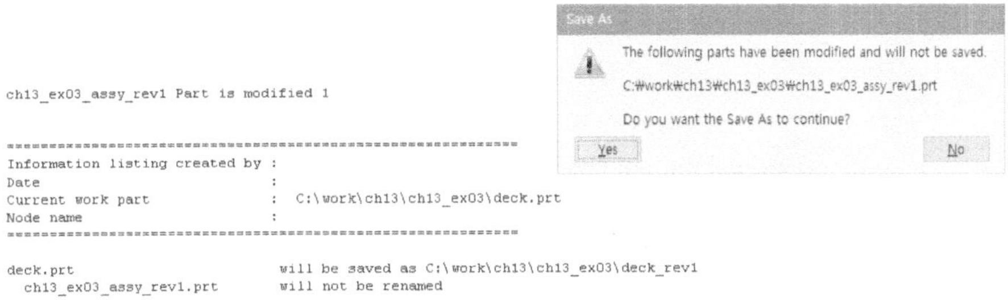

Fig 13-67 Executing the Save As Operation

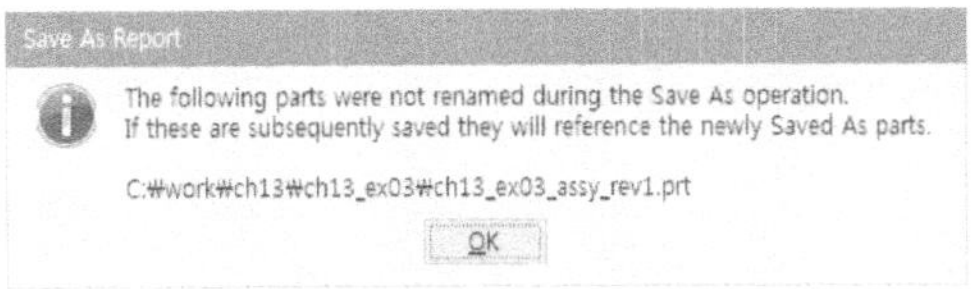

Fig 13-68 Save As Report

4. Read the message in the **Save As Report** information box as shown in Fig 13-68.

5. Close the information box.

The assembly navigator is as shown in Fig 13-69. The name of the **Deck** component has been changed while the name of the top assembly is not changed.

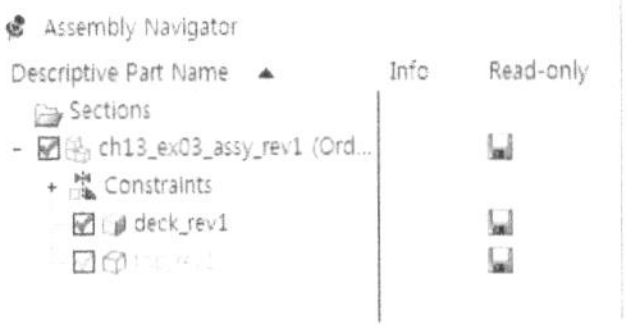

Fig 13-69 Assembly Navigator

Modifying Assembly

Let's modify the assembly configuration for interference check.

1. Double click the top assembly (ch13_ex03_assy_rev1) to make it a work part.

2. Show the **Top_rev1** component.

3. Delete the **Touch** constraint in the assembly navigator.

4. Click the **Assembly Constraints** in the **Assemblies** icon group, reset the dialog box and drag the **Top** component to rotate as shown in Fig 13-70.

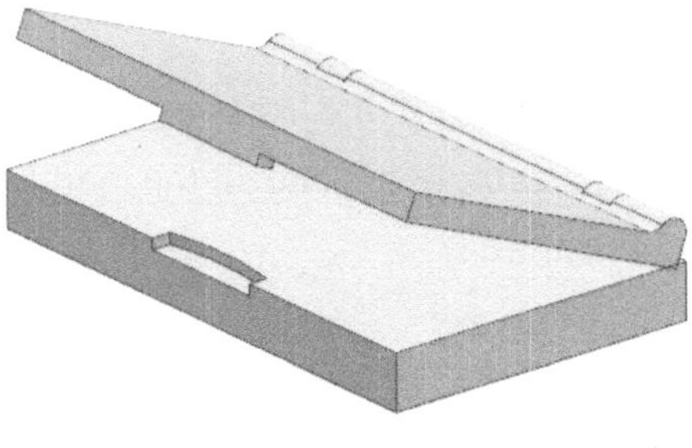

Fig 13-70 Rotate the Top Component

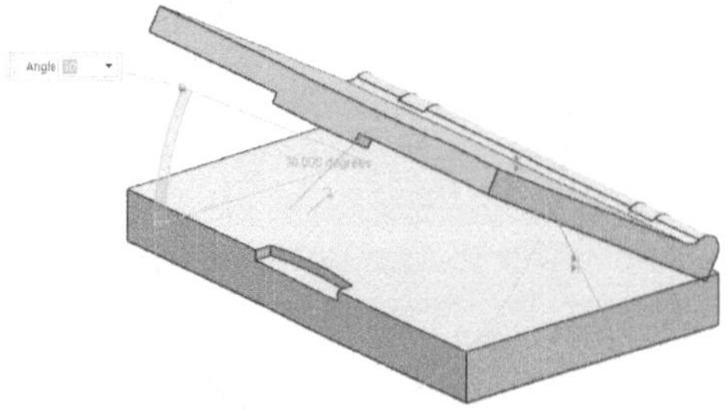

Fig 13-71 Applying the Angle Constraint

5. Apply the 30° **Angle** constraint between the faces as shown in Fig 13-71.

Checking Interference

1. Choose **Analysis > Assembly Clearance > Clearance Browser** in the **Menu** button.

Verify that the interference occurs as shown in Fig 13-72.

2. Close the **Clearance Browser**.

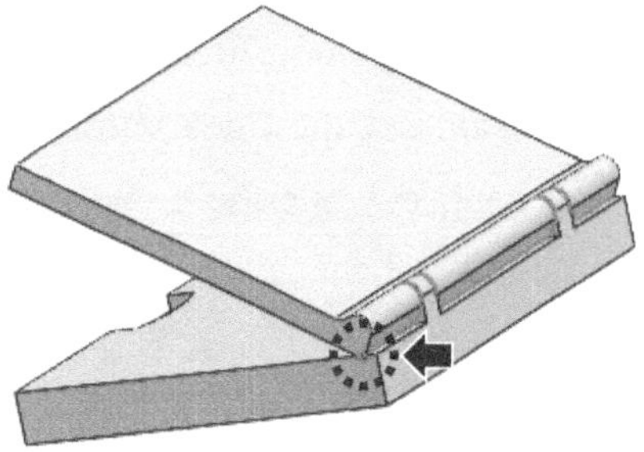

Fig 13-72 Interference Detected

Modifying the Top Component

1. Make the **Top_rev1** component a work part.

2. Apply the R5 edge blend on the edges as specified in Fig 13-73.

3. Create a φ3 mm through hole as shown in Fig 13-73.

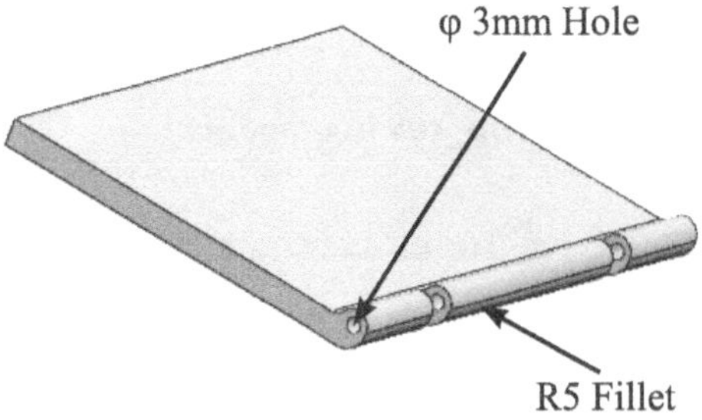

Fig 13-73 Pin Hole

Saving Files

When the assembly file is in work, you can save the assembly file and all the modified component files.

1. Double click the assembly to make it a work part.

Note that the status of the **Modified** column in the assembly navigator is as shown in Fig 13-74.

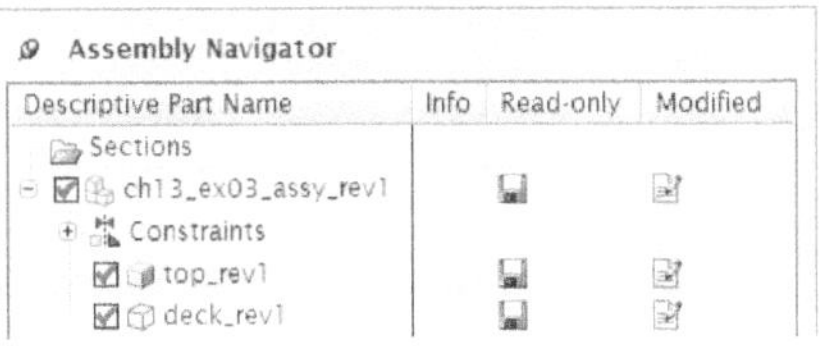

Fig 13-74 Assembly Navigator (Before Saving)

2. Choose **File > Save > Save.**

Verify that the symbol in the **Modified** column has disappeared.

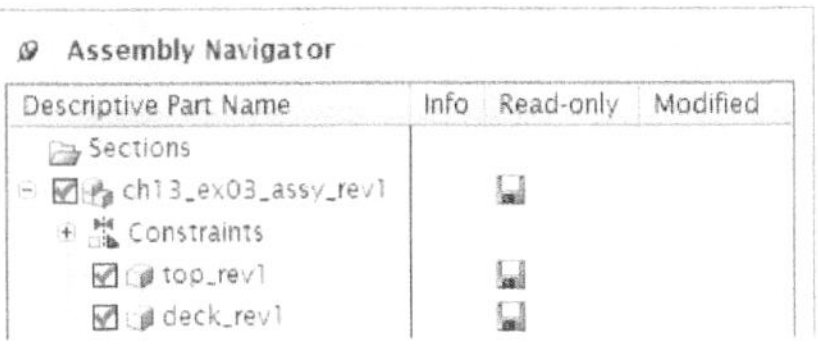

Fig 13-75 Assembly Navigator (After Saving)

3. Choose **File > Close > All Parts**.

END of Exercise

13.4 Creating a New Component

You can create a new component in an assembly by creating a new part file and creating geometry in the new file. Make the assembly a work part and click the **Create New** icon in the **Assemblies** icon group as shown in Fig 13-76.

Note that a component has a corresponding master part. Therefore, you have to create the master part first when you create a new component in an assembly. You will create the master part with the **Model** template and will select no object for the new component. The procedure for creating geometry in the empty component is the same as the general top-down modeling process.

Fig 13-76 Create New Icon

Exercise 05 Creating the Pin Component

Folder: ch13_ex05
File: ch13_ex05_assy.prt

Create a new component in the given assembly file and create a geometry in the new component. Then we will complete the assembly by fully constraining the components.

Creating the Pin Component

1. Open the given assembly file ch13_ex05_assy.prt.

2. Hide the symbols of constraints.

3. Click the **Create New** icon in the **Assemblies** icon group.

4. Select the **Model** template in the **New Component File** dialog box. Confirm the folder and enter the name of the master part as shown in Fig 13-77 and click **OK**.

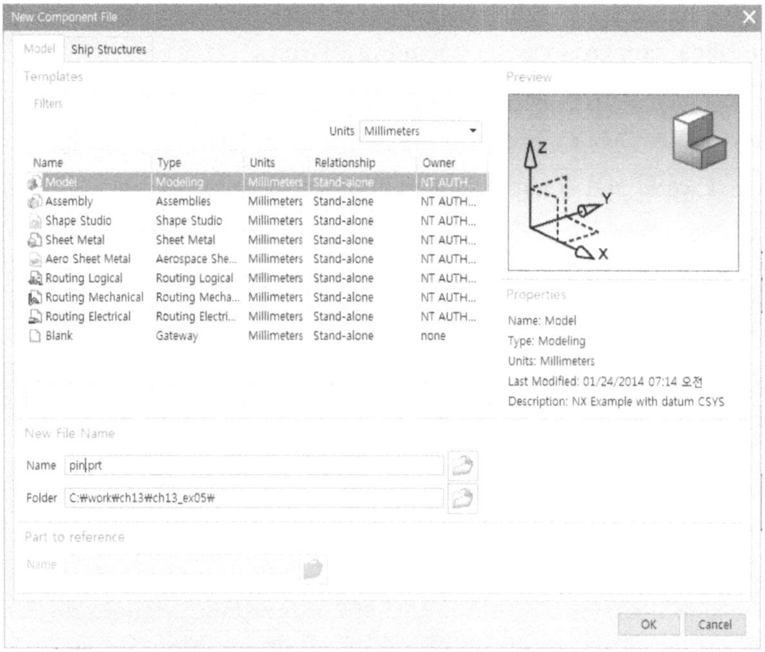

Fig 13-77 Creating Master Part for the New Component

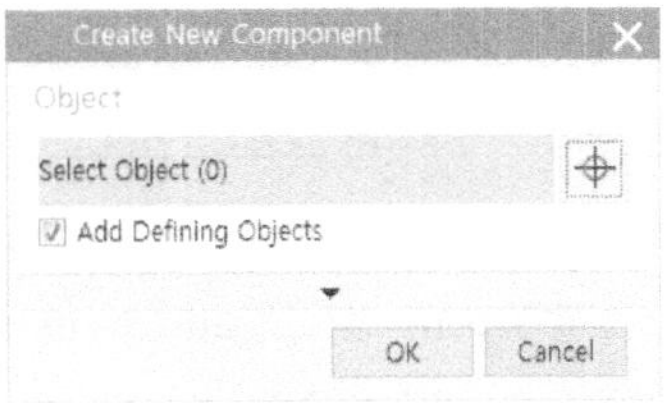

Fig 13-78 Create New Component Dialog Box

Fig 13-79 Pin Component Created

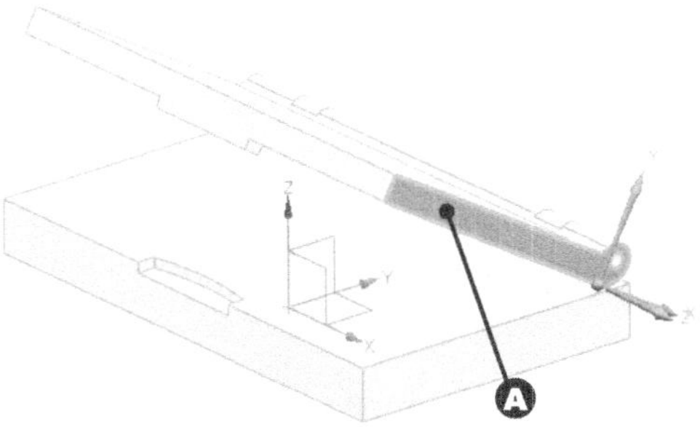

Fig 13-80 Sketch Plane

5. The **Create New Component** dialog box is invoked and you are prompted to select objects for the new component. Do not select any object and click **OK** in the dialog box.

The **Pin** component is created in the assembly navigator as shown in Fig 13-79. Note that the reference set is set to **Entire Part**.

Selecting Objects

If you have already created geometry for the **Pin** component in the assembly file, you can select the geometry when you are prompted to select objects for the component. We will start from an empty part for this exercise.

Modeling the Pin Component

1. Make the **Pin** component a work part.

2. Click the **Sketch** icon.

3. Choose **Entire Assembly** in the **Selection Scope** dropdown list.

4. Select the side face of the **Top** component designated by **A** in Fig 13-80.

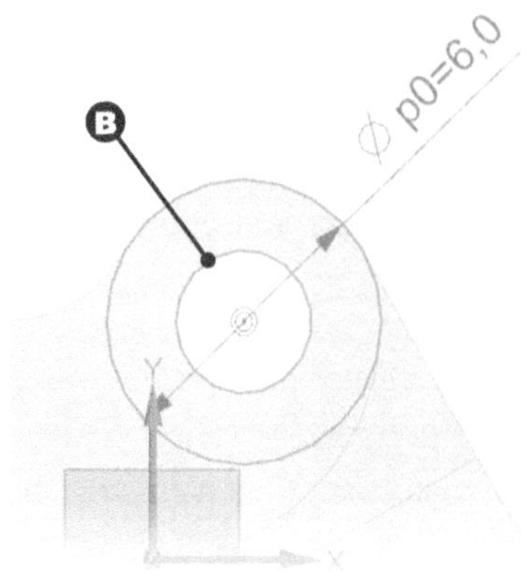

Fig 13-81 Sketch

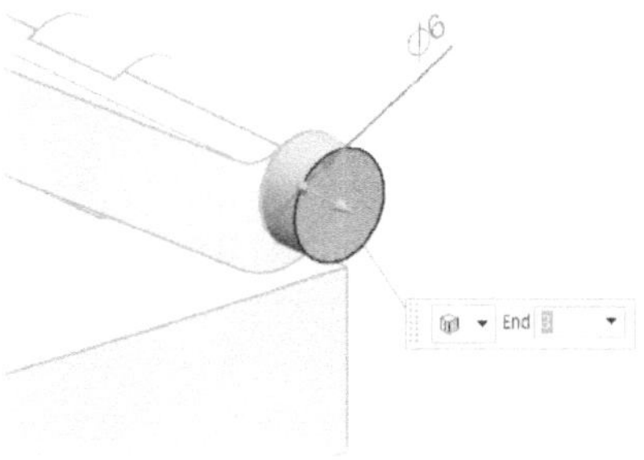

Fig 13-82 Extruding Pin Head

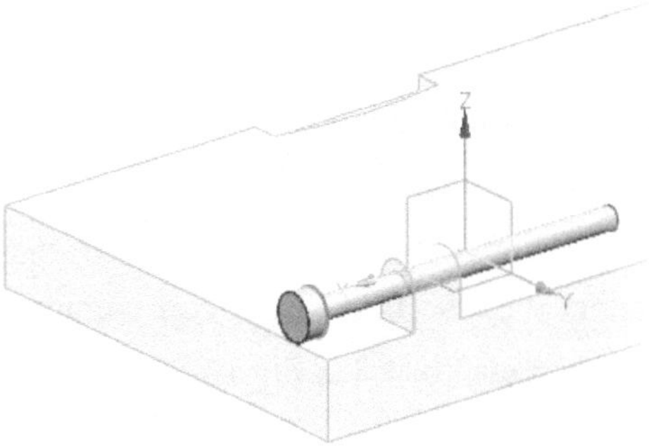

Fig 13-83 Completed Pin

5. Project the circular edge designated by Ⓑ in Fig 13-81 on the sketch plane.

6. Create a ϕ6 mm circle and constrain it fully as shown in Fig 13-81.

7. Finish the sketch.

Constraining Sketch

Note that you cannot select the objects of other component in constraining sketch. Therefore, you have to project the object on the sketch plane first and then constrain the sketch with respect to the projected curve.

Extruding

1. Extrude the circle by 3mm as shown in Fig 13-82. Choose **None** in the **Boolean** option.

Creating the Shank

1. Hide the **Top** component.

2. Extrude the curve Ⓑ in Fig 13-81 by 35 mm and unite to the pin head.

Constraining the Pin Component

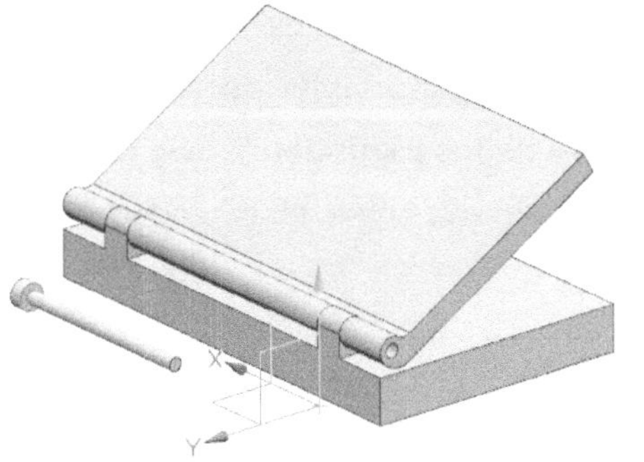

Fig 13-84 Dragged Pin Component

1. Double click **ch13_ex05_assy** in the assembly navigator to make it a work part.

2. Confirm that the reference set of the **Pin** component is **Entire Part**.

3. Show the **Top** component.

4. Click the **Assembly Constraint** icon and drag the **Pin** component as shown in Fig 13-84.

Make sure that the datum coordinate system moves together.

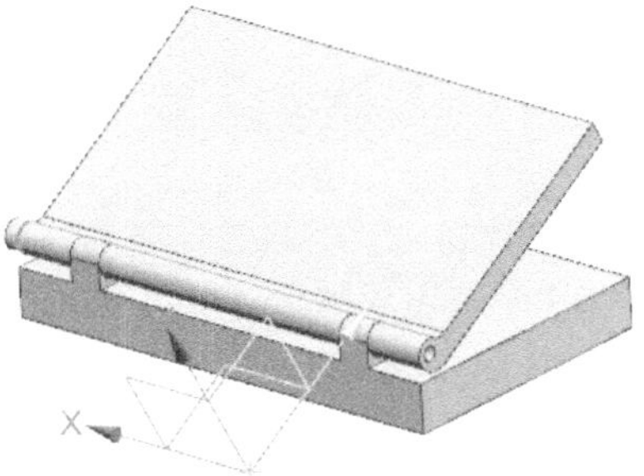

Fig 13-85 Constraining the Pin Component

5. Fully constrain the **Pin** component.

6. Copy the **Pin** component and assembly on the other side of the **Top** component.

7. Change the reference set to **Model** for the two **Pin** components.

Fig 13-86 shows the completed assembly.

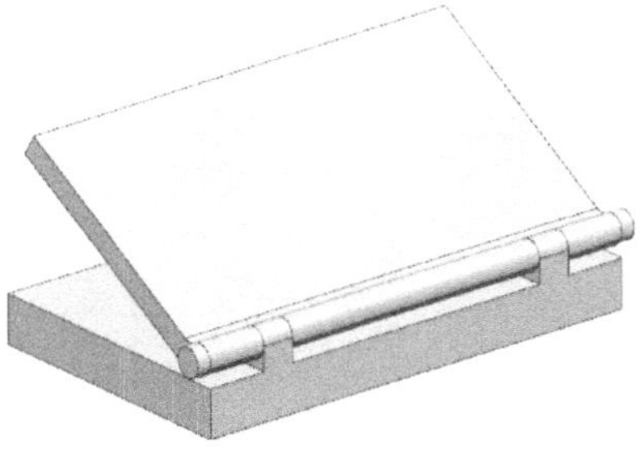

Fig 13-86 Completed Assembly

8. Choose **File > Save > Save**. All the modified files including the **Pin** component are saved.

9. Close all parts.

END of Exercise

13.5 Disassembling an Assembly

A product is an assembly of many components. After constraining each component, we can disassemble the components so that we can explain the assembly structure and create an assembly drawing. In NX, you can disassemble with the **Exploded Views** command. You can create as many explosions as required and you can create an exploded drawing view which will be explained in Chapter 15.

The exploded view can be created according to the following procedure. Each step number corresponds to those in Fig 13-87.

① Click the **Exploded Views** icon in the **Assemblies** tab.
② Create a new explosion.
③ Move or rotate components with the **Edit Explosion** icon in the **Exploded Views** icon group.
④ Create tracelines.

You can create the exploded view in the **Assemblies** tab. Click MB3 on an empty area in the ribbon bar and choose **Assemblies** in the pop-up menu as shown in Fig 13-87. Fig 13-88 shows the icon groups that are available in the **Assemblies** tab. The location of the **Exploded View** icon is designated by the arrow.

Fig 13-87 Adding the Assemblies Tab

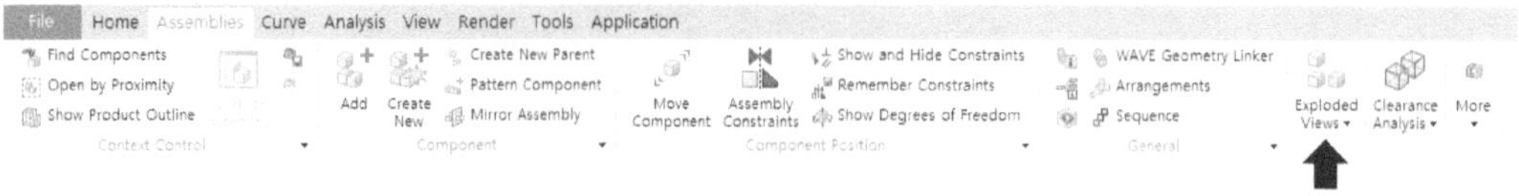

Fig 13-88 Icon Groups in the Assemblies Tab

Create an exploded view and tracelines for the given assembly.

Creating an Exploded View

1. Open the given assembly file ch13_ex06_assy.prt.

2. Add the **Assemblies** tab and click the **Exploded View** icon.

3. Click **New Explosion** icon in the Exploded Views icon group.

4. Enter the name of the explosion in the **New Explosion** dialog box shown in Fig 13-90 and click **OK**. Confirm that other icons in the **Exploded Views** icon group are activated.

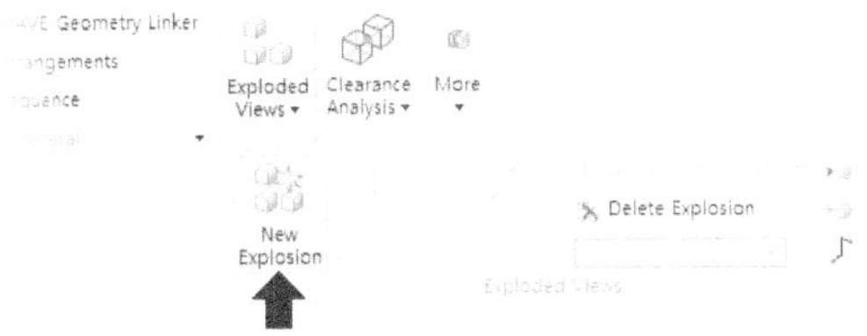

Fig 13-89 Naming the Explosion

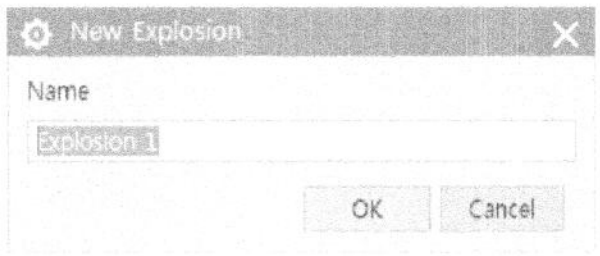

Fig 13-90 New Explosion Dialog Box

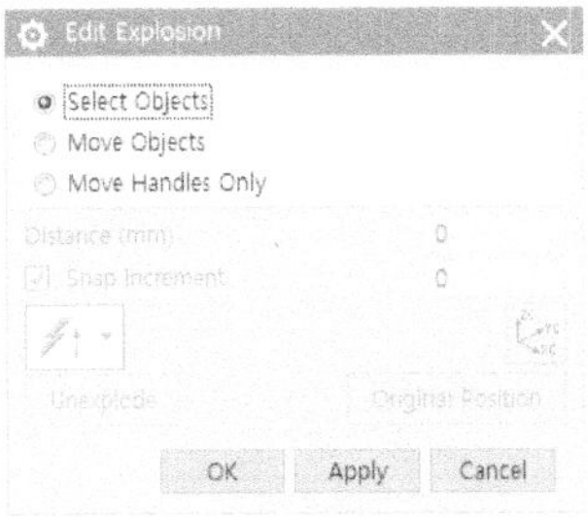

Fig 13-91 Edit Explosion Dialog Box

5. Click the **Edit Explosion** icon in the **Exploded Views** icon group. Confirm that the **Select Objects** radio button is selected in the **Edit Explosion** dialog box as shown in Fig 13-91. You are prompted to select the components to explode.

6. Select the **Pin** component in the graphics window and click MB2. Confirm that the **Move Objects** radio button is selected in the **Edit Explosion** dialog box and the move handle appears as shown in Fig 13-92.

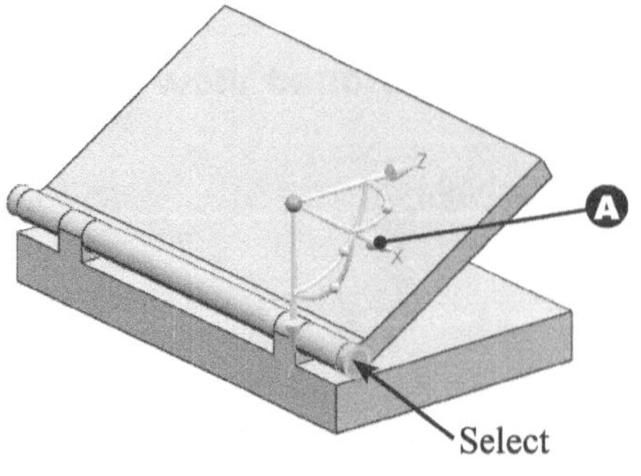

Fig 13-92 Moving Component

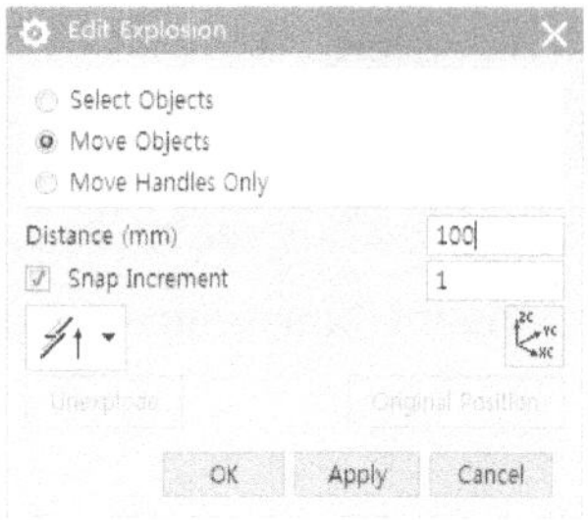

Fig 13-93 Entering Distance

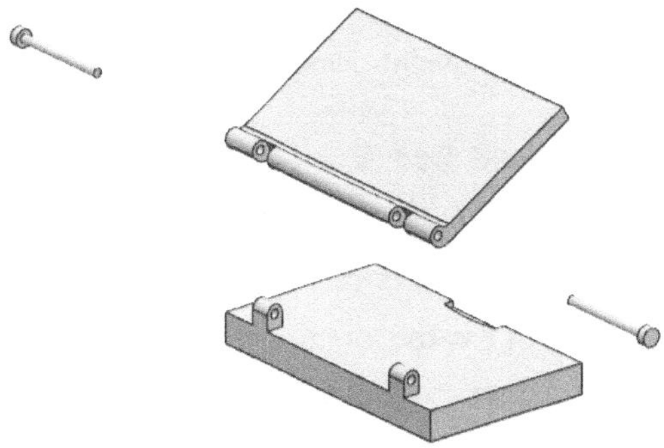

Fig 13-94 Exploded Assembly

Fig 13-95 Tracelines Icon

7. Click the arrow head designated by Ⓐ in Fig 13-92. Enter 100 in the **Distance** input box in the **Edit Explosion** dialog box and click **Apply**.

8. Choose the **Select Objects** radio button in the **Edit Explosion** dialog box. Deselect the **Pin** component that has just been moved by selecting it with **Shift + MB1** and select the **Pin** component at the other side.

9. Click MB2. Next the **Move Objects** radio button is selected.

10. Move the **Pin** component 100 mm and click **Apply**.

11. Select the **Top_modified** component and the two **Pin** components and move along the Z direction of WCS by 50 mm as shown in Fig 13-94.

12. Click **OK** in the **Edit Explosion** dialog box.

Creating Traceline

1. Click the **Tracelines** icon in the **Exploded Views** icon group.

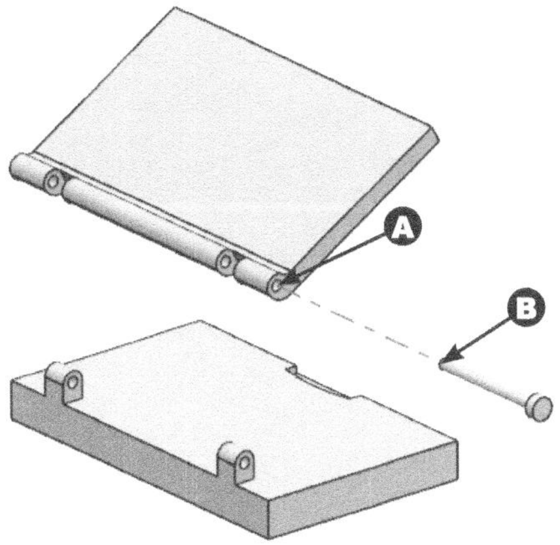

Fig 13-96 Traceline

2. Select the center points Ⓐ and Ⓑ to create the traceline as shown in Fig 13-96. You can use the snap point option properly.

3. Create other tracelines as shown in Fig 13-97.

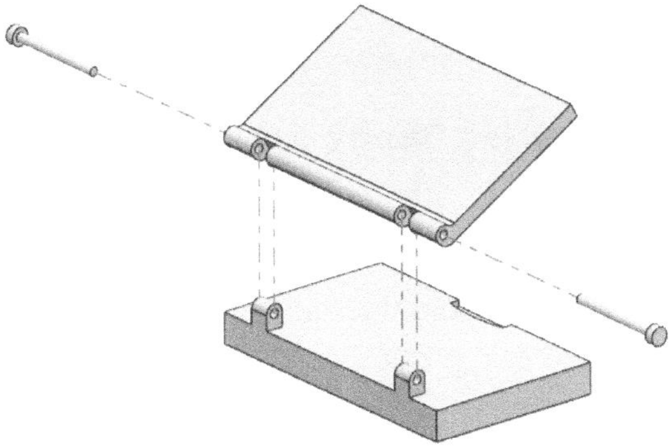

Fig 13-97 Completed Tracelines

Fig 13-98 Selecting Work View Explosion

4. Select **(No Explosion)** in the **Work View Explosion** dropdown list as shown in Fig 13-98. The assembly turns to the assembled state and the traceline becomes invalid.

5. Select **Explosion 1** in the **Work View Explosion** dropdown list.

6. Save the assembly file as a new part ch13_ex06_assy_exploded.prt.

7. Close all parts.

END of Exercise

13.6 Additional Assemblies Commands

13.6.1 Display of Components

Using the **Edit Object Display** icon in the **View** tab > **Visualization** icon group, you can modify the color, opacity, line font, etc. of the components. Note that the change of appearance applies only to the components of the current displayed assembly.

Keep to the following process.

① Press MB3 on the component in the graphics window and choose **Edit Display** in the pop-up menu.

② Set the options in the **Edit Object Display** dialog box and click **OK**.

Fig 13-99 shows the assembly with various display states. Note that the two **Pin** components which get their geometry from the same master part can have different display properties.

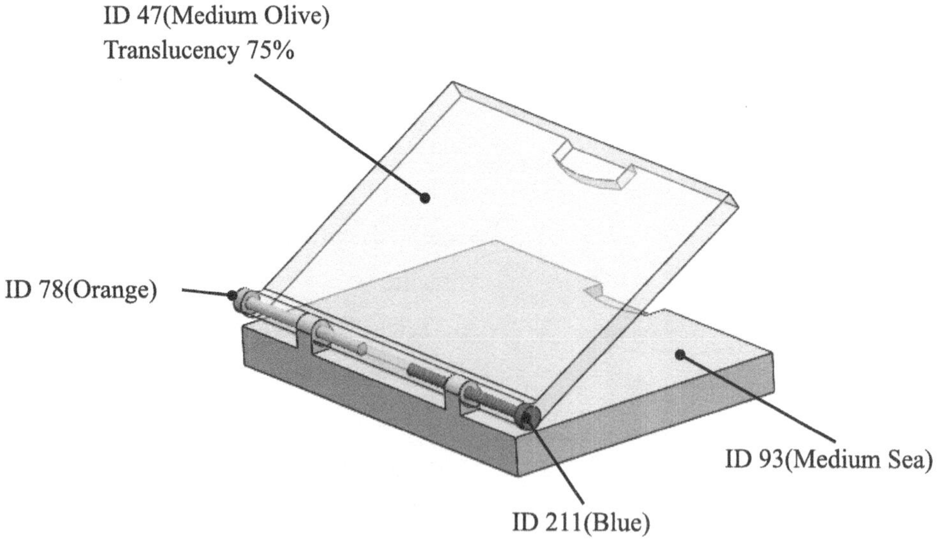

Fig 13-99 Various Display Properties

13.6.2 Sectioning

You can display a section of the components using the sectioning tools in the **View** tab.

► **Edit Work Section**: Set the options for the work section.

► **Clip Work Section**: If you click **OK** after setting the options of the work section with the **Edit Work Section** command, the **Clip Work Section** button is turned on. You can turn off the button by clicking it once again.

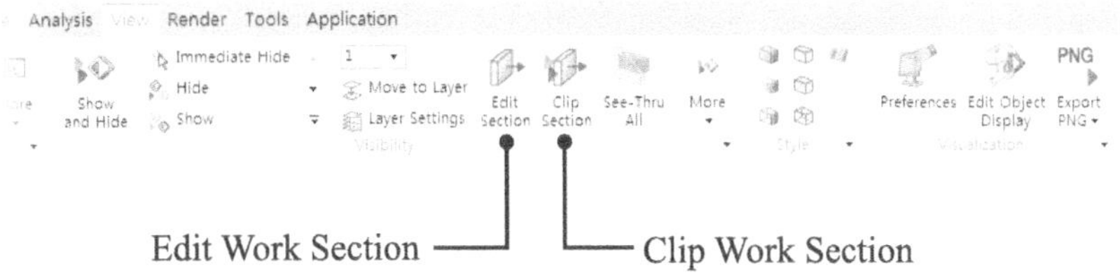

Fig 13-100 Sectioning Icons

Folder: ch13_ex07
File: ch13_ex07_assy.prt

Sectioning **Exercise 07**

Let's learn how to use the sectioning command and options through an exercise.

1. Open the given assembly file ch13_ex07_assy.prt in the given folder ch13_ex07.

2. Click the **Edit Work Section** icon in the **Visibility** icon group in the **View** tab.

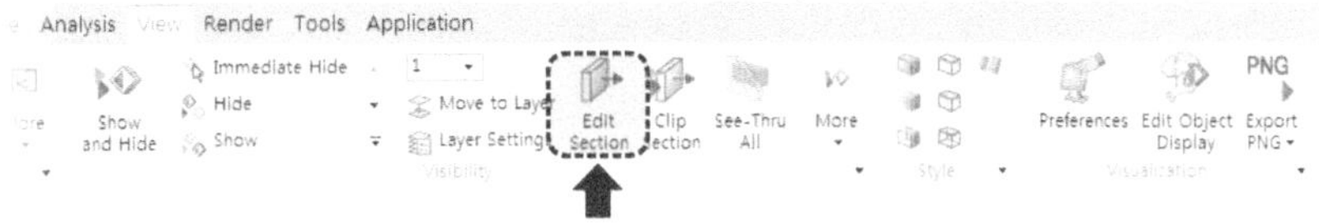

Fig 13-101 Edit Work Section Icon

3. Press the **X** button (❸ in Fig 13-102) in the **View Section** dialog box. The sectioning plane is set normal to the XC direction.

4. Move the scroll bar in the dialog box as designated by ❹ in Fig 13-102.

5. Click **OK** in the dialog box. The section is displayed as shown in Fig 13-103. Identify that the **Clip Work Section** icon is turned on in the **Visibility** icon group.

6. Press the **Clip Work Section** icon to turn off sectioning.

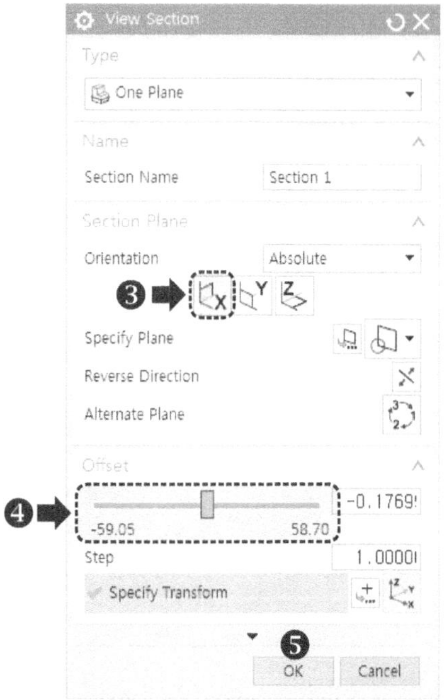

Fig 13-102 Setting the Section Plane

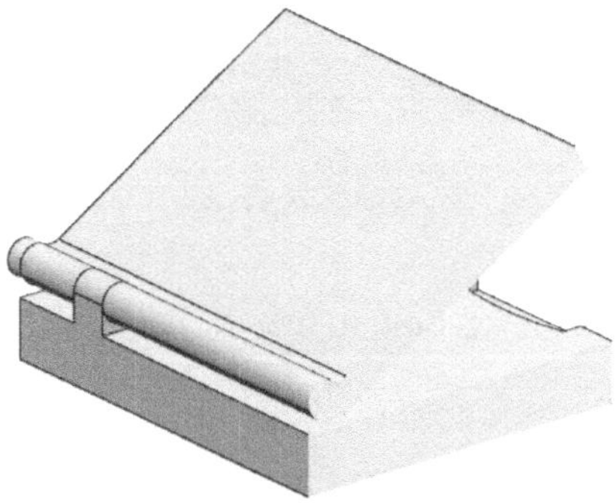

Fig 13-103 Sectioned Assembly

7. Choose **View > Section > New Section** in the **Menu** button.

8. Drag the arrow head of the handle as shown in Fig 13-104.

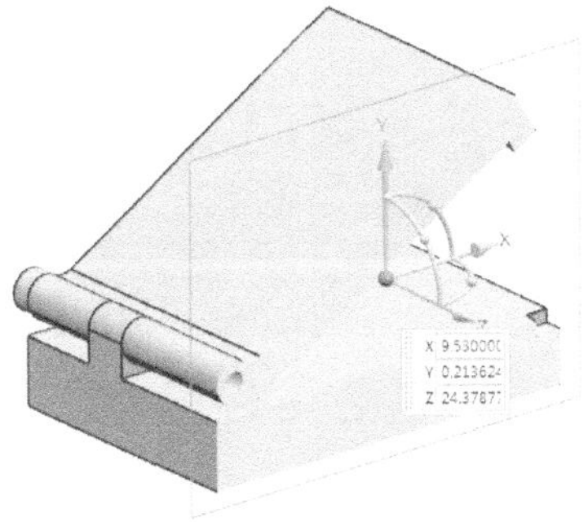

Fig 13-104 Creating a New Section Plane

9. Check the option **Show 2D Viewer** in the **View Sections** dialog box as shown in Fig 13-105. Section lines are displayed in the **2D Section Viewer** as shown in Fig 13-105.

10. Click **OK** in the dialog box and turn off the **Clip Work View** button in the **Visibility** icon group.

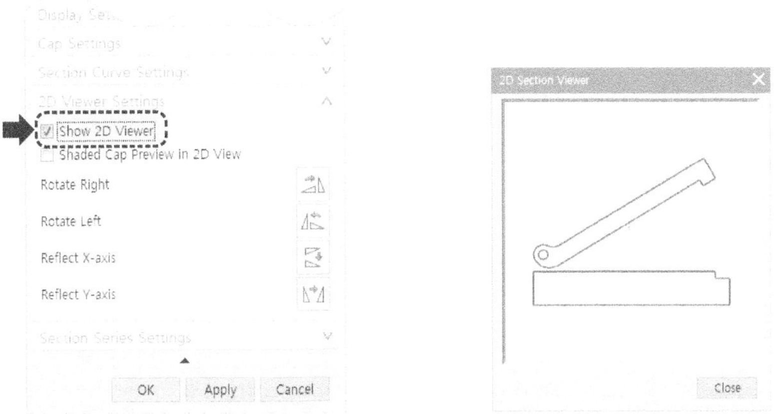

Fig 13-105 2D Section Viewer

11. Expand the **Sections** container in the **Assembly Navigator** by clicking the ⊞ symbol. The section created in the second is marked as **(Work)** as shown in Fig 13-106.

12. Check the boxes in front of the two sections in the **Assembly Navigator**.

13. Verify that the sections are displayed as shown in Fig 13-107.

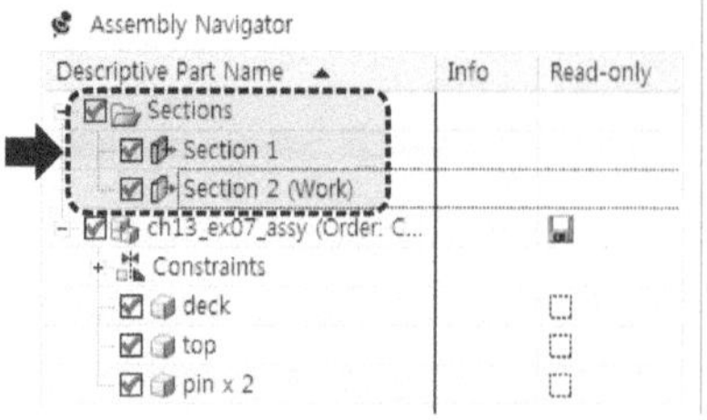

Fig 13-106 Expanded Sections Container

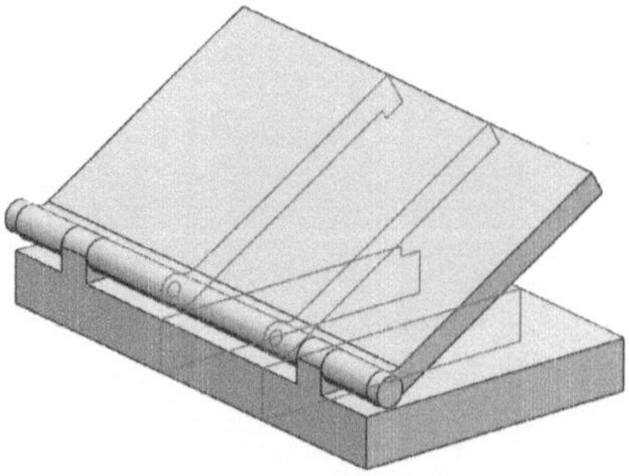

Fig 13-107 Sections

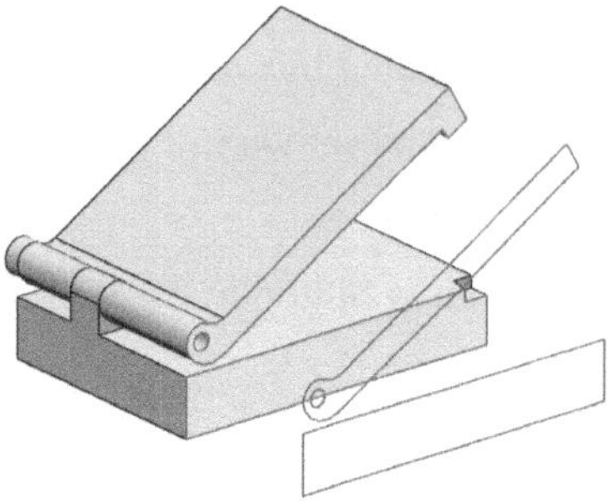

Fig 13-108 Cut Section

14. Click the **Clip Work Section** icon in the **Visibility** icon group. The current work section is displayed in the graphics window.

15. Close without saving the file.

END of Exercise

! Checking Interference

You can identify the location of interference by checking the **Show Interference** option in the **Cap Settings** option group.

Fig 13-109 Cap Settings Option

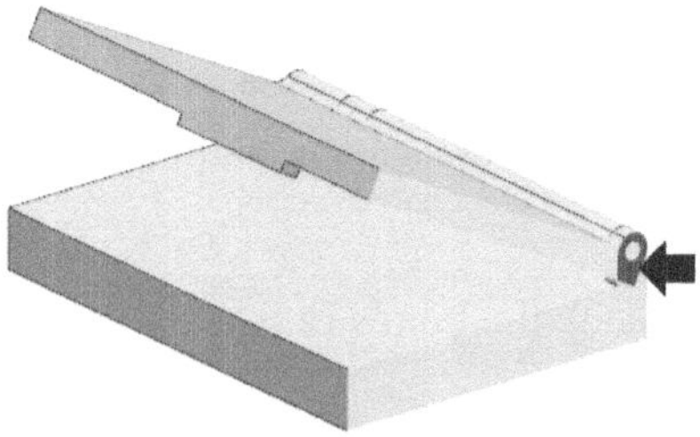

Fig 13-110 Interference

13.6.3 Measuring Mass

You can measure the mass of assembly and its components.

Folder: ch13_ex08
File: ch13_ex08_assy.prt

Measuring Mass **Exercise 08**

Let's measure the mass of assembly and display the mass of each component.

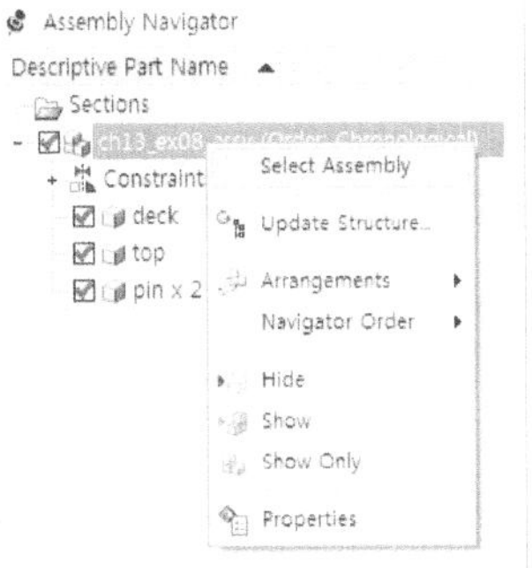

Fig 13-111 Selecting the Assembly to Measure

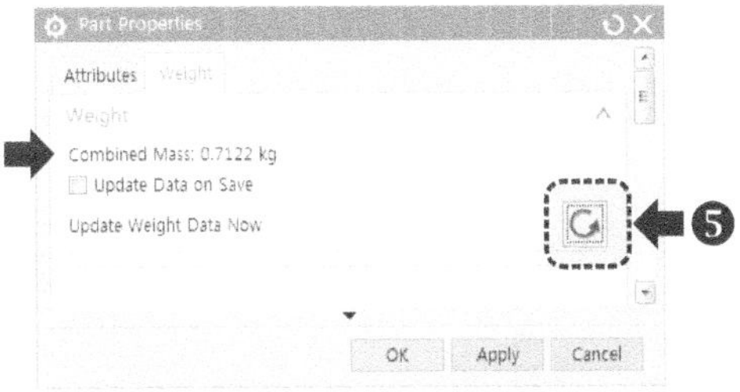

Fig 13-112 Updating Mass

1. Open the given assembly file ch13_ex08_assy.prt.

2. Click MB3 on the top assembly and choose **Select Assembly** in the pop-up menu.

3. Click MB3 on the selected assembly and choose **Properties** in the pop-up menu.

4. Click the **Weight** tab in the **Part Properties** dialog box.

5. Click the **Update Weight Data Now** button in the dialog box as shown in Fig 13-110.

The combined mass is displayed in the dialog box as specified by the arrow in Fig 13-110.

6. Click **OK** in the dialog box.

Assigning Material

Let's assign material for the Top component and measure the weight.

1. Make the **Top** component a work part.
2. Choose **Tools > Materials > Assign Material** in the **Menu** button.
3. Select the solid body of the **Top** part in the **Select Body** option.
4. Select **ABS** in the **Materials** list and click OK in the **Assign Material** dialog box.
5. Make the assembly a work part by double clicking the assembly in the partnavigator.
6. Measure the weight of the assembly according to the steps described previously. The result is shown as Fig 13-115.
7. Click **OK** in the **Part Properties** dialog box.

Fig 13-113 Assign Materials Menu

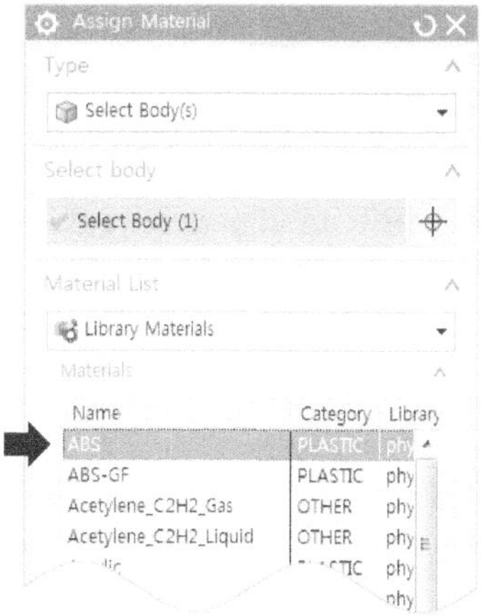

Fig 13-114 Assign Material Dialog Box

Displaying Weight

1. Click MB3 on an empty area in the assembly navigator and choose **Columns > Weight (g)** in the pop-up menu as shown in Fig 13-116.

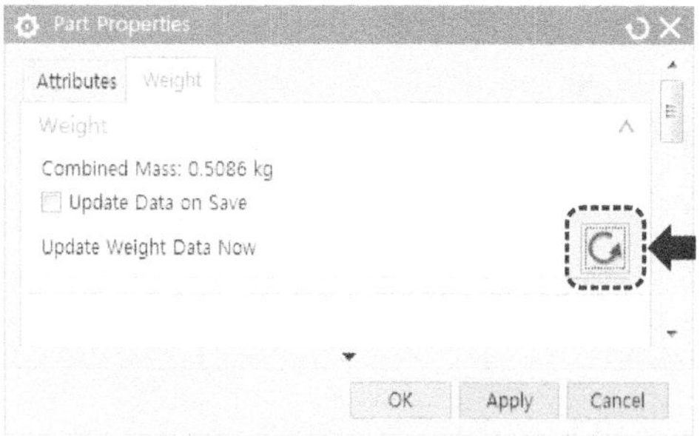

Fig 13-115 Updated Mass

The **Weight (g)** column is included in the assembly navigator as shown in Fig 13-117 and you can identify the mass of each component.

7. Close without saving the file.

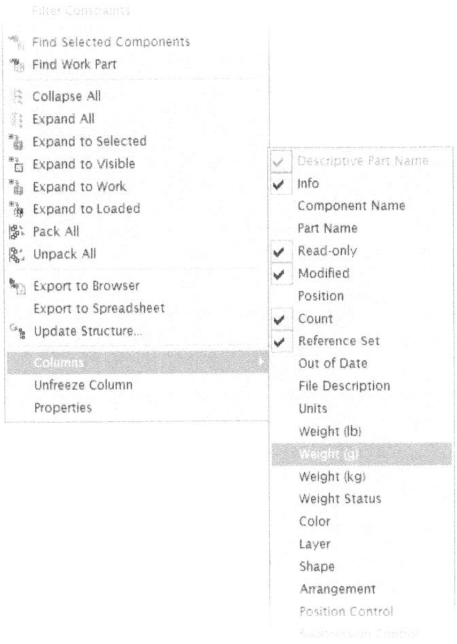

Fig 13-116 Adding the Weight Column

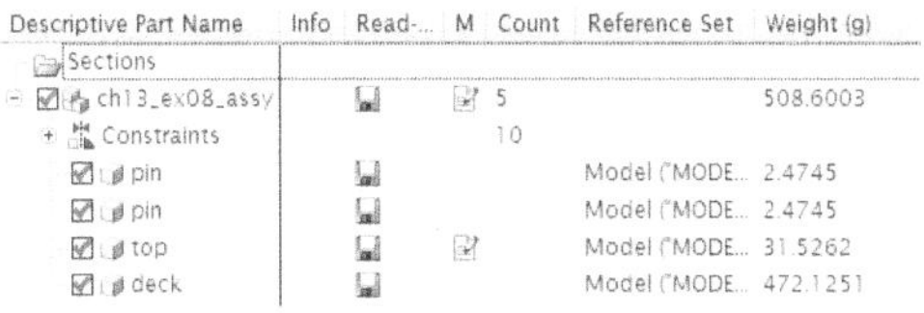

Fig 13-117 Weight (g) Column

END of Exercise

Folder: ch13_ex09_assy
File: ch13_ex09_assy.prt

Creating a Part in Context of Assembly — Exercise 09

1. Create the **Driving Assembly** referring to the assembly drawing shown in Fig 13-118. Note that there is no part file for the **Link** in the given folder.

2. Create the part with the name of link.prt in the corresponding folder. Determine your own dimensions for the part unless the part does not interfere with other components.

3. Complete the assembly and constrain it such that the eccentric axle can rotate and the **Connector** can move up and down as a result.

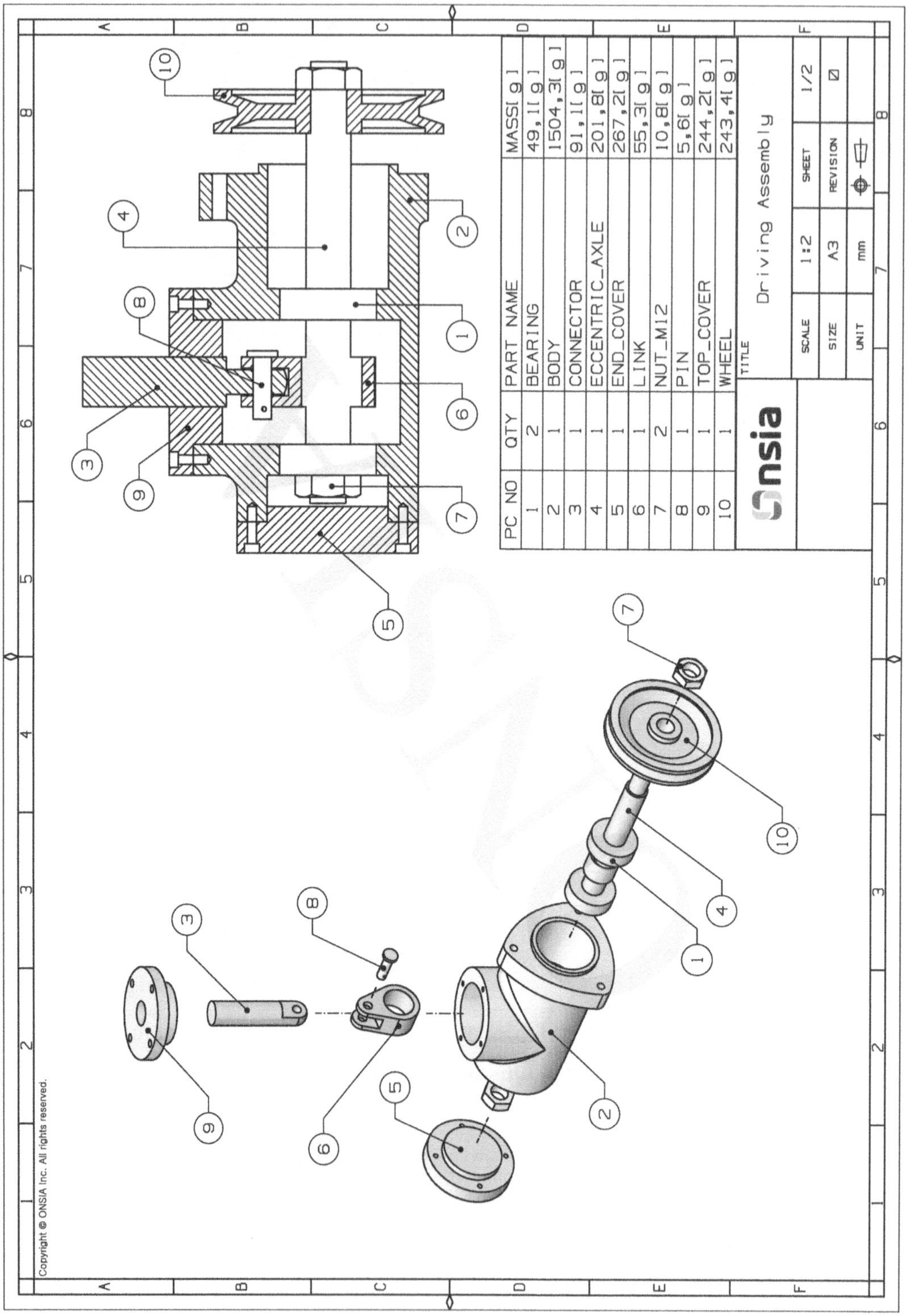

Fig 13-118 Driving Assembly

Chapter 14

Creating Drawing Views

After completing this chapter you will understand

- objectives and types of drawings.
- projection methods.
- the process of creating each drawing view in NX.
- types of various drawing views and how to create them in NX.

14.1 Introduction

These days, three dimensional design is widely adopted by manufacturing industries in designing products. If a product is designed using a three dimensional modeling program such as NX and manufactured on the basis of automation, there should be utilities available in the factory so that the manufacturing process can refer to the three dimensional design data.

If the manufacturing process is based on a manual, such utilities to deal with three dimensional data are not required. In those cases, traditional drawings explaining the shapes and manufacturing methods of a part or product will be sufficient. Therefore, we have to be able to create drawings in three dimensional modeling programs.

There are two types of drawings based on the underlying objectives of drawings; a part drawing and an assembly drawing. A part drawing is created to manufacture individual parts. An assembly drawing is created for assembly. The assembly sequence and path can be illustrated in a disassembled drawing view. Names, quantity, material, etc. of each component of an assembly can be included in the parts list.

In NX, we can create each drawing view by referencing a three dimensional part geometry. This is called **Model-Based Drawing**. If the part geometry is modified, the drawing can be updated to reflect the design changes. You can create a drawing without a 3D model, which is called a **Stand-Alone Drawing**. This type of drawing falls outside the scope of this textbook.

The general process to create a drawing is as follows.

① Determine a part or assembly for which to create the drawing.
② Create a drawing file.
③ Create drawing views required to explain the three dimensional shape of the part.
④ Create dimensions, annotations, symbols, etc. in the drawing.

14.2 Terms and Definitions

14.2.1 Drawing View

The three dimensional part geometry can be viewed from various directions or can be cut or magnified to express its shape completely in two dimensions.

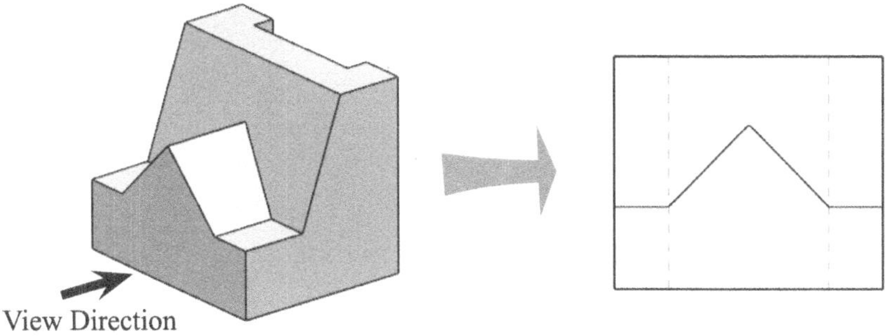

Fig 14-1 Drawing View

14.2.2 Title Block

The basic information for a drawing is recorded in the title block which is located in the bottom right of the drawing sheet. Fig 14-2 shows a typical title block that is available by default in NX.

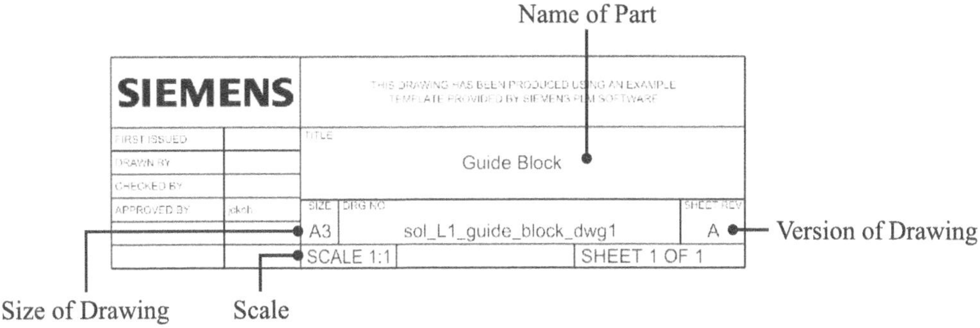

Fig 14-2 Title Block

14.2.3 Drawing Sheet

A manual drawing is created on a sheet. In a 2D drawing created with a CAD program, the size of the drawing, scale, drawing standard, projection method, etc. are defined in the drawing sheet.

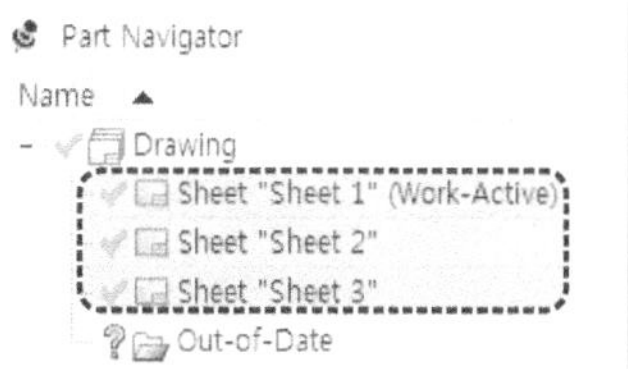

Fig 14-3 Drawing Sheet

14.3 Drawing File

Drawing files in NX have an extension of .prt. The three dimensional part for which you will create a drawing is called a master part. That is to say, the three dimensional geometry is managed as a component in a drawing file. You can modify the 3D geometry while you are creating a drawing the same way that you have modified a master part in the context of an assembly.

14.3.1 Creating a Drawing File

You can create a drawing file for the specified master part according to the following procedure. Suppose that there is no part open in the NX session.

1. Click the **New** icon in the **Home** tab.

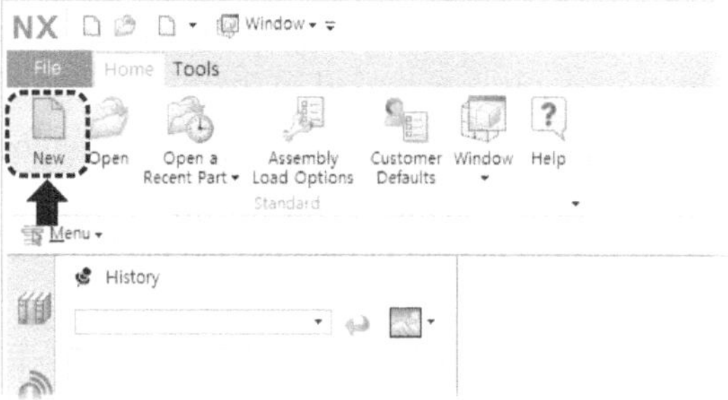

Fig 14-4 New Icon

2. Click the **Drawing** tab in the **New** dialog box (❷ in Fig 14-5).

3. Select **Reference Existing Part** in the **Relationship** dropdown list (❸ in Fig 14-5).

4. Select the **Unit** option (❹ in Fig 14-5).

5. Choose a size for the drawing (❺ in Fig 14-5).

6. Click the **Open** button in the **Part to create a drawing of** option (❻ in Fig 14-5).

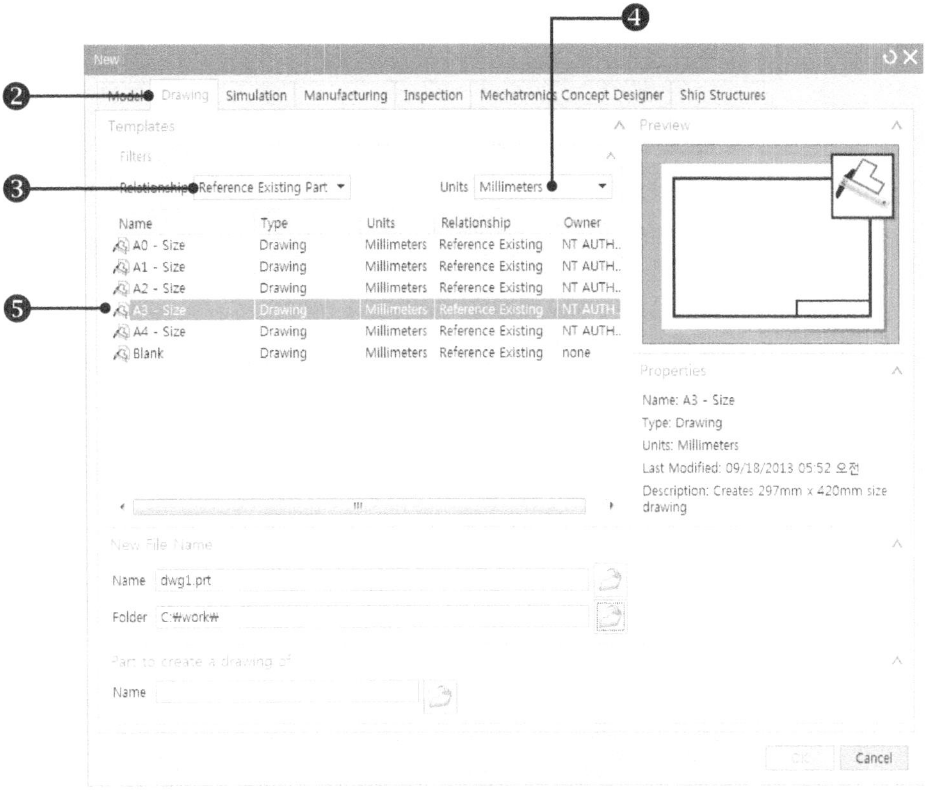

Fig 14-5 New Dialog Box

7. Select the part for which to create a drawing by clicking the **Open** button in the **Select master part** dialog box and click **OK** in the dialog box.

Fig 14-6 Specifying the Master Part

8. Confirm that the folder and the name of the part file are specified automatically.

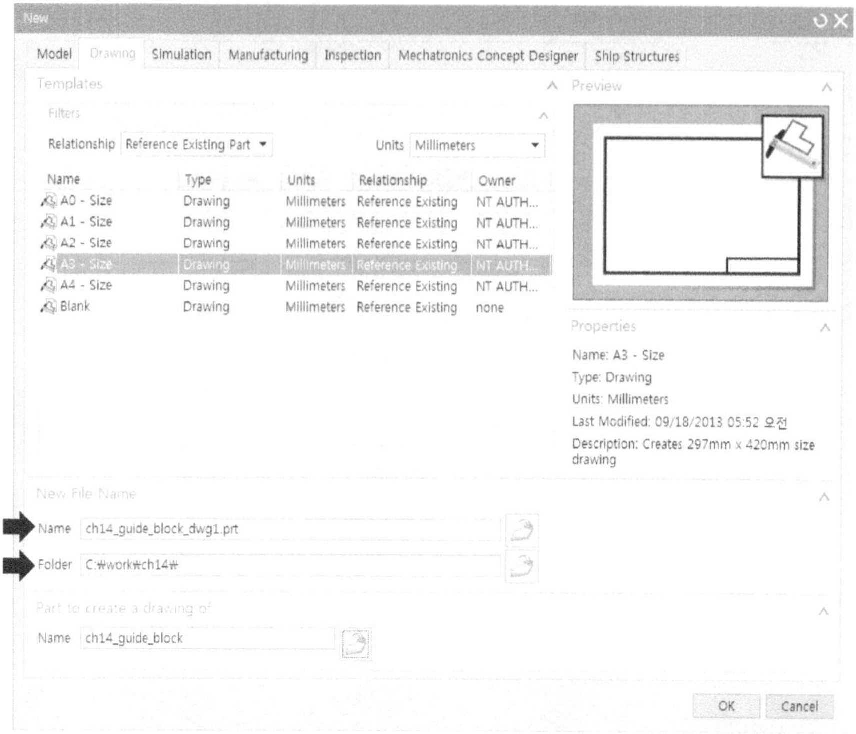

Fig 14-7 New Dialog Box

9. Click the **OK** button in the **New** dialog box. The **Populate Title Block** dialog box is invoked as shown in Fig 14-8. You can enter the name of the people who have responsibility for the drawing. Click **Close** after entering the names.

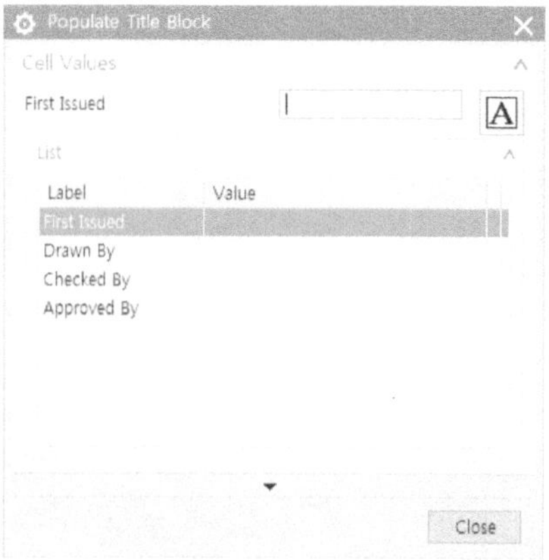

Fig 14-8 Populate Title Block Dialog Box

10. The **View Creation Wizard** as shown in Fig 14-9 is invoked. You can create four drawing views automatically with the wizard. Click **Cancel** because we will create each drawing view manually.

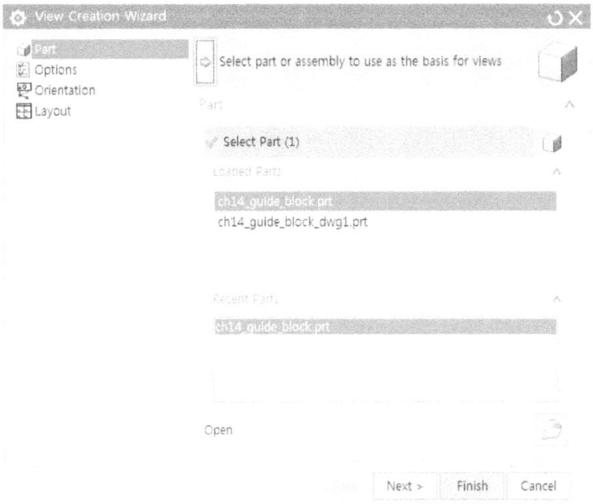

Fig 14-9 View Creation Wizard Dialog Box

The drawing screen is shown as in Fig 14-10.

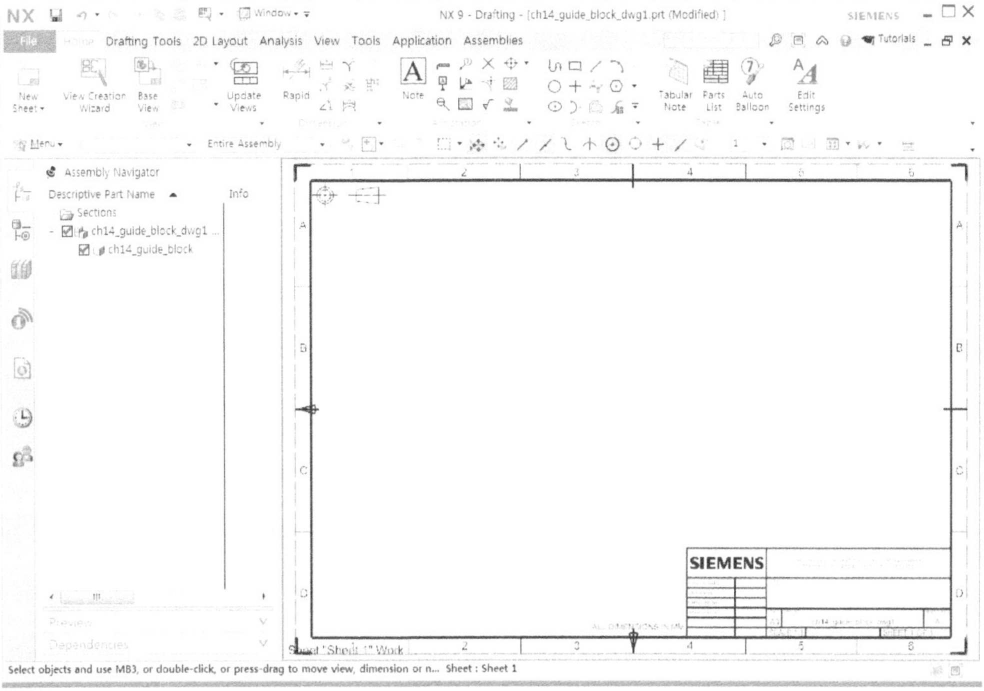

Fig 14-10 Drawing Screen

14.3.2 Understanding the Drawing Screen

Let's understand the meaning and usage of the items in the drawing screen.

Ⓐ **Part Navigator**: Records the drawing sheets, drawing views in the drawing sheet, drawng sketches, etc.

Ⓑ **Assembly Navigator**: Shows the structure of the drawing file as the form of assembly. Note that the geometry for which to create the drawing is a component of the drawing file.

Ⓒ **Title Bar**: Notifies the current application and the file name.

Ⓓ **Title Block**: Basic information such as the name of the part and revisions of the drawing is recorded.

Ⓔ Shows the unit of length.

Ⓕ Explains the projection method.

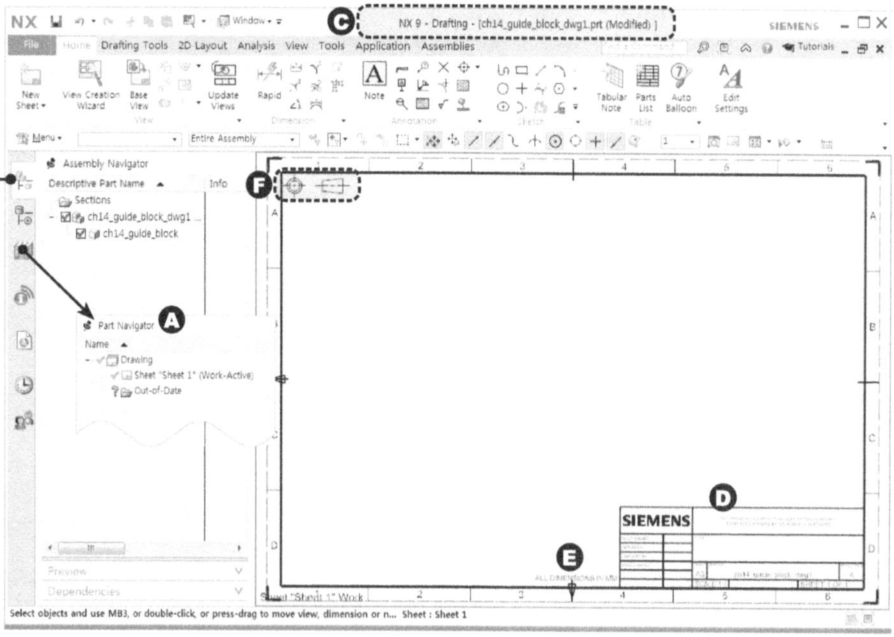

Fig 14-11 Drawing Screen

Default Action in Creating a New File

There are some default actions that are performed in creating a new drawing file.

Ⓐ A sheet is created automatically.

Ⓑ The **View Creation Wizard** is activated automatically.

Ⓒ The **Projected View** command is executed automatically after inserting a **Base View**.

You can set the options in the **Menu** button by choosing **Preferences > Drafting** and selecting the **Workflow** option as shown in Fig 14-12.

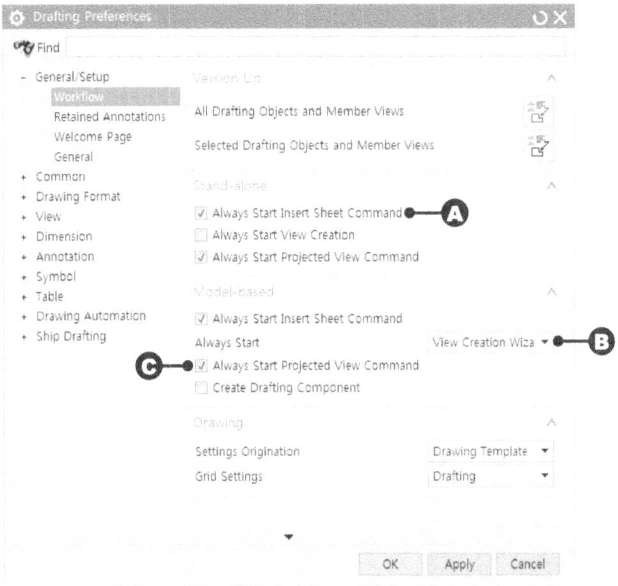

Fig 14-12 Drafting Preferences

14.4.2 Saving the Drawing File

You can save the drawing file by clicking the **Save** icon in the **Quick Access** toolbar. When you are saving the file for the first time, a dialog box is invoked as shown in Fig 14-13 and you can modify the folder and file name.

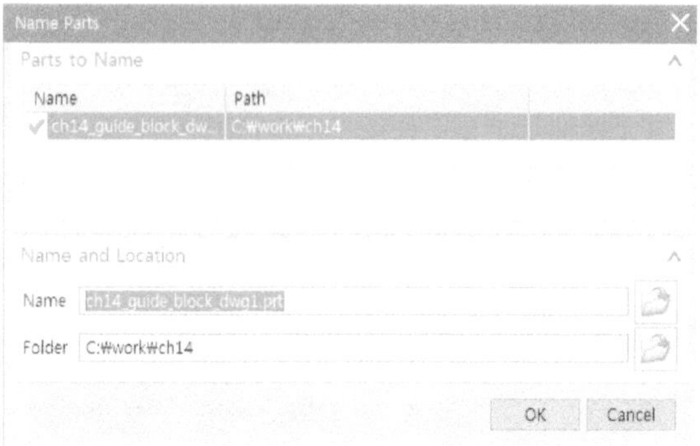

Fig 14-13 Name Part Dialog Box

14.4 Drawing Sheet

The largest standard size of a sheet is **A0** of which the dimension is 1189 mm x 841 mm. However, we cannot draw all necessary drawing views and annotations in a single sheet because we need to ensure that the texts and views are not too small. Bearing in mind that we have to print out the drawing in the end, the size of the texts and drawing views have to be easy and comfortable to read. What, then, should we do in cases where we have to create a drawing for a part with great complexity in its geometry? All necessary drawing entities for those parts cannot be created in a single **A0** sheet. We need to insert more drawing sheets and arrange the drawing views in several drawing sheets.

14.4.1 Creating a Drawing Sheet

In NX, you can insert additional drawing sheets in the following way.

① Click the **New Sheet** icon in the **Home** tab.

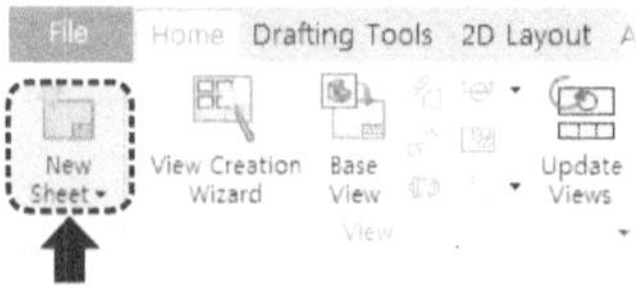

Fig 14-14 New Sheet Icon

② Click MB3 on **Drawing** in the part navigator and choose **Insert Sheet** in the pop-up menu.

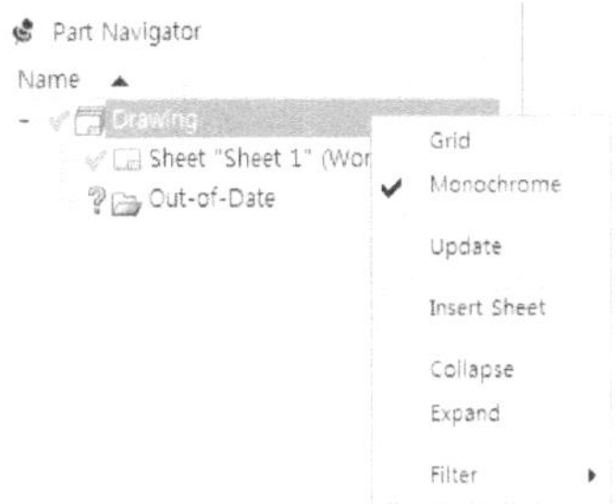

Fig 14-15 Drawing Pop-up Menu

14.4.3 Setting a Drawing Sheet

Click MB3 on the **Sheet** in the part navigator and choose **Edit Sheet** in the pop-up menu as shown in Fig 14-16. The **Sheet** dialog box as shown in Fig 14-17 appears and the basic settings for the sheet can be defined or modified. You can modify the name of the sheet, scale, drawing size, projection method, etc. in the dialog box.

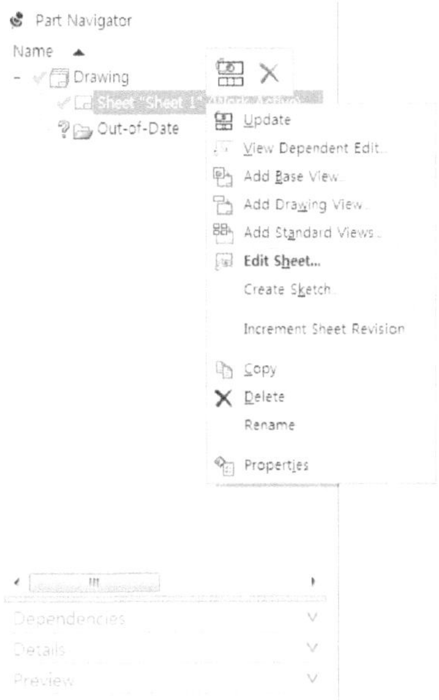

Fig 14-16 Edit Sheet Menu

The **Projection** option is set as the **3rd Angle Projection** by default. Note that we will choose the third angle projection method to create drawing views in this textbook.

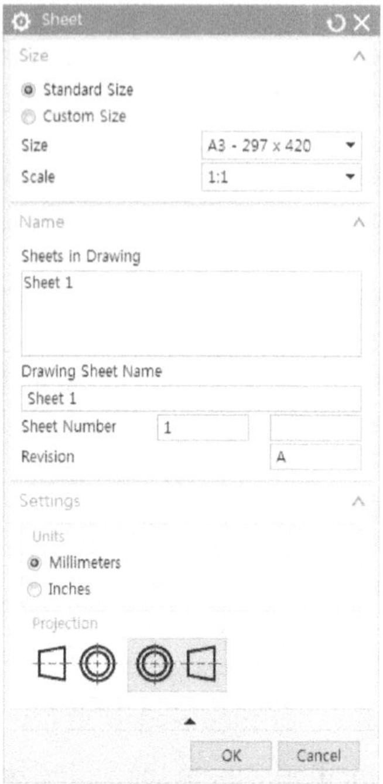

Fig 14-17 Sheet Dialog Box(More Option)

Drawing Standard

Drawings in this textbook are explained depending on the **ISO** standard. You can modify the drawing standard by choosing **Tools > Drafting Standard** in the **Menu** button.

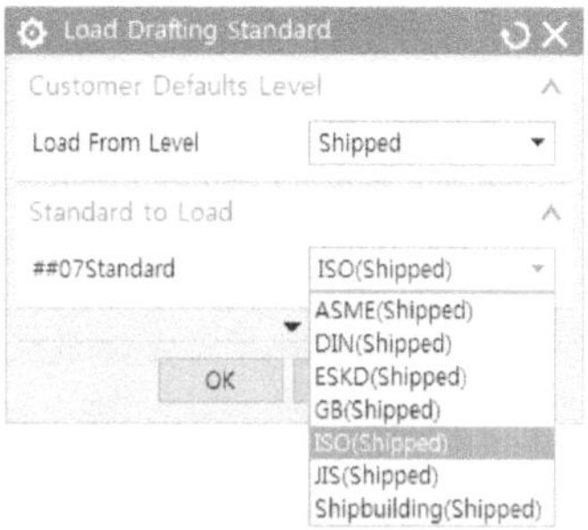

Fig 14-18 Drawing Standard

Projection Methods

► **1st Angle Projection**: A part is placed in the 1st quadrant in the space and is projected on each plane along the projection direction. The plane of projection is unfolded to arrange each projection view as shown in Fig 14-19.

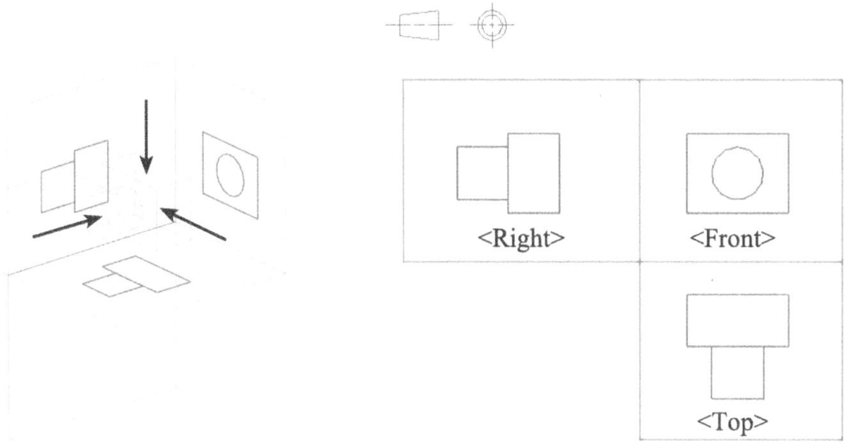

Fig 14-19 1st Angle Projection

► **3rd Angle Projection**: A part is placed in the 3rd quadrant in the space and is projected on each plane along the projection direction. The plane of projection is unfolded to arrange each projection view as shown in Fig 14-20.

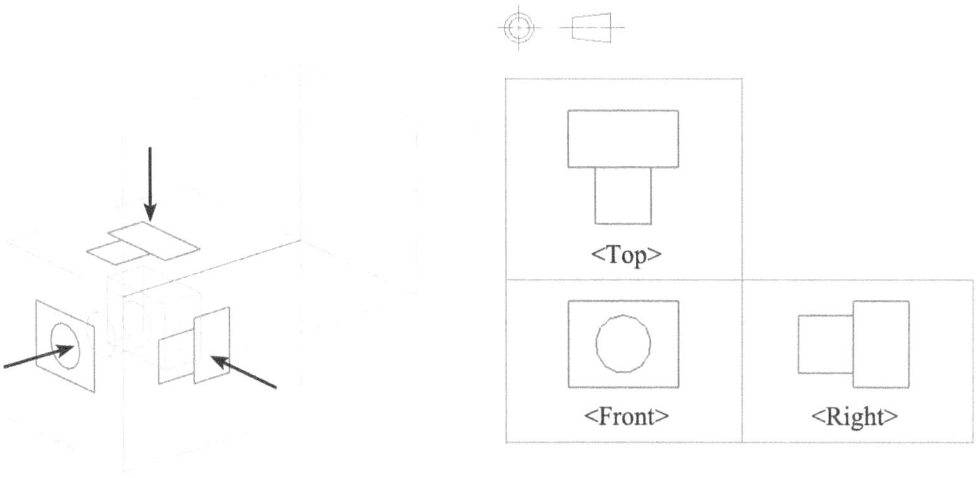

Fig 14-20 3rd Angle Projection

14.5 Drawing View

To illustrate a three dimensional shape in a 2D sheet, we can create various types of drawing views to express the full shape without missing any aspect of it. Note that a smaller number of drawing views is preferable for the simplicity of the drawing. After creating all necessary drawing views, we create the dimensions and drawing symbols.

Various drawing views can be created with the icons in the **View** icon group.

- ► **Base View**: You can create a drawing view according to the orientation of the model view.
- ► **Projected View**: An existing drawing view is projected along a specified direction and viewed according to the projection view.
- ► **Section View**: An existing drawing view is cut at a location and is viewed along a specified direction.
- ► **Detail View**: A complex portion of another view is magnified.
- ► **Break-out Section View**: A portion of an existing view is cut out at a specified depth.
- ► **Broken View**: A long uniform part can be cut short.

14.5.1 Base View

You can create a drawing view according to the orientation of the model view. You can use the standard view direction of the drawing file or you can choose an arbitrary view direction. Note also that you can create as many base views as required.

Fig 14-21 Base View Icon

Fig 14-22 shows the default **Base View** dialog box. If you click the **Base View** icon, the **Specify Location** option is activated and the **Top** base view is previewed on the mouse pointer. You can create the base view by clicking MB1 on a location in the drawing sheet. Of course, you can choose another model view in the **Model View to Use** dropdown list.

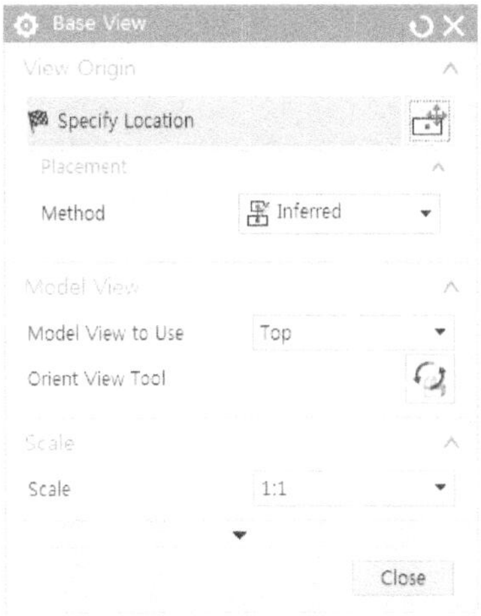

Fig 14-22 Base View Dialog Box

If you click the **Orient View Tool** button in the **Model View** option group, the geometry of the component is shown in the **Orient View** window as shown in Fig 14-23. You can set the view direction of the base view by clicking MB2 and rotating the 3D geometry. You can also use the options **Normal Direction** and **X Direction** in the **Orient View Tool** dialog box. Click **OK** in the dialog box after setting the view direction.

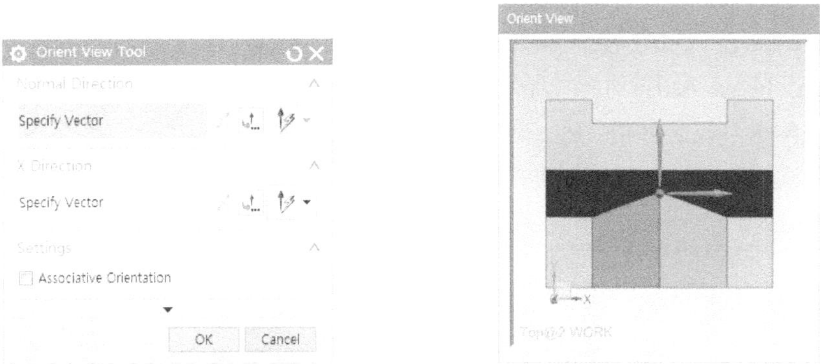

Fig 14-23 Using the Orient View Tool

Model View

Basic model views are created automatically in 3D in the part file, and they appear in the Model View dropdown list when you are creating a base view. You can create your own model view according to your requirements in the 3D part file, which will be explained in Exercise 07 in Chapter 15.

14.5.2 Projected View

You can create a view projected along a specified direction. The new view is created according to the specified projection angle. Fig 14-24 shows the preview of the projected view, where the left view is projected on the right.

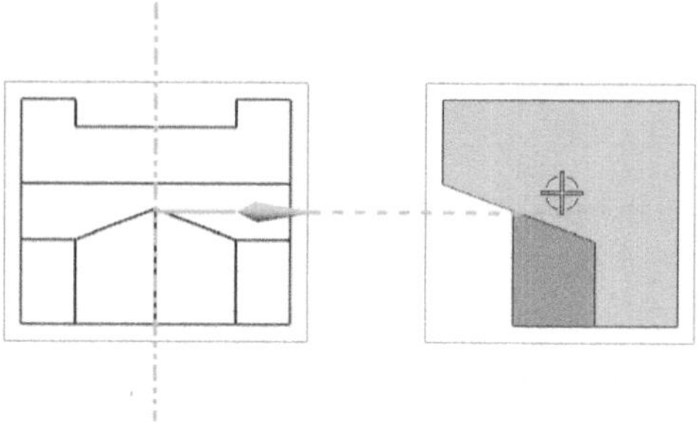

Fig 14-24 Preview of the Projected View

Exercise 01 Creating Drawing Views

ch14_ex01.prt

Create drawing views for the given part.

1. Create the top view using the **Base View** command.
2. Create the projected view on the right of the top view.
3. Create the isometric view using the **Base View** command.
4. Modify the scale of the drawing sheet.
5. Create a projected view under the right projected view.

Creating a Drawing File

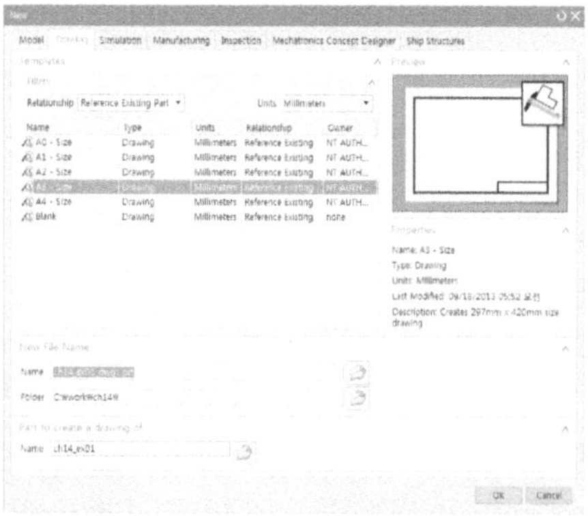

Fig 14-25 Creating a Drawing File

1. Close all open parts by choosing **File > Close > All Parts.**
2. Open the given file ch14_ex01.prt.
3. Click the **New** icon. Confirm that the master part is designated automatically in the **New** dialog box as shown in Fig 14-25.
4. Specify the folder and click **OK**. Refer to section 14.3.1 on Page 548 for the detailed process of creating the drawing file.

Creating Top View and Projected View

Fig 14-26 Base View Icon

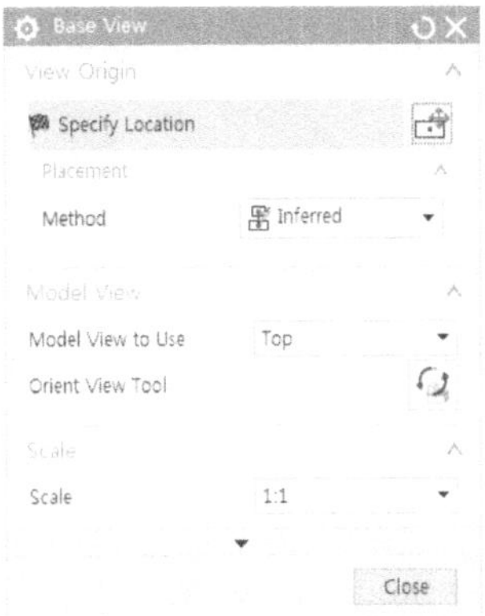

Fig 14-27 Base View Dialog Box

1. Click the **Base View** icon in the **View** icon group

2. Choose **Top** in the **Model View to Use** option in the **Base View** dialog box.

3. Click MB1 at the location shown in Fig 14-28 to create the top view.

The **Projected View** dialog box is invoked as shown in Fig 14-29 and the projected view is previewed according to the location of the mouse pointer.

4. Move the mouse pointer on the right of the top view and click MB1 to create the projected view.

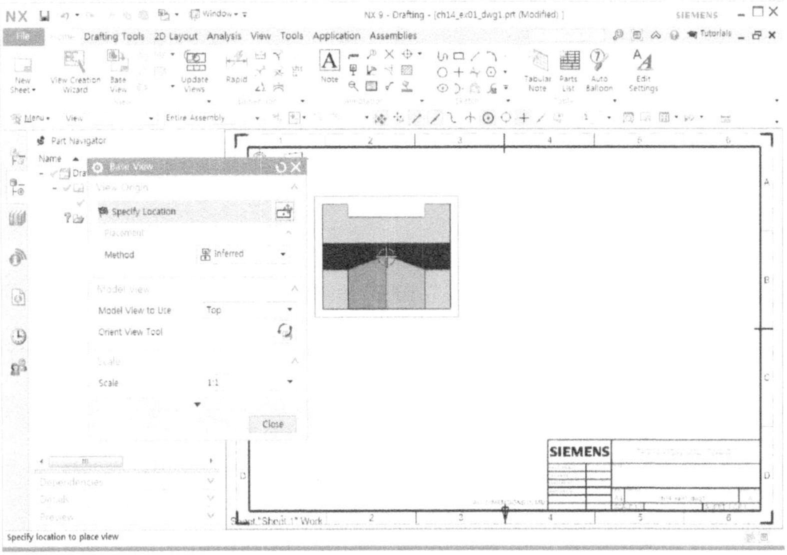

Fig 14-28 Preview of the Top View

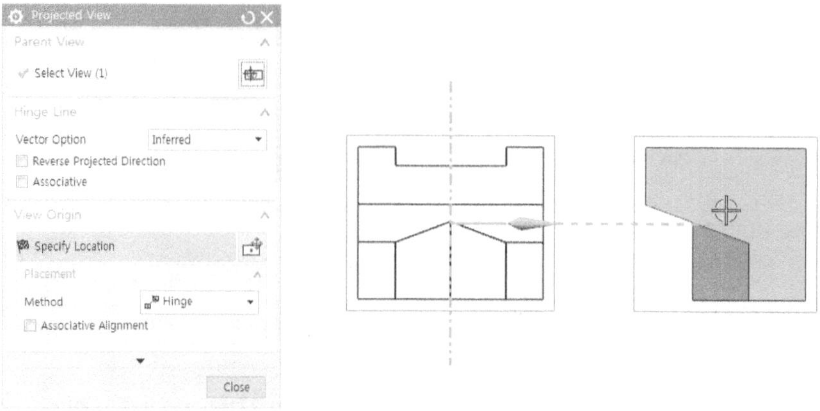

Fig 14-29 Preview of the Projected View

5. Close the **Projected View** dialog box.

Creating Trimetric View

1. Click the **Base View** icon in the **View** icon group.

2. Choose **Trimetric** in the **Model View to Use** option in the **Base View** dialog box.

3. Click MB1 at the location as shown in Fig 14-31 to create the trimetric view.

4. Close the **Projected View** dialog box.

Fig 14-30 Specifying the View to Use

! *Automatic Execution of Projected View*

Note that the **Projected View** command is executed automatically after creating a base view on account of the option set in Fig 14-12.

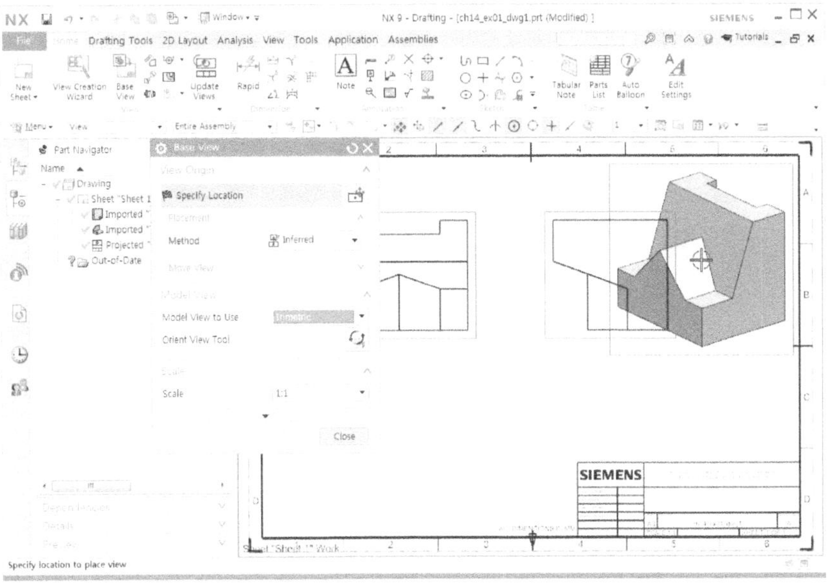

Fig 14-31 Creating the Trimetric View

Fig 14-32 Part Navigator

Fig 14-33 Modifying the Scale

Modifying Scale of the Sheet

1. Double click the **Sheet 1** in the part navigator.

2. Modify the scale to 2:3.

3. Click **OK** in the dialog box.

4. Place the mouse pointer on the boundary of the view and drag the view by clicking MB1 to arrange the views as shown in Fig 14-34.

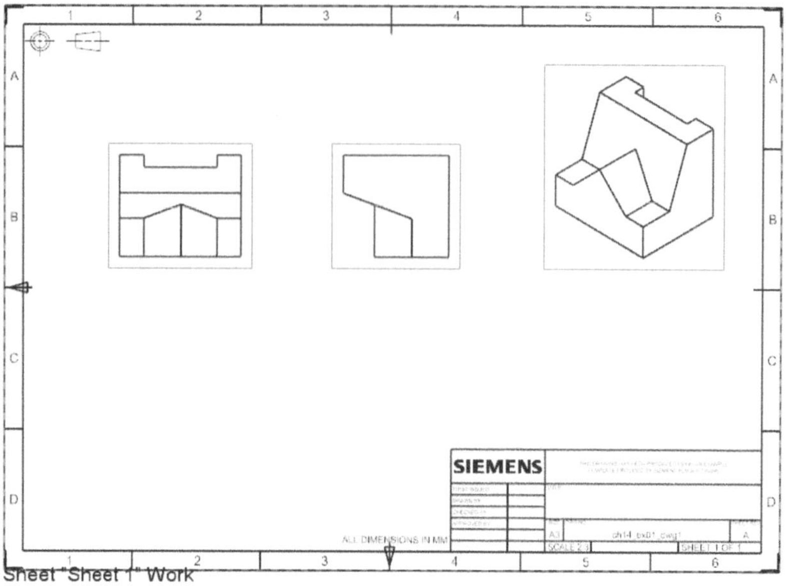

Fig 14-34 Arranged Views

Fig 14-35 Projected View Icon

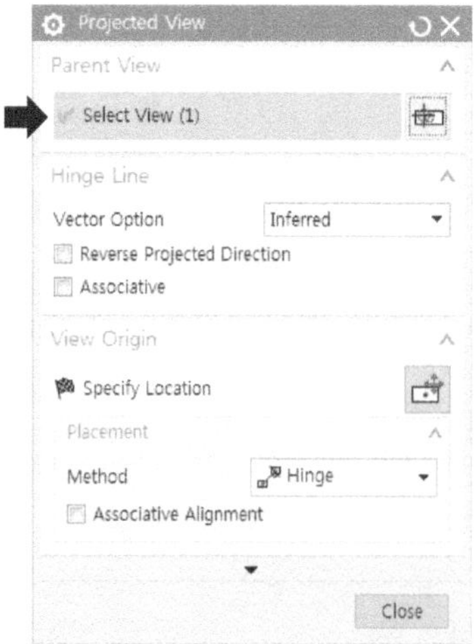

Fig 14-36 Projected View Dialog Box

Creating the Projected View

1. Click the **Projected View** icon in the **View** icon group.

The projected view for the top view is pre-viewed by default.

2. Click the **Select View** option field in the **Projected View** dialog box as shown in Fig 14-36.

3. Select the right projected view with MB1.

4. Move the mouse pointer under the right projected view as shown in Fig 14-37 and click MB1 to create the view.

5. Close the **Projected View** dialog box.

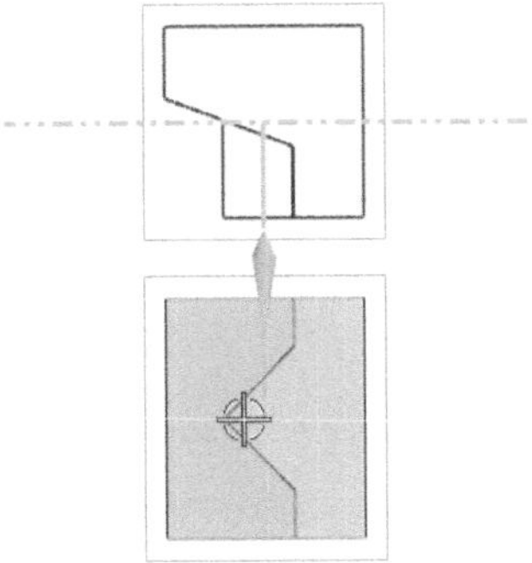

Fig 14-38 shows the drawing sheet which has four drawing views.

6. Save the drawing file and close the file.

Fig 14-37 Preview of the Projected View

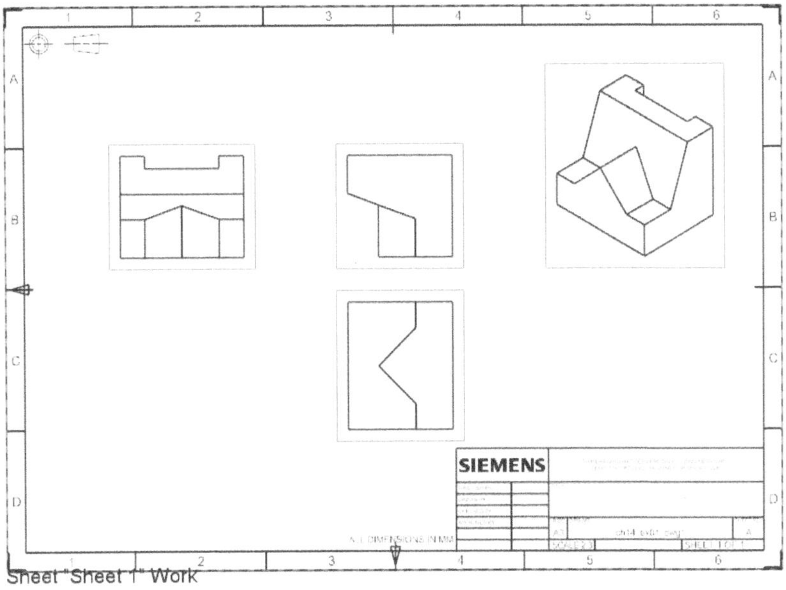

Fig 14-38 Drawing Views Created

END of Exercise

Hiding the View Border

Choose **Preferences > Drafting** in the **Menu** button and click the **View** tab. You can hide the view border by unchecking the **Border > Display** option in the **View > Workflow** item.

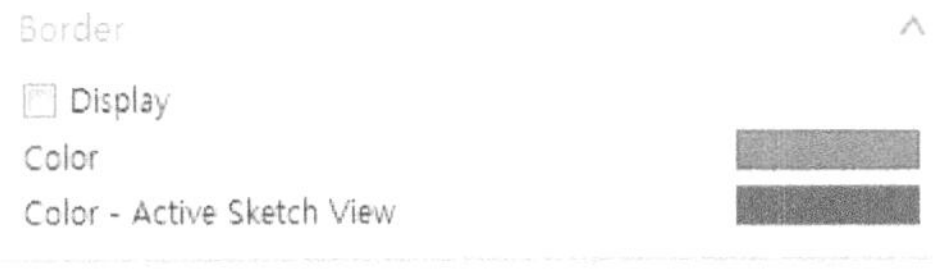

Fig 14-39 Border Option

You can specify the projection direction by using the **Hinge Line** option. Keep to the following procedure.

① Click the **Projected View** icon and select the parent view.

② Choose **Defined** in the **Vector Option** dropdown list in the **Hinge Line** option group.

③ Specify the projection direction in the parent view. If you choose line 3 in Fig 14-40, the direction is defined normal to the line. Check the **Reverse Projected Direction** option if required.

④ Click the location to place the view.

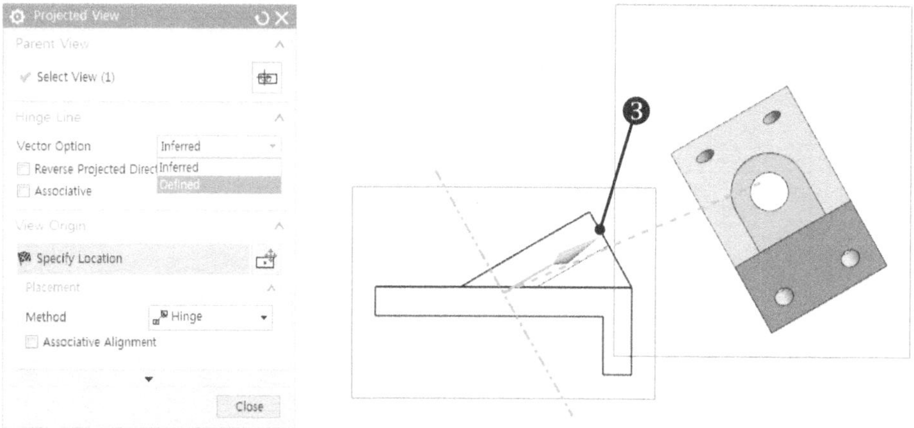

Fig 14-40 Specifying the Projection Direction

Setting the Title Block

If you have skipped setting the title block while creating the drawing file, you can set it by choosing **Tools > Drawing Format > Populate Title Block** in the **Menu** button as shown in Fig 14-41. You can also use the corresponding icon in the **Drafting Tools** tab.

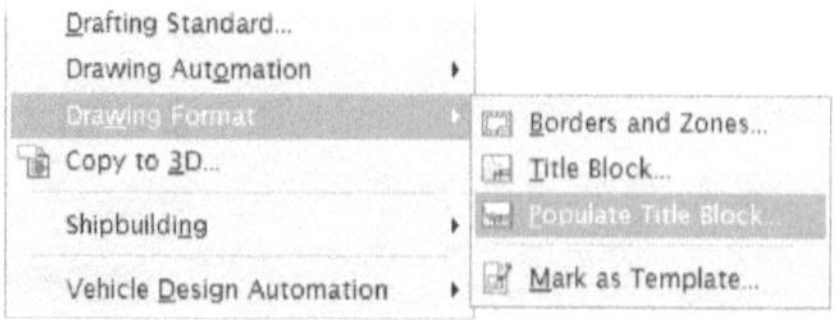

Fig 14-41 Populate Title Block Menu

14.5.3 View Style

Press **MB3 > Settings** on the view boundary as shown in Fig 14-42 The **Settings** dialog box as shown in Fig 14-43 appears and you can set the options for the drawing view. The dialog box is also invoked by pressing **MB3 > Settings** on a view in the part navigator.

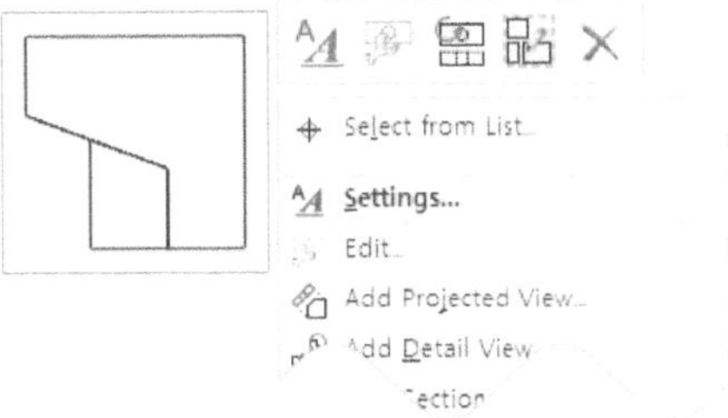

Fig 14-42 Settings Option

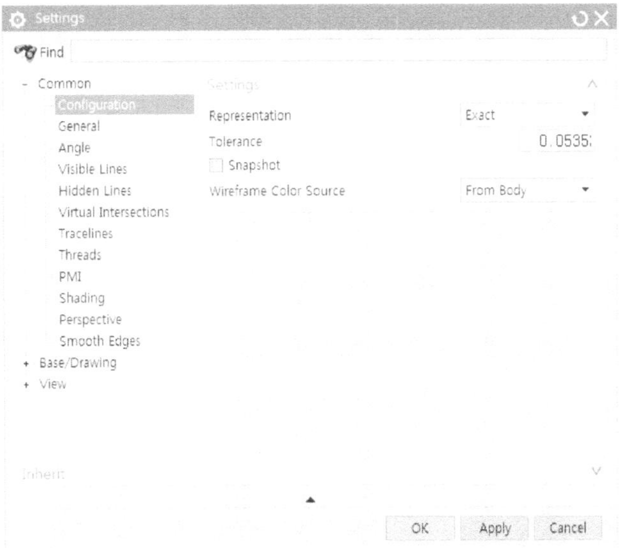

Fig 14-43 Settings Dialog Box of Drawing View

If you would like to have a shaded isometric drawing view, set the **Rendering Style** option in the **Shading** tab to **Fully Shaded** as shown in Fig 14-44.

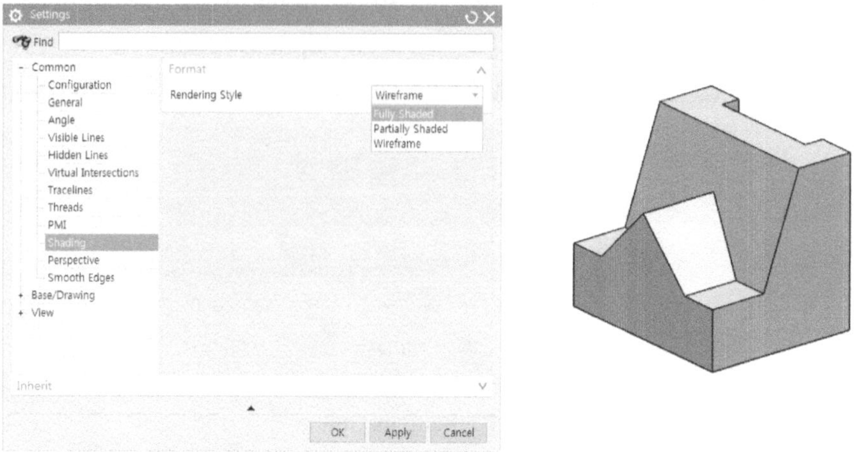

Fig 14-44 Fully Shaded Trimetric Drawing View

You can show the hidden edges with the dashed line by setting the **Hidden Line** option as shown in Fig 14-45.

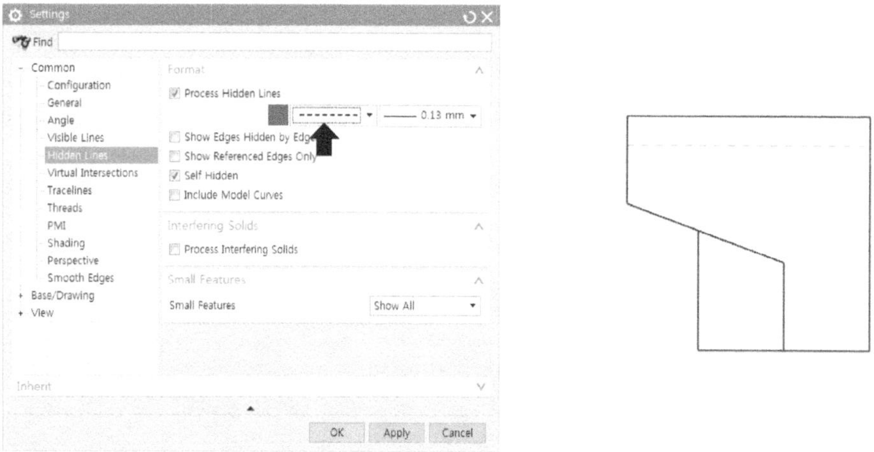

Fig 14-45 Hidden Line Option

! *Parent View*

The projected view can be created for the existing drawing view. The view which is used as the reference for creating another view is called a **Parent View**. The view style is inherited from the parent view. You can modify the view style independent of the parent view after creating it.

14.5.4 Section View

By defining a section line that passes through a specific location in the 3D geometry, you can express a complex shape exactly and effectively. In NX, you can create four types of section views; **Section View, Half Section View, Revolved Section View** and **Break-out Section View**, etc.

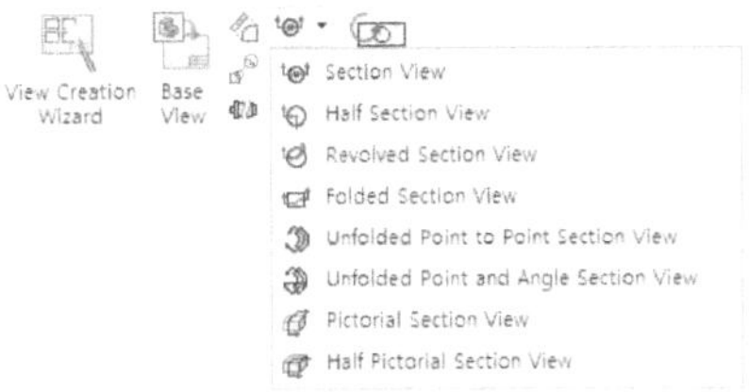

Fig 14-46 Icons Group for Section View

With the **Section View** icon, you can create either a simple section view or a stepped section view as shown in Fig 14-47.

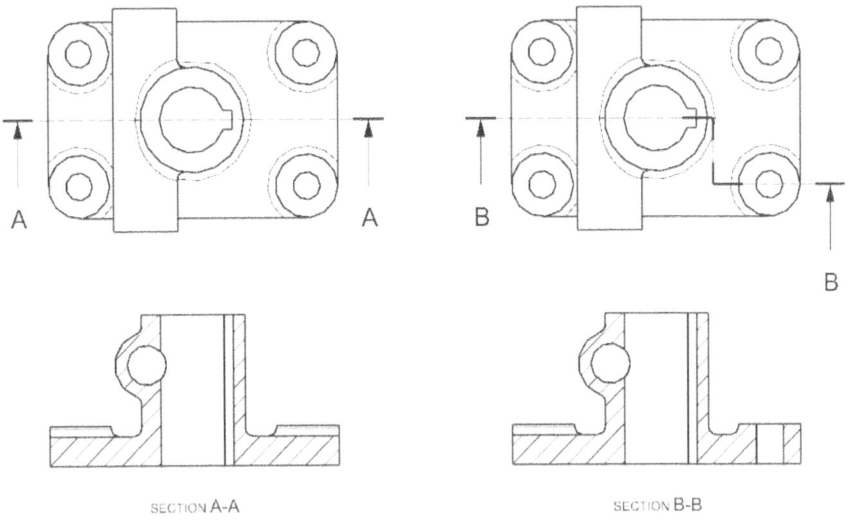

<Full Section View> <Stepped Section View>

Fig 14-47 Section Views

Using the **Half Section View** icon, you can create a section for the specified portion of the parent view as shown in Fig 14-48.

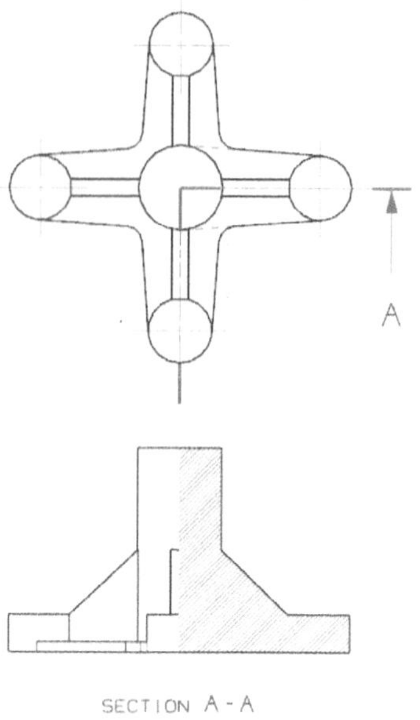

Fig 14-48 Half Section View

Using the **Revolved Section View** icon, an angled section line can be defined as shown in Fig 14-49. The section lines are revolved about the rotation point depending on the location of the section view. Fig 14-49 shows a revolved section where the angle section line is rotated until the horizontal line because the location of the section view is defined normal to the horizontal line.

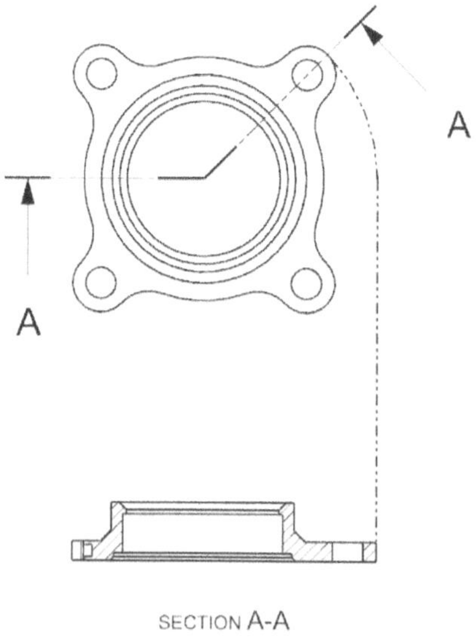

Fig 14-49 Revolved Section View

If you click the **Section View** icon, a **Section View** option bar is invoked and you are prompted to select a parent view. If you select the parent view and a point for the section line to pass through, the **Section View** option bar is changed as shown in Fig 14-50. Each option is explained next.

Ⓐ **Infer Hinge Line**: The direction of the section line is defined by the location of the mouse pointer.

Ⓑ **Define Hinge Line**: If you click the **Define Hinge Line** button in the option bar, you can specify the direction of the section line explicitly. You can use the vector tool on the right of the button or you can select an object in the view to specify the direction.

Ⓒ **Segment Option**: You can add, delete or move a section line segment. This option is required when you are creating a stepped section view or half section view.

Ⓓ **Section Line Style**: You can specify the style of the section line.

Ⓔ **View Style**: You can specify the style of the section view.

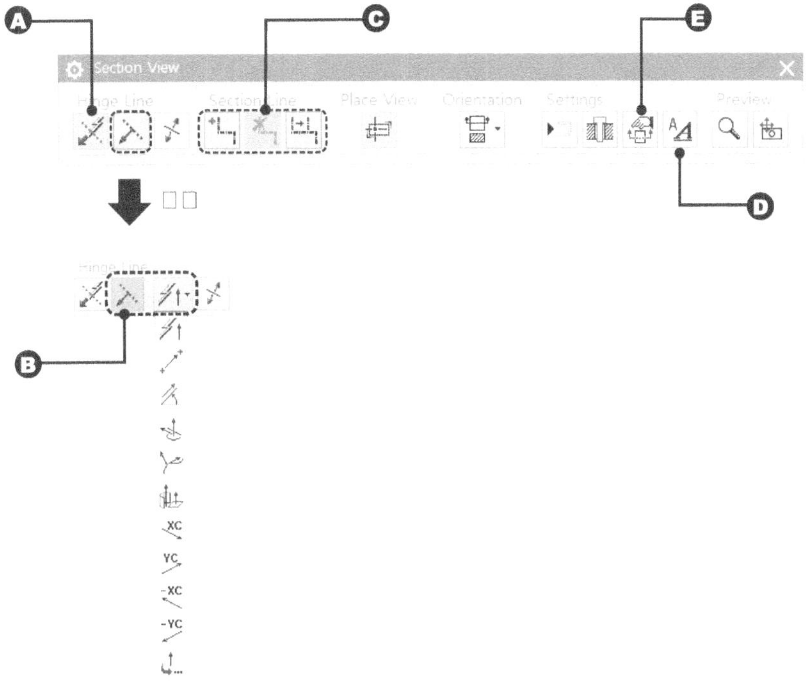

Fig 14-50 Section View Option Bar

Exercise 02 Stepped Section View

ch14_ex02.prt

Let's learn how to create a stepped section view by using the appropriate options in the **Section View** option bar.

Creating a File

Create a drawing file by specifying the given part file ch14_ex02.prt as the master part.

We will not enter the title block or use the view creation wizard.

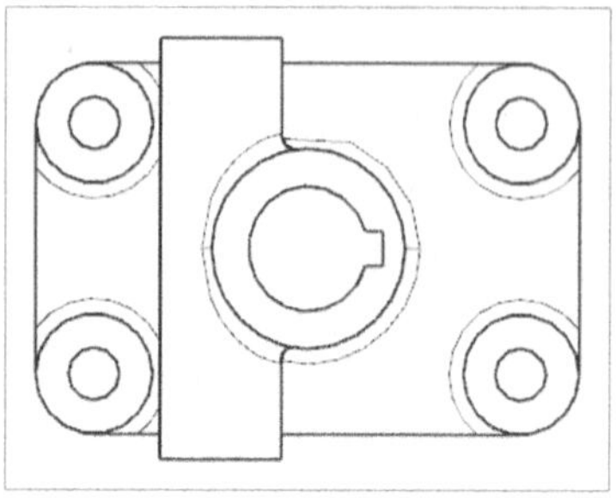

Fig 14-51 Top View

Creating Top View

1. Click the **Base View** icon in the **View** icon group.

2. Create the top view as shown in Fig 14-51.

3. Close the **Base View** dialog box.

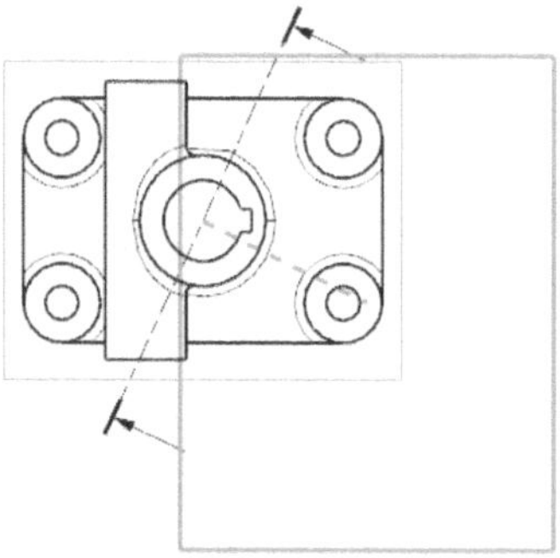

Fig 14-52 Point for Section Line

Creating Section View

1. Click MB3 on the boundary of the top view and choose **Add Section View** in the pop-up menu.

2. Select the center point using the snap point option. The direction of the section line is inferred by the location of the mouse pointer as shown in Fig 14-52.

3. Move the mouse pointer under the parent view, press MB3 and choose **Lock Alignment** in the pop-up menu.

The direction of the section is fixed as shown in Fig 14-54.

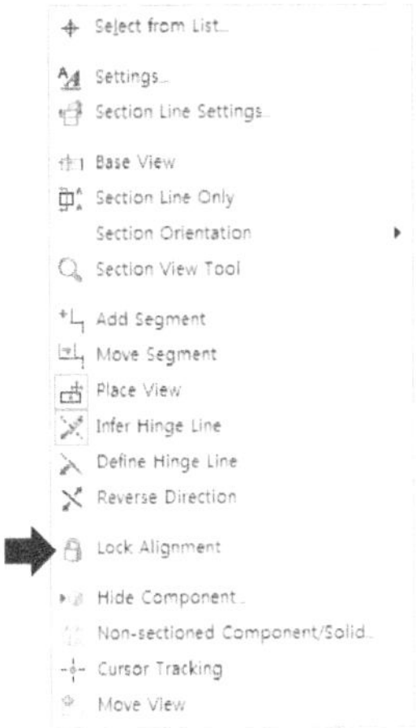

Fig 14-53 Lock Alignment Option

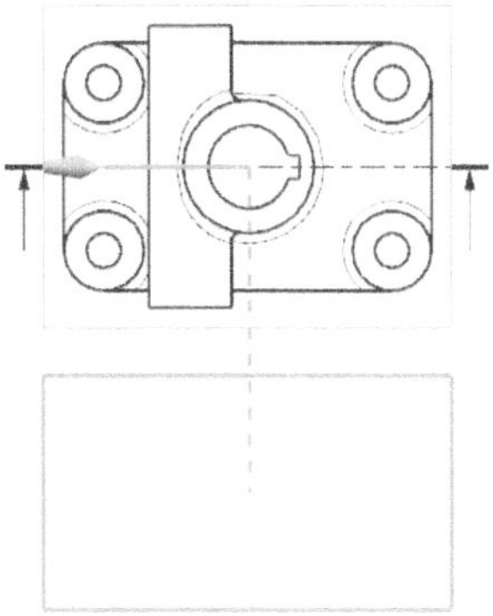

Fig 14-54 Fixed Section Line

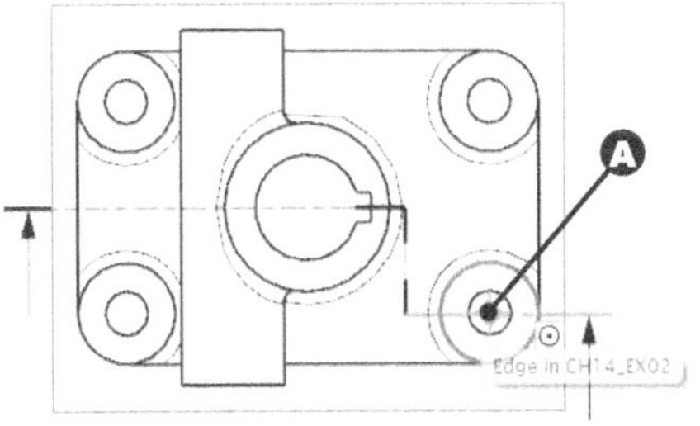

Fig 14-55 Adding Section Line Segment

4. Press MB3 and choose **Add Segment** in the pop-up menu.

5. Select the point Ⓐ specified in Fig 14-55. Use the appropriate snap point option.

6. Click MB2. You may click the **Place View** icon in the **Section View** option bar.

You are prompted to indicate the center of the section view and the graphics window appears as in Fig 14-56.

Moving the Section Line Segment

Let's move the section line segment before placing the section view.

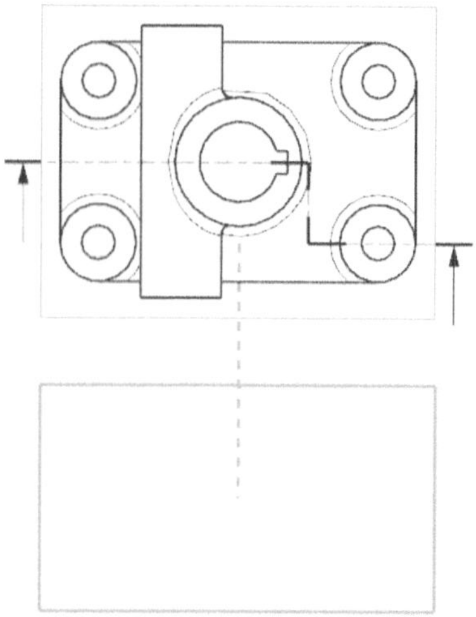

Fig 14-56 Preview of the Section View

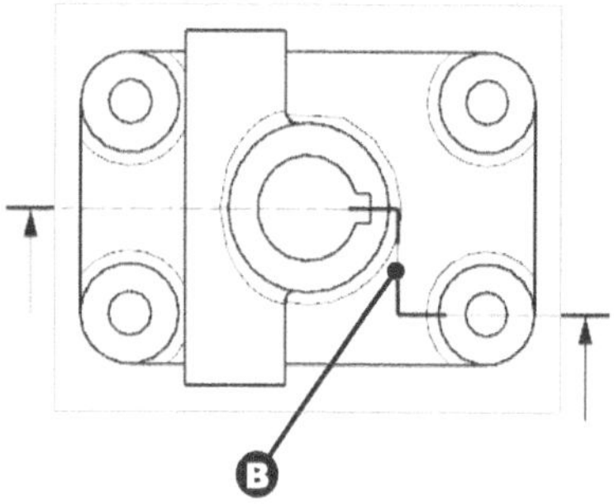

Fig 14-57 Selecting the Segment

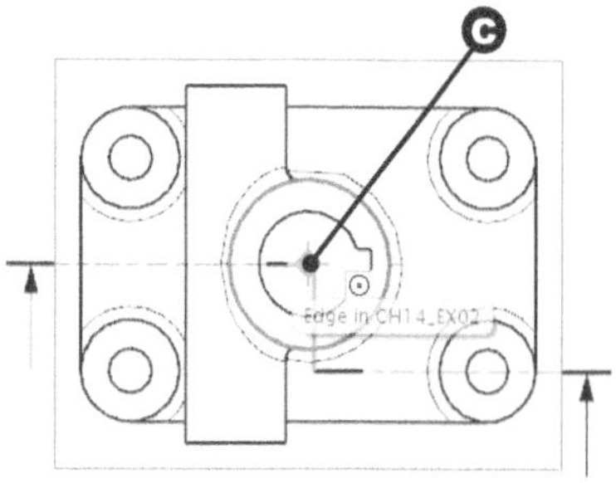

Fig 14-58 Location of the Segment

1. Press MB3 and choose **Move Segment** in the pop-up menu.

2. Select the section line segment **B** specified in Fig 14-57.

3. Select the point **C** in Fig 14-58 by using the appropriate snap point option.

4. Click MB2 or select the **Place View** button in the **Section View** option bar.

5. Click MB1 at the location to create the stepped section view as shown in Fig 14-59.

6. Press the **ESC** key to finish the **Section View** command.

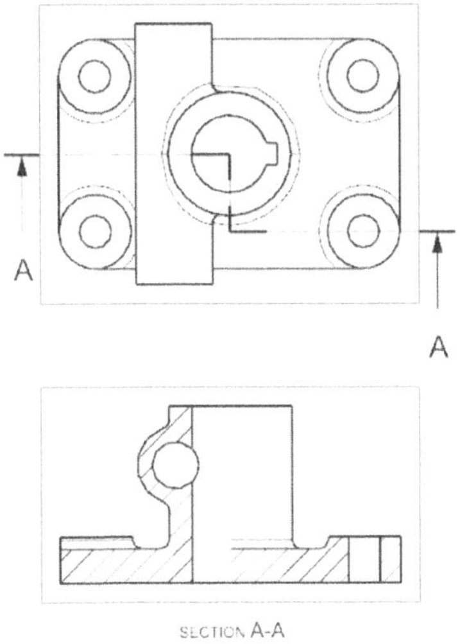

Fig 14-59 Stepped Section View Created

END of Exercise

If you double click the section line in the parent view, the **Section Line** dialog box as shown in Fig 14-60 is invoked, and you can modify the section line after creation. Note that the watch symbol is shown after modifying the section line. This means that you have to update the corresponding views. You can update all views in the drawing or sheet or you can update the selected view by pressing MB3 on the respective item in the part navigator.

Fig 14-60 Section Line Dialog Box

Fig 14-61 Update Option

Press MB3 on the section line in the parent view and choose **Settings** in the pop-up menu. The **Section Line Style** dialog box as shown in Fig 14-62 is invoked and you can modify the style of the section line. You can set a thicker bend line with the **Bend and End Segment Width Factor** option.

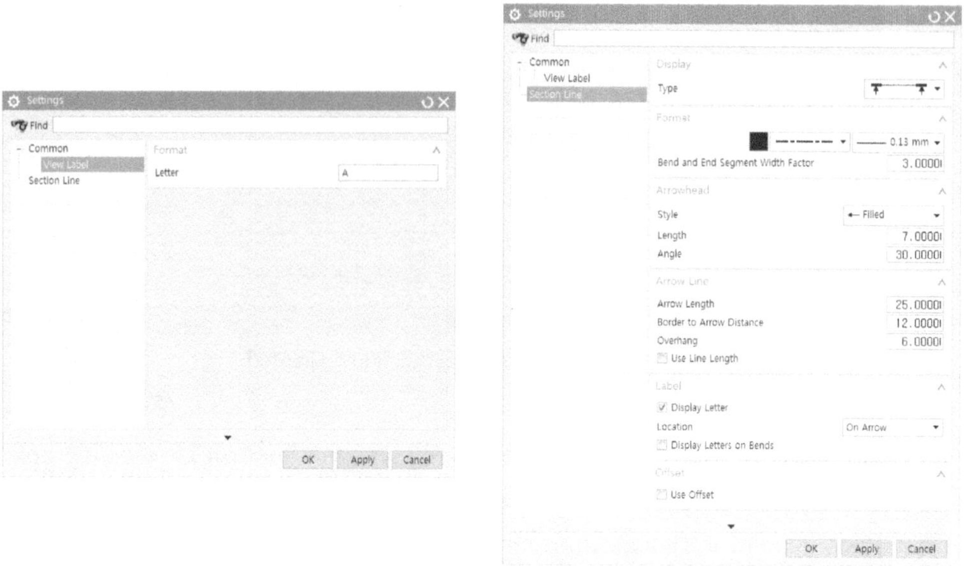

Fig 14-62 Settings Dialog Box of Section Line

Press MB3 on the boundary of the section view and choose **Settings** in the pop-up menu. The **Settings** dialog box as shown in Fig 14-63 is invoked and you can modify the style of the section view. Fig 14-63 shows the section view where the **Show Background** option is unchecked.

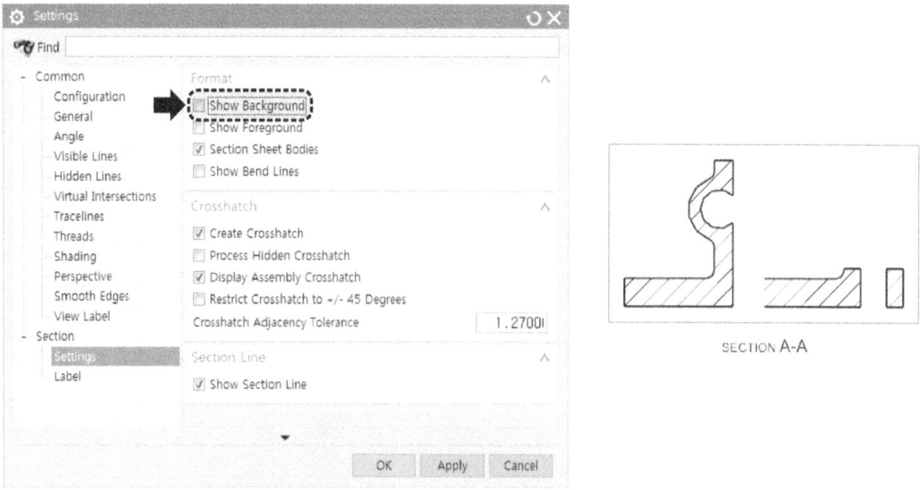

Fig 14-63 Background Option Unchecked

If you double click the crosshatch line on the section, the **Crosshatch** dialog box is invoked, and you can modify the properties of the crosshatch line such as pattern, distance, angle, color, etc.

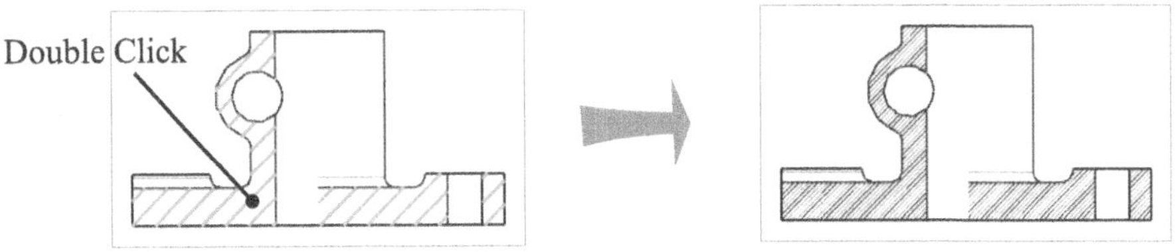

Fig 14-64 Modified Distance of Hatching Line

The crosshatch line is not properly applied with the 5 mm default distance for the case of small parts, which means that you cannot modify the crosshatch distance by double clicking it. In this case, you have to set a smaller crosshatch distance in the drafting preferences by choosing **Menu** button > **Preferences > Drafting** as shown in Fig 14-65.

Fig 14-65 Crosshatch/Area Fill Option

14.5.5 Detail View

You can magnify a region of a drawing view to create a detail view by applying a higher scaling ratio. You can even create another detail view for an existing detail view.

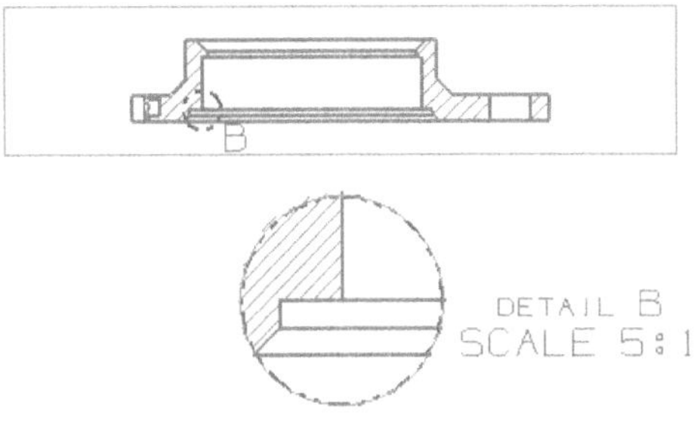

Fig 14-66 Detail View

Exercise 03 **Revolved Section View and Detail View** *ch14_ex03_dwg1.prt*

Let's create the revolved section view and the detail view by using the given parent view.

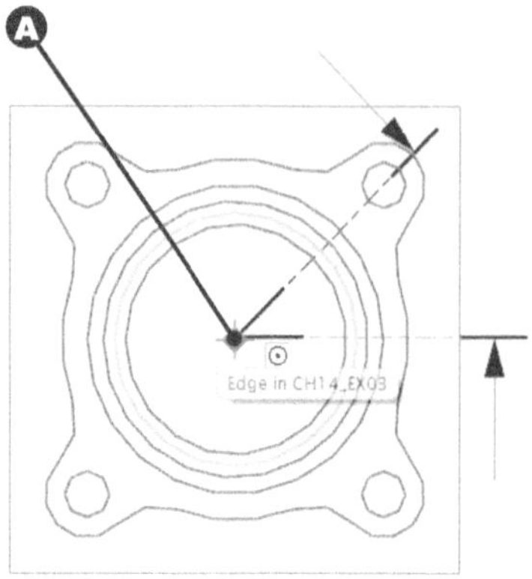

Fig 14-67 Center of Revolution

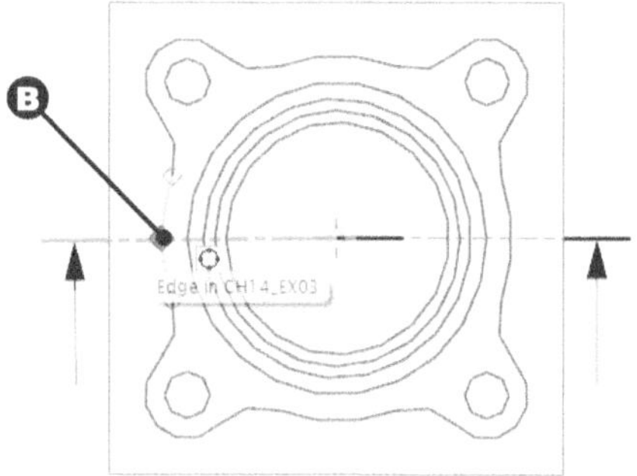

Fig 14-68 Start Point

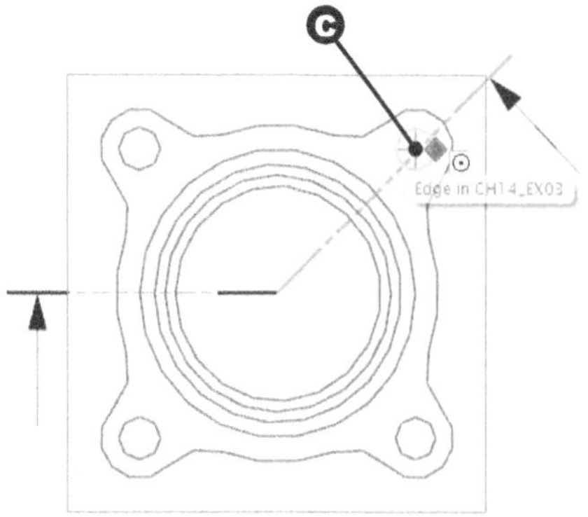

Fig 14-69 End Point

Revolved Section View

1. Open the given drawing file ch14_ex03_dwg1.prt.

2. Select the view by clicking it with MB1 and click MB3 on the view boundary. Then choose **Add Revolved Section View** in the pop-up menu.

3. Select the center of the revolution by using the appropriate snap point option (A in Fig 14-67).

4. Select the start point of the revolution by using the **Quadrant Point** option (B in Fig 14-68).

5. Select the end point of the revolution by using the **Arc Center** option (C in Fig 14-69).

6. Move the mouse pointer below the parent view as shown in Fig 14-70.

7. Click MB1 to locate the revolved section view.

8. Press **ESC** to finish creating the revolved section view.

9. Modify the hatching distance to 1 mm.

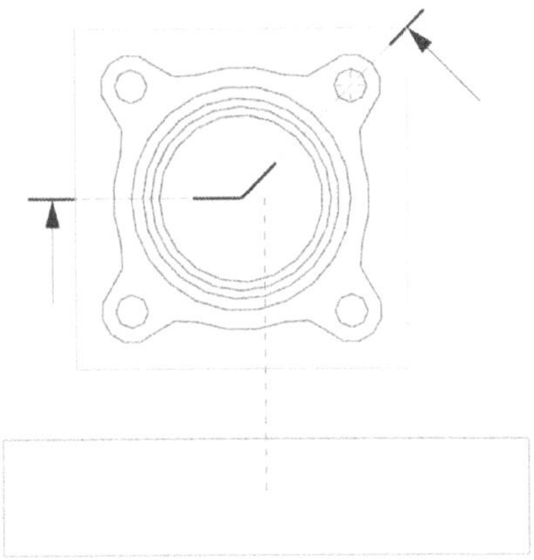

Fig 14-70 Locating the Revolved Section View

Detail View

1. Click MB3 on the boundary of the revolved section view and choose **Add Detail View** in the pop-up menu.

2. Reset the dialog box and select the center of circular region to magnify (A in Fig 14-71).

3. Select the radius point (B in Fig 14-72).

4. Enter 3:1 in the **Scale** option.

5. Click MB1 to locate the detail view.

6. Close the **Detail View** dialog box.

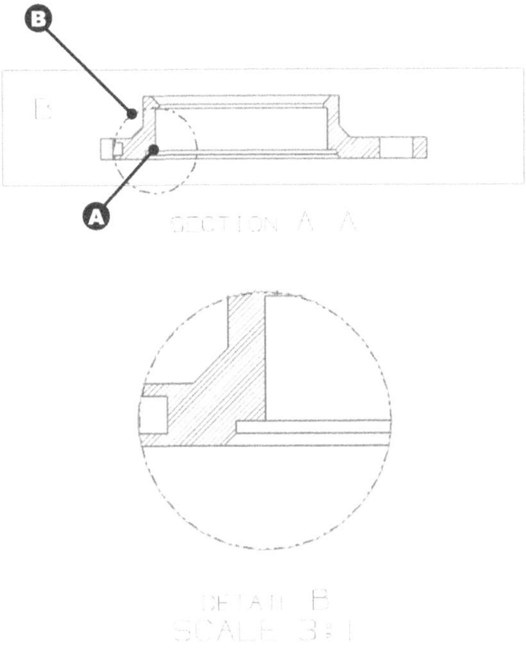

Fig 14-71 Detail View

END of Exercise

Click **MB3 > Edit** on the boundary of the detail view. The **Detail View** dialog box is invoked as shown in Fig 14-72 and you can modify options in defining the detail view.

Click **MB3 > Settings** on the magnification boundary on the parent view. The **Settings** dialog box as shown in Fig 14-73 is invoked and you can modify the style of the view label.

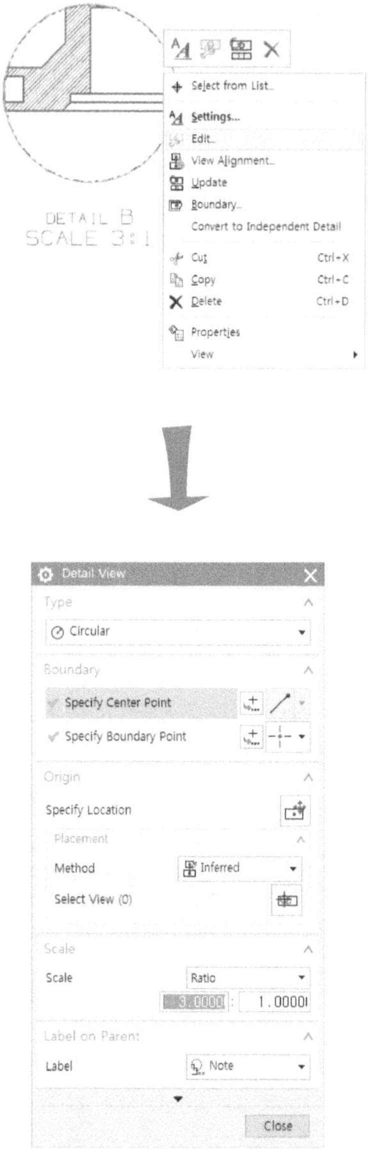

Fig 14-72 Detail View Dialog Box

Fig 14-73 Settings Dialog Box

14.5.6 Break-out Section View

A portion of an existing view is cut out at a specified depth.

Fig 14-74 Break-out Section View

To create a break-out section view, you have to define the region to break-out first. The break-out region can be created using the sketch tools. Note that the region curves have to be included in the view to break-out.

If you want to create curves in a view, you have to specify the view as an active sketch view. Click MB3 on the boundary of the view and choose **Active Sketch View** in the pop-up menu. If a view is designated as an active sketch view, you can identify it in the part navigator as shown in Fig 14-76. Fig 14-77 shows a view in which the break-out region is created. If you create the curves out of the current view boundary, the boundary is extended so that it can contain the sketch curves.

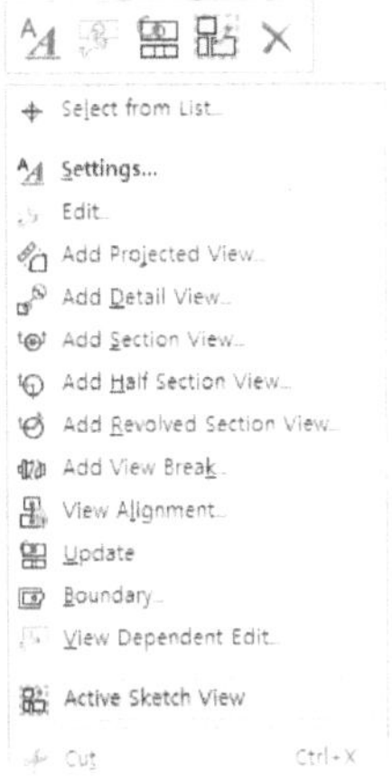

Fig 14-75 Active Sketch View Menu

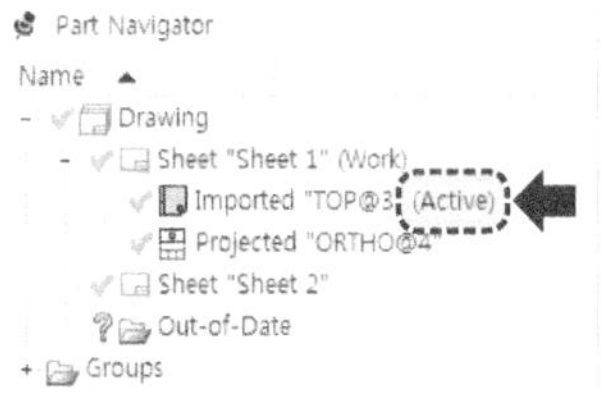

Fig 14-76 Active Sketch View

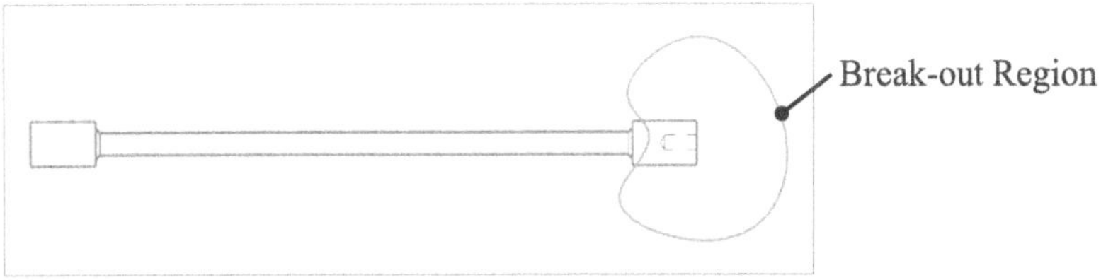

Fig 14-77 Break-Out Region

14.5.7 Break View

A long uniform part can be cut short. You can create the break view using the **Break View** icon in the **View** icon group. Note that you can create the break view for the break-out view, but not vice versa.

Fig 14-78 Break View Icon

Fig 14-79 Broken View

Exercise 04 **Break-out View and Break View** *ch14_ex04_dwg1.prt*

Create a break-out section view for the given drawing and create the break view to remove the central region of the break-out section view.

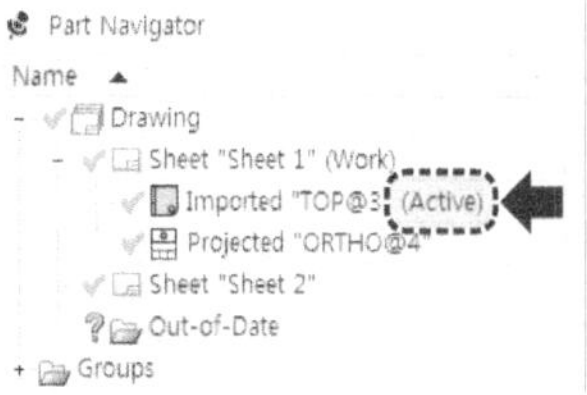

Fig 14-80 Active Sketch View

Defining the Break-out Region

1. Open the given drawing file ch14_ex04_dwg1.prt.

2. Click MB3 on the boundary of the top view and choose **Active Sketch View** in the pop-up menu.

3. Press '**S**' in the keyboard. The **Studio Spline** command is activated. You can click the **Studio Spline** icon in the **Sketch** icon group.

4. Create a spline by defining the points as shown in Fig 14-81. Note that you have to check the **Closed** option in the **Studio Spline** dialog box after defining the last point to create a closed spline. You can modify the shape of the spline by dragging the defining points. You can delete the defining point by pressing MB3 on the point, and add the defining points by pressing MB1 on the spline.

5. Click **OK** in the **Studio Spline** dialog box. Be sure that the view boundary is extended so that it contains the spline. Also, the sketch feature is defined in the top view in the part navigator.

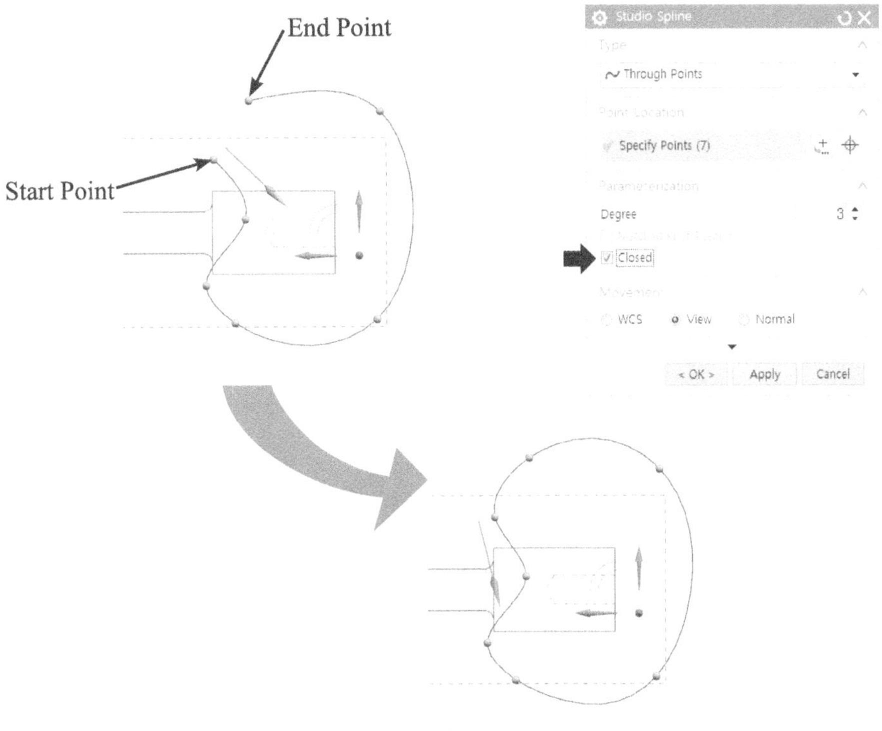

Fig 14-81 Defining Break-out Region

6. Press '**Q**' to finish the sketch.

Fig 14-82 shows the top view in which the break-out region has been defined.

Fig 14-82 Break-out Region Defined

Fig 14-83 Break-out Section Icon

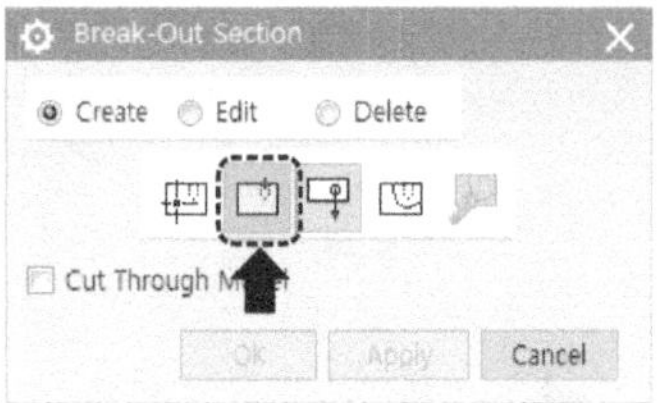

Fig 14-84 Base Point Option

Fig 14-85 Base Point

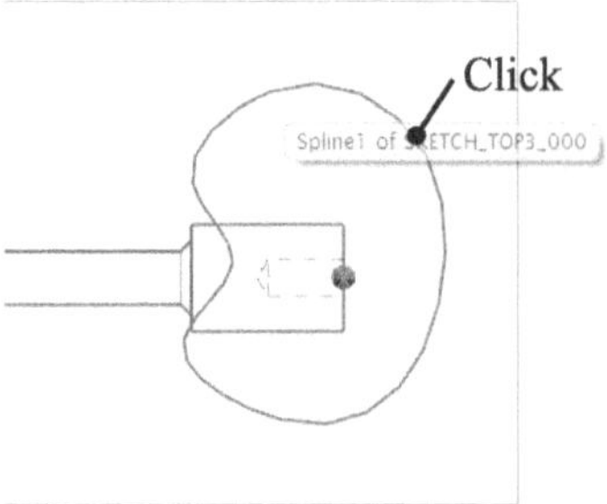

Fig 14-86 Break-out Region

Creating Break-out Section View

1. Click the **Break-out Section View** icon in the **View** icon group.

2. Select the top view. You can select the view boundary or select the top view in the dialog box.

The dialog box is changed as shown in Fig 14-84 and you are prompted to indicate the base point which defines the break-out depth.

3. Select the center point on the right view.

An arrow is displayed and the third icon is highlighted in the dialog box. The arrow indicates the break-out direction.

4. Confirm the direction and click MB2 if it is correct. The fourth icon is highlighted.

5. Select the break-out region which is created by the sketch in the top view.

6. Click the **Apply** button in the dialog box.

7. Close the dialog box.

8. Modify the hatching distance to 1 mm. Fig 14-87 shows the result of the break-out section.

Fig 14-87 Break-out Section Created

Creating Break View

1. Click the **View Break** icon in the **View** icon group.

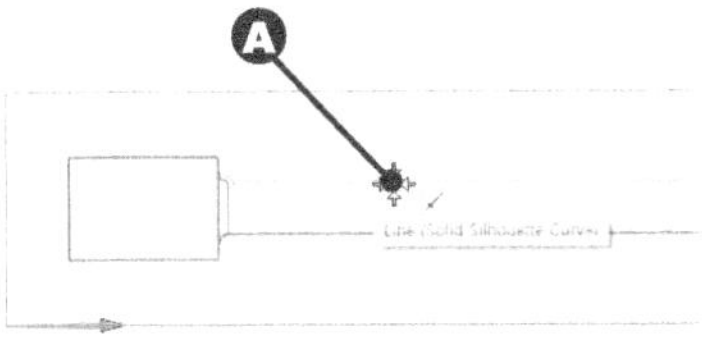

Fig 14-88 Break Line 1 Point

2. Select the top view as the master view.

3. Turn on the **Point on Curve** snap point option.

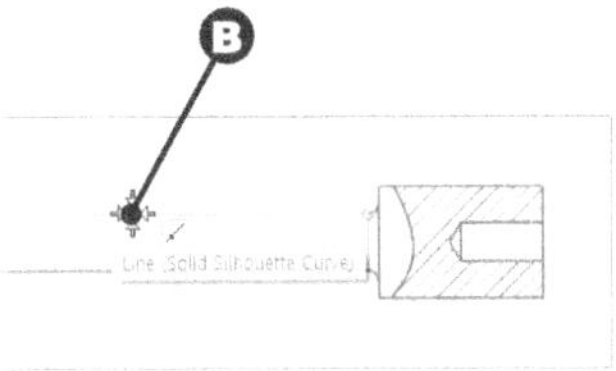

Fig 14-89 Break Line 2 Point

4. Select the point for break line 1 as designated by Ⓐ in Fig 14-88.

5. Select the point for break line 2 as designated by Ⓑ in Fig 14-89.

6. Click **OK** in the **View Break** dialog box.

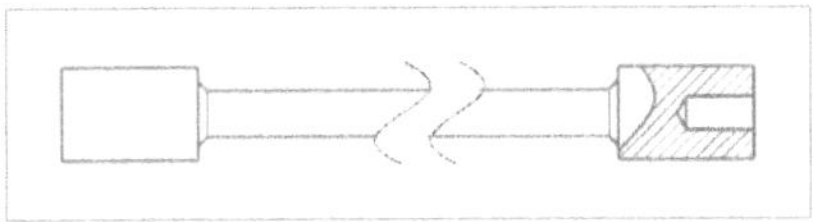

Fig 14-90 Break View Created

The view is shortened as shown in Fig 14-90. Note that the length dimension will show an actual value.

END of Exercise

14.6 View Dependent Edit

The curves for the three dimensional geometry in the drawing view cannot be deleted. However, you can hide or modify attributes of the geometry curves by using the **View Dependent Edit** command.

Fig 14-91 shows a projected view.

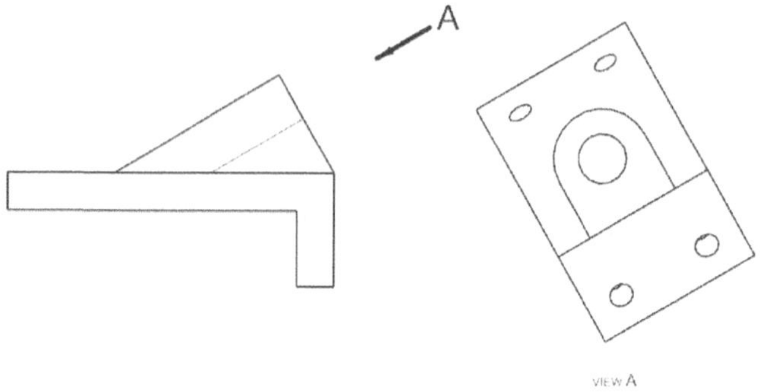

Fig 14-91 Projected View

Click **MB3 > View Dependent Edit** on the boundary of the projected view. The **View Dependent Edit** dialog box as shown in Fig 14-93 is invoked. Click the **Erase Objects** button (Ⓐ in Fig 14-93) and select the curves to erase in the projected view to create the local projected view as shown in Fig 14-94.

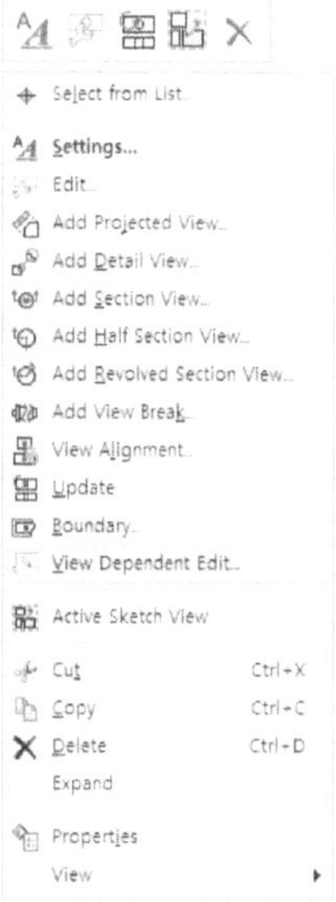

Fig 14-92 View Dependent Edit Option

Fig 14-93 View Dependent Edit Dialog Box

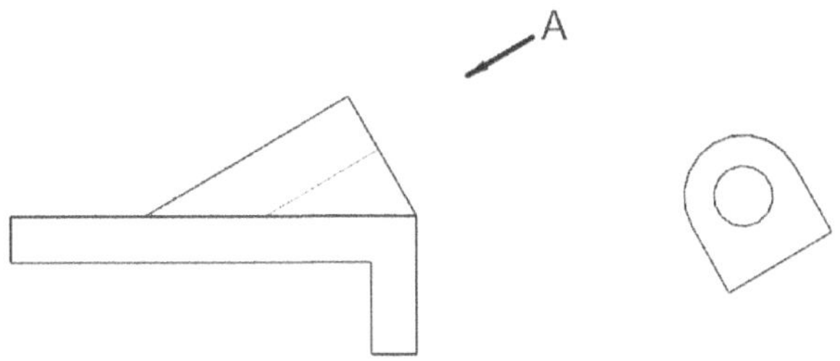

Fig 14-94 Local Projected View

14.7 Resizing View Boundary

The view boundary is defined automatically depending on the geometry in the view. You can resize the view boundary if required. Click **MB3 > Boundary** on a view boundary. The View Boundary dialog box as shown in Fig 14-95 is invoked. Choose **Manual Rectangle** in the dropdown list, click MB1 and drag to define a rectangle. Fig 14-96 shows a resized view boundary for the local projected view.

Fig 14-95 View Boundary Dialog Box

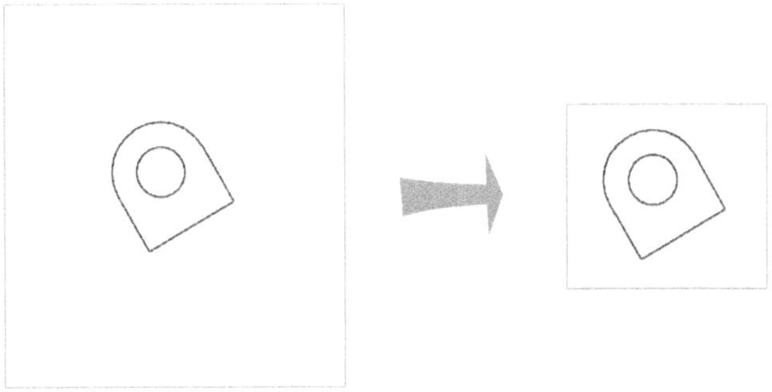

Fig 14-96 Resizing View Boundary

14.8 Modifying the Master Part and Component Orientation

In model based drafting in NX, the master part is added to the drawing file as a component and you are creating a drawing for the component geometry. The drawing part file is called a non-master part, which does not have information in constructing the geometry.

Remember that you can move or rotate the component in an assembly and that the drawing file can be considered as an assembly file. Therefore, you can set the standard view that is available in the **Base View** dialog box by rotating the component in the drawing file.

If you want to modify the geometry of the master part, you have to enter the **Modeling** application. Remember that you have to make the component master part a work part, which has been explained in Chapter 13. After modifying the master part, you have to return to the **Drafting** application and update the drawing views.

Exercise 05 Modifying View Orientation and Master Part Geometry

ch14_ex05_dwg1.prt

1. Rotate the component of the drawing file.
2. Switch to the **Modeling** application and modify the geometry of the master part.

Rotating the Component

Let's rotate the component of drawing to modify the standard view orientation.

1. Open the given drawing file ch14_ex05_dwg1.prt.

2. Press the **Modeling** icon in the **Application** tab as shown in Fig 14-97.

Confirm that you have entered the **Modeling** application.

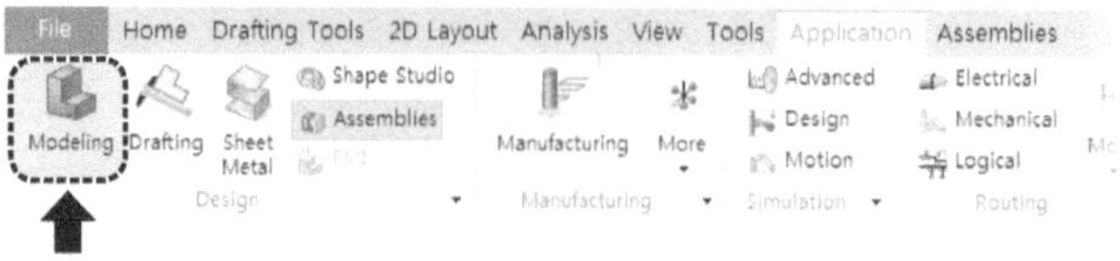

Fig 14-97 Start Menu

Fig 14-98 Modeling Application

The drawing sheet is removed in the graphics window and the 3D model, which is the component, is displayed.

3. Press the **Home** key in the keyboard to display the trimetric view.

4. Click the **Move Component** icon in the **Assemblies** icon group.

5. Select the component and rotate it 180° about the ZC axis so that the trimetric view is shown as in Fig 14-99.

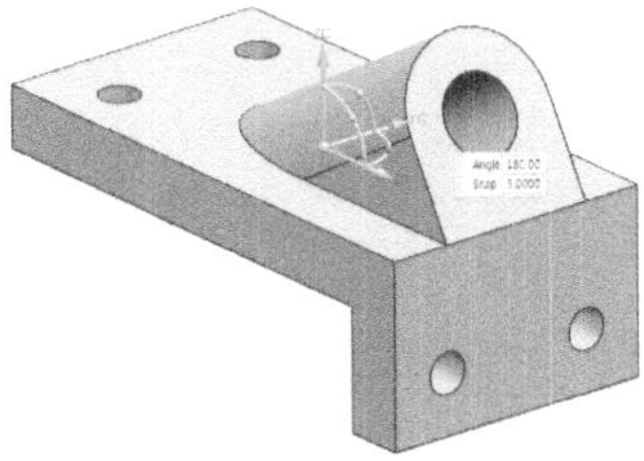

Fig 14-99 Modified Trimetric View

6. Press the **Drafting** icon in the **Application** tab.

Drawing sheets are displayed in the graphics window.

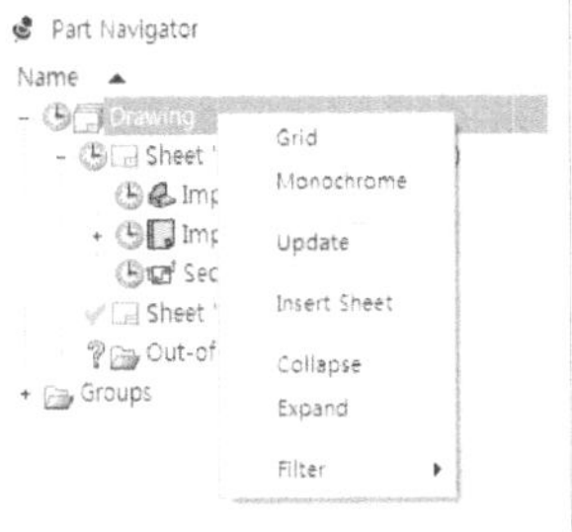

Fig 14-100 Update Option

7. Click **MB3 > Update** in the **Drawing** in the part navigator to update the drawing views as shown in Fig 14-102.

Which is Modified?

Looking at the assembly navigator, you can recognize that only the drawing file is modified.

Fig 14-101 Assembly Navigator

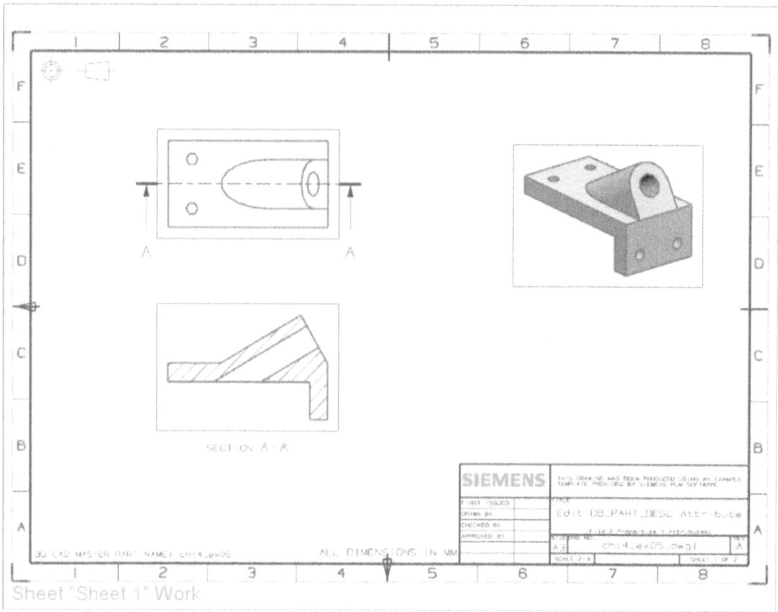

Fig 14-102 Modified Drawing

Modifying the Master Part

1. Press the **Modeling** icon in the **Application** tab.

The 3D geometry is shown in the graphics window. Note that the geometry is of the component because the current work part is the drawing file.

Fig 14-103 Component in Work Part

2. Double click the component in the assembly navigator to make it a work part.

3. Double click **Datum Plane (4)** in the part navigator and modify the angle to 45˚.

4. Double click the drawing part in the assembly navigator to make it a work part.

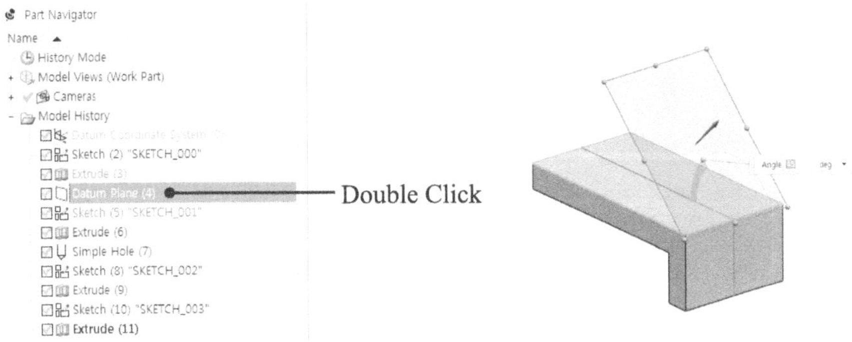

Fig 14-104 Modifying the Master Part

5. Switch back to the **Drafting** application.

6. Update the drawing in the part navigator. Fig 14-105 shows the drawing for the modified part.

7. Verify in the assembly navigator that the master part has been modified. You can save the drawing file and the master part file by choosing **File > Save > Save**.

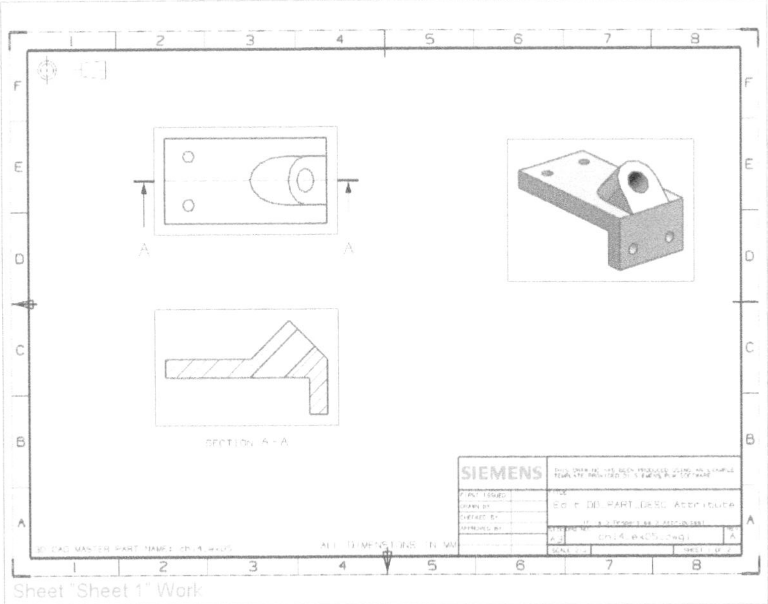

Fig 14-105 Updated Drawing

END of Exercise

This page left blank intentionally.

Chapter 15

Dimension, Annotation and Assembly Drawing

■ After completing this chapter you will understand

- how to create dimensions and modify their setting.
- how to create annotations and modify their setting.
- types of center lines.
- major topics in assembly drawing.

15.1 General Procedure of Creating Drawings

The major interest of Chapter 14 was explaining how to create various types of drawing views. The general procedure for creating drawings in NX is as follows.

① Determine a part or assembly for which to create the drawing.
② Create a drawing file.
③ Create drawing views.
④ Create dimensions, annotations, symbols, etc. in the drawing.

In this chapter, we will learn how to create center lines, dimensions and annotations and how to set the options to improve their appearances. Basic topics in creating assembly drawings will also be explained in this chapter.

15.2 Creating Dimensions

You can create various types of dimensions by clicking the **Rapid Dimension** icon in the **Dimension** icon group.

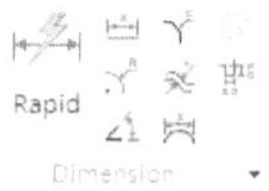

Fig 15-1 Dimensions Icon Group

If you click **Rapid Dimension** in the **Dimensions** icon group, the **Rapid Dimension** dialog box as shown in Fig 15-2 appears. You can create a dimension by choosing the **First Object** and the **Second Object**. The type of dimension is determined in the **Measurement** option. If you choose **Inferred** in the **Measurement Method** dropdown list, the type of dimension is determined according to the objects you select.

In the **Driving** option, you can choose to create a driving or driven dimension. For the curves that are created in association with the three dimensional model, you can create only the driven dimension. For the curves that are created in the **Drafting** application, if you select **Driving** in the **Method** dropdown list, you can modify the curve by modifying the dimension value.

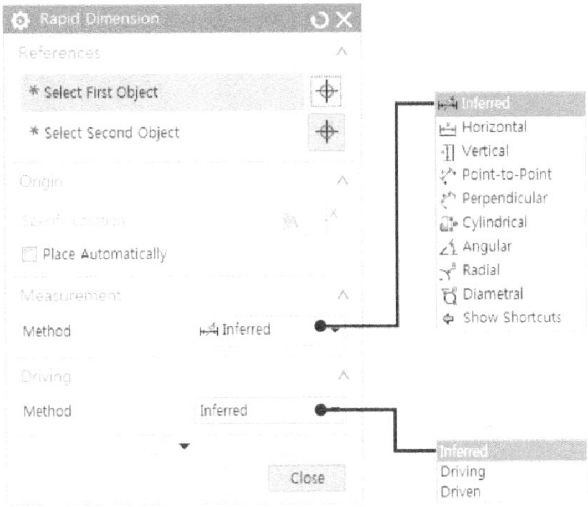

Fig 15-2 Rapid Dimension Dialog Box

If you click the **More** button on the lower part of the dialog box, the **Origin** and the **Settings** options are available as shown in Fig 15-3.

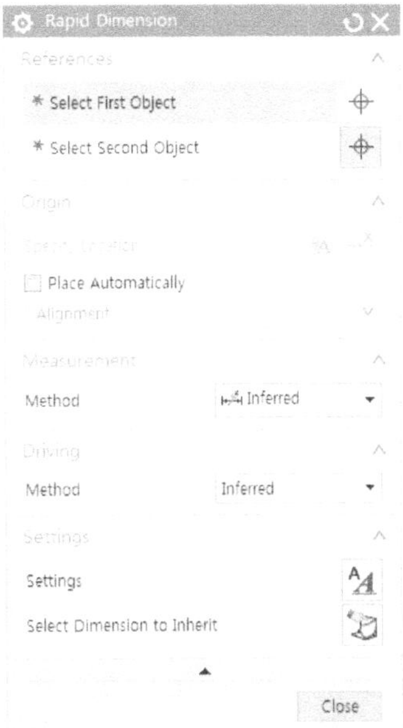

Fig 15-3 Rapid Dimension Dialog Box (More Options)

If you wait for a moment when you are creating a dimension, a pop-up toolbar appears as shown in Fig 15-4. The dropdown list that is shown in the first place is the same as the **Measurement Method** dropdown list in the **Rapid Dimension** dialog box.

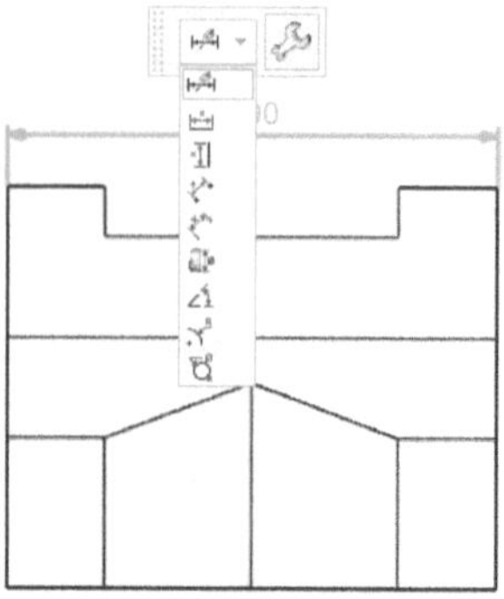

Fig 15-4 Pop-up Toolbar

If you click the icon in the second place of the pop-up toolbar, the edit mode is invoked as shown in Fig 15-5, where point A is clicked. If you click point A that is attached to the dimension line, you can modify the settings of the dimension line that is being created. If you click the **Settings** button (B in Fig 15-5), the **Settings** dialog box is invoked as shown in Fig 15-6. You can modify appearances such as color, font, thickness, etc. of the dimension line and arrow.

If you click point C in edit mode, you can set the extension line in the pop-up toolbar as shown in Fig 15-7. You can hide the extension line by clicking button E in Fig 15-7. If

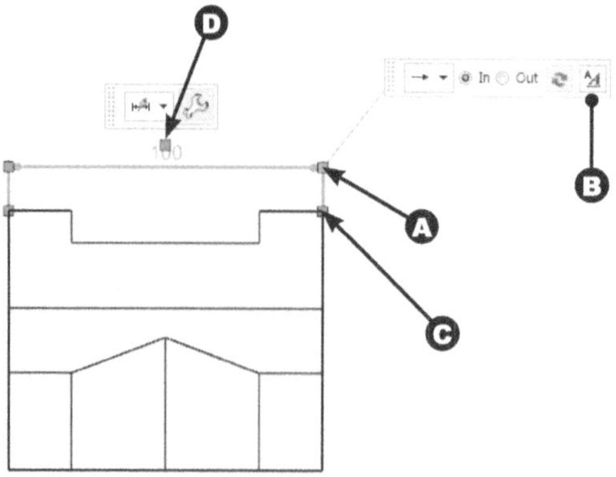

Fig 15-5 Edit Mode

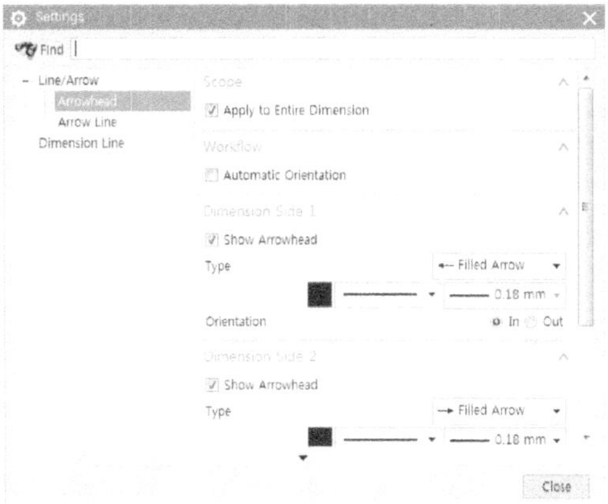

Fig 15-6 Settings Dialog Box of the Dimension Line and Arrow

you click the **Settings** button (F in Fig 15-7), the **Settings** dialog box is invoked where you can set the appearance of the extension line.

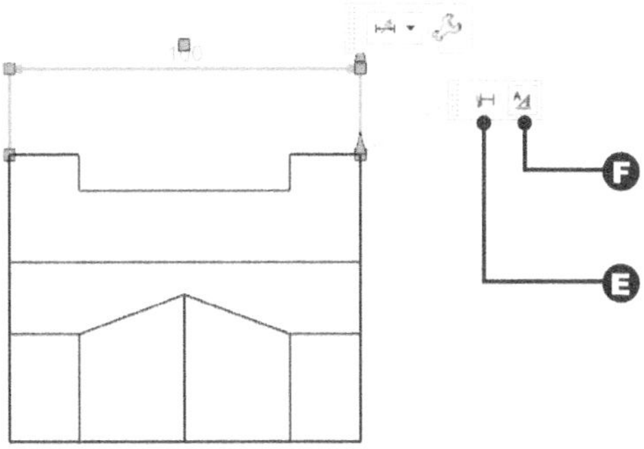

Fig 15-7 Setting of the Extension Line

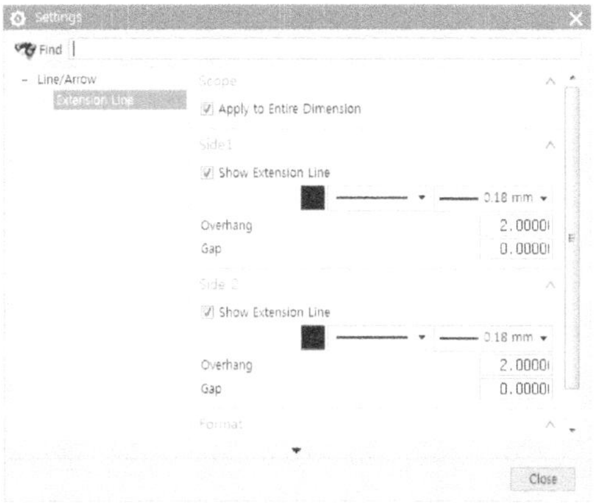

Fig 15-8 Settings Dialog Box of the Extension Line

You can modify the **Gap** and **Overhang** by clicking and dragging the corresponding arrow in the edit mode of the extension line. Fig 15-9 shows dragging of the gap arrow.

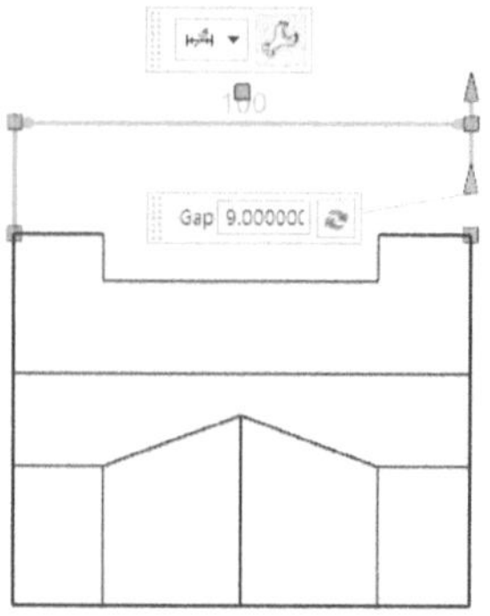

Fig 15-9 Gap Setting

If you click point **D** in Fig 15-5, a pop-up toolbar appears as shown in Fig 15-10 where you can set the appearance of the dimension text. You can set the tolerance type in the dropdown list **A** in Fig 15-10 and the decimal places in the dropdown list **B**.

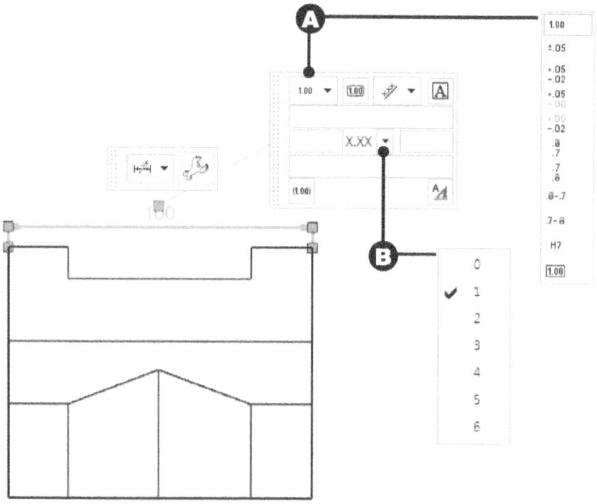

Fig 15-10 Setting the Dimension Text

You can enter the appended texts in the input boxes in the dimension pop-up toolbar. Fig 15-11 shows the appended texts a, b, c and d in the respective input boxes and the results in the dimension text where a, b, c and d appears in the upper, front, rear and lower part of the dimension value, respectively.

If you click button **C** in Fig 15-11, you can create a reference dimension.

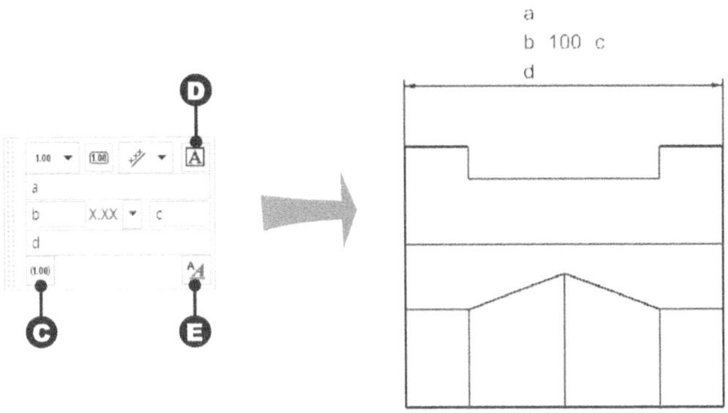

Fig 15-11 Setting the Appended Text

If you click button D in Fig 15-11, the **Appended Text** dialog box appears as shown in Fig 15-12 where you can enter various drafting symbols in the upper, front, rear and lower part of the dimension value. Note that local languages can be chosen in the **Font** dropdown list.

Fig 15-12 Appended Text Dialog Box

If you click button E in Fig 15-11, the Settings dialog box appears as shown in Fig 15-13. You can set the appearances of the **Lettering**, **Stacking**, **Tolerance**, etc.

Fig 15-13 Settings Dialog Box of the Dimension Text

In the **Text / Units** option shown in Fig 15-14, you can set units, decimal places, type of decimal point, etc. You can specify whether to use a dot or a comma as the decimal point and whether to display the leading or trailing zeroes in the dimension value or not.

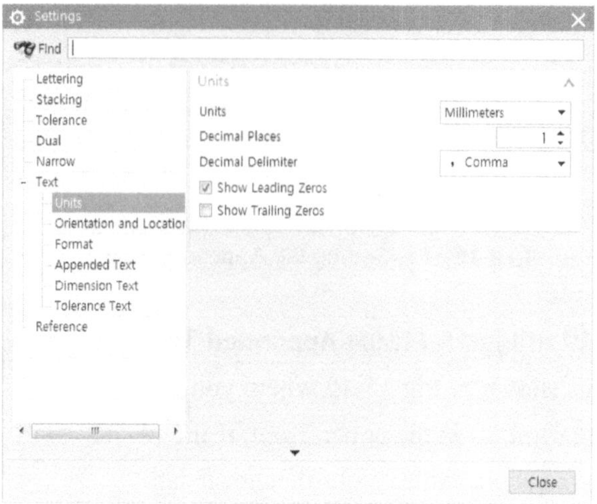

Fig 15-14 Units Option

In the **Text / Appended Text** option shown in Fig 15-15, you can set height, font gap factor, aspect ratio, etc. of the appended text. You can set the appearance of the dimension text and the tolerance text in the corresponding option.

If you have modified the appearances of the dimension related objects with the **Edit** button, you have to release the button after setting and click MB1 to create the dimension.

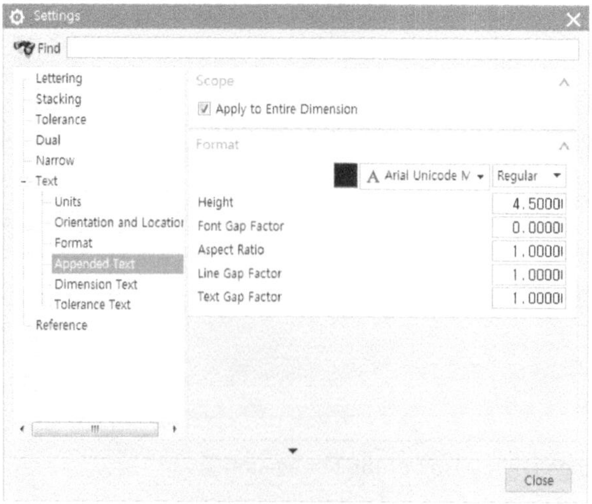

Fig 15-15 Text Option

When the dimension options are set, you can create the dimensions of the same option consecutively.

15.2.1 Linear Dimension

If you click the **Linear** icon in the **Dimension** icon group, the **Linear Dimension** dialog box appear as shown in Fig 15-16. You can specify the desired dimension type in the **Measurement Method** option or you can create a dimension with the inferred option. You can create a hole dimension with the **Hole Callout** option when the hole has been created with the **Hole** command in the **Modeling** application. Fig 15-17 shows examples of the linear dimension.

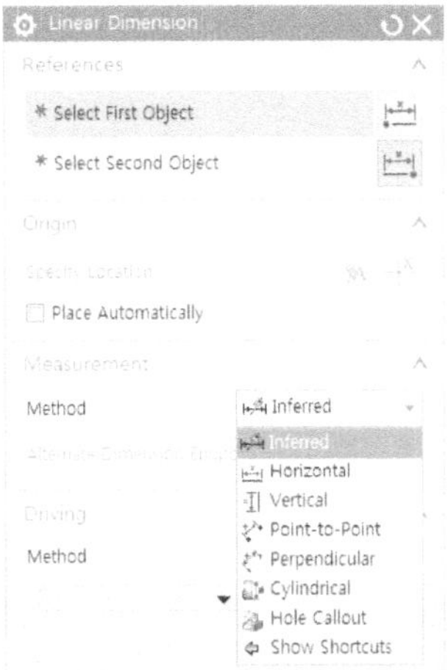

Fig 15-16 Linear Dimension Dialog Box

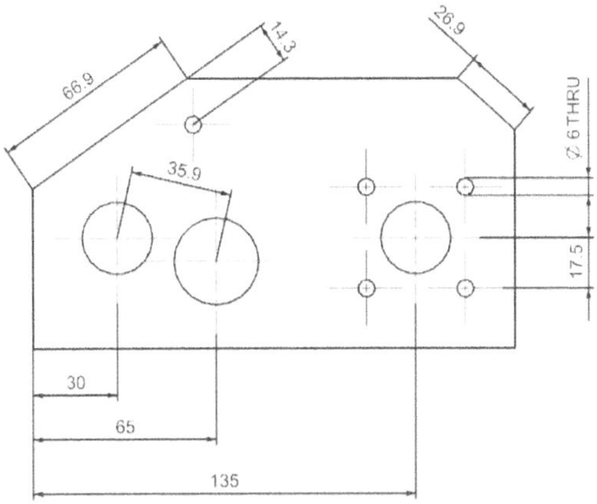

Fig 15-17 Examples of Linear Dimension

15.2.2 Radial Dimension

You can create a radial or diametral dimension with the **Radial** icon in the **Dimension** icon group. Fig 15-18 shows the **Radial Dimension** dialog box. You can create one of the three types of radial dimension with the **Inferred** option. Fig 15-19 shows examples of the radial dimension.

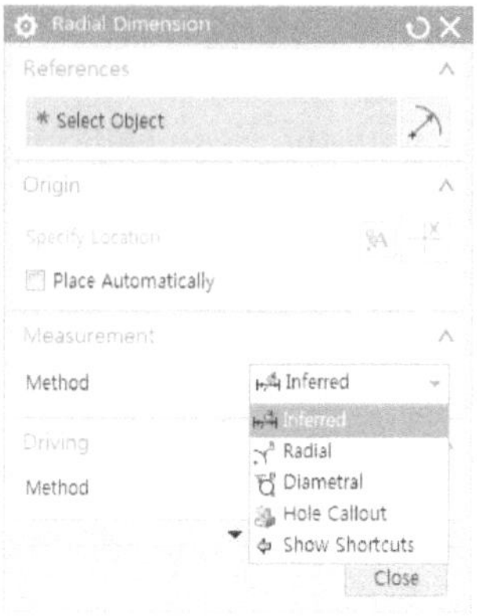

Fig 15-18 Radial Dimension Dialog Box

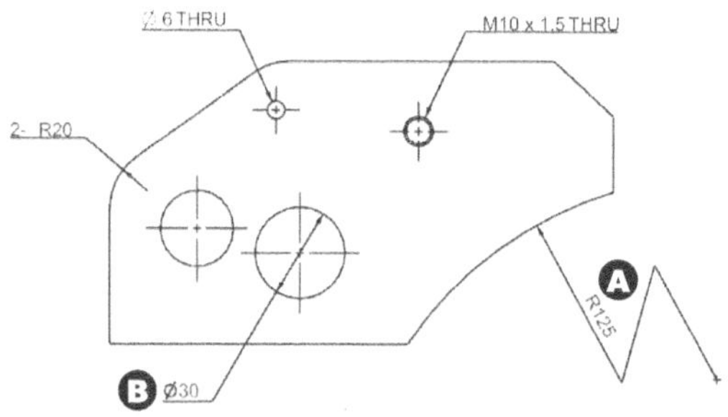

Fig 15-19 Example of Radial Dimension

Dimension Ⓐ shown in Fig 15-19 is created with the **Create Folded Radius** option in the **Radial Dimension** dialog box which appears when you have chosen **Radial** in the **Measurement Method** option. Note that you have to create the center point of the arc in advance. Refer to "15.7.5 Offset Center Point Symbol" on Page 615 to create the center point of a large radius arc.

Types of dimension Ⓑ shown in Fig 15-19 can be created with the **Horizontal Text** option and the **Text above Stub** option as shown in Fig 15-20. Note that the options in the **Settings** dialog box varies according to the types of dimension.

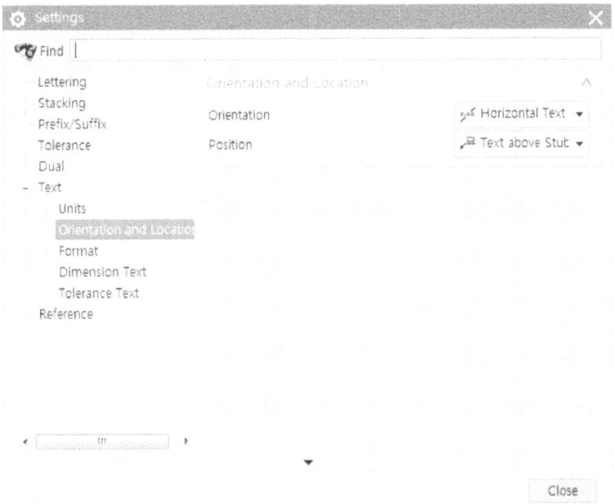

Fig 15-20 Setting Options of Radial Dimension

15.2.3 Angular Dimension

With the **Angular** icon in the **Dimension** icon group, you can create an angular dimension. Note that you can create the angular dimension with the **Rapid Dimension** command. With the **Alternate Angle** option in the **Angular Dimension** dialog box, you can create an alternate angle of the current angle. If you press MB3 while creating the angular dimension, a pop-up menu is available as shown in Fig 15-22. You can choose **Lock Angle** in the pop-up menu to lock the quadrant of the angular dimension.

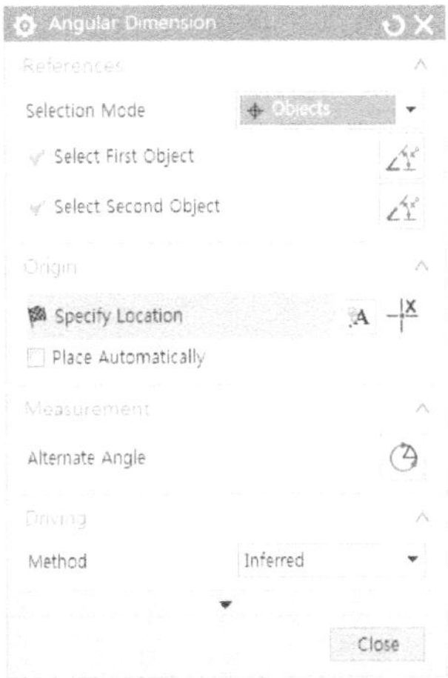

Fig 15-21 Angular Dimension Dialog Box

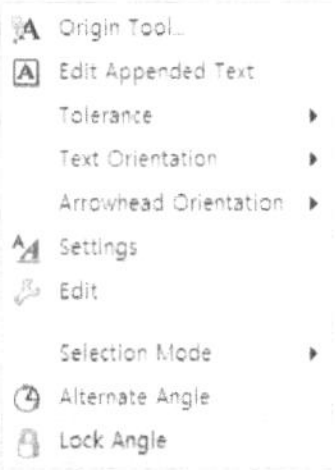

Fig 15-22 Pop-up Menu of the Angular Dimension

15.2.4 Setting Options

Setting options of a dimension varies according to the type of dimensions. Fig 15-23 shows the pop-up toolbar of a radial dimension. The **Radius to Center** option and the **Create Folded Radius** option become available and you can choose the symbol of the radius.

You can set the **Settings** options by pressing the **Settings** button ( ) in the pop-up toolbar. Note that the setting options vary according to where you have chosen the **Settings** option.

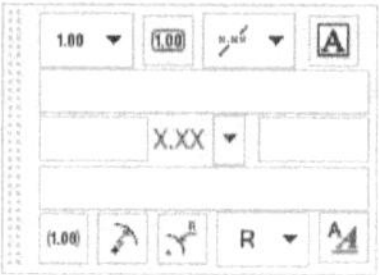

Fig 15-23 Pop-up Toolbar of Radial Dimension

15.2.5 Inherit of Settings

You can apply the same settings of another dimension when you are creating or modifying a dimension. Press the **Select Dimension to Inherit** button in the **Settings** option group of the dimension dialog box and select the dimension from which to inherit the settings.

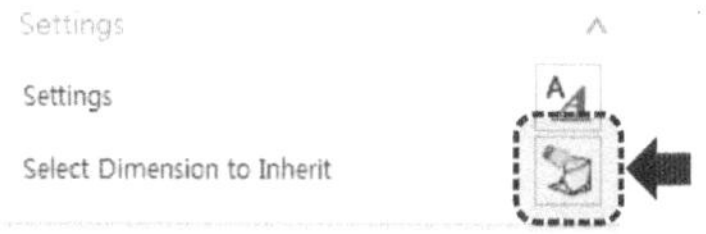

Fig 15-24 Select Dimension to Inherit Option

15.3 Modifying the Dimension Settings after Creation

You can modify settings of the dimension, dimension lines, etc. after creation.

15.3.1 Dimension Dialog Box

If you double click a dimension after creation, the dialog box corresponding to the type of dimension appears and you can modify the options in the dialog box. If you press the **Settings** button in the dialog box, you can modify all the settings of the selected dimension.

15.3.2 Pop-up Toolbar

If you double click a dimension after creation, the pop-up toolbar becomes available as shown Fig 15-25, and the setting options are available by pressing the **Settings** button in the pop-up toolbar. Note that only the options corresponding to the selected setting point appear in the **Settings** dialog box.

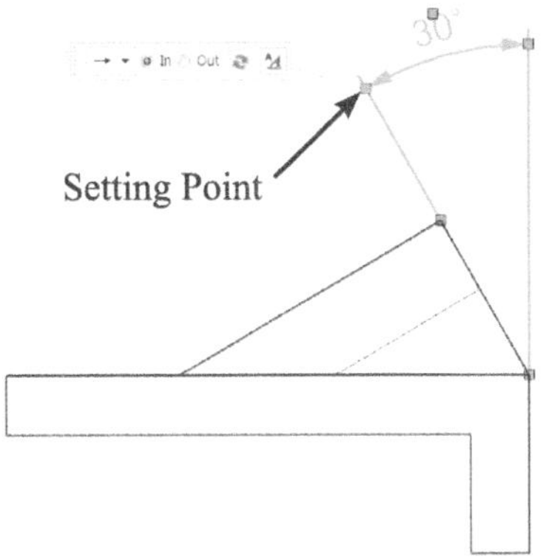

Fig 15-25 Pop-up Toolbar

15.3.3 Pop-up Menu

If you press MB3 after double clicking a dimension, a pop-up menu is available as shown in Fig 15-26 and you can set the frequently used options. If you choose **Settings** in the pop-up menu, the same settings options as the settings options in the dialog box appear in the **Settings** dialog box. You can modify all the settings of the selected dimension.

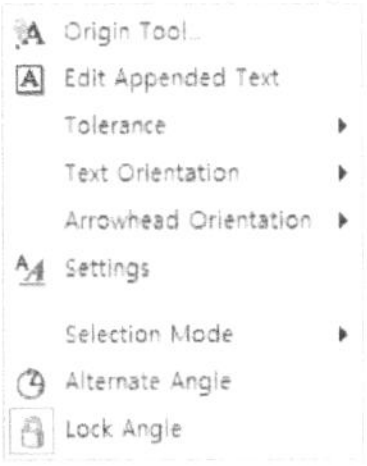

Fig 15-26 Pop-up Menu

15.4 Drafting Preferences

If you want to apply settings of drawing views or dimension for all drawings in the current NX session, you have to set the corresponding options in the drafting preferences. You can access the **Drafting Preferences** dialog box by choosing **Preferences > Drafting** in the **Menu** button. You can set the options for the items on the left panel. Note that the options are reset when you re-start NX.

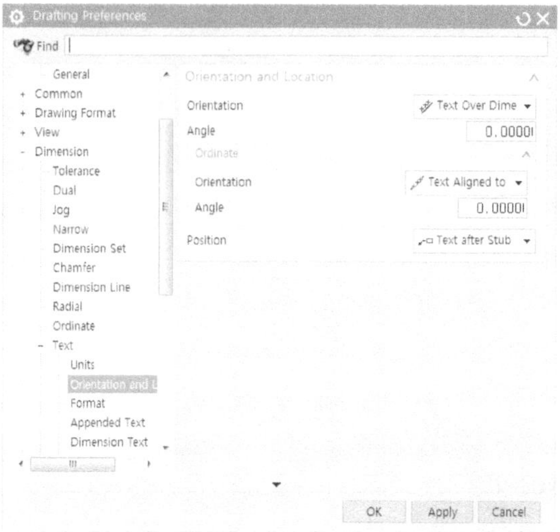

Fig 15-27 Drafting Preferences Dialog Box

You have to set the options in the **Customer Defaults** to make the settings be applied whenever you execute NX. You can access the **Customer Defaults** dialog box by choosing **Utilities > Customer Defaults** in the **File** tab.

Modifying Settings for Several Dimensions

Press the **Edit Settings** icon in the **Home** tab and select the dimensions to modify the settings of the selected dimensions.

15.5 Aligning Dimension

When you are creating a vertical dimension between the two points Ⓐ and Ⓑ in Fig 15-28, you can align the dimension to the existing dimension Ⓒ by placing the mouse pointer on the dimension. If you move the dimension Ⓒ, the aligned dimension will move. If you drag the latter dimension, the alignment is cancelled.

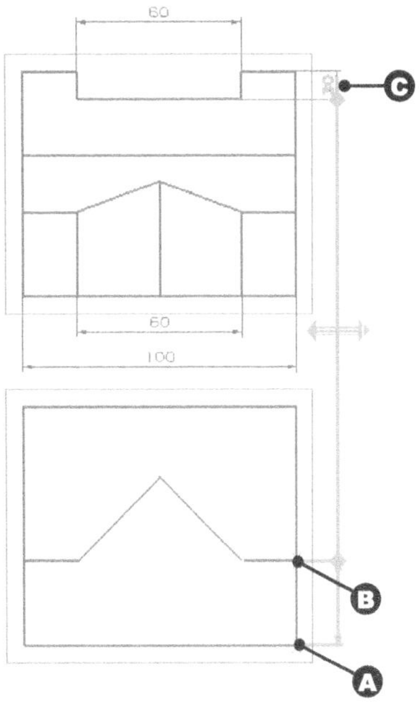

Fig 15-28 Aligning Dimension

If you want to align the dimension after creating the dimension, click MB3 on the existing dimension and choose **Origin** in the pop-up menu. You can align the dimension by using the options in the **Origin Tool** dialog box.

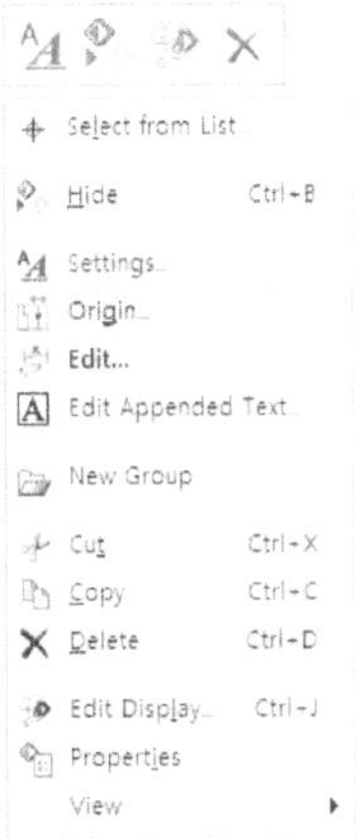

Fig 15-29 Origin Option

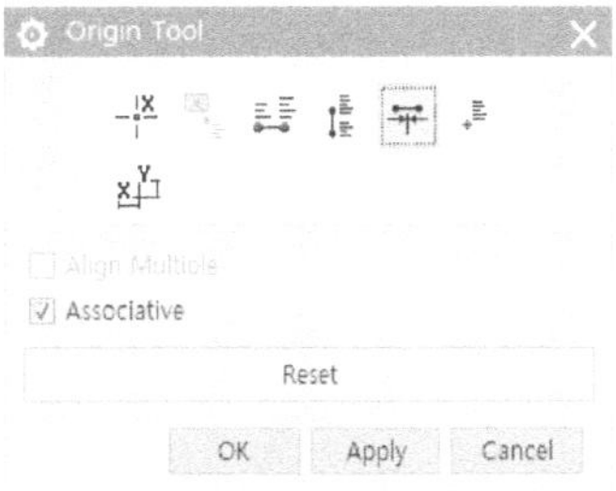

Fig 15-30 Origin Tool Dialog Box

Exercise 01 Creating Linear Dimensions *ch15_ex01.prt*

Create dimensions for the given part as shown in Fig 15-31. Use the **Hole Callout** method to create a dimension for the hole. Set the height of dimensions to 4.5mm.

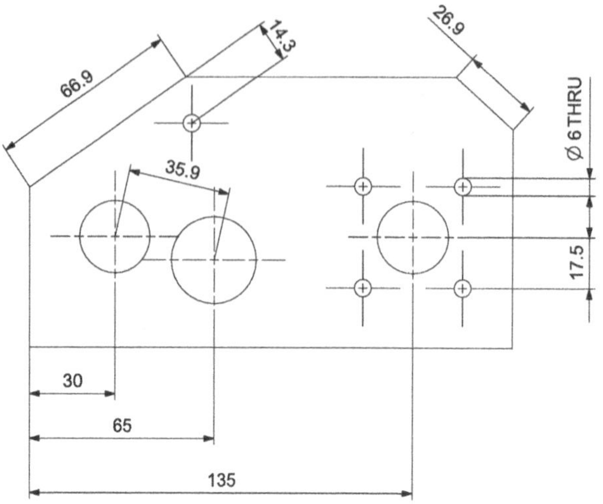

Fig 15-31 Drawing for Exercise 01

Exercise 02 Creating Radial Dimensions *ch15_ex02.prt*

Create dimensions for the given part as shown in Fig 15-32. Use the **Hole Callout** method to create a dimension for the hole. Set the height of dimensions to 4.5mm.

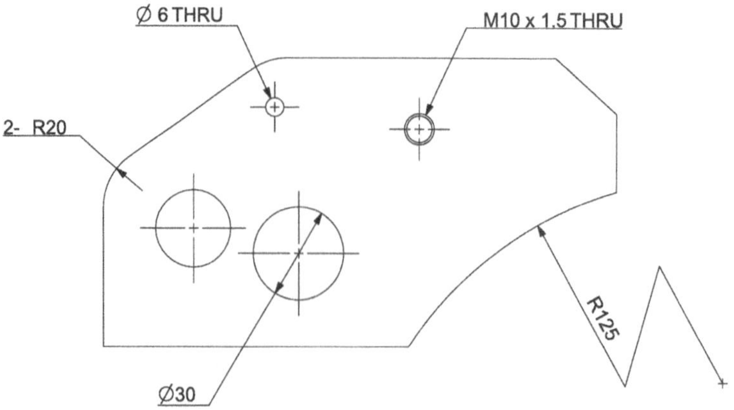

Fig 15-32 Drawing for Exercise 01

15.6 Notes

Drawing objects such as notes, weld and roughness symbols, balloon and datum target symbols and center marks are called annotations. You can create annotations using the icons in the **Annotation** icon group. General texts and leader type texts can be created with the **Note** command.

Fig 15-33 Annotation Icon Group

Procedure for Creating Notes

① Click the **Note** icon in the **Annotation** icon group.

② Enter texts in the **Note** dialog box.

③ Click MB1 at the location where to create the note.

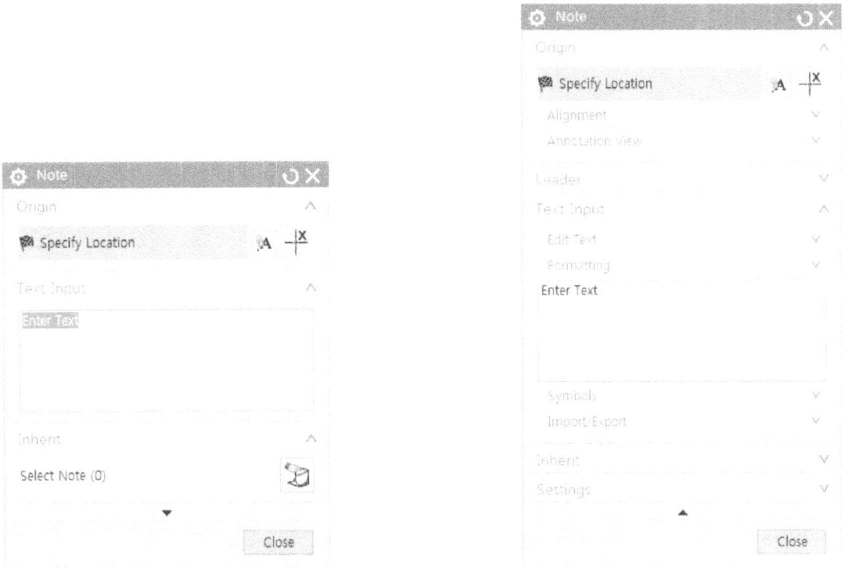

Fig 15-34 Note Dialog Box

You can snap the note to the existing text or dimension by moving the mouse pointer as shown in Fig 15-35. If you do not want it to be snapped, press the **Alt** key.

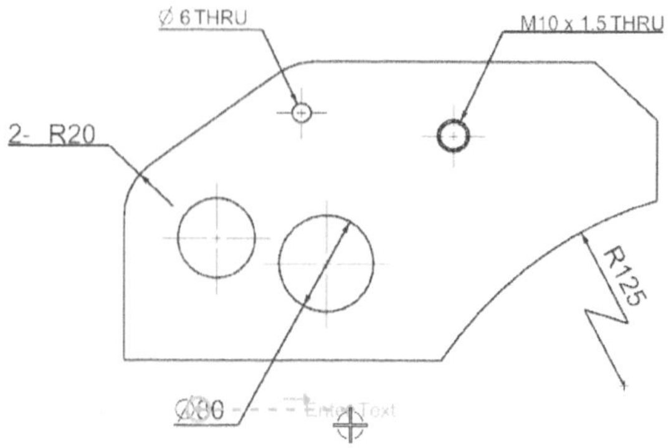

Fig 15-35 The Snapped Text

The leader type text can be created as shown in Fig 15-36. Move the mouse pointer to place the leader and wait for a second. The mouse pointer changes as designated by the arrow in Fig 15-36 (a). Click MB1 and drag, then the leader type text is previewed as shown in Fig 15-36 (b).

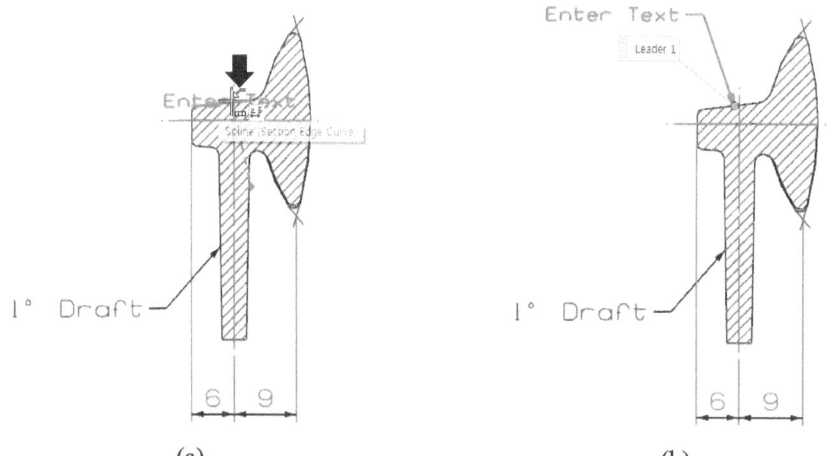

(a) (b)

Fig 15-36 Creating the Leader Type Note

Changing General Note to Leader Type

Double click the general note. The **Select Terminating Object** option is activated and you can select the terminating object for the leader type note.

15.6.1 Modifying the Note

Double click the leader type note. The **Note** dialog box is invoked and you can expand the **Leader** options group as shown in Fig 15-37.

A : You can re-select the target object to designate by the leader arrow.

B : The leader arrow can be bent to avoid crossing other drawing objects. You can drag the bent point, and can add or remove the bent point by pressing MB3 on the point.

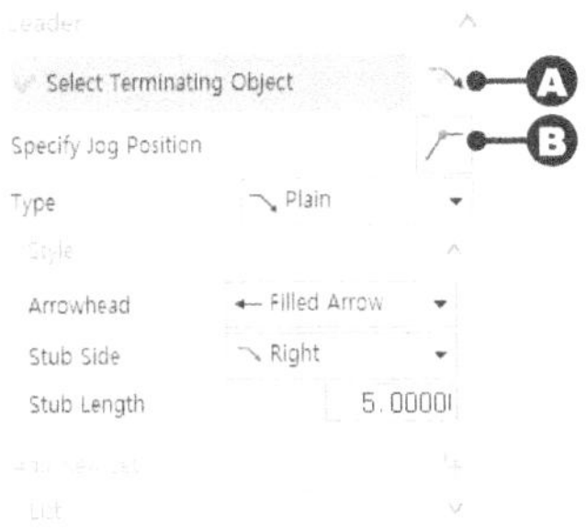

Fig 15-37 Leader Option

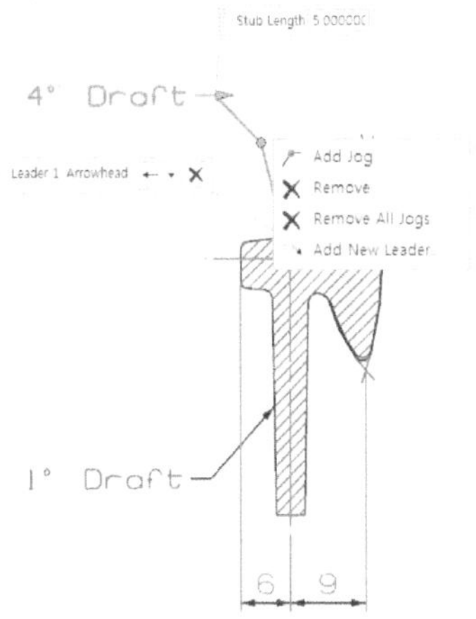

Fig 15-38 Modifying the Leader

If you press MB3 on the leader, a pop-up menu is available as shown in Fig 15-39. You can add a new leader, align the leader or modify the settings.

You can enter various types of special characters by expanding the **Symbols** option group below the **Text Input** area.

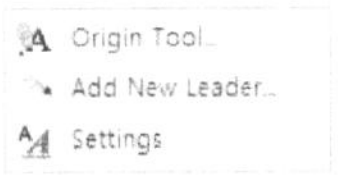

Fig 15-39 Leader Pop-up Menu

Fig 15-40 Symbols Option

15.6.2 Multiple Terminating Objects

If you want to specify multiple objects with a leader type note, keep to the following procedure.

① Double click the already created note and press MB3. Choose **Add New Leader** in the pop-up menu and select an object to create a leader.
② Expand the **List** in the **Leader** option group and select the **New** item in the list. You are prompted to select an object to create a leader.

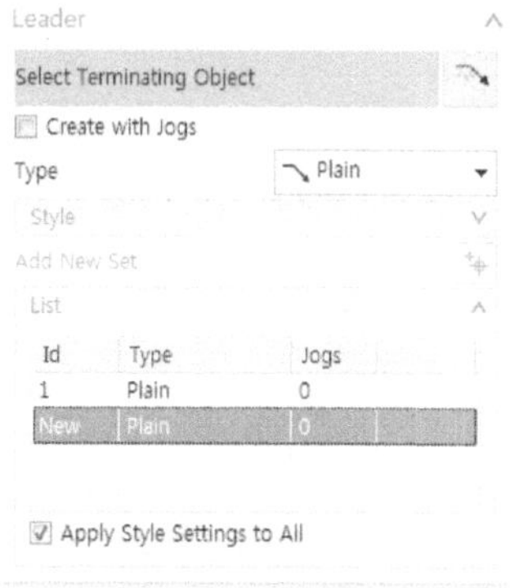

Fig 15-41 List of Leaders

When you are changing a general note into the leader type, you can select multiple objects one by one. You can modify each leader by double clicking the note and choosing a desired leader in the list or by choosing the arrow in the graphics window. You can modify the terminating object or define a jog for the selected leader.

15.7 Center Lines

You can create several types of center lines using the icons in the **Annotation** icon group.

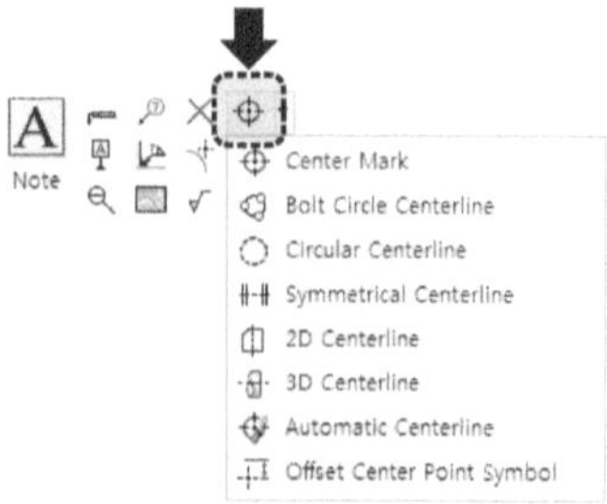

Fig 15-42 Icons for Center Lines

15.7.1 Center Mark

You can create two crossed center lines for the holes viewed on the top. If you select several holes, the center marks are connected linearly. Turn on the **Create Multiple Center Marks** option to create individual center marks that are not linear connected as shown in Fig 15-43.

You can resize the center lines by dragging the arrow head designated by Ⓐ in Fig 15-43. You can also set the **Gap** and **Center Cross** options in the **Settings** option group. If you want to resize the two crossed center lines individually, check the **Set Extension Individually** option in the **Settings** option group.

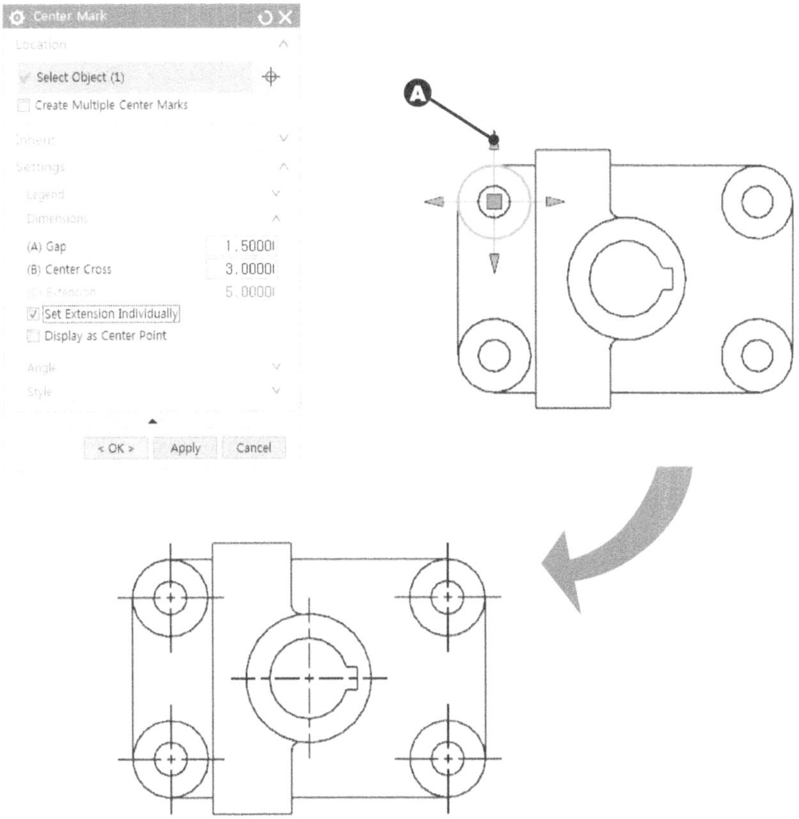

Fig 15-43 Creating Center Marks

15.7.2 Bolt Circle Centerline

The **Bolt Circle Centerline**, which connects the center of holes by circle, can be created for the holes that can be patterned circular. You can create P.C.D (Pitch Circle Diameter) as shown in Fig 15-44.

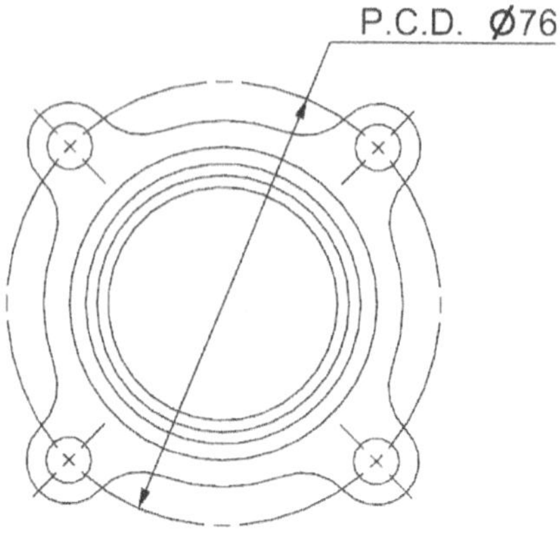

Fig 15-44 Bolt Circle Centerline

15.7.3 2D Centerline

You can create a single centerline between two curves or by connecting two points. Note that the curves are not confined to lines but you can select splines. This type of centerline is used to specify the center of geometries viewed in front.

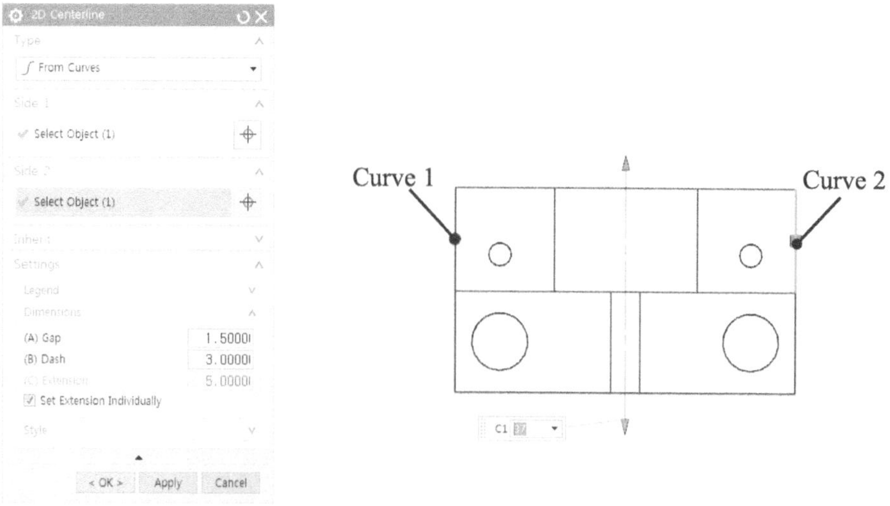

Fig 15-45 2D Centerline

15.7.4 3D Centerline

The side view of the hole centerline can be created by selecting the cylindrical face. Note that you have to click MB1 when the 3D face is recognized in orange.

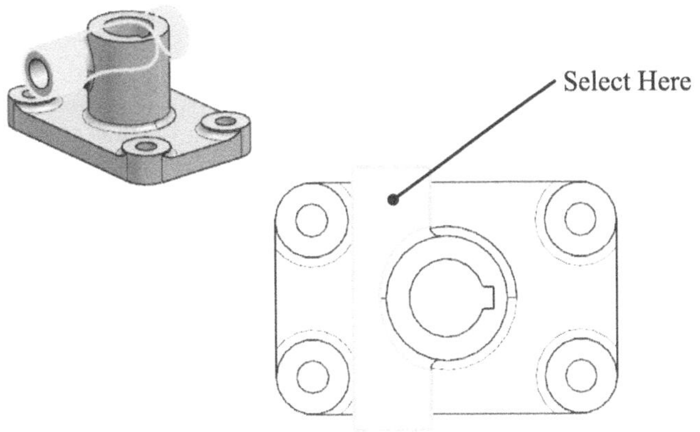

Fig 15-46 3D Centerline

15.7.5 Offset Center Point Symbol

When you create a radial dimension for a large arc, you can create an offset center point and create a folded radius. Fig 15-47 shows offsetting the center point 50mm vertically from the upper quadrant point of the arc.

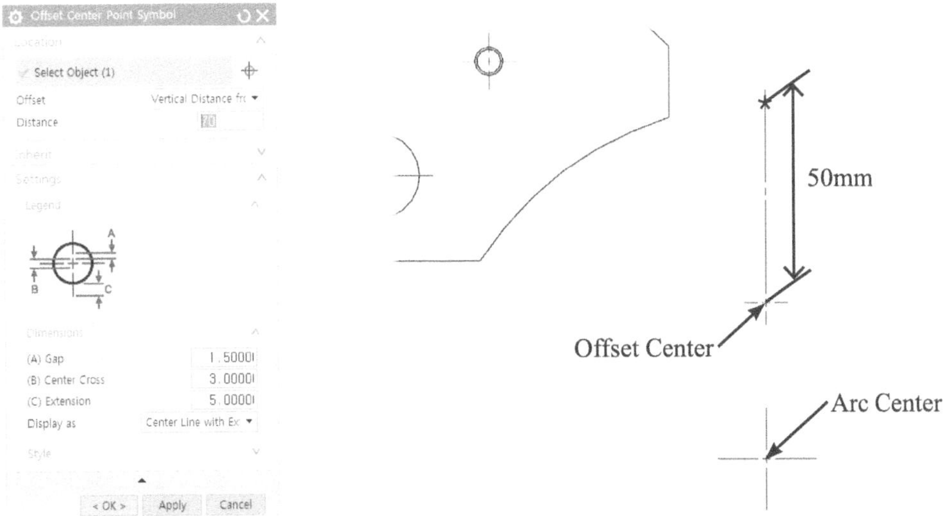

Fig 15-47 Offset Center Point

15.8 Intersection Symbol

After creating an intersection symbol, you can create a linear dimension for the vertex before applying a fillet.

Fig 15-48 Intersection Symbol Icon

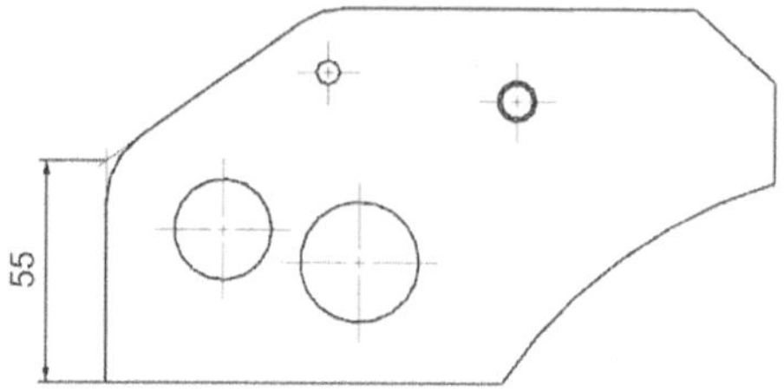

Fig 15-49 Linear Dimension for Intersection Point

15.9 View Dependent Edit

You can remove or modify the type of curves in a specific drawing view. Press MB3 on the view boundary and choose **View Dependent Edit** in the pop-up menu. You can remove curves, modify the font of curves or modify the color of faces with the icons in the **Add Edits** option. You can delete the modification with the icons in the **Delete Edits** option.

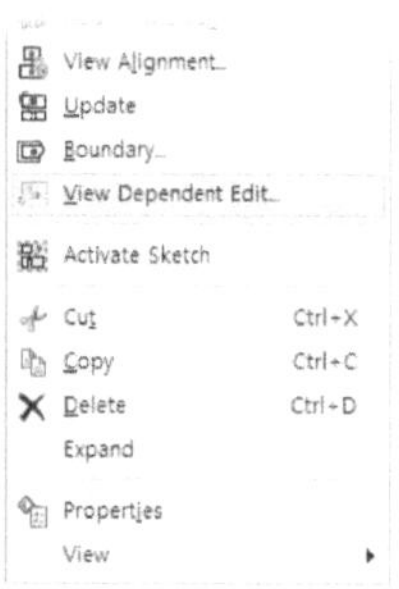

Fig 15-50 View Dependent Edit Menu

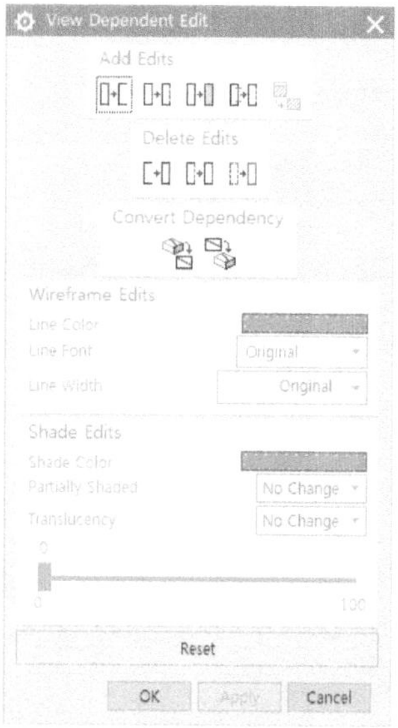

Fig 15-51 View Dependent Edit Dialog Box

Create a drawing as shown in Fig 15-52 for the given part.

Remarks

1. Create the drawing exactly the same as the given drawing.
2. Refer to the size of sheet and scale.
3. Height of dimensions and appended texts is 5mm.

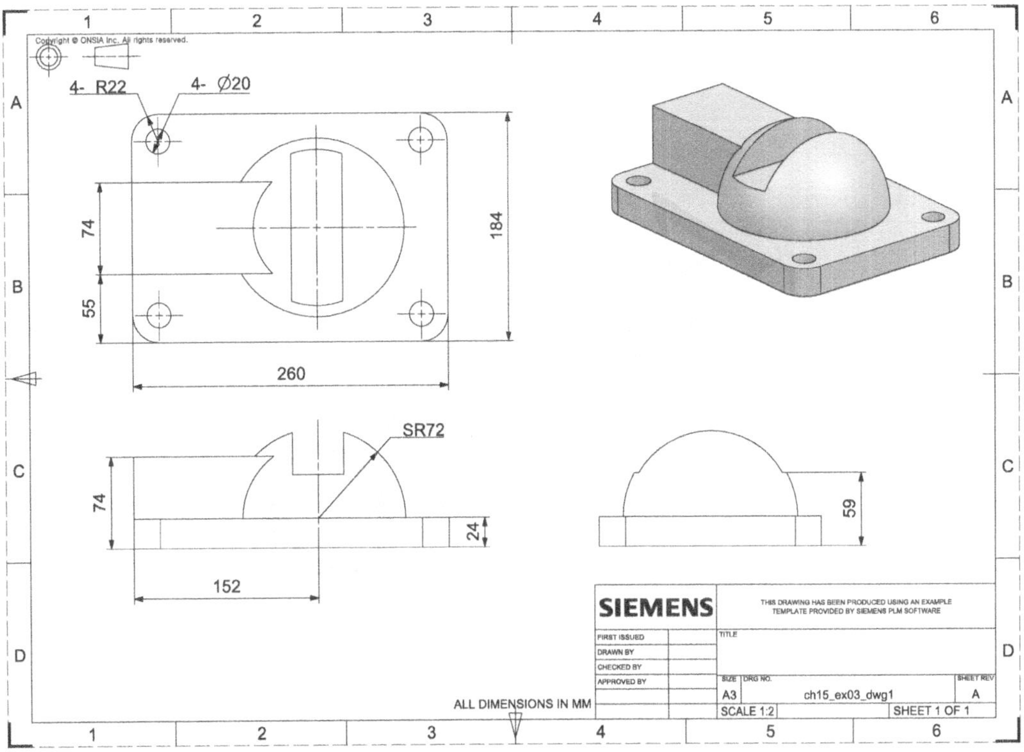

Fig 15-52 Drawing for Exercise 03

END of Exercise

Exercise 04

ch15_ex04.prt

Create a drawing as shown in Fig 15-53 for the given part.

Remarks

1. Create the drawing exactly the same as the given drawing.
2. Refer to the size of sheet and scale.
3. Height of dimensions and appended texts is 5mm.

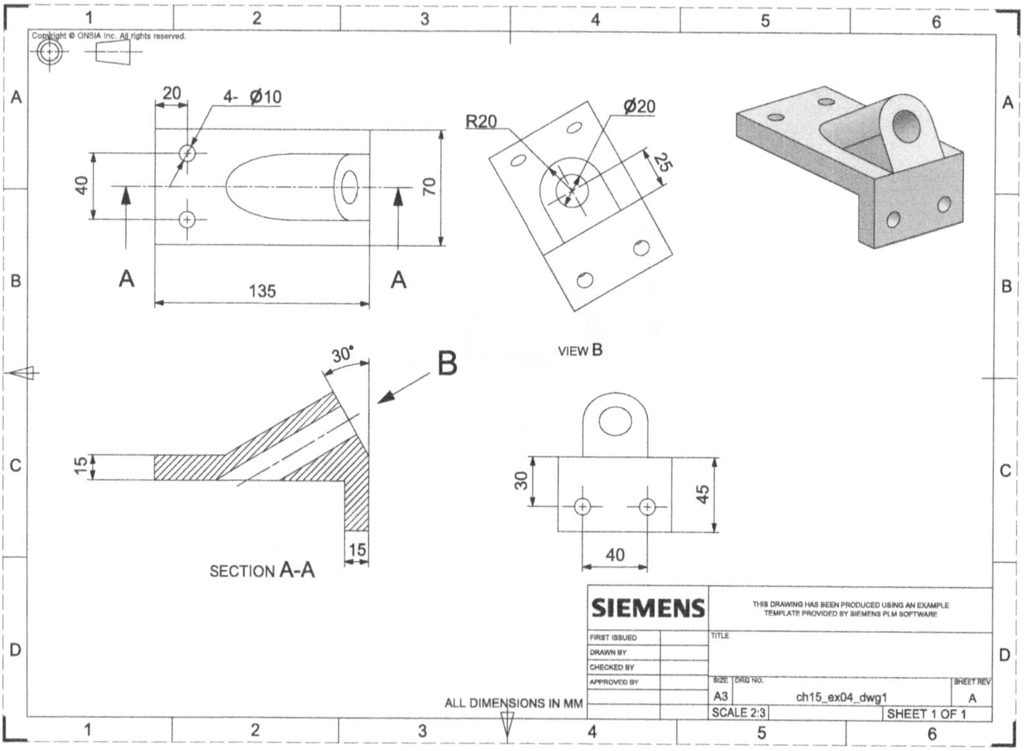

Fig 15-53 Drawing for Exercise 04

END of Exercise

15.10 Assembly Drawing

You can create a drawing for an assembly. The purpose of creating an assembly drawing is to provide the information required for assembling a product. The assembly sequence and path can be illustrated in a disassembled drawing view. Names, quantity, material, etc. of each component of an assembly can be included in the parts list.

To create an assembly drawing, open the assembly part file, create a drawing file and insert the drawing views as shown in Fig 15-54 as you have done for the part drawings. You can create a disassembled drawing view, apply balloon annotations and include a parts list. In this chapter, we will learn the following topics.

① Excluding specific components in the assembly drawing view.
② Creating a break-out section view for an assembly drawing view.
③ Creating a disassembled view and inserting a parts list and balloon annotation.

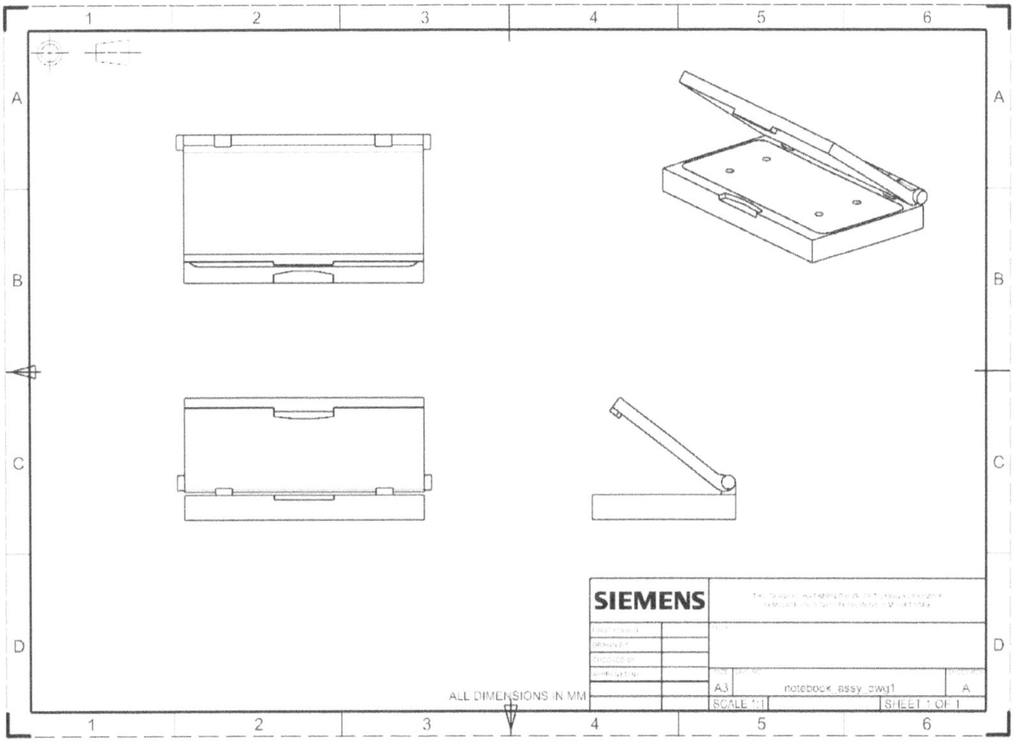

Fig 15-54 Drawing for Notebook_assy

15.10.1 Excluding Components in a Drawing View

Press the **More** button in the **Base View** or **Projected View** dialog box and expand the **Settings** option as shown in Fig 15-55. You can hide a specific component in a drawing view and exclude components from being sectioned.

① The **Hidden Components** Option

Press MB3 on the boundary of a drawing view and choose **Edit** in the pop-up menu. Click the **Select Object** option field in the **Hidden Components** option and select the components in the drawing sheet or in the assembly navigator to hide in the drawing view.

② The **Non-Sectioned** Option

When you create a section view for an assembly, you can exclude certain components from being cut. Note that the essential components such as bolts and nuts are not cut in the section view of the assembly drawing in general. You can select the non-sectioned components in the assembly navigator effectively.

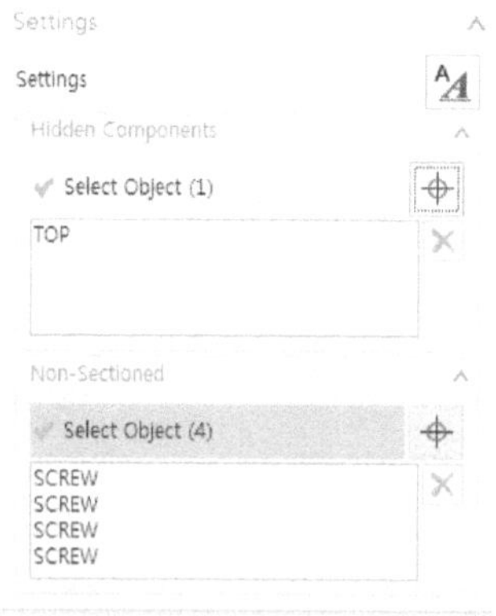

Fig 15-55 Settings Option

Let's create a drawing view for the given assembly and exclude a component in a view. Then, we will exclude the **Screw** component from being cut in the section view.

Option in the Base View

1. Create the drawing file named notebook_assy_dwg1.prt for the given assembly file notebook_assy.prt in the folder notebook_assy.

2. Create the front view using the **Base View** command as shown in Fig 15-56.

3. Create the top view by projecting the front view.

4. Click **MB3 > Edit** on the top view in the part navigator.

5. Expand the **Settings** option group in the **Projected View** dialog box.

6. Click the **Select Object** option field of the **Hidden Components** option.

7. Select the **Top** component in the top view as designated in Fig 15-56.

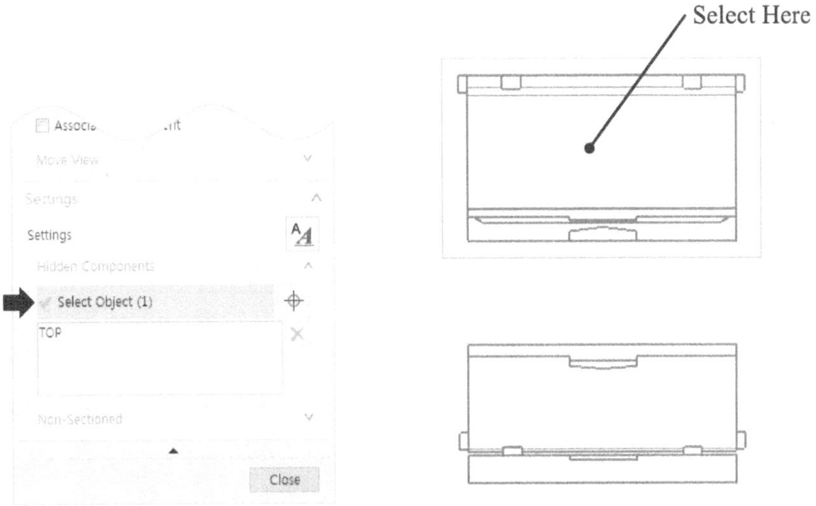

Fig 15-56 Selecting the Component to Hide

8. Click the **Select Object** option field of the **Non-Sectioned** option in the **Projected View** dialog box.

9. Show the components in the assembly navigator and select the four **Screw** components as shown in Fig 15-57 (a). The selected components are listed in the list box as shown in Fig 15-57 (b).

10. Close the dialog box.

(a) (b)

Fig 15-57 Components to be Non-Sectioned

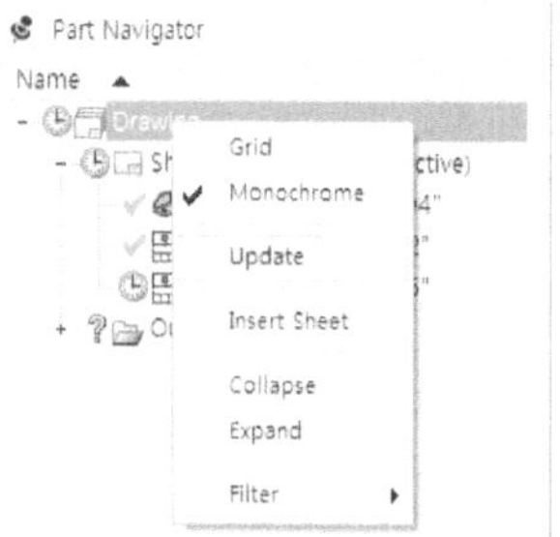

Fig 15-58 Update Option

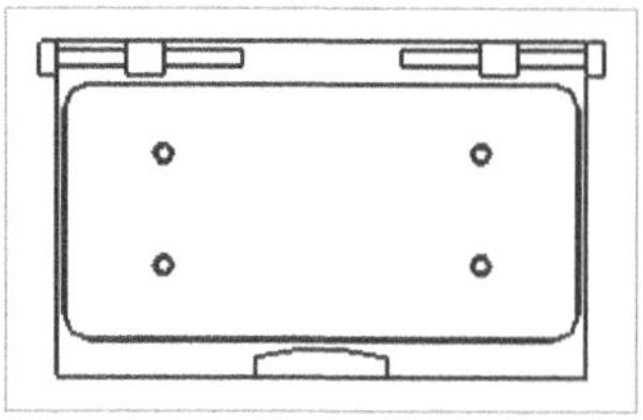

Fig 15-59 Top View Updated

Updating the Views

1. Select the part navigator in the resource bar. Identify the update symbol in the part navigator.

2. Click **MB3 > Update** on the **Drawing**. You can click the update symbol.

The **Top** component is hidden only in the top view as shown in Fig 15-59.

Creating Section View

1. Click **MB3 > Add Section View** on the **Top** view.
2. Select the mid point as designated by ❶ in Fig 15-60.
3. Move the mouse cursor on the right of the **Top** view and choose MB3 > **Lock Alignment.**
4. Click the button ❷ in the **Section View** option bar and select the hole center designated by ❸ in Fig 15-60 to define the stepped section line.
5. Click MB2. Or you can click the **Place View** button in the **Section View** option bar.
6. Click the location ❹ with MB1 to create the section view as shown in Fig 15-61.

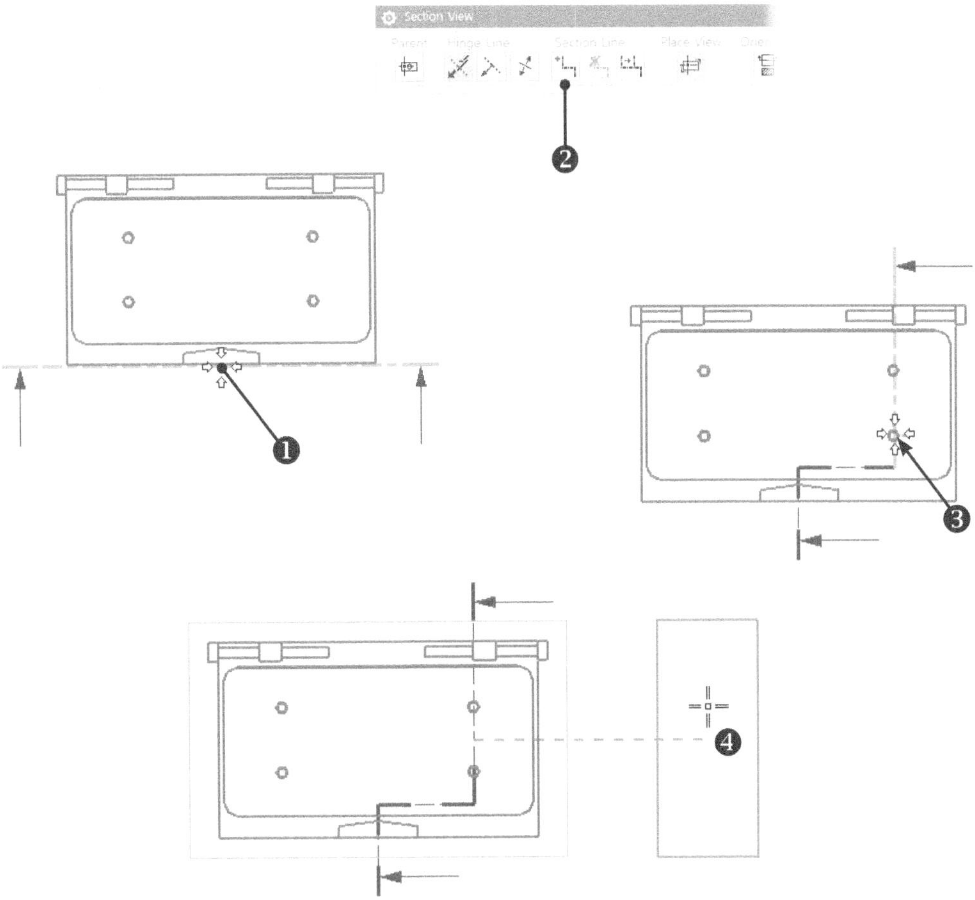

Fig 15-60 Defining Stepped Section Line

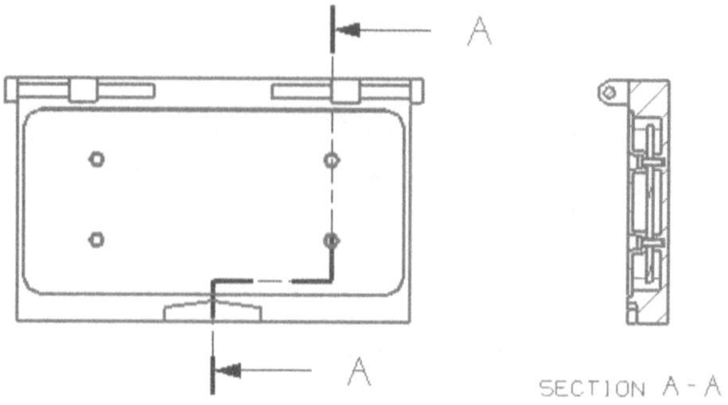

Fig 15-61 Stepped Section View

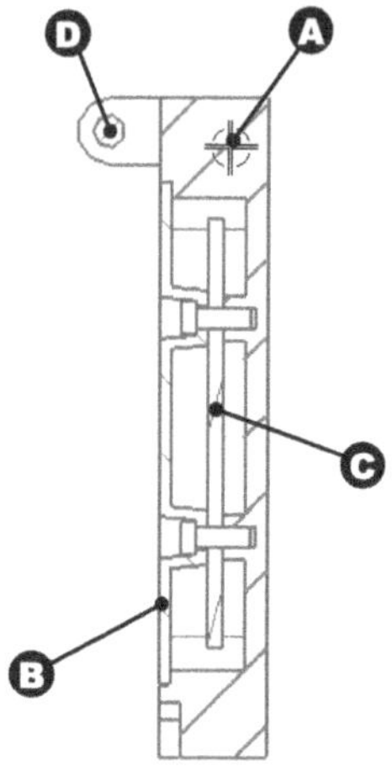

Fig 15-62 Crosshatch to Modify

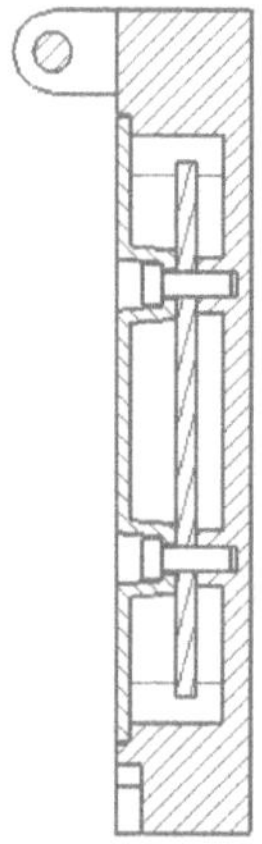

Fig 15-63 Modified Hatching Distance

7. Double click the crosshatch Ⓐ designated in Fig 15-62 and enter 1mm in the **Distance** input box.

8. Set the hatching distance to 1mm for the crosshatches Ⓑ, Ⓒ and Ⓓ.

9. Click **OK** in the **Crosshatch** dialog box.

The hatching distance is shown like in Fig 15-63. Verify that there is no hatching line in the **Screw** components.

10. Save the drawing file.

It is recommended to do the next exercise to create a break-out section view.

END of Exercise

15.10.2 Break-out Section View for an Assembly Drawing View

It is hard to describe the assembly state for interior components. In this case, the break out section view can be helpful. The procedure is the same as that for the part drawing. Fig 15-64 shows the break out section view of the notebook assembly. The disassembled view, which will be explained later, shows the individual components in an arbitrary disassembled position. It does not show the components in the assembled position.

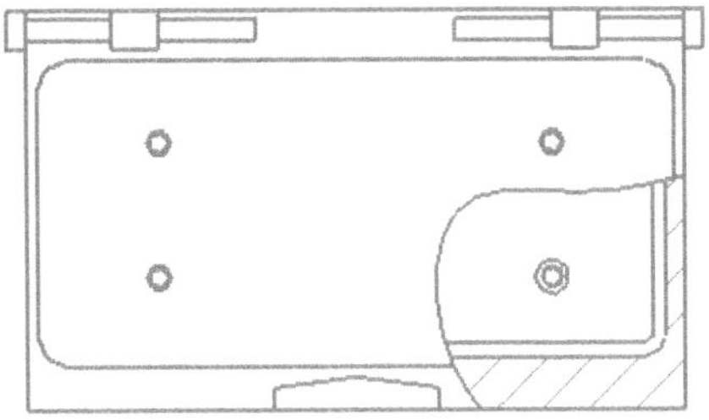

Fig 15-64 Break-out Section View

Folder: notebook_assy
File: notebook_assy_dwg1.prt

Creating Break-Out Section View **Exercise 06**

Let's create a break-out section view for the top view created in Exercise 05.

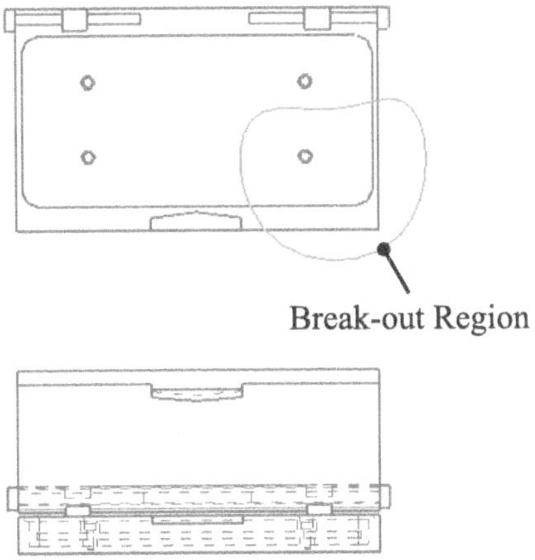

Fig 15-65 Break-out Region

Creating the Break-Out Region

1. Delete the section view in the drawing created in Exercise 04.

2. Display the hidden line for the front view to specify the break-out depth later.

3. Click **MB3 > Active Sketch View** on the top view.

4. Using the **Studio Spline** command in the **Sketch** icon group, create the break-out region as shown in Fig 15-65.

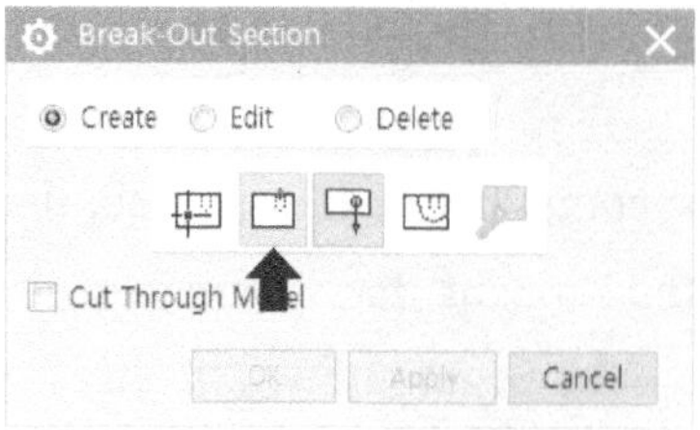

Fig 15-66 Break-Out Section Dialog Box

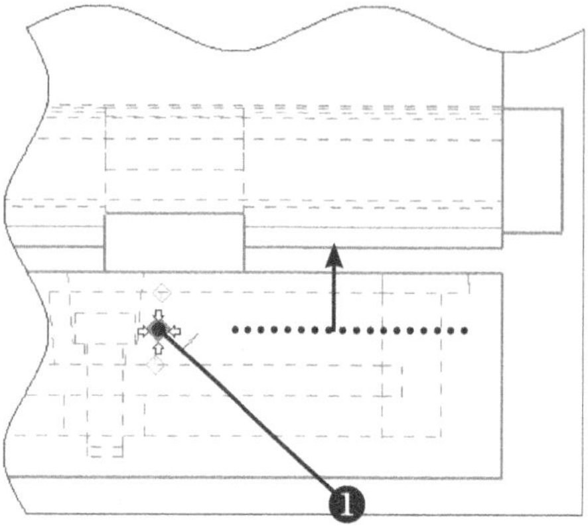

Fig 15-67 Base Point

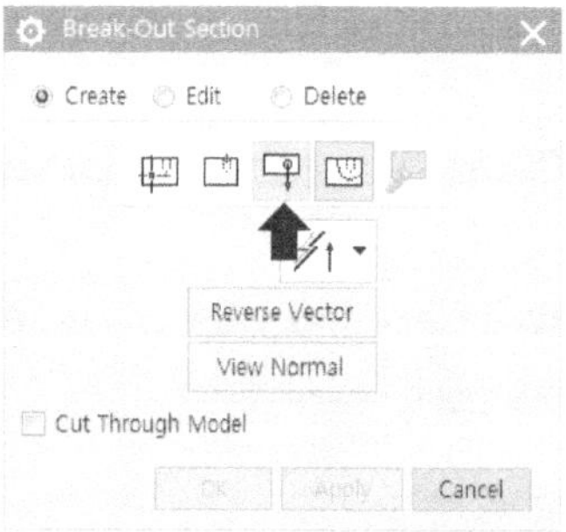

Fig 15-68 Extrusion Vector

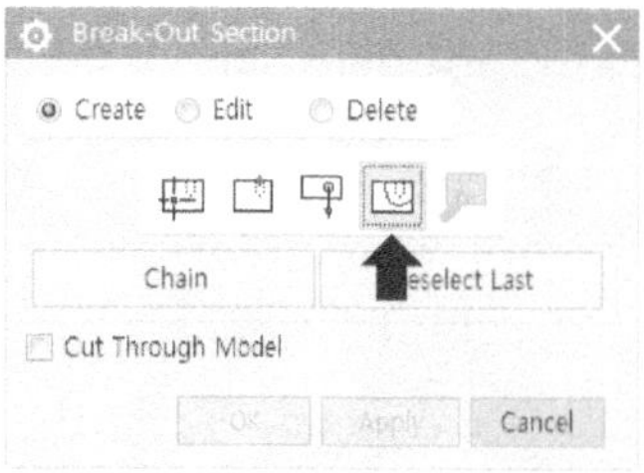

Fig 15-69 Break-out Region

5. Finish the sketch.

Creating Break-out Section View

1. Click the **Break-out Section View** icon in the **View** icon group.

2. Select the top view. The dialog box changes as shown in Fig 15-66. We have to specify the base point.

3. Select the point ❶ designated in Fig 15-67. We will break-out above this point.

4. The dialog box changes as shown in Fig 15-68. Confirm the vector as the break-out direction and click MB2.

5. The dialog box changes as shown in Fig 15-69. We have to specify the region to break-out.

6. Select the region created in Fig 15-65. Make sure that the curves have to be created in the top view to break-out.

7. Click the **Apply** button and click **Cancel** to close the dialog box.

The top view is broken-out as shown in Fig 15-70 and you can see the interior components of the assembly.

8. Save the drawing file and close all parts.

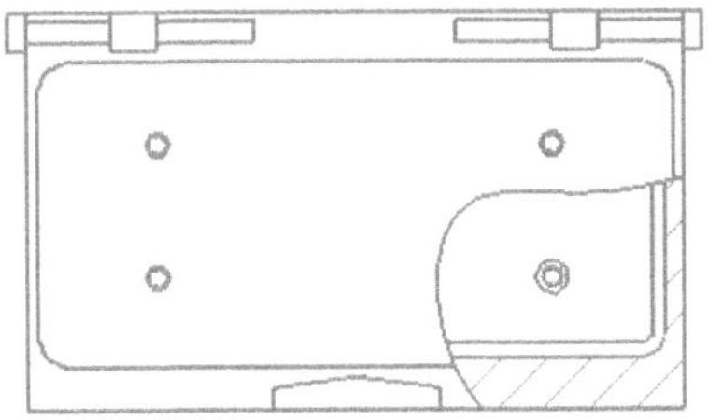

Fig 15-70 Break-out Section Created

END of Exercise

15.10.3 Disassembled Drawing View

The purpose of the disassembled drawing view is to illustrate the assembling position of each component. Therefore, the components are not located in the assembled position, but they are moved in a manner to illustrate the assembling relationship effectively.

You can create a parts list automatically for the assembly drawing view and you can create balloon annotations in the assembly drawing view.

Fig 15-71 shows the disassembled drawing view with a parts list and balloon annotation.

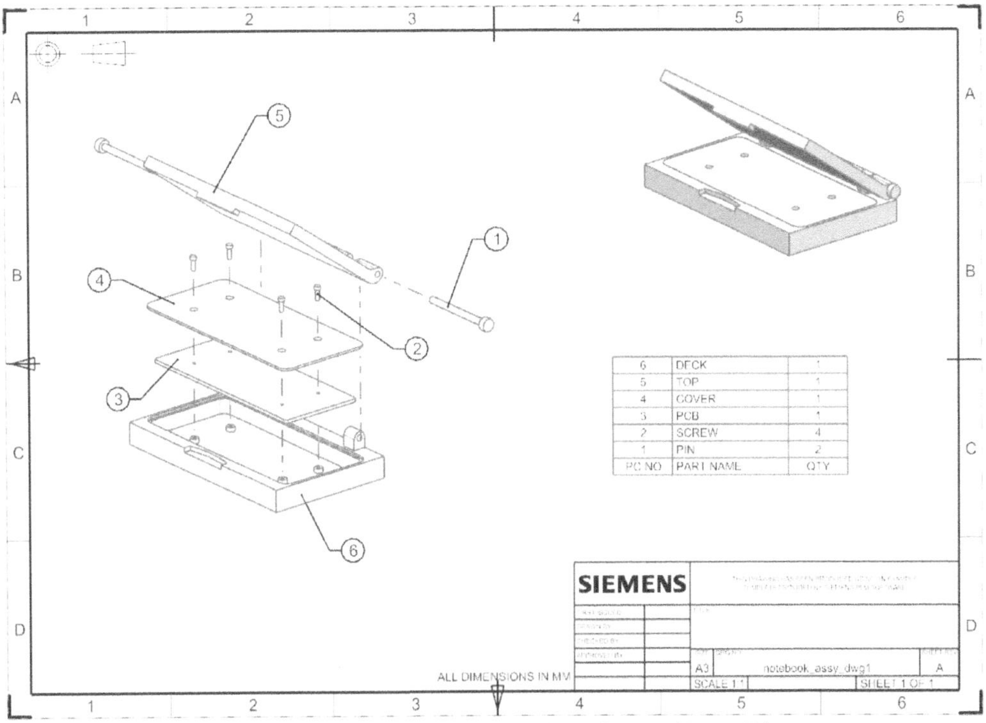

Fig 15-71 Disassembled Drawing View and Parts List

Exercise 06 Disassembled Drawing View and Parts List

Folder: notebook_assy
File: notebook_assy.prt

Let's create a disassembled drawing view, then create a parts list and balloon annotation.

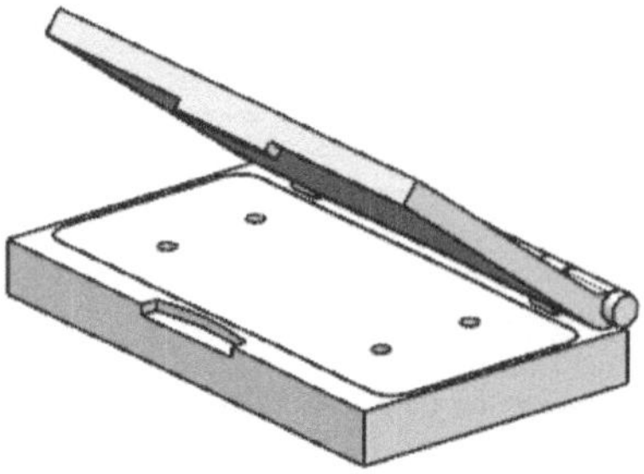

Fig 15-72 Trimetric Drawing View

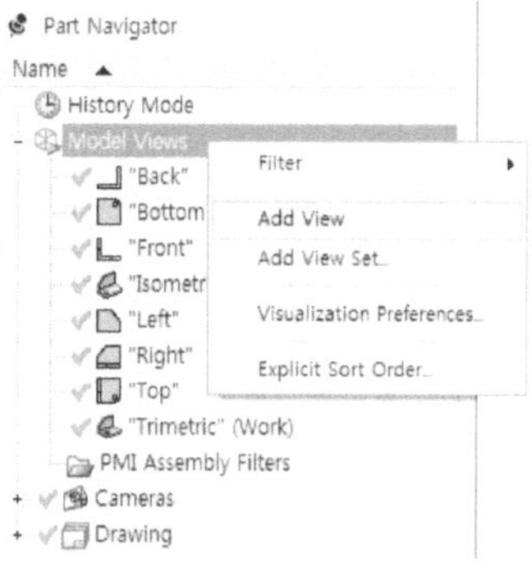

Fig 15-73 Creating the Model View

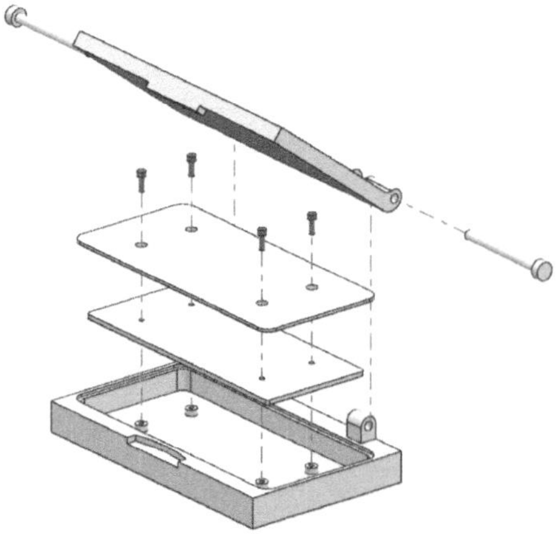

Fig 15-74 Disassembled Status

Creating Drawing File and Disassembling

1. Create a drawing file for the given assembly file notebook_assy.prt. Use the **A3 - Size** drawing template. The name of the drawing file will be notebook_assy_dwg2.prt.
2. Create a trimetric drawing view on the top right of the drawing sheet as shown in Fig 15-72.
3. Close the **Base View** dialog box.
4. Choose **Modeling** in the **Application** tab.
5. Display the **Part Navigator** and expand the **Model View** as shown in Fig 15-73.
6. Click MB3 on the **Model View** and choose **Add View** in the pop-up menu.
7. Name the view as "exploded" and press the **Enter** key.

Confirm that the newly added view is designated as **Work**.

8. Disassemble the assembly according to the method which has been explained in "13.5 Disassembling an Assembly" on Page 532. Fig 15-74 shows the disassembled status. You may have to move the handle only to move the top component properly. Refer to the next page to move only the handle.

Moving Only the Handles

If the handle is not orientated properly while you are moving components, you can move only the handles by checking the **Move Handles Only** option in the **Edit Explosion** dialog box. You can re-orient the handle as shown in Fig 15-75 according to the following procedure. Each number corresponds to those in Fig 15-75.

① Check the **Move Handles Only** option.
② Click the head of the move handle with MB1.
③ Select a vector to align the arrow.

After aligning the handle, select the **Move Objects** in the **Edit Explosion** dialog box and move the component by dragging the handle.

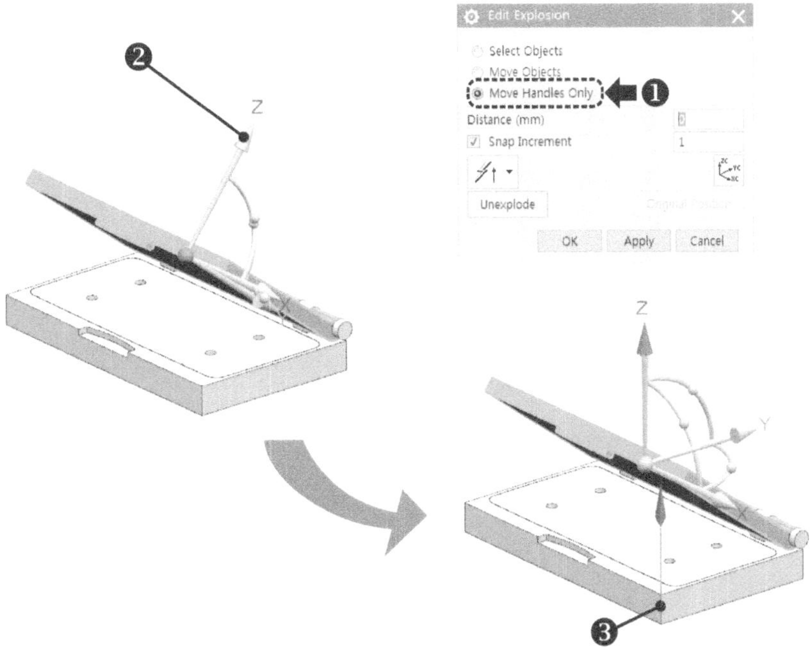

Fig 15-75 Moving Only the Handle

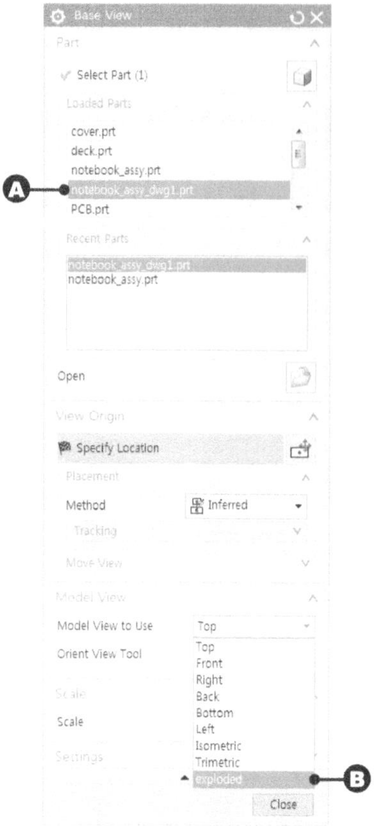

Fig 15-76 Adding the Disassembled Drawing View

Disassembled Drawing View

1. Switch the application to **Drafting**.

2. Click the **Base View** icon and press the **More** button in the dialog box.

3. Select the drawing file in the **Loaded Parts** selection area as designated by **A** in Fig 15-76.

4. Select "**exploded**" in the **Model View to Use** dropdown list as designated by **B** in Fig 15-76.

5. Locate the disassembled drawing view as shown in Fig 15-77.

6. Close the **Base View** dialog box.

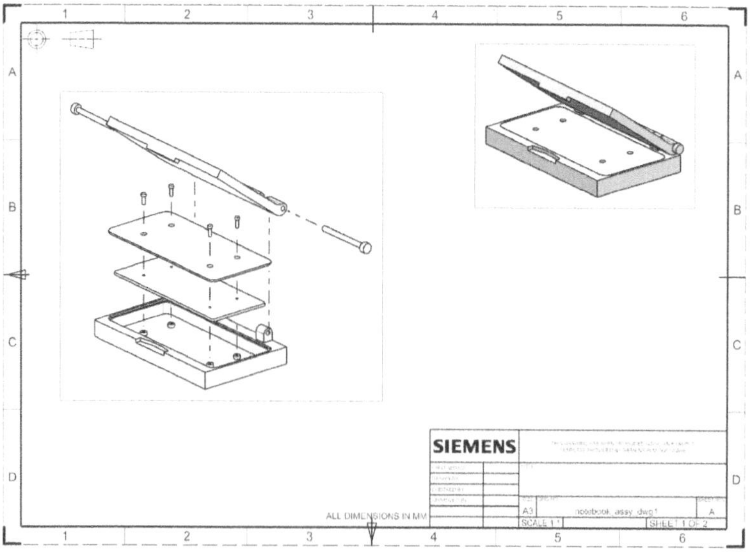

Fig 15-77 Added Disassembled Drawing View

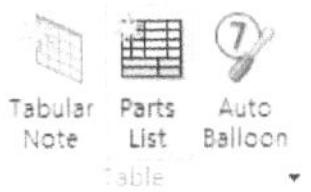

Fig 15-78 Parts List Icon

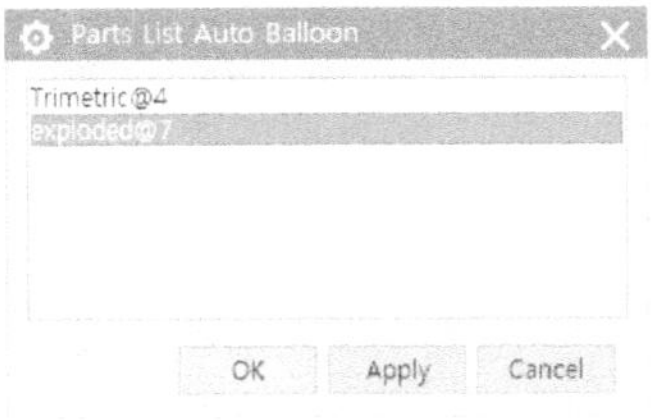

Fig 15-79 Selecting the View

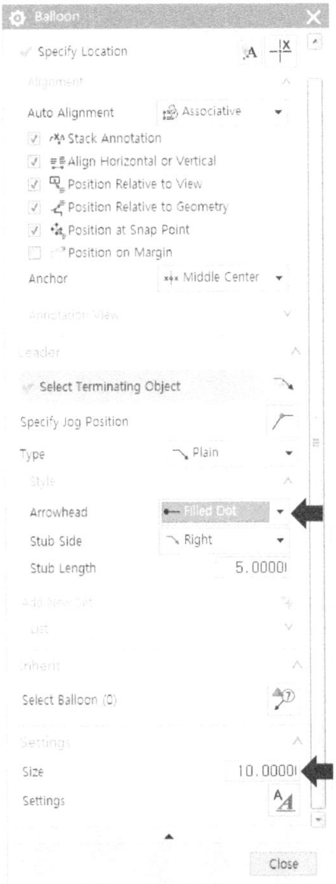

Fig 15-80 Identification Symbol Option

Parts List and Balloon Annotation

1. Click the **Parts List** icon in the **Table** icon group as shown in Fig 15-78.

2. A box is attached at the mouse pointer. Click MB1 at the lower part of the **Trimetric** drawing view to create the parts list.

3. Click the **Auto Balloon** icon in the **Table** icon group.

4. Select the parts list.

5. Click **OK** in the dialog box.

6. Select the drawing view to create the annotation, i.e. the disassembled view, and press **OK** in the dialog box.

7. Double click the leader of the annotation and modify its shape one by one as shown in Fig 15-80. Set the height of the annotation to 5mm and the circle size to 10. Choose **Filled Dot** as the **Arrowhead** option. When you modify the pointing location, use the snap point option of **Point on Face**.

8. Save the drawing file.

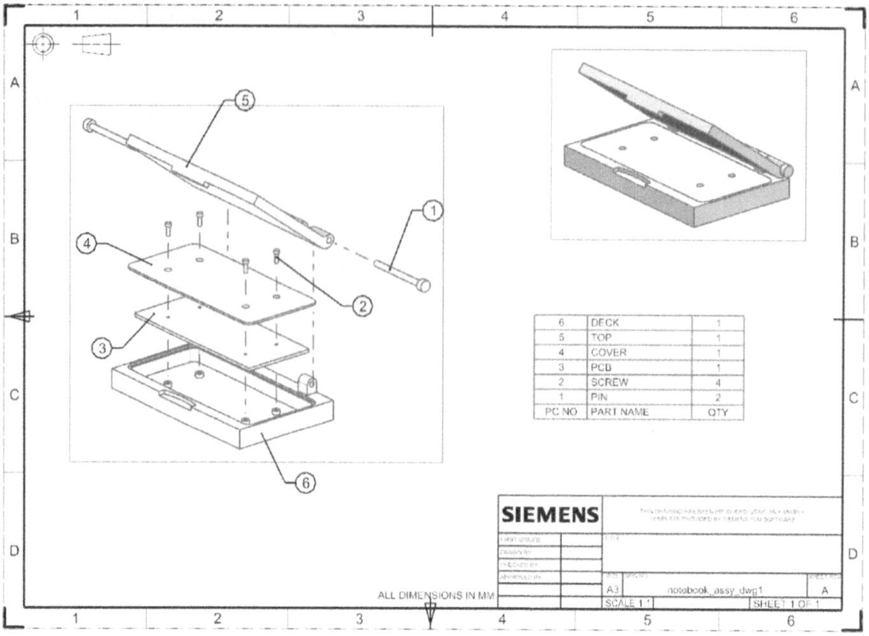

6	DECK	1
5	TOP	1
4	COVER	1
3	PCB	1
2	SCREW	4
1	PIN	2
PC NO	PART NAME	QTY

Fig 15-81 Completed Assembly Drawing

END of Exercise

Appendix A

Selecting Objects

■ After completing this chapter you will understand

- the importance and cautions in selecting objects while using a command.

A.1 Selection Steps in Dialog Box

The selection steps in a dialog box are marked by a red asterisk (*). If you do not select an object for the selection steps, the **OK** and **Apply** buttons in the dialog box are not activated and the preview of the result is not shown. If you select an appropriate object for the selection step, the asterisk mark changes to a green check mark as shown in Fig A-1.

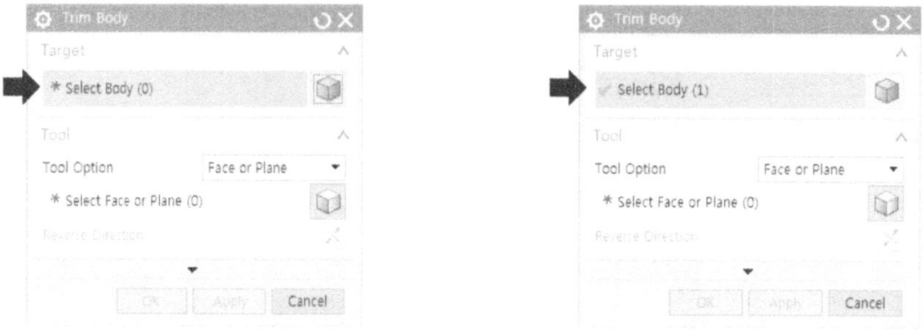

Fig A-1 Target Option Before and After the Selection

A.2 Number of Selected Objects

The number of selected objects is displayed in the parenthesis of the selection option. For options where you can select only one object, the next selection step is proceeded to automatically. For options where you can select several objects, you have to press MB2 or press the corresponding selection option to proceed to the selection step. Because only one target body is allowed for the **Unite** command, you are prompted to select the tool body immediately after you select the target body. On the other hand, you can select several target bodies in the **Trim Body** command. Therefore, you have to press MB2 or press the **Tool** option button so that you can select the tool body.

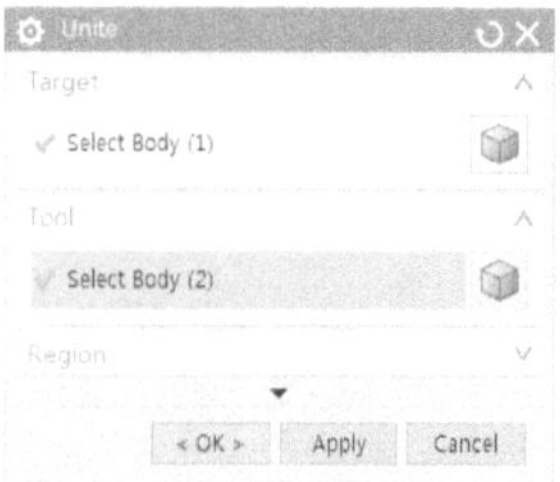

Fig A-2 Unite Dialog Box

A.3 Type Filter

When you select objects, you can filter the types of objects in the **Type Filter** dropdown list as shown in Fig A-3.

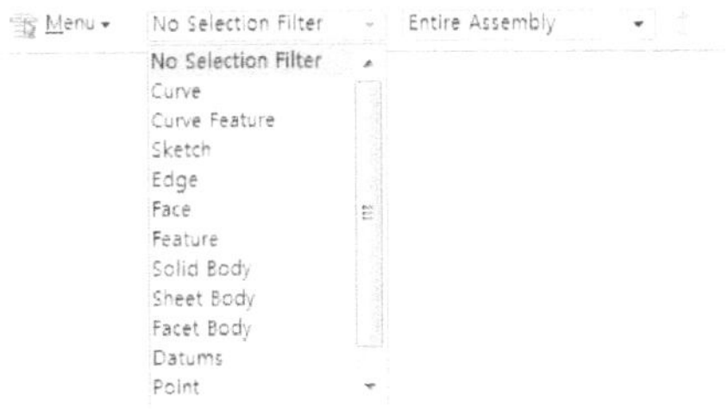

Fig A-3 Type Filter

Note that the list of the **Type Filter** is confined automatically for a selection step. This means that you can identify which type of objects you can select for the current selection step by looking at the **Type Filter** dropdown list. Fig A-4 **B** shows the types of object that you can select as the **Tool** object in the **Trim Body** command.

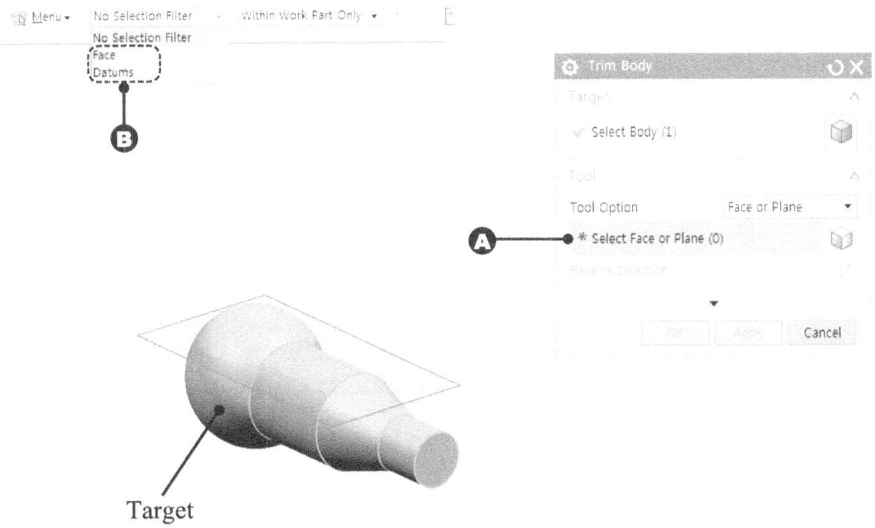

Fig A-4 Type Filter for the Tool Option in the Trim Body Command

A.4 Selecting Points, Lines and Faces

You can use the **Snap Point** option, **Curve Rule** and **Face Rule** to facilitate selecting points, curves and faces, respectively.

A.4.1 Snap Point Option

Using the **Snap Point** option as shown in Fig A-5, you can select points conveniently. Here, the points include the end points of a curve, center point of a circle, end point of an arc, quadrant point of a circle, a point on a face, etc., which are called control points.

Fig A-5 Snap Point Option

Note that the **Control Point** option is always activated in the selection steps where you have to select points. Fig A-6 shows the step for selecting the **Through Point** for defining the **Point and Direction** type datum axis. You can invoke the **Point** dialog box or you can use the snap point drop-down list. Note that the **Snap Point** option is not activated if you designate a point type in the snap point dropdown list, i.e., the **Snap Point** option is activated when the **Inferred Point** is selected in the dropdown list.

Fig A-6 Through Point Option in Defining a Datum Axis

A.4.2 Curve Rule

The **Curve Rule** is available when you are selecting curves. Using the curve rule, you can select curves efficiently and correctly. Here, the curves include the sketch curves, edges, three dimensional curves, etc. Note that the **Curve Rule** dropdown list is not shown or activated when you are in a selection step where you cannot select curves.

The section in the **Extrude** command is defined using curves. Therefore, the curve rule is activated when you are selecting the section as shown in Fig A-7. If you choose the

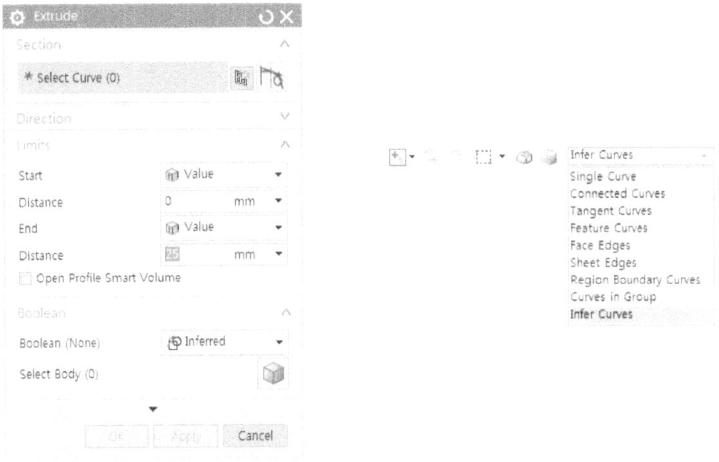

Fig A-7 Section Option in the Extrude Command

Inferred Curves in the dropdown list, a proper type is designated according to your first selection of a curve. For example, if you select a curve in a sketch feature with the **Inferred Curves** curve rule, all the curves in that sketch feature are selected together to define a section.

Some additional options are available with the **Curve Rule**.

If you press the **Stop At Intersection** button as shown in Fig A-8, you can choose which path to follow by stopping at an intersection. This option is available for the curve rules of **Single Curve, Connected Curves** and **Tangent Curves**. Fig A-9 shows defining a section with the **Stop At Intersection** option.

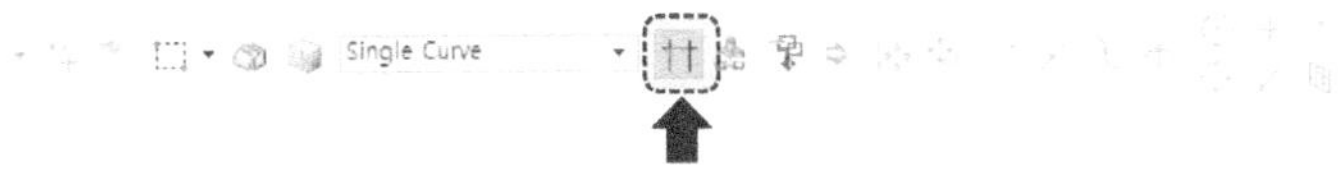

Fig A-8 The Stop At Intersection Option

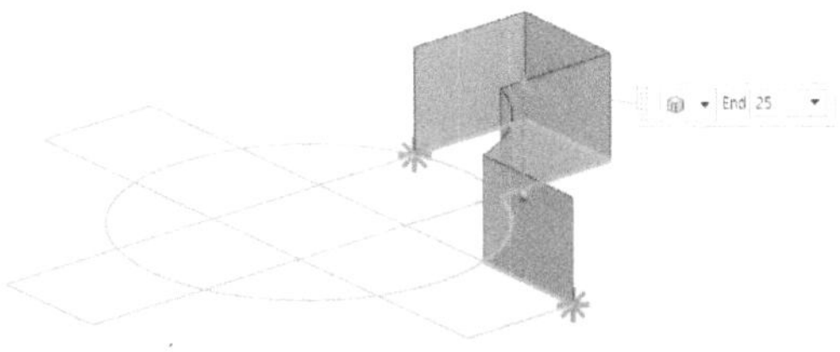

Fig A-9 Selecting Curves with the Stop At Intersection Option

The **Follow Fillet** option is available when you have selected the **Connected Curves** or the **Tangent Curves** curve rule. You can select curves by following the fillet at a single click as shown in Fig A-10.

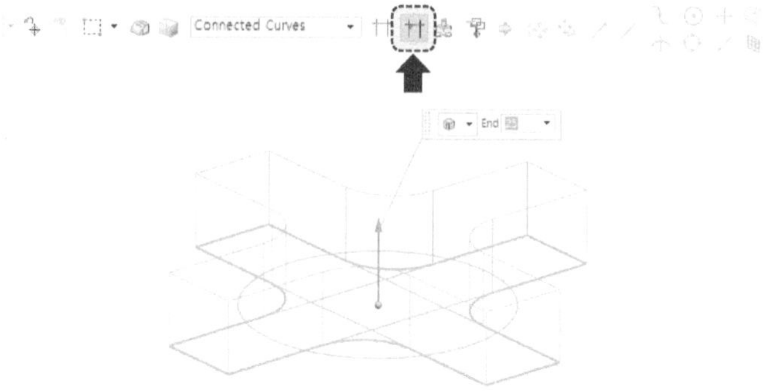

Fig A-10 Selecting Curves Using the Follow Fillet Option

If you use the **Chain Within Feature** option, the curve chain is valid only within the feature where the first selected curve belongs. The circle and the crossed rectangle shown in Fig A-11 are created in the respective sketches. If you select the **Stop At Intersection** option and the **Chain Within Feature** option at the same time and select a line in the rectangle, the section does not stop at the intersection with the circle because the circle is defined in another sketch feature.

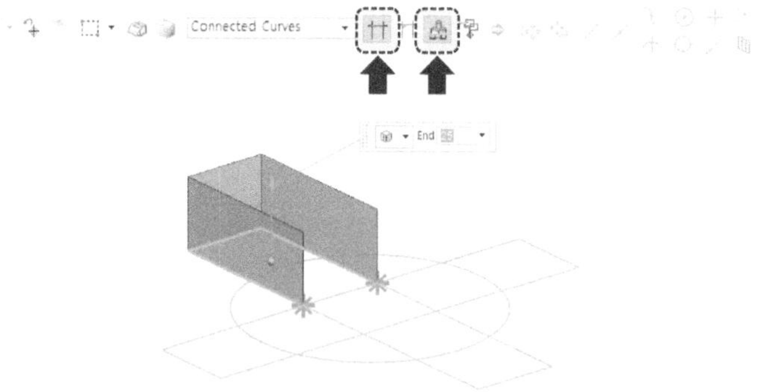

Fig A-11 Selecting Curves Using the Chain Within Feature Option

Using the **Path Selection** option, you can select curves preselected by the path which depends on the cursor location. Select the line ❶ as specified in Fig A-12 and place the mouse cursor on the line ❷ at the location as specified in Fig A-12. The path is highlighted and you can select the highlighted curves by clicking mouse button 1.

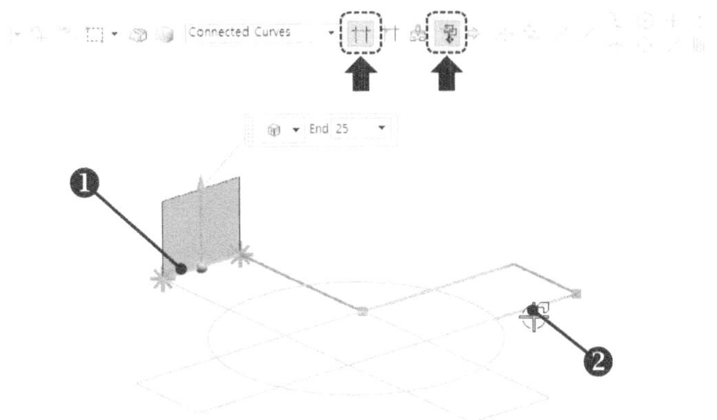

Fig A-12 Selecting Curves Using the Path Selection Option

You can add, remove or replace the through point of the path by pressing MB3 on the through point and you can turn on or off the **Path Selection** option during the selection period. The **Path Selection** option is generally used in combination with the **Stop At Intersection** option.

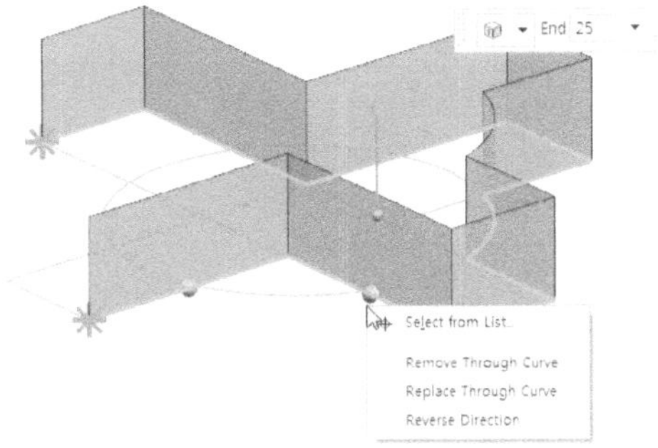

Fig A-13 Options for Modifying Path

A.4.3 Face Rule

The **Face Rule** is available when you are selecting faces. Using the face rule, you can select faces efficiently and correctly. Note that the **Face Rule** dropdown list is not shown or activated when you are in a selection step where you cannot select faces.

Fig A-14 shows the selection bar and the dialog box in the selection step for the stationary face in the **Draft** command. Note that both the **Face Rule** and the **Snap Point** option are activated because you can select faces or points to define the stationary face. Also note that the **Point Dialog** button is shown in the dialog box.

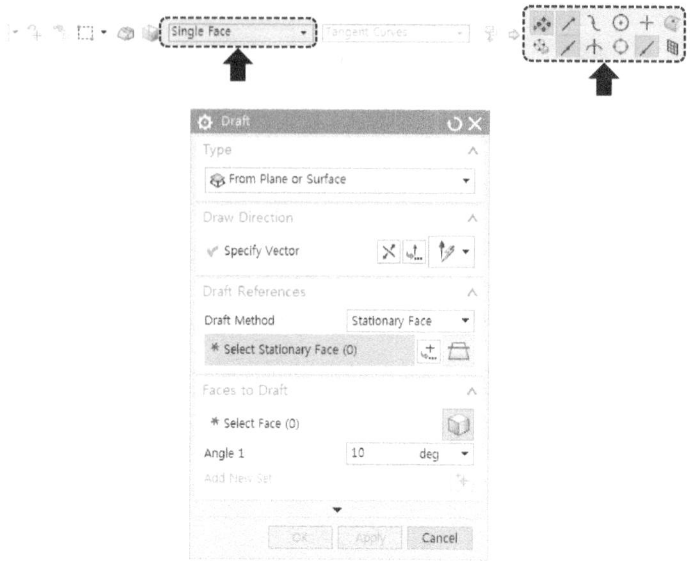

Fig A-14 Stationary Face Option in Draft

If you press the **Select Face** in the Faces to **Draft** option area, only the **Face Rule** is activated as shown in Fig A-15.

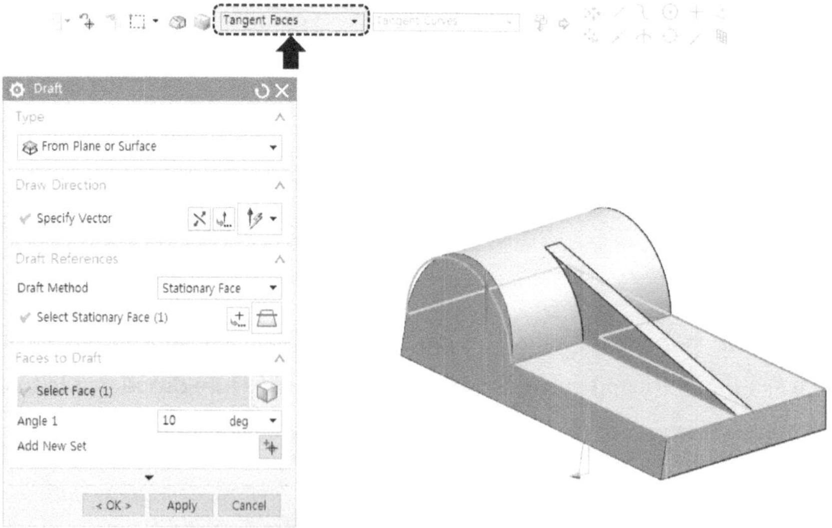

Fig A-15 Face to Draft Option in Draft

A.5 Deselecting Objects

You can deselect all selected objects or deselect one by one.

A.5.1 Deselecting All Objects

You can deselect all selected objects by pressing the ESC key in the keyboard or by resetting the dialog box. Note that, if you reset the dialog box, all other options in the dialog box are reset and all other selections are deselected.

If you press the **Deselect All** button in the selection bar as shown in Fig A-16, you can deselect all objects selected in the current active selection step.

Fig A-16 Deselect All Button

A.5.2 Deselecting One by One

You can deselect selected objects one by one by selecting the objects again with the **Shift** key pressed.

A.6 Detail Filtering and Other Tools

You can use the **Detail Filtering** and other tools in the **Selection Bar** as shown in Fig A-17. If you choose the **Detail Filtering** option in the dropdown, the **Detail Filtering** dialog box is invoked as shown in Fig A-18. You can filter objects by their colors using the **Color Filter** tool.

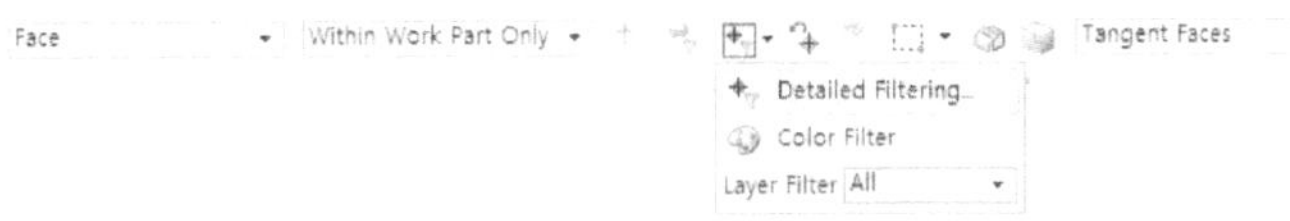

Fig A-17 Detail Filtering and Other Filtering Tools

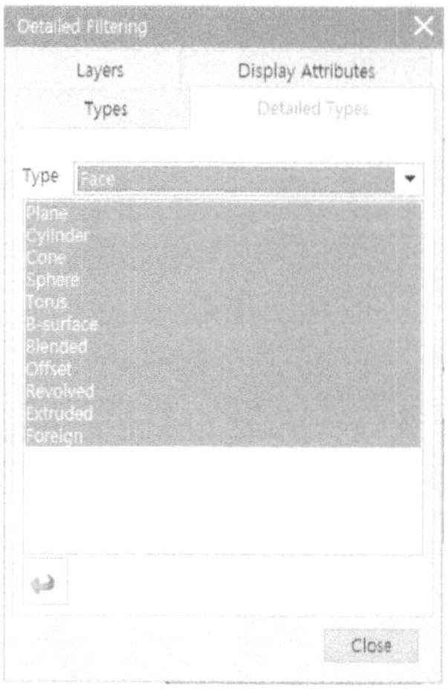

Fig A-18 Detail Filtering Dialog Box

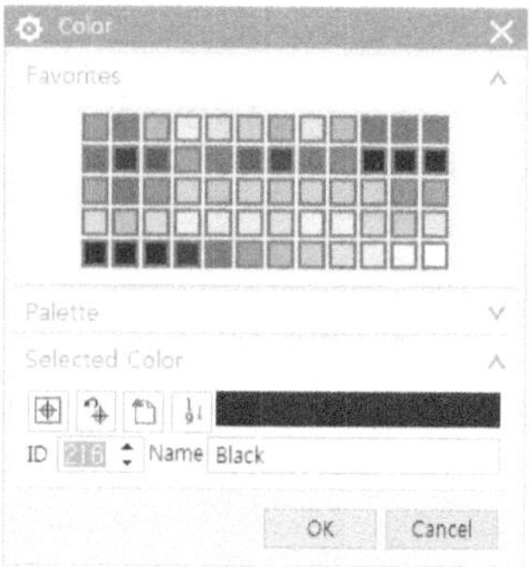

Fig A-19 Color Dialog Box

Do not forget to reset the filters by pressing the **Reset Filters** button in the **Selection Bar**.

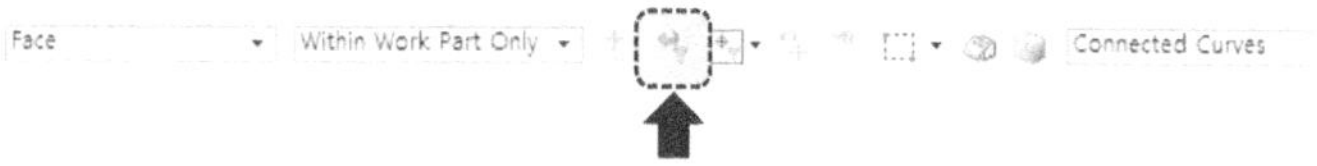

Fig A-20 Resetting the Filter

A.7 Selection Scope

You can specify the scope of selection according to where the objects belong. For example, an edge belongs to a part and a sketch curve belongs to a sketch feature. A sketch curve can also belong to the scope of a part. A solid body or a sheet body can belong to the scope of a part or to the scope of an assembly.

Fig A-21 shows the **Selection Scope** dropdown. If you choose **Within Work Part Only**, you can select objects that belong to the current work part. If you choose **Within Work Part and Component**, the selection scope is extended to the components of the current work part or assembly, but you cannot select objects from other components that are in the same level of assembly structure. If you choose **Entire Assembly**, the selection scope is extended to the components that are in the same level of assembly structure.

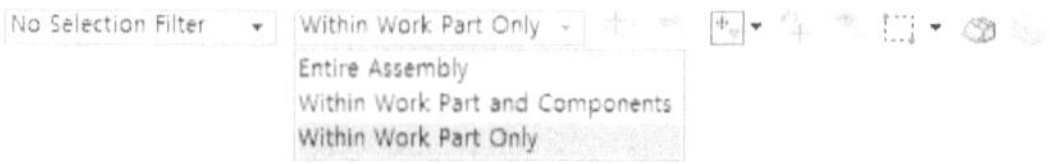

Fig A-21 Selection Scope in Modeling

When you are drawing a sketch, the **Within Active Sketch Only** option is available. Using this scope, you can confine the object selection to the current active sketch. As a result, you can refrain from selecting objects beyond the sketch when you are applying geometric constraints.

Fig A-22 Selection Scope in Sketch

A.8 Selection Priority

If you place the mouse pointer on a part, the feature is highlighted as shown in Fig A-23 and the feature is selected by clicking MB1. You cannot select a solid body or an edge by pressing MB1 directly. The reason is because the selection priority is set to feature by default. You can change the selection priority in the **Menu** button > **Edit** > **Selection** by choosing the desired top selection priority. If you choose the Top **Selection Priority - Face** (Shortcut: Shift + G), you can select a face by clicking MB1 directly as shown in Fig A-24.

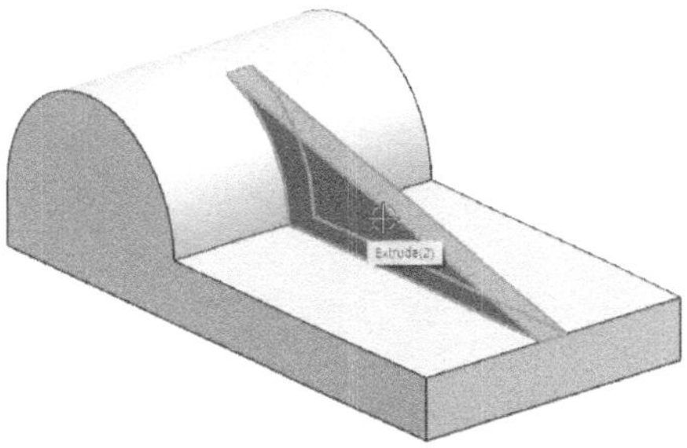

Fig A-23 Highlighted Feature

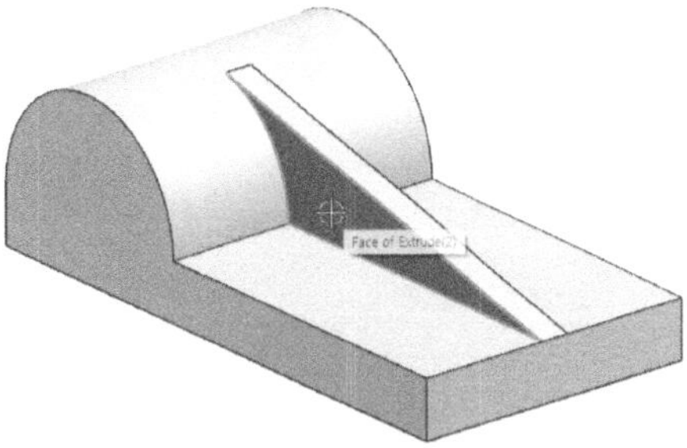

Fig A-24 Highlighted Face

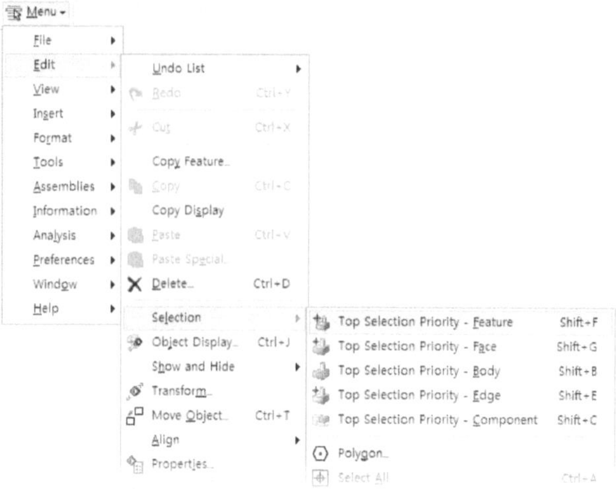

Fig A-25 Selection Priority

A.9 QuickPick

You can select your desired object when some objects are overlapped without the help of the filter. Place the mouse pointer on the overlapped objects and wait for one or two seconds. The cursor changes to the **QuickPick** cursor as shown in Fig A-26. If you click MB1 at this moment, the **QuickPick** dialog box is invoked as shown in Fig A-27 and you can select the desired object in the list. You can invoke the **QuickPick** dialog box by pressing MB1 on the overlapped objects for one or two seconds and releasing the button.

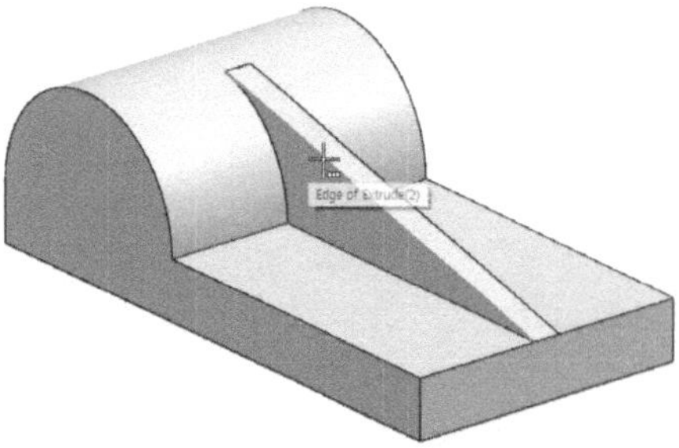

Fig A-26 QuickPick Cursor

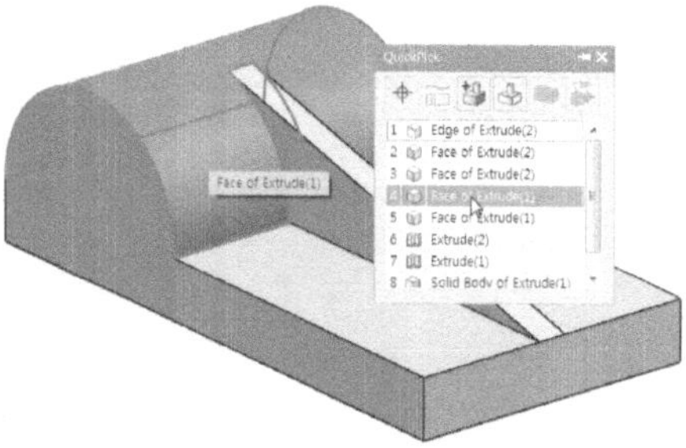

Fig A-27 QuickPick Dialog Box

Index

Symbols

A

B

C

Thank You !

This page left blank intentionally.

This page left blank intentionally.

This page left blank intentionally.

Made in United States
Cleveland, OH
04 November 2026

47642463R00366